Second Edition

The Encyclopedia of Technical Market Indicators

Robert W. Colby, CMT

McGraw-Hill

New York Chicago San Francisco
Lisbon London Madrid Mexico City Milan
New Delhi San Juan Seoul Singapore
Sydney Toronto

The McGraw-Hill Companies

Library of Congress Cataloging-in-Publication Data

Colby, Robert W.
The encyclopedia of technical market indicators / Robert W. Colby.—2nd ed.
p. cm.
Includes index.
ISBN 0-07-012057-9
1. Stock price indexes—United States. 2. Stocks—Prices—United States—Charts, diagrams, etc. 1. Title.

HG4915 .C56 2002
332.63'222'0973—dc21

2001055786

1 2 3 4 5 6 7 8 9 0 DOC/DOC 0 9 8 7 6 5 4 3 2

ISBN 0-07-012057-9

Disclaimer

This publication is designed to provide accurate and authoritative information in regard to the subject matter covered. It is sold with the understanding that the publisher is not engaged in rendering legal, accounting, or other professional service. If legal advice or other expert assistance is required, the services of a competent professional person should be sought.

From a Declaration of Principles jointly adopted by a Committee of the American Bar Association and a Committee of Publishers.

 This book is printed on recycled, acid-free paper containing a minimum of 50% recycled de-inked fiber.

To my wife Carolyn

Preface

The world's top traders and investors use Technical Market Indicators. This small minority of smart-money investors substantially outperforms the market, growing wealthy from their investments. The evidence in this book strongly suggests that the most probable way to join this successful minority is to adopt a strictly realistic investment approach based on objective performance measurement applied to actual past market behavior.

This book offers an accumulated treasury of more than one hundred of the best Technical Market Indicators. These indicators were developed over decades of close daily observation of market price behavior by intensely involved market participants. Technical Market Indicators are designed to make the highly complex investment decision-making process relatively simple and effective.

We tested all available historical data to show you precisely how to establish specific indicator parameters, clear rules for buying and selling securities, with the objective of maximizing profit while minimizing risk of loss. You will be able to judge for yourself the most suitable indicators to apply to your own investment decision making, consistent with your objectives, whether they involve short-term trading, long-term investing, aggressive speculation, or conservation of capital. You will gain a realistic understanding of the actual forecasting value, the strengths, and the weaknesses of a wide range of possible indicator formulas.

This book will save the intelligent user years of time and effort attempting to rediscover the best approaches to trading and investing. The wheel has been invented; you don't have to reinvent it. Many ideas in this book will inspire independent hypothesis testing by the imaginative market student, as established concepts may be dissected and recombined in a wide variety of new ways. With relatively inexpensive computers, software, and data, any intelligent investor can now access affordable tools to conduct original research. This book provides a rich source of tested ideas for adapting a trading system that is right for you.

Robert W. Colby, CMT

www.robertwcolby.com

Acknowledgements

"If I have seen further, it is by standing on the shoulders of giants." Isaac Newton

Many have struggled long and hard to gain practical understanding of the way markets actually behave, and some have generously shared their valuable and hard-earned experience so that we might benefit. Whenever possible, they are acknowledged by name in these pages.

Equis International provided the powerful MetaStock® software used for all historical testing and charts in this book, except where noted. Contact Equis International, Inc., 3950 South 700 East, Suite 100, Salt Lake City, Utah 84107, phone (800) 882-3040 or (801) 265-8886, fax (801) 265-3999, www.equis.com. MetaStock® is a registered trademark of Equis International, Inc., a Reuters Company.

Except where noted, long-term data extending several decades back in time was supplied by UST Securities Corporation, 5 Vaughn Drive, CN5209, Princeton, NJ 08543-5209, phone (201) 734-7747. This institutional broker has long been a preferred supplier of technical analysis and reliable data on market breadth (advance-decline and high-low), sentiment (short sales, advisory service opinion, put/call ratios), volume, price indexes, and individual stock data. UST is widely recognized as "the source" of accurate and detailed point-and-figure charts for institutional investors.

Numerous excellent charts and indicator studies were provided by Ned Davis Research, Inc., 600 Bird Bay Drive West, Venice, FL 34292, phone (941) 484-6107, fax (941) 484-6221, www.ndr.com. For several decades, Ned Davis Research has offered extensive research services for professional and institutional investors.

Reuters DataLink at www.equis.com provided fast and reliable end-of-day data updates and more than 20 years of historical data for individual stocks, various price indexes, volume, breadth, yields, and futures prices.

CSI's Unfair Advantage supplied clean historical data and fast current end-of-day updates for the S&P 500 Composite Stock Price Index futures contract used in many of our strategy examples. CSI is the widely acknowledged leader in supplying accurate futures price data. CSI also provides stock price and volume data. Contact Commodity Systems, Inc., 200 West Palmetto Park Road, Boca Raton, FL 33432, phone (561) 392-8663, www.csidata.com.

The Board of Governors of the Federal Reserve System, www.federalreserve.gov, and the St. Louis Federal Reserve Bank, www.stls.frb.org/fred/data/business.html, offer free historical and current economic data on their internet web sites.

We are indebted to our former co-author, Thomas A. Meyers, CPA, who showed us that it is possible to compile an encyclopedia of technical research. And we are indebted to Stephen Isaacs, Executive Editor, and his colleagues at McGraw-Hill Publishing for producing this encyclopedia.

Finally, we are grateful for countless contributions by our fellow members of the Market Technicians Association, 74 Main Street, 3rd Floor, Woodbridge, NJ 07095, phone (732) 596-9399, fax (732) 596-9392, www.mta.org. This professional organization of the top technical analysts has a journal, newsletter, library, web site, e-mail chat list, meetings, and seminars that inspire many stimulating ideas. New members are welcome.

Contents

PART II Technical Market Indicators 45

Part I

Evaluating Technic
Market Indicators

Chapter 1

Introducing Technical Market Indicators

24 Advantages of Using Technical Market Indicators

1. Technical Market Indicators can be selected or discarded based on logic, common sense, and practical workability based on past performance.
2. Technical Market Indicators can be approached in a systematic, scientific way.
3. Technical Market Indicators provide a precisely quantified framework for organizing information about actual observed market behavior.
4. Technical Market Indicators can provide a firm foundation for making speculative decisions, grounded on historical precedent.
5. Technical Market Indicators save precious time. We do not need to spend decades of time personally observing the market to learn to take advantage of its behavioral patterns. Effective indicator testing and selection is an easier, quicker, and less costly way to learn from historical precedent.
6. Different Technical Market Indicators can be tailored for each of the three possible trend directions: up, down, and sideways.
7. Technical Market Indicators can be tailored to detect trends in any time frame. Due to the fractal nature of markets, trends unfold in a similar fashion in various time intervals. So, Technical Market Indicators can be adapted to the dominant major trends that typically last for years, the intermediate-term movements that typically last for a few weeks to a few months, the day-to-day minor trends, and the momentary fluctuations that concern very short-term traders.
8. Technical Market Indicators can be applied to the full range of financial instruments: stocks, futures, commodities, currencies, and anything else that trades in an open market.
9. Technical Market Indicators can be designed to detect trends and probable changes in trends in the timeliest manner available. Markets anticipate the

probable future trends, and Technical Market Indicators put us on the leading edge of market trends. In contrast, most investors react too late because they are focusing on lagging fundamentals, including current news.

10. Technical Market Indicators allow us to make clear-cut decisions without uncertainty, guesswork, confusion, anxiety, and stress because they can be precisely defined and tested.
11. Technical Market Indicators offer precise and objective signals that can free us from forecasts, opinion, bias, ego, hope, greed, and fear, which interfere with accurate perception of developing market trends. By acting on objective Technical Market Indicator signals with a dispassionate attitude and a minimum of emotional and mental involvement, we can maximize our chances of success.
12. Our Nine Steps to Walk-Forward Simulation of Technical Market Indicators offer an objective and orderly procedure for selecting reasonable and specific Technical Market Indicator parameters. These Nine Steps allow us to establish precise decision rules based on entirely objective back-testing of actual past market behavior.
13. Tested and precisely defined Technical Market Indicator rules give us specific signals that allow us to confidently execute trades. We can feel confident because these are the rules that would have maximized reward/risk performance over actual past market behavior.
14. Although the future is unlikely to exactly mirror the past, assuming that future market behavior will resemble the past is the best available assumption on which to base our current decisions. Thus, we can select specific Technical Market Indicator parameters that would have worked best in the past.
15. Technical Market Indicators can offer more flexibility and adaptability than alternative decision-making methods. Technical analysis can be stretched to include data extraneous to the market being analyzed, such as inter-market comparisons, sentiment surveys, and cycle studies, along with data considered fundamental, such as economic and monetary data. Technical analytical tools can detect trends and trend changes in any data series.
16. Technical Market Indicators can be relatively quick and easy to use compared to alternative decision-making methods. All too often investment strategy is incompletely defined or excessively complex with an overwhelming number of hard-to-quantify variables. Many complex systems are impossible to understand and monitor. In contrast, many Technical Market Indicators offer simple, sensible, intuitively obvious, easy-to-understand, and precisely defined formulas based on a manageable number of variables. These qualities can enable us to execute decisions with the timely and disciplined consistency that is vital for success in the financial markets.

17. Technical Market Indicator research always produces valuable information. Even when an indicator fails to produce an obviously useful result, we benefit because we can discard that indicator and free our attention for research in other directions. And for very bad indicators that lose money, we can try reversing their signals, buying when they turn negative and selling when they turn positive, if logic permits.
18. Traditional Technical Market Indicators can be adapted to incorporate the most up-to-date and sophisticated mathematical and statistical tools.
19. Conservation of capital is the first rule of any prudent investment strategy, and the probability of large losses can be effectively reduced by the disciplined application of tested Technical Market Indicators. Historical research can allow us to precisely define our methods for risk control. Risk reduction means greater consistency of profitable returns.
20. Playing the probabilities based on historically tested Technical Market Indicators, with risk controls to limit damage when the improbable happens, is the best we can do. The alternatives (to search in vain for consistently accurate forecasts of the future, to react to news developments, or to follow the latest market guru) do not work.
21. Technical Market Indicators are more accessible than ever before. Thanks to improving technology, the historical data necessary for independent research is easy to acquire and process.
22. Increasingly, Technical Market Indicators are the preferred decision-making tools of well-informed market participants. Technical Market Indicators are used by the majority of the most successful investors and traders.
23. The same Technical Market Indicators used by top-performing traders and investors are available now. This book offers the necessary knowledge on how to formulate and test Technical Market Indicators in an orderly, step-by-step fashion.
24. Specific Technical Market Indicator parameters offered in this book would have maximized reward/risk performance over actual market history.

Trends Are the Most Important Considerations in Trading and Investing

Market prices move in trends. Many variables influence trends. Market prices lead actual developments in underlying fundamental conditions. Therefore, why trends occur is not always evident in real time. Sometimes, the reasons are not clear even well after the trend is over. Technical Market Indicators are designed simply to identify trends and trend changes without concern for underlying causes and effects.

Trends persist. We do not need to know how long a trend will last. We only need to know that trends continue until something changes in the supply and demand balance for the financial instrument in the marketplace. And we need to identify trend changes in a timely manner.

The market's response to a significant new force unfolds over time as investors of different abilities and various constraints perceive and react to new developments at different rates. Market trends begin like rippling rings of water after a pebble has been tossed into the center of a still pond. At the beginning, the most knowledgeable and best informed players transact their business based on the new reality, and their transactions create the first ripple in the market. Following closely, the second best informed react to create a second ring. Soon after, the third best informed investors make their trades to create a third ring. And so on, until finally the least sophisticated investors respond to the changed environment. By then the trend is over, and a trend reversal is at hand. This is the way directional-price trends unfold in waves of buying and selling.

Human beings buy and sell stocks, and people are moved by their emotions. The emotional state of the crowd, investor psychology, apart from all rational fundamental economic considerations, is the most important determinant of investors' decision-making and therefore of actual market behavior. Investor psychology is revealed in Tape Indicators and in specialized Sentiment Indicators in this book.

Trends are detectable in several different time frames, ranging from years to moments. There are three possible trend directions: up, down, or sideways. These trend directions differ in different time frames: major long-term trends that last for years; significant intermediate-term trends that last from a few weeks to a few months; minor short-term trends that last for days; and noisy momentary trends that concern only short-term traders. Different trend directions and different time frames require different specific Technical Market Indicator parameters to maximize reward/risk performance. This may seem complex, but this complexity can be managed with an orderly identification of appropriate investment objectives and an orderly research method as shown in this book.

Back-Testing Technical Market Indicators Has Proved to Be Effective

One of the great advantages of Technical Market Indicators is that they can be tested against actual market history. Some of the world's top-performing traders and investors use back-testing to determine their trading strategies. (See Schwager, Jack D., *Market Wizards, Interviews with Top Traders,* New York Institute of Finance, New York, 1989, 458 pages.) For example, Richard Dennis ran $400 to $200,000,000 in 16 years of trading on the Chicago futures markets. (Futures "speculation" is about the same as stock market "investing" except for high leverage, which greatly magnifies gains and losses.) Like nearly all great futures traders, Dennis is a technician who studies the behavior of the market itself. Dennis employs mathematicians and computer experts to help him test all known Technical Market Indicators. Based on his research, he established a set of trading rules that capitalizes on price trends, cuts losses quickly, and identifies unsustainable excesses. To prove that his methods are valid and not unique to his personal attributes, Dennis taught his trading rules to 23 raw trainees, whom he called his *Turtles.* Although they had no previous trading experience, 20 of the 23 averaged returns of 100% annually. These results suggest that back-testing precisely defined trading rules on historical data is a reasonable way to select trading strategies.

Back-testing Technical Market Indicators has proved to be useful in actual practice because the market's behavior patterns do not change dramatically over time. As Fed Chairman Alan Greenspan said, "Human psychology molds the value system that drives a competitive market economy. And that process is inextricably linked to human nature, which appears essentially immutable and, thus, anchors the future to the past." And as philosopher George Santayana wrote, in *Life of Reason* (1906), "Those who cannot remember the past are condemned to repeat it."

Traditionally, most investors make decisions based on some combination of their instincts and the "conventional wisdom" readily available from popular information sources. Unfortunately, a subjective consideration of widely discounted known facts leads to poor decisions and below average results. By relying on shifting subjective impressions based on an unsystematic sampling of unfiltered information, the actual decision process becomes impossibly confused. When we cannot analyze or even identify exactly what went wrong, we cannot learn from mistakes and improve. This may not seem to be a problem when the market is in a generous mood and it is easy to make money, but when the hard times come—as they always do—a haphazard, untested approach quickly becomes a serious hazard to wealth.

Back-testing Technical Market Indicators provides practical alternatives that offer much better probabilities of success. A tested, objective and systematic strategy does not rely on forecasts or subjective judgments, and it leaves no room for guesswork or doubt. Instead, it offers a precise set of instructions that tightly control investment risks while allowing maximum profits to accumulate. Moreover, by testing substantial historical data covering many market cycles, we can design a model to maximize reward and risk tradeoffs in all kinds of market environments.

Types of Technical Market Indicators: Trend, Momentum, Sentiment

Early technicians observed and catalogued all kinds of transaction data. In time, repetitive patterns were identified and general theories emerged. Trend (price movement: up, down, or sideways) emerged as the primary consideration in technical analysis.

Momentum (price velocity, or rate of change of price movement) is a leading indicator of a change in price trend direction. Momentum change usually precedes price trend change. In a typical major market cycle, price begins a new uptrend with very high and rising momentum, the signal for a new bull market. Over the next months to years, this positive velocity gradually diminishes, and the slope of the price advance lessens. Usually, momentum hits its peak well before the price hits its ultimate high. Then, velocity gradually tapers off as price begins to make little upward progress on rally attempts. Momentum forms a pattern of decreasing peaks as price rallies to or slightly beyond previous peaks. This is known as *negative divergence*. The end of the bull market is at hand when price begins to fall short of previous peaks on minor rally attempts—a clear evidence of bullish exhaustion. When price drops below previous minor lows and momentum breaks sharply into negative territory, it is the beginning of the downward part of the cycle, the bear market. Finally, after a long decline, price velocity bottoms out before actual price hits its ultimate low. Gradually, price velocity becomes less and less negative on minor price declines. Price may make a lower low, but momentum is not as negative as it was previously at higher price lows, and that is called *positive divergence.* As negative momentum diminishes, the stage is being set for a new upward cycle. Finally, quite likely following one or many tests of the lows, or a prolonged period of dull, sideways price fluctuation at depressed levels, price breaks to a new multi-month high on large volume and high price velocity to signal a new bull market. This full cycle repeats endlessly.

Basic chart analysis is supplemented by a variety of statistical formulas known as *Tape Indicators.* (The ticker tape is the streaming, almost real-time report listing each stock transaction in sequence on the floor of the stock exchange. "The tape tells all," is a time-honored axiom on Wall Street.) Tape Indicators quantify the market's direction (trend) and velocity (momentum) using price, volume, and breadth data. Tape Indicators offer clues about the potential for trend change.

Sentiment Indicators are based on the Theory of Contrary Opinion: when investors swing to emotional extremes they are likely to be overreacting. These indicators include short sales, put and call activity, and investment advisory service opinion polls. Sentiment is used to highlight junctures of *bullish excess (overbought)* and *bearish excess (oversold),* which are useful leading indicators of trend exhaustion.

Other kinds of indicators not classified as technical also have wide followings as indicators of stock prices. Monetary, Interest Rate, Economic and Fundamental Indicators can be back-tested using the same objective methods we use to test Technical Market Indicators. Technical analysts are practical and consider any data that might help them win. Monetary, Interest Rate, Economic, and Fundamental indicators are covered separately in Colby, Robert W., *Investment Strategies,* www.robertwcolby.com, 2002.

Criteria for Judging Technical Market Indicators, Trading Systems, Investment Timing Models

Percentage accuracy (profitable trades to total trades) is an obsession of novice traders, but it is not a very important criterion for judging a trading system. Some highly effective technical timing models are wrong more often than they are right, while some marginal models are right more often than they are wrong.

The key performance measure is the ratio of total net profit to maximum equity drawdown, also known as the reward/risk ratio. Maximum equity drawdown determines the practical workability of a strategy. A model that sustains large losses is not practical, even if total profits are high in the end.

Maximum equity drawdown is the largest overall downtrend in capital from peak to trough. Maximum equity drawdown is not just the largest cumulative loss of consecutive losing trades, since a bad performance period could be interrupted by a small profit, only to be followed by a resumption of the cumulative net equity downtrend to a still lower low.

The best and simplest way to grasp reward versus risk is to visually inspect the graph of Cumulative Equity. Large equity drawdowns become obvious on a chart. If these drawdowns are severe when compared to the drawdowns of other indicators, we should discard that trading system and choose an alternative strategy.

There are many other performance measures, some of which involve extremely complex statistical manipulations, but these do not tell us as much as the chart of Cumulative Equity. "Keep it simple" is still the best advice.

Chapter 2

Walk-Forward Simulation of Technical Market Indicators Offers the Potential for Consistent Profits Through Time

Simulation, or historical back-testing, is one of the most powerful analytical techniques ever devised. It is a crucial step in finding effective market strategies. Through simulation, we can isolate timing models that would have been consistently profitable over actual past market history. Powerful computers, specialized software, and reliable historical data make simulation increasingly accessible.

Simulation is much more sensible than the alternatives: using untested decision-making models or using systems that would have failed to produce consistent profits in the past. Yet critics point out that future market behavioral patterns may not match those of the past. True, but perfect match-ups are not necessary. A worthwhile advantage may be gained by quantifying imperfect similarities, patterns, or tendencies. If a market is a manifestation of human crowd psychology, and if mass human behavior has some underlying order and characteristic repetitive patterns, then effective historical testing may find these patterns.

The correct way to test Technical Market Indicators is to use *walk-forward, blind simulation,* also known as *ex-ante cross validation.* This is an orderly, systematic procedure for realistically testing a hypothesis that can be performed in nine steps.

Nine Steps to Walk-Forward Simulation of Technical Market Indicators

1. **Form Hypothesis.** Start with a reasonable hypothesis about market behavior, one well-founded in logic and observation. There are more than a hundred promising and clearly defined hypotheses (Technical Market Indicators) to choose from in this book.
2. **Get Data.** We acquire the largest quantity of accurate historical data on a tradable financial instrument of interest that we can find. The more data, the greater the significance of our test results.

or not our hypothesis is accepted or rejected. As Thomas Edison pointed out, a rejected hypothesis is very useful information that allows us to turn our resources to other approaches that may produce better results. The process of doing the research often rewards us with more realistic insights into market behavior and inspires new ideas.

A Specific Example of a Walk-Forward Simulation of a Simple Technical Indicator: The Evolving Exponential Moving Average Crossover Strategy

The Evolving Exponential Moving Average Crossover Strategy is one of the simplest trend-following Technical Market Indicators. We choose exponential moving averages crossovers for this demonstration because of their simplicity and attractive theoretical and practical advantages. We prefer exponential smoothing as a moving average method because it is more responsive to newer data and less dependent on older data than simple moving averages. Also, exponential smoothing is less sensitive to newer data and less dependent on older data than weighted moving averages. Compared to other methods, exponential smoothing is more stable.

This strategy buys long and covers short when price crosses above its own trailing exponential moving average, and then it sells long and sells short when price crosses under its own trailing exponential moving average. In this example, using weekly data, if this Friday's closing price is above the previous week's exponential moving average, we buy long the Dow-Jones Industrial Average at this Friday's close. On the other hand, if the most recent end-of-week price is below last week's exponential moving average, we sell our long position and also sell short the Dow-Jones Industrial Average. This strategy is always in the market, either long or short. The clearly and precisely defined buy and sell signals leave absolutely no room for uncertainty, subjective judgment, or interpretation, which can be sources of problems. Moving average smoothing is the basis of many trend-following approaches and systems, and our unqualified crossover rule is its simplest form.

Avoid hindsight bias. We go both long and short because we must be very careful not to inadvertently introduce a bullish bias, which is a common but incorrect unspoken assumption of those who choose a long or cash strategy without selling short. It is only obvious in hindsight that the stock market has had a strong bullish (upward) bias over the past century, but that information was not at all available a century ago. Note that a random long or short strategy would have lost very substantially on the short side, due to the market's unusual uptrend from years 1982 to 2000. So, a long and short strategy is a good test, since any indicator that survives equal-opportunity short selling and still performs strongly has to be good.

The only parameter that can be varied is the period length, *n*. With such a simple, unbiased approach, there is only one parameter (variable) to optimize: the number of time periods (in this case, the number of weeks) used to estimate our exponential smoothing constant. To translate the number of time periods into an exponential smoothing constant, use the formula $2/(n+1)$, where n represents the number of time periods.

The greater n:

- the greater the number of time periods,
- the greater the length of the exponential moving average,
- the more loosely the exponential moving average follows the raw data,
- the longer the lag time in following the raw data,
- the lower the sensitivity of the decision rule,
- the smaller the number of buy and sell signals,
- the greater the tolerance for random movement without triggering a trade signal, and
- the greater the price change required to signal a change in existing long or short positions.

A large n means a slow, insensitive, and inactive indicator that generates few trading signals.

The smaller n:

- the smaller the number of time periods,
- the smaller the length of the exponential moving average,
- the more tightly the exponential moving average follows the raw data,
- the shorter the lag time in following the raw data,
- the higher the sensitivity of the decision rule,
- the greater the number of buy and sell signals,
- the smaller the tolerance for random movement without triggering a trade signal, and
- the smaller the price change required to signal a change in existing long or short positions.

A small n means a fast, sensitive, and active indicator that generates many trading signals.

Transaction costs, dividends, margin, and interest can vary substantially and complicate the analysis. These costs are not included in this example, solely in the interest of simplicity of presentation, and not at all because they are insignificant in reality. On the contrary, these deserve careful consideration when choosing an investment strategy. The more frequent the trading signals, the greater the transaction costs, which not only include commissions but also *slippage*—the price you actually receive on an order compared to the price you hoped to receive. Slippage can be highly variable, and it can exceed the bid-ask spread, especially in fast markets. Slippage is usually a negative number, and therefore a cost. Because margin and leverage can greatly magnify profits and losses, they are another major consideration.

Example of Using the Nine Steps to Walk-Forward Simulation on the Dow-Jones Industrial Average

1. **Form Hypothesis.** We choose a one-parameter (period length) Exponential Moving Average Crossover Strategy.
2. **Get Data.** We acquire historical data on the Dow-Jones Industrial Average back to 1900 from UST Securities. (This data also is available from other sources.) To simplify our work for this example, we sample end-of-week data only.
3. **Check Data.** We carefully examine data to insure its accuracy, by visual inspection of the chart looking for outliers (odd excursions) and by systematic spot checks. We correct any data errors.
4. **Segment the Data.** We choose to segment the data into 1-year time intervals, from January 1 to December 31 each year. Therefore, we will walk forward by one year at a time, and our seen database will grow in size by 52 Friday closing prices each year, while our unseen database available for future walk-forward simulation will shrink by 52 Friday closing prices each year. We select 16 years of weekly closing prices from January 1, 1900 to December 31, 1915 for our initial (earliest) data segment. This initial segment must include a minimum of 30 trades and cover an integer multiple of a full low frequency cycle (for example, the well-known 4-year cycle) in order to eliminate a buy or sell bias. Two 4-year cycles are eight years, and two 8-year cycles are 16 years. *(See Cycles.)*
5. **Optimize.** We conduct a brute-force optimization on our initial segment of data (the 16 years of weekly price closes), systematically trying all Exponential Moving Average period lengths from 1 week to 50 weeks. We make note of which parameter would have produced the best reward/risk performance results. All this initial data is considered to be seen data, so it will not be counted in our walk-forward, blind simulation performance evaluation in Step 9.
6. **Walk Forward.** We apply the best parameter from our optimization in Step 5 to unseen data for the next year-ahead data segment. We carefully record the results of this walk-forward, real-time simulation for evaluation in Step 9.
7. **Add.** We add that just-simulated data from Step 6 to the previously optimized, seen database (from Step 5), so our original 16 years of weekly price closes is now 17 years. We retain all the old seen data in our optimization database, never deleting any seen data from our ever-growing optimization database, even as we add new, just-seen data each year. The length in years of our optimization database will grow from 16 years, to 17 years, to 18, to 19, 20, 21, 22, 23, 24, 25, 26 . . . and so on to the end of all our data.

8. **Repeat.** We repeat Steps 5, 6, and 7, over and over again, one year at a time, until all unseen data is used in our walk-forward simulation.
9. **Evaluate Results.** We evaluate the cumulative results of our walk-forward simulation performed on unseen data only. This will provide us with a realistic perspective on how our method would have evolved and performed in real-time through many iterations over the years.

This walk-forward simulation, year by year, will allow our optimized indicator parameter to adapt over time to any possible evolutionary change in the market's cyclic rhythms. We carefully record the profits and losses of each walk-forward simulation on unseen data each year so that we can build a realistic, simulated cumulative track record of the performance results of our indicator over time.

At this point, we have selected our hypothesis, acquired our data, thoroughly checked our data, segmented our data, and are now ready for our next step, Step 5, Optimize.

5. **Optimize.** We systematically try every exponential moving average period length from 1 to 50 against the weekly closing prices for the first 16 years of the past century. We find that all the period lengths tested would have been profitable. The maximum profit would have been recorded by the 4-week exponential moving average crossover.
6. **Walk Forward.** We measure the simulated performance of this 4-week exponential moving average crossover strategy over the next 52 weeks of unseen data, from January 1, 1916, through December 31, 1916. We record the result for future evaluation (in Step 9).
7. **Add.** We add that just-simulated data (from Step 6, data for January 1, 1916, through December 31, 1916) to our previously optimized, seen database (from Step 5), such that our original 16 years of weekly price closes is now 17 years.
8. **Repeat.** We repeat Steps 5, 6, and 7.
5. **Optimize.** We apply systematic brute-force number crunching to 17 years of data (now from January 1, 1900 through December 31, 1916). Again, we find that the maximum profit would have been recorded by the 4-week exponential moving average crossover.
6. **Walk Forward.** We walk forward with this 4-week exponential moving average crossover strategy over the next 52 weeks of unseen data, from January 1, 1917, through December 31, 1917. We record the result for future evaluation (in Step 9).
7. **Add.** We add that just-simulated data (from January 1, 1917, through December 31, 1917, from Step 6) to our previously optimized, seen database (from Step 5). Our original 16 years of weekly price closes has now grown

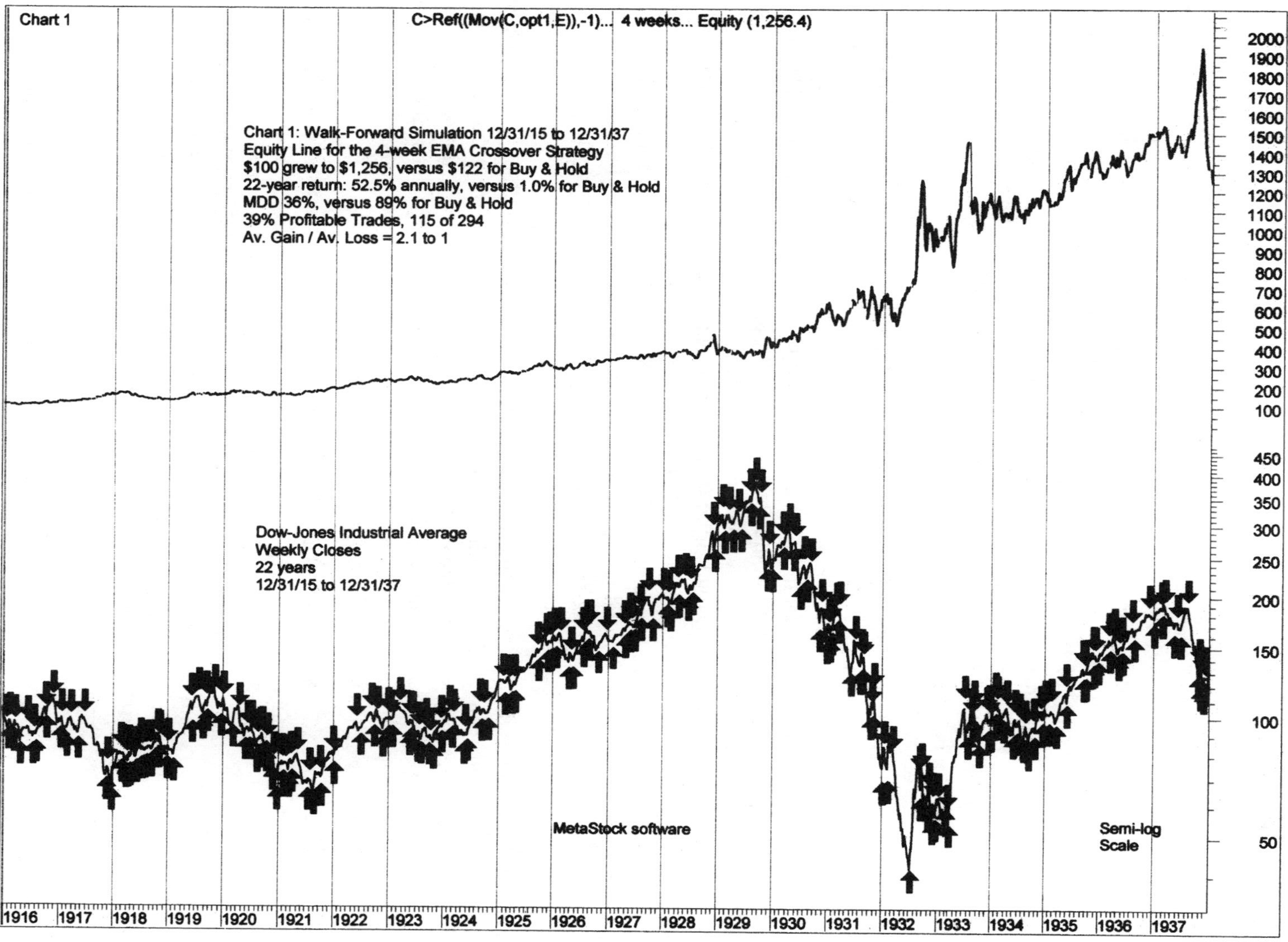

Chart 1
C>Ref((Mov(C,opt1,E)),-1)... 4 weeks... Equity (1,256.4)
Chart 1: Walk-Forward Simulation 12/31/15 to 12/31/37
Equity Line for the 4-week EMA Crossover Strategy
$100 grew to $1,256, versus $122 for Buy & Hold
22-year return: 52.5% annually, versus 1.0% for Buy & Hold
MDD 36%, versus 89% for Buy & Hold
39% Profitable Trades, 115 of 294
Av. Gain / Av. Loss = 2.1 to 1
Dow-Jones Industrial Average
Weekly Closes
22 years
12/31/15 to 12/31/37
MetaStock software
Semi-log
Scale
2000
1900
1800
1700
1600
1500
1400
1300
1200
1100
1000
900
800
700
600
500
400
300
200
100
450
400
350
300
250
200
150
100
50
1916
1917
1918
1919
1920
1921
1922
1923
1924
1925
1926
1927
1928
1929
1930
1931
1932
1933
1934
1935
1936
1937

to 18 years. We retain all the original 16 years of data in our optimization database, and we keep adding to it all simulated data each year. Thus, our optimization database grows larger by 52 weeks every year, at year end.

8. **Repeat.** We again repeat Steps 5, 6, and 7. We continue to optimize, we project forward, then add back that data to the seen database at year-end on 1918, 1919, 1920 . . . and so on to year-end 1936.

5. **Optimize.** Each yearend from December 1915 to December 1936, we find the same result: all the period lengths tested would have been profitable, and maximum profit would have been recorded with a 4-week exponential moving average crossover strategy.

6. **Walk Forward.** Since with the addition of all 22 1-year increments the exponential moving average period length remained unchanged at 4 weeks, we can summarize the walk-forward simulation results in Chart 1 as one continuous Cumulative Equity Line from 12/31/15 to 12/31/37. The real-time simulated profit for this 22-year period would have been 52.52% annually. Total simulated profit would have been 1156%, which would have been 32.1 times the maximum drawdown of 36%. Maximum drawdown is the worst-case scenario we would suffer if we started trading our strategy at the worst possible time; that is, if we started at a peak in the Cumulative Equity Line just before the beginning of the worst cumulative loss periods. Only 39% or 115 of the 294 total number trades would have been profitable, which is fairly typical of long-term trend-following strategies; however, the gains would have been bigger than the losses.

Note the sharp drop in the Equity Line at the end of 1937. Such a large decline in Equity can be taken as a hint that the exponential moving average that fit the market's behavior so well in the past might need to be updated. In actual practice, whenever we see such an equity drop, we can take it as a message from the market to rerun our Step 5 Optimization to see if anything has changed—even if such an optimization is not yet "scheduled" by our predefined procedure.

7. **Add.** We add simulated data (from Step 6) to our previously optimized, seen database (from Step 5). That is, to prepare for our next routine brute-force optimization (Step 5), according to our predefined procedure, we load all data from January 1, 1900 through December 31, 1937. All that seen data already has been used either in our previous year-end optimizations or, in the case of data for 1937, in our most recent 52-week, walk-forward simulation.

8. **Repeat.** We again repeat Steps 5, 6, and 7.

5. **Optimize.** Repeating this longer new 38-year brute-force optimization provides us with our first change of period length in our whole 22 years of simulated, real-time experience: the best reward/risk performance now would have been recorded by the 17-week exponential moving average crossover rule.

   Note that although this back-search for an optimal period length has found a new period length of 17 weeks as of December 31, 1937, this new parameter does not change our simulated track record over the past 22 years of real-time simulation. That simulated performance is recorded separately in an entirely separate step, Step 6, Walk Forward. Our simulated track record of the past stands as is and cannot be revised, no matter what later back-search optimizations may reveal. We take care to separate "the past" from "the future."
6. **Walk Forward.** The important question remains: How well might this new optimized decision rule perform in the future, over the next year of fresh, new, untested, untouched, unknown, unseen data? For the answer, we project our walk-forward simulation ahead onto the next 52 weeks of unseen data. We load unseen data from 1/1/38 to 12/31/38, apply the 17-week exponential moving average crossover strategy to this unseen data, then carefully record the results.
7. **Add.** We add the data from 1/1/38 to 12/31/38 that we just used for our Step 6 Walk Forward to our previously optimized, seen database (now 39 years long) in order to prepare for our next routine Step 5 Optimization. All that 39-year seen data already has been used either in our previous optimization or, in the case of data for 1938, in walk-forward simulation.

We continue with this procedure, again and again, every year at year-end, optimizing (Step 5), walking forward (Step 6), adding (Step 7) and repeating (Step 8). We follow the same routine at year-end 1939, 1940, 1941, 1942, 1943, 1944, 1945, 1946, 1947 . . . and so on through year-end 1991. Each time, we find that all the period lengths in the optimization would have been profitable, and maximum profit would have been recorded every year with the same 17-week exponential moving average crossover strategy.

6. **Walk Forward.** Since over all 54 of these 1-year increments the exponential moving average period length remains unchanged at 17 weeks, we can show the walk-forward simulation results in Chart 2 as one continuous Cumulative Equity Line from 12/31/37 to 12/31/92. The real-time simulated profit for this period would have been 10.58% annually. Total simulated profit would have been 582%, which would have been 14.6 times the maximum drawdown of 40%. (Maximum drawdown is the worst-case scenario we would suffer if we started trading our strategy at the worst possible time.) Only 29% or 107 of the 375 total number trades would have been profitable.
7. **Add.** We add back all simulated data to our previously optimized, seen database.
5. **Optimize.** We load all seen data from January 1, 1900, through December 31, 1992, for our routine brute-force optimization. All that data already has been seen either in our initial optimization or in one of our walk-forward simulations at the end of each year. Our new optimization on all 93 years of seen data provides us with our first change of period length in 55 years: the best reward/risk performance would have been produced by using a 40-week exponential moving average crossover rule.
6. **Walk Forward.** We load into our computer's memory the next 52 weeks of previously unseen data, from 1/1/93 to 12/31/93, and then we apply the 40-week exponential moving average crossover strategy to this unseen data. We carefully record the results.

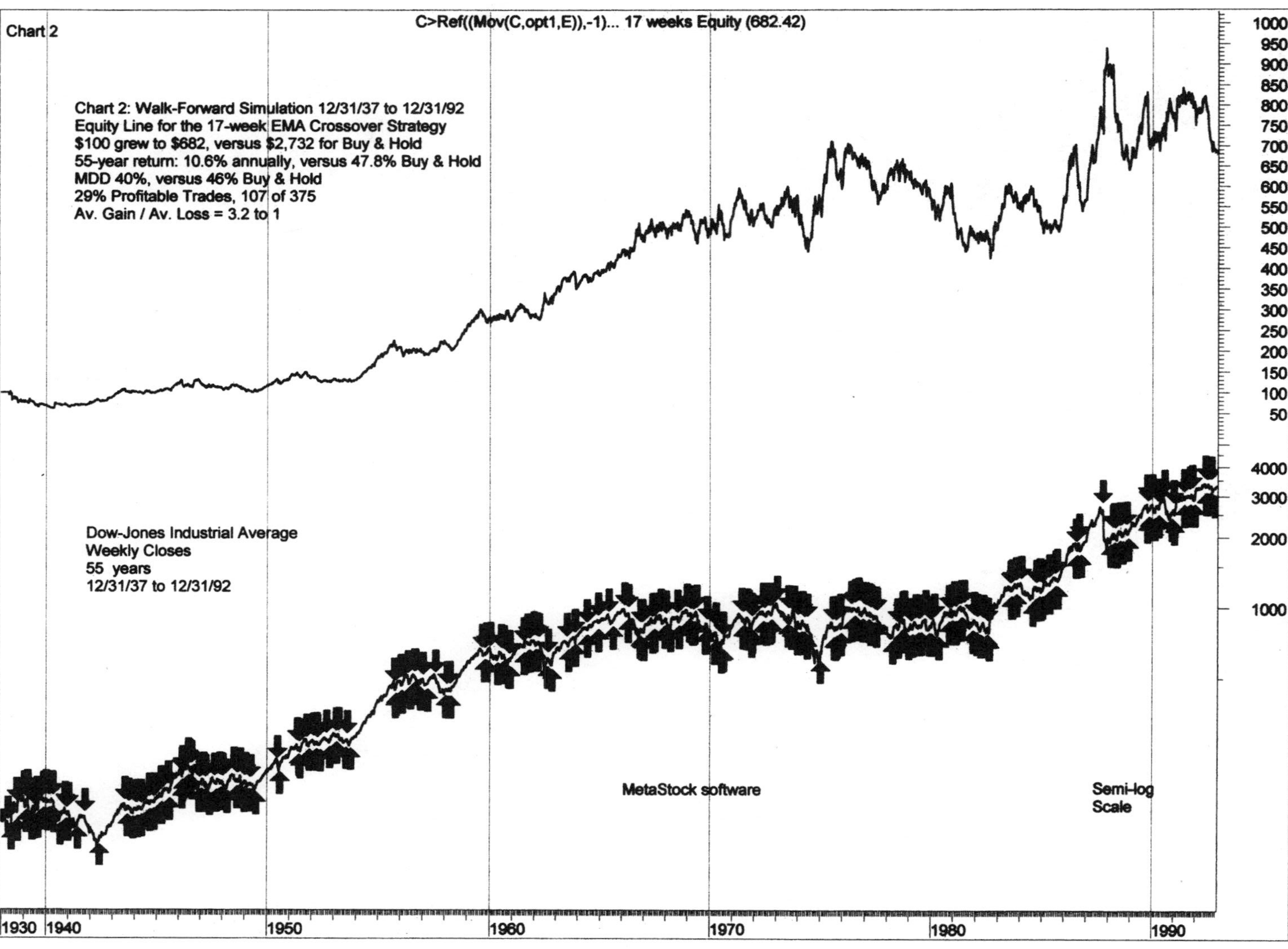
Chart 2
C>Ref((Mov(C,opt1,E)),-1)... 17 weeks Equity (682.42)
Chart 2: Walk-Forward Simulation 12/31/37 to 12/31/92
Equity Line for the 17-week EMA Crossover Strategy
$100 grew to $682, versus $2,732 for Buy & Hold
55-year return: 10.6% annually, versus 47.8% Buy & Hold
MDD 40%, versus 46% Buy & Hold
29% Profitable Trades, 107 of 375
Av. Gain / Av. Loss = 3.2 to 1
Dow-Jones Industrial Average
Weekly Closes
55 years
12/31/37 to 12/31/92
MetaStock software
Semi-log
Scale
1000
950
900
850
800
750
700
650
600
550
500
450
400
350
300
250
200
150
100
50
4000
3000
2000
1000
1930
1940
1950
1960
1970
1980
1990

At year-end of 1994, 1995, 1996 and 1997, we find that all 50 tested period lengths would have been profitable, and the best reward/risk performance would have been produced using a 40-week exponential moving average crossover strategy. Since over all four of these 1-year increments, the exponential moving average period length would have remained unchanged at 40 weeks, we can show the walk-forward simulation results in Chart 3 as one continuous Cumulative Equity Line from 1/1/93 to 10/30/98 (our cut-off date for this demonstration). The real-time simulated profit for this 5.8-year period would have been 18.48% annually. Total simulated profit would have been 221%, which would have been 6.4 times the maximum draw down of 19%. Only 38% or 3 of the 8 total number trades would have been profitable.

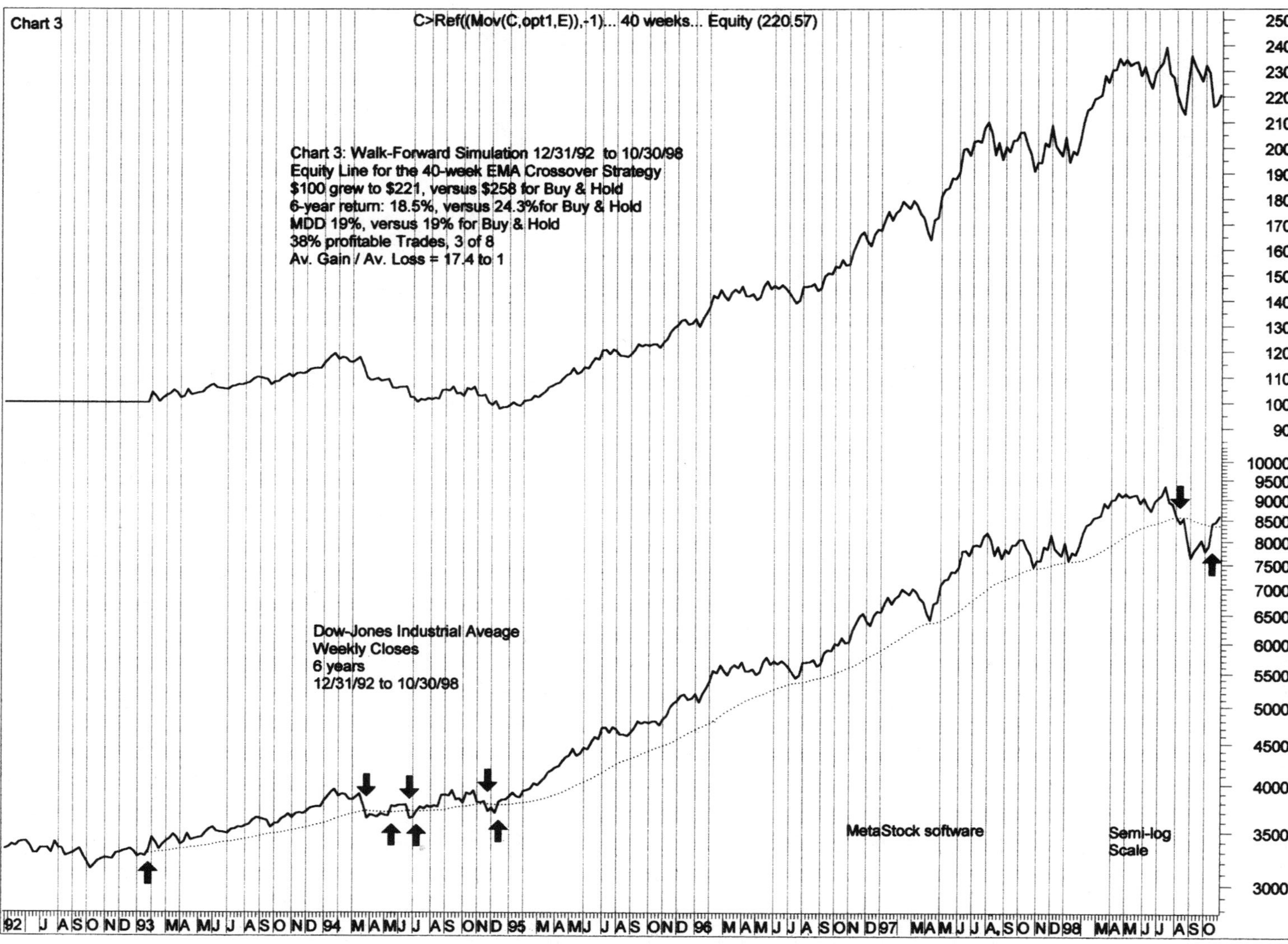
Chart 3
C>Ref((Mov(C,opt1,E)),-1)... 40 weeks... Equity (220.57)
Chart 3: Walk-Forward Simulation 12/31/92 to 10/30/98
Equity Line for the 40-week EMA Crossover Strategy
$100 grew to $221, versus $258 for Buy & Hold
6-year return: 18.5%, versus 24.3%for Buy & Hold
MDD 19%, versus 19% for Buy & Hold
38% profitable Trades, 3 of 8
Av. Gain / Av. Loss = 17.4 to 1
Dow-Jones Industrial Aveage
Weekly Closes
6 years
12/31/92 to 10/30/98
MetaStock software
Semi-log
Scale
250 240 230 220 210 200 190 180 170 160 150 140 130 120 110 100 90
10000 9500 9000 8500 8000 7500 7000 6500 6000 5500 5000 4500 4000 3500 3000
92 J A S O N D 93 M A M J J A S O N D 94 M A M J J A S O N D 95 M A M J J A S O N D 96 M A M J J A S O N D97 M A M J J A S O N D98 M A M J J A S O

The following two tables show the simulated real-time results of The Evolving Exponential Moving Average Crossover Strategy and the passive Buy-and-Hold Strategy. The dynamic Evolving Exponential Moving Average Crossover Strategy produced significantly greater profit (Total Reinvested P&L%) with smaller risk (Total MDD%, where MDD% is maximum drawdown as a percentage of Cumulative Equity), as compared to the static Buy-and-Hold Strategy.

EMA: Walk-Forward, Blind Simulation for the Dow-Jones Industrial Average

REAL-TIME DATES	*EMA WEEKS*	*EMA P & L %*	*P & L % ANNUALLY*	*EMA MDD%*	*EMA P & L % / MDD*	*REINVESTED P & L % START@$100*
1915–1937	4	1291.20	58.75	36.00	35.87	1391.20
1937–1992	17	627.90	11.43	40.00	15.70	10126.54
1992–1998	40	174.41	24.91	19.00	9.18	27788.25
Totals	61	2093.51	95.09	95.00	60.74	27788.25
Averages	20.33	697.84	31.70	31.67	20.25	334.80

Buy-and-Hold Strategy Fully Invested in the Dow-Jones Industrial Average

REAL-TIME DATES	*B & H WEEKS*	*B & H P & L %*	*B & H P & L % ANNUALLY*	*B & H MDD%*	*B&H P&L % / MDD*	*REINVESTED P & L % START@$100*
1915–1937	ALL	25.17	1.15	89.00	0.28	125.17
1937–1992	ALL	2586.45	47.08	46.00	56.23	3362.63
1992–1998	ALL	221.55	31.64	19.00	11.66	10812.54
Totals		2833.17	79.87	154.00	68.17	10812.54
Averages		944.39	26.62	51.33	22.72	130.27

Given the fact that the overall market trend has been strongly biased upward much of the time since 1932, and especially from years 1982 to 1998, it is perhaps remarkable that our simple trend-following strategy's results were not penalized more by short selling. Although profitability suffers noticeably in choppy, sideways, trendless periods, this disadvantage is overcome in markets that experienced both up and down price movements of significance. In a prolonged and deep bear market, like 1929–1932, the popular buy-and-hold strategy would lose substantially, while a long or short exponential moving average crossover strategy would offer the possibility of significant short side profits.

A brute-force optimization number crunching of all the available data from 1900 to 1998 yields some interesting additional findings. Over that 98.8 years, crossover signals for all exponential moving average lengths between 1 and 100 weeks would have been profitable. The fact that all would have been profitable suggests the robustness of the basic trend-following concept, one that is well established in technical analysis. In addition, all exponential moving average lengths from 10 to 50 weeks would have outperformed the buy-and-hold strategy. The profitability of the best performing exponential moving average of 40 weeks in length would have beaten the buy-and-hold strategy by more than six to one, while suffering much less risk. The 40-week exponential moving average crossover strategy maximum drawdown would have been 44% smaller than the buy-and-hold drawdown. That is a worthwhile reduction in risk.

Even the best 40-week exponential moving average crossover strategy would have been wrong on 72% of its transactions. But the bottom line shows that, in this case at least, "often wrong but never in doubt" can be a virtue, because we automatically cut our losses and let our profits run. We avoid confusion, indecision, hesitation, and anxiety. We always know precisely what action to take and when to take it. We always know exactly what our position in the market should be, according to our entirely objective, unemotional, unbiased, predetermined formula. These are worthwhile benefits.

With one eye steadily fixed on the rear view mirror, most investors avoid the short side. For 60 years, from 1938 to 1998, short selling would have lost money using the Evolving Exponential Moving Average Crossover Strategy. The number of transactions could have been cut in half and profits could have been larger by totally ignoring the short side.

But, that is precisely the kind of hindsight over-fitting we should avoid. Unbiased objectivity requires both buying long and selling short. That is why all of our tests of the Evolving Exponential Moving Average Crossover Strategy assumed unbiased long buying and short selling: either we were 100% invested on the long side in the DJIA, or we were 100% short. Take care that bias does not creep into your research when you are not thinking.

Summary and Conclusions about Walk-Forward Simulation

It may seem to be only common sense that the most rational approach to forecasting the future requires a careful study of the past. However, this historical testing procedure remains underutilized by the great majority of investors.

There is no assurance that future results will resemble past performance, of course. Nevertheless, correctly performed, walk-forward simulation offers a logical, consistent, and totally objective approach for selecting effective decision rules and practical investment strategies. Both logic and experience suggest that this approach offers a reasonably good chance of future success. Besides, there is no other alternative for selecting investment strategy that is so firmly grounded in actual market behavior.

It bears repeating that we should test substantial quantities of historical data that cover all kinds of market environments. Also, we should guard against excessive curve fitting that involves too many conditions or rules or, worse, biased or conditional rules designed with hindsight for the sole conscious or unconscious purpose of filtering out a specific bad period. We should make certain that our research is truly blind, honest, and objective. Complexity makes our research difficult to comprehend. Keeping it simple helps us understand and have confidence in our indicator.

This highly simplified demonstration is strictly for educational purposes and is not a recommendation of any particular trading strategy. It is intended to show how to simulate real-world experience with a clearly defined walk-forward simulation method. The example and assumptions were purposely simplified to a bare minimum for the sake of clarity. To be more realistic, transactions costs, which were not reflected in these numbers, must be subtracted from simulated profits. Also, better simulated results could have been obtained using daily instead of weekly data sampling.

Chapter 3

Finding a Technical Market Indicator That Is Right for You

There are hundreds of Technical Market Indicators, trading systems, investment timing models, and other strategies. Some are effective, while others are not. How can we tell the difference? How can we select a method without risking capital? How and when might we use the best indicators? How can we really make a system our own? How can we avoid common mistakes? How can we identify and steer clear of flawed ideas? How can we separate the wheat from the chaff, fact from fiction, myth from reality? How can we find appropriate tools for different market environments and different investment objectives?

The best answer to all these questions is walk-forward simulation based on actual historical market data. (See Chapter 2.) With simulation, we can develop and test a precise set of trading rules to deal with all kinds of market behavior–rules that leave no room for uncertainty or confusion. We can find specific decision rules that would have maximized profit and minimized risk of significant loss in the past. By testing our ideas in all kinds of market conditions, we can uncover the vitally important information we need about the nature of markets and trading methods. And with this knowledge, we can trade with confidence. Confidence makes the difference in how we are able to trade, not as weak hands, battered about by our own very human emotions of greed and fear, but as strong hands, acting boldly and calmly based on solid knowledge of verifiable facts established on actual market behavior.

Six Common Errors to Avoid

Many investment ideas are logically flawed from their conception. Logic and common sense can save time and effort. There are six common errors that can be easily avoided.

1. Avoid indicators that signal twice based on the same data, once when new data enters the calculation and once again when that same data drops out of

the moving window of the calculation period. Stochastics, Rate-of-Change, Momentum, even Simple Moving Averages (particularly the fast, sensitive ones) all signal twice, particularly when the data entering and exiting the moving time window represents a big change. Obviously, the market does not care about our so-called take-away number, or drop-off number, the stale data being passed by the moving time window. The market looks ahead, not behind. Any indicator that responds to stale data from the past will introduce random errors into our analysis. We need to be independent of old data and on the forward edge with fresh data representing the latest realities in the marketplace.

2. Be aware of structural changes in a market over time. In the equity markets, odd-lot trading data has not been the same since options became popular. Also, Specialist and Member Short Sales ratios do not match the levels of several years ago. There are substantially greater numbers of issues traded today than there were several decades ago, destroying the comparability over time of the advance-decline line, new highs-new lows and volume. This data needs to be statistically normalized, but all too commonly it is not. Rather than working with absolute indicator levels, try reworking the indicator into various ratios, such as advances minus declines divided by total issues traded. Also, try a deviation from trend ratio: divide the current indicator level by its own trailing 1-year or half-year moving average. Often, these variations will normalize an indicator so that it appears more stable over time.
3. Avoid working with dollars or points after a big price move. Use percentage changes instead. For example, 100-point price movements in a single day for the Dow-Jones Industrial Average have been quite common since 1997, but 100-point days were totally unheard of 10 years previous, before 1987. It would be a serious mistake to compare Momentum (generally defined as today's close *minus* the close *n*-days ago) levels now to Momentum levels years ago when the Dow was much lower. They are not comparable. Of course momentum readings are more extreme now, both higher and lower, expressed in price or index points, because absolute price index levels are so much higher. Working with dollar or point differences, rather than with ratios or percentages, destroys comparability over time, making it impossible to compare accurately today's behavior with past behavior.
4. Avoid too much complexity and curve fitting. A model with many parts, several different types of data, and several different methods of calculation is hard, if not impossible, to comprehend. If we cannot comprehend our indicator, we will not be confident enough to execute its signals in times of uncertainty, confusion, anxiety, and high stress. By adding curve fitting on top

of complexity, the practical value of any statistical model will collapse. Overly complex and overly processed models have poor records in real time.

5. Do not expect experience to be a good or kind teacher. In the market, the old saying, "Experience is the best teacher," is not true. Experience is knowledge learned too late. Experience is what you get when you don't get what you want. Learning from actual experience has substantial disadvantages. Experience is too often unsystematic, even haphazard, and all but impossible to learn from. Without sufficient knowledge going in, unstructured trading can be overwhelmingly confusing in real-time, with ever-changing distractions, including events, opinions, and moment to moment price fluctuations. Making matters worse, our own emotional reactions color and distort our perceptions of objective reality. Even if we could learn from experience, experience takes forever. It takes too many years to see the markets in all their many phases. At best, experience is an inefficient way to collect data and formulate decision rules. Wrong decisions in trading and investing can be extremely expensive. It is far less costly to simulate experience through historical back-testing than to attempt to acquire experience slowly and painfully in real-time.
6. Avoid "Trader's Hell." We must make certain than our trading rules cover all bases, leaving no gaps that can turn into yawning chasms of uncertainty, indecision, hesitation, and dysfunctional emotional excesses. We need to know at all times exactly what we must do to take the kind of timely and effective actions that lead to success in trading and investing.

Do Your Own Work: Generate Your Own Decisions Based on What You Know

Take the time to determine appropriate, realistic objectives that are right for you. One size does not fit all. The best trading system for a well-capitalized, unleveraged long-term investor seeking to maximize profits from riding long-term trends is very different from the best trading system for an undercapitalized, highly leveraged speculator hoping to scalp modest profits with minimal risk. The trend-following big investor can tolerate the significant equity drawdowns associated with Secondary Reactions against the long-term Major Trend. On the other hand, the small trader trying to profit from the waves and ripples in prices needs a sensitive, short-term trading system that tightly controls equity drawdowns while offering consistent profitability.

Both big investors and small traders need to take the real costs of trading into account. Sophisticated big investors try to keep costs down by not trying to catch every wave. Many try to minimize their trading. They worry about *market impact,* when the size of their transactions moves prices away from them. Impact can be minimized by timing transactions contrary to the minor ripples: buying dips when most traders are cutting losses and dumping positions, and selling rallies when many traders are chasing prices up with market orders to buy. Trading the same way as the majority, *trend chasing,* assures the worst fills possible.

For the novice small trader, transactions costs come as a big shock—beginners cannot possibly imagine how seemingly small commissions and slippage can eat up equity. We all must learn to control our trading, not to overtrade, to wait for opportunities, and not to act impulsively at the wrong time. A thorough understanding of trading systems, real-time executions, and computer simulation can provide the facts needed by both investors and traders.

The long-term trend follower is well equipped to capitalize on big trends that develop gradually over substantial periods of time. This is not such a hard thing to do, since the Major Trend is usually obvious to anyone with a long-term chart and a good basic book on technical analysis.

The short-term trader has more of a challenge. He is subject to the sudden shifts in crowd psychology that frequently occur, seemingly for no reason. He also will be caught by unforeseeable information events, changing expectations, and rumors. These strike without warning, making the results of trading systems tailored to the very short-term hit-and-miss.

Because profits can vanish swiftly in the short-term, the short-term trader tends to take profits quickly before they go away. It feels good to be right and ring the cash register. But that cuts the probability of big gains. On the other hand, the deep-seated psychological drive not to be wrong, and to fall into denial when we are wrong, too often tends to make short-term discretionary traders carry losing positions longer than they should. As a rule of thumb, tolerated losses only get worse. And the longer the losses are tolerated, the worse they get.

Short-term trading offers challenge and action and a chance to make something from practically nothing, quickly. Therefore, there will always be a market for short-term trading systems.

If we want to be successful, we must study and learn and do our own work. We cannot simply buy someone else's black box system (a system in which the decision rules are not disclosed) because we cannot develop enough confidence in it to follow it when uncertainty, stress, and losses mount. Unless we thoroughly understand and believe in it, the best black box trading system in the world is of little value to us. In contrast, a system that we deeply understand and have tested ourselves over substantial actual history would be much more useful to us, even if it is actually less effective than another system that we do not thoroughly understand and believe in. Confidence makes the difference.

Too many investors have wasted fortunes and years of time being battered about by the markets while using vaguely defined notions they merely heard or read somewhere but never tested themselves. They eventually quit in confusion and defeat, blaming everyone but themselves, and often after losing most of their capital. The cause of their problems cannot even be identified in hindsight because of their haphazard decision-making process. They learn nothing from their experience.

To function effectively on the firing line, amid all the confusion and noise, we must generate our own plan of action while shutting out all external opinions, advice, rumors, news reports, and other harmful noise. When we feel like asking someone else what is going on or what we should do, that is a good indication that we have become confused and lost our discipline. We must immediately close out our positions and systematically analyze what has gone wrong. Unless we internalize our trading strategy based on well-tested Technical Market Indicator signals, our strategy does not really belong to us, and it will not be there for us when we need it.

Walk-forward historical simulation and systematic execution of tested Technical Market Indicator signals offer an orderly way to quantify and apply the lessons given by actual past market behavior. We know precisely what would have worked and what would not have worked. We can move forward into the future with confidence based on this knowledge.

For this *Encyclopedia of Technical Market Indicators,* Second Edition, we tested 127 technical indicators, on a comparable basis, over all available historical data. Our test results are offered as a preliminary screen for your own research. The following table should help you find Technical Market Indicators that are right for you.

Comparably Measured Technical Market Indicators

	Versus Buy & Hold	*Annual Relative Advantage*	*L&S % Win*	*Short % Win*	*Trades per Year*	*Profit Loss Index*
Absolute Breadth Index	35.13	0.00	56.42	N / A	27.23	34.49
Accumulation/Distribution (AD)	327898.38	4554.84	49.00	41.27	86.05	10.81
Accumulation Swing Index (ASI)	429129.83	5961.04	44.99	37.33	74.22	23.58
Advance-Decline Line, A-D Line	3075777.61	45084.89	51.36	43.28	104.67	31.80
Advance-Decline Non-Cumulative (Hughes)	4624210.92	67454.12	50.90	43.15	102.65	100.00
Percentage Hughes AD Oscillator with 8 Parameters	12800398.17	186721.50	53.57	45.62	148.79	32.71
Advance/Decline Ratio	7055813.92	102924.31	51.36	43.17	105.30	31.57
Advisory Sentiment Index	70.27	1.85	47.54	45.90	3.21	87.10
Arms' Ease of Movement Value (EMV)	4944.66	68.69	43.43	35.32	57.74	15.60
Arms' Short-Term Trading Index (TRIN, MKDS)	80.47	4.94	79.79	74.47	11.55	88.43
Aroon, Aroon Oscillator	55.89	0.78	44.12	N / A	35.42	25.37
Aroon 270	5.20	0.07	63.33	N / A	0.42	91.88
Bollinger Bands	−35.10	−1.88	88.61	N / A	4.24	80.62
Breadth A/D Indicator: Breadth Thrust	17122.14	249.76	52.26	44.19	104.39	23.36
Buy-and-Hold Strategy: the Passive Strategy	0.00	0.00	N / A	N / A	0.00	100.00
Call-Put Dollar Value Flow Line (CPFL)	−12.94	−0.53	100.00	N / A	0.12	100.00
Call-Put Dollar Value Ratio	101.65	5.95	60.00	61.90	2.40	81.91
Call-Put Premium Ratio	41.17	2.10	66.67	50.00	0.61	96.76
Call-Put Volume Ratio	116.41	4.79	58.13	49.89	74.84	24.74
Chande Momentum Oscillator (CMO)	−26.67	−1.43	77.46	N / A	11.40	60.26
Commodity Channel Index (CCI)	136.42	1.90	43.31	38.99	29.24	16.18
Commodity Channel Index Crossing Zero: Zero CCI	26967.33	374.60	46.83	38.57	101.21	24.88
Coppock Curve (Coppock Guide)	−11.80	−0.12	51.22	N / A	0.81	75.74
Smoothed Momentum Slope Indicator	263.49	2.60	62.50	N / A	0.63	85.06
Days of the Month	650.85	6.45	61.63	N / A	11.93	47.24
Days of the Month and the Months of the Year	3013.58	29.85	67.68	56.00	1.97	88.53
Days of the Week	239.05	4.93	56.82	N / A	50.16	15.58
Demand Index (DI)	1728.18	24.01	34.32	28.27	25.25	19.58
Directional Movement Index	118.32	1.64	44.43	38.92	52.65	15.16
Double Exponential Moving Averages (DEMA)	−47.24	−2.53	46.74	N / A	56.50	31.95

Dow Theory	3920.98	38.75	87.10	63.33	0.60	68.28
Dow Theory: 90-Day Price Channels	114.21	1.13	61.82	N / A	0.54	88.31
Dow Theory: 8 Different Price Channels	5637.10	55.71	54.84	53.85	1.26	83.10
Dow Theory: using 3-day EMA	2349788.11	23220.51	44.36	36.93	57.47	20.30
Envelopes, Moving Average Envelopes	3.35	0.18	84.09	N / A	4.72	85.56
Exponential Moving Average (120 days)	2430.53	23.98	25.59	17.97	10.87	33.76
Exponential Moving Average (5 days)	77865725.02	766849.86	42.28	34.38	62.10	22.27
General Motors as a Market Bellwether Stock	−55.05	−2.66	51.45	N / A	48.16	26.91
Haurlan Index	5699.64	83.14	54.53	34.21	70.19	22.38
Herrick Payoff Index	−57.00	−3.05	47.92	N / A	41.16	32.84
Indicator Seasons, Colby's Variation	17919.98	176.82	49.14	40.97	44.26	17.73
Indicator Seasons, Colby's—Optimized	8348307.47	82374.96	51.46	43.36	85.39	23.60
Insiders' Sell/Buy Ratio	29.22	0.98	76.74	N / A	1.44	94.37
Keltner Channel with EMA filter	−20.06	−0.98	77.00	60.00	11.75	64.97
Key Reversal Day	−35.56	−1.73	70.97	N / A	1.51	90.39
KST (Know Sure Thing)	−57.89	−0.57	60.00	N / A	0.39	83.34
KST with 33% faster parameters	63.64	0.63	58.93	N / A	0.55	76.57
Linear Regression Line, 5-days	−26.04	−1.39	49.38	N / A	55.71	34.74
Linear Regression Slope, 244 days	−49.19	−2.63	100.00	N / A	0.27	100.00
Lowry's Buying Power Minus Selling Pressure	1216146.87	19916.26	49.88	45.02	110.10	28.56
Lowry's Short-term Buying Power	1220638.12	19989.81	50.73	46.37	108.15	26.04
Margin Debt Overbought/Oversold Bracket Rule	111.56	3.20	100.00	66.67	0.20	98.71
Margin Debt crosses trailing 13-month EMA	−43.71	−1.24	69.23	N / A	0.37	96.56
McClellan Oscillator Crossing Zero, Long and Short	7087.84	103.39	47.45	34.66	30.88	30.28
McClellan Summation Crossing Zero, Long Only	−27.13	−0.40	44.09	N / A	1.36	77.99
McClellan Summation Index Direction, Long and Short	7129.19	103.99	47.45	34.75	30.88	30.28
Member Short Ratio (Envelope, 25 EMA & 10%)	0.05	0.00	80.33	N / A	1.11	96.58
Months of the Year (a seasonal strategy)	643.83	6.39	64.65	56.00	1.97	77.25
Moving Average Convergence-Divergence (MACD)	0.99	0.01	58.62	N / A	0.40	86.58
Multiple Time Frame Analysis (10, 50, 200)	14324.15	141.18	38.36	31.57	24.29	23.46
Negative Volume Index (NVI)	−32.31	−0.45	46.27	N / A	30.74	32.62
New Highs-New Lows	960.51	15.82	43.89	39.81	24.24	34.79
(New Highs-New Lows) / Total Issues Traded	382.20	6.29	48.51	36.57	4.41	71.78
New Highs/Total Issues Traded >< 1.55%	78.20	1.29	42.20	39.11	28.72	21.48

Continued

Comparably Measured Technical Market Indicators—*Continued*

	Versus Buy & Hold	*Annual Relative Advantage*	*L&S % Win*	*Short % Win*	*Trades per Year*	*Profit Loss Index*
New Lows/Total Issues Traded <> 3.53%	2002.46	32.97	43.98	41.36	18.87	52.58
Ninety Percent Days, Nine to One Days	−53.17	−1.43	57.89	N / A	1.02	84.77
Number of Advancing Issues	2515162.84	36689.09	54.08	44.84	129.85	23.29
Number of Declining Issues	1122877.16	16379.59	53.47	46.18	141.44	18.34
Odd Lot Sales / Purchases	31.07	0.80	55.34	N / A	43.18	25.68
Odd Lot Short Ratio	221.06	5.66	51.06	49.18	109.15	12.34
Open Interest	16.85	0.90	65.00	50.31	17.05	53.61
Open Interest Trend-following Strategy	20.27	1.08	78.18	56.36	5.88	72.42
Parabolic Time/Price System (Contrary)	20.19	1.06	76.19	59.10	35.12	42.53
Percentage 30-week Simple Moving Averages	467.45	13.36	58.06	50.54	5.32	78.41
Percentage 10-week Simple Moving Averages	245.24	7.01	57.53	46.58	4.17	59.39
Pivot Point Reverse Trading System	13463.27	133.22	43.97	36.86	68.24	22.28
Positive Volume Index VS 1-year EMA	44.08	0.61	33.33	N / A	1.50	75.93
Presidential Election Cycle	−73.63	−1.07	94.12	N / A	0.25	99.30
Price Channel Trading Range Breakout Rule	45.96	2.47	38.46	30.77	2.80	81.70
Price Oscillators: Moving Average Oscillators	331.86	3.28	29.94	N / A	1.75	67.41
Projection Bands	−21.99	−1.18	77.24	N / A	6.58	72.36
Projection Oscillator	16.57	0.89	76.64	N / A	11.45	73.16
Public Short Ratio	123.20	2.24	83.33	72.22	0.65	95.25
Public/Specialist Short Ratio	61.59	1.12	100.00	80.00	0.18	99.70
Put/Call Premium Ratio	143.47	6.73	76.67	55.00	5.63	69.28
Put/Call Volume Ratio Jump Strategy	141.37	6.14	89.47	90.00	1.69	98.65
Qstick 1, Trend-following	−78.32	−4.19	49.19	N / A	75.61	22.47
Qstick 9, Counter-trend	4.33	0.23	74.04	N / A	19.59	67.81
R-squared	−47.00	−2.52	100.00	N / A	0.27	100.00
Random Walk Index (RWI)	−65.05	−3.48	53.19	N / A	2.52	74.81
The Range Indicator (TRI)	−49.82	−2.67	33.33	N / A	1.28	92.55
Rate of Change, 18 weeks	305.37	3.02	43.06	N / A	2.07	60.43
Relative Strength Index (RSI)	−31.39	−1.68	85.94	N / A	6.86	78.13
Relative Volatility Index (RVI)	1.33	0.07	100.00	0.00	0.25	98.67

Schultz Advances/Total Issues Traded (A/T)	3779846.12	55137.23	53.56	43.26	117.22	29.55
Short Interest Ratio	−57.89	−0.84	72.97	N / A	1.07	90.38
Sign of the Bear	83908.87	1223.99	42.90	45.00	54.00	30.67
Simple Moving Average (126-days)	2022.54	19.96	24.83	16.93	8.74	32.96
Specialist Short Ratio	−7.43	−0.14	100.00	N / A	0.15	100.00
STIX: The Polymetric Short-term Indicator	1814.19	26.46	40.78	32.42	22.32	26.99
Stochastics (7 days, 3 SMA, B 30, S 70)	52.12	2.55	77.29	63.97	26.63	42.84
Stochastics with EMA Filter	3.32	0.16	78.13	45.10	13.44	64.18
TICK (Crossing 11-day EMA)	12905.09	368.28	51.88	46.50	119.92	18.28
Total Issues Traded (270-day EMA)	79.15	1.15	54.28	N / A	27.07	52.04
Triple EMA (TEMA), 6-days	−21.19	−1.13	46.97	N / A	47.58	36.76
TRIX (triple exponential smoothing)	−32.86	−1.76	48.10	N / A	56.13	35.01
25-Day Plurality Index	−93.32	−1.36	92.86	N / A	0.20	97.33
25-Day Plurality with Bollinger Bands (324, 2sd)	45.61	0.67	93.33	N / A	0.22	99.80
Ultimate Oscillator	31.20	1.67	96.00	57.14	2.46	93.20
Unchanged Issues Index	−25.01	−0.36	59.38	48.45	18.83	25.06
Upside/Downside Ratio	26.91	1.65	54.72	40.38	130.27	20.30
Volatility, CBOE Volatility Index (VIX)	−46.65	−3.17	63.43	N / A	29.40	46.79
Volatility & Price Channel	109.29	5.72	75.00	50.00	1.68	80.04
Volume	177.21	2.47	51.84	44.55	54.40	7.63
Volume Acceleration	1767385.88	24350.59	52.37	46.96	101.02	23.20
Volume Accumulation Oscillator	457807.44	6307.55	49.22	41.96	97.46	10.39
Volume: Cumulative Volume Index	66357.02	1789.85	47.88	45.49	101.74	28.93
Volume: Klinger Oscillator (KO)	−74.73	−3.99	46.30	N / A	36.14	27.18
Volume: On-Balance Volume (OBV)	1165062.91	16051.94	43.47	35.67	104.21	17.76
Volume * Price Momentum Oscillator (V*PMO)	1495436.39	20603.74	44.05	35.66	69.00	19.15
Volume Reversal	90.06	1.24	45.80	35.88	40.69	4.03
Volume: Williams' Variable Accumulation Distribution	515047.90	7096.20	44.07	35.61	67.79	10.86
Weighted Moving Average (6-days)	51712052.38	510822.71	42.63	34.34	62.02	18.41

Chapter 4

What Others Say about Technical Market Indicators, Models, and Trading Systems

A Useful Guide to Decision Making: Bierman, Bonini, and Hausman

The following general process of finding a mathematical solution is common to all types of decision-making situations:

1. Establish the criterion to be used (for example, maximize profits relative to risks).
2. Select a set of alternatives for consideration.
3. Determine the model to be used and the values of the parameters of the process.
4. Determine which alternative optimizes the criterion established in Step 1.

Critical variables are combined in a logical manner to form a model of the actual problem. A model is a simplified representation of an empirical situation. Ideally, it strips a natural phenomenon of its bewildering complexity and duplicates the essential behavior of the natural phenomenon with a few variables, simply related. The simpler the model, the better it is, as long as the model serves as a reasonably reliable counterpart of the empirical problem. A simple model is:

- Economical of time and thought.
- Readily understood by the decision maker.
- Capable of being modified quickly and effectively when necessary.

The object is not to construct a model that is as close as possible to reality in every respect. Such a model would require an excessive length of time to construct, and then it might be beyond human comprehension. Rather, we want the simplest model that predicts outcomes reasonably well and is consistent with effective action.

If our variables can be quantified, then mathematics facilitates the decision-making process. Mathematics is an inherently rigorous discipline that ensures an orderly procedure. We must be specific about what variables we select and what relationships we assume to exist among them. Mathematics is a powerful technique for relating variables and for deriving logical conclusions from given premises. Mathematics and computers make it possible to handle problems of great complexity.

Solving a model means obtaining logical conclusions. If the model is designed and solved properly, such conclusions ought to be a useful guide to decision making.

Adapted with permission of the publisher from Bierman, Bonini, and Hausman, *Quantitative Analysis for Business Decisions,* 7th Edition, Richard D. Irwin, Inc., Homewood, IL 60430, 1986, pages 4–19.

Effective Application of Pattern Recognition Decision Rules: Ted C. Earle

In finance and economics, controlled experimental data cannot be generated in a laboratory, and formal theoretical models have not proved to be effective for practical investment application. Therefore, our only practical alternative for developing useable investment decision rules is historical data testing using statistical standards for validation. Empirical modeling applies scientific methods to investment decision making. We need not be concerned about complex causes and effects; we simply test the statistical correlation between observed events. With empirical modeling, we identify events that are related to other events in a way that makes sense and is effective for practical investment application.

Modeling with pattern recognition decision rules is a practical application of empirical modeling:

- We relate patterns in an indicator data series to patterns in a forecast data series.
- We look for quantifiable correlation using time series data from the past.
- We discover patterns by observing changes in the indicator data series that occur at about the same time as the events that we want to predict.
- We test any indicator data that we think might be reasonably relevant.
- We test our decision rules over long histories, so that we can ascertain statistical validity to accept or reject indicators.
- We base our acceptance criteria on the degree of statistical reliability. When a pattern recognition decision rule tested over a sufficiently long period of time consistently yields statistically significant results, it earns our confidence.

We need to define our decision rules precisely, so that they may be applied unambiguously by any user. Empirical models need to be objective, so that results can be duplicated independently when the decision rules are applied to the same historical time series data.

There are six phases of research that are general to all types of mathematical modeling:

1. Formulating the problem.
2. Collecting the data series to be used for identifying patterns.
3. Developing decision rules to identify patterns in the indicator series.
4. Testing decision rules and evaluating the predictive results on the forecast series.
5. Establishing control over the use of the decision rules.
6. Proceeding to implement the actual use of the decision rules.

Each of these six phases consists of several steps that are subject to frequent reevaluation and reworking as our research progresses. In investing, there are an infinite number of relationships from which to choose. We narrow down relationships to test based on reason and common sense. Our research process is facilitated by experience with the empirical approach, familiarity with the variables, and the ability to identify odd or unexpected quirks in the data. We adapt future testing in light of feedback from our past test results.

Establishing controls over the use of the decision rules is necessary. No matter how well rules may work on historical data, rules may not work exactly the same way in the future. Relationships between variables are subject to change without notice. Therefore, we should establish guidelines in advance to tell us what to do in the event that our decision rules do not work as expected. These guidelines should cover protective closing of open positions whenever a specified, predetermined percentage loss is attained. Also, a pre-specified number of consecutive losing trades might trigger suspension of our decision rules until we can revise them to work successfully with both the original data and the new data.

Ted C. Earle, editor of Market Timing Report (P.O. Box 225, Tucson, AZ 85702), holds advanced degrees in engineering and finance, and he approaches investment decision making with a highly disciplined, scientific perspective. Earle's methods seem to be working, for he has been named the most accurate market analyst in the U.S. by Timer Digest (Fort Lauderdale, FL). Earle's thoughts were adapted with permission of the publisher from Earle's extensive article "Modeling with Pattern Recognition Decision Rules," *Technical Analysis of Stocks & Commodities,* April 1986, p. 30-39, www.traders.com.

The Advantages of Developing Your Own Trading System: Joe Krutsinger

A trading system must be adapted to the individual objectives of each trader. It must be designed with simplicity, so that we can understand exactly how it operates. It must make sense to us, so that we can be comfortable with it. It must have a basic logic that fits our convictions about how the markets work. It must fit our psychological needs, temperament, preferences, reward/risk comfort levels, and capital and time constraints. It must offer trading frequency, or lack thereof, that is comfortable for us.

Each individual must decide what feels best. No one cares more for our money and personal comfort than we do, so we must depend on ourselves to design a trading system custom fitted to our personal needs. If we skip this step, we will not be able to execute a trading system consistently without second-guessing.

Joe Krutsinger shares many practical insights in his book, *The Trading Systems Toolkit, How to Build, Test and Apply Money-Making Stock and Futures Trading Systems,* Probus Publishing Company, Chicago, Illinois, 1994, 246 pages. Adapted with permission of the publisher.

Keep It Simple and Do Adequate Testing: Robert C. Pelletier

Be aware of the concept of loss of freedom in statistical testing and model building. Each additional parameter introduced into a model represents a measure of control that detracts from the predictive reliability of the model with unseen data. The greater the imposition of constraints (indicator signals), the less predictive reliability of the results.

Test the association present in the independent variables chosen. A well-designed statistical experiment will test for joint correlation. It will exclude redundant variables in order to avoid overstating results. The best trading models use a very low number of variables, no more than two to five.

A timing model should be tested over a long sample database, long enough to allow a minimum of 30 trades, thus approaching normality according to the Central Limit Theorem. The test period should include an integer multiple of a full low frequency cycle in order to eliminate a buy or sell bias. For example, given the well-known 4-year stock market cycle, the analyst should test at least eight years of data (twice the cycle length) in order to eliminate performance bias. Models developed over shorter test periods or with more than five parameters are not trustworthy.

Robert C. Pelletier, a former professional statistician, is president of Commodity Systems, Inc., 200 West Palmetto Park Road, Boca Raton, FL 33432, www.csidata.com. His company sells current and historical data useful for research, and his data has gained recognition for its accuracy. Adapted with permission of the publisher, CSI News Journal, February, 1986.

The Cells Method of Indicator Evaluation: David R. Aronson

The cells method for evaluating the utility of technical indicators is different from and complementary to the more common signal event method, which evaluates the net profit or loss that would have resulted over past data had we acted on the buy and sell signals. The cells method ranks and sorts historical data into *cells* (also known as *bins* or *ranges*) in such a way that observations with similar indicator readings will be grouped together. Sorting observations into a typical ten cells, for example, the top two cells will contain 20% of the total number of observations, those with the highest indicator readings; the middle six cells will contain 60% of the total number of observations; and the lowest two cells will contain 20% of the total number of the observations, those with the lowest indicator readings.

The cells method focuses directly on an indicator's ability to forecast future market changes rather than the profitability of trading signals derived from the indicator. Second, the cells method evaluates the predictive information content of an indicator over its entire range of possible values rather than only at "signal event" points. Third, no buy/sell rules need to be defined to conduct cells method analysis. This avoids the problem of overly complex rules. Fourth, since our analysis is no longer limited to specific action points, we have a larger sample of data points. Fifth, the indicator is evaluated with respect to a specific prediction horizon. For example, an indicator may be useful in forecasting the trend over the next 50 days, but useless for purposes of predicting it over the next 10 days. The cells method will reveal this. Typically, the analyst will examine an indicator with respect to a number of different horizons during the same analysis (for example, over the next 10, 20, 60, 120, and 250 days.)

The cells method determines the predictive power of the indicator by measuring the degree of association between the indicator's current level and the subsequent percentage change in the market. In other words, it discovers to what degree the market's future change depends upon or is predicted from the current level of the indicator.

The cells method rates the strength of this dependence on a continuous scale anywhere from 0% to 100%. A reading of 100% would imply the ability to predict perfectly, while 0% indicates a total lack of predictive information. This rating is called *variance reduction.*

Financial markets are too complex and too subject to random shocks to permit a single indicator to contain high degrees of predictive power. Indicators typically score in the range of 0% to 10%, with many more scoring closer to zero than to 10. Achieving higher levels of variance reduction requires the proper integration of several complementary indicators into a multivariate model.

A prime benefit of the cells method is that it permits a ranked comparison of many indicators with respect to specific time horizons. This is important as the market analyst often has a whole library of indicators but lacks an objective way of comparing predictive power for short-term, intermediate-term, and long-term forecasting.

To illustrate how the cells method is performed, we choose the New York Stock Exchange smoothed advance/decline ratio (SADR). The ratio is defined as the *net difference between the number of stocks advancing and the number of stocks declining divided by total issues traded.* We apply a 10-day exponential moving average to the erratic daily ratio. We select the 60-day future percent change in the Standard & Poor's

500 Index (S&P 500) for our prediction horizon, our dependent variable. In the parlance of statistical data analysis, this future change in the S&P 500 is known as the *dependent variable.* The implication of the word *dependent* is that the value of this variable depends to some degree on the current value of the indicator. The variance reduction rating provided by the cells method measures the strength of this dependence.

Variance reduction is determined statistically from historical data. We sampled 5,354 days of historical data. Each of these past 5,354 observations was characterized by two pieces of information: the value of the SADR indicator on the given day and the value of the percent change in the S&P 500 over the following 60 days.

Central to the cells method is the grouping of observations with similar indicator values into bins. There are an almost unlimited number of ways of grouping data, but one common way is based on deciles. Decile grouping creates 10 equally populated cells, with 10% of the population in each cell. Since the number of cells created can influence the results of the analysis, it is recommended that a number of different cell structures be tried. Typically, the strongest indicators will rank well for a variety of cell resolutions.

The grouping process begins by ranking all 5,354 days according to their SADR values. Those days in the top decile (the 535 days with the highest SADR values) are placed in cell 10. Of the remaining 4,819 cases, those 535 with the next highest SADR readings are placed in cell 9. Cell 8 gets the third highest SADR group. The process of grouping continues until the 535 observations with the lowest SADR reading are placed in cell 1.

After all 5,354 observations have been placed in their proper cells based on the associated SADR value, the cells method turns its attention to the dependent variable, the market's future percentage change. First, a "grand sample" dependent variable average for all 5,354 observations is calculated. For the data set used in this analysis, for all 5,354 cases, the average 60-day percent change for the S&P 500 was +1.85%. This positive value merely reflects the long-term upward trend in stock prices since 1945.

It so happens that this grand sample average can serve as the basis of a simplistic type of forecast, or *naïve prediction,* which on any given day is history's best estimate of what the market is likely to do over the next 60 days.

Next, the dependent variable average in each individual cell is calculated. In other words, an average dependent variable for just the 535 cases in cell 10 is calculated. The same is done for cell 9, cell 8, and so on until an average dependent variable has been computed for each cell.

The cases falling into cell 10 had an average dependent variable of +3.22%. This means that for all 535 cases qualifying for cell 10, the average 60-day future change in the S&P 500 was +3.22%. The cell dependent variable can serve as the basis for a conditional forecast, which is conditioned on information other than the grand dependent variable average. In this case, the conditional forecast of +3.22% is higher than the naïve forecast, which was +1.85%, the grand dependent variable average.

Whether or not conditional forecast is truly better than the naïve forecast is determined by the variance reduction measure. A naïve forecast is often more accurate than one based on an indicator, in which case the variance reduction is zero or a negative number. *Variance reduction is the degree to which the conditional prediction is less erroneous than the naïve forecast.* The higher the variance reduction, the higher the predictive information content will be. Variance reduction measures indicate how much less error-prone our predictions will be when using the dependent variable average of each decile cell, as compared to the naïve forecast. *The definition of an indicator with predictive information is one that can provide more accurate forecasts than the naïve forecast.*

Care must be taken to guard against accidental variance reduction, which can be achieved by chance. The larger the number of indicators being tested, the greater this risk. Cross-validation and significance testing can minimize this risk.

Cross-validation involves breaking the data up into two independent sets for learning and testing. The learning set is used to derive the cell dependent variable values. These values are then used to predict on the independent test set. In other words, we require that the predictive power be found in two independent sets of data. Thus, indicators that look good by chance on one set of data will be revealed as bogus when they fail to predict well on the test set.

Despite the inherent rigor of the cross-validation method, there is still a small probability of a bogus indicator doing well in both test and learning sets. So, as an additional form of insurance, the variance reduction achieved by an indicator must exceed a threshold of significance. The threshold is derived by a complex statistical theory that calculates the amount of variance reduction that can be achieved by a useless indicator by chance alone 5% of the time. Indicators that can pass these two tests are likely to contain valid predictive information.

Informational synergy, when indicators are permitted to act in concert, can be significant. Indicators that show no predictive power individually can, when properly combined, demonstrate a high level of predictive power. An entire branch of data analysis, known as *multivariate analysis,* is devoted to the discovery of such effects. Potential indicators can easily number in the thousands, and the process of reducing the candidate indicators to a manageable number is referred to as *feature selection.*

Raden Research Group's EXAMINE program determined the variance reduction of 284 indicators used to forecast the S&P 500. Each indicator was evaluated with respect to five different dependent variables, which were prediction time horizons: the percent change in the S&P 500 over the following 10, 20, 60, 120, and 250 days. Results of this test suggest the following four indicators may contain useful predictive information: Change in the Slope of the Yield Curve; Smoothed Change in

Long-Term Government Bond Yields; Smoothed Change in 3-Month Treasury Bill Yields; and Smoothed Yield Curve Slope. In addition, Raden's analysis suggests that the longer time horizons were the most predictable: variance reductions of more than 10% were achieved for 120- and 250-day prediction, while the maximum variance reductions achieved for 10- and 20-day prediction was less than 3%. Sixty-day forecasting was the shortest horizon that seemed feasible with individual indicators. While time horizons of less than 120 days are very difficult to forecast with single indicators, multiple indicators may be able to forecast short-term horizons to a meaningful degree. Long-term exponential smoothings (approximately equal to a 150-day simple moving average) produced better results than short-term smoothings in enhancing the information of various indicators, even for short horizon prediction.

Objective evaluation of an indicator's predictive power is crucial to the development of sound prediction systems. This is best left to a computer programmed with rigorous data analysis methods, employing cross-validation and significance testing.

Adapted with permission of the publisher, David R. Aronson, President, Raden Research Group, P.O. Box 1809, Madison Square Station, New York, NY 10159.

Part 2

Technical Market Indicators

Absolute Breadth Index

The Absolute Breadth Index is a modestly effective measure of stock price movement, regardless of direction, up or down. This indicator was developed by Norman Fosback (The Institute for Econometric Research, 3471 North Federal Highway, Fort Lauderdale, FL 33306). The Absolute Breadth Index uses daily New York Stock Exchange data. Weekly data, available in weekend news sources, such as Barron's, might also be employed.

The Absolute Breadth Index is the absolute value of the number of advancing issues minus the number of declining issues. To make the data comparable over time, absolute difference must be divided by total issues traded. There was a 1080% increase in the number of stocks listed on the NYSE over 59 years, from a low of 303 total issues traded on 8/24/40 to a high of 3574 on 11/30/99. Such growth could distort the meaning of a breadth indicator over time, unless the technical analyst normalized the data. We can convert the data to a percentage by dividing the absolute value of the number of net changed issues traded by the total number of issues traded, which is the sum of number of stocks ending the day higher, lower, and unchanged on any given day.

The calculation may be expressed mathematically as follows:

$$N = ((|A - D|)/(A + D + U)) * 100$$

where

N = today's 1-day ratio of the absolute value of net changed issues traded to total issues traded
A = number of advancing issues
D = number of declining issues
U = number of unchanged issues
A + D + U = total number of issues traded each day
* 100 = multiply by one hundred to convert a fractional ratio to a percentage

Absolute value ignores either the plus or minus sign. So, for example, if the day's market movement is moderately bullish (with the number of advancing issues 1500 and the number of declining issues 1300) the Absolute Breadth Index numerator is 200. On the other hand, if the next day's market trend is reversed to moderately bearish (with the number of advancing issues 1300 and the number of declining issues 1500) the Absolute Breadth Index numerator still equals 200, because absolute value only counts the difference, without regard to whether the imbalance is to the advancing or declining side. In contrast, most other breadth indicators assign a plus sign to advances and a minus sign to declines, and they retain the sign.

When the absolute difference between the number of advancing and declining stocks is relatively high, it shows that a large proportion of stocks are changed in price. Fosback's accurate observation behind the Absolute Breadth Index is that the market is more likely to be near a market bottom when the number of changed issues is high. Significant market price lows are often more extreme, more intensely emotional, with most stocks affected by general pessimism, fear, and forced selling to meet margin calls. The prices of most stocks are changing near a market bottom.

Conversely, when the absolute difference between the number of advancing and declining stocks is low, many stocks must be unchanged. Significant market price tops are more likely to be dull, slowly unfolding affairs, as ready cash reserves for buying stock are gradually drawn down until they are eventually exhausted. Stock uptrends begin to stall out on an stock by stock basis, one by one, as the whole topping process stretches out over time. At the end of a long bull market, as the bull becomes increasingly exhausted, demand and supply for stocks eventually reach equilibrium, and so more stocks are likely to end the day unchanged.

Indicator Strategy Example of the Absolute Breadth Index

Based on a 68-year file of daily data for the number of shares advancing, declining and unchanged each day on the New York Stock Exchange and the Dow-Jones Industrial Average since 1932, we found that extreme levels above and below a trailing 2-day exponential moving average would have produced a positive result on a purely mechanical signal basis with no subjectivity, no sophisticated technical analysis, and no judgement:

Enter Long (Buy) at the current daily price close of the Dow-Jones Industrial Average when the current Absolute Breadth Index today is greater than its own previous day's 2-day exponential moving average plus 81%.

Close Long (Sell) at the current daily price close of the Dow-Jones Industrial Average when the current Absolute Breadth Index today is less than its own previous day's 2-day exponential moving average minus 81%.

Sell Short never.

Starting with $100 and reinvesting profits, total net profits for this Absolute Breadth Index trend-following strategy would have been $17,675.90, assuming a fully invested strategy, reinvestment of profits, no transactions costs and no taxes. This would have been 35.13% better than buy-and-hold. Short selling would have lost a small amount. Trading would have been active, with one trade every 13 calendar days. This indicator would have been right more often than it is wrong, with 56.42% winning trades.

Absolute Breadth Index

Total net profit	17675.9	Open position value	−142.58	Net Profit/Buy&Hold %	35.13
Percent gain/loss	17675.9	Annual percent gain/loss	257.65	Annual Net %/B&H %	35.14
Initial investment	100	Interest earned	0		
Current position	Long	Date position entered	9/6/00		
Buy/Hold profit	13080.55	Days in test	25041	# of days per trade	13.41
Buy/Hold pct gain/loss	13080.55	Annual B/H pct gain/loss	190.66		
Total closed trades	1868	Commissions paid	0		
Avg profit per trade	9.54	Avg Win/Avg Loss ratio	1.18		
Total long trades	1868	Total short trades	0	Long Win Trade %	56.42
Winning long trades	1054	Winning short trades	0	Short Win Trade %	#DIV/0!
Total winning trades	1054	Total losing trades	814	Total Win Trade %	56.42
Amount of winning trades	51394.28	Amount of losing trades	−33575.81	Net Profit Margin %	20.97
Average win	48.76	Average loss	−41.25	Average P. Margin %	8.34
Largest win	1661.07	Largest loss	−2749.01	% Net/(Win + Loss)	−24.67
Average length of win	8.79	Average length of loss	8.31	(Win − Loss)/Loss %	5.78
Longest winning trade	64	Longest losing trade	48	(Win − Loss)/Loss %	33.33
Most consecutive wins	11	Most consecutive losses	7	(Win − Loss)/Loss %	57.14
Total bars out	5820	Average length out	3.11		
Longest out period	16				
System close drawdown	−44.08	Profit/Loss index	34.49	% Net Profit/SODD	40099.59
System open drawdown	−44.08	Reward/Risk index	99.75	(Net P. − SODD)/Net P.	99.75
Max open trade drawdown	−2930.24	Buy/Hold index	34.04	% SODD/Net Profit	−0.25

In the Equis MetaStock® "System Report" (profit and loss summary statistics), the *Total net profit* is the sum of profits minus the sum of losses, including open positions marked to the market. In contrast, the *Amount of Winning Trades* is the sum of realized profits (the total of all gains on closed-out trades only, excluding any open positions). Similarly, the *Amount of Losing Trades* is the sum of realized losses (the total of all losses on closed-out trades only, excluding any open positions). *System close drawdown* is the largest decline in the cumulative equity line below the initial investment, based on closed-out positions only. *System open drawdown (SODD)* is the largest decline in the cumulative equity line below the initial investment when a position is open. *Max open trade drawdown* is the largest decline in the cumulative equity line below the trade entry price during the worst single trade. The *Profit/Loss Index* is a complex calculation that relates the Amount of Winning Trades to the Amount of Losing Trades on a scale of −100 (worst possible performance) to +100 (best possible performance), with zero representing profits equal to losses. *Reward/Risk Index* is the Total net profit minus System open drawdown. The resulting difference is then divided by the Total net profit. The *Buy/Hold Index* is the Total net profit minus the buy-and-hold strategy's net profit. The resulting difference is then divided by the buy-and-hold net profit. In this exercise, initial equity is assumed to be $100. Both long and short positions are taken unless otherwise noted. Trades are executed at the closing price on the signal date. Transaction costs, interest expenses, and margins are not included in the statistics.

The Equis International MetaStock® System Testing rules, where the current Absolute Breadth Index is inserted into the data field normally reserved for Volume (V), are written as follows:

Enter long: V > (Ref(Mov(V,opt1,E),−1) + ((opt2/100)) * Ref(Mov(V,opt1,E),−1))

Close long: V < (Ref(Mov(V,opt1,E),−1) − ((opt2/100)) * Ref(Mov(V,opt1,E),−1))

OPT1 Current value: 2

OPT2 Current value: 81

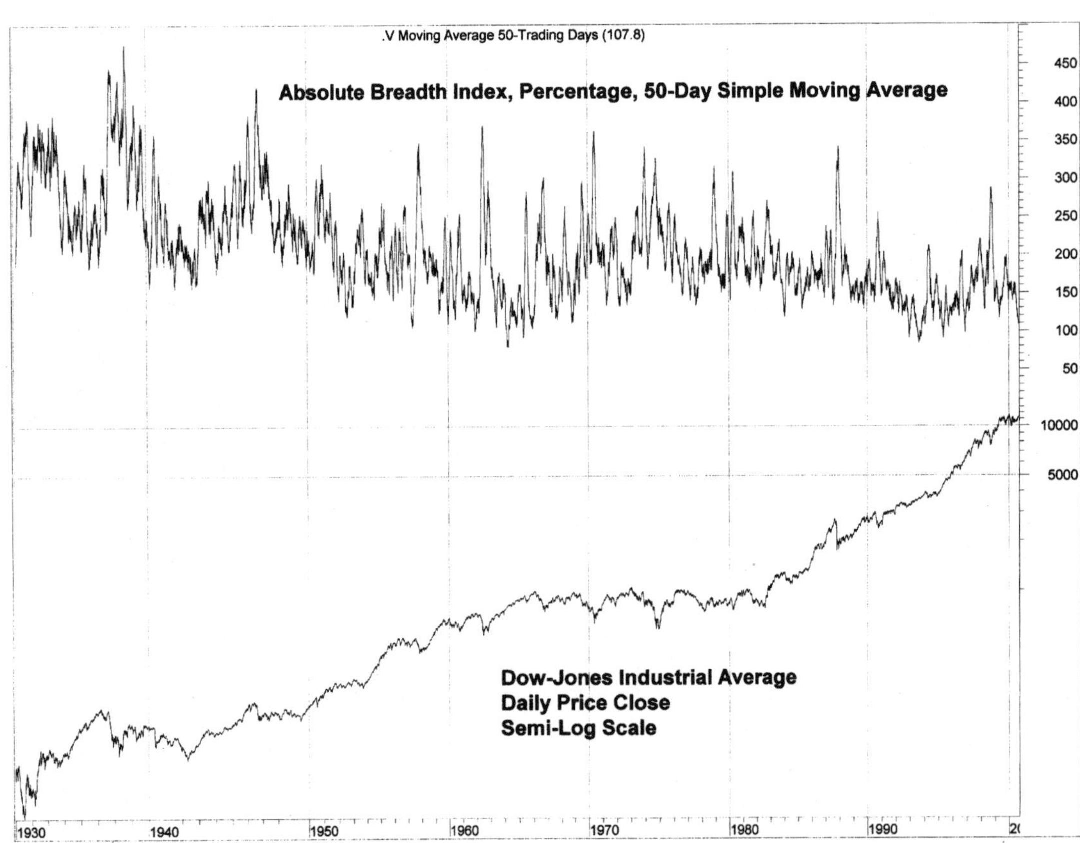

Accumulation/Distribution (AD)

The Accumulation/Distribution (AD) is a variation on the basic theme of On Balance Volume (OBV), but the AD appears to be less effective than OBV. The AD difference is that daily volume is weighted by the position of the closing price relative to the price range. The indicator was developed by Marc Chaikin (177 E. 77th Street, New York, NY 10021), and it is the basis for the Chaikin Oscillator, which measures price-weighted volume momentum.

We illustrate this indicator using daily data, although a similar Accumulation/Distribution line may be calculated on any time frame for which volume and prices (for high, low and last) are available from minutes to months.

The Accumulation/Distribution measures the position of the daily price close within the daily price range, expressed as a fraction of that range. This fraction is multiplied by total daily volume, and gives a quantification of net daily Accumulation (buying pressure identified by a plus sign, +) or Distribution (selling pressure identified by a minus sign, −). These net daily pressures are cumulated into a running total and plotted as a line. A rising trend would be bullish, while a falling trend would be bearish.

Mathematically, Accumulation/Distribution may be expressed as follows:

$$AD = cum((((C - L) - (H - C))/(H - L)) * V)$$

where

AD = the Accumulation/Distribution cumulative running total line.
cum = the abbreviation for "calculate a cumulative running total line."
C = the daily closing price.
H = the daily high price.
L = the daily low price.
V = the daily total volume.

Standard technical analysis tools may be used on the cumulative Accumulation/Distribution line, including trendlines, recognition of higher highs and lower lows, and divergence analysis as compared to the plain price chart. Accumulation/Distribution could also be compared to its own trailing moving average to generate buy and sell signals.

Indicator Strategy Example for Cumulative Accumulation/Distribution

Historical data shows that the Accumulation/Distribution used to be an effective indicator on both the long and short sides, but particularly on the long side. Based on the daily prices for the Dow-Jones Industrial Average for 72 years from 1928 to 2000,

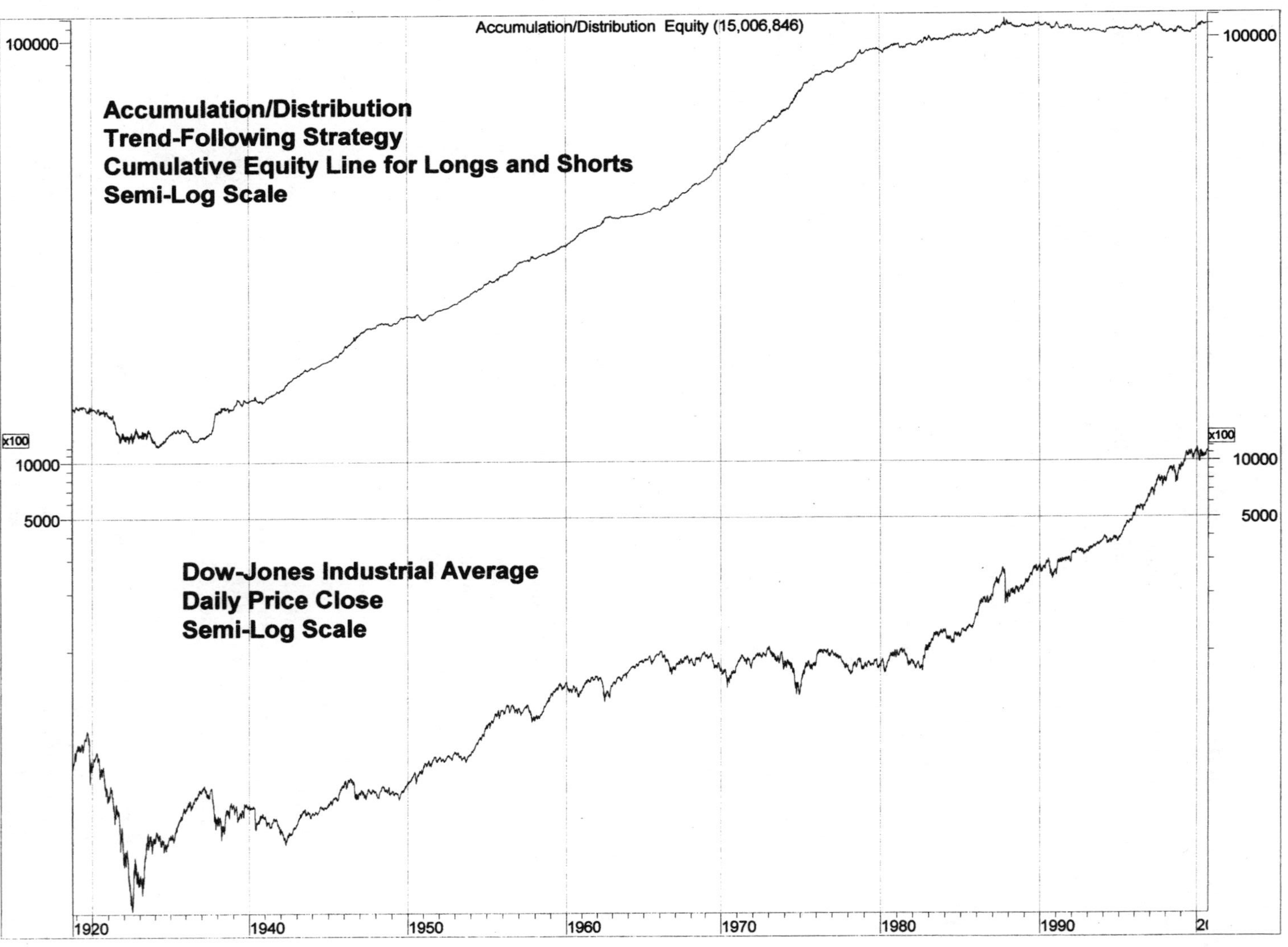

Accumulation/Distribution Equity (15,006,846)
Accumulation/Distribution
Trend-Following Strategy
Cumulative Equity Line for Longs and Shorts
Semi-Log Scale
Dow-Jones Industrial Average
Daily Price Close
Semi-Log Scale
100000
x100
10000
5000
1920
1940
1950
1960
1970
1980
1990

Accumulation/Distribution

Total net profit	15006746	Open position value	−7363.12	Net Profit/Buy&Hold %	327898.38
Percent gain/loss	15006746	Annual percent gain/loss	208458.76	Annual Net %/B&H %	327923.23
Initial investment	100	Interest earned	0		
Current position	Short	Date position entered	8/29/00		
Buy/Hold profit	4575.25	Days in test	26276	# of days per trade	4.24
Buy/Hold pct gain/loss	4575.25	Annual B/H pct gain/loss	63.55		
Total closed trades	6195	Commissions paid	0		
Avg profit per trade	2423.59	Avg Win/Avg Loss ratio	1.36		
Total long trades	3098	Total short trades	3097	Long Win Trade %	49.00
Winning long trades	1518	Winning short trades	1278	Short Win Trade %	41.27
Total winning trades	2796	Total losing trades	3399	Total Win Trade %	45.13
Amount of winning trades	138793616	Amount of losing trades	−123779512	Net Profit Margin %	5.72
Average win	49640.06	Average loss	−36416.45	Average P. Margin %	15.37
Largest win	2783770	Largest loss	−1389113	% Net/(Win + Loss)	33.42
Average length of win	5.28	Average length of loss	2.79	(Win − Loss)/Loss %	89.25
Longest winning trade	33	Longest losing trade	15	(Win − Loss)/Loss %	120.00
Most consecutive wins	11	Most consecutive losses	14	(Win − Loss)/Loss %	−21.43
Total bars out	4	Average length out	4		
Longest out period	4				
System close drawdown	−68.74	Profit/Loss index	10.81	% Net Profit/SODD	21726865.50
System open drawdown	−69.07	Reward/Risk index	100	(Net P. − SODD)/Net P.	100.00
Max open trade drawdown	−1389113	Buy/Hold index	327737.45	% SODD/Net Profit	0.00

In the Equis MetaStock® "System Report" (profit and loss summary statistics), the *Total net profit* is the sum of profits minus the sum of losses, including open positions marked to the market. In contrast, the *Amount of Winning Trades* is the sum of realized profits (the total of all gains on closed-out trades only, excluding any open positions). Similarly, the *Amount of Losing Trades* is the sum of realized losses (the total of all losses on closed-out trades only, excluding any open positions). *System close drawdown* is the largest decline in the cumulative equity line below the initial investment, based on closed-out positions only. *System open drawdown (SODD)* is the largest decline in the cumulative equity line below the initial investment when a position is open. *Max open trade drawdown* is the largest decline in the cumulative equity line below the trade entry price during the worst single trade. The *Profit/Loss Index* is a complex calculation that relates the Amount of Winning Trades to the Amount of Losing Trades on a scale of −100 (worst possible performance) to +100 (best possible performance), with zero representing profits equal to losses. *Reward/Risk Index* is the Total net profit minus System open drawdown. The resulting difference is then divided by the Total net profit. The *Buy/Hold Index* is the Total net profit minus the buy-and-hold strategy's net profit. The resulting difference is then divided by the buy-and-hold net profit. In this exercise, initial equity is assumed to be $100. Both long and short positions are taken unless otherwise noted. Trades are executed at the closing price on the signal date. Transaction costs, interest expenses, and margins are not included in the statistics.

we found that the following parameters would have produced a positive result on a purely mechanical trend-following signal basis with no subjectivity, no sophisticated technical analysis, and no judgement:

Enter Long (Buy) at the current daily price close of the Dow-Jones Industrial Average when the current Accumulation/Distribution is greater than yesterday's 3-day exponential moving average of Accumulation/Distribution.

Close Long (Sell) at the current daily price close of the Dow-Jones Industrial Average when the current Accumulation/Distribution is less than yesterday's 3-day exponential moving average of Accumulation/Distribution.

Enter Short (Sell Short) at the current daily price close of the Dow-Jones Industrial Average when the current Accumulation/Distribution is less than yesterday's 3-day exponential moving average of Accumulation/Distribution.

Close Short (Cover) at the current daily price close of the Dow-Jones Industrial Average when the current Accumulation/Distribution is greater than yesterday's 3-day exponential moving average of Accumulation/Distribution.

Starting with $100 and reinvesting profits, total net profits for this Accumulation/Distribution strategy would have been $15,006,746, assuming a fully invested strategy, reinvestment of profits, no transactions costs, and no taxes. This would have been 327,898.38 percent better than buy-and-hold. Short selling, which was included in this strategy, would have lost money since August, 1982, but nevertheless would have been profitable over the entire 72 years as a whole. Short selling would have been such a drag that this Accumulation/Distribution strategy would have actually lost money on balance since October 19, 1987, despite net profitable long trades.

The Equis International MetaStock® System Testing rules are written as follows:

Enter long: AD() > Ref(Mov(AD(),opt1,E),−1)

Close long: AD() < Ref(Mov(AD(),opt1,E),−1)

Enter short: AD() < Ref(Mov(AD(),opt1,E),−1)

Close short: AD() > Ref(Mov(AD(),opt1,E),−1)

OPT1 Current value: 3

Accumulation Swing Index (ASI)

The Accumulation Swing Index (ASI) is a cumulative total of the Swing Index (SI), which is a complex trend-confirmation/divergence indicator published by J. Welles Wilder, Jr., in his 1978 book *New Concepts in Technical Trading Systems* (Trend Research, PO Box 128, McLeansville, NC 27301). Wilder designed SI to be a better representation of the true market trend. SI compares relationships between current prices (including open, high, low, and close) and the previous period's prices. Mathematically, SI may be expressed as follows:

$$SI = ((50 * K)/M) * ((C - Cp) + .5 (C - O) + .25(Cp - Op))/R)$$

where

K = the larger of H − Cp *or* L − Cp.
H = the highest price of the current period.
Cp = the closing price of the previous period.
L = the lowest price of the current period.
M = the value of a limit move set by the futures exchange.
C = the closing price of the current period.
O = the opening price of the current period.
Op = the opening price of the previous period.
R = defined by the following two steps:

Step 1: Determine which is the largest of the following three values:

$$H - Cp, \textit{ or}$$

$$L - Cp, \textit{ or}$$

$$H - L.$$

Step 2: Calculate R according to one of following:

If the largest value in Step 1 is H − Cp, then

$$R = (H - Cp) - .5(L - C) + .25(Cp - Op).$$

If the largest value in Step 1 is L − Cp, then

$$R = (L - Cp) - .5(H - C) + .25(Cp - Op).$$

If the largest value in Step 1 is H − L, then

$$R = (H - L) + .25(Cp - Op).$$

Stocks do not have daily price movement limits. Therefore, when using MetaStock® software, we use the maximum number of 30,000 for the "limit move parameter."

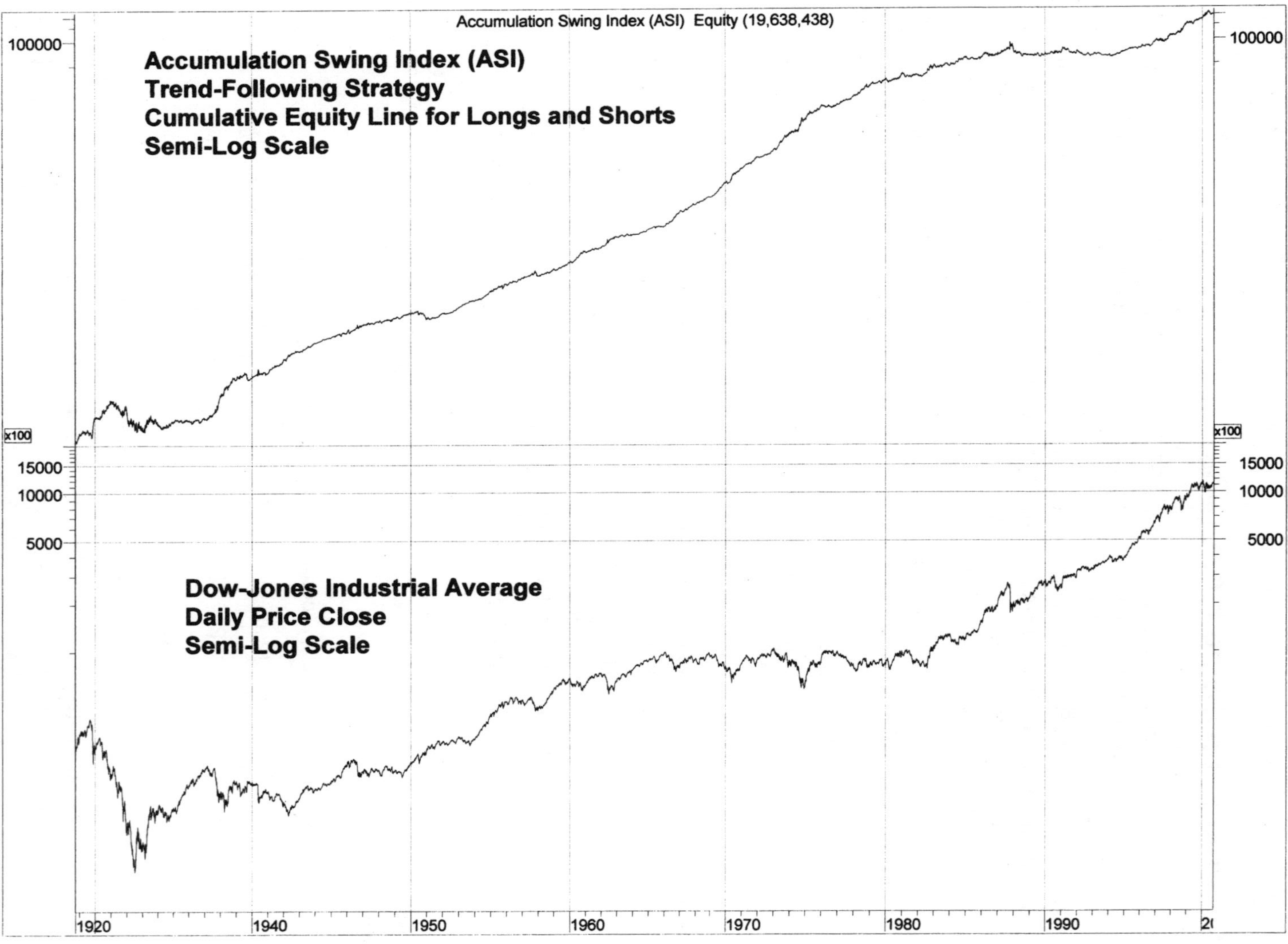
Accumulation Swing Index (ASI) Equity (19,638,438)
Accumulation Swing Index (ASI)
Trend-Following Strategy
Cumulative Equity Line for Longs and Shorts
Semi-Log Scale
Dow-Jones Industrial Average
Daily Price Close
Semi-Log Scale
100000
x100
15000
10000
5000
1920
1940
1950
1960
1970
1980
1990

Accumulation Swing Index (ASI)

Total net profit	19638338	Open position value	68306.24	Net Profit/Buy&Hold %	429129.83
Percent gain/loss	19638338	Annual percent gain/loss	272796.22	Annual Net %/B&H %	429162.34
Initial investment	100	Interest earned	0		
Current position	Short	Date position entered	9/7/00		
Buy/Hold profit	4575.25	Days in test	26276	# of days per trade	4.92
Buy/Hold pct gain/loss	4575.25	Annual B/H pct gain/loss	63.55		
Total closed trades	5343	Commissions paid	0		
Avg profit per trade	3662.74	Avg Win/Avg Loss ratio	1.87		
Total long trades	2672	Total short trades	2671	Long Win Trade %	44.99
Winning long trades	1202	Winning short trades	997	Short Win Trade %	37.33
Total winning trades	2199	Total losing trades	3144	Total Win Trade %	41.16
Amount of winning trades	83200696	Amount of losing trades	−63630736	Net Profit Margin %	13.33
Average win	37835.7	Average loss	−20238.78	Average P. Margin %	30.30
Largest win	1622776	Largest loss	−620164	% Net/(Win + Loss)	44.70
Average length of win	6.52	Average length of loss	2.88	(Win − Loss)/Loss %	126.39
Longest winning trade	22	Longest losing trade	11	(Win − Loss)/Loss %	100.00
Most consecutive wins	8	Most consecutive losses	12	(Win − Loss)/Loss %	−33.33
Total bars out	5	Average length out	5		
Longest out period	5				
System close drawdown	0	Profit/Loss index	23.58	% Net Profit/SODD	5951011515.15
System open drawdown	−0.33	Reward/Risk index	100	(Net P. − SODD)/Net P.	100.00
Max open trade drawdown	−620164	Buy/Hold index	430622.79	% SODD/Net Profit	0.00

In the Equis MetaStock® "System Report" (profit and loss summary statistics), the *Total net profit* is the sum of profits minus the sum of losses, including open positions marked to the market. In contrast, the *Amount of Winning Trades* is the sum of realized profits (the total of all gains on closed-out trades only, excluding any open positions). Similarly, the *Amount of Losing Trades* is the sum of realized losses (the total of all losses on closed-out trades only, excluding any open positions). *System close drawdown* is the largest decline in the cumulative equity line below the initial investment, based on closed-out positions only. *System open drawdown (SODD)* is the largest decline in the cumulative equity line below the initial investment when a position is open. *Max open trade drawdown* is the largest decline in the cumulative equity line below the trade entry price during the worst single trade. The *Profit/Loss Index* is a complex calculation that relates the Amount of Winning Trades to the Amount of Losing Trades on a scale of −100 (worst possible performance) to +100 (best possible performance), with zero representing profits equal to losses. *Reward/Risk Index* is the Total net profit minus System open drawdown. The resulting difference is then divided by the Total net profit. The *Buy/Hold Index* is the Total net profit minus the buy-and-hold strategy's net profit. The resulting difference is then divided by the buy-and-hold net profit. In this exercise, initial equity is assumed to be $100. Both long and short positions are taken unless otherwise noted. Trades are executed at the closing price on the signal date. Transaction costs, interest expenses, and margins are not included in the statistics.

The ASI may be plotted as a line chart. Standard technical analysis tools may be used on the ASI, including trendlines, higher highs and lower lows, and divergence analysis as compared to the plain price chart. ASI also could be compared to its own trailing moving average to generate buy and sell signals.

Indicator Strategy Example for the Accumulation Swing Index (ASI)

Historical data shows that the ASI can be an effective indicator on both the long and short sides, but particularly on the long side. Based on the daily prices for the Dow-Jones Industrial Average for 72 years from 1928 to 2000, we found that the following parameters would have produced a significantly positive result on a purely mechanical trend-following signal basis with no subjectivity, no sophisticated technical analysis, and no judgement:

Enter Long (Buy) at the current daily price close of the Dow-Jones Industrial Average when the current ASI is greater than yesterday's 2-day exponential moving average of ASI.

Close Long (Sell) at the current daily price close of the Dow-Jones Industrial Average when the current ASI is less than yesterday's 2-day exponential moving average of ASI.

Enter Short (Sell Short) at the current daily price close of the Dow-Jones Industrial Average when the current ASI is less than yesterday's 2-day exponential moving average of ASI.

Close Short (Cover) at the current daily price close of the Dow-Jones Industrial Average when the current ASI is greater than yesterday's 2-day exponential moving average of ASI.

Starting with $100 and reinvesting profits, total net profits for this ASI strategy would have been $19,638,338, assuming a fully invested strategy, reinvestment of profits, no transactions costs and no taxes. This would have been 429,129.83 percent better than buy-and-hold. Short selling, which was included in this strategy, would have lost money since December, 1984, but nevertheless would have been profitable over the entire 72 years as a whole.

The Equis International MetaStock® System Testing rules are written as follows:

Enter long: ASwing(30000) > Ref(Mov(ASwing(30000),opt1,E),−1)

Close long: ASwing(30000) < Ref(Mov(ASwing(30000),opt1,E),−1)

Enter short: ASwing(30000) < Ref(Mov(ASwing(30000),opt1,E),−1)

Close short: ASwing(30000) > Ref(Mov(ASwing(30000),opt1,E),−1)

OPT1 Current value: 2

Adaptive Moving Average

An Adaptive Moving Average employs a continuously changing exponential moving average smoothing constant that increases as the price trend slope approaches the vertical and decreases as the price trend slope approaches zero. In other words, in a steep and accelerating price trend, the exponential moving average period length grows shorter or more sensitive to new data entering the calculation. In a flattening price trend, the exponential moving average period length grows longer or less sensitive to new data entering the calculation.

Although the Adaptive Moving Average is an interesting newer idea with considerable intellectual appeal, our preliminary tests fail to show any real practical advantage to this more complex trend smoothing method. After all, the data that determines the smoothing constant is still the same old past data that is used for any other smoothing method, so it is still looking into the rear-view mirror rather than into the ever unknowable future. Also, it is quite normal and common for steep price trends to pause and form minor continuation patterns, in which case an Adaptive Moving Average would be more likely to produce unprofitable whipsaws than a non-adaptive moving average. Finally, an Adaptive Moving Average is much more calculation intensive so takes longer to compute, though this should become less of a consideration with ever faster computer hardware and software.

Advance/Decline Divergence Oscillator (ADDO)

A popular method of interpreting the Advance-Decline Line is to visually compare it to a market price index, such as the Dow Jones Industrial Average (DJIA). For example, if the Advance-Decline Line enters a falling trend while the DJIA is still in a rising trend, such a negative divergence (sometimes) increases the probability of an eventual change to a bearish price trend, a move to the downside. There is usually a variable lead time, and another risk in this type of visual analysis judgment call is that subjectivity could creep in.

Arthur A. Merrill, CMT, created his Advance/Decline Divergence Oscillator (ADDO) to bypass this risk of subjectivity. He calculates and interprets ADDO in ten steps.

1. Convert daily breadth data to weekly data for all New York Stock Exchange issues in three sub-steps: sum the daily number of advancing issues for each day of the week; separately, sum the number of declining issues; and sum the number of unchanged issues for each day.
2. Subtract the sum of declining issues from the sum of advancing issues. Respect the sign. This is net advancing issues.

3. Place that net difference in the numerator of a weekly (A − D)/U ratio, which is the net advancing issues divided by the number of unchanged issues. Merrill credits Edmund Tabell for developing that indicator, which gives emphasis to the level of the market's confidence (small unchanged) or indecisiveness (large unchanged).
4. Sum that weekly (A − D)/U ratio's values over the most recent trailing 52 weeks. This is a *moving total* of (A − D)/U.
5. Using the weekly closing price of the DJIA and the moving sum of (A − D)/U compute a linear regression of the two over the most recent 52 weeks.
6. Plot the regression line, with the DJIA on the *Y* axis and the moving sum of the (A − D)/U ratio on the *X* axis.
7. To determine the expected value of the DJIA for a given value of the moving sum (A − D)/U ratio, locate the point on the regression line that is directly above the current (A − D)/U ratio value.
8. Express ADDO as the percentage deviation of the current closing price of the DJIA minus its expected value.
9. Positive deviations of DJIA versus its expected value increase bearish probabilities for the future.
10. Negative deviations of DJIA versus its expected value increase bullish probabilities for the future.

Advance-Decline Line, A-D Line

The Cumulative Daily Advance-Decline Line, perhaps the most widely known market breadth indicator, traditionally has been used to spot divergences relative to a general market price index, such as the S&P 500 or the Dow Jones Industrial Average.

Most commonly, the Cumulative A-D Line is calculated as a running total of daily net advancing minus declining stock issues on the New York Stock Exchange. Similar indicators may be calculated for other markets, such as the NASDAQ, and weekly data also may be used. There are only two steps to compute this indicator.

1. From the number of advancing issues, subtract the number of declining issues each day, respecting sign. This is *net advancing issues*, and it is often a negative number.
2. Add that daily advances-declines difference to a cumulative total of the daily *net* advancing issues. This forms a continuous line that rises and falls with breadth trends on the NYSE.

For example, our calculations for one month, from August 8 to September 8, 2000, are shown. These calculations are anchored to a starting value at the all-time low of the A-D Line on 12/24/74 set to zero. By starting on that date, we avoid handling negative cumulative numbers. Alternately, if one does not mind graphing large negative numbers, one could set the 12/24/74 low to −124,484, following the precedent of the *Daily Stock Price Record*, Standard & Poor's, 25 Broadway, New York, NY 10004. Business libraries carry this data source.

Calculating the A-D Line

Date	*Advances*	*Declines*	*Difference*	*Cumulative*	*DJIA*
8/8/00	1588	1256	332	60121	10976.90
8/9/00	1440	1400	40	60161	10905.80
8/10/00	1347	1473	−126	60035	10908.80
8/11/00	1998	853	1145	61180	11027.80
8/14/00	1835	1038	797	61977	11176.10
8/15/00	1161	1690	−529	61448	11067.00
8/16/00	1594	1243	351	61799	11008.40
8/17/00	1602	1220	382	62181	11055.60
8/18/00	1170	1603	−433	61748	11046.50
8/21/00	1325	1477	−152	61596	11079.80
8/22/00	1435	1329	106	61702	11139.10
8/23/00	1287	1496	−209	61493	11144.60
8/24/00	1431	1381	50	61543	11182.70
8/25/00	1420	1329	91	61634	11192.60
8/28/00	1378	1426	−48	61586	11252.80
8/29/00	1325	1470	−145	61441	11215.10
8/30/00	1408	1410	−2	61439	11103.00
8/31/00	1716	1149	567	62006	11215.10
9/1/00	1626	1164	462	62468	11238.80
9/5/00	1417	1446	−29	62439	11260.60
9/6/00	1592	1235	357	62796	11310.60
9/7/00	1529	1269	260	63056	11259.90
9/8/00	1304	1514	−210	62846	11220.60

For another perspective, weekly New York Stock Exchange data, published in weekend news sources such as *Barron's,* also can be used for a separate calculation. Weekly data produces a much different looking cumulative line than the more popular daily cumulative total.

Technical analysts have long been aware that the most common subtraction calculation fails to compensate for a distortion that inflates the number of issues traded over the years, namely, the ever growing number of issues listed on the exchange. To regain analytical comparability over time, some analysts normalize the daily data, before cumulating a running total, as follows:

$$N = (A - D)/(A + D)$$

or

$$T = (A - D)/(A + D + U)$$

where

N = today's 1-day ratio of net advances to total issues exhibiting any price change at all

A = number of advancing issues

D = number of declining issues

T = today's 1-day ratio of net advances to total issues traded

U = number of unchanged issues

A + D + U = total number of issues traded each day

Neither of these adjustments appear to make any substantial difference to the behavior of the basic A-D Line, however. A simple subtraction of declines from advances has always been the most popular and widely used method of calculation.

Interpretation of the Cumulative Daily Advance-Decline Line

Trends and divergences of the Cumulative Daily Advance-Decline Line relative to a broad-based market price index have long been the most popular techniques of interpretation. (There may be a better way to view this data, however, as we shall see, below.) For example, if the market price index is rising at a time when the Cumulative Advance-Decline Line is declining, underlying market weakness is suggested, and that is a bearish warning, and sometimes an early warning, for stock prices. Conversely, if the market price index is declining while the Cumulative Advance-Decline Line is rising, underlying market strength is evident, and that is a bullish indication for stock prices. The following table shows a traditional interpretation of the Advance-Decline Line compared to a broad-based market price index, specifically, the Standard & Poor's 500 Index (S&P).

Interpretation of the Cumulative Advance-Decline Line

Market Index (S&P 500)	*Advance-Decline Line*	*Interpretation*
Rising	Falling	Bearish
Near or at previous top	Significantly below corresponding top	Bearish
Near or at previous top	Significantly above corresponding top	Bullish
Falling	Rising	Bullish
Near or at previous bottom	Significantly above previous bottom	Bullish
Near or at previous bottom	Significantly below previous bottom	Bearish

Indicator Strategy Example for the Cumulative Daily Advance-Decline Line

The Cumulative Daily Advance-Decline Line can be an effective indicator on a purely objective basis. Based on a 68-year file of daily data for the number of shares advancing and declining each day on the New York Stock Exchange and the Dow-Jones Industrial Average since its all-time low of 41.22 on July 8, 1932, we found that the simplest possible trend-following rule would have produced a positive result on a purely mechanical signal basis with no subjectivity, no sophisticated technical analysis, and no judgement:

Enter Long (Buy) at the current daily price close of the Dow-Jones Industrial Average when the Cumulative Daily Advance-Decline Line rises relative to its level the previous day.

Close Long (Sell) at the current daily price close of the Dow-Jones Industrial Average when the Cumulative Daily Advance-Decline Line falls relative to its level the previous day.

Enter Short (Sell Short) at the current daily price close of the Dow-Jones Industrial Average when the Cumulative Daily Advance-Decline Line falls relative to its level the previous day.

Close Short (Cover) at the current daily price close of the Dow-Jones Industrial Average when the Cumulative Daily Advance-Decline Line rises relative to its level the previous day.

Starting with $100 and reinvesting profits, total net profits for this Cumulative Advance-Decline Line trend-following strategy would have been $822.4 million, assuming a fully invested strategy, reinvestment of profits, no transactions costs, and no taxes. This would have been 3.08 million percent better than buy-and-hold. Even short selling would have been profitable. Trading would have been hyperactive with one trade every 3.49 calendar days.

The Equis International MetaStock® System Testing rules, where the current Cumulative Daily A-D Line is inserted into the data field normally reserved for Volume (V), are written as follows:

Enter long: V > Ref(V,−1)

Close long: V < Ref(V,−1)

Enter short: V < Ref(V,−1)

Close short: V > Ref(V,−1)

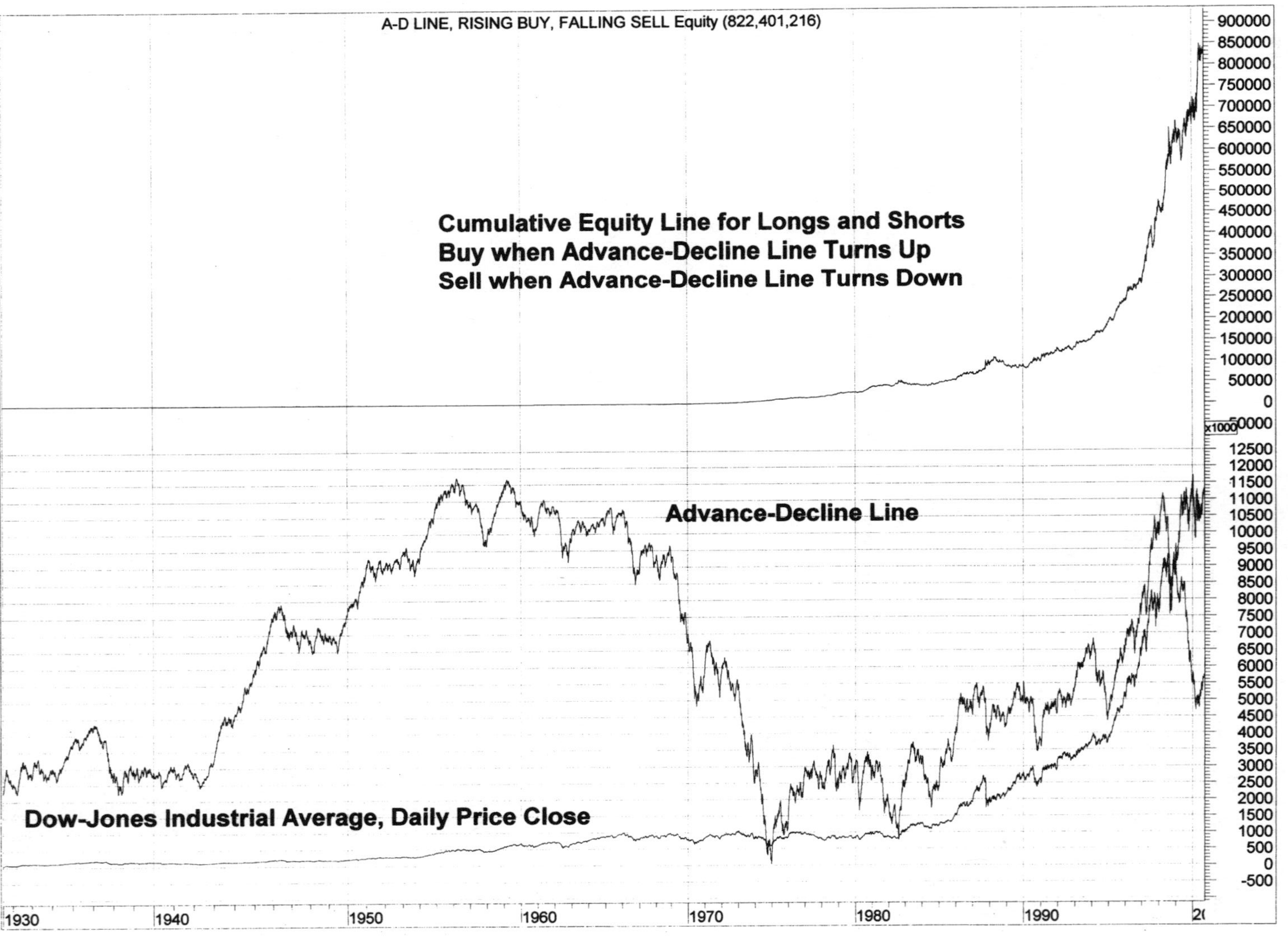
A-D LINE, RISING BUY, FALLING SELL Equity (822,401,216)
Cumulative Equity Line for Longs and Shorts
Buy when Advance-Decline Line Turns Up
Sell when Advance-Decline Line Turns Down
Advance-Decline Line
Dow-Jones Industrial Average, Daily Price Close
900000
850000
800000
750000
700000
650000
600000
550000
500000
450000
400000
350000
300000
250000
200000
150000
100000
50000
0
x1000
12500
12000
11500
11000
10500
10000
9500
9000
8500
8000
7500
7000
6500
6000
5500
5000
4500
4000
3500
3000
2500
2000
1500
1000
500
0
-500
1930
1940
1950
1960
1970
1980
1990

Cumulative A-D Line, Buy +, Sell –

Total net profit	822401088	Open position value	0	Net Profit/Buy&Hold %	3075777.61
Percent gain/loss	822401088	Annual percent gain/loss	12054792.9	Annual Net %/B&H %	3075808.46
Initial investment	100	Interest earned	0		
Current position	Short	Date position entered	9/8/00		
Buy/Hold profit	26737.12	Days in test	24901	# of days per trade	3.49
Buy/Hold pct gain/loss	26737.12	Annual B/H pct gain/loss	391.91		
Total closed trades	7141	Commissions paid	0		
Avg profit per trade	115166.1	Avg Win/Avg Loss ratio	1.63		
Total long trades	3571	Total short trades	3570	Long Win Trade %	51.36
Winning long trades	1834	Winning short trades	1545	Short Win Trade %	43.28
Total winning trades	3379	Total losing trades	3762	Total Win Trade %	47.32
Amount of winning trades	2.586E+09	Amount of losing trades	−1.764E+09	Net Profit Margin %	18.90
Average win	765454.09	Average loss	−468918	Average P. Margin %	24.02
Largest win	57249344	Largest loss	−27337728	% Net/(Win + Loss)	35.36
Average length of win	4.6	Average length of loss	2.55	(Win − Loss)/Loss %	80.39
Longest winning trade	20	Longest losing trade	12	(Win − Loss)/Loss %	66.67
Most consecutive wins	9	Most consecutive losses	11	(Win − Loss)/Loss %	−18.18
Total bars out	3	Average length out	3		
Longest out period	3				
System close drawdown	0	Profit/Loss index	31.8	% Net Profit/SODD	#DIV/0!
System open drawdown	0	Reward/Risk index	100	(Net P. − SODD)/Net P.	100.00
Max open trade drawdown	−27337728	Buy/Hold index	3075777.71	% SODD/Net Profit	0.00

In the Equis MetaStock® "System Report" (profit and loss summary statistics), the *Total net profit* is the sum of profits minus the sum of losses, including open positions marked to the market. In contrast, the *Amount of Winning Trades* is the sum of realized profits (the total of all gains on closed-out trades only, excluding any open positions). Similarly, the *Amount of Losing Trades* is the sum of realized losses (the total of all losses on closed-out trades only, excluding any open positions). *System close drawdown* is the largest decline in the cumulative equity line below the initial investment, based on closed-out positions only. *System open drawdown (SODD)* is the largest decline in the cumulative equity line below the initial investment when a position is open. *Max open trade drawdown* is the largest decline in the cumulative equity line below the trade entry price during the worst single trade. The *Profit/Loss Index* is a complex calculation that relates the Amount of Winning Trades to the Amount of Losing Trades on a scale of −100 (worst possible performance) to +100 (best possible performance), with zero representing profits equal to losses. *Reward/Risk Index* is the Total net profit minus System open drawdown. The resulting difference is then divided by the Total net profit. The *Buy/Hold Index* is the Total net profit minus the buy-and-hold strategy's net profit. The resulting difference is then divided by the buy-and-hold net profit. In this exercise, initial equity is assumed to be $100. Both long and short positions are taken unless otherwise noted. Trades are executed at the closing price on the signal date. Transaction costs, interest expenses, and margins are not included in the statistics.

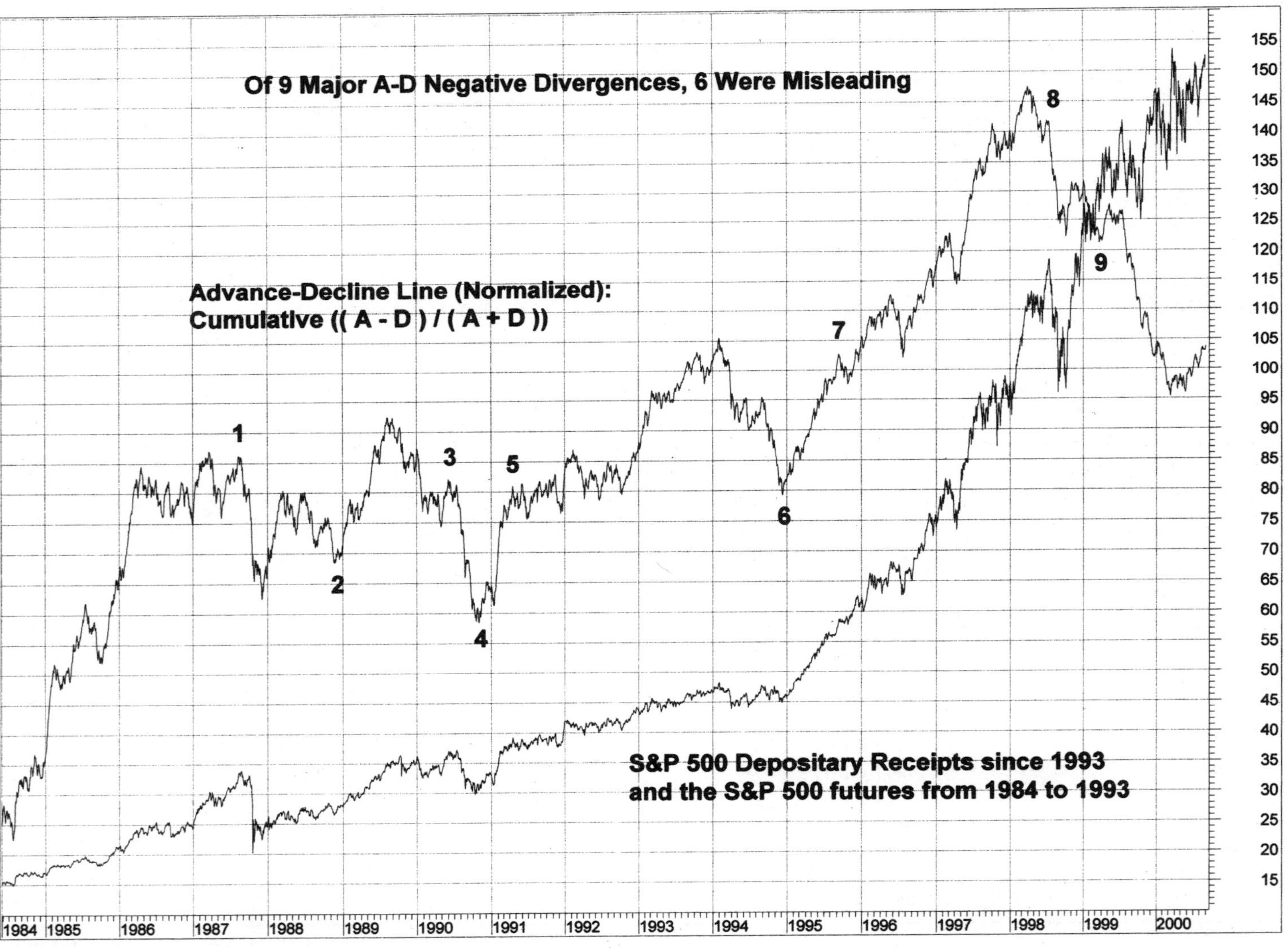

Of 9 Major A-D Negative Divergences, 6 Were Misleading
Advance-Decline Line (Normalized):
Cumulative ((A - D) / (A + D))
S&P 500 Depositary Receipts since 1993
and the S&P 500 futures from 1984 to 1993
1
2
3
4
5
6
7
8
9
1984
1985
1986
1987
1988
1989
1990
1991
1992
1993
1994
1995
1996
1997
1998
1999
2000
155
150
145
140
135
130
125
120
115
110
105
100
95
90
85
80
75
70
65
60
55
50
45
40
35
30
25
20
15

Traditional methods of chart interpretation are only as good as the experience, judgement, and objectivity of the technician doing the analysis. A risk for the novice is that human judgement can be influenced by subjectivity, including position bias, which inclines the observer to interpret an indicator as bullish if he is long and bearish if he is short. Moreover, significant divergences between the Advance-Decline Line and a market price index are sometimes clear only in retrospect.

The Cumulative Daily Advance-Decline Line has called every major market decline in history. The problem is that it has done *nothing but* call for major declines. A cursory glance at the accompanying graph illustrates the problem. At each of the nine junctures labeled on the graph, the Advance-Decline Line showed obvious negative divergences (in hindsight at least). The table, Nine Major A-D Divergences, shows the less-than-impressive results of these bearish warnings. A two-thirds majority of the Advance-Decline Line divergences proved to be ill timed or outright misleading from 1987 to 2000.

Nine Major A-D Divergences

Symbol	*Year*	*Divergence*	*Forecast*	*Outcome*	*Score*
1	1987	Negative	Bearish	Right	1
2	1988	Negative	Bearish	Wrong	0
3	1990	Negative	Bearish	Right	1
4	1990	Negative	Bearish	Wrong	0
5	1991	Negative	Bearish	Wrong	0
6	1994	Negative	Bearish	Wrong	0
7	1995	Negative	Bearish	Wrong	0
8	1998	Negative	Bearish	Right	1
9	1999	Negative	Bearish	Wrong	0
Average					33%

There have been few examples of positive divergences in the Advance-Decline Line relative to the major price indexes over the past 40 years—the years of the greatest bull market in history. The Advance-Decline Line topped out in 1959 and has remained mostly bearish ever since. This is a serious shortcoming of the standard divergence analysis approach to this data.

Advance-Decline Non-Cumulative: Hughes Breadth-Momentum Oscillator

The Hughes Breadth-Momentum Oscillator, named for a pioneering technical analyst in the early part of the twentieth century, is calculated in three easy steps:

1. Subtract the number of declining issues each day from the number of advancing issues.
2. Divide that difference (from Step 1) by the total number of issues traded each day.
3. Finally, tame minor, erratic daily movement by smoothing the ratio (calculated in Step 2) with a moving average.

Calculations in Steps 1 and 2 are written:

$$H = (A - D)/(A + D + U)$$

where

H = today's 1-day ratio of net advances to total issues traded
A = number of advancing issues
D = number of declining issues
U = number of unchanged issues
A + D + U = total number of issues traded each day

Raw data is gathered from daily newspapers or electronic data services and is most commonly based on New York Stock Exchange daily trading statistics. Similar indicators may be calculated for other markets, such as the NASDAQ. For another perspective, weekly data, published in weekend news sources, also can be used for a separate calculation. Weekly data produces a much different indicator than the more popular daily oscillator.

The traditional method of chart interpretation examines the oscillator's trend, absolute level and level relative to a market price index. However, much depends on the experience, judgement, and objectivity of the technical analyst. A risk for the novice is that human judgement can be influenced by subjectivity, including position bias, which inclines the observer to interpret an indicator as bullish if he is long and bearish if he is short. Moreover, significant divergences between the oscillator and a market index are sometimes clear only in retrospect; but there is another way.

Indicator Strategy Example of the Hughes Breadth-Momentum Oscillator, Advance-Decline Non-Cumulative

The Hughes Breadth-Momentum Oscillator is a useful indicator even without any data smoothing or other manipulation. Based on a 68-year file of daily data for the number of shares advancing and declining each day on the New York Stock Exchange and the Dow-Jones Industrial Average since March 8, 1932, we found that one of the simplest possible trend-following rules would have produced a positive result on a purely mechanical signal basis with no subjectivity, no sophisticated technical analysis, and no judgement:

Enter Long (Buy) at the current daily price close of the Dow-Jones Industrial Average when the Hughes Breadth-Momentum Oscillator rises to cross above zero.

Close Long (Sell) at the current daily price close of the Dow-Jones Industrial Average when the Hughes Breadth-Momentum Oscillator falls to cross below zero.

Enter Short (Sell Short) at the current daily price close of the Dow-Jones Industrial Average when the Hughes Breadth-Momentum Oscillator falls to cross below zero.

Close Short (Cover) at the current daily price close of the Dow-Jones Industrial Average when the Hughes Breadth-Momentum Oscillator rises to cross above zero.

Starting with $100 and reinvesting profits, total net profits for this Hughes Breadth-Momentum Oscillator trend-following strategy would have been $579,826,624, assuming a fully invested strategy, reinvestment of profits, no transactions costs and no taxes. This would have been 4,624,210.92 percent better than buy-and-hold. Even short selling would have been profitable. Trading would have been hyperactive with one trade every 3.56 calendar days.

The Equis International MetaStock® System Testing rules, where the current Hughes Breadth-Momentum Oscillator is inserted into the data field normally reserved for Volume (V), are written as follows:

Enter long: V > 0

Close long: V < 0

Enter short: V < 0

Close short: V > 0

Percentage Hughes Breadth-Momentum Oscillator with Eight Parameters

There are a large number of possible permutations that could be created from the basic Hughes Breadth-Momentum Oscillator. These could fill this book. Tens of thousands of parameter sets could be created from the following example algorithm alone, which appears to have some profitable potential. For this algorithm, in order to avoid

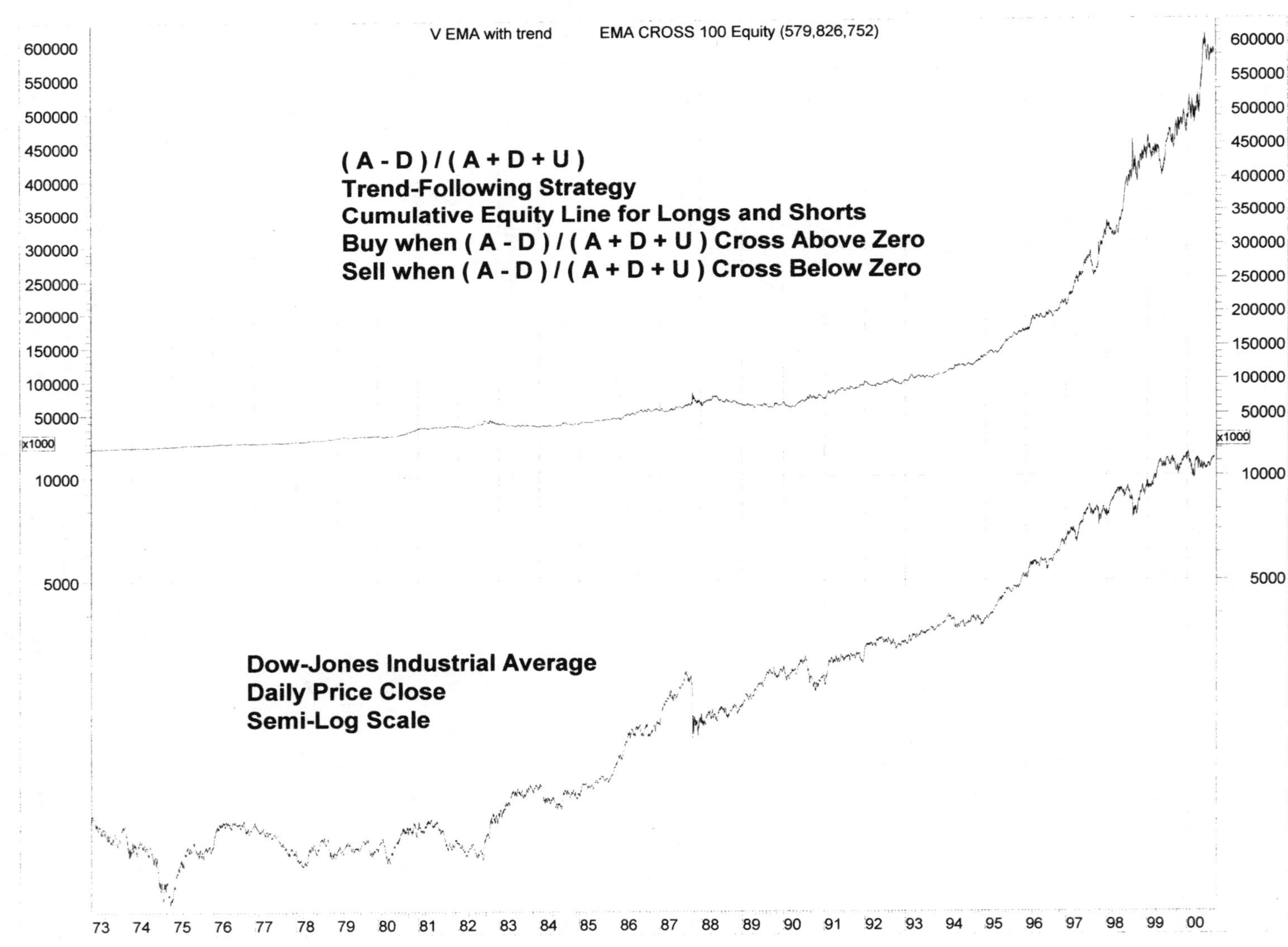

V EMA with trend
EMA CROSS 100 Equity (579,826,752)
(A - D) / (A + D + U)
Trend-Following Strategy
Cumulative Equity Line for Longs and Shorts
Buy when (A - D) / (A + D + U) Cross Above Zero
Sell when (A - D) / (A + D + U) Cross Below Zero
Dow-Jones Industrial Average
Daily Price Close
Semi-Log Scale
600000
550000
500000
450000
400000
350000
300000
250000
200000
150000
100000
50000
x1000
10000
5000
73
74
75
76
77
78
79
80
81
82
83
84
85
86
87
88
89
90
91
92
93
94
95
96
97
98
99
00

(A − D)/(A + D + U) Cross Zero

Total net profit	579826624	Open position value	0	Net Profit/Buy&Hold %	4624210.92
Percent gain/loss	579826624	Annual percent gain/loss	8458025.65	Annual Net %/B&H %	4624298.93
Initial investment	100	Interest earned	0		
Current position	Short	Date position entered	9/8/00		
Buy/Hold profit	12538.66	Days in test	25022	# of days per trade	3.56
Buy/Hold pct gain/loss	12538.66	Annual B/H pct gain/loss	182.9		
Total closed trades	7037	Commissions paid	0		
Avg profit per trade	82396.85	Avg Win/Avg Loss ratio	1.64		
Total long trades	3519	Total short trades	3518	Long Win Trade %	50.90
Winning long trades	1791	Winning short trades	1518	Short Win Trade %	43.15
Total winning trades	3309	Total losing trades	3728	Total Win Trade %	47.02
Amount of winning trades	1.849E+09	Amount of losing trades	−1.269E+09	Net Profit Margin %	18.59
Average win	558864.36	Average loss	−340519.42	Average P. Margin %	24.28
Largest win	40027968	Largest loss	−19114144	% Net/(Win + Loss)	35.36
Average length of win	4.69	Average length of loss	2.58	(Win − Loss)/Loss %	81.78
Longest winning trade	20	Longest losing trade	12	(Win − Loss)/Loss %	66.67
Most consecutive wins	9	Most consecutive losses	11	(Win − Loss)/Loss %	−18.18
Total bars out	0	Average length out	N/A		
Longest out period	0				
System close drawdown	−11.57	Profit/Loss index	31.35	% Net Profit/SODD	579826624.00
System open drawdown	−100	Reward/Risk index	100	(Net P.-SODD)/Net P.	100.00
Max open trade drawdown	−19114144	Buy/Hold index	4624211.95	% SODD/Net Profit	0.00

In the Equis MetaStock® "System Report" (profit and loss summary statistics), the *Total net profit* is the sum of profits minus the sum of losses, including open positions marked to the market. In contrast, the *Amount of Winning Trades* is the sum of realized profits (the total of all gains on closed-out trades only, excluding any open positions). Similarly, the *Amount of Losing Trades* is the sum of realized losses (the total of all losses on closed-out trades only, excluding any open positions). *System close drawdown* is the largest decline in the cumulative equity line below the initial investment, based on closed-out positions only. *System open drawdown (SODD)* is the largest decline in the cumulative equity line below the initial investment when a position is open. *Max open trade drawdown* is the largest decline in the cumulative equity line below the trade entry price during the worst single trade. The *Profit/Loss Index* is a complex calculation that relates the Amount of Winning Trades to the Amount of Losing Trades on a scale of −100 (worst possible performance) to +100 (best possible performance), with zero representing profits equal to losses. *Reward/Risk Index* is the Total net profit minus System open drawdown. The resulting difference is then divided by the Total net profit. The *Buy/Hold Index* is the Total net profit minus the buy-and-hold strategy's net profit. The resulting difference is then divided by the buy-and-hold net profit. In this exercise, initial equity is assumed to be $100. Both long and short positions are taken unless otherwise noted. Trades are executed at the closing price on the signal date. Transaction costs, interest expenses, and margins are not included in the statistics.

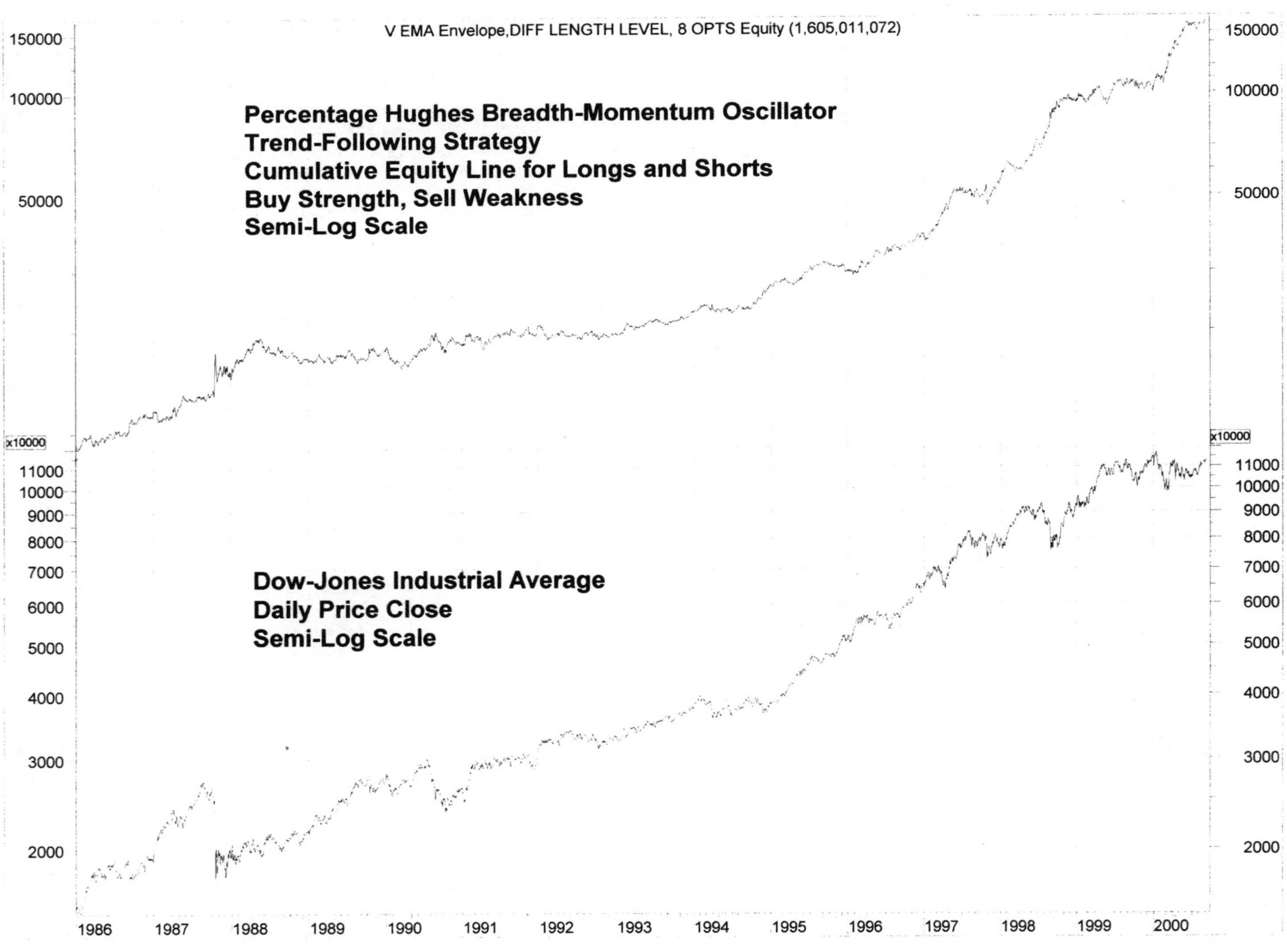
V EMA Envelope,DIFF LENGTH LEVEL, 8 OPTS Equity (1,605,011,072)
Percentage Hughes Breadth-Momentum Oscillator
Trend-Following Strategy
Cumulative Equity Line for Longs and Shorts
Buy Strength, Sell Weakness
Semi-Log Scale
Dow-Jones Industrial Average
Daily Price Close
Semi-Log Scale
150000
100000
50000
x10000
11000
10000
9000
8000
7000
6000
5000
4000
3000
2000
1986
1987
1988
1989
1990
1991
1992
1993
1994
1995
1996
1997
1998
1999
2000

Percentage Hughes Breadth-Momentum Oscillator

Total net profit	1.605E+09	Open position value	5582535	Net Profit/Buy&Hold %	12800398.17
Percent gain/loss	1.605E+09	Annual percent gain/loss	23412556.7	Annual Net %/B&H %	12800641.79
Initial investment	100	Interest earned	0		
Current position	Short	Date position entered	9/7/00		
Buy/Hold profit	12538.66	Days in test	25022	# of days per trade	2.45
Buy/Hold pct gain/loss	12538.66	Annual B/H pct gain/loss	182.9		
Total closed trades	10200	Commissions paid	0		
Avg profit per trade	156806.71	Avg Win/Avg Loss ratio	1.5		
Total long trades	5393	Total short trades	4807	Long Win Trade %	53.57
Winning long trades	2889	Winning short trades	2193	Short Win Trade %	45.62
Total winning trades	5082	Total losing trades	5118	Total Win Trade %	49.82
Amount of winning trades	4.901E+09	Amount of losing trades	−3.301E+09	Net Profit Margin %	19.50
Average win	964299.71	Average loss	−645006.56	Average P. Margin %	19.84
Largest win	93997312	Largest loss	−38615808	% Net/(Win + Loss)	41.76
Average length of win	3.06	Average length of loss	2.22	(Win − Loss)/Loss %	37.84
Longest winning trade	9	Longest losing trade	6	(Win − Loss)/Loss %	50.00
Most consecutive wins	11	Most consecutive losses	12	(Win − Loss)/Loss %	−8.33
Total bars out	2760	Average length out	2.01		
Longest out period	10				
System close drawdown	−3.42	Profit/Loss index	32.71	% Net Profit/SODD	46930144561.40
System open drawdown	−3.42	Reward/Risk index	100	(Net P. − SODD)/Net P.	100.00
Max open trade drawdown	−38615808	Buy/Hold index	12844923.6	% SODD/Net Profit	0.00

In the Equis MetaStock® "System Report" (profit and loss summary statistics), the *Total net profit* is the sum of profits minus the sum of losses, including open positions marked to the market. In contrast, the *Amount of Winning Trades* is the sum of realized profits (the total of all gains on closed-out trades only, excluding any open positions). Similarly, the *Amount of Losing Trades* is the sum of realized losses (the total of all losses on closed-out trades only, excluding any open positions). *System close drawdown* is the largest decline in the cumulative equity line below the initial investment, based on closed-out positions only. *System open drawdown (SODD)* is the largest decline in the cumulative equity line below the initial investment when a position is open. *Max open trade drawdown* is the largest decline in the cumulative equity line below the trade entry price during the worst single trade. The *Profit/Loss Index* is a complex calculation that relates the Amount of Winning Trades to the Amount of Losing Trades on a scale of −100 (worst possible performance) to +100 (best possible performance), with zero representing profits equal to losses. *Reward/Risk Index* is the Total net profit minus System open drawdown. The resulting difference is then divided by the Total net profit. The *Buy/Hold Index* is the Total net profit minus the buy-and-hold strategy's net profit. The resulting difference is then divided by the buy-and-hold net profit. In this exercise, initial equity is assumed to be $100. Both long and short positions are taken unless otherwise noted. Trades are executed at the closing price on the signal date. Transaction costs, interest expenses, and margins are not included in the statistics.

dealing with negative numbers and fractions and to create an oscillator that fluctuates around 100%, we first converted the basic Hughes Breadth-Momentum Oscillator to percentages from fractions, and then we added 100%. The conversion can be expressed as follows:

$$\text{Percentage Hughes Breadth-Momentum Oscillator} = (H * 100) + 100 = (((A - D)/(A + D + U)) * 100) + 100$$

where

H = today's 1-day ratio of net advances to total issues traded
A = number of advancing issues
D = number of declining issues
U = number of unchanged issues
A + D + U = total number of issues traded each day

Enter Long (Buy) at the current daily price close of the Dow-Jones Industrial Average when the Percentage Hughes Breadth-Momentum Oscillator is greater than 92% of its own previous day's 12-day exponential moving average.

Close Long (Sell) at the current daily price close of the Dow-Jones Industrial Average when the Percentage Hughes Breadth-Momentum Oscillator is less than 104% of its own previous day's 2-day exponential moving average.

Enter Short (Sell Short) at the current daily price close of the Dow-Jones Industrial Average when the Percentage Hughes Breadth-Momentum Oscillator is less than 104% of its own previous day's 8-day exponential moving average.

Close Short (Cover) at the current daily price close of the Dow-Jones Industrial Average when the Percentage Hughes Breadth-Momentum Oscillator is greater than 92% of its own previous day's 46-day exponential moving average.

Starting with $100 and reinvesting profits, total net profits for this Percentage Hughes Breadth-Momentum Oscillator trend-following strategy would have been $1.6 billion, assuming a fully invested strategy, reinvestment of profits, no transactions costs, and no taxes. This would have been 12.8 million percent better than buy-and-hold. Even short selling would have been profitable. Trading would have been hyperactive with one trade every 2.45 calendar days. Despite its profitability, with such active trading and such a complex calculation, this indicator will not suit everyone.

The Equis International MetaStock® System Testing rules, where the current Percentage Hughes Breadth-Momentum Oscillator is inserted into the data field normally reserved for Volume (V), are written as follows:

Enter long: V > Ref(Mov(V,opt1,E),−1) * (opt5/100)

Close long: V < Ref(Mov(V,opt2,E),−1) * (opt6/100)

Enter short: V < Ref(Mov(V,opt3,E),−1) * (opt7/100)

Close short: V > Ref(Mov(V,opt4,E),−1) * (opt8/100)

OPT1 Current value: 12
OPT2 Current value: 2
OPT3 Current value: 8
OPT4 Current value: 46
OPT5 Current value: 92
OPT6 Current value: 104
OPT7 Current value: 104
OPT8 Current value: 92

Advance/Decline Ratio

The Advance/Decline Ratio is a breadth-momentum oscillator calculated by first dividing the number of advancing issues by the number of declining issues each day; and then by smoothing the previously derived fraction by using a moving average to tame some of the erratic daily movement. The basic calculation before smoothing is given by the following formula:

$$R = A/D$$

where

R = today's 1-day ratio of advancing issues to declining issues
A = number of advancing issues
D = number of declining issues

Indicator Strategy Example of the Advance/Decline Ratio Oscillator

The Advance/Decline Ratio is a useful indicator even without any data smoothing or other manipulation. Based on a 68-year file of daily data for the number of shares advancing and declining each day on the New York Stock Exchange and the Dow-Jones

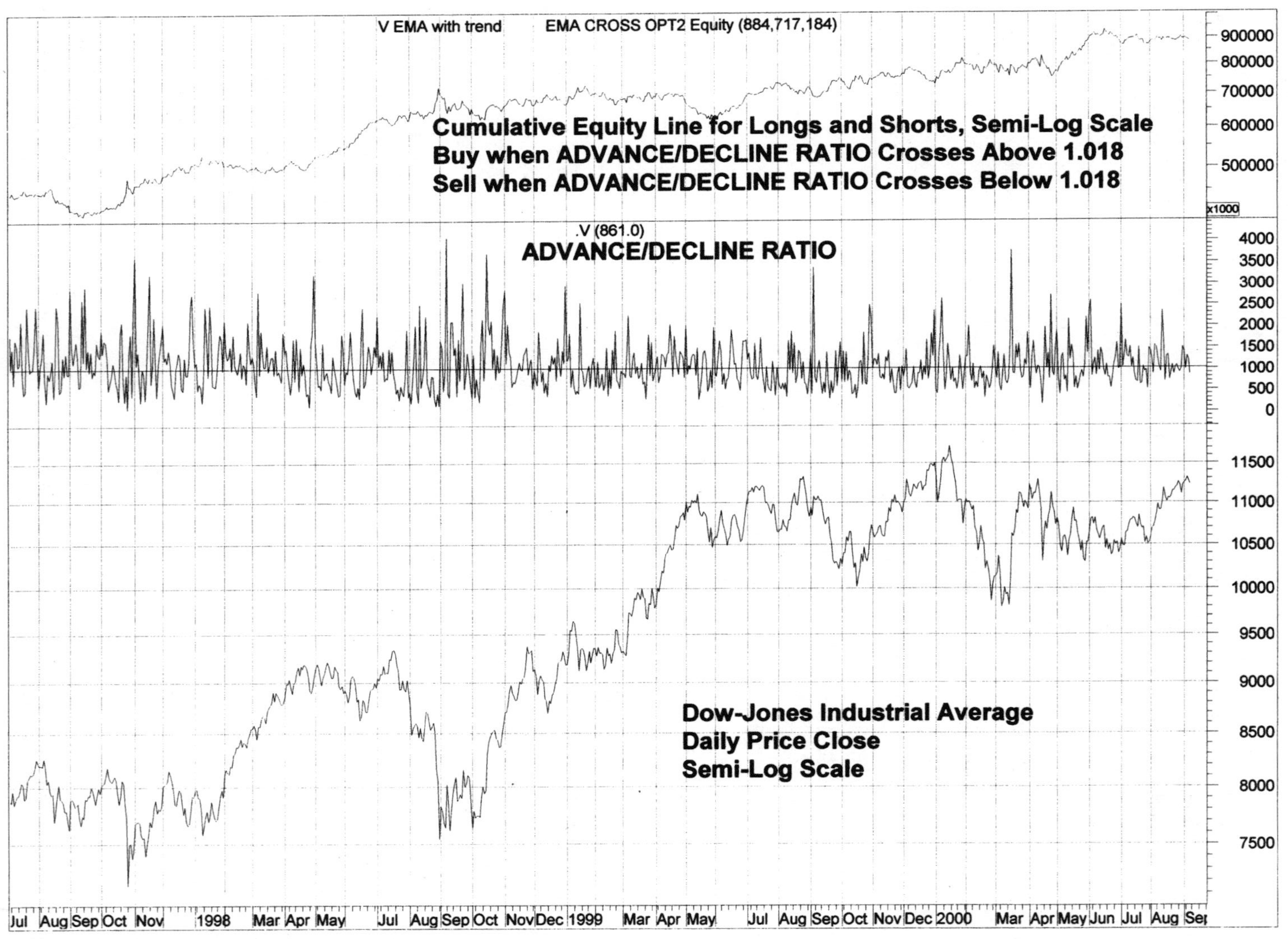
V EMA with trend
EMA CROSS OPT2 Equity (884,717,184)
Cumulative Equity Line for Longs and Shorts, Semi-Log Scale
Buy when ADVANCE/DECLINE RATIO Crosses Above 1.018
Sell when ADVANCE/DECLINE RATIO Crosses Below 1.018
900000
800000
700000
600000
500000
x1000
.V (861.0)
ADVANCE/DECLINE RATIO
4000
3500
3000
2500
2000
1500
1000
500
0
Dow-Jones Industrial Average
Daily Price Close
Semi-Log Scale
11500
11000
10500
10000
9500
9000
8500
8000
7500
Jul Aug Sep Oct Nov 1998 Mar Apr May Jul Aug Sep Oct Nov Dec 1999 Mar Apr May Jul Aug Sep Oct Nov Dec 2000 Mar Apr May Jun Jul Aug Sep

Advance/Decline Ratio Crossing 1.018

Total net profit	884717056	Open position value	0	Net Profit/Buy&Hold %	7055813.92
Percent gain/loss	884717056	Annual percent gain/loss	12905512.2	Annual Net %/B&H %	7055948.21
Initial investment	100	Interest earned	0		
Current position	Short	Date position entered	9/8/00		
Buy/Hold profit	12538.66	Days in test	25022	# of days per trade	3.47
Buy/Hold pct gain/loss	12538.66	Annual B/H pct gain/loss	182.9		
Total closed trades	7219	Commissions paid	0		
Avg profit per trade	122553.96	Avg Win/Avg Loss ratio	1.63		
Total long trades	3610	Total short trades	3609	Long Win Trade %	51.36
Winning long trades	1854	Winning short trades	1558	Short Win Trade %	43.17
Total winning trades	3412	Total losing trades	3807	Total Win Trade %	47.26
Amount of winning trades	2.802E+09	Amount of losing trades	−1.918E+09	Net Profit Margin %	18.74
Average win	821294.74	Average loss	−503688.1	Average P. Margin %	23.97
Largest win	63495616	Largest loss	−30320448	% Net/(Win + Loss)	35.36
Average length of win	4.57	Average length of loss	2.55	(Win − Loss)/Loss %	79.22
Longest winning trade	20	Longest losing trade	12	(Win − Loss)/Loss %	66.67
Most consecutive wins	10	Most consecutive losses	11	(Win − Loss)/Loss %	−9.09
Total bars out	0	Average length out	N/A		
Longest out period	0				
System close drawdown	−10.67	Profit/Loss index	31.57	% Net Profit/SODD	884717056.00
System open drawdown	−100	Reward/Risk index	100	(Net P. − SODD)/Net P.	100.00
Max open trade drawdown	−30320448	Buy/Hold index	7055815.48	% SODD/Net Profit	0.00

In the Equis MetaStock® "System Report" (profit and loss summary statistics), the *Total net profit* is the sum of profits minus the sum of losses, including open positions marked to the market. In contrast, the *Amount of Winning Trades* is the sum of realized profits (the total of all gains on closed-out trades only, excluding any open positions). Similarly, the *Amount of Losing Trades* is the sum of realized losses (the total of all losses on closed-out trades only, excluding any open positions). *System close drawdown* is the largest decline in the cumulative equity line below the initial investment, based on closed-out positions only. *System open drawdown (SODD)* is the largest decline in the cumulative equity line below the initial investment when a position is open. *Max open trade drawdown* is the largest decline in the cumulative equity line below the trade entry price during the worst single trade. The *Profit/Loss Index* is a complex calculation that relates the Amount of Winning Trades to the Amount of Losing Trades on a scale of −100 (worst possible performance) to +100 (best possible performance), with zero representing profits equal to losses. *Reward/Risk Index* is the Total net profit minus System open drawdown. The resulting difference is then divided by the Total net profit. The *Buy/Hold Index* is the Total net profit minus the buy-and-hold strategy's net profit. The resulting difference is then divided by the buy-and-hold net profit. In this exercise, initial equity is assumed to be $100. Both long and short positions are taken unless otherwise noted. Trades are executed at the closing price on the signal date. Transaction costs, interest expenses, and margins are not included in the statistics.

Industrial Average since March 8, 1932, we found that a simple crossover, trend-following rule would have produced a positive result on a purely mechanical signal basis with no subjectivity, no sophisticated technical analysis, and no judgement:

Enter Long (Buy) at the current daily price close of the Dow-Jones Industrial Average when the Advance/Decline Ratio rises to cross above 1.018.

Close Long (Sell) at the current daily price close of the Dow-Jones Industrial Average when the Advance/Decline Ratio falls to cross below 1.018.

Enter Short (Sell Short) at the current daily price close of the Dow-Jones Industrial Average when the Advance/Decline Ratio falls to cross below 1.018.

Close Short (Cover) at the current daily price close of the Dow-Jones Industrial Average when the Advance/Decline Ratio rises to cross above 1.018.

Starting with $100 and reinvesting profits, total net profits for this Advance/Decline Ratio trend-following strategy would have been $884,717,056, assuming a fully invested strategy, reinvestment of profits, no transactions costs and no taxes. This would have been 7,055,813.92 percent better than buy-and-hold. Even short selling would have been profitable. Trading would have been hyperactive with one trade every 3.47 calendar days.

The Equis International MetaStock® System Testing rules, where the current Advance/Decline Ratio multiplied by 1000 (to avoid handling fractions) is inserted into the data field normally reserved for Volume (V), are written as follows:

Enter long: Mov(V,opt1,E) > opt2

Close long: Mov(V,opt1,E) < opt2

Enter short: Mov(V,opt1,E) < opt2

Close short: Mov(V,opt1,E) > opt2

OPT1 Current value: 1
OPT2 Current value: 1018

Advisory Sentiment Index

This indicator may refer to any one of four different sentiment polls or surveys conducted by investment advisory service newsletters and is generally made available to subscribers via telephone recording. The data is also printed in *Barron's* weekly financial newspaper, which is available every Saturday. The four surveys are conducted by Investors Intelligence, Market Vane, American Association of Individual Investors (AAII), and Bullish Consensus.

The original Advisory Sentiment Index is an overbought/oversold sentiment indicator based on the so-called Theory of Contrary Opinion: whatever the majority thinks is *supposed to be wrong*. Since 1962, Abraham W. Cohen and his successors, the editors of the stock market newsletter, *Investors Intelligence* (1 West Avenue, Larchmont, NY 10538), have read about 100 different stock market newsletters and have tallied the percentages expressing clear bullish, bearish, and correction opinions as to the stock market's future trend.

Over the past 35 years, the average percentage of bulls has been 42.96%, bears 33.60%, and corrections 23.44%. By general consensus, the most important number is the percentage of bears. Most people talk bullish most of the time, while the precise meaning of correction can be nebulous. But to state a clear bearish opinion is to say something that stands out clearly.

Contrary to popular Contrary Opinion, however, buying when the percentage of bears has been above average, and selling and selling short when the percentage of bears has been below average would *not* have been a profitable strategy. In fact, crossovers of all exponential moving average lengths from 1 to 1000 weeks would have *lost* money. Even though there was a majority of correct signals for each exponential moving average length, losses were larger than gains. Actually fading the contrary crowd, that is, going contrary to the contrarians, would have been a profitable strategy.

Die-hard contrarians will protest that this indicator should be counted only when it reaches extremes. But the problem with that is that it is difficult to quantify what is meant by *extremes* because the ranges of the observed data have narrowed since 1974, and especially since 1994 such that the indicator has been growing less and less volatile. This is evident simply by inspecting the chart of the reported data. Because the observed ranges have been changing, interpretation of this indicator generally has become dangerously subjective.

Contrary opinion is a popular idea, known even to television commentators, whose general level of understanding of technical analysis is superficial, at best. Many experienced technical analysts use sentiment, but more as a supplement to trend, momentum, and other technical indicators than as a stand-alone, signal generator. Sentiment typically shows overbought and oversold levels well before the directional price move is over and, therefore, can be misleading when viewed in isolation. In general, sentiment is more of a background indicator that is not suitable for precise timing.

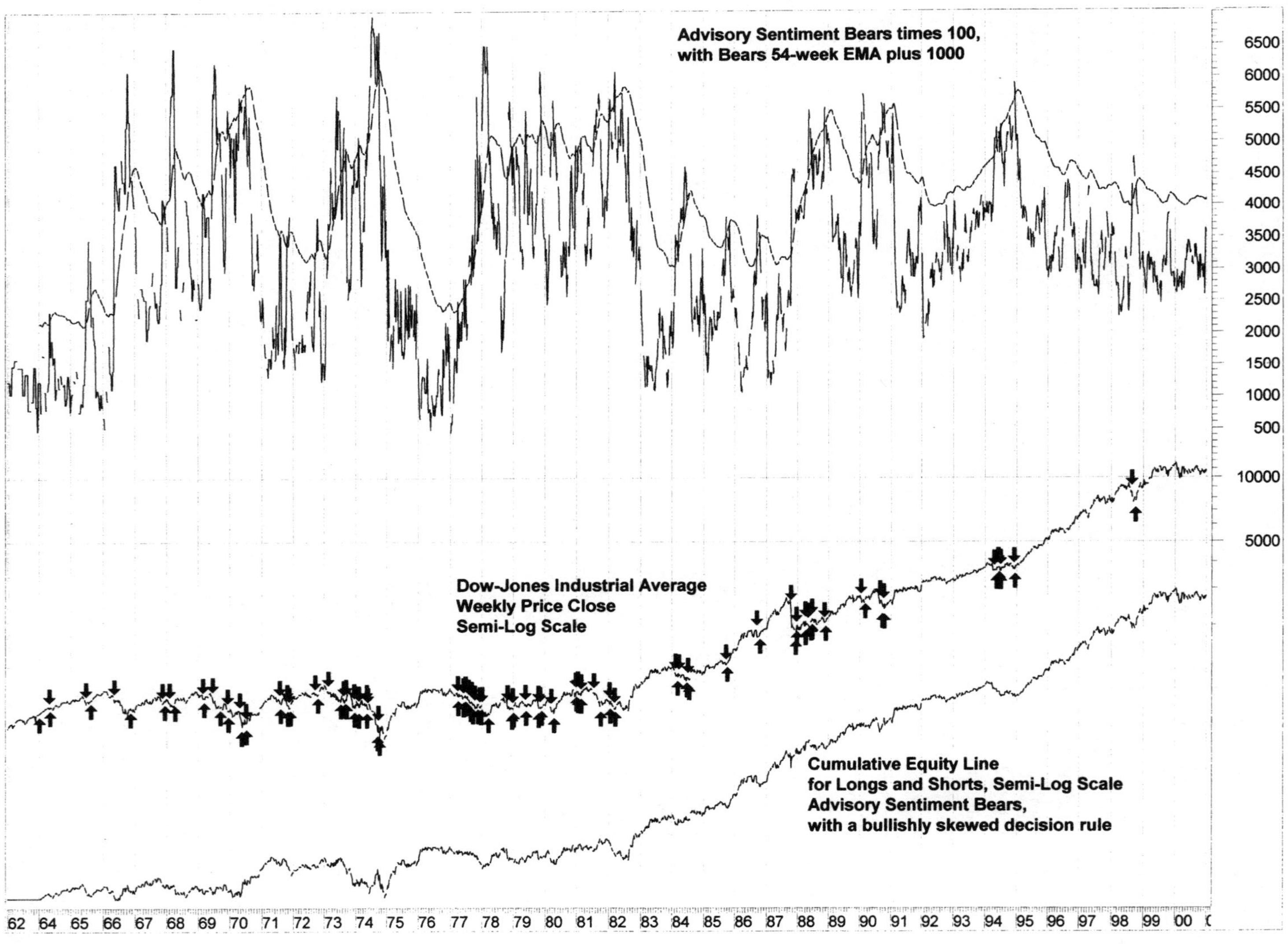
Advisory Sentiment Bears times 100,
with Bears 54-week EMA plus 1000
6500
6000
5500
5000
4500
4000
3500
3000
2500
2000
1500
1000
500
10000
5000
Dow-Jones Industrial Average
Weekly Price Close
Semi-Log Scale
Cumulative Equity Line
for Longs and Shorts, Semi-Log Scale
Advisory Sentiment Bears,
with a bullishly skewed decision rule
62 64 65 66 67 68 69 70 71 72 73 74 75 76 77 78 79 80 81 82 83 84 85 86 87 88 89 90 91 92 93 94 95 96 97 98 99 00

Advisory Sentiment Bears, Crossing 54-week EMA + 10% Points

Total net profit	2649.57	Open position value	765.46	Net Profit/Buy&Hold %	70.27
Percent gain/loss	2649.57	Annual percent gain/loss	69.67	Annual Net %/B&H %	70.26
Initial investment	100	Interest earned	0		
Current position	Long	Date position entered	10/2/98		
Buy/Hold profit	1556.12	Days in test	13882	# of days per trade	113.79
Buy/Hold pct gain/loss	1556.12	Annual B/H pct gain/loss	40.92		
Total closed trades	122	Commissions paid	0		
Avg profit per trade	15.44	Avg Win/Avg Loss ratio	6.61		
Total long trades	61	Total short trades	61	Long Win Trade %	47.54
Winning long trades	29	Winning short trades	28	Short Win Trade %	45.90
Total winning trades	57	Total losing trades	65	Total Win Trade %	46.72
Amount of winning trades	2276.6	Amount of losing trades	−392.49	Net Profit Margin %	70.59
Average win	39.94	Average loss	−6.04	Average P. Margin %	73.73
Largest win	1012.36	Largest loss	−33.21	% Net/(Win + Loss)	93.65
Average length of win	25.09	Average length of loss	7.75	(Win − Loss)/Loss %	223.74
Longest winning trade	194	Longest losing trade	47	(Win − Loss)/Loss %	312.77
Most consecutive wins	4	Most consecutive losses	6	(Win − Loss)/Loss %	−33.33
Total bars out	55	Average length out	55		
Longest out period	55				
System close drawdown	0	Profit/Loss index	87.1	% Net Profit/SODD	420566.67
System open drawdown	−0.63	Reward/Risk index	99.98	(Net P. − SODD)/Net P.	99.98
Max open trade drawdown	−36.53	Buy/Hold index	119.46	% SODD/Net Profit	−0.02

In the Equis MetaStock® "System Report" (profit and loss summary statistics), the *Total net profit* is the sum of profits minus the sum of losses, including open positions marked to the market. In contrast, the *Amount of Winning Trades* is the sum of realized profits (the total of all gains on closed-out trades only, excluding any open positions). Similarly, the *Amount of Losing Trades* is the sum of realized losses (the total of all losses on closed-out trades only, excluding any open positions). *System close drawdown* is the largest decline in the cumulative equity line below the initial investment, based on closed-out positions only. *System open drawdown (SODD)* is the largest decline in the cumulative equity line below the initial investment when a position is open. *Max open trade drawdown* is the largest decline in the cumulative equity line below the trade entry price during the worst single trade. The *Profit/Loss Index* is a complex calculation that relates the Amount of Winning Trades to the Amount of Losing Trades on a scale of −100 (worst possible performance) to +100 (best possible performance), with zero representing profits equal to losses. *Reward/Risk Index* is the Total net profit minus System open drawdown. The resulting difference is then divided by the Total net profit. The *Buy/Hold Index* is the Total net profit minus the buy-and-hold strategy's net profit. The resulting difference is then divided by the buy-and-hold net profit. In this exercise, initial equity is assumed to be $100. Both long and short positions are taken unless otherwise noted. Trades are executed at the closing price on the signal date. Transaction costs, interest expenses, and margins are not included in the statistics.

Indicator Strategy Example for Advisory Sentiment Bears, with a Bullishly Skewed Decision Rule

This skewed strategy would not have spent much time on the short side, but when short it would have been profitable on balance. That is, for those brief periods when there were an extraordinary proportion of bears, the market performed poorly. Based on a 38-year file of weekly data for Advisory Sentiment Bears and the Dow-Jones Industrial Average from 1/28/62 to 12/29/00, we found a bullishly skewed decision rule that would have been profitable on a purely mechanical contrary signal basis with no subjectivity, no sophisticated technical analysis, and no judgement:

Enter Long (Buy) at the current weekly price close of the Dow-Jones Industrial Average when the current level of Advisory Sentiment Bears is less than its previous week's 54-week exponential moving average plus 10 percentage points.

Close Long (Sell) at the current weekly price close of the Dow-Jones Industrial Average when the current level of Advisory Sentiment Bears is greater than its previous week's 54-week exponential moving average plus 10 percentage points.

Enter Short (Sell Short) at the current weekly price close of the Dow-Jones Industrial Average when the current level of Advisory Sentiment Bears is greater than its previous week's 54-week exponential moving average plus 10 percentage points.

Close Short (Cover) at the current weekly price close of the Dow-Jones Industrial Average when the current level of Advisory Sentiment Bears is less than its previous week's 54-week exponential moving average plus 10 percentage points.

Starting with $100 and reinvesting profits, total net profits for this Advisory Sentiment Bears bullishly skewed strategy would have been $2,649.57, assuming a fully invested strategy, reinvestment of profits, no transactions costs, and no taxes. This would have been 70.27% better than buy-and-hold. Even short selling would have been profitable, and it was included in the strategy. The indicator would have given profitable buy signals only 46.72% of the time. Trading would have been relatively inactive at one trade every 113.79 calendar days. Although the majority of signals wound have been unprofitable, note that the average winning trade would have been 6.61 times as large as the average losing trade.

The Equis International MetaStock® System Testing rules, where Advisory Sentiment Bears data (multiplied by 100 to avoid handling decimals) are inserted into the field normally reserved for Volume, are written as follows:

Enter long: V < (Ref(Mov(V ,opt1,E),−1) + opt2)

Close long: V > (Ref(Mov(V ,opt1,E),−1) + opt2)

Enter short: V > (Ref(Mov(V ,opt1,E),−1) + opt2)

Close short: V < (Ref(Mov(V ,opt1,E),−1) + opt2)

OPT1 Current value: 54
OPT2 Current value: 1000

ADX (Average Directional Movement)

(See Directional Movement.)

American Association of Individual Investors Survey

The American Association of Individual Investors (AAII), of Chicago, IL, mails 25 survey postcards daily asking small retail investors their opinions of the stock market for the next six months. This indicator is one of four different sentiment polls or surveys conducted by investment advisory service newsletters, which are generally made available to subscribers via telephone recording. After a moderate time lag, the data is also printed in *Barron's* weekly financial newspaper, which is available every Saturday. Popular interpretation is generally contrarian. (See Contrary Opinion and Advisory Service Sentiment.) Opinion polls can be tricky to interpret, and they are useful more for background than for precise timing.

Over an 11-year period measured, Ned Davis Research found extraordinarily high returns when a 2-week smoothing of this data falls to 44% bulls, indicating extreme pessimism. Below-average returns followed when the smoothing moved above 61%, indicating excessive optimism.

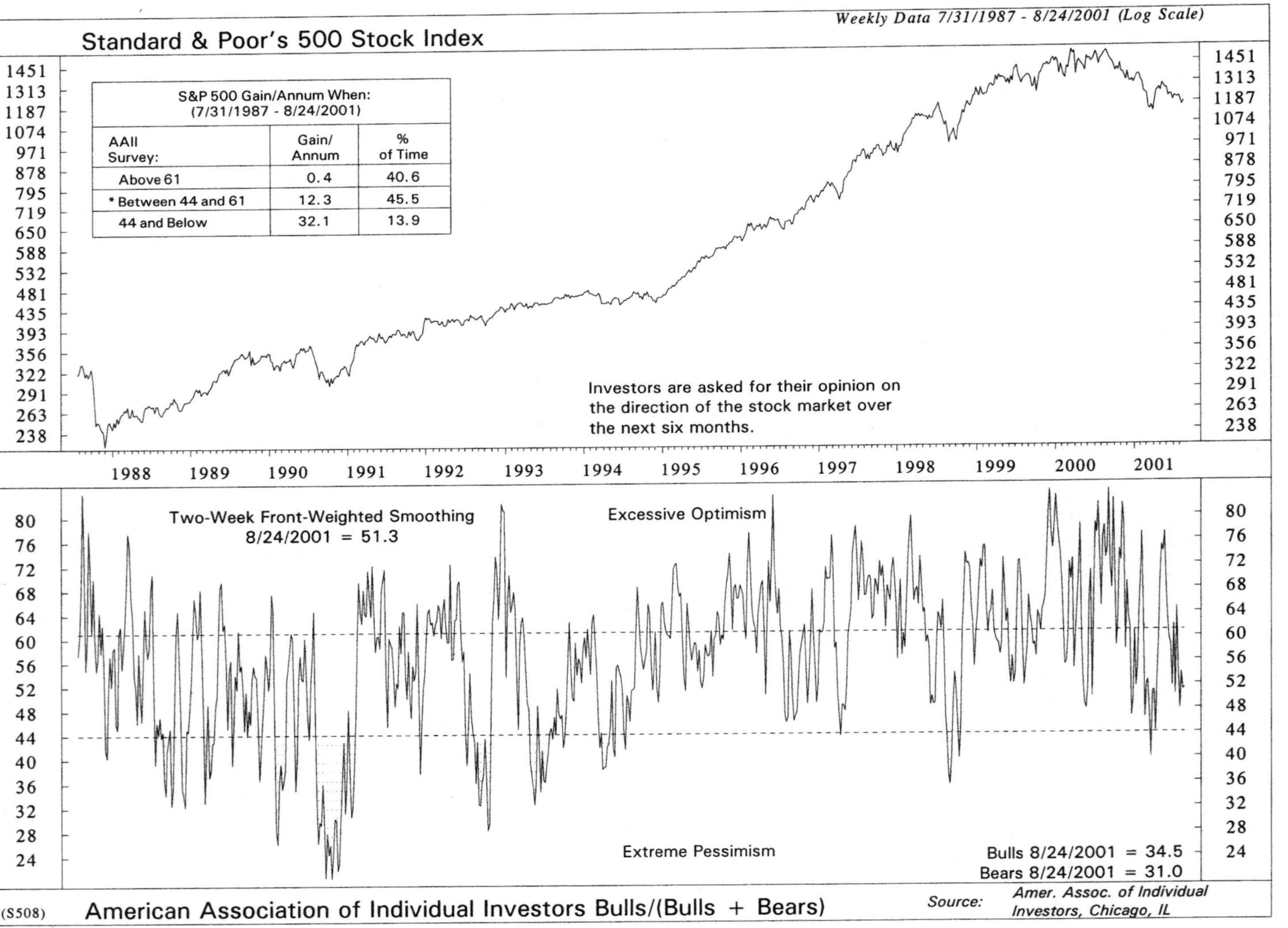

AAII Survey:	Gain/ Annum	% of Time
Above 61	0.4	40.6
* Between 44 and 61	12.3	45.5
44 and Below	32.1	13.9

Chart by permission of Ned Davis Research.

Andrews' Pitchfork: Median Line Method

Andrews' Pitchfork, or Median Line Method, is a chart-based visual tool used to judge trend strength, support, and resistance. It was developed by Alan Hall Andrews for use on arithmetic-scaled bar-charts.

Andrews' Pitchfork requires three price pivot points separated by time and price: an early high (or low), a subsequent reaction low (or high), and a still later high (or low). Andrews' Pitchfork may be drawn after any price reaction; that is, after any correction against an existing trend. From the midpoint between the reaction high and low (the second and third dates in time), extend a line backward in time (into the past) to the original price extreme (either a high or a low) that marked the beginning of the trend at hand. Next, using that midpoint line, draw two parallel lines, one from the recent reaction high, and one from the recent reaction low. Extend all three parallel lines forward into the future.

Highs and lows may be defined as price pivot points. On a daily bar chart, a pivot point high is a daily high immediately preceded by a lower daily high and followed by a lower daily high. A pivot point low is a low immediately preceded by a higher low and followed by a higher low.

Any three pivot points can be used to draw Andrews' Pitchfork. To keep it simple, select obvious points that mark substantial and consecutive directional changes of similar magnitude. If you become confused by too many pivot points, switch to a bar chart of the next larger time frame, and move from the daily to the weekly bar chart.

Although traditionally technical analysts use their judgement to select appropriate price pivot points, various quantitative filters rules can be devised to define appropriate price pivot points. For example, Envelopes, Bollinger Bands, and Price Channels can be used. A significant price pivot point is identified when price tags an extreme boundary line and then reverses below the low of the previous bar or bars. Also, momentum divergences could be used for identifying pivot points.

Three specific criteria for constructing Andrews' Pitchfork were developed by Barbara Star in her 1995 article, "Support and Resistance with the Andrews Pitchfork," *Technical Analysis of Stocks & Commodities,* Vol. 13, www.traders.com.

- First, identify a new trend after a successful retest of a price low or high.
- Second, identify a subsequent reaction (a corrective move against the trend) that breaks the conventional trendline.
- Third, quickly identify when the trend resumes. At that point, there is a trend and a countertrend reaction from which to draw the median line and two parallel lines.

Another way to view this method is sequentially in time. When viewing an uptrend, first select the low that marks the end of the previous downtrend and the beginning of the current uptrend. Second, select a subsequent price high. Third, select a still later reaction low. When viewing a downtrend, select the high that marks the end of the previous uptrend and the beginning of the current downtrend, select a subsequent low, and select a still later reaction high. In either an uptrend or downtrend, the median line connects the earliest of three outstanding price pivot points to a point midway between the two more recent price pivot points—one a high and the other a low. This median line becomes the handle of the pitchfork. The second and third lines are drawn parallel to the handle of the pitchfork from the two more recent price pivot points, the high and the low. These two parallel lines, extending forward in time, are the tines of the pitchfork.

All three parallel lines, the handle and the two tines, may offer support and resistance *before* the fact, making them useful in trading. Often, price will approach, meet or even slightly exceed a line, but fail to close beyond it. Such failures at support and resistance offer low-risk trading opportunities: close stop-loss orders may be placed just beyond the extreme price of the failure bar.

A recent example is shown on the chart. First, the DJIA made a new all-time high at 11909 on 1/14/00, and that obvious high was selected as point one. Second, the DJIA fell to an obvious low of 9612 on 3/8/00, and that obvious low was selected as point two. Third, the DJIA rose to an obvious high of 11600 on 4/12/00, and that obvious high was selected as point three. Note how the next decline found support near the pitchfork handle, and the next two rally attempts found resistance near the upper pitchfork tine. Once resistance at the upper tine was penetrated on a closing basis, it switched roles and became support.

The S&P 500 futures made an obvious price low in October 1998, and that was selected as an obvious point one. The all-time high in July 1999 was an obvious point two. The low in October 1999 stood out as an obvious point three. Note how the subsequent rallies found resistance near the pitchfork handle. Also, the lower pitchfork tine offered both support and resistance. Past April 2000, it became increasingly evident that the bull trend was unable to recover its upward momentum, having failed to overcome that lower pitchfork tine by increasingly larger amounts on each rally attempt.

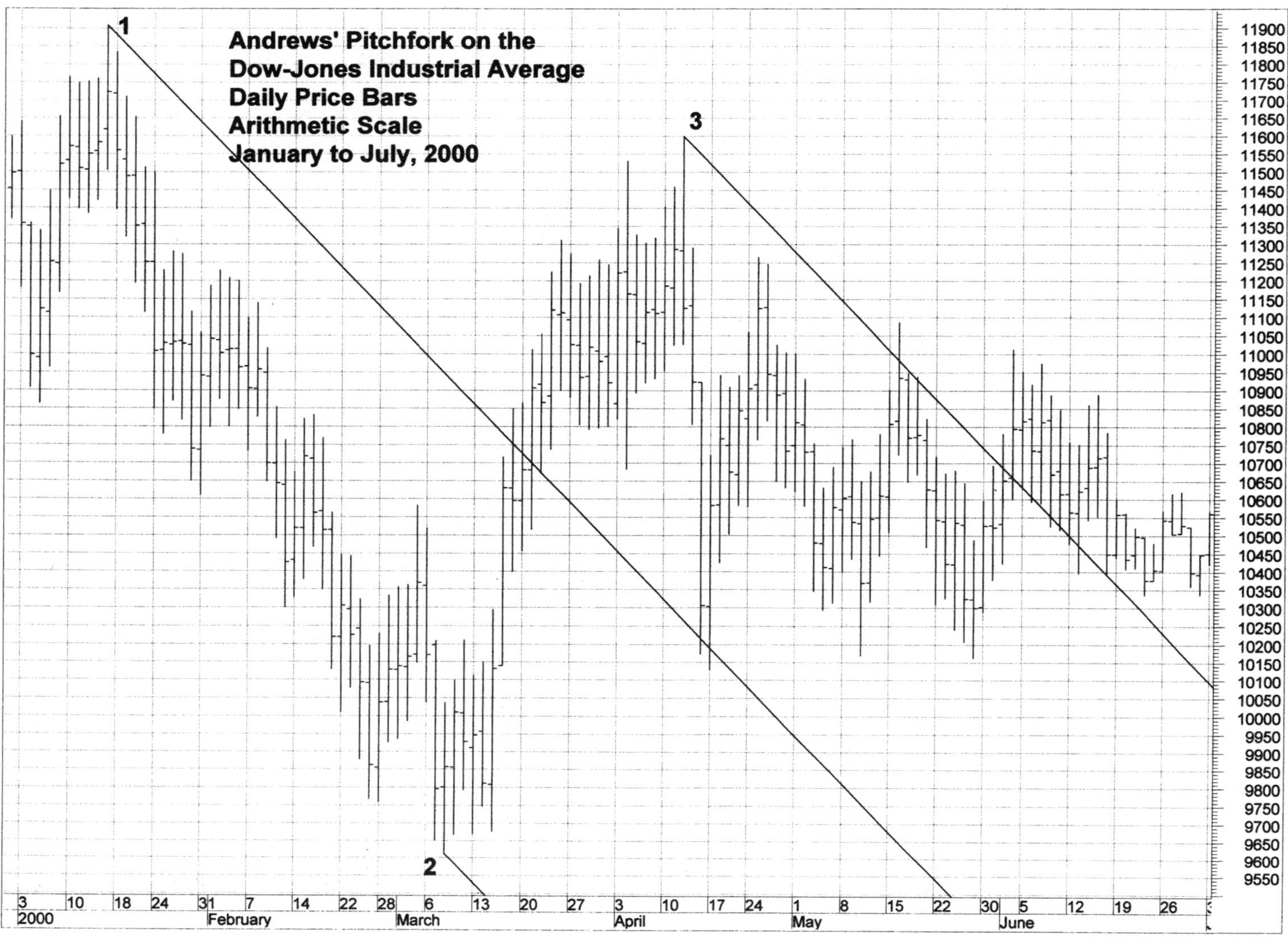
Andrews' Pitchfork on the
Dow-Jones Industrial Average
Daily Price Bars
Arithmetic Scale
January to July, 2000
1
2
3
11900
11850
11800
11750
11700
11650
11600
11550
11500
11450
11400
11350
11300
11250
11200
11150
11100
11050
11000
10950
10900
10850
10800
10750
10700
10650
10600
10550
10500
10450
10400
10350
10300
10250
10200
10150
10100
10050
10000
9950
9900
9850
9800
9750
9700
9650
9600
9550
3
10
18
24
31
7
14
22
28
6
13
20
27
3
10
17
24
1
8
15
22
30
5
12
19
26
2000
February
March
April
May
June

Andrews' Pitchfork on the
S&P 500 Futures Contract (CSI Perpetual)
Daily Price Bars
Arithmetic Scale
1
2
3
1550
1500
1450
1400
1350
1300
1250
1200
1150
1100
1050
1000
950
Oct
Nov
Dec
1999
Feb
Mar
Apr
May
Jun
Jul
Aug
Sep
Oct
Nov
Dec
2000
Feb
Mar
Apr
May
Jun
Jul
Aug
Sep

Arms' Ease of Movement Value (EMV)

Arms' Ease of Movement Value (EMV) quantifies the ease with which prices are moving. EMV is a moderately effective price and volume momentum indicator developed by Richard W. Arms, Jr. (Arms Advisory, 800 Wagontrain Drive S. E., Albuquerque, NM 87102).

The larger the price change and the lighter the volume, the easier the movement. EMV is simply price change (using midpoints of the range) divided by the ratio of volume divided by range. Mathematically, EMV may be expressed as follows:

$$\text{EVM} = (((H + L)/2) - ((Hp + Lp)/2)))/(V/(H - L))$$

where

H = the current period's high price.
L = the current period's low price.
Hp = the previous period's high price.
Lp = the previous period's low price.
V = the current period's volume.

The raw EMV may be smoothed by a moving average, and that average may produce a buy signal when it crosses above zero, and a sell signal when it crosses below the zero. High readings on smoothed EMV imply easy upward price movement, so the path of least resistance is bullish. Low readings on smoothed EMV imply easy downward price movement, so the path of least resistance is bearish.

Indicator Strategy Example for the Arms' Ease of Movement Value (EMV)

Historical data shows that the EMV can be a moderately effective indicator on both the long and short sides, but particularly on the long side. Based on the daily prices for the Dow-Jones Industrial Average for 72 years from 1928 to 2000, we found that the following parameters would have produced a positive result on a purely mechanical trend-following signal basis with no subjectivity, no sophisticated technical analysis, and no judgement:

Enter Long (Buy) at the current daily price close of the Dow-Jones Industrial Average when EMV smoothed by a 4-period exponential moving average rises above zero.

Close Long (Sell) at the current daily price close of the Dow-Jones Industrial Average when EMV smoothed by a 4-period exponential moving average falls below zero.

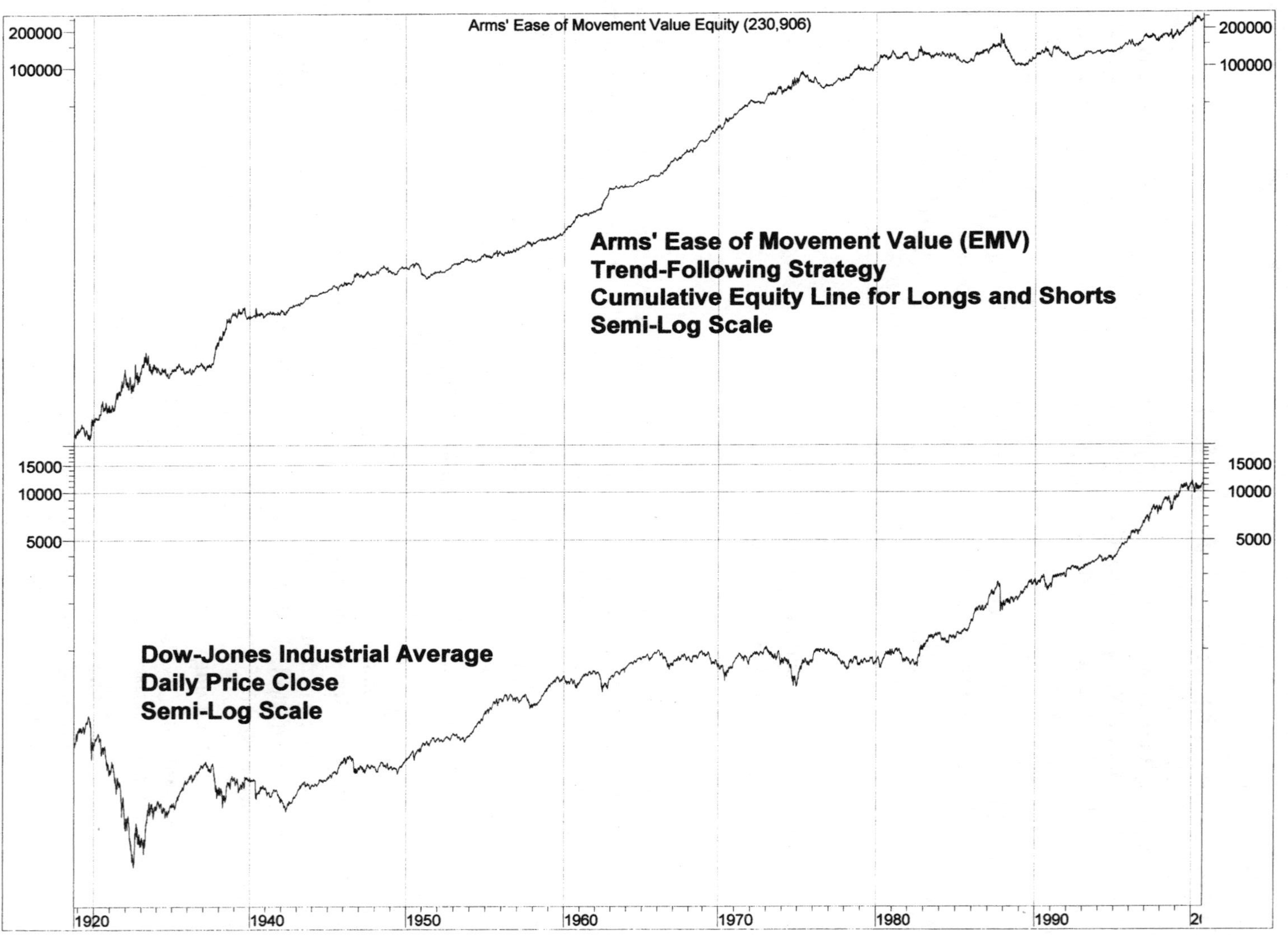

Arms' Ease of Movement Value Equity (230,906)
200000
100000
Arms' Ease of Movement Value (EMV)
Trend-Following Strategy
Cumulative Equity Line for Longs and Shorts
Semi-Log Scale
15000
10000
5000
Dow-Jones Industrial Average
Daily Price Close
Semi-Log Scale
1920
1940
1950
1960
1970
1980
1990

Arms' Ease of Movement Value (EMV)

Total net profit	230805.78	Open position value	0	Net Profit/Buy&Hold %	4944.66
Percent gain/loss	230805.78	Annual percent gain/loss	3206.12	Annual Net %/B&H %	4945.04
Initial investment	100	Interest earned	0		
Current position	Short	Date position entered	9/8/00		
Buy/Hold profit	4575.25	Days in test	26276	# of days per trade	6.32
Buy/Hold pct gain/loss	4575.25	Annual B/H pct gain/loss	63.55		
Total closed trades	4157	Commissions paid	0		
Avg profit per trade	55.52	Avg Win/Avg Loss ratio	1.82		
Total long trades	2079	Total short trades	2078	Long Win Trade %	43.43
Winning long trades	903	Winning short trades	734	Short Win Trade %	35.32
Total winning trades	1637	Total losing trades	2520	Total Win Trade %	39.38
Amount of winning trades	1479696.5	Amount of losing trades	−1248890	Net Profit Margin %	8.46
Average win	903.91	Average loss	−495.59	Average P. Margin %	29.18
Largest win	33302.14	Largest loss	−9382.08	% Net/(Win + Loss)	56.04
Average length of win	8.32	Average length of loss	3.41	(Win − Loss)/Loss %	143.99
Longest winning trade	35	Longest losing trade	24	(Win − Loss)/Loss %	45.83
Most consecutive wins	9	Most consecutive losses	12	(Win − Loss)/Loss %	−25.00
Total bars out	5	Average length out	5		
Longest out period	5				
System close drawdown	−7.83	Profit/Loss index	15.6	% Net Profit/SODD	2947711.11
System open drawdown	−7.83	Reward/Risk index	100	(Net P. − SODD)/Net P.	100.00
Max open trade drawdown	−9382.08	Buy/Hold index	4944.66	% SODD/Net Profit	0.00

In the Equis MetaStock® "System Report" (profit and loss summary statistics), the *Total net profit* is the sum of profits minus the sum of losses, including open positions marked to the market. In contrast, the *Amount of Winning Trades* is the sum of realized profits (the total of all gains on closed-out trades only, excluding any open positions). Similarly, the *Amount of Losing Trades* is the sum of realized losses (the total of all losses on closed-out trades only, excluding any open positions). *System close drawdown* is the largest decline in the cumulative equity line below the initial investment, based on closed-out positions only. *System open drawdown (SODD)* is the largest decline in the cumulative equity line below the initial investment when a position is open. *Max open trade drawdown* is the largest decline in the cumulative equity line below the trade entry price during the worst single trade. The *Profit/Loss Index* is a complex calculation that relates the Amount of Winning Trades to the Amount of Losing Trades on a scale of −100 (worst possible performance) to +100 (best possible performance), with zero representing profits equal to losses. *Reward/Risk Index* is the Total net profit minus System open drawdown. The resulting difference is then divided by the Total net profit. The *Buy/Hold Index* is the Total net profit minus the buy-and-hold strategy's net profit. The resulting difference is then divided by the buy-and-hold net profit. In this exercise, initial equity is assumed to be $100. Both long and short positions are taken unless otherwise noted. Trades are executed at the closing price on the signal date. Transaction costs, interest expenses, and margins are not included in the statistics.

Enter Short (Sell Short) at the current daily price close of the Dow-Jones Industrial Average when EMV smoothed by a 4-period exponential moving average falls below zero.

Close Short (Cover) at the current daily price close of the Dow-Jones Industrial Average when EMV smoothed by a 4-period exponential moving average rises above zero.

Starting with $100 and reinvesting profits, total net profits for this EMV strategy would have been $230,805.78, assuming a fully invested strategy, reinvestment of profits, no transactions costs and no taxes. This would have been 4,944.66 percent better than buy-and-hold. Short selling, which was included in this strategy, would have lost money since March, 1980, but nevertheless would have been profitable over the entire 72-years as a whole.

The Equis International MetaStock® System Testing rules are written as follows:

Enter long: EMV(opt1,E) > 0

Close long: EMV(opt1,E) < 0

Enter short: EMV(opt1,E) < 0

Close short: EMV(opt1,E) > 0

OPT1 Current value: 4

Arms' Short-Term Trading Index (TRIN, MKDS)

Arms' Short-Term Trading Index is a popular overbought/oversold oscillator developed in the 1960's by Richard W. Arms, Jr. (Arms Advisory, 800 Wagontrain Drive S. E., Albuquerque, NM 87102). Arms' Index is also commonly referred to by its quote machine symbols, TRIN and MKDS. Mathematically, Arms' Index is calculated as follows:

(Advances/Declines)/(Advancing Volume/Declining Volume)

Thus, Arms' Index is calculated using four numbers combined into three ratios. These three ratios use four numbers derived from closing price and volume data for all issues traded each day on the New York Stock Exchange (NYSE). This data is readily available from online sources such as Reuters. Also, the data is published in many daily newspapers. For example, in the Wall Street Journal, this data appears on page C2, under STOCK MARKET DATA BANK, DIARIES, NYSE.

The four required numbers are:

- Advances, or advancing issues, are the number of NYSE listed stocks with a positive, upward price change for the day;
- Declines, or declining issues, are the number of NYSE listed stocks with a negative, downward price change for the day;
- zAdv vol (000), the volume of advancing issues, or Advancing Volume; and
- zDec vol (000), the volume of declining issues, or Declining Volume.

After gathering this data, the Arms' Index is computed in three steps:

1. Divide the number of advancing issues by the number of declining issues; that is, Advances/Declines;
2. Divide the volume of advancing issues by the volume of declining issues; that is, zAdv vol/zDec vol;
3. Divide the ratio obtained in Step 1 by the ratio obtained in Step 2; that is, (Advances/Declines)/(zAdv vol/zDec vol).

Arms' Index effectively quantifies the intensity of buying pressure relative to the intensity of selling pressure for the market as a whole. We found that both extremely high Arms' Index levels greater than 1.444 and extremely low Arms' Index levels of 0.523 or less were bullish and statistically significant at the 99% confidence level over a 1-year holding period (or forward window of time). This means that there was less than an one in 100 probability that the stock market rose by chance alone after extreme readings in the daily Arm's Index.

Although at first impression it may seem odd that both extremely high and extremely low levels would be bullish, we can understand this as we reflect on how markets bottom and reverse trend. Important trend reversals are characterized by extreme swings in market sentiment. First, sentiment is extremely bearish as the market falls (to extremely oversold) at the end of a substantial market price drop. When selling is exhausted, meaning everyone who can sell has already sold, selling pressure dries up, and bargain hunters move in. Prices start to move up causing short sellers to cut losses, and portfolio managers must quickly jump on board the rise so they will not fall behind their performance benchmarks. A powerful rebound effect emerges from the ruins left by the bear. There is a price reversion to the mean (for example, to a 50-day or 200-day moving average), or perhaps beyond. The sudden imbalance of buying pressure over selling pressure produces distorted ratios of buying relative to selling at the beginning of a new bull wave. Thus, extremely high and extremely low levels of the Arms' Index are both bullish, first with high levels on the panic selling climax then followed by low levels on the one-sided, snap-back rally.

Intense selling pressure was bullish. If there was significantly more selling pressure than buying pressure on any given day, the Arms' Index rose to 1.444 or higher, and it was probable at the 99% confidence level that the market would be higher in a year.

Intense buying pressure was bullish. If there was significantly more buying pressure than selling pressure on any given day, the Arms' Index fell to 0.523 or lower, and it was probable at the 99% confidence level that the market would be higher in 6-month and 1-year holding periods. For shorter-term forward time windows of 1 month and 3 months, readings of 0.523 or lower also were bullish, but at the lesser 95% confidence level. Arms' Index levels above 0.523, but below 1.444, had no statistical significance.

Technical analysts traditionally have smoothed raw data with their standard 10-period simple moving average of the daily readings. They have done this in order to even out erratic day-to-day movements. The results of 10-day simple moving averages greater than 1.266 were very bullish over 1-year holding periods (forward time windows). These results were statistically highly significant at the 99.9% confidence level, which means that there was less than an one in 1000 probability that the stock market rose by chance alone after a high 10-day Arms' Index reading in excess of 1.266.

The following table, Out-of-Sample Simulation for Arms' 10-day SMA > 1.266, shows out-of-sample testing without hindsight bias. It shows all of the completed round-turn long trades signaled by Arms' Index 10-day simple moving average greater than 1.266. (The 1988 edition of this book established these specific parameters.) Because these parameters were established on available data before 1987, the performance statistics in the table represent a simulation of what realistically might have been achieved using this indicator, excluding transactions costs, taxes and dividends. An initial $100.00 would have grown to $454.95 without a losing trade.

Note that in our testing, a repeated buy signal (that is, Arm's 10-day SMA > 1.266) within one year of the previous buy signal extended the 1-year holding period to one year from the repeated buy signal. Thus, a series of repeated buy signals extended the holding period substantially. For example, the long-side trade that was opened on 10/16/87 remained open more than 5 years until 12/3/92 because of repeated buy signals before the previous buy signal was yet one year old. Note also that the actual reading of Arms' Index on 7/16/86 was 1.2663, which rounds down to 1.266, but is actually greater than 1.266, as our strict decision rule demands.

Out-of-Sample Simulation for Arms' 10-day SMA > 1.266

Arms' 10	*Date*	*S&P 500*	*+ 1 Year*	*S&P 500*	*Net Profit*	*Net P. %*	*Compound*
1.266	7/16/86	235.00	7/16/87	312.70	77.70	33.06	133.06
1.681	10/16/87	282.70	*12/3/92	409.55	126.85	44.87	192.77
1.284	2/23/93	434.80	2/23/94	470.69	35.89	8.25	208.68
1.267	7/16/96	628.37	7/16/97	936.59	308.22	49.05	311.04
1.904	10/27/97	876.98	*9/30/99	1282.71	405.73	46.26	454.95

*1-year holding period extended by repeated buy signals: Arms' 10-day SMA > 1.266.

Our original testing method divided Arm's Index readings for the 59-year test period from January 1928 to March 1987 into 20 ranges with approximately the same number of occurrences in each range. For each reading in a range, the gain or loss in four subsequent time periods (1 month later, 3 months later, 6 months later, and 12 months later) was calculated. The combined results for readings within each range were statistically compared, using chi-squared tests, to the performance of the overall market (as measured by the Standard & Poor's 500). Varying degrees of bullish and bearish significance were noted on the basis of that comparison.

Countless variations for manipulating this fascinating indicator are too numerous to test here. The "Open 10 TRIN" or "Open 10 Trading Index" is calculated by dividing a ratio of a 10-day total of the number of advancing issues to a 10-day total of the number of declining issues by a ratio of a 10-day total of volume of advancing issues to a 10-day total of the volume of declining issues. The "Open 30 TRIN" or "Open 30 Trading Index" are similar, and they use 30-day totals. Analysts have experimented with Fibonacci numbers, other number progressions and optimization for the day totals, and they have varied the signal threshold levels in a wide variety of increments, not necessarily symmetrically, since observed raw data are not distributed symmetrically around the balanced ratio of 1.00.

A single day's Arms' Index reading at 2.65 and higher was found to be a useful threshold in 1986. (See Alphier, J., & Kuhn, B., "A helping hand from the Arms Index," *Technical Analysis of Stocks & Commodities,* Vol. 5:4, pp. 142–143, www.traders.com.) If we bought the S&P 500 Composite Stock Price Index on the close of every day when the Arms' Index was 2.65 or higher and held for one year, we would have made a profit 11 out of 12 times over the past 35 years: 92% of the signals were profitable. Because these parameters were established on available data before 1987, the performance statistics in the table on trades closed out after 1987 represent a simulation of what realistically might have been achieved using this indicator, excluding transactions costs, taxes and dividends. An initial $100.00 in 1986 would have grown to $273.25 without a losing trade. Like our Arms' Index 10-day simple moving average greater than 1.266 rule, 100% accuracy in a 14-year, out-of-sample simulation with different parameters suggests that the underlying idea behind the Arms' Index may well be worthwhile.

Note that in our testing a repeated buy signal (that is, an Arm's Index 1-day reading greater than 2.65), within one year of the previous buy signal, extended the 1-year holding period to one year from the repeated buy signal. Thus, a series of repeated buy signals extended the holding period substantially. For example, the long-side trade opened on 7/7/86 and remained open more than 5 years until 10/10/91 because of repeated buy signals before the previous buy signal was yet one year old.

Updated Arms' Index > 2.65, Out-of-Sample Since 10/14/86

Arms'	*Date*	*S&P 500*	*+ 1 Yr.*	*S&P 500*	*Net Profit*	*Net P. %*	*Compound*	*Since '86*
2.82	6/24/65	83.56	6/24/66	86.58	3.02	3.61	103.61	
2.99	10/3/66	74.90	10/3/67	96.65	21.75	29.04	133.70	
3.16	3/14/68	88.32	3/14/69	98.00	9.68	10.96	148.35	
3.50	5/4/70	79.37	5/4/71	103.79	24.42	30.77	193.99	
2.81	9/27/74	64.94	*12/2/75	89.33	24.39	37.56	266.85	
2.66	10/14/76	100.88	*11/18/77	95.33	−5.55	−5.50	252.17	
3.06	5/7/79	99.02	*10/25/83	166.45	67.43	68.10	423.90	
2.78	2/8/84	155.85	*1/2/86	209.59	53.74	34.48	570.06	
2.81	7/7/86	244.05	*10/10/91	380.55	136.50	55.93	888.90	155.93
4.02	11/15/91	382.60	11/16/92	420.70	38.10	9.96	977.42	171.46
2.85	2/16/93	433.91	2/16/94	472.79	38.88	8.96	1065.00	186.82
8.82	10/27/97	876.98	*9/30/99	1282.71	405.73	46.26	1557.72	273.25
4.01	4/14/00	1356.56	4/14/01					

*1-year holding period extended by repeat buy signals: Arms' Index > 2.65.

Shorter-term trading with the Arms' Index is an irresistible temptation. After all, the full name of the indicator is "the Arms' Short-Term Trading Index." In the real-world, few traders would have the patience to hold for a year based on a historical study of the data.

We searched for a mechanical long and short decision rule that would be adaptive to the current action of the market. Based on a 16-year file of daily data for the Arms' Short-Term Trading Index, and for an adjusted series of price data for the S&P 500 Depositary Receipts from inception in 1993 and the S&P futures from 1984 to 1993, we found that the following parameters would have produced a positive result on a purely mechanical signal basis with no subjectivity, no sophisticated technical analysis, and no judgement:

Enter Long (Buy) at the current daily price close when the 11-day exponential moving average of the daily Arms' Short-Term Trading Index is greater than 0.800.

Close Long (Sell) at the current daily price close when the 11-day exponential moving average of the daily Arms' Short-Term Trading Index is less than 0.800.

Sell Long and Sell Short at the current daily price close when the 11-day exponential moving average of the daily Arms' Short-Term Trading Index is less than 0.800.

Cover Short and Buy Long at the current daily price close when the 11-day exponential moving average of the daily Arms' Short-Term Trading Index is greater than 0.800.

Starting with $100 and reinvesting profits, total net profits for this strategy would have been $1,640.39, with 77.13% winning trades, assuming a fully invested strategy, reinvestment of profits, no transactions costs and no taxes. This would have been 80.47% better than buy-and-hold. Also, the worst drawdowns would have been milder than buy-and-hold.

The Equis International MetaStock® System Testing rules are written as follows, with the Arms' Short-Term Trading Index multiplied by 1000 and placed in the data field normally reserved for volume:

Enter long: Mov(V,opt1,E) > opt2

Close long: Mov(V,opt1,E) < opt2

Enter short: Mov(V,opt1,E) < opt2

Close short: Mov(V,opt1,E) > opt2

OPT1 Current value: 11
OPT2 Current value: 800

Also, the exact same parameters outperformed buy-and-hold using Dow-Jones Industrial Average daily data over the same 16 years from 1984 to 2000, as shown in the final table for this topic.

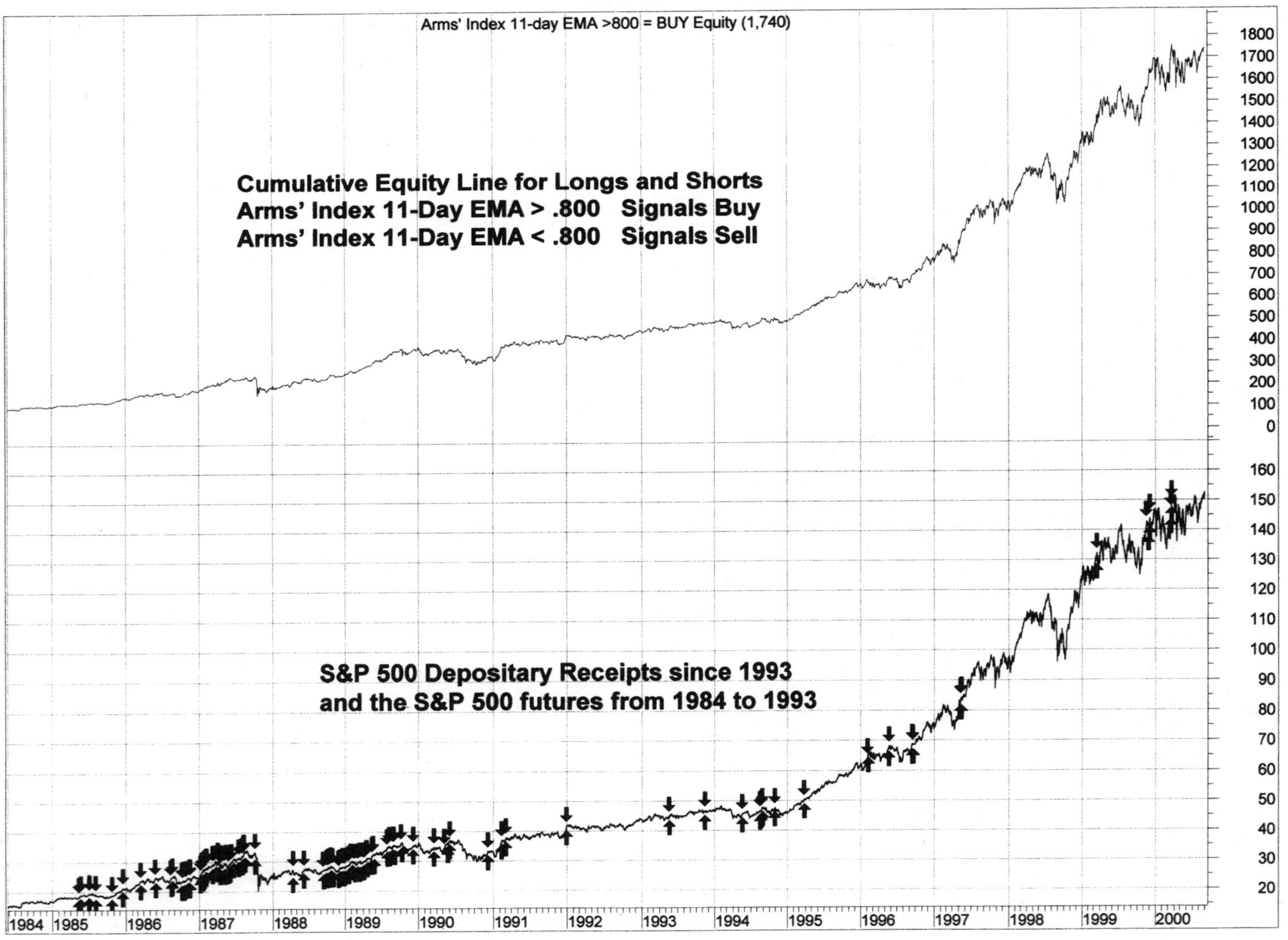
Arms' Index 11-day EMA >800 = BUY Equity (1,740)
Cumulative Equity Line for Longs and Shorts
Arms' Index 11-Day EMA > .800 Signals Buy
Arms' Index 11-Day EMA < .800 Signals Sell
S&P 500 Depositary Receipts since 1993
and the S&P 500 futures from 1984 to 1993
1800
1700
1600
1500
1400
1300
1200
1100
1000
900
800
700
600
500
400
300
200
100
0
160
150
140
130
120
110
100
90
80
70
60
50
40
30
20
1984
1985
1986
1987
1988
1989
1990
1991
1992
1993
1994
1995
1996
1997
1998
1999
2000

Arms' Index 11-Day EMA > .800, Signals Buy S&P

Total net profit	1640.39	Open position value	27.46	Net Profit/Buy&Hold %	80.47
Percent gain/loss	1640.39	Annual percent gain/loss	100.8	Annual Net %/B&H %	80.48
Initial investment	100	Interest earned	0		
Current position	Long	Date position entered	3/22/00		
Buy/Hold profit	908.93	Days in test	5940	# of days per trade	31.60
Buy/Hold pct gain/loss	908.93	Annual B/H pct gain/loss	55.85		
Total closed trades	188	Commissions paid	0		
Avg profit per trade	8.58	Avg Win/Avg Loss ratio	2.53		
Total long trades	94	Total short trades	94	Long Win Trade %	79.79
Winning long trades	75	Winning short trades	70	Short Win Trade %	74.47
Total winning trades	145	Total losing trades	43	Total Win Trade %	77.13
Amount of winning trades	1827.51	Amount of losing trades	−214.58	Net Profit Margin %	78.98
Average win	12.6	Average loss	−4.99	Average P. Margin %	43.26
Largest win	521	Largest loss	−37.24	% Net/(Win + Loss)	86.66
Average length of win	22.48	Average length of loss	21.21	(Win − Loss)/Loss %	5.99
Longest winning trade	463	Longest losing trade	132	(Win − Loss)/Loss %	250.76
Most consecutive wins	19	Most consecutive losses	3	(Win − Loss)/Loss %	533.33
Total bars out	11	Average length out	11		
Longest out period	11				
System close drawdown	0	Profit/Loss index	88.43	% Net Profit/SODD	54138.28
System open drawdown	−3.03	Reward/Risk index	99.82	(Net P. − SODD)/Net P.	99.82
Max open trade drawdown	−160.85	Buy/Hold index	83.5	% SODD/Net Profit	−0.18

In the Equis MetaStock® "System Report" (profit and loss summary statistics), the *Total net profit* is the sum of profits minus the sum of losses, including open positions marked to the market. In contrast, the *Amount of Winning Trades* is the sum of realized profits (the total of all gains on closed-out trades only, excluding any open positions). Similarly, the *Amount of Losing Trades* is the sum of realized losses (the total of all losses on closed-out trades only, excluding any open positions). *System close drawdown* is the largest decline in the cumulative equity line below the initial investment, based on closed-out positions only. *System open drawdown (SODD)* is the largest decline in the cumulative equity line below the initial investment when a position is open. *Max open trade drawdown* is the largest decline in the cumulative equity line below the trade entry price during the worst single trade. The *Profit/Loss Index* is a complex calculation that relates the Amount of Winning Trades to the Amount of Losing Trades on a scale of −100 (worst possible performance) to +100 (best possible performance), with zero representing profits equal to losses. *Reward/Risk Index* is the Total net profit minus System open drawdown. The resulting difference is then divided by the Total net profit. The *Buy/Hold Index* is the Total net profit minus the buy-and-hold strategy's net profit. The resulting difference is then divided by the buy-and-hold net profit. In this exercise, initial equity is assumed to be $100. Both long and short positions are taken unless otherwise noted. Trades are executed at the closing price on the signal date. Transaction costs, interest expenses, and margins are not included in the statistics.

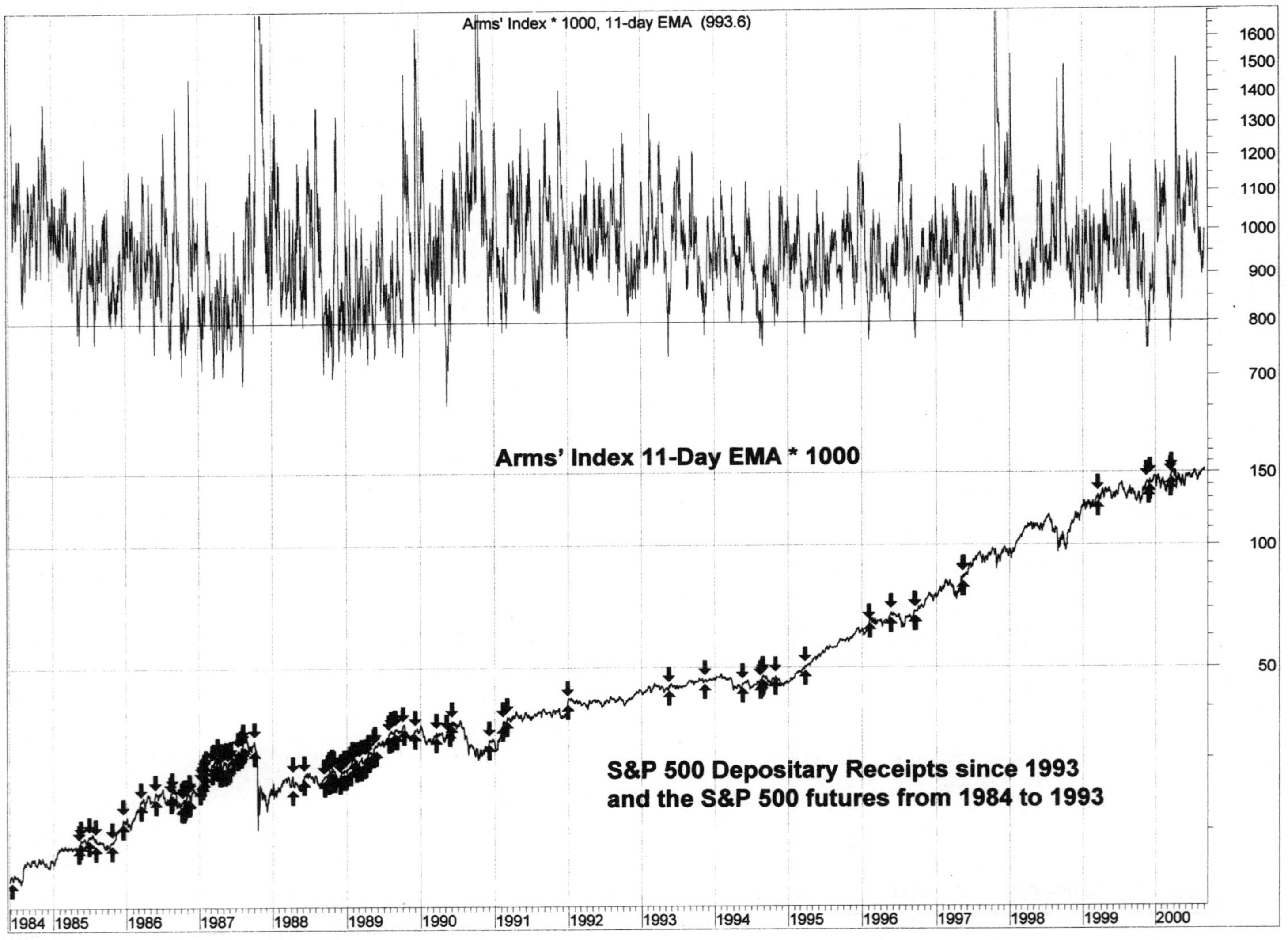

Arms' Index * 1000, 11-day EMA (993.6)
Arms' Index 11-Day EMA * 1000
S&P 500 Depositary Receipts since 1993
and the S&P 500 futures from 1984 to 1993
1600
1500
1400
1300
1200
1100
1000
900
800
700
150
100
50
1984
1985
1986
1987
1988
1989
1990
1991
1992
1993
1994
1995
1996
1997
1998
1999
2000

Arms' Index 11-Day EMA > .800, Signals Buy DJIA

Total net profit	1253.93	Open position value	42.7	Net Profit/Buy&Hold %	36.43
Percent gain/loss	1253.93	Annual percent gain/loss	76.96	Annual Net %/B&H %	36.43
Initial investment	100	Interest earned	0		
Current position	Long	Date position entered	3/22/00		
Buy/Hold profit	919.13	Days in test	5947	# of days per trade	31.97
Buy/Hold pct gain/loss	919.13	Annual B/H pct gain/loss	56.41		
Total closed trades	186	Commissions paid	0		
Avg profit per trade	6.51	Avg Win/Avg Loss ratio	2.17		
Total long trades	93	Total short trades	93	Long Win Trade %	81.72
Winning long trades	76	Winning short trades	58	Short Win Trade %	62.37
Total winning trades	134	Total losing trades	52	Total Win Trade %	72.04
Amount of winning trades	1475.28	Amount of losing trades	−264.05	Net Profit Margin %	69.64
Average win	11.01	Average loss	−5.08	Average P. Margin %	36.86
Largest win	328.63	Largest loss	−71.86	% Net/(Win + Loss)	64.11
Average length of win	25.1	Average length of loss	15.56	(Win − Loss)/Loss %	61.31
Longest winning trade	463	Longest losing trade	132	(Win − Loss)/Loss %	250.76
Most consecutive wins	10	Most consecutive losses	4	(Win − Loss)/Loss %	150.00
Total bars out	11	Average length out	11		
Longest out period	11				
System close drawdown	0	Profit/Loss index	82.61	% Net Profit/SODD	58052.31
System open drawdown	−2.16	Reward/Risk index	99.83	(Net P. − SODD)/Net P.	99.83
Max open trade drawdown	−172.75	Buy/Hold index	41.07	% SODD/Net Profit	−0.17

In the Equis MetaStock® "System Report" (profit and loss summary statistics), the *Total net profit* is the sum of profits minus the sum of losses, including open positions marked to the market. In contrast, the *Amount of Winning Trades* is the sum of realized profits (the total of all gains on closed-out trades only, excluding any open positions). Similarly, the *Amount of Losing Trades* is the sum of realized losses (the total of all losses on closed-out trades only, excluding any open positions). *System close drawdown* is the largest decline in the cumulative equity line below the initial investment, based on closed-out positions only. *System open drawdown (SODD)* is the largest decline in the cumulative equity line below the initial investment when a position is open. *Max open trade drawdown* is the largest decline in the cumulative equity line below the trade entry price during the worst single trade. The *Profit/Loss Index* is a complex calculation that relates the Amount of Winning Trades to the Amount of Losing Trades on a scale of −100 (worst possible performance) to +100 (best possible performance), with zero representing profits equal to losses. *Reward/Risk Index* is the Total net profit minus System open drawdown. The resulting difference is then divided by the Total net profit. The *Buy/Hold Index* is the Total net profit minus the buy-and-hold strategy's net profit. The resulting difference is then divided by the buy-and-hold net profit. In this exercise, initial equity is assumed to be $100. Both long and short positions are taken unless otherwise noted. Trades are executed at the closing price on the signal date. Transaction costs, interest expenses, and margins are not included in the statistics.

Aroon, Aroon Oscillator

Aroon was designed by Tushar S. Chande in his 1995 article, "A Time Price Oscillator," *Technical Analysis of Stocks & Commodities* (Vol. 13, pp. 369–374), www.traders.com. The idea was to quickly detect the change from price directional trend to flat trading range (and vice versa) by measuring the number of time periods within a defined moving time window of n-periods that have passed since the most recent n-period high and n-period low. Aroon Oscillator is the difference between Aroon Up minus Aroon Down.

Mathematically, Aroon may be expressed as follows:

$$\text{Aroon Up} = 100 * ((n - \text{H})/n)$$

$$\text{Aroon Down} = 100 * ((n - \text{L})/n)$$

where

Aroon Up = the number of periods since the most recent n-period high, expressed as a percentage of the total number of periods, n.

Aroon Down = the number of periods since the most recent n-period low, expressed as a percentage of the total number of periods, n.

H = the number of periods within a defined moving time window of n-periods since the most recent n-period high.

L = the number of periods within a defined moving time window of n-periods since the most recent n-period low.

n = the total number of periods in the moving time window being evaluated.

Aroon has two parts, each of which range from 0 to 100. Aroon Up measures the number of periods since the most recent n-period high. When price makes a new n-period high, Aroon Up equals 100, and that indicates a strong price trend. When price has not made a new high for n-periods, Aroon Up equals 0, indicating that the uptrend has lost bullish momentum.

Aroon Down measures the number of periods since the most recent n-period low. When price makes a new n-period low, Aroon Down equals 100, indicating a weak price trend. When price has not made a new low for n-periods, Aroon Down equals 0, and that indicates that the downtrend has lost bearish momentum.

A strong uptrend is indicated when the Aroon Up line persistently remains between 70 and 100 while the Aroon Down line persistently remains between 0 and 30. A significant downtrend is indicated when the Aroon Down line persistently remains between 70 and 100 while the Aroon Up line persistently remains between 0 and 30.

A clear and simple decision rule is: buy when the Aroon Up line crosses above the Aroon Down line; sell when the Aroon Down line crosses above the Aroon Up line. This is the same as the Aroon Oscillator crossing zero.

Indicator Strategy Example for Aroon Up Crossing Aroon Down

Historical data shows that Aroon can be a moderately effective indicator on long side only. It lost money on the short side. Based on the daily prices for the Dow-Jones Industrial Average for 72 years from 1928 to 2000, we found that the following parameters would have produced a positive result on a purely mechanical trend-following signal basis with no subjectivity, no sophisticated technical analysis, and no judgement:

Enter Long (Buy) at the current daily price close of the Dow-Jones Industrial Average when the 2-day Aroon Up is greater than the 2-day Aroon Down.

Close Long (Sell) at the current daily price close of the Dow-Jones Industrial Average when the 2-day Aroon Up is less than the 2-day Aroon Down.

Enter Short (Sell Short) never.

Starting with $100 and reinvesting profits, total net profits for this Aroon long-only strategy would have been $7,132.30, assuming a fully invested strategy, reinvestment of profits, no transactions costs, and no taxes. This would have been 55.89 percent better than buy-and-hold. Short selling, which was not included in this strategy, would have lost money over the entire 72-years as a whole, but those short-side losses would not have exceeded long-side profits.

The Equis International MetaStock® System Testing rules are written as follows:

Enter long: AroonUp(opt1) > AroonDown(opt1)

Close long: AroonUp(opt1) < AroonDown(opt1)

OPT1 Current value: 2

Another Indicator Strategy Example for Aroon, as a Long-term Bull Market Indicator

There is always a good demand for an indicator that is right all the time, and this one has not made a bad trade since 1982. The signals are not the most timely, and profits would have been only 5.2% greater than the passive buy-and-hold strategy. But some people would rather be right than rich.

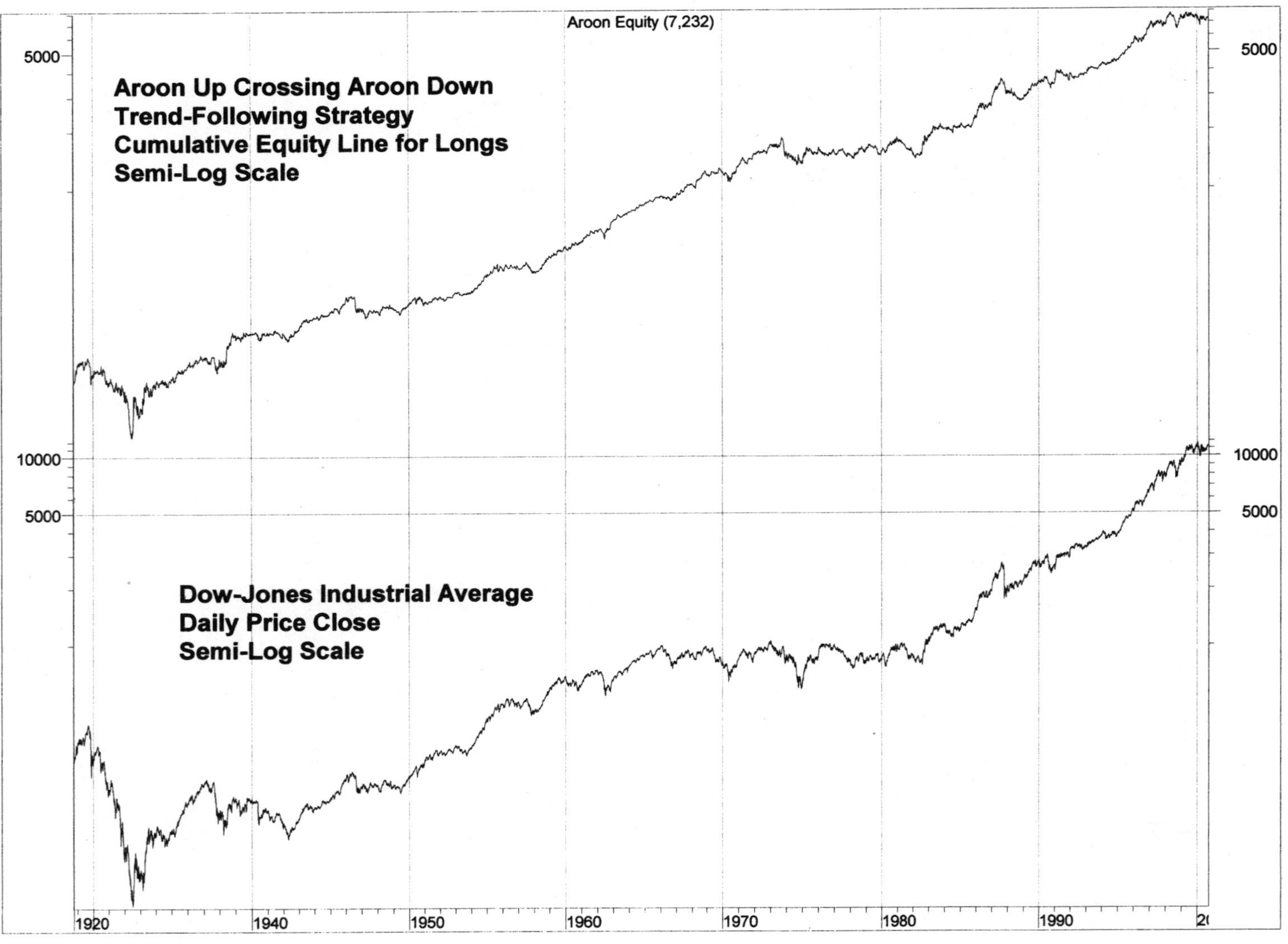
Aroon Equity (7,232)
Aroon Up Crossing Aroon Down
Trend-Following Strategy
Cumulative Equity Line for Longs
Semi-Log Scale
Dow-Jones Industrial Average
Daily Price Close
Semi-Log Scale
5000
10000
5000
1920
1940
1950
1960
1970
1980
1990

Aroon

Total net profit	7132.3	Open position value	N/A	Net Profit/Buy&Hold %	55.89
Percent gain/loss	7132.3	Annual percent gain/loss	99.07	Annual Net %/B&H %	55.89
Initial investment	100	Interest earned	0		
Current position	Out	Date position entered	9/8/00		
Buy/Hold profit	4575.25	Days in test	26276	# of days per trade	10.30
Buy/Hold pct gain/loss	4575.25	Annual B/H pct gain/loss	63.55		
Total closed trades	2550	Commissions paid	0		
Avg profit per trade	2.8	Avg Win/Avg Loss ratio	1.7		
Total long trades	2550	Total short trades	0	Long Win Trade %	44.12
Winning long trades	1125	Winning short trades	0	Short Win Trade %	#DIV/0!
Total winning trades	1125	Total losing trades	1425	Total Win Trade %	44.12
Amount of winning trades	28115.33	Amount of losing trades	−20983.02	Net Profit Margin %	14.53
Average win	24.99	Average loss	−14.72	Average P. Margin %	25.86
Largest win	529.28	Largest loss	−350.01	% Net/(Win + Loss)	20.39
Average length of win	6.75	Average length of loss	3.33	(Win − Loss)/Loss %	102.70
Longest winning trade	21	Longest losing trade	12	(Win − Loss)/Loss %	75.00
Most consecutive wins	9	Most consecutive losses	12	(Win − Loss)/Loss %	−25.00
Total bars out	10826	Average length out	4.24		
Longest out period	20				
System close drawdown	−47.28	Profit/Loss index	25.37	% Net Profit/SODD	15085.24
System open drawdown	−47.28	Reward/Risk index	99.34	(Net P. − SODD)/Net P.	99.34
Max open trade drawdown	−350.01	Buy/Hold index	55.89	% SODD/Net Profit	−0.66

In the Equis MetaStock® "System Report" (profit and loss summary statistics), the *Total net profit* is the sum of profits minus the sum of losses, including open positions marked to the market. In contrast, the *Amount of Winning Trades* is the sum of realized profits (the total of all gains on closed-out trades only, excluding any open positions). Similarly, the *Amount of Losing Trades* is the sum of realized losses (the total of all losses on closed-out trades only, excluding any open positions). *System close drawdown* is the largest decline in the cumulative equity line below the initial investment, based on closed-out positions only. *System open drawdown (SODD)* is the largest decline in the cumulative equity line below the initial investment when a position is open. *Max open trade drawdown* is the largest decline in the cumulative equity line below the trade entry price during the worst single trade. The *Profit/Loss Index* is a complex calculation that relates the Amount of Winning Trades to the Amount of Losing Trades on a scale of −100 (worst possible performance) to +100 (best possible performance), with zero representing profits equal to losses. *Reward/Risk Index* is the Total net profit minus System open drawdown. The resulting difference is then divided by the Total net profit. The *Buy/Hold Index* is the Total net profit minus the buy-and-hold strategy's net profit. The resulting difference is then divided by the buy-and-hold net profit. In this exercise, initial equity is assumed to be $100. Both long and short positions are taken unless otherwise noted. Trades are executed at the closing price on the signal date. Transaction costs, interest expenses, and margins are not included in the statistics.

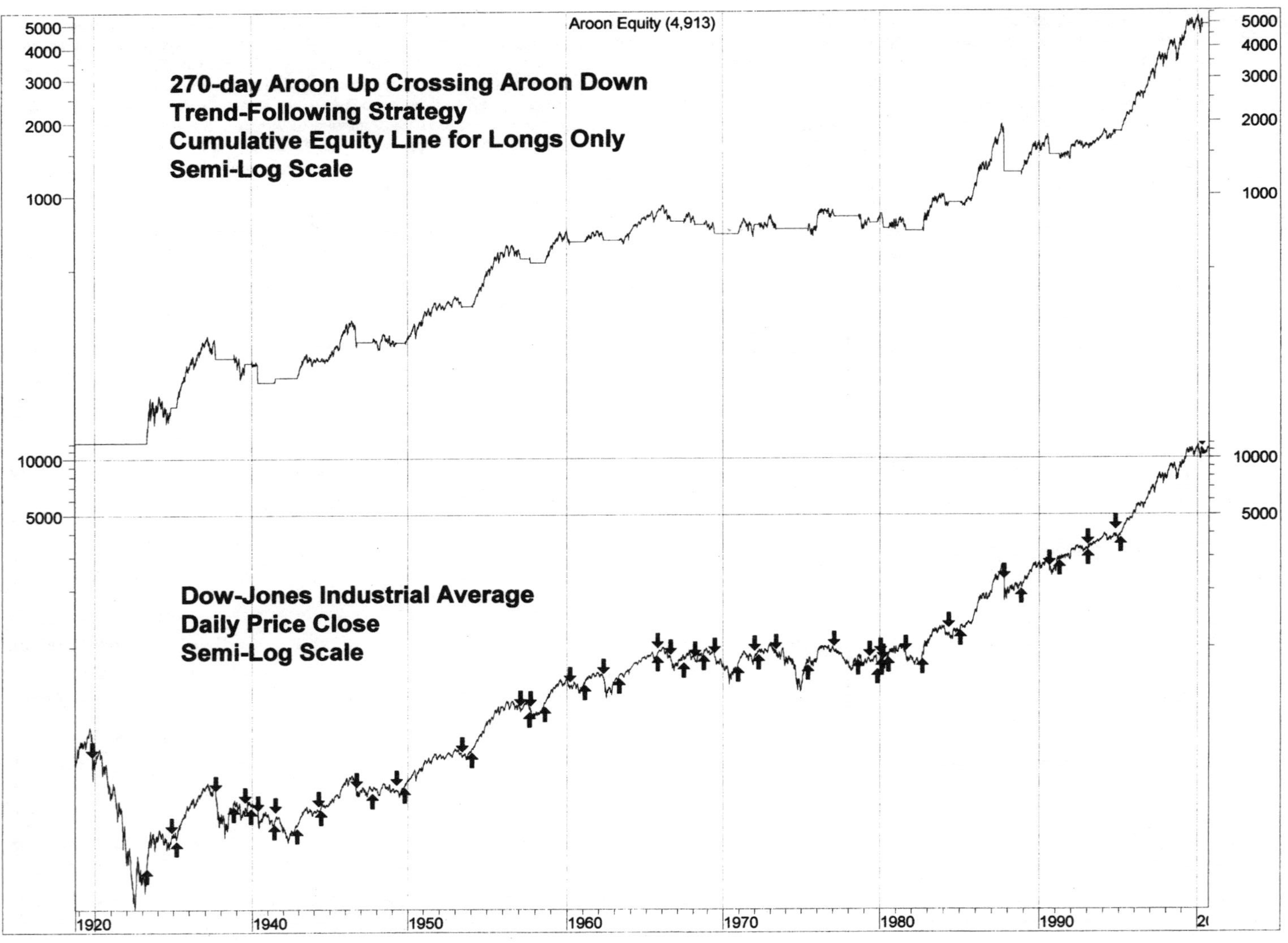

Aroon Equity (4,913)
270-day Aroon Up Crossing Aroon Down
Trend-Following Strategy
Cumulative Equity Line for Longs Only
Semi-Log Scale
Dow-Jones Industrial Average
Daily Price Close
Semi-Log Scale
5000
4000
3000
2000
1000
10000
5000
1920
1940
1950
1960
1970
1980
1990

Aroon 270

Total net profit	4813.25	Open position value	N/A	Net Profit/Buy&Hold %	5.20
Percent gain/loss	4813.25	Annual percent gain/loss	66.86	Annual Net %/B&H %	5.21
Initial investment	100	Interest earned	0		
Current position	Out	Date position entered	4/18/00	# of days per trade	8.01
Buy/Hold profit	4575.25	Days in test	26276		
Buy/Hold pct gain/loss	4575.25	Annual B/H pct gain/loss	63.55		
Total closed trades	30	Commissions paid	0		
Avg profit per trade	160.44	Avg Win/Avg Loss ratio	7.13		
Total long trades	30	Total short trades	0	Long Win Trade %	63.33
Winning long trades	19	Winning short trades	0	Short Win Trade %	#DIV/0!
Total winning trades	19	Total losing trades	11	Total Win Trade %	63.33
Amount of winning trades	5238.73	Amount of losing trades	−425.48	Net Profit Margin %	84.98
Average win	275.72	Average loss	−38.68	Average P. Margin %	75.39
Largest win	3094.32	Largest loss	−106.5	% Net/(Win + Loss)	93.35
Average length of win	494.53	Average length of loss	182.45	(Win − Loss)/Loss %	171.05
Longest winning trade	1307	Longest losing trade	386	(Win − Loss)/Loss %	238.60
Most consecutive wins	6	Most consecutive losses	3	(Win − Loss)/Loss %	100.00
Total bars out	6720	Average length out	216.77		
Longest out period	1137				
System close drawdown	0	Profit/Loss index	91.88	% Net Profit/SODD	#DIV/0!
System open drawdown	0	Reward/Risk index	100	(Net P. − SODD)/Net P.	100.00
Max open trade drawdown	−106.5	Buy/Hold index	5.2	% SODD/Net Profit	0.00

In the Equis MetaStock® "System Report" (profit and loss summary statistics), the *Total net profit* is the sum of profits minus the sum of losses, including open positions marked to the market. In contrast, the *Amount of Winning Trades* is the sum of realized profits (the total of all gains on closed-out trades only, excluding any open positions). Similarly, the *Amount of Losing Trades* is the sum of realized losses (the total of all losses on closed-out trades only, excluding any open positions). *System close drawdown* is the largest decline in the cumulative equity line below the initial investment, based on closed-out positions only. *System open drawdown (SODD)* is the largest decline in the cumulative equity line below the initial investment when a position is open. *Max open trade drawdown* is the largest decline in the cumulative equity line below the trade entry price during the worst single trade. The *Profit/Loss Index* is a complex calculation that relates the Amount of Winning Trades to the Amount of Losing Trades on a scale of −100 (worst possible performance) to +100 (best possible performance), with zero representing profits equal to losses. *Reward/Risk Index* is the Total net profit minus System open drawdown. The resulting difference is then divided by the Total net profit. The *Buy/Hold Index* is the Total net profit minus the buy-and-hold strategy's net profit. The resulting difference is then divided by the buy-and-hold net profit. In this exercise, initial equity is assumed to be $100. Both long and short positions are taken unless otherwise noted. Trades are executed at the closing price on the signal date. Transaction costs, interest expenses, and margins are not included in the statistics.

Buy,Date	*Sell,Date*	*Points,Gained*
9/10/82	5/3/84	215.76
1/29/85	10/19/87	320.27
11/10/88	8/23/90	217.64
4/17/91	1/22/93	123.1
2/4/93	10/20/94	229.93
2/15/95	4/18/00	3094.32

Enter Long (Buy) at the current daily price close of the Dow-Jones Industrial Average when the 270-day Aroon Up is greater than the 270-day Aroon Down.

Close Long (Sell) at the current daily price close of the Dow-Jones Industrial Average when the 270-day Aroon Up is less than the 270-day Aroon Down.

Enter Short (Sell Short) never.

Starting with $100 in 1928 and reinvesting profits, total net profits for this Aroon long-only strategy would have been $4,813.25, assuming a fully invested strategy, reinvestment of profits, no transactions costs and no taxes. This would have been 5.20 percent better than buy-and-hold. Short selling, which was not included in this strategy, would have lost money since 1938 and over the entire 72-years as a whole, but those short-side losses would not have exceeded long-side profits.

The Equis International MetaStock® System Testing rules are written as follows:

Enter long: AroonUp(opt1) > AroonDown(opt1)

Close long: AroonUp(opt1) < AroonDown(opt1)

OPT1 Current value: 270

Astrology, Financial Applications of Astronomical Cycles

The use of Astrology and Astronomical Cycles applied to analysis of financial markets is complex and controversial. It is well known that W. D. Gann, a highly influential technician and trader who practiced in the first half of the 20th century, intensely applied astrology to market timing, reportedly with remarkable success. Unfortunately, Gann's methods are not fully disclosed in his writings.

Astrological literature accumulated over the past 4000 years could fill whole libraries. It was an important academic discipline taught in major universities until just a few hundred years ago. Today, astrology has fallen out of fashion on campus, but retains a wide following off campus.

Few market technicians acknowledge any attempt to incorporate astrology into their work. Some unknowable number of large money managers take an active but secret interest in the subject. Arch Crawford and Bill Meridian are the most prominent technical analysts who openly use astrology in their work.

Arch Crawford has been named "Wall Street's best known astrologer" by Barron's financial weekly, based on his many uncanny predictions over the past 40 years. He is famous for calling the Crash of '87 months in advance, and he correctly predicted bear markets in July 1990 and March 2000. Crawford also has pinpointed in advance many minor trend change dates, such as the temporary bottom on April 4, 2001. And his forecasts extend beyond market turns. In his newsletter dated September 4, 2001, just seven days before the World Trade Center was hit in New York on 9/11, Crawford specifically identified two separate Mars aspects that could lead to war and a steep drop in stock prices in days ahead.

Crawford offers a popular investment advisory service focusing on market timing for the U.S. general stock market price indexes (primarily the S&P 500, the Dow-Jones Industrial Average, and the NASDAQ 100) as well as futures, including U.S. Treasuries, Gold, Oil, and Foreign Currencies. For more than two decades he has published a monthly newsletter, *Crawford Perspectives*, 6890 E. Sunrise Drive, #120-70, Tucson, Arizona 85750-0840, phone (520) 577-1158, fax (520) 577-1110, www.Astromoney.com. He also updates a twice-daily phone hotline, (900) 776-3449. Crawford's combination of astronomical cycles and technical analysis to make market calls have earned him top ratings in market timing in the Hulbert and Timer Digest surveys.

Bill Meridian is an internationally renowned financial researcher, fund manager, and designer of analytical software, including the first program developed for researching the correlation between time series data (including stock prices) and planetary cycles. Also, he compiled an authoritative collection of first trade charts for 1062 individual stocks in the 1998 edition of his book, *Planetary Stock Trading*. Meridian found that the astrological chart of the date of the initial trade in a stock correlates with subsequent changes in the stock's price trend. His 55 case studies of widely held stocks show precisely how progressions and transits correlate with changes in price. Meridian's latest book, *Planetary Economic Forecasting,* correlates a monthly index of industrial production with planetary cycles over 200 years. His 1994 study of the effect of the lunar cycle on the DJIA was confirmed by an analysis at the University of Michigan in 2001. He also demonstrated a 3.8-year Mars cycle whose signals outperformed the market. Meridian's studies and market timing advisory services are available through www.billmeridian.com, or write to Cycles Research, 666 Fifth Avenue, Suite 402, Lower Arcade, New York, NY 10103.

The following study, updated by Bill Meridian and reprinted here with his permission, previously was published in the *Journal of the Astrological Association of Great Britain* in 1985, *NCGR* in 1986, and Llewellyn's *Financial Astrology for the 1990s.*

The Mars Vesta Cycle in U.S. Stock Prices, by Bill Meridian

One of the dominant rhythms in common stock prices is a cycle of approximately four years in length. Examples of lows in this cycle are 1974, 1978, 1982, 1986, 1990, 1994, and 1998.

When this cycle first came under scrutiny, analysts attributed the phenomenon to the four years in the presidential cycle. They theorized that the government stimulated the economy through the Federal Reserve at election time to provide the illusion of prosperity and ensure the reelection of the incumbent. However, closer analysis reveals that the cycle also exists in countries where elections are held every six or eight years. And yet, local media people continue to describe bull and bear markets in terms of their own economies and local events. They do not see that there is some larger force at work, known as the principle of commonality. In addition, the cycle existed well before the establishment of the Fed in 1913.

The powerful Rothschild banking family is said to have been the first to exploit the 4-year cycle for profitable trading in the 1800's. On June 30, 1952, Veryl L. Dunbar described a 3.84-year cycle in Barron's.

There is a planetary correlation to this cycle. In order to determine the length of a synodic planetary period in longitude (the length of time that elapses from the conjunction of two bodies to their next conjunction), substitute the sidereal periods in the following formula:

$$(A \times B/(A - B) = \text{Synodic Cycle}$$

(where A and B are the sidereal periods of the two planets involved)

Substitution of the sidereal periods of the planet Mars and the asteroid Vesta (which is usually prominent in the natal horoscopes of professional stock traders) into this formula gives a cycle of 3.90 years.

The stock market tops out at the 90-degree aspect of Mars-Vesta, and it bottoms out at the 240-degree angle of Mars-Vesta. The table on the next page shows the results since 1903 of a mechanical buy-and-sell strategy based on Mars-Vesta Cycle timing versus the passive buy-and-hold strategy. The portfolio bought the Dow Jones Industrial Average whenever Mars and Vesta were 240 degrees apart and then sold the DJIA when Mars and Vesta were 90 degrees apart. In cases where the aspect occurred more than once due to retrograde motion, the latest aspect was selected as the buy or sell signal.

Following the signals of this Mars-Vesta cycle market timing rule, a $1,000 portfolio would have grown to $283,472, versus $117,645 for the buy-and-hold strategy. This outperformance is better then 2.4 to 1. Moreover, the performance of the cycle has been improving since our first publication, since the cycle outperformed by only 1.9 to 1 up to 1985.

The Mars-Vesta cycle market timing rule generated 19 gains and six losses, for 76% correct signals. Again, performance has been improving: four of the six losses were before 1942, there have been only two moderately incorrect buy signals since 1942, and all the buy signals since 1982 have been profitable. For simplicity of presentation, these figures ignore trading costs, interest rates, dividends, and leverage.

Trade #	*$ Equity*	*Buy on*	*DJIA*	*Sell on*	*DJIA*	*% Change*
1	1000	12/11/1903	46	05/11/1906	93	102%
2	2016	12/22/1907	58	06/03/1909	94	61%
3	3256	02/10/1911	85	07/09/1913	75	−12%
4	2859	02/09/1915	57	08/14/1917	92	61%
5	4613	02/20/1919	83	09/11/1921	71	−14%
6	3949	03/16/1923	104	10/02/1925	146	40%
7	5548	05/04/1927	169	10/15/1929	347	106%
8	11425	07/08/1931	144	11/16/1932	63	−56%
9	5005	08/26/1935	129	12/09/1936	181	40%
10	7022	07/13/1938	137	01/04/1941	132	−4%
11	6771	09/15/1942	106	02/02/1945	154	45%
12	9792	10/27/1946	166	03/02/1949	174	5%
13	10261	11/20/1950	232	03/22/1953	287	24%
14	12720	12/01/1954	384	04/23/1956	507	32%
15	16792	01/13/1958	440	06/02/1960	628	43%
16	23983	01/19/1962	701	07/11/1964	846	21%
17	28956	01/29/1966	984	08/11/1968	881	−10%
18	25938	02/16/1970	754	09/02/1972	969	29%
19	33347	03/22/1974	878	09/13/1976	983	12%
20	37329	05/21/1978	855	10/19/1979	815	−5%
21	35565	07/20/1982	833	11/13/1983	1254	50%
22	53513	05/28/1985	1302	12/07/1987	1812	39%
23	74501	08/01/1989	2641	12/31/1991	3169	20%
24	89396	09/25/1993	3543	01/21/1996	6884	94%
25	173695	01/10/1997	6704	01/31/2000	10941	63%
26	283472	11/13/2000*		03/17/2003		

*There were 3 buy signal trines within a 1-year period: on 11/13/2000, on 5/14/2001, and on 11/10/2001.

Mars-Vesta Buy/Sell Strategy Yields: $283,472
Buy and Hold Strategy Yields: $117,645

Astrology, Long-Term Cycles

According to David McMinn (*Financial Crises & The 56-Year Cycle*, Twin Palms, Blue Knob 2480, Australia), a 56-year cycle has been established in trends of U.S. and Western European financial crises since 1760 (Funk, 1932; McMinn, 1995). Mills (1867) speculated that the "mental mood of businessmen tends to run in cycles." Throughout economic history, generations of human beings appear to repeat cycles of manic optimism and depressed pessimism. Crises occur when there is a sudden shift in sentiment from greed to fear. The 56-year cycle correlates closely with cycles of the sun and the moon. It is well established that these cycles have a direct impact on planet earth and its all its life forms, including human beings. The sun and moon directly impact the following earthly phenomena: gravitational pull causes tides in the sea, atmosphere, and land surface; earthquake and volcanic activity; weather; magnetic and electromagnetic energy fields; the four seasons; the 24-hour day; sexual/breeding cycles (human average menstrual cycle is the same as the synodic month of 29.5 days and the average human gestation period is 9 synodic months); reproduction, molting, and many physiological rhythms in mammals are regulated by seasonal changes in the photo period (variation in hours of daylight); and gravity effects biological tides of bodily liquids in life forms, and that may impinge on physical functions and emotions. The 56-year cycle appears to correlate with angular relationships between the sun and moon: the angles 0° and 180° between the sun, moon, and nodes repeat to within one degree every 56 and 9 solar years. Perfect correlations exist between the 36 year sub-cycles and: 1) zodiacal placement of the conjunctions of the sun and moon's north node; 2) the moon angles to these sun and moon's north node conjunctions; 3) the position of the moon's north node on a specific date of the year. Major financial crises are most likely to occur when the moon's north node is in the quadrants: Aries-Taurus-Gemini and Libra-Scorpio-Sagittarius. Several variables combine to give rise to complex cyclical behavior. Specific patterns never repeat exactly but vary and change progressively over long time spans. McMinn's ideas presented here were adapted from the Technical Securities Analysts Association of San Francisco monthly newsletter, April, 1996.

"New Evidence of Precise Long-Wave Stock Cycles," was presented by Christopher L. Carolan, of Calendar Research, Inc., PO Box 680666, Marietta, GA 30068, (770) 579-5804, www.calendarresearch.com. From his position on the floor of the options exchange, Carolan witnessed first hand the effects of the 1987 crash, which occurred on precisely the same date on the lunar calendar as the 1929 crash, according to Carolan's Spiral Calendar. This tool identifies potential turning points in the stock market that provide highly significant correlations by chi-squared tests. Basically, solar and lunar eclipses offer significant market timing dates, although not all eclipses have an impact on the market. Tops and panics are associated with eclipses that occur with a cycle of approximately 36- and 58-years since 1763. Carolan's Spiral Calendar enabled him to identify in advance large-but-quick "pothole" declines of

20–30% in July 1998 (the actual drop began on 7/17/98) and on April 14, 2000, which was a selling climax day. Looking ahead, Carolan identified a potential top in the stock market in December 2001 and a potential 1987-style panic in July 2023. This is a brief summary of Carolan's talk given at the Market Technicians Association's 25th Annual Seminar in May 2000, adapted from the notes of Mike Carr, which were posted on the MTA web site, www.mta.org.

It is interesting to note how the same or similar cycle lengths appear in the work of independent researchers using differing approaches. *(See Cycles.)*

Average Directional Movement (ADX)

(See Directional Movement.)

Average True Range

The Average True Range is simply the average of the True Ranges over the past *n*-periods. True Range is the full price range of a period, including gaps. Gaps are price points where there were no actual trades executed. Gaps often occur overnight, and often in reaction to news events, although gaps can occur within any time interval and without any event.

J. Welles Wilder, Jr., in his 1978 book *New Concepts in Technical Trading Systems* (Trend Research, PO Box 128, McLeansville, NC 27301) defined True Range as the largest value of the following three possibilities:

$$T = H - L$$
$$T = H - P$$
$$T = P - L$$

where

T = True Range.
H = the highest price of the current period.
L = the lowest price of the current period.
P = the closing price of the previous period.

Wilder defined Average True Range (ATR) as a exponential smoothing (or exponential moving average) of True Range. Most frequently, Wilder uses examples with an exponential smoothing constant of 1/14, or 0.07143, which is roughly equivalent to a 27-day simple moving average. For his Volatility Index, Wilder uses an exponential smoothing constant of 1/7, or 0.14286, which is roughly equivalent to a 13-day simple moving average.

Black-Box Systems

These are proprietary indicators offered without documentation. The algorithm or formula needed to calculate the result is not divulged. The quite understandable business reason for such non-disclosure is to preserve the uniqueness of the analysis, to prevent widespread imitation, and to maintain trade secrets. Unfortunately for the user, however, such secrecy also prevents him from understanding and developing confidence in the indicator output. If a trader cannot understand exactly what an indicator is saying and why, then he is likely to abandon all discipline based on such an indicator after a few losing signals. Although strings of losing signals are common to most indicators, good indicators overcome this problem if the trader sticks with the discipline of following every signal. But such persistence is less likely with a black box. Also, if the underlying assumptions on which the indicator relies should be changed by any powerful external development, the user would not be equipped to comprehend a problem before substantial losses are incurred. Furthermore, relying on a proprietary indicator does not contribute to intellectual development, enhanced trading skills or growth of wisdom of its user. Therefore, most thoughtful technicians avoid all proprietary indicators. There are, after all, many interesting and useful concepts to explore that are fully available for thorough analysis. And, no matter if an indicator is accepted or rejected, a thorough analysis of the workings and the past performance of an indicator offers beneficial insights into the nature of market movements.

Bollinger Bands

This popular indicator is similar to the older moving average envelope. It was developed by John A. Bollinger, CFA, CMT, Bollinger Capital Management, Inc., PO Box 3358, Manhattan Beach, CA 90266, (310) 798-8855, www.bollingerbands.com.

In contrast to the moving average envelope, instead of plotting a "resistance" line some fixed percentage above a moving average and another "support" line the same fixed percentage below a moving average, Bollinger plots a resistance line two standard deviations above and a support line two standard deviations below a 20-day simple moving average.

Bollinger Bands are versatile and can be adapted to any time frame, from minutes to months. They are designed to quickly react to large moves in the market, and to show whether prices are high or low relative to normal trading ranges. Bollinger uses his bands with other indicators to confirm price action.

Bollinger suggests the 20-day simple moving average with plus and minus two standard deviations to be descriptive of the intermediate-term trend. These have become the most popular default settings. For analysis of the short-term trend, Bollinger suggests a 10-day simple moving average with one and a half standard deviations. For analysis of the long-term trend, Bollinger suggests a 50-day simple moving average with two and a half standard deviations.

Bollinger notes that the moving average length should be descriptive of the chosen time frame, and that this moving average is almost always a different length than the one that proves most useful for crossover buys and sells. Also, Bollinger suggests that a way to identify an appropriate moving average length is to choose one that provides support to the correction of the first move up off a bottom. If the average is penetrated by the correction, then the average is too short; and if the correction falls short of the average, then the average is too long. The moving average ought to provide support far more often than it is broken.

Bollinger does not recommend applying his Bands for absolute buy and sell signals when price touches or crosses the Bands. Rather, he uses Bands to provide a framework within which price may be related to other, independent technical indicators, such as on-balance volume or money flow. For example, if price touches the upper band and the chosen independent technical indicator confirms such price strength, no sell signal is generated—instead a continuation buy confirmation is recognized. On the other hand, if price tags the upper band and the independent indicator does not confirm such price strength (that is, the indicator diverges negatively), a sell signal is recognized. Another example of a sell signal is after a series of higher price highs, all pushing to or outside the upper band, a final new price high is unable to meet the upper band, thus indicating a loss of upward price momentum and offering a sell signal.

A mirror-image analysis would apply to the use of the lower bands for recognizing buy signals. For example, if price touches the lower band and the chosen independent technical indicator confirms such price weakness, no buy signal is generated, but instead, a continuation sell confirmation is recognized. On the other hand, if price tags the lower band and the independent indicator does not confirm such price weakness (that is, the indicator diverges positively), a buy signal is recognized. Another example of a buy signal is after a series of lower price lows, all pushing to or below the lower band, a final new price low is unable to meet the lower band, thus indicating a loss of downward price momentum and offering a buy signal.

Indicator Strategy Example for Bollinger Bands

Bollinger Bands require experience and judgement to use as Bollinger intended. But even naïve testing assumptions suggest that Bollinger Bands may have some objective potential value as a purely mechanical, contra-trend technical indicator. The great majority of oversold buy signals would have been profitable. Moreover, these buy signals would have been robust, with all simple moving average lengths from 6 to 50 days, minus and plus two standard-deviations, profitable and right most of the time, again for long trades only.

As attractive as a high percentage of profitable trades may seem, it is important to note that this, like other contra-trend strategies, failed to provide any protection in the Crash of '87, the decline of 1998, and other market price drops. As the chart shows, there are sharp equity drawdowns. Using Bollinger Bands for contra-trend oversold and overbought signals would have underperformed the passive buy-and-hold strategy. Short selling would not have been profitable in the past.

Based on a 18-year file of daily data for the entire history of the S&P 500 Composite Stock Price Index futures *CSI Perpetual Contract* from 4/21/82 to 12/08/00 collected from www.csidata.com, we found that the following parameters, suggested by Bollinger, would have produced profits most of the time (for long-side trades only) on a purely mechanical overbought/oversold signal basis with no subjectivity, no sophisticated technical analysis, and no judgement:

Enter Long (Buy) at the current daily price close when the S&P 500 Composite Stock Price Index *CSI Perpetual Contract* closing price is less than the current 10-day simple moving average of the daily closing prices minus two standard deviations.

Close Long (Sell) at the current daily price close when the S&P 500 Composite Stock Price Index *CSI Perpetual Contract* closing price is greater than the current 10-day simple moving average of the daily closing prices plus two standard deviations.

Enter Short (Sell Short) never.

Starting with $100 and reinvesting profits, total net profits for this Bollinger Bands counter-trend strategy would have been $678.60, assuming a fully invested strategy, reinvestment of profits, no transactions costs, and no taxes. This would have been 35.10 percent less than buy-and-hold. No short selling would have been profitable, and no short selling was included in the strategy. Short selling would have cut the profit in half. Although this strategy would have not kept pace with the passive buy-and-hold strategy, the long-only Bollinger Bands as an indicator would have given profitable buy signals 88.61% of the time. Trading would have been relatively inactive at one trade every 86.16 calendar days. Note that this strategy considers closing prices only, while ignoring intraday highs and lows.

The Equis International MetaStock® System Testing rules are written as follows:

Enter long: CLOSE < BBandBot(CLOSE,opt1,S,opt2)

Close long: CLOSE > BBandTop(CLOSE,opt1,S,opt2)

OPT1 Current value: 10

OPT2 Current value: 2

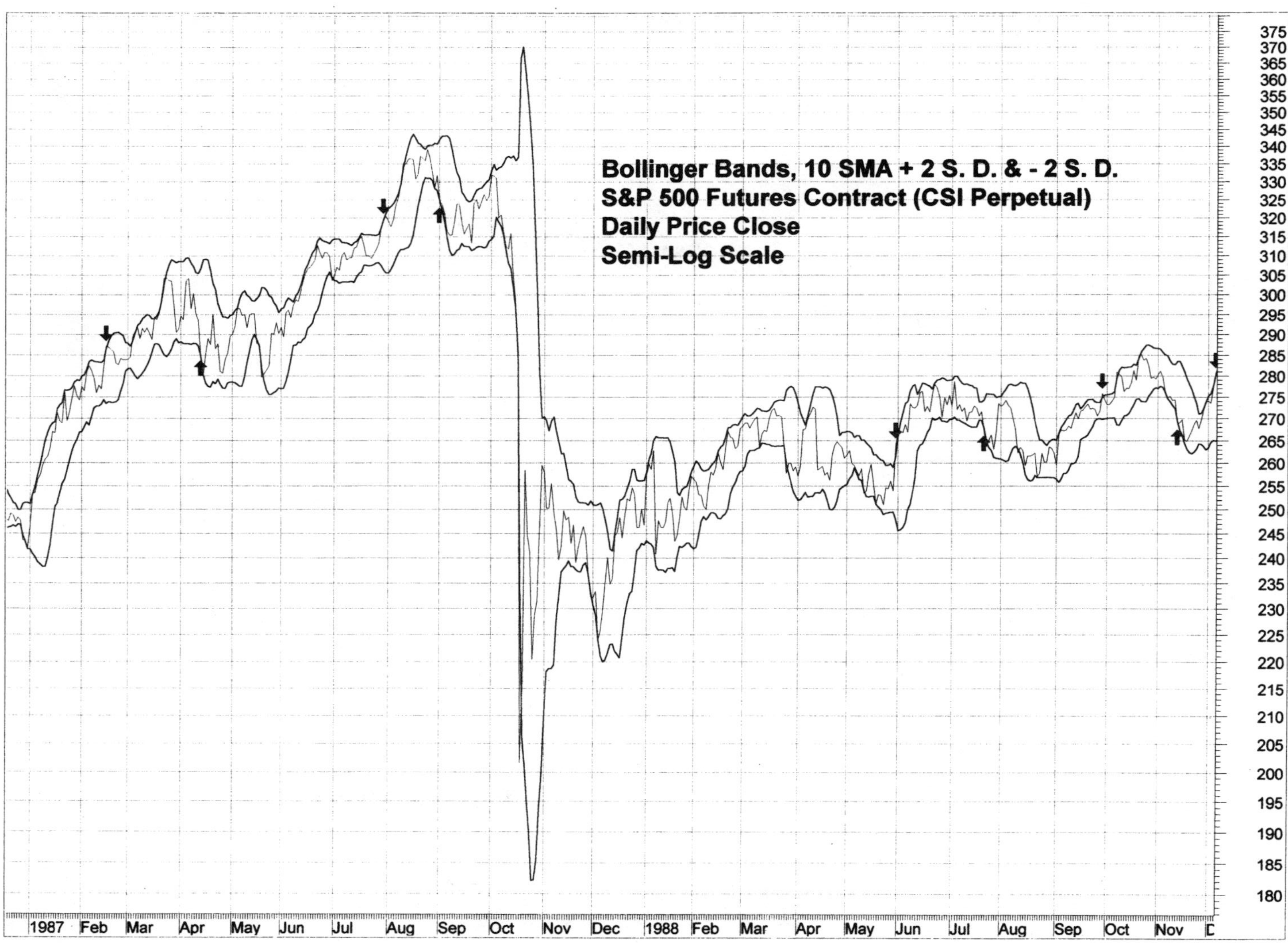
Bollinger Bands, 10 SMA + 2 S. D. & - 2 S. D.
S&P 500 Futures Contract (CSI Perpetual)
Daily Price Close
Semi-Log Scale
1987 Feb Mar Apr May Jun Jul Aug Sep Oct Nov Dec 1988 Feb Mar Apr May Jun Jul Aug Sep Oct Nov
375 370 365 360 355 350 345 340 335 330 325 320 315 310 305 300 295 290 285 280 275 270 265 260 255 250 245 240 235 230 225 220 215 210 205 200 195 190 185 180

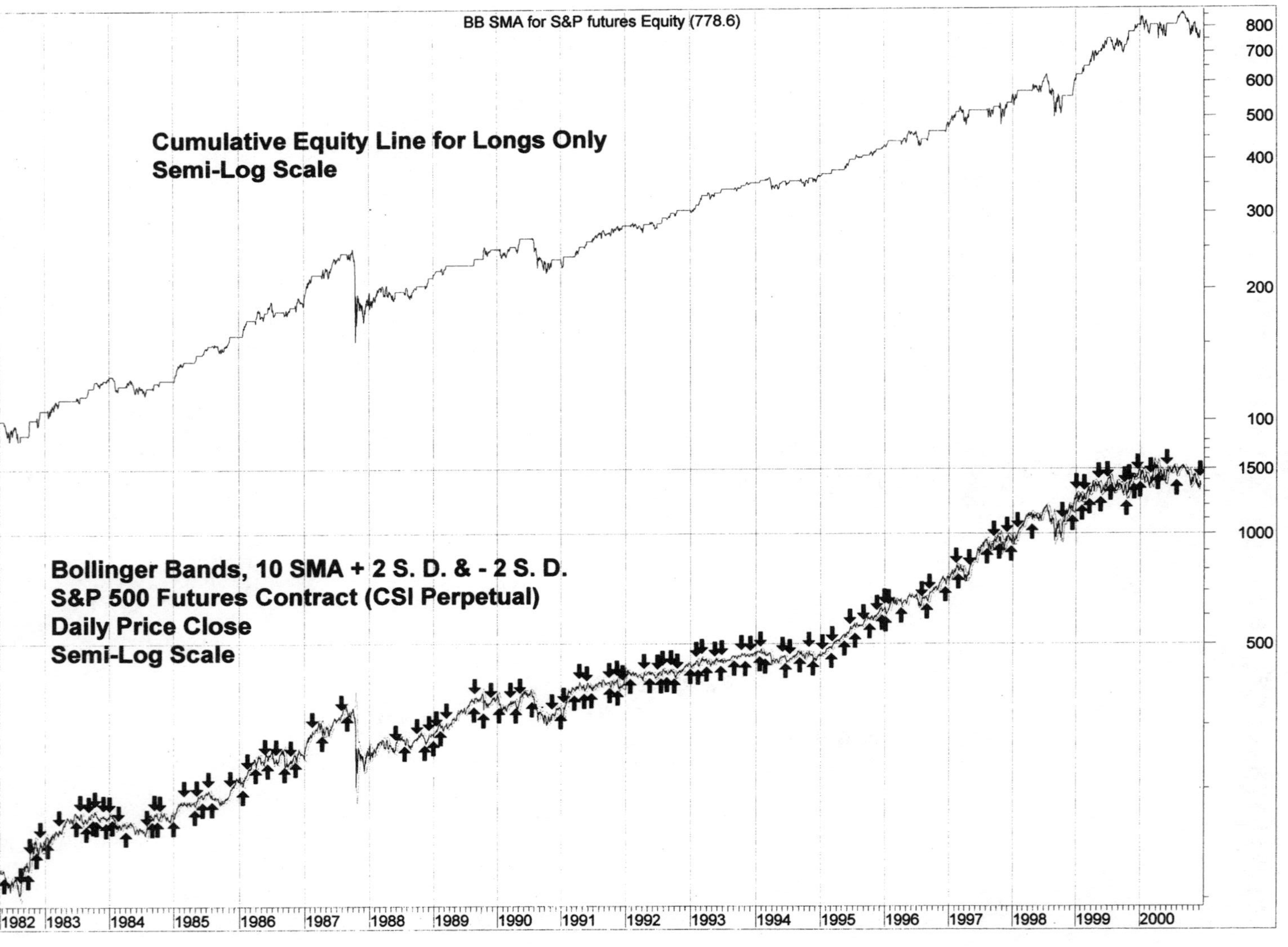

BB SMA for S&P futures Equity (778.6)
Cumulative Equity Line for Longs Only
Semi-Log Scale
Bollinger Bands, 10 SMA + 2 S. D. & - 2 S. D.
S&P 500 Futures Contract (CSI Perpetual)
Daily Price Close
Semi-Log Scale
800
700
600
500
400
300
200
100
1500
1000
500
1982
1983
1984
1985
1986
1987
1988
1989
1990
1991
1992
1993
1994
1995
1996
1997
1998
1999
2000

Bollinger Bands, 10 Simple Moving Average, Plus and Minus Two Standard Deviations

Total net profit	678.6	Open position value	N/A	Net Profit/Buy&Hold %	−35.10
Percent gain/loss	678.6	Annual percent gain/loss	36.39	Annual Net %/B&H %	−35.09
Initial investment	100	Interest earned	0		
Current position	Out	Date position entered	12/5/00		
Buy/Hold profit	1045.54	Days in test	6807	# of days per trade	86.16
Buy/Hold pct gain/loss	1045.54	Annual B/H pct gain/loss	56.06		
Total closed trades	79	Commissions paid	0		
Avg profit per trade	8.59	Avg Win/Avg Loss ratio	0.66		
Total long trades	79	Total short trades	0	Long Win Trade %	88.61
Winning long trades	70	Winning short trades	0	Short Win Trade %	#DIV/0!
Total winning trades	70	Total losing trades	9	Total Win Trade %	88.61
Amount of winning trades	841.73	Amount of losing trades	−163.13	Net Profit Margin %	67.53
Average win	12.02	Average loss	−18.13	Average P. Margin %	−20.27
Largest win	66.37	Largest loss	−45.73	% Net/(Win + Loss)	18.41
Average length of win	25.94	Average length of loss	86.44	(Win − Loss)/Loss %	−69.99
Longest winning trade	82	Longest losing trade	189	(Win − Loss)/Loss %	−56.61
Most consecutive wins	18	Most consecutive losses	2	(Win − Loss)/Loss %	800.00
Total bars out	2277	Average length out	28.46		
Longest out period	110				
System close drawdown	−7.23	Profit/Loss index	80.62	% Net Profit/SODD	5415.80
System open drawdown	−12.53	Reward/Risk index	98.19	(Net P. − SODD)/Net P.	98.15
Max open trade drawdown	−92.13	Buy/Hold index	−35.1	% SODD/Net Profit	−1.85

In the Equis MetaStock® "System Report" (profit and loss summary statistics), the *Total net profit* is the sum of profits minus the sum of losses, including open positions marked to the market. In contrast, the *Amount of Winning Trades* is the sum of realized profits (the total of all gains on closed-out trades only, excluding any open positions). Similarly, the *Amount of Losing Trades* is the sum of realized losses (the total of all losses on closed-out trades only, excluding any open positions). *System close drawdown* is the largest decline in the cumulative equity line below the initial investment, based on closed-out positions only. *System open drawdown (SODD)* is the largest decline in the cumulative equity line below the initial investment when a position is open. *Max open trade drawdown* is the largest decline in the cumulative equity line below the trade entry price during the worst single trade. The *Profit/Loss Index* is a complex calculation that relates the Amount of Winning Trades to the Amount of Losing Trades on a scale of −100 (worst possible performance) to +100 (best possible performance), with zero representing profits equal to losses. *Reward/Risk Index* is the Total net profit minus System open drawdown. The resulting difference is then divided by the Total net profit. The *Buy/Hold Index* is the Total net profit minus the buy-and-hold strategy's net profit. The resulting difference is then divided by the buy-and-hold net profit. In this exercise, initial equity is assumed to be $100. Both long and short positions are taken unless otherwise noted. Trades are executed at the closing price on the signal date. Transaction costs, interest expenses, and margins are not included in the statistics.

%b

Based on Bollinger Bands and inspired by the formula for Stochastics, John Bollinger, CFA, CMT, developed %b as a price-momentum oscillator. Just as Stochastics quantifies the position of the latest price close within its recent price range, so %b quantifies the position of the latest price close within the Bollinger Bands. But, unlike Stochastics, which is bounded by 0 and 100, %b moves beyond these boundaries when prices are outside of the bands.

- %b below 0 is below the lower band.
- %b at 0 is at the lower band.
- %b at 50 is mid-way between the upper and lower bands.
- %b at 100 is at the upper band.
- %b above 100 is above the upper band.

The %b indicator can be used for overbought/oversold signals, and %b invites comparison to the price itself and to other indicators for confirmation and divergence analysis.

Bollinger Band Width Index

The Bollinger Band Width Index is four times the 20-day standard deviation of the daily price closes. According to John A. Bollinger, CFA, CMT, volatility is cyclical, and unusually low volatility periods alternate with periods of unusually high volatility. The Bollinger Band Width Index quantifies this volatility. Bollinger uses it to identify periods of unusual and unsustainable volatility, which can lead to the opposite condition. For example, Bollinger notes that a drop in band width below 2% for the Standard & Poor's 500 has led to large moves. Also, Bollinger uses Band Width to identify the end of trends. The Bollinger Band Width Index is given by the following:

$$\text{Bollinger Band Width Index} = (\text{UpperBB} - \text{LowerBB})/\text{MiddleBB}$$

where the UpperBB is the moving average of close plus two standard deviations, the LowerBB is the moving average of close minus two standard deviations, and the MiddleBB is the moving average itself.

Assuming the default parameters suggested by John Bollinger of plus or minus two standard deviation bands around a 20-day simple moving average, the above formula reduces to:

$$\text{Bollinger Band Width Index} = (4 * \text{20-day sigma})/\text{20-day mean}$$

where sigma is the 20-day standard deviation of the closing price around the 20-day simple moving average.

Bolton-Tremblay Indicator

The Bolton-Tremblay Indicator is a cumulative advance-decline indicator that uses the number of unchanged issues as a basic component. Because of its greater computational complexity, the Bolton-Tremblay Indicator is not nearly as popular as the simpler breadth calculations. Only the basics of its calculation are presented here.

The Bolton-Tremblay Indicator is computed in five steps.

1. Divide the number of advancing issues by the number of unchanged issues.
2. Divide the number of declining issues by the number of unchanged issues.
3. Subtract the declining ratio from the advancing ratio.
4. Calculate the square root of the difference.
5. Add the square root to the previous day's Bolton-Tremblay Indicator, respecting the sign (plus if there were more advances, minus if more declines).

The indicator is expressed by using the following two formulas:

If there are a greater number of advances than declines, then:

$$T = Y + (\text{Square Root } ((A/U) - (D/U)))$$

But if there are a lesser number of advances than declines, then:

$$T = Y - (\text{Square Root } |\, (A/U) - (D/U) \,|)$$

where

T = today's Bolton-Tremblay Indicator
Y = yesterday's Bolton-Tremblay Indicator
A = number of advancing issues
D = number of declining issues
U = number of unchanged issues
$|x|$ = absolute value of x

For example, if yesterday's Bolton-Tremblay Indicator was 1000, and today's market is strong, with 1400 advancing issues, 600 declining issues, and 200 unchanged issues, today's Bolton-Tremblay Indicator is calculated as follows:

$$T = 1000 + (\text{Square Root } ((A/U) - (D/U)))$$
$$T = 1000 + (\text{Square Root } ((1400/200) - (600/200)))$$
$$T = 1000 + (\text{Square Root } ((7) - (3)))$$
$$T = 1000 + (\text{Square Root } (4))$$
$$T = 1002$$

But if today's market is weak, with 600 advancing issues, 1400 declining issues, and 200 unchanged issues, today's Bolton-Tremblay Indicator is calculated as follows:

T = 1000 − (Square Root | (600/200) − (1400/200) |)
T = 1000 − (Square Root | (3) − (7) |)
T = 1000 − (Square Root (4))
T = 1000 − (2)
T = 998

Begin calculating the Bolton-Tremblay Indicator at any arbitrary start date. Starting with a positive value for *Y* (for example, 1000) is recommended in order to avoid the extra effort of working with cumulative negative numbers.

The Bolton-Tremblay Indicator can be charted and interpreted in a manner similar to the Advance-Decline Line. Traditionally, technical analysts focused on indicator divergences from a market price index, such as the Dow Jones Industrial Average, to gauge underlying strength or weakness in the market. The absolute and relative levels of the indicator are less important than its trend.

Bracketing, Brackets, Dynamic Brackets

Bracketing is an extremely flexible and adaptive analytical tool that can be used to identify extremes at absolute or relative levels in otherwise hard-to-tame data. Bracketing is a primary tool of Ned Davis Research, Inc., 600 Bird Bay Drive West, Venice, FL 34292, phone (941) 484-6107, fax (941) 484-6221, www.ndr.com.

Some source data is so orderly that it offers obvious and stable extremes in high and low values that possess good predictive capacity. It is a simple exercise to fit horizontal lines to mark these extremes, which can be identified as high and low cut-off points, or thresholds. For example, extreme zones are used for partitioning the information into one of three brackets: bullish, neutral, and bearish. For those who prefer subtle gradations, any number of zones could be identified and weighted according to historical statistical significance.

But most source data is so "noisy" that it needs to be smoothed or normalized first. If the data migrates over time, trending higher or lower, moving average bands may be fitted around the data to mark extremes. (*See Envelopes.*)

Further, if the source data contains wide variations in volatility, adaptable standard deviation bands may be fitted to the data to mark extremes. (*See Bollinger Bands.*)

Overbought/oversold models frequently rely on Bracket Rules. Such indicators often give extreme signals in advance of an actual top or bottom. This leading indicator characteristic can allow overbought/oversold models to be used as *screens*, or *permission filters*, permitting other models' signals to be acted upon only when both are in the same mode, either both bullish for a buy signal or both bearish for a sell signal.

Since a market sometimes hits an overbought/oversold extreme and the extreme trend still continues, a variation on overbought/oversold zones is to recognize a signal only when two conditions are observed: first, there must have been an extreme reading (overbought/oversold) for *n* periods (with the value of *n* to be determined by historical research); and second, the actual buy or sell signal is recognized when the data finally exits the extreme zone. Thus, this method acts only when the pressure producing the extreme level lifts. This may offer a safer entry point more closely timed to an actual trend reversal.

Another variation is shifting or *dynamic bracket* levels, which change according to the readings of a separate model used to modify and to filter the bracket rule.

Breadth Advance/Decline Indicator: Breadth Thrust

The Breadth Advance/Decline Indicator was developed by Martin Zweig. It is a 10-day simple moving average of the ratio of the number of advancing issues divided by the sum of the number of advancing issues plus declining issues. It is usually calculated based on issues listed on the New York Stock Exchanges, and similar indicators may be calculated for other markets, such as the NASDAQ. The indicator can be expressed by the following formula, before applying the 10-day simple moving average:

$$Z = (A)/(A + D)$$

where

Z = today's 1-day ratio of advances to total issues exhibiting any price change at all

A = number of advancing issues

D = number of declining issues

The cumulative equity graph shows that from 7/22/32 to 3/30/94 (for long trades only with no shorting) the Breadth Advance/Decline Indicator gave steadily profitable buy and sell signals when it made an extreme directional thrust, thus confirming powerful market momentum. When the 10-day simple moving average reached extremes, rising above 0.659 for a buy signal, and falling below 3.66 for a sell signal, it paid to follow the momentum. Account equity rose steadily, with no drawdowns.

However, since 3/30/94, there have been no signals. The chart of the indicator shows that it has not reached as high as 0.66 since 1/6/92. It is apparent that the behavior of the underlying statistics have changed so that the 10-day moving average of the A/(A + D) no longer reaches the high levels it had. We must conclude that this formerly useful indicator, which depended more on the level rather than the trend of the underlying data, has not adapted to the changing behavior of the breadth data.

Trend is More Important than Level for the Breadth Advance/Decline Indicator

The trend of the Breadth Advance/Decline Indicator is an effective indicator, although not as profitable as the Advance-Decline Line. Based on a 68-year file of daily data for the number of shares advancing and declining each day on the New York Stock Exchange and the Dow-Jones Industrial Average since March 8, 1932, we found that the simplest possible trend-following rule would have produced a positive result on a purely mechanical signal basis with no subjectivity, no sophisticated technical analysis, and no judgement:

Enter Long (Buy) at the current daily price close of the Dow-Jones Industrial Average when Breadth Advance/Decline Indicator rises relative to its level the previous day.

Close Long (Sell) at the current daily price close of the Dow-Jones Industrial Average when the Breadth Advance/Decline Indicator falls relative to its level the previous day.

Enter Short (Sell Short) at the current daily price close of the Dow-Jones Industrial Average when the Breadth Advance/Decline Indicator falls relative to its level the previous day.

Close Short (Cover) at the current daily price close of the Dow-Jones Industrial Average when the Breadth Advance/Decline Indicator rises relative to its level the previous day.

Starting with $100 and reinvesting profits, total net profits for this Breadth Advance/Decline Indicator trend-following strategy would have been $2,159,426, assuming a fully invested strategy, reinvestment of profits, no transactions costs and no taxes. This would have been 17,122 percent better than buy-and-hold. Even short selling would have been profitable. Trading would have been hyperactive with one trade every 3.50 calendar days.

The Equis International MetaStock® System Testing rules, where the current the Breadth Advance/Decline Indicator Line is inserted into the data field normally reserved for Volume (V), are written as follows:

Enter long: V > Ref(V,−1)

Close long: V < Ref(V,−1)

Enter short: V < Ref(V,−1)

Close short: V > Ref(V,−1)

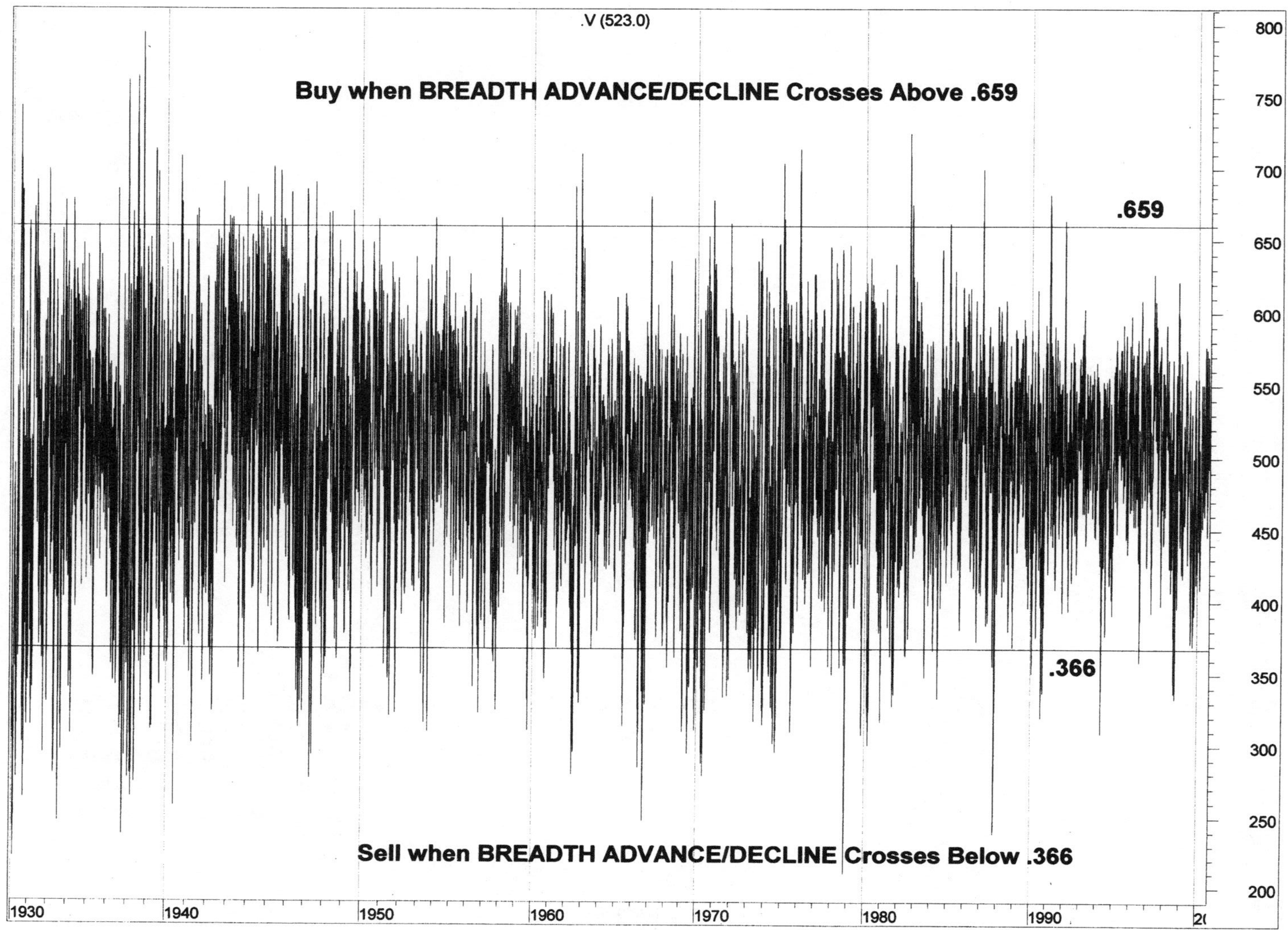
.V (523.0)
Buy when BREADTH ADVANCE/DECLINE Crosses Above .659
.659
.366
Sell when BREADTH ADVANCE/DECLINE Crosses Below .366
800
750
700
650
600
550
500
450
400
350
300
250
200
1930
1940
1950
1960
1970
1980
1990

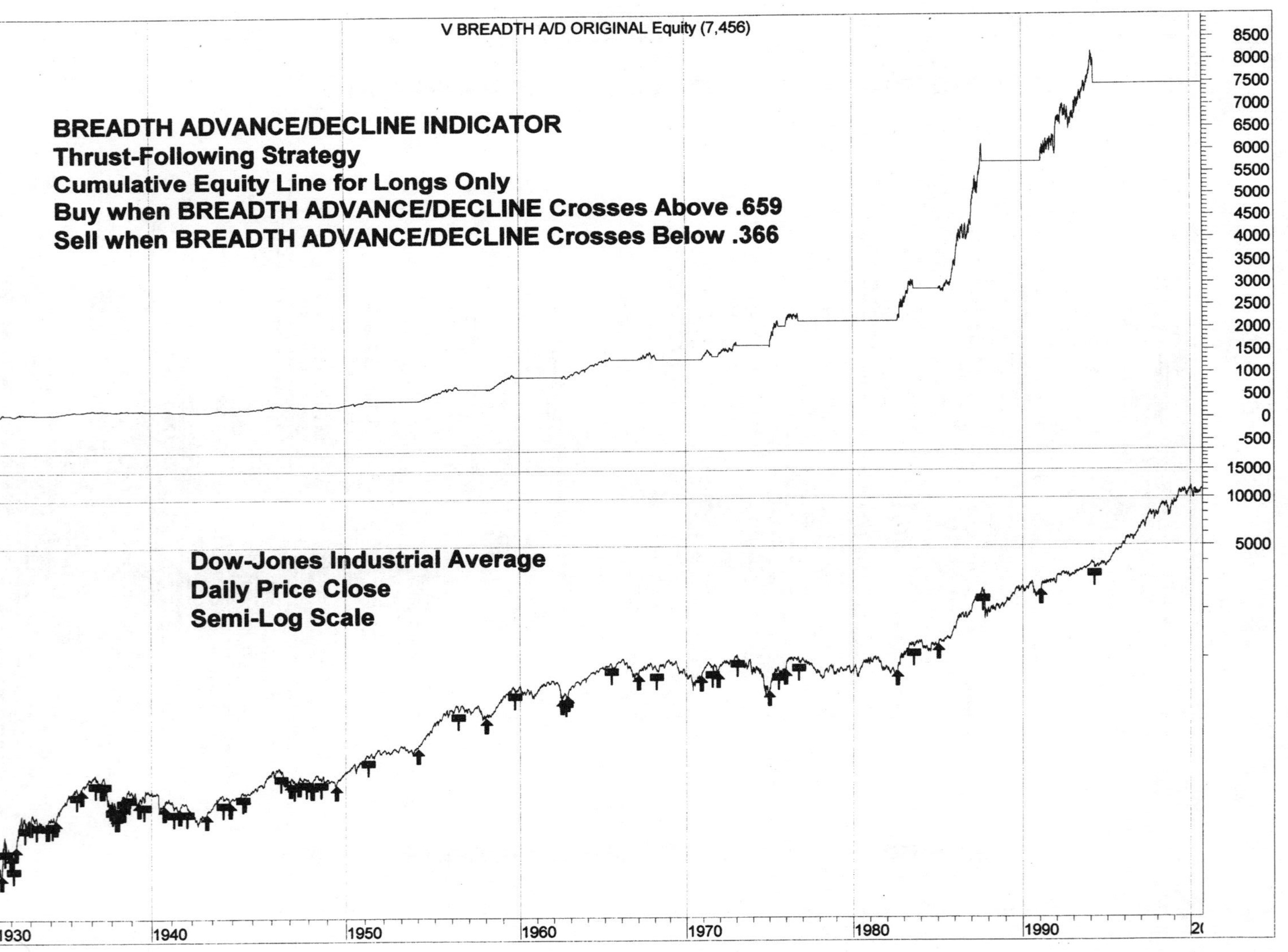
V BREADTH A/D ORIGINAL Equity (7,456)
BREADTH ADVANCE/DECLINE INDICATOR
Thrust-Following Strategy
Cumulative Equity Line for Longs Only
Buy when BREADTH ADVANCE/DECLINE Crosses Above .659
Sell when BREADTH ADVANCE/DECLINE Crosses Below .366
Dow-Jones Industrial Average
Daily Price Close
Semi-Log Scale
8500
8000
7500
7000
6500
6000
5500
5000
4500
4000
3500
3000
2500
2000
1500
1000
500
0
-500
15000
10000
5000
1930
1940
1950
1960
1970
1980
1990

Breadth Advance/Decline Indicator

Total net profit	2159426	Open position value	0	Net Profit/Buy&Hold %	17122.14
Percent gain/loss	2159426	Annual percent gain/loss	31499.9	Annual Net %/B&H %	17122.47
Initial investment	100	Interest earned	0		
Current position	Short	Date position entered	9/8/00		
Buy/Hold profit	12538.66	Days in test	25022	# of days per trade	3.50
Buy/Hold pct gain/loss	12538.66	Annual B/H pct gain/loss	182.9		
Total closed trades	7156	Commissions paid	0		
Avg profit per trade	301.76	Avg Win/Avg Loss ratio	1.4		
Total long trades	3578	Total short trades	3578	Long Win Trade %	52.26
Winning long trades	1870	Winning short trades	1581	Short Win Trade %	44.19
Total winning trades	3451	Total losing trades	3705	Total Win Trade %	48.23
Amount of winning trades	9244850	Amount of losing trades	−7085419.5	Net Profit Margin %	13.22
Average win	2678.89	Average loss	−1912.39	Average P. Margin %	16.69
Largest win	116321.25	Largest loss	−98349.75	% Net/(Win + Loss)	8.37
Average length of win	4.22	Average length of loss	2.88	(Win − Loss)/Loss %	46.53
Longest winning trade	18	Longest losing trade	12	(Win − Loss)/Loss %	50.00
Most consecutive wins	10	Most consecutive losses	11	(Win − Loss)/Loss %	−9.09
Total bars out	2	Average length out	2		
Longest out period	2				
System close drawdown	−27.53	Profit/Loss index	23.36	% Net Profit/SODD	7682056.21
System open drawdown	−28.11	Reward/Risk index	100	(Net P. − SODD)/Net P.	100.00
Max open trade drawdown	−98349.75	Buy/Hold index	17122.15	% SODD/Net Profit	0.00

In the Equis MetaStock® "System Report" (profit and loss summary statistics), the *Total net profit* is the sum of profits minus the sum of losses, including open positions marked to the market. In contrast, the *Amount of Winning Trades* is the sum of realized profits (the total of all gains on closed-out trades only, excluding any open positions). Similarly, the *Amount of Losing Trades* is the sum of realized losses (the total of all losses on closed-out trades only, excluding any open positions). *System close drawdown* is the largest decline in the cumulative equity line below the initial investment, based on closed-out positions only. *System open drawdown (SODD)* is the largest decline in the cumulative equity line below the initial investment when a position is open. *Max open trade drawdown* is the largest decline in the cumulative equity line below the trade entry price during the worst single trade. The *Profit/Loss Index* is a complex calculation that relates the Amount of Winning Trades to the Amount of Losing Trades on a scale of −100 (worst possible performance) to +100 (best possible performance), with zero representing profits equal to losses. *Reward/Risk Index* is the Total net profit minus System open drawdown. The resulting difference is then divided by the Total net profit. The *Buy/Hold Index* is the Total net profit minus the buy-and-hold strategy's net profit. The resulting difference is then divided by the buy-and-hold net profit. In this exercise, initial equity is assumed to be $100. Both long and short positions are taken unless otherwise noted. Trades are executed at the closing price on the signal date. Transaction costs, interest expenses, and margins are not included in the statistics.

Bullish Consensus

Consensus, Inc., of Kansas City, MO, offers one of four different sentiment polls (surveys conducted by investment advisory service newsletters) and is available to subscribers via telephone recording. After a moderate time lag the data is also printed in *Barron's* weekly financial newspaper, which is available every Saturday. Popular interpretation is generally contrarian. (*See Contrary Opinion and Advisory Service Sentiment.*)

Bullish Consensus is tabulation of market opinions expressed in published market letters distributed widely by futures brokers and advisors. Opinions are quantified, weighed by influence, and interpreted as follows:

90%–100% excessive optimism, extremely overbought, an end to the uptrend is imminent

80%–90% unbalanced optimism, overbought, a downside reversal is possible

60%–80% moderate, an uptrend can continue; but if near a bottom look for new lows

50%–60% neutral

30%–50% moderate, a downtrend can continue; but if near a top look for new highs

20%–30% unbalanced pessimism, an upside reversal is possible

0%–20% excessive pessimism, an end to the downtrend is imminent

Contrary opinion is a popular idea, known even to television commentators, whose general level of understanding of technical analysis is superficial at best. Many experienced technical analysts use sentiment, but more as a supplement to trend, momentum, and other technical indicators than as a stand-alone, signal generator. Sentiment typically shows overbought and oversold levels well *before* the directional price move is over and, therefore, can be misleading. In general, sentiment is more of a background indicator that is not suitable for precise timing.

As the chart shows, over the 14-year period, Ned Davis found extraordinarily high returns of 25.1% per annum when data fell below its lower dynamic bracket (*See Bollinger Bands*), indicating excessive pessimism. Interestingly, using both extremes for buy and sell signals produced long-only returns only 6% greater than buy-and-hold.

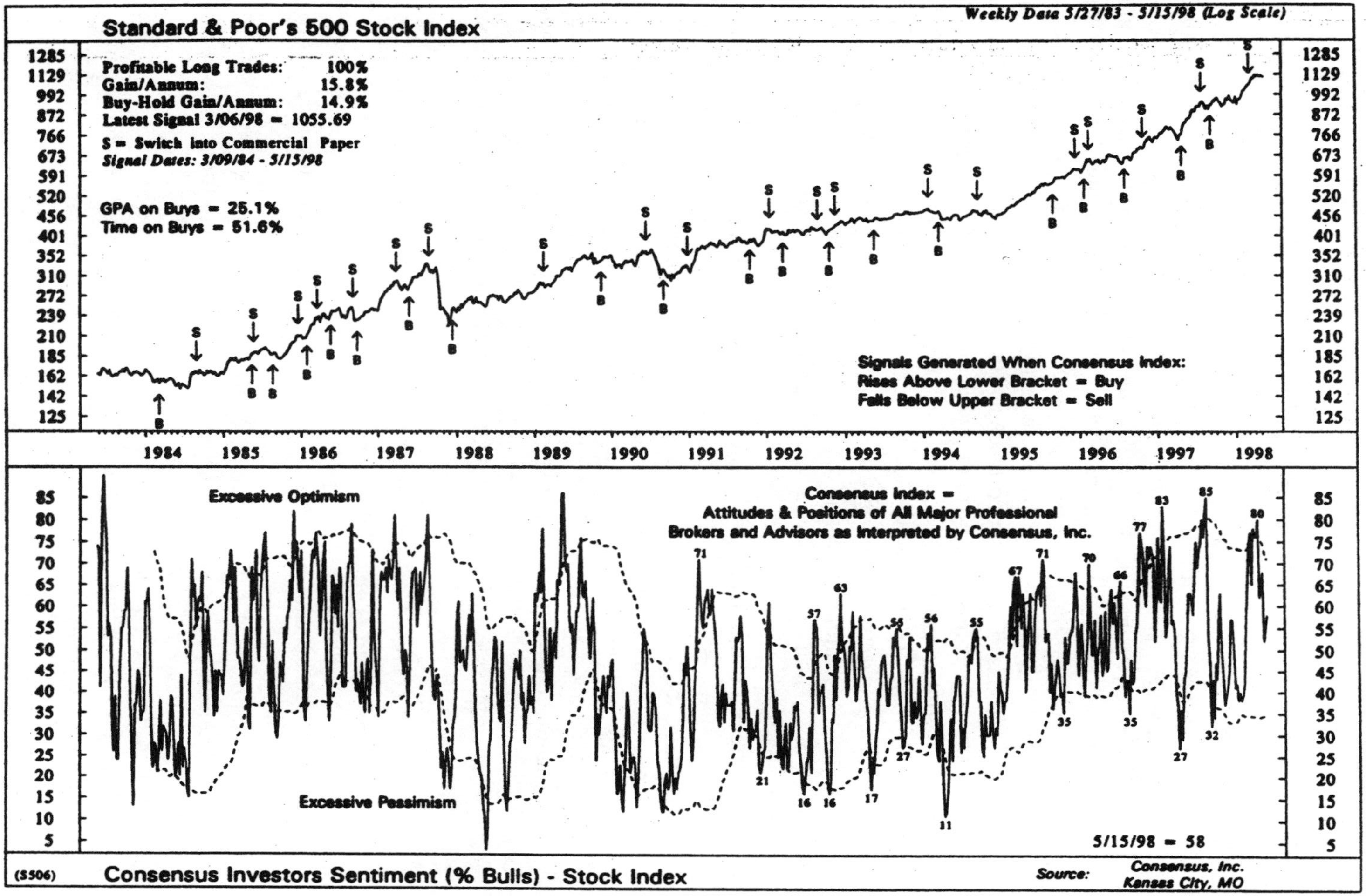
Standard & Poor's 500 Stock Index
Weekly Data 5/27/83 - 5/15/98 (Log Scale)
Profitable Long Trades: 100%
Gain/Annum: 15.8%
Buy-Hold Gain/Annum: 14.9%
Latest Signal 3/06/98 = 1055.69
S = Switch into Commercial Paper
Signal Dates: 3/09/84 - 5/15/98
GPA on Buys = 25.1%
Time on Buys = 51.6%
Signals Generated When Consensus Index:
Rises Above Lower Bracket = Buy
Falls Below Upper Bracket = Sell
1285
1129
992
872
766
673
591
520
456
401
352
310
272
239
210
185
162
142
125
1984
1985
1986
1987
1988
1989
1990
1991
1992
1993
1994
1995
1996
1997
1998
Excessive Optimism
Excessive Pessimism
Consensus Index =
Attitudes & Positions of All Major Professional
Brokers and Advisors as Interpreted by Consensus, Inc.
5/15/98 = 58
(S506)
Consensus Investors Sentiment (% Bulls) - Stock Index
Source: Consensus, Inc. Kansas City, MO

Chart by permission of Ned Davis Research.

Call-Put Dollar Value Flow Line (CPFL)

The Call-Put Dollar Value Flow Line (CPFL) is a sentiment and price-direction confirmation indicator created by Robert B. McCurtain. It may be computed using daily or weekly data.

McCurtain designed CPFL to reflect the direction option money is flowing. The relative importance of an options transaction needs to be weighted by the dollar value of the transaction—that is, price times volume. In contrast, conventional Call-Put analysis treats all call and put volume equally; that is, 1000 contracts of an option trading at 1/16 has the same importance as 1000 contracts of an option priced at 25. McCurtain corrects this error by multiplying the option price by the option volume to arrive at the dollar value of the transaction. One thousand contracts at 25 would have a dollar value of $250,000, which is 400 times greater than the dollar value of $6,250 for the option at 1/16. Assuming that the option at 1/16 is more likely to reflect the hopes of a wild gambler, while the option at 25 is more likely to reflect the considered strategy of a serious professional, McCurtain's price times volume weighting places the emphasis where it belongs.

If stock volume leads price, and option volume offers further clues to future stock price movements, then McCurtain reasoned that when CPFL starts a new trend before the price of the underlying issue, the stock price should follow. Also, if the stock price rallies to new highs while CPFL fails to rise, option dollar flows are relatively weak, and price strength should not continue. Similarly, if the stock price falls to new lows and CPFL does not confirm that price weakness by also making new lows, option dollar flows are relatively strong, and the stock price decline should be temporary.

McCurtain's Call-Put Dollar Value Flow Line (CPFL) may be computed in seven steps:

1. Collect end-of-day closing price and volume data for all call and all put options of the underlying stock, index, or commodity to be analyzed. Since most publications do not publish complete details for all options, McCurtain collects his data electronically for all strike prices and all maturities for each issue.
2. Multiply each call option's volume by its closing price.
3. Sum the products (from Step 2) for each call option for each issue to arrive at the day's *Call Dollar Value.*
4. Multiply each put option's volume by its closing price.
5. Sum the products (from Step 4) for each put option for each issue to arrive at the day's *Put Dollar Value.*

6. Subtract the Put Dollar Value from the Call Dollar Value, for the *Net Call-Put Dollar Value.* Respect the sign, so if Call Dollar Value is less than Put Dollar Value, the Net Call-Put Dollar Value will carry a minus sign.
7. Calculate a cumulative total of the Net Call-Put Dollar Values (from Step 6). This cumulative total will rise when Call Dollar Value is greater than Put Dollar Value, and it will decline when Call Dollar Value is less than Put Dollar Value.

Indicator Strategy Example for McCurtain's Call-Put Dollar Value Flow Line

Historical data shows that the Call-Put Dollar Value Flow Line can offer accurate signals on the long side. Based on the weekly call and put data for S&P 100 Stock Price Index and the Dow-Jones Industrial Average for 18 years from March 1983 to January 2001, we found that the following parameters would have produced (for long trades only) a moderately positive result on a purely mechanical trend-following signal basis with no subjectivity, no sophisticated technical analysis, and no judgement:

Enter Long (Buy) at the current weekly price close of the Dow-Jones Industrial when the weekly Call-Put Dollar Value Flow Line crosses above its previous week's trailing 114-week Exponential Moving Average of the weekly Call-Put Dollar Value Flow Line.

Close Long (Sell) at the current weekly price close of the Dow-Jones Industrial when the weekly Call-Put Dollar Value Flow Line crosses below its previous week's trailing 114-week Exponential Moving Average of the weekly Call-Put Dollar Value Flow Line.

Enter Short (Sell Short) never.

Starting with $100 and reinvesting profits, total net profits for this Call-Put Dollar Value Flow Line strategy would have been $832.45, assuming a fully invested strategy, reinvestment of profits, no transactions costs and no taxes. This would have been 12.94 percent less than buy-and-hold. Short selling was not included in this strategy and would have lowered total net profit by 2.69%. The long-only Call-Put Dollar Value Flow Line would have given profitable buy signals 3 times out of 3. Trading would have been inactive at one trade every 2,963.67 calendar days.

The Equis International MetaStock® System Testing rules, where the Call-Put Dollar Value Flow Line is inserted in the field normally reserved for volume, are written as follows:

Enter long: V > Ref(Mov(V,opt1,E),−1)

Close long: V < Ref(Mov(V,opt1,E),−1)

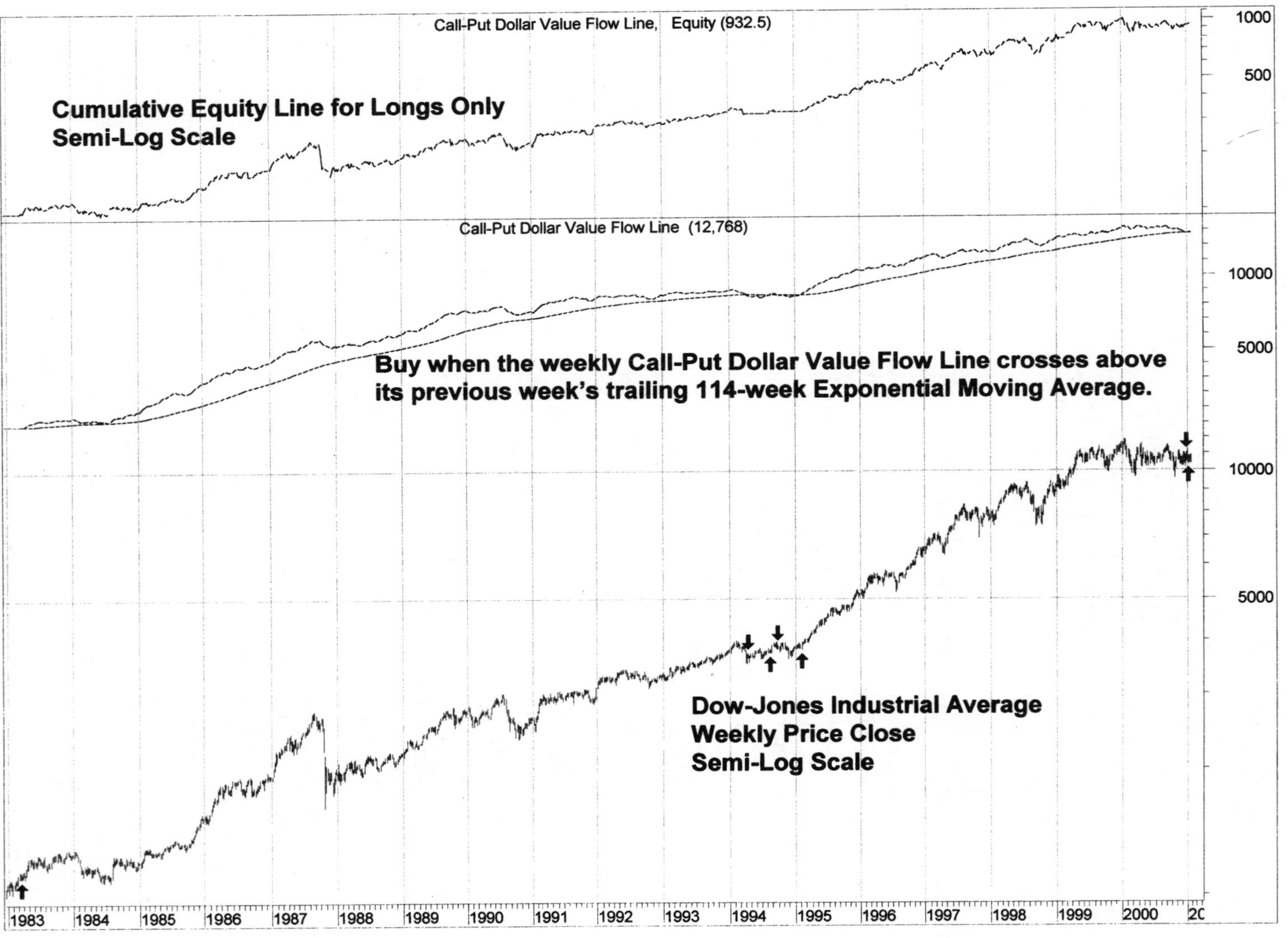
Call-Put Dollar Value Flow Line, Equity (932.5)
Cumulative Equity Line for Longs Only
Semi-Log Scale
1000
500
Call-Put Dollar Value Flow Line (12,768)
10000
5000
Buy when the weekly Call-Put Dollar Value Flow Line crosses above
its previous week's trailing 114-week Exponential Moving Average.
10000
5000
Dow-Jones Industrial Average
Weekly Price Close
Semi-Log Scale
1983
1984
1985
1986
1987
1988
1989
1990
1991
1992
1993
1994
1995
1996
1997
1998
1999
2000
2C

Call-Put Dollar Value Flow Line

Total net profit	832.45	Open position value	11.77	Net Profit/Buy&Hold %	−12.94
Percent gain/loss	832.45	Annual percent gain/loss	34.17	Annual Net %/B&H %	−12.94
Initial investment	100	Interest earned	0		
Current position	Long	Date position entered	1/12/01		
Buy/Hold profit	956.18	Days in test	8891	# of days per trade	2963.67
Buy/Hold pct gain/loss	956.18	Annual B/H pct gain/loss	39.25		
Total closed trades	3	Commissions paid	0		
Avg profit per trade	273.56	Avg Win/Avg Loss ratio	N/A		
Total long trades	3	Total short trades	0	Long Win Trade %	100.00
Winning long trades	3	Winning short trades	0	Short Win Trade %	#DIV/0!
Total winning trades	3	Total losing trades	0	Total Win Trade %	100.00
Amount of winning trades	820.68	Amount of losing trades	0	Net Profit Margin %	100.00
Average win	273.56	Average loss	N/A	Average P. Margin %	#VALUE!
Largest win	585.4	Largest loss	0	% Net/(Win + Loss)	100.00
Average length of win	298.33	Average length of loss	N/A	(Win − Loss)/Loss %	#VALUE!
Longest winning trade	579	Longest losing trade	0	(Win − Loss)/Loss %	#DIV/0!
Most consecutive wins	3	Most consecutive losses	0	(Win − Loss)/Loss %	#DIV/0!
Total bars out	380	Average length out	95		
Longest out period	339				
System close drawdown	0	Profit/Loss index	100	% Net Profit/SODD	30161.23
System open drawdown	−2.76	Reward/Risk index	99.67	(Net P. − SODD)/Net P.	99.67
Max open trade drawdown	−2.76	Buy/Hold index	−11.71	% SODD/Net Profit	−0.33

In the Equis MetaStock® "System Report" (profit and loss summary statistics), the *Total net profit* is the sum of profits minus the sum of losses, including open positions marked to the market. In contrast, the *Amount of Winning Trades* is the sum of realized profits (the total of all gains on closed-out trades only, excluding any open positions). Similarly, the *Amount of Losing Trades* is the sum of realized losses (the total of all losses on closed-out trades only, excluding any open positions). *System close drawdown* is the largest decline in the cumulative equity line below the initial investment, based on closed-out positions only. *System open drawdown (SODD)* is the largest decline in the cumulative equity line below the initial investment when a position is open. *Max open trade drawdown* is the largest decline in the cumulative equity line below the trade entry price during the worst single trade. The *Profit/Loss Index* is a complex calculation that relates the Amount of Winning Trades to the Amount of Losing Trades on a scale of −100 (worst possible performance) to +100 (best possible performance), with zero representing profits equal to losses. *Reward/Risk Index* is the Total net profit minus System open drawdown. The resulting difference is then divided by the Total net profit. The *Buy/Hold Index* is the Total net profit minus the buy-and-hold strategy's net profit. The resulting difference is then divided by the buy-and-hold net profit. In this exercise, initial equity is assumed to be $100. Both long and short positions are taken unless otherwise noted. Trades are executed at the closing price on the signal date. Transaction costs, interest expenses, and margins are not included in the statistics.

Enter short: V < Ref(Mov(V,opt1,E),−1)

Close short: V > Ref(Mov(V,opt1,E),−1)

OPT1 Current value: 114

Call-Put Dollar Value Ratio

The Call-Put Dollar Value Ratio is a sentiment oscillator created by Robert B. McCurtain. It may be computed using daily or weekly data. This ratio can be scaled to oscillate up and down around 100, within a range of zero to 200.

To calculate, normalize and scale this Call-Put Dollar Value Ratio, start with Steps 1 through 6 for the Call-Put Dollar Value Flow Line.

7. Divide the net difference of Call Dollar Value minus Put Dollar Value by the sum of Call Dollar Value plus Put Dollar Value.
8. Multiply the ratio in Step 7 by 100, to arrive at the percentage of net call-put dollar volume relative to the total call plus put dollar volume.
9. Add the product of Step 8 to a constant of 100 (for scaling).
10. Compute a 3-period Exponential Moving Average of the weekly sums in Step 9.
11. Plot that 3-period Exponential Moving Average.

Indicator Strategy Example for McCurtain's Call-Put Dollar Value Ratio

Historical data shows that the Call-Put Dollar Value Ratio can be an effective indicator on both the long and short sides, and particularly on the long side. Based on the weekly call and put data for S&P 100 Stock Price Index and the Dow-Jones Industrial Average for 17 years from January 1984 to January 2001, we found that the following parameters would have produced a significantly positive result on a purely mechanical trend-following signal basis with no subjectivity, no sophisticated technical analysis, and no judgement:

Enter Long (Buy) at the current weekly price close of the Dow-Jones Industrial Average when 3-period Exponential Moving Average of the weekly sums (from Step 10) rises from below to above 60.

Close Long (Sell) at the current weekly price close of the Dow-Jones Industrial Average when 3-period Exponential Moving Average of the weekly sums (from Step 10) falls from above to below 61.

Enter Short (Sell Short) at the current weekly price close of the Dow-Jones Industrial Average when 3-period Exponential Moving Average of the weekly sums (from Step 10) falls from above to below 61.

Close Short (Cover) at the current weekly price close of the Dow-Jones Industrial Average when 3-period Exponential Moving Average of the weekly sums (from Step 10) rises from below to above 52.

Starting with $100 and reinvesting profits, total net profits for this Call-Put Dollar Value Ratio strategy would have been $1,469.11, assuming a fully invested strategy, reinvestment of profits, no transactions costs and no taxes. This would have been 101.65 percent better than buy-and-hold. Short selling, which was included in this strategy, would have lost money since October, 1990, but would have been profitable over the entire 17 years. The long-and-short Call-Put Dollar Value Ratio would have given profitable signals 60.98% of the time. Trading would have been more active but still modest at one trade every 151.98 calendar days.

The Equis International MetaStock® System Testing rules, where the pre-smoothed Call-Put Dollar Value Ratio is inserted in the field normally reserved for volume, are written as follows:

Enter long: Ref(Mov(V,opt1,E),−1) < opt2 AND Mov(V,opt1,E) > opt2

Close long: Ref(Mov(V,opt1,E),−1) > opt3 AND Mov(V,opt1,E) < opt3

Enter short: Ref(Mov(V,opt1,E),−1) > opt4 AND Mov(V,opt1,E) < opt4

Close short: Ref(Mov(V,opt1,E),−1) < opt5 AND Mov(V,opt1,E) > opt5

OPT1 Current value: 3
OPT2 Current value: 60
OPT3 Current value: 61
OPT4 Current value: 61
OPT5 Current value: 52

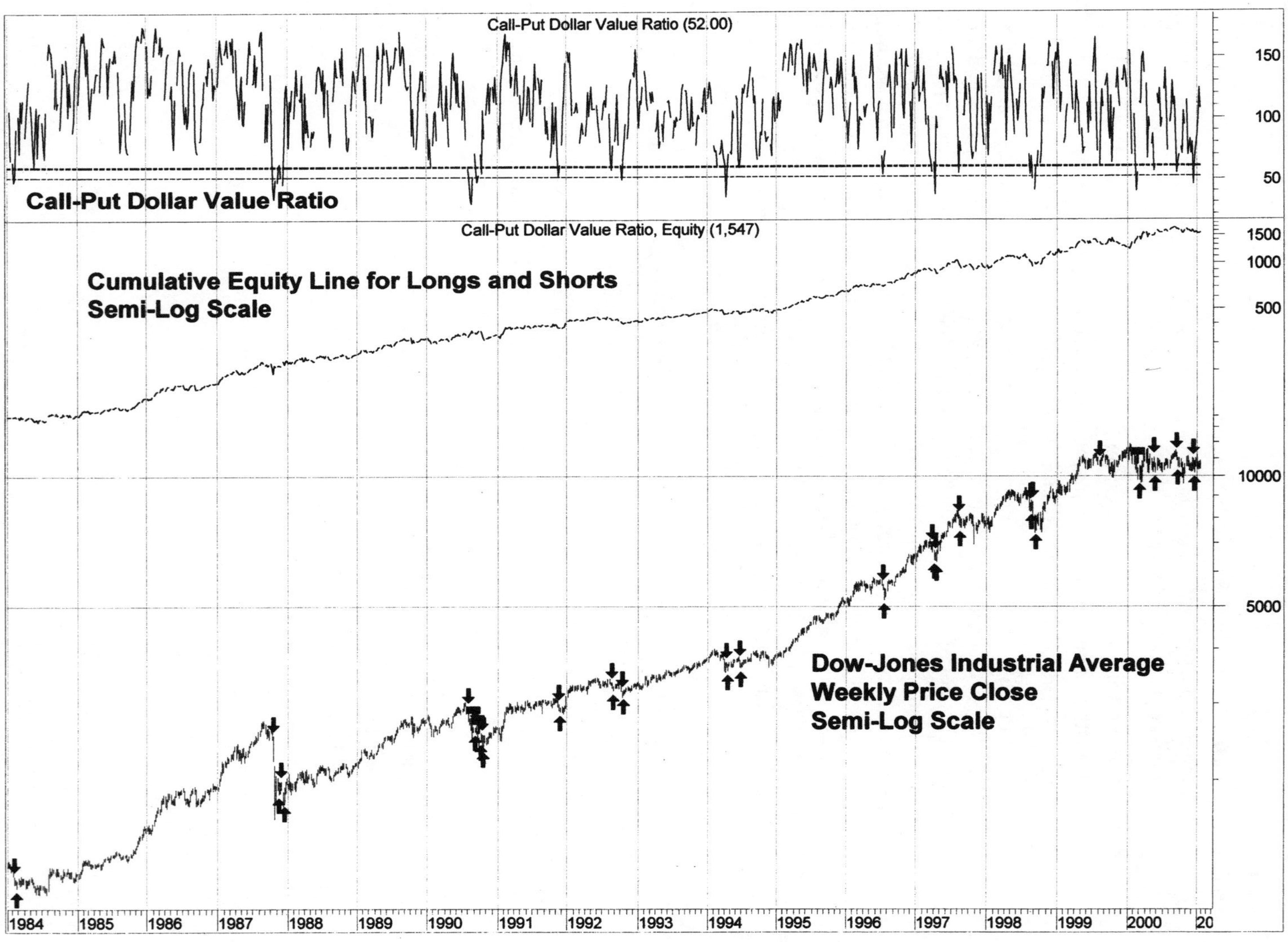
Call-Put Dollar Value Ratio (52.00)
Call-Put Dollar Value Ratio
Call-Put Dollar Value Ratio, Equity (1,547)
Cumulative Equity Line for Longs and Shorts
Semi-Log Scale
Dow-Jones Industrial Average
Weekly Price Close
Semi-Log Scale
150
100
50
1500
1000
500
10000
5000
1984
1985
1986
1987
1988
1989
1990
1991
1992
1993
1994
1995
1996
1997
1998
1999
2000
20

Call-Put Dollar Value Ratio

Total net profit	1469.11	Open position value	3.59	Net Profit/Buy&Hold %	101.65
Percent gain/loss	1469.11	Annual percent gain/loss	86.06	Annual Net %/B&H %	101.64
Initial investment	100	Interest earned	0		
Current position	Long	Date position entered	12/22/00		
Buy/Hold profit	728.54	Days in test	6231	# of days per trade	151.98
Buy/Hold pct gain/loss	728.54	Annual B/H pct gain/loss	42.68		
Total closed trades	41	Commissions paid	0		
Avg profit per trade	35.74	Avg Win/Avg Loss ratio	3.53		
Total long trades	20	Total short trades	21	Long Win Trade %	60.00
Winning long trades	12	Winning short trades	13	Short Win Trade %	61.90
Total winning trades	25	Total losing trades	16	Total Win Trade %	60.98
Amount of winning trades	1790.02	Amount of losing trades	−324.51	**Net Profit Margin %**	**69.31**
Average win	**71.6**	**Average loss**	**−20.28**	**Average P. Margin %**	**55.86**
Largest win	**370.79**	**Largest loss**	**−63.08**	**% Net/(Win + Loss)**	**70.92**
Average length of win	**34.4**	**Average length of loss**	**3.56**	**(Win − Loss)/Loss %**	**866.29**
Longest winning trade	**191**	**Longest losing trade**	**13**	**(Win − Loss)/Loss %**	**1369.23**
Most consecutive wins	**7**	**Most consecutive losses**	**3**	**(Win − Loss)/Loss %**	**133.33**
Total bars out	**14**	**Average length out**	**2.8**		
Longest out period	**6**				
System close drawdown	**0**	**Profit/Loss index**	**81.91**	**% Net Profit/SODD**	**25505.38**
System open drawdown	**−5.76**	**Reward/Risk index**	**99.61**	**(Net P. − SODD)/Net P.**	**99.61**
Max open trade drawdown	**−128.18**	**Buy/Hold index**	**102.14**	**% SODD/Net Profit**	**−0.39**

In the Equis MetaStock® "System Report" (profit and loss summary statistics), the *Total net profit* is the sum of profits minus the sum of losses, including open positions marked to the market. In contrast, the *Amount of Winning Trades* is the sum of realized profits (the total of all gains on closed-out trades only, excluding any open positions). Similarly, the *Amount of Losing Trades* is the sum of realized losses (the total of all losses on closed-out trades only, excluding any open positions). *System close drawdown* is the largest decline in the cumulative equity line below the initial investment, based on closed-out positions only. *System open drawdown (SODD)* is the largest decline in the cumulative equity line below the initial investment when a position is open. *Max open trade drawdown* is the largest decline in the cumulative equity line below the trade entry price during the worst single trade. The *Profit/Loss Index* is a complex calculation that relates the Amount of Winning Trades to the Amount of Losing Trades on a scale of −100 (worst possible performance) to +100 (best possible performance), with zero representing profits equal to losses. *Reward/Risk Index* is the Total net profit minus System open drawdown. The resulting difference is then divided by the Total net profit. The *Buy/Hold Index* is the Total net profit minus the buy-and-hold strategy's net profit. The resulting difference is then divided by the buy-and-hold net profit. In this exercise, initial equity is assumed to be $100. Both long and short positions are taken unless otherwise noted. Trades are executed at the closing price on the signal date. Transaction costs, interest expenses, and margins are not included in the statistics.

Call-Put Premium Ratio

The Call-Put Premium Ratio is a sentiment oscillator. It is usually computed using daily data, although it may be used on weekly data.

This ratio can be normalized and scaled to oscillate up and down around 100 within a range of zero to 200 in seven steps, as follows:

1. Using Options Clearing Corporation's Equity Average Premium Per Contract Totals, subtract put premiums from call premiums.
2. Add call premiums and put premiums.
3. Divide the subtraction from Step 1 by the addition from Step 2.
4. Multiply the ratio in Step 3 by 100, to arrive at the percentage of net call minus put premiums relative to the total call plus put premiums.
5. Add the percentage from Step 4 to a constant of 100 (for scaling).
6. Compute a 5-period Exponential Moving Average of the newly scaled percentages in Step 5.
7. Plot that 5-period Exponential Moving Average.

Historical data for this indicator is available to institutional investors through UST Securities Corporation, 5 Vaughn Drive, CN5209, Princeton, NJ 08543-5209, phone (609) 734-7788.

Indicator Strategy Example for the Call-Put Premium Ratio

The Call-Put Premium Ratio can be an effective indicator on both the long and short sides, particularly on the long side. Based on the weekly Options Clearing Corporation's Equity Average Premium Per Contract Totals for call and put premium data and the Dow-Jones Industrial Average for 20 years from April 1981 to January 2001, we found that the following parameters would have produced a positive result on a purely mechanical trend-following signal basis with no subjectivity, no sophisticated technical analysis, and no judgement:

Enter Long (Buy) at the current weekly price close of the Dow-Jones Industrial Average when the 5-period Exponential Moving Average of the weekly Call-Put Premium Ratio rises from below 80 to above 80.

Close Long (Sell) at the current weekly price close of the Dow-Jones Industrial Average when the 5-period Exponential Moving Average of the weekly Call-Put Premium Ratio falls from above 80 to below 80.

Enter Short (Sell Short) at the current weekly price close of the Dow-Jones Industrial Average when the 5-period Exponential Moving Average of the weekly Call-Put Premium Ratio falls from above 80 to below 80.

Close Short (Cover) at the current weekly price close of the Dow-Jones Industrial Average when 5-period Exponential Moving Average of the weekly Call-Put Premium Ratio rises from below 80 to above 80.

Starting with $100 and reinvesting profits, total net profits for this Call-Put Premium Ratio strategy would have been $1,307.40, assuming a fully invested strategy, reinvestment of profits, no transactions costs and no taxes. This would have been 41.17 percent better than buy-and-hold. Even short selling would have been slightly profitable and was included in this strategy. The long-and-short Call-Put Premium Ratio would have given profitable signals 58.33% of the time. Trading would have been inactive at one trade every 596.25 calendar days.

The Equis International MetaStock® System Testing rules, where the pre-smoothed Call-Put Premium Ratio is inserted in the field normally reserved for volume, are written as follows:

Enter long: Ref(Mov(V,opt1,E),−1) < opt2 AND Mov(V,opt1,E) > opt2

Close long: Ref(Mov(V,opt1,E),−1) > opt3 AND Mov(V,opt1,E) < opt3

Enter short: Ref(Mov(V,opt1,E),−1) > opt4 AND Mov(V,opt1,E) < opt4

Close short: Ref(Mov(V,opt1,E),−1) < opt5 AND Mov(V,opt1,E) > opt5

OPT1 Current value: 5
OPT2 Current value: 80
OPT3 Current value: 80
OPT4 Current value: 80
OPT5 Current value: 80

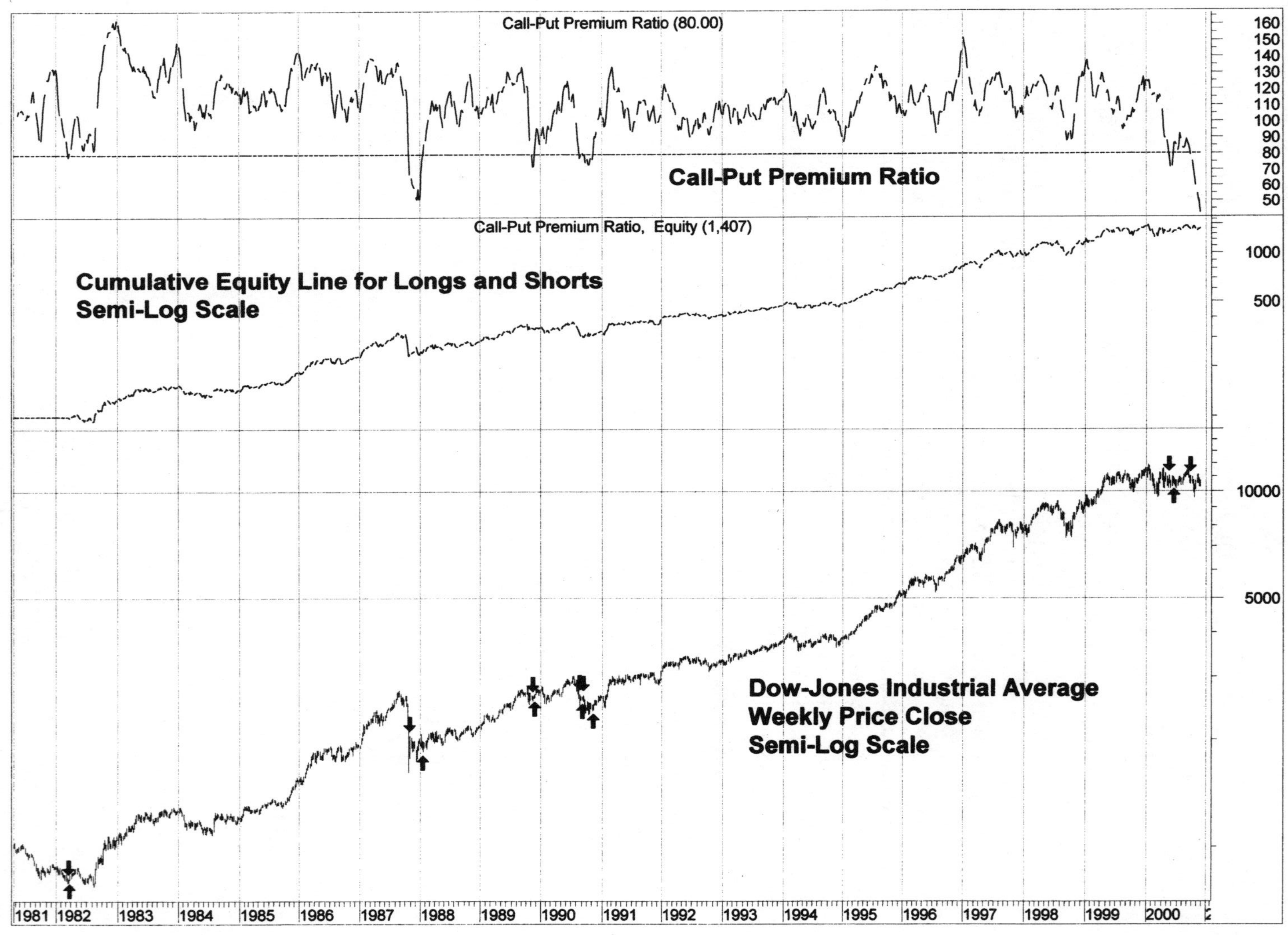

Call-Put Premium Ratio (80.00)
Call-Put Premium Ratio
Call-Put Premium Ratio, Equity (1,407)
Cumulative Equity Line for Longs and Shorts
Semi-Log Scale
Dow-Jones Industrial Average
Weekly Price Close
Semi-Log Scale
160
150
140
130
120
110
100
90
80
70
60
50
1000
500
10000
5000
1981
1982
1983
1984
1985
1986
1987
1988
1989
1990
1991
1992
1993
1994
1995
1996
1997
1998
1999
2000

Call-Put Premium Ratio

Total net profit	1307.4	Open position value	23.48	Net Profit/Buy&Hold %	41.17
Percent gain/loss	1307.4	Annual percent gain/loss	66.69	Annual Net %/B&H %	41.17
Initial investment	100	Interest earned	0		
Current position	Short	Date position entered	9/29/00		
Buy/Hold profit	926.09	Days in test	7155	# of days per trade	596.25
Buy/Hold pct gain/loss	926.09	Annual B/H pct gain/loss	47.24		
Total closed trades	12	Commissions paid	0		
Avg profit per trade	106.99	Avg Win/Avg Loss ratio	21.66		
Total long trades	6	Total short trades	6	Long Win Trade %	66.67
Winning long trades	4	Winning short trades	3	Short Win Trade %	50.00
Total winning trades	7	Total losing trades	5	Total Win Trade %	58.33
Amount of winning trades	1327.71	Amount of losing trades	−43.78	**Net Profit Margin %**	**93.62**
Average win	**189.67**	**Average loss**	**−8.76**	**Average P. Margin %**	**91.17**
Largest win	**1022.69**	**Largest loss**	**−18.1**	**% Net/(Win + Loss)**	**96.52**
Average length of win	**132.71**	**Average length of loss**	**10**	**(Win − Loss)/Loss %**	**1227.10**
Longest winning trade	**498**	**Longest losing trade**	**40**	**(Win − Loss)/Loss %**	**1145.00**
Most consecutive wins	**4**	**Most consecutive losses**	**4**	**(Win − Loss)/Loss %**	**0.00**
Total bars out	**48**	**Average length out**	**48**		
Longest out period	**48**				
System close drawdown	**−1.51**	**Profit/Loss index**	**96.76**	**% Net Profit/SODD**	**23514.39**
System open drawdown	**−5.56**	**Reward/Risk index**	**99.58**	**(Net P. − SODD)/Net P.**	**99.57**
Max open trade drawdown	**−21.7**	**Buy/Hold index**	**43.71**	**% SODD/Net Profit**	**−0.43**

In the Equis MetaStock® "System Report" (profit and loss summary statistics), the *Total net profit* is the sum of profits minus the sum of losses, including open positions marked to the market. In contrast, the *Amount of Winning Trades* is the sum of realized profits (the total of all gains on closed-out trades only, excluding any open positions). Similarly, the *Amount of Losing Trades* is the sum of realized losses (the total of all losses on closed-out trades only, excluding any open positions). *System close drawdown* is the largest decline in the cumulative equity line below the initial investment, based on closed-out positions only. *System open drawdown (SODD)* is the largest decline in the cumulative equity line below the initial investment when a position is open. *Max open trade drawdown* is the largest decline in the cumulative equity line below the trade entry price during the worst single trade. The *Profit/Loss Index* is a complex calculation that relates the Amount of Winning Trades to the Amount of Losing Trades on a scale of −100 (worst possible performance) to +100 (best possible performance), with zero representing profits equal to losses. *Reward/Risk Index* is the Total net profit minus System open drawdown. The resulting difference is then divided by the Total net profit. The *Buy/Hold Index* is the Total net profit minus the buy-and-hold strategy's net profit. The resulting difference is then divided by the buy-and-hold net profit. In this exercise, initial equity is assumed to be $100. Both long and short positions are taken unless otherwise noted. Trades are executed at the closing price on the signal date. Transaction costs, interest expenses, and margins are not included in the statistics.

Call-Put Volume Ratio

The Call-Put Volume Ratio, another sentiment oscillator, is an inverse variation of the popular Put/Call Ratio. Call and Put volume statistics are reported by Chicago Board Options Exchange (CBOE). It may be computed using daily or weekly data.

This ratio can be normalized and scaled to oscillate up and down around 100 within a range of zero to 200 in five steps, as follows:

1. Using Chicago Board Options Exchange volume data, subtract put volume from call volume.
2. Add call volume and put volume.
3. Divide the subtraction from Step 1 by the addition from Step 2.
4. Multiply the ratio in Step 3 by 100, to arrive at the percentage of net call minus put volume relative to the total call plus put volume.
5. Add the percentage from Step 4 to a constant of 100 (for scaling).

According to the *Theory of Contrary Opinion*, option speculators are usually wrong when they go to extremes. Therefore, above-average Call-Put Volume Ratio levels are bearish. Below-average Call-Put Volume Ratios are bullish. Because it takes time for traders' emotional extremes to run their course, it is advantageous to build in a 3-day lag.

Indicator Strategy Example for the Call-Put Volume Ratio

The Call-Put Volume Ratio can be an effective indicator on both the long and short sides, and particularly on the long side. Based on the daily Chicago Board Options Exchange call and put volume data and the Dow-Jones Industrial Average (for 23 years from January 1978 to January 2001), we found that the following parameters would have produced a positive result on a purely mechanical trend-following signal basis with no subjectivity, no sophisticated technical analysis, and no judgement:

Enter Long (Buy) at the current daily price close of the Dow-Jones Industrial Average when the Call-Put Volume Ratio (as of three trading days ago) is less than the current 88-day Exponential Moving Average of the daily Call-Put Volume Ratio. This indicates a relatively low call volume.

Close Long (Sell) at the current daily price close of the Dow-Jones Industrial Average when the Call-Put Volume Ratio (as of three trading days ago) is greater than the current 88-day Exponential Moving Average of the daily Call-Put Volume Ratio. This indicates a relatively high call volume.

Enter Short (Sell Short) at the current daily price close of the Dow-Jones Industrial Average when the Call-Put Volume Ratio (as of three trading days ago) is greater than the current 88-day Exponential Moving Average of the daily Call-Put Volume Ratio. This indicates a relatively high call volume.

Close Short (Cover) at the current daily price close of the Dow-Jones Industrial Average when the Call-Put Volume Ratio (as of three trading days ago) is less than the current 88-day Exponential Moving Average of the daily Call-Put Volume Ratio, thus indicating relatively low call volume.

Starting with $100 and reinvesting profits, total net profits for this Call-Put Volume Ratio contrary strategy would have been $2,048.64, assuming a fully invested strategy, reinvestment of profits, no transactions costs and no taxes. This would have been 116.41 percent better than buy-and-hold. Even short selling would have been slightly profitable and is included in this strategy. The long-and-short Call-Put Volume Ratio would have given profitable signals 54.01% of the time. Trading would have been hyperactive at one trade every 4.88 calendar days.

The Equis International MetaStock® System Testing rules, where the pre-smoothed Call-Put Volume Ratio is inserted in the field normally reserved for volume, are written as follows:

Enter long: Ref(Mov(V,opt1,E),−opt3) > Ref(Mov(V,opt2,E),−opt4)

Close long: Ref(Mov(V,opt1,E),−opt3) < Ref(Mov(V,opt2,E),−opt5)

Enter short: Ref(Mov(V,opt1,E),−opt3) < Ref(Mov(V,opt2,E),−opt5)

Close short: Ref(Mov(V,opt1,E),−opt3) > Ref(Mov(V,opt2,E),−opt4)

OPT1 Current value: 88

OPT2 Current value: 1

OPT3 Current value: 0

OPT4 Current value: 3

OPT5 Current value: 3

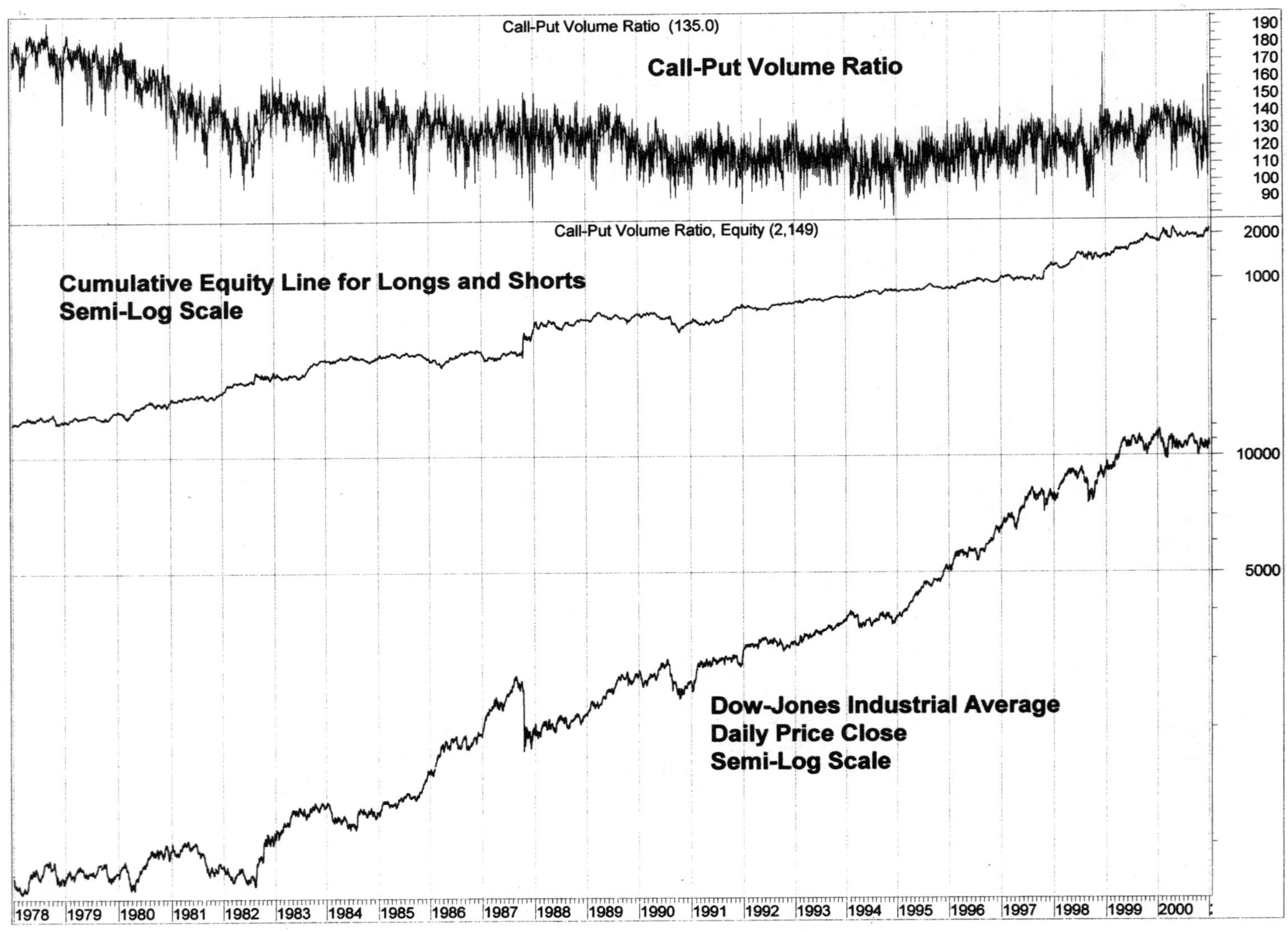

Call-Put Volume Ratio (135.0)
Call-Put Volume Ratio
190
180
170
160
150
140
130
120
110
100
90
Call-Put Volume Ratio, Equity (2,149)
Cumulative Equity Line for Longs and Shorts
Semi-Log Scale
2000
1000
10000
5000
Dow-Jones Industrial Average
Daily Price Close
Semi-Log Scale
1978
1979
1980
1981
1982
1983
1984
1985
1986
1987
1988
1989
1990
1991
1992
1993
1994
1995
1996
1997
1998
1999
2000

Call-Put Volume Ratio

Total net profit	2048.64	Open position value	0	Net Profit/Buy&Hold %	116.41
Percent gain/loss	2048.64	Annual percent gain/loss	84.24	Annual Net %/B&H %	116.39
Initial investment	100	Interest earned	0		
Current position	Short	Date position entered	1/8/01		
Buy/Hold profit	946.66	Days in test	8876	# of days per trade	4.88
Buy/Hold pct gain/loss	946.66	Annual B/H pct gain/loss	38.93		
Total closed trades	1820	Commissions paid	0		
Avg profit per trade	1.13	Avg Win/Avg Loss ratio	1.13		
Total long trades	910	Total short trades	910	Long Win Trade %	58.13
Winning long trades	529	Winning short trades	454	Short Win Trade %	49.89
Total winning trades	983	Total losing trades	837	Total Win Trade %	54.01
Amount of winning trades	8281.02	Amount of losing trades	−6232.38	**Net Profit Margin %**	**14.12**
Average win	**8.42**	**Average loss**	**−7.45**	**Average P. Margin %**	**6.11**
Largest win	**163.02**	**Largest loss**	**−167.89**	**% Net/(Win + Loss)**	**−1.47**
Average length of win	**4.12**	**Average length of loss**	**4.28**	**(Win − Loss)/Loss %**	**−3.74**
Longest winning trade	**42**	**Longest losing trade**	**30**	**(Win − Loss)/Loss %**	**40.00**
Most consecutive wins	**11**	**Most consecutive losses**	**7**	**(Win − Loss)/Loss %**	**57.14**
Total bars out	**324**	**Average length out**	**324**		
Longest out period	**324**				
System close drawdown	**0**	**Profit/Loss index**	**24.74**	**% Net Profit/SODD**	**#DIV/0!**
System open drawdown	**0**	**Reward/Risk index**	**100**	**(Net P. − SODD)/Net P.**	**100.00**
Max open trade drawdown	**−167.89**	**Buy/Hold index**	**116.41**	**% SODD/Net Profit**	**0.00**

In the Equis MetaStock® "System Report" (profit and loss summary statistics), the *Total net profit* is the sum of profits minus the sum of losses, including open positions marked to the market. In contrast, the *Amount of Winning Trades* is the sum of realized profits (the total of all gains on closed-out trades only, excluding any open positions). Similarly, the *Amount of Losing Trades* is the sum of realized losses (the total of all losses on closed-out trades only, excluding any open positions). *System close drawdown* is the largest decline in the cumulative equity line below the initial investment, based on closed-out positions only. *System open drawdown (SODD)* is the largest decline in the cumulative equity line below the initial investment when a position is open. *Max open trade drawdown* is the largest decline in the cumulative equity line below the trade entry price during the worst single trade. The *Profit/Loss Index* is a complex calculation that relates the Amount of Winning Trades to the Amount of Losing Trades on a scale of −100 (worst possible performance) to +100 (best possible performance), with zero representing profits equal to losses. *Reward/Risk Index* is the Total net profit minus System open drawdown. The resulting difference is then divided by the Total net profit. The *Buy/Hold Index* is the Total net profit minus the buy-and-hold strategy's net profit. The resulting difference is then divided by the buy-and-hold net profit. In this exercise, initial equity is assumed to be $100. Both long and short positions are taken unless otherwise noted. Trades are executed at the closing price on the signal date. Transaction costs, interest expenses, and margins are not included in the statistics.

Chaikin's Money Flow

(*See Volume Accumulation Oscillator, Volume Accumulation Trend.*)

Chande Momentum Oscillator (CMO)

The Chande Momentum Oscillator (CMO) is a price momentum oscillator that is closely related to RSI (Relative Strength Index) in its method of calculation: CMO uses data for both up days and down days in its numerator, calculations are applied on unsmoothed data, then the ratio is smoothed. But in contrast to RSI, which is bounded within a range of 100 to 0, the CMO indicator scale is bounded by +100 and −100, with default overbought/oversold thresholds at +50/−50. Like other oscillators, CMO may be interpreted in a variety of ways. CMO was presented by Tushar Chande and Stanley Kroll, *The New Technical Trader*, John Wiley & Sons, New York, 1994, 256 pages.

Indicator Strategy Example for CMO

CMO appears to produce results similar to RSI. Naïve testing assumptions suggest that CMO may have some objective value as a purely mechanical, contra-trend technical indicator, using −50 as a buy signal and +50 as a sell signal. The majority of oversold buy signals would have been profitable, although the winning percentage is less than that of RSI. Moreover, these buy signals would have been robust, with all CMO lengths from 1 to 31 days profitable and right most of the time (for long trades only).

As attractive as a high percentage of profitable trades may seem, it is important to note that CMO (like other contra-trend strategies) failed to provide any protection in the Crash of '87, the decline of 1998, and other significant market price drops. As the chart shows, there are sharp equity drawdowns. Using CMO for contratrend oversold and overbought signals underperformed the passive buy-and-hold strategy for long trades only, while short selling would not have been profitable.

Based on an 18-year file of daily data for the entire history of the S&P 500 Composite Stock Price Index futures *CSI Perpetual Contract* from 4/21/82 to 12/08/00 collected from www.csidata.com, we found that the following parameters would have produced a positive result on a purely mechanical overbought/oversold signal basis with no subjectivity, no sophisticated technical analysis, and no judgement:

Enter Long (Buy) at the current daily price close of the S&P 500 Composite Stock Price Index futures *CSI Perpetual Contract* when the 5-day CMO is less than −50.

Close Long (Sell) at the current daily price close of the S&P 500 Composite Stock Price Index futures *CSI Perpetual Contract* when the 5-day CMO is greater than +50.

Enter Short (Sell Short) never.

Starting with $100 and reinvesting profits, total net profits for this CMO counter-trend strategy would have been $753.39, assuming a fully invested strategy, reinvestment of profits, no transactions costs and no taxes. This would have been 26.68 percent less than buy-and-hold. No short selling would have been profitable, and no short selling was included in the strategy. Short selling would have cut the profit in half. Long-only CMO as an indicator would have given profitable buy signals 77.46% of the time. Trading would have been moderately active at one trade every 32.02 calendar days.

The Equis International MetaStock® System Testing rules are written as follows:

Enter long: CMO(C,opt1) < −50

Close long: CMO(C,opt1) > 50

OPT1 Current value: 5

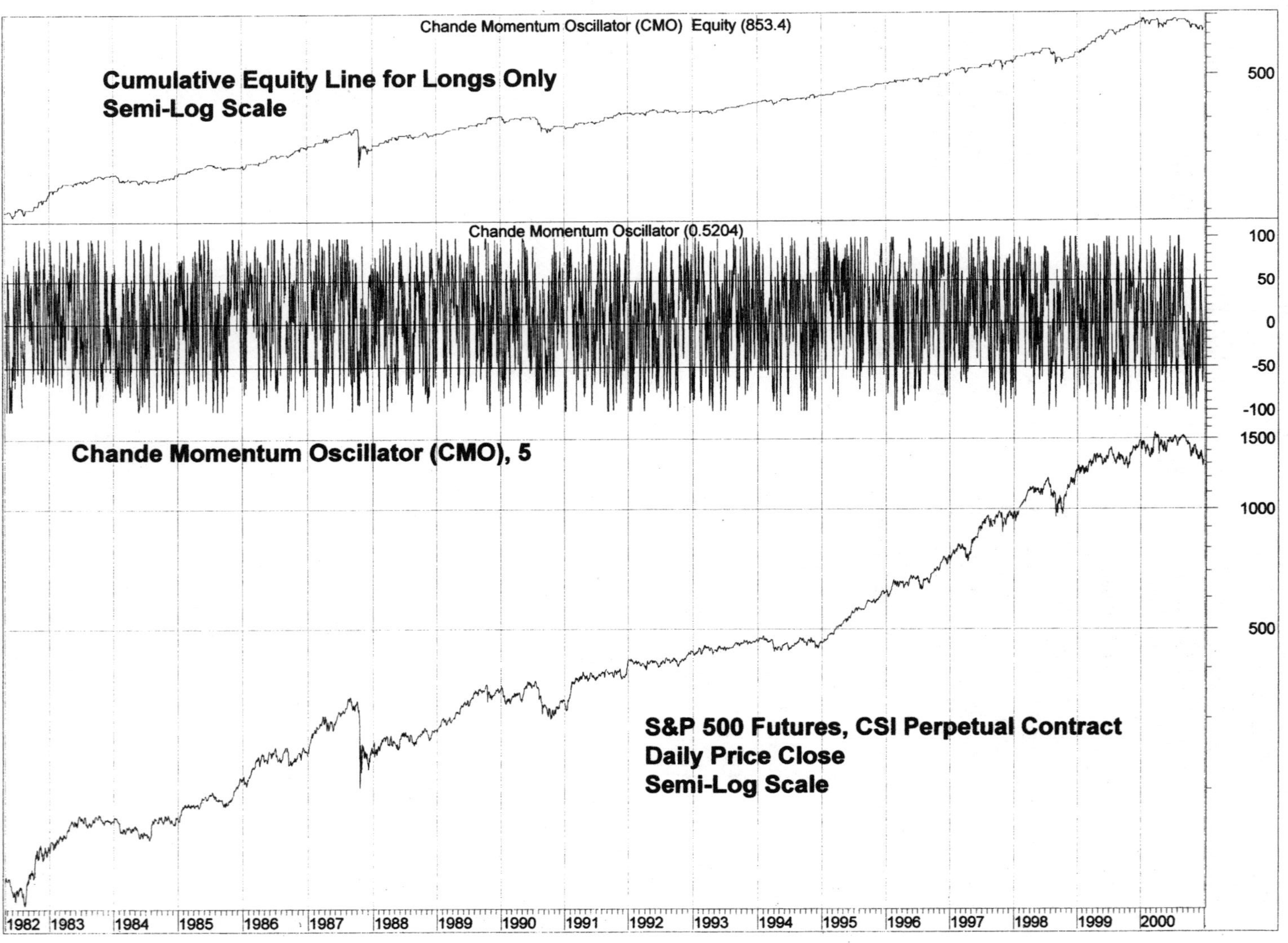

Chande Momentum Oscillator (CMO) Equity (853.4)
Cumulative Equity Line for Longs Only
Semi-Log Scale
500
Chande Momentum Oscillator (0.5204)
100
50
0
-50
-100
Chande Momentum Oscillator (CMO), 5
1500
1000
500
S&P 500 Futures, CSI Perpetual Contract
Daily Price Close
Semi-Log Scale
1982
1983
1984
1985
1986
1987
1988
1989
1990
1991
1992
1993
1994
1995
1996
1997
1998
1999
2000

Chande Momentum Oscillator (CMO), Five Day

Total net profit	753.39	Open position value	−12.73	Net Profit/Buy&Hold %	−26.67
Percent gain/loss	753.39	Annual percent gain/loss	40.31	Annual Net %/B&H %	−26.68
Initial investment	100	Interest earned	0		
Current position	Long	Date position entered	12/18/00		
Buy/Hold profit	1027.4	Days in test	6821	# of days per trade	32.02
Buy/Hold pct gain/loss	1027.4	Annual B/H pct gain/loss	54.98		
Total closed trades	213	Commissions paid	0		
Avg profit per trade	3.6	Avg Win/Avg Loss ratio	0.74		
Total long trades	213	Total short trades	0	Long Win Trade %	77.46
Winning long trades	165	Winning short trades	0	Short Win Trade %	#DIV/0!
Total winning trades	165	Total losing trades	48	Total Win Trade %	77.46
Amount of winning trades	1262.88	Amount of losing trades	−496.75	Net Profit Margin %	43.54
Average win	7.65	Average loss	−10.35	Average P. Margin %	−15.00
Largest win	38.09	Largest loss	−69.21	% Net/(Win + Loss)	−29.00
Average length of win	8.01	Average length of loss	17.83	(Win − Loss)/Loss %	−55.08
Longest winning trade	25	Longest losing trade	43	(Win − Loss)/Loss %	−41.86
Most consecutive wins	15	Most consecutive losses	4	(Win − Loss)/Loss %	275.00
Total bars out	2968	Average length out	13.87		
Longest out period	51				
System close drawdown	−2.55	Profit/Loss index	60.26	% Net Profit/SODD	13648.37
System open drawdown	−5.52	Reward/Risk index	99.27	(Net P. − SODD)/Net P.	99.27
Max open trade drawdown	−113.21	Buy/Hold index	−27.91	% SODD/Net Profit	−0.73

In the Equis MetaStock® "System Report" (profit and loss summary statistics), the *Total net profit* is the sum of profits minus the sum of losses, including open positions marked to the market. In contrast, the *Amount of Winning Trades* is the sum of realized profits (the total of all gains on closed-out trades only, excluding any open positions). Similarly, the *Amount of Losing Trades* is the sum of realized losses (the total of all losses on closed-out trades only, excluding any open positions). *System close drawdown* is the largest decline in the cumulative equity line below the initial investment, based on closed-out positions only. *System open drawdown (SODD)* is the largest decline in the cumulative equity line below the initial investment when a position is open. *Max open trade drawdown* is the largest decline in the cumulative equity line below the trade entry price during the worst single trade. The *Profit/Loss Index* is a complex calculation that relates the Amount of Winning Trades to the Amount of Losing Trades on a scale of −100 (worst possible performance) to +100 (best possible performance), with zero representing profits equal to losses. *Reward/Risk Index* is the Total net profit minus System open drawdown. The resulting difference is then divided by the Total net profit. The *Buy/Hold Index* is the Total net profit minus the buy-and-hold strategy's net profit. The resulting difference is then divided by the buy-and-hold net profit. In this exercise, initial equity is assumed to be $100. Both long and short positions are taken unless otherwise noted. Trades are executed at the closing price on the signal date. Transaction costs, interest expenses, and margins are not included in the statistics.

Chi-Squared Test of Statistical Significance

The chi-squared test tells us how reliable an indicator is, according to Arthur A. Merrill, CMT, who has many decades of experience as both a professional statistician and technical analyst. The chi-squared test is a standard statistical test used to determine if the patterns exhibited by data could have been produced by chance. For a simple two-way test (one with only two possible outcomes such as right or wrong), the formula for the chi-square test with the Yates Correction is:

$$(((|a1 - e1| - 0.5)^2)/e1) + (((|a2 - e2| - 0.5)^2)/e2)$$

where

|...| = the absolute value of the expression within, that is, ignoring sign

a1 = actual observed frequency of outcome 1
e1 = expected or theoretical frequency of outcome 1
a2 = actual observed frequency of outcome 2
e2 = expected or theoretical frequency of outcome 2

Merrill offers an actual example based on all trading days for 31 years from 1952 to 1983. The number of actual observed Mondays when the market rose was 669. The number of actual observed Mondays when the market fell was 865. The total number of all Mondays was 1534. Since 52.1% of all trading days were up over this period, the expected frequency of up Mondays would be the total number of all Mondays multiplied by that expected frequency, which is 1534 multiplied by 52.1%, or 799. The expected frequency of down Mondays would be the total number of all Mondays at 1534 multiplied by 47.9% (that is, 100% minus 52.1%), which is 735. This is all the data we need to plug into the above chi-squared formula:

$$(((|a1 - e1| - 0.5)^2)/e1) + (((|a2 - e2| - 0.5)^2)/e2) =$$

$$(((|669 - 799| - 0.5)^2)/799) + (((|865 - 735| - 0.5)^2)/735) =$$

$$((129.5^2)/799) + ((129.5^2)/735) =$$

$$(16770.25/799) + ((16770.25)/735) = 20.99 + 22.82 = 43.81$$

The chi-squared test result, 43.81, is highly significant at the 99.9% confidence level; that is, the probability is less than 1 in 1000 that the actual observed outcome was due to random chance alone.

Generally, chi-squared test results are interpreted as follows:

Chi-squared test results from zero to and including 3.84 are insignificant; that is, the probability is at least 1 in 20 that the actual observed outcome was due to random chance alone.

Chi-squared test results above 3.84 are probably significant at the 95% confidence level; that is, the probability is less than 1 in 20 that the actual observed outcome was due to random chance alone.

Chi-squared test results above 6.64 are significant at the 99% confidence level; that is, the probability is less than 1 in 100 that the actual observed outcome was due to random chance alone.

Chi-squared test results above 10.83 are highly significant at the 99.9% confidence level; that is, the probability is less than 1 in 1000 that the actual observed outcome was due to random chance alone.

Generally, cross tabulations allow identification of relationships between variables, and the Pearson chi-square test is the most common test of significance to determine the relationship between variables. Basically, we observe actual outcomes and compare them with expected frequencies assuming no relationship between variables.

As a trivial example of a simple binomial experiment, suppose we flip a fair coin to forecast the direction of the stock market. Since there could be no relationship between this naïve forecast and any actual outcome, we expect about an equal number of correct and incorrect forecasts. In other words, the difference between actual observed outcomes and expected outcomes should approach zero as we increase our sample size. (When the expected outcome is 50/50, chi-squared reduces to the square of the difference of the actual observed number of heads minus the actual observed number of tails; then that squared difference is divided by the sum of the actual observed number of heads plus the actual number of observed tails.)

If we next test an actual technical indicator, the difference between actual observed outcomes and expected outcomes should be significant if the indicator has any real value. The actual observed outcomes should deviate from a 50/50 pattern expected for a naïve forecast. Statistical significance increases proportionately to the degree that actual observed outcomes and expected outcomes differ from an equal number of correct and incorrect forecasts.

The chi-square test depends on the overall number of observations. Relatively small deviations of actual observed frequencies from the expected pattern prove more significant as the number of observations increases. On the other hand, when the expected cell frequencies fall below 5, probabilities cannot be estimated with sufficient precision. For small samples with expected frequencies less than 10, accuracy can be improved by using the Yates Correction, which reduces the absolute value of differences between expected and observed frequencies by 0.5 before squaring.

Circuit Breakers, Daily Price Limits, Trading Halts, Curbs

The United States Securities and Exchange Commission (SEC), reacting to the 23% stock market crash of October 19, 1987, imposed circuit breakers or trading limits designed to cap maximum stock market price declines in a single day. These limits inhibit price declines in phases, first curbing New York Stock Exchange (NYSE) program trades then, if the decline continues, eventually halting all U.S. equity, options and futures trading activity. The purpose of these limits is to put a break on emotional panic that may occur within any single day, giving investors time to calmly assess the situation. Circuit breakers do not prevent prices from dropping more than 30 percent spread out over any time period greater than one day.

NYSE Rule 80A states that when the Dow Jones Industrial Average (DJIA) falls or rises 2% from its previous day's close, index arbitrage orders in S&P 500 stocks must be stabilizing; that is, *sell plus* (sell orders on plus ticks) in a weak market, or *buy minus* (buy orders on minus ticks) in a strong market. The 2% value is reset at the beginning of each quarter based on averaged levels of the DJIA over the previous quarter.

Further, the NYSE declares trading halts at minus 10%, 20% and 30%. If the DJIA declines 10% before 2:00 p.m. (eastern time), trading halts for one-hour. If the DJIA declines 10% between 2:00 p.m. and 2:30 p.m., trading halts for thirty minutes. After 2:30 p.m., the 10% limit is not in effect. If the DJIA declines 20% before 1:00 p.m., trading halts for two-hours. If the DJIA declines 20% after 2:00 p.m., trading halts for the rest of the day. Also, if the DJIA declines 30% at any time of day, trading halts for the rest of the day.

The Chicago Mercantile Exchange (CME) imposes 10-minute halts when the S&P 500 index futures fall 2.5% and again when the futures fall 5%. Halts are longer for larger price drops. At minus 10% before 2:30 p.m. (eastern time), futures trading is permitted only at or above this 10% limit. If the primary futures contract is limit offer and the NYSE has declared a trading halt (due to a 10% decline in the DJIA), futures trading also will halt. Futures trading may resume when 50% of the total capitalization weight of the underlying S&P 500 stocks reopen. At minus 10% after 2:30 p.m. (eastern time), futures trading may occur only at or above this 10% limit for 102 minutes. Then, trading will halt for two minutes if the primary futures contract is limit offer at the end of 102 minutes. A similar halt takes effect at minus 15%. At minus 20%, futures trading halts for the rest of the day.

Combining Multiple Technical Indicators

Criteria for including, excluding, and weighting indicators in combinations should be based on the investor's objectives, logic, common sense, and historical risk-adjusted returns simulated over many decades of unseen historical data. Also, each component indicator should be analyzed and followed separately to allow the technical analyst to perceive possible changes in each indicator's behavior, which have been substantial over time for some indicators, due to structural changes in the trading environment.

An overwhelmingly large number of possible technical indicator combinations exist. For example, assume we pick just 10 indicators from this book and we choose to examine all combinations of these indicators. We would need to examine 10 to the 10th power number of combinations, or 10 billion combinations.

Commodex Trend Index is an example of how complex indicator combinations can become. This index employs crossovers of a fast and a slow moving average, volume and open interest momentum for trend confirmation, a trading band for a stop, overbought/oversold levels for profit taking, liquidation based on money management, and inverse pyramiding. Moreover, the components of the system are weighted differently, with the longer term elements given greater weight.

There are many other combined indicator systems that are even more complex. And the more complex the indicator combinations, the more difficult the final system is to comprehend and to work with. It is quite easy to combine different indicators in a way that prevents understanding of how the combination actually works. Moreover, a chain of indicators is no stronger than its weakest link.

The number of possibilities mushrooms when we assign variable weights to different indicators. William Eckhardt, a trader and mathematician, stated that assigning weights tends to be assumption-laden regarding the relationship among the indicators. The literature on robust statistics implies that the best strategy is not an optimized weighting scheme, but is a system to weight each indicator by 1 or 0. If the indicator is good enough to be used, it is weighted equally. If not good, it is excluded entirely. For a stimulating interview with Eckhardt, see Schwager, J., *The New Market Wizards,* 1995, New York: Harper-Collins, 512 pages, p. 109.

An alternate approach is used by Arthur A. Merrill, CMT, who has many decades of experience as both a professional statistician and technical analyst. Merrill observes that at any given time some indicators are bullish while others are bearish, and it is only human nature to see only those that confirm our preconceived opinion. Merrill's solution to this problem is to objectively weight the indicators by past performance. First, he measures each indicator by its accuracy in forecasting the direction of the Dow-Jones Industrial Average over 1, 5, 13, 26, and 52 weeks ahead, giving progressively greater weight to the longer time periods, which generally provide the most accurate forecasts. Then, Merrill defines accuracy by the number of correct forecasts divided by the total number of forecasts. He further quantifies accuracy by the chi-squared test of statistical significance with one degree of freedom. Merrill translates this significance data for all of his indicators into weights proportional to the logs of chi-square, which is his own original innovation. Finally, he divides the sum of all bullish weights by the sums of all bullish plus all bearish weights for a totally objective weight of the statistical evidence he calls the Technical Trend Balance.

Pruden's Suggested Framework for Combining Indicators

Element	*Unit*	*Indicators**	*Weighting*
Price	Momentum Extent Form		
Volume	Total Upside/Downside On-Balance		
Time	Cycle Duration Season		
Sentiment	News Opinion Speculation		

*Specific indicators to select depend on time frame and market.

A framework for combining indicators has been suggested by Henry O. Pruden, Ph.D., professor of business and executive director of the Institute for Technical Market Analysis at Golden Gate University, 536 Mission Street, San Francisco, CA 94105, phone 415-442-6583, fax 415-442-6579, e-mail: hpruden@ggu.edu. Reprints of his four-page article, *Life Cycle Model of Crowd Behavior,* 1999, are available from *Technical Analysis of Stocks & Commodities* magazine, www.traders.com.

Commitment of Traders Report

Since large commercial hedgers are professionals with the deepest pockets and best insights into supply and demand, they are considered to be the "smart money" in the commodities markets. When the commercials are longer than normal, it is bullish. When they are shorter than normal, it is bearish. Large speculators are also generally correct, although less so. Small speculators, like the public and the odd-lot trader in the stock market, are usually wrong. The Commodity Futures Trading Commission

(CFTC) releases the Commitment of Traders data only once a month on the eleventh day of each month, and the data is reported with a lag of 11 days. Therefore, it is more useful for longer-term trend background analysis rather than for short-term trading.

Commodity Channel Index (CCI)

Commodity Channel Index (CCI) is a price momentum indicator developed by Donald R. Lambert. CCI is equally applicable to stocks despite the word commodity in its name. Mathematically, the CCI formula is represented as:

$$CCI = (M - A)/(0.015 * D)$$

where

M = (H + L + C)/3 = simple mean price for a period.
H = highest price for a period.
L = lowest price for a period.
C = closing price for a period.
A = *n*-period simple moving average of M.
D = mean deviation of the absolute value of the difference between mean price and simple moving average of mean prices, M − A.

CCI creates an index similar to a statistical standard score measuring the price excursions from the mean price as a statistical variation. It may be calculated in six steps:

1. Calculate each period's mean—the high plus low plus close divided by 3.
2. Calculate the *n*-period simple moving average of the means from results derived in Step 1.
3. From each period's mean price (calculated in Step 1), subtract the *n*-period simple moving average of the mean prices (calculated in Step 2).
4. Compute the mean deviation, which is the sum of the absolute values of the differences in Step 3.
5. Multiply the mean deviations by 0.015.
6. Divide the result of Step 3 by the result of Step 5. (The mean price-moving average differences are divided by 0.015 times the mean deviations.)

Most of the random fluctuations of the CCI are supposed to fall within a +100% to −100% channel. Movements beyond +100% to −100% are supposed to be nonrandom. Therefore, such large movements may create trading opportunities.

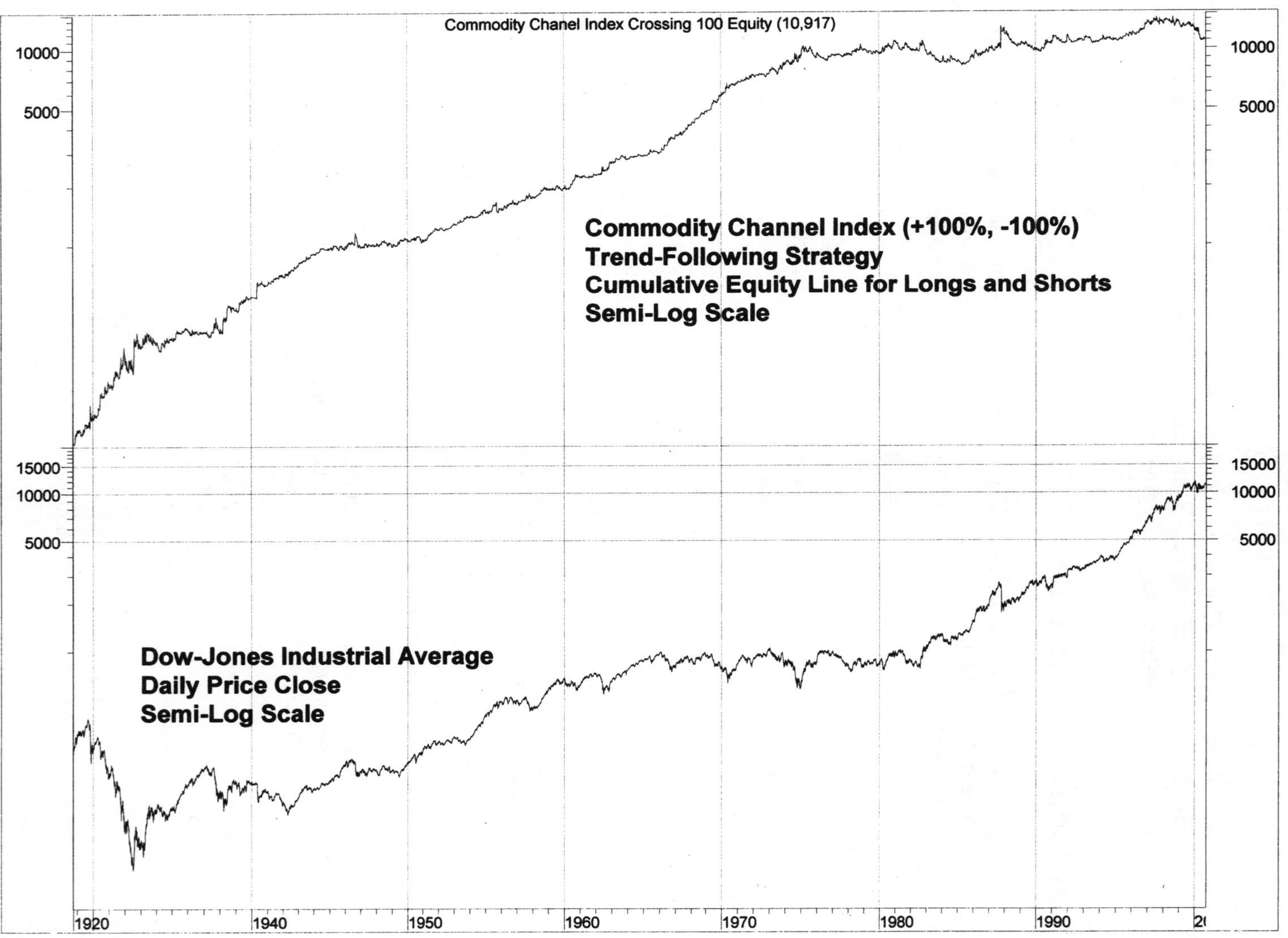

Commodity Chanel Index Crossing 100 Equity (10,917)
Commodity Channel Index (+100%, -100%)
Trend-Following Strategy
Cumulative Equity Line for Longs and Shorts
Semi-Log Scale
Dow-Jones Industrial Average
Daily Price Close
Semi-Log Scale
10000
5000
15000
10000
5000
1920
1940
1950
1960
1970
1980
1990

Commodity Channel Index

Total net profit	10816.84	Open position value	N/A	Net Profit/Buy&Hold %	136.42
Percent gain/loss	10816.84	Annual percent gain/loss	150.26	Annual Net %/B&H %	136.44
Initial investment	100	Interest earned	0		
Current position	Out	Date position entered	9/7/00		
Buy/Hold profit	4575.25	Days in test	26276	# of days per trade	12.48
Buy/Hold pct gain/loss	4575.25	Annual B/H pct gain/loss	63.55		
Total closed trades	2105	Commissions paid	0		
Avg profit per trade	5.14	Avg Win/Avg Loss ratio	1.68		
Total long trades	1210	Total short trades	895	Long Win Trade %	43.31
Winning long trades	524	Winning short trades	349	Short Win Trade %	38.99
Total winning trades	873	Total losing trades	1232	Total Win Trade %	41.47
Amount of winning trades	66846.78	Amount of losing trades	−56029.91	**Net Profit Margin %**	**8.80**
Average win	**76.57**	**Average loss**	**−45.48**	**Average P. Margin %**	**25.47**
Largest win	**2226.53**	**Largest loss**	**−643.44**	**% Net/(Win + Loss)**	**55.16**
Average length of win	**6.85**	**Average length of loss**	**3.23**	**(Win − Loss)/Loss %**	**112.07**
Longest winning trade	**21**	**Longest losing trade**	**9**	**(Win − Loss)/Loss %**	**133.33**
Most consecutive wins	**8**	**Most consecutive losses**	**12**	**(Win − Loss)/Loss %**	**−33.33**
Total bars out	**12307**	**Average length out**	**5.86**		
Longest out period	**26**				
System close drawdown	**−2.76**	**Profit/Loss index**	**16.18**	**% Net Profit/SODD**	**391914.49**
System open drawdown	**−2.76**	**Reward/Risk index**	**99.97**	**(Net P. − SODD)/Net P.**	**99.97**
Max open trade drawdown	**−643.44**	**Buy/Hold index**	**136.42**	**% SODD/Net Profit**	**−0.03**

In the Equis MetaStock® "System Report" (profit and loss summary statistics), the *Total net profit* is the sum of profits minus the sum of losses, including open positions marked to the market. In contrast, the *Amount of Winning Trades* is the sum of realized profits (the total of all gains on closed-out trades only, excluding any open positions). Similarly, the *Amount of Losing Trades* is the sum of realized losses (the total of all losses on closed-out trades only, excluding any open positions). *System close drawdown* is the largest decline in the cumulative equity line below the initial investment, based on closed-out positions only. *System open drawdown (SODD)* is the largest decline in the cumulative equity line below the initial investment when a position is open. *Max open trade drawdown* is the largest decline in the cumulative equity line below the trade entry price during the worst single trade. The *Profit/Loss Index* is a complex calculation that relates the Amount of Winning Trades to the Amount of Losing Trades on a scale of −100 (worst possible performance) to +100 (best possible performance), with zero representing profits equal to losses. *Reward/Risk Index* is the Total net profit minus System open drawdown. The resulting difference is then divided by the Total net profit. The *Buy/Hold Index* is the Total net profit minus the buy-and-hold strategy's net profit. The resulting difference is then divided by the buy-and-hold net profit. In this exercise, initial equity is assumed to be $100. Both long and short positions are taken unless otherwise noted. Trades are executed at the closing price on the signal date. Transaction costs, interest expenses, and margins are not included in the statistics.

The trading rules are simple:

- Buy long when CCI rises above +100%.
- Sell long when CCI falls below +100%.
- Sell short when CCI falls below −100%.
- Cover short when CCI rises above −100%.

Indicator Strategy Example for the Commodity Channel Index

Historical data shows that the Commodity Channel Index can be an effective indicator on both the long and short sides, but particularly on the long side. Based on the daily prices for the Dow-Jones Industrial Average for 72 years from 1928 to 2000, we found that the following parameters would have produced a positive result on a purely mechanical trend-following signal basis with no subjectivity, no sophisticated technical analysis, and no judgement:

Enter Long (Buy) at the current daily price close of the Dow-Jones Industrial Average when CCI (14) rises above +100%.

Close Long (Sell) at the current daily price close of the Dow-Jones Industrial Average when CCI (14) falls below +100%.

Enter Short (Sell Short) at the current daily price close of the Dow-Jones Industrial Average when CCI (14) falls below −100%.

Close Short (Cover) at the current daily price close of the Dow-Jones Industrial Average when CCI (14) rises above −100%.

Starting with $100 and reinvesting profits, total net profits for this CCI strategy would have been $10816.84, assuming a fully invested strategy, reinvestment of profits, no transactions costs and no taxes. This would have been 136.42 percent better than buy-and-hold. Short selling, which was included in this strategy, would have lost money since October, 1987, but nevertheless, would have been profitable over the entire 72-years as a whole. Trading would have been active at one trade every 12.49 calendar days.

The Equis International MetaStock® System Testing rules are written as follows:

Enter long: CCI(opt1) > 100

Close long: CCI(opt1) < 100

Enter short: CCI(opt1) < −100

Close short: CCI(opt1) > −100

OPT1 Current value: 14

Commodity Channel Index Crossing Zero: Zero CCI

Lambert's original Commodity Channel Index (CCI) was designed with a large neutral zone between +100% and −100%. This keeps the CCI system out of the market a substantial part of the time, most importantly at some critical turning points, when price can move rapidly. Thus, CCI misses the very early phases of new trends. These early phases are often the most dynamic.

By relaxing the plus and minus one hundred filter (+100% and −100%) and switching to crossings of the neutral zero line for buy and sell signals, the problem of lag is overcome. Under our assumptions, results would have been more profitable.

Indicator Strategy Example for ZERO CCI

Historical data shows that the ZERO CCI can be an effective indicator on both the long and short sides, but particularly on the long side. Based on the daily prices of the Dow-Jones Industrial Average for 72 years from 1928 to 2000, we found that the following parameters would have produced a positive result on a purely mechanical trend-following signal basis with no subjectivity, no sophisticated technical analysis, and no judgement:

Enter Long (Buy) at the current daily price close of the Dow-Jones Industrial Average when ZERO CCI (2) rises above 0%.

Close Long (Sell) at the current daily price close of the Dow-Jones Industrial Average when ZERO CCI (2) falls below 0%.

Enter Short (Sell Short) at the current daily price close of the Dow-Jones Industrial Average ZERO CCI (2) falls below 0%.

Close Short (Cover) at the current daily price close of the Dow-Jones Industrial Average when ZERO CCI (2) rises above 0%.

Starting with $100 and reinvesting profits, total net profits for this ZERO CCI strategy would have been $1,238,397.90, assuming a fully invested strategy, reinvestment of profits, no transactions costs and no taxes. This would have been 26,967.33 percent better than buy-and-hold. Short selling, which was included in this strategy, would have lost money since August, 1982, but nevertheless, would have been profitable over the entire 72-years. Trading would have been hyperactive at one trade every 3.61 calendar days.

The Equis International MetaStock® System Testing rules are written as follows:

Enter long: CCI(opt1) > 0

Close long: CCI(opt1) < 0

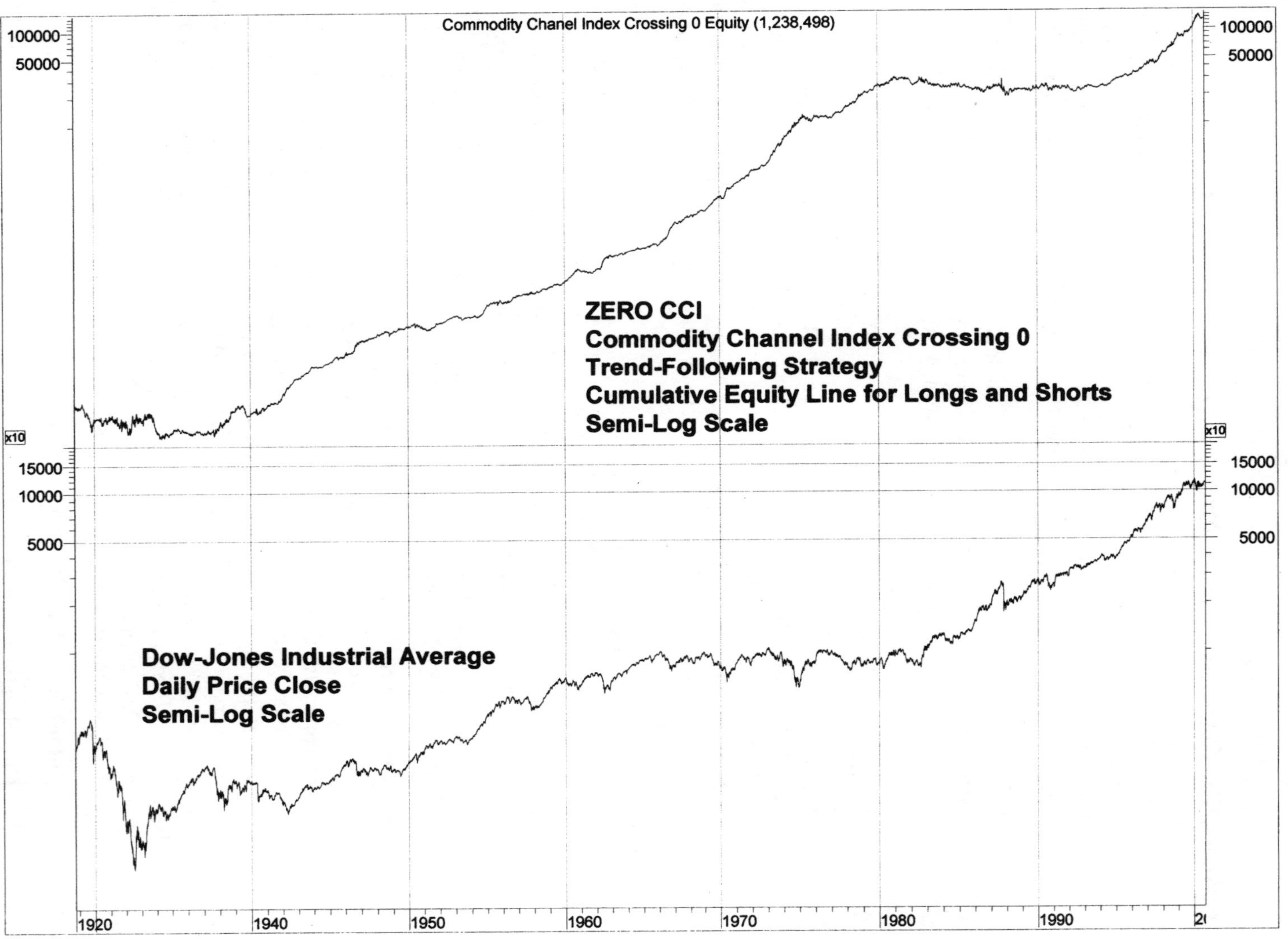

Commodity Chanel Index Crossing 0 Equity (1,238,498)
100000
50000
ZERO CCI
Commodity Channel Index Crossing 0
Trend-Following Strategy
Cumulative Equity Line for Longs and Shorts
Semi-Log Scale
x10
15000
10000
5000
Dow-Jones Industrial Average
Daily Price Close
Semi-Log Scale
1920
1940
1950
1960
1970
1980
1990

ZERO CCI

Total net profit	1238397.9	Open position value	4307.73	Net Profit/Buy&Hold %	26967.33
Percent gain/loss	1238397.9	Annual percent gain/loss	17202.59	Annual Net %/B&H %	26969.38
Initial investment	100	Interest earned	0		
Current position	Short	Date position entered	9/7/00		
Buy/Hold profit	4575.25	Days in test	26276	# of days per trade	3.61
Buy/Hold pct gain/loss	4575.25	Annual B/H pct gain/loss	63.55		
Total closed trades	7286	Commissions paid	0		
Avg profit per trade	169.38	Avg Win/Avg Loss ratio	1.78		
Total long trades	3643	Total short trades	3643	Long Win Trade %	46.83
Winning long trades	1706	Winning short trades	1405	Short Win Trade %	38.57
Total winning trades	3111	Total losing trades	4175	Total Win Trade %	42.70
Amount of winning trades	4973692	Amount of losing trades	−3739598	**Net Profit Margin %**	**14.16**
Average win	**1598.74**	**Average loss**	**−895.71**	**Average P. Margin %**	**28.18**
Largest win	**105713.25**	**Largest loss**	**−35504.13**	**% Net/(Win + Loss)**	**49.72**
Average length of win	**4.71**	**Average length of loss**	**2.56**	**(Win − Loss)/Loss %**	**83.98**
Longest winning trade	**18**	**Longest losing trade**	**8**	**(Win − Loss)/Loss %**	**125.00**
Most consecutive wins	**10**	**Most consecutive losses**	**13**	**(Win − Loss)/Loss %**	**−23.08**
Total bars out	**2**	**Average length out**	**2**		
Longest out period	**2**				
System close drawdown	**−54.03**	**Profit/Loss index**	**24.88**	**% Net Profit/SODD**	**2292056.04**
System open drawdown	**−54.03**	**Reward/Risk index**	**100**	**(Net P. − SODD)/Net P.**	**100.00**
Max open trade drawdown	**−35504.13**	**Buy/Hold index**	**27061.48**	**% SODD/Net Profit**	**0.00**

In the Equis MetaStock® "System Report" (profit and loss summary statistics), the *Total net profit* is the sum of profits minus the sum of losses, including open positions marked to the market. In contrast, the *Amount of Winning Trades* is the sum of realized profits (the total of all gains on closed-out trades only, excluding any open positions). Similarly, the *Amount of Losing Trades* is the sum of realized losses (the total of all losses on closed-out trades only, excluding any open positions). *System close drawdown* is the largest decline in the cumulative equity line below the initial investment, based on closed-out positions only. *System open drawdown (SODD)* is the largest decline in the cumulative equity line below the initial investment when a position is open. *Max open trade drawdown* is the largest decline in the cumulative equity line below the trade entry price during the worst single trade. The *Profit/Loss Index* is a complex calculation that relates the Amount of Winning Trades to the Amount of Losing Trades on a scale of −100 (worst possible performance) to +100 (best possible performance), with zero representing profits equal to losses. *Reward/Risk Index* is the Total net profit minus System open drawdown. The resulting difference is then divided by the Total net profit. The *Buy/Hold Index* is the Total net profit minus the buy-and-hold strategy's net profit. The resulting difference is then divided by the buy-and-hold net profit. In this exercise, initial equity is assumed to be $100. Both long and short positions are taken unless otherwise noted. Trades are executed at the closing price on the signal date. Transaction costs, interest expenses, and margins are not included in the statistics.

Enter short: CCI(opt1) < 0

Close short: CCI(opt1) > 0

OPT1 Current value: 2

Commodity Selection Index (CSI)

The Commodity Selection Index (CSI) is a formula designed to determine which futures contracts are most likely to make the greatest moves for each dollar invested. It was originally published by J. Welles Wilder, Jr., in his 1978 book, *New Concepts in Technical Trading Systems,* McLeansville, NC: Trend Research. CSI is derived from Wilder's Directional Movement Index (DMI).

The CSI is the Average Directional Movement Index Rating (ADXR) multiplied by the Smoothed True Range (STR) multiplied by a constant that represents the monetary movement potential for each futures contract (K):

$$CSI = ADXR * STR * K$$

The CSI begins with Directional Movement (DM), defined as the largest part of the current period's price range that lies outside the previous period's price range. Thus,

$$PDM = H - Hp$$

$$MDM = Lp - L$$

where

PDM = positive or plus DM.
MDM = negative or minus DM.
H = highest price of the current period.
Hp = highest price of the previous period.
Lp = lowest price of the previous period.
L = lowest price of the current period.

The lesser of the above two values is reset to equal zero. That is, if PDM is greater than MDM, then MDM is reset to equal zero. Or, if MDM is greater than PDM, then PDM is reset to equal zero. Also, any negative number is reset to equal zero. Therefore, on an inside day (with lower high and higher low), both PDM and MDM are negative numbers, so both are reset to equal zero.

True Range (TR) is defined as the largest value of the following three possibilities:

$$TR = H - L, \text{ or}$$

$$TR = H - Cp, \text{ or}$$

$$TR = Cp - L$$

where Cp is the closing price of the previous period.

Before proceeding, all data is smoothed by an exponential smoothing constant. Wilder suggests an exponential smoothing constant of 1/14, or 0.07143, which is roughly equivalent to a 27-day simple moving average. (This smoothing is used in all of the following calculations.)

The Positive Directional Indicator (PDI) is the exponentially smoothed Plus Directional Movement divided by the smoothed True Range. Thus,

$$PDI = SPDM/STR = \text{Smoothed PDM/Smoothed TR}$$

Remember, when Lp − L is greater than H − Hp, then PDM is reset to zero, so PDI must decline.

The Minus Directional Indicator (MDI) is defined by the following exponentially smoothed data:

$$MDI = SMDM/STR = \text{Smoothed MDM/Smoothed TR}$$

Remember, when Lp − L is less than H − Hp, then MDM is reset to zero, so MDI must decline.

Next, Directional Movement (DX) is defined as one hundred times the absolute value of the daily difference of PDI minus MDI divided by the sum of PDI plus MDI:

$$DX = 100 * |PDI - MDI|/(PDI + MDI)$$

Average Directional Movement (ADX) is a 0.07143 exponential smoothing of DX.

The Average Directional Movement Index Rating (ADXR) smoothes the ADX. So, it further smoothes an already smoothed indicator. ADXR is the sum of the most recent ADX plus the ADX reading 14 periods previous, and then that sum is divided by two.

Next, we look up specific futures contract information needed to calculate K, a constant that represents the monetary movement potential for each futures contract, according to the following formula:

$$K = V/M * (1/(150 + C)) * 100$$

where

V = the value of a one cent price fluctuation, expressed in dollars

M = margin, expressed in dollars

C = commissions, expressed in dollars

The CSI is the ADXR multiplied by the STR (Smoothed True Range), and the resulting product is multiplied by K, leading us to the formula for CSI:

$$CSI = ADXR * STR * K$$

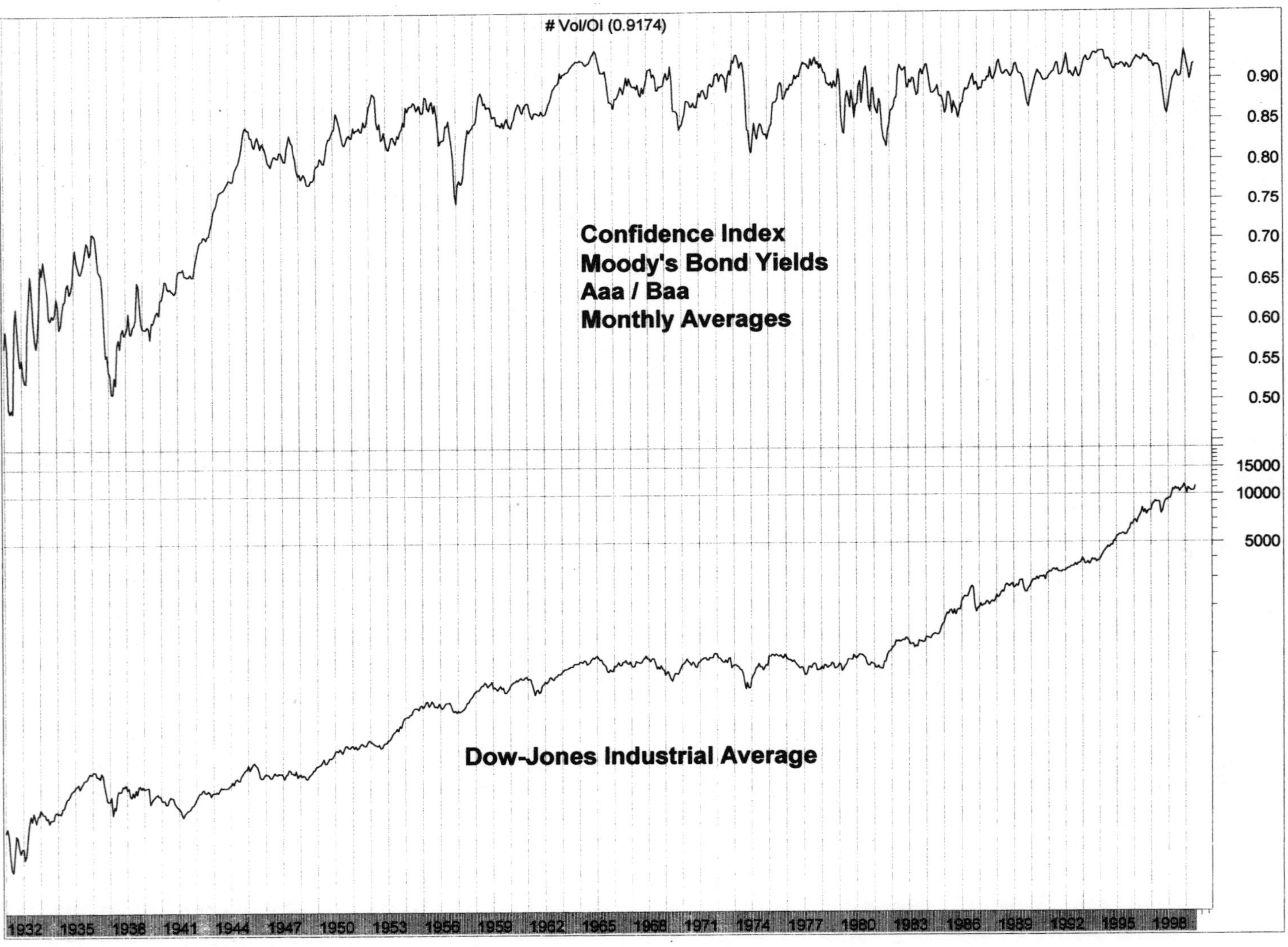

Vol/OI (0.9174)
Confidence Index
Moody's Bond Yields
Aaa / Baa
Monthly Averages
Dow-Jones Industrial Average
0.90
0.85
0.80
0.75
0.70
0.65
0.60
0.55
0.50
15000
10000
5000
1932
1935
1938
1941
1944
1947
1950
1953
1956
1959
1962
1965
1968
1971
1974
1977
1980
1983
1986
1989
1992
1995
1998

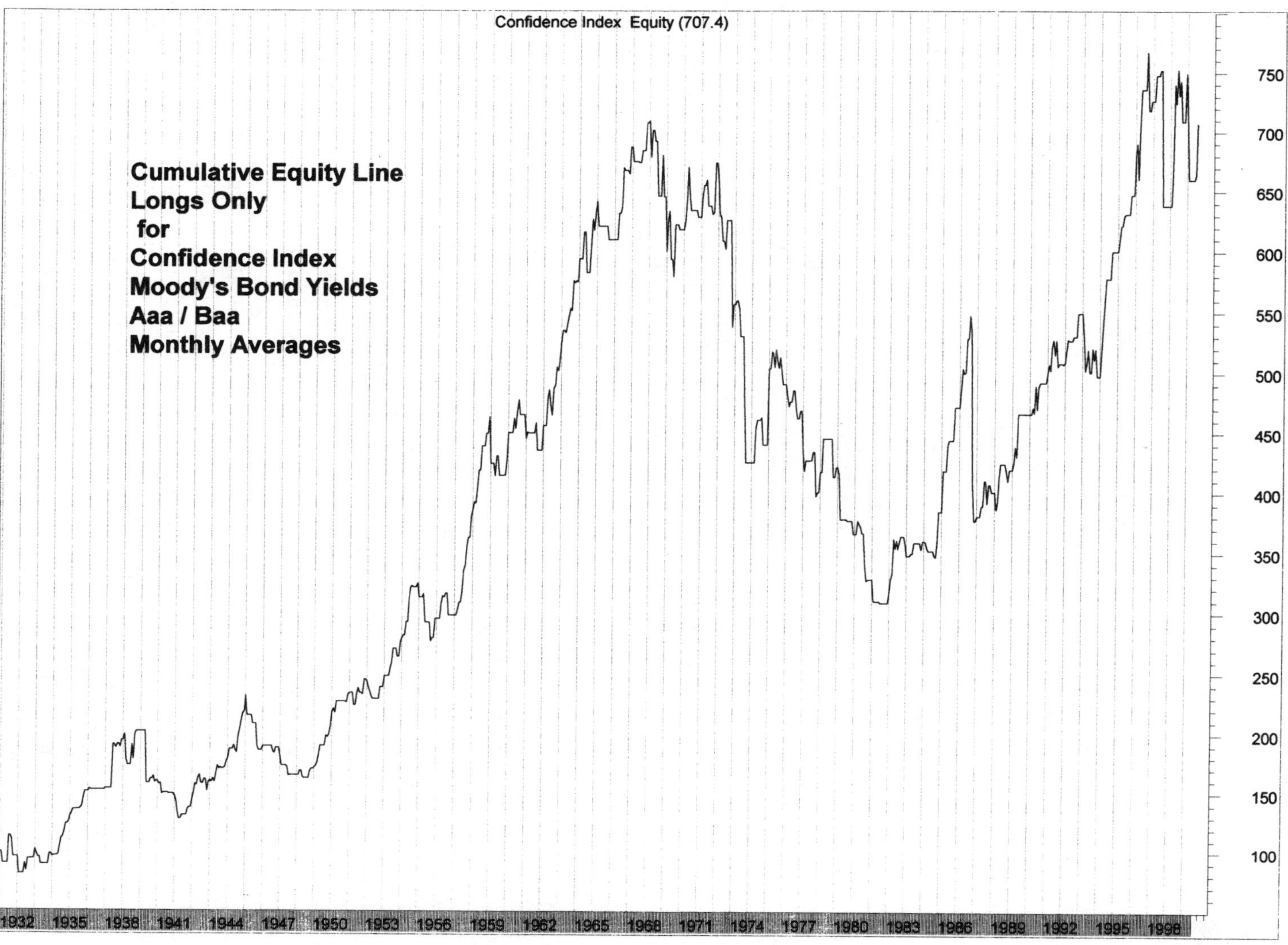
Confidence Index Equity (707.4)
Cumulative Equity Line
Longs Only
for
Confidence Index
Moody's Bond Yields
Aaa / Baa
Monthly Averages
750
700
650
600
550
500
450
400
350
300
250
200
150
100
1932
1935
1938
1941
1944
1947
1950
1953
1956
1959
1962
1965
1968
1971
1974
1977
1980
1983
1986
1989
1992
1995
1998

Confidence Index

The Confidence Index, developed in 1932 by *Barron's,* is one of the oldest sentiment indicators. It is calculated by dividing the average yield of high grade conservative bonds by the average yield of intermediate grade speculative bonds.

The Confidence Index is based on a logical observation: when investors feel confident about future economic conditions, they are more willing to put their money in riskier, more speculative bonds. As a result, yields on lower grade bonds decrease, and so the Confidence Index rises. But when investors worry about the future of the economy, they shift their funds from speculative bonds to safer, higher-grade bonds. Thus, yields on lower grade bonds rise relative to yields on higher grade bonds, and so the Confidence Index falls.

Furthermore, it seems logical that there should be a positive correlation between bond confidence and stock market sentiment. When investors are confident, they take chances on riskier bonds and stocks, which are also quite dependent on future economic conditions.

We tested these ideas using the ratio of Aaa bond yields on the highest rated corporate bonds divided by Baa bond yields on lower grade corporate bonds from Moody's Investor Service. Refer to the charts on the preceding two pages.

We examined monthly average yields back to January 1932. The chart on page 164 shows the ratio of Aaa yields to Baa yields fell to a low of 0.4873 in May, 1932, during the dark days of the Great Depression, when investor confidence was at an extreme low. High grade bond yields were less than half of lower grade bonds, and lower grade bond yields were more than double the yields of the highest grade bonds.

By January 1966, confidence was running high, and the ratio of Aaa to Baa corporate bond yields rose to 0.9368. High grade Aaa bond yields were only 6.32% less than lower grade Baa bond yields.

In the 36 years from 1932 to 1968, the Cumulative Equity Line shows an upward change in the trend of the Confidence Index as a profitable indicator for a long-only strategy. We buy the Dow-Jones Industrial Average at month end when the Confidence Index turns higher, and we exit long positions and go into cash when the Confidence Index turns down.

Over the most recent 32 years, after testing a variety of trend filters, we found that a strategy of trading equities based on the rises (buying long) and declines (exiting long positions and going into cash) in the Confidence Index would not have been profitable. For a long or cash strategy, the chart shows the Cumulative Equity Line in August, 2000, was actually lower than it was in December, 1968. Selling equities short based on a falling Confidence Index would have been extremely unprofitable.

Although the Confidence Index produced profits for a long-only strategy in the distant past, it no longer offers worthwhile possibilities for timing the equity market.

Contrary Opinion: The Art of Contrary Thinking

Sometimes called the Theory of Contrary Opinion, the idea that we should do the opposite of what the majority is doing might more properly be called *The Art of Contrary Thinking,* after the book by Humphrey B. Neill. (Neill, H. B. (1954). *The Art of Contrary Thinking,* Caldwell, Idaho: Caxton Printers.)

Thanks to the influence of Robert J. Farrell, technician at Merrill Lynch for several decades, contrary thinking has become popular—perhaps excessively so. Application of contrary thinking is not simple, and it is widely misused. In the words of top-performing hedge-fund manager, George Soros, "There are many events that actually occur in spite of the fact that they were widely anticipated . . . It has become fashionable to be a contrarian, but to bet against prevailing expectations is far from safe . . . Events tend to reinforce prevailing expectations most of the time and contradict them only at the inflection points, and inflection points are notoriously difficult to identify. Now that the contrarian viewpoint has become the prevailing bias, I have become a confirmed anti-contrarian." (Soros, George, *The Alchemy of Finance,* John Wiley, New York, 1994, 378 pages, pages 307-308.) Indeed, we have confirmed some basis in fact for fading contrarians. (*See Advisory Service Index.*)

"Contrary opinion is usually ahead of time," according to Humphrey B. Neill. "The public is perhaps right more of the time than not . . . The public is right during the trends but wrong at both ends . . ." Identifying the right spot to go against the thundering herd is not always easy. Momentum can carry prices much further than is reasonable. That is where the *Art* comes in.

Neill advised us to look at all sides of any question and challenge the popular view, saying "The weight of popular predictions causes their own downfall." The underling logic is that a market cannot accommodate the vast majority of participants thinking the same way and doing the same thing. When everybody is bullish, there is no one left to buy, and when everyone is bearish, there is no one left to sell. So, it is time for a trend reversal. The problem in actual practice is that there is never anything close to a 100% consensus of opinion to fade.

Scientists who study human behavior confirm that people lose their individuality and critical faculties when they join a large crowd or mob. A crowd functions on an extremely primitive, emotional, impulsive, and irrational level. Herd behavior is unthinking. There is a basic part of the human makeup that is social, gregarious, and so people are willing to bond to the group and follow it unquestioningly and thoughtlessly. Perhaps this quality has some group survival value under certain circumstances, but it can be quite costly to the individual when engaged in trading markets.

The point at which the crowd seems to reach its height of emotional frenzy is sometimes a turning point, but the precise timing is not easy to determine. One clever trader bought call options the Friday before the Monday Crash of '87. He was convinced that the stock market was oversold, everyone was bearish, and stock prices were overdue for a rebound. He was right within two trading days, but that two days made all the difference. He lost most of his money as the market totally collapsed the very next trading day. Instead, if he had waited two trading days, ideally buying on Tuesday after lunch, he would have made a fast and large fortune instead of losing one.

There are many technical indicators of the Sentiment and Overbought/Oversold classes that attempt to objectively quantify excessive crowd opinion and, perhaps more importantly, behavior, since people do not always do what they say.

So, contrary opinion has become a popular notion, bandied about loosely by television commentators, whose general level of understanding of technical analysis is superficial. Many experienced technical analysts use sentiment, but more as a supplement to trend, momentum, and other technical indicators than as a stand-alone, signal generator. Sentiment typically shows overbought and oversold levels well *before* the directional price move is over and, therefore, can be misleading. In general, sentiment is a background indicator that is not useful for precise timing.

John Bollinger points out that thinking contrary alone is not sufficient. Rather, effective use depends on a crowd held together by a falsity until something startles them. There must be a widely held opinion that is incorrect or becomes incorrect, and a catalyst that creates the conditions for a reversal of that opinion. (John A. Bollinger, CFA, CMT, Bollinger Capital Management, Inc., PO Box 3358, Manhattan Beach, CA 90266, (310) 798-8855, www.bollingerbands.com.)

Coppock Curve (Coppock Guide)

The Coppock Curve quantifies changes in longer-term smoothed price momentum in order to identify significant stock market bottoms. It was designed by Edwin Sedgewick Coppock, who published it in *Barron's* in 1962. Coppock's original expression is a 10-month weighted moving average of the sum of the 14-month rate of change plus the 11-month rate of change for the S&P 500. Signals are recognized when this smoothed price momentum changes direction from down to up (buy) and from up to down (sell). Divergences of smoothed price momentum versus price itself are also analyzed.

Using daily closing price data and 21 trading days for an average month, the MetaStock® custom formula language for the Coppock Curve could be expressed as follows:

((Mov((ROC(Mov(C,21,S),231,%) + ROC(Mov(C,21,S),294,%))/2

,210,W)));Input("Plot a horizontal line at",−100,100,0);

Indicator Strategy Example for Coppock Curve Changing Direction

Using the Coppock Curve formula applied to a 101-year file of daily data for the Dow-Jones Industrial Average from January 1900 to May 2001, we found that the following parameters would have produced a modest result on a purely mechanical trend-following signal basis with no subjectivity, no sophisticated technical analysis, and no judgement:

Enter Long (Buy) at the current daily price close of the Dow-Jones Industrial Average when the Coppock Curve is greater than the previous day's 5-day exponential moving average of the Coppock Curve.

Close Long (Sell) at the current daily price close of the Dow-Jones Industrial Average when the Coppock Curve is less than the previous day's 5-day exponential moving average of the Coppock Curve.

Enter Short (Sell Short) never.

Starting with $100 and reinvesting profits, total net profits for this Coppock Curve Changing Direction trend-following strategy would have been $19,091.66, assuming a fully invested strategy, reinvestment of profits, no transactions costs and no taxes. This would have been 11.80 percent less than buy-and-hold. No short selling would have been profitable, so no short selling was included in the strategy. Long-only Coppock Curve Changing Direction as an indicator would have given profitable buy signals 51.22% of the time. Trading would have been inactive at one trade every 451.51 calendar days. Note that Equity drawdowns would have been moderate relative to buy-and-hold.

The Equis International MetaStock® System Testing rules are written as follows:

Enter long: (Mov((ROC(Mov(C,opt1,S),opt1*opt2,%) +
ROC(Mov(C,opt1,S),opt1*opt3,%))/2,
opt1*opt4,W)) > Ref(Mov(
(Mov((ROC(Mov(C,opt1,S),opt1*opt2,%) +
ROC(Mov(C,opt1,S),opt1*opt3,%))/2,
opt1*opt4,W)),opt5,E),−1)

Close long: (Mov((ROC(Mov(C,opt1,S),opt1*opt2,%) +
ROC(Mov(C,opt1,S),opt1*opt3,%))/2,
opt1*opt4,W)) < Ref(Mov(
(Mov((ROC(Mov(C,opt1,S),opt1*opt2,%) +
ROC(Mov(C,opt1,S),opt1*opt3,%))/2,
opt1*opt4,W)),opt5,E),−1)

OPT1 Current value: 21

OPT2 Current value: 11

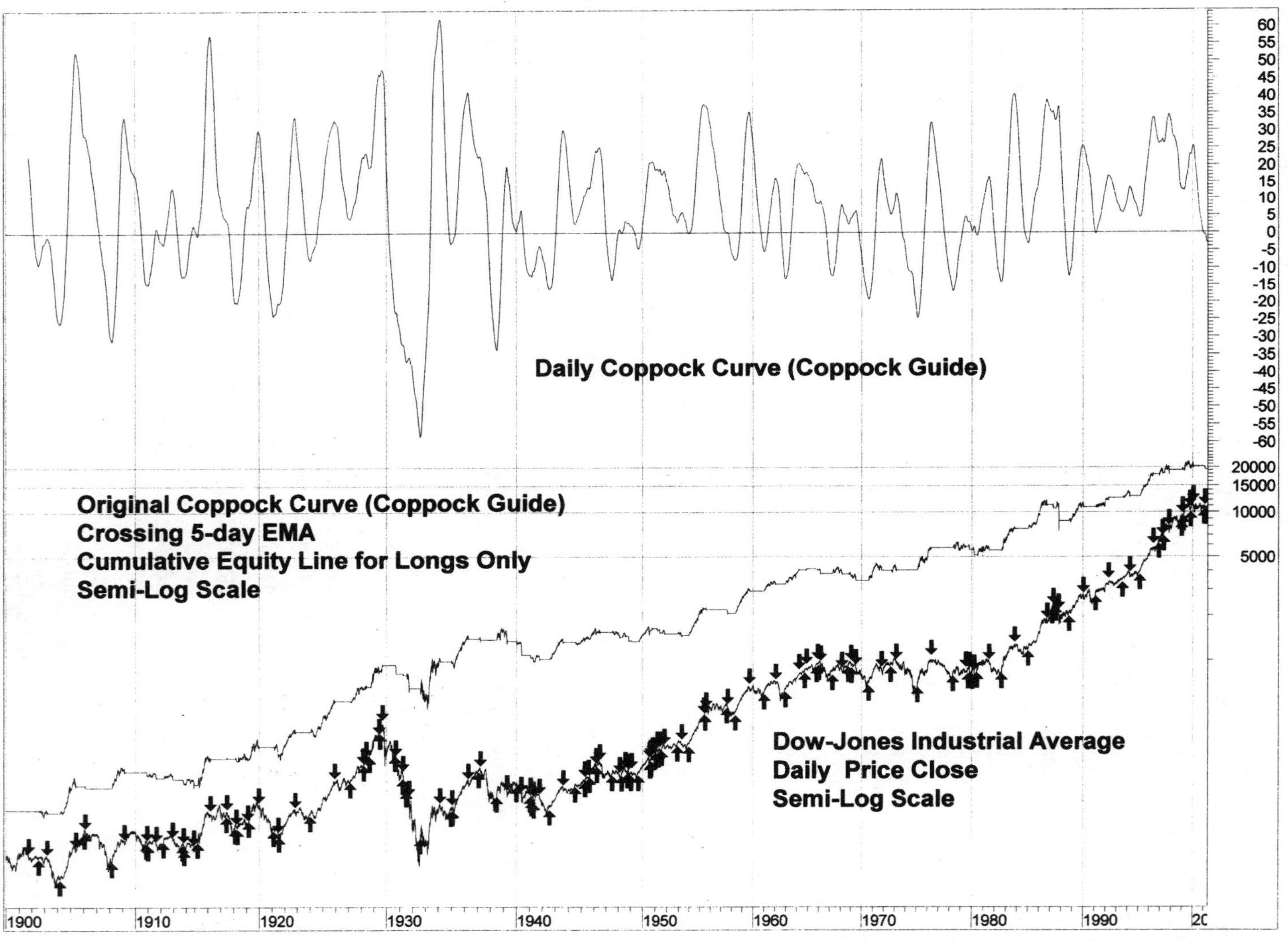
Daily Coppock Curve (Coppock Guide)
Original Coppock Curve (Coppock Guide)
Crossing 5-day EMA
Cumulative Equity Line for Longs Only
Semi-Log Scale
Dow-Jones Industrial Average
Daily Price Close
Semi-Log Scale
60 55 50 45 40 35 30 25 20 15 10 5 0 -5 -10 -15 -20 -25 -30 -35 -40 -45 -50 -55 -60
20000 15000 10000 5000
1900 1910 1920 1930 1940 1950 1960 1970 1980 1990 20

Coppock Curve Crossing 5-day EMA

Total net profit	19091.66	Open position value	−109.79	Net Profit/Buy&Hold %	−11.80
Percent gain/loss	19091.66	Annual percent gain/loss	188.21	Annual Net %/B&H %	−11.80
Initial investment	100	Interest earned	0		
Current position	Long	Date position entered	5/7/01		
Buy/Hold profit	21646	Days in test	37024	# of days per trade	451.51
Buy/Hold pct gain/loss	21646	Annual B/H pct gain/loss	213.4		
Total closed trades	82	Commissions paid	0		
Avg profit per trade	234.16	Avg Win/Avg Loss ratio	3.94		
Total long trades	82	Total short trades	0	Long Win Trade %	51.22
Winning long trades	42	Winning short trades	0	Short Win Trade %	#DIV/0!
Total winning trades	42	Total losing trades	40	Total Win Trade %	51.22
Amount of winning trades	25317.04	Amount of losing trades	−6115.59	Net Profit Margin %	61.09
Average win	602.79	Average loss	−152.89	Average P. Margin %	59.54
Largest win	5150.14	Largest loss	−1820.33	% Net/(Win + Loss)	47.77
Average length of win	235.79	Average length of loss	70.78	(Win − Loss)/Loss %	233.13
Longest winning trade	575	Longest losing trade	241	(Win − Loss)/Loss %	138.59
Most consecutive wins	9	Most consecutive losses	5	(Win − Loss)/Loss %	80.00
Total bars out	15215	Average length out	183.31		
Longest out period	759				
System close drawdown	−3.52	Profit/Loss index	75.74	% Net Profit/SODD	183397.31
System open drawdown	−10.41	Reward/Risk index	99.95	(Net P. − SODD)/Net P.	99.95
Max open trade drawdown	−3064	Buy/Hold index	−12.31	% SODD/Net Profit	−0.05

In the Equis MetaStock® "System Report" (profit and loss summary statistics), the *Total net profit* is the sum of profits minus the sum of losses, including open positions marked to the market. In contrast, the *Amount of Winning Trades* is the sum of realized profits (the total of all gains on closed-out trades only, excluding any open positions). Similarly, the *Amount of Losing Trades* is the sum of realized losses (the total of all losses on closed-out trades only, excluding any open positions). *System close drawdown* is the largest decline in the cumulative equity line below the initial investment, based on closed-out positions only. *System open drawdown (SODD)* is the largest decline in the cumulative equity line below the initial investment when a position is open. *Max open trade drawdown* is the largest decline in the cumulative equity line below the trade entry price during the worst single trade. The *Profit/Loss Index* is a complex calculation that relates the Amount of Winning Trades to the Amount of Losing Trades on a scale of −100 (worst possible performance) to +100 (best possible performance), with zero representing profits equal to losses. *Reward/Risk Index* is the Total net profit minus System open drawdown. The resulting difference is then divided by the Total net profit. The *Buy/Hold Index* is the Total net profit minus the buy-and-hold strategy's net profit. The resulting difference is then divided by the buy-and-hold net profit. In this exercise, initial equity is assumed to be $100. Both long and short positions are taken unless otherwise noted. Trades are executed at the closing price on the signal date. Transaction costs, interest expenses, and margins are not included in the statistics.

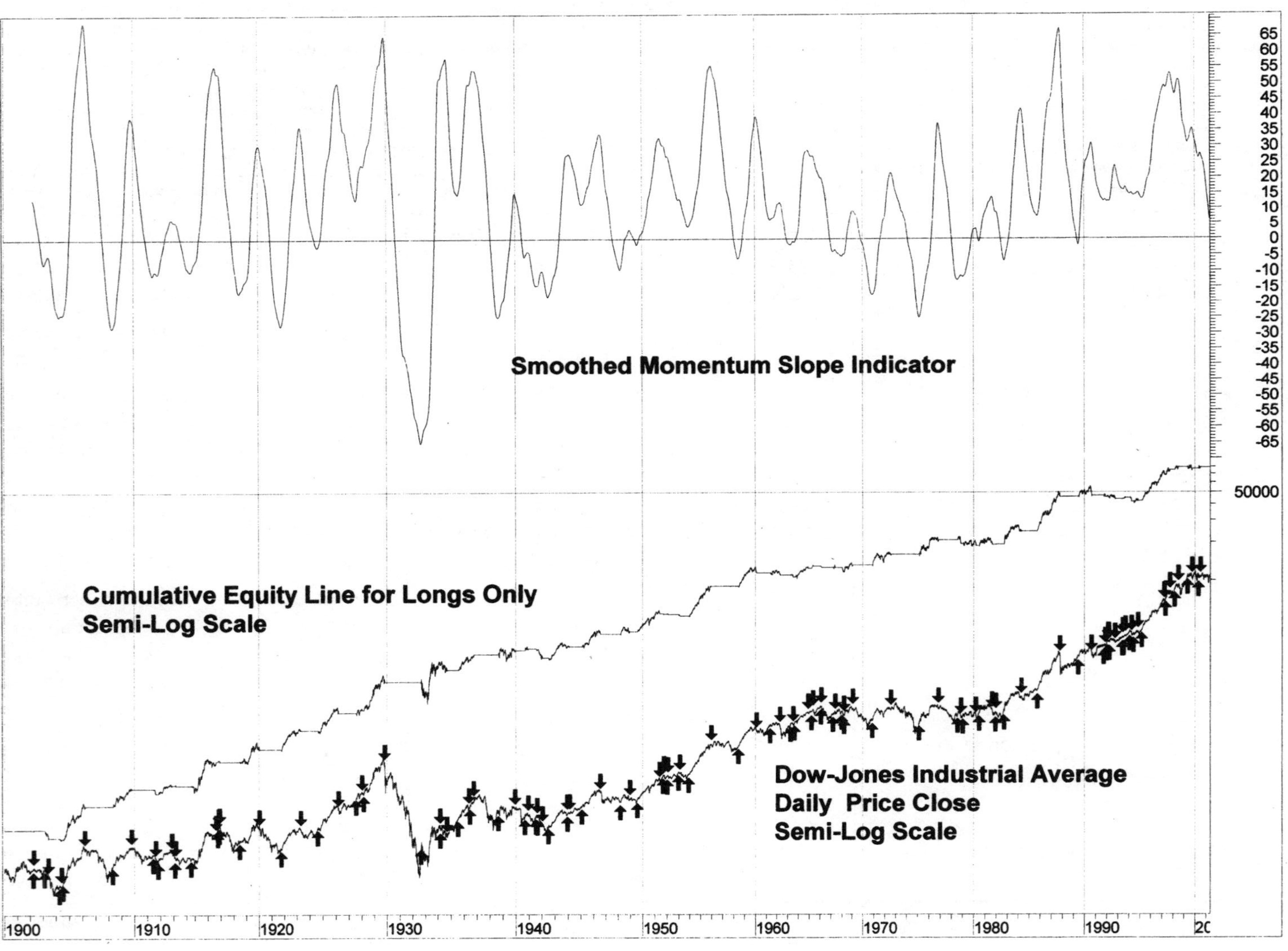
Smoothed Momentum Slope Indicator
Cumulative Equity Line for Longs Only
Semi-Log Scale
Dow-Jones Industrial Average
Daily Price Close
Semi-Log Scale
65
60
55
50
45
40
35
30
25
20
15
10
5
0
-5
-10
-15
-20
-25
-30
-35
-40
-45
-50
-55
-60
-65
50000
1900
1910
1920
1930
1940
1950
1960
1970
1980
1990
20

Smoothed Momentum Slope Indicator

Total net profit	78681.33	Open position value	N/A	Net Profit/Buy&Hold %	263.49
Percent gain/loss	78681.33	Annual percent gain/loss	775.68	Annual Net %/B&H %	263.49
Initial investment	100	Interest earned	0		
Current position	Out	Date position entered	7/7/00		
Buy/Hold profit	21646	Days in test	37024	# of days per trade	578.50
Buy/Hold pct gain/loss	21646	Annual B/H pct gain/loss	213.4		
Total closed trades	64	Commissions paid	0		
Avg profit per trade	1229.4	Avg Win/Avg Loss ratio	4.02		
Total long trades	64	Total short trades	0	Long Win Trade %	62.50
Winning long trades	40	Winning short trades	0	Short Win Trade %	#DIV/0!
Total winning trades	40	Total losing trades	24	Total Win Trade %	62.50
Amount of winning trades	92505.03	Amount of losing trades	−13823.7	**Net Profit Margin %**	**74.00**
Average win	**2312.63**	**Average loss**	**−575.99**	**Average P. Margin %**	**60.12**
Largest win	**25975.73**	**Largest loss**	**−3109.47**	**% Net/(Win + Loss)**	**78.62**
Average length of win	**287.45**	**Average length of loss**	**72.08**	**(Win − Loss)/Loss %**	**298.79**
Longest winning trade	**577**	**Longest losing trade**	**292**	**(Win − Loss)/Loss %**	**97.60**
Most consecutive wins	**6**	**Most consecutive losses**	**3**	**(Win − Loss)/Loss %**	**100.00**
Total bars out	**14691**	**Average length out**	**226.02**		
Longest out period	**855**				
System close drawdown	**−15.21**	**Profit/Loss index**	**85.06**	**% Net Profit/SODD**	**456123.65**
System open drawdown	**−17.25**	**Reward/Risk index**	**99.98**	**(Net P. − SODD)/Net P.**	**99.98**
Max open trade drawdown	**−5310.55**	**Buy/Hold index**	**263.49**	**% SODD/Net Profit**	**−0.02**

In the Equis MetaStock® "System Report" (profit and loss summary statistics), the *Total net profit* is the sum of profits minus the sum of losses, including open positions marked to the market. In contrast, the *Amount of Winning Trades* is the sum of realized profits (the total of all gains on closed-out trades only, excluding any open positions). Similarly, the *Amount of Losing Trades* is the sum of realized losses (the total of all losses on closed-out trades only, excluding any open positions). *System close drawdown* is the largest decline in the cumulative equity line below the initial investment, based on closed-out positions only. *System open drawdown (SODD)* is the largest decline in the cumulative equity line below the initial investment when a position is open. *Max open trade drawdown* is the largest decline in the cumulative equity line below the trade entry price during the worst single trade. The *Profit/Loss Index* is a complex calculation that relates the Amount of Winning Trades to the Amount of Losing Trades on a scale of −100 (worst possible performance) to +100 (best possible performance), with zero representing profits equal to losses. *Reward/Risk Index* is the Total net profit minus System open drawdown. The resulting difference is then divided by the Total net profit. The *Buy/Hold Index* is the Total net profit minus the buy-and-hold strategy's net profit. The resulting difference is then divided by the buy-and-hold net profit. In this exercise, initial equity is assumed to be $100. Both long and short positions are taken unless otherwise noted. Trades are executed at the closing price on the signal date. Transaction costs, interest expenses, and margins are not included in the statistics.

OPT3 Current value: 14

OPT4 Current value: 10

OPT5 Current value: 5

Indicator Strategy Example of a Smoothed Momentum Slope Indicator

The general idea of using the slope of a smoothed momentum curve can be simplified and adapted to any market over any time frame. Of course, a very large number of variations are possible. Coppock's original formula had five variables, but we can reduce this number to three and obtain more robust and more profitable results with fewer and milder drawdowns in cumulative net equity. Using MetaStock® formula language, the following might be just one possible adaptation of smoothed momentum slope with fewer variables (three versus five) for use with daily data:

```
Mov(ROC(Mov(C,21*2,E),21*2*2*5,%),21*2*5,E) ;

Input("Plot a horizontal line at ",-100,100,0);
```

Any of these parameters can be allowed to vary. In this specific example, this formula translates into just three steps:

1. Compute a 42-day Exponential Moving Average of the daily closing prices.
2. Compute a 420-day percentage Rate of Change of the 42-day Exponential Moving Average from the first step.
3. Compute a 210-day Exponential Moving Average of the 420-day Rate of Change from the second step.

A buy signal is recognized when the slope of the smoothed rate of change (from the third step) turns from down to up. A sell signal is recognized when the slope of the smoothed rate of change (from the third step) turns from up to down. The result is plotted on the chart two pages previous, page 172.

Based on the same 101-year file of daily data for the Dow-Jones Industrial Average from January 1900 to May 2001, we found that these three parameters would have produced a positive result on a purely mechanical trend-following signal basis with no subjectivity, no sophisticated technical analysis, and no judgement:

Enter Long (Buy) at the current daily price close of the Dow-Jones Industrial Average when the slope of the smoothed rate of change turns from down to up.

Close Long (Sell) at the current daily price close of the Dow-Jones Industrial Average when the slope of the smoothed rate of change turns from up to down.

Enter Short (Sell Short) never.

Starting with $100 and reinvesting profits, total net profits for this Smoothed Momentum Slope Indicator trend-following strategy would have been $78,681.33, assuming a fully invested strategy, reinvestment of profits, no transactions costs and no taxes. This would have been 263.49 percent greater than buy-and-hold. No short selling would have been profitable, so no short selling was included in the strategy. Long-only Smoothed Momentum Slope as an indicator would have given profitable buy signals 62.50% of the time. Trading would have been relatively inactive at one trade every 578.50 calendar days. Note on the chart that there are fewer and milder drawdowns in cumulative net equity than with the Coppock Curve.

The Equis International MetaStock® System Testing rules are written as follows:

Enter long: Mov(ROC(Mov(C,opt1*opt2,E),opt1*opt2*opt2*opt3,%), opt1*opt2*opt3,E) > Ref(Mov(Mov(ROC(Mov(C,opt1*opt2,E),opt1*opt2*opt2*opt3,%), opt1*opt2*opt3,E),1,E),−1)

Close long: Mov(ROC(Mov(C,opt1*opt2,E),opt1*opt2*opt2*opt3,%), opt1*opt2*opt3,E) < Ref(Mov(Mov(ROC(Mov(C,opt1*opt2,E),opt1*opt2*opt2*opt3,%), opt1*opt2*opt3,E),1,E),−1)

OPT1 Current value: 21

OPT2 Current value: 2

OPT3 Current value: 5

Cumulative Equity Line

The Cumulative Equity Line for an indicator is the running total of the performance of all the signals (the cumulative sum of all profits minus all losses), including open positions marked to the market. For illustration purposes in this book, we consistently start with $100 and reinvest net profits after every closed-out long or short transaction. A loss on a trade causes the Cumulative Equity Line to fall proportionately. To simplify our analyses, we exclude variables such as transactions costs, margin, interest and taxes. In the real world of trading, the Cumulative Equity Line would be a graphical representation of our account's net worth, and net of variable costs. In this book, the Cumulative Equity Line rises and falls strictly according to the indicator's efficiency in correctly identifying price direction.

Technical analysis of the Cumulative Equity Line can be a useful money management tool. When the Cumulative Equity Line is trending upward, our indicator is working as expected, and the market environment is friendly to our style of trading. We could devise an indicator to signal an uptrending Cumulative Equity Line, then increase position size, commitment of cash reserves, and leverage. On the other hand, when the trend of the Cumulative Equity Line reverses (from up to down), we could decrease position size, total capital exposure, and leverage. While we use basic indicators to exploit trends in market prices, we can apply similar indicators to our Cumulative Equity Line, exploiting trends in the performance of basic indicators to take full advantage of friendly market environments as they appear.

The Cumulative Equity Line also could be used to select among basic indicators. A visual inspection of the direction, slope and smoothness of the Cumulative Equity Line chart and the relative size of drawdowns offers a chart reader a quick, but very good sense of the critical Reward/Risk performance characteristics of an indicator. Also, standard statistical tests of the variance of the Cumulative Equity Line of an indicator can be used as a supplement to visual inspection. This quantifies the performance to allow different indicators (tested over different time periods and under somewhat different assumptions) to be objectively compared by a common standard.

Cumulative Volume Index

The Cumulative Volume Index is a running total of the daily net differences between Advancing minus Declining stock volume, similar to the Cumulative Daily Advance-Decline Line. A rising trend in the index indicates increasing net demand relative to supply for stocks, and that is bullish. A falling trend in the index indicates increasing net supply relative to demand for stocks, and that is bearish. Technical analysts generally use New York Stock Exchange data published on page C2 of *The Wall Street Journal* and other major newspapers. *(See Volume: Cumulative Volume Index of the Volume of Advancing Issues Minus the Volume of Declining Issues.)*

Cycles of Time and Price

Cycle analysts study time as it relates to data generated by the markets. *Cycle* is derived from the Greek word *kuklos,* which means circle. A cycle is a recurring interval of time within which a round of regularly repeated events is completed. Cycle analysts apply past precedents of time duration between past events, such as the time between market price lows, in order to estimate the probabilities of the future course of prices and to make educated estimates of how long a particular trend might last.

Only approximately 15% of the members of the Market Technicians Association admit to using cycles in their work. Some technicians think cycles should be considered a separate area of study. Indeed, the subject is deep, and the following discussion is necessarily limited to only a few of the more well-known financial cycles. (*See Astrology and Fibonacci Numbers.*)

Many modern urban people choose to deny the existence of cycles, either because they cannot find a satisfyingly logical reason why cycles should exist, or because they do not like to acknowledge the role of cycles in their lives. Western culture prefers the illusion that each individual can completely control his life. Yet our lives are inevitably shaped, even predetermined, by cycles. Every living being's life is prescheduled and pre-scripted within actuarially predictable ranges of time.

Planet earth undergoes cyclical changes daily, seasonally and over vast expanses of time. Geophysicists, drilling into rock layers deep down in the earth, can measure these changes in thousands and tens of thousands of years. Some scientists hypothesize that our ancestors endured periodic ice ages, and our progeny will deal with future recurrences. Also, the earth's orbit takes it through an asteroid belt that has caused collisions responsible for mass extinctions of earthly life forms, and the earth will pass through this asteroid belt again and again according to very long-term cycles.

Ancient people were closely tied to the natural world and accepted the cyclical facts of life. Survival demanded sowing, reaping, and engaging in animal husbandry in conformance with natural cycles, although most modern urban dwellers do not give it much thought. More than two millennia ago, Pythagoras of Samos recognized the cyclical nature of the vibrations known as *music*, which he extended to *music of the spheres*, the harmonic motion of the lights in the sky that are more regular than clocks. The movements of the sun, the moon and the stars literally define our notions of time here on earth. Our ancestors made extraordinary efforts to build remarkable monuments, such as Stonehenge, to mark the cycles of these lights in the sky.

Observed Stock Market Cycles

Market cycles are fractal, with smaller cycles within larger cycles. There are extremely long and extremely short cycles. With many cycles in different time frames at work at the same time, cycle analysis can become extremely complex. Shorter-term cycles are subordinate to longer cycles. The intraday market price cycles, measured in minutes, are subject to minor cycles, measured in days. These are subject to directional domination by intermediate secondary cycles measured in weeks, which in turn are dominated by the long-term major cycles measured in months, which are subject to still longer cycles measured in years, decades, centuries, millennia, and so on.

Limiting ourselves to daily close-only data over the past 52 years, from 1949 to 2001, the Dow-Jones Industrial Average has changed direction every 3.39 calendar days, on average. Twice that is 6.78 calendar days. Therefore, a short-term daily cycle trader might look to make a transaction about twice a week.

Next, if we filter out price movements of less than 1%, the Dow-Jones Industrial Average has changed direction every 10.09 calendar days, on average. Twice that is 20.19 calendar days for the full cycle. Therefore, a minor-cycle trader might look for a trading system that signals about three times a month.

As the Observed Cycle Lengths table (on the facing page) shows, trading frequency declines exponentially as we increase our percentage price filter linearly. There appears to be a break point at the 8% filter. Filters larger than 8% produce diminishing reductions in average days of trade duration. Therefore, a price movement of 8% might be considered an objective for an investor who wishes to maximize returns without being glued to the daily fluctuations. If we filter out price movements of less than 8%, the Dow-Jones Industrial Average has changed direction every 186.97 calendar days, on average. Twice that is 373.94 calendar days for the full cycle. That also translates to 53.42 weeks, or 12.29 months, or 1.02 years. This 1-year cycle is popular with intermediate-term cycle traders, who try to capture 8% price movements and seek a trading system that signals about twice a year. The 8% filter table (on page 180) shows the dates of all 8% filter, 1.02-year cycle high and low turning points.

The Observed Cycle Lengths table (on the facing page) illustrates various actual average cycle lengths between significant market price lows (bottoms) in the Dow-Jones Industrial Average, again over the past 52 years, using price change filters of various sizes to reduce noise. Average cycle lengths give us only a rough estimation of underlying cyclical rhythms, since there is a great deal of variability hidden by averaging. Therefore, these cycles should be regarded as mere tendencies rather than as any kind of accurate clocks.

Nesting Cycles: Cycles Within Cycles

Nesting cycles were described by J.M. Hurst, *Profit Magic of Stock Market Transaction Timing,* Prentice Hall, New York, 1960. Combinations of cycles of different lengths account for some of the observed variability in cycles. Hurst observes that cycles of different lengths tend to converge at significant market price bottoms. The more different cycles that coincide, the greater the tendency for an important cyclic bottom to form. Hurst suggests that different cycle intervals can be averaged to form a model that might suggest possible turning points for price trends.

Hurst demonstrates a proportionate relationship between the following cycles: the 10-week cycle, two of which make a 20-week cycle; a 20-week cycle, two of which make a 40-week cycle; and a 40-week cycle, two of which make an 80-week cycle. Cycle lengths fairly close to these appear in our table of Observed Cycle Lengths.

In addition, from the same table, we note proportionate relationships between the following Observed Cycle Lengths:

Observed Cycle Lengths

Size of Filter	Number of Trades	Average Days Duration	Full Cycle in Days	Full Cycle in Weeks	Full Cycle in Months	Full Cycle in Years
0%	5569	3.39	6.78	0.97	0.22	0.02
1%	1871	10.09	20.19	2.88	0.66	0.06
2%	943	20.03	40.05	5.72	1.32	0.11
3%	581	32.50	65.01	9.29	2.14	0.18
4%	395	47.81	95.62	13.66	3.14	0.26
5%	271	69.68	139.37	19.91	4.58	0.38
6%	195	96.84	193.68	27.67	6.36	0.53
7%	143	132.06	264.11	37.73	8.68	0.72
8%	101	186.97	373.94	53.42	12.29	1.02
9%	83	227.52	455.04	65.01	14.95	1.25
10%	65	290.52	581.05	83.01	19.09	1.59
11%	60	314.73	629.47	89.92	20.68	1.72
12%	51	370.27	740.55	105.79	24.33	2.03
13%	43	439.16	878.33	125.48	28.86	2.40
14%	35	539.54	1079.09	154.16	35.45	2.95
15%	33	572.24	1144.48	163.50	37.60	3.13
16%	28	674.43	1348.86	192.69	44.32	3.69
17%	23	821.04	1642.09	234.58	53.95	4.50
18%	21	899.24	1798.48	256.93	59.09	4.92
19%	21	899.24	1798.48	256.93	59.09	4.92
20%	17	1110.82	2221.65	317.38	72.99	6.08
25%	13	1452.62	2905.23	415.03	95.45	7.95
30%	7	2697.71	5395.43	770.78	177.26	14.77
35%	7	2697.71	5395.43	770.78	177.26	14.77
40%	3	6294.67	12589.33	1798.48	413.61	34.47

Two cycles of 1.02-years (based on an 8% price filter) sum to 2.04 years, which compares to the observed 2.03-year cycle (based on a 12% price filter).

Three cycles of 2.03-years (based on a 12% price filter) sum to 6.09 years, which compares to the observed 6.08-year cycle (based on a 20% price filter).

Three cycles of 6.08-years (based on a 20% price filter) sum to 18.24 years, which compares to the approximate 17.7-year to 18-year cycles observed in several data series (see page 184).

Three cycles of 17.7 years to 18.24 years sum to 53.10 years to 54.72 years, which is within the range of the Long Wave (see page 181).

One-half the cycle of 17.7 years to 18.24 years would be the Juglar Wave of 8 to 10 years (see page 180).

All 8% filter high and low pivot dates, marking important turns.

Trade #	Trade	Entry Date	Trade #	Trade	Entry Date	Trade #	Trade	Entry Date
1	Long	6/13/49	35	Long	11/23/71	69	Long	6/15/84
2	Short	6/12/50	36	Short	1/11/73	70	Short	9/4/86
3	Long	7/13/50	37	Long	8/22/73	71	Long	9/29/86
4	Short	1/5/53	38	Short	10/26/73	72	Short	8/25/87
5	Long	9/14/53	39	Long	12/5/73	73	Long	10/19/87
6	Short	9/23/55	40	Short	1/3/74	74	Short	10/21/87
7	Long	10/11/55	41	Long	2/11/74	75	Long	10/26/87
8	Short	4/6/56	42	Short	3/13/74	76	Short	11/2/87
9	Long	5/28/56	43	Long	5/29/74	77	Long	12/4/87
10	Short	8/2/56	44	Short	6/10/74	78	Short	1/7/88
11	Long	2/12/57	45	Long	10/4/74	79	Long	1/20/88
12	Short	7/12/57	46	Short	11/5/74	80	Short	1/2/90
13	Long	10/22/57	47	Long	12/6/74	81	Long	1/30/90
14	Short	8/3/59	48	Short	7/15/75	82	Short	7/16/90
15	Long	9/22/59	49	Long	10/1/75	83	Long	10/11/90
16	Short	1/5/60	50	Short	9/21/76	84	Short	6/1/92
17	Long	3/8/60	51	Long	11/10/76	85	Long	10/9/92
18	Short	6/9/60	52	Short	12/31/76	86	Short	1/31/94
19	Long	10/25/60	53	Long	2/28/78	87	Long	4/4/94
20	Short	12/13/61	54	Short	9/8/78	88	Short	3/11/97
21	Long	6/26/62	55	Long	11/14/78	89	Long	4/11/97
22	Short	8/22/62	56	Short	10/5/79	90	Short	8/6/97
23	Long	10/23/62	57	Long	11/7/79	91	Long	10/27/97
24	Short	5/14/65	58	Short	2/13/80	92	Short	7/17/98
25	Long	6/28/65	59	Long	4/21/80	93	Long	8/31/98
26	Short	2/9/66	60	Short	11/20/80	94	Short	8/25/99
27	Long	10/7/66	61	Long	12/11/80	95	Long	10/15/99
28	Short	9/25/67	62	Short	4/27/81	96	Short	1/14/00
29	Long	3/21/68	63	Long	9/25/81	97	Long	3/7/00
30	Short	11/29/68	64	Short	12/4/81	98	Short	4/11/00
31	Long	5/26/70	65	Long	3/8/82	99	Long	5/26/00
32	Short	4/28/71	66	Short	5/7/82	100	Short	9/6/00
33	Long	8/10/71	67	Long	8/11/82	101	Long	10/18/00
34	Short	9/8/71	68	Short	11/29/83			
35	**Long**	**11/23/71**	**69**	**Long**	**6/15/84**			

Juglar Wave, a Cycle of 8 to 10 Years

In 1860, Clemant Juglar first observed a general economic cycle lasting 8 to 10 years, based on his study of data on banking, interest rates, stock prices, business failures, patents issued, pig iron prices, and a variety of other phenomena. Juglar's cycle forms the basis of the Decennial Pattern, a 10-year cycle, and of the Juglar Wave, a 9.25-year cycle in stock prices. This cycle has repeated 16 times since 1834. Ian Notley, using the Bartels test of probability, found that the 9.25-year cycle could not occur by chance more than once in 5000 times. Note that 8 to 10 years is about half the 17.70 cycle of war. *(See Cycles of War.)*

Every 9 solar years, the angles 0° and 180° between the sun, moon, and the moon's nodes repeat to within one degree, according to David McMinn, author of *Financial Crises & The 56-Year Cycle,* Twin Palms, Blue Knob 2480, Australia. (*See Astrology, Financial Applications of Astronomical Cycles.*)

Our 25% filter (from our table Observed Cycle Lengths) reveals a 7.95-year cycle. This 7.95-year cycle is about twice the well-known 4-year cycle. A simple moving average of 7.95-years effectively smoothes out nesting cycles of 7.95-years or less.

The 4-Year Cycle (Kitchin Wave) and the 49- to 58-Year Long Wave (Kondratieff Wave)

Two cycles of 2.03 years (from our table Observed Cycle Lengths) sum to 4.06 years, and four cycles of 1.02 years sum to 4.08 years. The 4-year cycle was known by traders such as the Rothschilds for more than a century. In 1923, Harvard Professor Joseph Kitchin showed 4-year cyclic influences in bank clearings, wholesale prices, and interest rates in Great Britain and in the U.S. for the period 1890 to 1922. Bill Meridian relates the 4-year cycle to both the U.S. presidential election cycle and the Mars-Vesta cycle. (*See Astrology, Financial Applications of Astronomical Cycles.*)

The **4-Year Cycle** table (on the next page) illustrates actual observed cycle lengths between significant market price lows for the Dow-Jones Industrial Average from 1896. These bottoms mostly appear before mid-term elections in the US. The column labeled *Time (years)* represents the time duration between important lows expressed in years (including fractions of years converted to decimals) and is the difference between the more recent date and the previous date listed on the line immediately above.

Approximately thirteen 4-year cycles make up the Long Wave, which ranges from 49- to 58-years. This cycle in economic data was discovered in 1847 by Clarke. Later, it was rediscovered by W.S. Jevons and N.D. Kondratieff. We already noted (in Nesting Cycles) that three cycles of 17.7 years to 18.24 years sum to 53.10 years to 54.72 years, which is well within the range of the Long Wave.

Since 1885, the Long Wave has averaged 53.94 years between market price lows or bottoms for the U.S. stock market. The Long Wave table (on page 183) shows all of the available data. The table is based on the daily Dow-Jones Industrial Average from 1896. The earliest three dates (1885, 1890, and 1893) are for monthly average

The 4-Year Cycle

Date of Low			DJIA	Time
Month	*Day*	*Year*	*Price*	*(years)*
8	10	1896	29.64	
6	23	1900	53.68	3.87
11	9	1903	42.15	3.38
11	15	1907	53.00	4.02
9	25	1911	72.94	3.86
12	24	1914	53.17	3.25
12	19	1917	65.95	2.99
8	24	1921	63.90	3.68
3	30	1926	135.20	4.60
7	8	1932	40.60	6.27
3	31	1938	97.50	5.73
4	28	1942	92.70	4.08
10	30	1946	160.50	4.51
6	14	1949	160.60	2.62
9	15	1953	254.40	4.25
10	22	1957	416.20	4.10
6	25	1962	524.60	4.68
10	10	1966	735.70	4.29
5	26	1970	627.50	3.63
12	9	1974	570.00	4.54
3	1	1978	736.75	3.23
8	9	1982	770.00	4.44
8	4	1986	1730.60	3.99
10	11	1990	2344.31	4.19
4	4	1994	3520.80	3.48
9	1	1998	7400.30	4.41
			Average	4.08

prices published by Standard & Poor's, and here we assume the lowest points occurred mid-month, on the fifteenth day.

Long Waves of Interest Rates and Stock Prices

Charles D. Kirkpatrick, CMT, in his Charles H. Dow Award winning paper, "Long Waves of Interest Rates and Stock Prices," found that over the past 200 years, every period when long-term interest rates decline and the stock market rises has *always* been followed by a major stock market collapse. Declining long-term interest rates

The Long Wave

Date of Low			Add Number	Date of Low		
Month	*Day*	*Year*	*of Years*	*Month*	*Day*	*Year*
1	15	1885	53.21	3	31	1938
12	15	1890	51.37	4	28	1942
8	15	1893	53.21	10	30	1946
8	10	1896	52.84	6	14	1949
6	23	1900	53.23	9	15	1953
11	9	1903	53.95	10	22	1957
11	15	1907	54.61	6	25	1962
9	25	1911	55.04	10	10	1966
12	24	1914	55.42	5	26	1970
12	19	1917	56.97	12	9	1974
8	24	1921	56.52	3	1	1978
3	30	1926	56.36	8	9	1982
7	8	1932	54.07	8	4	1986
3	31	1938	52.53	10	11	1990
4	28	1942	51.93	4	4	1994
10	30	1946	51.84	9	1	1998
		Average	53.94			

signal deflation, which ultimately proves harmful to the stock market. The stock market collapse is confirmed when the market violates its previous 4-year (40-month) cycle price low. For example, the latest 40-month cycle bottom was made on August 31, 1998, at a low closing price of 7539.07 on the DJIA. If that bottom is violated, it could suggest substantial downside risk for U.S. equity markets. Kirkpatrick's research is available through Kirkpatrick & Company, Inc., 7669 County Road 502, Bayfield, CO, 81122, e-mail: kirkco@capecod.net.

Cycles of War and the Long Wave of 49 to 58 years

Cycles of war relate to economic and financial cycles, particularly cycles of inflation, deflation, recession, and depression. Anticipation of war, particularly *fear* of war, is bearish for stock prices. Investors obviously *hate* war. Although the number of observations is far from sufficient to establish statistical validity, there may be a Long Wave ranging from 49 to 58 years for U.S. involvement in wars:

- 58 years after the outbreak of the French and Indian War of 1754 followed the outbreak of the War of 1812 between the U.S. and Britain.

- 49 years after the outbreak of the War of 1812 followed the outbreak of U.S. Civil War in 1861.
- 53 years after the outbreak of the U.S. Civil War in 1861 followed the outbreak of World War I in 1914.
- 52 years after the outbreak of Spanish-American War in 1898 followed the outbreak of Korean War in 1950.
- 53 years after the outbreak of World War I in 1914 followed the major U.S. Vietnam War offensive and the Middle East War, both in 1967.
- 51 years after Germany invaded Poland on September 1, 1939, thereby igniting World War II, Iraq invaded Kuwait on August 2, 1990. Both were followed by U.S. war preparations and subsequent U.S. participation in war.
- 49 years and 41 days after the Japanese bombed Pearl Harbor on December 7, 1941, an US-led coalition bombed Iraq on January 17, 1991.

Cycles of War and the 17.70-Year Cycle

The Foundation for the Study of Cycles has substantiated the periodicity of the following historic data sets, some of which may be related:

- 17.70-year cycle in War, dating back to 600 BC.
- 17.50-year cycle in U.S. Wholesale Prices.
- 18.00-year cycle in Bituminous Coal Production.
- 17.33-year cycle in the Flood Stages of the River Nile.

Three cycles of 17.70 years are 53.10 years (17.70 times 3 is 53.10), which coincides fairly closely with the Long Wave in U.S. stock prices, averaging 53.94 years. One third of the 53.94-year Long Wave in U.S. stock prices is 17.98 years.

Confining our investigation to the U.S. only, starting with the American colonial militiamens' first Revolutionary War battle with British troops at Lexington and Concord, Massachusetts, on April 19, 1775, and counting forward in time, there have been 12 full cycles of 17.70 years:

- The U.S. was involved in the Civil War in 1863, at the end of the fifth cycle of 17.70 years (17.70 times 5 is 88.50 years).
- The U.S. was involved in World War I in 1916, at the end of the eighth cycle of 17.70 years (17.70 times 8 is 141.60 years).
- The U.S. was involved in the Korean War in 1952, at the end of the tenth cycle of 17.70 years (17.70 times 10 is 177.00 years).
- The U.S. was involved in the Vietnam War in 1970, at the end of the eleventh cycle of 17.70 years (17.70 times 11 is 194.70 years).
- The thirteenth cycle of 17.70 years (17.70 times 13 is 230.10 years) ends in 2005. War on terrorism started on September 11, 2001.

Three-Year Cycle in Long-Term Interest Rates

The 3-Year Cycle in Long-Term Interest Rates table (on the next page) suggests that there may be a 3.02-year cycle (median) in the U.S. Bond Treasury futures contract, including both the advancing and declining phases, over the entire past 23-year history of bond futures trading. The advancing, upward part of the cycle at 1.79 years has lasted 59% of the typical 3.02-year full cycle, while the declining, downward part of the cycle at 1.23 years has lasted 41% of the 3.02 years.

We also examined Moody's Investor Service monthly average Aaa corporate long-term bond yield data for 68 years from 1932 to 2000. We found 28 directional up or down trends of 10% or greater. These 10% yield swings lasted a median time duration of 609 calendar days or 20.01 months, or 1.67 years. Twice the swing duration of 1.67 years gives a full cycle of 3.34 years. Although the median gives us one pleasing and precise number, it is important to note that there has been a great deal of variation in the time duration of the yield swings, from a minimum of 0.17 years maximum of 12.09 years.

Fibonacci Time Cycles

Robert C. Miner proportions future time by Fibonacci ratios. First, Miner applies Fibonacci Time-Cycle Ratios to the time duration of the latest completed price swing, using both trading days and calendar days. The most important Fibonacci ratios are: 0.382, 0.500, 0.618, 1.000, 1.618, 2.000, and 2.618.

Miner's Alternative Time Projections are calculated as time ratios of the previous price swing in the same direction, that is, up swings are measured out as proportions of previous up swings, while down swings are measured out as proportions of previous down swings. Also, Alternative Time Projections may be derived from same-direction price swings earlier than the latest one.

Miner points out that there is a very high probability of trend change when both price and time ratios coincide.

Miner's Trend Vibration™ method is based on two directional movements early in a trend: the initial thrust and the initial corrective wave of that thrust. Together, these two movements are Elliot Waves one and two, and Miner calls them the *initial vibration*. Fibonacci ratios of that initial vibration time projected forward coincide with subsequent turning dates, including the end point of the completed trend.

Of secondary importance are the day counts, numbering each day in straight numerical sequence from outstanding turning points, using both trading days and calendar days. When one or more day counts is a number in the Fibonacci sequence, the probability of a directional trend change is heightened. The more hits on Fibonacci numbers, the greater the confirmation and power of that date.

Three-Year Cycle in Long-Term Interest Rates

Bond Advances						Bond Declines					
Price Low Date	*Price Low*	*Price High Date*	*Price High*	*Price % Gain*	*Time in Years*	*Price High Date*	*Price High*	*Price Low Date*	*Price Low*	*Price % Loss*	*Time in Years*
2/22/80	51.8873	6/13/80	72.0126	38.79	0.31	9/6/77	85.5065	2/22/80	51.8873	−39.32	2.46
9/28/81	46.9591	5/5/83	66.0524	40.66	1.60	6/13/80	72.0126	9/28/81	46.9591	−34.79	1.29
7/2/84	49.0233	4/17/86	87.0810	77.63	1.79	5/5/83	66.0524	7/2/84	49.0233	−25.78	1.16
10/19/87	62.9304	10/16/89	83.1591	32.14	1.99	4/17/86	87.0810	10/19/87	62.9304	−27.73	1.51
9/24/90	71.7288	9/7/93	100.9870	40.79	2.96	10/16/89	83.1591	9/24/90	71.7288	−13.75	0.94
11/11/94	79.2886	1/4/96	100.8330	27.17	1.15	9/7/93	100.9870	11/11/94	79.2886	−21.49	1.18
6/13/96	87.5706	10/5/98	111.6700	27.52	2.31	1/4/96	100.8330	6/13/96	87.5706	−13.15	0.44
1/18/00	89.8438	*Nov-01*	*124.6942*	*38.79*	*1.79*	10/5/98	111.6700	1/18/00	89.8438	−19.55	1.29

Last line above is projected based on past median performance.

Mean				40.67	1.73					−24.44	1.28
Median				38.79	1.79					−23.63	1.23

Data based on CSI's Perpetual, time-weighted nearest two futures contracts. Also, data adjusted for contract change in December 1999.

Moody's Aaa Long-Term Bond Yields: 10% Swings

#	*Direction*	*Turn Date*	*Days*	*Months*	*Years*
	Down	6/30/32			
1	Up	12/31/36	1645	54.04	4.51
2	Down	4/30/37	120	3.94	0.33
3	Up	7/31/39	822	27.00	2.25
4	Down	9/30/39	61	2.00	0.17
5	Up	4/30/46	2404	78.98	6.59
6	Down	12/31/47	610	20.04	1.67
7	Up	1/31/50	762	25.03	2.09
8	Down	6/30/53	1246	40.93	3.41
9	Up	4/30/54	304	9.99	0.83
10	Down	9/30/57	1249	41.03	3.42
11	Up	5/31/58	243	7.98	0.67
12	Down	6/30/70	4413	144.97	12.09
13	Up	2/28/71	243	7.98	0.67
14	Down	10/31/74	1341	44.05	3.67
15	Up	9/30/77	1065	34.99	2.92
16	Down	3/31/80	913	29.99	2.50
17	Up	6/30/80	91	2.99	0.25
18	Down	9/30/81	457	15.01	1.25
19	Up	5/31/83	608	19.97	1.67
20	Down	6/30/84	396	13.01	1.08
21	Up	1/31/87	945	31.04	2.59
22	Down	10/31/87	273	8.97	0.75
23	Up	9/30/93	2161	70.99	5.92
24	Down	11/30/94	426	13.99	1.17
25	Up	1/31/96	427	14.03	1.17
26	Down	4/30/97	455	14.95	1.25
27	Up	12/31/98	610	20.04	1.67
28	Down	5/31/00	517	16.98	1.42

	Days	*Months*	*Years*
Median	609	20.01	1.67
Mean	886	29.11	2.43
Min	61	2.00	0.17
Max	4413	144.97	12.09

As suggested by W. D. Gann, Miner also uses multiples of 30 (specifically, 30, 60, 90, 120, 150, 180, 210, 240, 270, 300, 330, and 360), and multiples of 36 (specifically, 36, 72, 108, 144, 180, 216, 252, 288, 324, and 360) in his day counts. Anniversary dates of previous turning points in history also add value to his analysis of time.

Miner also uses Bollinger Bands (which are also known as Standard Deviation Bands and Volatility Bands) to help identify and confirm time/price turning points. Two standard deviations above and below a moving average create a channel that encloses 95% of the price action. In relatively low volatility, sideways trading-range markets, such bands reliably indicate support and resistance. In trending markets, where the trend is strong and continuing, reactions against the trend often do not exceed the moving average mid-way between the upper and lower bands. In a bullish trend, price spends more of the time testing the upper band and the moving average. In a bearish trend, price spends more of the time testing the lower band and the moving average.

At the independently determined cyclical time of probable trend change, Miner has observed that price is often near one extreme band or the other. Then, to confirm the trend change, price moves quickly to the opposite band, in the direction of the new trend, showing a relatively high degree of absolute price velocity. Trend, Elliott Wave and Chart Pattern interpretation complement and complete Miner's cycle analysis.

The time and price projection methods cited here are adapted with permission from Miner, Robert C., *Dynamic Trading,* Dynamic Traders Group, Inc., 6336 N. Oracle, Suite 326-346, Tucson, AZ 85704. This recommended book offers practical guidelines for interpretation and a large number of actual trading examples. Miner also develops software to efficiently make calculations of the Fibonacci relationships, including time as well as price, in any market.

Data

With any kind of technical analysis, accurate data is critical. At a minimum, make a thorough visual inspection of the data in graphic form. The most obvious outliers and errors should stand out and away from the rest of the data and can be checked on a case by case basis. Spot check the rest of the data against an independent data source.

The rule for back testing is to search out the most data and the most accurate data available. We can never have too much data. A long data base allows Walk-Forward Simulation, a powerful analytical technique.

When working with different independent data series, such as a sentiment indicator used for buy and sell signals to be used against stock prices, take special care that the data points line up in correct order. Pasting both data series onto a spread sheet makes misalignment easy to see.

Economic data are usually reported with a lag, such that data labeled for the month of January are actually reported in February or March. Therefore, we must advance the data as of the labeled date forward by the amount of the time lag in reporting. The dates of actual market prices must line up with the dates the economic data were actually reported, and not the labeled dates. We must not paper trade on data that is not yet available at the time of the signal. We must insist that our simulations are realistic, otherwise, we are fooling ourselves. For example, buying on the date of the end of an economic recession and selling on the date of the beginning of an economic recession would have been a profitable strategy, if we could actually execute it, but we cannot. Adjusting for the lag in economic data reporting, profits for a recession-timing strategy evaporate.

Data Exploration, Data Mining

Data exploration is an inevitable part of the discovery process. We must establish specific, well-defined analytic procedures designed to explore large amounts of raw data to find trends, patterns or relationships between variables. If an algorithm is found, it can be applied to detect signals in out-of-sample, unseen data. Then, if that is fruitful, an actual trading program might be launched. An example of one of our most used data exploration routines is the *Exponential Moving Average* crossover rule to detect elementary directional trends. When data mining is used properly, it is an important step in the development of a technical indicator.

Days of the Month

Arthur A. Merrill, CMT, pioneered the study of seasonal behavior of stock market prices in his classic book, Merrill, A. (1984) *Behavior of Prices on Wall Street,* Second Edition. Chappaqua, New York: Analysis Press.

Days of the Month

Day of Month	*Percentage Gain (−Loss)*	*Total # of Trades*	*Winning Trades*	*Losing Trades*	*# Win/ # Total*	*Ratio Avg $ Win/ Avg $ Loss*
1	177.32	848	445	403	0.5248	1.3447
2	233.92	893	460	433	0.5151	1.4312
3	111.66	905	437	468	0.4829	1.3038
4	2.17	831	387	444	0.4657	1.1567
5	213.69	891	441	450	0.4949	1.4400
6	−39.20	919	407	512	0.4429	1.0529
7	−16.07	912	416	496	0.4561	1.1140
8	−24.20	937	408	529	0.4354	1.1985
9	24.05	937	442	495	0.4717	1.1922
10	−7.10	938	435	503	0.4638	1.1252
11	−43.81	918	389	529	0.4237	1.1257
12	−12.00	853	393	460	0.4607	1.1239
13	69.05	927	458	469	0.4941	1.2048
14	30.30	934	443	491	0.4743	1.2110
15	40.35	941	449	492	0.4772	1.2067
16	−11.51	937	426	511	0.4546	1.1625
17	−14.84	939	430	509	0.4579	1.1228
18	−41.91	936	414	522	0.4423	1.0699
19	62.54	932	422	510	0.4528	1.3960
20	−18.60	940	406	534	0.4319	1.2415
21	−47.72	928	406	522	0.4375	1.0531
22	2.53	880	387	493	0.4398	1.2838
23	−13.69	919	411	508	0.4472	1.1751
24	−23.18	916	410	506	0.4476	1.1416
25	−14.97	841	391	450	0.4649	1.0900
26	15.88	902	410	492	0.4545	1.2587
27	21.81	925	441	484	0.4768	1.1678
28	40.99	914	436	478	0.4770	1.2266
29	172.17	867	422	445	0.4867	1.4802
30	185.49	787	408	379	0.5184	1.3322
31	79.58	523	271	252	0.5182	1.3036
Avg 16.00	37.25	892.58	416.16	476.42	0.47	1.22

Using the calendar and daily price changes for the Dow-Jones Industrial Average, he counted the number of times the DJIA rose or fell for each day of the month over an 87-year period, from 1897 to 1983.

Measuring each specific date of the month, from the 1st to the 31st, Merrill found a significant bullish bias in the first six calendar days of the month and in the last three days calendar days of the month. He found that the stock market lagged in the middle of the month, in terms of in winning frequency, the percentage of "up" days.

We independently collected our own statistics for the past 100 years from 1900 to 2000. Our findings support the study Merrill conducted 17-years earlier. Our numbers (on the facing page) show a probable rise in each of the last two and first two calendar days of each month. The rest of the days were more likely to go down than to go up.

Although losing days were more frequent, the size of the gains were bigger than the size of the losses. As shown in the *Percentage Gain (-Loss)* column, only 14 of 31 calendar days actually would have lost money (on average), while 17 of the 31 calendar days would have gained money for long transactions. And the losing days would have lost less money per day than the winning days would have made money per day. So, not only do we need to consider the *frequency* of an observation, but also the *magnitude* of a price movement.

Note some variability in the total number of trades is due to leap years, holidays, and weekends. The New York Stock Exchange was closed from July 31 to December 11, 1914, due to fears of selling imbalances as a result of the outbreak of World War I. Also, before May 26, 1952, the market was open on Saturdays.

Indicator Strategy Example for the Days of the Month

Historical data shows that a simple strategy based on the day of the month can produce positive results, but only on the long side. The short side would have lost money over the past 100 years and especially since 1974. Based on the daily closing prices for the Dow-Jones Industrial Average for 100 years from 1900 to 2000, we found that the following parameters would have produced a positive result on a purely mechanical trend-following signal basis with no subjectivity, no sophisticated technical analysis, and no judgement:

Enter Long (Buy) at the current daily price close of the DJIA each month when the calendar says the day is the 26th, or buy on the next trading session if the market is closed on the 26th.

Close Long (Sell) at the current daily price close of the DJIA each month when the calendar says the day is the 6th, or sell on the next trading session if the market is closed on the 6th.

Enter Short (Sell Short) never.

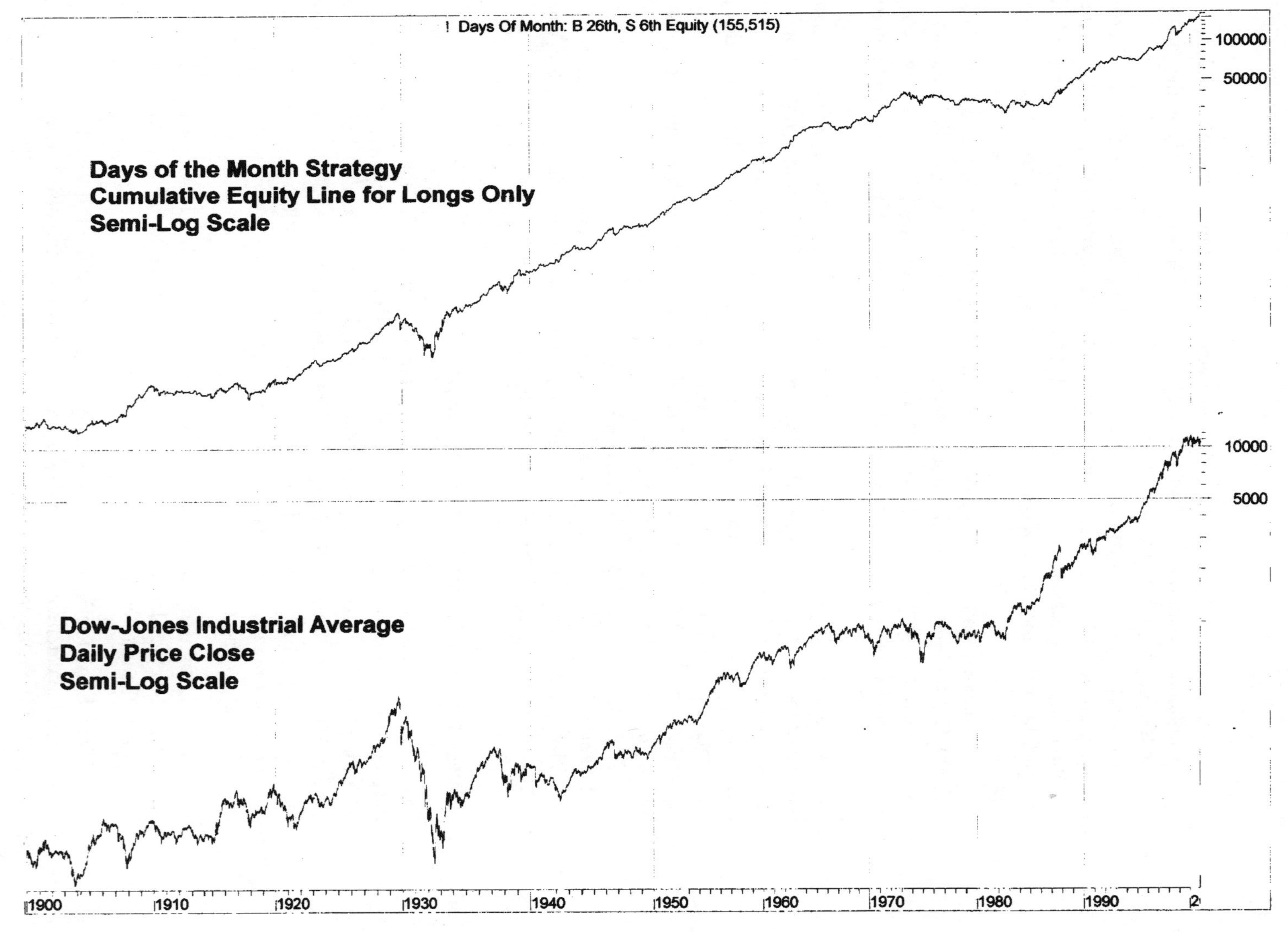

! Days Of Month: B 26th, S 6th Equity (155,515)
Days of the Month Strategy
Cumulative Equity Line for Longs Only
Semi-Log Scale
Dow-Jones Industrial Average
Daily Price Close
Semi-Log Scale
100000
50000
10000
5000
1900
1910
1920
1930
1940
1950
1960
1970
1980
1990

Days of the Month, Buy on the 26th, Sell on the 6th

Total net profit	155414.94	Open position value	N/A	Net Profit/Buy&Hold %	650.85
Percent gain/loss	155414.94	Annual percent gain/loss	1539.39	Annual Net %/B&H %	650.85
Initial investment	100	Interest earned	0		
Current position	Out	Date position entered	11/6/00		
Buy/Hold profit	20698.6	Days in test	36850	# of days per trade	30.61
Buy/Hold pct gain/loss	20698.6	Annual B/H pct gain/loss	205.02		
Total closed trades	1204	Commissions paid	0		
Avg profit per trade	129.08	Avg Win/Avg Loss ratio	1.18		
Total long trades	1204	Total short trades	0	Long Win Trade %	61.63
Winning long trades	742	Winning short trades	0	Short Win Trade %	#DIV/0!
Total winning trades	742	Total losing trades	462	Total Win Trade %	61.63
Amount of winning trades	328986.31	Amount of losing trades	−173571.44	Net Profit Margin %	30.92
Average win	443.38	Average loss	−375.7	Average P. Margin %	8.26
Largest win	8459.17	Largest loss	−7131.32	% Net/(Win + Loss)	8.52
Average length of win	8.68	Average length of loss	8.8	(Win − Loss)/Loss %	−1.36
Longest winning trade	25	Longest losing trade	22	(Win − Loss)/Loss %	13.64
Most consecutive wins	15	Most consecutive losses	9	(Win − Loss)/Loss %	66.67
Total bars out	19573	Average length out	16.24		
Longest out period	22				
System close drawdown	−6.64	Profit/Loss index	47.24	% Net Profit/SODD	2295641.65
System open drawdown	−6.77	Reward/Risk index	100	(Net P. − SODD)/Net P.	100.00
Max open trade drawdown	−13966.65	Buy/Hold index	650.85	% SODD/Net Profit	0.00

In the Equis MetaStock® "System Report" (profit and loss summary statistics), the *Total net profit* is the sum of profits minus the sum of losses, including open positions marked to the market. In contrast, the *Amount of Winning Trades* is the sum of realized profits (the total of all gains on closed-out trades only, excluding any open positions). Similarly, the *Amount of Losing Trades* is the sum of realized losses (the total of all losses on closed-out trades only, excluding any open positions). *System close drawdown* is the largest decline in the cumulative equity line below the initial investment, based on closed-out positions only. *System open drawdown (SODD)* is the largest decline in the cumulative equity line below the initial investment when a position is open. *Max open trade drawdown* is the largest decline in the cumulative equity line below the trade entry price during the worst single trade. The *Profit/Loss Index* is a complex calculation that relates the Amount of Winning Trades to the Amount of Losing Trades on a scale of −100 (worst possible performance) to +100 (best possible performance), with zero representing profits equal to losses. *Reward/Risk Index* is the Total net profit minus System open drawdown. The resulting difference is then divided by the Total net profit. The *Buy/Hold Index* is the Total net profit minus the buy-and-hold strategy's net profit. The resulting difference is then divided by the buy-and-hold net profit. In this exercise, initial equity is assumed to be $100. Both long and short positions are taken unless otherwise noted. Trades are executed at the closing price on the signal date. Transaction costs, interest expenses, and margins are not included in the statistics.

Starting with $100 and reinvesting profits, total net profits, long only, for this Days of the Month strategy would have been $155,414.94, assuming a fully invested strategy, reinvestment of profits, no transactions costs and no taxes. This would have been 650.85 percent greater than buy-and-hold. About 61.63 percent of the 1204 signals would have produced winning trades. Short selling, which was not included in this strategy, would have lost money over the past 100 years, and especially since 1974. Note that results would have been much better when we also considered what month it was. *(See Months of the Year.)*

The Equis International MetaStock® System Testing rules are written as follows:

Enter long: DayOfMonth()=opt1 OR
DayOfMonth()=opt1+1 OR
DayOfMonth()=opt1+2 OR
DayOfMonth()=opt1+3

Close long: DayOfMonth()=opt2 OR
DayOfMonth()=opt2+1 OR
DayOfMonth()=opt2+2 OR
DayOfMonth()=opt2+3

OPT1 Current value: 26
OPT2 Current value: 6

Indicator Strategy Example for the Days of the Month and the Months of the Year

A more complex strategy, considering both the specific days of the month and the months of the year, would have produced a much more positive result on a purely mechanical trend-following signal basis with no subjectivity, no sophisticated technical analysis, and no judgement:

Enter Long (Buy) at the current daily price close of the DJIA every year on October 27th, or on the next trading session if the market is closed on October 27th.

Close Long (Sell) at the current daily price close of the DJIA every year on September 5th, or on the next trading session if the market is closed on September 5th.

Enter Short (Sell Short) at the current daily price close of the DJIA every year on September 5th, or on the next trading session if the market is closed on September 5th.

Close Short (Cover) at the current daily price close of the DJIA every year on October 27th, or on the next trading session if the market is closed on October 27th.

Starting with $100 and reinvesting profits, total net profits, long and short, for this seasonal strategy would have been $644,466.56, assuming a fully invested strategy, reinvestment of profits, no transactions costs and no taxes. This would have been 3,013.58 percent greater than buy-and-hold. About 61.81 percent of the 199 signals would have produced winning trades. Even short selling, which was included in this strategy, would have made money during the great bull market since 1982.

The Equis International MetaStock® System Testing rules are written as follows:

Enter long: (Month()=opt1 AND DayOfMonth()=(opt2+0)) OR
(Month()=opt1 AND DayOfMonth()=(opt2+1)) OR
(Month()=opt1 AND DayOfMonth()=(opt2+2)) OR
(Month()=opt1 AND DayOfMonth()=(opt2+3)) OR
(Month()=opt1 AND DayOfMonth()=(opt2+4))

Close long: (Month()=opt3 AND DayOfMonth()=(opt4+0)) OR
(Month()=opt3 AND DayOfMonth()=(opt4+1)) OR
(Month()=opt3 AND DayOfMonth()=(opt4+2)) OR
(Month()=opt3 AND DayOfMonth()=(opt4+3)) OR
(Month()=opt3 AND DayOfMonth()=(opt4+4))

Enter short: (Month()=opt3 AND DayOfMonth()=(opt4+0)) OR
(Month()=opt3 AND DayOfMonth()=(opt4+1)) OR
(Month()=opt3 AND DayOfMonth()=(opt4+2)) OR
(Month()=opt3 AND DayOfMonth()=(opt4+3)) OR
(Month()=opt3 AND DayOfMonth()=(opt4+4))

Close short: (Month()=opt1 AND DayOfMonth()=(opt2+0)) OR
(Month()=opt1 AND DayOfMonth()=(opt2+1)) OR
(Month()=opt1 AND DayOfMonth()=(opt2+2)) OR
(Month()=opt1 AND DayOfMonth()=(opt2+3)) OR
(Month()=opt1 AND DayOfMonth()=(opt2+4))

OPT1 Current value: 10

OPT2 Current value: 27

OPT3 Current value: 9

OPT4 Current value: 5

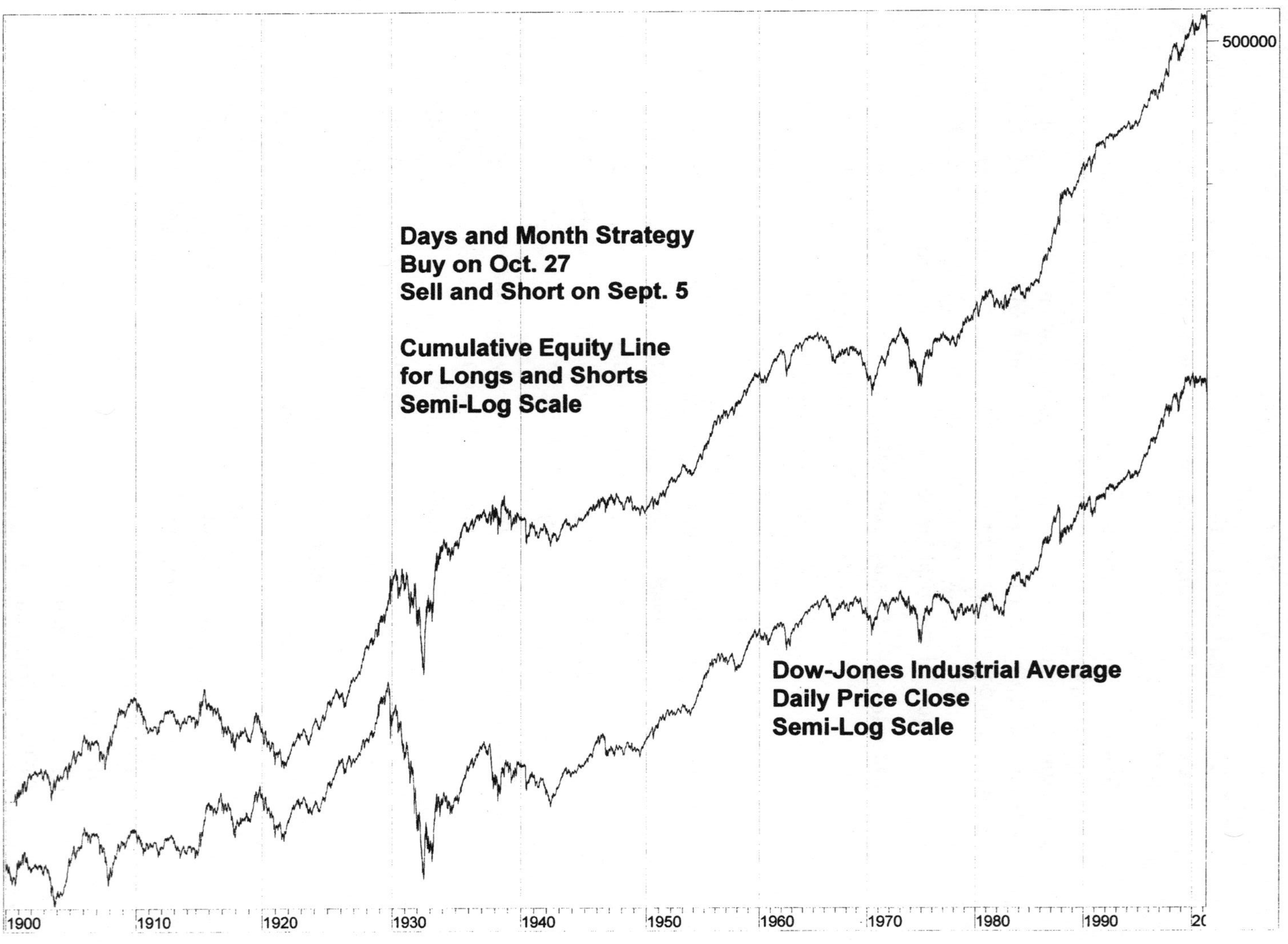

500000
Days and Month Strategy
Buy on Oct. 27
Sell and Short on Sept. 5
Cumulative Equity Line
for Longs and Shorts
Semi-Log Scale
Dow-Jones Industrial Average
Daily Price Close
Semi-Log Scale
1900
1910
1920
1930
1940
1950
1960
1970
1980
1990
20

Buy October 27th, Sell September 5th

Total net profit	644466.56	Open position value	-11857.09	Net Profit/Buy&Hold %	3013.58
Percent gain/loss	644466.56	Annual percent gain/loss	6383.45	Annual Net %/B&H %	3013.57
Initial investment	100	Interest earned	0		
Current position	Long	Date position entered	10/27/00		
Buy/Hold profit	20698.6	Days in test	36850	# of days per trade	185.18
Buy/Hold pct gain/loss	20698.6	Annual B/H pct gain/loss	205.02		
Total closed trades	199	Commissions paid	0		
Avg profit per trade	3298.11	Avg Win/Avg Loss ratio	5.47		
Total long trades	99	Total short trades	100	Long Win Trade %	67.68
Winning long trades	67	Winning short trades	56	Short Win Trade %	56.00
Total winning trades	123	Total losing trades	76	Total Win Trade %	61.81
Amount of winning trades	739821.5	Amount of losing trades	-83497.89	Net Profit Margin %	79.72
Average win	6014.81	Average loss	-1098.66	Average P. Margin %	69.11
Largest win	130720.66	Largest loss	-18789.31	% Net/(Win + Loss)	74.87
Average length of win	147.6	Average length of loss	124.91	(Win − Loss)/Loss %	18.17
Longest winning trade	450	Longest losing trade	264	(Win − Loss)/Loss %	70.45
Most consecutive wins	7	Most consecutive losses	4	(Win − Loss)/Loss %	75.00
Total bars out	204	Average length out	204		
Longest out period	204				
System close drawdown	-2.56	Profit/Loss index	88.53	% Net Profit/SODD	15199683.02
System open drawdown	-4.24	Reward/Risk index	100	(Net P. − SODD)/Net P.	100.00
Max open trade drawdown	-32949.94	Buy/Hold index	2956.29	% SODD/Net Profit	0.00

In the Equis MetaStock® "System Report" (profit and loss summary statistics), the *Total net profit* is the sum of profits minus the sum of losses, including open positions marked to the market. In contrast, the *Amount of Winning Trades* is the sum of realized profits (the total of all gains on closed-out trades only, excluding any open positions). Similarly, the *Amount of Losing Trades* is the sum of realized losses (the total of all losses on closed-out trades only, excluding any open positions). *System close drawdown* is the largest decline in the cumulative equity line below the initial investment, based on closed-out positions only. *System open drawdown (SODD)* is the largest decline in the cumulative equity line below the initial investment when a position is open. *Max open trade drawdown* is the largest decline in the cumulative equity line below the trade entry price during the worst single trade. The *Profit/Loss Index* is a complex calculation that relates the Amount of Winning Trades to the Amount of Losing Trades on a scale of −100 (worst possible performance) to +100 (best possible performance), with zero representing profits equal to losses. *Reward/Risk Index* is the Total net profit minus System open drawdown. The resulting difference is then divided by the Total net profit. The *Buy/Hold Index* is the Total net profit minus the buy-and-hold strategy's net profit. The resulting difference is then divided by the buy-and-hold net profit. In this exercise, initial equity is assumed to be $100. Both long and short positions are taken unless otherwise noted. Trades are executed at the closing price on the signal date. Transaction costs, interest expenses, and margins are not included in the statistics.

Independent Study of Days Each Month from Yale Hirsch's *Stock Traders Almanac*

The actual historical performance data (on the facing page), quantifying the percentage of times the S&P 500 Index rose in price on each specific Day of each Month, are updated each year in Yale Hirsch's, *Stock Traders Almanac,* The Hirsch Organization, Inc., 184 Central Avenue, Old Tappan, NJ 07675, page 138, www.stocktradersalmanac.com. Hirsch's *Almanac* provides annual updates on a variety of interesting calendar-based statistical studies.

Days of the Week

Arthur A. Merrill, CMT, pioneered the study of seasonal behavior of stock market prices in his classic book, Merrill, A. (1984), *Behavior of Prices on Wall Street,* Second Edition, Chappaqua, New York: The Analysis Press.

Using the calendar and daily price changes for the Dow-Jones Industrial Average, he counted the number of times the market rose or fell for each day of the week over a 31-year period, from 1952 to 1983.

Measuring each specific day of the week (Monday, Tuesday, Wednesday, Thursday, and Friday), Merrill found a strong bullish bias on the last three calendar days of the trading week, namely Friday, Wednesday and Thursday—in that order. He found Tuesday to be only slightly positive, while Monday was a losing day more often than not.

Merrill found that on average the DJIA increased 52.1% of the time each day of the week. Tuesdays, Wednesdays, and Thursdays did not deviate significantly from the norm, respectively rising 50.5%, 55.2%, and 53.2% of the time. Mondays and Fridays were more significant: Mondays were bearish with the market rising only 43.6% of the time; and Fridays were bullish with the market up 57.7% of the time.

We independently calculated our own statistics for the past 48 years from Monday, May 26, 1952, through Wednesday, November 22, 2000.

Our findings completely supported Merrill's findings on the frequency of winning days. Results conformed precisely to the order of his ranking. Friday was the best day, followed by Wednesday, Thursday, and Tuesday, which, again, was only slightly positive. Monday was still a losing day more often than not, and Monday was only negative day of the week. However, the frequency of losing Mondays was not quite as bad as Merrill found in his test 17 years earlier, probably because of the great bullish stock market uptrend from 1982 to 2000.

S&P 500 MARKET PROBABILITY CHART 2001

THE CHANCE OF THE MARKET RISING ON ANY TRADING DAY OF THE YEAR*

(Based on the number of times the S&P 500 rose on a particular trading day during January 1953-December 1999)

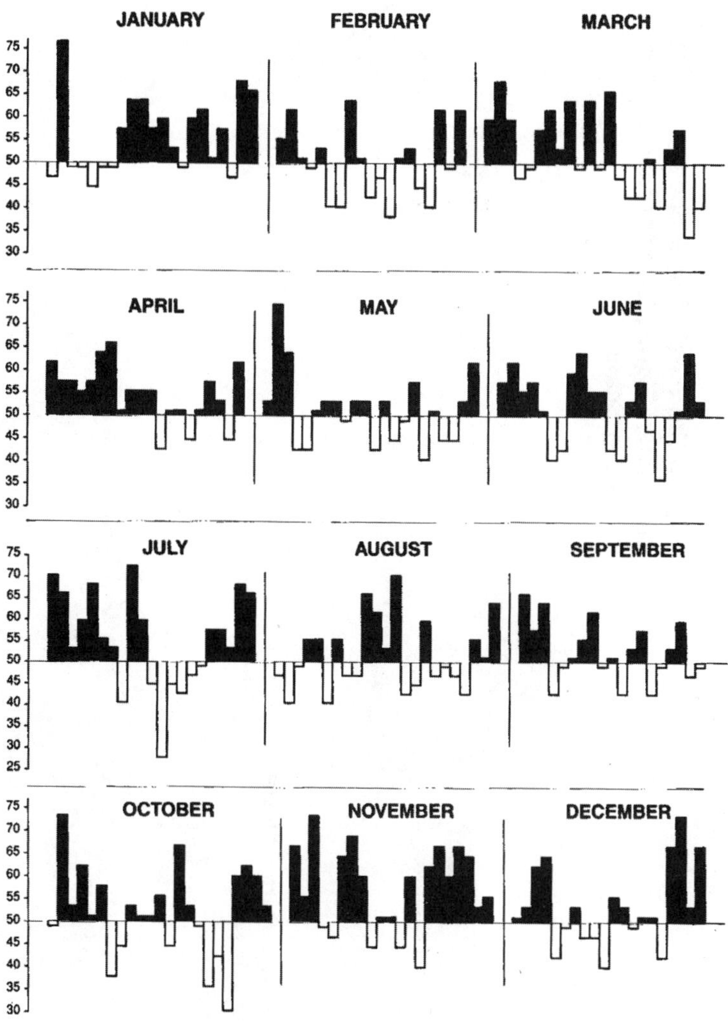

Shows the number of trading days in each month (Saturdays, Sundays, and holidays excluded) for 2001
Graphic representation of page 188

** See new trends developing on pages 76, 94, 96 and 134*

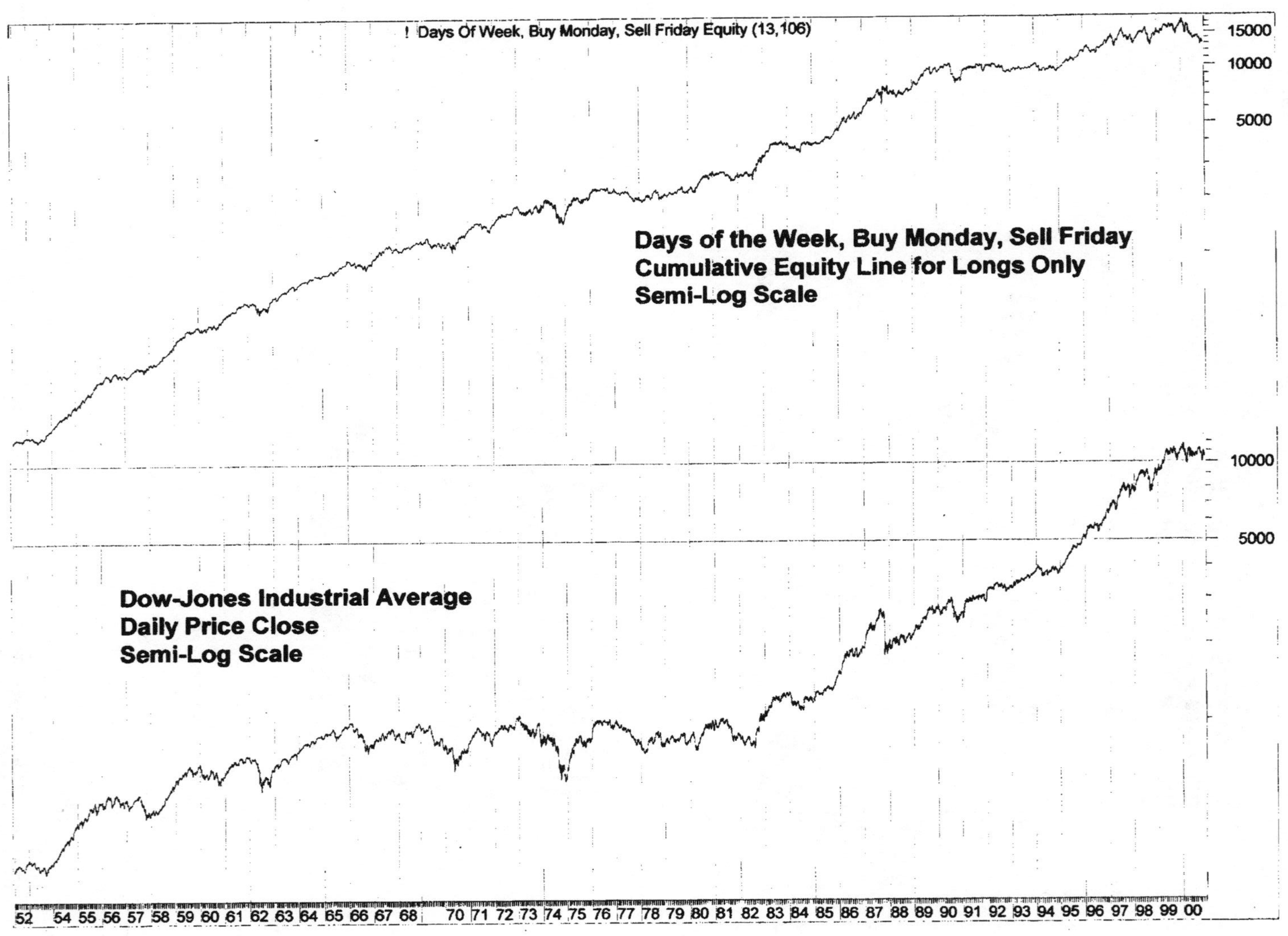
! Days Of Week, Buy Monday, Sell Friday Equity (13,106)
15000
10000
5000
Days of the Week, Buy Monday, Sell Friday
Cumulative Equity Line for Longs Only
Semi-Log Scale
10000
5000
Dow-Jones Industrial Average
Daily Price Close
Semi-Log Scale
52 54 55 56 57 58 59 60 61 62 63 64 65 66 67 68 70 71 72 73 74 75 76 77 78 79 80 81 82 83 84 85 86 87 88 89 90 91 92 93 94 95 96 97 98 99 00

Days of the Week, Buy Friday, Sell Monday

Total net profit	13006.5	Open position value	−79.78	Net Profit/Buy&Hold %	239.05
Percent gain/loss	13006.5	Annual percent gain/loss	268.02	Annual Net %/B&H %	239.05
Initial investment	100	Interest earned	0		
Current position	Long	Date position entered	11/20/00		
Buy/Hold profit	3836.15	Days in test	17713	# of days per trade	7.28
Buy/Hold pct gain/loss	3836.15	Annual B/H pct gain/loss	79.05		
Total closed trades	2434	Commissions paid	0		
Avg profit per trade	5.38	Avg Win/Avg Loss ratio	0.9		
Total long trades	2434	Total short trades	0	Long Win Trade %	56.82
Winning long trades	1383	Winning short trades	0	Short Win Trade %	#DIV/0!
Total winning trades	1383	Total losing trades	1051	Total Win Trade %	56.82
Amount of winning trades	83575.84	Amount of losing trades	−70489.59	Net Profit Margin %	8.49
Average win	60.43	Average loss	−67.07	Average P. Margin %	−5.21
Largest win	1051.41	Largest loss	−1273.47	% Net/(Win + Loss)	−9.55
Average length of win	5.01	Average length of loss	5.02	(Win − Loss)/Loss %	−0.20
Longest winning trade	13	Longest losing trade	13	(Win − Loss)/Loss %	0.00
Most consecutive wins	12	Most consecutive losses	6	(Win − Loss)/Loss %	100.00
Total bars out	4868	Average length out	2		
Longest out period	2				
System close drawdown	0	Profit/Loss index	15.58	% Net Profit/SODD	13006.50
System open drawdown	−100	Reward/Risk index	99.24	(Net P. − SODD)/Net P.	99.23
Max open trade drawdown	−1273.47	Buy/Hold index	236.97	% SODD/Net Profit	−0.77

In the Equis MetaStock® "System Report" (profit and loss summary statistics), the *Total net profit* is the sum of profits minus the sum of losses, including open positions marked to the market. In contrast, the *Amount of Winning Trades* is the sum of realized profits (the total of all gains on closed-out trades only, excluding any open positions). Similarly, the *Amount of Losing Trades* is the sum of realized losses (the total of all losses on closed-out trades only, excluding any open positions). *System close drawdown* is the largest decline in the cumulative equity line below the initial investment, based on closed-out positions only. *System open drawdown (SODD)* is the largest decline in the cumulative equity line below the initial investment when a position is open. *Max open trade drawdown* is the largest decline in the cumulative equity line below the trade entry price during the worst single trade. The *Profit/Loss Index* is a complex calculation that relates the Amount of Winning Trades to the Amount of Losing Trades on a scale of −100 (worst possible performance) to +100 (best possible performance), with zero representing profits equal to losses. *Reward/Risk Index* is the Total net profit minus System open drawdown. The resulting difference is then divided by the Total net profit. The *Buy/Hold Index* is the Total net profit minus the buy-and-hold strategy's net profit. The resulting difference is then divided by the buy-and-hold net profit. In this exercise, initial equity is assumed to be $100. Both long and short positions are taken unless otherwise noted. Trades are executed at the closing price on the signal date. Transaction costs, interest expenses, and margins are not included in the statistics.

In terms of the *magnitude* of price movement, Wednesday showed the best gains. Monday was the only day of the week that lost money.

Note that before Monday, May 26, 1952, there was trading on Saturdays. Including data before 5/26/52 would have distorted test results. Therefore, the earliest data before 5/26/52 was excluded from this study.

Day of Week	*Percentage Gain (−Loss)*	*Total # of Trades*	*Winning Trades*	*Losing Trades*	*# Win/ # Total*	*Ratio Avg $ Win/ Avg $ Loss*
Monday	−69.97	2434	1170	1264	0.4807	0.7994
Tuesday	155.77	2358	1190	1168	0.5047	1.1256
Wednesday	518.41	2486	1345	1141	0.5410	1.0315
Thursday	109.52	2480	1296	1184	0.5226	0.9858
Friday	295.48	2452	1329	1123	0.5420	0.9703
Average	201.84	2442	1266	1176	0.5182	0.9825

Note there is some variability in the total number of trades due to leap years, holidays, and weekends. There are fewer Tuesdays in the count, reflecting the frequency of holidays which fall on Mondays: our rule buys on Monday's close and sells on Tuesday's close. When the market is closed on Monday, it does not enter a trade.

Indicator Strategy Example for the Days of the Week

The best strategy is obvious from the table: buy on Monday's close, and sell on Friday's close. Historical data shows that this simple strategy (based on the day of the week) can produce positive results, on the long side only. Although the short side would have made money over the past 48 years, short selling would have lost money since 11/30/87, and so short selling was not included in the results shown. Based on the daily closing prices for the Dow-Jones Industrial Average for 48 years from May 26, 1952, through November 22, 2000, we found that the following parameters would have produced a positive result on a purely mechanical trend-following signal basis with no subjectivity, no sophisticated technical analysis, and no judgement:

Enter Long (Buy) at the current daily price close of the DJIA each week when the calendar says the day is Monday, Tuesday, Wednesday, or Thursday, whichever comes first. This range of dates is necessary to avoid skipping trading in a week because Monday falls on a holiday.

Close Long (Sell) at the current daily price close of the DJIA each week when the calendar says the day is Friday. If there is no Friday in a week due to a holiday, hold until the next Friday.

Enter Short (Sell Short) never.

Starting with \$100 and reinvesting profits, total net profits, long only, for this Days of the Week strategy would have been \$13,006.50, assuming a fully invested strategy, reinvestment of profits, no transactions costs and no taxes. This would have been 239.05 percent greater than buy-and-hold. About 56.82 percent of the 2434 signals would have produced winning trades. Short selling, which was not included in this strategy, would have been made money from 1952 to 1987 but would have lost money since 11/30/87

The Equis International MetaStock® System Testing rules are written as follows:

Enter long: DayOfWeek()=opt1 OR
DayOfWeek()=opt1+1 OR
DayOfWeek()=opt1+2 OR
DayOfWeek()=opt1+3

Close long: DayOfWeek()=opt2

OPT1 Current value: 1
OPT2 Current value: 5

Decennial Pattern, Decennial Cycle

By tradition, each year is numbered. The Decennial Cycle is based on the observation that the digit that is at the end of the year marker may have something to do with stock price performance. This calendar study was pioneered by Edgar Lawrence Smith. (Smith, E. L. (1932), *Tides and the Affairs of Men,* New York: Macmillan (1959) and *Common Stocks and Business Cycles,* William-Frederick Press.) Anthony Gaubis contributed to the research.

A later study by Edson Gould, covering 89 years from 1881 through 1970, compiled the average tendencies for each year of the decade. As the chart by Ned Davis Research on page 205 shows, there has been a fairly steady and substantial declining trend from a top in the fourth quarter of year nine to a major market low in the middle of year two. There has been a brief but sharp rally in the third quarter of year two. Following that brief rally, stock prices have worked higher into year four. Year five has been strongly up without significant corrections. There have been moderate corrections in year six. Stock prices have moved modestly higher into the third quarter of year seven, then a sharp correction into year end. Year eight and the first three quarters of year nine have been strongly up again without significant corrections. From the fourth quarter of year nine, the pattern starts over again with a fairly steady

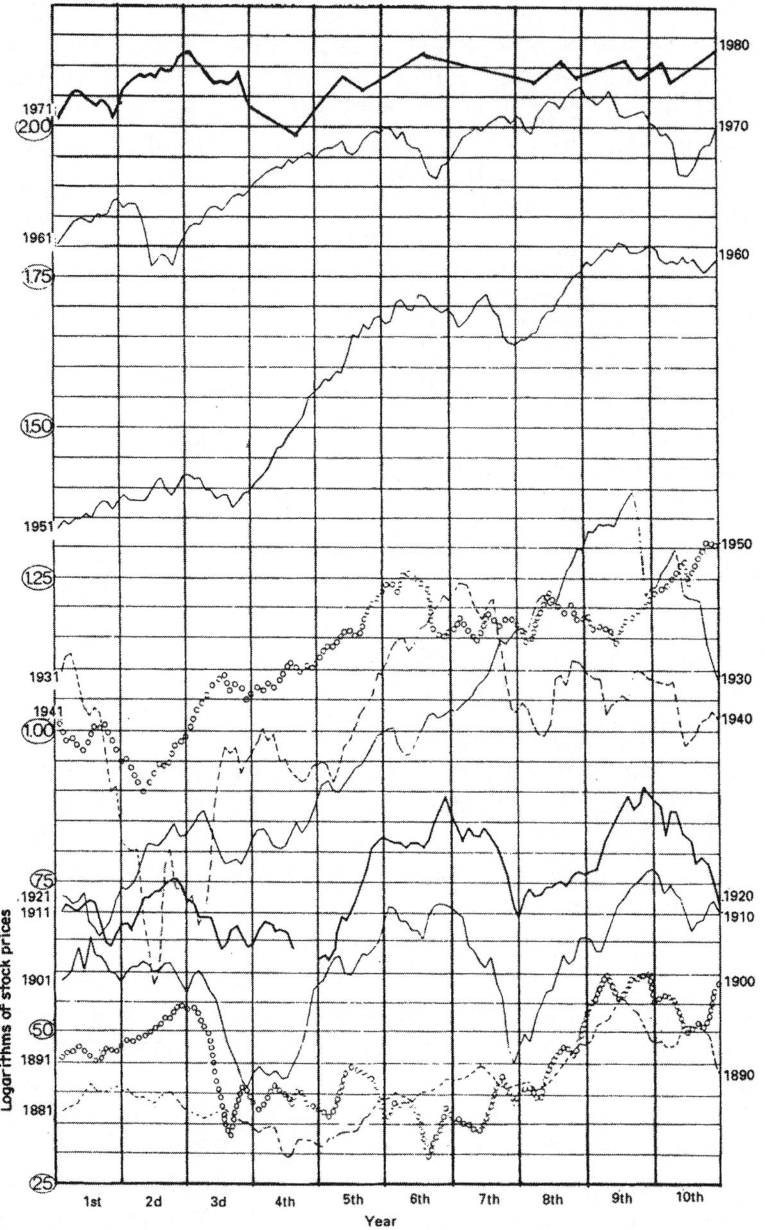

Original chart by Gould, Edson, *1974 Stock Market Forecast.* Adapted and updated 1974–1980 by Martin J. Pring. Reprinted with permission of Pring, Martin J., *Technical Analysis Explained: The Successful Investor's Guide to Spotting Investment Trends and Turning Points,* Fourth Edition, McGraw-Hill, 2002, 560 pages, page 379.

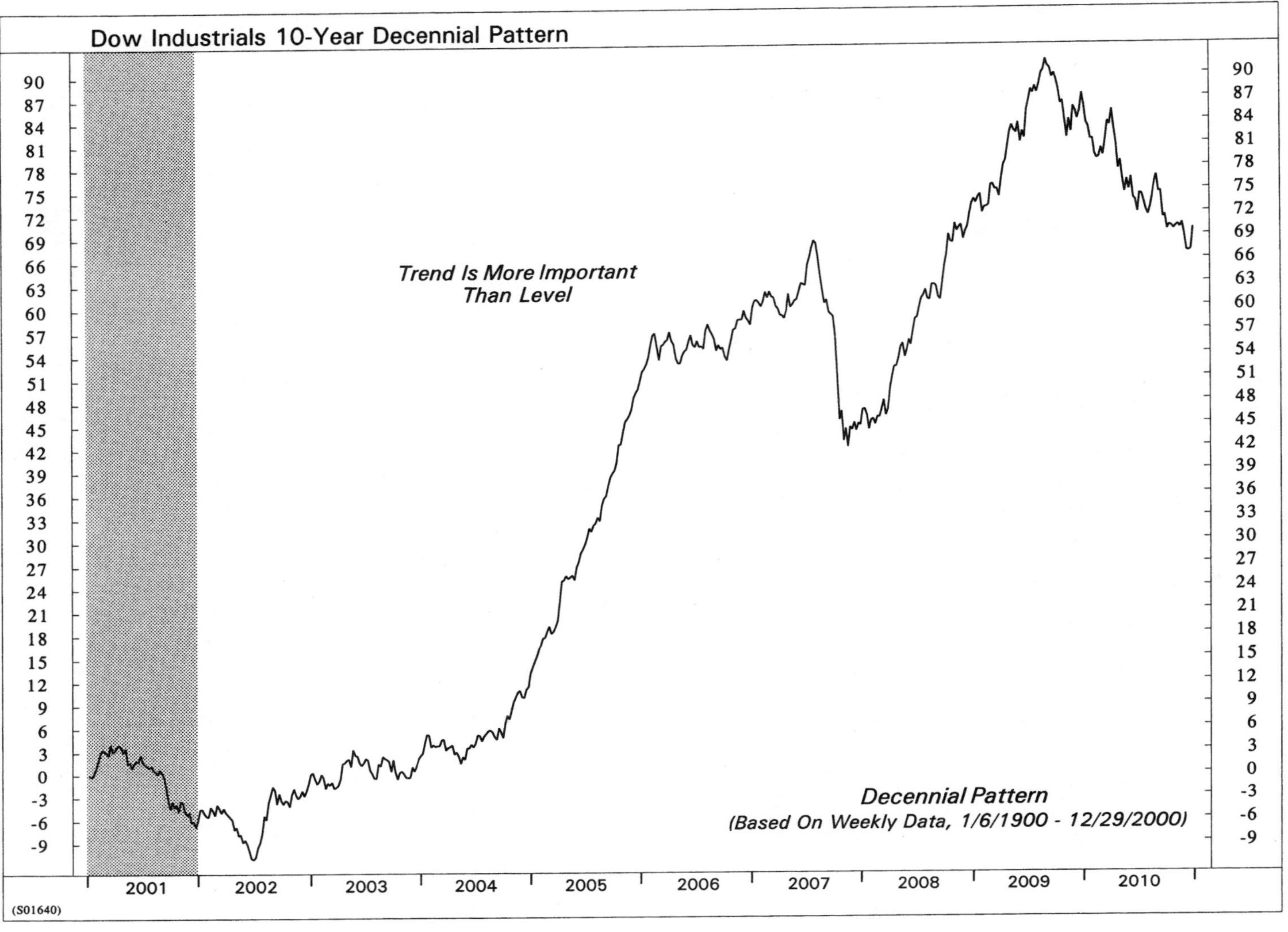

Chart by permission of Ned Davis Research

THE TEN-YEAR STOCK MARKET CYCLE

Annual % Change In Dow Jones Industrial Average
Year Of Decade

DECADES	1st	2nd	3rd	4th	5th	6th	7th	8th	9th	10th
1881-1890	3.0	– 2.9	– 8.5	–18.8	20.1	12.4	– 8.4	4.8	5.5	–14.1
1891-1900	17.6	– 6.6	–24.6	– 0.6	2.3	– 1.7	21.3	22.5	9.2	7.0
1901-1910	– 8.7	– 0.4	–23.6	41.7	38.2	– 1.9	–37.7	46.6	15.0	–18.0
1911-1920	0.5	7.6	–10.3	– 5.1	81.7	– 4.2	–21.7	10.5	30.5	–32.9
1921-1930	12.7	21.7	– 3.3	26.2	30.0	0.3	28.8	48.2	–17.2	–33.8
1931-1940	–52.7	–23.1	66.7	4.1	38.5	24.8	–32.8	28.1	– 2.9	–12.7
1941-1950	–15.4	7.6	13.8	12.1	26.6	– 8.1	2.2	– 2.1	12.9	17.6
1951-1960	14.4	8.4	– 3.8	44.0	20.8	2.3	–12.8	34.0	16.4	– 9.3
1961-1970	18.7	–10.8	17.0	14.6	10.9	–18.9	15.2	4.3	–15.2	4.8
1971-1980	6.1	14.6	–16.6	–27.6	38.3	17.9	–17.3	– 3.1	4.2	14.9
1981-1990	– 9.2	19.6	20.3	– 3.7	27.7	22.6	2.3	11.8	27.0	– 4.3
1991-2000	20.3	4.2	13.7	2.1	33.5	26.0	22.6	16.1	25.2	
Total % Change	**7%**	**40%**	**41%**	**89%**	**369%**	**72%**	**–38%**	**222%**	**111%**	**–81%**
Up Years	8	7	5	7	12	7	6	10	9	4
Down Years	4	5	7	5	0	5	6	2	3	7

Based on annual close
Cowles indices 1881–1885

Reprinted by permission of Yale Hirsch, *Stock Traders Almanac,* The Hirsch Organization, Inc., 184 Central Avenue, Old Tappan, NJ 07675, www.stocktradersalmanac.com.

and substantial declining trend to a low in the middle of year two. Note that these are only average tendencies of past performance and not strict laws of the market. Still, they might have had some value in preparing for the major market low in the middle of 1982, the sharp correction starting in the third quarter of 1987, and the substantial declining trends of 2000 into 2002.

The historical performance statistics for the Decennial Cycle are updated each year in Yale Hirsch's, *Stock Traders Almanac,* The Hirsch Organization, Inc., 184 Central Avenue, Old Tappan, NJ 07675, www.stocktradersalmanac.com. This *Almanac* provides annual updates on the Decennial Cycle as well as other curious and helpful calendar-based statistics updated each year.

Years that end in five, such as 2005, have been by far the best years for the Dow-Jones Industrial Average. The 5-year has been up 12 times in a row, up every decade since 1881. The 12 gains ranged from 2% to 82%, with a median gain of 29%.

Years that end in eight, such as 2008, have been the next best years for the Dow-Jones Industrials. The 8-year has been up 10 times out of 12 since 1881. The only exceptions to the rising trend of eight years were mildly declining years in 1948 and 1978, which lost only 2% and 3%, respectively. The median performance for years ending in eight is a gain of 14%.

The ninth year deserves honorable mention, up 75% of the time. The first year has been up two-thirds of the time.

Years that end in zero, such as 2000 and 2010, have been by far the worst years for the Dow-Jones Industrial Average. The zero year has been down eight times out of 12 since 1881, including most recently 1990 and 2000. The eight declines were in the range of 4% to 34%, with a median loss of 13%.

Years that end in three, such as 2003, have been the next worst years. The 3-year has been down seven times out of 12 since 1881. Three of the 7 down years have lost 17% to 25%. The median performance for years ending in three is a loss of 4%.

Years that end in seven, such as 2007, also have been relatively poor years for the Dow-Jones Industrial Average. The 7-year has been down half of the time (six times out of 12) since 1881. Four of these six down years have been real bears, losing 17% to 38%. The median performance for years ending in seven is a loss of 3%.

Years ending in four, six and two, in that order, have been more mixed, but net slightly positive on balance. The market has been up single digits, on average. These years have been up seven times out of 12.

DEMA

(See Double Exponential Moving Averages.)

Demand Index (DI)

The Demand Index is a momentum oscillator based on price change, volume, and volatility. It was designed by James Sibbet to be a leading indicator of price change. According to Thomas E. Aspray. ("Fine-Tuning the Demand Index," *Technical Analysis of Stocks & Commodities,* Vol. 4:4, pp. 141–143, www.traders.com), DI is based the ratio of Buying Pressure (BP) to Selling Pressure (SP). If BP is greater than SP, then the ratio is assigned a positive sign. But if SP is greater than BP, then the ratio is assigned a negative sign. If today's price rises, Buying Pressure (BP) is defined as total volume, while Selling Pressure (SP) is defined as today's total volume divided by today's adjusted change in price. On the other hand, if today's price declines, SP is defined as today's total volume, while BP is defined as today's total volume divided by today's adjusted change in price. Today's adjusted change in price is defined in two parts: first, compute the percentage price change from yesterday's close to today's close; second, multiply this percentage price change by three times today's volatility-adjusted price. Today's volatility-adjusted price is today's closing price divided by a 10-day average of price range. Price range is defined as the highest high minus the lowest low for the latest two trading days.

Fortunately, the complex formula for DI is preprogrammed in the MetaStock® software exactly the same as Sibbet's original, except for different *y*-axis scaling from +100 to −100. (The original was plotted on a scale labeled +0 at the top, 1 in the middle, and −0 at the bottom.)

DI is interpreted in standard momentum oscillator fashion. DI crossing zero confirms price trend change. More subjectively, a divergence between DI and price suggests a change in trend. Extreme high readings in DI indicate very strong demand, and in that case, further rally attempts are probable. When DI hovers near zero for a long time, demand and supply have reached a balance, and minor price fluctuations do not last long or amount to much.

Indicator Strategy Example for the Demand Index (DI)

Historical data shows that the simple Demand Index crossing zero would have produced positive results, mainly on the long side. The short side would have lost money over the past 18-year bull market. Based on the number of shares traded each day on the New York Stock Exchange and the daily prices for the Dow-Jones Industrial Average for 72 years from 1928 to 2000, we found that the following parameters would have produced a positive result on a purely mechanical trend-following signal basis with no subjectivity, no sophisticated technical analysis, and no judgement:

Enter Long (Buy) at the current daily price close of the DJIA when the current Demand Index is greater than zero.

Close Long (Sell) at the current daily price close of the DJIA when the current Demand Index is less than zero.

Enter Short (Sell Short) at the current daily price close of the DJIA when the current Demand Index is less than zero.

Close Short (Cover) at the current daily price close of the DJIA when the current Demand Index is greater than zero.

Starting with $100 and reinvesting profits, total net profits, long and short, for this Demand Index strategy would have been $83,643.62, assuming a fully invested strategy, reinvestment of profits, no transactions costs and no taxes. This would have been 1,728.18 percent greater than buy-and-hold. Only about 31.30 percent of the 1818 signals would have produced winning trades, and the average open trade would have lasted 14.45 calendar days on average. Short selling, which was included in this strategy, would have lost money since 1982.

The Equis International MetaStock® System Testing rules are written as follows:

Enter long: DI()>0

Close long: DI()<0

Enter short: DI()<0

Close short: DI()>0

Dev-Stop, Kase Adaptive Dev-Stop

(See Kase Indicators.)

DiNapoli Levels, Fibonacci Profit Objectives

(See Fibonacci Numbers.) Fibonacci numbers can be applied to price in an attempt to project support, resistance, and objectives. Also, see www.coast@fibtrader.com/, or Coast Investment Software, 8851 Albatross Dr., Huntington Beach, CA 92646, (714) 968-1978.

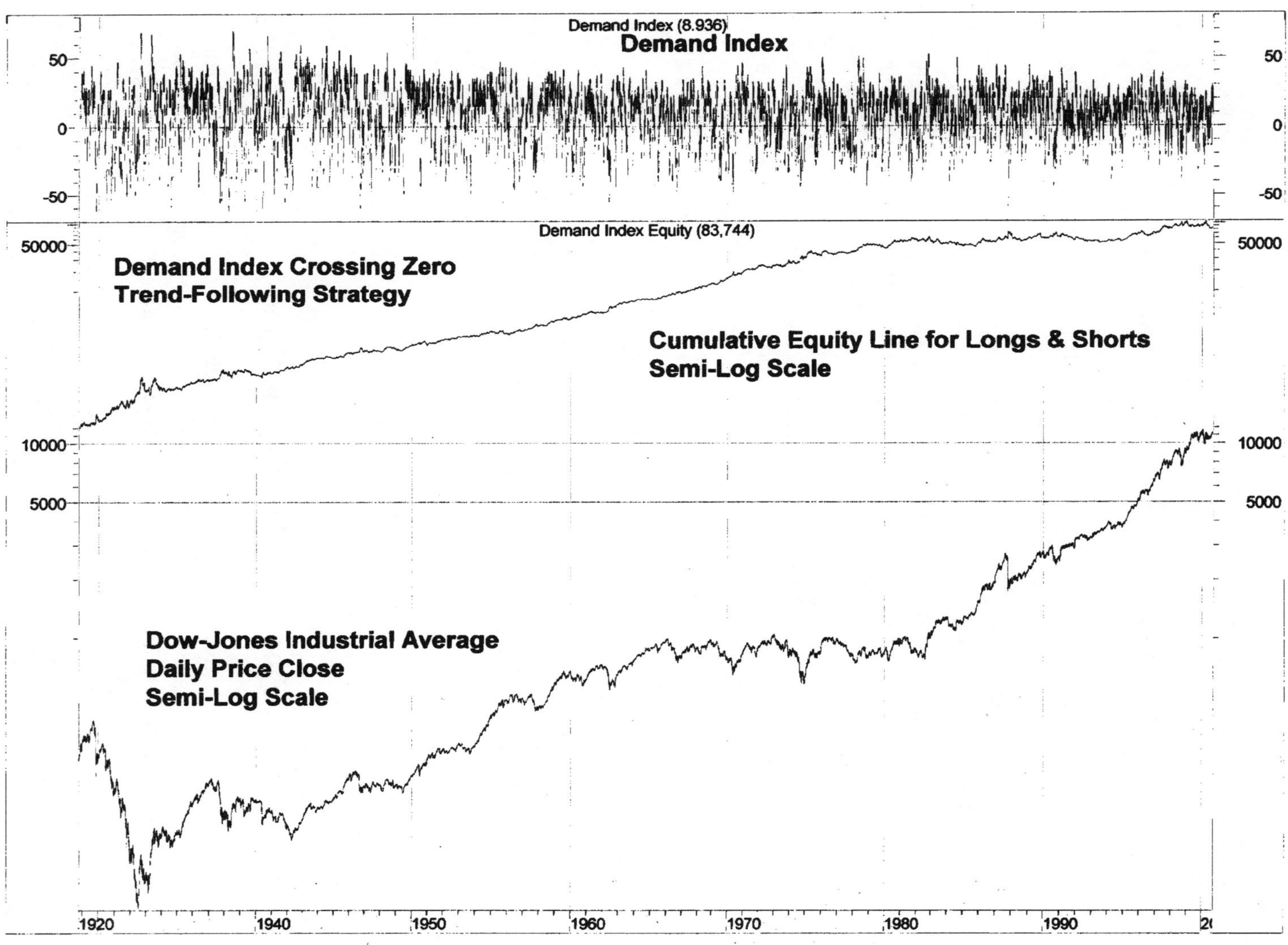
Demand Index (8.936)
Demand Index
50
0
-50
Demand Index Equity (83,744)
50000
Demand Index Crossing Zero
Trend-Following Strategy
Cumulative Equity Line for Longs & Shorts
Semi-Log Scale
10000
5000
Dow-Jones Industrial Average
Daily Price Close
Semi-Log Scale
1920
1940
1950
1960
1970
1980
1990

Demand Index

Total net profit	83643.62	Open position value	3978.73	Net Profit/Buy&Hold %	1728.18
Percent gain/loss	83643.62	Annual percent gain/loss	1161.89	Annual Net %/B&H %	1728.31
Initial investment	100	Interest earned	0		
Current position	Long	Date position entered	8/2/00		
Buy/Hold profit	4575.25	Days in test	26276	# of days per trade	14.45
Buy/Hold pct gain/loss	4575.25	Annual B/H pct gain/loss	63.55		
Total closed trades	1818	Commissions paid	0		
Avg profit per trade	43.82	Avg Win/Avg Loss ratio	2.7		
Total long trades	909	Total short trades	909	Long Win Trade %	34.32
Winning long trades	312	Winning short trades	257	Short Win Trade %	28.27
Total winning trades	569	Total losing trades	1249	Total Win Trade %	31.30
Amount of winning trades	423115.28	Amount of losing trades	−343450.31	Net Profit Margin %	10.39
Average win	743.61	Average loss	−274.98	Average P. Margin %	46.01
Largest win	13907.58	Largest loss	−4294.28	% Net/(Win + Loss)	52.81
Average length of win	24.38	Average length of loss	4.78	(Win − Loss)/Loss %	410.04
Longest winning trade	112	Longest losing trade	24	(Win − Loss)/Loss %	366.67
Most consecutive wins	5	Most consecutive losses	15	(Win − Loss)/Loss %	−66.67
Total bars out	10	Average length out	10		
Longest out period	10				
System close drawdown	0	Profit/Loss index	19.58	% Net Profit/SODD	41821810.00
System open drawdown	−0.2	Reward/Risk index	100	(Net P. − SODD)/Net P.	100.00
Max open trade drawdown	−4294.28	Buy/Hold index	1815.14	% SODD/Net Profit	0.00

In the Equis MetaStock® "System Report" (profit and loss summary statistics), the *Total net profit* is the sum of profits minus the sum of losses, including open positions marked to the market. In contrast, the *Amount of Winning Trades* is the sum of realized profits (the total of all gains on closed-out trades only, excluding any open positions). Similarly, the *Amount of Losing Trades* is the sum of realized losses (the total of all losses on closed-out trades only, excluding any open positions). *System close drawdown* is the largest decline in the cumulative equity line below the initial investment, based on closed-out positions only. *System open drawdown (SODD)* is the largest decline in the cumulative equity line below the initial investment when a position is open. *Max open trade drawdown* is the largest decline in the cumulative equity line below the trade entry price during the worst single trade. The *Profit/Loss Index* is a complex calculation that relates the Amount of Winning Trades to the Amount of Losing Trades on a scale of −100 (worst possible performance) to +100 (best possible performance), with zero representing profits equal to losses. *Reward/Risk Index* is the Total net profit minus System open drawdown. The resulting difference is then divided by the Total net profit. The *Buy/Hold Index* is the Total net profit minus the buy-and-hold strategy's net profit. The resulting difference is then divided by the buy-and-hold net profit. In this exercise, initial equity is assumed to be $100. Both long and short positions are taken unless otherwise noted. Trades are executed at the closing price on the signal date. Transaction costs, interest expenses, and margins are not included in the statistics.

Directional Movement Index (DMI)

The Directional Movement Index (DMI) is a unique filtered momentum indicator published by J. Welles Wilder, Jr., in his 1978 book *New Concepts in Technical Trading Systems* (Trend Research, PO Box 128, McLeansville, NC 27301). DMI is a rather complex trend-following indicator. Wilder has asserted that markets exhibit strong trends only about 30% of the time. To avoid the unprofitable frustration of attempting to follow trends in a sideways market, Wilder devised DMI as a filter that permits entry into trades only when markets exhibit significant trending characteristics. When a market fails to exhibit significant trending or directional behavior, DMI keeps investors out of the market.

By use of exponential moving averages and ratios, DMI tames high, low, and close price data down to a scale that ranges from zero to 100. Directional Movement (DM) is defined as the largest part of the current period's price range that lies outside the previous period's price range. Thus,

$$PDM = H - Hp$$
$$MDM = Lp - L$$

where

PDM = positive or plus DM.
MDM = negative or minus DM.
H = the highest price of the current period.
Hp = the highest price of the previous period.
Lp = the lowest price of the previous period.
L = the lowest price of the current period.

The *lesser* of the above two values is reset to equal zero. That is, if PDM > MDM, then MDM is reset to equal zero. Or, if MDM > PDM, then PDM is reset to equal zero. Also, any negative number is reset to equal zero. Therefore, on an inside day (with lower high and higher low), both PDM and MDM are negative numbers, so both are reset to equal zero.

True Range (TR) is defined as the largest value of the following three possibilities:

$$TR = H - L$$
$$TR = H - Cp$$
$$TR = Cp - L$$

where Cp is the closing price of the previous period.

Before proceeding, the PDM, MDM and TR are smoothed with an exponential smoothing constant. Wilder suggests an exponential smoothing constant of 1/14, or

0.07143, which is roughly equivalent to a 27-day simple moving average. This smoothing is used in all of the following calculations.

The Positive Directional Indicator (PDI) is the exponentially Smoothed Plus Directional Movement divided by the exponentially Smoothed True Range. Thus,

$$PDI = SPDM/STR = \text{Smoothed PDM/Smoothed TR}$$

Remember, when Lp − L is greater than H − Hp, then PDM is reset to zero, so PDI must decline.

The Minus Directional Indicator (MDI) is defined by the following exponentially smoothed data:

$$MDI = SMDM/STR = \text{Smoothed MDM/Smoothed TR}$$

Remember, when Lp − L is less than H − Hp, then MDM is reset to zero, so MDI must decline.

Next, Directional Movement (DX) is defined as one hundred times the absolute value of the daily difference of PDI *minus* MDI divided by the sum of PDI *plus* MDI:

$$DX = 100 * | PDI - MDI | /(PDI + MDI)$$

DX must be always contained in a range from zero (representing equality of PDI and MDI) to 100 (representing all of one and none of the other).

Average directional movement (ADX) is a *n*-period exponential smoothing of DX. (Again, Wilder suggests the same exponential smoothing constant, 1/14 or 0.07143.)

Directional Movement Rating (ADXR) is defined as the average of today's ADX plus the ADX of 14 days ago, that is, the current ADX plus the 14-day-old ADX readings divided by two.

Wilder suggests that high and rising levels on ADX and its average, ADXR, indicate a healthy and forceful major trend, either up or down. Low and falling levels on ADX and its average, ADXR, indicate a trendless market, going nowhere. As a general guide, ADXR readings less than 20 might indicate a trendless market, while ADXR readings greater than 25 might indicate a market that is trending.

Indicator Strategy Example for the Directional Movement Index

Historical data shows that Directional Movement can be effective on both the long and short sides, but particularly on the long side. Based on the daily prices for the Dow-Jones Industrial Average for 72 years from 1928 to 2000, we found that the following parameters would have produced a significantly positive result on a purely mechanical trend-following signal basis with no subjectivity, no sophisticated technical analysis, and no judgement:

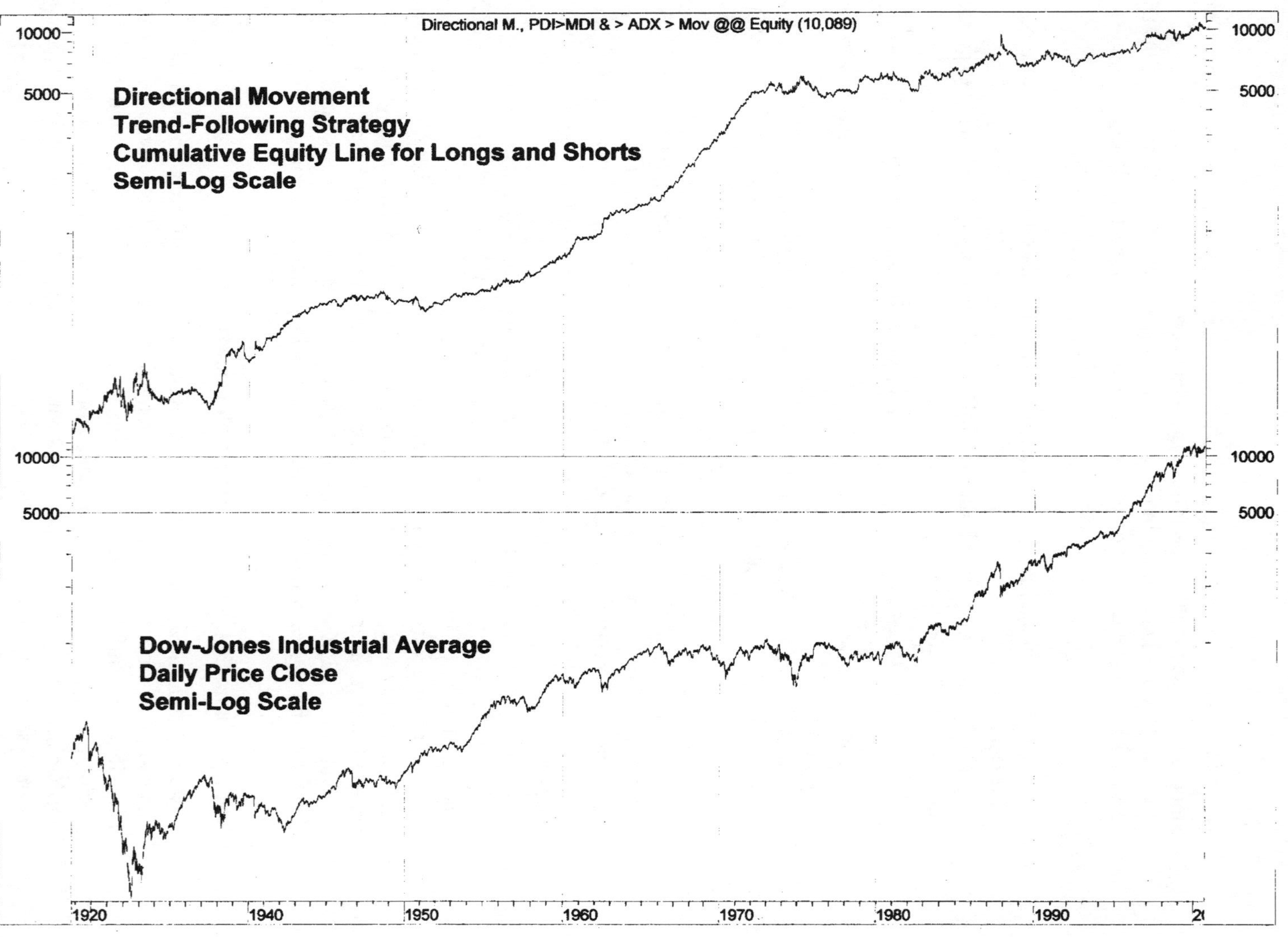
Directional M., PDI>MDI & > ADX > Mov @@ Equity (10,089)
Directional Movement
Trend-Following Strategy
Cumulative Equity Line for Longs and Shorts
Semi-Log Scale
Dow-Jones Industrial Average
Daily Price Close
Semi-Log Scale
10000
5000
10000
5000
1920
1940
1950
1960
1970
1980
1990
2(

Directional Movement

Total net profit	9988.57	Open position value	N/A	Net Profit/Buy&Hold %	118.32
Percent gain/loss	9988.57	Annual percent gain/loss	138.75	Annual Net %/B&H %	118.33
Initial investment	100	Interest earned	0		
Current position	Out	Date position entered	9/7/00		
Buy/Hold profit	4575.25	Days in test	26276	# of days per trade	6.93
Buy/Hold pct gain/loss	4575.25	Annual B/H pct gain/loss	63.55		
Total closed trades	3790	Commissions paid	0		
Avg profit per trade	2.64	Avg Win/Avg Loss ratio	1.64		
Total long trades	2030	Total short trades	1760	Long Win Trade %	44.43
Winning long trades	902	Winning short trades	685	Short Win Trade %	38.92
Total winning trades	1587	Total losing trades	2203	Total Win Trade %	41.87
Amount of winning trades	65866.3	Amount of losing trades	−55877.76	Net Profit Margin %	8.20
Average win	41.5	Average loss	−25.36	Average P. Margin %	24.14
Largest win	1052.32	Largest loss	−486.09	% Net/(Win + Loss)	36.81
Average length of win	5.12	Average length of loss	2.87	(Win − Loss)/Loss %	78.40
Longest winning trade	20	Longest losing trade	12	(Win − Loss)/Loss %	66.67
Most consecutive wins	8	Most consecutive losses	13	(Win − Loss)/Loss %	−38.46
Total bars out	10888	Average length out	3.13		
Longest out period	9				
System close drawdown	−0.05	Profit/Loss index	15.16	% Net Profit/SODD	3567346.43
System open drawdown	−0.28	Reward/Risk index	100	(Net P. − SODD)/Net P.	100.00
Max open trade drawdown	−486.09	Buy/Hold index	118.32	% SODD/Net Profit	0.00

In the Equis MetaStock® "System Report" (profit and loss summary statistics), the *Total net profit* is the sum of profits minus the sum of losses, including open positions marked to the market. In contrast, the *Amount of Winning Trades* is the sum of realized profits (the total of all gains on closed-out trades only, excluding any open positions). Similarly, the *Amount of Losing Trades* is the sum of realized losses (the total of all losses on closed-out trades only, excluding any open positions). *System close drawdown* is the largest decline in the cumulative equity line below the initial investment, based on closed-out positions only. *System open drawdown (SODD)* is the largest decline in the cumulative equity line below the initial investment when a position is open. *Max open trade drawdown* is the largest decline in the cumulative equity line below the trade entry price during the worst single trade. The *Profit/Loss Index* is a complex calculation that relates the Amount of Winning Trades to the Amount of Losing Trades on a scale of −100 (worst possible performance) to +100 (best possible performance), with zero representing profits equal to losses. *Reward/Risk Index* is the Total net profit minus System open drawdown. The resulting difference is then divided by the Total net profit. The *Buy/Hold Index* is the Total net profit minus the buy-and-hold strategy's net profit. The resulting difference is then divided by the buy-and-hold net profit. In this exercise, initial equity is assumed to be $100. Both long and short positions are taken unless otherwise noted. Trades are executed at the closing price on the signal date. Transaction costs, interest expenses, and margins are not included in the statistics.

Enter Long (Buy) at the current daily price close of the Dow-Jones Industrial Average when PDI (2) is greater than MDI (2) and ADX (2) is greater than its own 2-day exponential moving average.

Close Long (Sell) at the current daily price close of the Dow-Jones Industrial Average when PDI (2) is less than MDI (2) or ADX (2) is less than its own 2-day exponential moving average.

Enter Short (Sell Short) at the current daily price close of the Dow-Jones Industrial Average when PDI (2) is less than MDI (2) and ADX (2) is greater than its own 2-day exponential moving average.

Close Short (Cover) at the current daily price close of the Dow-Jones Industrial Average when PDI (2) is greater than MDI (2) or ADX (2) is less than its own 2-day exponential moving average.

Starting with $100 and reinvesting profits, total net profits for this Directional Movement strategy would have been $9,988.57, assuming a fully invested strategy, reinvestment of profits, no transactions costs and no taxes. This is 118.32 percent better than buy-and-hold. Short selling, which was included in this strategy, would have lost money since October, 1987, but nevertheless would have been profitable over the entire 72-years as a whole.

The Equis International MetaStock® System Testing rules are written as follows:

Enter long: PDI(opt1)>MDI(opt1) AND
ADX(opt1)>Mov(ADX(opt1),opt1,E)

Close long: PDI(opt1)<MDI(opt1) OR
ADX(opt1)<Mov(ADX(opt1),opt1,E)

Enter short: PDI(opt1)<MDI(opt1) AND
ADX(opt1)>Mov(ADX(opt1),opt1,E)

Close short: PDI(opt1)>MDI(opt1) OR
ADX(opt1)<Mov(ADX(opt1),opt1,E)

OPT1 Current value: 2

Low Average Directional Movement (ADX): The Calm Before the Storm

Dan Chesler observes a tendency toward marked contraction in volatility and diminution of volume immediately before a breakout of chart pattern boundaries. Chesler uses ADX (with Wilder's suggested exponential smoothing constant of 1/14 or

0.07143) as a tool for identifying such junctures. ADX levels below 15 indicate an absence of trend and a conspicuous decrease in volatility—the calm before the storm—which tends to precede trending moves in both bull and bear markets, in both stocks and commodities, and in both daily and intraday charts. Adapted with permission of Daniel L. Chesler, CTA, CMT, 2075 Polo Gardens Drive, No. 302, Wellington, Florida 33414, phone (561) 793-6867, e-mail: dan@crowd-control.com.

Divergence Analysis

Divergence analysis offers the potential for timely signals of impending trend change. But not all divergences are followed by trend change, and response times may be delayed. In current practice, a wide variety of indexes and indicators are compared against one another to look for technical divergences.

Studies suggest that the larger the number of logically selected technical indicators that diverge, the more likely a trend reversal. Conversely, the larger the number of indicators that confirm an existing trend, the more likely that trend is to continue.

A technical divergence is present when the price of any instrument (stock, index, or contract) makes a significant price movement unconfirmed or unaccompanied by a similar movement in a logically selected companion indicator.

For example, when the Dow-Jones Industrial Average makes a new high but the Dow-Jones Transportation Average and the cumulative Daily Advance-Decline Line do not confirm this strength by making new highs, then negative divergences are present, and these could have bearish implications for the near future. Conversely, if the Industrials make a new low and the Transports and A-D Line do not confirm this weakness by making new lows, then positive divergences are present, and these could have bullish implications for the immediate future.

Indeed, in narrow and rigorous chi-squared statistical testing, David A. Glickstein and Rolf Wubbels ("Dow Theory is Alive and Well!", *Journal of Portfolio Management,* Spring 1983) concluded that daily relationships from 1971 through 1980 between the Dow Jones Industrials and Transports and the cumulative Daily Advance-Decline Line were not random but instead were statistically significant.

Independently, Kalish found similar divergences that also were highly statistically significant, beyond the 0.005 level, so the probability is less is than 5 in 1000 that the actual observed outcome was due to random chance alone. This also means, of course, that it is more than 99.5% certain than these relationships did not occur by chance. (See Kalish, Joseph E., "Divergence Analysis: Several Empirical Tests," *Market Technicians Association Journal,* May 1986.) Kalish sampled weekly data from 1961 through 1980 to identify divergences between the Dow-Jones Industrial Average, the Dow-Jones Transports, the New York Stock Exchange Cumulative Daily Advance-Decline Line, the 20 Most Active Stocks, the Cumulative Weekly Advance-

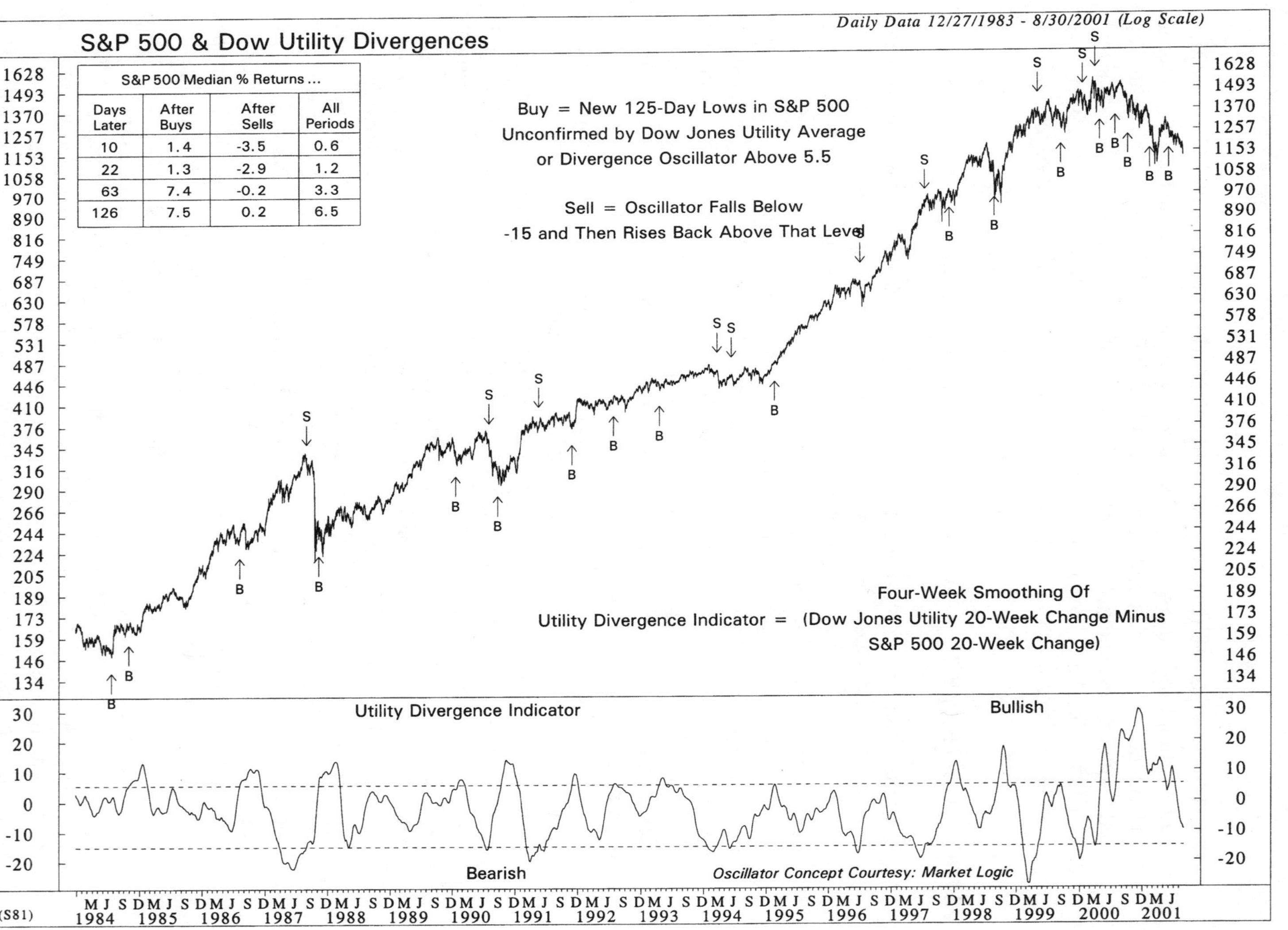

S&P 500 Median % Returns ...			
Days Later	After Buys	After Sells	All Periods
10	1.4	-3.5	0.6
22	1.3	-2.9	1.2
63	7.4	-0.2	3.3
126	7.5	0.2	6.5

Chart by permission of Ned Davis Research

Decline Line, and 5% and 10% reversals of Trendline's Percentage of Stocks Above Their Own 30-Week Moving Averages. Kalish's composite chi-squared test showed that the greater the number of indicators confirming or diverging, the more likely it is that the market will move in the direction expected by these confirming or diverging indicators.

A Utility Divergence Indicator was developed by the Market Logic newsletter. It is computed and interpreted in the following seven steps.

1. Using weekly data, calculate 20-week percentage rates of change for the S&P 500 Composite Stock Price Index and the Dow-Jones Utility Average.
2. Subtract the S&P 500 rate of change, from the Dow-Jones Utility Average rate of change.
3. Smooth that difference with a 4-week moving average.
4. Plot that smoothing.
5. Draw horizontal signal lines at 5.5 and −15.
6. Buy the S&P 500 when the S&P 500 makes a new 125-day low but the Utility Average does not make a new 125-day low, or when the Utility Divergence Oscillator rises above 5.5.
7. Sell when the Utility Divergence Indicator falls below −15 and then rises above −15. As the chart shows, this Utility Divergence Indicator gave profitable signals in the past.

Donchian's 4-Week Rule

This rule is a specific form of the more general *Price Channel Trading Range Breakout Rule,* where the period length is set at four weeks. Buy when the current price high rises above the highest price high over the most recent four weeks by the minimum unit of price measurement. Sell when the current price low falls below the lowest price low over the previous four weeks by the minimum unit of price measurement.

Double Exponential Moving Averages (DEMA)

DEMA was designed to respond faster than EMA. DEMA is a composite implementation of single and double Exponential Moving Averages (EMAs) producing another EMA with less lag than either of the original two EMAs. DEMA was introduced by Patrick G. Mulloy in 1994, "Smoothing Data With Faster Moving Averages," *Technical Analysis of Stocks & Commodities* magazine, V. 12:1, www.traders.com.

In our independent observations, at short period lengths, DEMA does appear to respond more effectively to changing new data than does an ordinary EMA. At longer period lengths, however, DEMA responds much less effectively than the equivalent length EMA. As the table shows, DEMA underperforms EMA at period lengths of 23 days and higher. Therefore, DEMA should not be assumed to be a substitute for any other moving average. Rather, DEMA may best be considered to be an unfamiliar new tool to be approached with appropriately cautious respect.

The following table shows a comparison of the signal performance of a standard moving average crossover rule using DEMA and an ordinary EMA of the same length, expressed in trading days, as measured against the S&P 500 Composite Stock Price Index futures *CSI Perpetual Contract* from 4/21/82 to 12/29/00. The data reflects long trades only.

Comparison of Signal Performance

DEMA Length in days	*Total Net Profit*	*# of Trades Total*	*Win*	*Lose*	*% Wins*	*Avg Win/ Avg Loss*
2	421.17	1243	590	653	47.47	1.49
3	545.79	1057	494	563	46.74	1.67
4	516.49	945	425	520	44.97	1.78
5	399.46	868	383	485	44.12	1.79
6	339.45	813	351	462	43.17	1.86
7	240.32	762	319	443	41.86	1.84
8	276.58	711	296	415	41.63	1.93
9	277.35	664	285	379	42.92	1.81
10	239.35	631	257	374	40.73	1.97
11	198.83	594	238	356	40.07	1.97
12	192.75	568	223	345	39.26	2.08
13	202.92	543	208	335	38.31	2.21
14	218.71	518	198	320	38.22	2.29
15	232.26	513	200	313	38.99	2.23
16	198.51	504	191	313	37.90	2.25
17	180.76	490	185	305	37.76	2.21
18	146.84	483	180	303	37.27	2.17
19	133.69	471	174	297	36.94	2.20
20	137.85	452	165	287	36.50	2.27
21	158.59	440	160	280	36.36	2.36
22	129.72	437	155	282	35.47	2.37
23	101.30	435	155	280	35.63	2.26
24	93.91	426	147	279	34.51	2.34
25	68.51	428	142	286	33.18	2.37

Indicator Strategy Example for DEMA

Based on a 18-year file of daily data for the entire history of the S&P 500 Composite Stock Price Index futures *CSI Perpetual Contract* from 4/21/82 to 12/29/00 collected from www.csi.com, we found that the following parameters would have produced a positive result on a purely mechanical signal basis with no subjectivity, no sophisticated technical analysis, and no judgement:

Enter Long (Buy) at the current daily price close of the S&P 500 Composite Stock Price Index futures *CSI Perpetual Contract* when that price close is greater than the 3-day DEMA, signifying a short-term price uptrend.

Close Long (Sell) at the current daily price close of the S&P 500 Composite Stock Price Index futures *CSI Perpetual Contract* when that price close is less than the 3-day DEMA, signifying a short-term price downtrend.

Enter Short (Sell Short) never.

Comparison of Signal Performance

EMA Length in days	*Total Net Profit*	*# of Trades Total*	*Win*	*Lose*	*% Wins*	*Avg Win/ Avg Loss*
2	311.97	917	382	535	41.66	2.01
3	260.03	768	311	457	40.49	2.06
4	182.53	669	261	408	39.01	2.09
5	139.26	606	226	380	37.29	2.15
6	136.28	563	208	355	36.94	2.17
7	115.31	538	195	343	36.25	2.22
8	116.75	508	179	329	35.24	2.32
9	105.67	480	161	319	33.54	2.45
10	106.24	454	145	309	31.94	2.63
11	87.03	443	134	309	30.25	2.77
12	76.94	422	122	300	28.91	2.90
13	61.87	415	117	298	28.19	2.93
14	67.75	395	111	284	28.10	3.01
15	91.22	376	109	267	28.99	3.02
16	121.09	359	102	257	28.41	3.27
17	105.64	359	104	255	28.97	3.10
18	117.50	348	100	248	28.74	3.20
19	108.23	343	99	244	28.86	3.15
20	111.52	334	95	239	28.44	3.23
21	115.76	329	93	236	28.27	3.29
22	123.31	318	89	229	27.99	3.33
23	144.92	305	86	219	28.20	3.41
24	140.92	299	85	214	28.43	3.34
25	168.71	290	80	210	27.59	3.59

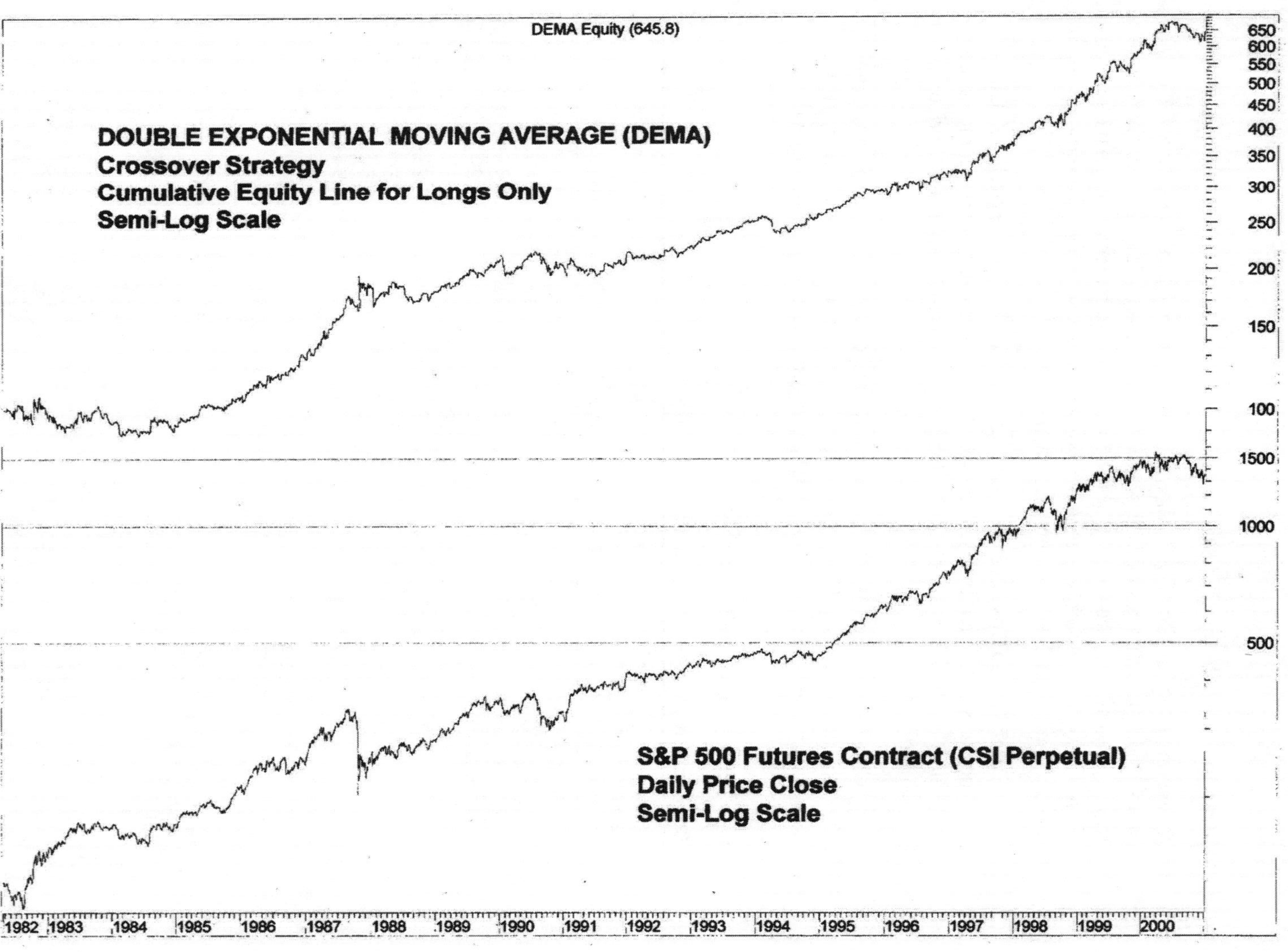
DEMA Equity (645.8)
DOUBLE EXPONENTIAL MOVING AVERAGE (DEMA)
Crossover Strategy
Cumulative Equity Line for Longs Only
Semi-Log Scale
S&P 500 Futures Contract (CSI Perpetual)
Daily Price Close
Semi-Log Scale
650
600
550
500
450
400
350
300
250
200
150
100
1500
1000
500
1982
1983
1984
1985
1986
1987
1988
1989
1990
1991
1992
1993
1994
1995
1996
1997
1998
1999
2000

DEMA Crossover, 3 days

Total net profit	545.79	Open position value	N/A	Net Profit/Buy&Hold %	−47.24
Percent gain/loss	545.79	Annual percent gain/loss	29.18	Annual Net %/B&H %	−47.23
Initial investment	100	Interest earned	0		
Current position	Out	Date position entered	12/28/00		
Buy/Hold profit	1034.49	Days in test	6828	# of days per trade	6.46
Buy/Hold pct gain/loss	1034.49	Annual B/H pct gain/loss	55.3		
Total closed trades	1057	Commissions paid	0		
Avg profit per trade	0.52	Avg Win/Avg Loss ratio	1.67		
Total long trades	1057	Total short trades	0	Long Win Trade %	46.74
Winning long trades	494	Winning short trades	0	Short Win Trade %	#DIV/0!
Total winning trades	494	Total losing trades	563	Total Win Trade %	46.74
Amount of winning trades	1708.35	Amount of losing trades	−1162.56	Net Profit Margin %	19.01
Average win	3.46	Average loss	−2.06	Average P. Margin %	25.36
Largest win	31.13	Largest loss	−22.62	% Net/(Win + Loss)	15.83
Average length of win	4.02	Average length of loss	2.44	(Win − Loss)/Loss %	64.75
Longest winning trade	9	Longest losing trade	7	(Win − Loss)/Loss %	28.57
Most consecutive wins	7	Most consecutive losses	10	(Win − Loss)/Loss %	−30.00
Total bars out	3481	Average length out	3.29		
Longest out period	10				
System close drawdown	−11.96	Profit/Loss index	31.95	% Net Profit/SODD	4563.46
System open drawdown	−11.96	Reward/Risk index	97.86	(Net P. − SODD)/Net P.	97.81
Max open trade drawdown	−22.62	Buy/Hold index	−47.24	% SODD/Net Profit	−2.19

In the Equis MetaStock® "System Report" (profit and loss summary statistics), the *Total net profit* is the sum of profits minus the sum of losses, including open positions marked to the market. In contrast, the *Amount of Winning Trades* is the sum of realized profits (the total of all gains on closed-out trades only, excluding any open positions). Similarly, the *Amount of Losing Trades* is the sum of realized losses (the total of all losses on closed-out trades only, excluding any open positions). *System close drawdown* is the largest decline in the cumulative equity line below the initial investment, based on closed-out positions only. *System open drawdown (SODD)* is the largest decline in the cumulative equity line below the initial investment when a position is open. *Max open trade drawdown* is the largest decline in the cumulative equity line below the trade entry price during the worst single trade. The *Profit/Loss Index* is a complex calculation that relates the Amount of Winning Trades to the Amount of Losing Trades on a scale of −100 (worst possible performance) to +100 (best possible performance), with zero representing profits equal to losses. *Reward/Risk Index* is the Total net profit minus System open drawdown. The resulting difference is then divided by the Total net profit. The *Buy/Hold Index* is the Total net profit minus the buy-and-hold strategy's net profit. The resulting difference is then divided by the buy-and-hold net profit. In this exercise, initial equity is assumed to be $100. Both long and short positions are taken unless otherwise noted. Trades are executed at the closing price on the signal date. Transaction costs, interest expenses, and margins are not included in the statistics.

Starting with $100 and reinvesting profits, total net profits for this DEMA trend-following strategy would have been $545.79, assuming a fully invested strategy, reinvestment of profits, no transactions costs and no taxes. This would have been 47.24 percent less than buy-and-hold. No short selling would have been profitable, and no short selling was included in the strategy. This long-only DEMA would have given profitable buy signals 46.74% of the time. Trading would have been very active at one trade every 6.46 calendar days.

The Equis International MetaStock® System Testing rules are written as follows:

Enter long: CLOSE > Dema(CLOSE,opt1)

Close long: CLOSE < Dema(CLOSE,opt1)

OPT1 Current value: 3

Dow Theory*

The Dow Theory is a major corner stone of technical analysis. It is one of the oldest and best known methods used to determine the major trend of stock prices. It was derived from the writings of Charles H. Dow from 1900 to 1902 published in the daily newspaper he founded, *The Wall Street Journal.* Dow's Theory was further refined by analysts and writers S. A. Nelson, William P. Hamilton, and Robert Rhea in the first few decades of the 20th century.

Seven Basic Principles of Dow's Theory:

1. Everything is discounted by the price Averages, specifically, the Dow-Jones Industrial Average and the Dow-Jones Transportation Average. Since the Averages reflect all information, experience, knowledge, opinions, and activities of all stock market investors, everything that could possibly affect the demand for or supply of stocks is discounted by the Averages.
2. There are three trends in stock prices. The Primary Tide is the major long-term trend. But no trend moves in a straight line for long, and Secondary Reactions are the intermediate-term corrections that interrupt and move in an opposite direction against the Primary Tide. Ripples are the very minor day-to-day fluctuations that are of concern only to short-term traders and not at all to Dow Theorists.
3. *Primary Tides going up,* also known as *Bull Markets,* usually have three up moves in stock prices. The first move up is the result of far-sighted investors accumulating stocks at a time when business is slow but anticipated to improve. The second move up is a result of investors buying stocks in reaction

to improved fundamental business conditions and increasing corporate earnings. The final up move occurs when the general public finally notices that all the financial news is good. During the final up move, speculation runs rampant.

4. *Primary Tides going down,* also known as *Bear Markets,* usually have three down moves. The first move down occurs when far-sighted investors sell based on their experienced judgement that high valuations and booming corporate earnings are unsustainable. The second move down reflects panic as a now fearful public dumps at any price the same stock they just recently bought at much higher prices. The final move down results from distress selling and the need to raise cash.
5. The two Averages must confirm each other. To signal a Primary Tide Bull Market major trend, both Averages must rise above their respective highs of previous upward Secondary Reactions. To signal a Primary Tide Bear Market major trend, both the Dow-Jones Industrial Average and the Dow-Jones Transportation Average must drop below their respective lows of previous Secondary Reactions. A move to a new high or low by just one Average alone is not meaningful. Also, it is not uncommon for one Average to signal a change in trend before the other. The Dow Theory does not stipulate any time limit on trend confirmation by both Averages.
6. Only end-of-day, closing prices on the Averages are considered. Price movements during the day are ignored.
7. The Primary Tide remains in effect until a Dow Theory reversal has been signaled by both Averages.

Further Helpful Elaboration on the Dow Theory

The whole point of this time-honored theory is the identification of major movements of the stock market. Such major moves take quite some time to unfold, and prices change by a considerable amount. Although not specified by the Dow Theory, the Primary Tide usually lasts a year to several years. Bull Markets typically run toward the longer length, while Bear Markets are shorter in duration but more violent in the velocity of downward price movement.

Victor Sperandeo has quantified Dow Theory definitions. (See Sperandeo, Victor, *Trader Vic—Methods of a Wall Street Master,* John Wiley & Sons, New York, 1991.) He found that 75% of Primary Tide Bear Markets declined from 20.4% to 47.1% in price. Also, 75% of Bear Markets lasted between 0.8 and 2.8 years. Bull Markets lasted much longer: 67% lasted between 1.8 and 4.1 years.

The Secondary Wave is a reaction or correction in the opposite direction to the Primary Tide. This intermediate-term Secondary Wave typically lasts from 3 to 13 weeks. It typically retraces one-third, one-half, or two-thirds of the preceding Primary Tide swing. Sperandeo found that 65% last from 3 weeks to 3 months, and 98% last from 2 weeks to 8 months. Further, Sperandeo found that 61% retrace between 30% and 70% of the previous Primary Swing in price.

The Minor Ripple typically lasts only 1 day to 3 weeks. It is ignored as insignificant noise by the Dow Theory. Sperandeo found that 98.7% last less than 2 weeks.

A *Line* is a narrow sideways price range, extending ten calendar days or longer, the longer in time the more significant. The usual guideline to define a narrow range is approximately 5%, although William Hamilton classified a price range in excess of 11% from February to June 1929 as a Line. The Averages usually break out of a Line in the same direction as the Primary Tide. These breakouts are quite reliable. Although a Line can mark a reversal to a new direction opposite to the established Primary Tide, such reversal signals are much less reliable.

No matter how large a move in just one Average, it would not be sufficient to indicate a change in the Primary Tide unless the other Average confirmed. Nonconfirmations (divergences where one Average exceeds a preceding Secondary Wave reaction price extreme on a closing price basis but the other Average fails to confirm) function only as warnings to be alert for the possibility of an actual signal ahead.

It is not necessary that both Averages confirm on the same day or even the same month, though some authorities believe the closer the better and become more wary as the days pass without confirmation. In the absence of joint confirmation by both Averages, there is no signal of major trend change—in fact, there is nonconfirmation.

As a final important detail, the most minimal unit of price measure for the Averages (down to a penny, that is, 0.01, with no rounding off) strictly counts, when comparing the current closing price of each Average to its previous Secondary Wave extreme close.

There are six phases of the full bull through bear cycle: Skepticism, Growing Recognition, Enthusiasm, Disbelief, Shock and Fear, and Disgust.

In a major Bull Market, the first phase is *accumulation* of stocks at bargain prices by the "smart money" (the most knowledgeable and experienced investors). Meanwhile, the mass mood toward the stock market ranges from disgust to general skepticism. Stocks are depressed, and may have been for a long time. Still, some investors know that the cycle always turns up, even while fundamental business conditions still appear grim. The smart money begins to bid for out-of-favor stocks, which are selling at temptingly low bargain prices. Transactional volume, which has been low, starts to improve on rallies reflecting the entrance into the market by these forward-looking, patient investors.

The second Bull phase is known as the *mark-up phase.* Stock prices rise on increasing transactional volume. There is growing recognition that fundamental business conditions will improve. Stocks move up big. It is a very rewarding time to be in the market.

The third Bull phase is marked by popular enthusiasm and speculation. Sentiment indicators are near record levels. Fundamentals now appear extremely positive. There even may be widespread talk of a "new era" of rapid economic growth and never-ending prosperity. Stories of speculators making millions in the market flood the media. Everybody is optimistic and is buying, so transactional volume is extremely heavy. Late in this third phase, however, volume starts to diminish on rallies, as greedy buyers shoot their wads and become fully invested, usually on margin. Also, the smart money has reminded itself that "no tree grows to the sky" and all good things must eventually come to an end. Consequently, those knowledgeable investors, who bought early at wholesale prices, stop buying. Moreover, they begin the *distribution* phase, parceling out their stocks at retail prices. Smart selling intensifies as the greedy but unsophisticated mob snaps up overvalued stocks at absurdly high prices. Late in this game, tell-tale bearish technical cracks start to appear under the "obviously" bullish surface. Technical divergences in stocks and groups are caused by irrational buying of the wrong stocks by unsophisticated players while the smart money liquidates the best stocks. Stocks churn and make little net progress.

The first Bear Market phase is marked by clear and widespread technical deterioration, even while almost everybody is still feeling extremely bullish. But when everyone who ever is going to buy has already bought, there is only one direction for prices to go—down. When buying power is used up, there is insufficient demand to absorb the accelerating distribution of stocks by the smart money at current prices, so prices have to move lower. An ever increasing number of stocks already have stalled out and formed potentially bearish chart patterns. But even as stocks break critical chart support levels, this clear bearish technical evidence is widely ignored by the uninformed masses. After all, fundamental business conditions are still rosy, and "buy the dips" is still the advice of the brokers and the dealers and their paid spokesmen in the media. The public hopes and believes that the "conventional wisdom" of all the highly compensated Wall Street analysts, strategists and economists is right. Besides, the public has been told that they bought for the long term, and over the long term stock prices always go up. So, stock price declines are met with general disbelief. The public would buy more, if only they were not already fully margined. But they are. So they can't.

The second Bear phase is marked by a sudden mood change, from optimism and hope to shock and fear. One day, the public wakes up and sees, much to its surprise, that "the emperor has no clothes." Actual fundamental business conditions are not panning out to be as positive as previously hoped. In fact, there may be a little problem. The smart money is long gone, and there is no one left to buy when the public wants out. Stock prices drop steeply in a vacuum. Fear quickly replaces greed. Repeated waves of panic may sweep the market. Transactional volume swells as the unsophisticated investor screams, "Get me out at any price!" Sharp professional traders are willing to bid way down in price for stocks when prices drop too far too fast. The best that can be expected, however, is a dead-cat bounce that recovers only a fraction of the steep loss.

The third Bear phase is marked by discouraged selling and, finally, total disgust toward stocks. Fundamentals clearly have deteriorated and the outlook is bleak. Downward price movement continues but the negative rate of change eventually begins to slow as potential sellers liquidate holdings at distress prices. Even the best stocks, which initially resist the downtrend, succumb to the persistence of the Bear. Transactional volume, which was high in the panic phase, starts to diminish on price declines as liquidation runs its course. Eventually, after everyone who is capable of selling has sold already, the Bear Market is exhausted. The discouraged public lament is, "never again." After stocks are totally sold out, the stage is then set for the cycle to begin again. When everyone who ever is going to sell has already sold, there is only one direction for prices to go—up.

These phases are no secret. They have been written about by Dow and his successors for more than a century. These phases repeat endlessly, over and over again. Still, the public never learns. It is all too easy, it is merely human nature, to get caught up in the mass mood of the moment, lose all perspective and run with the emotions of the crowd. If you do not learn how to recognize the technical indications, and if you are not disciplined, the easiest thing in the world to do is to allow yourself to be pulled along by the mass mood, the "group think." But that is the way to be wrong at the critical turning points, to buy at tops and sell at bottoms, and to consistently underperform the market. To make money and outperform the market, we need to do the opposite. The Dow Theory tells us how.

Indicator Strategy Example for the Dow Theory

The venerable Dow Theory after a century has stood the *test of time.* Our tests of the Dow Theory against the actual historical data covering the past 101 years from January 1900 to February 2001 confirms the importance of this major contribution to technical analysis. We attempted to minimize subjectivity and judgement, and we added no other forms of analysis. We checked and rechecked our signals against available published sources. Based on trend confirming closing prices only for the Dow-Jones Industrial Average and the Dow-Jones Transportation Average, using only the Seven Basic Principles of Dow's Theory exactly as enumerated above, we found very positive results for both long and short signals.

At Arthur A. Merrill's suggestion (on page 84 of his *Behavior of Prices on Wall Street,* Second Edition, The Analysis Press, Chappaqua, NY, 1984, 147 pages), we multiplied by 0.7339 all closing prices for the old 12-stock Dow-Jones Industrial Average series prior to December 12, 1914, in order to make it comparable with the new

20-stock Industrial Average introduced at that time. (Previous compilers of Dow Theory signals failed to make this adjustment, throwing off their tabulations of hypothetical profits.)

Starting with $100 and reinvesting profits, total net profits, long and short, for this Dow Theory strategy wound have been $864,494.25, assuming a fully invested strategy, reinvestment of profits, no transactions costs and no taxes. This would have been 3920.98 percent greater than buy-and-hold. More than three out of four signals, 75.41 percent of the 41 signals, would have produced winning trades. Trading was inactive with only one trade every 605.5 days on Average. Even short selling, which is included in this strategy, would have been profitable, though not since Black Monday, October 19, 1987.

Dow Theory Signals

Trade #	*Trade Type*	*Entry Date*	*Close Date*	*Profit & Loss*	*MAE*
	Out	1/2/00	10/20/00	0	0
1	Long	10/20/00	6/4/03	−1.14	0
2	Short	6/4/03	7/12/04	12.59	60.81
3	Long	7/12/04	4/26/06	89.09	0
4	Short	4/26/06	4/24/08	48.66	70
5	Long	4/24/08	5/3/10	52.38	0
6	Short	5/3/10	10/10/10	10.04	61.14
7	Long	10/10/10	1/14/13	11.61	0
8	Short	1/14/13	4/9/15	−13.84	53.58
9	Long	4/9/15	8/28/17	100.4	0
10	Short	8/28/17	5/13/18	18.84	4.41
11	Long	5/13/18	2/3/20	92.86	0
12	Short	2/3/20	2/6/22	84.83	0
13	Long	2/6/22	6/20/23	51.5	0
14	Short	6/20/23	12/7/23	−21.66	0
15	Long	12/7/23	10/23/29	1438.14	9.47
16	Short	10/23/29	5/24/33	1502.63	0
17	Long	5/24/33	9/7/37	3399.12	69.83
18	Short	9/7/37	6/23/38	1569.71	0
19	Long	6/23/38	3/31/39	297.83	110.15
20	Short	3/31/39	7/17/39	−720.42	0
21	Long	7/17/39	5/13/40	−282.01	120.06
22	Short	5/13/40	2/1/43	670.57	0
23	Long	2/1/43	8/27/46	4408.02	109.5
24	Short	8/27/46	5/14/48	165.01	0
25	Long	5/14/48	11/9/48	−1017.09	155.34

Dow Theory Signals—*Continued*

Trade #	*Trade Type*	*Entry Date*	*Close Date*	*Profit & Loss*	*MAE*
26	Short	11/9/48	10/11/49	−888.04	0
27	Long	10/11/49	4/2/53	5585.02	149.34
28	Short	4/2/53	1/19/54	−493.31	0
29	Long	1/19/54	10/1/56	10184.33	234.6
30	Short	10/1/56	4/21/58	1014.88	0
31	Long	4/21/58	3/3/60	9832.76	374.29
32	Short	3/3/60	11/4/60	973.95	0
33	Long	11/4/60	4/26/62	5304.89	502.98
34	Short	4/26/62	11/9/62	4016.71	0
35	Long	11/9/62	5/5/66	21912.49	494.92
36	Short	5/5/66	1/11/67	5970.23	0
37	Long	1/11/67	6/12/69	6432.3	702.7
38	Short	6/12/69	12/23/70	6375.41	0
39	Long	12/23/70	4/27/73	10627.63	718.05
40	Short	4/27/73	1/27/75	24620.09	0
41	Long	1/27/75	7/27/77	34915.9	618.62
42	Short	7/27/77	8/2/78	881.06	0
43	Long	8/2/78	7/2/81	13652.2	787.45
44	Short	7/2/81	8/31/82	10438.44	0
45	Long	8/31/82	2/1/84	63291.28	786.83
46	Short	2/1/84	8/3/84	2081.92	0
47	Long	8/3/84	10/16/87	216216.19	1077.03
48	Short	10/16/87	2/29/88	36245.03	0
49	Long	2/29/88	1/25/90	118422.34	1904.54
50	Short	1/25/90	6/4/90	−90531.06	0
51	Long	6/4/90	8/17/90	−52350.94	2734.99
52	Short	8/17/90	1/18/91	−356.94	0
53	Long	1/18/91	8/21/92	109322.69	2451.61
54	Short	8/21/92	2/3/93	−21545.19	0
55	Long	2/3/93	3/30/94	42304.06	3175.79
56	Short	3/30/94	2/13/95	−54763.19	0
57	Long	2/13/95	7/15/96	194625.63	3768.6
58	Short	7/15/96	11/11/96	−126504.75	0
59	Long	11/11/96	8/4/98	251020.56	6046.13
60	Short	8/4/98	1/6/99	−52184	0
61	Long	1/6/99	9/23/99	88167.94	9028.98
62	Open/Short	9/23/99	2/16/01	−42291.94	1589.9
Sums				864494.24	37971.64

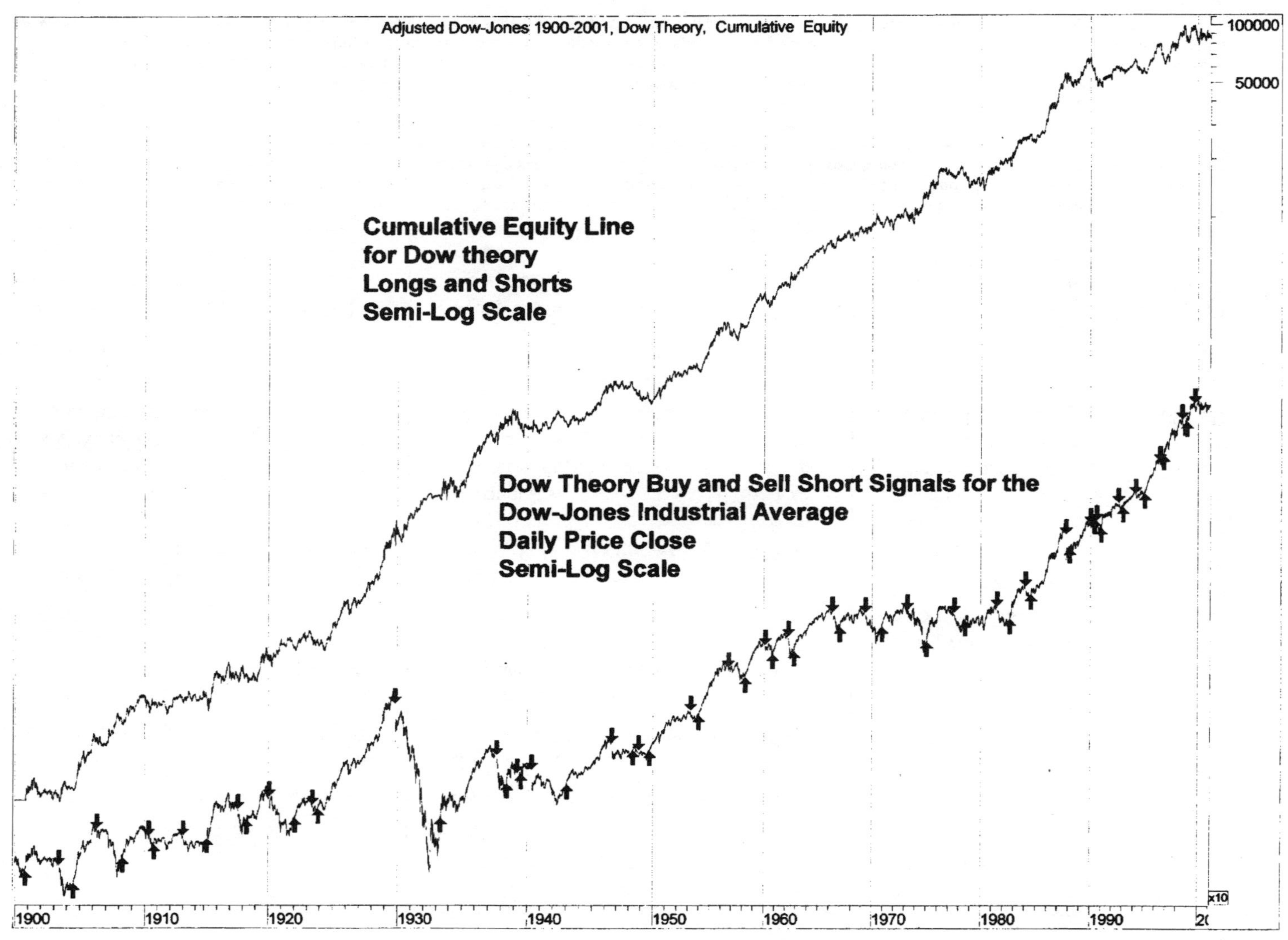

Adjusted Dow-Jones 1900-2001, Dow Theory, Cumulative Equity
100000
50000
Cumulative Equity Line
for Dow theory
Longs and Shorts
Semi-Log Scale
Dow Theory Buy and Sell Short Signals for the
Dow-Jones Industrial Average
Daily Price Close
Semi-Log Scale
x10
1900
1910
1920
1930
1940
1950
1960
1970
1980
1990

Dow Theory

Total net profit	864494.25	Open position value	−42291.96	Net Profit/Buy&Hold %	3920.98
Percent gain/loss	864494.25	Annual percent gain/loss	8542.9	Annual Net %/B&H %	3920.95
Initial investment	100	Interest earned	0		
Current position	Short	Date position entered	9/23/99		
Buy/Hold profit	21499.6	Days in test	36936	# of days per trade	605.51
Buy/Hold pct gain/loss	21499.6	Annual B/H pct gain/loss	212.46		
Total closed trades	61	Commissions paid	0		
Avg profit per trade	14865.35	Avg Win/Avg Loss ratio	1.06		
Total long trades	31	Total short trades	30	Long Win Trade %	87.10
Winning long trades	27	Winning short trades	19	Short Win Trade %	63.33
Total winning trades	46	Total losing trades	15	Total Win Trade %	75.41
Amount of winning trades	1308459.8	Amount of losing trades	−401673.56	Net Profit Margin %	53.02
Average win	28444.78	Average loss	−26778.24	Average P. Margin %	3.02
Largest win	251020.56	Largest loss	−126504.75	% Net/(Win + Loss)	32.98
Average length of win	521.57	Average length of loss	212.4	(Win − Loss)/Loss %	145.56
Longest winning trade	1760	Longest losing trade	774	(Win − Loss)/Loss %	127.39
Most consecutive wins	21	Most consecutive losses	3	(Win − Loss)/Loss %	600.00
Total bars out	243	Average length out	243		
Longest out period	243				
System close drawdown	−1.14	Profit/Loss index	68.28	% Net Profit/SODD	43009664.18
System open drawdown	−2.01	Reward/Risk index	100	(Net P. − SODD)/Net P.	100.00
Max open trade drawdown	−126504.8	Buy/Hold index	3724.27	% SODD/Net Profit	0.00

In the Equis MetaStock® "System Report" (profit and loss summary statistics), the *Total net profit* is the sum of profits minus the sum of losses, including open positions marked to the market. In contrast, the *Amount of Winning Trades* is the sum of realized profits (the total of all gains on closed-out trades only, excluding any open positions). Similarly, the *Amount of Losing Trades* is the sum of realized losses (the total of all losses on closed-out trades only, excluding any open positions). *System close drawdown* is the largest decline in the cumulative equity line below the initial investment, based on closed-out positions only. *System open drawdown (SODD)* is the largest decline in the cumulative equity line below the initial investment when a position is open. *Max open trade drawdown* is the largest decline in the cumulative equity line below the trade entry price during the worst single trade. The *Profit/Loss Index* is a complex calculation that relates the Amount of Winning Trades to the Amount of Losing Trades on a scale of −100 (worst possible performance) to +100 (best possible performance), with zero representing profits equal to losses. *Reward/Risk Index* is the Total net profit minus System open drawdown. The resulting difference is then divided by the Total net profit. The *Buy/Hold Index* is the Total net profit minus the buy-and-hold strategy's net profit. The resulting difference is then divided by the buy-and-hold net profit. In this exercise, initial equity is assumed to be $100. Both long and short positions are taken unless otherwise noted. Trades are executed at the closing price on the signal date. Transaction costs, interest expenses, and margins are not included in the statistics.

Criticisms of Dow's Theory

Despite its impressive record, Dow's Theory has been subjected to its share of criticism. The main one is that imprecision in the definition of a Secondary Reaction has produced some confusion as to the precise timing of Dow Theory signals. This is a significant criticism, but not an insurmountable one, as we shall see.

"The wish must never be allowed to father the thought," Robert Rhea cautioned in *The Story of the Averages,* 1934. "Perhaps no two students have identical ideas as to the proper classification and forecasting authority of the various price patterns which Dow and Hamilton recognized; consequently, any attempt to record and classify them seemed likely to provoke controversy." Rhea warned of the dangers of self-delusion in interpreting Dow's Theory: "Critics will properly point out that it is easy to produce a good argument in favor of Dow's Theory in such a study as we are undertaking, because it is easy to be wise after the event, and this contention is true . . . I hope that my respect for Dow's Theory is such that I will treat the subject as an impartial observer pointing out, so far as it lies within my ability to do so, the places where the Averages either gave no clue to future trends or afforded erroneous implications . . . It was painful work writing confessions about one trading episode in each of the years '17, '26, and '30." Dow's Theory gave false signals in each of these years.

Dow's Theory lacks specificity, according to Norman G. Fosback, *Stock Market Logic,* The Institute for Econometric Research Incorporated, 3471 North Federal Highway, Fort Lauderdale, Florida, 33306, 1976, pages 9–12. "Unfortunately, because stock prices seldom seem to move in uniform, perfectly defined cyclical patterns, it is difficult to develop [specific] criteria. In fact, different Dow theorists have derived radically different criteria for Dow Theory buy and sell signals . . . and have consequently derived different signal dates as well . . . "

"The Secondary Trend is often confusing . . . its correct appraisal . . . poses the Dow Theorist's most difficult problem . . . " Minor Trends are also difficult, and " . . . inferences drawn from these day-to-day fluctuations are quite apt to be misleading . . . The charge of second guessing will continue to crop up as long as opinions differ among Dow Theorists at critical periods (which is, unfortunately, often the case). Even the most experienced and careful Dow analysts find it necessary occasionally to change their interpretations when a stand first ventured is rendered untenable by some subsequent market action," according to Robert D. Edwards and John Magee, *Technical Analysis of Stock Trends,* Seventh Edition, John Magee, Inc., 103 State Street, Chicago, 1997, 624 pages.

The Dow Theory "doesn't always give a correct forecast, and the forecast isn't always clear," according to Arthur A. Merrill, CMT, *Behavior of Prices on Wall Street,* Second Edition, The Analysis Press, Chappaqua, NY, 1984, 147 pages, page 81.

"The most difficult task for a Dow theorist, or any trend-follower for that matter, is being able to distinguish between a normal secondary correction in an existing trend and the first leg of a new trend in the opposite direction. Dow Theorists often disagree as when the market gives an actual reversal signal," according to John J. Murphy, CMT, *Technical Analysis of the Financial Markets,* New York Institute of Finance, New York, 1999, 542 pages, page 29.

"When considering the results, note that these signals are the result of interpretation, in some cases with the benefit of hindsight. Some Dow Theorists would disagree with my interpretation," according to Martin J. Pring, *Technical Analysis Explained,* Third Edition, McGraw-Hill, New York, 1991, 521 pages, page 40 footnote.

"Making the distinction between minor reactions and secondary corrections isn't always this clear cut, however, and is the only somewhat subjective element of Dow Theory," according to Victor Sperandeo, *Trader Vic—Methods of a Wall Street Master,* John Wiley & Sons, New York, 1991, page 46.

All criticisms considered, the strengths of Dow's Theory far outweigh any weaknesses. Dow's Theory has proven itself over the past 100 years to be a useful, sound and profitable investment approach. Dow's Theory has made extremely important contributions to the development technical analysis. Technical students would benefit greatly from a thorough study of the Dow Theory, including the detailed historical performance of its signals. It would be time well invested.

New Frontiers for Dow's Theory

Considering its absence of evolutionary change, it is all the more remarkable that the Dow Theory has survived the test of time over the past turbulent century of unprecedented events, which included two world wars, a world-wide economic depression, and mind boggling triumphs of science and technology unimaginable in Charles H. Dow's day. Consider too that Dow created from scratch a predictive stock market barometer over a period of just a few years, with only a small quantity of primitive data and with no computer. If Charles H. Dow and his successors, S. A. Nelson, William P. Hamilton, and Robert Rhea, were alive today, they might extend their pioneering work with the help of vastly more data and power to analyze that data than they ever could have imagined.

Properly governed by sensible discipline to insure valid procedures and logic, the computer can handle complex data far more efficiently than our unaided mental capabilities ever could. It can quickly find patterns in reams of confusing data, patterns that the human eye could never see and the human mind could never grasp. Since it has no emotions, and it does not care if our pet hypothesis is accepted or rejected, the computer does not see signals that are not really there, and it does not ignore signals that are really there. We can not match the computer's ability to be coldly calculating. It can help us to precisely define decision rules, with which we can then actually execute precisely defined actions. We must always remember, however, that because the computer lacks judgement and common sense, we must impose on it reasonable limitations, lest it spew forth more misleading noise than we already have to deal with.

New Dow Theory Hypotheses for Computer-Assisted Testing

Hypothesis One: We can use objective and precise analysis to identify a signal. Since distinguishing between Primary Tides, Secondary Reactions, and Minor Ripples is the biggest problem human analysts have with Dow's Theory, let us program our computer to define these movements by the criterion of maximization of profits.

At its most basic level, excluding any qualifications or subtleties, Dow's Theory requires an advance that rises above a previous high for a buy signal and a decline that falls below a previous low for a sell signal, for both Averages. This simplest possible definition is similar to what has been called a *Price Channel Trading Range Breakout Rule.* (This is also known by futures traders as Richard D. Donchian's *n*-period trading rule and one of Richard Dennis's Turtle trading rules. *See Price Channel.*) It is one of the oldest and simplest trend following models: we buy when the daily closing price moves up to a new *n*-period high; then we sell long and sell short when the daily closing price moves down to a new *n*-period low. This is a precisely definable model that leaves no room for doubt or fuzzy thinking. We can work with such a model.

With a little imaginative database manipulation and much persistence, we were able to analyze the daily closing prices of both the Dow-Jones Industrial and Transportation Averages simultaneously in a single test, rather than just one at a time, like we had to do in the good old days. Specifically, we created an artificial file in Microsoft Excel, where we copied the Transportation Average's closing price (multiplied by 100 to avoid handling decimals) into the field (column) normally reserved for the Industrial Average's daily Volume, then we copied this file into a data file management software program, DownLoader for Windows, by Equis International, Salt Lake City, www.equis.com.

With this prepared data and MetaStock® for Windows software, also from Equis, running on a pentium-class computer, we are able to search up to 32,000 different period lengths applied to the entire century's daily market data (more than 25,000 days) in a single test. Our exact testing program is printed on page 238.

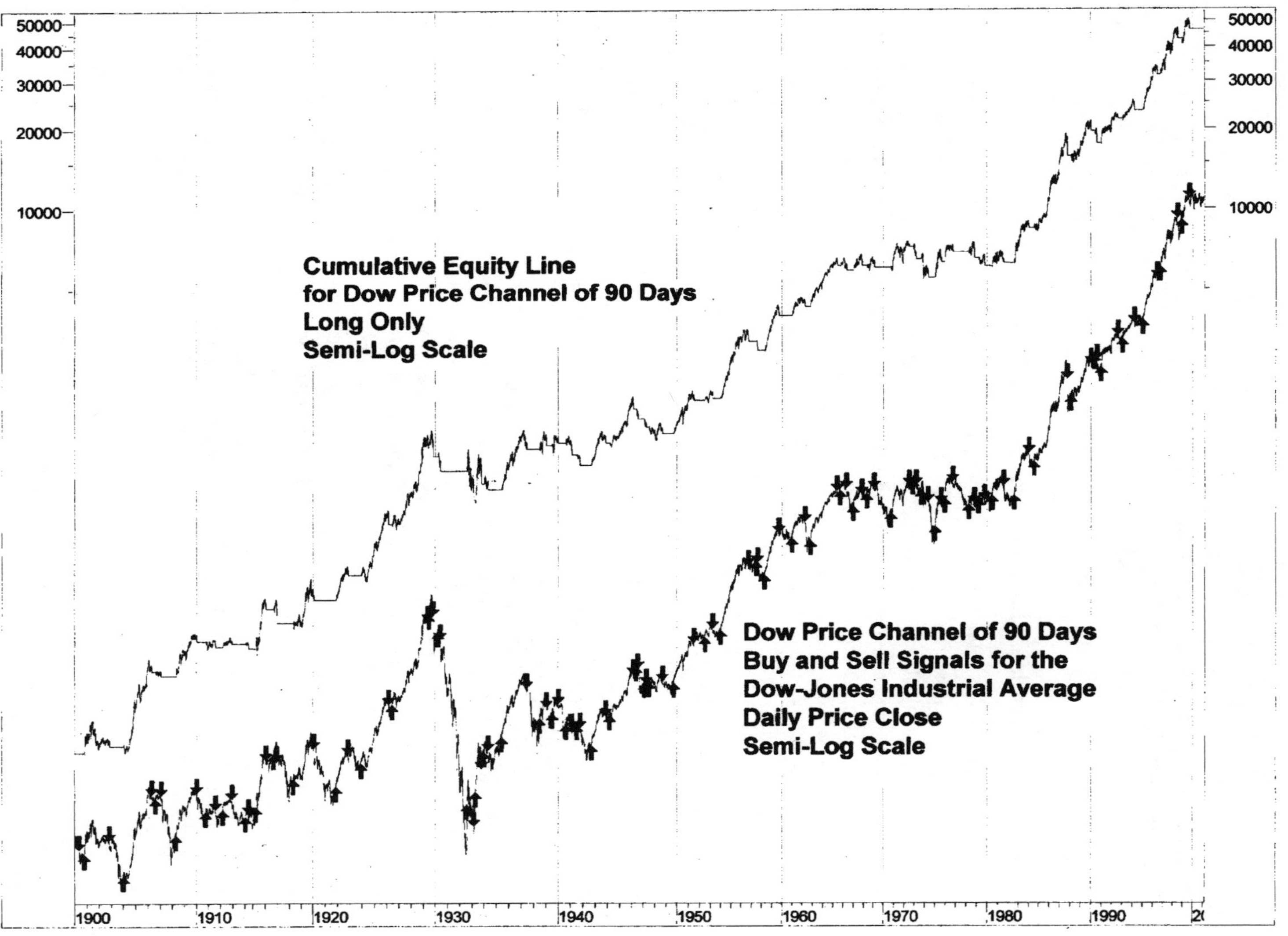

50000
40000
30000
20000
10000
Cumulative Equity Line
for Dow Price Channel of 90 Days
Long Only
Semi-Log Scale
Dow Price Channel of 90 Days
Buy and Sell Signals for the
Dow-Jones Industrial Average
Daily Price Close
Semi-Log Scale
1900
1910
1920
1930
1940
1950
1960
1970
1980
1990

Dow-Jones Industrials & Transports versus 90-Day Price Channels

Total net profit	46055.3	Open position value	N/A	Net Profit/Buy&Hold %	114.21
Percent gain/loss	46055.3	Annual percent gain/loss	455.12	Annual Net %/B&H %	114.21
Initial investment	100	Interest earned	0		
Current position	Out	Date position entered	9/23/99		
Buy/Hold profit	21499.6	Days in test	36936	# of days per trade	671.56
Buy/Hold pct gain/loss	21499.6	Annual B/H pct gain/loss	212.46		
Total closed trades	55	Commissions paid	0		
Avg profit per trade	837.37	Avg Win/Avg Loss ratio	5.28		
Total long trades	55	Total short trades	0	Long Win Trade %	61.82
Winning long trades	34	Winning short trades	0	Short Win Trade %	#DIV/0!
Total winning trades	34	Total losing trades	21	Total Win Trade %	61.82
Amount of winning trades	52151.64	Amount of losing trades	−6096.34	Net Profit Margin %	79.07
Average win	1533.87	Average loss	−290.3	Average P. Margin %	68.17
Largest win	11226.46	Largest loss	−1932.58	% Net/(Win + Loss)	70.63
Average length of win	408.97	Average length of loss	120.1	(Win − Loss)/Loss %	240.52
Longest winning trade	877	Longest losing trade	336	(Win − Loss)/Loss %	161.01
Most consecutive wins	5	Most consecutive losses	3	(Win − Loss)/Loss %	66.67
Total bars out	11397	Average length out	203.52		
Longest out period	650				
System close drawdown	0	Profit/Loss index	88.31	% Net Profit/SODD	5418270.59
System open drawdown	−0.85	Reward/Risk index	100	(Net P. − SODD)/Net P.	100.00
Max open trade drawdown	−1932.58	Buy/Hold index	114.21	% SODD/Net Profit	0.00

In the Equis MetaStock® "System Report" (profit and loss summary statistics), the *Total net profit* is the sum of profits minus the sum of losses, including open positions marked to the market. In contrast, the *Amount of Winning Trades* is the sum of realized profits (the total of all gains on closed-out trades only, excluding any open positions). Similarly, the *Amount of Losing Trades* is the sum of realized losses (the total of all losses on closed-out trades only, excluding any open positions). *System close drawdown* is the largest decline in the cumulative equity line below the initial investment, based on closed-out positions only. *System open drawdown (SODD)* is the largest decline in the cumulative equity line below the initial investment when a position is open. *Max open trade drawdown* is the largest decline in the cumulative equity line below the trade entry price during the worst single trade. The *Profit/Loss Index* is a complex calculation that relates the Amount of Winning Trades to the Amount of Losing Trades on a scale of −100 (worst possible performance) to +100 (best possible performance), with zero representing profits equal to losses. *Reward/Risk Index* is the Total net profit minus System open drawdown. The resulting difference is then divided by the Total net profit. The *Buy/Hold Index* is the Total net profit minus the buy-and-hold strategy's net profit. The resulting difference is then divided by the buy-and-hold net profit. In this exercise, initial equity is assumed to be $100. Both long and short positions are taken unless otherwise noted. Trades are executed at the closing price on the signal date. Transaction costs, interest expenses, and margins are not included in the statistics.

Indicator Strategy Examples for Price Channel Trading Range Breakout Rules Applied to Both Averages

We tested our Price Channel hypothesis twice: first, on the Dow-Jones Industrial Average alone; second, on both Industrials and Transports together, requiring joint confirmation. We found that Charles H. Dow was correct in stating that confirmation by both Averages is more significant and produces a better outcome than a breakout by one Average alone.

Testing only one variable period length (in trading days) applied equally to both Industrials and Transports over the past 101 years, for a long-only strategy with no short selling, hypothetical net profits were highest at a 90-day period length. Profits would have been more than double those of the passive buy-and-hold strategy, as shown below. But because this strategy did not approach the traditional Dow Theory's results, we keep trying.

The Equis International MetaStock® System Testing rules, where the current Dow-Jones Transportation Average (multiplied by 100 to eliminate the fraction) is inserted into the data field normally reserved for Volume (V), are written as follows:

Enter long: C>Ref(HHV(C,opt1) ,-1)
AND V>Ref(HHV(V,opt1) ,-1)

Close long: C<Ref(LLV(C,opt1) ,-1)
AND V<Ref(LLV(V,opt1) ,-1)

Enter short: C<Ref(LLV(C,opt1) ,-1)
AND V<Ref(LLV(V,opt1) ,-1)

Close short: C>Ref(HHV(C,opt1) ,-1)
AND V>Ref(HHV(V,opt1) ,-1)

OPT1 Current value: 90

Dow Price Channels of 90 Days

Trade #	*Trade Type*	*Entry Date*	*Close Date*	*Profit & Loss*	*MAE*
—	Out	1/2/00	10/20/00	0	0
1	Long	10/20/00	11/8/02	5.63	0.37
—	Out	11/8/02	1/21/04	0	0
2	Long	1/21/04	4/26/06	92.1	2.18
—	Out	4/26/06	8/18/06	0	0
3	Long	8/18/06	1/28/07	−7.15	2.53
—	Out	1/28/07	4/24/08	0	0
4	Long	4/24/08	1/14/10	64.47	0.34

Dow Price Channels of 90 Days—*Continued*

Trade #	*Trade Type*	*Entry Date*	*Close Date*	*Profit & Loss*	*MAE*
—	Out	1/14/10	10/15/10	0	0
5	Long	10/15/10	8/10/11	−11.49	4.1
—	Out	8/10/11	3/20/12	0	0
6	Long	3/20/12	12/4/12	6.86	0
—	Out	12/4/12	1/21/14	0	0
7	Long	1/21/14	4/23/14	−9.75	2.34
—	Out	4/23/14	4/9/15	0	0
8	Long	4/9/15	1/31/16	94.61	4.64
—	Out	1/31/16	9/26/16	0	0
9	Long	9/26/16	12/21/16	−37.14	11.23
—	Out	12/21/16	5/13/18	0	0
10	Long	5/13/18	2/3/20	64.59	4.23
—	Out	2/3/20	11/25/21	0	0
11	Long	11/25/21	11/13/22	84.74	0.01
—	Out	11/13/22	12/7/23	0	0
12	Long	12/7/23	3/3/26	241.58	5.47
—	Out	3/3/26	6/17/26	0	0
13	Long	6/17/26	5/27/29	628.62	7.78
—	Out	5/27/29	6/26/29	0	0
14	Long	6/26/29	10/23/29	−91.23	22.75
—	Out	10/23/29	3/28/30	0	0
15	Long	3/28/30	6/9/30	−142.89	33.07
—	Out	6/9/30	8/6/32	0	0
16	Long	8/6/32	2/23/33	−238.01	14.62
—	Out	2/23/33	4/24/33	0	0
17	Long	4/24/33	10/19/33	122.66	1.98
—	Out	10/19/33	1/15/34	0	0
18	Long	1/15/34	5/5/34	−46.82	4.99
—	Out	5/5/34	6/11/35	0	0
19	Long	6/11/35	6/14/37	381.14	0
—	Out	6/14/37	7/1/38	0	0
20	Long	7/1/38	1/25/39	39.97	6.62
—	Out	1/25/39	7/17/39	0	0
21	Long	7/17/39	1/13/40	24.58	11.25
—	Out	1/13/40	9/3/40	0	0
22	Long	9/3/40	2/14/41	−127.29	12.08
—	Out	2/14/41	7/21/41	0	0
23	Long	7/21/41	10/16/41	−105.21	10.99
—	Out	10/16/41	9/24/42	0	0
24	Long	9/24/42	11/8/43	234.7	0

Dow Price Channels of 90 Days—*Continued*

Trade #	*Trade Type*	*Entry Date*	*Close Date*	*Profit & Loss*	*MAE*
—	Out	11/8/43	3/11/44	0	0
25	Long	3/11/44	2/26/46	444.41	5.44
—	Out	2/26/46	5/28/46	0	0
26	Long	5/28/46	7/23/46	−141.19	16.48
—	Out	7/23/46	2/7/47	0	0
27	Long	2/7/47	4/12/47	−109.05	11.98
—	Out	4/12/47	7/14/47	0	0
28	Long	7/14/47	9/27/48	−80.95	20.21
—	Out	9/27/48	10/4/49	0	0
29	Long	10/4/49	6/29/51	471.09	0
—	Out	6/29/51	6/25/52	0	0
30	Long	6/25/52	4/6/53	26.37	7.39
—	Out	4/6/53	1/19/54	0	0
31	Long	1/19/54	10/1/56	1239.27	0
—	Out	10/1/56	7/5/57	0	0
32	Long	7/5/57	8/19/57	−236.29	37.94
—	Out	8/19/57	5/2/58	0	0
33	Long	5/2/58	9/22/59	1018.35	4.11
—	Out	9/22/59	1/12/61	0	0
34	Long	1/12/61	4/26/62	319.47	0
—	Out	4/26/62	11/9/62	0	0
35	Long	11/9/62	6/9/65	1849.33	0
—	Out	6/9/65	9/27/65	0	0
36	Long	9/27/65	5/5/66	−250.72	38.11
—	Out	5/5/66	1/11/67	0	0
37	Long	1/11/67	11/3/67	245.63	0
—	Out	11/3/67	5/1/68	0	0
38	Long	5/1/68	2/25/69	−90.46	43.55
—	Out	2/25/69	10/5/70	0	0
39	Long	10/5/70	7/12/72	1149.6	23.14
—	Out	7/12/72	12/4/72	0	0
40	Long	12/4/72	3/22/73	−716.21	101.82
—	Out	3/22/73	9/25/73	0	0
41	Long	9/25/73	5/22/74	−954.72	152.24
—	Out	5/22/74	1/27/75	0	0
42	Long	1/27/75	8/20/75	806.53	0
—	Out	8/20/75	1/5/76	0	0
43	Long	1/5/76	10/8/76	540.1	0
—	Out	10/8/76	4/25/78	0	0
44	Long	4/25/78	10/31/78	−340.53	41.14

Dow Price Channels of 90 Days—*Continued*

Trade #	*Trade Type*	*Entry Date*	*Close Date*	*Profit & Loss*	*MAE*
—	Out	10/31/78	3/27/79	0	0
45	Long	3/27/79	10/19/79	−426.67	56.68
—	Out	10/19/79	7/7/80	0	0
46	Long	7/7/80	8/21/81	152.67	12.29
—	Out	8/21/81	8/31/82	0	0
47	Long	8/31/82	2/1/84	2168.77	6.26
—	Out	2/1/84	8/3/84	0	0
48	Long	8/3/84	10/16/87	7346.97	38.87
—	Out	10/16/87	2/29/88	0	0
49	Long	2/29/88	1/25/90	3733	130.14
—	Out	1/25/90	6/4/90	0	0
50	Long	6/4/90	8/17/90	−1932.58	290.39
—	Out	8/17/90	1/18/91	0	0
51	Long	1/18/91	8/21/92	4038.77	43.56
—	Out	8/21/92	2/3/93	0	0
52	Long	2/3/93	3/30/94	1622.54	71.6
—	Out	3/30/94	2/13/95	0	0
53	Long	2/13/95	7/15/96	8205.6	0.67
—	Out	7/15/96	11/11/96	0	0
54	Long	11/11/96	8/4/98	11226.46	0
—	Out	8/4/98	1/6/99	0	0
55	Long	1/6/99	9/23/99	3460.46	481.71
—	Out	9/23/99	2/16/01	0	0
Sums	46055.29	1799.29			

Hypothesis Two: Period lengths should be allowed to vary according to the long or short nature of the signal. The statistical tabulations published by Robert Rhea in the 1930's and Victor Sperandeo in 1991 show that Bull Markets and Bear Markets have been much different in extent and duration. Therefore, look-back period lengths for buy and sell signals should not be the same. Furthermore, the requirements for each of the four possible market actions (buy long, sell long, sell short, and cover short) need not necessarily be the same. Therefore, we will allow these parameters to vary.

Hypothesis Three: Period lengths for each Average should be allowed to vary independently. Since the historical behaviors of the Dow-Jones Industrial and Transportation Averages obviously differ, with the two Averages even trending in opposite directions occasionally, let us allow different parameters for each Average.

Combining the three hypotheses, we completely cover all trading possibilities. We allow two separate period lengths for each of the four possible market actions (buy long, sell long, sell short, and cover short), one period length applied to the closing prices of the Dow-Jones Industrial Average (INDU) and a separate period length applied to the closing prices of the Dow-Jones Transportation Average (TRAN).

With four possible actions (buy long, sell long, sell short, and cover short) and two price Averages to test, there are eight indicators (4 × 2 = 8) to test for each model. We can vary the number of specific period length values (more generally known as parameter sets) for each indicator. As Louis B. Mendelsohn ("Designing and Testing Trading Systems: How to Avoid Costly Mistakes," Mendelsohn Enterprises, 25941 Apple Blossom Lane, Wesley Chapel, FL 33544, www.profittaker.com) has pointed out, as we allow an arithmetic increase in the number of parameter sets (period lengths), the number of models tested increases geometrically. For example, if we allow three period lengths for our eight indicators, we test three to the eighth power = 3 × 3 × 3 × 3 × 3 × 3 × 3 × 3 = 6561 models. But if we attempt to add just one more period length to our test, we jump up to four to the eighth power = 4 × 4 × 4 × 4 × 4 × 4 × 4 × 4 = 65,536 models. Adding just that one extra period length overwhelms our present software resources, which limits us to 32,000 models in a single test. Although our computing power is great compared to the past, it is still quite limited for testing complex models.

Fortunately, we are not forced to limit ourselves to very coarse testing with only three broad parameters. As an alternative, we can break our testing into two halves, longs only and shorts only, testing each separately. This cuts the number of indicators in each test in half, from eight to four. With only four indicators, we can test thirteen period lengths in one pass, since thirteen to the fourth power = 13 × 13 × 13 × 13 = 28,561 models. After we develop the long and short models separately, we can combine both models into one long and short model. Then we can do some final fine tuning of that combined model, indicator by indicator. Because we break apart our testing into pieces, however, we may well miss the best combination of parameter sets and our findings may be sub-optimal.

After many iterations, here is what our search uncovered:

Enter Long (Buy) when INDU rises to a new 9 trading day high and TRAN rises to a new 39 trading day high.

Close Long (Sell) when INDU falls to a new 22 trading day low and TRAN falls to a new 166 trading day low.

Enter Short (Sell Short) when INDU falls to a new 22 trading day low and TRAN falls to a new 166 trading day low.

Close Short (Cover) when INDU rises to a new 36 trading day high and TRAN rises to a new 32 trading day high.

The results are enlightening. The asymmetry of these rules means that we do not always have a position. Note that we buy on a very sensitive, short-term price confirmation, only a new 9-day high for the INDU confirmed by a 39-day new high for TRAN. Thus, it is relatively easy to get a buy signal. In contrast, note that it is relatively hard to get sell and sell short signals: we have to wait for the INDU to fall to a new 22-day low confirmed by the TRAN falling to a new 166-day low. Thus, this non-thinking model has correctly recognized the long-term bullish bias of a stock market that spends more time going up than down and has bigger rallies than declines.

Looking at the entire period from the beginning of January 2, 1900 to February 16, 2001, the above decision rules do a consistent job of precisely defining the buy and sell signals. There is absolutely no doubt as to what the signals are and when and at what price level the signals occur. If we could have executed this strategy over the past 101 years, we would have beaten the buy-and-hold strategy by a staggering 5637.10%. Total net profit would have been $1,233,454.40. This more complex trend-following rule was more active at one trade every 290.83 days on Average. Of the 127 total number of trades, 69 or 54.84% were winning trades (69 of 127 total number of trades).

The Equis International MetaStock® System Testing rules, where the current Dow-Jones Transportation Average (multiplied by 100 to eliminate the fraction) is inserted into the data field normally reserved for Volume (V), are written as follows:

Enter long: C>Ref(HHV(C,opt1) ,-1)
AND V>Ref(HHV(V,opt5) ,-1)

Close long: C<Ref(LLV(C,opt2) ,-1)
AND V<Ref(LLV(V,opt6) ,-1)

Enter short: C<Ref(LLV(C,opt3) ,-1)
AND V<Ref(LLV(V,opt7) ,-1)

Close short: C>Ref(HHV(C,opt4) ,-1)
AND V>Ref(HHV(V,opt8) ,-1)

OPT1 Current value: 9
OPT2 Current value: 22
OPT3 Current value: 22
OPT4 Current value: 36
OPT5 Current value: 39
OPT6 Current value: 166
OPT7 Current value: 166
OPT8 Current value: 32

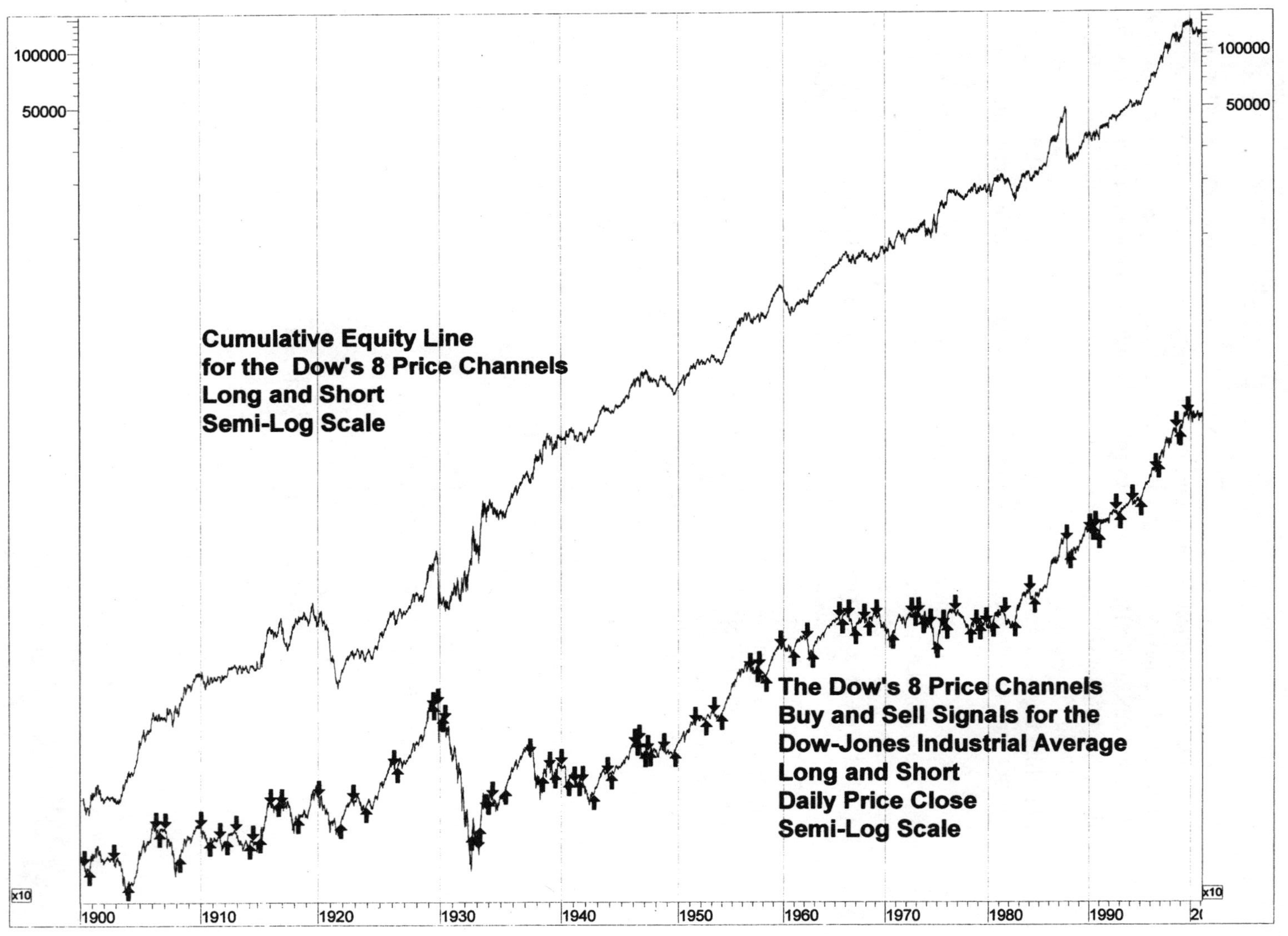
Cumulative Equity Line
for the Dow's 8 Price Channels
Long and Short
Semi-Log Scale
The Dow's 8 Price Channels
Buy and Sell Signals for the
Dow-Jones Industrial Average
Long and Short
Daily Price Close
Semi-Log Scale
100000
50000
x10
1900
1910
1920
1930
1940
1950
1960
1970
1980
1990

Dow-Jones Industrials & Transports versus 8 Different Price Channels

Total net profit	1233454.4	Open position value	−36561.93	Net Profit/Buy&Hold %	5637.10
Percent gain/loss	1233454.4	Annual percent gain/loss	12188.94	Annual Net %/B&H %	5637.05
Initial investment	100	Interest earned	0		
Current position	Long	Date position entered	3/23/00		
Buy/Hold profit	21499.6	Days in test	36936	# of days per trade	290.83
Buy/Hold pct gain/loss	21499.6	Annual B/H pct gain/loss	212.46		
Total closed trades	127	Commissions paid	0		
Avg profit per trade	10000.13	Avg Win/Avg Loss ratio	5.1		
Total long trades	62	Total short trades	65	Long Win Trade %	54.84
Winning long trades	34	Winning short trades	35	Short Win Trade %	53.85
Total winning trades	69	Total losing trades	58	Total Win Trade %	54.33
Amount of winning trades	1520814.4	Amount of losing trades	−250798.14	Net Profit Margin %	71.69
Average win	22040.79	Average loss	−4324.11	Average P. Margin %	67.20
Largest win	600036.56	Largest loss	−53044.61	% Net/(Win + Loss)	83.76
Average length of win	317.62	Average length of loss	92.78	(Win − Loss)/Loss %	242.34
Longest winning trade	1334	Longest losing trade	780	(Win − Loss)/Loss %	71.03
Most consecutive wins	5	Most consecutive losses	7	(Win − Loss)/Loss %	−28.57
Total bars out	337	Average length out	15.32		
Longest out period	69				
System close drawdown	−4.28	Profit/Loss index	83.1	% Net Profit/SODD	7016236.52
System open drawdown	−17.58	Reward/Risk index	100	(Net P. − SODD)/Net P.	100.00
Max open trade drawdown	−130768.4	Buy/Hold index	5467.05	% SODD/Net Profit	0.00

In the Equis MetaStock® "System Report" (profit and loss summary statistics), the *Total net profit* is the sum of profits minus the sum of losses, including open positions marked to the market. In contrast, the *Amount of Winning Trades* is the sum of realized profits (the total of all gains on closed-out trades only, excluding any open positions). Similarly, the *Amount of Losing Trades* is the sum of realized losses (the total of all losses on closed-out trades only, excluding any open positions). *System close drawdown* is the largest decline in the cumulative equity line below the initial investment, based on closed-out positions only. *System open drawdown (SODD)* is the largest decline in the cumulative equity line below the initial investment when a position is open. *Max open trade drawdown* is the largest decline in the cumulative equity line below the trade entry price during the worst single trade. The *Profit/Loss Index* is a complex calculation that relates the Amount of Winning Trades to the Amount of Losing Trades on a scale of −100 (worst possible performance) to +100 (best possible performance), with zero representing profits equal to losses. *Reward/Risk Index* is the Total net profit minus System open drawdown. The resulting difference is then divided by the Total net profit. The *Buy/Hold Index* is the Total net profit minus the buy-and-hold strategy's net profit. The resulting difference is then divided by the buy-and-hold net profit. In this exercise, initial equity is assumed to be $100. Both long and short positions are taken unless otherwise noted. Trades are executed at the closing price on the signal date. Transaction costs, interest expenses, and margins are not included in the statistics.

Dow Versus 8 Price Channels

Trade #	Trade Type	Entry Date	Close Date	Profit & Loss	MAE
—	Out	1/2/00	3/24/00	0	0
1	Long	3/24/00	11/8/02	−2.12	8.29
2	Short	11/8/02	12/31/02	−2.16	1.02
3	Long	12/31/02	3/5/03	0.61	0.07
4	Short	3/5/03	11/19/03	30.03	0.77
5	Long	11/19/03	4/23/06	138.84	0.65
6	Short	4/23/06	7/31/06	2.98	1.28
—	Out	7/31/06	8/1/06	0	0
7	Long	8/1/06	1/28/07	−5.22	1.5
8	Short	1/28/07	7/5/07	28.73	1.1
9	Long	7/5/07	8/12/07	−38.02	7.83
10	Short	8/12/07	12/5/07	35.69	1.99
—	Out	12/5/07	1/6/08	0	0
11	Long	1/6/08	1/14/10	149.65	2.3
12	Short	1/14/10	3/7/10	−3.06	0.61
13	Long	3/7/10	4/28/10	−37.21	5.91
14	Short	4/28/10	8/16/10	24.24	2.47
15	Long	8/16/10	8/11/11	−1.78	1.98
16	Short	8/11/11	11/3/11	13.16	0.49
17	Long	11/3/11	12/9/12	43.6	0.03
18	Short	12/9/12	4/1/13	22.86	1.86
—	Out	4/1/13	4/3/13	0	0
19	Long	4/3/13	4/29/13	−23.01	2.77
20	Short	4/29/13	7/18/13	7.89	1.15
—	Out	7/18/13	7/21/13	0	0
21	Long	7/21/13	4/17/14	9.74	2.12
22	Short	4/17/14	1/21/15	0	1.55
—	Out	1/21/15	3/23/15	0	0
23	Long	3/23/15	2/1/17	246.62	0
24	Short	2/1/17	3/19/17	−70.84	8.45
—	Out	3/19/17	4/10/17	0	0
25	Short	4/10/17	12/28/17	140.35	7.88
26	Long	12/28/17	1/20/19	90.12	0
27	Short	1/20/19	2/24/19	−50.41	4.48
—	Out	2/24/19	2/26/19	0	0
28	Long	2/26/19	8/7/19	151.16	1.56
29	Short	8/7/19	10/6/19	−111.78	11.24
30	Long	10/6/19	11/12/19	−38.87	4.89
31	Short	11/12/19	3/8/20	77.67	3.54
32	Long	3/8/20	12/21/20	−292.35	30.63

Dow Versus 8 Price Channels—*Continued*

Trade #	*Trade Type*	*Entry Date*	*Close Date*	*Profit & Loss*	*MAE*
33	Short	12/21/20	5/5/21	−126.75	13.28
34	Long	5/5/21	6/18/21	−81.5	12.78
35	Short	6/18/21	7/23/21	−12.63	2.61
36	Long	7/23/21	5/7/23	157.4	5.33
37	Short	5/7/23	9/11/23	10.82	2.78
38	Long	9/11/23	2/17/28	617.29	7.85
39	Short	2/17/28	3/12/28	−67.74	10.85
—	Out	3/12/28	3/16/28	0	0
40	Long	3/16/28	10/29/29	140.55	2.74
41	Short	10/29/29	1/29/30	−177.88	43.44
—	Out	1/29/30	2/4/30	0	0
42	Long	2/4/30	6/12/30	−87	21.3
43	Short	6/12/30	9/9/30	11.8	2.51
—	Out	9/9/30	9/27/30	0	0
44	Short	9/27/30	1/22/31	211.77	1.66
45	Long	1/22/31	4/15/31	−27.82	3.8
46	Short	4/15/31	6/24/31	95.61	0
—	Out	6/24/31	6/26/31	0	0
47	Long	6/26/31	9/3/31	−176.52	20.9
48	Short	9/3/31	1/15/32	399.16	0
49	Long	1/15/32	3/28/32	−191.43	14.08
50	Short	3/28/32	7/25/32	449.04	2.06
51	Long	7/25/32	7/23/34	1510.04	0.74
52	Short	7/23/34	10/11/34	−125.96	3.73
—	Out	10/11/34	10/24/34	0	0
53	Long	10/24/34	2/6/35	153.3	3.07
54	Short	2/6/35	4/12/35	−139.73	6.94
—	Out	4/12/35	4/25/35	0	0
55	Long	4/25/35	8/27/37	1883.13	1.76
56	Short	8/27/37	5/9/38	1625.29	1.97
57	Long	5/9/38	5/13/40	1019.09	11.69
58	Short	5/13/40	7/16/40	812.47	0
59	Long	7/16/40	11/12/41	−531.39	7.82
60	Short	11/12/41	7/2/42	810.24	1.86
61	Long	7/2/42	11/5/43	2692	0
62	Short	11/5/43	1/4/44	−142.49	1.68
63	Long	1/4/44	7/23/46	4804.49	2.93
64	Short	7/23/46	11/2/46	1877.28	9.3
65	Long	11/2/46	4/14/47	−610.27	8.98
66	Short	4/14/47	6/19/47	−987.51	9.45

Dow Versus 8 Price Channels—*Continued*

Trade #	*Trade Type*	*Entry Date*	*Close Date*	*Profit & Loss*	*MAE*
—	Out	6/19/47	6/20/47	0	0
67	Long	6/20/47	11/10/48	−275.66	11.05
68	Short	11/10/48	1/7/49	−729.18	7.83
—	Out	1/7/49	2/4/49	0	0
69	Short	2/4/49	3/30/49	−45.95	0.53
70	Long	3/30/49	5/31/49	−869.65	10.09
71	Short	5/31/49	7/19/49	−599.02	6.95
—	Out	7/19/49	7/26/49	0	0
72	Long	7/26/49	8/26/53	7110.11	0.45
73	Short	8/26/53	10/19/53	−536.37	6.8
—	Out	10/19/53	10/29/53	0	0
74	Long	10/29/53	9/28/56	14749.36	2.43
75	Short	9/28/56	3/28/57	17.79	24.22
—	Out	3/28/57	4/9/57	0	0
76	Long	4/9/57	8/23/57	−505.43	6.92
77	Short	8/23/57	1/24/58	1831.8	10.39
78	Long	1/24/58	9/8/59	15586.65	13.77
79	Short	9/8/59	1/5/60	−3472.36	42.78
80	Long	1/5/60	3/4/60	−5376.04	75.68
81	Short	3/4/60	6/8/60	−2881.24	40.56
82	Long	6/8/60	7/21/60	−2096.57	33.72
83	Short	7/21/60	11/10/60	287.25	24.93
—	Out	11/10/60	1/4/61	0	0
84	Long	1/4/61	4/26/62	3554.47	0
85	Short	4/26/62	11/2/62	4605.45	0
86	Long	11/2/62	5/27/65	23884.76	0
87	Short	5/27/65	7/30/65	2436.15	4.82
88	Long	7/30/65	7/26/66	−2451.73	29.57
89	Short	7/26/66	11/16/66	2595.17	4.06
90	Long	11/16/66	2/8/68	2628	35.18
91	Short	2/8/68	4/8/68	−3042.94	34.1
92	Long	4/8/68	6/2/69	4014.79	14.77
93	Short	6/2/69	10/24/69	5839.77	0
94	Long	10/24/69	11/21/69	−3752.56	39.13
95	Short	11/21/69	8/24/70	6094.44	0
96	Long	8/24/70	9/12/72	20873.59	12.11
97	Short	9/12/72	11/1/72	−2518.8	22.5
—	Out	11/1/72	11/13/72	0	0
98	Long	11/13/72	1/29/73	−63.25	0.61
99	Short	1/29/73	9/19/73	8926.77	2.56

Dow Versus 8 Price Channels—*Continued*

Trade #	*Trade Type*	*Entry Date*	*Close Date*	*Profit & Loss*	*MAE*
100	Long	9/19/73	5/17/74	−11285.87	122.06
101	Short	5/17/74	10/14/74	17920.78	40.83
102	Long	10/14/74	8/11/77	35997.58	95.9
103	Short	8/11/77	4/14/78	14527.53	0
104	Long	4/14/78	8/27/81	20017.05	36
105	Short	8/27/81	10/30/81	7783.11	3.14
106	Long	10/30/81	3/4/82	−10409.36	45
107	Short	3/4/82	4/8/82	−8186.39	35.39
—	Out	4/8/82	4/26/82	0	0
108	Long	4/26/82	6/8/82	−13072.48	63.35
109	Short	6/8/82	8/20/82	−13838.05	67.06
110	Long	8/20/82	2/8/84	50087.77	0
111	Short	2/8/84	8/1/84	3785.25	30.26
112	Long	8/1/84	10/19/87	109461.14	0
113	Short	10/19/87	1/5/88	−53044.61	292.76
114	Long	1/5/88	1/15/90	82263.52	152.36
115	Short	1/15/90	3/19/90	−11124.56	86.26
116	Long	3/19/90	8/6/90	−4749.81	110.58
117	Short	8/6/90	12/5/90	12807.31	42.57
118	Long	12/5/90	8/21/92	84134.44	140.1
119	Short	8/21/92	10/23/92	6072.56	122.12
120	Long	10/23/92	10/4/94	79818.88	14.32
121	Short	10/4/94	1/6/95	−8914.06	134.91
122	Long	1/6/95	8/4/98	600036.56	35.33
123	Short	8/4/98	11/2/98	−28423.25	266.47
124	Long	11/2/98	9/16/99	250569.88	30.12
125	Short	9/16/99	11/12/99	−3922.5	123.4
126	Long	11/12/99	1/28/00	−3727.63	57.2
127	Short	1/28/00	3/23/00	−46719.38	397.7
128	Open	Long	3/23/00	2/16/01	−36561.88
1468.22					
Sums	1233454.4	4892.22			

Indicator Strategy Example with Just One Exponential Moving Average Crossover Applied to Both Averages

Hypothesis Four: While Price Channel is good at defining breakouts from horizontal trading ranges, often the market moves in a steeply sloping direction, either up or down. In these cases, at least, the use of sloping lines may be more productive for sig-

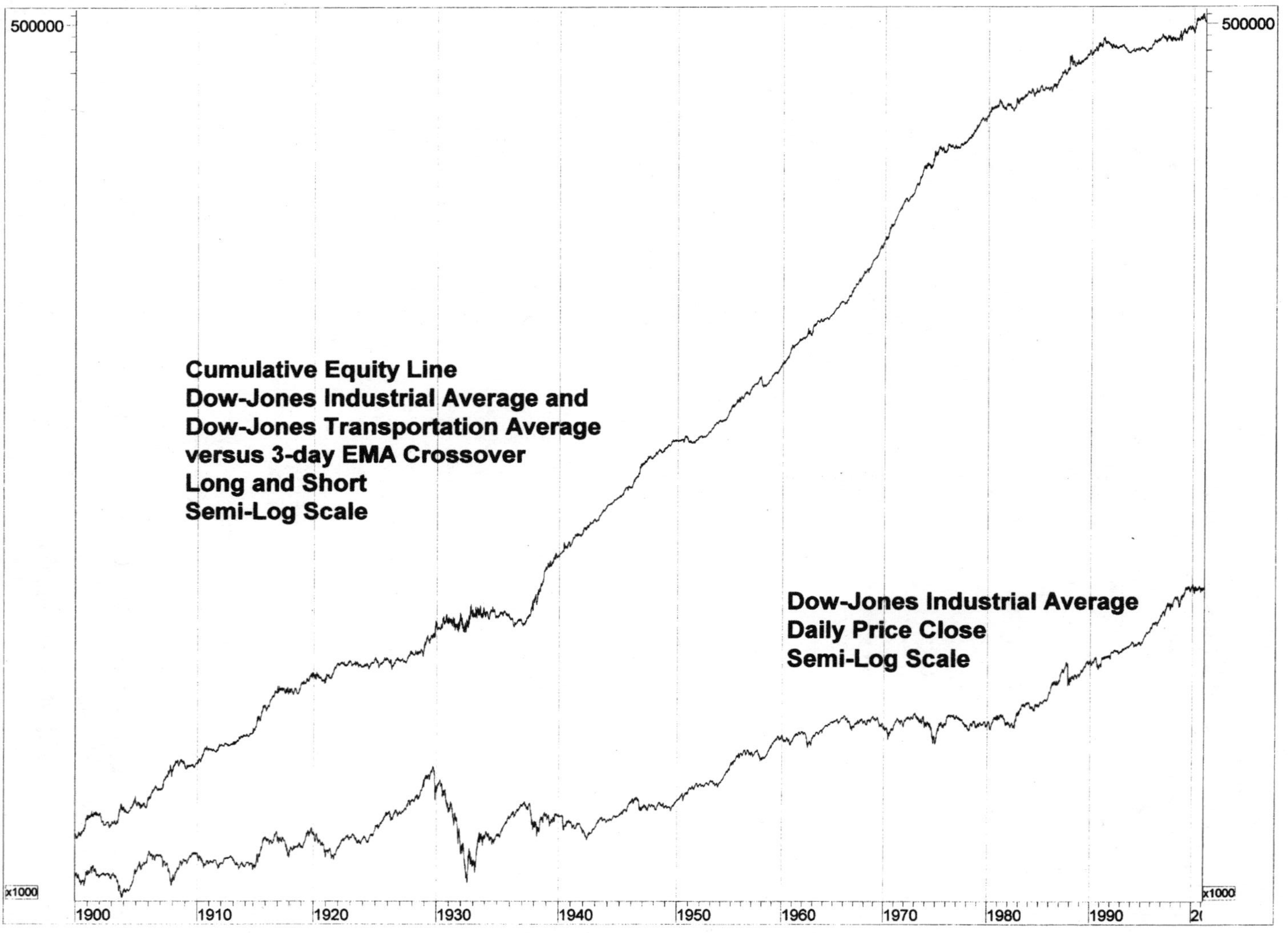

500000
500000
Cumulative Equity Line
Dow-Jones Industrial Average and
Dow-Jones Transportation Average
versus 3-day EMA Crossover
Long and Short
Semi-Log Scale
Dow-Jones Industrial Average
Daily Price Close
Semi-Log Scale
x1000
x1000
1900
1910
1920
1930
1940
1950
1960
1970
1980
1990

Dow Industrials & Transports versus 3-day EMA

Total net profit	505216544	Open position value	0	Net Profit/Buy&Hold %	2349788.11
Percent gain/loss	505216544	Annual percent gain/loss	4992528.66	Annual Net %/B&H %	2349767.58
Initial investment	100	Interest earned	0		
Current position	Short	Date position entered	2/16/01		
Buy/Hold profit	21499.6	Days in test	36936	# of days per trade	6.35
Buy/Hold pct gain/loss	21499.6	Annual B/H pct gain/loss	212.46		
Total closed trades	5816	Commissions paid	0		
Avg profit per trade	86866.67	Avg Win/Avg Loss ratio	1.83		
Total long trades	2908	Total short trades	2908	Long Win Trade %	44.36
Winning long trades	1290	Winning short trades	1074	Short Win Trade %	36.93
Total winning trades	2364	Total losing trades	3452	Total Win Trade %	40.65
Amount of winning trades	2488249344	Amount of losing trades	−1983032960	Net Profit Margin %	11.30
Average win	1052558.94	Average loss	−574459.14	Average P. Margin %	29.39
Largest win	49968768	Largest loss	−27665024	% Net/(Win + Loss)	28.73
Average length of win	8.91	Average length of loss	3.61	(Win − Loss)/Loss %	146.81
Longest winning trade	36	Longest losing trade	19	(Win − Loss)/Loss %	89.47
Most consecutive wins	8	Most consecutive losses	18	(Win − Loss)/Loss %	−55.56
Total bars out	4	Average length out	4		
Longest out period	4				
System close drawdown	−4.36	Profit/Loss index	20.3	% Net Profit/SODD	11202140665.19
System open drawdown	−4.51	Reward/Risk index	100	(Net P. − SODD)/Net P.	100.00
Max open trade drawdown	−27665024	Buy/Hold index	2349788.15	% SODD/Net Profit	0.00

In the Equis MetaStock® "System Report" (profit and loss summary statistics), the *Total net profit* is the sum of profits minus the sum of losses, including open positions marked to the market. In contrast, the *Amount of Winning Trades* is the sum of realized profits (the total of all gains on closed-out trades only, excluding any open positions). Similarly, the *Amount of Losing Trades* is the sum of realized losses (the total of all losses on closed-out trades only, excluding any open positions). *System close drawdown* is the largest decline in the cumulative equity line below the initial investment, based on closed-out positions only. *System open drawdown (SODD)* is the largest decline in the cumulative equity line below the initial investment when a position is open. *Max open trade drawdown* is the largest decline in the cumulative equity line below the trade entry price during the worst single trade. The *Profit/Loss Index* is a complex calculation that relates the Amount of Winning Trades to the Amount of Losing Trades on a scale of −100 (worst possible performance) to +100 (best possible performance), with zero representing profits equal to losses. *Reward/Risk Index* is the Total net profit minus System open drawdown. The resulting difference is then divided by the Total net profit. The *Buy/Hold Index* is the Total net profit minus the buy-and-hold strategy's net profit. The resulting difference is then divided by the buy-and-hold net profit. In this exercise, initial equity is assumed to be $100. Both long and short positions are taken unless otherwise noted. Trades are executed at the closing price on the signal date. Transaction costs, interest expenses, and margins are not included in the statistics.

nal generation. An Exponential Moving Average crossover (see Exponential Moving Average) could be one example of a sloping line that could be applied to both the Dow-Jones Industrial and Transportation Averages to define a trend and a trend change signal.

The exponential moving Average crossover rule would have been a profitable indicator over all time frames and, particularly, over the shorter ones. All lengths in the range of 100-days or less would have outperformed the passive buy-and-hold strategy. For traders with very low transactions costs, exponential moving Average lengths around three days would have been best. Based on the daily closing prices for the Dow-Jones Industrial and Transportation Averages for 101 years from 1900 to 2001, we found that the following parameters would have produced a significantly positive result on a purely mechanical trend-following signal basis with no subjectivity, no sophisticated technical analysis, and no judgement:

Enter Long (Buy) at the current daily price close of the Dow-Jones Industrial Average when this daily closing price crosses above yesterday's 3-day exponential moving Average of the daily closes and when the close of the Dow-Jones Transportation Average also crosses above yesterday's 3-day exponential moving Average of its daily closes.

Close Long (Sell) at the current daily price close of the Dow-Jones Industrial Average when this daily closing price crosses below yesterday's 3-day exponential moving Average of the daily closes and when the close of the Dow-Jones Transportation Average also crosses below yesterday's 3-day exponential moving Average of its daily closes.

Enter Short (Sell Short) at the current daily price close of the Dow-Jones Industrial Average when this daily closing price crosses below yesterday's 3-day exponential moving Average of the daily closes and when the close of the Dow-Jones Transportation Average also crosses below yesterday's 3-day exponential moving Average of its daily closes.

Close Short (Cover) at the current daily price close of the Dow-Jones Industrial Average when this daily closing price crosses above yesterday's 3-day exponential moving Average of the daily closes and when the close of the Dow-Jones Transportation Average also crosses above yesterday's 3-day exponential moving Average of its daily closes.

Starting with $100 and reinvesting profits, total net profits for this exponential moving Average crossover strategy would have been more than $505 million, assuming a fully invested strategy, reinvestment of profits, no transactions costs and no taxes. This would have been more than two million percent better than a passive buy-and-hold strategy. Short selling would have been profitable and was included in the strategy. Typical of other trend-following strategies, however, short selling would have been unprofitable in the unusually large bull market from 1980 to 2000. Note that this strategy is right on only 40.36% of its signals, but the size of the a Average winning trade is 1.83 times the size of the Average losing trade. This exponential moving Average crossover strategy is very active at one trade every 6.35 days.

The Equis International MetaStock® System Testing rules, where the current Dow-Jones Transportation Average (multiplied by 100 to eliminate the fraction) is inserted into the data field normally reserved for Volume (V), are written as follows:

Enter long: CLOSE > Ref(Mov(CLOSE,opt1,E),-1) AND
V > Ref(Mov(V,opt1,E),-1)

Close long: CLOSE < Ref(Mov(CLOSE,opt1,E),-1) AND
V < Ref(Mov(V,opt1,E),-1)

Enter short: CLOSE < Ref(Mov(CLOSE,opt1,E),-1) AND
V < Ref(Mov(V,opt1,E),-1)

Close short: CLOSE > Ref(Mov(CLOSE,opt1,E),-1) AND
V > Ref(Mov(V,opt1,E),-1)

OPT1 Current value: 3

An Evolutionary Future for the Dow Theory?

Our purpose here is not to offer any particular fix or remake of the Dow Theory. We merely hope to stimulate thinking as to how the theory might be allowed to evolve. You might use ideas herein to launch your own research. You might find your own unique guidelines in harmony with your own particular objectives and limitations. You might develop your own individual variations and interpretations, all based on the actual historical evidence. There are a very large number of indicators in this book that could be used to supplement basic Dow Theory concepts.

Think of how a theory evolves. An observer ponders the data, forms a hypothesis, then tests the hypothesis. The hypothesis may be adjusted many times to better fit the data. The hypothesis also may change as new data becomes available. The hypothesis is allowed to evolve so that it describes observed phenomena better and better.

Merely pondering data without testing it could lead to erroneous hypotheses, misconceptions, false conclusions and general confusion. Things that seem like they ought to be true often are not when you rigorously test the hypothesis against the actual data. Testing helps us clarify our thinking. Without testing, we can miss subtleties in the data and evolutionary changes in the nature of underlying phenomena over time. In the absence of testing, delusions may persist. Obsolete beliefs may lead to flawed decisions.

Over the years Dow's Theory has been subjected to misunderstanding due to imprecise definitions and the absence of continuous evolutionary testing. Change is constant, and no theory should be taken as etched in stone.

Our testing must be objective, precise, and unbiased. We must maintain strict logical control over what and how we are testing at all times. Our testing must make sense. This is where experienced judgement will never be obsolete.

There is a compelling logic to defining and continuously redefining through back testing a set of decision rules that would have performed best in the past. In fact, there is no acceptable alternative. You can theorize all you want, but without historical back testing you could be on shaky ground and not know it. An objective approach based on simulated performance against actual historical data simply offers the best hard factual backing available.

Dunnigan's One-Way Formula

Dunnigan's One-Way Formula requires a test of a previous bottom followed by an upward thrust for a buy signal. And it requires a test of a previous top followed by a downward thrust for a sell signal. In addition, the entire range of the thrust day must be away from the range of the previous day, that is, both the high and the low of the thrust day must be above the high of the previous day for a buy signal, and both the low and the high of the thrust day must be below the low of the previous day for a sell signal. These strict criteria are designed to give fewer but more significant signals.

For further discussion, see Dunnigan, W. (1954), *Select Studies in Speculation,* San Francisco: Dunnigan. Also, see Dunnigan, W. (1956, 1997), *New Blueprints for Gains in Stocks and Grains & One-Way Formula for Trading in Stocks and Commodities,* London: Pitman.

Dunnigan's Thrust Method

Dunnigan's Thrust Method is a trend reversal signal that is triggered by any one of five different price setups on any given day, confirmed the next day by a *thrust,* which is a relatively large price move. The optimal size of the thrust can be determined by back-testing.

In a downswing, which is defined as lower highs and lower lows, there are five preconditions that set-up a trend reversal buy-signal using daily data:

1. A test of a previous daily bottom.
2. A closing price reversal (a lower daily low followed by a reversal to a higher daily close).
3. A narrow daily range of less than half the largest daily range for the current downswing.
4. An inside day, with both a lower daily high and a higher daily low than the previous day.

For each of these four preconditions, the buy signal is given if there is a thrust in an upward direction the very next day. The fifth precondition is a fail-safe that assures us that we shall never miss a major trend: an upside penetration of a previous upswing high sets up an upward trend-change signal. In this fifth case, there is no time limit on confirmation by a thrust—the thrust may confirm the fifth setup many days later to complete the buy signal.

In an upswing, which is defined as higher highs and higher lows, there are five preconditions that set-up a swing reversal sell signal using daily data:

1. A test of a previous daily high.
2. A closing price reversal (a higher daily high followed by a reversal to a lower daily close).
3. A narrow daily range of less than half the largest daily range for the current upswing.
4. An inside day, with both a lower daily high and a higher daily low than the previous day.

For each of these four preconditions, the sell signal is given if there is a thrust in a downward direction the very next day. Again, the fifth precondition is a fail-safe in that it assures us that we shall never miss a major trend: a downside penetration of a previous downswing low sets up a downward trend-change signal. In this fifth case, there is no time limit on confirmation by a thrust—the thrust may confirm the fifth setup many days later to complete the sell signal.

Repeat signals, especially the test of the previous bottom or top and the closing price reversal, offer even more significant confirmation. Especially significant are double thrusts, when one thrust is immediately followed by another, or when the first thrust is followed by a brief hesitation then another thrust.

Efficient Market Hypothesis

The Efficient Market Hypothesis is the opposite of technical analysis. It is a toned-down version of the more strongly stated Random Walk Hypothesis. *(See Random Walk Hypothesis.)* Basically, the idea is that the market is so efficient that it instantly discounts all known information, which is instantly reflected in stock prices. So, there is nothing anyone can do to beat the markets, since anything knowable will already be reflected in the current price.

The Efficient Market Hypothesis has never been proved and appears to be slowly dying out. Contradictory research evidence has been accumulating. Moreover, it is impossible to find practical market professionals, traders and investors, willing to even entertain the idea. Consistently successful traders express absolute certainty that their profits are a direct reflection of their skill and have nothing whatsoever to do with random outcomes. Remember, if the markets really were efficient, the strong performances by many indicators shown in these pages would not to be possible.

Elder-Ray

Elder-Ray was developed in 1989 by Alexander Elder and presented in his popular book, *Trading for a Living: Psychology, Trading Tactics, Money Management,* John Wiley & Sons, New York, 1993.

Using daily data, Elder computes a 13-day exponential moving average (EMA) of the daily close. He defines Bull Power as the daily high price minus this 13-day EMA. He defines Bear Power as the daily low price minus this 13-day EMA.

$$\text{Bull Power} = \text{High} - \text{EMA}$$
$$\text{Bear Power} = \text{Low} - \text{EMA}$$

Elder's basic trading rules for Elder-Ray are:

Buy when the longer-term trend is up and Bear Power is negative but rising; that is, beginning to become less negative. It is also helpful, though not essential, if there is a positive divergence in Bear Power; that is, if price is making lower lows but Bear Power is making higher lows. Liquidate long positions on a negative divergence in Bull Power.

Sell short when the longer-term trend is down and Bull Power is positive but falling, that is, beginning to become less positive. It is also helpful, though not essential, if there is a negative divergence in Bull Power; that is, if price is making higher highs but Bull Power is making lower highs. If Bull Power is already negative, it is too late to initiate short positions. Cover short positions on a positive divergence in Bear Power.

End Point Moving Average (EPMA)

This term is a misnomer, strictly speaking, because the actual indicator is not computed like a moving average. Rather, EPMA is the ending value of a Linear Regression trendline plus its slope. *(See Time Series Forecast (TSF).)*

Envelopes, Moving Average Envelopes, and Trading Bands

Envelopes are plotted a fixed percentage above and below a moving average. Envelopes are commonly used for overbought and oversold signals: a sell signal is generated when the security reaches the upper band; and a buy signal is generated at the lower band. The length of the moving average and the appropriate percentage plus and minus shift of the moving average both depend on the trading characteristics and the volatility of the security. In general, a greater volatility results in a larger percentage shift. When overzealous buyers and sellers push prices to extremes, the upper and lower bands provide resistance and support levels for price to reverse trend and revert to the mean (the moving average) or even the opposite extreme.

The parameters for Envelopes can vary widely according to a security's individual observed historical habits and volatility. For example, Jerry Favors, a well-known market newsletter writer, calculates a 21-day exponential moving average (EMA) for the general stock market indexes, such as the Dow-Jones Industrial Average. For a vertical shift percentage, Jerry favors plus and minus 3.5%. That is, he adds 3.5% to each point on this 21-day EMA to derive the upper envelope. Then he subtracts 3.5% from each point on this 21-day EMA to plot the lower envelope.

Indicator Strategy Example for Envelopes

Even naïve testing assumptions suggest that Envelopes have potential value as a purely mechanical, contra-trend technical indicator. The great majority of oversold buy signals would have been profitable. Moreover, these buy signals would have been robust, with all exponential moving average lengths from 1 to 50 days, minus and plus two percent, profitable and right most of the time, for long trades only.

As attractive as a high percentage of profitable trades may seem, however, it is important to note that this (like other contra-trend strategies) failed to provide any protection in the Crash of '87, the decline of 1998 and other market price drops. As the chart shows, there are sharp equity drawdowns. Using Envelopes for contra-trend oversold and overbought signals slightly outperformed the passive buy-and-hold strategy for long trades only, while short selling would not have been profitable in the past.

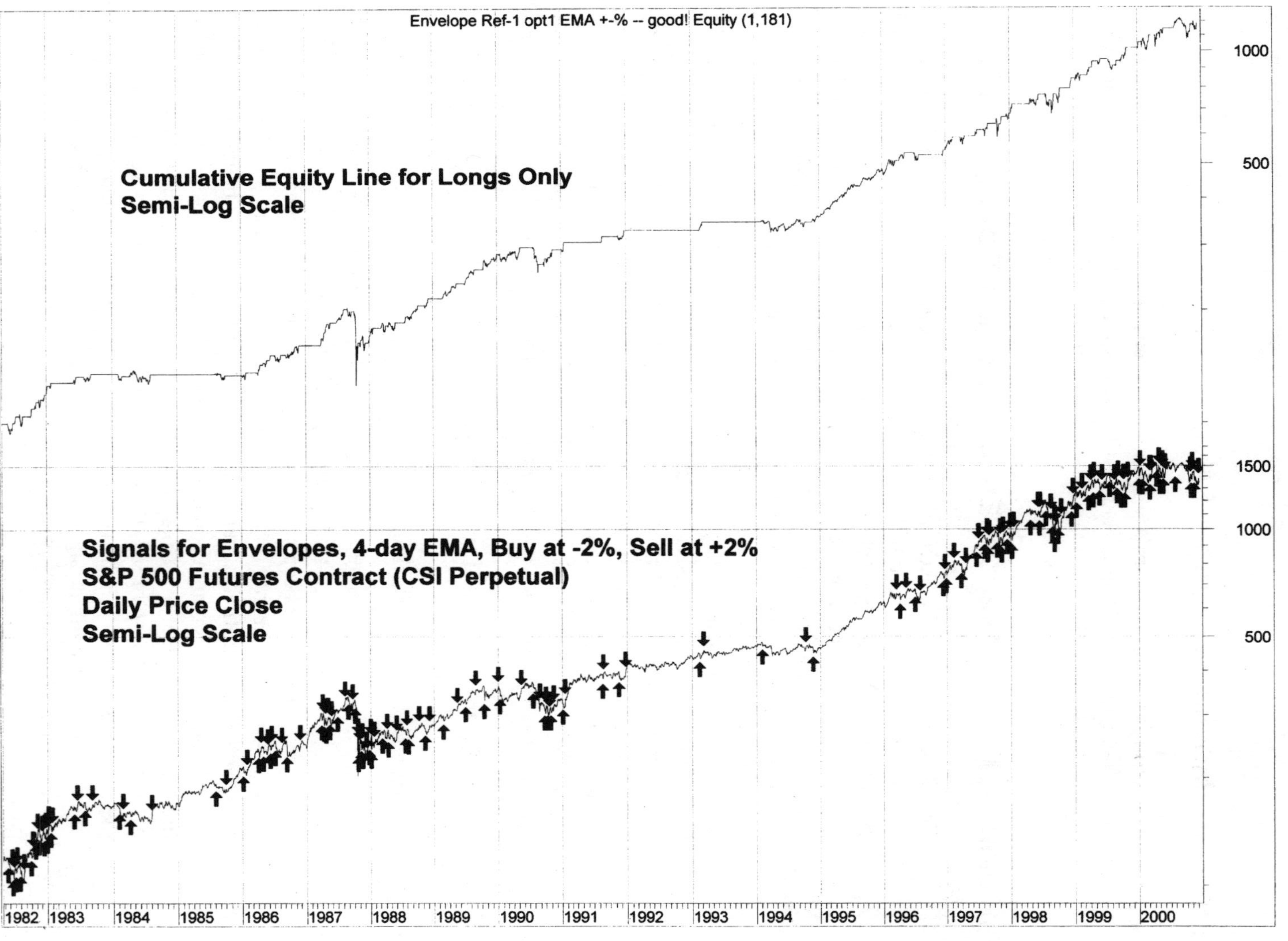

Envelope Ref-1 opt1 EMA +-% -- good! Equity (1,181)
Cumulative Equity Line for Longs Only
Semi-Log Scale
Signals for Envelopes, 4-day EMA, Buy at -2%, Sell at +2%
S&P 500 Futures Contract (CSI Perpetual)
Daily Price Close
Semi-Log Scale
1000
500
1500
1000
500
1982
1983
1984
1985
1986
1987
1988
1989
1990
1991
1992
1993
1994
1995
1996
1997
1998
1999
2000

Envelopes, Four EMA & Two-Percent

Total net profit	1080.61	Open position value	N/A	Net Profit/Buy&Hold %	3.35
Percent gain/loss	1080.61	Annual percent gain/loss	57.94	Annual Net %/B&H %	3.35
Initial investment	100	Interest earned	0		
Current position	Out	Date position entered	12/5/00	# of days per trade	35.26
Buy/Hold profit	1045.54	Days in test	6807		
Buy/Hold pct gain/loss	1045.54	Annual B/H pct gain/loss	56.06		
Total closed trades	88	Commissions paid	0		
Avg profit per trade	12.28	Avg Win/Avg Loss ratio	1.31		
Total long trades	88	Total short trades	0	Long Win Trade %	84.09
Winning long trades	74	Winning short trades	0	Short Win Trade %	#DIV/0!
Total winning trades	74	Total losing trades	14	Total Win Trade %	84.09
Amount of winning trades	1263.05	Amount of losing trades	−182.44	Net Profit Margin %	74.76
Average win	17.07	Average loss	−13.03	Average P. Margin %	13.42
Largest win	163.8	Largest loss	−38.44	% Net/(Win + Loss)	61.99
Average length of win	20.08	Average length of loss	32.07	(Win − Loss)/Loss %	−37.39
Longest winning trade	333	Longest losing trade	172	(Win − Loss)/Loss %	93.60
Most consecutive wins	11	Most consecutive losses	2	(Win − Loss)/Loss %	450.00
Total bars out	2954	Average length out	33.19		
Longest out period	291				
System close drawdown	−3.09	Profit/Loss index	85.56	% Net Profit/SODD	17861.32
System open drawdown	−6.05	Reward/Risk index	99.44	(Net P. − SODD)/Net P.	99.44
Max open trade drawdown	−81.19	Buy/Hold index	3.35	% SODD/Net Profit	−0.56

In the Equis MetaStock® "System Report" (profit and loss summary statistics), the *Total net profit* is the sum of profits minus the sum of losses, including open positions marked to the market. In contrast, the *Amount of Winning Trades* is the sum of realized profits (the total of all gains on closed-out trades only, excluding any open positions). Similarly, the *Amount of Losing Trades* is the sum of realized losses (the total of all losses on closed-out trades only, excluding any open positions). *System close drawdown* is the largest decline in the cumulative equity line below the initial investment, based on closed-out positions only. *System open drawdown (SODD)* is the largest decline in the cumulative equity line below the initial investment when a position is open. *Max open trade drawdown* is the largest decline in the cumulative equity line below the trade entry price during the worst single trade. The *Profit/Loss Index* is a complex calculation that relates the Amount of Winning Trades to the Amount of Losing Trades on a scale of −100 (worst possible performance) to +100 (best possible performance), with zero representing profits equal to losses. *Reward/Risk Index* is the Total net profit minus System open drawdown. The resulting difference is then divided by the Total net profit. The *Buy/Hold Index* is the Total net profit minus the buy-and-hold strategy's net profit. The resulting difference is then divided by the buy-and-hold net profit. In this exercise, initial equity is assumed to be $100. Both long and short positions are taken unless otherwise noted. Trades are executed at the closing price on the signal date. Transaction costs, interest expenses, and margins are not included in the statistics.

Based on a 18-year file of daily data for the entire history of the S&P 500 Composite Stock Price Index futures contract from 4/21/82 to 12/08/00 collected from www.csidata.com, we found that the following parameters would have produced a positive result on a purely mechanical overbought/oversold signal basis with no subjectivity, no sophisticated technical analysis, and no judgement:

Enter Long (Buy) at the current daily price close when the S&P 500 Composite Stock Price Index futures contract closing price is less than yesterday's 4-day exponential moving average of the daily closing prices minus 2%.

Close Long (Sell) at the current daily price close when the S&P 500 Composite Stock Price Index futures contract closing price is greater than yesterday's 4-day exponential moving average of the daily closing prices plus 2%.

Enter Short (Sell Short) never.

Starting with $100 and reinvesting profits, total net profits for this Envelopes counter-trend strategy would have been $1,080.61, assuming a fully invested strategy, reinvestment of profits, no transactions costs and no taxes. This would have been 3.35 percent greater than buy-and-hold. No short selling would have been profitable, and no short selling was included in the strategy. Short selling would have cut the profit to less than buy-and-hold. Long-only Envelopes as an indicator would have given profitable buy signals 84.09% of the time. Trading would have been only moderately active at one trade every 35.26 calendar days. Note that this strategy considers closing prices only while ignoring intraday highs and lows.

The Equis International MetaStock® System Testing rules for Envelopes are written as follows:

Enter long: CLOSE < (Ref(Mov(CLOSE,opt1,E),-1)-
((opt2/1000))*Ref(Mov(CLOSE,opt1,E),-1))

Close long: CLOSE > (Ref(Mov(CLOSE,opt1,E),-1)+
((opt2/1000))*Ref(Mov(CLOSE,opt1,E),-1))

OPT1 Current value: 4

OPT2 Current value: 20

Equity Drop Ratio

The Equity Drop Ratio, a measure of risk, is the annualized return divided by the standard deviation of the equity drops of the Cumulative Equity Line.

Exploratory Data Analysis

Exploratory Data Analysis is the process of identifying systematic relations between variables when there are no (or not complete) *a priori* expectations as to the nature of those relations. In a typical exploratory data analysis process, many variables are taken into account and compared, using a variety of techniques, in a search for systematic patterns. We require variables found to be related to pass tests of logic and common sense before we proceed to the next step in model building.

Exponential Moving Average (EMA), Exponential Smoothing

The Exponential Moving Average (EMA) is also referred to as Exponential Smoothing. The EMA is the best of the moving average techniques, and it is increasingly preferred by technical analysts over other moving average methods. Behaviorally, in its responsiveness to new data being generated by the markets, the EMA represents an excellent compromise between the overly sensitive weighted moving average and the overly sluggish simple moving average. Compared to other averaging techniques, the EMA follows the trend of the current data smoothly and seamlessly, minimizing jumps, wiggles, and lags.

Computationally, the EMA is the simplest and most streamlined of all moving average techniques. The EMA requires the fewest calculations, the least data handling, and the least data history. The EMA requires numerical values for only two data periods: the most recently available raw data and the immediate past period's EMA. For example, working with daily data, we need only today's observed, unprocessed data and yesterday's EMA in order to calculate today's EMA. Thus, the EMA eliminates the need to keep and handle long lists of historical data.

A significant advantage of this superior computational method is that the EMA is never distorted by old data suddenly dropping out of the calculation. Old data is never suddenly dropped because it is not actually part of the calculation. For practical purposes, the effect of past data fades away gradually due to the ever decreasing weighting of yesterday's EMA. The EMA's method of calculation correctly avoids the problem of erratic current movement caused solely by irrelevant and obsolete data dropping out of the calculation.

An Exponential Moving Average is calculated as follows:

$$EMA = (C - Ep)K + Ep$$

where

EMA = the Exponential Moving Average for the current period.
C = the closing price for the current period.
Ep = the Exponential Moving Average for the previous period.
K = the exponential smoothing constant, equal to $2/(n + 1)$.
n = the total number of periods in a simple moving average to be roughly approximated by the EMA.

The exponential smoothing constant formula, $K = 2/(n + 1)$, allows an approximate comparison of any EMA to the more sluggish Simple Moving Average of length n. As the number of days n increases, the value of K grows ever smaller, and the EMA becomes increasingly less sensitive to the newer data.

Use this table to quickly convert from simple n days to exponential smoothing constants (K), and back.

n days	*K = 2/(n + 1)*	*n days*	*K = 2/(n + 1)*	*n days*	*K = 2/(n + 1)*	*n days*	*K = 2/(n + 1)*
1	1.00000	10	0.18182	100	0.01980	1000	0.00200
2	0.66667	20	0.09524	200	0.00995	2000	0.00100
3	0.50000	30	0.06452	300	0.00664	3000	0.00067
4	0.40000	40	0.04878	400	0.00499	4000	0.00050
5	0.33333	50	0.03922	500	0.00399	5000	0.00040
6	0.28571	60	0.03279	600	0.00333	6000	0.00033
7	0.25000	70	0.02817	700	0.00285	7000	0.00029
8	0.22222	80	0.02469	800	0.00250	8000	0.00025
9	0.20000	90	0.02198	900	0.00222	9000	0.00022
10	0.18182	100	0.01980	1000	0.00200	10000	0.00020

When first starting a new EMA, it takes approximately n days of calculations for an accurate reading. For a quick startup of a EMA, on the first day of calculation we may use a n day simple moving average to approximate the previous day's EMA (Ep) in the formula,

$$EMA = (C - Ep)K + Ep$$

After that first day, we will never need any data other than yesterday's EMA and today's fresh data to maintain our EMA.

The table on the facing page illustrates how to compute an EMA of four periods, which is also known as a 40% EMA, named for the exponential smoothing constant, K.

Example of Exponential Smoothing
Approximating a 4-Period Simple Moving Average

Year End	*NYSE Close*	*Previous Period's EMA*	*Difference = Close Minus EMA Previous (D)*	*Multiply by*	*Smoothing Constant (K) Equals 2÷ (n + 1) = 2÷ (4 + 1) =*		*Difference Times Smoothing Constant D × K*	*Add Previous Period's EMA*		*Current New EMA*
1968	58.90	58.90	0.00	×	.4	=	0.00	58.90	=	58.90
1969	51.53	58.90	−7.37	×	.4	=	−2.95	+58.90	=	55.95
1970	50.23	55.95	−5.72	×	.4	=	−2.95	+55.95	=	53.66
1971	56.43	53.66	+2.77	×	.4	=	+1.11	+53.66	=	54.77
1972	64.48	54.77	+9.71	×	.4	=	+3.88	+54.77	=	58.65
1973	51.82	58.65	−6.83	×	.4	=	−2.73	+58.65	=	55.92
1974	36.13	55.92	−19.79	×	.4	=	−7.92	+55.92	=	48.00
1975	47.64	48.00	−0.36	×	.4	=	−0.14	+48.00	=	47.86
1976	57.88	47.86	+10.02	×	.4	=	+4.01	+47.86	=	51.87
1977	52.50	51.87	+0.63	×	.4	=	+0.25	+51.87	=	52.12
1978	53.62	52.12	+1.51	×	.4	=	+0.60	+52.12	=	52.72
1979	61.95	52.72	+9.23	×	.4	=	+3.69	+52.72	=	56.41
1980	77.86	56.41	+21.45	×	.4	=	+8.58	+56.41	=	64.99
1981	71.11	64.99	+6.12	×	.4	=	+2.45	+64.99	=	67.44
1982	81.03	67.44	+13.59	×	.4	=	+5.44	+67.44	=	72.88
1983	95.18	72.88	+22.30	×	.4	=	+8.92	+72.88	=	81.80
1984	96.38	81.80	+14.58	×	.4	=	+5.83	+81.80	=	87.63
1985	121.58	87.63	+33.95	×	.4	=	+13.58	+87.63	=	101.21
1986	138.58	101.21	+37.37	×	.4	=	+14.95	+101.21	=	116.16
1987		116.16		×	.4	=		+116.16	=	

Indicator Strategy Example for the Exponential Moving Average (EMA), 120-days

Based on the daily closing prices for the DJIA from 1900 to 2001, Exponential Moving Average Crossover Strategies of all lengths from 1 day to 300 days would have been profitable and would have beaten the passive buy-and-hold-strategy by at least 69%. The 5-, 3- and 2-day EMA would have produced maximum net profits in excess of six billion dollars, assuming we start with one hundred dollars in 1900. All EMA period lengths of 1 to 20 days would have produced net profits in excess of ten million dollars, and all 20 lengths would have outperformed buy-and-hold by more than 540 to one. All EMA period lengths of 1 to 60 days would have produced net profits in excess of one million dollars, and all 60 lengths would have outperformed buy-and-hold by more than 64 to one. Of the "intermediate-term" lengths, the 44-day EMA would have produced the best results, net profit of $3,251,721, which would have been more than 162 times the buy-and-hold-strategy's $20,105. Performance deteriorated as the moving average period length increased. The popular 200-day EMA Crossover Strategy would have produced much less profit of $109,158, which would have been only 5.4 times the buy-and-hold-strategy's $20,105 net profit.

Of the "long-term" EMA period lengths in excess of 100 days, the 120-day EMA Crossover Strategy would have produced the maximum profit on a purely mechanical trend-following signal basis with no subjectivity, no sophisticated technical analysis, and no judgement:

Enter Long (Buy) at the current daily price close of the DJIA when this close is greater than the previous day's 120-day exponential moving average of the daily closing prices.

Close Long (Sell) at the current daily price close of the DJIA when this close is less than the previous day's 120-day exponential moving average of the daily closing prices.

Enter Short (Sell Short) at the current daily price close of the DJIA when this close is less than the previous day's 120-day exponential moving average of the daily closing prices.

Close Short (Cover) at the current daily price close of the DJIA when this close is greater than the previous day's 120-day exponential moving average of the daily closing prices.

Starting with $100 and reinvesting profits, total net profits for this 120-day EMA Crossover Strategy would have been $508,772.91, assuming a fully invested strategy, reinvestment of profits, no transactions costs and no taxes. This would have been 2,430.53 percent better than buy-and-hold. Short selling would have been profitable, but not since the Crash of '87. Trading frequency would have been moderate with one trade every 33.57 calendar days. There would have been 240 profitable trades and 862 losing trades, for a winning percentage of only 21.78% profitable. But because this trend-following strategy cuts losses and lets profits run, it makes money despite being wrong on most of its signals. This is typical of the longer-term trend-following strategies. Such a strategy may be used alone, and it also can be useful as a filter to other trading systems.

The Equis International MetaStock® System Testing rules are written as follows:

Enter long: CLOSE > Ref(Mov(CLOSE,opt1,E),-1)

Close long: CLOSE < Ref(Mov(CLOSE,opt1,E),-1)

Enter short: CLOSE < Ref(Mov(CLOSE,opt1,E),-1)

Close short: CLOSE > Ref(Mov(CLOSE,opt1,E),-1)

OPT1 Current value: 120

Indicator Strategy Example for the Exponential Moving Average (EMA), 5-days

This is the best simple trend-following indicator we tested against daily DJIA data. Substituting 5-days for 120-days in the same formula (above), and starting with $100 and reinvesting profits, total net profits for this 5-day EMA Crossover Strategy would have been $16 billion, assuming a fully invested strategy, reinvestment of profits, no transactions costs and no taxes. This would have been 78 million percent better than buy-and-hold. Short selling would have been profitable. Trading frequency would have been hyperactive with one trade every 5.88 calendar days. There would have been 2417 profitable trades and 3889 losing trades, for a winning percentage of only 38.33% profitable.

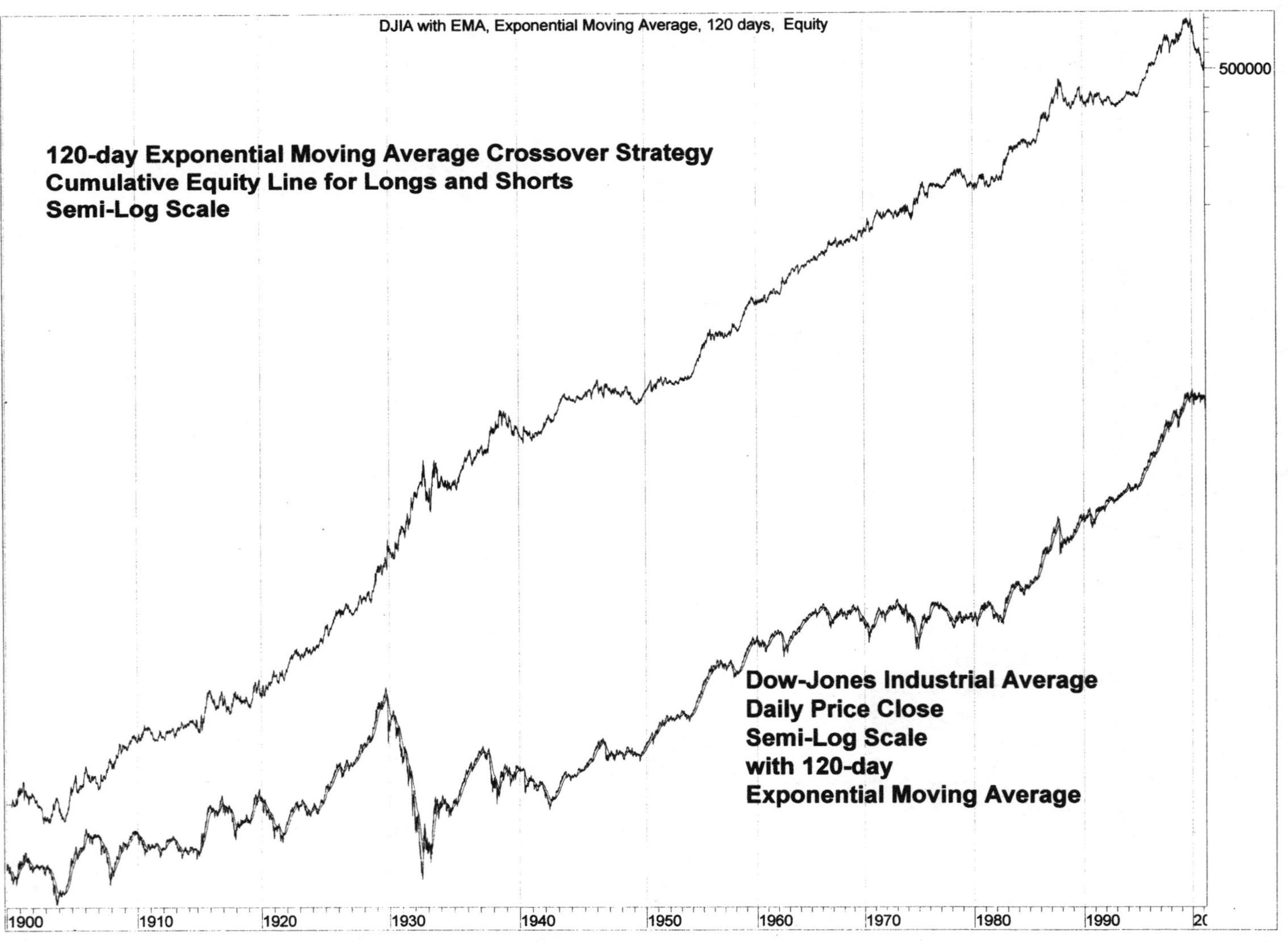
DJIA with EMA, Exponential Moving Average, 120 days, Equity
120-day Exponential Moving Average Crossover Strategy
Cumulative Equity Line for Longs and Shorts
Semi-Log Scale
500000
Dow-Jones Industrial Average
Daily Price Close
Semi-Log Scale
with 120-day
Exponential Moving Average
1900
1910
1920
1930
1940
1950
1960
1970
1980
1990

120-day EMA Crossover Strategy

Total net profit	508772.91	Open position value	24650.96	Net Profit/Buy&Hold %	2430.53
Percent gain/loss	508772.91	Annual percent gain/loss	5020.47	Annual Net %/B&H %	2430.48
Initial investment	100	Interest earned	0		
Current position	Short	Date position entered	3/9/01		
Buy/Hold profit	20105.4	Days in test	36989	# of days per trade	33.57
Buy/Hold pct gain/loss	20105.4	Annual B/H pct gain/loss	198.4		
Total closed trades	1102	Commissions paid	0		
Avg profit per trade	439.31	Avg Win/Avg Loss ratio	5.33		
Total long trades	551	Total short trades	551	Long Win Trade %	25.59
Winning long trades	141	Winning short trades	99	Short Win Trade %	17.97
Total winning trades	240	Total losing trades	862	Total Win Trade %	21.78
Amount of winning trades	1482363.63	Amount of losing trades	−998241.63	Net Profit Margin %	19.52
Average win	6176.52	Average loss	−1158.05	Average P. Margin %	68.42
Largest win	167218.81	Largest loss	−41004.06	% Net/(Win + Loss)	60.62
Average length of win	95.11	Average length of loss	6.82	(Win − Loss)/Loss %	1294.57
Longest winning trade	500	Longest losing trade	68	(Win − Loss)/Loss %	635.29
Most consecutive wins	4	Most consecutive losses	28	(Win − Loss)/Loss %	−85.71
Total bars out	121	Average length out	121		
Longest out period	121				
System close drawdown	−20.12	Profit/Loss index	33.76	% Net Profit/SODD	2528692.40
System open drawdown	−20.12	Reward/Risk index	100	(Net P. − SODD)/Net P.	100.00
Max open trade drawdown	−41004.06	Buy/Hold index	2553.14	% SODD/Net Profit	0.00

In the Equis MetaStock® "System Report" (profit and loss summary statistics), the *Total net profit* is the sum of profits minus the sum of losses, including open positions marked to the market. In contrast, the *Amount of Winning Trades* is the sum of realized profits (the total of all gains on closed-out trades only, excluding any open positions). Similarly, the *Amount of Losing Trades* is the sum of realized losses (the total of all losses on closed-out trades only, excluding any open positions). *System close drawdown* is the largest decline in the cumulative equity line below the initial investment, based on closed-out positions only. *System open drawdown (SODD)* is the largest decline in the cumulative equity line below the initial investment when a position is open. *Max open trade drawdown* is the largest decline in the cumulative equity line below the trade entry price during the worst single trade. The *Profit/Loss Index* is a complex calculation that relates the Amount of Winning Trades to the Amount of Losing Trades on a scale of −100 (worst possible performance) to +100 (best possible performance), with zero representing profits equal to losses. *Reward/Risk Index* is the Total net profit minus System open drawdown. The resulting difference is then divided by the Total net profit. The *Buy/Hold Index* is the Total net profit minus the buy-and-hold strategy's net profit. The resulting difference is then divided by the buy-and-hold net profit. In this exercise, initial equity is assumed to be $100. Both long and short positions are taken unless otherwise noted. Trades are executed at the closing price on the signal date. Transaction costs, interest expenses, and margins are not included in the statistics.

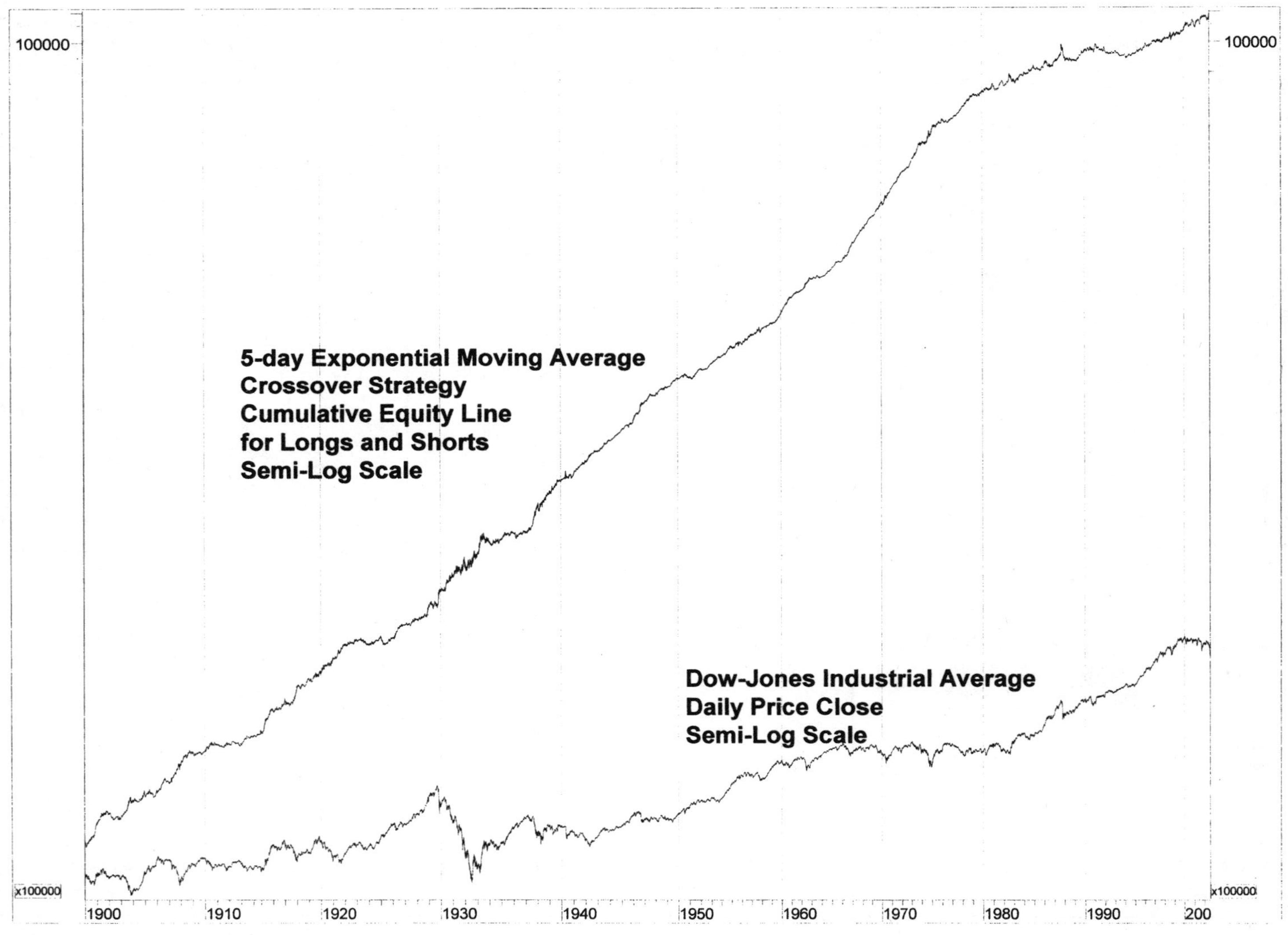

5-day Exponential Moving Average
Crossover Strategy
Cumulative Equity Line
for Longs and Shorts
Semi-Log Scale
Dow-Jones Industrial Average
Daily Price Close
Semi-Log Scale
100000
100000
x100000
x100000
1900
1910
1920
1930
1940
1950
1960
1970
1980
1990
200

5-Day EMA Crossover Strategy

Total net profit	16437 mm	Open position value	0	Net Profit/Buy&Hold %	77865725.02
Percent gain/loss	16437 mm	Annual percent gain/loss	161876079.2	Annual Net %/B&H %	77866117.35
Initial investment	100	Interest earned	0		
Current position	Short	Date position entered	6/22/01		
Buy/Hold profit	21109.2	Days in test	37062	# of days per trade	5.88
Buy/Hold pct gain/loss	21109.2	Annual B/H pct gain/loss	207.89		
Total closed trades	6306	Commissions paid	0		
Avg profit per trade	2606541.82	Avg Win/Avg Loss ratio	2.07		
Total long trades	3153	Total short trades	3153	Long Win Trade %	42.28
Winning long trades	1333	Winning short trades	1084	Short Win Trade %	34.38
Total winning trades	2417	Total losing trades	3889	Total Win Trade %	38.33
Amount of winning trades	73800 mm	Amount of losing trades	−57362 mm	Net Profit Margin %	12.53
Average win	30533627.8	Average loss	−14750053	Average P. Margin %	34.85
Largest win	1737168384	Largest loss	−603679744	% Net/(Win + Loss)	48.42
Average length of win	9.09	Average length of loss	3.12	(Win − Loss)/Loss %	191.35
Longest winning trade	39	Longest losing trade	24	(Win − Loss)/Loss %	62.50
Most consecutive wins	6	Most consecutive losses	13	(Win − Loss)/Loss %	−53.85
Total bars out	6	Average length out	6		
Longest out period	6				
System close drawdown	−7.71	Profit/Loss index	22.27	% Net Profit/SODD	213189 mm
System open drawdown	−7.71	Reward/Risk index	100	(Net P. − SODD)/Net P.	100.00
Max open trade drawdown	−603680064	Buy/Hold index	77865727.91	% SODD/Net Profit	0.00

In the Equis MetaStock® "System Report" (profit and loss summary statistics), the *Total net profit* is the sum of profits minus the sum of losses, including open positions marked to the market. In contrast, the *Amount of Winning Trades* is the sum of realized profits (the total of all gains on closed-out trades only, excluding any open positions). Similarly, the *Amount of Losing Trades* is the sum of realized losses (the total of all losses on closed-out trades only, excluding any open positions). *System close drawdown* is the largest decline in the cumulative equity line below the initial investment, based on closed-out positions only. *System open drawdown (SODD)* is the largest decline in the cumulative equity line below the initial investment when a position is open. *Max open trade drawdown* is the largest decline in the cumulative equity line below the trade entry price during the worst single trade. The *Profit/Loss Index* is a complex calculation that relates the Amount of Winning Trades to the Amount of Losing Trades on a scale of −100 (worst possible performance) to +100 (best possible performance), with zero representing profits equal to losses. *Reward/Risk Index* is the Total net profit minus System open drawdown. The resulting difference is then divided by the Total net profit. The *Buy/Hold Index* is the Total net profit minus the buy-and-hold strategy's net profit. The resulting difference is then divided by the buy-and-hold net profit. In this exercise, initial equity is assumed to be $100. Both long and short positions are taken unless otherwise noted. Trades are executed at the closing price on the signal date. Transaction costs, interest expenses, and margins are not included in the statistics.

Fibonacci Numbers, Fibonacci Cycles

Leonardo Fibonacci of Piza, Italy, (1170–1250) was a number theorist who has been credited with rediscovering the two-term difference sequence that has became known as Fibonacci numbers. He reportedly found it while studying the Great Pyramid of Giza in Egypt, which is said to be based on these numbers and ratios. It is believed that the sequence was well known to the Egyptians and to Pythagoras long before their rediscovery by Leonardo.

Fibonacci numbers are a sequence where each successive number is the sum of the two previous numbers:

0, 1, 1, 2, 3, 5, 8, 13, 21, 34, 55, 89, 144, 233, 377, 610, 987, and so forth.

These numbers possess intriguing interrelationships. It is an eye-opening exercise to play with them in a spread sheet (see table). First, we number down each row in column A to make a reference label. Second, we create the Fibonacci sequence in column B, starting with zero in cell B1 and one in cell B2, then add each cell's value to the previous cell's value. Third, in column C, divide each number in the Fibonacci sequence in column B by the previous number in the Fibonacci sequence, immediately above in column B. Fourth, in column D, divide each number in the Fibonacci sequence by the number two cells up. Fifth, in column E, divide each number in the Fibonacci sequence by the number three cells up. This is the Fibonacci expansion sequence, where subsequent numbers are 1.618 times the previous number, are 2.618 times the next previous number, and are 4.236 times the number three cells up.

The next three columns (F, G, H) show the Fibonacci contraction sequence, where the ratio of the current Fibonacci number to the next one is 0.618 times, then the ratio to the one after that is 0.382 times, and the ratio to the number three cells down is 0.236 times.

In addition you will find 0.5000, 1.000, and 2.000 in the table, and these are also useful. Finally, please note that the square roots of the key ratios of 0.618 and 1.618 are 0.786 and 1.272.

When projecting price targets forward, in ascending order, the most important Fibonacci ratios are: 0.236, 0.382, 0.500, 0.618, 0.786, 1.000, 1.272, 1.618, 2.000, 2.618, and 4.236. These ratios are useful in comparing market price movements to one another.

In technical analysis, the interpretation of Fibonacci numbers is based on experienced judgement. Popular computer software, such as MetaStock®, offers visual studies based on the Fibonacci sequence. Fibonacci Arcs, Fans and Retracements are based on a line that the user may draw connecting any significant price low and high. If that line is rising, the arcs and fan lines point upward; if that line is falling, the arcs and fan lines point downward.

A	B	C	D	E	F	G	H
row #	*Fib. #*	*Fib. # Divided by cell B# − 1*	*Fib. # Divided by cell B# − 2*	*Fib. # Divided by cell B# − 3*	*Fib. # Divided by cell B# + 1*	*Fib. # Divided by cell B# + 2*	*Fib. # Divided by cell B# + 3*
1	0				0.000	0.000	0.000
2	1				1.000	0.500	0.333
3	1	1.000			0.500	0.333	0.200
4	2	2.000	2.000		0.667	0.400	0.250
5	3	1.500	3.000	3.000	0.600	0.375	0.231
6	5	1.667	2.500	5.000	0.625	0.385	0.238
7	8	1.600	2.667	4.000	0.615	0.381	0.235
8	13	1.625	2.600	4.333	0.619	0.382	0.236
9	21	1.615	2.625	4.200	0.618	0.382	0.236
10	34	1.619	2.615	4.250	0.618	0.382	0.236
11	55	1.618	2.619	4.231	0.618	0.382	0.236
12	89	1.618	2.618	4.238	0.618	0.382	0.236
13	144	1.618	2.618	4.235	0.618	0.382	0.236
14	233	1.618	2.618	4.236	0.618	0.382	0.236
15	377	1.618	2.618	4.236	0.618	0.382	0.236
16	610	1.618	2.618	4.236	0.618	0.382	0.236
17	987	1.618	2.618	4.236	0.618	0.382	0.236
18	1597	1.618	2.618	4.236	0.618	0.382	0.236
19	2584	1.618	2.618	4.236	0.618	0.382	0.236
20	4181	1.618	2.618	4.236	0.618	0.382	0.236
21	6765	1.618	2.618	4.236	0.618	0.382	0.236

Fibonacci Arcs and Fibonacci Circles offer support and resistance as well as possible trend change times. These bisect a straight line connecting an early low to a subsequent high at points on that line that are 61.8%, 50%, and 38.2% of the length of the line. Anchor a compass point at the subsequent high, then draw a circle through these points. When a future price move meets a curving Arc and Circle line extended out to the right of the chart, look for support, resistance and/or trend change. Similarly, Arcs and Circles also are drawn through a Fibonacci proportioned straight line from an early high to a subsequent low.

Fibonacci Fans also offer support and resistance. Fans are computed and drawn on a chart in five steps:

1. Subtract an early significant low price from a subsequent significant high price.
2. Multiply that difference by 61.8%, 50%, and 38.2%.
3. Add these products to the early low price.

4. Plot those points (from Step 3) directly beneath and on the same date as the subsequent high price.
5. Connect the early low price to the plotted points (from Step 4) with straight lines extending forward in time.

The resulting ascending Fibonacci Fans are estimates of future support and resistance. A similar method is used to plot descending Fibonacci Fans, based on the distance from a significant price high to a subsequent significant price low, and with the Fibonacci price points plotted directly above the subsequent low.

Fibonacci Retracements also are based on a line that the user may draw connecting significant price troughs and peaks. If that line is rising, the retracement lines will project downward; if that line is falling, the retracement lines will project upward. These Retracement lines offer support and resistance. Note on the graph of the NASDAQ 100 futures contract that the 0.618 retracement ratio based on the steep 2-month price decline from 3/24/00 to 5/24/00 worked well as resistance to rallies on 7/17/00 and 9/1/00. The 0.236 retracement ratio was effective support on 8/3/00.

The **Fibonacci Pentagon/Star** can be overlaid on top of a price chart, such that one of the sides of either the pentagon or the star connects by a straight line a significant price bottom and a significant price top. Then the other lines that make up the Pentagon/Star can be used to anticipate potential levels of support and resistance before they might appear in actual price data. The Pentagon/Star begins with a regular pentagon. To reveal the five-pointed star within the pentagon, draw five straight diagonal lines through the body of the pentagon from each corner to the second next corner (that is, skipping over the adjacent corners). Each line in the star has a length that is 1.618 times the length of each side of the pentagon.

Fibonacci Time Zones are vertical lines placed at time intervals separated by Fibonacci numbers. Starting with an obvious turning point high or low, labeled day zero, MetaStock® will count and mark the subsequent trading days (skipping weekends and holidays) according to the Fibonacci sequence: 0, 1, 1, 2, 3, 5, 8, 13, 21, 34, 55, 89, 144, 233, 377, 610, 987, and so forth. Be alert for possible directional price trend changes at or near these vertical lines marking the Fibonacci Time Zones.

Robert C. Miner* proportions future time by Fibonacci ratios. First, Miner applies **Fibonacci Time-Cycle Ratios** to the time duration of the latest completed price swing, using both trading days and calendar days. The most important Fibonacci ratios are: 0.382, 0.500, 0.618, 1.000, 1.618, 2.000, and 2.618.

Miner's Alternative Time Projections are calculated as time ratios of the previous price swing in the same direction: up swings are measured out as proportions of previous up swings, while down swings are measured out as proportions of previous down swings. Alternative Time Projections may also be derived from same-direction price swings earlier than the latest one.

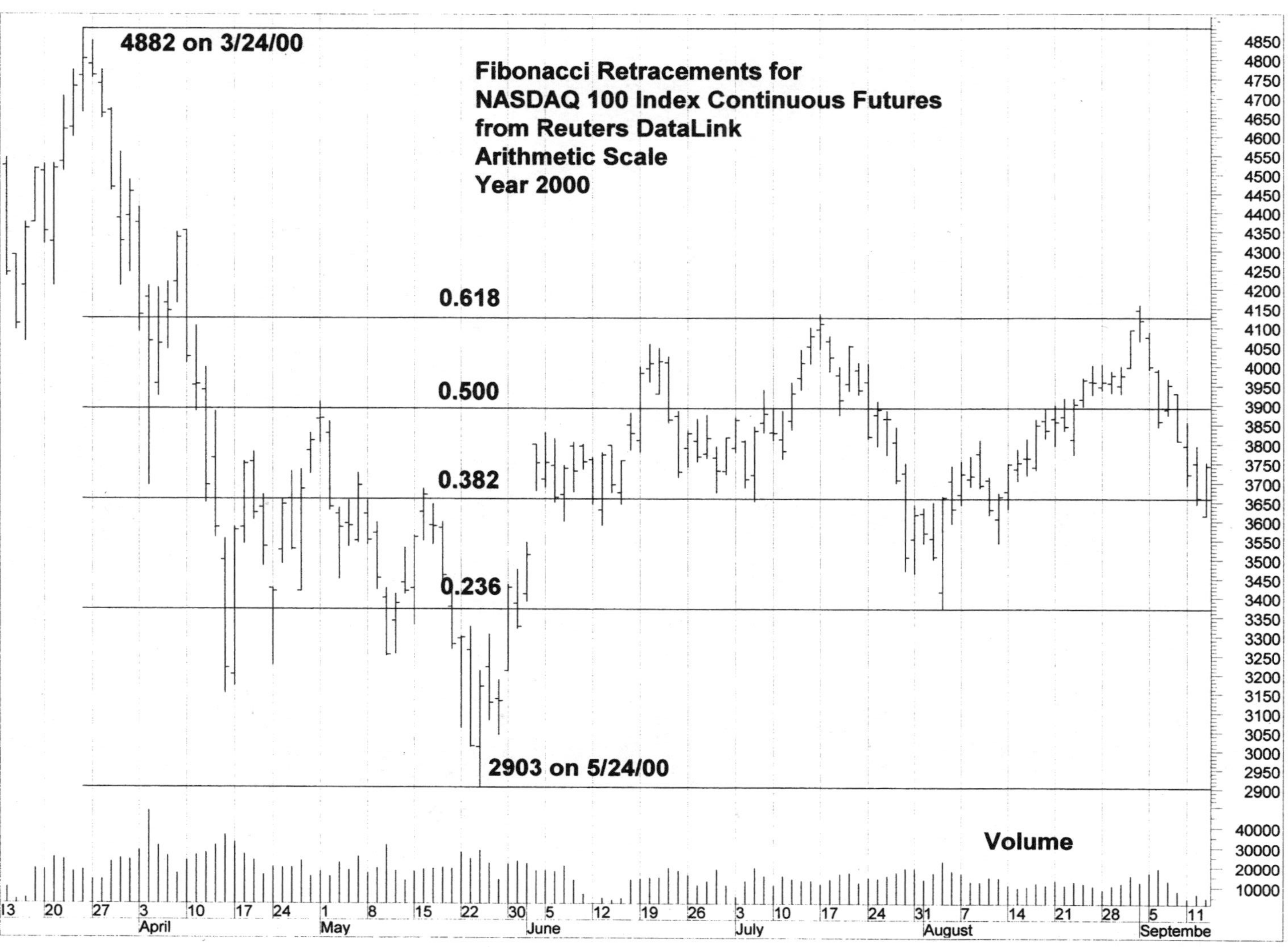

Fibonacci Retracements for
NASDAQ 100 Index Continuous Futures
from Reuters DataLink
Arithmetic Scale
Year 2000
4882 on 3/24/00
0.618
0.500
0.382
0.236
2903 on 5/24/00
Volume
4850
4800
4750
4700
4650
4600
4550
4500
4450
4400
4350
4300
4250
4200
4150
4100
4050
4000
3950
3900
3850
3800
3750
3700
3650
3600
3550
3500
3450
3400
3350
3300
3250
3200
3150
3100
3050
3000
2950
2900
40000
30000
20000
10000
13
20
27
3
April
10
17
24
1
May
8
15
22
30
5
June
12
19
26
3
July
10
17
24
31
August
7
14
21
28
5
Septembe
11

Miner points out that there is a very high probability of trend change when *both* price and time ratios coincide (page 5-36)*.

Miner's Trend Vibration™ method is based on two directional movements early in a trend: the initial thrust and the initial corrective wave of that thrust. Together these two movements are Elliot Waves one and two, and Miner calls them the *initial vibration.* Fibonacci ratios of that initial vibration time projected forward coincide with subsequent turning dates, including the end point of the completed trend (page 5-38)*.

Of secondary importance are the day counts, numbering each day in straight numerical sequence from outstanding turning points, using both trading days and calendar days. When one or more day counts is a number in the Fibonacci sequence, the probability of a directional trend change is heightened. The more hits on Fibonacci numbers, the greater the confirmation and power of that date.

As suggested by **W. D. Gann,** Miner also uses multiples of 30 (specifically, 30, 60, 90, 120, 150, 180, 210, 240, 270, 300, 330, and 360), and multiples of 36 (specifically, 36, 72, 108, 144, 180, 216, 252, 288, 324, and 360) in his day counts. **Anniversary dates** of previous turning points in history also add value to his analysis of time.

Miner also uses **Bollinger Bands** (which are also known as Standard Deviation Bands and Volatility Bands) to help identify and confirm time/price turning points. Two standard deviations above and below a moving average create a channel that encloses 95% of the price action. In relatively low volatility, sideways trading-range markets, such bands reliably indicate support and resistance. In trending markets, where the trend is strong and continuing, reactions against the trend often do not exceed the moving average mid-way between the upper and lower bands. In a bullish trend, price spends more of the time testing the upper band and the moving average. In a bearish trend, price spends more of the time testing the lower band and the moving average.

At the independently determined cyclical time of probable trend change, Miner has observed that price is often near one extreme band or the other. To confirm the trend change, price moves quickly to the opposite band in the direction of the new trend, showing a relatively high degree of absolute price velocity. Trend, Elliott Wave and Chart Pattern interpretation complement and complete Miner's cycle analysis.

---

*The time and price projection methods cited here are an incomplete sampling from Miner's book, which is one of the more productive and practical Fibonacci studies to emerge in years. Miner also offers guidelines for combining these studies, putting them into useful perspective, as well as a large number of real-world examples. We recommend his book: Miner, Robert C., *Dynamic Trading,* Dynamic Traders Group, Inc., 6336 N. Oracle, Suite 326-346, Tucson, AZ 85704. Miner also has developed software to efficiently make the calculations of the Fibonacci relationships, including time as well as price, in any market. Adapted with permission.

First Five Days in January: an "Early Warning" System

(See January's First Five Days.)

Force Index

The Force Index is a smoothed price change times volume velocity oscillator presented by Alexander Elder in his popular book, *Trading for a Living: Psychology, Trading Tactics, Money Management,* John Wiley & Sons, Inc., New York, 1993. The Force Index is calculated precisely the same way as a much older indicator *(see Volume * Price Momentum Oscillator (V*PMO)).*

Elder offers five pages covering a number of rather complex interpretations of what he re-names the Force Index. Basically he fades a very short-term version when it is contrary to the larger trend, and he looks for divergences of the Force Index versus the underlying price series.

As a purely mechanical indicator, however, our tests suggest that the Force Index is better used as a trend-following indicator than faded as a contra-trend indicator.

Fourier Analysis: Fast Fourier Transform

Fourier Analysis is said to be ideally suited for finding precise recurring cycles in the physical sciences. Thus it is tempting for well-educated analysts with strong mathematical backgrounds to apply this method to market data. The problem is that unlike data from the physical sciences, market data is relatively irregular. The market is not a pendulum. Although we are able to obtain precise and seemingly scientific answers using Fourier Analysis, we cannot rely on the underlying assumptions and, therefore, we can have no confidence about any value in forecasting. In fact, our research suggests that it is not fruitful to apply Fourier Analysis to cyclical analysis of financial markets.

In the words of Richard Mogey and Jack Schwager (*Schwager on Futures, Technical Analysis,* John Wiley, New York, 1996, 775 pages, pages 591-2), " . . . cycles are only one market force and can at times be swamped by other market influences. Moreover, even the most consistent cycles will deviate from their mathematical representations. Therefore, the rigid application of cycle projections in making trading decisions (to the exclusion of other methods and considerations) is a recipe for disaster."

Fourier transform (FT) is a frequency description of time domain events. *FT is designed to study repetitious phenomena.* FT is named for French analyst and physicist, Jean Baptiste Joseph Fourier (1768–1830), whose study of the conduction of heat had a profound influence on mathematical physics and on the study of real functions. In 1822, Fourier was the first to represent any function as an infinite summation of sine and cosine terms. FT decomposes or separates a waveform or function into sinusoids of different frequency which sum to the original waveform. It identifies or distinguishes the different frequency sinusoids and their respective amplitudes. FT is an integral transform that sends function *f* to another function *F.* Under reasonable conditions the FT is invertible. The Fourier transform of $f(x)$ can be expressed as follows:

$$F(y) = \int_{-\infty}^{\infty} f(x) \exp(-i\, y\, x)\, dx$$

where

exp = the symbol for the exponential function

$\int_{-\infty}^{\infty}$ = the symbol for the imaginary number the square root of -1

dx denotes an element, the derivative of *x*

Fast Fourier Transform (FFT) is an efficient algorithm for digital computation of the Fourier transform. FFT is an abbreviated calculation that computes quickly, in seconds rather than minutes. The FFT sacrifices phase relationships and concentrates only on cycle length and amplitude (strength). The benefit of FFT is its ability to extract the predominate cycle from a series of data, such as a security's price.

FFTs are based on the principal that any finite, time-ordered set of data can be approximated by decomposing the data into a set of sine waves. Each sine wave has a specific cycle length, amplitude, and phase relationship to the other sine waves. Because FFTs were designed to be applied to non-trending, periodic data and security price data tends to be trending, the raw price data must be detrended, commonly by using a linear regression trendline. Also, security price data is not truly periodic, since securities are not traded on weekends and some holidays. These discontinuities must be removed by passing the data through a smoothing function, such as a Hamming window, which is based on binary codes that correct transmission errors on the presumption that the chance of a very high proportion of errors is negligible.

Equis MetaStock® software program can extract the predominate FFT cycle from price data and display cycle length and amplitude (cycle strength). Copy the following "default" FFT formula into the MetaStock® Indicator Builder:

fft(CLOSE, 100, 1, DETREND, POWER)

where

fft = Fast Fourier Transform
CLOSE = the closing price of the day
100 = the PERIOD of time to analyze, in days
DETREND = the linear regression smoothing method used to remove trends from the data
POWER = the type of analysis display, the power spectrum, which is a plot in histogram form of the cycle power (y-axis) versus cycle length or frequency (x-axis). Cycle power (the y-axis) of a Fourier power spectrum is the cycle amplitude squared.

This FFT formula plots a graph, and the highest peak on that graphed line, as measured against the vertical y-axis, is the "typical" dominant cycle length. Rather than interpreting this time cycle length as a precise number of days, experience suggests that it might be more practical to think of it as "plus or minus a few days", because of the typical variability of cycles as long observed in markets.

On his website (www.mesasoftware.com) John F. Ehlers, professional engineer and market cycles researcher, points out that the correct use of Fourier Transforms requires relatively long databases, and the data must be stationary (non-shifting) over the observation period. For short databases, he has concluded that "the use of FFTs for trading is not advisable." Ehlers designed his Maximum Entropy Spectral Analysis (MESA) software program to be a better solution than FFTs for identifying short, shifting cycles on relatively small quantities of data.

Loading the Dow-Jones Industrial Average daily closing prices for the past 100 years from 1900 to 2000 and employing the Equis MetaStock® formula fft(CLOSE, 100, 1, DETREND, POWER), the FFT dominant cycle length for the daily DJIA for the past century is about 22.57 days on average, give or take a few days.

In Column 3 of the table, we ran FFT on the actual daily closing price of the DJIA. We relied on the FFT formula to de-trend this data.

In Column 4, we first detrended the actual DJIA by dividing the daily close by a 170-day exponential moving average of the close, then we tested that ratio. (See our section on *Exponential Moving Average.*) The FFT formula, using a linear regression trendline, detrended that close/EMA ratio. Therefore, we could say the raw closing price data was twice detrended. As expected from reading the literature, the second, twice de-trended method resulted in somewhat less variability and greater stability of the cycle length.

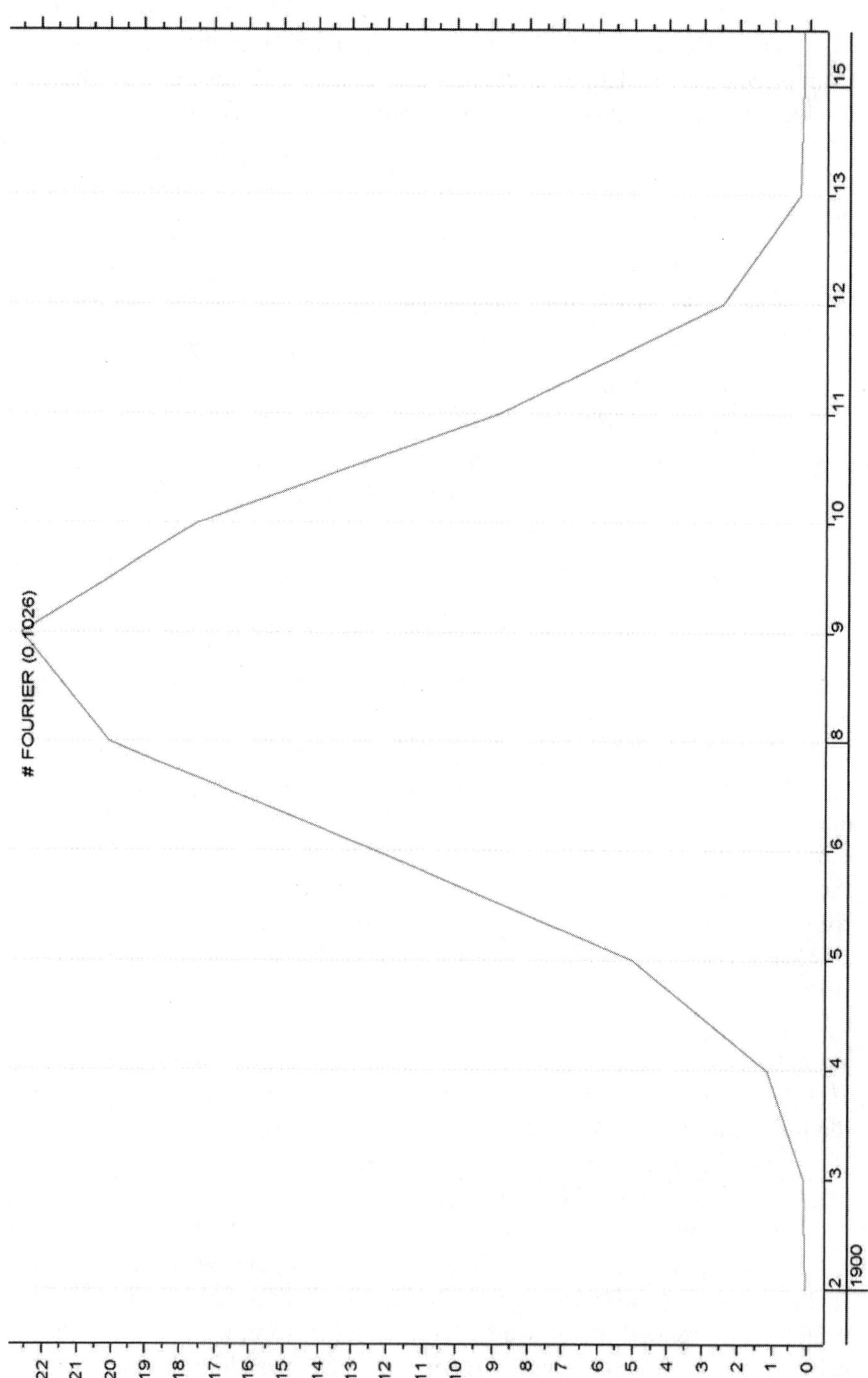

FOURIER (0,1026)
1900

The table shows how the FFT cycle length at various start dates has shifted over the past 70 years. We arbitrarily broke the database into 14 overlapping test windows. Each test period ends on September 8, 2000. Each test period begins on January 2nd of the years shown in the table. After we tested the longest window, starting on 1/2/30, we then shifted *forward in time* in 5-year time increments in an effort to measure how shifts in the starting date would impact the calculated FFT dominant cycle length.

FFT Cycle Lengths for Different Time Windows

Start Date Jan. 2	*End Date Sept. 8*	*Close FFT in days*	*C/170 EMA FFT in days*
1930	2000	21	12
1935	2000	27	19
1940	2000	13	11
1945	2000	16	14
1950	2000	16	8
1955	2000	21	15
1960	2000	23	20
1965	2000	15	17
1970	2000	17	13
1975	2000	24	15
1980	2000	23	21
1985	2000	16	13
1990	2000	15	14
1995	2000	11	9
Range		11 to 27	8 to 21
Mean		18	14
Median		17	14

It is perhaps an interesting coincidence that FFT critic, John F. Ehlers, using his Maximum Entropy Spectral Analysis (MESA) program, found that for the S&P 500 futures contract as of 6/13/93 the measured dominant cycle length was about 14 days—the same mean and median number of days we found over 70 years of history using the twice detrended FFT method in Column 4. (See John F. Ehlers, "Creating Indicators With Physics", *Technical Analysis of Stocks & Commodities* V. 11:10 (pages 395–400), www.traders.com.) On previous occasions, Ehlers found 9-day, 14-day and 22-day dominant cycle lengths for the S&P 500 futures, which were within the historical FFT ranges we found in the table above. (See John F. Ehlers, "How to use Maximum Entropy", *Technical Analysis of Stocks & Commodities* V. 5:10

(pages 334–339), and "Cyclic Personalities", *Technical Analysis of Stocks & Commodities* V. 7:4 (pages 132–134), www.traders.com.) Ehlers found the S&P to be the best futures contract in terms of its statistical cyclic behavior, followed by U.S. Treasury Bonds (with a dominant cycle of 9 days). Of 12 contracts examined, all showed dominant cycles within a range of 7 to 19 days.

Funds Net Purchases Index

The Funds Net Purchases Index is a sentiment indicator developed by Arthur A. Merrill, CMT. Merrill found that professionally managed mutual fund net buy-sell activity was a highly significant indicator of future stock market direction over forward periods of 13, 26, and 52 weeks.

Data on mutual fund purchases and sales of common stocks and on total fund assets for stock, bond and income funds is published by *Barron's* financial weekly newspaper on a monthly basis, with about a 1-month lag. More timely data is available on a subscription basis from the Investment Company Institute, 1600 M Street NW, Washington, DC 20036.

To compute Merrill's indicator, first subtract sales of common stock from purchases of common stock. Second, divide that difference by total fund assets, including stock, bond and income funds. Third, smooth that ratio with a 33% exponential smoothing constant, which is roughly the equivalent of a 5-month simple moving average. Fourth, normalize the smoothed ratio by dividing it by the standard deviation.

Over a 10-year back-test period, Merrill found that his Funds Net Purchases Index was bullish when it was greater than two thirds of one standard deviation above the mean. It was bearish when more than two thirds of one standard deviation below the mean. Forward predictions were highly significant statistically, measured against the Dow-Jones Industrial Average over three different time intervals, 13, 26, and 52 weeks, into the future.

Futures Algorithm of Rollovers for CSI's Perpetual Contract®

CSI's Perpetual Contract® data is computed by a proprietary CSI formula that makes historical futures data useful for long-term technical analysis studies. Historical data needs to be adjusted because of price gaps between contracts with different expiration dates.

CSI Perpetual Contract is a time-weighted average price of the two nearest active contracts. As the nearest contract approaches expiration, it is allocated progressively less weight, according to a straight linear formula reflecting the number of days remaining until expiration (or roll date). Meanwhile, the next contract forward in time is allocated progressively greater weight each day. Add the two time-weighted contract values each day to arrive at the *CSI Perpetual Contract*.

The *CSI Perpetual Contract* is actually simpler than it may seem at first glance, as illustrated by the following practical example. For the Standard & Poor's 500 Stock Composite Index Futures Contracts, there are three months between contracts. Three months is about 63 trading days on average, depending on the distribution of holidays and other minor quirks of the calendar. There are four contracts each calendar year, one expiring each quarter on the third Friday of March, June, September, and December.

Assume it is the second Thursday of June. The nearest contract, the June contact, will expire a week from tomorrow, on a Friday one week and one day from today. This Thursday is the traditionally predetermined roll date, when the pit-trader members of the Chicago Mercantile Exchange name the next contract (in this case the September contract) the front month. Therefore, as of today, the prime real estate on the trading floor is now reserved for trading the September contract. According to the *CSI Perpetual Contract* formula, on this Thursday roll date, the nearest contract, the soon-expiring June contract, is weighted at 0/63 times the June contract price (and zero divided by sixty three equals zero). Meanwhile, the new "front-month" September contract is weighted 63/63 times the September contract price (that is, 100% of the September contract price).

The next trading day, Friday, the September contract is weighted 62/63 times the September contract price and the December contract is weighted 1/63 times the December contract price. The third trading day, Monday, the September contract is weighted 61/63 times the September contract price and the December is weighted 2/63 times the December contract price. The fourth trading day, Tuesday, the September is weighted 60/63 times the September price and the December is weighted 3/63 times the December price.

And so on, until at the September contract roll date (on the second Thursday of September), the September contract is weighted 0/63 times the September contract price and the December contract is weighted 63/63 times the December contract price. The next day December is weighted 62/63 and the March is weighted 1/63 times the March price. The second day, the December contract is weighted 61/63 and the March is weighted 2/63 times the March price. Add the two weighted contracts to arrive at the *CSI Perpetual Contract*.

An alternative is to weight the nearest two contracts by their respective open interests, rolling forward and excluding the nearest contract when heaviest open interest shifts to the subsequent delivery month.

For long-term computer studies in technical analysis, this *CSI Perpetual Contract* is probably the best solution for handling rollovers of contracts. The only disadvantage of *CSI Perpetual Contract* is that we cannot actually buy or sell it or use it for precise support and resistance levels for short-term trading.

An alternate method is backward-adjusted contracts. Here, at the roll date, if the next contract is trading, say, 10 points above the expiring June contract, then add 10 points to all historical data. On the other hand, if the next contract is trading 10 points below the expiring June contract, then subtract 10 points from all historical data to fill the gap. Unfortunately, this method can produce negative prices way back in time, and such negative numbers can cause problems in back testing of technical strategies. Also, long-term chart trend analysis may be substantially distorted.

So, CSI invented their Perpetual Contract to eliminate historical negative numbers. And the long-term charts look right. But, of course, you cannot call your broker and actually place an order for a *CSI Perpetual Contract,* since they do not trade.

Futures Contracts: Expiration Months and Symbols

Futures contracts generally become most actively traded a few months before they expire. Trading activity dries up, however, in the month of expiration or in some cases the month before expiration, depending on the traditions of the particular contract. Futures traders must pay attention to the calendar and to shifts in volume and open interest. It generally pays to trade only in the most active contracts in order to avoid getting caught by a lack of liquidity which increases slippage. (Slippage is the difference between the price you expect to get on your order and the price you actually get.)

Stock index options expire on the Saturday following the third Friday of each month. Those third Fridays in March, June, September, and December are referred to as "triple witching," because futures, index options and individual stock options all expire. The days before and after such simultaneous expirations have been unusually volatile. Generally, it is better to exit expiring options well before expiration, since the time premiums and liquidity erode in an accelerating fashion in the days and weeks before expiration.

Symbol	*Month*
F	January
G	February
H	March
J	April
K	May
M	June
N	July
Q	August
U	September
V	October
X	November
Z	December

Gann Angles*

W. D. Gann (1878–1955) developed the use of what he called "Geometric Angles," now commonly referred to as Gann Angles, used to determine trend direction and strength, support and resistance, as well as probabilities of price reversal.

Gann was fascinated by the relation of time (T) and price (P). Gann drew his angles from all significant price pivot point highs and lows. He used just one pivot point to draw an angle that rose (or fell) at predetermined and fixed rates of speed, as follows:

T × P	*n* degrees
1 × 8	82.5 degrees
1 × 4	75 degrees
1 × 3	71.25 degrees
1 × 2	63.75 degrees
1 × 1	45 degrees
2 × 1	26.25 degrees
3 × 1	18.75 degrees
4 × 1	15 degrees
8 × 1	7.5 degrees

where

T = the number of units of time, graphically plotted on the horizontal x-axis.

P = the number of units of price, graphically plotted on the vertical y-axis.

× = read as *by.*

n degrees specifies the slope of the Gann angle, measured in degrees.

Translating time by price into degrees assumes a *square grid,* where one unit of time on the x-axis takes up the same amount of horizontal space as the one unit of price on the y-axis takes up vertical space. For example, 1/16 of an inch might be set to one week of time on the horizontal x-axis, and 1/16 of an inch might be set to one dollar of price on the vertical y-axis. On such a proportionally scaled chart, the 1 × 1 geometric angle, which for every one unit of time rises one point in price, is a 45 degree angle.

Without this equality of time and price scaling, Gann angles stated in degrees do not work out correctly. That would not prevent correct Gann angles from being drawn on oddly proportioned grids; it would only prevent the translation of time by price angles into correctly displayed degrees. But that would not affect the interpretation of the Gann angles if we avoid thinking in terms of degrees. Rather than thinking in terms of degrees, it is simpler to express Gann angles in terms of units of *time by price.*

For practical purposes, weekly Gann angles, drawn on a weekly bar chart, appear to offer the most useful perspective. Gann often said that the weekly chart was more important than the daily chart. Nevertheless, Gann angles are flexible and can be used on any time-scale, so long as the time by price proportions are correctly calculated.

Gann angles offer indications of support and resistance that may not be evident based on any other method. For example, during an up-trend, the 1 × 1 angle tends to provide major support. A major reversal is signaled when prices fall below the 1 × 1 angle. According to Gann, prices should then be expected to fall to the next angle below—the 2 × 1 angle. In other words, as one angle is penetrated, expect prices to test the next angle, which is less steep.

Gann placed special emphasis on the 1 × 1 angle. On a perfectly proportioned time by price grid, in an uptrend, the 1 × 1 angle extends "northeast" from a price pivot point low at a precise 45 degree angle. This 1 × 1 angle is the most significant angle: it represents a sustainable, perfectly balanced trend, not too fast and not too slow, but just right. In a bullish uptrend, the 1 × 1 angle tends to provide major support. When this 1 × 1 angle is broken, a significant price trend reversal is signaled. The price should then drop down to test the 2 × 1 angle.

In a downtrend, the 1 × 1 angle extends "southeast" from a price pivot point high at a precise 45 degree angle. Eventually after a downtrend, when price moves above and stays above the 1 × 1 angle (which is sloping down and to the left at 45 degrees), price should then make its way up to test the next, less-steep Gann angle—the declining 2 × 1 angle. An angle that provided resistance, once decisively broken, should provide support.

Furthermore, when a 1 × 1 angle crosses a horizontal line extending forward in time from a significant past pivot point price (an obvious high or low), then *time and price are square* relative to that past pivot point, and that is a likely time for a change in trend or an acceleration of the existing trend. Also, when a geometric angle crosses zero or another geometric angle, a trend change is likely.

Identification of the most important Gann angle is dependent of the price level of the instrument analyzed: very high and very low priced instruments will follow steeper and shallower Gann angles, respectively. In other words, the best functioning Gann angle for support and resistance depends on the price level of the instrument being analyzed.

For the S&P 500 Composite Stock Price Index, a relevant support and resistance price channel was well defined by 2 × 1 weekly Gann angles from the 8/9/82 price low at 102.20 until 1995. After the 12/9/94 low at 442.88, the S&P price level quickly rose so high that the bull market trend was better defined by the rising 1 × 4 weekly

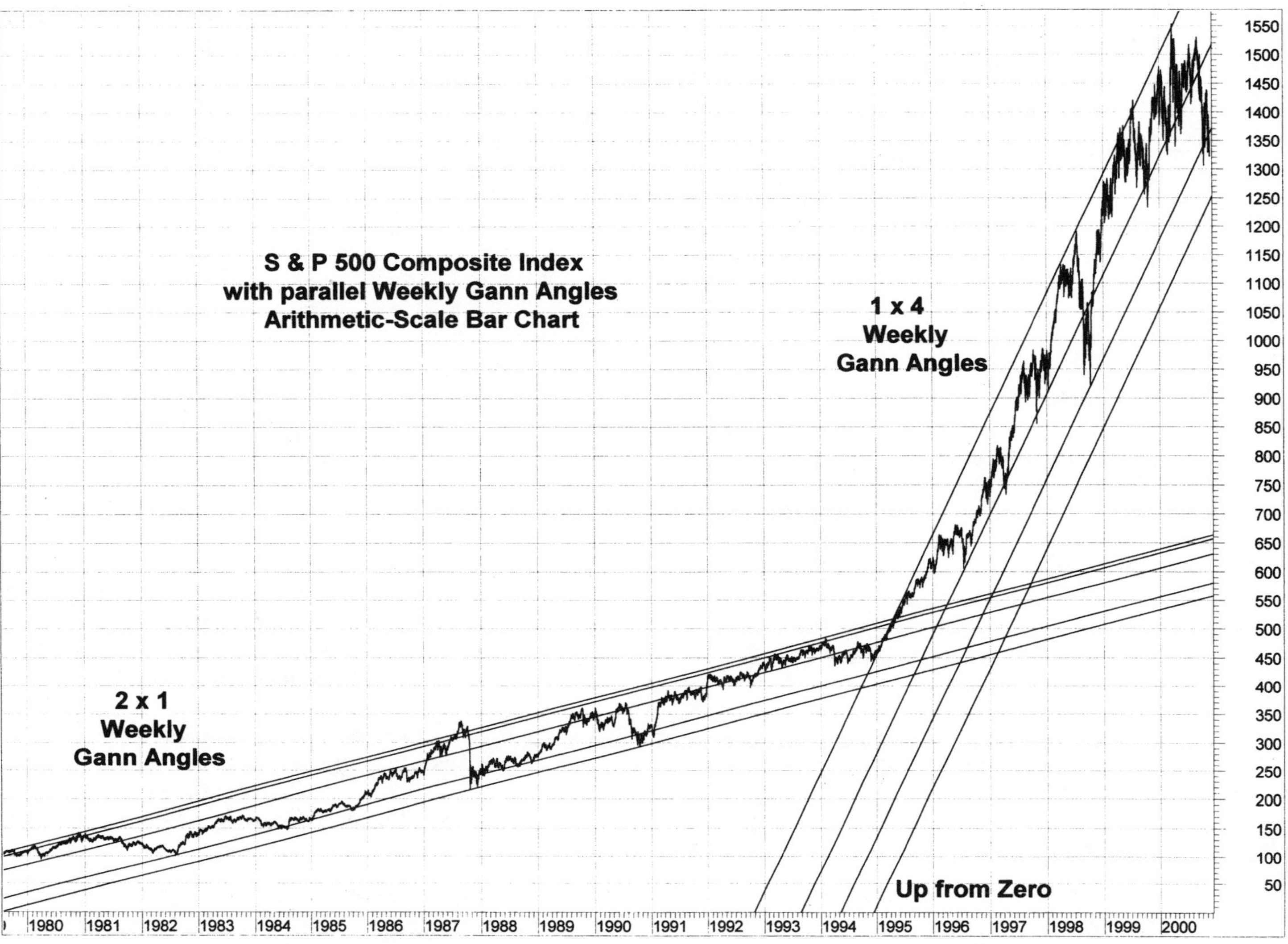
S & P 500 Composite Index
with parallel Weekly Gann Angles
Arithmetic-Scale Bar Chart
1 x 4
Weekly
Gann Angles
2 x 1
Weekly
Gann Angles
Up from Zero
1550
1500
1450
1400
1350
1300
1250
1200
1150
1100
1050
1000
950
900
850
800
750
700
650
600
550
500
450
400
350
300
250
200
150
100
50
1980
1981
1982
1983
1984
1985
1986
1987
1988
1989
1990
1991
1992
1993
1994
1995
1996
1997
1998
1999
2000

Cisco Systems (CSCO)
Weekly Bars
Weekly 2 X 1 Gann Angles,
drawn from any high or low,
and rising at the rate of
one point every two weeks,
would have been useful
for identifying
support and resistance.
When the last
Gann Angle broke,
in September 2000,
price fell quickly.
80
75
70
65
60
55
50
45
40
35
30
25
20
15
10
5
500000
x10
1997 M A M J J A S O N D 1998 M A M J J A S O N D 1999 M A M J J A S O N D 2000 M A M J J A S O N D 2001 M

Gann angles. A glance at the chart should make obvious the value of these Gann angles, which can be drawn *before* the fact, as soon as the user can identify a pivot point high or low.

Gann also divided significant price and time ranges and previous highs and lows into eighths, and looked for support and resistance there. For example, dividing the low to high price range after a substantial upswing, the most important divisions would be 8/8 (or the high), 1/2 (the midpoint), and 0/8 (the low). Next most important would be 3/8 and 5/8. Expressed in decimals, 3/8 is 0.375 and 5/8 is 0.625, which are only .007 away from the Fibonacci ratios of 0.382 and 0.618.

Gann's Square of Nine

W.D. Gann's Square of Nine number cycle has been related to a number of natural cycles, relationships and structures, including those that appear in the structure of the Great Pyramid, Fibonacci spirals, various harmonic frequencies, the celestial and acoustic vibrations of Pythagoras, Galileo's Theorem of Equivalence and his conception of solar system motion, and the equal tempered twelve-tone musical scale of Leonard Euler, as pointed out by Constance Brown, CMT, CPO, of Aerodynamic Investments Inc., on her web site, www.aeroinvest.com.

The illustration here, based on the work of Gann expert Peter Suarez, has been corrected for errors that appear in popular published sources. The best way to learn about it is to study it in detail. From one at the center, it expands in a linear progression, spiraling around and outward in a clockwise fashion. One of the interesting things to note are the squares of the even numbers ascending on a diagonal to the *northeast* (parallel to the 45 degree angle) and squares of the odd numbers descending on a diagonal to the *southwest* (parallel to the 225 degree angle).

The degrees of a 360 degree full circle are marked in a counter-clockwise fashion, with major emphasis on the horizontal, vertical and diagonal angles, specifically 45, 90, 135, 180, 225, 270, 315, and 360 degrees. When a significant price high or low appears in a tradable instrument of interest, we look to the next numbers along these major angles for potential support, resistance and price targets.

For example, when the S&P 500 Stock Index futures contract set its all-time low at 101 on 8/9/82 and reversed upward, we might have looked to numbers on the major angles up from 45 degrees (on which that 101 low lies) for upside targets, specifically 106, 111, 116, 122, 127, 133, 139, 145 (which is a full number cycle of 360 degrees at this price level), and so on, upward and outward around the spiral. As price increases, the numerical distance between angles grows larger.

Trial and error experimentation is the only way to learn this method. Constructing your own spreadsheet might help you begin to comprehend Gann's Square of Nine number cycle spiral.

135 90 45

993	994	995	996	997	998	999																									
992	871	872	873	874	875	876	877	878	879	880	881	882	883	884	885	886	887	888	889	890	891	892	893	894	895	896	897	898	899	900	901
991	870	757	758	759	760	761	762	763	764	765	766	767	768	769	770	771	772	773	774	775	776	777	778	779	780	781	782	783	784	785	902
990	869	756	651	652	653	654	655	656	657	658	659	660	661	662	663	664	665	666	667	668	669	670	671	672	673	674	675	676	677	786	903
989	868	755	650	553	554	555	556	557	558	559	560	561	562	563	564	565	566	567	568	569	570	571	572	573	574	575	576	577	678	787	904
988	867	754	649	552	463	464	465	466	467	468	469	470	471	472	473	474	475	476	477	478	479	480	481	482	483	484	485	578	679	788	905
987	866	753	648	551	462	381	382	383	384	385	386	387	388	389	390	391	392	393	394	395	396	397	398	399	400	401	486	579	680	789	906
986	865	752	647	550	461	380	307	308	309	310	311	312	313	314	315	316	317	318	319	320	321	322	323	324	325	402	487	580	681	790	907
985	864	751	646	549	460	379	306	241	242	243	244	245	246	247	248	249	250	251	252	253	254	255	256	257	326	403	488	581	682	791	908
984	863	750	645	548	459	378	305	240	183	184	185	186	187	188	189	190	191	192	193	194	195	196	197	258	327	404	489	582	683	792	909
983	862	749	644	547	458	377	304	239	182	133	134	135	136	137	138	139	140	141	142	143	144	145	198	259	328	405	490	583	684	793	910
982	861	748	643	546	457	376	303	238	181	132	91	92	93	94	95	96	97	98	99	100	101	146	199	260	329	406	491	584	685	794	911
981	860	747	642	545	456	375	302	237	180	131	90	57	58	59	60	61	62	63	64	65	102	147	200	261	330	407	492	585	686	795	912
980	859	746	641	544	455	374	301	236	179	130	89	56	31	32	33	34	35	36	37	66	103	148	201	262	331	408	493	586	687	796	913
979	858	745	640	543	454	373	300	235	178	129	88	55	30	13	14	15	16	17	38	67	104	149	202	263	332	409	494	587	688	797	914
978	857	744	639	542	453	372	299	234	177	128	87	54	29	12	3	4	5	18	39	68	105	150	203	264	333	410	495	588	689	798	915
977	856	743	638	541	452	371	298	233	176	127	86	53	28	11	2	1	6	19	40	69	106	151	204	265	334	411	496	589	690	799	916
976	855	742	637	540	451	370	297	232	175	126	85	52	27	10	9	8	7	20	41	70	107	152	205	266	335	412	497	590	691	800	917
975	854	741	636	539	450	369	296	231	174	125	84	51	26	25	24	23	22	21	42	71	108	153	206	267	336	413	498	591	692	801	918
974	853	740	635	538	449	368	295	230	173	124	83	50	49	48	47	46	45	44	43	72	109	154	207	268	337	414	499	592	693	802	919
973	852	739	634	537	448	367	294	229	172	123	82	81	80	79	78	77	76	75	74	73	110	155	208	269	338	415	500	593	694	803	920
972	851	738	633	536	447	366	293	228	171	122	121	120	119	118	117	116	115	114	113	112	111	156	209	270	339	416	501	594	695	804	921
971	850	737	632	535	446	365	292	227	170	169	168	167	166	165	164	163	162	161	160	159	158	157	210	271	340	417	502	595	696	805	922
970	849	736	631	534	445	364	291	226	225	224	223	222	221	220	219	218	217	216	215	214	213	212	211	272	341	418	503	596	697	806	923
969	848	735	630	533	444	363	290	289	288	287	286	285	284	283	282	281	280	279	278	277	276	275	274	273	342	419	504	597	698	807	924
968	847	734	629	532	443	362	361	360	359	358	357	356	355	354	353	352	351	350	349	348	347	346	345	344	343	420	505	598	699	808	925
967	846	733	628	531	442	441	440	439	438	437	436	435	434	433	432	431	430	429	428	427	426	425	424	423	422	421	506	599	700	809	926
966	845	732	627	530	529	528	527	526	525	524	523	522	521	520	519	518	517	516	515	514	513	512	511	510	509	508	507	600	701	810	927
965	844	731	626	625	624	623	622	621	620	619	618	617	616	615	614	613	612	611	610	609	608	607	606	605	604	603	602	601	702	811	928
964	843	730	729	728	727	726	725	724	723	722	721	720	719	718	717	716	715	714	713	712	711	710	709	708	707	706	705	704	703	812	929
963	842	841	840	839	838	837	836	835	834	833	832	831	830	829	828	827	826	825	824	823	822	821	820	819	818	817	816	815	814	813	930
962	961	960	959	958	957	956	955	954	953	952	951	950	949	948	947	946	945	944	943	942	941	940	939	938	937	936	935	934	933	932	931

180 0

225 270 315

General Motors as a Market Bellwether Stock

"What's good for General Motors is good for the country," a past CEO of GM reportedly asserted many years ago. Indeed, GM used to be one of the largest and most powerful corporations in America, and GM stock was a speculative favorite on Wall Street. The movements of GM stock were closely followed as a *bellwether* (leading indicator) of the dominant forces of demand (bullish) and supply (bearish) for the stock market in general.

The General Motors Bellwether rule is defined by the failure of the existing trend of GM stock to continue in the same direction. A signal is recognized when the prevailing price trend stalls out for four consecutive months. On the bullish side, following a general market decline, buy when GM stock fails to reach a new low within a 4-month time period. On the bearish side, following a general market rise, sell when GM stock fails to reach a new high for four consecutive months.

This simple rule worked like a charm from 1929 to 1958: of ten signals, ten were profitable. A losing signal in 1959 was followed by three more good ones in 1961–2.

Sadly, the General Motors Bellwether went haywire from 1962 to 1976, batting only 50/50 while underperforming the naïve buy-and-hold strategy, according to Norman Fosback, *Stock Market Logic,* The Institute for Econometric Research, 3471 North Federal Highway, Fort Lauderdale, FL 33306, 1976, 384 pages.

Data gathered by Thomas A. Meyers and published in the first edition of this book indicated that in the ten years from April 1974 to May 1984, the General Motors Bellwether produced six winning signals and nine losing signals, and it actually would have lost money.

The price chart shows that GM has not kept pace with the market over the past twenty years. Its days as a market leader ended a long time ago.

Indicator Strategy Example for General Motors as a Bellwether

Based on a 20-year file of daily data for the closing price of GM and the DJIA from March 17, 1980, to November 22, 2000, a systematic search failed to uncover any strategy that beat the market. Short selling would have lost heavily and consistently. However, for long trades only, GM crossovers of various length exponential moving averages would have produced slightly profitable results on a purely mechanical signal basis with no subjectivity, no sophisticated technical analysis, and no judgement:

> **Enter Long (Buy)** at the current daily price close of the DJIA when the closing price of GM stock today is greater than its own previous day's 2-day exponential moving average.

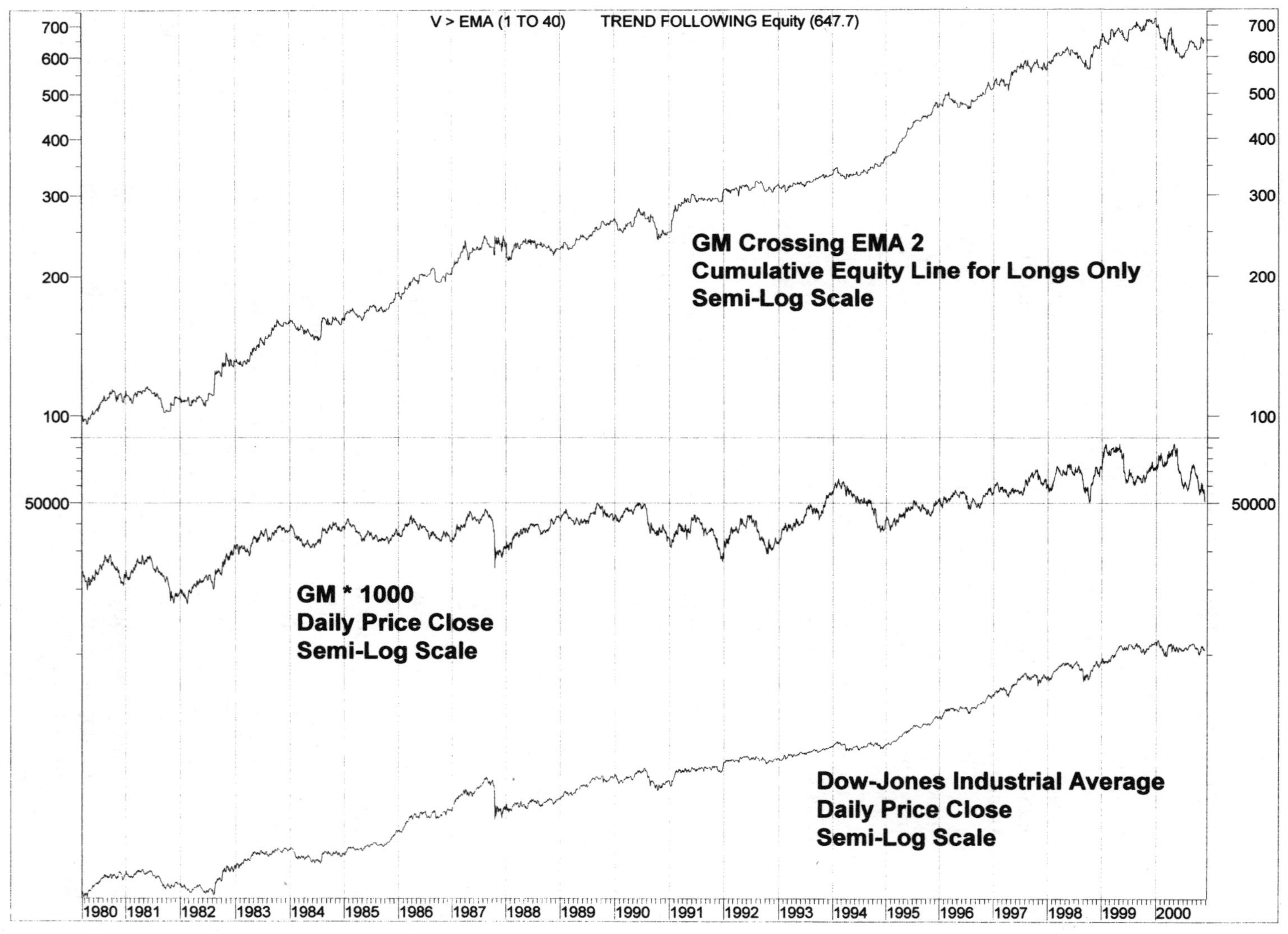

V > EMA (1 TO 40)
TREND FOLLOWING Equity (647.7)
GM Crossing EMA 2
Cumulative Equity Line for Longs Only
Semi-Log Scale
GM * 1000
Daily Price Close
Semi-Log Scale
Dow-Jones Industrial Average
Daily Price Close
Semi-Log Scale
700
600
500
400
300
200
100
50000
1980
1981
1982
1983
1984
1985
1986
1987
1988
1989
1990
1991
1992
1993
1994
1995
1996
1997
1998
1999
2000

General Motors Bellwether

Total net profit	547.68	Open position value	N/A	Net Profit/Buy&Hold %	−55.05
Percent gain/loss	547.68	Annual percent gain/loss	26.46	Annual Net %/B&H %	−55.05
Initial investment	100	Interest earned	0		
Current position	Out	Date position entered	11/16/00		
Buy/Hold profit	1218.54	Days in test	7556	# of days per trade	7.58
Buy/Hold pct gain/loss	1218.54	Annual B/H pct gain/loss	58.86		
Total closed trades	997	Commissions paid	0		
Avg profit per trade	0.55	Avg Win/Avg Loss ratio	1.29		
Total long trades	997	Total short trades	0	Long Win Trade %	51.45
Winning long trades	513	Winning short trades	0	Short Win Trade %	#DIV/0!
Total winning trades	513	Total losing trades	484	Total Win Trade %	51.45
Amount of winning trades	2035.06	Amount of losing trades	−1487.39	Net Profit Margin %	15.55
Average win	3.97	Average loss	−3.07	Average P. Margin %	12.78
Largest win	39.96	Largest loss	−49.69	% Net/(Win + Loss)	−10.85
Average length of win	4.25	Average length of loss	2.92	(Win − Loss)/Loss %	45.55
Longest winning trade	14	Longest losing trade	11	(Win − Loss)/Loss %	27.27
Most consecutive wins	10	Most consecutive losses	8	(Win − Loss)/Loss %	25.00
Total bars out	3630	Average length out	3.64		
Longest out period	18				
System close drawdown	−3.85	Profit/Loss index	26.91	% Net Profit/SODD	13971.43
System open drawdown	−3.92	Reward/Risk index	99.29	(Net P.-SODD)/Net P.	99.28
Max open trade drawdown	−49.69	Buy/Hold index	−55.05	% SODD/Net Profit	−0.72

In the Equis MetaStock® "System Report" (profit and loss summary statistics), the *Total net profit* is the sum of profits minus the sum of losses, including open positions marked to the market. In contrast, the *Amount of Winning Trades* is the sum of realized profits (the total of all gains on closed-out trades only, excluding any open positions). Similarly, the *Amount of Losing Trades* is the sum of realized losses (the total of all losses on closed-out trades only, excluding any open positions). *System close drawdown* is the largest decline in the cumulative equity line below the initial investment, based on closed-out positions only. *System open drawdown (SODD)* is the largest decline in the cumulative equity line below the initial investment when a position is open. *Max open trade drawdown* is the largest decline in the cumulative equity line below the trade entry price during the worst single trade. The *Profit/Loss Index* is a complex calculation that relates the Amount of Winning Trades to the Amount of Losing Trades on a scale of −100 (worst possible performance) to +100 (best possible performance), with zero representing profits equal to losses. *Reward/Risk Index* is the Total net profit minus System open drawdown. The resulting difference is then divided by the Total net profit. The *Buy/Hold Index* is the Total net profit minus the buy-and-hold strategy's net profit. The resulting difference is then divided by the buy-and-hold net profit. In this exercise, initial equity is assumed to be $100. Both long and short positions are taken unless otherwise noted. Trades are executed at the closing price on the signal date. Transaction costs, interest expenses, and margins are not included in the statistics.

Close Long (Sell) at the current daily price close of the DJIA when the closing price of GM stock today is less than its own previous day's 2-day exponential moving average.

Sell Short never.

Starting with $100 and reinvesting profits, total net profits for this General Motors Bellwether trend-following strategy would have been $547.68, assuming a long-only, fully invested strategy, reinvestment of profits, no transactions costs and no taxes. This would have been 55.05% less than buy-and-hold. Short selling would have lost heavily and consistently. Trading would have been active, with one trade every 7.58 calendar days. This indicator would have been right slightly more often than wrong, with 51.45% winning trades.

The Equis International MetaStock® System Testing rules, where the closing price of GM is inserted into the data field normally reserved for Volume (V), are written as follows:

Enter long: V > Ref(Mov(V,opt1,E),−1)

Close long: V < Ref(Mov(V,opt1,E),−1)

Enter short: V < Ref(Mov(V,opt1,E),−1)

Close short: V > Ref(Mov(V,opt1,E),−1)

OPT1 Current value: 2

General Motors Bellwether 4-Month Rule

Buy-and-Sell Signal Results from 1942 to 1984

Buy Signals			*Sell Signals*		
Buy Date	*DJIA*	*% Drop*	*Sell Date*	*DJIA*	*% Rise*
Apr-42	96.92	34.5	Jun-46	211.47	118.2
Jul-48	185.90	12.1	Mar-56	503.88	171.0
Apr-58	450.72	10.5	Nov-59	650.92	44.4
Apr-61	672.66	−3.3	Apr-62	687.90	2.3
Oct-62	569.02	17.3	Mar-64	802.75	41.1
Aug-64	840.35	−4.7	Feb-66	951.89	13.3
May-67	892.93	6.2	Jan-68	863.67	−3.3
Jul-68	883.36	2.3	Feb-69	903.97	2.3
Sep-70	758.97	16.0	Aug-71	901.43	18.8
Mar-72	928.66	−3.0	Aug-72	953.12	2.6
Apr-74	847.54	11.1	Oct-74	658.17	−22.3
Apr-75	842.88	−28.1	Apr-76	986.00	17.0
Dec-76	996.09	−1.0	May-77	931.22	−6.5
Jun-78	836.97	10.1	Dec-78	817.65	−2.3
Jun-79	843.04	−3.1	Jan-80	879.95	4.4
Aug-80	955.03	−8.5	Jan-81	970.99	1.7
May-81	976.86	−0.6	Oct-81	851.69	−12.8
Mar-82	805.65	5.4	May-84	1167.19	44.9
Averages		4.1			24.2

Gross Trinity Index

This sentiment indicator, which compares professional short selling activity with public shorting each week, was developed by the late Robert Gross, who was editor of the *Professional Investor* market newsletter (P.O. Box 2144, Pompano Beach, FL 33061). It is also known as the *Professional Investor's* Trinity Index. The Gross Trinity Index may be calculated and interpreted in five steps. First, calculate the three basic component ratios that make up the index:

Specialist Short Ratio = Specialist Shorts/Total Shorts
Member Short Ratio = Member Shorts/Total Shorts
Public Short Ratio = Public Shorts/Total Shorts

Each of these short sales ratios are explained separately herein.

Second, smooth each of these three component ratios using the following exponential smoothing constants (for calculation examples, see exponential moving averages): an 18% smoothing constant (roughly equivalent to a 10-week simple moving Average) applied to both the Specialist Short Ratio and the Public Short Ratio; and a 29% exponential smoothing constant (roughly equivalent to a 6-week simple moving average) applied to the Member Short Ratio.

Third, add the smoothed Specialist and Member Short Ratios.

Fourth, divide that sum by the smoothed Public Short Ratio.

Fifth, Bob Gross interpreted high readings as bearish, since these represented relatively heavy professional shorting compared to public shorting. Low readings were bullish, since they represented relatively light professional shorting compared to public shorting.

Haurlan Index

The Haurlan Index is a multiple-timeframe market breadth indicator developed by P.N. Haurlan, Trade Levels, Inc., 22801 Ventura Boulevard, Suite 210, Woodland Hills, CA 91364. Generally, NYSE daily data is used, although the same analysis could be applied to daily and weekly data from other exchanges.

The Haurlan Index consists of three components, each with a different purpose and interpretation. The short-term component is a 3-day exponential moving average of the net difference between the number of advancing issues and the number of declining issues. The intermediate-term component is a 20-day exponential moving average of the net difference between the number of advancing issues and the number of declining issues. The long-term component is a 200-day exponential moving average of the net difference between the number of advancing issues and the number of declining issues.

Each of the three components is interpreted differently. The intermediate-component (20-day exponential moving average) is interpreted subjectively with buy and sell signals given when trend lines or support and resistance levels are crossed.

The long-term component (200-day exponential moving average) is not used to generate specific buy and sell signals. Rather, it is intended to be used to determine the primary trend of stock prices.

When the short-term component (3-day exponential moving average) moves above +100, a buy signal is given. The buy signal remains in effect until a level of −150 is reached. At that time, a short-term sell signal is generated and remains in effect until the next short-term buy signal.

The graph shows that the levels of the Haurlan Index are expanding over time, reflecting an increasing number of issues traded on the New York Stock Exchange. The traditional Haurlan parameters have not allowed for this expansion in levels, but it probably ought to be adjusted for this fact.

Indicator Strategy Example for The Haurlan Index, 3-day exponential moving average

The already-established, short-term rules lend themselves to objective testing. Based on a 68-year file of daily data for the number of shares advancing and declining each day on the NYSE and the DJIA since March 8, 1932, we found that the stated parameters would have produced a positive result on a purely mechanical signal basis with no subjectivity, no sophisticated technical analysis, and no judgement:

Enter Long (Buy) at the current daily price close of the DJIA when the 3-day exponential moving average of the advances minus declines rises above 100.

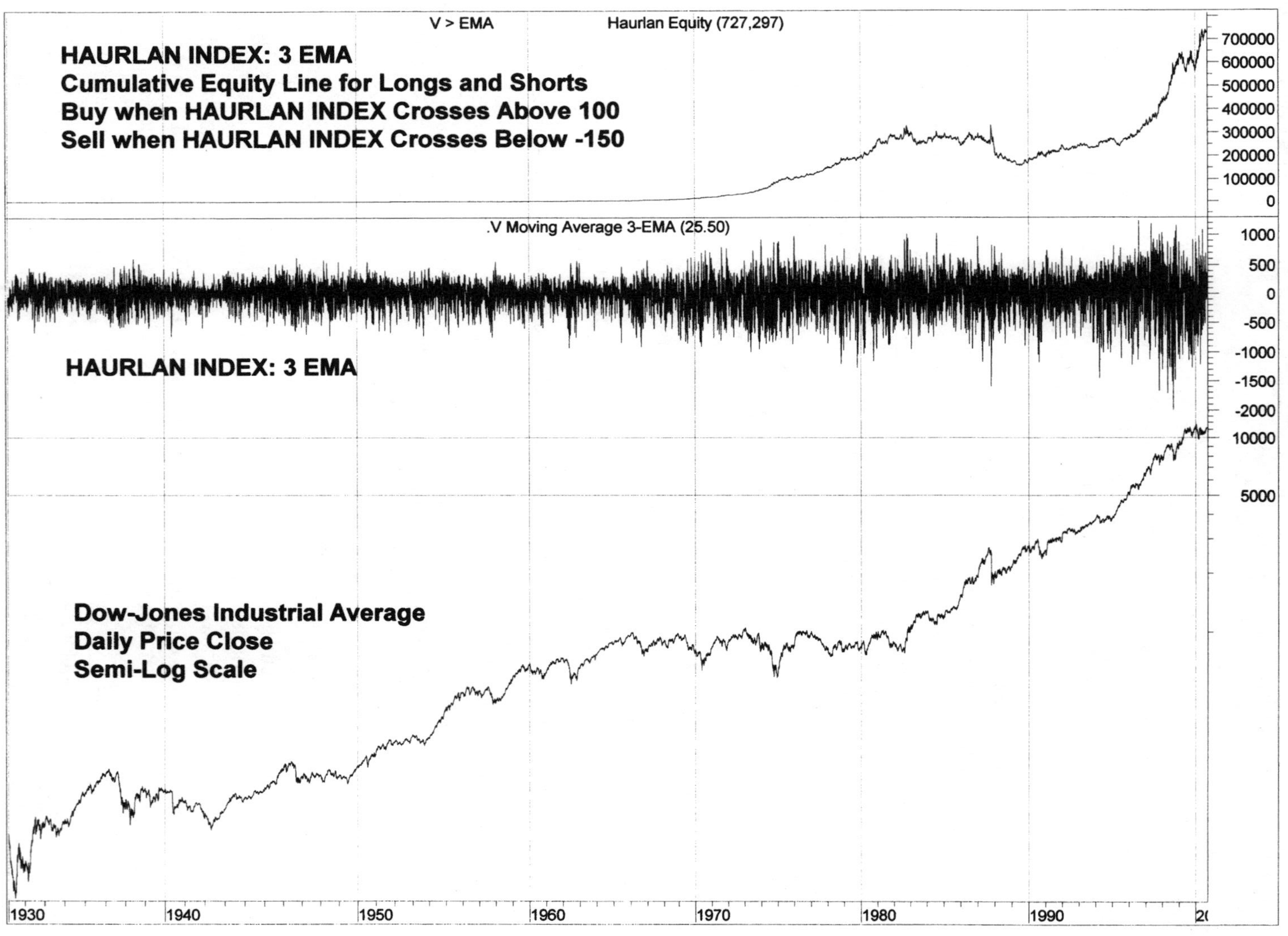
V > EMA
Haurlan Equity (727,297)
HAURLAN INDEX: 3 EMA
Cumulative Equity Line for Longs and Shorts
Buy when HAURLAN INDEX Crosses Above 100
Sell when HAURLAN INDEX Crosses Below -150
700000
600000
500000
400000
300000
200000
100000
0
.V Moving Average 3-EMA (25.50)
HAURLAN INDEX: 3 EMA
1000
500
0
-500
-1000
-1500
-2000
10000
5000
Dow-Jones Industrial Average
Daily Price Close
Semi-Log Scale
1930
1940
1950
1960
1970
1980
1990

Haurlan Index: 3-day EMA

Total net profit	727197	Open position value	0	Net Profit/Buy&Hold %	5699.64
Percent gain/loss	727197	Annual percent gain/loss	10607.74	Annual Net %/B&H %	5699.75
Initial investment	100	Interest earned	0		
Current position	Short	Date position entered	9/8/00		
Buy/Hold profit	12538.66	Days in test	25022	# of days per trade	5.20
Buy/Hold pct gain/loss	12538.66	Annual B/H pct gain/loss	182.9		
Total closed trades	4812	Commissions paid	0		
Avg profit per trade	151.12	Avg Win/Avg Loss ratio	1.62		
Total long trades	2406	Total short trades	2406	Long Win Trade %	54.53
Winning long trades	1312	Winning short trades	823	Short Win Trade %	34.21
Total winning trades	2135	Total losing trades	2677	Total Win Trade %	44.37
Amount of winning trades	3248707	Amount of losing trades	−2521506.3	Net Profit Margin %	12.60
Average win	1521.64	Average loss	−941.91	Average P. Margin %	23.53
Largest win	57467.2	Largest loss	−22480.06	% Net/(Win + Loss)	43.76
Average length of win	6.51	Average length of loss	3.36	(Win − Loss)/Loss %	93.75
Longest winning trade	45	Longest losing trade	30	(Win − Loss)/Loss %	50.00
Most consecutive wins	9	Most consecutive losses	14	(Win − Loss)/Loss %	−35.71
Total bars out	3	Average length out	3		
Longest out period	3				
System close drawdown	−60.6	Profit/Loss index	22.38	% Net Profit/SODD	1199995.05
System open drawdown	−60.6	Reward/Risk index	99.99	(Net P.-SODD)/Net P.	99.99
Max open trade drawdown	−22480.06	Buy/Hold index	5699.64	% SODD/Net Profit	−0.01

In the Equis MetaStock® "System Report" (profit and loss summary statistics), the *Total net profit* is the sum of profits minus the sum of losses, including open positions marked to the market. In contrast, the *Amount of Winning Trades* is the sum of realized profits (the total of all gains on closed-out trades only, excluding any open positions). Similarly, the *Amount of Losing Trades* is the sum of realized losses (the total of all losses on closed-out trades only, excluding any open positions). *System close drawdown* is the largest decline in the cumulative equity line below the initial investment, based on closed-out positions only. *System open drawdown (SODD)* is the largest decline in the cumulative equity line below the initial investment when a position is open. *Max open trade drawdown* is the largest decline in the cumulative equity line below the trade entry price during the worst single trade. The *Profit/Loss Index* is a complex calculation that relates the Amount of Winning Trades to the Amount of Losing Trades on a scale of −100 (worst possible performance) to +100 (best possible performance), with zero representing profits equal to losses. *Reward/Risk Index* is the Total net profit minus System open drawdown. The resulting difference is then divided by the Total net profit. The *Buy/Hold Index* is the Total net profit minus the buy-and-hold strategy's net profit. The resulting difference is then divided by the buy-and-hold net profit. In this exercise, initial equity is assumed to be $100. Both long and short positions are taken unless otherwise noted. Trades are executed at the closing price on the signal date. Transaction costs, interest expenses, and margins are not included in the statistics.

Close Long (Sell) at the current daily price close of the DJIA when the 3-day exponential moving average of the advances minus declines falls below −150.

Enter Short (Sell Short) at the current daily price close of the DJIA when the 3-day exponential moving average of the advances minus declines falls below −150.

Close Short (Cover) at the current daily price close of the DJIA when the 3-day exponential moving average of the advances minus declines rises above 100.

Starting with $100 and reinvesting profits, total net profits for 3-day Haurlan Index trend-following strategy would have been $727,197, assuming a fully invested strategy, reinvestment of profits, no transactions costs and no taxes. This would have been 5,699.64 percent better than buy-and-hold. Even short selling would have been profitable. Trading would have been hyperactive with one trade every 5.20 calendar days.

The Equis International MetaStock® System Testing rules, where the current Haurlan Index is inserted into the data field normally reserved for Volume (V), are written as follows:

Enter long: Mov(V,opt1,E) > 100

Close long: Mov(V,opt1,E) < 150

Enter short: Mov(V,opt1,E) < 150

Close short: Mov(V,opt1,E) > 100

OPT1 Current value: 3

Herrick Payoff Index

The Herrick Payoff Index is a momentum oscillator used to analyze futures. John Herrick developed the complex formula, which is based on changes in price, volume and open interest. Since it requires data on open interest, it cannot be applied to common stocks.

Begin with price velocity times volume, which is called *Money Flow.* Money Flow is multiplied by the absolute value of the daily percentage change in the open interest, and the result is called *Modulated Dollar Amount.* Finally, that Modulated Dollar Amount is smoothed with an exponential moving average. The resulting oscillator moves above and below a horizontal reference line at zero.

The formula for the Herrick Payoff Index is preprogrammed and appears on the MetaStock® indicator drop-down window. The value of a *One Cent Move* has a default parameter of 100, but allowing that value to vary makes little difference. In contrast the *Multiplying Factor* appears to be the critical variable. This determines the length of the *Exponential Moving Average,* roughly approximated in days, with small values near the default setting of 10 producing a sensitive short-term trading oscillator, while large values approaching the maximum setting of 100 produce a slow-moving, long-term oscillator.

Possible interpretations of the Herrick Payoff Index include its own rising or falling trend direction. Also, levels in the oscillator are compared to levels in the price of the underlying security, to identify divergences and convergences. Crossings of the horizontal reference line at zero do not appear to be significant.

Indicator Strategy Example for Herrick Payoff Index

Based on a 18-year file of daily data for the entire history of the S&P 500 Composite Stock Price Index Futures Contract from 4/21/82 to 12/29/00 (*CSI Perpetual Contract* collected from www.csi.com), we found that the following parameters would have produced a positive result on a purely mechanical overbought/oversold signal basis with no subjectivity, no sophisticated technical analysis, and no judgement:

Enter Long (Buy) at the current daily price close of the S&P 500 Composite Stock Price Index futures *CSI Perpetual Contract* when the current Herrick Payoff Index (using default parameters of 100 for the value of a *One Cent Move* and 10 as the value of the *Multiplying Factor*) crosses above its own trailing 2-day exponential moving average computed as of the previous day's close.

Close Long (Sell) at the current daily price close of the S&P 500 Composite Stock Price Index futures *CSI Perpetual Contract* when the current Herrick Payoff Index (using default parameters of 100 for the value of a *One Cent Move* and 10 as the value of the *Multiplying Factor*) crosses below its own trailing 2-day exponential moving average computed as of the previous day's close.

Enter Short (Sell Short) never.

Starting with $100 and reinvesting profits, total net profits for this Herrick Payoff Index trend-following strategy would have been $444.84, assuming a fully invested strategy, reinvestment of profits, no transactions costs and no taxes. This would have been 57.00 percent less than buy-and-hold. No short selling would have been profitable, and no short selling was included in the strategy. Short selling would have cut the profit further. The long-only Herrick Payoff Index as an indicator would have given profitable buy signals 47.92% of the time. Trading would have been hyperactive at one trade every 8.87 calendar days.

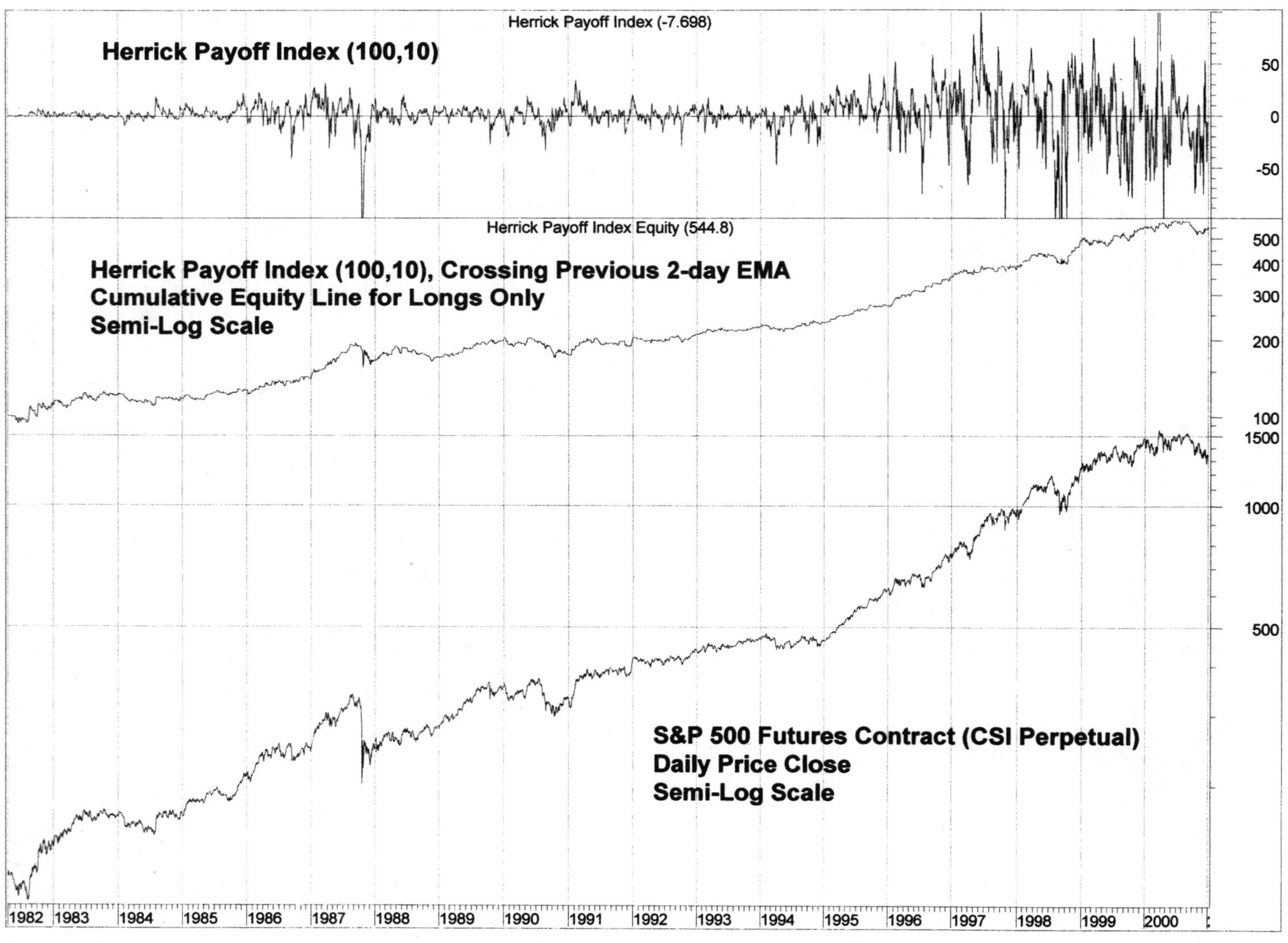

Herrick Payoff Index (-7.698)
Herrick Payoff Index (100,10)
50
0
-50
Herrick Payoff Index Equity (544.8)
Herrick Payoff Index (100,10), Crossing Previous 2-day EMA
Cumulative Equity Line for Longs Only
Semi-Log Scale
500
400
300
200
100
1500
1000
500
S&P 500 Futures Contract (CSI Perpetual)
Daily Price Close
Semi-Log Scale
1982
1983
1984
1985
1986
1987
1988
1989
1990
1991
1992
1993
1994
1995
1996
1997
1998
1999
2000

Herrick Payoff Index (100,10), Cross Previous 2 EMA

Total net profit	444.84	Open position value	3.41	Net Profit/Buy&Hold %	−57.00
Percent gain/loss	444.84	Annual percent gain/loss	23.78	Annual Net %/B&H %	−57.00
Initial investment	100	Interest earned	0		
Current position	Long	Date position entered	12/22/00		
Buy/Hold profit	1034.49	Days in test	6828	# of days per trade	8.87
Buy/Hold pct gain/loss	1034.49	Annual B/H pct gain/loss	55.3		
Total closed trades	770	Commissions paid	0		
Avg profit per trade	0.57	Avg Win/Avg Loss ratio	1.61		
Total long trades	770	Total short trades	0	Long Win Trade %	47.92
Winning long trades	369	Winning short trades	0	Short Win Trade %	#DIV/0!
Total winning trades	369	Total losing trades	401	Total Win Trade %	47.92
Amount of winning trades	1351.03	Amount of losing trades	−909.59	Net Profit Margin %	19.53
Average win	3.66	Average loss	−2.27	Average P. Margin %	23.44
Largest win	32.87	Largest loss	−12.77	% Net/(Win + Loss)	44.04
Average length of win	5.2	Average length of loss	2.89	(Win − Loss)/Loss %	79.93
Longest winning trade	16	Longest losing trade	14	(Win − Loss)/Loss %	14.29
Most consecutive wins	7	Most consecutive losses	7	(Win − Loss)/Loss %	0.00
Total bars out	3183	Average length out	4.13		
Longest out period	15				
System close drawdown	−6.33	Profit/Loss index	32.84	% Net Profit/SODD	7027.49
System open drawdown	−6.33	Reward/Risk index	98.6	(Net P.-SODD)/Net P.	98.58
Max open trade drawdown	−26.84	Buy/Hold index	−56.67	% SODD/Net Profit	−1.42

In the Equis MetaStock® "System Report" (profit and loss summary statistics), the *Total net profit* is the sum of profits minus the sum of losses, including open positions marked to the market. In contrast, the *Amount of Winning Trades* is the sum of realized profits (the total of all gains on closed-out trades only, excluding any open positions). Similarly, the *Amount of Losing Trades* is the sum of realized losses (the total of all losses on closed-out trades only, excluding any open positions). *System close drawdown* is the largest decline in the cumulative equity line below the initial investment, based on closed-out positions only. *System open drawdown (SODD)* is the largest decline in the cumulative equity line below the initial investment when a position is open. *Max open trade drawdown* is the largest decline in the cumulative equity line below the trade entry price during the worst single trade. The *Profit/Loss Index* is a complex calculation that relates the Amount of Winning Trades to the Amount of Losing Trades on a scale of −100 (worst possible performance) to +100 (best possible performance), with zero representing profits equal to losses. *Reward/Risk Index* is the Total net profit minus System open drawdown. The resulting difference is then divided by the Total net profit. The *Buy/Hold Index* is the Total net profit minus the buy-and-hold strategy's net profit. The resulting difference is then divided by the buy-and-hold net profit. In this exercise, initial equity is assumed to be $100. Both long and short positions are taken unless otherwise noted. Trades are executed at the closing price on the signal date. Transaction costs, interest expenses, and margins are not included in the statistics.

The Equis International MetaStock® System Testing rules are written as follows:

Enter long: HPI(100,opt1)>Ref(Mov(HPI(100,opt1),opt2,E),−1)

Close long: HPI(100,opt1)<Ref(Mov(HPI(100,opt1),opt2,E),−1)

OPT1 Current value: 10
OPT2 Current value: 2

Hi Mom System, High Momentum System

The Hi Mom System identifies unusually high short-term momentum (price velocity) and early signs of a change in that velocity to trade in a contrary manner. Using intraday data divided into workable time intervals, first identify an extremely high velocity spike that stands out from the rest. Subsequently, when price makes one or two more higher highs while velocity fails to make higher highs (a negative momentum divergence), the trader fades the move as it begins to stall. Place a protective stop just above the highest price high, then trail your stop down to eventually take profits if the price declines as expected.

An opposite long strategy could be devised for extremely negative price momentum followed by positive divergences. It could be named "Lo Mom System". The two together would make a contra-trend trading system that attempts to fade extremes and plays for a reversion to the mean, which is actually quite common in all but the most strongly trending markets.

For a further discussion, see LeBeau, Charles, and Lucas, David W., *Technical Traders Guide to Computer Analysis of the Futures Market,* Business One Irwin, Homewood, IL., 1992, 234 pages.

High Low Logic Index

The High Low Logic Index was developed by Normal Fosback of The Institute for Econometric Research, 3471 North Federal Highway, Fort Lauderdale, FL 33306. Using NYSE data, the index is defined as the lesser of two ratios: the number of new highs divided by the total number of issues traded; or the number of new lows divided by the total number of issues traded. Low levels on this index might imply a strongly trending market in one direction, with many new highs and few new lows, or with few new highs and many new lows. Similarly, high levels on this index might imply a mixed-up two-way market, with many new highs and many new lows, with many stocks trending up while many other stocks are trending down.

Fosback tested the NYSE weekly High Low Logic Index over a 40-year period. He first smoothed the raw data with a 10-week exponential moving average. He found that smoothed index levels above 0.050 were bearish, while levels below 0.010 were bullish.

In the first edition of this book, Thomas A. Meyers confirmed Fosback's findings. Using chi-squared statistical testing, he independently examined the NYSE weekly High Low Logic Index over a longer 50-year period (1937–1987). Meyers found that the following results were highly significant at the 99.9% confidence level: there is not one chance in a thousand that these results could have been obtained by chance alone.

Meyers first smoothed the raw weekly data with a 10-week simple moving average. He found that the highest 5% of observed smoothed weekly index levels above 0.058 were bearish for a 3-months forward time window. On the other side, the lowest 5% of observed smoothed weekly index levels of less than or equal to 0.005 were bullish for both 3- and 12-months forward time windows.

Meyers also found that the top 10% of raw (not smoothed by moving averages) *daily* index levels above 0.020 were bearish for both 1- and 3-months forward time windows. The bottom 10%, raw daily levels less than or equal to 0.002, were bullish for 1-, 3-, and 6-months forward time windows.

Smoothing the daily data with a 10-day simple moving average, Meyers found that the lowest 10% of levels less than or equal to 0.002 were bullish over all time frames tested, 1-, 3-, 6- and 12-months forward time windows.

The Hindenberg Omen

This compound indicator was designed as a warning of major stock market trouble ahead. It was developed by Jim Mikkea of The Sudbury Bull and Bear Report, and it was named by Kennedy Gammage of the Richland Report in remembrance of the Hindenberg disaster. (The Hindenberg was a German zeppelin filled with hydrogen gas that exploded and burned, killing 36 people, on May 6, 1937, on arrival at Lakehurst, New Jersey.) The Hindenberg Omen requires that all three of the following conditions are met: 1) The lessor of the number of new highs or the number of new lows is more than 2.4% of total issues traded. 2) The 10-week simple moving average of the NYSE Composite Index is rising. 3) The McClellan oscillator is negative.

Holidays

The stock market is scheduled to open from 9:30 AM to 4 PM Monday through Friday, except for holidays. It used to be open on Saturdays before May 26, 1952. The market may occasionally close because of an extreme snow storm or the funeral of a former U.S. president, but it is rare. The market closed for more than four months from 7/13/14 through 12/11/14, because of panic on the outbreak of World War I, and for four trading days following the terrorist attack on the World Trade Towers in New York on Tuesday, 9/11/01.

From 1991 through 1999, the stock market was open for trading 252, 253 or 254 days, depending on the calendar. On average the stock market was open for trading 252.7778 days a year.

The stock market is regularly closed for holidays nine weekdays a year—New Year's Day, Martin Luther King, Jr. Day, Washington's Birthday, Good Friday, Memorial Day, Independence Day, Labor Day, Thanksgiving Day and Christmas Day. Martin Luther King, Jr. Day, Washington's Birthday and Memorial Day are celebrated on the third Mondays in January, February and May, respectively. When any holiday falls on a Saturday, the market is closed on the preceding Friday. When any holiday falls on a Sunday, the market is closed on the succeeding Monday.

Arthur A. Merrill, CMT, pioneered the study of seasonal behavior of stock market prices in his classic book, *Behavior of Prices on Wall Street, Second Edition,* The Analysis Press, Chappaqua, New York, 1984, 147 pages.

Merrill found that the market has a strong tendency to rise the day *before* most holidays. On average, the DJIA has been up a statistically highly significant 68% of the time the day before a holiday. Merrill found that the best days (up 81% to 72% of the time) were the day before Labor Day, Independence Day, Memorial Day, Christmas Day and New Years Day, in that order.

The day before Election Day, the second Tuesday of November, was up 71% of the time.

The day before Good Friday and the day before Thanksgiving, however, were only slightly better than average and were, therefore, not significant statistically. There is insufficient data to make any conclusions about market behavior around the newest holiday, Martin Luther King, Jr. Day.

A glaring exception to the bullish holiday rule–the trading day before Presidents' Day in February–was actually down slightly more often than not. The day after Presidents' Day was up only 40% of the time, which was significantly bearish.

The day *after* a holiday was generally not significant, except for the very bullish day after Thanksgiving, up 66% of the time. Also, the day after Independence Day was up 60% of the time.

"Sell Rosh Hashanah, buy Yom Kippur," would have been correct most of the time: the market has been up only 46% of the time between these two High Holy Days. (Rosh Hashanah, the Jewish New Year, is the day after the new moon in late September or early October. Yom Kippur, the Jewish Day of Atonement, follows nine days later, on the tenth day of the Jewish New Year.)

"Buy on July Fourth and sell on Labor Day and pay your expenses for the year," would have been profitable a statistically significant 66% of the time.

Merrill coined the phrase, "Buy at Thanksgiving and sell at the New Years and pay your Christmas bills." This strategy would have had a highly significant success rate of 72% from 1897 to 1983.

Our tests suggest another one: "Sell Labor Day, buy Halloween." More specifically, "Sell on September 5th, buy on October 27th." This one has a quite a good record (see Months of the Year).

Holy Grail

Holy Grail is a particular price setup: within a strong price uptrend making new highs, and after a minor price pullback to the 20-day exponential moving average, buy when the price moves above the previous day's high. A strong price uptrend is defined by a Average Directional Movement (14) above 30 and rising. Place a protective stop just below the recent pullback low and trail the stop upward. Look to book profits at the recent swing high. For further details on this setup, see Connors, Laurence A., and Raschke, Linda Bradford, *Street Smarts, High Probability Short-Term Trading Strategies,* M. Gordon Publishing Group, Malibu, California, 1995, 239 pages.

Hook

A Hook occurs when price breaks out above or below a resistance or support level but immediately reverses with a forceful move in the opposite direction. This *hooks* or *traps* trend-followers who went with the breakout. These trend-followers must now cut losses, which adds fuel to the new directional momentum. The resulting fast move is of interest to short-term traders. A Hook is also known as a *Springboard.*

Hypothesis Testing

Traditional hypothesis testing is designed to verify a priori hypotheses about relations between variables.

In the world of academic finance, controlled laboratory experiments are not possible; historical data may be subject to errors and biases or not be available in sufficient quantities; computer testing programs may be vulnerable to certain hidden assumptions, bugs and biases; mathematical theories and formulas may be dependent on unrealistic assumptions; and assumptions must be made about difficult-to-quantify variables such as transactions costs.

Contrast that to the gradual evolution of classic technical analysis, which has been tested with no assumptions, in real time, every day, in all kinds of market conditions, over many decades, by many thousands of traders, and with real money. Technical analysis has been hammered out on the hard anvil of harsh market reality every day that traders do their jobs, buying and selling.

Indicator Seasons, Elder's Concept

There is a time to sow and a time to reap. Indicator Seasons can show a trader where he is in the market cycle, according to Alexander Elder (*Trading for a Living: Psychology, Trading Tactics, Money Management,* John Wiley & Sons, Inc., New York, 1993). Elder's idea of Indicator Seasons is based on Gerald Appel's Moving Average Convergence Divergence (MACD) indicator. *(See Moving Average Convergence Divergence.)*

To signal trades, Elder uses the position relative to the zero line (above or below) and the slope (rising or falling) of the Moving Average Convergence Divergence Histogram (MACDH). Slope is defined as the relationship between the current MACDH and the previous period's MACDH.

When the weekly MACDH is below zero and its slope turns positive, it is springtime in the market and time to buy. Hold a long position until the weekly MACDH moves above zero–it is now summer and time to start selling.

When the weekly MACDH is above zero and its slope turns negative, it is fall in the market and time to sell short. Hold a short position until the weekly MACDH moves below zero–it is now winter and time to start covering shorts.

Indicator Seasons, Colby's Variation

Elder's original concept, as outlined on pages 188–192 of his book, did not perform well in our independent tests. But we found a variation using daily data and modified rules for interpretation that would have substantially outperformed the market, without any optimization.

When the daily MACDH is above zero and its slope is positive, it is springtime in the market and time to buy. Hold a long position as long as the daily MACDH remains above zero and its slope is positive. Liquidate longs when either the daily MACDH crosses under zero or its slope turns downward.

When the daily MACDH is below zero and its slope is negative, it is time for the market to fall. Therefore, it is time to sell short. Hold a short position as long as the daily MACDH remains below zero and its slope is negative. Liquidate shorts when either the daily MACDH crosses above zero or its slope turns upward.

Indicator Strategy Example for Indicator Seasons, Colby's Variation

After the 1930's, the cumulative equity line for Indicator Seasons, Colby's Variation, shows few drawdown periods. Based on a 101-year file, from January 1900 to April 2001, of the MACDH at the end of each day and the DJIA daily closing price, the following parameters would have produced a positive result on a purely mechanical signal basis with no subjectivity, no sophisticated technical analysis, and no judgement:

Enter Long (Buy) at the current daily price close of the DJIA when current MACDH is both greater than zero and above its previous day's level, thus showing positive and rising price velocity.

Close Long (Sell) at the current daily price close of the DJIA when current MACDH is either less than zero or below its previous day's level, thus showing deteriorating price velocity.

Enter Short (Sell Short) at the current daily price close of the DJIA when current MACDH is both less than zero and below its previous day's level, thus showing negative and worsening price velocity.

Close Short (Cover) at the current daily price close of the DJIA when current MACDH is either greater than zero or above its previous day's level, thus showing positively changing price velocity.

Starting with $100 and reinvesting profits, total net profits for this Indicator Seasons, Colby's Variation, trend-following strategy would have been $3,631,710.75, assuming a fully invested strategy, reinvestment of profits, no transactions costs and no taxes. This would have been 17,919.98 percent greater than buy-and-hold. Short selling would have been profitable, and short selling was included in the strategy. Despite its high profitability, the strategy would have been wrong more often than it was right, with only 45.07% winning trades. Trading would have been hyperactive at one trade every 8.25 calendar days.

The Equis International MetaStock® System Testing rules for Indicator Seasons, Colby's Variation, are written as follows:

Enter long:

```
((Mov(C,12,E)-Mov(C,26,E))-
(Mov(Mov(C,12,E)-Mov(C,26,E),9,E)))>0 AND
((Mov(C,12,E)-Mov(C,26,E))-
(Mov(Mov(C,12,E)-Mov(C,26,E),9,E)))>
Ref(((Mov(C,12,E)-Mov(C,26,E))-
(Mov(Mov(C,12,E)-Mov(C,26,E),9,E))),-1)
```

Close long:

```
((Mov(C,12,E)-Mov(C,26,E))-
(Mov(Mov(C,12,E)-Mov(C,26,E),9,E)))<0 OR
((Mov(C,12,E)-Mov(C,26,E))-
(Mov(Mov(C,12,E)-Mov(C,26,E),9,E)))<
Ref(((Mov(C,12,E)-Mov(C,26,E))-
(Mov(Mov(C,12,E)-Mov(C,26,E),9,E))),-1)
```

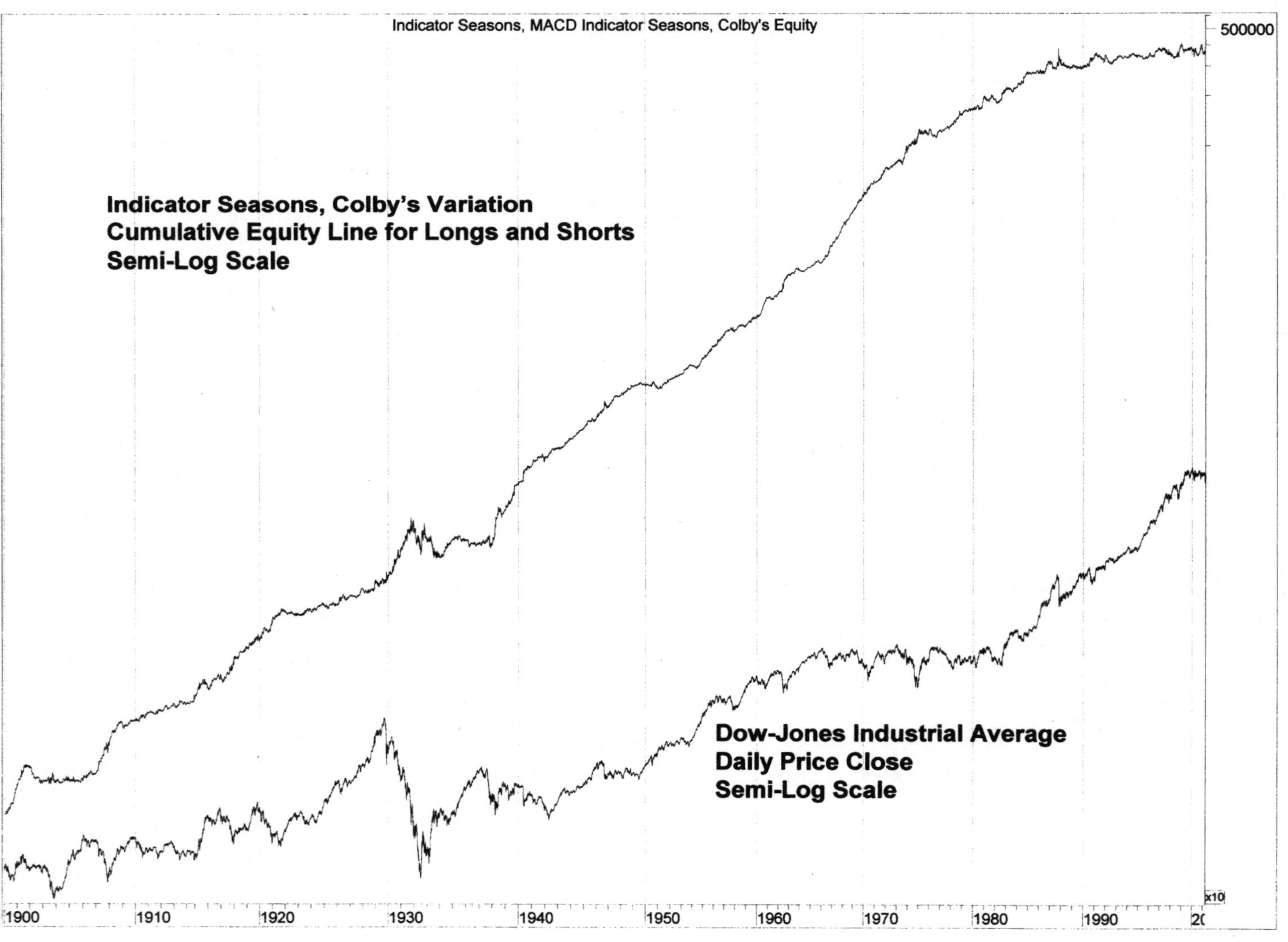
Indicator Seasons, MACD Indicator Seasons, Colby's Equity
500000
Indicator Seasons, Colby's Variation
Cumulative Equity Line for Longs and Shorts
Semi-Log Scale
Dow-Jones Industrial Average
Daily Price Close
Semi-Log Scale
x10
1900
1910
1920
1930
1940
1950
1960
1970
1980
1990
2(

Indicator Seasons, Colby's Variation

Total net profit	3631710.75	Open position value	74900.09	Net Profit/Buy&Hold %	17919.98
Percent gain/loss	3631710.75	Annual percent gain/loss	35835.05	Annual Net %/B&H %	17920.24
Initial investment	100	Interest earned	0		
Current position	Long	Date position entered	4/5/01		
Buy/Hold profit	20153.8	Days in test	36991	# of days per trade	8.25
Buy/Hold pct gain/loss	20153.8	Annual B/H pct gain/loss	198.86		
Total closed trades	4486	Commissions paid	0		
Avg profit per trade	792.87	Avg Win/Avg Loss ratio	1.48		
Total long trades	2255	Total short trades	2231	Long Win Trade %	49.14
Winning long trades	1108	Winning short trades	914	Short Win Trade %	40.97
Total winning trades	2022	Total losing trades	2464	Total Win Trade %	45.07
Amount of winning trades	20408018	Amount of losing trades	−16851206	Net Profit Margin %	9.55
Average win	10092.99	Average loss	−6838.96	Average P. Margin %	19.22
Largest win	481084.5	Largest loss	−206704.25	% Net/(Win + Loss)	39.89
Average length of win	5.73	Average length of loss	3.09	(Win − Loss)/Loss %	85.44
Longest winning trade	14	Longest losing trade	11	(Win − Loss)/Loss %	27.27
Most consecutive wins	10	Most consecutive losses	11	(Win − Loss)/Loss %	−9.09
Total bars out	17263	Average length out	4.08		
Longest out period	39				
System close drawdown	0	Profit/Loss index	17.73	% Net Profit/SODD	#DIV/0!
System open drawdown	0	Reward/Risk index	100	(Net P.-SODD)/Net P.	100.00
Max open trade drawdown	−206704.25	Buy/Hold index	18291.62	% SODD/Net Profit	0.00

In the Equis MetaStock® "System Report" (profit and loss summary statistics), the *Total net profit* is the sum of profits minus the sum of losses, including open positions marked to the market. In contrast, the *Amount of Winning Trades* is the sum of realized profits (the total of all gains on closed-out trades only, excluding any open positions). Similarly, the *Amount of Losing Trades* is the sum of realized losses (the total of all losses on closed-out trades only, excluding any open positions). *System close drawdown* is the largest decline in the cumulative equity line below the initial investment, based on closed-out positions only. *System open drawdown (SODD)* is the largest decline in the cumulative equity line below the initial investment when a position is open. *Max open trade drawdown* is the largest decline in the cumulative equity line below the trade entry price during the worst single trade. The *Profit/Loss Index* is a complex calculation that relates the Amount of Winning Trades to the Amount of Losing Trades on a scale of −100 (worst possible performance) to +100 (best possible performance), with zero representing profits equal to losses. *Reward/Risk Index* is the Total net profit minus System open drawdown. The resulting difference is then divided by the Total net profit. The *Buy/Hold Index* is the Total net profit minus the buy-and-hold strategy's net profit. The resulting difference is then divided by the buy-and-hold net profit. In this exercise, initial equity is assumed to be $100. Both long and short positions are taken unless otherwise noted. Trades are executed at the closing price on the signal date. Transaction costs, interest expenses, and margins are not included in the statistics.

Enter short:

```
((Mov(C,12,E)-Mov(C,26,E))-
(Mov(Mov(C,12,E)-Mov(C,26,E),9,E)))<0 AND
((Mov(C,12,E)-Mov(C,26,E))-
(Mov(Mov(C,12,E)-Mov(C,26,E),9,E)))<
Ref(((Mov(C,12,E)-Mov(C,26,E))-
(Mov(Mov(C,12,E)-Mov(C,26,E),9,E))),-1)
```

Close short:

```
((Mov(C,12,E)-Mov(C,26,E))-
(Mov(Mov(C,12,E)-Mov(C,26,E),9,E)))>0 OR
((Mov(C,12,E)-Mov(C,26,E))-
(Mov(Mov(C,12,E)-Mov(C,26,E),9,E)))>
Ref(((Mov(C,12,E)-Mov(C,26,E))-
(Mov(Mov(C,12,E)-Mov(C,26,E),9,E))),-1)
```

Indicator Strategy Example for Indicator Seasons, Colby's Variation–Optimized

In our view, indicator parameters never need to be taken as given. Rather than using the default settings of 12, 26, and 9 for MACDH, we can allow these to vary. Remarkably, profitability increases nearly five fold when we plug in 3, 33, and 3 in place of the default 12, 26, and 9 for MACDH.

Starting with $100 and reinvesting profits, total net profits for this Indicator Seasons, Colby's Variation–Optimized, trend-following strategy would have been $1,682,521,344, assuming a fully invested strategy, reinvestment of profits, no transactions costs and no taxes. This would have been 8,348,307.47 percent greater than buy-and-hold. Short selling would have been profitable, and short selling was included in the strategy. Despite its high profitability, the strategy would have been wrong more often than it was right, with only 47.42% winning trades. Trading would have been even more hyperactive at one trade every 4.27 calendar days.

The Equis International MetaStock® System Testing rules for Indicator Seasons, Colby's Variation–Optimized, are written as follows:

Enter long:

```
((Mov(C,opt1,E)-Mov(C,opt1*opt2,E))-
(Mov(Mov(C,opt1,E)-Mov(C,opt1*opt2,E),opt1,E)))>0 AND
((Mov(C,opt1,E)-Mov(C,opt1*opt2,E))-
(Mov(Mov(C,opt1,E)-Mov(C,opt1*opt2,E),opt1,E)))>
Ref(((Mov(C,opt1,E)-Mov(C,opt1*opt2,E))-
(Mov(Mov(C,opt1,E)-Mov(C,opt1*opt2,E),opt1,E))),-1)
```

Close long:

```
((Mov(C,opt1,E)-Mov(C,opt1*opt2,E))-
(Mov(Mov(C,opt1,E)-Mov(C,opt1*opt2,E),opt1,E)))<0 OR
((Mov(C,opt1,E)-Mov(C,opt1*opt2,E))-
(Mov(Mov(C,opt1,E)-Mov(C,opt1*opt2,E),opt1,E)))<
Ref(((Mov(C,opt1,E)-Mov(C,opt1*opt2,E))-
(Mov(Mov(C,opt1,E)-Mov(C,opt1*opt2,E),opt1,E))),-1)
```

Enter short:

```
((Mov(C,opt1,E)-Mov(C,opt1*opt2,E))-
(Mov(Mov(C,opt1,E)-Mov(C,opt1*opt2,E),opt1,E)))<0 AND
((Mov(C,opt1,E)-Mov(C,opt1*opt2,E))-
(Mov(Mov(C,opt1,E)-Mov(C,opt1*opt2,E),opt1,E)))<
Ref(((Mov(C,opt1,E)-Mov(C,opt1*opt2,E))-
(Mov(Mov(C,opt1,E)-Mov(C,opt1*opt2,E),opt1,E))),-1)
```

Close short:

```
((Mov(C,opt1,E)-Mov(C,opt1*opt2,E))-
(Mov(Mov(C,opt1,E)-Mov(C,opt1*opt2,E),opt1,E)))>0 OR
((Mov(C,opt1,E)-Mov(C,opt1*opt2,E))-
(Mov(Mov(C,opt1,E)-Mov(C,opt1*opt2,E),opt1,E)))>
Ref(((Mov(C,opt1,E)-Mov(C,opt1*opt2,E))-
(Mov(Mov(C,opt1,E)-Mov(C,opt1*opt2,E),opt1,E))),-1)
```

OPT1 Current value: 3
OPT2 Current value: 11

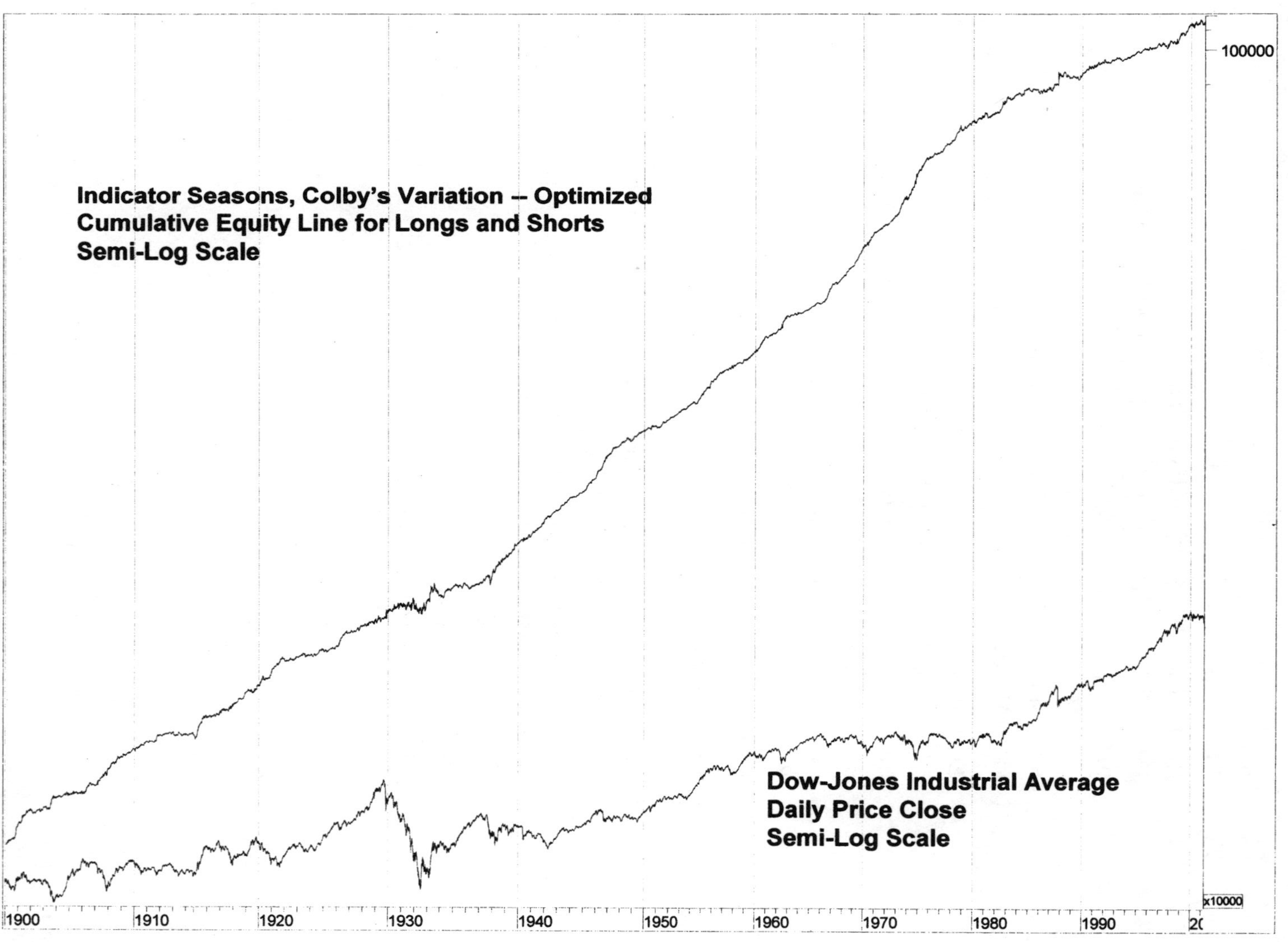
Indicator Seasons, Colby's Variation -- Optimized
Cumulative Equity Line for Longs and Shorts
Semi-Log Scale
Dow-Jones Industrial Average
Daily Price Close
Semi-Log Scale
100000
x10000
1900
1910
1920
1930
1940
1950
1960
1970
1980
1990

Indicator Seasons, Colby's Variation–Optimized

Total net profit	1682521344	Open position value	0	Net Profit/Buy&Hold %	8348307.47
Percent gain/loss	1682521344	Annual percent gain/loss	16601883.99	Annual Net %/B&H %	8348428.61
Initial investment	100	Interest earned	0		
Current position	Long	Date position entered	4/12/01		
Buy/Hold profit	20153.8	Days in test	36991	# of days per trade	4.27
Buy/Hold pct gain/loss	20153.8	Annual B/H pct gain/loss	198.86		
Total closed trades	8654	Commissions paid	0		
Avg profit per trade	194421.23	Avg Win/Avg Loss ratio	1.45		
Total long trades	4339	Total short trades	4315	Long Win Trade %	51.46
Winning long trades	2233	Winning short trades	1871	Short Win Trade %	43.36
Total winning trades	4104	Total losing trades	4550	Total Win Trade %	47.42
Amount of winning trades	7130662912	Amount of losing trades	−5448136704	Net Profit Margin %	13.38
Average win	1737490.96	Average loss	−1197392.68	Average P. Margin %	18.40
Largest win	120703136	Largest loss	−53168256	% Net/(Win + Loss)	38.84
Average length of win	3.48	Average length of loss	2.31	(Win − Loss)/Loss %	50.65
Longest winning trade	9	Longest losing trade	6	(Win − Loss)/Loss %	50.00
Most consecutive wins	13	Most consecutive losses	12	(Win − Loss)/Loss %	8.33
Total bars out	18404	Average length out	2.71		
Longest out period	37				
System close drawdown	−0.26	Profit/Loss index	23.6	% Net Profit/SODD	647123593846.15
System open drawdown	−0.26	Reward/Risk index	100	(Net P.-SODD)/Net P.	100.00
Max open trade drawdown	−53168256	Buy/Hold index	8348307.14	% SODD/Net Profit	0.00

In the Equis MetaStock® "System Report" (profit and loss summary statistics), the *Total net profit* is the sum of profits minus the sum of losses, including open positions marked to the market. In contrast, the *Amount of Winning Trades* is the sum of realized profits (the total of all gains on closed-out trades only, excluding any open positions). Similarly, the *Amount of Losing Trades* is the sum of realized losses (the total of all losses on closed-out trades only, excluding any open positions). *System close drawdown* is the largest decline in the cumulative equity line below the initial investment, based on closed-out positions only. *System open drawdown (SODD)* is the largest decline in the cumulative equity line below the initial investment when a position is open. *Max open trade drawdown* is the largest decline in the cumulative equity line below the trade entry price during the worst single trade. The *Profit/Loss Index* is a complex calculation that relates the Amount of Winning Trades to the Amount of Losing Trades on a scale of −100 (worst possible performance) to +100 (best possible performance), with zero representing profits equal to losses. *Reward/Risk Index* is the Total net profit minus System open drawdown. The resulting difference is then divided by the Total net profit. The *Buy/Hold Index* is the Total net profit minus the buy-and-hold strategy's net profit. The resulting difference is then divided by the buy-and-hold net profit. In this exercise, initial equity is assumed to be $100. Both long and short positions are taken unless otherwise noted. Trades are executed at the closing price on the signal date. Transaction costs, interest expenses, and margins are not included in the statistics.

Inertia

In physics, inertia is the tendency of matter at rest to remain at rest or, if moving, to keep moving in the same direction unless affected by some outside force. This idea has long been attractive to market technicians, some of whom are also highly trained in the physical sciences.

The Inertia indicator was developed by Donald G. Dorsey and first introduced in the September 1995 issue of *Technical Analysis of Stocks & Commodities* magazine (www.traders.com). Dorsey's Inertia indicator is simply a smoothed version of his Relative Volatility Index *(see Relative Volatility Index).*

Dorsey reasoned that it takes significantly more energy for a market to reverse direction than to continue along the same path. He used price momentum to quantify the direction of price motion and volatility as a measurement of inertia. Dorsey defined Inertia as a smoothed Relative Volatility Index (RVI). His preferred smoothing mechanism is Linear Regression *(see Linear Regression).* The RVI measures the general direction of volatility.

If the Inertia indicator is above 50, positive inertia is indicated. The long-term trend is up and should remain up as long as the indicator is above 50.

If Inertia is below 50, negative inertia is indicated. The long-term trend is down and should remain down as long as the indicator is below 50.

Our Indicator Strategy testing for Dorsey's Inertia indicator confirms that Inertia indeed lives up to its name—it is inert. By smoothing the RVI, Inertia filters out even more signals than RVI. In fact, it eliminates nearly all signals. Meanwhile it produces a level of profitability not significantly better than the passive buy-and-hold strategy. *(See Relative Volatility Index (RVI)).*

Insiders' Sell/Buy Ratio

An insider is an officer, director, or beneficial owner of a company's stock. Insiders of companies with publicly traded securities are required to report any changes in direct or indirect holdings to the Securities and Exchange Commission no later than the tenth day of the month following the month of the transaction.

In an effort to prevent insiders from taking advantage of access to materially significant information before it is made available to the public, insiders are legally prohibited from realizing a profit from their transactions within at least six months. If an insider should realize a profit within six months, any shareholder may challenge the publicly reported transaction, and the insider could be required to return any such short-term gains to the company.

Insiders are in a position to acquire superior information and insight into the prospects for their companies. Therefore, it is logical that they would buy when their company's fortunes are about to improve, or when the stock price has fallen irresistibly far below its intrinsic value. People buy a stock when they have positive expectations about the stock's future performance.

Logically, Insiders ought to be motivated to sell their stock when the company's future prospects are likely to deteriorate, or when the stock price has risen too far above its intrinsic value.

It is said that insiders sometimes sell stocks in order to diversify, to raise funds for personal and family expenditures, for philanthropy, for estate planning and for other reasons not necessarily related to a stock's investments merits. As a result insiders' future expectations for their company's stock may be not always completely obvious judging by their stock sales.

Vickers' weekly Insider Sell/Buy Ratio rates each company's insider transactions for the past six months, taking into account the following, weighted by relative importance:

1. The number of insider buy and sell transactions for each company.
2. The percentage change in an insider's holdings with each purchase or sale.
3. Unanimity among a given company's insiders, either all buys or all sells.
4. Reversals in insiders buying patterns, either a change from buying to selling, or a change from selling to buying.
5. Transactions involving $250,000 or more dollar value are given added weight.

Vickers publishes its weekly Insider Sell/Buy Ratio and an 8-week moving average of the ratio. Vickers considers a ratio of 2.25 neutral, under 2.25 suggests a rising market, and greater than 2.25 suggests heavy insider selling and a weakening market. The average Insider Sell/Buy Ratio is 1.99 over the past quarter century.

The original source of data on insider trading is Vickers Stock Research Corporation, a wholly owned subsidiary of the Argus Research Group, www.argusgroup.com. Vickers provides updates on transactions and holdings of corporate officials, significant shareholders and institutions. Vickers' data are available electronically, via hard copy, and on magnetic tape.

Indicator Strategy Example for the weekly Insiders' Sell/Buy Ratio

The data shows that the Insiders' Sell/Buy Ratio can be an effective indicator, but on the long side only. Short selling would not have been profitable. Based on the weekly Insiders' Sell/Buy Ratio and the DJIA for nearly 30 years from April 1971 to January 2001, we found that the following parameters would have produced a significantly positive result on a purely mechanical trend-following signal basis with no subjectivity, no sophisticated technical analysis, and no judgement:

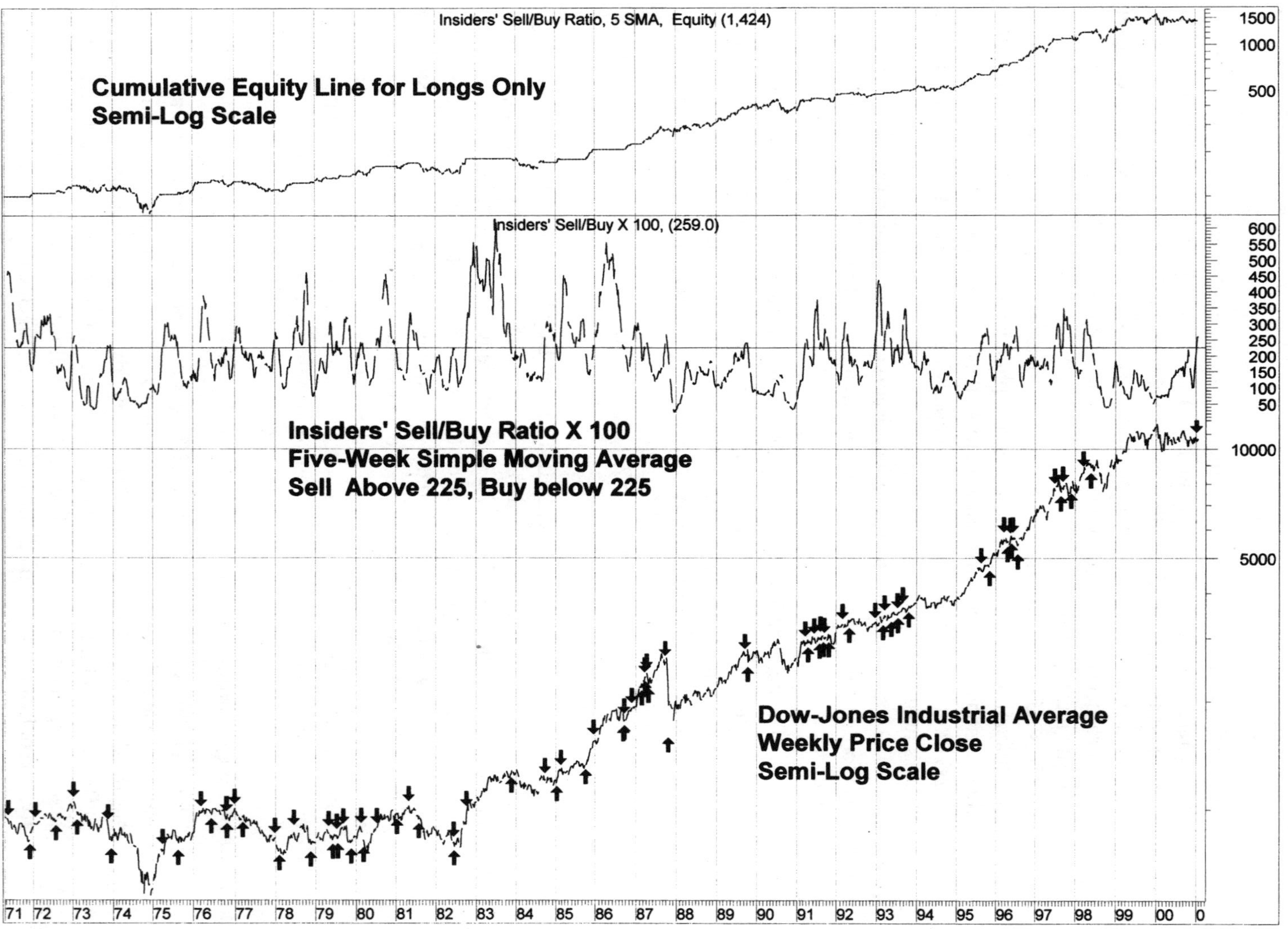

Insiders' Sell/Buy Ratio, 5 SMA, Equity (1,424)
Cumulative Equity Line for Longs Only
Semi-Log Scale
1500
1000
500
Insiders' Sell/Buy X 100, (259.0)
600
550
500
450
400
350
300
250
200
150
100
50
Insiders' Sell/Buy Ratio X 100
Five-Week Simple Moving Average
Sell Above 225, Buy below 225
10000
5000
Dow-Jones Industrial Average
Weekly Price Close
Semi-Log Scale
71 72 73 74 75 76 77 78 79 80 81 82 83 84 85 86 87 88 89 90 91 92 93 94 95 96 97 98 99 00 0

Insiders' Sell/Buy Ratio

Total net profit	1324.14	Open position value	N/A	Net Profit/Buy&Hold %	29.22
Percent gain/loss	1324.14	Annual percent gain/loss	44.45	Annual Net %/B&H %	29.22
Initial investment	100	Interest earned	0		
Current position	Out	Date position entered	1/12/01		
Buy/Hold profit	1024.71	Days in test	10872	# of days per trade	252.84
Buy/Hold pct gain/loss	1024.71	Annual B/H pct gain/loss	34.4		
Total closed trades	43	Commissions paid	0		
Avg profit per trade	30.79	Avg Win/Avg Loss ratio	5.38		
Total long trades	43	Total short trades	0	Long Win Trade %	76.74
Winning long trades	33	Winning short trades	0	Short Win Trade %	#DIV/0!
Total winning trades	33	Total losing trades	10	Total Win Trade %	76.74
Amount of winning trades	1403.17	Amount of losing trades	−79.03	Net Profit Margin %	89.34
Average win	42.52	Average loss	−7.9	Average P. Margin %	68.66
Largest win	310.55	Largest loss	−25.63	% Net/(Win + Loss)	84.75
Average length of win	24.06	Average length of loss	30.8	(Win − Loss)/Loss %	−21.88
Longest winning trade	138	Longest losing trade	68	(Win − Loss)/Loss %	102.94
Most consecutive wins	11	Most consecutive losses	2	(Win − Loss)/Loss %	450.00
Total bars out	538	Average length out	12.23		
Longest out period	60				
System close drawdown	0	Profit/Loss index	94.37	% Net Profit/SODD	5980.76
System open drawdown	−22.14	Reward/Risk index	98.36	(Net P.-SODD)/Net P.	98.33
Max open trade drawdown	−170.44	Buy/Hold index	29.22	% SODD/Net Profit	−1.67

In the Equis MetaStock® "System Report" (profit and loss summary statistics), the *Total net profit* is the sum of profits minus the sum of losses, including open positions marked to the market. In contrast, the *Amount of Winning Trades* is the sum of realized profits (the total of all gains on closed-out trades only, excluding any open positions). Similarly, the *Amount of Losing Trades* is the sum of realized losses (the total of all losses on closed-out trades only, excluding any open positions). *System close drawdown* is the largest decline in the cumulative equity line below the initial investment, based on closed-out positions only. *System open drawdown (SODD)* is the largest decline in the cumulative equity line below the initial investment when a position is open. *Max open trade drawdown* is the largest decline in the cumulative equity line below the trade entry price during the worst single trade. The *Profit/Loss Index* is a complex calculation that relates the Amount of Winning Trades to the Amount of Losing Trades on a scale of −100 (worst possible performance) to +100 (best possible performance), with zero representing profits equal to losses. *Reward/Risk Index* is the Total net profit minus System open drawdown. The resulting difference is then divided by the Total net profit. The *Buy/Hold Index* is the Total net profit minus the buy-and-hold strategy's net profit. The resulting difference is then divided by the buy-and-hold net profit. In this exercise, initial equity is assumed to be $100. Both long and short positions are taken unless otherwise noted. Trades are executed at the closing price on the signal date. Transaction costs, interest expenses, and margins are not included in the statistics.

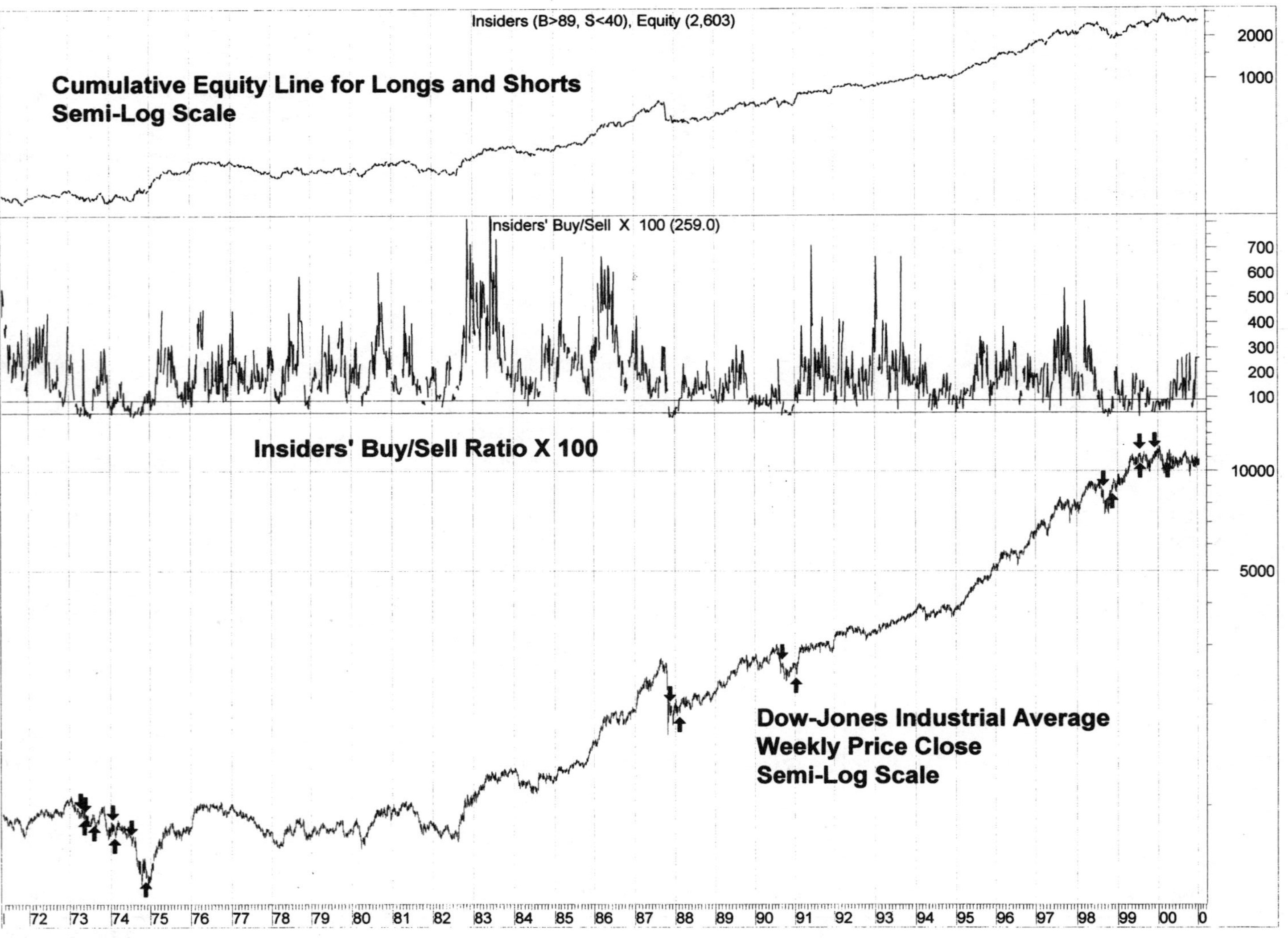
Insiders (B>89, S<40), Equity (2,603)
Cumulative Equity Line for Longs and Shorts
Semi-Log Scale
2000
1000
Insiders' Buy/Sell X 100 (259.0)
700
600
500
400
300
200
100
Insiders' Buy/Sell Ratio X 100
10000
5000
Dow-Jones Industrial Average
Weekly Price Close
Semi-Log Scale
72
73
74
75
76
77
78
79
80
81
82
83
84
85
86
87
88
89
90
91
92
93
94
95
96
97
98
99
00
0

Enter Long (Buy) at the current weekly price close of the DJIA when the 5-week Simple Moving Average of the Insiders' Sell/Buy Ratio is less than 2.25, thus indicating relatively low Insiders' Selling.

Close Long (Sell) at the current weekly price close of the DJIA when the 5-week Simple Moving Average of the Insiders' Sell/Buy Ratio is greater than 2.25, thus indicating relatively high Insiders' Selling.

Enter Short (Sell Short) never.

Starting with $100 and reinvesting profits, total net profits for this Insiders' Sell/Buy Ratio contrary strategy would have been $1324.14, assuming a fully invested strategy, reinvestment of profits, no transactions costs and no taxes. This would have been 29.22 percent better than buy-and-hold. Short selling would have been unprofitable and was not included in this strategy. The long-only Insiders' Sell/Buy Ratio would have given profitable signals 76.74% of the time. Trading would have been inactive at one trade every 252.84 calendar days.

The Equis International MetaStock® System Testing rules, where the Insiders' Sell/Buy Ratio is inserted into the field normally reserved for volume, are written as follows:

Enter long: Mov(V,opt1,S) < opt2

Close long: Mov(V,opt1,S) > opt2

OPT1 Current value: 5
OPT2 Current value: 225

An Independent Indicator Strategy Example: Corporate Insiders' Big Block Transactions

The following is an abbreviated summary of a paper, "Corporate Insiders' Big Block Transactions", written in 1999 by Eric Bjorgen and Steve Leuthold of the Leuthold Group. The paper won the annual Charles H. Dow Award for market analysis.

Unusually low insider selling is bullish and unusually high insider selling is bearish. Insiders normally are net sellers on balance, in increasing amounts over time. To normalize the data for their analysis, the authors used a 10-week average dollar amount of net insider selling as a percentage of total market capitalization.

From 1983 into 1999, a period of 16.3 years, the normalized 10-week average dollar amount of net insider selling spent 85.6% of its time within a normal range from 0.01% to 0.07% of total market capitalization. This means that the normalized average spent 14.4% of its time outside that normal range. Of that outside normal range-time (100.0%), insiders spent more time engaging in unusually high selling (60.4%) than engaging in unusually low selling (39.6%). In other words, the normalized average spent 1.4 years or 74 weeks or 8.7% of the total time of 16.3 years in the high selling zone. The normalized average spent 0.9 years or 48 weeks or 5.7% of the total time of 16.3 years in the low selling zone.

From 1983 to late 1990, the normalized average showed net buying on only three occasions, and each time a bear market bottom occurred within weeks. When insider net selling has been unusually low, the S&P 500 has outperformed its average performance by several percentage points going forward 3, 6, 9 and 12 months ahead. Low selling identified the market bottoms of 1984, 1987 and 1990 within several weeks. But there was not a single instance of an unusually low level of insider selling from late 1990 to the time of the paper in 1999.

Insider's Net Selling Levels	**S&P 500 Average Return**			
	3 Months	*6 Months*	*9 Months*	*12 Months*
High	−0.6%	3.5%	7.0%	0.3%
Normal	3.7%	7.2%	10.7%	14.8%
Low	6.0%	10.4%	13.5%	17.7%

The "Insider's Net Selling Levels" table shows that when insider selling has been "High," the S&P 500 underperformed "Normal" substantially, especially 12 months ahead. A rapid increase in insider net selling often preceded or coincided with market weakness and price volatility. However, the signals were 6 to 12 months early. For example, insider net selling peaked in March 1987, but the market did not crash until 7 months later in October 1987. Also, the insider selling spike in the fall of 1989 was immediately followed by a choppy market, but the S&P 500 did not collapse until August 1990.

The table also shows that when insider selling has been "Low," the S&P 500 has outperformed "Normal" by 2.3 to 3.2 percentage points.

Big Block transactions were defined as those involving more than 100,000 shares or a total transaction value greater than $1,000,000.

Corporate insiders increased selling following the SEC's 1997 code revision shortening the holding period of restricted shares. Also in 1997, there was a long-term maximum capital gains tax rate cut to 20%. Both of these changes have encouraged increasing selling by insiders.

Normalizing the data by adjusting for the growth of the stock market over time allows a better historical perspective. This also shows net insider selling increasing since 1991.

Insider trading laws prohibit using "material, non-public information" for financial gain. Still, insiders' insights into the probable success or failure of future corporate plans naturally influence insiders decisions about when and whether to buy or sell company stock. Consequently, insider transactions reflect insights that might not be available in cautiously worded company news releases. Since the stock market is the sum of all public firms, it follows that the aggregate buying and selling patterns of all insiders could offer insights into future prospects of the stock market.

The SEC makes information on insider's transactions available weekly. By law, all corporate insiders (and beneficial owners who hold 10% or more of outstanding shares) are required to file Form 4 by the tenth day of the month following a transaction. Each week the latest filings are compiled and published in Vicker's Weekly Insider. The transactions of corporations, foundations, trusts and other institutional shareholders are ignored, since these transactions are often motivated by factors that have nothing to do with the financial prospects of a company.

Insiders buy and sell transactions are summed for a weekly aggregate net dollar amount of selling and buying. Most of the time, selling is much greater than buying. Weeks of net selling outnumber weeks of net buying 12 to 1. Insiders' sell transactions include the sale of stock resulting from the exercise of options, although no corresponding buy transaction occurs when options are issued. In the seven years from 1992 to 1999, the sell/buy ratio climbed to 50 to 1, partly due to increasing use of options to compensate corporate insiders. As option issuance and market capitalization increased, net selling has drifted upward, so the data must be normalized by dividing by total market capitalization.

While the dollar amount measures the magnitude of insider's transactions, the net number of transactions measures the breadth of net sells/buys. Normally the two data series move together. Occasionally, the weekly net dollar amount of net selling surges, but the net number of sell transactions remains flat. This indicates that there were one or more unusually large transactions during that particular week, for example, huge blocks of Texaco in July 1989, Duracell in May 1995, and Microsoft in March 1998. When insider data shows both record dollar amounts and record numbers of net sell transactions, a market peak follows. In 1983, 1987, 1993 and late 1989, selling surges foreshadowed significant price drops. Three later selling surges in the 1990s were followed by market price consolidation. A set of sell signals occurred during Q2 of 1998, offering a timely warning of the market price decline during Q3 of 1998.

Intermarket Divergences

The trader first identifies two (or more) closely equivalent financial instruments that trade separately. When two prices diverge, by one not moving to a proportionately similar extent or in a similar direction as the other, the trader initiates a trade. He may buy one and short the other in an attempt to take advantage of possible price movement if the two instruments come back into alignment, as they usually do.

The risk is that on occasion there is a good reason for the divergence and the misalignment persists or even intensifies. This happened in a dramatic way to Long Term Capital Management, which quickly lost so many billions of dollars betting on *normality* that it required a massive government-sponsored financial bailout in 1998.

Intraday Trading, Day Trading, Behavior of Prices Through the Day

Arthur A. Merrill, CMT, pioneered the study of seasonal behavior of stock market prices in his classic book, *Behavior of Prices on Wall Street, Second Edition,* The Analysis Press, Chappaqua, New York, 1984, 147 pages. On pages 10-11, he revealed the "Behavior Through the Day," based on a tally of hourly price changes from January 1962 through December 1974. It may be significant to note that during this period the Dow-Jones Industrial Average fell from 731.14 to 616.24, a decline of 18.65%.

Merrill found that the hour-by-hour pattern today depends on the trend yesterday. If the DJIA rose yesterday, then the market opened higher 70% of the time. Next, during the first hour of trading, 62% of the time the market continued to move higher. After that bullish first full hour of trading, during the middle of the day, 53% to 55% of the time there was profit taking and downward price movement. During the next to last hour of trading, 53% of the time there was upside price movement. Finally, during the last hour of trading, 54% of the time there was downward price movement, presumably as day traders closed out long positions.

The daily pattern was much different following a down day. Merrill found that if the DJIA fell the previous day, then the next day the market opened lower 65% of the time. After the open, there was a slight tendency for the market to continue to decline, on average, although that depended on the particular day of the week. On Mondays, there was a definite tendency for the market to continue to move lower through the close. But this clear bearish bias was less pronounced on Wednesdays and Thursdays. In contrast, on Tuesdays there was no bearish tendency after the open, and on Fridays, the market was slightly (but not significantly) more likely to rise after the open and through the rest of the day.

The performance of the DJIA at half-hour intervals is updated each year in Yale Hirsch's, *Stock Traders Almanac,* The Hirsch Organization, Inc., 184 Central Avenue, Old Tappan, NJ 07675, pages 128-129, www.stocktradersalmanac.com. His statistical charts are reprinted here with permission. Hirsch's *Almanac* provides annual updates on seasonal tendencies and other interesting calendar-based statistics.

MARKET PERFORMANCE EACH HALF-HOUR OF THE DAY (JANUARY 1987–DECEMBER 1999)

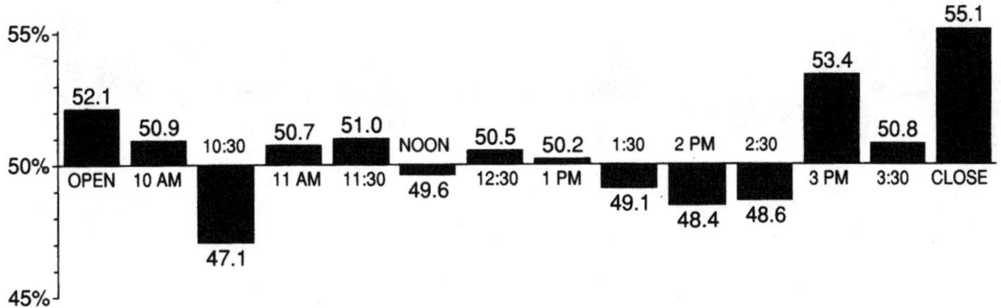

Based on the number of times the Dow Jones industrial average increased over previous half-hour

MARKET PERFORMANCE EACH HOUR OF THE DAY (NOVEMBER 1963–JUNE 1985)

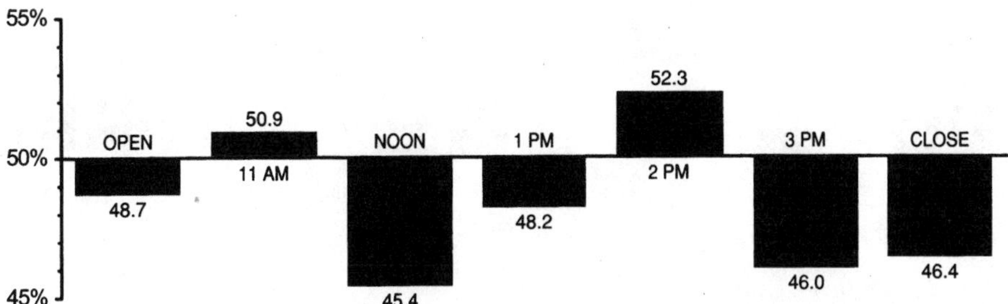

Based on the number of times the Dow Jones industrial average increased over previous hour

---

Reprinted by permission of Yale Hirsch, Stock Traders Almanac, The Hirsch Organization, Inc., 184 Central Avenue, Old Tappan, NJ 07675, www.stocktradersalmanac.com.

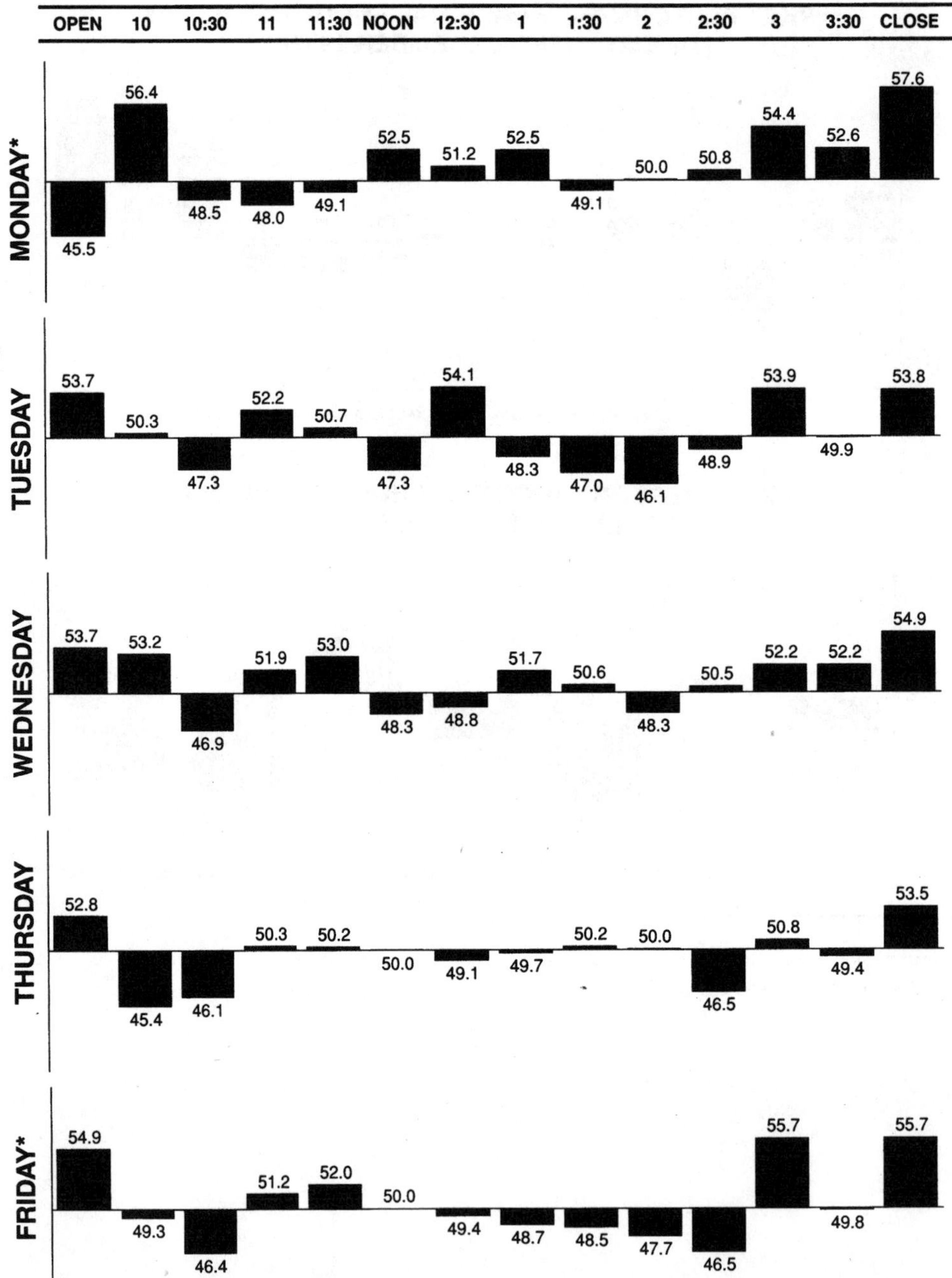

**Research indicates that where Tuesday is the first trading day of the week, it follows the Monday pattern. Therefore, all such Tuesdays were combined with the Mondays here. Thursdays that are the final trading day of a given week behave like Fridays, and were similarly grouped with Fridays.*

Hirsch recently published a study of half-hourly price changes from January 1987 through December 1999. It may be significant to note that during this period the DJIA rose from 1895.95 to 11497.12, a remarkable increase of 506.40%. Based on this bullish bias, we reasonably might expect to find significantly bullish tendencies, but such was hardly the case.

The most consistent tendency was to rise late in the day, particularly the last half hour from 3:30 to the close at 4 PM, but even that occurred only 55% of the time. Also, the half hour from 2:30 to 3 PM was bullish every day of the week, on average, but only 53% of the time. On balance, the last 1.5 hours from 2:30 to the close at 4 PM were up a bit more than half of the time.

The open tended to be higher about 54% of the time, every day but Monday, when it was down 54% of the time. There was a decline from 10 to 10:30 AM, about 53% of the time. The rest of the day the market action was remarkable only for its complete statistical insignificance.

Tendencies evident a little more or less than half the time are hardly better than flipping a coin and far from enough to inspire confidence in trading. Moreover, intraday tendencies are easily overwhelmed by news reports and rumors that surface at unpredictable times during the day.

"Day traders die broke," is an old saying on Wall Street. An August 1999, study by the North American Securities Administration Association (NASAA) found that 70% of the customers at a day-trading firm surveyed lost money. Only 11.5% of the traders in the sampling showed they had the ability to conduct profitable short-term trading, even during a record-breaking bull market trend.

Day traders exchange limited risk for limited reward. At the end of the month, a long list of small gains and small losses have to offset commissions, slippage, fees, and taxes and other expenses that the trader must pay. Trading is a highly competitive business with many thousands of competitors fighting hard with each other trying to win small fractions of a dollar. The advantage lies with the house and the market makers. But even their jobs are far from easy, and they have been known to lose large sums in difficult market environments.

It has long been said that the typical investor is much more likely to profit from major price trends that last for months or even years, as opposed to the relatively insignificant price ripples that occur within a typical trading day. Even short-term traders can benefit from stepping back from the confusion of daily fluctuations to see the bigger picture, the major trends beyond the reach of day-to-day random noise.

The value of a major trend perspective has long been recognized by astute technical analysts. Nearly seven decades ago, Richard W. Schabacker emphasized that short-term traders are likely to be more successful when they trade in harmony with the direction of the major trend, rather than trying to capture every minor move. The technical trader "will seldom if ever lose very much by holding himself aloof from constant communication with the ticker and, indeed, he is much more likely to benefit by divorcing himself from the excitement, the conversation, the gossip, the impetuosities, and the nerve strain, which emanate from watching the erratic fluctuations within the day's market from the dubious vantage point of the board-room. Many professional operators are past masters in the art of so splitting or bunching their orders in order to make the tape produce the effect they desire at a certain time of the day on the crowds who are watching in the board-room. The ideal aim of the chart student is to let the action of the market speak for itself in forecasting its own technical position, and it is exceedingly difficult to assume the calm open-mindedness necessary for such an ideal, while exposed to the psychological tides of board-room gossip, news, hopes and fears."—Schabacker, Richard W., *Technical Analysis and Stock Market Profits, A Course in Forecasting,* Pitman Publishing, 128 Long Acre, London WC2C9AN, 1932 and 1997, 451 pages, page 372.

January Barometer

As January goes, so goes the year. The January Barometer historical performance statistics are updated each year in Yale Hirsch's, *Stock Traders Almanac,* The Hirsch Organization, Inc., 184 Central Avenue, Old Tappan, NJ 07675, www.stocktradersalmanac.com. His statistical table is reprinted here with permission. Hirsch's *Almanac* provides annual updates on the January Barometer and a variety of other interesting calendar-based statistical studies.

The January Barometer is simply the up or down direction of the S&P 500 Composite Stock Price Index in the month of January, from the closing price level of the last trading day of December to the last trading day of January just one month later.

From 1950 through 2000, the January Barometer has correctly predicted *all* of the 25 S&P moves in excess of 14% for the full-year.

For all 51 years, this simple January direction has effectively predicted the full-year direction of stock market prices 82% of the time: it has been right 42 times out of the past 51 years.

Years beginning with January gains were followed by up full years 31 out of 33 times, or 94% of the time. In 1994, the indicator missed by only 1.5%. The only other loss was in 1966, when a January gain was followed by a full-year decline of 13.1%, which was not a major market loss.

In general, the larger the gain in January, the larger the gain for the full year.

The indicator is not quite as accurate on its bearish forecasts. Following 18 January losses, the full year was down 11 times, or 61% of the time. The unusually persistent and powerful bull market that started in 1982 overwhelmed this indicator to some extent, accounting for three of the wrong bearish forecasts that were followed by price gains by year end.

Following its small error in 1994, the January Barometer has been back on track, 100% correct, for the most recent six years.

Oddly, over the past 51 years, the January Barometer has never missed in odd-numbered years, such as 2001. So, for years ending in an odd number, it has a *perfect* record.

Of course, perfect records always have a special allure. Everyone would like to be right all of the time. But if we choose to live in reality, we must ask ourselves if the January Barometer might be just some statistical quirk, a mere historical coincidence. Thoughtful analysts are troubled by the absence of any compelling and logical rationale behind this indicator.

A prudent analyst might look to other indicators for confirmation. In fact, that is a good idea when using any one indicator, no matter how logical and accurate it may seem. Times change and markets change. Few indicators, no matter how impressive, can be expected to sustain overwhelming accuracy through the years. Long experience with markets clearly shows that the search for perfection will no doubt remain elusive and in all probability counter productive.

JANUARY BAROMETER IN GRAPHIC FORM

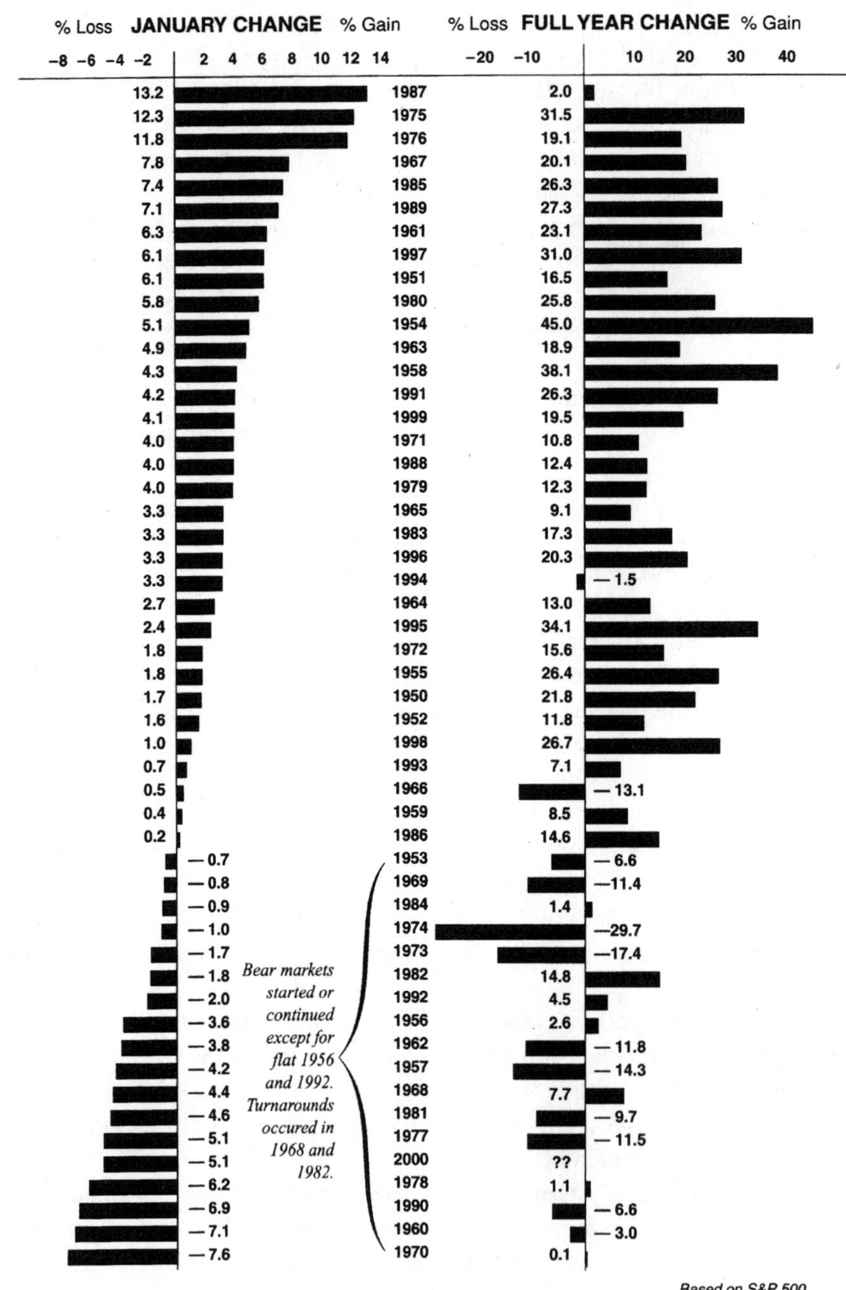

Reprinted with permission of Yale Hirsch, *Stock Traders Almanac,* The Hirsch Organization, Inc., 184 Central Avenue, Old Tappan, NJ 07675, www.stocktradersalmanac.com.

ONLY THREE SIGNIFICANT ERRORS IN 50 YEARS

Since 1950, the January Barometer has predicted the annual course of the stock market with amazing accuracy. Based on whether Standard & Poor's 500 index is up or down in January, most years (excluding four flat years 1970, 1978, 1984, and 1994) have, in essence, followed suit—45 out of 50 times—for a 90% batting average. However, there were **no errors in odd years** when new congresses convened. Bear markets began or continued when Januarys had a loss. Both 1956 and 1992 were flat years.

January performance chronologically and by rank is shown below. The top 29 Januarys (except 1994) had gains of 1% and launched the best market years. Twenty-two Januarys were losers or had miniscule gains. Only one very good year—1982—followed a January loss. Of the three significant errors 1966, 1968, and 1982, Vietnam affected the first two.

AS JANUARY GOES, SO GOES THE YEAR

Market Performance In January

	Previous Year's Close	January Close	January Change
1950	16.76	17.05	1.7%
1951	20.41	21.66	6.1
1952	23.77	24.14	1.6
1953	26.57	26.38	- 0.7
1954	24.81	26.08	5.1
1955	35.98	36.63	1.8
1956	45.48	43.82	- 3.6
1957	46.67	44.72	- 4.2
1958	39.99	41.70	4.3
1959	55.21	55.42	0.4
1960	59.89	55.61	- 7.1
1961	58.11	61.78	6.3
1962	71.55	68.84	- 3.8
1963	63.10	66.20	4.9
1964	75.02	77.04	2.7
1965	84.75	87.56	3.3
1966	92.43	92.88	0.5
1967	80.33	86.61	7.8
1968	96.47	92.24	- 4.4
1969	103.86	103.01	- 0.8
1970	92.06	85.02	- 7.6
1971	92.15	95.88	4.0
1972	102.09	103.94	1.8
1973	118.05	116.03	- 1.7
1974	97.55	96.57	- 1.0
1975	68.56	76.98	12.3
1976	90.19	100.86	11.8
1977	107.46	102.03	- 5.1
1978	95.10	89.25	- 6.2
1979	96.11	99.93	4.0
1980	107.94	114.16	5.8
1981	135.76	129.55	- 4.6
1982	122.55	120.40	- 1.8
1983	140.64	145.30	3.3
1984	164.93	163.42	- 0.9
1985	167.24	179.63	7.4
1986	211.28	211.78	0.2
1987	242.16	274.08	13.2
1988	247.09	257.07	4.0
1989	277.72	297.48	7.1
1990	353.40	329.07	- 6.9
1991	330.23	343.93	4.2
1992	417.09	408.79	- 2.0
1993	435.71	438.78	0.7
1994	466.45	481.61	3.3
1995	459.27	470.42	2.4
1996	615.93	636.02	3.3
1997	740.74	786.16	6.1
1998	970.43	980.28	1.0
1999	1229.23	1279.64	4.1
2000	1469.25	1394.46	- 5.1

January Performance By Rank

Rank		January Change	Year's Change
1	1987	13.2%	2.0%
2	1975	12.3	31.5
3	1976	11.8	19.1
4	1967	7.8	20.1
5	1985	7.4	26.3
6	1989	7.1	27.3
7	1961	6.3	23.1
8	1997	6.1	31.0
9	1951	6.1	16.5
10	1980	5.8	25.8
11	1954	5.1	45.0
12	1963	4.9	18.9
13	1958	4.3	38.1
14	1991	4.2	26.3
15	1999	4.1	19.5
16	1971	4.0	10.8
17	1988	4.0	12.4
18	1979	4.0	12.3
19	1965	3.3	9.1
20	1983	3.3	17.3
21	1996	3.3	20.3
22	1994	3.3	- 1.5
23	1964	2.7	13.0
24	1995	2.4	34.1
25	1972	1.8	15.6
26	1955	1.8	26.4
27	1950	1.7	21.8
28	1952	1.6	11.8
29	1998	1.0	26.7
30	1993	0.7	7.1
31	1966	0.5	- 13.1
32	1959	0.4	8.5
33	1986	0.2	14.6
34	1953	- 0.7	- 6.6
35	1969	- 0.8	- 11.4
36	1984	- 0.9	1.4
37	1974	- 1.0	- 29.7
38	1973	- 1.7	- 17.4
39	1982	- 1.8	14.8
40	1992	- 2.0	4.5
41	1956	- 3.6	2.6
42	1962	- 3.8	- 11.8
43	1957	- 4.2	- 14.3
44	1968	- 4.4	7.7
45	1981	- 4.6	- 9.7
46	2000	- 5.1	??
47	1977	- 5.1	- 11.5
48	1978	- 6.2	1.1
49	1990	- 6.9	- 6.6
50	1960	- 7.1	- 3.0
51	1970	- 7.6	0.1

Based on S&P 500

Reprinted with permission of Yale Hirsch, *Stock Traders Almanac,* The Hirsch Organization, Inc., 184 Central Avenue, Old Tappan, NJ 07675, www.stocktradersalmanac.com.

For a discussion of a similar indicator, refer to the section on the First Five Days in January.

January Effect

The January Effect is the tendency of small, cheap stocks beaten down by year-end tax-loss selling to make bottoms around the third week of December. After that, these stocks tend to rebound strongly for a month or so, until the third week of January. Data published by Yale Hirsch suggests that this happens most years. Hirsch's observations are reprinted here with permission. For an update, see *Stock Traders Almanac,* The Hirsch Organization, Inc., 184 Central Avenue, Old Tappan, NJ 07675, page 112, www.stocktradersalmanac.com.

JANUARY EFFECT STARTS IN MID-DECEMBER

We always hear about the January Effect, but now we have a graph revealing that it does indeed exist. Ned Davis Research has taken the 20 years of daily data of the Russell 2000 index of smaller companies and divided it by the Russell 1000 index of largest companies. Then they compressed the 20 years into a single year to show an idealized yearly pattern. When the graph is descending, big blue chips are outperforming smaller companies; when the graph is rising, smaller companies are moving up faster than their larger brethren.

In a typical year the smaller fry stay on the sidelines while the big boys are on the field, suddenly in mid-December the smaller fry take over and take off. This is known as the "January Effect." Many year-end dividends, payouts and bonuses could be a factor. Another major move is quite evident just before Labor Day. Possibly because individual investors are back from vacations.

RUSSELL 2000/RUSSELL 1000 A ONE-YEAR SEASONAL PATTERN

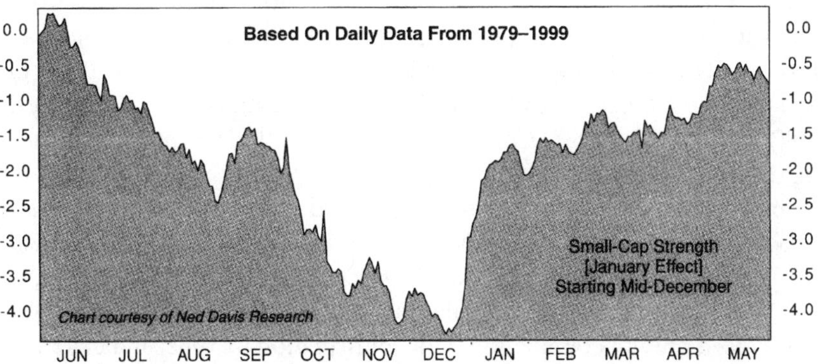

The data for the bottom graph was provided by Global Financial Data and shows the actual ratio of the Russell 2000 divided by the Russell 1000 from 1979. We see the smaller companies having the upper hand for five years into 1983, then falling behind for about eight years, coming back after the Persian Gulf War and moving up more until 1994. For six years the picture had been bleak as the blue chips and tech stocks moved into stratospheric PE ratios. But note the small-cap spike that begins in late 1999. Perhaps we are poised for some years of outperformance from stocks with lower market capitalizations.

RUSSELL 2000/RUSSELL 1000 (1979–JULY 2000)

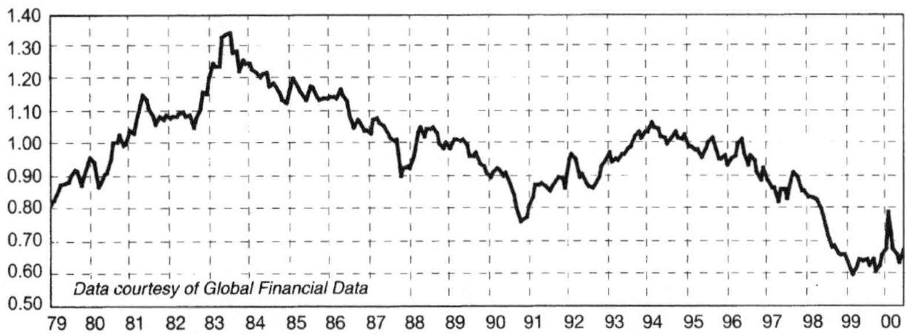

Reprinted with permission of Yale Hirsch, *Stock Traders Almanac,* The Hirsch Organization, Inc., 184 Central Avenue, Old Tappan, NJ 07675, www.stocktradersalmanac.com.

January's First Five Days, an "Early Warning" System

As early January goes, so goes the year. January's First Five Days Early Warning System's historical performance statistics are updated each year in Yale Hirsch's, *Stock Traders Almanac,* The Hirsch Organization, Inc., 184 Central Avenue, Old Tappan, NJ 07675, www.stocktradersalmanac.com. His statistical table is reprinted here with permission. Hirsch's *Almanac* provides annual updates on a variety of interesting calendar-based statistical studies.

If the S&P 500 Composite Stock Price Index goes up during the first five trading days of the year, the market for the whole year tends to go up. Since 1950, this bullish Early Warning has worked 27 out of 31 times, or 87% of the time. Yale Hirsch suggests that three of the four misses might have been thrown off by war news–Vietnam in 1966 and 1973, and Iraq-Kuwait in 1990. Indeed, history strongly suggests that war often coincides with jittery, unpredictable stock market movements. The opposite side of the early January coin has not been accurate since 1950; that is, bearish signals have not been significant. But before the unusual bull market that started in 1982, when the S&P 500 Composite Stock Price Index fell during the first five trading days of the year, the market for the whole year went down 73% of the time. Alas, the powerful bullish trend since 1982 reduced that tendency to less-than coin-flip accuracy. The statistics for the indicator are now correct only 47% of the time, with the full-year S&P down only 9 of the 19 early decline years. With eroding accuracy rates and no logical underlying rationale, January's First Five Days Early Warning System is best used only in conjunction with confirmation by other indicators.

JANUARY'S FIRST FIVE DAYS AN "EARLY WARNING" SYSTEM

Market action during the first five trading days of the month often serve as an excellent "early warning" system for the year as a whole.

Early January gains since 1950 (excluding 1994) were matched by whole-year gains with just three war related exceptions: The start of the Vietnam war triggered big military spending which delayed the start of the 1966 bear market; and the imminence of a final ceasefire raised stock prices temporarily in early January 1973; Saddam Hussein's actions in Kuwait brought the market down in 1990. Eighteen Januarys got off to a bad start and eight of those ended on the downside. The ten that didn't follow suit were 1955, 1956, 1978, 1982, 1985, 1986, 1988, 1991, 1993 and 1998.

Remember that five days is a brief span and some extraordinary event could sidetrack this indicator as it did on the fifth day of 1986 and 1998.

THE FIRST-FIVE-DAYS-IN-JANUARY INDICATOR

Chronological Data

	Previous Year's Close	5th Day In January	Change 1st 5 Days
1950	16.76	17.09	2.0%
1951	20.41	20.88	2.3
1952	23.77	23.91	0.6
1953	26.57	26.22	−1.3
1954	24.81	24.93	0.5
1955	35.98	35.33	−1.8
1956	45.48	44.51	−2.1
1957	46.67	46.25	−0.9
1958	39.99	40.99	2.5
1959	55.21	55.40	0.3
1960	59.89	59.50	−0.7
1961	58.11	58.81	1.2
1962	71.55	69.12	−3.4
1963	63.10	64.74	2.6
1964	75.02	76.00	1.3
1965	84.75	85.37	0.7
1966	92.43	93.14	0.8
1967	80.33	82.81	3.1
1968	96.47	96.62	0.2
1969	103.86	100.80	−2.9
1970	92.06	92.68	0.7
1971	92.15	92.19	0.0
1972	102.09	103.47	1.4
1973	118.05	119.85	1.5
1974	97.55	96.12	−1.5
1975	68.56	70.04	2.2
1976	90.19	94.58	4.9
1977	107.46	105.01	−2.3
1978	95.10	90.64	−4.7
1979	96.11	98.80	2.8
1980	107.94	108.95	0.9
1981	135.76	133.06	−2.0
1982	122.55	119.55	−2.4
1983	140.64	145.23	3.3
1984	164.93	168.90	2.4
1985	167.24	163.99	−1.9
1986	211.28	207.97	−1.6
1987	242.16	257.28	6.2
1988	247.09	243.40	−1.5
1989	277.72	280.98	1.2
1990	353.40	353.79	0.1
1991	330.23	314.90	−4.6
1992	417.09	418.10	0.2
1993	435.71	429.05	−1.5
1994	466.45	469.90	0.7
1995	459.27	460.83	0.3
1996	615.93	618.46	0.4
1997	740.74	748.41	1.0
1998	970.43	956.04	−1.5
1999	1229.23	1275.09	3.7
2000	1469.25	1441.46	−1.9

Ranked By Performance

Rank		Change 1st 5 Days	Change For Year
1	1987	6.2%	2.0%
2	1976	4.9	19.1
3	1999	3.7	19.5
4	1983	3.3	17.3
5	1967	3.1	20.1
6	1979	2.8	12.3
7	1963	2.6	18.9
8	1958	2.5	38.1
9	1984	2.4	1.4
10	1951	2.3	16.5
11	1975	2.2	31.5
12	1950	2.0	21.8
13	1973	1.5	−17.4
14	1972	1.4	15.6
15	1964	1.3	13.0
16	1961	1.2	23.1
17	1989	1.2	27.3
18	1997	1.0	31.0
19	1980	0.9	25.8
20	1966	0.8	−13.1
21	1994	0.7	− 1.5
22	1965	0.7	9.1
23	1970	0.7	0.1
24	1952	0.6	11.8
25	1954	0.5	45.0
26	1996	0.4	20.3
27	1959	0.3	8.5
28	1995	0.3	34.1
29	1992	0.2	4.5
30	1968	0.2	7.7
31	1990	0.1	− 6.6
32	1971	0.0	10.8
33	1960	−0.7	− 3.0
34	1957	−0.9	−14.3
35	1953	−1.3	− 6.6
36	1974	−1.5	−29.7
37	1998	−1.5	26.7
38	1988	−1.5	12.4
39	1993	−1.5	7.1
40	1986	−1.6	14.6
41	1955	−1.8	26.4
42	2000	−1.9	??
43	1985	−1.9	26.3
44	1981	−2.0	− 9.7
45	1956	−2.1	2.6
46	1977	−2.3	−11.5
47	1982	−2.4	14.8
48	1969	−2.9	−11.4
49	1962	−3.4	−11.8
50	1991	−4.6	26.3
51	1978	−4.7	1.1

Based on S&P 500

Reprinted with permission of Yale Hirsch, *Stock Traders Almanac,* The Hirsch Organization, Inc., 184 Central Avenue, Old Tappan, NJ 07675, www.stocktradersalmanac.com.

Kagi Charts

The Japanese Kagi Chart is a unique kind of a line chart designed to filter out minor, short-term market noise. It is similar to the western Point-and-Figure technique in that price movement (and not the passage of time) determines the progress along the horizontal *x*-axis.

For trend continuation, a Kagi line is extended in the prevailing trend direction whenever the current closing price continues to progress in the same direction as the latest vertical Kagi line, no matter how small the price movement.

For a trend reversal, a new Kagi line heading in the opposite direction is drawn in a new column to the right only when the closing price reverses direction by a fixed and predetermined amount, called a *reversal amount.* This reversal amount is usually expressed in a some obvious unit of local currency, such as one dollar, though it could be set to any amount. Alternately, the reversal amount could be defined as a percentage price change. But when the closing price moves in the opposite direction by less than the reversal amount, no new lines are drawn on the Kagi Chart.

When the current closing price moves beyond the previous column's high or low, the thickness of the Kagi line changes. Specifically, when a thin Kagi line penetrates (rises above) the previous high point on the Kagi chart, the line becomes thick. In contrast, when a thick Kagi line violates (falls below) a previous low point on the Kagi chart, the line becomes thin.

The chart shows the one dollar reversal amount Kagi Chart for the S&P Depositary Receipts (SPY) for the full year 2000, January through December, drawn with MetaStock® software. See Renko Chart to compare this Kagi Chart to the similar 1 point box size Renko Chart and to the 1 point box size and 1 point reversal Point-and-Figure Chart for the same stock over the same time. For a further discussion of Kagi charts, see Nison, Steven, *Beyond Candlesticks,* Wiley, New York, NY, 1994.

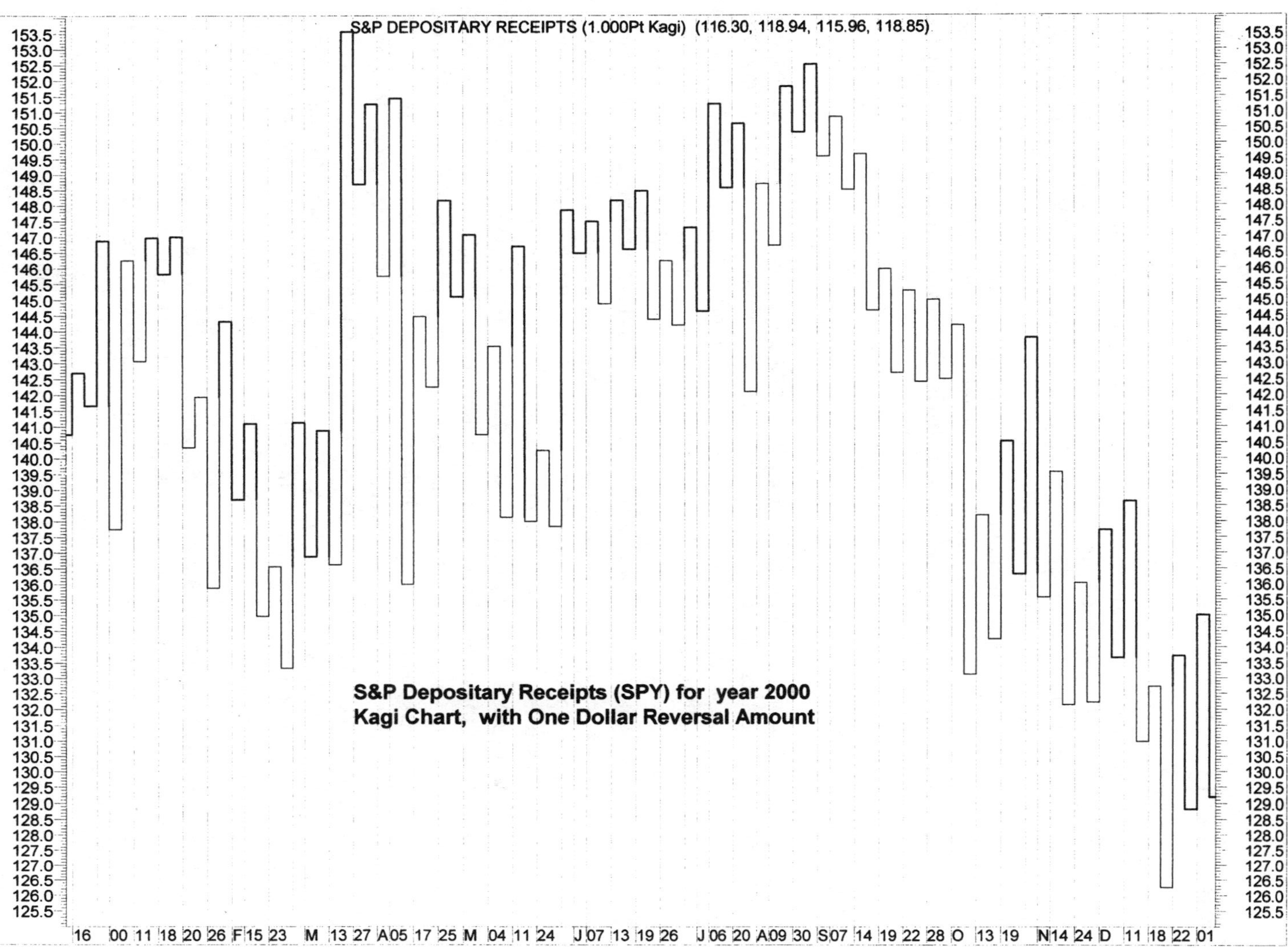
S&P DEPOSITARY RECEIPTS (1.000Pt Kagi) (116.30, 118.94, 115.96, 118.85)
S&P Depositary Receipts (SPY) for year 2000
Kagi Chart, with One Dollar Reversal Amount
16 00 11 18 20 26 F15 23 M 13 27 A05 17 25 M 04 11 24 J07 13 19 26 J 06 20 A09 30 S07 14 19 22 28 O 13 19 N14 24 D 11 18 22 01

Kane's % K Hooks

Kane's % K Hooks are based on Stochastics slow %K *(see Stochastics).* Long trades are initiated when the hourly trading trend is up, there is a dip in the five-minute bar chart slow %K to oversold levels, then slow %K turns up indicating the price dip is ending. Short trades are initiated when the hourly trading trend is down, there is a pop in the five-minute bar chart slow %K to overbought levels, then slow %K turns down, indicating the price rally is ending. For a further discussion of Kane's % K Hooks, see LeBeau, Charles, and Lucas, David W., *Technical Traders Guide to Computer Analysis of the Futures Market,* Business One Irwin, Homewood, IL., 1992, 234 pages.

Kase Indicators

Cynthia A. Kase, an engineer by education and a technical analyst by profession, defined several technical/quantitative indicators in her book, *Trading with the Odds: Using the Power of Probability to Profit in the Futures Market,* Irwin Professional Publishing, 1996, 149 pages. The following has been adapted with permission of the publisher.

Kase Adaptive Dev-Stop sets a protective stop-loss order price according to the standard deviation of price and price skew. Skew is the amount at which range can spike in the opposite direction of the trend. In a trending market, a moving average may be used as an early warning line, and one, two and three standard deviations may function as stops. Further, these standard deviations may be corrected for skew. Skew is biased to the upside in price because there is an absolute limit to how far down price can fall. Optionally, the user may weight these stops by the volatility of the market and by risk tolerance. For example, when a market becomes unusually volatile or uncertain, the user may reduce risk by shifting to a tighter stop level. Reasonable volatility trends may allow a stop at three standard deviations.

Kase PeakOscillator (KPO) is an adaptive momentum oscillator that automatically searches for the most significant cycle length. KPO is designed to express price velocity in terms that have common meaning across time frames, instruments, and units of measure

Kase PeakOut Lines are overbought and oversold extremes at the 90th percentile on the distribution curve. When the Kase PeakOscillator (KPO) peaks through the PeakOut Line and then pulls back, there is a 90% chance of a trend change or a penultimate peak preceding a divergence.

KaseCD (KCD) is a convergence/divergence histogram very similar to MACD. The KCD histogram (KCDH) subtracts an average of KPO from KPO.

Keltner Channel with EMA Filter

A Keltner Channel is based on two bands, plotted above and below a moving average. It is similar to Envelopes and Bollinger Bands except it uses Average True Range instead of percentages (Envelopes) or standard deviations (Bollinger Bands). The upper band is the moving average plus some multiple of the Average True Range (ATR). The lower band is the moving average minus a multiple of the Average True Range. Typically, the upper band is used to define an overbought market that may be due for a downward correction. The lower band defines an oversold market that may be due for an upward correction. For example, we might buy a long position when the current closing price is less than the previous day's 4-day exponential average minus 77% of the previous day's 4-day ATR. We might sell and sell short when the current closing price is greater than the previous day's 4-day exponential average plus 77% of the previous day's 4-day ATR. To filter out some losing trades and thus improve overall results, various longer-term filters could be added to force the system to trade only with the major trend.

Indicator Strategy Example for Keltner Channel with EMA Filter

Keltner Channel with EMA Filter is a moderately profitable indicator with moderate drawdowns and a large majority of profitable trades. It is based on mechanical overbought/oversold signals filtered by a long-term moving average to define the more significant trend and weed out many countertrend trades. Based on daily data for the S&P 500 Stock Index Futures *CSI Perpetual Contract* (www.csidata.com) from 4/21/82 to 4/27/01, we found that the following parameters would have produced a positive result with no subjectivity, no sophisticated technical analysis, and no judgement:

Enter Long (Buy) at the current daily price close when the S&P 500 Composite Stock Price Index futures *CSI Perpetual Contract* closing price is less than yesterday's 4-day exponential moving average of the daily closing prices minus 77% of Average True Range (ATR) also measured over the past four-trading days and the close is above the long-term 274-day exponential moving average of the daily closing prices.

Close Long (Sell) at the current daily price close when the S&P 500 Composite Stock Price Index futures *CSI Perpetual Contract* closing price is greater than yesterday's 4-day exponential moving average of the daily closing prices plus 77% of Average True Range (ATR) also measured over the past four-trading days or the close is below the long-term 274-day exponential moving average of the daily closing prices.

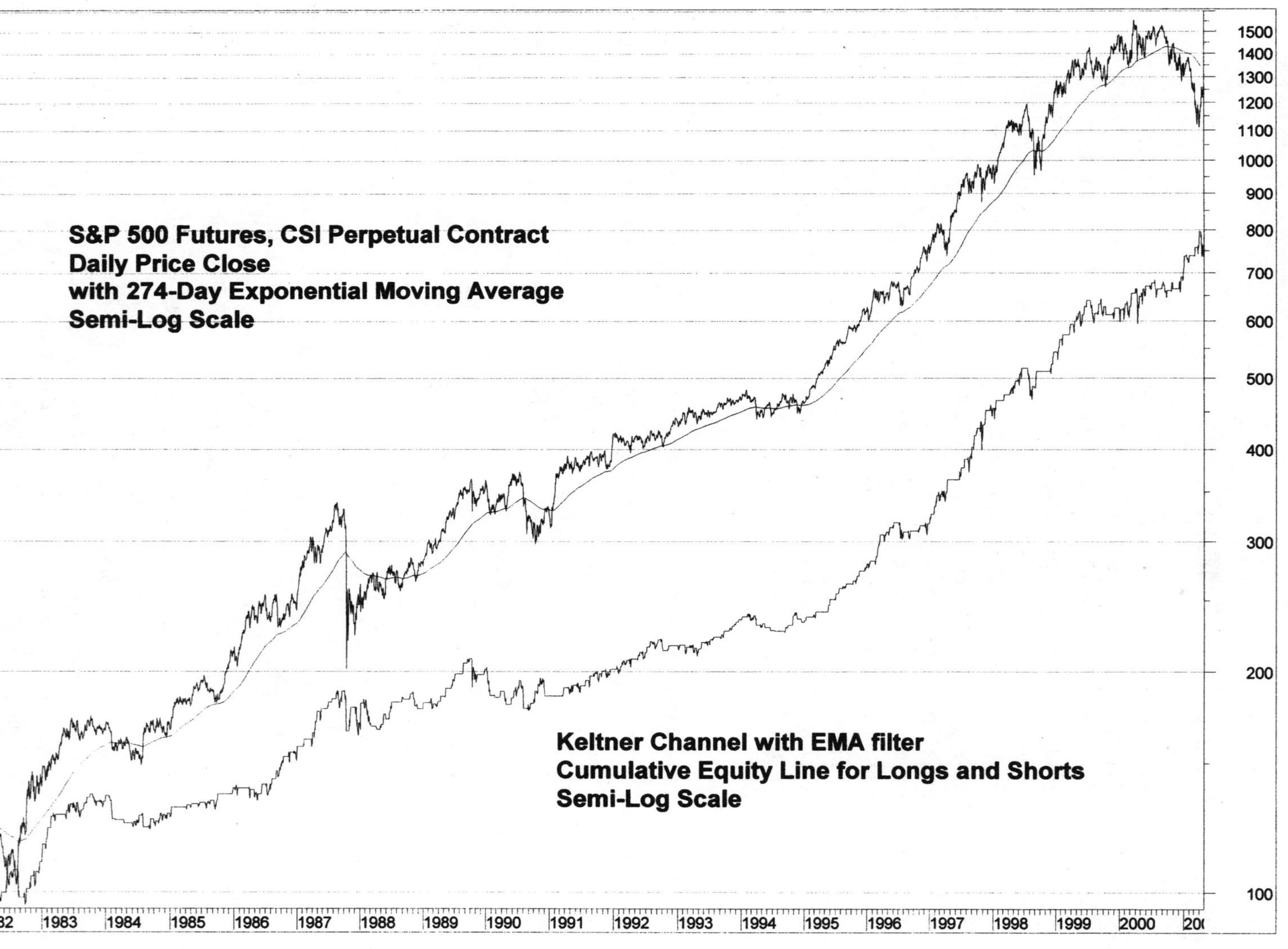
S&P 500 Futures, CSI Perpetual Contract
Daily Price Close
with 274-Day Exponential Moving Average
Semi-Log Scale
Keltner Channel with EMA filter
Cumulative Equity Line for Longs and Shorts
Semi-Log Scale
1500
1400
1300
1200
1100
1000
900
800
700
600
500
400
300
200
100
82
1983
1984
1985
1986
1987
1988
1989
1990
1991
1992
1993
1994
1995
1996
1997
1998
1999
2000
20(

Keltner Channel with EMA filter

Total net profit	636.75	Open position value	−58.84	Net Profit/Buy&Hold %	−20.06
Percent gain/loss	636.75	Annual percent gain/loss	31.17	Annual Net %/B&H %	−20.08
Initial investment	100	Interest earned	0		
Current position	Short	Date position entered	4/10/01		
Buy/Hold profit	796.58	Days in test	7456	# of days per trade	31.07
Buy/Hold pct gain/loss	796.58	Annual B/H pct gain/loss	39		
Total closed trades	240	Commissions paid	0		
Avg profit per trade	2.9	Avg Win/Avg Loss ratio	1.05		
Total long trades	200	Total short trades	40	Long Win Trade %	77.00
Winning long trades	154	Winning short trades	24	Short Win Trade %	60.00
Total winning trades	178	Total losing trades	62	Total Win Trade %	74.17
Amount of winning trades	1038.97	Amount of losing trades	−343.38	Net Profit Margin %	50.32
Average win	5.84	Average loss	−5.54	Average P. Margin %	2.64
Largest win	37.86	Largest loss	−29.32	% Net/(Win + Loss)	12.71
Average length of win	7.2	Average length of loss	11.27	(Win − Loss)/Loss %	−36.11
Longest winning trade	28	Longest losing trade	40	(Win − Loss)/Loss %	−30.00
Most consecutive wins	18	Most consecutive losses	4	(Win − Loss)/Loss %	350.00
Total bars out	3647	Average length out	15.13		
Longest out period	295				
System close drawdown	−1.75	Profit/Loss index	64.97	% Net Profit/SODD	15761.14
System open drawdown	−4.04	Reward/Risk index	99.37	(Net P.-SODD)/Net P.	99.37
Max open trade drawdown	−59.53	Buy/Hold index	−27.45	% SODD/Net Profit	−0.63

In the Equis MetaStock® "System Report" (profit and loss summary statistics), the *Total net profit* is the sum of profits minus the sum of losses, including open positions marked to the market. In contrast, the *Amount of Winning Trades* is the sum of realized profits (the total of all gains on closed-out trades only, excluding any open positions). Similarly, the *Amount of Losing Trades* is the sum of realized losses (the total of all losses on closed-out trades only, excluding any open positions). *System close drawdown* is the largest decline in the cumulative equity line below the initial investment, based on closed-out positions only. *System open drawdown (SODD)* is the largest decline in the cumulative equity line below the initial investment when a position is open. *Max open trade drawdown* is the largest decline in the cumulative equity line below the trade entry price during the worst single trade. The *Profit/Loss Index* is a complex calculation that relates the Amount of Winning Trades to the Amount of Losing Trades on a scale of −100 (worst possible performance) to +100 (best possible performance), with zero representing profits equal to losses. *Reward/Risk Index* is the Total net profit minus System open drawdown. The resulting difference is then divided by the Total net profit. The *Buy/Hold Index* is the Total net profit minus the buy-and-hold strategy's net profit. The resulting difference is then divided by the buy-and-hold net profit. In this exercise, initial equity is assumed to be $100. Both long and short positions are taken unless otherwise noted. Trades are executed at the closing price on the signal date. Transaction costs, interest expenses, and margins are not included in the statistics.

Enter Short (Sell Short) at the current daily price close when the S&P 500 Composite Stock Price Index futures *CSI Perpetual Contract* closing price is greater than yesterday's 4-day exponential moving average of the daily closing prices plus 77% of Average True Range (ATR) also measured over the past four-trading days and the close is below the long-term 274-day exponential moving average of the daily closing prices.

Close Short (Cover) at the current daily price close when the S&P 500 Composite Stock Price Index futures *CSI Perpetual Contract* closing price is less than yesterday's 4-day exponential moving average of the daily closing prices minus 77% of Average True Range (ATR) also measured over the past four-trading days or the close is above the long-term 274-day exponential moving average of the daily closing prices.

Starting with $100 and reinvesting profits, total net profits for this indicator short-term trend-fading and long-term trend-following strategy would have been $636.75, assuming a fully invested strategy, reinvestment of profits, no transactions costs and no taxes. This would have been 20.06 percent less than buy-and-hold. Short selling would have been profitable, and short selling was included in the strategy. Its sub-par profitability would have been offset by moderate equity drawdowns. And, this strategy would have been right much more often than it was wrong, with 74.17% winning trades. Trading would have been reasonably active at one trade every 31.07 calendar days.

The Equis International MetaStock® System Testing rules for Keltner Channel with EMA filter are written as follows:

Enter long: C < (Ref(Mov(C,opt1,E),-1) - (.01*opt2*Ref(ATR(opt1),-1))) AND C > Ref(Mov(C,opt3,E),-1)

Close long: C > (Ref(Mov(C,opt1,E),-2) + (.01*opt2*Ref(ATR(opt1),-2))) OR C < Ref(Mov(C,opt3,E),-1)

Enter short: C > (Ref(Mov(C,opt1,E),-2) + (.01*opt2*Ref(ATR(opt1),-2))) AND C < Ref(Mov(C,opt3,E),-1)

Close short: C < (Ref(Mov(C,opt1,E),-1) - (.01*opt2*Ref(ATR(opt1),-1))) OR C > Ref(Mov(C,opt3,E),-1)

OPT1 Current value: 4

OPT2 Current value: 77

OPT3 Current value: 274

Keltner's Minor Trend Rule

Keltner's Minor Trend Rule is one of the simplest of all trend-following methods. Buy when H is greater than Hp. That is, buy when the current price high rises above the previous period's price high by the minimum unit of price measurement. Sell when L is less than Lp. That is, sell when the current price low falls below the previous period's price low by the minimum unit of price measurement. Although this simple system looks good at times in simulation, in actual trading it can be a surprisingly costly strategy when transaction costs are significant and the price action is choppy. (See Keltner, Chester W., *How to Make Money in Commodities,* The Keltner Statistical Service, Kansas City, 1960.)

Keltner's 10-Day Moving Average Rule

Keltner's 10-Day Moving Average Rule buys when the current day's high crosses an upper band and sells when the current day's low crosses a lower band. The upper and lower bands are the 10-day simple moving average of the daily price range (high minus low) added to and subtracted from the 10-day simple moving average of the Typical Price, which is the day's high plus the low plus the close, divided by three. (See Keltner, Chester W., *How to Make Money in Commodities,* The Keltner Statistical Service, Kansas City, 1960.)

Key Reversal Day

A bullish Key Reversal is defined as a day where the current day's low is below the previous day's low and the current day's close is above the previous day's close. Long positions are closed on the first lower close. A bearish Key Reversal is defined as a day where the current day's high is above the previous day's high and the current day's close is below the previous day's close. Short position are closed on the first higher close.

This would have been an unprofitable trading strategy, on both the long and short sides, over 19-years of S&P 500 futures trading.

The Equis International MetaStock® System Testing rules are written as follows:

Enter long: L < Ref(L,-1) AND C > Ref(C,-1)

Close long: C < Ref(C,-1)

Enter short: H > Ref(H,-1) AND C < Ref(C,-1)

Close short: C > Ref(C,-1)

Key Reversal Day with Filters

A Key Reversal with Filters might begin as a simple Key Reversal and, in addition, require that in order to enter long the current day's low must be a minimum amount below the previous day's low and the longer-term trend must be bullish. Similar filters could be added for the specific sell rule. This may be best illustrated with a specific example.

Indicator Strategy Example for a Key Reversal with Filters, a Trend-Following Strategy

Based on daily data for the S&P 500 Stock Index Futures *CSI Perpetual Contract* (www.csidata.com) from 4/21/82 to 5/23/01, we found that the following specific parameters would have produced a positive result on a purely mechanical trend-following signal basis with no subjectivity, no sophisticated technical analysis, and no judgement:

Enter Long (Buy) at the current daily price close of the S&P 500 Stock Index Futures *CSI Perpetual Contract* when the daily price close is greater than the previous day's close and the current daily low is below the previous day's low by at least 45% of the current 3-day Average True Range (calculated over the most recent three trading days, including the current day). In addition, the long-term trend must be up, as indicated by the current day's close above the previous day's 328-day exponential moving average of the close.

Close Long (Sell) at the current daily price close of the S&P 500 Stock Index Futures *CSI Perpetual Contract* when the daily price close is less than the previous day's close and the current day's high is above the previous day's high plus 45% of the current 3-day Average True Range (calculated over the most recent three trading days, including the current day). Alternately, sell long anytime the current day's close falls below the previous day's 1640-day exponential moving average of the close.

Enter Short (Sell Short) at the current daily price close of the S&P 500 Stock Index Futures *CSI Perpetual Contract* when the daily price close is less than the previous day's close and the current day's high is above the previous day's high plus 45% of the Average True Range. In addition, the current day's close must be below the previous day's 1640-day exponential moving average of the close.

Close Short (Cover) at the current daily price close of the S&P 500 Stock Index Futures *CSI Perpetual Contract* when the daily price close is greater than the previous day's close and the current daily low is below the previous day's low by at least 45% of the current day's Average True Range. Alternately, cover shorts anytime the current day's close rises above the previous day's 328-day exponential moving average of the close.

Starting with $100 and reinvesting profits, total net profits for this Key Reversal with Filters Trend-Following Strategy would have been $528.37, assuming a fully invested strategy, reinvestment of profits, no transactions costs and no taxes. This would have been 35.56 percent less than buy-and-hold. Short selling would have been totally eliminated by the long-term moving average filter. This trend-following indicator would have given profitable buy signals 70.97% of the time. Trading would have been inactive at one trade every 241.35 calendar days. The chart shows how Cumulative Equity, which started at 100, grew with milder drawdowns than the passive buy-and-hold strategy, represented by the price chart itself. Milder equity drawdowns are a desirable quality in an indicator.

The Equis International MetaStock® System Testing rules are written as follows:

Enter long: C > Ref(C,-1) AND L < Ref(L,-1)-ATR(opt1)*opt2/100
AND C > Ref(Mov(C,opt3,E),-1)

Close long: (C < Ref(C,-1) AND H > Ref(H,-1)+ATR(opt1)*opt2/100)
OR C < Ref(Mov(C,opt4*opt3,E),-1)

Enter short: C < Ref(C,-1) AND H > Ref(H,-1)+ATR(opt1)*opt2/100
AND C < Ref(Mov(C,opt4*opt3,E),-1)

Close short: (C > Ref(C,-1) AND (L < Ref(L,-1)-ATR(opt1)*opt2/100))
OR C > Ref(Mov(C,opt3,E),-1)

OPT1 Current value: 3

OPT2 Current value: 45

OPT3 Current value: 328

OPT4 Current value: 5

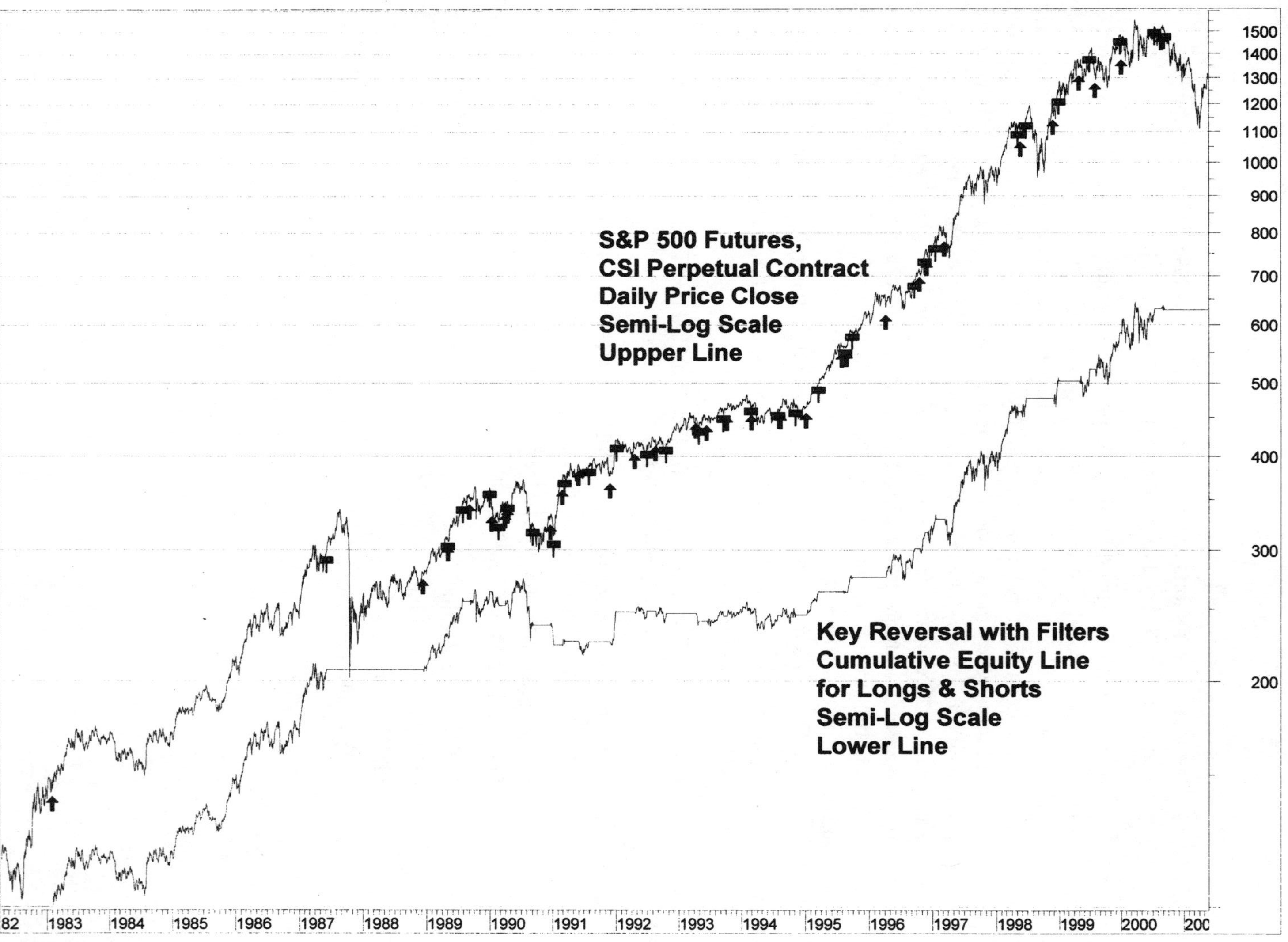
S&P 500 Futures,
CSI Perpetual Contract
Daily Price Close
Semi-Log Scale
Uppper Line
Key Reversal with Filters
Cumulative Equity Line
for Longs & Shorts
Semi-Log Scale
Lower Line
1500
1400
1300
1200
1100
1000
900
800
700
600
500
400
300
200
82
1983
1984
1985
1986
1987
1988
1989
1990
1991
1992
1993
1994
1995
1996
1997
1998
1999
2000
200

Key Reversal with Filters

Total net profit	528.37	Open position value	N/A	Net Profit/Buy&Hold %	−35.56
Percent gain/loss	528.37	Annual percent gain/loss	25.78	Annual Net %/B&H %	−35.55
Initial investment	100	Interest earned	0		
Current position	Out	Date position entered	9/11/00		
Buy/Hold profit	819.93	Days in test	7482	# of days per trade	241.35
Buy/Hold pct gain/loss	819.93	Annual B/H pct gain/loss	40		
Total closed trades	31	Commissions paid	0		
Avg profit per trade	17.04	Avg Win/Avg Loss ratio	4.26		
Total long trades	31	Total short trades	0	Long Win Trade %	70.97
Winning long trades	22	Winning short trades	0	Short Win Trade %	#DIV/0!
Total winning trades	22	Total losing trades	9	Total Win Trade %	70.97
Amount of winning trades	584.56	Amount of losing trades	−56.19	Net Profit Margin %	82.46
Average win	26.57	Average loss	−6.24	Average P. Margin %	61.96
Largest win	128.23	Largest loss	−18.24	% Net/(Win + Loss)	75.09
Average length of win	114.73	Average length of loss	41.33	(Win − Loss)/Loss %	177.59
Longest winning trade	1100	Longest losing trade	106	(Win − Loss)/Loss %	937.74
Most consecutive wins	10	Most consecutive losses	2	(Win − Loss)/Loss %	400.00
Total bars out	2343	Average length out	73.22		
Longest out period	552				
System close drawdown	0	Profit/Loss index	90.39	% Net Profit/SODD	#DIV/0!
System open drawdown	0	Reward/Risk index	100	(Net P.-SODD)/Net P.	100.00
Max open trade drawdown	−30.69	Buy/Hold index	−35.56	% SODD/Net Profit	0.00

In the Equis MetaStock® "System Report" (profit and loss summary statistics), the *Total net profit* is the sum of profits minus the sum of losses, including open positions marked to the market. In contrast, the *Amount of Winning Trades* is the sum of realized profits (the total of all gains on closed-out trades only, excluding any open positions). Similarly, the *Amount of Losing Trades* is the sum of realized losses (the total of all losses on closed-out trades only, excluding any open positions). *System close drawdown* is the largest decline in the cumulative equity line below the initial investment, based on closed-out positions only. *System open drawdown (SODD)* is the largest decline in the cumulative equity line below the initial investment when a position is open. *Max open trade drawdown* is the largest decline in the cumulative equity line below the trade entry price during the worst single trade. The *Profit/Loss Index* is a complex calculation that relates the Amount of Winning Trades to the Amount of Losing Trades on a scale of −100 (worst possible performance) to +100 (best possible performance), with zero representing profits equal to losses. *Reward/Risk Index* is the Total net profit minus System open drawdown. The resulting difference is then divided by the Total net profit. The *Buy/Hold Index* is the Total net profit minus the buy-and-hold strategy's net profit. The resulting difference is then divided by the buy-and-hold net profit. In this exercise, initial equity is assumed to be $100. Both long and short positions are taken unless otherwise noted. Trades are executed at the closing price on the signal date. Transaction costs, interest expenses, and margins are not included in the statistics.

Klinger Oscillator (KO)

This volume-based oscillator was developed by Stephen J. Klinger. It is computed in seven steps:

1. Find the average price of the day by summing the high, low and close, then dividing by three.
2. If today's average price is greater than the previous day's average price, assign a plus sign to today's volume.
3. If today's average price is less than the previous day's average price, assign a minus sign to today's volume.
4. Calculate a 34-period period exponential moving average of the signed volume from Steps 2 and 3.
5. Calculate a 55-period period exponential moving average of the signed volume from Steps 2 and 3.
6. Subtract the 34-period exponential moving average from the 55-period exponential moving average, and plot the difference.
7. Calculate and plot a 13-period exponential moving average of the daily differences from Step 6.

When today's average price is greater than yesterday's average price, that is accumulation. Conversely, when today's average price is less than yesterday's average price, that is distribution. When the sums are equal, the forces of demand and supply are in balance. The average difference between the number of shares being accumulated and distributed each day is the volume force. A rising trend of volume force is bullish, while a falling trend of volume force is bearish. The Klinger Oscillator is compared to price to identify divergences. (See Volume: Klinger Oscillator (KO).)

KST (Know Sure Thing)

KST (Know Sure Thing) is a complex, smoothed price velocity indicator developed by Martin J. Pring and described in *Martin Pring on Market Momentum,* McGraw-Hill, New York 1993, 335 pages. It is a combined indicator, with an enormous number of possible combinations. Just in case we become too excited by the "Sure Thing" implied promise in the name of this indicator, Pring points out (on page 155), "it's also important to know that this approach is not a sure thing." Clearly, there can be no sure thing in investing, but some indicators are better than others, so we continue our search for the best ones. *(See Rate-of-Change, Exponential Moving Averages, and Combined Indicators for a complete description of elements of this indicator.)*

KST may be computed in 6 steps:

1. Compute four different, progressively longer length, rates of change of price, for four different measures of price velocity. Pring suggests increasing the period lengths by about one-third to one-half each time. For example, Pring uses rates of change of 9, 12, 18, and 24 months for his long-term version of KST, which he says is most reliable.
2. Smooth the first three shorter price velocities with a 26-month Exponential Moving Average. Smooth the longest 24-month rate of change with a 39-month Exponential Moving Average.
3. Weight each of the four smoothed price velocities with progressively higher weight assigned to the longer period-length smoothed velocities. Specifically, weight the shortest by 1, weight the next shortest by 2, weight the third length by 3, and weight the longest by 4.
4. Sum these four weighted and smoothed price velocities (from Step 3), then divide by the sum of the weights, which is 10. This is the basic KST.
5. Compute a 9-month Exponential Moving Average of the basic KST (from Step 4) for use as a *signal line.*
6. Plot the basic KST (from Step 4) and its 9-month EMA signal line (from Step 5) on a graph under the price.

Interpretation of KST depends on:

- KST crossing the signal line (the 9-month Exponential Moving Averages of itself): crossing above is bullish, crossing below is bearish.
- KST direction (slope): rising is bullish, falling is bearish.
- 9-month EMA signal line direction (slope): rising is bullish, falling is bearish.
- Trendline breaks on KST and/or its 9-month EMA signal line.
- Divergence analysis of KST and its 9-month EMA signal line versus raw price itself.
- Pattern analysis of raw price, KST and its 9-month EMA signal line.
- Directional confirmation by raw price.
- Overbought/Oversold considerations.
- "Generally speaking, the monthly KST is far more reliable than its daily and weekly counterparts," Pring wrote in *Technical Analysis Explained,* McGraw-Hill, New York 1993, 521 pages, page 169.

Given the variety of interpretation possibilities and possible parameter sets, it is clear that our analysis using KST could become exceedingly complex.

The Equis International MetaStock® Indicator Builder formula for Pring's suggested long-term monthly KST may be written as follows:

```
Periods:= Input("Enter the number of periods", 1,9999,1);
((1*Mov(((C/Ref(C,-(9*periods)))*100),(6*periods),E)
+2*(Mov(((C/Ref(C,-(12*periods)))*100),(6*periods),E))
+3*(Mov(((C/Ref(C,-(18*periods)))*100),(6*periods),E))
+4*(Mov(((C/Ref(C,-(24*periods)))*100),(9*periods),E)))
/10)-100;Mov(
((1*Mov(((C/Ref(C,-(9*periods)))*100),(6*periods),E)
+2*(Mov(((C/Ref(C,-(12*+periods)))*100),(6*periods),E))
+3*(Mov(((C/Ref(C,-(18*periods)))*100),(6*periods),E))
+4*(Mov(((C/Ref(C,-(24*periods)))*100),(9*periods),E))
)/10)-100,(9*periods),E);Input("Plot a horizontal line at ",-100,100,0);
{KST (Know Sure Thing) formula for Equis International MetaStock®
Indicator Builder}
```

Indicator Strategy Example for KST (monthly, with Pring's suggested parameters)

Using mechanical rules only, and based on month-end data for the DJIA for 101 years from January 1900 to May 2001, we found that the following specific parameters suggested by Pring would have produced a modestly profitable result *for long-side trades only* (shorts would have lost) on a purely mechanical trend-following signal basis with no subjectivity, no sophisticated technical analysis, and no judgement:

Enter Long (Buy) at the current month-end closing price for the DJIA when the monthly basic KST crosses above its signal line (the 9-month Exponential Moving Averages of itself).

Close Long (Sell) at the current month-end closing price for the DJIA when the monthly basic KST crosses below its signal line (the 9-month Exponential Moving Averages of itself).

Enter Short (Sell Short) never.

Starting with $100 and reinvesting profits, total net profits for this KST Trend-Following Strategy would have been would have been $9,493.46, assuming a fully invested strategy, reinvestment of profits, no transactions costs and no taxes. This would have been 57.89 percent less than buy-and-hold. Short selling would have been unprofitable and was excluded from the strategy. This trend-following indicator would have given profitable buy signals 60.00% of the time. Trading would have been inactive at one trade every 925.30 calendar days.

The Equis International MetaStock® System Testing rules are written as follows:

Enter long:

```
((1*Mov(((C/Ref(C,-(3*opt1)))*100),(2*opt1),E)
+2*(Mov(((C/Ref(C,-(4*opt1)))*100),(2*opt1),E))
+3*(Mov(((C/Ref(C,-(6*opt1)))*100),(2*opt1),E))
+4*(Mov(((C/Ref(C,-(8*opt1)))*100),(3*opt1),E)))/10)-100 > Mov(
((1*Mov(((C/Ref(C,-(3*opt1)))*100),(2*opt1),E)
+2*(Mov(((C/Ref(C,-(4*opt1)))*100),(2*opt1),E))
+3*(Mov(((C/Ref(C,-(6*opt1)))*100),(2*opt1),E))
+4*(Mov(((C/Ref(C,-(8*opt1)))*100),(3*opt1),E)))/10)-100,(3*opt1),E)
```

Close long:

```
((1*Mov(((C/Ref(C,-(3*opt1)))*100),(2*opt1),E)
+2*(Mov(((C/Ref(C,-(4*opt1)))*100),(2*opt1),E))
+3*(Mov(((C/Ref(C,-(6*opt1)))*100),(2*opt1),E))
+4*(Mov(((C/Ref(C,-(8*opt1)))*100),(3*opt1),E)))/10)-100 < Mov(
((1*Mov(((C/Ref(C,-(3*opt1)))*100),(2*opt1),E)
+2*(Mov(((C/Ref(C,-(4*opt1)))*100),(2*opt1),E))
+3*(Mov(((C/Ref(C,-(6*opt1)))*100),(2*opt1),E))
+4*(Mov(((C/Ref(C,-(8*opt1)))*100),(3*opt1),E)))/10)-100,(3*
opt1),E)
```

Enter short:

```
((1*Mov(((C/Ref(C,-(3*opt1)))*100),(2*opt1),E)
+2*(Mov(((C/Ref(C,-(4*opt1)))*100),(2*opt1),E))
+3*(Mov(((C/Ref(C,-(6*opt1)))*100),(2*opt1),E))
+4*(Mov(((C/Ref(C,-(8*opt1)))*100),(3*opt1),E)))/10)-100 < Mov(
((1*Mov(((C/Ref(C,-(3*opt1)))*100),(2*opt1),E)
+2*(Mov(((C/Ref(C,-(4*opt1)))*100),(2*opt1),E))
+3*(Mov(((C/Ref(C,-(6*opt1)))*100),(2*opt1),E))
+4*(Mov(((C/Ref(C,-(8*opt1)))*100),(3*opt1),E)))/10)-100,(3*
opt1),E)
```

Close short:

```
((1*Mov(((C/Ref(C,-(3*opt1)))*100),(2*opt1),E)
+2*(Mov(((C/Ref(C,-(4*opt1)))*100),(2*opt1),E))
+3*(Mov(((C/Ref(C,-(6*opt1)))*100),(2*opt1),E))
+4*(Mov(((C/Ref(C,-(8*opt1)))*100),(3*opt1),E)))/10)-100 > Mov(
```

```
((1*Mov(((C/Ref(C,-(3*opt1)))*100),(2*opt1),E)
+2*(Mov(((C/Ref(C,-(4*opt1)))*100),(2*opt1),E))
+3*(Mov(((C/Ref(C,-(6*opt1)))*100),(2*opt1),E))
+4*(Mov(((C/Ref(C,-(8*opt1)))*100),(3*opt1),E)))/10)-100,(3*opt1),E)
OPT1 Current value: 3
```

Indicator Strategy Example for a *Faster* KST (monthly, with 33% faster parameters, across the board: "OPT1 Current value: 2")

Substituting "OPT1 Current value: 2" for "OPT1 Current value: 3" in the MetaStock® System Testing rules, and again starting with $100 and reinvesting profits, total net profits for this faster and more sensitive version of the otherwise same KST Trend-Following Strategy would have been $36,894.75, assuming a fully invested strategy, reinvestment of profits, no transactions costs and no taxes. This would have been 63.64 percent greater than buy-and-hold. Short selling would have been unprofitable and was excluded from the strategy. This trend-following indicator would have given profitable buy signals 58.93% of the time. Trading would have been a bit more active at one trade every 660.93 calendar days. The chart shows how Cumulative Equity, which started at 100, grew with milder drawdowns than the passive buy-and-hold strategy, represented by the price chart itself. Milder equity drawdowns are a desirable quality in an indictor.

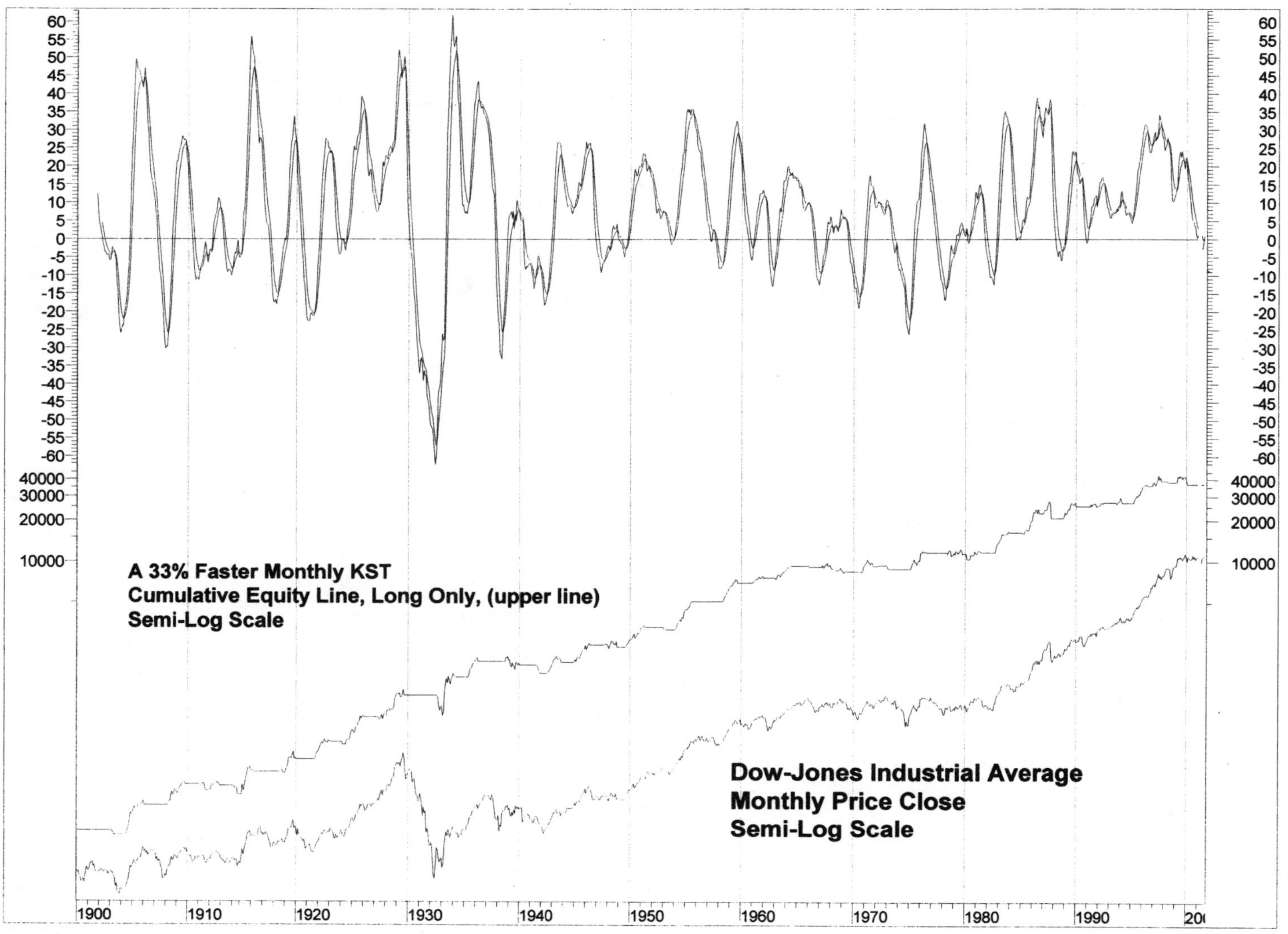
A 33% Faster Monthly KST
Cumulative Equity Line, Long Only, (upper line)
Semi-Log Scale
Dow-Jones Industrial Average
Monthly Price Close
Semi-Log Scale
60
55
50
45
40
35
30
25
20
15
10
5
0
-5
-10
-15
-20
-25
-30
-35
-40
-45
-50
-55
-60
40000
30000
20000
10000
1900
1910
1920
1930
1940
1950
1960
1970
1980
1990
20

KST (monthly, with 33% faster parameters: "OPT1 Current value: 2")

Total net profit	36894.75	Open position value	0	Net Profit / Buy&Hold %	63.64
Percent gain/loss	36894.75	Annual percent gain/loss	363.84	Annual Net % / B&H %	63.63
Initial investment	100	Interest earned 0			
Current position	Long	Date position entered	6/1/01		
Buy/Hold profit	22546.61	Days in test	37012	# of days per trade	660.93
Buy/Hold pct gain/loss	22546.61	Annual B/H pct gain/loss	222.35		
Total closed trades	56	Commissions paid	0		
Avg profit per trade	658.83	Avg Win/Avg Loss ratio	2.97		
Total long trades	56	Total short trades	0	Long Win Trade %	58.93
Winning long trades	33	Winning short trades	0	Short Win Trade %	#DIV/0!
Total winning trades	33	Total losing trades	23	Total Win Trade %	58.93
Amount of winning trades	48187.09	Amount of losing trades	−11292.35	Net Profit Margin %	62.03
Average win	1460.21	Average loss	−490.97	Average P. Margin %	49.67
Largest win	8923.37	Largest loss	−4999.73	% Net / (Win + Loss)	28.18
Average length of win	14.24	Average length of loss	6.43	(Win - Loss) / Loss %	121.46
Longest winning trade	22	Longest losing trade	19	(Win - Loss) / Loss %	15.79
Most consecutive wins	5	Most consecutive losses	4	(Win - Loss) / Loss %	25.00
Total bars out	708	Average length out	12.42		
Longest out period	37				
System close drawdown	−7.55	Profit/Loss index	76.57	% Net Profit / SODD	395866.42
System open drawdown	−9.32	Reward/Risk index	99.97	(Net P.-SODD)/Net P.	99.97
Max open trade drawdown	−4999.73	Buy/Hold index	63.64	% SODD / Net Profit	−0.03

In the Equis MetaStock® "System Report" (profit and loss summary statistics), the *Total net profit* is the sum of profits minus the sum of losses, including open positions marked to the market. In contrast, the *Amount of Winning Trades* is the sum of realized profits (the total of all gains on closed-out trades only, excluding any open positions). Similarly, the *Amount of Losing Trades* is the sum of realized losses (the total of all losses on closed-out trades only, excluding any open positions). *System close drawdown* is the largest decline in the cumulative equity line below the initial investment, based on closed-out positions only. *System open drawdown (SODD)* is the largest decline in the cumulative equity line below the initial investment when a position is open. *Max open trade drawdown* is the largest decline in the cumulative equity line below the trade entry price during the worst single trade. The *Profit/Loss Index* is a complex calculation that relates the Amount of Winning Trades to the Amount of Losing Trades on a scale of −100 (worst possible performance) to +100 (best possible performance), with zero representing profits equal to losses. *Reward/Risk Index* is the Total net profit minus System open drawdown. The resulting difference is then divided by the Total net profit. The *Buy/Hold Index* is the Total net profit minus the buy-and-hold strategy's net profit. The resulting difference is then divided by the buy-and-hold net profit. In this exercise, initial equity is assumed to be $100. Both long and short positions are taken unless otherwise noted. Trades are executed at the closing price on the signal date. Transaction costs, interest expenses, and margins are not included in the statistics.

KST (monthly, with Pring's suggested parameters)

Total net profit	9493.46	Open position value	N/A	Net Profit/Buy&Hold %	−57.89
Percent gain/loss	9493.46	Annual percent gain/loss	93.62	Annual Net %/B&H %	−57.90
Initial investment	100	Interest earned	0		
Current position	Out	Date position entered	9/30/99		
Buy/Hold profit	22546.61	Days in test	37012	# of days per trade	925.30
Buy/Hold pct gain/loss	22546.61	Annual B/H pct gain/loss	222.35		
Total closed trades	40	Commissions paid	0		
Avg profit per trade	237.34	Avg Win/Avg Loss ratio	4		
Total long trades	40	Total short trades	0	Long Win Trade %	60.00
Winning long trades	24	Winning short trades	0	Short Win Trade %	#DIV/0!
Total winning trades	24	Total losing trades	16	Total Win Trade %	60.00
Amount of winning trades	11390.59	Amount of losing trades	−1897.14	Net Profit Margin %	71.45
Average win	474.61	Average loss	−118.57	Average P. Margin %	60.02
Largest win	4404.5	Largest loss	−311.99	% Net/(Win + Loss)	86.77
Average length of win	21.08	Average length of loss	6.69	(Win − Loss)/Loss %	215.10
Longest winning trade	32	Longest losing trade	20	(Win − Loss)/Loss %	60.00
Most consecutive wins	4	Most consecutive losses	2	(Win − Loss)/Loss %	100.00
Total bars out	681	Average length out	16.61		
Longest out period	55				
System close drawdown	0	Profit/Loss index	83.34	% Net Profit/SODD	#DIV/0!
System open drawdown	0	Reward/Risk index	100	(Net P.-SODD)/Net P.	100.00
Max open trade drawdown	−311.99	Buy/Hold index	−57.89	% SODD/Net Profit	0.00

In the Equis MetaStock® "System Report" (profit and loss summary statistics), the *Total net profit* is the sum of profits minus the sum of losses, including open positions marked to the market. In contrast, the *Amount of Winning Trades* is the sum of realized profits (the total of all gains on closed-out trades only, excluding any open positions). Similarly, the *Amount of Losing Trades* is the sum of realized losses (the total of all losses on closed-out trades only, excluding any open positions). *System close drawdown* is the largest decline in the cumulative equity line below the initial investment, based on closed-out positions only. *System open drawdown (SODD)* is the largest decline in the cumulative equity line below the initial investment when a position is open. *Max open trade drawdown* is the largest decline in the cumulative equity line below the trade entry price during the worst single trade. The *Profit/Loss Index* is a complex calculation that relates the Amount of Winning Trades to the Amount of Losing Trades on a scale of −100 (worst possible performance) to +100 (best possible performance), with zero representing profits equal to losses. *Reward/Risk Index* is the Total net profit minus System open drawdown. The resulting difference is then divided by the Total net profit. The *Buy/Hold Index* is the Total net profit minus the buy-and-hold strategy's net profit. The resulting difference is then divided by the buy-and-hold net profit. In this exercise, initial equity is assumed to be $100. Both long and short positions are taken unless otherwise noted. Trades are executed at the closing price on the signal date. Transaction costs, interest expenses, and margins are not included in the statistics.

Large Block Ratio

Large blocks are defined as transactions of more than 10,000 shares on the New York Stock Exchange. The Large Block Ratio (also known as the Big Block Index) is calculated by dividing the volume of large block trades by the total volume on the New York Stock Exchange. The ratio may be smoothed by moving averages of various lengths to reduce noise and identify signals.

There are two very different approaches to interpreting this indicator. According to Contrary Opinion adherents, the Large Block Ratio can be viewed as an overbought/oversold sentiment indicator that reflects feelings of either enthusiasm or disgust of the usually wrong institutional investors. Since institutional portfolios do not keep up with unmanaged market indexes, contrarians look to "fade" them—that is, to sell when institutions are buying and buy when institutions are selling. The problem with that reasoning is that institutions are ***not** usually wrong,* they are merely *relatively* poor performers. Even though institutional performance (in the aggregate) has been below average, institutions do earn positive returns, so doing the opposite of the institutions will earn negative returns. Nevertheless, to contrarians a high level on this ratio implies an unsustainable level of optimism, while a low level implies institutional apathy or discouragement. Contrarians believe that indicator extremes and excesses precede reversals in the financial markets.

Our tests of the data contradict this contrary view: the relationship between large block activity and subsequent market performance is a positive one, and high Big Block ratios are bullish while low ratios are not.

Using data and software provided by Equis International, www.equis.com, we tested daily data compressed into weekly format from 1983 to 2001. We found that when the Large Block Ratio crossed above its own trailing 104-week exponential moving average, it gave buy signals that would have been profitable 70% of the time with a net profit of 511% *for long trades only.* This strategy exited longs when the ratio crossed below this trailing 104-week exponential moving average. But crossing below the 104-week exponential moving average would have given short sale signals that would have been profitable only 40% of the time with a net loss of 39%. Shorter moving average lengths would have produced similar but less profitable results.

Seasoned traders know that volume is a weapon of the bull: it takes volume to push prices higher, but prices can fall of their own weight in the absence of the buying interest reflected in the volume data. Likewise, high Large Block activity is bullish and low Large Block activity is not so bullish. Reaching a similar conclusion, Arthur A. Merrill, CMT, found his version of Large Block Transactions was profitable and highly significant statistically.

Large Block Transactions

Arthur A. Merrill, CMT, defines large blocks as transactions of more than 50,000 shares. Using daily data published in *Barron's* at the end of each week, Merrill quantifies the behavior of the large operators in 8 steps.

1. Using data for a full week (usually five but sometimes only four trading days), separately sum the daily numbers of large blocks traded on upticks, on downticks, and on unchanged ticks. Do this for three different weekly totals.
2. Smooth these three different weekly totals with 13-weeks exponential moving averages.
3. Subtract the downtick average from the uptick average (using the results from Step 2).
4. Divide that difference (from Step 3) by the unchanged average (from Step 2).
5. Compute a 52-weeks moving average of that ratio.
6. Calculate deviations of the current ratio (from Step 4) from its 52-weeks moving average (from Step 5).
7. Divide these deviations by their trailing standard deviation over the preceding 52 weeks.
8. Interpret resulting ratios as follows:
   - a ratio above 0.67 is bullish
   - a ratio below 0.67 is bearish

Using a chi-squared test of significance, Merrill found that these ratios correctly predicted the direction of the general market 66% of the time over the next 13 weeks, 81% of the time over the next 26 weeks, and 76% of the time over the next 52 weeks. All of these results are highly significant statistically. However, market behavior over the next one and five weeks was insignificant.

Least Squares Method

The Least Squares Method is a statistical technique for fitting a straight line to an independent variable, or observed data, such that the sum of the squares of the deviations of the observed data points from the straight line are minimized. (See Linear Regression.)

$$L = \Sigma(y\text{-}e)^2$$

where

L = the least squares line (at any given position).

Σ = Summation symbol.

y = independent variable, observed data point, at any given position.

e = the expected value of the independent, observed data point, according to the fitted straight line (at any given position).

^{2} = raised to the power of two, that is, squared, or multiplied by itself.

Linear Regression Line

Linear regression is a mathematical method for quantifying a straight-line relationship between one independent and one dependent variable, or any two variables. It is commonly used with price and time data to identify trends.

Mathematically the linear regression formula is represented as:

$$y = a + bx$$

where

y = the closing price.

x = the position of the current time period in the database.

a = $1/n\ (\Sigma y - b\Sigma x)$.

b = $(n\Sigma xy - \Sigma x\Sigma y)/n\Sigma x^2 - (\Sigma x)^2$

n = number of time periods in the summations.

Σ = Summation symbol, sum over n periods.

Linear Regression uses the *least squares* method to fit a trendline to the data. It arrives at the best fit by minimizing the distance between the given data points and the fitted Linear Regression trendline.

MetaStock® software (www.equis.com) predefines the formula for the Linear Regression trendline on its indicator menu. The software plots any n-day Linear Regression Line at the end date of the calculation. Thus, the current n-day Linear Regression Line is plotted at today's date. For all practical purposes, this Linear Regression Line changes every day, trailing and tracking the current price, much like a trailing moving average. Therefore, this indicator may be interpreted much like the better known moving average.

Also, the current relationship between price and the current n-day Linear Regression Line may be viewed as an oscillator. As shown in the chart, we may divide the current price close by the current trailing 5-day Linear Regression Line of the most recent 5-day closing prices. In MetaStock® formula language, that could be expressed as CLOSE/LinearReg(CLOSE,5).

Indicator Strategy Example for Linear Regression Line

Linear Regression Line is robust, with all period lengths between 2 and 700 days profitable for long trades only (no short selling). Based on an 18-year file of daily data for the entire history of the S&P 500 Composite Stock Price Index futures *CSI Perpetual Contract* (www.csidata.com) from 4/21/82 to 12/22/00, we found that the following parameters would have produced a positive result on a purely mechanical signal basis with no subjectivity, no sophisticated technical analysis, and no judgement:

Enter Long (Buy) at the current daily price close of the S&P 500 Composite Stock Price Index futures *CSI Perpetual Contract* when the close is greater than the 5-day Linear Regression Line.

Close Long (Sell) at the current daily price close of the S&P 500 Composite Stock Price Index futures *CSI Perpetual Contract* when the close is less than the 5-day Linear Regression Line.

Enter Short (Sell Short) never.

Starting with $100 and reinvesting profits, total net profits for this Linear Regression Slope trend-following strategy would have been $759.88, assuming a fully invested strategy, reinvestment of profits, no transactions costs and no taxes. This would have been 26.04 percent less than buy-and-hold. No short selling would have been profitable, and no short selling was included in the strategy. This long-only Linear Regression Slope variation would have given profitable buy signals 49.38% of the time. Trading would have been hyperactive at one trade every 6.55 calendar days.

The Equis International MetaStock® System Testing rules are written as follows:

Enter long: CLOSE>LinearReg(CLOSE,opt1)

Close long: CLOSE<LinearReg(CLOSE,opt1)

OPT1 Current value: 5

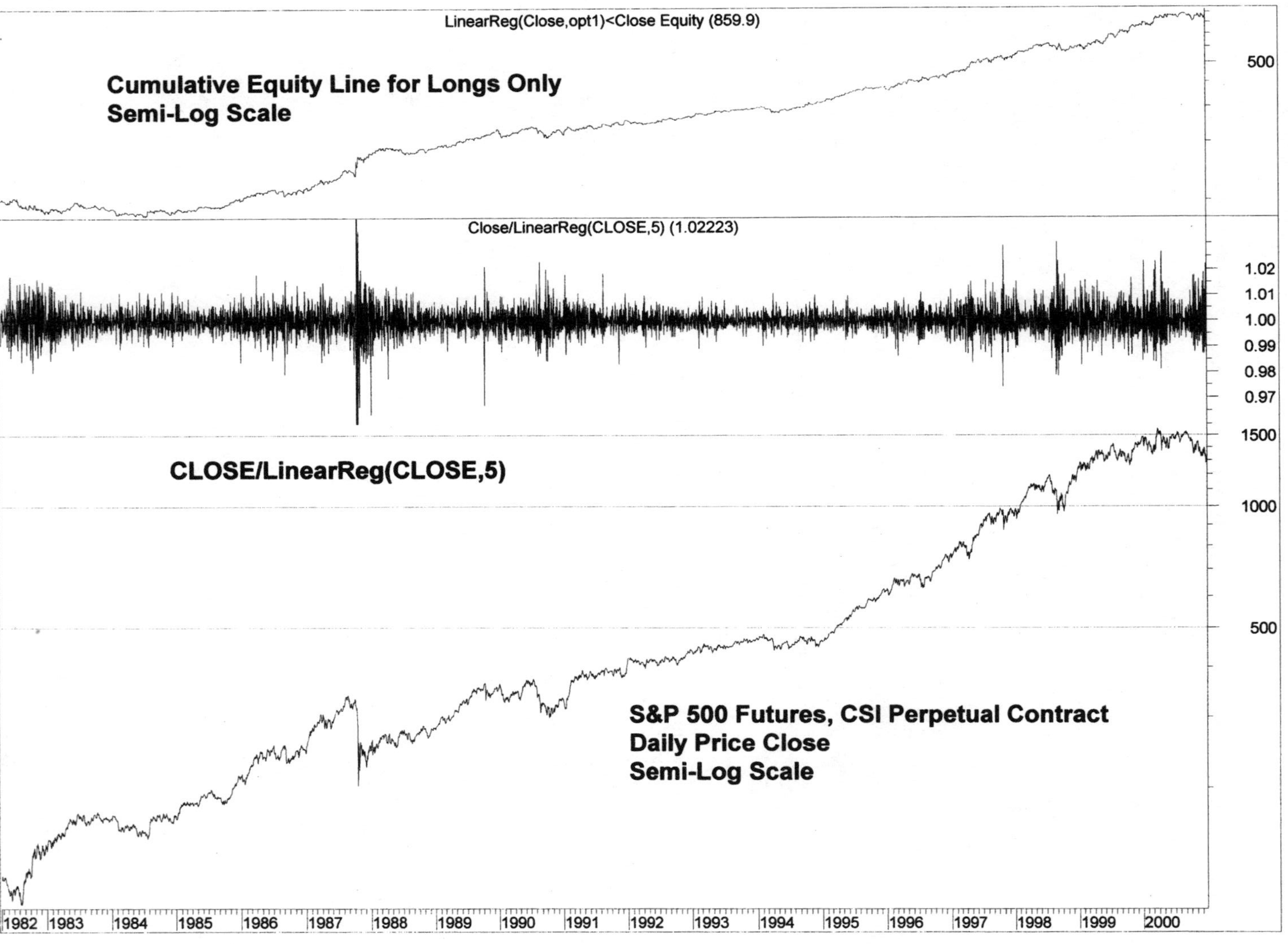

LinearReg(Close,opt1)<Close Equity (859.9)
Cumulative Equity Line for Longs Only
Semi-Log Scale
500
Close/LinearReg(CLOSE,5) (1.02223)
1.02
1.01
1.00
0.99
0.98
0.97
CLOSE/LinearReg(CLOSE,5)
1500
1000
500
S&P 500 Futures, CSI Perpetual Contract
Daily Price Close
Semi-Log Scale
1982
1983
1984
1985
1986
1987
1988
1989
1990
1991
1992
1993
1994
1995
1996
1997
1998
1999
2000

Linear Regression Line, 5-days

Total net profit	759.88	Open position value	25.08	Net Profit / Buy&Hold %	-26.04
Percent gain/loss	759.88	Annual percent gain/loss	40.66	Annual Net % / B&H %	-26.05
Initial investment	100	Interest earned	0		
Current position	Long	Date position entered	12/21/00		
Buy/Hold profit	1027.4	Days in test	6821	# of days per trade	6.55
Buy/Hold pct gain/loss	1027.4	Annual B/H pct gain/loss	54.98		
Total closed trades	1041	Commissions paid	0		
Avg profit per trade	0.71	Avg Win/Avg Loss ratio	1.55		
Total long trades	1041	Total short trades	0	Long Win Trade %	49.38
Winning long trades	514	Winning short trades	0	Short Win Trade %	#DIV/0!
Total winning trades	514	Total losing trades	527	Total Win Trade %	49.38
Amount of winning trades	2162.49	Amount of losing trades	-1427.68	Net Profit Margin %	20.47
Average win	4.21	Average loss	-2.71	Average P. Margin %	21.68
Largest win	38.38	Largest loss	-29.23	% Net / (Win + Loss)	13.53
Average length of win	3.87	Average length of loss	2.59	(Win - Loss) / Loss %	49.42
Longest winning trade	8	Longest losing trade	6	(Win - Loss) / Loss %	33.33
Most consecutive wins	7	Most consecutive losses	8	(Win - Loss) / Loss %	-12.50
Total bars out	3448	Average length out	3.31		
Longest out period	10				
System close drawdown	-16.92	Profit/Loss index	34.74	%Net Profit / SODD	4491.02
System open drawdown	-16.92	Reward/Risk index	97.82	(Net P.-SODD)/Net P.	97.77
Max open trade drawdown	-29.23	Buy/Hold index	-23.6	% SODD / Net Profit	-2.23

In the Equis MetaStock® "System Report" (profit and loss summary statistics), the *Total net profit* is the sum of profits minus the sum of losses, including open positions marked to the market. In contrast, the *Amount of Winning Trades* is the sum of realized profits (the total of all gains on closed-out trades only, excluding any open positions). Similarly, the *Amount of Losing Trades* is the sum of realized losses (the total of all losses on closed-out trades only, excluding any open positions). *System close drawdown* is the largest decline in the cumulative equity line below the initial investment, based on closed-out positions only. *System open drawdown (SODD)* is the largest decline in the cumulative equity line below the initial investment when a position is open. *Max open trade drawdown* is the largest decline in the cumulative equity line below the trade entry price during the worst single trade. The *Profit/Loss Index* is a complex calculation that relates the Amount of Winning Trades to the Amount of Losing Trades on a scale of −100 (worst possible performance) to +100 (best possible performance), with zero representing profits equal to losses. *Reward/Risk Index* is the Total net profit minus System open drawdown. The resulting difference is then divided by the Total net profit. The *Buy/Hold Index* is the Total net profit minus the buy-and-hold strategy's net profit. The resulting difference is then divided by the buy-and-hold net profit. In this exercise, initial equity is assumed to be $100. Both long and short positions are taken unless otherwise noted. Trades are executed at the closing price on the signal date. Transaction costs, interest expenses, and margins are not included in the statistics.

Linear Regression Slope

Linear Regression is a mathematical method for expressing a straight-line relationship between any two variables. It is commonly used with price and time data to identify trends. The Linear Regression Slope shows how much prices have changed per unit of time.

One possible trend-following decision rule is to use the Linear Regression Slope of the linear regression line for trend following signals. A positive slope (and, therefore, a rising linear regression line) is bullish, so buy when slope is above zero. A negative slope (and, therefore, a falling linear regression line) is bearish, so sell when slope is above zero.

Indicator Strategy Example for Linear Regression Slope

Linear Regression Slope is robust, with all period lengths between 2 and 300 days profitable for long trades only (no short selling). Based on a 18-year file of daily data for the entire history of the S&P 500 Composite Stock Price Index futures *CSI Perpetual Contract* from 4/21/82 to 12/22/00 collected from www.csidata.com, we found that the following parameters would have produced a positive result on a purely mechanical signal basis with no subjectivity, no sophisticated technical analysis, and no judgement:

Enter Long (Buy) at the current daily price close of the S&P 500 Composite Stock Price Index futures *CSI Perpetual Contract* when the 244-day Linear Regression Slope is greater than zero.

Close Long (Sell) at the current daily price close of the S&P 500 Composite Stock Price Index futures *CSI Perpetual Contract* when the 244-day Linear Regression Slope is less than zero.

Enter Short (Sell Short) never.

Starting with $100 and reinvesting profits, total net profits for this Linear Regression Slope trend-following strategy would have been $521.98, assuming a fully invested strategy, reinvestment of profits, no transactions costs and no taxes. This would have been 49.19 percent less than buy-and-hold. No short selling would have been profitable, and no short selling was included in the strategy. This long-only Linear Regression Slope variation would have given profitable buy signals 100% of the time, though the sample size of only five trades would not have been significant. Trading would have been inactive at one trade every 1364.20 calendar days.

The Equis International MetaStock® System Testing rules are written as follows:

Enter long: LinRegSlope(C,opt1)>0

Close long: LinRegSlope(C,opt1)<0

OPT1 Current value: 244

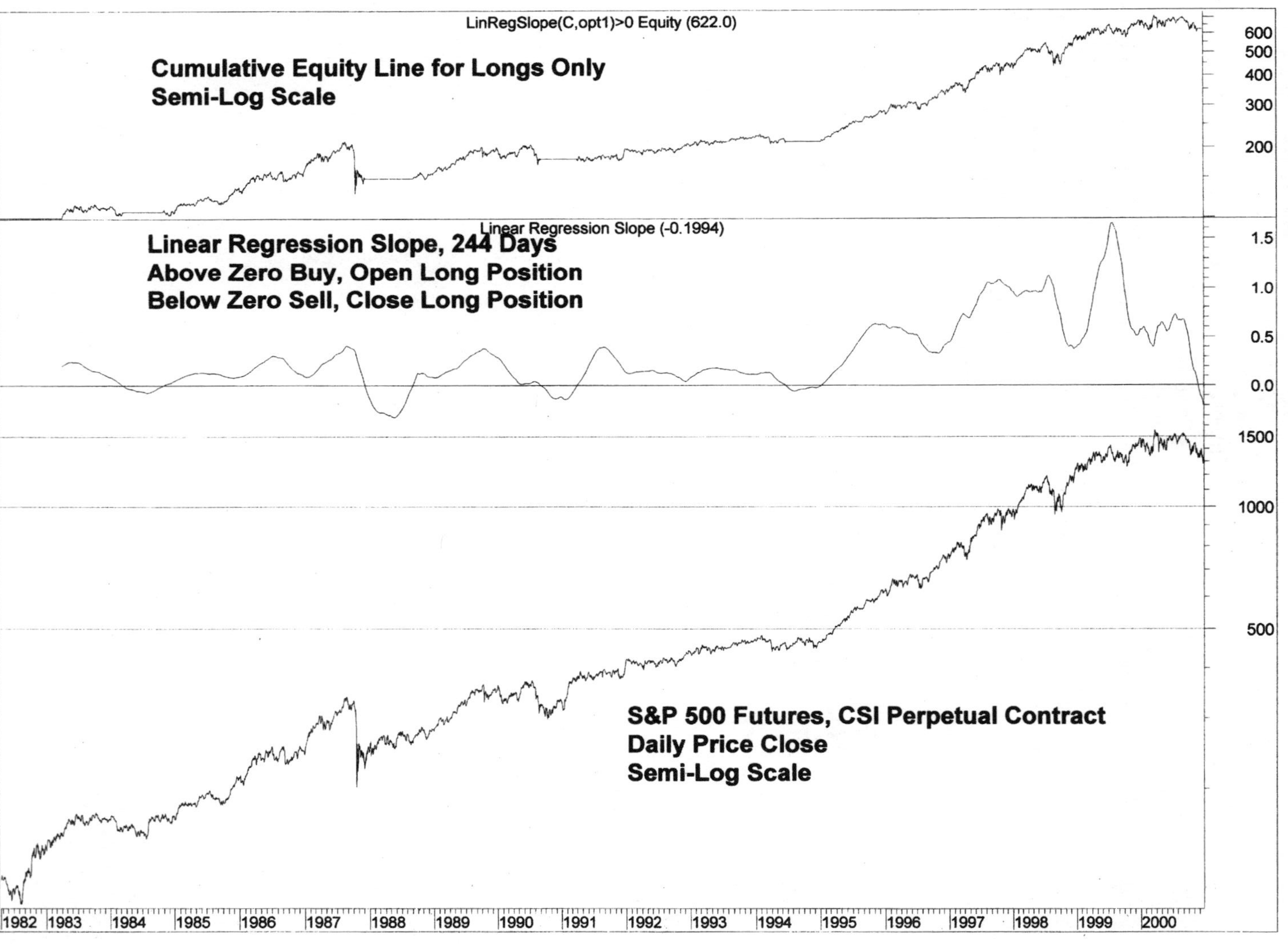
LinRegSlope(C,opt1)>0 Equity (622.0)
Cumulative Equity Line for Longs Only
Semi-Log Scale
600
500
400
300
200
Linear Regression Slope (-0.1994)
Linear Regression Slope, 244 Days
Above Zero Buy, Open Long Position
Below Zero Sell, Close Long Position
1.5
1.0
0.5
0.0
1500
1000
500
S&P 500 Futures, CSI Perpetual Contract
Daily Price Close
Semi-Log Scale
1982
1983
1984
1985
1986
1987
1988
1989
1990
1991
1992
1993
1994
1995
1996
1997
1998
1999
2000

Linear Regression Slope, 244 days

Total net profit	521.98	Open position value	N/A	Net Profit / Buy&Hold %	-49.19
Percent gain/loss	521.98	Annual percent gain/loss	27.93	Annual Net % / B&H %	-49.20
Initial investment	100	Interest earned	0		
Current position	Out	Date position entered	11/27/00		
Buy/Hold profit	1027	4 Days in test	6821	# of days per trade	1364.20
Buy/Hold pct gain/loss	1027	4 Annual B/H pct gain/loss	54.98		
Total closed trades	5	Commissions paid	0		
Avg profit per trade	104.4	Avg Win/Avg Loss ratio	N/A		
Total long trades	5	Total short trades	0	Long Win Trade %	100.00
Winning long trades	5	Winning short trades	0	Short Win Trade %	#DIV/0!
Total winning trades	5	Total losing trades	0	Total Win Trade %	100.00
Amount of winning trades	521.98	Amount of losing trades	0	Net Profit Margin %	100.00
Average win	104.4	Average loss	N/A	Average P. Margin %	#VALUE!
Largest win	409.59	Largest loss	0	% Net / (Win + Loss)	100.00
Average length of win	769	Average length of loss	N/A	(Win - Loss) / Loss %	#VALUE!
Longest winning trade	1486	Longest losing trade	0	(Win - Loss) / Loss %	#DIV/0!
Most consecutive wins	5	Most consecutive losses	0	(Win - Loss) / Loss %	#DIV/0!
Total bars out	888	Average length out	148		
Longest out period	244				
System close drawdown	0	Profit/Loss index	100	% Net Profit / SODD	#DIV/0!
System open drawdown	0	Reward/Risk index	100	(Net P.-SODD)/Net P.	100.00
Max open trade drawdown	-5.08	Buy/Hold index	-49.19	% SODD / Net Profit	0.00

In the Equis MetaStock® "System Report" (profit and loss summary statistics), the *Total net profit* is the sum of profits minus the sum of losses, including open positions marked to the market. In contrast, the *Amount of Winning Trades* is the sum of realized profits (the total of all gains on closed-out trades only, excluding any open positions). Similarly, the *Amount of Losing Trades* is the sum of realized losses (the total of all losses on closed-out trades only, excluding any open positions). *System close drawdown* is the largest decline in the cumulative equity line below the initial investment, based on closed-out positions only. *System open drawdown (SODD)* is the largest decline in the cumulative equity line below the initial investment when a position is open. *Max open trade drawdown* is the largest decline in the cumulative equity line below the trade entry price during the worst single trade. The *Profit/Loss Index* is a complex calculation that relates the Amount of Winning Trades to the Amount of Losing Trades on a scale of −100 (worst possible performance) to +100 (best possible performance), with zero representing profits equal to losses. *Reward/Risk Index* is the Total net profit minus System open drawdown. The resulting difference is then divided by the Total net profit. The *Buy/Hold Index* is the Total net profit minus the buy-and-hold strategy's net profit. The resulting difference is then divided by the buy-and-hold net profit. In this exercise, initial equity is assumed to be $100. Both long and short positions are taken unless otherwise noted. Trades are executed at the closing price on the signal date. Transaction costs, interest expenses, and margins are not included in the statistics.

Liquidity

In technical analysis, *liquidity* refers to the amount of investable cash and cash equivalents held on the sidelines in reserve for future commitment to the market. *(See Mutual Fund Cash.)* Large liquidity represents future buying power and is potentially bullish. On the other hand, low liquidity suggests that buying power is used up and that relatively little cash is in reserve to support prices at current levels, and that is potentially bearish. Far-sighted technical analysts (such as Ralph Acampora, CMT, who quite correctly forecasted Dow 7,000 then 10,000, years in advance) take into account distant future liquidity and money flows based on long-term demographic projections.

Trading liquidity refers to the amount of trading activity, the ease and rapidity of executions, the narrowness of spreads, the size of real bids and offers (*depth* of the market), and the absence of slippage on market orders. Active traders who act on short-term timing signals should focus only on active and deep markets, otherwise slippage on executions could erode theoretical paper profits.

Even the most liquid markets suffer from occasional order imbalances in so called "fast markets." Trading at times of big news events or other general mass emotional excess can be surprisingly costly. In fast markets, going with the majority, buying when everyone else wants to buy, or selling when everyone else wants to sell, often results in shockingly bad fills (executions). It also offers a good probability of buying at the top and selling at the bottom, which is the formula for instant losses. Conversely, doing just the opposite, going *against* the majority at times of general emotional excessive reactions, if timed well, can result in unusually good fills. Good or bad executions make a very big difference real trading.

Inactive markets with low volume and few participants generally have the widest bid-ask spreads and largest slippage on market orders. Executions on market orders for inactive, illiquid instruments in fast markets can be extremely costly, with very large slippage. Patience and limit orders may limit the damage.

Livermore Swing System, Livermore Penetration Filter

The Livermore Swing System was developed by a famous speculator, Jesse Livermore, in the 1920's. This system uses two filters: a *swing filter* of x%, and a *penetration filter* of one-half the size of the swing filter. An uptrend is defined on the *swing chart* by higher highs and higher lows. A downtrend is defined on the swing chart by lower lows and lower highs.

For example, assume a swing filter 4% and a penetration filter of 2%. After a downtrend, which is a series of lower lows and lower highs, close out short positions when price rises by the amount of the swing filter (4%) *and* exceeds the most recent previous swing high by the amount of the penetration filter (2%). Next, establish new long positions when the next most recent previous swing high is exceeded by the amount of the penetration filter (2%). Thus, the two most recent swing highs each must be exceeded by 2% in order to completely reverse from short to long.

Conversely, after an uptrend, which is a series of higher highs and higher lows, close out long positions when price falls by the amount of the swing filter (4%) *and* breaks the most recent previous swing low by the amount of the penetration filter (2%). Next, establish new short positions when the next most recent previous swing low is broken by the amount of the penetration filter (2%). Thus, the two most recent swing lows each must be broken by 2% in order to completely reverse from long to short.

Lowry's Reports

In 1938, the late Lyman M. Lowry originated the idea of compiling Upside and Downside Volume statistics in an effort to objectively quantify the basic forces of demand and supply for stocks and the underlying condition of the stock market in general. The company he founded, Lowry's Reports, publishes proprietary indices of *Buying Power and Selling Pressure,* NYSE Operating-Companies-Only Statistics, Advance-Decline, Points Gained and Lost, and Upside and Downside Volume. These indices use raw statistics for all domestic, ordinary New York Stock Exchange listed common stock issues, while specifically excluding all preferred stocks, ADRS, closed end mutual funds, REITS and other non-ordinary issues. In addition, Lowry offers proprietary *Power Ratings* to analyze sectors, industry groups, and individual stocks. Preprocessed technical indicators, both current and historical data, but not the actual proprietary algorithms, may be purchased from Lowry's Reports, Inc., 631 U.S. Highway 1, #305, North Palm Beach, FL 33408, Phone (561) 842-3514, www.lowryreports.com.

The chart (courtesy of Ned Davis Research), shows that Lowry's Short-Term Buying Power oscillator fully oversold levels below 60 appear to have effectively identified major market bottoms. Also, this oscillator has given some useful divergence signals, such as a higher low at the 1982 market bottom and a lower high at the 1987 market top. In contrast, reflecting the increasing levels of price and volume, the longer-term Buying Power and Selling Pressure lines have shown a distinct upward bias, but that still did not prevent them from giving misleading negative divergences at the bottoms of 1987, 1990, 1992, 1994, 1996, and 1997. Obviously, these lines require a different and more complex interpretation, compared to most other indicators.

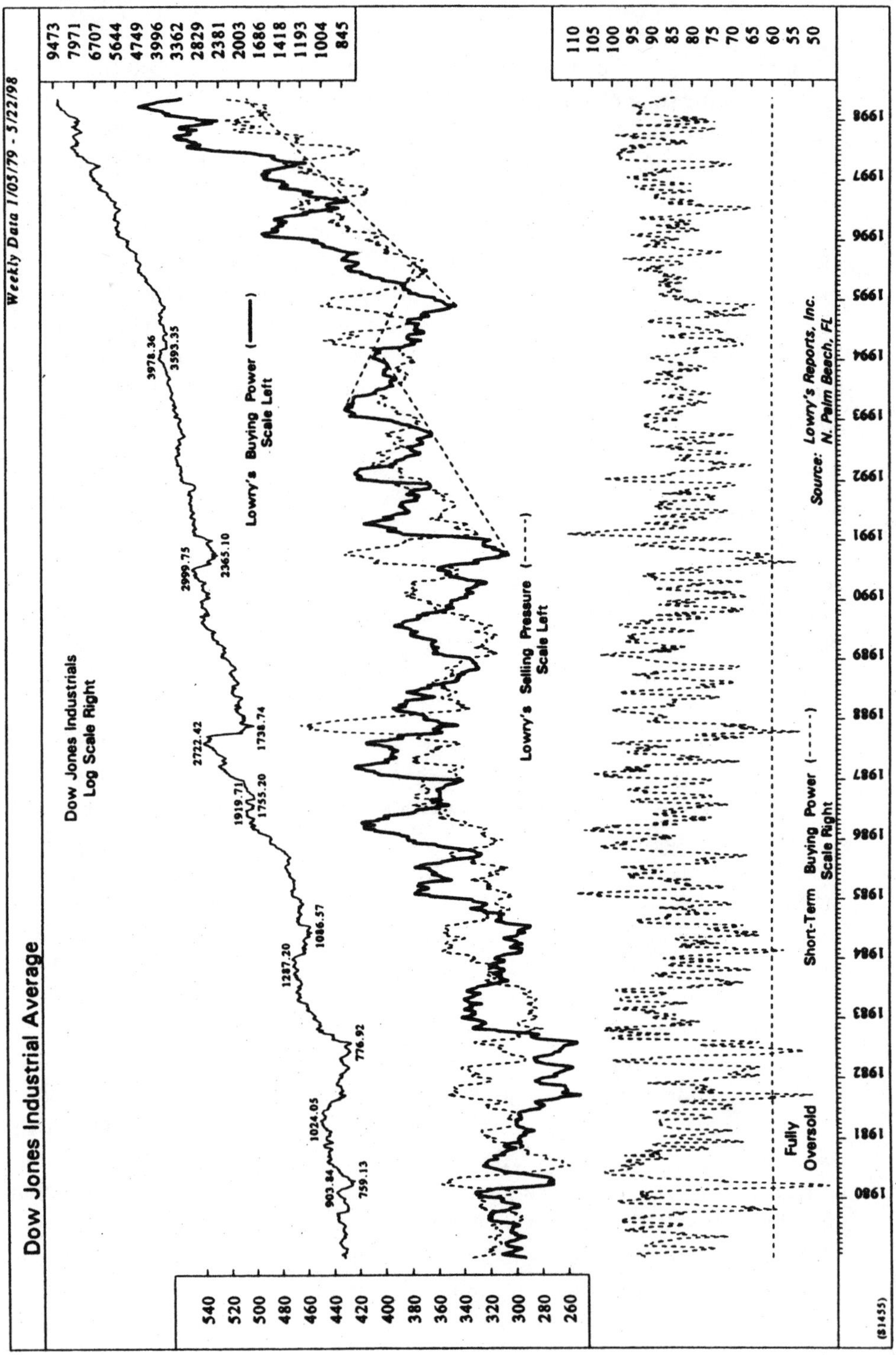

Dow Jones Industrial Average

Weekly Data 1/05/79 - 5/22/98

Dow Jones Industrials
Log Scale Right

903.84
759.13
1024.05
776.92
1287.20
1086.57
1919.71
1755.20
2722.42
1738.74
2999.75
2365.10
3978.36
3593.35

Lowry's Buying Power (——)
Scale Left

Lowry's Selling Pressure (- - - -)
Scale Left

Fully
Oversold

Short-Term Buying Power (- - - -)
Scale Right

Source: Lowry's Reports, Inc.
N. Palm Beach, FL

540
520
500
480
460
440
420
400
380
360
340
320
300
280
260

9473
7971
6707
5644
4749
3996
3362
2829
2381
2003
1686
1418
1193
1004
845

110
105
100
95
90
85
80
75
70
65
60
55
50

1980
1981
1982
1983
1984
1985
1986
1987
1988
1989
1990
1991
1992
1993
1994
1995
1996
1997
1998

(S1455)

Chart by permission of Ned Davis Research

According to Bishop and Rollins, general market activity can be reduced to four basic totals:

- Total dollars gained each day;
- Total volume of transactions for stocks moving up;
- Total dollars lost each day;
- Total volume of transactions for stocks moving down.

To smooth out short-term fluctuations, Lowry's aggregates these totals over approximately 50 and 15 trading days to produce long and short term indices of supply and demand. Lowry's employs specific rules for interpretation, involving overbought and oversold conditions, signs showing when prevailing pressures are dissipating, and Safety Controls to alert users when to cut losses on existing positions. In a study using 25 years of past daily data applying all of Lowry's interpretation rules, Bishop and Rollins concluded that the Lowry's Reports signals "led to returns significantly in excess of those achieved by naïve buy-and-hold programs" from 1950 to 1975. Also, ". . . this study indicated that extraordinary gains can be achieved by sophisticated technical analysis . . . " For complete details, see Bishop, E. L., & Rollins, J. R. (1975: Dec). *Validity of Technical Stock Market Analysis: A Study of Lowry's Reports, Inc.* An Advanced Study Project, The Wharton School.

Indicator Strategy Example of Lowry's Buying Power minus Selling Pressure

The full array of Lowry's proprietary indicators and complex decision rules for interpretation are beyond the scope of this book. Even a simple computer scan of Lowry's data indicates information of value. Historical data provided by UST Securities shows that for Buying Power minus Selling Pressure, the most basic form of trend following would have been effective, on both the long side and the short side. We emphasize that Lowry's never intended for its indicators to be used this way. Nevertheless, based on the daily prices for the Dow-Jones Industrial Average for 61 years from 1940 to 2001, we found that the following parameters would have produced a positive result on a purely mechanical trend-following signal basis with no subjectivity, no sophisticated technical analysis, and no judgement:

Enter Long (Buy) at the current daily price close of the DJIA when the current net of Lowry's Buying Power minus Selling Pressure rises to a level equal to or above yesterday's net reading.

Close Long (Sell) at the current daily price close of the DJIA when the current net of Lowry's Buying Power minus Selling Pressure falls below yesterday's net reading.

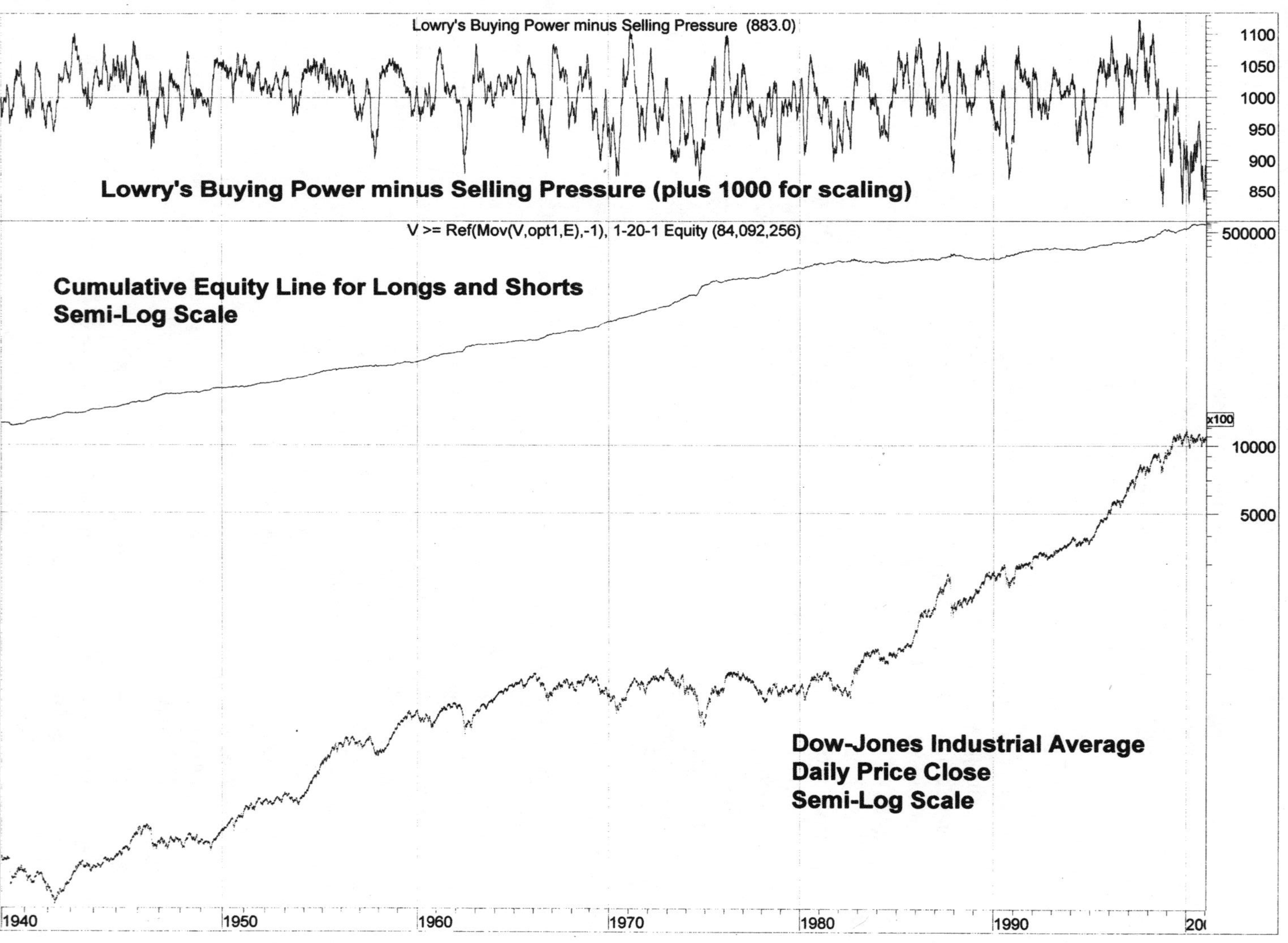

Lowry's Buying Power minus Selling Pressure (883.0)
1100
1050
1000
950
900
850
Lowry's Buying Power minus Selling Pressure (plus 1000 for scaling)
V >= Ref(Mov(V,opt1,E),-1), 1-20-1 Equity (84,092,256)
500000
Cumulative Equity Line for Longs and Shorts
Semi-Log Scale
x100
10000
5000
Dow-Jones Industrial Average
Daily Price Close
Semi-Log Scale
1940
1950
1960
1970
1980
1990
20

Lowry's Buying Power minus Selling Pressure

Total net profit	84092160	Open position value	318998.44	Net Profit/Buy&Hold %	1216146.87
Percent gain/loss	84092160	Annual percent gain/loss	1377137.4	Annual Net %/B&H %	1216130.15
Initial investment	100	Interest earned	0		
Current position	Short	Date position entered	1/5/01		
Buy/Hold profit	6914.07	Days in test	22288	# of days per trade	3.32
Buy/Hold pct gain/loss	6914.07	Annual B/H pct gain/loss	113.23		
Total closed trades	6723	Commissions paid	0		
Avg profit per trade	12460.68	Avg Win/Avg Loss ratio	1.55		
Total long trades	3362	Total short trades	3361	Long Win Trade %	49.88
Winning long trades	1677	Winning short trades	1513	Short Win Trade %	45.02
Total winning trades	3190	Total losing trades	3533	Total Win Trade %	47.45
Amount of winning trades	294089536	Amount of losing trades	−210316224	Net Profit Margin %	16.61
Average win	92191.08	Average loss	−59529.08	Average P. Margin %	21.53
Largest win	4350448	Largest loss	−2956960	% Net/(Win + Loss)	19.07
Average length of win	4.27	Average length of loss	2.53	(Win − Loss)/Loss %	68.77
Longest winning trade	19	Longest losing trade	10	(Win − Loss)/Loss %	90.00
Most consecutive wins	9	Most consecutive losses	12	(Win − Loss)/Loss %	−25.00
Total bars out	2	Average length out	2		
Longest out period	2				
System close drawdown	−19.01	Profit/Loss index	28.56	% Net Profit/SODD	442357496.05
System open drawdown	−19.01	Reward/Risk index	100	(Net P.-SODD)/Net P.	100.00
Max open trade drawdown	−2956960	Buy/Hold index	1220761.26	% SODD/Net Profit	0.00

In the Equis MetaStock® "System Report" (profit and loss summary statistics), the *Total net profit* is the sum of profits minus the sum of losses, including open positions marked to the market. In contrast, the *Amount of Winning Trades* is the sum of realized profits (the total of all gains on closed-out trades only, excluding any open positions). Similarly, the *Amount of Losing Trades* is the sum of realized losses (the total of all losses on closed-out trades only, excluding any open positions). *System close drawdown* is the largest decline in the cumulative equity line below the initial investment, based on closed-out positions only. *System open drawdown (SODD)* is the largest decline in the cumulative equity line below the initial investment when a position is open. *Max open trade drawdown* is the largest decline in the cumulative equity line below the trade entry price during the worst single trade. The *Profit/Loss Index* is a complex calculation that relates the Amount of Winning Trades to the Amount of Losing Trades on a scale of −100 (worst possible performance) to +100 (best possible performance), with zero representing profits equal to losses. *Reward/Risk Index* is the Total net profit minus System open drawdown. The resulting difference is then divided by the Total net profit. The *Buy/Hold Index* is the Total net profit minus the buy-and-hold strategy's net profit. The resulting difference is then divided by the buy-and-hold net profit. In this exercise, initial equity is assumed to be $100. Both long and short positions are taken unless otherwise noted. Trades are executed at the closing price on the signal date. Transaction costs, interest expenses, and margins are not included in the statistics.

Enter Short (Sell Short) at the current daily price close of the DJIA when the current net of Lowry's Buying Power minus Selling Pressure falls below yesterday's net reading.

Close Short (Cover) at the current daily price close of the DJIA when the current net of Lowry's Buying Power minus Selling Pressure rises to a level equal to or above yesterday's net reading.

Starting with $100 and reinvesting profits, total net profits for this Lowry's Buying Power minus Selling Pressure short-term trend following strategy would have been $84,092,160, assuming a fully invested strategy, reinvestment of profits, no transactions costs and no taxes. This would have been 1,216,146.87 percent better than buy-and-hold. Even short selling would have been profitable, and short selling was included in the strategy. Trading would have been hyperactive at one trade every 3.32 calendar days.

The Equis International MetaStock® System Testing rules, where Lowry's Buying Power minus Selling Pressure is inserted into the data field normally reserved for volume, are written as follows:

Enter long: V >= Ref(Mov(V,opt1,E),-1)

Close long: V < Ref(Mov(V,opt1,E),-1)

Enter short: V < Ref(Mov(V,opt1,E),-1)

Close short: V >= Ref(Mov(V,opt1,E),-1)

OPT1 Current value: 1

Indicator Strategy Example Using Lowry's Short-Term Buying Power

Lowry's also offers a short-term version of Buying Power. Using the exact same primitive trend rule as above, results would have been slightly better for this more sensitive version. Based on the daily prices for the DJIA for 61 years from 1940 to 2001, we found that the following parameters would have produced a positive result on a purely mechanical trend-following signal basis with no subjectivity, no sophisticated technical analysis, and no judgement:

Enter Long (Buy) at the current daily price close of the DJIA when the current Lowry's Short-Term Buying Power rises to a level equal to or above yesterday's reading.

Close Long (Sell) at the current daily price close of the DJIA when the current Lowry's Short-Term Buying Power falls below yesterday's reading.

Enter Short (Sell Short) at the current daily price close of the DJIA when the current Lowry's Short-Term Buying Power falls below yesterday's reading.

Close Short (Cover) at the current daily price close of the DJIA when the current Lowry's Short-Term Buying Power rises to a level equal to or above yesterday's reading.

Starting with $100 and reinvesting profits, total net profits for this Lowry's Short-Term Buying Power trend following strategy would have been $84,402,688, assuming a fully invested strategy, reinvestment of profits, no transactions costs and no taxes. This would have been 1,220,638.12 percent better than buy-and-hold. Even short selling would have been profitable, and short selling was included in the strategy. Trading would have been hyperactive at one trade every 3.37 calendar days.

The Equis International MetaStock® System Testing rules, where Lowry's Short-Term Buying Power is inserted into the data field normally reserved for volume, are written as follows:

Enter long: V >= Ref(Mov(V,opt1,E),-1)

Close long: V < Ref(Mov(V,opt1,E),-1)

Enter short: V < Ref(Mov(V,opt1,E),-1)

Close short: V >= Ref(Mov(V,opt1,E),-1)

OPT1 Current value: 1

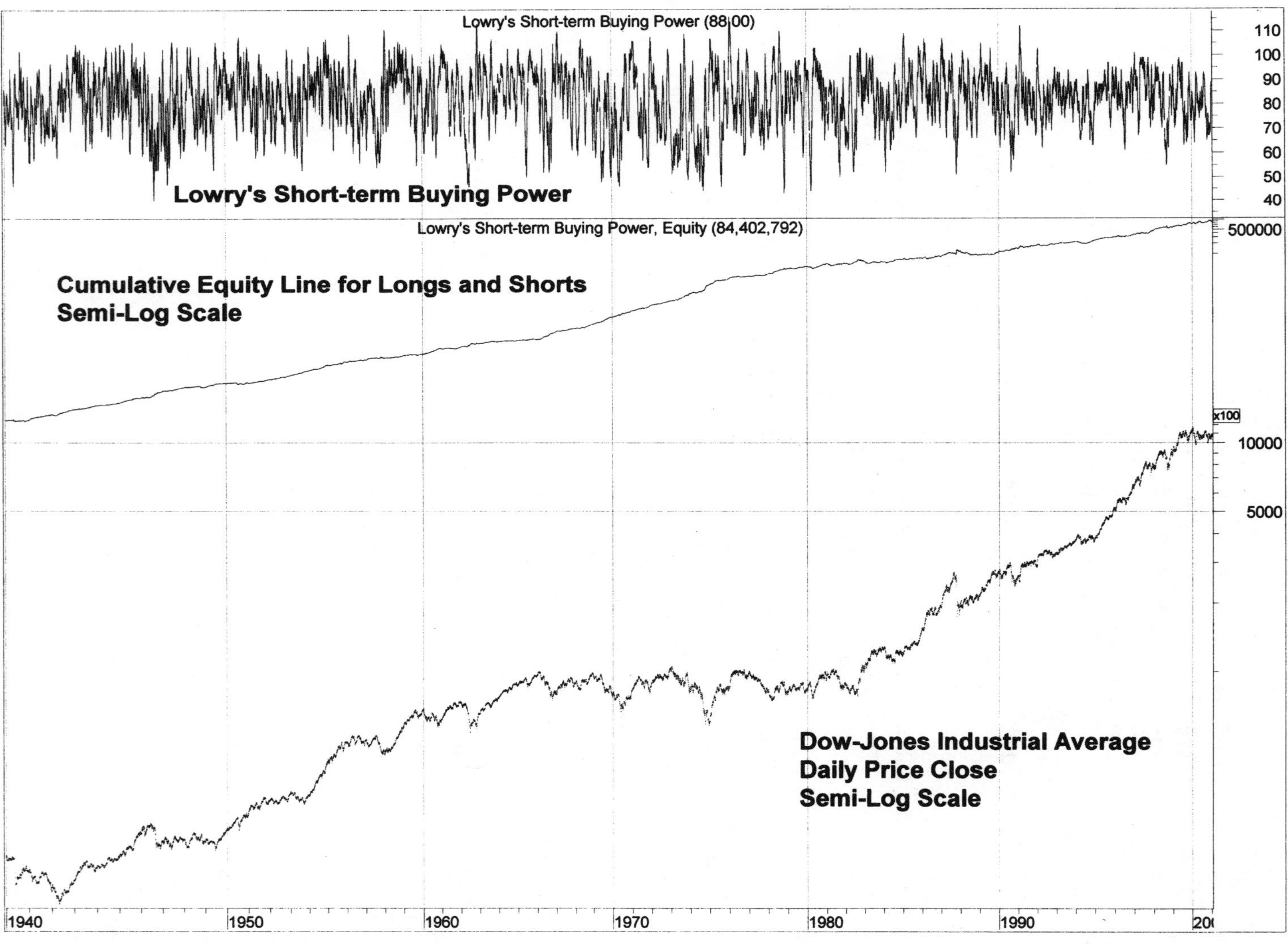

Lowry's Short-term Buying Power (88.00)
Lowry's Short-term Buying Power
Lowry's Short-term Buying Power, Equity (84,402,792)
Cumulative Equity Line for Longs and Shorts
Semi-Log Scale
Dow-Jones Industrial Average
Daily Price Close
Semi-Log Scale
110
100
90
80
70
60
50
40
500000
x100
10000
5000
1940
1950
1960
1970
1980
1990

Lowry's Short-term Buying Power

Total net profit	84402688	Open position value	0	Net Profit/Buy&Hold %	1220638.12
Percent gain/loss	84402688	Annual percent gain/loss	1382222.77	Annual Net %/B&H %	1220621.34
Initial investment	100	Interest earned	0		
Current position	Long	Date position entered	1/8/01		
Buy/Hold profit	6914.07	Days in test	22288	# of days per trade	3.37
Buy/Hold pct gain/loss	6914.07	Annual B/H pct gain/loss	113.23		
Total closed trades	6604	Commissions paid	0		
Avg profit per trade	12780.54	Avg Win/Avg Loss ratio	1.43		
Total long trades	3302	Total short trades	3302	Long Win Trade %	50.73
Winning long trades	1675	Winning short trades	1531	Short Win Trade %	46.37
Total winning trades	3206	Total losing trades	3398	Total Win Trade %	48.55
Amount of winning trades	324074880	Amount of losing trades	−239672256	Net Profit Margin %	14.97
Average win	101083.87	Average loss	−70533.33	Average P. Margin %	17.80
Largest win	5760244	Largest loss	−3009856	% Net/(Win + Loss)	31.36
Average length of win	4.29	Average length of loss	2.56	(Win − Loss)/Loss %	67.58
Longest winning trade	21	Longest losing trade	11	(Win − Loss)/Loss %	90.91
Most consecutive wins	13	Most consecutive losses	10	(Win − Loss)/Loss %	30.00
Total bars out	2	Average length out	2		
Longest out period	2				
System close drawdown	−7.91	Profit/Loss index	26.04	% Net Profit/SODD	1067037774.97
System open drawdown	−7.91	Reward/Risk index	100	(Net P.-SODD)/Net P.	100.00
Max open trade drawdown	−3009856	Buy/Hold index	1220638.75	% SODD/Net Profit	0.00

In the Equis MetaStock® "System Report" (profit and loss summary statistics), the *Total net profit* is the sum of profits minus the sum of losses, including open positions marked to the market. In contrast, the *Amount of Winning Trades* is the sum of realized profits (the total of all gains on closed-out trades only, excluding any open positions). Similarly, the *Amount of Losing Trades* is the sum of realized losses (the total of all losses on closed-out trades only, excluding any open positions). *System close drawdown* is the largest decline in the cumulative equity line below the initial investment, based on closed-out positions only. *System open drawdown (SODD)* is the largest decline in the cumulative equity line below the initial investment when a position is open. *Max open trade drawdown* is the largest decline in the cumulative equity line below the trade entry price during the worst single trade. The *Profit/Loss Index* is a complex calculation that relates the Amount of Winning Trades to the Amount of Losing Trades on a scale of −100 (worst possible performance) to +100 (best possible performance), with zero representing profits equal to losses. *Reward/Risk Index* is the Total net profit minus System open drawdown. The resulting difference is then divided by the Total net profit. The *Buy/Hold Index* is the Total net profit minus the buy-and-hold strategy's net profit. The resulting difference is then divided by the buy-and-hold net profit. In this exercise, initial equity is assumed to be $100. Both long and short positions are taken unless otherwise noted. Trades are executed at the closing price on the signal date. Transaction costs, interest expenses, and margins are not included in the statistics.

Lucas Numbers

French mathematician Edouard Lucas (1842–91) described a two-term difference sequence of integers similar to the Fibonacci number sequence, where the next number in the sequence is the sum of the previous two numbers. The Lucas difference is the starting point or the initial values, which are the integers 2 and 1, in that *reverse* order. Thus, Lucas derived the following sequence: 2, 1, 3, 4, 7, 11, 18, 29, 47, 76, 123, 199, 322, 421, 743, 1164, . . . Lucas Numbers are not as well-known nor as widely used as the much more popular Fibonacci Numbers.

Margin

The initial margin requirement is set by the Fed or the exchange. For most stocks, 50% of the purchase price is required. (For the riskiest stocks 100% is required.) The investor lays out half of the total purchase price, and his broker lends him the remaining 50% with interest. The initial margin requirement is usually much less for most futures contracts. Margin offers both opportunity and substantial danger. *Leverage* is defined as 100% minus margin. Leverage and margin are two-edged swords that must be handled with care.

Margin Debt

Margin Debt represents the total amount that customers owe their brokerage firms as a result of borrowing through their stock margin accounts. Margin Debt statistics are released on a monthly basis by the New York Stock Exchange.

Most of the time, margin debt follows the trend of the market and yields few significant clues for market timing. In a general bull market trend, the percentage of *troubled* margin accounts, with equity less than 40%, drops to a low level. Such a market is healthy and not vulnerable to involuntary margin selling on normal price pullbacks.

In the later stages of a bear market, however, margin debt becomes more interesting. After stock prices already have dropped substantially, the percentage of margin debt in troubled accounts, with equity less than 40%, rises to high levels. In the event of any further significant decline in stock prices, such accounts are vulnerable to forced liquidation through margin calls. This can create an avalanche of selling, producing a selling climax, and a final clean-out of the weak hands. Once the selling runs its course and troubled margin accounts are fully liquidated, stock prices spring back, up sharply from a deeply oversold condition.

Indicator Strategy Example for Margin Debt, with Overbought/Oversold Brackets

Based on a 36-year file of monthly data for Margin Debt on the New York Stock Exchange and the DJIA since January, 1965, we found that a Overbought/Oversold Bracket Rule would have produced a positive result on a purely mechanical signal basis with no subjectivity, no sophisticated technical analysis, and no judgement:

> **Enter Long (Buy)** at the current month-end price close of the DJIA when the current month's annual rate of change of Margin Debt crosses from below −1% to above −1%.

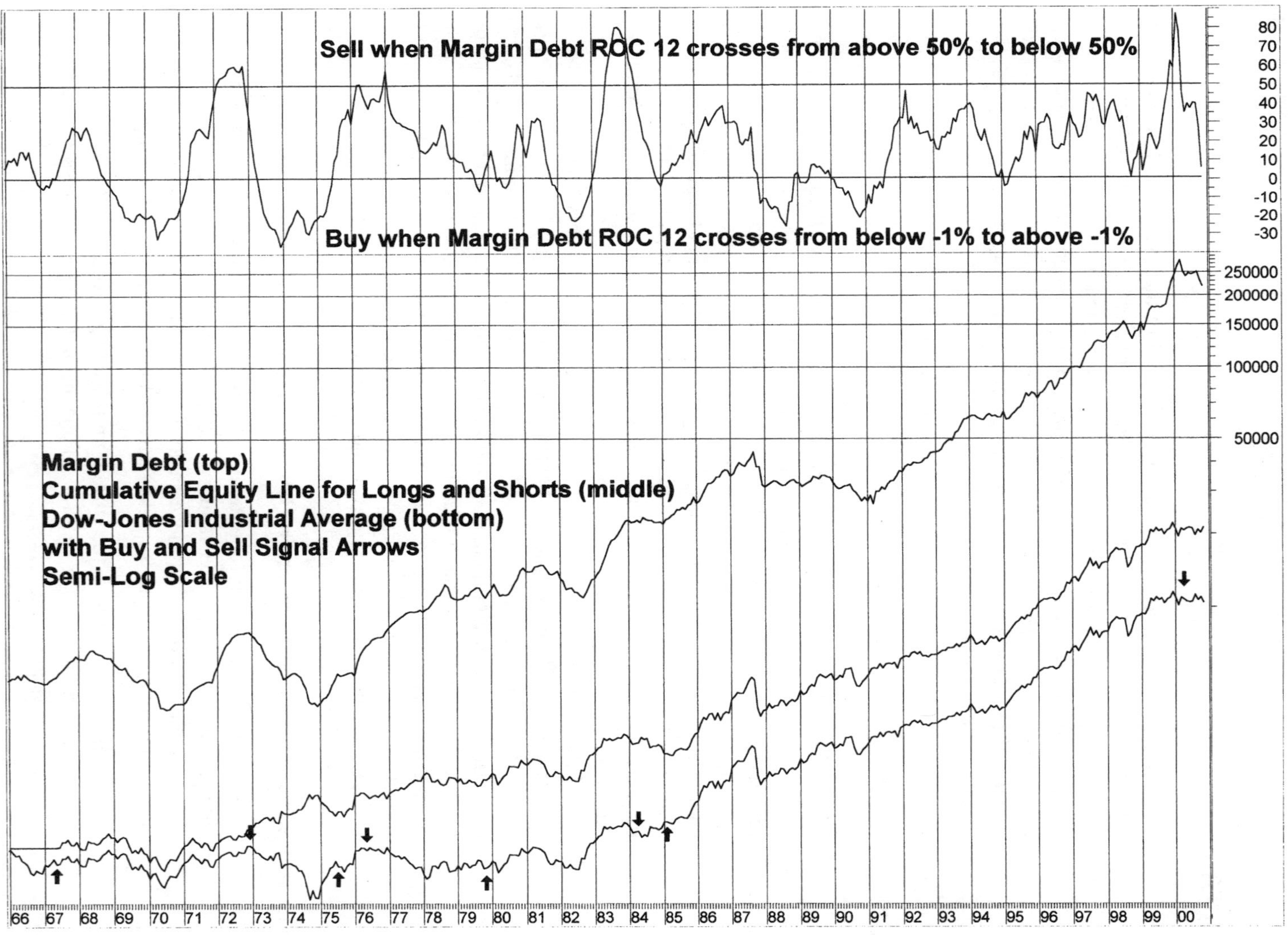

Sell when Margin Debt ROC 12 crosses from above 50% to below 50%
Buy when Margin Debt ROC 12 crosses from below -1% to above -1%
Margin Debt (top)
Cumulative Equity Line for Longs and Shorts (middle)
Dow-Jones Industrial Average (bottom)
with Buy and Sell Signal Arrows
Semi-Log Scale
80
70
60
50
40
30
20
10
0
-10
-20
-30
250000
200000
150000
100000
50000
66
67
68
69
70
71
72
73
74
75
76
77
78
79
80
81
82
83
84
85
86
87
88
89
90
91
92
93
94
95
96
97
98
99
00

Margin Debt Overbought/Oversold Bracket Rule

Total net profit	2028.7	Open position value	61.51	Net Profit / Buy&Hold %	111.56
Percent gain/loss	2028.7	Annual percent gain/loss	58.2	Annual Net % / B&H %	111.56
Initial investment	100	Interest earned	0		
Current position	Short	Date position entered	4/1/00		
Buy/Hold profit	958.92	Days in test	12724	# of days per trade	1817.71
Buy/Hold pct gain/loss	958.92	Annual B/H pct gain/loss	27.51		
Total closed trades	7	Commissions paid	0		
Avg profit per trade	281.03	Avg Win/Avg Loss ratio	12.55		
Total long trades	4	Total short trades	3	Long Win Trade %	100.00
Winning long trades	4	Winning short trades	2	Short Win Trade %	66.67
Total winning trades	6	Total losing trades	1	Total Win Trade %	85.71
Amount of winning trades	1993.65	Amount of losing trades	−26.47	Net Profit Margin %	97.38
Average win	332.28	Average loss	−26.47	Average P. Margin %	85.24
Largest win	1819.91	Largest loss	−26.47	% Net / (Win + Loss)	97.13
Average length of win	65.17	Average length of loss	11	(Win − Loss) / Loss %	492.45
Longest winning trade	183	Longest losing trade	11	(Win − Loss) / Loss %	1563.64
Most consecutive wins	5	Most consecutive losses	1	(Win − Loss) / Loss %	400.00
Total bars out	17	Average length out	17		
Longest out period	17				
System close drawdown	0	Profit/Loss index	98.71	% Net Profit / SODD	10230.46
System open drawdown	−19.83	Reward/Risk index	99.03	(Net P.-SODD)/Net P.	99.02
Max open trade drawdown	−92.67	Buy/Hold index	117.98	% SODD / Net Profit	−0.98

In the Equis MetaStock® "System Report" (profit and loss summary statistics), the *Total net profit* is the sum of profits minus the sum of losses, including open positions marked to the market. In contrast, the *Amount of Winning Trades* is the sum of realized profits (the total of all gains on closed-out trades only, excluding any open positions). Similarly, the *Amount of Losing Trades* is the sum of realized losses (the total of all losses on closed-out trades only, excluding any open positions). *System close drawdown* is the largest decline in the cumulative equity line below the initial investment, based on closed-out positions only. *System open drawdown (SODD)* is the largest decline in the cumulative equity line below the initial investment when a position is open. *Max open trade drawdown* is the largest decline in the cumulative equity line below the trade entry price during the worst single trade. The *Profit/Loss Index* is a complex calculation that relates the Amount of Winning Trades to the Amount of Losing Trades on a scale of −100 (worst possible performance) to +100 (best possible performance), with zero representing profits equal to losses. *Reward/Risk Index* is the Total net profit minus System open drawdown. The resulting difference is then divided by the Total net profit. The *Buy/Hold Index* is the Total net profit minus the buy-and-hold strategy's net profit. The resulting difference is then divided by the buy-and-hold net profit. In this exercise, initial equity is assumed to be $100. Both long and short positions are taken unless otherwise noted. Trades are executed at the closing price on the signal date. Transaction costs, interest expenses, and margins are not included in the statistics.

Close Long (Sell) at the current month-end price close of the DJIA when the current month's annual rate of change of Margin Debt crosses from above 50% to below 50%.

Enter Short (Sell Short) at the current month-end price close of the DJIA when the current month's annual rate of change of Margin Debt crosses from above 50% to below 50%.

Close Short (Cover) at the current month-end price close of the DJIA when the current month's annual rate of change of Margin Debt crosses from below −1% to above −1%.

Starting with $100 and reinvesting profits, total net profits for the Margin Debt Brackets strategy would have been $2,028.70, assuming a fully invested strategy, reinvestment of profits, no transactions costs and no taxes. This would have been 111.56 percent greater than buy-and-hold. Even short selling would have been profitable, and short selling was included in the strategy. Two-thirds of the short sales would have been profitable, while 100% of the long trades would have been profitable. Trading would have been inactive at one trade every 1817.71 calendar days.

The Equis International MetaStock® System Testing rules, where the Margin Debt is inserted into the data field normally reserved for Volume (V), are written as follows:

Enter long: Ref((((V-Ref(V,-12))/Ref(V,-12))*100),-1)<49-opt2

AND (((V-Ref(V,-12))/Ref(V,-12))*100)>49-opt2

Close long: Ref((((V-Ref(V,-12))/Ref(V,-12))*100),-1)>opt1

AND (((V-Ref(V,-12))/Ref(V,-12))*100)<opt1

Enter short: Ref((((V-Ref(V,-12))/Ref(V,-12))*100),-1)>opt1

AND (((V-Ref(V,-12))/Ref(V,-12))*100)<opt1

Close short: Ref((((V-Ref(V,-12))/Ref(V,-12))*100),-1)<49-opt2

AND (((V-Ref(V,-12))/Ref(V,-12))*100)>49-opt2

OPT1 Current value: 50
OPT2 Current value: 50

Indicator Strategy Example for Margin Debt–Trend Following

As the chart shows, the trend of Margin Debt appears to correlate with the trend of the stock market. Based on a 34-year file of monthly data for Margin Debt on the New York Stock Exchange and the DJIA since March, 1967, we found that all simple

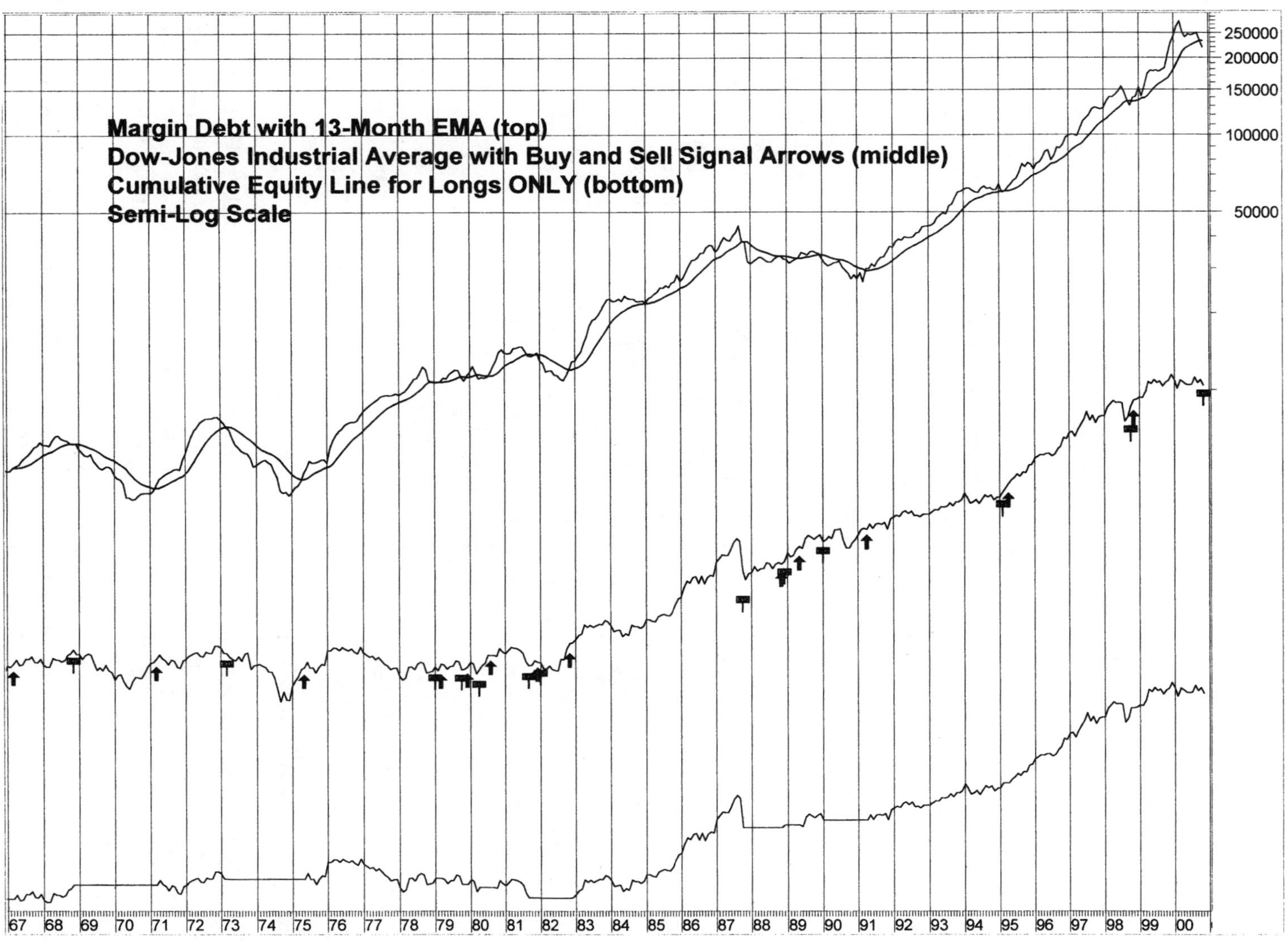

Margin Debt with 13-Month EMA (top)
Dow-Jones Industrial Average with Buy and Sell Signal Arrows (middle)
Cumulative Equity Line for Longs ONLY (bottom)
Semi-Log Scale
250000
200000
150000
100000
50000
67
68
69
70
71
72
73
74
75
76
77
78
79
80
81
82
83
84
85
86
87
88
89
90
91
92
93
94
95
96
97
98
99
00

trend-following rules would have produced positive results on a purely mechanical signal basis with no subjectivity, no sophisticated technical analysis, and no judgement:

Enter Long (Buy) at the current month-end price close of the DJIA when the current month's Margin Debt crosses above its own trailing 13-month Exponential Moving Average as of the previous month.

Close Long (Sell) at the current month-end price close of the DJIA when the current month's Margin Debt crosses below its own trailing 13-month Exponential Moving Average as of the previous month.

Enter Short (Sell Short) never.

Starting with $100 and reinvesting profits, total net profits for this Margin Debt trend-following strategy would have been $553.83, assuming a fully invested strategy, reinvestment of profits, no transactions costs and no taxes. This would have been 43.71 percent less than buy-and-hold. No short selling would have been profitable, and no short selling was included in the strategy. Short selling would have cut net profit by 64%. Although this strategy does not keep pace with the passive buy-and-hold strategy, Margin Debt as a trend-following strategy would have been right on 9 of 13 signals, for 69.23% winning trades. Trading would have been inactive at one trade every 985.85 calendar days.

The Equis International MetaStock® System Testing rules, where the Margin Debt is inserted into the data field normally reserved for Volume (V), are written as follows:

Enter long: V > Ref(Mov(V,opt1,E),-1)

Close long: V < Ref(Mov(V,opt1,E),-1)

OPT1 Current value: 13

Margin Requirement

The Margin Requirement is the minimum percentage of the total value of a position that an investor is required to put down as equity or collateral. With the Margin Requirement at 50%, the investor is required to put down at least half of the total purchase price. His broker will lend him the remaining 50%, and charge him interest on it.

The Federal Reserve Board Fed has kept the Margin Requirement unchanged at 50% since January 1974. So, it appears that the Fed no longer uses the Margin Requirement as a tool of monetary policy. Between 1934 to 1974, the Fed increased the

Margin Requirement 12 times and lowered it 10 times. The Fed raised the Margin Requirement to force investors to put up more money to buy stock and to dampen speculation. The Fed cut the Margin Requirement after significant declines in the stock market to make it easier for investors to hold and buy more stock. Critics of the Fed insist that the Fed should not be in the business of manipulating stock prices.

Although this indicator has been gathering dust for decades, the stock market used to react to changes in the Margin Requirement. Norman Fosback, in his 1976 book, *Stock Market Logic* (The Institute for Econometric Research, 3471 North Federal Highway, Fort Lauderdale, FL 33306), found that the stock market's initial reaction to increases in the Margin Requirement has been negative. But by the end of the first month after such an increase, the stock market recovered, rising 1.1% on average, as measured by the Standard & Poor's 500 Index. One year after an increase, the market rose 14.4%, a rate of gain significantly above normal.

Furthermore, Fosback discovered that the market initially declined an average of 2.3% three months after a reduction in the Margin Requirement, contrary to what one might expect. This might imply that in a bear market, the downward momentum is not quickly stemmed. But following that short-term decline, the market reversed to the upside, gaining above-average amounts of 12.5%, 16.3%, and 18.5%, in the 12 months, 15 months, and 18 months following a Margin Requirement reduction, respectively. So, longer term, after an initial disappointment, cuts in the Margin Requirement indeed have been bullish.

Market Profile

Market Profile is a statistical frequency distribution of tick data designed to reveal how many trades occurred at each specific price during each trading session. It reveals the market balance or imbalance as well as precise levels of support and resistance on a micro level. When there is a significant quantity of trading activity at a specific price, that price becomes established as the *value* in traders' minds. When price moves away from value then returns to value, price finds support or resistance at value. Market Profile gained a dedicated following among some sophisticated short-term traders but has not attained widespread use among investors or technicians. Source: Steidlemayer, J. P., & Koy, K. (1986). *Markets and Market Logic.* Chicago: Porcupine Press.

Market Vane

Market Vane Corp. of Pasadena, CA, weekly surveys 100 investment advisors from brokerage firms. This indicator is one of four different sentiment polls or surveys conducted by investment advisory service newsletters and generally made available to subscribers via telephone recording. The data is also printed in *Barron's* weekly financial newspaper, which is available every Saturday. Popular interpretation is generally contrarian. *(See Contrary Opinion* and *Advisory Service Sentiment.)*

Many experienced technical analysts use sentiment, but more as a supplement to trend, momentum, and other technical indicators than as a stand-alone, signal generator. Sentiment typically shows overbought and oversold levels well *before* the directional price move is over and, therefore, can be misleading. In general, sentiment is more of a background indicator that is not suitable for precise timing.

Using dynamic brackets *(see Bollinger Bands)* placed above and below a 15-day moving average of the daily Market Vane sentiment data, Ned Davis Research found a majority of profitable signals, while beating buy-and-hold by 33.8% per annum, for long trades only over the period shown on the chart. Buy when excessive pessimism abates, signaled by the 15-day moving average crossing above the lower bracket. Sell after a period of extreme optimism runs out, signaled by the 15-day moving average crossing under the upper bracket.

Mart's Master Trading Formula

Mart's Master Trading Formula is a complex variation on moving average trading bands. Using Average True Range to determine volatility, this indicator uses volatility to determine the exponential smoothing constant for the exponential moving average. The bands above and below the exponential moving average vary inversely with volatility, such that the bands are narrowly spaced when volatility is high and widely spaced when volatility is low. Buy when the current day's high crosses the upper band, and sell when the current day's low crosses the lower band. Source: Kaufman, P. J. (1987). *The New Commodity Trading Systems and Methods,* New York: John Wiley & Sons.

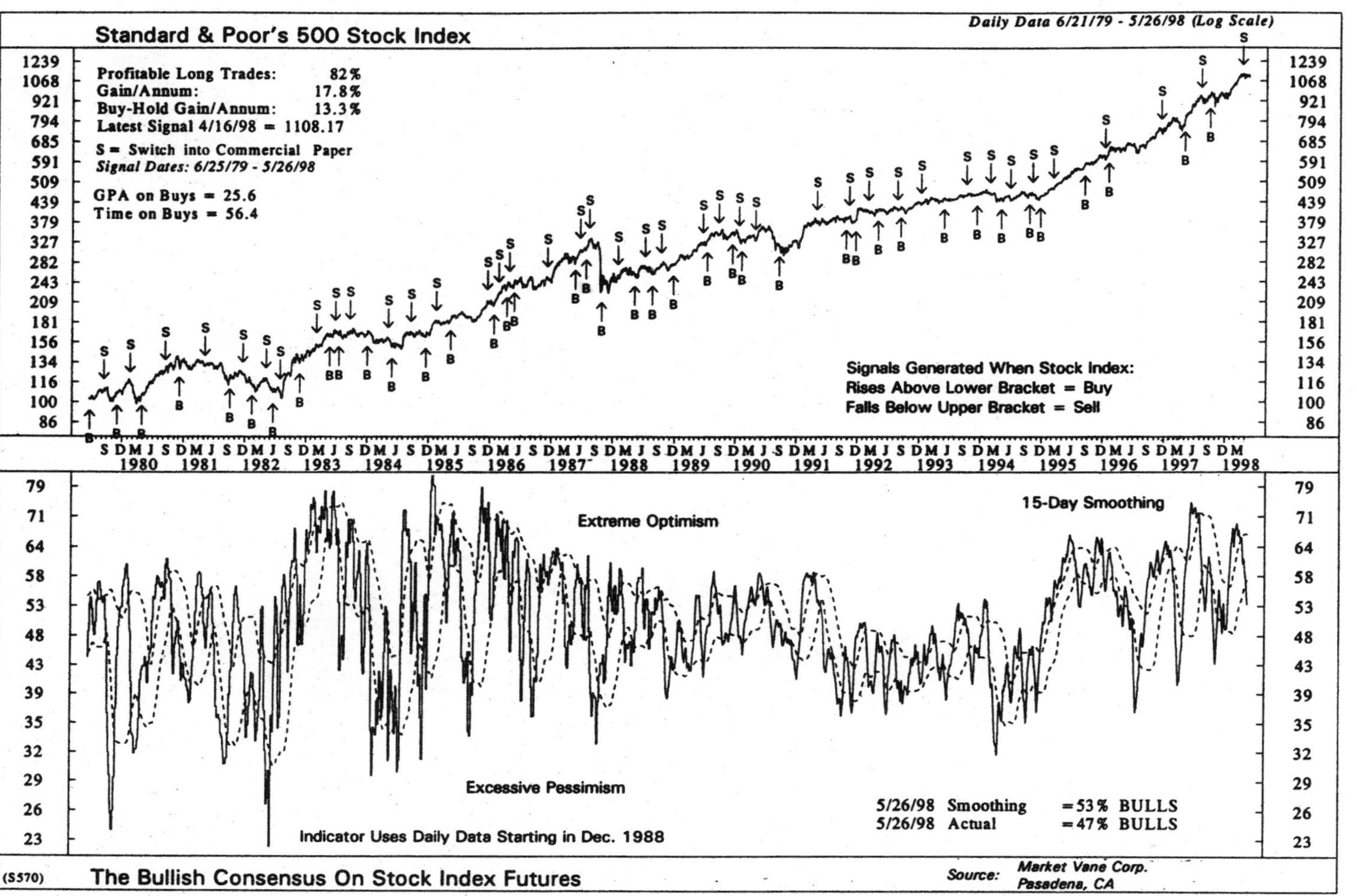

Standard & Poor's 500 Stock Index
Daily Data 6/21/79 - 5/26/98 (Log Scale)
Profitable Long Trades: 82%
Gain/Annum: 17.8%
Buy-Hold Gain/Annum: 13.3%
Latest Signal 4/16/98 = 1108.17
S = Switch into Commercial Paper
Signal Dates: 6/25/79 - 5/26/98
GPA on Buys = 25.6
Time on Buys = 56.4
Signals Generated When Stock Index:
Rises Above Lower Bracket = Buy
Falls Below Upper Bracket = Sell
Extreme Optimism
15-Day Smoothing
Excessive Pessimism
Indicator Uses Daily Data Starting in Dec. 1988
5/26/98 Smoothing =53% BULLS
5/26/98 Actual =47% BULLS
(S570)
The Bullish Consensus On Stock Index Futures
Source: Market Vane Corp. Pasadena, CA

Chart by permission of Ned Davis Research.

Mathematical Models

The technical indicators presented in this book are simple mathematical models. Being simple, they are easy to understand, compute, and implement. A mathematical model is simply an idealized representation of reality in the form of a clearly defined formula, or more than one formula, combined into a system. Fortunately, simple models actually work better than complex systems. If you can't understand it, don't use it.

Maximum Entropy Spectral Analysis (MESA)
Maximum Entropy Spectrum Analysis (MESA)
Maximum Entropy Method (MEM)

The names for MESA have been used interchangeably, even by the same writer. MESA, which was developed by a geophysics scientist, extracts short-term cycles using adaptive algorithms applied to short data lengths. Short-term cycles in financial markets, which generally are irregular and always shifting, seemingly offer almost unlimited promise to anyone who could forecast them. Naturally, traders are tempted to use minimal market price data and any available technique in a wishful attempt to identify the precise junctures when cycles shift. Unfortunately, market behavior is even more irregular over shorter time frames than it is over longer periods. And, of course, the irregular market data generated by mass psychological mood swings is not at all comparable to the regular data produced by physical phenomena, for which MESA was designed. Therefore, the application of MESA to market data is questionable.

MESA is based on the Burg algorithm. (See the Ph.D. thesis by John Parker Burg, Stanford University, 1975.) Burg pioneered high-resolution spectral estimation from limited time sequences, using minimal data.

Burg's ideas caught the imagination of traders and analysts. In 1978, John Ehlers, an aerospace signals engineer, was the first to write a software program to use MESA on market price data. On Ehlers' website, www.mesasoftware.com, he writes that his MESA2000 program employs adaptive filters and feedback loops to adjust to changing cycles. The output of the filter is compared with the samples of actual market price data, and the result of the comparison is repeatedly fed back to adjust the filter so that the filter output moves toward the observed data. A fraction of yesterday's dominant cycle is today's data length, and the filter parameters are fixed by the price data. The adaptive data length avoids measurement latency, or lag, usually produced by a fixed length data window.

Ehlers has written that it is not sound method to trade based solely on cycles, because tradable cycles are present only about 15% of the time. A sound trading strategy must incorporate trend-following techniques, such as moving averages.

(See "Cycle Measurements," *Technical Analysis of Stocks & Commodities,* Vol. 15:11, pp. 505–509, www.traders.com.)

Perry Kaufman has suggested that optimized cycles based on a small amount of data must have low reliability. (See "Kaufman on Commodity Trading," *Technical Analysis of Stocks & Commodities,* Vol. 6:4, pp. 123–128, www.traders.com.)

According to Jeffrey Katz and Donna McCormick, *The Encyclopedia of Trading Strategies,* McGraw Hill, New York, 2000, 376 pages, page 203–4, "A number of problems, however, exist with the maximum entropy method, as well as with many other mathematical methods for determining cycles. MEM, for example, is somewhat finicky. It can be extremely sensitive to small changes in the data or in such parameters as the number of poles and the look-back period. In addition, the price data must not only be de-trended or differenced, but also it must be passed through a low-pass filter for smoothing before the data can be handed to the maximum entropy algorithm; the algorithm does not work very well on noisy, raw data. The problem with passing the data through a filter, prior to the maximum entropy cycle extraction, is that lag and phase shifts are induced. Consequently, extrapolations of the cycles detected can be incorrect in terms of phase and timing unless additional analyses are employed."

Katz and McCormick conclude their Chapter 10, "Cycle-Based Entries", with the following observation: "The markets appear to have become more efficient relative to cycle models . . . Obvious market behavior (such as clear, tradable cycles) are traded away before most traders can capitalize on them." Quoted with permission.

McClellan Oscillator

The McClellan Oscillator is a breadth-momentum oscillator. It is computed in three steps.

1. Subtract the number of declining issues from the number of advancing issues each day, and respect the sign (so that more declines than advances will be a negative number).
2. Smooth this daily advance-decline difference with two different exponential moving averages (EMAs), a 19-day EMA and a 39-day EMA.
3. Subtract the 39-day EMA from the 19-day EMA.

The resulting plot of the McClellan Oscillator oscillates around zero. Like other momentum oscillators, the McClellan Oscillator sometimes reaches an extreme reading before a change in the trend of stock prices. NYSE data is usually used, though data for other exchanges could be used also.

Traditionally, the McClellan Oscillator was thought to signal overbought and oversold general market conditions. A bear market selling climax or a bull market buying climax was thought to be indicated by extreme oscillator readings. As the following chart shows, however, levels have been shifting to greater extremes over time, due to the large increase in the number of total issues listed on the stock exchange. Therefore, McClellan Oscillator ought to be adjusted for this increase by, for example, dividing the daily net advances by total issues traded.

When the McClellan Oscillator moves from below zero to above zero, it signals a change to positive momentum, and that is a bullish sign for stock prices in the near future. When the McClellan Oscillator moves from above zero to below zero, that is bearish for the stock market.

A detailed description of how to interpret the McClellan Oscillator is included in *Patterns for Profit: The McClellan Oscillator and Summation Index,* (Trade Levels, Inc., 22801 Ventura Boulevard, Suite 210, Woodland Hills, CA 91364).

Indicator Strategy Example for the McClellan Oscillator

Based on a 68-year file of daily data for the number of shares advancing and declining each day on the New York Stock Exchange and the DJIA since March 8, 1932, we found that a simple trend-following rule would have produced a positive result on a purely mechanical signal basis with no subjectivity, no sophisticated technical analysis, and no judgement:

Enter Long (Buy) at the current daily price close of the DJIA when the McClellan Oscillator crosses above 0.

Close Long (Sell) at the current daily price close of the DJIA when the McClellan Oscillator crosses below 0.

Enter Short (Sell Short) at the current daily price close of the DJIA when the McClellan Oscillator crosses below 0.

Close Short (Cover) at the current daily price close of the DJIA the McClellan Oscillator crosses above 0.

Starting with $100 and reinvesting profits, total net profits for the McClellan Oscillator trend-following strategy would have been $901,259.31, assuming a fully invested strategy, reinvestment of profits, no transactions costs and no taxes. This would have been 7,087.84 percent better than buy-and-hold. Even short selling would have been profitable. Trading would have been active with one trade every 11.82 calendar days.

The Equis International MetaStock® System Testing rules, where the McClellan Oscillator is inserted into the data field normally reserved for Volume (V), are written as follows:

Enter long: (Mov(V,opt1,E))-(Mov(V,opt2,E))>0

Close long: (Mov(V,opt1,E))-(Mov(V,opt2,E))<0

Enter short: (Mov(V,opt1,E))-(Mov(V,opt2,E))<0

Close short: (Mov(V,opt1,E))-(Mov(V,opt2,E))>0

OPT1 Current value: 19
OPT2 Current value: 39

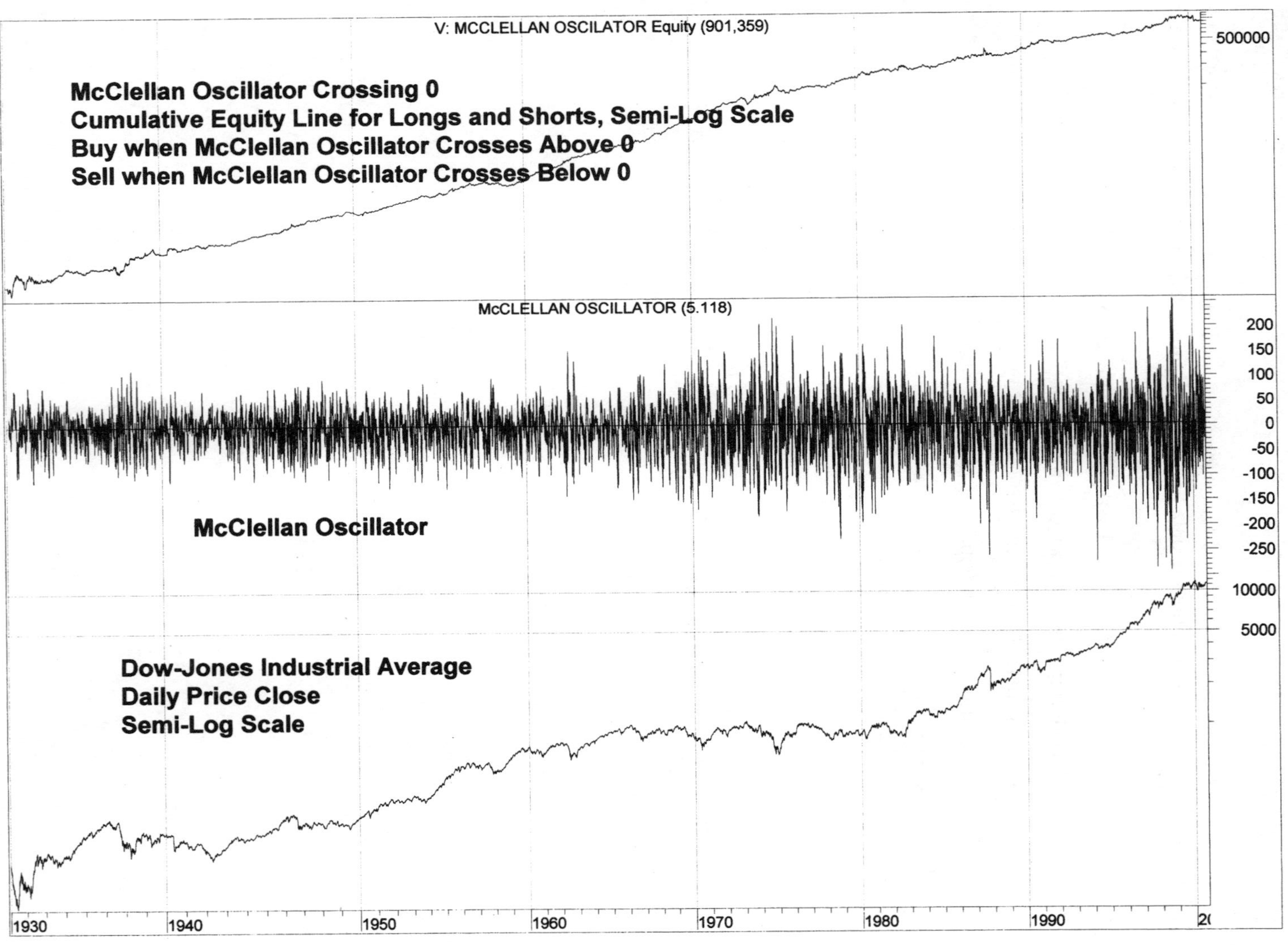
V: MCCLELLAN OSCILATOR Equity (901,359)
500000
McClellan Oscillator Crossing 0
Cumulative Equity Line for Longs and Shorts, Semi-Log Scale
Buy when McClellan Oscillator Crosses Above 0
Sell when McClellan Oscillator Crosses Below 0
McCLELLAN OSCILLATOR (5.118)
200
150
100
50
0
-50
-100
-150
-200
-250
McClellan Oscillator
10000
5000
Dow-Jones Industrial Average
Daily Price Close
Semi-Log Scale
1930
1940
1950
1960
1970
1980
1990

McClellan Oscillator Crossing Zero, Long and Short

Total net profit	901259.31	Open position value	−1462.04	Net Profit / Buy&Hold %	7087.84
Percent gain/loss	901259.31	Annual percent gain/loss	13146.82	Annual Net % / B&H %	7087.98
Initial investment	100	Interest earned	0		
Current position	Long	Date position entered	9/1/00		
Buy/Hold profit	12538.66	Days in test	25022	# of days per trade	11.82
Buy/Hold pct gain/loss	12538.66	Annual B/H pct gain/loss	182.9		
Total closed trades	2117	Commissions paid	0		
Avg profit per trade	426.42	Avg Win/Avg Loss ratio	2.06		
Total long trades	1058	Total short trades	1059	Long Win Trade %	47.45
Winning long trades	502	Winning short trades	367	Short Win Trade %	34.66
Total winning trades	869	Total losing trades	1248	Total Win Trade %	41.05
Amount of winning trades	2978256.8	Amount of losing trades	−2075535.5	Net Profit Margin %	17.86
Average win	3427.22	Average loss	−1663.09	Average P. Margin %	34.66
Largest win	117985.13	Largest loss	−53506.88	% Net / (Win + Loss)	37.60
Average length of win	15.12	Average length of loss	5.64	(Win − Loss) / Loss %	168.09
Longest winning trade	58	Longest losing trade	39	(Win − Loss) / Loss %	48.72
Most consecutive wins	7	Most consecutive losses	10	(Win − Loss) / Loss %	−30.00
Total bars out	39	Average length out	39		
Longest out period	39				
System close drawdown	−21.29	Profit/Loss index	30.28	% Net Profit / SODD	3349161.32
System open drawdown	−26.91	Reward/Risk index	100	(Net P.-SODD)/Net P.	100.00
Max open trade drawdown	−53506.88	Buy/Hold index	7076.19	% SODD / Net Profit	0.00

In the Equis MetaStock® "System Report" (profit and loss summary statistics), the *Total net profit* is the sum of profits minus the sum of losses, including open positions marked to the market. In contrast, the *Amount of Winning Trades* is the sum of realized profits (the total of all gains on closed-out trades only, excluding any open positions). Similarly, the *Amount of Losing Trades* is the sum of realized losses (the total of all losses on closed-out trades only, excluding any open positions). *System close drawdown* is the largest decline in the cumulative equity line below the initial investment, based on closed-out positions only. *System open drawdown (SODD)* is the largest decline in the cumulative equity line below the initial investment when a position is open. *Max open trade drawdown* is the largest decline in the cumulative equity line below the trade entry price during the worst single trade. The *Profit/Loss Index* is a complex calculation that relates the Amount of Winning Trades to the Amount of Losing Trades on a scale of −100 (worst possible performance) to +100 (best possible performance), with zero representing profits equal to losses. *Reward/Risk Index* is the Total net profit minus System open drawdown. The resulting difference is then divided by the Total net profit. The *Buy/Hold Index* is the Total net profit minus the buy-and-hold strategy's net profit. The resulting difference is then divided by the buy-and-hold net profit. In this exercise, initial equity is assumed to be $100. Both long and short positions are taken unless otherwise noted. Trades are executed at the closing price on the signal date. Transaction costs, interest expenses, and margins are not included in the statistics.

McClellan Summation Index

The McClellan Summation Index is the cumulative total of the McClellan Oscillator. It also is said to give buy and sell signals when it crosses zero: crossing above zero is bullish, while crossing below zero is bearish for the stock market. We found that this simple indicator, although profitable, is not one of the more productive ones explored in these pages.

A more thorough treatment of the McClellan Summation Index is included in *Patterns for Profit: The McClellan Oscillator and Summation Index* (Trade Levels, Inc., 22801 Ventura Boulevard, Suite 210, Woodland Hills, CA 91364).

Indicator Strategy Example for the McClellan Summation Index Crossing Zero

Based on a 68-year file of daily data for the number of shares advancing and declining each day on the NYSE and the DJIA since March 8, 1932, we found that the simple trend-following rule would have produced positive but somewhat sub-par results on a purely mechanical signal basis with no subjectivity, no sophisticated technical analysis, and no judgement:

Enter Long (Buy) at the current daily price close of the DJIA when the McClellan Summation Index crosses above 0.

Close Long (Sell) at the current daily price close of the DJIA when the McClellan Summation Index crosses below 0.

Enter Short (Sell Short) at the current daily price close of the DJIA when the McClellan Summation Index crosses below 0.

Close Short (Cover) at the current daily price close of the DJIA when the McClellan Summation Index crosses above 0.

Starting with $100 and reinvesting profits, total net profits for the McClellan Summation Index trend-following strategy would have been only $9,137.24, assuming a fully invested strategy, reinvestment of profits, no transactions costs and no taxes. This would have been 27.13 percent less than buy-and-hold. Short selling would have been unprofitable and was not included in these results. Trading was inactive, with one trade every 269 calendar days.

The Equis International MetaStock® System Testing rules, where the McClellan Summation Index is inserted into the data field normally reserved for Volume (V), are written as follows:

Enter long: Cum((Mov(V,opt1,E))-(Mov(V,opt2,E)))>0

Close long: Cum((Mov(V,opt1,E))-(Mov(V,opt2,E)))<0

Enter short: Cum((Mov(V,opt1,E))-(Mov(V,opt2,E)))<0

Close short: Cum((Mov(V,opt1,E))-(Mov(V,opt2,E)))>0

OPT1 Current value: 19
OPT2 Current value: 39

Indicator Strategy Example for the McClellan Summation Index Direction

Trend is more important than *level.* The slope or direction of the McClellan Summation Index, rising or falling, is a 99-times better indicator than crossing any level. This indicator is the equivalent of the McClellan Oscillator, since the Oscillator crosses zero when the Summation changes direction.

Based on a 68-year file of daily data for the number of shares advancing and declining each day on the NYSE and the DJIA since March 8, 1932, we found that the following simple trend-following rule would have produced a profitable result on a purely mechanical signal basis with no subjectivity, no sophisticated technical analysis, and no judgement:

Enter Long (Buy) at the current daily price close of the DJIA when the McClellan Summation Index changes direction from downward to upward.

Close Long (Sell) at the current daily price close of the DJIA when the McClellan Summation Index changes direction from upward to downward.

Enter Short (Sell Short) at the current daily price close of the DJIA when the McClellan Summation Index changes direction from upward to downward.

Close Short (Cover) at the current daily price close of the DJIA when the McClellan Summation Index changes direction from downward to upward.

Starting with $100 and reinvesting profits, total net profits for the McClellan Summation Index Direction trend-following strategy would have been $906,443.88, assuming a fully invested strategy, reinvestment of profits, no transactions costs and no taxes. This would have been 7,129.19 percent more than buy-and-hold. Even short selling would have been profitable and was included in these results. Trading would have been active, with one trade every 11.82 calendar days.

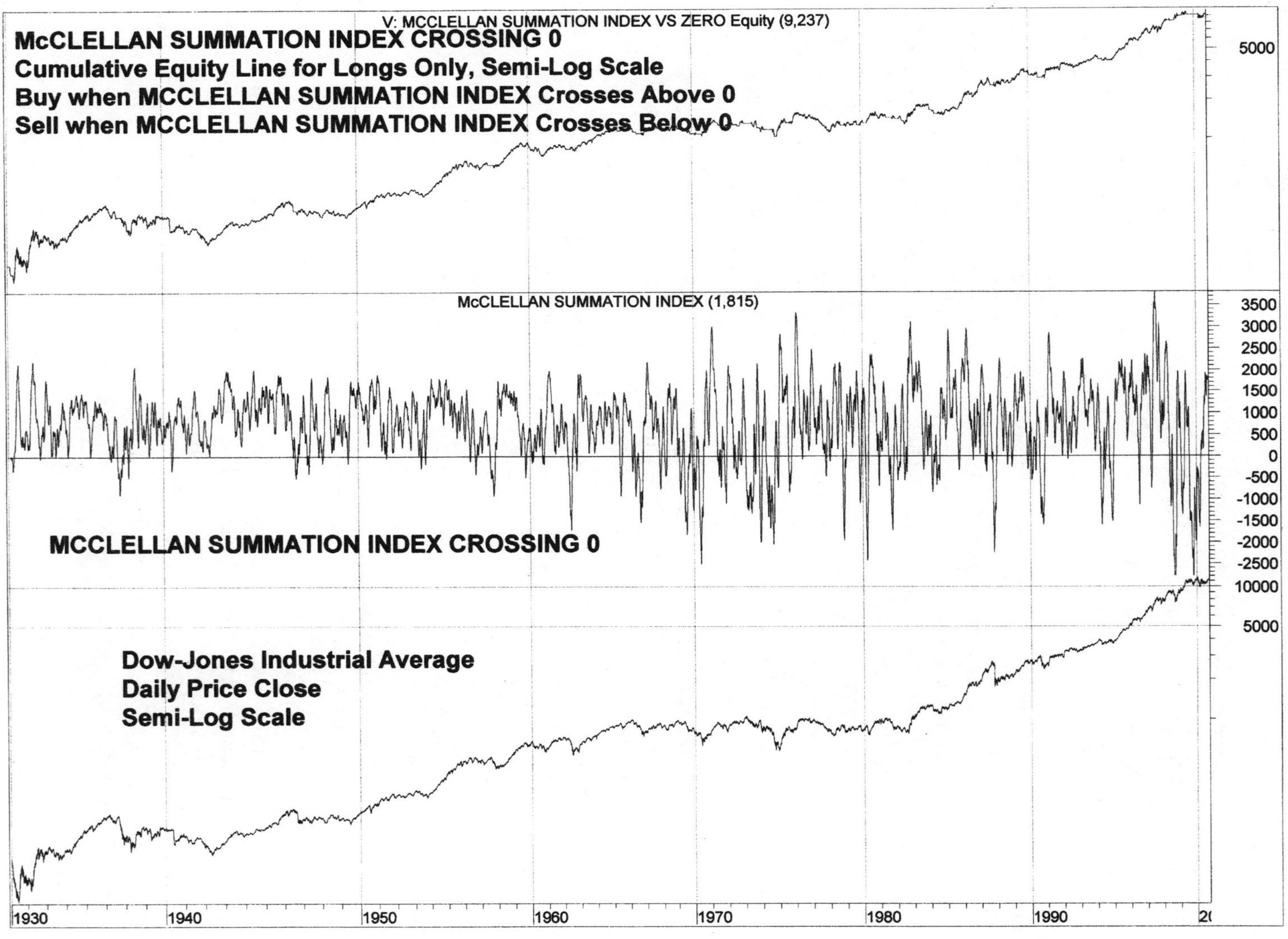
V: MCCLELLAN SUMMATION INDEX VS ZERO Equity (9,237)
McCLELLAN SUMMATION INDEX CROSSING 0
Cumulative Equity Line for Longs Only, Semi-Log Scale
Buy when MCCLELLAN SUMMATION INDEX Crosses Above 0
Sell when MCCLELLAN SUMMATION INDEX Crosses Below 0
5000
McCLELLAN SUMMATION INDEX (1,815)
3500
3000
2500
2000
1500
1000
500
0
-500
-1000
-1500
-2000
-2500
MCCLELLAN SUMMATION INDEX CROSSING 0
10000
5000
Dow-Jones Industrial Average
Daily Price Close
Semi-Log Scale
1930
1940
1950
1960
1970
1980
1990

McClellan Summation Index Crossing Zero, Long Only

Total net profit	9137.24	Open position value	87.51	Net Profit / Buy&Hold %	−27.13
Percent gain/loss	9137.24	Annual percent gain/loss	133.29	Annual Net % / B&H %	−27.12
Initial investment	100	Interest earned	0		
Current position	Long	Date position entered	4/6/00		
Buy/Hold profit	12538.66	Days in test	25022	# of days per trade	269.05
Buy/Hold pct gain/loss	12538.66	Annual B/H pct gain/loss	182.9		
Total closed trades	93	Commissions paid	0		
Avg profit per trade	97.31	Avg Win/Avg Loss ratio	5.72		
Total long trades	93	Total short trades	0	Long Win Trade %	44.09
Winning long trades	41	Winning short trades	0	Short Win Trade %	#DIV/0!
Total winning trades	41	Total losing trades	52	Total Win Trade %	44.09
Amount of winning trades	11629.12	Amount of losing trades	−2579.39	Net Profit Margin %	63.69
Average win	283.64	Average loss	−49.6	Average P. Margin %	70.23
Largest win	1725.03	Largest loss	−262.19	% Net / (Win + Loss)	73.61
Average length of win	292.59	Average length of loss	61.52	(Win − Loss) / Loss %	375.60
Longest winning trade	1814	Longest losing trade	634	(Win − Loss) / Loss %	186.12
Most consecutive wins	4	Most consecutive losses	6	(Win − Loss) / Loss %	−33.33
Total bars out	2981	Average length out	31.71		
Longest out period	174				
System close drawdown	−15.01	Profit/Loss index	77.99	% Net Profit / SODD	34702.77
System open drawdown	−26.33	Reward/Risk index	99.71	(Net P.-SODD)/Net P.	99.71
Max open trade drawdown	−671.02	Buy/Hold index	−26.43	% SODD / Net Profit	−0.29

In the Equis MetaStock® "System Report" (profit and loss summary statistics), the *Total net profit* is the sum of profits minus the sum of losses, including open positions marked to the market. In contrast, the *Amount of Winning Trades* is the sum of realized profits (the total of all gains on closed-out trades only, excluding any open positions). Similarly, the *Amount of Losing Trades* is the sum of realized losses (the total of all losses on closed-out trades only, excluding any open positions). *System close drawdown* is the largest decline in the cumulative equity line below the initial investment, based on closed-out positions only. *System open drawdown (SODD)* is the largest decline in the cumulative equity line below the initial investment when a position is open. *Max open trade drawdown* is the largest decline in the cumulative equity line below the trade entry price during the worst single trade. The *Profit/Loss Index* is a complex calculation that relates the Amount of Winning Trades to the Amount of Losing Trades on a scale of −100 (worst possible performance) to +100 (best possible performance), with zero representing profits equal to losses. *Reward/Risk Index* is the Total net profit minus System open drawdown. The resulting difference is then divided by the Total net profit. The *Buy/Hold Index* is the Total net profit minus the buy-and-hold strategy's net profit. The resulting difference is then divided by the buy-and-hold net profit. In this exercise, initial equity is assumed to be $100. Both long and short positions are taken unless otherwise noted. Trades are executed at the closing price on the signal date. Transaction costs, interest expenses, and margins are not included in the statistics.

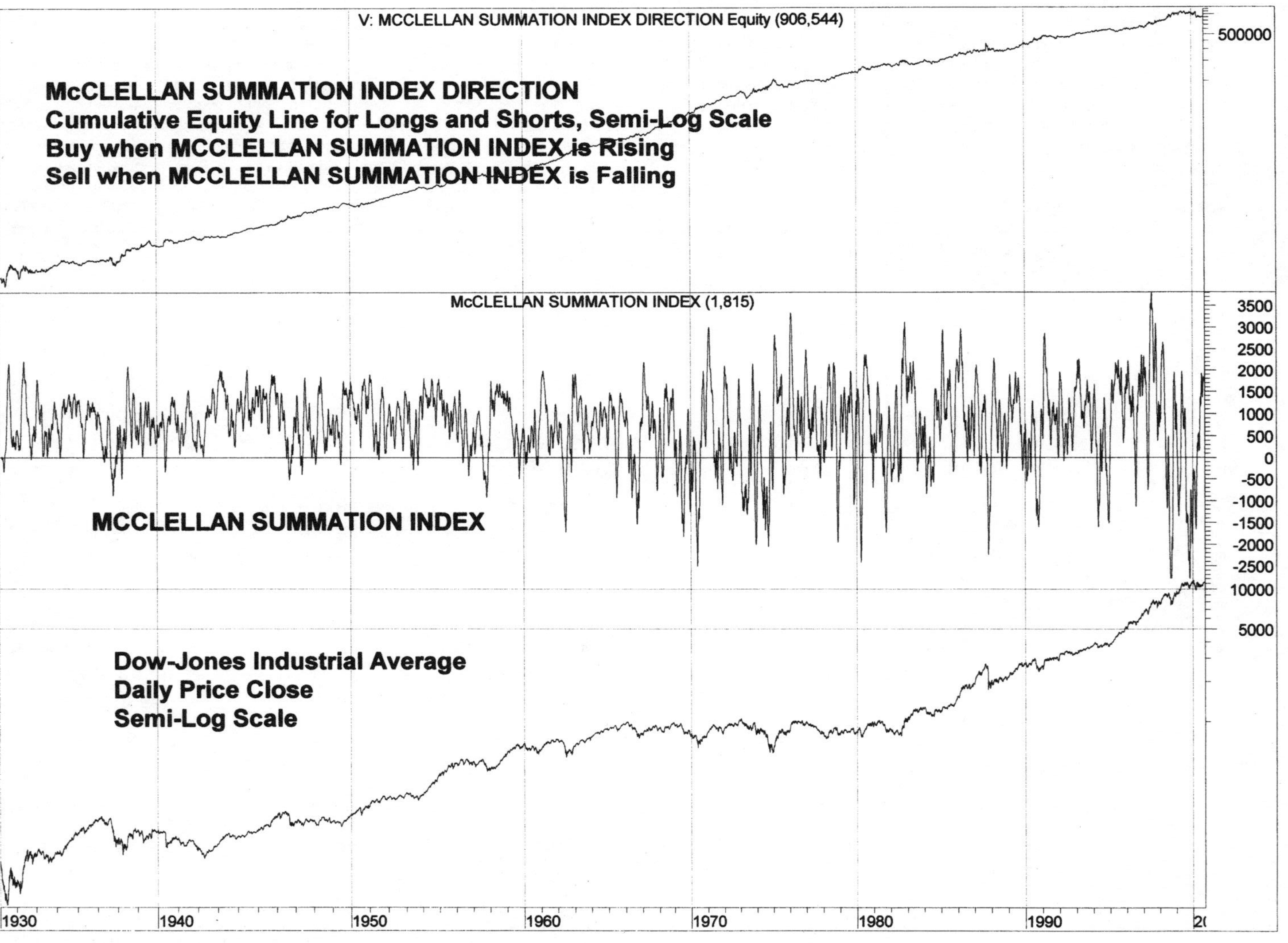

V: MCCLELLAN SUMMATION INDEX DIRECTION Equity (906,544)
500000
McCLELLAN SUMMATION INDEX DIRECTION
Cumulative Equity Line for Longs and Shorts, Semi-Log Scale
Buy when MCCLELLAN SUMMATION INDEX is Rising
Sell when MCCLELLAN SUMMATION INDEX is Falling
McCLELLAN SUMMATION INDEX (1,815)
3500
3000
2500
2000
1500
1000
500
0
-500
-1000
-1500
-2000
-2500
MCCLELLAN SUMMATION INDEX
10000
5000
Dow-Jones Industrial Average
Daily Price Close
Semi-Log Scale
1930
1940
1950
1960
1970
1980
1990

McClellan Summation Index Direction, Long and Short

Total net profit	906443.88	Open position value	−1470.45	Net Profit / Buy&Hold %	7129.19
Percent gain/loss	906443.87	Annual percent gain/loss	13222.44	Annual Net % / B&H %	7129.33
Initial investment	100	Interest earned	0		
Current position	Long	Date position entered	9/1/00		
Buy/Hold profit	12538.66	Days in test	25022	# of days per trade	11.82
Buy/Hold pct gain/loss	12538.66	Annual B/H pct gain/loss	182.9		
Total closed trades	2117	Commissions paid	0		
Avg profit per trade	428.87	Avg Win/Avg Loss ratio	2.06		
Total long trades	1058	Total short trades	1059	Long Win Trade %	47.45
Winning long trades	502	Winning short trades	368	Short Win Trade %	34.75
Total winning trades	870	Total losing trades	1247	Total Win Trade %	41.10
Amount of winning trades	2995385.5	Amount of losing trades	−2087471.8	Net Profit Margin %	17.86
Average win	3442.97	Average loss	−1673.99	Average P. Margin %	34.57
Largest win	118663.75	Largest loss	−53814.63	% Net / (Win + Loss)	37.60
Average length of win	15.1	Average length of loss	5.64	(Win − Loss) / Loss %	167.73
Longest winning trade	58	Longest losing trade	39	(Win − Loss) / Loss %	48.72
Most consecutive wins	7	Most consecutive losses	10	(Win − Loss) / Loss %	−30.00
Total bars out	40	Average length out	40		
Longest out period	40				
System close drawdown	−20.84	Profit/Loss index	30.28	% Net Profit / SODD	3421834.20
System open drawdown	−26.49	Reward/Risk index	100	(Net P.-SODD)/Net P.	100.00
Max open trade drawdown	−53814.63	Buy/Hold index	7117.47	% SODD / Net Profit	0.00

In the Equis MetaStock® "System Report" (profit and loss summary statistics), the *Total net profit* is the sum of profits minus the sum of losses, including open positions marked to the market. In contrast, the *Amount of Winning Trades* is the sum of realized profits (the total of all gains on closed-out trades only, excluding any open positions). Similarly, the *Amount of Losing Trades* is the sum of realized losses (the total of all losses on closed-out trades only, excluding any open positions). *System close drawdown* is the largest decline in the cumulative equity line below the initial investment, based on closed-out positions only. *System open drawdown (SODD)* is the largest decline in the cumulative equity line below the initial investment when a position is open. *Max open trade drawdown* is the largest decline in the cumulative equity line below the trade entry price during the worst single trade. The *Profit/Loss Index* is a complex calculation that relates the Amount of Winning Trades to the Amount of Losing Trades on a scale of −100 (worst possible performance) to +100 (best possible performance), with zero representing profits equal to losses. *Reward/Risk Index* is the Total net profit minus System open drawdown. The resulting difference is then divided by the Total net profit. The *Buy/Hold Index* is the Total net profit minus the buy-and-hold strategy's net profit. The resulting difference is then divided by the buy-and-hold net profit. In this exercise, initial equity is assumed to be $100. Both long and short positions are taken unless otherwise noted. Trades are executed at the closing price on the signal date. Transaction costs, interest expenses, and margins are not included in the statistics.

The Equis International MetaStock® System Testing rules, where the McClellan Summation Index is inserted into the data field normally reserved for Volume (V), are written as follows:

Enter long: Cum((Mov(V,opt1,E))-(Mov(V,opt2,E)))>Ref(Cum((Mov(V,opt1,E))- (Mov(V,opt2,E))),-1)

Close long: Cum((Mov(V,opt1,E))-(Mov(V,opt2,E)))<Ref(Cum((Mov(V,opt1,E))- (Mov(V,opt2,E))),-1)

Enter short: Cum((Mov(V,opt1,E))-(Mov(V,opt2,E)))<Ref(Cum((Mov(V,opt1,E))- (Mov(V,opt2,E))),-1)

Close short: Cum((Mov(V,opt1,E))-(Mov(V,opt2,E)))>Ref(Cum((Mov(V,opt1,E))- (Mov(V,opt2,E))),-1)

OPT1 Current value: 19

OPT2 Current value: 39

Meander

Meander uses the Typical Price in place of the closing price in Bollinger Bands overbought/oversold analysis. *(See Bollinger Bands.)* The Typical Price is calculated by adding the high, low, and closing prices together, and then dividing by three. The result is thought to be a rough estimate of the average or typical price for the period. The Typical Price may be used with many indicators in the place of the closing price. Any advantage of doing so is not apparent in out testing, however.

Member/Odd Lot Index

Arthur A. Merrill, CMT, compares the behavior of savvy professional traders to the little guy, the small-timer who can only afford to place orders of less than a round-lot of 100 shares.

Starting with the raw weekly data published in *Barron's,* in a complex series of basically simple calculations, Merrill manipulates the raw data to produce a smoothed ratio. Merrill's sentiment indicator may be calculated and interpreted in 9 steps.

1. Multiply member purchases by odd lot sales.
2. Multiply that product (from Step 1) by 100. Save this product for Step 6.
3. Add odd lot purchases to odd lot sales.
4. Subtract that sum (from Step 3) from member sales.
5. Multiply that difference (from Step 4) by odd lot purchases.
6. Divide that product (from Step 5) into the previous product (from Step 2).
7. Calculate a 5-period exponential moving average of that ratio (from Step 6).

8. Calculate plus and minus 67% of one standard deviation of the smoothed ratios (from Step 7). These should contain the middle quartiles, approximately.
9. Interpret these 5-week exponentially smoothed ratios (from Step 7) relative to their upper and lower 67% of one standard deviation bands (from Step 8) as follows: a ratio below 67% of one standard deviation is bullish; a ratio above 67% of one standard deviation is bearish.

Using a chi-squared test of significance and a test period covering 1976 to 1982, Merrill found that this indicator correctly predicted the direction of the general market only 41% of the time over the next 26 weeks. This result was probably significant statistically. Market behavior over the next one, five, 13, and 52 weeks was insignificant, however.

Member Short Ratio

Late Friday, after the close, the NYSE releases summary statistics on the total volume of short sales. Short sales by stock exchange members are separated from short sales by nonmembers (the public). Because the absolute levels of short selling have increased in all categories along with the general expansion in the total volume of trading activity, the data must be normalized somehow—hence the various short sales ratios.

The Member Short Ratio is computed by dividing total member short sales by total short sales. In theory, members, who are usually seasoned professional traders highly experienced in the ways of the market, are generally right about the trend of stock prices. If not, they won't be able to stay in business.

When the Member Short Ratio is high, members are shorting heavily relative to the public. This indicates smart money pros are pessimistic, and this is a bearish indicator for the future trend of stock prices.

Similarly, a low Member Short Ratio is bullish. The smart money pros are relatively optimistic. Thus, this indicator is interpreted in a manner similar to an Overbought/Oversold Oscillator.

Short Selling is an aggressive trading strategy designed to take advantage of declining prices. Speculators may *sell short* a stock when they anticipate a price decline. If the stock does drop, they may realize a profit equal to the difference between their sell-short price and the lower buy-back price. If they are wrong and the stock rises, their loss will equal the amount of the stock price appreciation, or the difference between their sell price and the higher buy-back price.

Indicator Strategy Example for Member Short Ratio

Based on a 55-year file of Member Short Ratios and weekly closing price data for the DJIA from January 1946 to December 2000, we found that the following parameters would have produced a positive result on a purely mechanical overbought/oversold

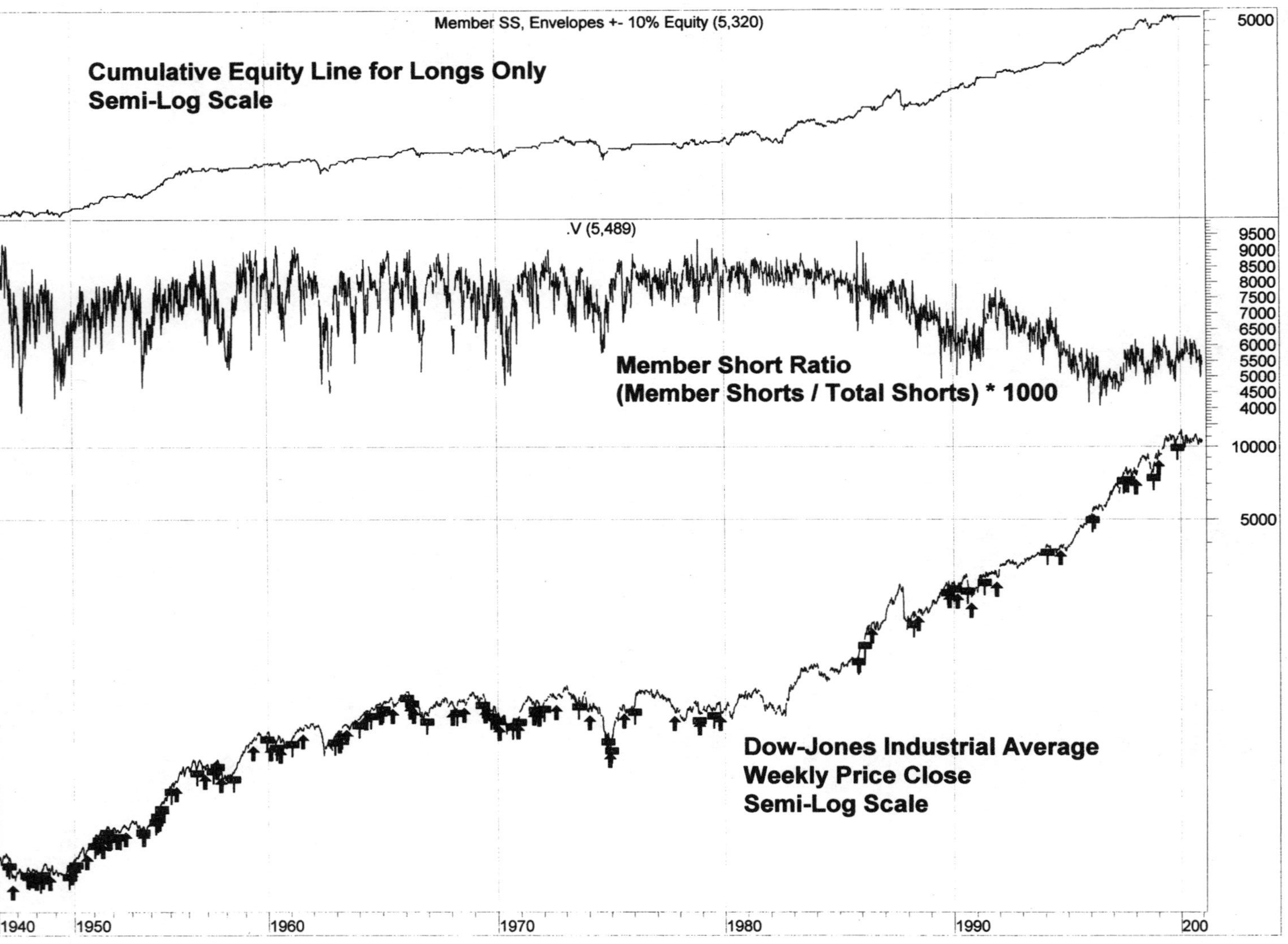
Member SS, Envelopes +- 10% Equity (5,320)
Cumulative Equity Line for Longs Only
Semi-Log Scale
5000
.V (5,489)
9500
9000
8500
8000
7500
7000
6500
6000
5500
5000
4500
4000
Member Short Ratio
(Member Shorts / Total Shorts) * 1000
10000
5000
Dow-Jones Industrial Average
Weekly Price Close
Semi-Log Scale
1940
1950
1960
1970
1980
1990
200

Member Short Ratio (Envelope)

Total net profit	5220.29	Open position value	N/A	Net Profit / Buy&Hold %	0.05
Percent gain/loss	5220.29	Annual percent gain/loss	94.94	Annual Net % / B&H %	0.05
Initial investment	100	Interest earned	0		
Current position	Out	Date position entered	11/12/99		
Buy/Hold profit	5217.78	Days in test	20070	# of days per trade	329.02
Buy/Hold pct gain/loss	5217.78	Annual B/H pct gain/loss	94.89		
Total closed trades	61	Commissions paid	0		
Avg profit per trade	85.58	Avg Win/Avg Loss ratio	7.16		
Total long trades	61	Total short trades	0	Long Win Trade %	80.33
Winning long trades	49	Winning short trades	0	Short Win Trade %	#DIV/0!
Total winning trades	49	Total losing trades	12	Total Win Trade %	80.33
Amount of winning trades	5405.12	Amount of losing trades	−184.83	Net Profit Margin %	93.39
Average win	110.31	Average loss	−15.4	Average P. Margin %	75.50
Largest win	1143.88	Largest loss	−92.57	% Net / (Win + Loss)	85.03
Average length of win	34.37	Average length of loss	22.33	(Win − Loss) / Loss %	53.92
Longest winning trade	317	Longest losing trade	74	(Win − Loss) / Loss %	328.38
Most consecutive wins	14	Most consecutive losses	3	(Win − Loss) / Loss %	366.67
Total bars out	1038	Average length out	16.74		
Longest out period	93				
System close drawdown	−0.69	Profit/Loss index	96.58	% Net Profit / SODD	141088.92
System open drawdown	−3.7	Reward/Risk index	99.93	(Net P.-SODD)/Net P.	99.93
Max open trade drawdown	−136.43	Buy/Hold index	0.05	% SODD / Net Profit	−0.07

In the Equis MetaStock® "System Report" (profit and loss summary statistics), the *Total net profit* is the sum of profits minus the sum of losses, including open positions marked to the market. In contrast, the *Amount of Winning Trades* is the sum of realized profits (the total of all gains on closed-out trades only, excluding any open positions). Similarly, the *Amount of Losing Trades* is the sum of realized losses (the total of all losses on closed-out trades only, excluding any open positions). *System close drawdown* is the largest decline in the cumulative equity line below the initial investment, based on closed-out positions only. *System open drawdown (SODD)* is the largest decline in the cumulative equity line below the initial investment when a position is open. *Max open trade drawdown* is the largest decline in the cumulative equity line below the trade entry price during the worst single trade. The *Profit/Loss Index* is a complex calculation that relates the Amount of Winning Trades to the Amount of Losing Trades on a scale of −100 (worst possible performance) to +100 (best possible performance), with zero representing profits equal to losses. *Reward/Risk Index* is the Total net profit minus System open drawdown. The resulting difference is then divided by the Total net profit. The *Buy/Hold Index* is the Total net profit minus the buy-and-hold strategy's net profit. The resulting difference is then divided by the buy-and-hold net profit. In this exercise, initial equity is assumed to be $100. Both long and short positions are taken unless otherwise noted. Trades are executed at the closing price on the signal date. Transaction costs, interest expenses, and margins are not included in the statistics.

signal basis with no subjectivity, no sophisticated technical analysis, and no judgement:

Enter Long (Buy) at the current weekly price close of the DJIA when the latest Member Short Ratio is less than 90% of its previous week's 3-week exponential moving average of the Member Short Ratio.

Close Long (Sell) at the current weekly price close of the DJIA when the latest Member Short Ratio is greater than 110% of its previous week's 25-week exponential moving average of the Member Short Ratio.

Enter Short (Sell Short) never.

Starting with $100 and reinvesting profits, total net profits for this Member Short Ratio counter-trend strategy would have been $5,220.29, assuming a fully invested strategy, reinvestment of profits, no transactions costs and no taxes. This would have been 0.05 percent greater than buy-and-hold. No short selling would have been profitable, and no short selling was included in the strategy. Short selling would have cut the profit by 90%. Long-only Member Short Ratio as an indicator would have given profitable buy signals 80.33% of the time. Trading would have been inactive at one trade every 329.02 calendar days. Note that this strategy considers weekend closing prices only while ignoring everything in between.

The Equis International MetaStock® System Testing rules for Member Short Ratio, where the ratio of Member Short Sales to Total Short Sales is inserted into the field normally reserved for volume, are written as follows:

Enter long: V < .9*Ref(Mov(V ,opt1,E),-1)

Close long: V > 1.1*Ref(Mov(V ,opt2,E),-1)

OPT1 Current value: 3
OPT2 Current value: 25

Momentum

Momentum measures the amount that a price has changed over a given time span. It is essentially the same indicator as *Rate-of-Change (ROC)*. Momentum can be defined as a difference or a ratio, with the ratio method much preferable in order to maintain comparability over time. The ratio method of calculating momentum can be expressed as follows:

$$\text{Momentum} = (C / Cn)\ 100$$

where C is the most recent closing price, and C*n* is the closing price *n* periods ago.

In the Equis MetaStock® Indicator Builder syntax, the popular 10-period momentum is represented as:

$$\text{Momentum} = (\text{C/Ref(C,-10)})100$$

where C is the most recent closing price, and Ref(C,-10) is the closing price 10 periods ago.

This formula produces a momentum ratio that fluctuates around 100.00. (Some analysts seem to prefer to subtract 100 so that the indicator fluctuates around zero.)

Momentum indicators are subject to irrelevant random noise when data outliers suddenly drop out of the moving time window on which the calculations are based, and for this reason we prefer other formulations of the same basic concept.

Trend followers buy when the momentum indicator:

- bottoms and turns up,
- crosses above some absolute threshold,
- crosses above some moving average of itself,
- shows some positive divergence relative to price.

Sell when the opposite conditions apply.

If the momentum indicator reaches extremely high or low values (relative to its historical values), it may imply a continuation of the current trend. For example, if the momentum indicator reaches extremely high levels that means the price trend is unusually strong and, therefore, price could trend still higher.

Divergences between momentum and price can be a leading indicator. As prices enter an important Top Reversal Pattern, or distribution phase, momentum begins to deteriorate as the advance slows. Similarly, at a market bottom, momentum often stabilizes before price.

The basic momentum concept is central to technical analysis. The velocity of price movement is a leading indicator of a change in trend direction. Momentum precedes price. In a typical major market cycle, price begins a new uptrend with very high and rising momentum. This positive velocity gradually diminishes as prices become fully valued, as buyers back away somewhat, and as sellers increase the supply of stock offered. The slope of the price advance lessens. Almost invariably, momentum hits its peak well before the price hits its ultimate high. Momentum tapers off further as price begins to make little further upward progress on rally attempts. Momentum decreases more dramatically as price rallies begin to fall short of previous peaks on minor rally attempts, depicting a very mature phase of bullish exhaustion. Suddenly, momentum breaks sharply into negative territory as price drops below previous minor lows, giving sell signals to chart readers. A new Bear Market (the downward phase of the full cycle) has begun. Eventually, after a long decline, price velocity typically bottoms out before price hits its ultimate low. When long margin accounts are liquidated and prices become cheap, or excessively undervalued, new buyers are attracted to tentatively bid for stocks in an atmosphere where sellers are already exhausted. As downward momentum becomes less negative on subsequent minor price declines, and as the negative rate of price change diminishes, the stage is set for a new upward cycle, which is clearly signaled when price breaks out to the upside of a chart bottom pattern on the best momentum seen since the last Bull Market. (See *Rate-of-Change (ROC)* for an Indicator Strategy Example.)

Money Flow (Chaikin's)

(See Volume Accumulation Oscillator, Volume Accumulation Trend.)

Months of the Year: Significant Seasonal Tendencies to Rise or Fall

Arthur A. Merrill, CMT, found that not all months of the year have been equally rewarding, and he proved it in his classic book, *Behavior of Prices on Wall Street, Second Edition,* The Analysis Press, Chappaqua, New York, 1984, 147 pages.

Using the calendar and price changes for the DJIA, he counted the number of times the market rose or fell for each month of the year over an 87-year period, from 1897 to 1983.

Eight of the 12 months saw higher stock prices most of the time. The market rose 55.5% of the time in the average month.

The best months were December (rising 68% of the time), August (rising 67% of the time), and January (rising 64.3% of the time). November, July, March, and April were strong, in that order, rising 58.8% to 57.1% of the time. October was below average, up only 51.6% of the time.

The worst months were September (rising 44.3% of the time), June (rising 44.9% of the time), February (rising 46.9% of the time), and May (rising 48.0% of the time).

We duplicated and updated Merrill's study using 101 years of month-end closing prices for the DJIA, from 1900 through 2000. Our findings closely match Merrill's. For the frequency of winning months of the year, the top three months are still December, August and January. The worst months are still September, February, May and June.

There have been some small shifts since Merrill's study 17 years ago. Thanks to the great bullish stock market uptrend over that time period, our most recent data shows that over the past century the average month rose 56.6% of the time, up from 55.5% in Merrill's study. December, the strongest month, is even stronger. Strong July, March and November have also gained further strength. June and May are still below average, but they are not as bad as they once were.

September, the worst month, has become even worse, rising only 42% of the time over the past century. April, though still up 53.5% of the time, has slipped from slightly above-average to slightly below average.

Our table offers additional insights. In terms of the *magnitude* of price movement, December, July, January, August, April, March, November and June showed the best gains. September, May, October and February showed the worst losses. Fortunately, *magnitude* is in harmony with *frequency,* and that adds to our confidence in our findings.

101 Years of Monthly Performance for the Dow-Jones Industrial Average, 1900 through 2000

Month of the Year	*Month of the Year*	*Percentage Gain (−Loss)*	*Total # of Trades*	*Winning Trades*	*Losing Trades*	*Win % of # Total*	*Ratio Avg $ Win / Avg $ Loss*
1	January	181.75	100	64	36	64.00%	1.09
2	February	−16.02	100	50	50	50.00%	0.88
3	March	93.93	101	61	40	60.40%	0.93
4	April	134.67	101	54	47	53.47%	1.53
5	May	−24.89	101	51	50	50.50%	0.83
6	June	38.96	101	51	50	50.50%	1.19
7	July	267.90	101	61	40	60.40%	1.26
8	August	151.98	101	64	37	63.37%	0.81
9	September	−67.58	100	42	58	42.00%	0.77
10	October	−16.64	100	52	48	52.00%	0.84
11	November	91.24	100	60	40	60.00%	0.91
12	December	326.80	100	72	28	72.00%	1.32
Average		96.84	101	57	44	56.55%	1.03

20 Years of Monthly Performance for the Dow-Jones Industrial Average, 1981 through 2000

Month of the Year	*Month of the Year*	*Percentage Gain (−Loss)*	*Total # of Trades*	*Winning Trades*	*Losing Trades*	*Win % of # Total*	*Ratio Avg $ Win / Avg $ Loss*
1	January	49.24	20	14	6	70.00%	1.46
2	February	23.12	20	13	7	65.00%	0.95
3	March	31.55	20	14	6	70.00%	1.17
4	April	46	20	11	9	55.00%	4.30
5	May	24.84	20	12	8	60.00%	1.54
6	June	14.48	20	12	8	60.00%	1.26
7	July	20.61	20	11	9	55.00%	1.67
8	August	−2.4	20	12	8	60.00%	0.64
9	September	−15.26	20	7	13	35.00%	1.04
10	October	9.18	20	12	8	60.00%	0.82
11	November	36.13	20	14	6	70.00%	0.91
12	December	49.64	20	15	5	75.00%	3.31
Average		23.93	20	12	8	61.25%	1.59

Indicator Strategy Example for the Months of the Year

The table suggests that September may be the worst month to be long stocks. Indeed, historical data shows that a strategy based on this insight alone can produce positive results, on both the long side and the short side. Based on the month-end closing prices for the DJIA for the past 100 years, we found that the following parameters would have produced a positive result on a purely mechanical trend-following signal basis with no subjectivity, no sophisticated technical analysis, and no judgement:

Enter Long (Buy) at the month end price close of the DJIA every year on the last trading day of September.

Close Long (Sell) at the month end price close of the DJIA every year on the last trading day of August.

Enter Short (Sell Short) at the month end price close of the DJIA every year on the last trading day of August.

Close Short (Cover) at the month end price close of the DJIA every year on the last trading day of September.

Starting with $100 and reinvesting profits, total net profits, long and short, for this seasonal strategy would have been $164,048.25, assuming a fully invested strategy, reinvestment of profits, no transactions costs and no taxes. This would have been 643.83 percent greater than buy-and-hold. About 60.30 percent of the 199 signals would have produced winning trades. Even short selling, which was included in this strategy, would have been made money.

The Equis International MetaStock® System Testing rules are written as follows:

Enter long: Month()=opt1

Close long: Month()=opt2

Enter short: Month()=opt2

Close short: Month()=opt1

OPT1 Current value: 9
OPT2 Current value: 8

Indicator Strategy Example for the Months and Days of the Year

A more complex strategy considering both months of the year and specific days of the month would have produced a more positive result on a purely mechanical trend-following signal basis with no subjectivity, no sophisticated technical analysis, and no judgement:

Enter Long (Buy) at the current daily price close of the DJIA every year on October 27th, or on the next trading session if the market is closed on October 27th.

Close Long (Sell) at the current daily price close of the DJIA every year on September 5th, or on the next trading session if the market is closed on September 5th.

Enter Short (Sell Short) at the current daily price close of the DJIA every year on September 5th, or on the next trading session if the market is closed on September 5th.

Close Short (Cover) at the current daily price close of the DJIA every year on October 27th, or on the next trading session if the market is closed on October 27th.

Starting with $100 and reinvesting profits, total net profits, long and short, for this seasonal strategy would have been $644,466.56, assuming a fully invested strategy, reinvestment of profits, no transactions costs and no taxes. This would have been 3,013.58 percent greater than buy-and-hold. About 61.81 percent of the 199 signals would have produced winning trades. Even short selling, which was included in this strategy, would have made money during the great bull market since 1982.

The Equis International MetaStock® System Testing rules are written as follows:

Enter long: (Month()=opt1 AND DayOfMonth()=(opt2+0)) OR
(Month()=opt1 AND DayOfMonth()=(opt2+1)) OR
(Month()=opt1 AND DayOfMonth()=(opt2+2)) OR
(Month()=opt1 AND DayOfMonth()=(opt2+3)) OR
(Month()=opt1 AND DayOfMonth()=(opt2+4))

Close long: (Month()=opt3 AND DayOfMonth()=(opt4+0)) OR
(Month()=opt3 AND DayOfMonth()=(opt4+1)) OR
(Month()=opt3 AND DayOfMonth()=(opt4+2)) OR
(Month()=opt3 AND DayOfMonth()=(opt4+3)) OR
(Month()=opt3 AND DayOfMonth()=(opt4+4))

Enter short: (Month()=opt3 AND DayOfMonth()=(opt4+0)) OR
(Month()=opt3 AND DayOfMonth()=(opt4+1)) OR
(Month()=opt3 AND DayOfMonth()=(opt4+2)) OR
(Month()=opt3 AND DayOfMonth()=(opt4+3)) OR
(Month()=opt3 AND DayOfMonth()=(opt4+4))

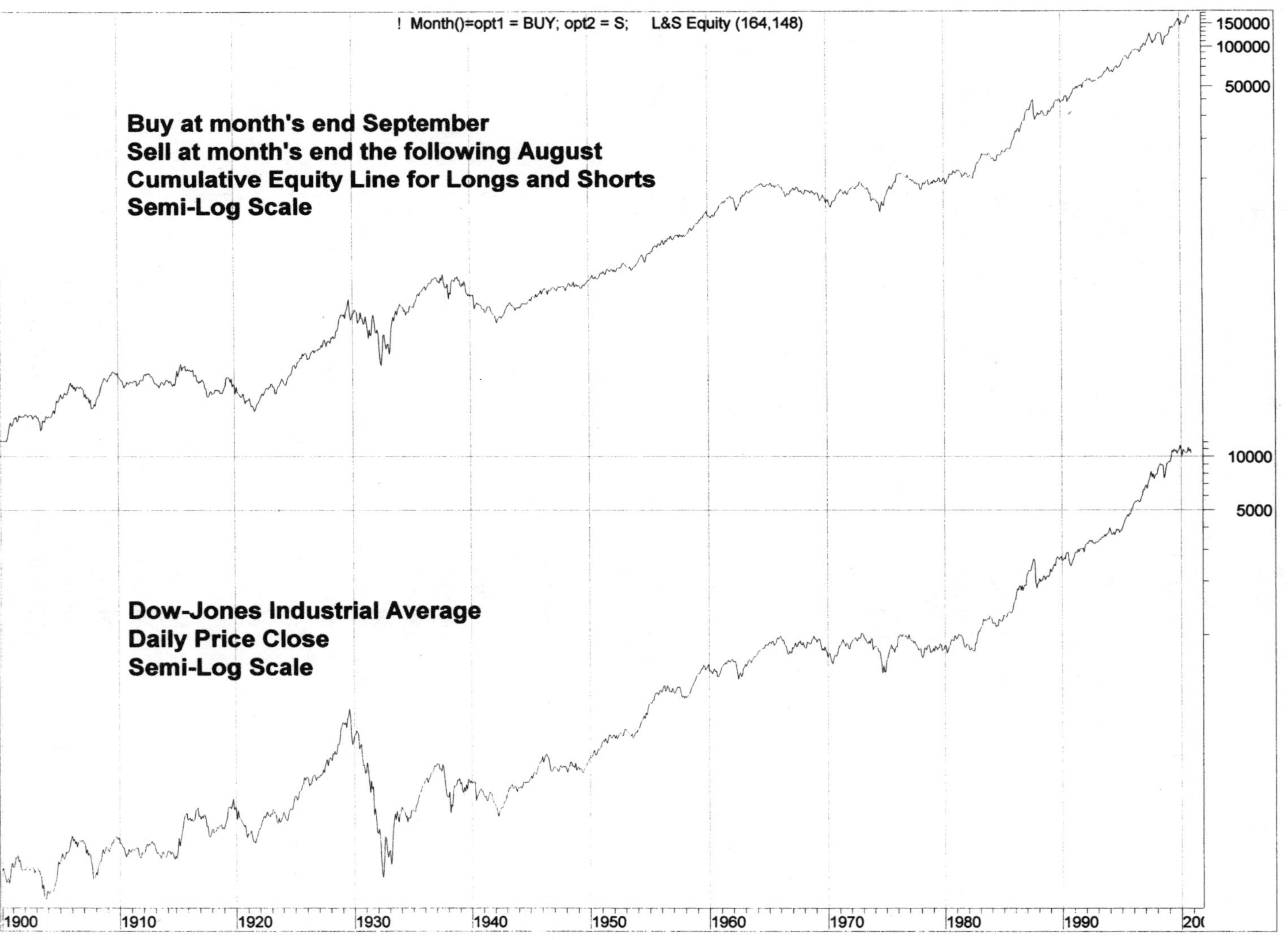
! Month()=opt1 = BUY; opt2 = S;
L&S Equity (164,148)
Buy at month's end September
Sell at month's end the following August
Cumulative Equity Line for Longs and Shorts
Semi-Log Scale
Dow-Jones Industrial Average
Daily Price Close
Semi-Log Scale
150000
100000
50000
10000
5000
1900
1910
1920
1930
1940
1950
1960
1970
1980
1990

Buy Last Day of September, Sell Next August on the Last Day

Total net profit	164048.25	Open position value	−3971.4	Net Profit / Buy&Hold %	643.83
Percent gain/loss	164048.25	Annual percent gain/loss	1627.42	Annual Net % / B&H %	643.83
Initial investment	100	Interest earned	0		
Current position	Long	Date position entered	9/29/00		
Buy/Hold profit	22054.45	Days in test	36793	# of days per trade	184.89
Buy/Hold pct gain/loss	22054.45	Annual B/H pct gain/loss	218.79		
Total closed trades	199	Commissions paid	0		
Avg profit per trade	844.32	Avg Win/Avg Loss ratio	2.95		
Total long trades	99	Total short trades	100	Long Win Trade %	64.65
Winning long trades	64	Winning short trades	56	Short Win Trade %	56.00
Total winning trades	120	Total losing trades	79	Total Win Trade %	60.30
Amount of winning trades	216326.58	Amount of losing trades	−48306.93	Net Profit Margin %	63.49
Average win	1802.72	Average loss	−611.48	Average P. Margin %	49.34
Largest win	38920.14	Largest loss	−8665.91	% Net / (Win + Loss)	63.58
Average length of win	7.4	Average length of loss	6.43	(Win − Loss) / Loss %	15.09
Longest winning trade	20	Longest losing trade	12	(Win − Loss) / Loss %	66.67
Most consecutive wins	7	Most consecutive losses	7	(Win − Loss) / Loss %	0.00
Total bars out	7	Average length out	7		
Longest out period	7				
System close drawdown	0	Profit/Loss index	77.25	% Net Profit / SODD	#DIV/0!
System open drawdown	0	Reward/Risk index	100	(Net P.-SODD)/Net P.	100.00
Max open trade drawdown	−11708.19	Buy/Hold index	625.83	% SODD / Net Profit	0.00

In the Equis MetaStock® "System Report" (profit and loss summary statistics), the *Total net profit* is the sum of profits minus the sum of losses, including open positions marked to the market. In contrast, the *Amount of Winning Trades* is the sum of realized profits (the total of all gains on closed-out trades only, excluding any open positions). Similarly, the *Amount of Losing Trades* is the sum of realized losses (the total of all losses on closed-out trades only, excluding any open positions). *System close drawdown* is the largest decline in the cumulative equity line below the initial investment, based on closed-out positions only. *System open drawdown (SODD)* is the largest decline in the cumulative equity line below the initial investment when a position is open. *Max open trade drawdown* is the largest decline in the cumulative equity line below the trade entry price during the worst single trade. The *Profit/Loss Index* is a complex calculation that relates the Amount of Winning Trades to the Amount of Losing Trades on a scale of −100 (worst possible performance) to +100 (best possible performance), with zero representing profits equal to losses. *Reward/Risk Index* is the Total net profit minus System open drawdown. The resulting difference is then divided by the Total net profit. The *Buy/Hold Index* is the Total net profit minus the buy-and-hold strategy's net profit. The resulting difference is then divided by the buy-and-hold net profit. In this exercise, initial equity is assumed to be $100. Both long and short positions are taken unless otherwise noted. Trades are executed at the closing price on the signal date. Transaction costs, interest expenses, and margins are not included in the statistics.

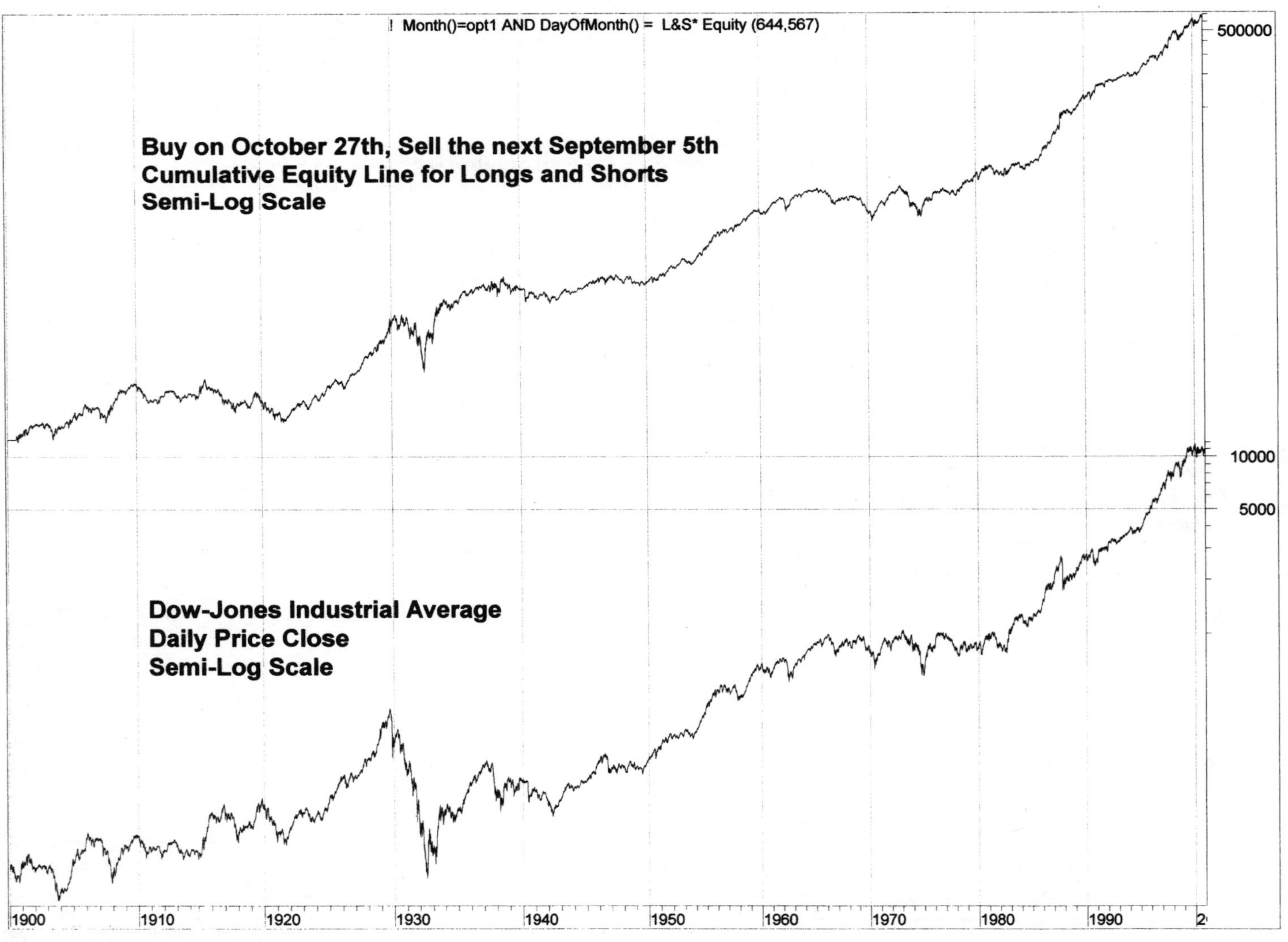
! Month()=opt1 AND DayOfMonth() = L&S* Equity (644,567)
Buy on October 27th, Sell the next September 5th
Cumulative Equity Line for Longs and Shorts
Semi-Log Scale
Dow-Jones Industrial Average
Daily Price Close
Semi-Log Scale
500000
10000
5000
1900
1910
1920
1930
1940
1950
1960
1970
1980
1990
2

Buy October 27th, Sell September 5th

Total net profit	644466.56	Open position value	−11857.09	Net Profit / Buy&Hold %	3013.58
Percent gain/loss	644466.56	Annual percent gain/loss	6383.45	Annual Net % / B&H %	3013.57
Initial investment	100	Interest earned	0		
Current position	Long	Date position entered	10/27/00		
Buy/Hold profit	20698.6	Days in test	36850	# of days per trade	185.18
Buy/Hold pct gain/loss	20698.6	Annual B/H pct gain/loss	205.02		
Total closed trades	199	Commissions paid	0		
Avg profit per trade	3298.11	Avg Win/Avg Loss ratio	5.47		
Total long trades	99	Total short trades	100	Long Win Trade %	67.68
Winning long trades	67	Winning short trades	56	Short Win Trade %	56.00
Total winning trades	123	Total losing trades	76	Total Win Trade %	61.81
Amount of winning trades	739821.5	Amount of losing trades	−83497.89	Net Profit Margin %	79.72
Average win	6014.81	Average loss	−1098.66	Average P. Margin %	69.11
Largest win	130720.66	Largest loss	−18789.31	% Net / (Win + Loss)	74.87
Average length of win	147.6	Average length of loss	124.91	(Win − Loss) / Loss %	18.17
Longest winning trade	450	Longest losing trade	264	(Win − Loss) / Loss %	70.45
Most consecutive wins	7	Most consecutive losses	4	(Win − Loss) / Loss %	75.00
Total bars out	204	Average length out	204		
Longest out period	204				
System close drawdown	−2.56	Profit/Loss index	88.53	% Net Profit / SODD	15199683.02
System open drawdown	−4.24	Reward/Risk index	100	(Net P.-SODD)/Net P.	100.00
Max open trade drawdown	−32949.94	Buy/Hold index	2956.29	% SODD / Net Profit	0.00

In the Equis MetaStock® "System Report" (profit and loss summary statistics), the *Total net profit* is the sum of profits minus the sum of losses, including open positions marked to the market. In contrast, the *Amount of Winning Trades* is the sum of realized profits (the total of all gains on closed-out trades only, excluding any open positions). Similarly, the *Amount of Losing Trades* is the sum of realized losses (the total of all losses on closed-out trades only, excluding any open positions). *System close drawdown* is the largest decline in the cumulative equity line below the initial investment, based on closed-out positions only. *System open drawdown (SODD)* is the largest decline in the cumulative equity line below the initial investment when a position is open. *Max open trade drawdown* is the largest decline in the cumulative equity line below the trade entry price during the worst single trade. The *Profit/Loss Index* is a complex calculation that relates the Amount of Winning Trades to the Amount of Losing Trades on a scale of −100 (worst possible performance) to +100 (best possible performance), with zero representing profits equal to losses. *Reward/Risk Index* is the Total net profit minus System open drawdown. The resulting difference is then divided by the Total net profit. The *Buy/Hold Index* is the Total net profit minus the buy-and-hold strategy's net profit. The resulting difference is then divided by the buy-and-hold net profit. In this exercise, initial equity is assumed to be $100. Both long and short positions are taken unless otherwise noted. Trades are executed at the closing price on the signal date. Transaction costs, interest expenses, and margins are not included in the statistics.

Close short: (Month()=opt1 AND DayOfMonth()=(opt2+0)) OR
(Month()=opt1 AND DayOfMonth()=(opt2+1)) OR
(Month()=opt1 AND DayOfMonth()=(opt2+2)) OR
(Month()=opt1 AND DayOfMonth()=(opt2+3)) OR
(Month()=opt1 AND DayOfMonth()=(opt2+4))

OPT1 Current value: 10
OPT2 Current value: 27
OPT3 Current value: 9
OPT4 Current value: 5

Most Active Stocks

The most actively traded stocks show where active traders focus their attention. There have been many versions of the basic concept over the decades. Ned Davis Research has developed a version that would have been highly accurate and would have outperformed the market substantially on the long side. It is calculated and interpreted in eight steps.

1. Using daily data for the NYSE 15 most actively traded stocks, count the net number of advances minus declines each day, (the number that rose minus the number that fell). Note that when a greater number of stocks decline than advance, the net is a negative number, and we retain that negative sign.
2. Using daily data for the ASE 10 most actively traded stocks, count a similar net number of most active advances minus declines each day.
3. Add the daily nets of the NYSE and ASE.
4. Calculate a 10-day moving total of the combined NYSE and ASE total.
5. Draw two standard deviation brackets *(see Bollinger Bands),* one above and one below this 10-day moving total.
6. Buy when the 10-day moving total crosses the lower bracket from below to above, thus, moving out of the oversold zone.
7. Sell when the 10-day moving total crosses the upper bracket from above to below, thus, moving out of the overbought zone.
8. Add a protective stop-loss: sell when the New York Stock Exchange Composite Stock Price Index falls 6% below its level at the time of the latest buy signal.

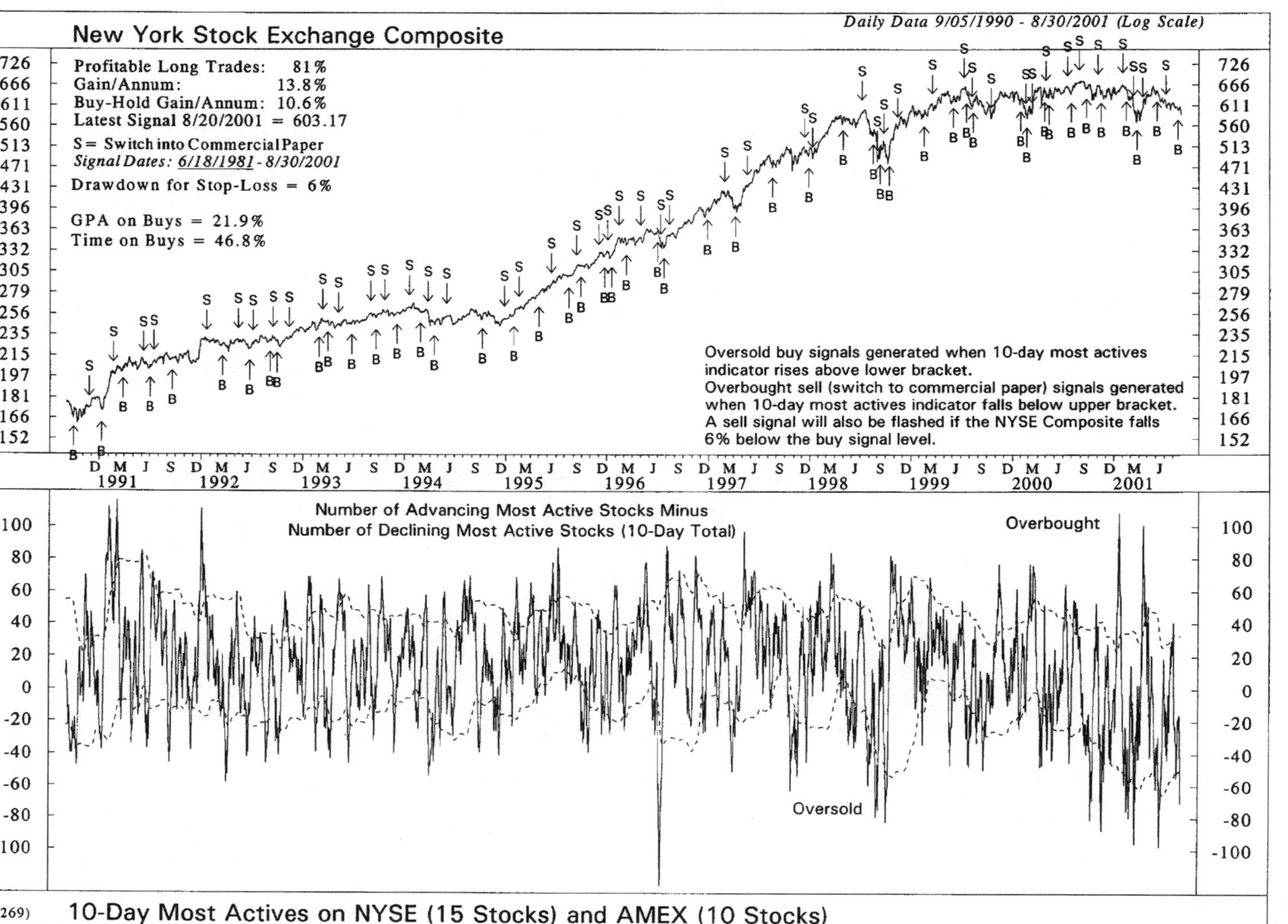
New York Stock Exchange Composite
Daily Data 9/05/1990 - 8/30/2001 (Log Scale)
Profitable Long Trades: 81%
Gain/Annum: 13.8%
Buy-Hold Gain/Annum: 10.6%
Latest Signal 8/20/2001 = 603.17
S= Switch into Commercial Paper
Signal Dates: 6/18/1981 - 8/30/2001
Drawdown for Stop-Loss = 6%
GPA on Buys = 21.9%
Time on Buys = 46.8%
Oversold buy signals generated when 10-day most actives indicator rises above lower bracket.
Overbought sell (switch to commercial paper) signals generated when 10-day most actives indicator falls below upper bracket.
A sell signal will also be flashed if the NYSE Composite falls 6% below the buy signal level.
Number of Advancing Most Active Stocks Minus
Number of Declining Most Active Stocks (10-Day Total)
Overbought
Oversold
(S269)
10-Day Most Actives on NYSE (15 Stocks) and AMEX (10 Stocks)

Chart by permission of Ned Davis Research.

Moving Average Convergence-Divergence Trading Method (MACD)

The Moving Average Convergence-Divergence Trading Method (MACD or MACDTM) is a price momentum oscillator developed by Gerald Appel, publisher of *Systems and Forecasts,* Signalert Corporation, 150 Great Neck Road, Great Neck, NY 11021, (516) 829-6444.

MACD is calculated in three steps:

1. Calculate the point spread difference between two Exponential Moving Averages (EMA) of the closing price: a slower, 26-day EMA (using a smoothing constant of .075) is subtracted from a faster 12-day EMA (using a smoothing constant of 0.15). Plot this differential oscillator, which measures *price velocity.*
2. Smooth this price velocity with an even faster 9-day EMA (with a smoothing constant of 0.2). Plot this *signal line.*
3. Calculate a second differential oscillator by subtracting the signal line from the price velocity. Plot this measure of *price acceleration* as a *histogram.*

Appel sometimes uses different lengths for the EMAs, depending on the behavior of the security and trading objectives, shorter or longer term. He also analyses longer-term perspectives using weekly data, based only on the closing price for the last day of each week. Appel has shown that his basic MACD concept is adaptable to any time-frame.

Appel does not advocate a simple mechanical rule for interpreting MACD. Rather, Appel has published proprietary decision rules he offers for sale in a research report and video tape.

Indicator Strategy Example for MACD

MACD requires experience and judgement to use as Appel intended. Even naïve testing assumptions suggest that MACD may have some objective potential value as a purely mechanical, trend-following technical indicator. The majority of monthly buy signals would have been profitable, for long trades only. MACD would have slightly outperformed the passive buy-and-hold strategy for long trades only, while short selling would not have been profitable.

Based on a 72-year file of month-end closing price data for the DJIA from 11/28 to 12/00, we found that the following parameters would have produced a positive result on a purely mechanical trend-following signal basis with no subjectivity, no sophisticated technical analysis, and no judgement:

Enter Long (Buy) at the current month-end price close of the DJIA when the MACD (the 12-month EMA minus the 26-month EMA) crosses above its own Signal Line (the 9-month EMA of the difference between the 12-month EMA minus the 26-month EMA).

Close Long (Sell) at the current month-end price close of the DJIA when the MACD (the 12-month EMA minus the 26-month EMA) crosses below its own Signal Line (the 9-month EMA of the difference between the 12-month EMA minus the 26-month EMA).

Enter Short (Sell Short) never.

Starting with $100 and reinvesting profits, total net profits for this MACD trend-following strategy would have been $3,586.55, assuming a fully invested strategy, reinvestment of profits, no transactions costs and no taxes. This would have been 0.99 percent greater than buy-and-hold. No short selling would have been profitable, and no short selling was included in the strategy. Short selling would have cut the profit by 84%, to much less than buy-and-hold. Long-only MACD as an indicator would have given profitable buy signals 58.62% of the time. Trading would have been extremely inactive at one trade every 907.14 calendar days. Note that this strategy considers month-end closing prices only while ignoring everything in between.

The Equis International MetaStock® System Testing rules for MACD are written as follows:

Enter long: Cross(MACD(),Mov(MACD(),opt1,E))

Close long: Cross(Mov(MACD(),opt1,E),MACD())

OPT1 Current value: 9

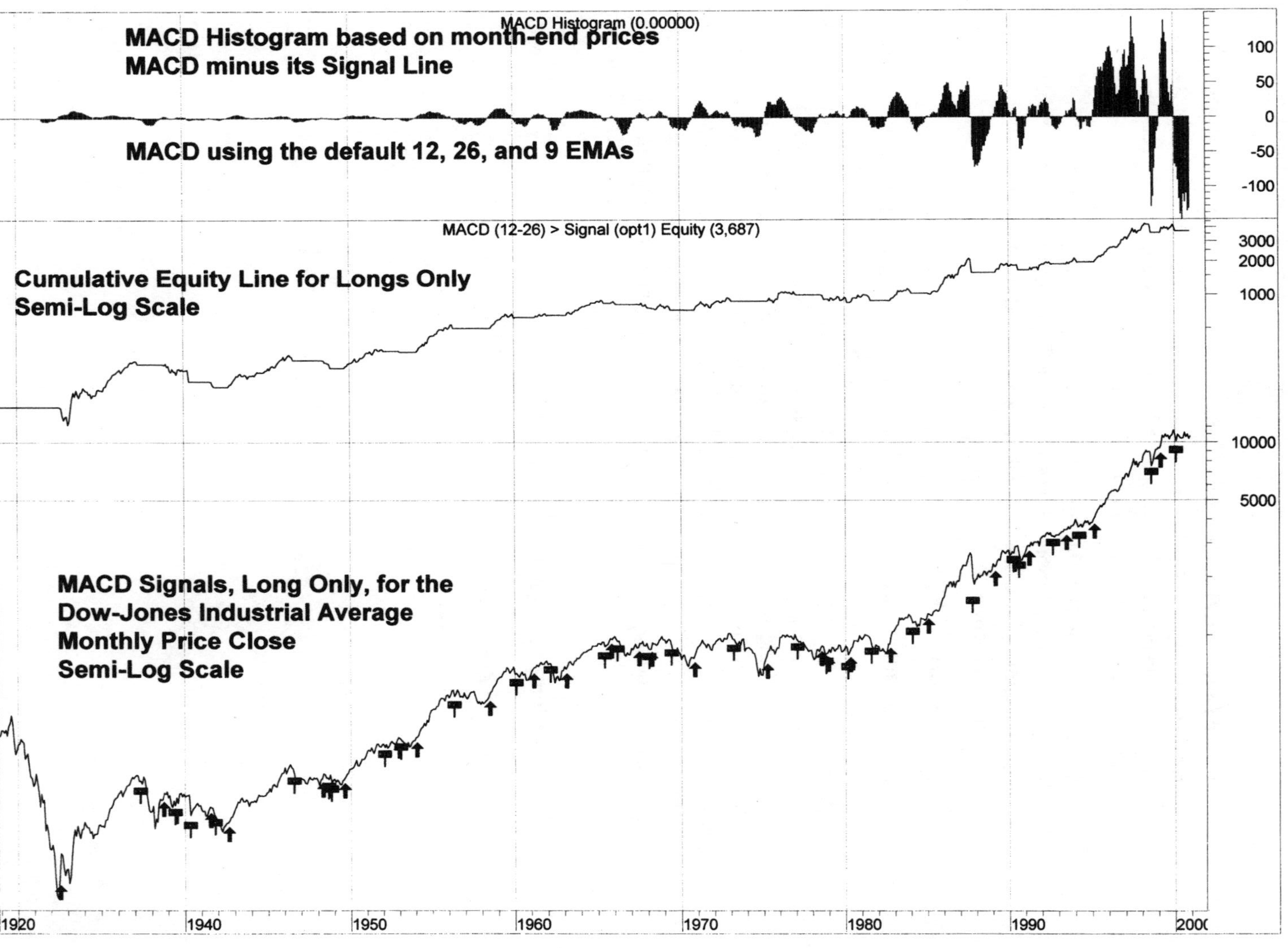

MACD Histogram (0.00000)
MACD Histogram based on month-end prices
MACD minus its Signal Line
MACD using the default 12, 26, and 9 EMAs
100
50
0
-50
-100
MACD (12-26) > Signal (opt1) Equity (3,687)
Cumulative Equity Line for Longs Only
Semi-Log Scale
3000
2000
1000
10000
5000
MACD Signals, Long Only, for the
Dow-Jones Industrial Average
Monthly Price Close
Semi-Log Scale
1920
1940
1950
1960
1970
1980
1990
2000

MACD Monthly (default EMAs: 12, 26 and 9)

Total net profit	3586.55	Open position value	N/A	Net Profit / Buy&Hold %	0.99
Percent gain/loss	3586.55	Annual percent gain/loss	49.76	Annual Net % / B&H %	0.99
Initial investment	100	Interest earned	0		
Current position	Out	Date position entered	2/29/00		
Buy/Hold profit	3551.3	Days in test	26307	# of days per trade	907.14
Buy/Hold pct gain/loss	3551.3	Annual B/H pct gain/loss	49.27		
Total closed trades	29	Commissions paid	0		
Avg profit per trade	123.67	Avg Win/Avg Loss ratio	5.26		
Total long trades	29	Total short trades	0	Long Win Trade %	58.62
Winning long trades	17	Winning short trades	0	Short Win Trade %	#DIV/0!
Total winning trades	17	Total losing trades	12	Total Win Trade %	58.62
Amount of winning trades	4142.25	Amount of losing trades	−555.7	Net Profit Margin %	76.34
Average win	243.66	Average loss	−46.31	Average P. Margin %	68.06
Largest win	1597.58	Largest loss	−167.25	% Net / (Win + Loss)	81.05
Average length of win	25.82	Average length of loss	7	(Win − Loss) / Loss %	268.86
Longest winning trade	58	Longest losing trade	15	(Win − Loss) / Loss %	286.67
Most consecutive wins	4	Most consecutive losses	3	(Win − Loss) / Loss %	33.33
Total bars out	401	Average length out	13.37		
Longest out period	46				
System close drawdown	0	Profit/Loss index	86.58	% Net Profit / SODD	12043.49
System open drawdown	−29.78	Reward/Risk index	99.18	(Net P.-SODD)/Net P.	99.17
Max open trade drawdown	−167.25	Buy/Hold index	0.99	% SODD / Net Profit	−0.83

In the Equis MetaStock® "System Report" (profit and loss summary statistics), the *Total net profit* is the sum of profits minus the sum of losses, including open positions marked to the market. In contrast, the *Amount of Winning Trades* is the sum of realized profits (the total of all gains on closed-out trades only, excluding any open positions). Similarly, the *Amount of Losing Trades* is the sum of realized losses (the total of all losses on closed-out trades only, excluding any open positions). *System close drawdown* is the largest decline in the cumulative equity line below the initial investment, based on closed-out positions only. *System open drawdown (SODD)* is the largest decline in the cumulative equity line below the initial investment when a position is open. *Max open trade drawdown* is the largest decline in the cumulative equity line below the trade entry price during the worst single trade. The *Profit/Loss Index* is a complex calculation that relates the Amount of Winning Trades to the Amount of Losing Trades on a scale of −100 (worst possible performance) to +100 (best possible performance), with zero representing profits equal to losses. *Reward/Risk Index* is the Total net profit minus System open drawdown. The resulting difference is then divided by the Total net profit. The *Buy/Hold Index* is the Total net profit minus the buy-and-hold strategy's net profit. The resulting difference is then divided by the buy-and-hold net profit. In this exercise, initial equity is assumed to be $100. Both long and short positions are taken unless otherwise noted. Trades are executed at the closing price on the signal date. Transaction costs, interest expenses, and margins are not included in the statistics.

Moving Average Filters and Multiple Confirmation

Moving Average Filters and Multiple Confirmation uses one or more longer moving averages to filter the signals of a shorter moving average. These reduce the trading frequency compared to using any one moving average alone.

For example, using just two different moving averages, one short-term and one long-term, buy when price is above the short-term moving average *and* is above the long-term moving average; and sell when price is below the short-term moving average *and* is below the long-term moving average.

A very different result is obtained when we substitute the word *or* for *and* in the decision rule above. Trading frequency is much higher for *or* than for *and.*

Moving Average Oscillators

(See Price Oscillator.)

Moving Average Slope

The Moving Average Slope subtracts the moving average level n-periods ago from the current moving average level. For example, a recent magazine article referred to slope as the 80-day simple moving average of the daily closing price minus the level of the same 80-day simple moving average 10-days previous. We have tried all the many variations on this theme, and we prefer the moving average crossover because it is more effective.

Some people fool themselves by using different indicators that are, in effect, the exact equivalent of one another. For example, it is curious to note that an exponential moving average changes slope from down to up or from up to down at the same time that the close crosses the exponential moving average. An n-period simple moving average changes slope from down to up or from up to down at the same time that an n-period rate of change crosses zero. An n-period weighted moving average changes slope from down to up or from up to down at the same time that the close crosses a simple moving average of length n-1 periods. Seemingly different indicators sometimes produce the same results. Watch out for multicolinearity.

Multicolinearity

John Bollinger, CFA, CMT, has correctly pointed out that multicolinearity is the dangerous illusion of weighing the same basic information in slightly different forms, while erroneously expecting independent verification. Smart analysts avoid this trap. Note that using several different momentum indicators derived from the same series of closing prices over the same time period to confirm each other is not correct independent verification, instead it is counting the same thing several times. For example, combining RSI, Stochastics, MACD, Momentum, and Rate-of-Change is not the same as weighing different independent indicators, since they are all based on closing price velocity.

To avoid this trap, an analyst could choose one indicator derived from closing prices, another from volume, another from price range, another from relative strength (not RSI), another from sentiment, and perhaps even another from a different market, such as using interest-rates in a stock model. A variety of time-frames, either short, intermediate, or long, may also add a valuable cross-check to the analysis.

Multiple Time Frame Analysis Using Exponential Moving Average Crossover Rules

Perhaps the most widely used technical indicator of all is the moving average crossover rule: buy when the daily price close crosses above the moving average and sell when the daily price close crosses under the moving average. This strategy predates computers and electronic calculators. It is probably no coincidence that the traditional moving average lengths are based on the number ten: 10 months (about 200 trading days), 10 weeks (about 50 trading days), and 10 days. It takes scant computing power to add together 10 numbers, then divide that sum by 10, which involves simply shifting the decimal point one place to the left. These specific lengths are well established in technical analysis literature and the popular media, so criticisms of hindsight curve fitting do not apply. (For a 65-year old reference citing these specific moving average lengths, see Gartley, H. M., *Profits in the Stock Market,* Lambert-Gann Publishing Co., Box O, Pomeroy WA., 1935.)

The use of three moving averages works well with the ancient (more than a century old) technical analysis approach of multiple time frame analysis for determining trends of three degrees. Borrowing the language of Charles Dow's theory,

- Start with the long-term, Primary Tide, which is fairly effectively captured by the 200-day moving average.
- Next, narrow your focus to the intermediate-term, Secondary Wave, which is captured by the 50-day moving average.
- Finally, fine tune with the short-term, Minor Ripple, captured by the 10-day moving average.

The decision rules for risk-averse profit maximization are clear and unambiguous:

- buy when the daily price close crosses above *all* three moving averages;
- sell long when the daily price close crosses under *any* of the three moving averages;
- sell short when the daily price close crosses under *all* three moving averages;
- cover short when the daily price close crosses above *any* of the three moving averages.

Indicator Strategy Example for Multiple Time Frame Exponential Moving Averages

To be consistent with our general testing protocol in this book, we substituted exponential moving averages for the more traditional simple moving averages of equivalent length. Also, we compared today's close with yesterday's exponential moving averages to recognize our trading signals (since we can't trade today based on a moving average we can't calculate yet because we don't yet have today's closing price). These small refinements not only offer greater realism in historical simulation, but also improve the performance of most systems by reducing the well-known lag-time associated with moving averages.

Historical data shows that this multiple time frame analysis for determining trends of three degrees outperformed the passive buy-and-hold strategy by an extremely large margin, more than 144 fold. Based on the daily closing prices for the DJIA for 101 years from 1900 to 2001, we found that the following parameters would have produced good results on a purely mechanical trend-following signal basis with no subjectivity, no sophisticated technical analysis, and no judgement:

Enter Long (Buy) at the current daily price close of the DJIA when that daily close is above all three exponential moving averages, specifically the 10-day, 50-day, and 200-day exponential moving averages of the daily closing price.

Close Long (Sell) at the current daily price close of the DJIA when that daily close is below any of the three exponential moving averages, specifically the 10-day, 50-day, or 200-day exponential moving averages of the daily closing price.

Enter Short (Sell Short) at the current daily price close of the DJIA when that daily close is below all three exponential moving averages, specifically the 10-day, 50-day, and 200-day exponential moving averages of the daily closing price.

Close Short (Cover) at the current daily price close of the DJIA when that daily close is above any of the three exponential moving averages, specifically the 10-day, 50-day, or 200-day exponential moving averages of the daily closing price.

Starting with $100 and reinvesting profits, total net profits for this multiple time frame trend-following strategy would have been $3,189,323.50, assuming a fully invested strategy, reinvestment of profits, no transactions costs and no taxes. This would have been 14,324.15 percent greater than buy-and-hold. Short selling would have been profitable, although not since 1987, and short selling was included in the strategy. Long and short signals together would have given profitable signals only 35.75% of the time, but winning trades were larger than losing trades. Trading would have been extremely active at one trade every 15.03 calendar days.

The Equis International MetaStock® System Testing rules are written as follows:

Enter long:

```
CLOSE > Ref(Mov(CLOSE,opt1,E),-1) AND
CLOSE > Ref(Mov(CLOSE,opt2,E),-1) AND
CLOSE > Ref(Mov(CLOSE,opt3,E),-1)
```

Close long:

```
CLOSE < Ref(Mov(CLOSE,opt1,E),-1) OR
CLOSE < Ref(Mov(CLOSE,opt2,E),-1) OR
CLOSE < Ref(Mov(CLOSE,opt3,E),-1)
```

Enter short:

```
CLOSE < Ref(Mov(CLOSE,opt1,E),-1) AND
CLOSE < Ref(Mov(CLOSE,opt2,E),-1) AND
CLOSE < Ref(Mov(CLOSE,opt3,E),-1)
```

Close short:

```
CLOSE > Ref(Mov(CLOSE,opt1,E),-1) OR
CLOSE > Ref(Mov(CLOSE,opt2,E),-1) OR
CLOSE > Ref(Mov(CLOSE,opt3,E),-1)
```

OPT1 Current value: 10

OPT2 Current value: 50

OPT3 Current value: 200

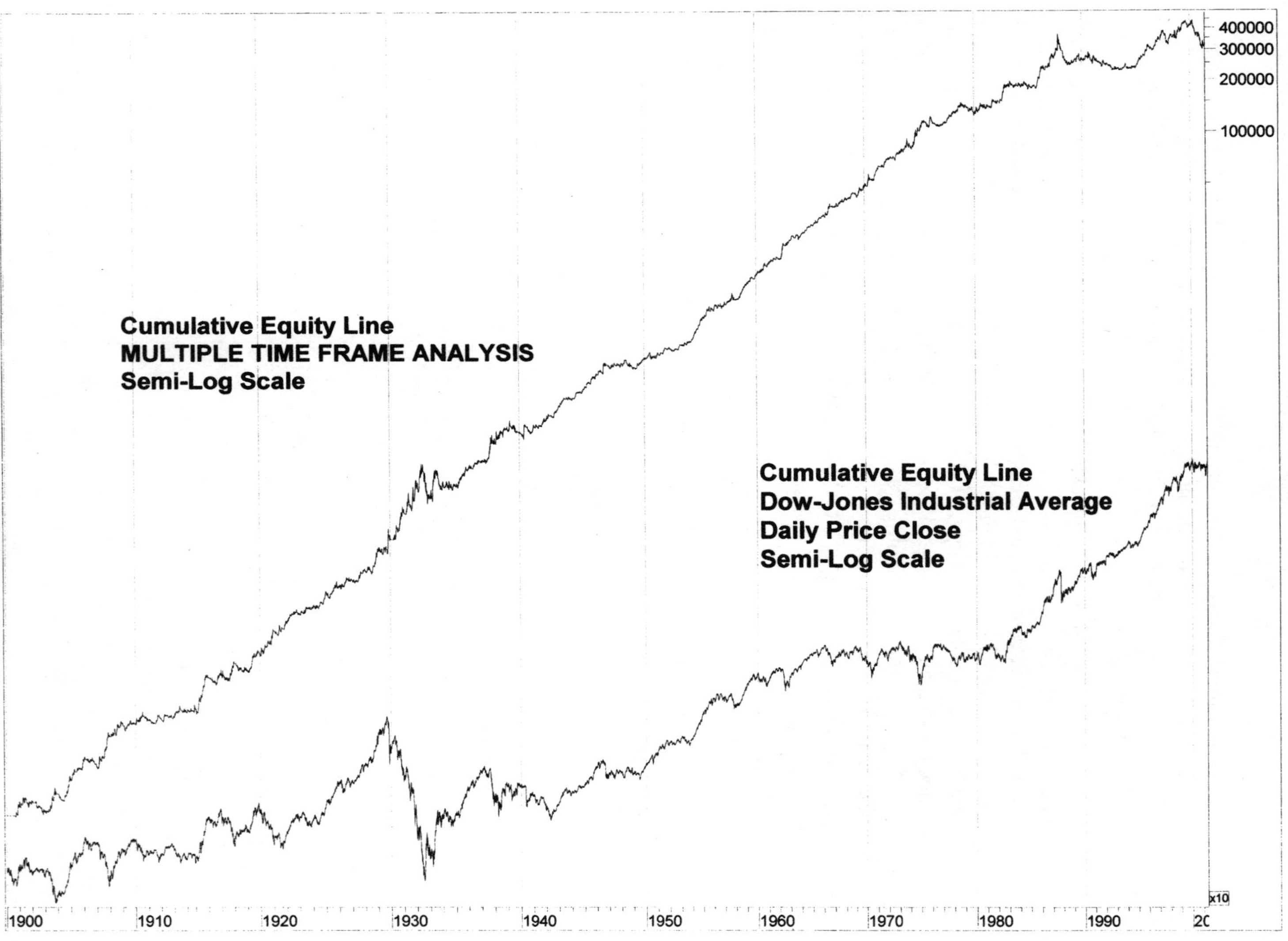
Cumulative Equity Line
MULTIPLE TIME FRAME ANALYSIS
Semi-Log Scale
Cumulative Equity Line
Dow-Jones Industrial Average
Daily Price Close
Semi-Log Scale
400000
300000
200000
100000
x10
1900
1910
1920
1930
1940
1950
1960
1970
1980
1990
2C

Multiple Time Frame Analysis

Total net profit	3189323.5	Open position value	N/A	Net Profit / Buy&Hold %	14324.15
Percent gain/loss	3189323.5	Annual percent gain/loss	31435.06	Annual Net % / B&H %	14324.38
Initial investment	100	Interest earned	0		
Current position	Out	Date position entered	5/23/01		
Buy/Hold profit	22111	Days in test	37032	# of days per trade	15.03
Buy/Hold pct gain/loss	22111	Annual B/H pct gain/loss	217.93		
Total closed trades	2464	Commissions paid	0		
Avg profit per trade	1294.37	Avg Win/Avg Loss ratio	2.35		
Total long trades	1520	Total short trades	944	Long Win Trade %	38.36
Winning long trades	583	Winning short trades	298	Short Win Trade %	31.57
Total winning trades	881	Total losing trades	1583	Total Win Trade %	35.75
Amount of winning trades	13597166	Amount of losing trades	−10407845	Net Profit Margin %	13.29
Average win	15433.79	Average loss	−6574.76	Average P. Margin %	40.25
Largest win	450190.5	Largest loss	−191684.75	% Net / (Win + Loss)	40.27
Average length of win	15	Average length of loss	3.93	(Win − Loss) / Loss %	281.68
Longest winning trade	63	Longest losing trade	24	(Win − Loss) / Loss %	162.50
Most consecutive wins	7	Most consecutive losses	11	(Win − Loss) / Loss %	−36.36
Total bars out	13214	Average length out	5.51		
Longest out period	202				
System close drawdown	−1.6	Profit/Loss index	23.46	% Net Profit / SODD	199332718.75
System open drawdown	−1.6	Reward/Risk index	100	(Net P.-SODD)/Net P.	100.00
Max open trade drawdown	−191684.75	Buy/Hold index	14324.15	% SODD / Net Profit	0.00

In the Equis MetaStock® "System Report" (profit and loss summary statistics), the *Total net profit* is the sum of profits minus the sum of losses, including open positions marked to the market. In contrast, the *Amount of Winning Trades* is the sum of realized profits (the total of all gains on closed-out trades only, excluding any open positions). Similarly, the *Amount of Losing Trades* is the sum of realized losses (the total of all losses on closed-out trades only, excluding any open positions). *System close drawdown* is the largest decline in the cumulative equity line below the initial investment, based on closed-out positions only. *System open drawdown (SODD)* is the largest decline in the cumulative equity line below the initial investment when a position is open. *Max open trade drawdown* is the largest decline in the cumulative equity line below the trade entry price during the worst single trade. The *Profit/Loss Index* is a complex calculation that relates the Amount of Winning Trades to the Amount of Losing Trades on a scale of −100 (worst possible performance) to +100 (best possible performance), with zero representing profits equal to losses. *Reward/Risk Index* is the Total net profit minus System open drawdown. The resulting difference is then divided by the Total net profit. The *Buy/Hold Index* is the Total net profit minus the buy-and-hold strategy's net profit. The resulting difference is then divided by the buy-and-hold net profit. In this exercise, initial equity is assumed to be $100. Both long and short positions are taken unless otherwise noted. Trades are executed at the closing price on the signal date. Transaction costs, interest expenses, and margins are not included in the statistics.

Mutual Funds Cash/Assets Ratio

The Mutual Funds Cash/Assets Ratio is cash and cash equivalents held by mutual funds divided by the total assets of mutual funds. Each month, the Investment Company Institute (1775 K Street, N.W., Washington, DC 20006) reports detailed statistics on the portfolio holdings of mutual funds.

The Mutual Funds Cash/Assets Ratio may be viewed as a sample of available buying power for the general stock market. Mutual Fund portfolio managers are similar to the broader universe of all professional money managers. When their Cash/Assets Ratio is relatively high as compared to historical norms, then relatively more cash is available to buy stocks, and that is potential fuel for a bullish trend, other things being equal. But when their Cash/Assets Ratio is relatively low, then relatively little cash is left to buy stocks or support prices, so the market may be vulnerable to a decline, other things being equal. It is important to note, however, that, other things are not always equal, and sentiment indicators should be used only as supplements to more precise technical timing indicators.

As the chart of Stock Mutual Funds Cash/Assets Ratio by Ned Davis Research shows, the S&P 500 has made strong gains of 20.1% per annum after cash rose above 9.5% of assets. In contrast, S&P 500 gains were only 2.1% per annum after cash fell to 6.9% of assets. This indicator has not given timely signals in recent years, however, and it appears that its characteristics may have changed.

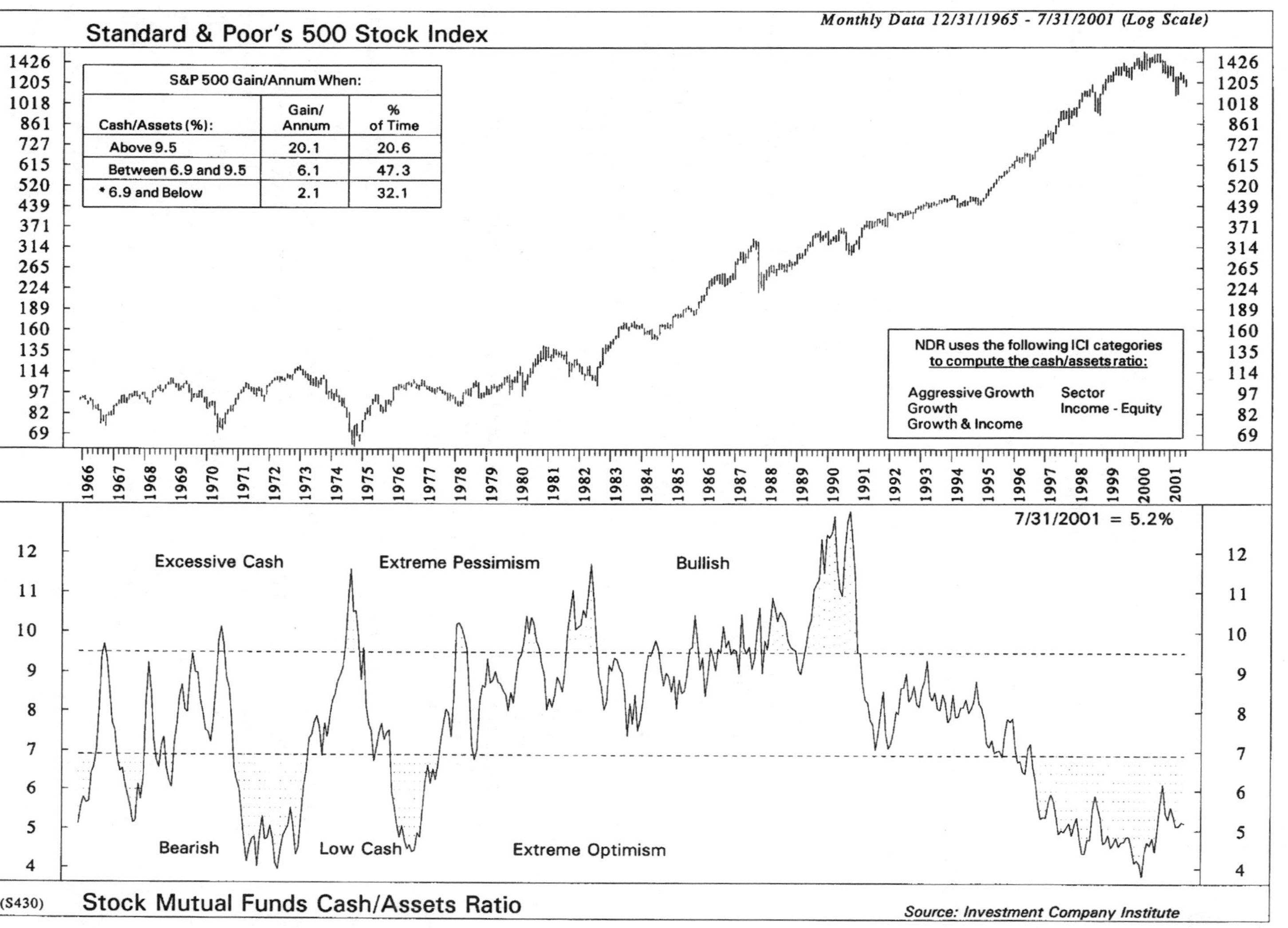
Standard & Poor's 500 Stock Index
Monthly Data 12/31/1965 - 7/31/2001 (Log Scale)
S&P 500 Gain/Annum When:
Cash/Assets (%): | Gain/Annum | % of Time
Above 9.5 | 20.1 | 20.6
Between 6.9 and 9.5 | 6.1 | 47.3
* 6.9 and Below | 2.1 | 32.1
NDR uses the following ICI categories to compute the cash/assets ratio:
Aggressive Growth
Growth
Growth & Income
Sector
Income - Equity
1426 1205 1018 861 727 615 520 439 371 314 265 224 189 160 135 114 97 82 69
1966 1967 1968 1969 1970 1971 1972 1973 1974 1975 1976 1977 1978 1979 1980 1981 1982 1983 1984 1985 1986 1987 1988 1989 1990 1991 1992 1993 1994 1995 1996 1997 1998 1999 2000 2001
7/31/2001 = 5.2%
Excessive Cash
Extreme Pessimism
Bullish
Bearish
Low Cash
Extreme Optimism
12 11 10 9 8 7 6 5 4
(S430)
Stock Mutual Funds Cash/Assets Ratio
Source: Investment Company Institute

Chart by permission of Ned Davis Research.

N-Day Rule

The *N*-Day Rule has us buy when the current price high rises above the previous *n* days' highest price high. Sell when the current price low falls below the previous *n* days' lowest price low. This is simply another name for the Price Channel Trading Range Breakout Rule. *(See Price Channel Trading Range Breakout Rule.)*

Negative Volume Index (NVI)

The Negative Volume Index, created by Paul Dysart, cumulates net price change for periods of declining volume only. The idea is that mainly smart professional traders buy and sell during relatively quiet periods of declining volume. In contrast, unprofessional, emotionally driven players are active on days when volume rises. Therefore, market activity on days when a negative change in volume occurs should better reflect the thinking of the smart-money professionals who treat trading as a serious business rather than as some wild casino game.

NVI may be calculated for any time interval, such as minutes, hourly, daily, weekly, and monthly. Moreover, NVI may be calculated using any market index, stock or commodity, as long as there is data for closing price and volume. The volume itself is used only as a qualifier to determine whether or not to include the day's net price change fractional ratio in the cumulative total. If volume today is less than volume yesterday, then today's net price change fractional ratio is included in the cumulative total. But if the volume today is greater than the volume of the previous day, then today's net price change fractional ratio is not included in the cumulative total. Thus, NVI is defined as a cumulative total of daily price change fractional ratios for declining volume days only.

To calculate the Negative Volume Index, compare the current day's volume to the previous day's volume. If today's volume is greater than yesterday's volume, then today does not qualify as a Negative Volume day; therefore today's net price change is assumed to be zero and the Negative Volume Index remains unchanged at yesterday's level. But, if today's volume is less than yesterday's volume, today does qualify as a Negative Volume day. Then, we divide the current day's net price change (respecting the sign, plus for a net gain, or minus for a net loss) by the closing price yesterday to arrive at today's net price change fractional ratio. Finally, we add today's plus or minus net price change fractional ratio to a cumulative total to arrive at the Negative Volume Index.

Thus, NVI rises on days of positive price change on lower volume, NVI falls on days of negative price change on lower volume, and NVI is unchanged on days of higher volume no matter what the price action.

In MetaStock®'s Indicator Builder dialogue, NVI may be expressed by the following:

`Cum(If(V<Ref(V,-1),ROC(C,1,%),0))`

The step-by-step literal translation is: "Cumulate the following: If the current volume is less than the previous period's volume, then compute the Rate-of-Change of the Closing price for one period, expressed as a percentage; otherwise (if the current volume is greater than the previous volume), set the day's Rate-of-Change of the Closing price to zero before cumulating."

Norman Fosback (The Institute for Econometric Research, 3471 North Federal Highway, Forth Lauderdale, FL 33306) found that when NVI was above its own trailing moving average, that indicated positive returns for the stock market. Our independent testing confirmed this across all moving average period lengths (see below).

Indicator Strategy Example for the Negative Volume Index (NVI)

Historical data shows that the Negative Volume Index produces a modestly positive result on the long side. NVI under performed the buy-and-hold strategy because of heavy long-side losses from 1929 to 1933. Short selling strategies all lost money. Based on the number of shares traded each day on the NYSE and the daily prices for the DJIA for 72 years from 1928 to 2000, we found that the following parameters would have produced a positive result on a purely mechanical trend-following signal basis with no subjectivity, no sophisticated technical analysis, and no judgement:

Enter Long (Buy) at the current daily price close of the DJIA when the current Negative Volume Index is greater than the previous day's Negative Volume Index.

Close Long (Sell) at the current daily price close of the DJIA when the current Negative Volume Index is less than the previous day's Negative Volume Index.

Enter Short (Sell Short) never.

Starting with $100 and reinvesting profits, total net profits for this Negative Volume Index strategy would have been $3,096.88, assuming a fully invested strategy, reinvestment of profits, no transactions costs and no taxes. This would have been 32.31 percent less than buy-and-hold. Only about 46.27 percent of the 2213 signals would have produced winning trades, and the average long trade lasted 11.87 trading days on average. Short selling, which was not included in this strategy, would have lost money.

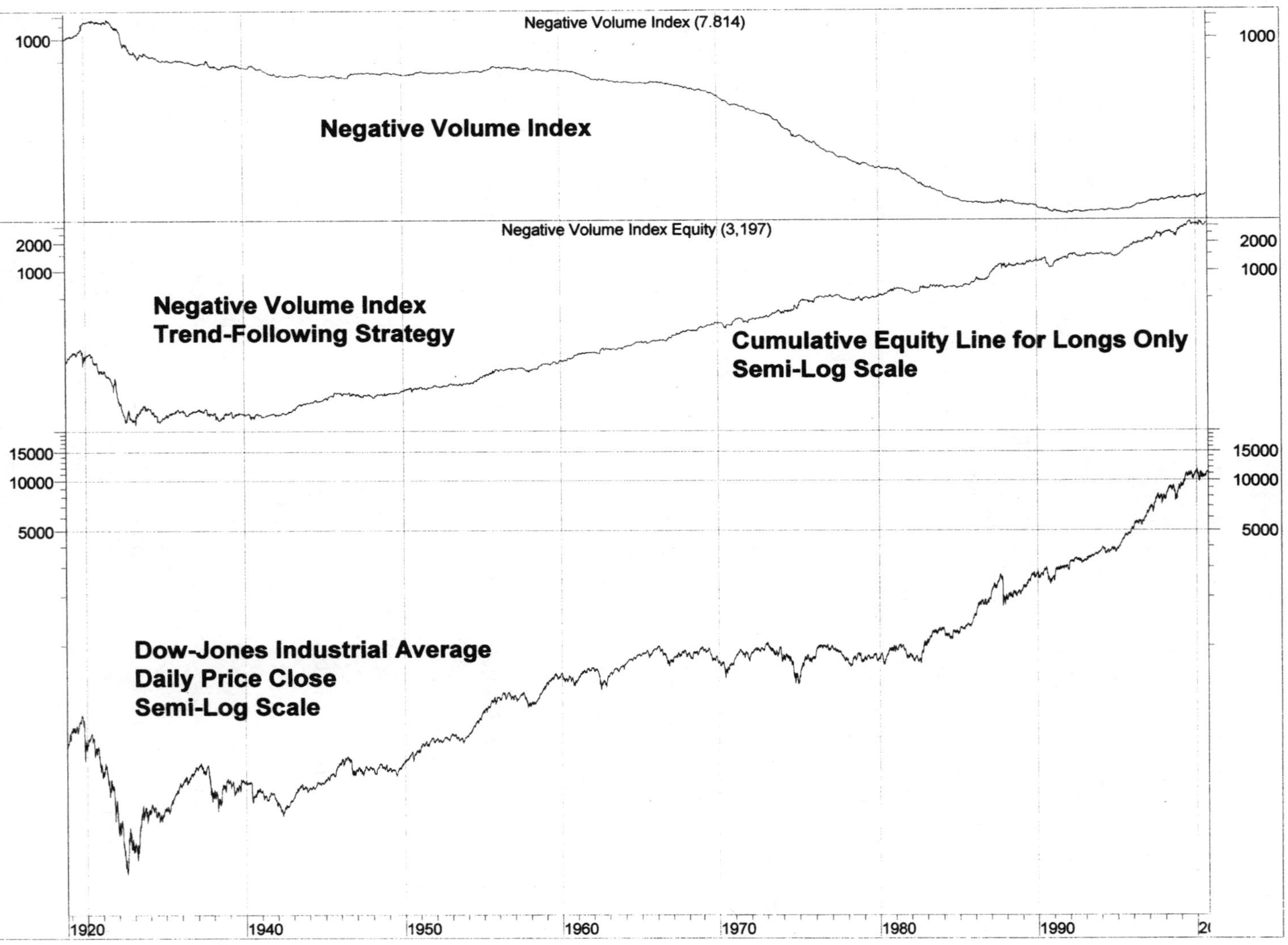

Negative Volume Index (7.814)
Negative Volume Index
Negative Volume Index Equity (3,197)
Negative Volume Index
Trend-Following Strategy
Cumulative Equity Line for Longs Only
Semi-Log Scale
Dow-Jones Industrial Average
Daily Price Close
Semi-Log Scale
1000
2000
15000
10000
5000
1920
1940
1950
1960
1970
1980
1990

Negative Volume Index

Total net profit	3096.88	Open position value	N/A	Net Profit / Buy&Hold %	−32.31
Percent gain/loss	3096.88	Annual percent gain/loss	43.02	Annual Net % / B&H %	−32.31
Initial investment	100	Interest earned	0		
Current position	Out	Date position entered	9/7/00		
Buy/Hold profit	4575.25	Days in test	26276	# of days per trade	11.87
Buy/Hold pct gain/loss	4575.25	Annual B/H pct gain/loss	63.55		
Total closed trades	2213	Commissions paid	0		
Avg profit per trade	1.4	Avg Win/Avg Loss ratio	1.72		
Total long trades	2213	Total short trades	0	Long Win Trade %	46.27
Winning long trades	1024	Winning short trades	0	Short Win Trade %	#DIV/0!
Total winning trades	1024	Total losing trades	1189	Total Win Trade %	46.27
Amount of winning trades	9493.05	Amount of losing trades	−6396.17	Net Profit Margin %	19.49
Average win	9.27	Average loss	−5.38	Average P. Margin %	26.55
Largest win	182.87	Largest loss	−165.69	% Net / (Win + Loss)	4.93
Average length of win	6.05	Average length of loss	3.63	(Win − Loss) / Loss %	66.67
Longest winning trade	22	Longest losing trade	20	(Win − Loss) / Loss %	10.00
Most consecutive wins	11	Most consecutive losses	14	(Win − Loss) / Loss %	−21.43
Total bars out	11986	Average length out	5.41		
Longest out period	41				
System close drawdown	−76.71	Profit/Loss index	32.62	% Net Profit / SODD	3966.29
System open drawdown	−78.08	Reward/Risk index	97.54	(Net P.-SODD)/Net P.	97.48
Max open trade drawdown	−233.38	Buy/Hold index	−32.31	% SODD / Net Profit	−2.52

In the Equis MetaStock® "System Report" (profit and loss summary statistics), the *Total net profit* is the sum of profits minus the sum of losses, including open positions marked to the market. In contrast, the *Amount of Winning Trades* is the sum of realized profits (the total of all gains on closed-out trades only, excluding any open positions). Similarly, the *Amount of Losing Trades* is the sum of realized losses (the total of all losses on closed-out trades only, excluding any open positions). *System close drawdown* is the largest decline in the cumulative equity line below the initial investment, based on closed-out positions only. *System open drawdown (SODD)* is the largest decline in the cumulative equity line below the initial investment when a position is open. *Max open trade drawdown* is the largest decline in the cumulative equity line below the trade entry price during the worst single trade. The *Profit/Loss Index* is a complex calculation that relates the Amount of Winning Trades to the Amount of Losing Trades on a scale of −100 (worst possible performance) to +100 (best possible performance), with zero representing profits equal to losses. *Reward/Risk Index* is the Total net profit minus System open drawdown. The resulting difference is then divided by the Total net profit. The *Buy/Hold Index* is the Total net profit minus the buy-and-hold strategy's net profit. The resulting difference is then divided by the buy-and-hold net profit. In this exercise, initial equity is assumed to be $100. Both long and short positions are taken unless otherwise noted. Trades are executed at the closing price on the signal date. Transaction costs, interest expenses, and margins are not included in the statistics.

The Equis International MetaStock® System Testing rules are written as follows:

Enter long: NVI()>Ref(Mov(NVI(),opt1,E),-1)

Close long: NVI()<Ref(Mov(NVI(),opt1,E),-1)

OPT1 Current value: 1

New Highs–New Lows

The difference between the number of New Highs minus the number of New Lows is a measure of the strength or weakness of the market. If New Highs outnumber New Lows, the demand for stocks is more intense than the supply of stocks, and that is bullish. But if New Lows outnumber New Highs, the supply of stocks is more intense than the demand for stocks, and that is bearish.

These numbers tally only those stocks on the move to new price extremes relative to their previous 1-year trading ranges. New Highs are the number of stock issues reaching new 52-week price highs; that is, attaining their highest intraday price extremes over the past year. New Lows are the number of issues reaching new 52-week price lows; that is, attaining their lowest intraday price extremes over the past year.

Daily data is published in many financial newspapers and electronic sources for New Highs and New Lows on three separate U.S. stock exchanges: New York, American, and NASDAQ. Our studies strongly suggest that daily data is more useful than weekly data for trading, so we limited our examples here to daily data only. Many technicians collect New Highs-New Lows data separately on a weekly basis for a long-term perspective, and such weekly indicators produce different results with fewer signals.

Note that although a simple subtraction of New Lows from New Highs has long been the more popular method, the difference between New Highs and New Lows is properly expressed as a percentage of Total Issues Traded each day on the NYSE. That stock exchange has promoted new business rather effectively, and so Total Issues Traded have increased 71% from 1971 issues on May 29, 1984, to 3371 issues on July 12, 2000. This adjustment is particularly important when comparing indicator *levels* over time. Without this normalization, the simple difference goes to great extremes as time goes by, simply because there are more stocks eligible for counting. This difference/ratio method preserves the comparability of data over time by automatically adjusting for the ever increasing number of stocks traded on the exchange. Thus, the levels on the chart remain comparable over the years. We show a chart of this difference/ratio in the next topic.

Also note that the method of counting New Highs and New Lows changed in early 1978. Since then, New Highs and New Lows are reported as the number of stock issues reaching new price high and new price low extremes over a trailing 52-week look-back period. Prior to 1978, the trailing look-back period varied from 2.5 to 14.5 months, according to the following arbitrary rule: for a date between January 1 and mid-March of any given year, a new high or new low was based on a look-back period from January 1 of the previous year to the current date; but for dates after mid-March, a new high or new low was based on a look-back period from January 1 of the current year to the current date. Theoretically, this inconsistent treatment destroyed proper comparability of the data. But for practical purposes of generating buy and sell signals, the data was useful as a market indicator both before and after the date of method change in early 1978. So, most technicians simply ignore this detail, as we do here in our testing.

Indicator Strategy Example of New Highs minus New Lows

Based on a 60-year file of daily data for the number of New Highs minus the number of New Lows and the DJIA since 1940, we found that the simplest possible trend-following rule would have produced a positive result on a purely mechanical signal basis with no subjectivity, no sophisticated technical analysis, and no judgement:

Enter Long (Buy) at the current daily price close of the DJIA when the number of New Highs minus the number of New Lows crosses above zero.

Close Long (Sell) at the current daily price close of the DJIA when the number of New Highs minus the number of New Lows crosses below zero.

Enter Short (Sell Short) at the current daily price close of the DJIA when the number of New Highs minus the number of New Lows crosses below zero.

Close Short (Cover) at the current daily price close of the DJIA when the number of New Highs minus the number of New Lows crosses above zero.

Starting with $100 and reinvesting profits, total net profits for this New Highs − New Lows trend-following strategy would have been $77,520.91, assuming a fully invested strategy, reinvestment of profits, no transactions costs and no taxes. This would have been 960.51 percent better than buy-and-hold. Even short selling would have been profitable, and short selling was included in this strategy. Trading would have been active with one trade every 15.06 calendar days.

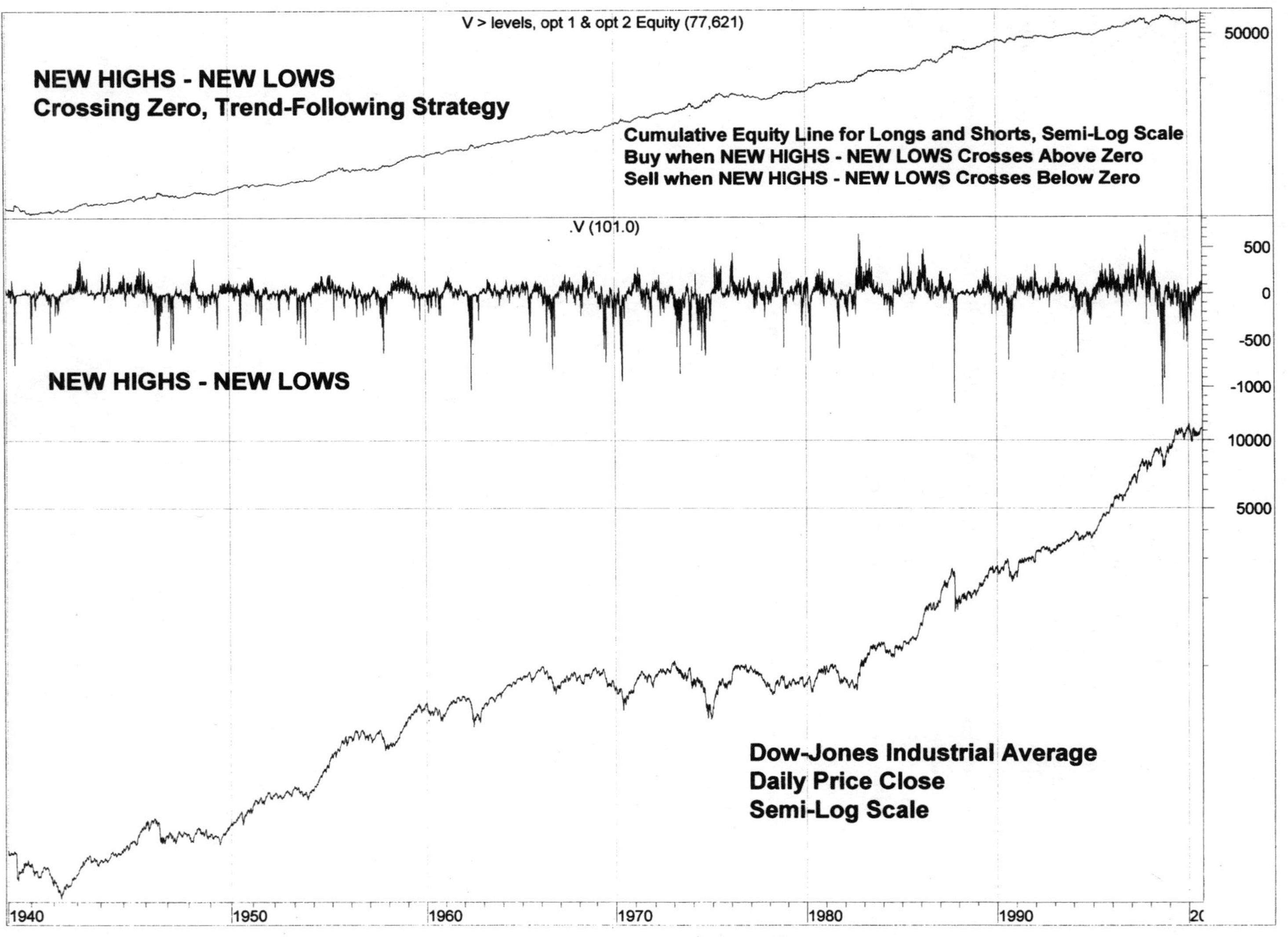

V > levels, opt 1 & opt 2 Equity (77,621)
NEW HIGHS - NEW LOWS
Crossing Zero, Trend-Following Strategy
Cumulative Equity Line for Longs and Shorts, Semi-Log Scale
Buy when NEW HIGHS - NEW LOWS Crosses Above Zero
Sell when NEW HIGHS - NEW LOWS Crosses Below Zero
50000
.V (101.0)
NEW HIGHS - NEW LOWS
500
0
-500
-1000
10000
5000
Dow-Jones Industrial Average
Daily Price Close
Semi-Log Scale
1940
1950
1960
1970
1980
1990

New Highs – New Lows Crossing Zero

Total net profit	77520.91	Open position value	4832.71	Net Profit / Buy&Hold %	960.51
Percent gain/loss	77520.91	Annual percent gain/loss	1276.51	Annual Net % / B&H %	960.49
Initial investment	100	Interest earned	0		
Current position	Long	Date position entered	7/31/00		
Buy/Hold profit	7309.76	Days in test	22166	# of days per trade	15.06
Buy/Hold pct gain/loss	7309.76	Annual B/H pct gain/loss	120.37		
Total closed trades	1472	Commissions paid	0		
Avg profit per trade	49.38	Avg Win/Avg Loss ratio	2.08		
Total long trades	736	Total short trades	736	Long Win Trade %	43.89
Winning long trades	323	Winning short trades	293	Short Win Trade %	39.81
Total winning trades	616	Total losing trades	856	Total Win Trade %	41.85
Amount of winning trades	217989.84	Amount of losing trades	−145301.63	Net Profit Margin %	20.01
Average win	353.88	Average loss	−169.74	Average P. Margin %	35.17
Largest win	10343.41	Largest loss	−5937.19	% Net / (Win + Loss)	27.06
Average length of win	20.79	Average length of loss	5.14	(Win − Loss) / Loss %	304.47
Longest winning trade	322	Longest losing trade	71	(Win − Loss) / Loss %	353.52
Most consecutive wins	6	Most consecutive losses	12	(Win − Loss) / Loss %	−50.00
Total bars out	0	Average length out	N/A		
Longest out period	0				
System close drawdown	−20.39	Profit/Loss index	34.79	% Net Profit / SODD	77520.91
System open drawdown	−100	Reward/Risk index	99.87	(Net P.-SODD)/Net P.	99.87
Max open trade drawdown	−5937.19	Buy/Hold index	1026.63	% SODD / Net Profit	−0.13

In the Equis MetaStock® "System Report" (profit and loss summary statistics), the *Total net profit* is the sum of profits minus the sum of losses, including open positions marked to the market. In contrast, the *Amount of Winning Trades* is the sum of realized profits (the total of all gains on closed-out trades only, excluding any open positions). Similarly, the *Amount of Losing Trades* is the sum of realized losses (the total of all losses on closed-out trades only, excluding any open positions). *System close drawdown* is the largest decline in the cumulative equity line below the initial investment, based on closed-out positions only. *System open drawdown (SODD)* is the largest decline in the cumulative equity line below the initial investment when a position is open. *Max open trade drawdown* is the largest decline in the cumulative equity line below the trade entry price during the worst single trade. The *Profit/Loss Index* is a complex calculation that relates the Amount of Winning Trades to the Amount of Losing Trades on a scale of −100 (worst possible performance) to +100 (best possible performance), with zero representing profits equal to losses. *Reward/Risk Index* is the Total net profit minus System open drawdown. The resulting difference is then divided by the Total net profit. The *Buy/Hold Index* is the Total net profit minus the buy-and-hold strategy's net profit. The resulting difference is then divided by the buy-and-hold net profit. In this exercise, initial equity is assumed to be $100. Both long and short positions are taken unless otherwise noted. Trades are executed at the closing price on the signal date. Transaction costs, interest expenses, and margins are not included in the statistics.

The Equis International MetaStock® System Testing rules, where the current net of New Highs minus New Lows is inserted into the data field normally reserved for Volume (V), are written as follows:

Enter long: V > opt1

Close long: V < opt2

Enter short: V < opt2

Close short: V > opt1

OPT1 Current value: 0
OPT2 Current value: 0

(New Highs–New Lows)/Total Issues Traded: New Highs/New Lows Ratio

As we noted in our discussion of New Highs − New Lows (above), a simple subtraction of New Lows from New Highs is a popular method of expressing the relationship. However, difference is more properly expressed as a percentage of Total Issues Traded because of the large increase in the total number of stocks traded each day on the NYSE. This means that the absolute difference between New Highs and New Lows increases over time, given constant market volatility. The ratio of the net difference of New Highs minus New Lows divided by the Total Issues Traded each day is plotted in the chart. The ratio normalizes the data and preserves the comparability of data over time by automatically adjusting for the ever increasing number of stocks traded. The *levels* on the chart remain comparable over the years. Without this adjustment, the data goes to ever greater extremes as time goes by, simply because there are more stocks eligible for counting, and that may result in a distortion of the meaning of the indicator over time.

Note that we cannot simply divide New Highs by New Lows because sometimes New Lows are zero, and division by zero is undefined. Therefore, the best way to normalize the data is to divide the net difference by Total Issues Traded.

Indicator Strategy Example of (New Highs − New Lows) / Total Issues Traded

Based on a 60-year file of daily data for the ratio of (New Highs − New Lows) / Total Issues Traded and the DJIA since 1940, we found that this ratio normalization permitted greater analytical flexibility than a simple subtraction. We multiplied the ratio by 1000 to make the numbers visually comparable to the simple subtraction. Levels of the indicator are directly comparable over time, and this allows us to experiment with different buy and sell rules at different levels. For example, for those paying substantial transactions costs or wishing less frequent trading, the following asymmetrical buy and sell rules, which create a neutral buffer zone, produce 82% fewer trades relative to a simple cross of zero:

Enter Long (Buy) at the current daily price close of the DJIA when the ratio of ((New Highs − New Lows) / Total Issues Traded) * 1000 crosses above 3.

Close Long (Sell) at the current daily price close of the DJIA when the ratio of ((New Highs − New Lows) / Total Issues Traded) * 1000 crosses below −47.

Enter Short (Sell Short) at the current daily price close of the DJIA when the ratio of ((New Highs − New Lows) / Total Issues Traded) * 1000 crosses below −47.

Close Short (Cover) at the current daily price close of the DJIA when the ratio of ((New Highs − New Lows) / Total Issues Traded) * 1000 crosses above 3.

Starting with $100 and reinvesting profits, total net profits for this New Highs − New Lows trend-following strategy would have been $35,247.34, assuming a fully invested strategy, reinvestment of profits, no transactions costs and no taxes. This would have been 382.20 percent better than buy-and-hold. Even short selling would have been profitable, and short selling was included in this strategy. Trading would have been relatively inactive with one trade every 82.71 calendar days.

The Equis International MetaStock® System Testing rules, where 1000 times the current ratio of New Highs-New Lows to Total Issues Traded is inserted into the data field normally reserved for Volume (V), are written as follows:

Enter long: V > opt1

Close long: V < opt2

Enter short: V < opt2

Close short: V > opt1

OPT1 Current value: 3
OPT2 Current value: −47

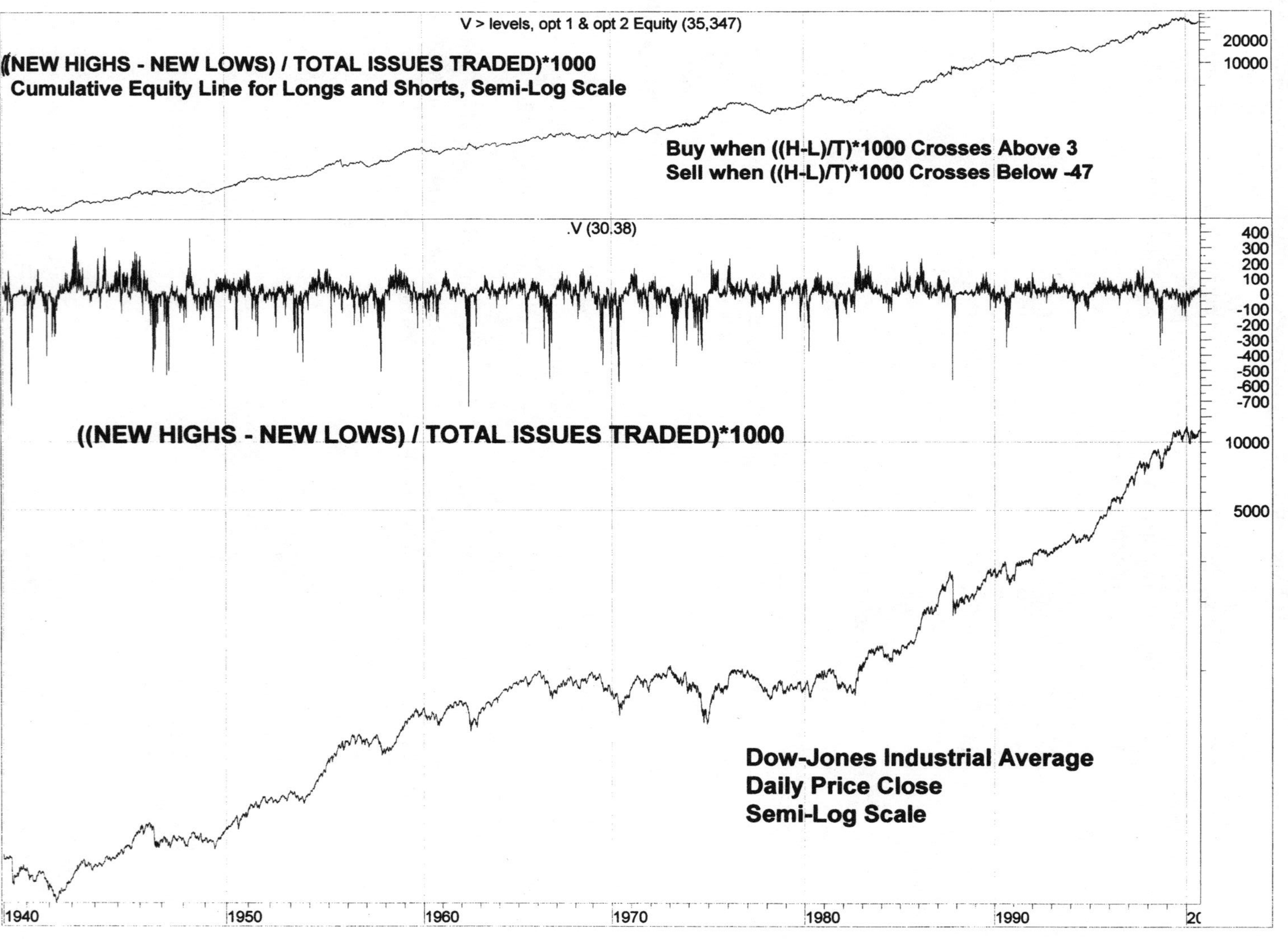

V > levels, opt 1 & opt 2 Equity (35,347)
((NEW HIGHS - NEW LOWS) / TOTAL ISSUES TRADED)*1000
Cumulative Equity Line for Longs and Shorts, Semi-Log Scale
Buy when ((H-L)/T)*1000 Crosses Above 3
Sell when ((H-L)/T)*1000 Crosses Below -47
20000
10000
.V (30.38)
400
300
200
100
0
-100
-200
-300
-400
-500
-600
-700
((NEW HIGHS - NEW LOWS) / TOTAL ISSUES TRADED)*1000
10000
5000
Dow-Jones Industrial Average
Daily Price Close
Semi-Log Scale
1940
1950
1960
1970
1980
1990

(New Highs–New Lows)/Total Issues Traded

Total net profit	35247.34	Open position value	1114.86	Net Profit / Buy&Hold %	382.20
Percent gain/loss	35247.34	Annual percent gain/loss	580.41	Annual Net % / B&H %	382.19
Initial investment	100	Interest earned	0		
Current position	Long	Date position entered	3/22/00		
Buy/Hold profit	7309.76	Days in test	22166	# of days per trade	82.71
Buy/Hold pct gain/loss	7309.76	Annual B/H pct gain/loss	120.37		
Total closed trades	268	Commissions paid	0		
Avg profit per trade	127.36	Avg Win/Avg Loss ratio	4.68		
Total long trades	134	Total short trades	134	Long Win Trade %	48.51
Winning long trades	65	Winning short trades	49	Short Win Trade %	36.57
Total winning trades	114	Total losing trades	154	Total Win Trade %	42.54
Amount of winning trades	47989.15	Amount of losing trades	−13856.67	Net Profit Margin %	55.19
Average win	420.96	Average loss	−89.98	Average P. Margin %	64.78
Largest win	7994.55	Largest loss	−2803.84	% Net / (Win + Loss)	48.07
Average length of win	112.08	Average length of loss	20.34	(Win − Loss) / Loss %	451.03
Longest winning trade	682	Longest losing trade	170	(Win − Loss) / Loss %	301.18
Most consecutive wins	7	Most consecutive losses	8	(Win − Loss) / Loss %	−12.50
Total bars out	0	Average length out	N/A		
Longest out period	0				
System close drawdown	−7.88	Profit/Loss index	71.78	% Net Profit / SODD	35247.34
System open drawdown	−100	Reward/Risk index	99.72	(Net P.-SODD)/Net P.	99.72
Max open trade drawdown	−2803.84	Buy/Hold index	397.45	% SODD / Net Profit	−0.28

In the Equis MetaStock® "System Report" (profit and loss summary statistics), the *Total net profit* is the sum of profits minus the sum of losses, including open positions marked to the market. In contrast, the *Amount of Winning Trades* is the sum of realized profits (the total of all gains on closed-out trades only, excluding any open positions). Similarly, the *Amount of Losing Trades* is the sum of realized losses (the total of all losses on closed-out trades only, excluding any open positions). *System close drawdown* is the largest decline in the cumulative equity line below the initial investment, based on closed-out positions only. *System open drawdown (SODD)* is the largest decline in the cumulative equity line below the initial investment when a position is open. *Max open trade drawdown* is the largest decline in the cumulative equity line below the trade entry price during the worst single trade. The *Profit/Loss Index* is a complex calculation that relates the Amount of Winning Trades to the Amount of Losing Trades on a scale of −100 (worst possible performance) to +100 (best possible performance), with zero representing profits equal to losses. *Reward/Risk Index* is the Total net profit minus System open drawdown. The resulting difference is then divided by the Total net profit. The *Buy/Hold Index* is the Total net profit minus the buy-and-hold strategy's net profit. The resulting difference is then divided by the buy-and-hold net profit. In this exercise, initial equity is assumed to be $100. Both long and short positions are taken unless otherwise noted. Trades are executed at the closing price on the signal date. Transaction costs, interest expenses, and margins are not included in the statistics.

New Highs/Total Issues Traded

The daily number of New Highs to Total Issues Traded ratio is a measure of the strength of the market. If the ratio of New Highs / Total Issues Traded is high and rising, the demand for stocks is strong and growing more intense, and that is bullish. But if the ratio of New Highs / Total Issues Traded is low and falling, the demand for stocks is weak and growing less intense, and that is bearish. The chart shows the ratio multiplied by 10,000 to avoid decimals.

New Highs are the sum of only those stocks on the move to new upward price extremes relative to their trailing 1-year trading ranges. In other words, New Highs are the total number of stock issues (listed on a predefined stock exchange) attaining their highest intraday prices relative to their own most recent past 52-week moving windows of time, that is, relative to the most recent 1-year look-back period.

Daily data is published in many financial newspapers and electronic sources for New Highs and New Lows on three separate U.S. stock exchanges: New York, American, and NASDAQ. Our studies strongly suggest that daily data is more useful than weekly data for trading, so we limited our examples to daily data only.

As we noted under the topic New Highs − New Lows, the method of counting New Highs and New Lows changed in early 1978, but for practical purposes most technicians simply ignore this detail, as we do here in our testing. Also, New Highs and New Lows data should be analyzed as a percentage of Total Issues Traded so that the levels of indicator readings displayed on the chart remain comparable over the years.

Indicator Strategy Example of New Highs / Total Issues Traded

Based on a 60-year file of daily data for the number of New Highs / Total Issues Traded and the DJIA since 1940, we found that using a very low threshold level of 1.55% for generating trend-following buy and sell signals would have produced a positive result on a purely mechanical signal basis with no subjectivity, no sophisticated technical analysis, and no judgement:

Enter Long (Buy) at the current daily price close of the DJIA when the number of New Highs to the number of Total Issues Traded crosses above 1.55%.

Close Long (Sell) at the current daily price close of the DJIA when the number of New Highs to the number of Total Issues Traded crosses below 1.55%.

Enter Short (Sell Short) at the current daily price close of the DJIA when the number of New Highs to the number of Total Issues Traded crosses below 1.55%.

Close Short (Cover) at the current daily price close of the DJIA when the number of New Highs to the number of Total Issues Traded crosses above 1.55%.

Starting with $100 and reinvesting profits, total net profits for this New Highs – New Lows trend-following strategy would have been $13,025.79, assuming a fully invested strategy, reinvestment of profits, no transactions costs and no taxes. This would have been 78.20 percent better than buy-and-hold. Even short selling would have been profitable, and short selling was included in this strategy. Trading would have been hyperactive with one trade every 5.02 calendar days.

The Equis International MetaStock® System Testing rules, where the current ratio of New Highs / Total Issues Traded times 10,000 is inserted into the data field normally reserved for Volume (V), are written as follows:

Enter long: V > opt1

Close long: V < opt2

Enter short: V < opt2

Close short: V > opt1

OPT1 Current value: 155
OPT2 Current value: 155

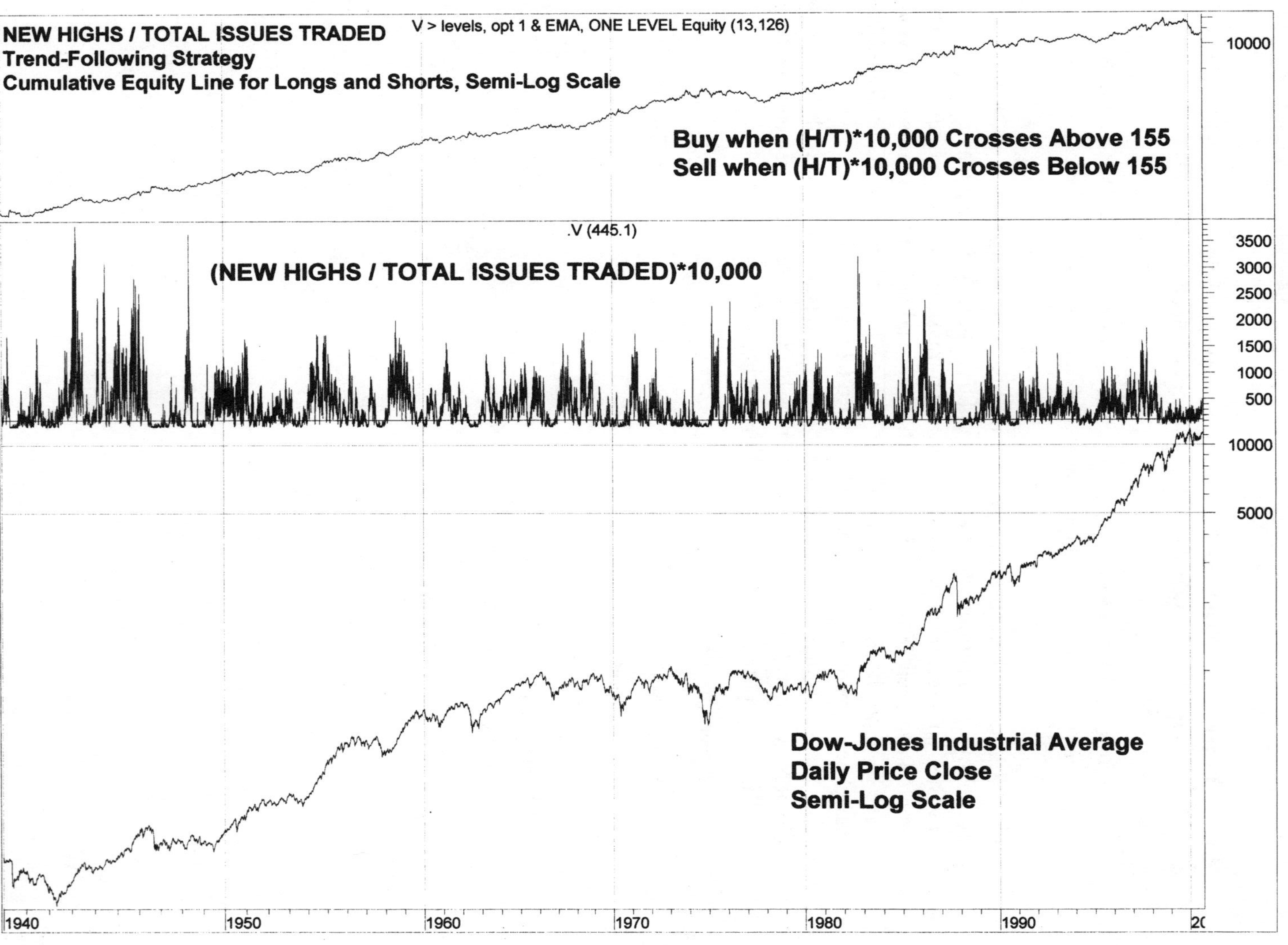
NEW HIGHS / TOTAL ISSUES TRADED
V > levels, opt 1 & EMA, ONE LEVEL Equity (13,126)
Trend-Following Strategy
Cumulative Equity Line for Longs and Shorts, Semi-Log Scale
10000
Buy when (H/T)*10,000 Crosses Above 155
Sell when (H/T)*10,000 Crosses Below 155
.V (445.1)
(NEW HIGHS / TOTAL ISSUES TRADED)*10,000
3500
3000
2500
2000
1500
1000
500
10000
5000
Dow-Jones Industrial Average
Daily Price Close
Semi-Log Scale
1940
1950
1960
1970
1980
1990
20

New Highs / Total Issues Traded >< 1.55%

Total net profit	13025.79	Open position value	440.66	Net Profit / Buy&Hold %	78.20
Percent gain/loss	13025.79	Annual percent gain/loss	214.49	Annual Net % / B&H %	78.19
Initial investment	100	Interest earned	0		
Current position	Long	Date position entered	7/20/00	# of days per trade	5.02
Buy/Hold profit	7309.76	Days in test	22166		
Buy/Hold pct gain/loss	7309.76	Annual B/H pct gain/loss	120.37		
Total closed trades	1744	Commissions paid	0		
Avg profit per trade	7.22	Avg Win/Avg Loss ratio	1.85		
Total long trades	872	Total short trades	872	Long Win Trade %	42.20
Winning long trades	368	Winning short trades	341	Short Win Trade %	39.11
Total winning trades	709	Total losing trades	1035	Total Win Trade %	40.65
Amount of winning trades	60193.97	Amount of losing trades	−47608.83	Net Profit Margin %	11.67
Average win	84.9	Average loss	−46	Average P. Margin %	29.72
Largest win	2849.72	Largest loss	−1552.95	% Net / (Win + Loss)	29.45
Average length of win	17.99	Average length of loss	4.56	(Win − Loss) / Loss %	294.52
Longest winning trade	184	Longest losing trade	70	(Win − Loss) / Loss %	162.86
Most consecutive wins	7	Most consecutive losses	15	(Win − Loss) / Loss %	−53.33
Total bars out	0	Average length out	N/A		
Longest out period	0				
System close drawdown	−7.48	Profit/Loss index	21.48	% Net Profit / SODD	13025.79
System open drawdown	−100	Reward/Risk index	99.24	(Net P.-SODD)/Net P.	99.23
Max open trade drawdown	−1552.95	Buy/Hold index	84.23	% SODD / Net Profit	−0.77

In the Equis MetaStock® "System Report" (profit and loss summary statistics), the *Total net profit* is the sum of profits minus the sum of losses, including open positions marked to the market. In contrast, the *Amount of Winning Trades* is the sum of realized profits (the total of all gains on closed-out trades only, excluding any open positions). Similarly, the *Amount of Losing Trades* is the sum of realized losses (the total of all losses on closed-out trades only, excluding any open positions). *System close drawdown* is the largest decline in the cumulative equity line below the initial investment, based on closed-out positions only. *System open drawdown (SODD)* is the largest decline in the cumulative equity line below the initial investment when a position is open. *Max open trade drawdown* is the largest decline in the cumulative equity line below the trade entry price during the worst single trade. The *Profit/Loss Index* is a complex calculation that relates the Amount of Winning Trades to the Amount of Losing Trades on a scale of −100 (worst possible performance) to +100 (best possible performance), with zero representing profits equal to losses. *Reward/Risk Index* is the Total net profit minus System open drawdown. The resulting difference is then divided by the Total net profit. The *Buy/Hold Index* is the Total net profit minus the buy-and-hold strategy's net profit. The resulting difference is then divided by the buy-and-hold net profit. In this exercise, initial equity is assumed to be $100. Both long and short positions are taken unless otherwise noted. Trades are executed at the closing price on the signal date. Transaction costs, interest expenses, and margins are not included in the statistics.

New Issue Thermometer (IPO Monthly Total)

New issue stock sales are initial public stock offerings by corporations without a previously existing public market for their stock. Such sales raise capital for future growth. Also, corporate officers may feel that the time is right to take advantage of generally overvalued stock market prices. When founders and other insiders offer a considerable amount of new issue stock, they may feel that the time is right to cash out. This indicator was developed by Norman Fosback, noted market analyst at the Institute for Econometric Research.

Ned Davis Research found that a spike up in initial public stock offerings from a low level of 27 to an extremely high level of 62 has been followed by below-average stock market returns and has preceded some major market declines, as the chart shows. The sell signal in late 1995 appears a bit more than premature, possibly because there are a greater number of corporations than in the past. Thus, this data may need to be statistically normalized relative to the number of companies. For an example of normalization, see *Insiders' Sell/Buy Ratio.*

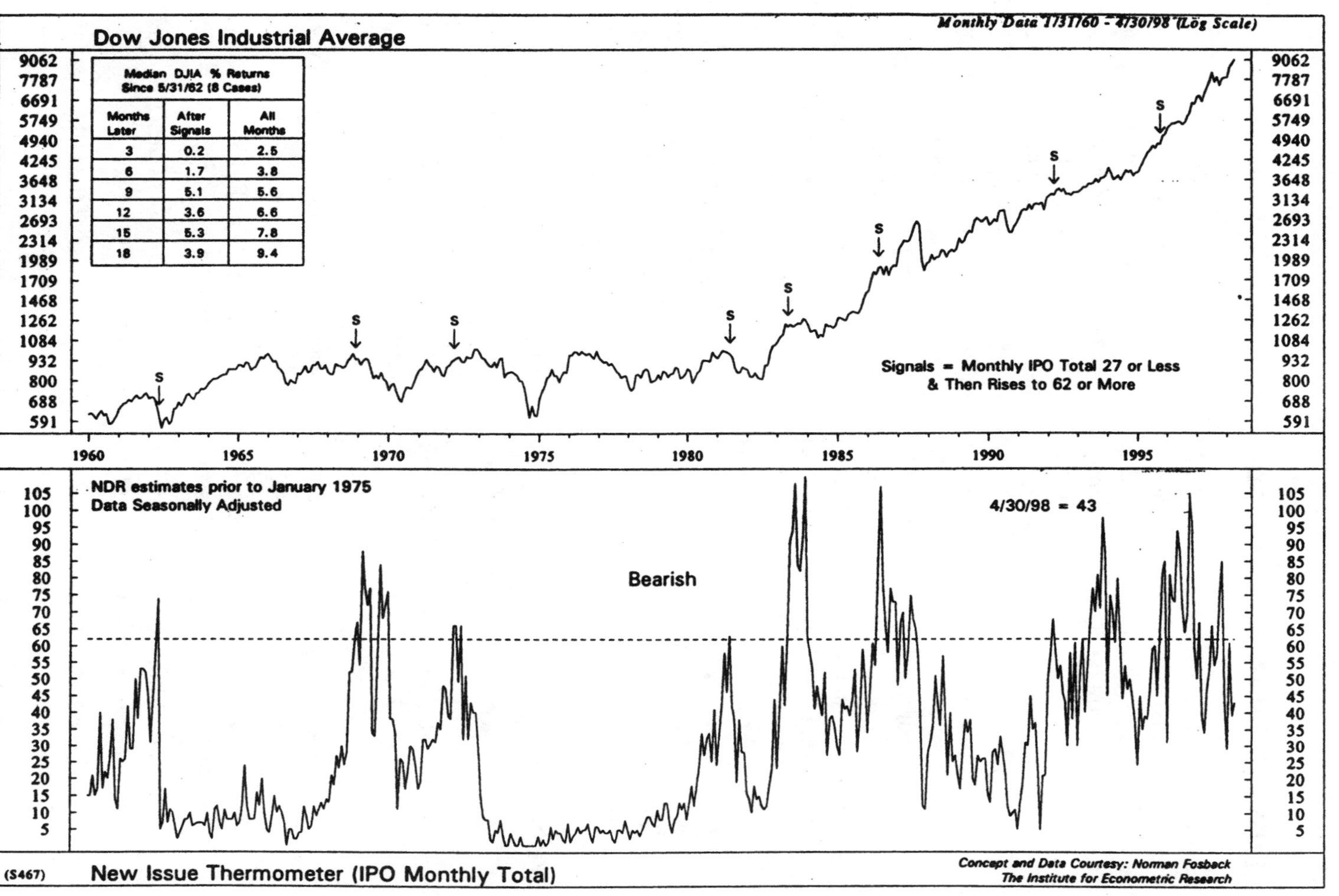
Dow Jones Industrial Average
Monthly Data 1/31/60 - 4/30/98 (Log Scale)
Median DJIA % Returns Since 5/31/62 (8 Cases)
Months Later | After Signals | All Months
3 | 0.2 | 2.5
6 | 1.7 | 3.8
9 | 5.1 | 5.6
12 | 3.6 | 6.6
15 | 5.3 | 7.8
18 | 3.9 | 9.4
9062 7787 6691 5749 4940 4245 3648 3134 2693 2314 1989 1709 1468 1262 1084 932 800 688 591
S
Signals = Monthly IPO Total 27 or Less & Then Rises to 62 or More
1960 1965 1970 1975 1980 1985 1990 1995
NDR estimates prior to January 1975
Data Seasonally Adjusted
4/30/98 = 43
Bearish
105 100 95 90 85 80 75 70 65 60 55 50 45 40 35 30 25 20 15 10 5
(S467)
New Issue Thermometer (IPO Monthly Total)
Concept and Data Courtesy: Norman Fosback
The Institute for Econometric Research
Chart by permission of Ned Davis Research.

New Lows/Total Issues Traded

The daily ratio of New Lows to Total Issues Traded is a measure of the strength of the market. If New Lows / Total Issues Traded are high and rising, the demand for stocks is weak and growing weaker, and that is bearish. But if New Lows / Total Issues Traded are low and falling, the demand for stocks is strong and growing more intense, and that is bullish. The chart shows the ratio multiplied by 10,000 to avoid decimals.

New Lows are the sum of only those stocks on the move to new downward price extremes relative to their trailing 1-year trading ranges. In other words, New Lows are the total number of stock issues (listed on a predefined stock exchange) attaining their lowest intraday prices relative to their own most recent past 52-week moving windows of time, the most recent 1-year look-back period.

Daily data is published in many financial newspapers and electronic sources for New Highs and New Lows on three separate U.S. stock exchanges: New York, American, and NASDAQ. Our studies strongly suggest that daily data is more useful than weekly data for trading, so we limited our examples here to daily data only.

The method of counting New Highs − New Lows changed in early 1978, but for practical purposes most technicians simply ignore this detail, as we do here in our testing. Also, New Highs − New Lows data should be analyzed as a percentage of Total Issues Traded so that the levels of indicator readings displayed on the chart remain comparable over the years.

Indicator Strategy Example of New Lows / Total Issues Traded

Based on a 60-year file of daily data for the ratio of New Lows to Total Issues Traded and the DJIA since 1940, we found that using a threshold level of 3.53% for generating trend-following buy and sell signals would have produced a positive result on a purely mechanical signal basis with no subjectivity, no sophisticated technical analysis, and no judgement:

Enter Long (Buy) at the current daily price close of the DJIA when the ratio of New Lows to Total Issues Traded crosses below 3.53%.

Close Long (Sell) at the current daily price close of the DJIA when the ratio of New Lows to Total Issues Traded crosses above 3.53%.

Enter Short (Sell Short) at the current daily price close of the DJIA when the ratio of New Lows to Total Issues Traded crosses above 3.53%.

Close Short (Cover) at the current daily price close of the DJIA when the ratio of New Lows to Total Issues Traded crosses below 3.53%.

Starting with $100 and reinvesting profits, total net profits for this ratio of New Lows to Total Issues Traded trend-following strategy would have been $153,684.44, assuming a fully invested strategy, reinvestment of profits, no transactions costs and no taxes. This would have been 2,002.46 percent better than buy-and-hold. Even short selling would have been profitable, and short selling was included in this strategy. Trading would have been moderately active with one trade every 19.34 calendar days.

The Equis International MetaStock® System Testing rules, where the current ratio of New Lows / Total Issues Traded times 10,000 is inserted into the data field normally reserved for Volume (V), are written as follows:

Enter long: V < opt2

Close long: V > opt2

Enter short: V > opt2

Close short: V < opt2

OPT1 Current value: 353

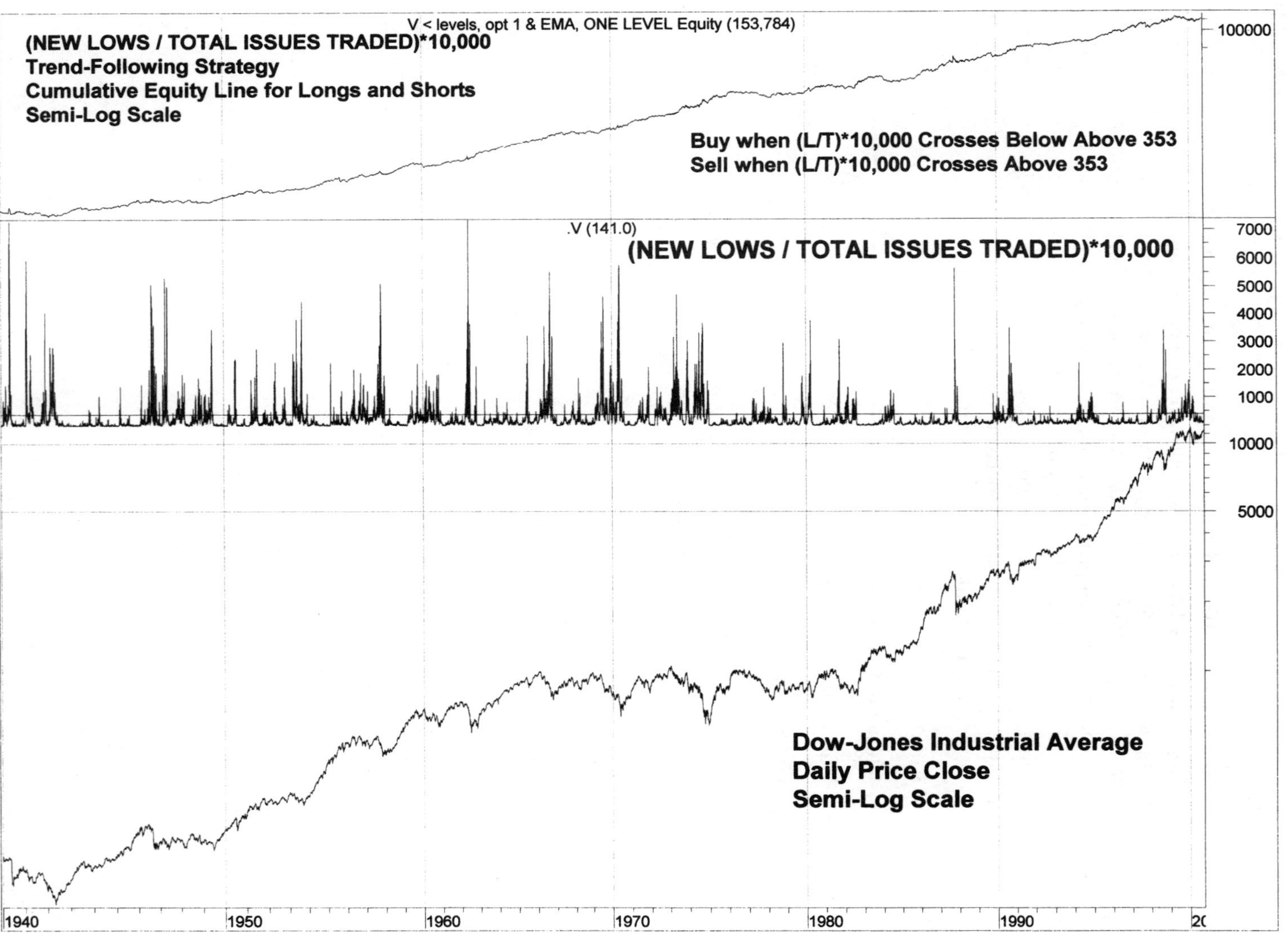
V < levels, opt 1 & EMA, ONE LEVEL Equity (153,784)
(NEW LOWS / TOTAL ISSUES TRADED)*10,000
Trend-Following Strategy
Cumulative Equity Line for Longs and Shorts
Semi-Log Scale
Buy when (L/T)*10,000 Crosses Below Above 353
Sell when (L/T)*10,000 Crosses Above 353
100000
.V (141.0)
(NEW LOWS / TOTAL ISSUES TRADED)*10,000
7000
6000
5000
4000
3000
2000
1000
10000
5000
Dow-Jones Industrial Average
Daily Price Close
Semi-Log Scale
1940
1950
1960
1970
1980
1990
20

New Lows / Total Issues Traded <> 3.53%

Total net profit	153684.44	Open position value	12289.75	Net Profit / Buy&Hold %	2002.46
Percent gain/loss	153684.44	Annual percent gain/loss	2530.67	Annual Net % / B&H %	2002.41
Initial investment	100	Interest earned	0		
Current position	Long	Date position entered	5/25/00		
Buy/Hold profit	7309.76	Days in test	22166	# of days per trade	19.34
Buy/Hold pct gain/loss	7309.76	Annual B/H pct gain/loss	120.37		
Total closed trades	1146	Commissions paid	0		
Avg profit per trade	123.38	Avg Win/Avg Loss ratio	2.71		
Total long trades	573	Total short trades	573	Long Win Trade %	43.98
Winning long trades	252	Winning short trades	237	Short Win Trade %	41.36
Total winning trades	489	Total losing trades	657	Total Win Trade %	42.67
Amount of winning trades	279986.41	Amount of losing trades	−138591.73	Net Profit Margin %	33.78
Average win	572.57	Average loss	−210.95	Average P. Margin %	46.15
Largest win	17372.34	Largest loss	−8502.08	% Net / (Win + Loss)	34.28
Average length of win	27.02	Average length of loss	5.51	(Win − Loss) / Loss %	390.38
Longest winning trade	465	Longest losing trade	124	(Win − Loss) / Loss %	275.00
Most consecutive wins	7	Most consecutive losses	8	(Win − Loss) / Loss %	−12.50
Total bars out	0	Average length out	N/A		
Longest out period	0				
System close drawdown	−19.7	Profit/Loss index	52.58	% Net Profit / SODD	153684.44
System open drawdown	−100	Reward/Risk index	99.93	(Net P.-SODD)/Net P.	99.93
Max open trade drawdown	−8502.08	Buy/Hold index	2170.58	% SODD / Net Profit	−0.07

In the Equis MetaStock® "System Report" (profit and loss summary statistics), the *Total net profit* is the sum of profits minus the sum of losses, including open positions marked to the market. In contrast, the *Amount of Winning Trades* is the sum of realized profits (the total of all gains on closed-out trades only, excluding any open positions). Similarly, the *Amount of Losing Trades* is the sum of realized losses (the total of all losses on closed-out trades only, excluding any open positions). *System close drawdown* is the largest decline in the cumulative equity line below the initial investment, based on closed-out positions only. *System open drawdown (SODD)* is the largest decline in the cumulative equity line below the initial investment when a position is open. *Max open trade drawdown* is the largest decline in the cumulative equity line below the trade entry price during the worst single trade. The *Profit/Loss Index* is a complex calculation that relates the Amount of Winning Trades to the Amount of Losing Trades on a scale of −100 (worst possible performance) to +100 (best possible performance), with zero representing profits equal to losses. *Reward/Risk Index* is the Total net profit minus System open drawdown. The resulting difference is then divided by the Total net profit. The *Buy/Hold Index* is the Total net profit minus the buy-and-hold strategy's net profit. The resulting difference is then divided by the buy-and-hold net profit. In this exercise, initial equity is assumed to be $100. Both long and short positions are taken unless otherwise noted. Trades are executed at the closing price on the signal date. Transaction costs, interest expenses, and margins are not included in the statistics.

Ninety Percent Days, Nine to One Days

Substantial stock market price declines tend to be marked by intense selling, signaled by 90% Downside Days, where the Volume of Declining Issues exceeds the Volume of Advancing Issues by a ratio of nine to one.

Substantial stock market price advances tend to be marked by intense buying, signaled by 90% Upside Days, where the Volume of Advancing Issues exceeds the Volume of Declining Issues by a ratio of nine to one.

Most commonly, data from the NYSE is used, although a similar analysis could be performed with data from other exchanges. Data appears on page C2 of *The Wall Street Journal* and is also widely available in many other newspapers, web sites, and subscription electronic data services.

Indicator Strategy Example for Ninety Percent Days, Nine to One Days

Nine to One Days offer moderately effective signals for long trades only, but perform poorly on the short side. Based on a 37-year file of daily data for the ratios of volume of shares advancing and declining each day on the NYSE and the DJIA since May 1, 1964, we found that the following simple trend-following rule would have produced a positive result on a purely mechanical signal basis with no subjectivity, no sophisticated technical analysis, and no judgement:

Enter Long (Buy) at the current daily price close of the DJIA when the Volume of Advancing Issues is at least nine times greater than the Volume of Declining Issues.

Close Long (Sell) at the current daily price close of the DJIA when the Volume of Declining Issues is at least nine times greater than the Volume of Advancing Issues.

Enter Short (Sell Short) never.

Starting with $100 and reinvesting profits, total net profits for this Ninety Percent Days trend-following strategy would have been $600.89, assuming a fully invested strategy, reinvestment of profits, no transactions costs and no taxes. This would have been 53.17 percent less than buy-and-hold. Short selling would have been unprofitable and is not included in this strategy. Most of the long trades, 57.89%, would have been profitable, and Cumulative Equity Line DrawDowns would have been very well contained. One might ask, if it underperforms buy-and-hold, why use it? The answer is because, with 50% margin, this strategy would have outperformed buy-and-hold and still have had more moderate Cumulative Equity Line DrawDowns. Trading would have been inactive with one trade every 356.11 calendar days.

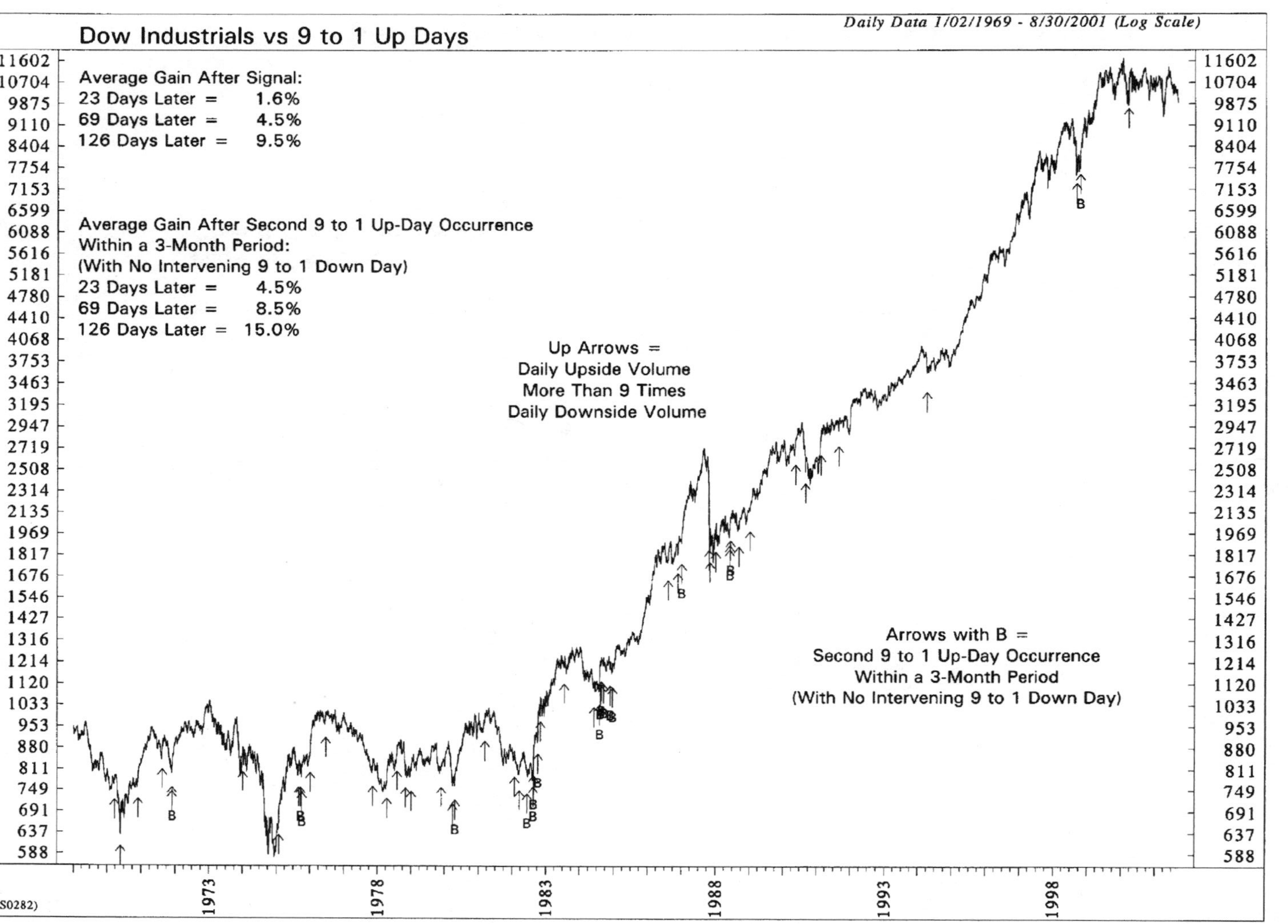
Dow Industrials vs 9 to 1 Up Days
Daily Data 1/02/1969 - 8/30/2001 (Log Scale)
Average Gain After Signal:
23 Days Later = 1.6%
69 Days Later = 4.5%
126 Days Later = 9.5%
Average Gain After Second 9 to 1 Up-Day Occurrence
Within a 3-Month Period:
(With No Intervening 9 to 1 Down Day)
23 Days Later = 4.5%
69 Days Later = 8.5%
126 Days Later = 15.0%
Up Arrows =
Daily Upside Volume
More Than 9 Times
Daily Downside Volume
Arrows with B =
Second 9 to 1 Up-Day Occurrence
Within a 3-Month Period
(With No Intervening 9 to 1 Down Day)
11602
10704
9875
9110
8404
7754
7153
6599
6088
5616
5181
4780
4410
4068
3753
3463
3195
2947
2719
2508
2314
2135
1969
1817
1676
1546
1427
1316
1214
1120
1033
953
880
811
749
691
637
588
1973
1978
1983
1988
1993
1998
(S0282)

Chart by permission of Ned Davis Research.

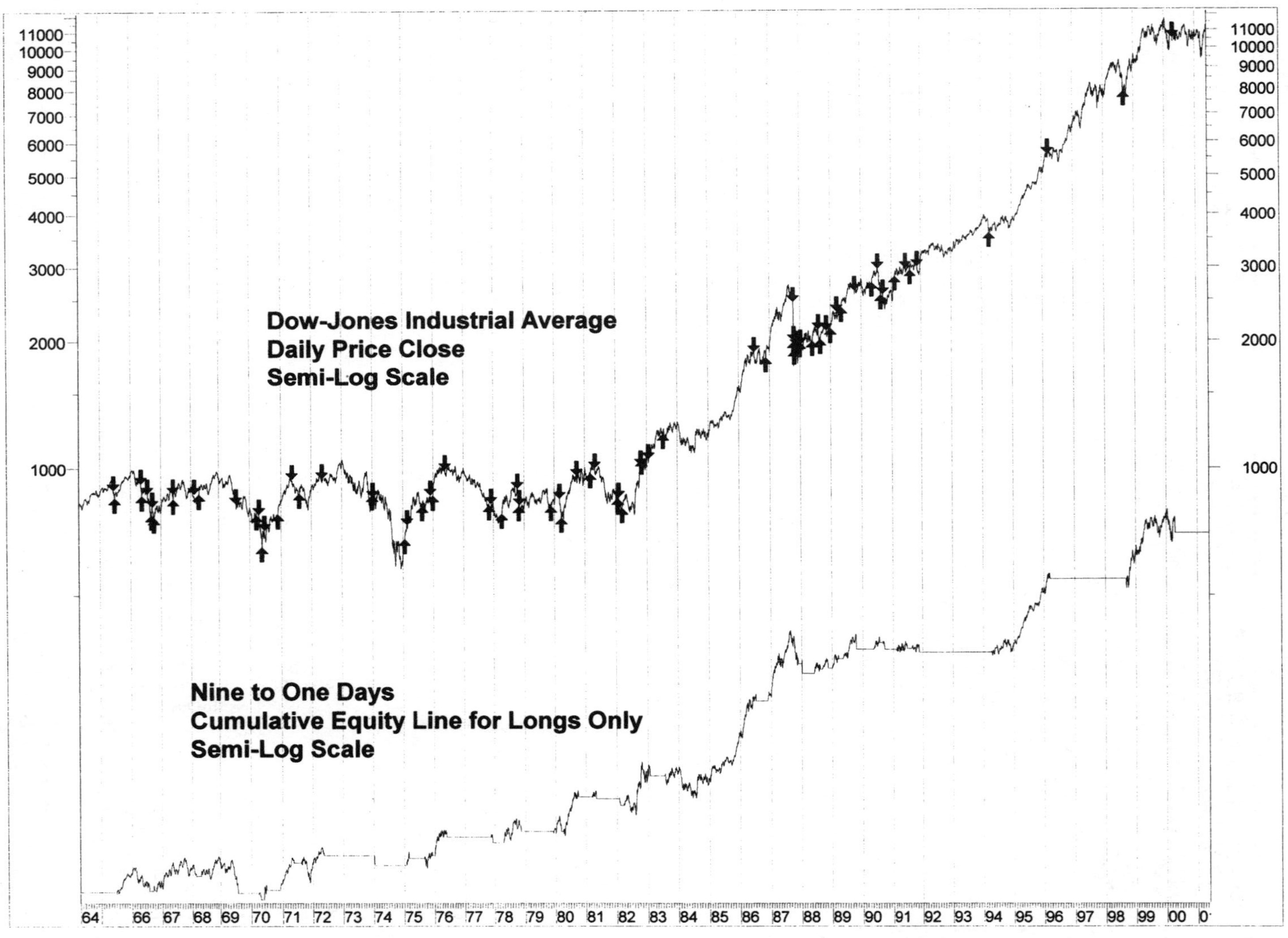

Dow-Jones Industrial Average
Daily Price Close
Semi-Log Scale
Nine to One Days
Cumulative Equity Line for Longs Only
Semi-Log Scale
11000
10000
9000
8000
7000
6000
5000
4000
3000
2000
1000
64
66
67
68
69
70
71
72
73
74
75
76
77
78
79
80
81
82
83
84
85
86
87
88
89
90
91
92
93
94
95
96
97
98
99
00
0

Ninety Percent Days, Nine to One Days

Total net profit	600.89	Open position value	N/A	Net Profit / Buy&Hold %	−53.17
Percent gain/loss	600.89	Annual percent gain/loss	16.21	Annual Net % / B&H %	−53.16
Initial investment	100	Interest earned	0		
Current position	Out	Date position entered	4/14/00		
Buy/Hold profit	1283.15	Days in test	13532	# of days per trade	356.11
Buy/Hold pct gain/loss	1283.15	Annual B/H pct gain/loss	34.61		
Total closed trades	38	Commissions paid	0		
Avg profit per trade	15.81	Avg Win/Avg Loss ratio	4.77		
Total long trades	38	Total short trades	0	Long Win Trade %	57.89
Winning long trades	22	Winning short trades	0	Short Win Trade %	#DIV/0!
Total winning trades	22	Total losing trades	16	Total Win Trade %	57.89
Amount of winning trades	708.88	Amount of losing trades	−107.99	Net Profit Margin %	73.56
Average win	32.22	Average loss	−6.75	Average P. Margin %	65.36
Largest win	178.99	Largest loss	−17.75	% Net / (Win + Loss)	81.96
Average length of win	162.45	Average length of loss	52.69	(Win − Loss) / Loss %	208.31
Longest winning trade	749	Longest losing trade	300	(Win − Loss) / Loss %	149.67
Most consecutive wins	5	Most consecutive losses	3	(Win − Loss) / Loss %	66.67
Total bars out	4989	Average length out	127.92		
Longest out period	632				
System close drawdown	−4.03	Profit/Loss index	84.77	% Net Profit / SODD	14910.42
System open drawdown	−4.03	Reward/Risk index	99.33	(Net P.-SODD)/Net P.	99.33
Max open trade drawdown	−27.56	Buy/Hold index	−53.17	% SODD / Net Profit	−0.67

In the Equis MetaStock® "System Report" (profit and loss summary statistics), the *Total net profit* is the sum of profits minus the sum of losses, including open positions marked to the market. In contrast, the *Amount of Winning Trades* is the sum of realized profits (the total of all gains on closed-out trades only, excluding any open positions). Similarly, the *Amount of Losing Trades* is the sum of realized losses (the total of all losses on closed-out trades only, excluding any open positions). *System close drawdown* is the largest decline in the cumulative equity line below the initial investment, based on closed-out positions only. *System open drawdown (SODD)* is the largest decline in the cumulative equity line below the initial investment when a position is open. *Max open trade drawdown* is the largest decline in the cumulative equity line below the trade entry price during the worst single trade. The *Profit/Loss Index* is a complex calculation that relates the Amount of Winning Trades to the Amount of Losing Trades on a scale of −100 (worst possible performance) to +100 (best possible performance), with zero representing profits equal to losses. *Reward/Risk Index* is the Total net profit minus System open drawdown. The resulting difference is then divided by the Total net profit. The *Buy/Hold Index* is the Total net profit minus the buy-and-hold strategy's net profit. The resulting difference is then divided by the buy-and-hold net profit. In this exercise, initial equity is assumed to be $100. Both long and short positions are taken unless otherwise noted. Trades are executed at the closing price on the signal date. Transaction costs, interest expenses, and margins are not included in the statistics.

The Equis International MetaStock® System Testing rules, where the current ratio of Volume of Advancing Issues divided by the Volume of Declining Issues is inserted into the data field normally reserved for Volume (V), where the current ratio of Volume of Declining Issues divided by the Volume of Advancing Issues is inserted into the data field normally reserved for Open Interest (OI), and with both ratios multiplied by 1000 for scaling, are written as follows:

Enter long: V >= 1000*opt1

Close long: OI >= 1000*opt1

OPT1 Current value: 9

Indicator Strategy Example for Ninety Percent Days, Nine to One Days, Using 50% Margin

With 50% margin this strategy would have outperformed buy-and-hold and still have had more moderate Cumulative Equity Line DrawDowns. Starting with the same $100 and reinvesting profits, leverage would have boosted total net profits to $2,933.33, assuming a fully invested strategy, reinvestment of profits, no transactions costs and no taxes. This would have been 14.30 percent greater than buy-and-hold using the same 50% margin. Short selling still is not included. Trading frequency and accuracy would have been unchanged from the 100% margined strategy. A record of each trade follows.

Ninety Percent Days with 50% Margin, a record of each trade

Trade #	*B/S Trade*	*Entry Date*	*Close Date*	*Net Profit*
—	Out	5/1/64	6/30/65	0.00
1	Long	6/30/65	5/5/66	7.31
—	Out	5/5/66	5/18/66	0.00
2	Long	5/18/66	7/25/66	−6.27
—	Out	7/25/66	9/12/66	0.00
3	Long	9/12/66	9/21/66	0.77
—	Out	9/21/66	10/12/66	0.00
4	Long	10/12/66	5/31/67	19.46
—	Out	5/31/67	6/6/67	0.00
5	Long	6/6/67	2/8/68	−3.48
—	Out	2/8/68	4/8/68	0.00
6	Long	4/8/68	7/28/69	−20.83
—	Out	7/28/69	3/25/70	0.00
7	Long	3/25/70	4/22/70	−6.75
—	Out	4/22/70	5/27/70	0.00
8	Long	5/27/70	6/23/70	9.50
—	Out	6/23/70	11/30/70	0.00
9	Long	11/30/70	5/17/71	31.94
—	Out	5/17/71	8/16/71	0.00
10	Long	8/16/71	5/9/72	10.71
—	Out	5/9/72	1/3/74	0.00
11	Long	1/3/74	1/9/74	−14.84
—	Out	1/9/74	1/27/75	0.00

12	Long	1/27/75	2/25/75	9.77
—	Out	2/25/75	8/28/75	0.00
13	Long	8/28/75	12/2/75	4.55
—	Out	12/2/75	1/5/76	0.00
14	Long	1/5/76	5/24/76	30.28
—	Out	5/24/76	11/10/77	0.00
15	Long	11/10/77	12/6/77	−10.60
—	Out	12/6/77	4/14/78	0.00
16	Long	4/14/78	10/16/78	32.52
—	Out	10/16/78	11/1/78	0.00
17	Long	11/1/78	11/7/78	−12.99
—	Out	11/7/78	11/26/79	0.00
18	Long	11/26/79	3/6/80	−0.30
—	Out	3/6/80	3/28/80	0.00
19	Long	3/28/80	9/26/80	75.51
—	Out	9/26/80	3/12/81	0.00
20	Long	3/12/81	5/4/81	−5.55
—	Out	5/4/81	1/28/82	0.00
21	Long	1/28/82	2/8/82	−17.88
—	Out	2/8/82	3/22/82	0.00
22	Long	3/22/82	10/25/82	99.77
—	Out	10/25/82	11/3/82	0.00
23	Long	11/3/82	1/24/83	−22.05
—	Out	1/24/83	7/20/83	0.00
24	Long	7/20/83	7/7/86	309.13
—	Out	7/7/86	11/20/86	0.00
25	Long	11/20/86	10/14/87	367.70
—	Out	10/14/87	10/21/87	0.00
26	Long	10/21/87	10/22/87	−75.39
—	Out	10/22/87	10/29/87	0.00
27	Long	10/29/87	11/19/87	−40.41
—	Out	11/19/87	1/4/88	0.00
28	Long	1/4/88	1/8/88	−89.90
—	Out	1/8/88	5/31/88	0.00
29	Long	5/31/88	8/9/88	36.95
—	Out	8/9/88	9/2/88	0.00
30	Long	9/2/88	11/11/88	9.91
—	Out	11/11/88	1/4/89	0.00
31	Long	1/4/89	3/17/89	87.10
—	Out	3/17/89	5/12/89	0.00
32	Long	5/12/89	10/13/89	97.25
—	Out	10/13/89	5/11/90	0.00
33	Long	5/11/90	7/23/90	74.56
—	Out	7/23/90	8/27/90	0.00
34	Long	8/27/90	9/20/90	−77.70
—	Out	9/20/90	2/11/91	0.00
35	Long	2/11/91	6/24/91	7.50
—	Out	6/24/91	8/21/91	0.00
36	Long	8/21/91	11/15/91	−39.71
—	Out	11/15/91	4/5/94	0.00
37	Long	4/5/94	3/8/96	954.82
—	Out	3/8/96	9/8/98	0.00
38	Long	9/8/98	4/14/00	1100.99
—	Out	4/14/00	5/18/01	0.00
			Sum	2933.35

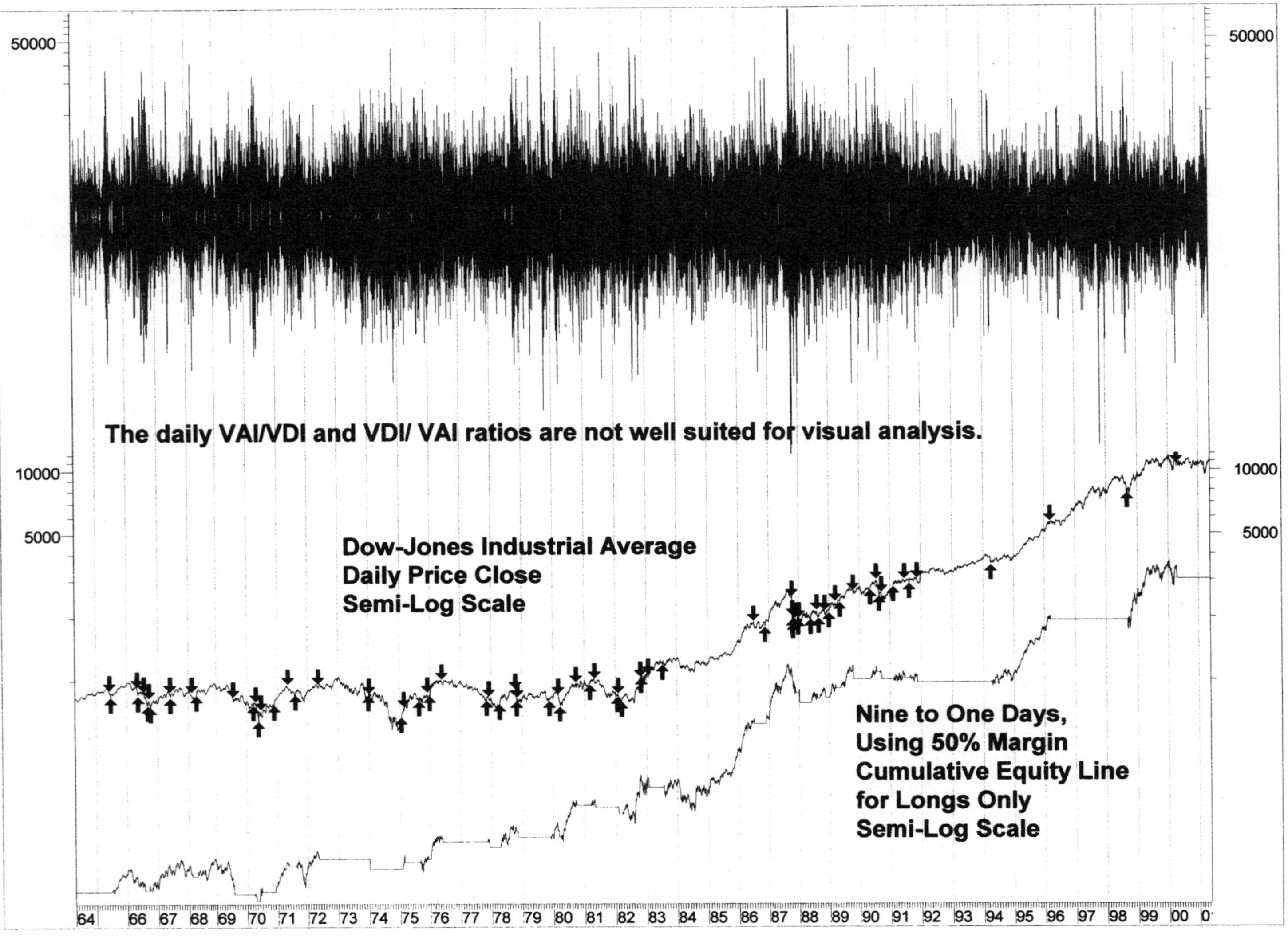

The daily VAI/VDI and VDI/ VAI ratios are not well suited for visual analysis.
Dow-Jones Industrial Average
Daily Price Close
Semi-Log Scale
Nine to One Days,
Using 50% Margin
Cumulative Equity Line
for Longs Only
Semi-Log Scale
50000
10000
5000
64 66 67 68 69 70 71 72 73 74 75 76 77 78 79 80 81 82 83 84 85 86 87 88 89 90 91 92 93 94 95 96 97 98 99 00 0

Ninety Percent Days, Using 50% Margin

Total net profit	2933.33	Open position value	N/A	Net Profit / Buy&Hold %	14.30
Percent gain/loss	2933.33	Annual percent gain/loss	79.12	Annual Net % / B&H %	14.30
Initial investment	100	Interest earned	0		
Current position	Out	Date position entered	4/14/00		
Buy/Hold profit	2566.3	Days in test	13532	# of days per trade	356.11
Buy/Hold pct gain/loss	2566.3	Annual B/H pct gain/loss	69.22		
Total closed trades	38	Commissions paid	0		
Avg profit per trade	77.19	Avg Win/Avg Loss ratio	5.52		
Total long trades	38	Total short trades	0	Long Win Trade %	57.89
Winning long trades	22	Winning short trades	0	Short Win Trade %	#DIV/0!
Total winning trades	22	Total losing trades	16	Total Win Trade %	57.89
Amount of winning trades	3377.99	Amount of losing trades	−444.66	Net Profit Margin %	76.74
Average win	153.54	Average loss	−27.79	Average P. Margin %	69.35
Largest win	1100.99	Largest loss	−89.9	% Net / (Win + Loss)	84.90
Average length of win	162.45	Average length of loss	52.69	(Win − Loss) / Loss %	208.31
Longest winning trade	749	Longest losing trade	300	(Win − Loss) / Loss %	149.67
Most consecutive wins	5	Most consecutive losses	3	(Win − Loss) / Loss %	66.67
Total bars out	4989	Average length out	127.92		
Longest out period	632				
System close drawdown	−9.79	Profit/Loss index	86.84	% Net Profit / SODD	29962.51
System open drawdown	−9.79	Reward/Risk index	99.67	(Net P.-SODD)/Net P.	99.67
Max open trade drawdown	−195.26	Buy/Hold index	14.3	% SODD / Net Profit	−0.33

In the Equis MetaStock® "System Report" (profit and loss summary statistics), the *Total net profit* is the sum of profits minus the sum of losses, including open positions marked to the market. In contrast, the *Amount of Winning Trades* is the sum of realized profits (the total of all gains on closed-out trades only, excluding any open positions). Similarly, the *Amount of Losing Trades* is the sum of realized losses (the total of all losses on closed-out trades only, excluding any open positions). *System close drawdown* is the largest decline in the cumulative equity line below the initial investment, based on closed-out positions only. *System open drawdown (SODD)* is the largest decline in the cumulative equity line below the initial investment when a position is open. *Max open trade drawdown* is the largest decline in the cumulative equity line below the trade entry price during the worst single trade. The *Profit/Loss Index* is a complex calculation that relates the Amount of Winning Trades to the Amount of Losing Trades on a scale of −100 (worst possible performance) to +100 (best possible performance), with zero representing profits equal to losses. *Reward/Risk Index* is the Total net profit minus System open drawdown. The resulting difference is then divided by the Total net profit. The *Buy/Hold Index* is the Total net profit minus the buy-and-hold strategy's net profit. The resulting difference is then divided by the buy-and-hold net profit. In this exercise, initial equity is assumed to be $100. Both long and short positions are taken unless otherwise noted. Trades are executed at the closing price on the signal date. Transaction costs, interest expenses, and margins are not included in the statistics.

Nofri's Congestion-Phase System

Most markets spend most of their time going sideways in narrow, non-trending, trading ranges known as congestion phases. Hence, a method that takes advantage of this tendency should show a high percentage of winning trades. Nofri's system, named for its developer Eugene Nofri, waits for a well-defined trading range to develop, then it fades the close after two consecutive directional days. This position is closed one day later, on the third day's close. That is, after two up days in a row, we sell short on the close, and we cover our short on the next day's close. Also, after two down days in a row, we buy on the close, and we close out our long position by selling on the next day's close. Many refinements and filters on top of this basic system are possible. For example, to produce fewer trades, defer action until the third consecutive directional day, and close out the position on the fourth day's close of trading. The optimal size of the time filter can be determined by back testing. In addition, we could use chart levels or percentage retracements as confirmation to either enter new positions or to exit positions.

Number of Advancing Issues

The number of advancing issues is the total number of stocks traded that ended the current day at a share price *higher* than the previous day's closing price. The number of advancing issues has risen steadily over the years along with the total number of stocks traded. Most commonly, data from the NYSE is used, though a similar analysis could be performed with data from other exchanges. Data appears on page C2 of *The Wall Street Journal* and is also widely available in many other newspapers, web sites, and subscription electronic data services.

Indicator Strategy Example for the Number of Advancing Issues

The trend of the Number of Advancing Issues is an effective indicator, producing steadily rising cumulative profits over many decades. Based on a 68-year file of daily data for the number of shares advancing each day on the NYSE and the DJIA since March 8, 1932, we found that a simple trend-following rule would have produced a positive result on a purely mechanical signal basis with no subjectivity, no sophisticated technical analysis, and no judgement:

Enter Long (Buy) at the current daily price close of the DJIA when the Number of Advancing Issues crosses above its own previous day's trailing 3-day EMA.

Close Long (Sell) at the current daily price close of the DJIA when the Number of Advancing Issues crosses below its own previous day's trailing 3-day EMA.

Enter Short (Sell Short) at the current daily price close of the DJIA when the Number of Advancing Issues crosses below its own previous day's trailing 3-day EMA.

Close Short (Cover) at the current daily price close of the DJIA when the Number of Advancing Issues crosses above its own previous day's trailing 3-day EMA.

Starting with $100 and reinvesting profits, total net profits for this Number of Advancing Issues trend-following strategy would have been $315,380,256, assuming a fully invested strategy, reinvestment of profits, no transactions costs and no taxes. This would have been 2,515,162 percent better than buy-and-hold. Even short selling would have been profitable. Trading would have been hyperactive with one trade every 2.81 calendar days.

The Equis International MetaStock® System Testing rules, where the current Number of Advancing Issues is inserted into the data field normally reserved for Volume (V), are written as follows:

Enter long: V > Ref(Mov(V,opt1,E),-1)

Close long: V < Ref(Mov(V,opt1,E),-1)

Enter short: V < Ref(Mov(V,opt1,E),-1)

Close short: V > Ref(Mov(V,opt1,E),-1)

OPT1 Current value: 3

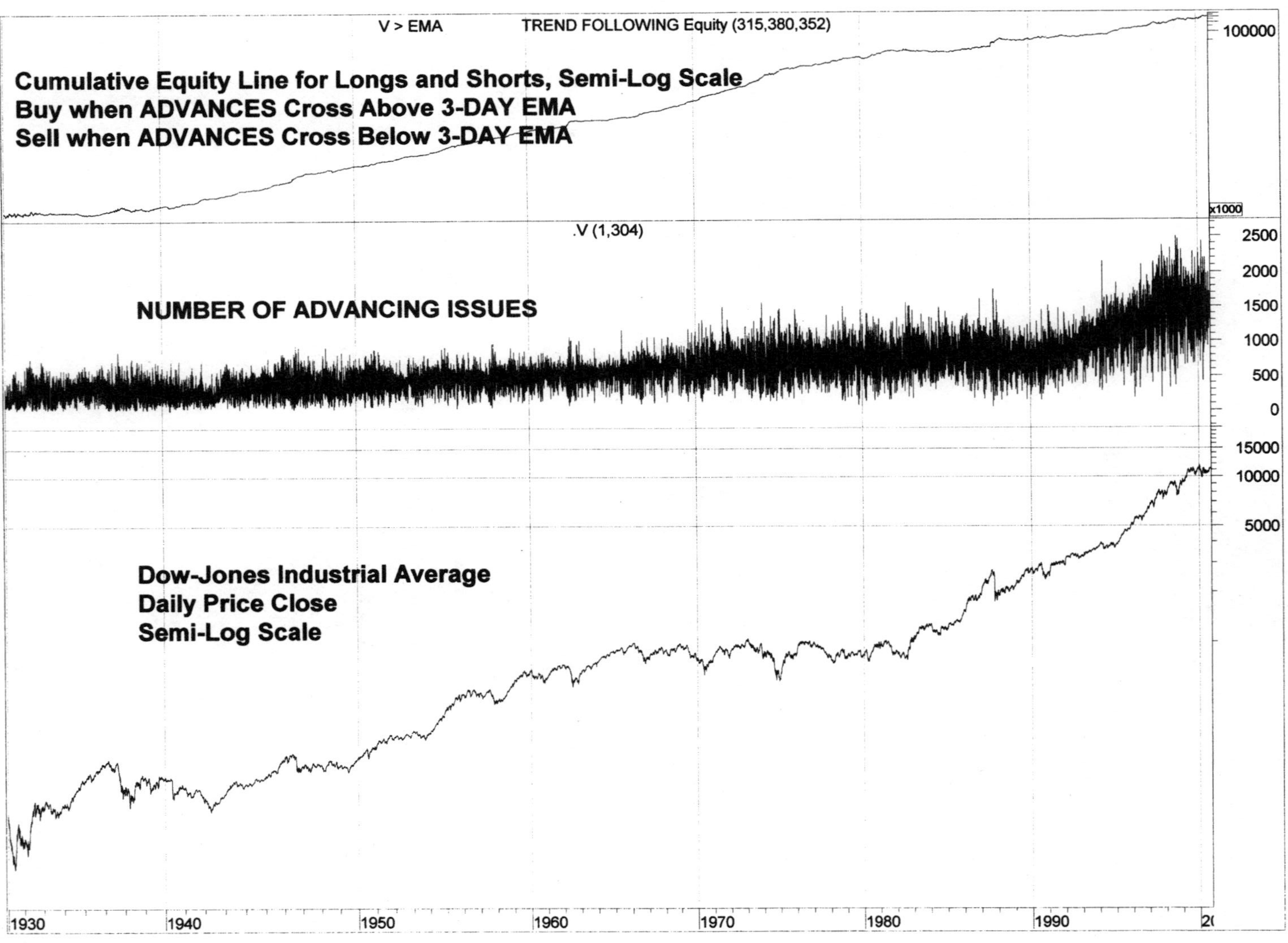
V > EMA
TREND FOLLOWING Equity (315,380,352)
Cumulative Equity Line for Longs and Shorts, Semi-Log Scale
Buy when ADVANCES Cross Above 3-DAY EMA
Sell when ADVANCES Cross Below 3-DAY EMA
100000
x1000
.V (1,304)
NUMBER OF ADVANCING ISSUES
2500
2000
1500
1000
500
0
Dow-Jones Industrial Average
Daily Price Close
Semi-Log Scale
15000
10000
5000
1930
1940
1950
1960
1970
1980
1990

Number of Advancing Issues Crossing 3-day EMA

Total net profit	315380256	Open position value	1096953.13	Net Profit / Buy&Hold %	2515162.84
Percent gain/loss	315380256	Annual percent gain/loss	4600503.29	Annual Net % / B&H %	2515210.71
Initial investment	100	Interest earned	0		
Current position	Short	Date position entered	9/7/00		
Buy/Hold profit	12538.66	Days in test	25022	# of days per trade	2.81
Buy/Hold pct gain/loss	12538.66	Annual B/H pct gain/loss	182.9		
Total closed trades	8902	Commissions paid	0		
Avg profit per trade	35304.8	Avg Win/Avg Loss ratio	1.33		
Total long trades	4451	Total short trades	4451	Long Win Trade %	54.08
Winning long trades	2407	Winning short trades	1996	Short Win Trade %	44.84
Total winning trades	4403	Total losing trades	4499	Total Win Trade %	49.46
Amount of winning trades	1.353E+09	Amount of losing trades	−1.038E+09	Net Profit Margin %	13.14
Average win	307237.09	Average loss	−230825.07	Average P. Margin %	14.20
Largest win	20820608	Largest loss	−15593024	% Net / (Win + Loss)	14.36
Average length of win	3.56	Average length of loss	2.52	(Win − Loss) / Loss %	41.27
Longest winning trade	10	Longest losing trade	8	(Win − Loss) / Loss %	25.00
Most consecutive wins	10	Most consecutive losses	13	(Win − Loss) / Loss %	−23.08
Total bars out	4	Average length out	4		
Longest out period	4				
System close drawdown	−25.3	Profit/Loss index	23.29	% Net Profit / SODD	1246562276.68
System open drawdown	−25.3	Reward/Risk index	100	(Net P.-SODD)/Net P.	100.00
Max open trade drawdown	−15593024	Buy/Hold index	2523911.97	% SODD / Net Profit	0.00

In the Equis MetaStock® "System Report" (profit and loss summary statistics), the *Total net profit* is the sum of profits minus the sum of losses, including open positions marked to the market. In contrast, the *Amount of Winning Trades* is the sum of realized profits (the total of all gains on closed-out trades only, excluding any open positions). Similarly, the *Amount of Losing Trades* is the sum of realized losses (the total of all losses on closed-out trades only, excluding any open positions). *System close drawdown* is the largest decline in the cumulative equity line below the initial investment, based on closed-out positions only. *System open drawdown (SODD)* is the largest decline in the cumulative equity line below the initial investment when a position is open. *Max open trade drawdown* is the largest decline in the cumulative equity line below the trade entry price during the worst single trade. The *Profit/Loss Index* is a complex calculation that relates the Amount of Winning Trades to the Amount of Losing Trades on a scale of −100 (worst possible performance) to +100 (best possible performance), with zero representing profits equal to losses. *Reward/Risk Index* is the Total net profit minus System open drawdown. The resulting difference is then divided by the Total net profit. The *Buy/Hold Index* is the Total net profit minus the buy-and-hold strategy's net profit. The resulting difference is then divided by the buy-and-hold net profit. In this exercise, initial equity is assumed to be $100. Both long and short positions are taken unless otherwise noted. Trades are executed at the closing price on the signal date. Transaction costs, interest expenses, and margins are not included in the statistics.

Number of Declining Issues

The number of declining issues is the total number of stocks traded that ended the current day at a share price *lower* than the previous day's closing price. The number of declining issues has risen steadily over the years along with the total number of stocks traded. Most commonly, data from the NYSE is used, though a similar analysis could be performed with data from other exchanges. Data appears on page C2 of *The Wall Street Journal* and is also widely available in many other newspapers, web sites, and subscription electronic data services.

Indicator Strategy Example for the Number of Declining Issues

The trend of the Number of Declining Issues is an effective indicator, producing steadily rising cumulative profits over many decades. Based on a 68-year file of daily data for the number of shares declining each day on the NYSE and the DJIA since March 8, 1932, we found that a simple trend-following rule would have produced a positive result on a purely mechanical signal basis with no subjectivity, no sophisticated technical analysis, and no judgement:

Enter Long (Buy) at the current daily price close of the DJIA when the Number of Declining Issues crosses below its own previous day's trailing 2-day EMA.

Close Long (Sell) at the current daily price close of the DJIA when the Number of Declining Issues crosses above its own previous day's trailing 2-day EMA.

Enter Short (Sell Short) at the current daily price close of the DJIA when the Number of Declining Issues crosses above its own previous day's trailing 2-day EMA.

Close Short (Cover) at the current daily price close of the DJIA when the Number of Declining Issues crosses below its own previous day's trailing 2-day EMA.

Starting with $100 and reinvesting profits, total net profits for this Number of Declining Issues trend-following strategy would have been $140,806,288, assuming a fully invested strategy, reinvestment of profits, no transactions costs and no taxes. This would have been 1,122,877 percent better than buy-and-hold. Even short selling would have been profitable and is included in this strategy. Trading would have been hyperactive with one trade every 2.58 calendar days.

The Equis International MetaStock® System Testing rules, where the current Number of Declining Issues is inserted into the data field normally reserved for Volume (V), are written as follows:

Enter long: V < Ref(Mov(V,opt1,E),-1)

Close long: V > Ref(Mov(V,opt1,E),-1)

Enter short: V > Ref(Mov(V,opt1,E),-1)

Close short: V < Ref(Mov(V,opt1,E),-1)

OPT1 Current value: 2

Number of Total Issues Traded

Total Issues Traded is the total number of stocks that have transactional activity on an exchange each day. It is the sum of advancing, declining, and unchanged issues. Since some listed stocks do not trade every day, total issues traded is less than total issues listed on an exchange.

Total issues traded on the New York, American, and NASDAQ stock exchanges appear on page C2 of *The Wall Street Journal.* These data are also widely available in many other newspapers, web sites, and subscription electronic data services. Some weekend news sources publish weekly data offering the number of stocks up, down, and unchanged for the week as a whole, usually from the previous Friday's close to the latest Friday's close, except when holidays fall on a Friday, in which case they use Thursday's close. Calculations based on this weekly data offer a different result from daily figures.

Total issues traded are important when analyzing *levels* in indicators that are derived from the total issues traded. These include advances, declines, new highs, and new lows, all of which are subsets of total issues traded. When total issues traded increase substantially, then these *dependent variables* also increase.

The chart on page 462 shows the substantial increase in the number of total issues traded on the NYSE, a growth of 1080% over 60 years, from a low of 303 on 8/24/40 to a high of 3574 on 11/30/99. This growth can distort the meaning of a breadth indicator over time, unless the technical analyst adjusts for the growth by converting his indicator to a percentage of total issues traded.

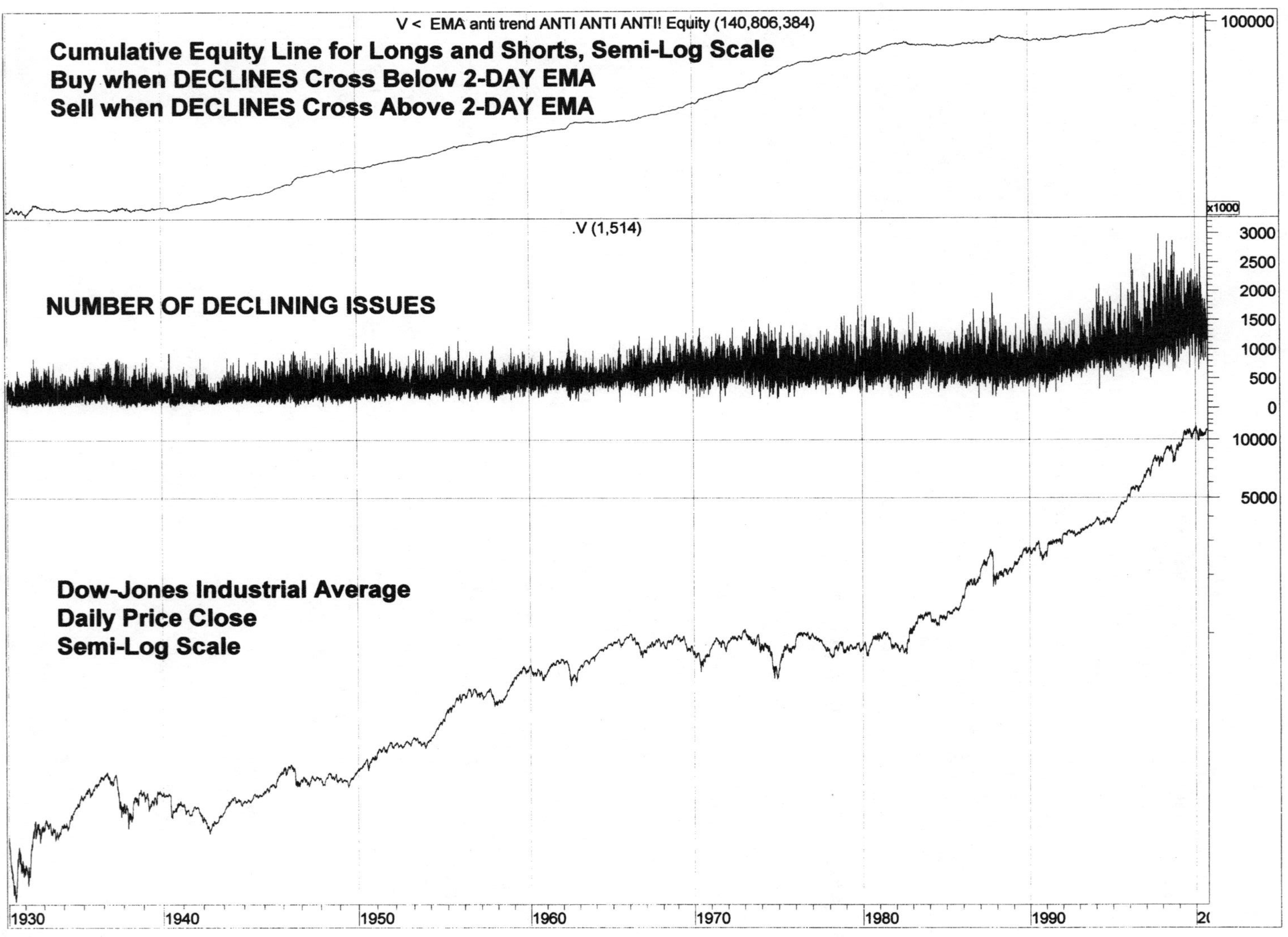
V < EMA anti trend ANTI ANTI ANTI! Equity (140,806,384)
Cumulative Equity Line for Longs and Shorts, Semi-Log Scale
Buy when DECLINES Cross Below 2-DAY EMA
Sell when DECLINES Cross Above 2-DAY EMA
100000
x1000
.V (1,514)
NUMBER OF DECLINING ISSUES
3000
2500
2000
1500
1000
500
0
10000
5000
Dow-Jones Industrial Average
Daily Price Close
Semi-Log Scale
1930
1940
1950
1960
1970
1980
1990

Number of Declining Issues Crossing Under 2-day EMA

Total net profit	140806288	Open position value	0	Net Profit / Buy&Hold %	1122877.16
Percent gain/loss	140806288	Annual percent gain/loss	2053964.32	Annual Net % / B&H %	1122898.53
Initial investment	100	Interest earned	0		
Current position	Short	Date position entered	9/8/00		
Buy/Hold profit	12538.66	Days in test	25022	# of days per trade	2.58
Buy/Hold pct gain/loss	12538.66	Annual B/H pct gain/loss	182.9		
Total closed trades	9696	Commissions paid	0		
Avg profit per trade	14522.1	Avg Win/Avg Loss ratio	1.23		
Total long trades	4848	Total short trades	4848	Long Win Trade %	53.47
Winning long trades	2592	Winning short trades	2239	Short Win Trade %	46.18
Total winning trades	4831	Total losing trades	4865	Total Win Trade %	49.82
Amount of winning trades	767836288	Amount of losing trades	−627030144	Net Profit Margin %	10.09
Average win	158939.41	Average loss	−128885.95	Average P. Margin %	10.44
Largest win	10446592	Largest loss	−8619320	% Net / (Win + Loss)	9.58
Average length of win	3.28	Average length of loss	2.45	(Win − Loss) / Loss %	33.88
Longest winning trade	10	Longest losing trade	8	(Win − Loss) / Loss %	25.00
Most consecutive wins	9	Most consecutive losses	14	(Win − Loss) / Loss %	−35.71
Total bars out	3	Average length out	3		
Longest out period	3				
System close drawdown	−31.5	Profit/Loss index	18.34	% Net Profit / SODD	447004088.89
System open drawdown	−31.5	Reward/Risk index	100	(Net P.-SODD)/Net P.	100.00
Max open trade drawdown	−8619320	Buy/Hold index	1122877.41	% SODD / Net Profit	0.00

In the Equis MetaStock® "System Report" (profit and loss summary statistics), the *Total net profit* is the sum of profits minus the sum of losses, including open positions marked to the market. In contrast, the *Amount of Winning Trades* is the sum of realized profits (the total of all gains on closed-out trades only, excluding any open positions). Similarly, the *Amount of Losing Trades* is the sum of realized losses (the total of all losses on closed-out trades only, excluding any open positions). *System close drawdown* is the largest decline in the cumulative equity line below the initial investment, based on closed-out positions only. *System open drawdown (SODD)* is the largest decline in the cumulative equity line below the initial investment when a position is open. *Max open trade drawdown* is the largest decline in the cumulative equity line below the trade entry price during the worst single trade. The *Profit/Loss Index* is a complex calculation that relates the Amount of Winning Trades to the Amount of Losing Trades on a scale of −100 (worst possible performance) to +100 (best possible performance), with zero representing profits equal to losses. *Reward/Risk Index* is the Total net profit minus System open drawdown. The resulting difference is then divided by the Total net profit. The *Buy/Hold Index* is the Total net profit minus the buy-and-hold strategy's net profit. The resulting difference is then divided by the buy-and-hold net profit. In this exercise, initial equity is assumed to be $100. Both long and short positions are taken unless otherwise noted. Trades are executed at the closing price on the signal date. Transaction costs, interest expenses, and margins are not included in the statistics.

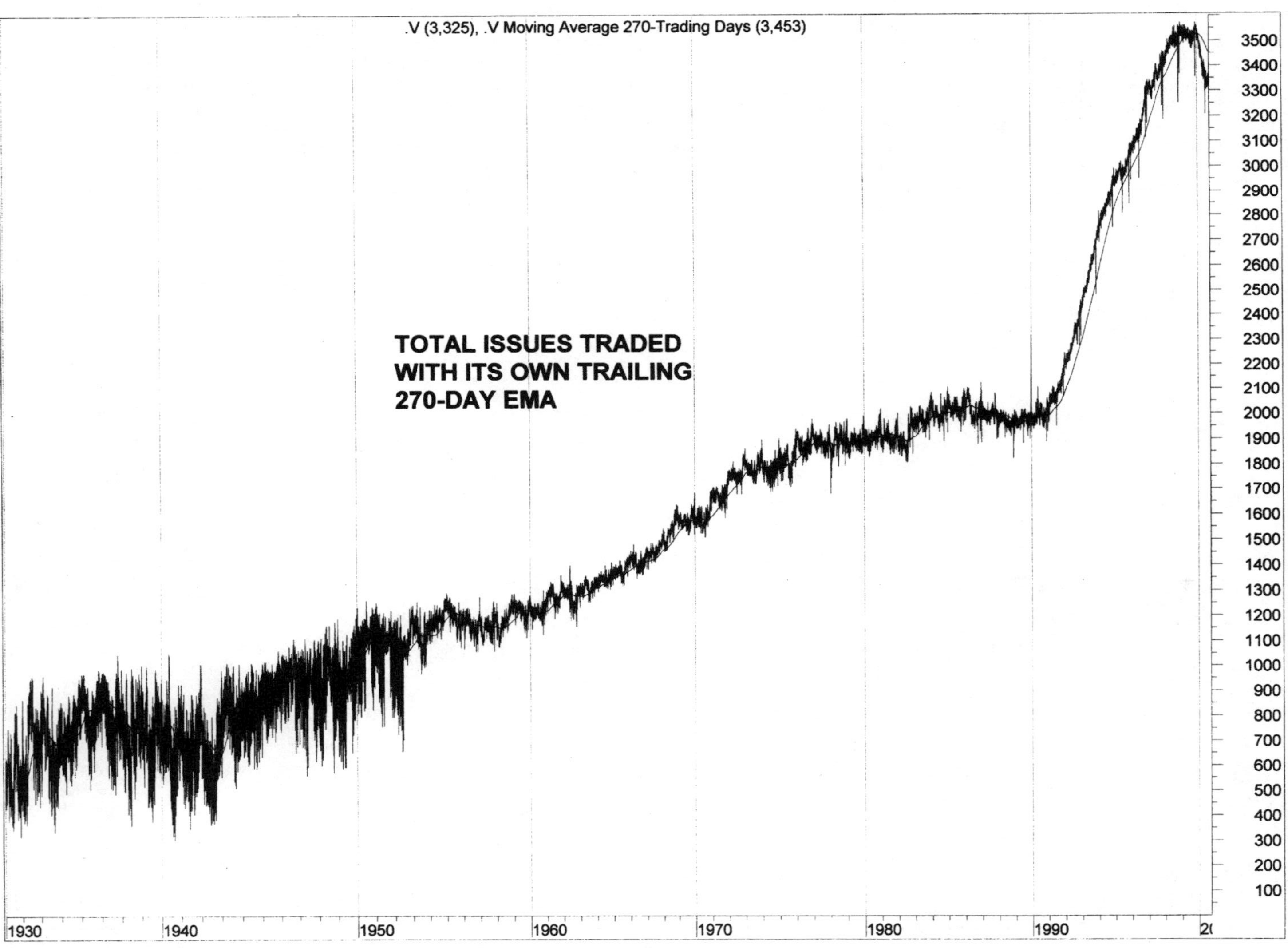
.V (3,325), .V Moving Average 270-Trading Days (3,453)
TOTAL ISSUES TRADED
WITH ITS OWN TRAILING
270-DAY EMA
3500
3400
3300
3200
3100
3000
2900
2800
2700
2600
2500
2400
2300
2200
2100
2000
1900
1800
1700
1600
1500
1400
1300
1200
1100
1000
900
800
700
600
500
400
300
200
100
1930
1940
1950
1960
1970
1980
1990

Odd Lot Balance Index
Odd Lot Total Sales/Odd Lot Total Purchases

The Odd Lot Balance Index is a *contrary opinion* market sentiment indicator. It is calculated by dividing Odd Lot Total Sales by Odd Lot Total Purchases. (Here, this ratio has been multiplied by 1000 for scaling.) The daily New York Stock Exchange data used in the calculation is published in many daily newspapers.

An *odd lot* is a small order to buy or sell a number of shares less than a *round lot* of 100 shares of a stock. The reasoning behind this indicator is that small speculators who cannot afford to buy 100 shares of stock are unsophisticated and uninformed. Therefore, these *little guys* are likely to be wrong about the future direction of stock prices.

Indeed, the record shows that generally this reasoning is correct. Therefore, it pays to do the opposite of what the Odd Lotter is doing: buy when the Odd Lot Balance Index is relatively high (indicating high odd lot selling), and sell when the Odd Lot Balance Index is relatively low (indicating greater odd lot buying).

Indicator Strategy Example for the Daily Odd Lot Balance Index Envelope

Based on a 39-year file of the daily Odd Lot Balance Index Envelope and the daily closing price data for the DJIA from January 1962 to January 2001, we found that the following parameters would have outperformed the passive buy-and-hold strategy and would have called the direction right most of the time, on a purely mechanical trend-following signal basis with no subjectivity, no sophisticated technical analysis, and no judgement:

Enter Long (Buy) at the current daily price close of the DJIA when the latest Odd Lot Balance Index is 3.1% above its previous day's 2-day EMA of the Odd Lot Balance Index.

Close Long (Sell) at the current daily price close of the DJIA when the latest Odd Lot Balance Index is 3.1% below its previous day's 9-day EMA of the Odd Lot Balance Index.

Enter Short (Sell Short) never.

Starting with $100 and reinvesting profits, total net profits for this Odd Lot Balance Index Envelope contrary strategy would have been $1,789.97, assuming a fully invested strategy, reinvestment of profits, no transactions costs and no taxes. This would have been 31.07 percent greater than buy-and-hold. No short selling would have been profitable, and no short selling was included in the strategy. Short selling would have cut the profit by 13%. Long-only Odd Lot Balance Index Envelope as an

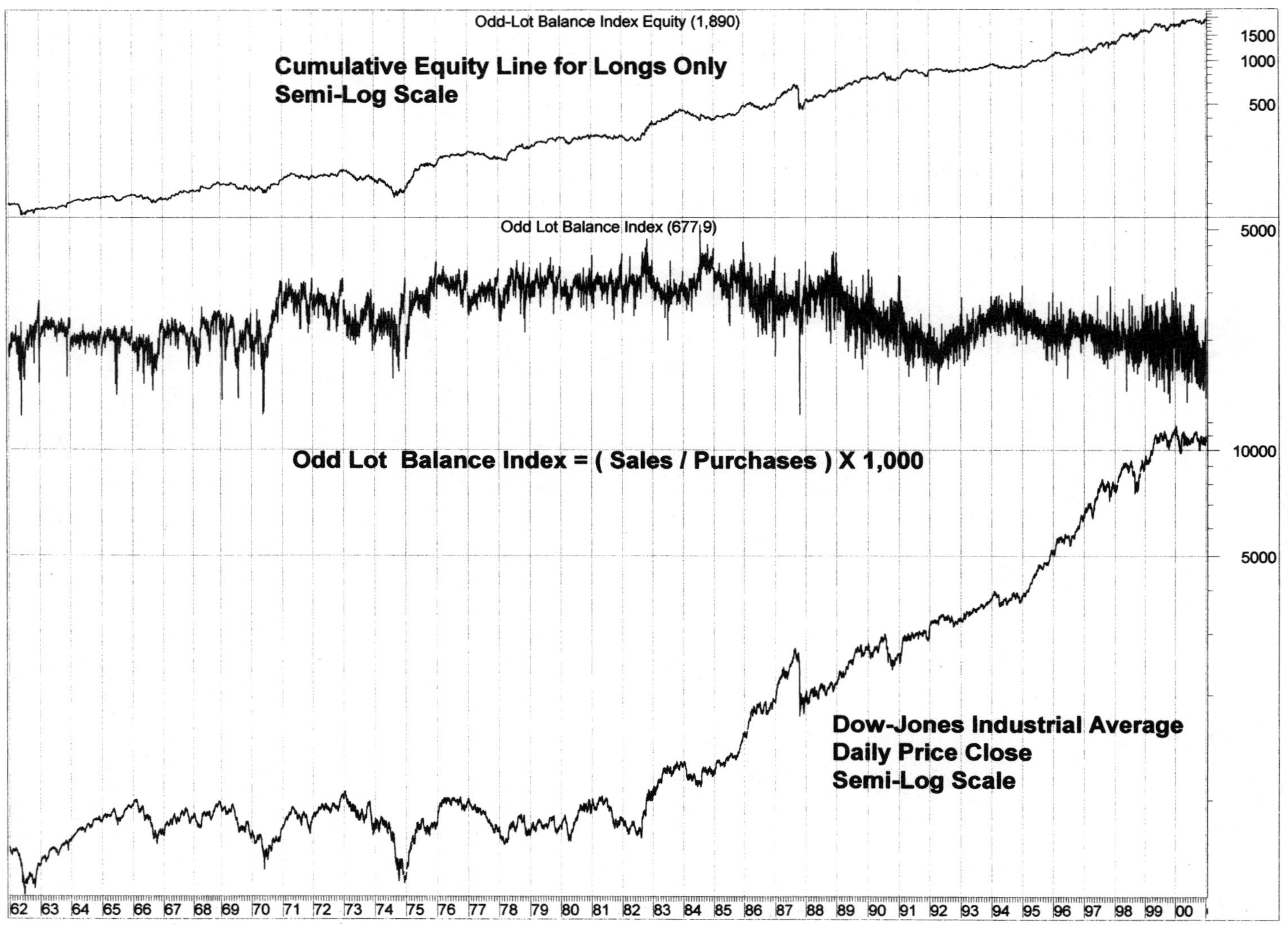

Odd-Lot Balance Index Equity (1,890)
Cumulative Equity Line for Longs Only
Semi-Log Scale
1500
1000
500
Odd Lot Balance Index (677.9)
5000
Odd Lot Balance Index = (Sales / Purchases) X 1,000
10000
5000
Dow-Jones Industrial Average
Daily Price Close
Semi-Log Scale
62 63 64 65 66 67 68 69 70 71 72 73 74 75 76 77 78 79 80 81 82 83 84 85 86 87 88 89 90 91 92 93 94 95 96 97 98 99 00

Odd Lot Balance Index Envelope

Total net profit	1789.97	Open position value	N/A	Net Profit / Buy&Hold %	31.07
Percent gain/loss	1789.97	Annual percent gain/loss	45.84	Annual Net % / B&H %	31.08
Initial investment	100	Interest earned	0		
Current position	Out	Date position entered	1/5/01		
Buy/Hold profit	1365.61	Days in test	14252	# of days per trade	8.45
Buy/Hold pct gain/loss	1365.61	Annual B/H pct gain/loss	34.97		
Total closed trades	1686	Commissions paid	0		
Avg profit per trade	1.06	Avg Win/Avg Loss ratio	1.09		
Total long trades	1686	Total short trades	0	Long Win Trade %	55.34
Winning long trades	933	Winning short trades	0	Short Win Trade %	#DIV/0!
Total winning trades	933	Total losing trades	753	Total Win Trade %	55.34
Amount of winning trades	6970.44	Amount of losing trades	−5180.48	Net Profit Margin %	14.73
Average win	7.47	Average loss	−6.88	Average P. Margin %	4.11
Largest win	92.53	Largest loss	−140.9	% Net / (Win + Loss)	−20.72
Average length of win	4.74	Average length of loss	4.44	(Win − Loss) / Loss %	6.76
Longest winning trade	30	Longest losing trade	26	(Win − Loss) / Loss %	15.38
Most consecutive wins	16	Most consecutive losses	9	(Win − Loss) / Loss %	77.78
Total bars out	5437	Average length out	3.22		
Longest out period	15				
System close drawdown	−15.32	Profit/Loss index	25.68	% Net Profit / SODD	10547.85
System open drawdown	−16.97	Reward/Risk index	99.06	(Net P.-SODD)/Net P.	99.05
Max open trade drawdown	−168.86	Buy/Hold index	31.07	% SODD / Net Profit	−0.95

In the Equis MetaStock® "System Report" (profit and loss summary statistics), the *Total net profit* is the sum of profits minus the sum of losses, including open positions marked to the market. In contrast, the *Amount of Winning Trades* is the sum of realized profits (the total of all gains on closed-out trades only, excluding any open positions). Similarly, the *Amount of Losing Trades* is the sum of realized losses (the total of all losses on closed-out trades only, excluding any open positions). *System close drawdown* is the largest decline in the cumulative equity line below the initial investment, based on closed-out positions only. *System open drawdown (SODD)* is the largest decline in the cumulative equity line below the initial investment when a position is open. *Max open trade drawdown* is the largest decline in the cumulative equity line below the trade entry price during the worst single trade. The *Profit/Loss Index* is a complex calculation that relates the Amount of Winning Trades to the Amount of Losing Trades on a scale of −100 (worst possible performance) to +100 (best possible performance), with zero representing profits equal to losses. *Reward/Risk Index* is the Total net profit minus System open drawdown. The resulting difference is then divided by the Total net profit. The *Buy/Hold Index* is the Total net profit minus the buy-and-hold strategy's net profit. The resulting difference is then divided by the buy-and-hold net profit. In this exercise, initial equity is assumed to be $100. Both long and short positions are taken unless otherwise noted. Trades are executed at the closing price on the signal date. Transaction costs, interest expenses, and margins are not included in the statistics.

indicator would have given profitable buy signals 55.34% of the time. Trading would have been active at one trade every 8.45 calendar days.

The Equis International MetaStock® System Testing rules for the Odd Lot Balance Index, where the ratio of 1,000 times the ratio of Odd Lot Total Sales to Odd Lot Total Purchases is inserted into the field normally reserved for open interest, are written as follows:

Enter long: OI>Ref(Mov(OI,opt1,E),-1) + ((opt2/1000))*Ref(Mov(OI,opt1,E),-1)

Close long: OI<Ref(Mov(OI,opt3,E),-1) − ((opt2/1000))*Ref(Mov(OI,opt3,E),-1)

OPT1 Current value: 2

OPT2 Current value: 31

OPT3 Current value: 9

Odd Lot Short Ratio

The Odd Lot Short Sales Ratio is an obsolete sentiment indicator that reflects the behavior of small, amateur speculators, who traditionally have been thought of as "usually wrong." *(See Contrary Opinion.)* Indeed odd-lot short sellers have been wrong more often than right. From January 1962 to January 2001, however, fading odd-lot short sellers would have lost dollars because losses would have been larger than gains. This discouraging result would have been obtained over any time horizon. Contrary Opinion would have been wrong.

Odd Lot Short Sales are the volume (stated in number of shares) of short sales transactions entered into by small traders who trade in odd lots. (An *odd lot* is any order size smaller than a *round lot* of 100 shares.) The Odd Lot Short Sales Ratio is a sample of data that precisely quantifies the behavior and sentiment of traders and investors dealing in small quantities of stock.

Odd Lot Short Sales Ratios are calculated in a variety of ways. The simplest and best way is to divide odd lot short sales by odd lot total sales, using daily data. Alternately, some divide odd lot short sales by odd lot total sales plus odd lot total purchases. The formulas are very similar so the results are very similar. A less profitable variation uses weekly data, dividing odd lot short sales by total short sales. NYSE data is used in the calculations.

As the weekly chart shows, on page 478, the ratio of odd lot short sales to total short sales has declined substantially over the past 55 years. Therefore, traditional benchmarks identifying absolute levels have become meaningless. The data needs to be normalized and related to an adaptive standard.

Generally, a speculator may *sell short* when he anticipates lower prices ahead. If the short seller is correct and the price falls, he may *cover his short position* at a profit, by buying the stock back at a price lower than what he sold it for. The difference (the short sale price minus the short cover price) is the profit. If the short seller is wrong and the price rises, he limits or cuts losses by *covering his short,* by buying back the stock at a price that is higher than the price he received when he sold it short. The price difference is taken as a loss.

Indicator Strategy Example for the Ratio of Daily Odd Lot Short Sales to Odd Lot Total Sales, Long and Short, an Inverted Strategy

Trading contrary to odd-lot short sellers lost most of our money over the past 39 years. Because results are dismal, we may reverse the logic by assuming that odd-lot short sellers reflect the opinion of the smart money.

Using daily data, we divided odd lot short sales by odd lot total sales. We multiplied that ratio by 1,000,000 for scaling. Based on a 39-year file of these daily Odd Lot Short Sales Ratios and daily closing price data for the DJIA from January 1962 to January 2001, we found that the following long and short parameters would have outperformed the passive buy-and-hold strategy on a purely mechanical trend-following signal basis with no subjectivity, no sophisticated technical analysis, and no judgement:

Enter Long (Buy) at the current daily price close of the DJIA when the latest Ratio of Daily Odd Lot Short Sales to Odd Lot Total Sales is below its previous day's value.

Close Long (Sell) at the current daily price close of the DJIA when the latest Ratio of Daily Odd Lot Short Sales to Odd Lot Total Sales is above its previous day's trailing 18-day EMA of the Ratio of Daily Odd Lot Short Sales to Odd Lot Total Sales.

Enter Short (Sell Short) at the current daily price close of the DJIA when the latest Ratio of Daily Odd Lot Short Sales to Odd Lot Total Sales is above its previous day's trailing 18-day EMA of the Ratio of Daily Odd Lot Short Sales to Odd Lot Total Sales.

Close Short (Cover) at the current daily price close of the DJIA when the latest Ratio of Daily Odd Lot Short Sales to Odd Lot Total Sales is below its previous day's value.

Starting with $100 and reinvesting profits, total net profits for this Ratio of Daily Odd Lot Short Sales to Odd Lot Total Sales Inverted Strategy would have been $4,384.41, assuming a fully invested strategy, reinvestment of profits, no transactions

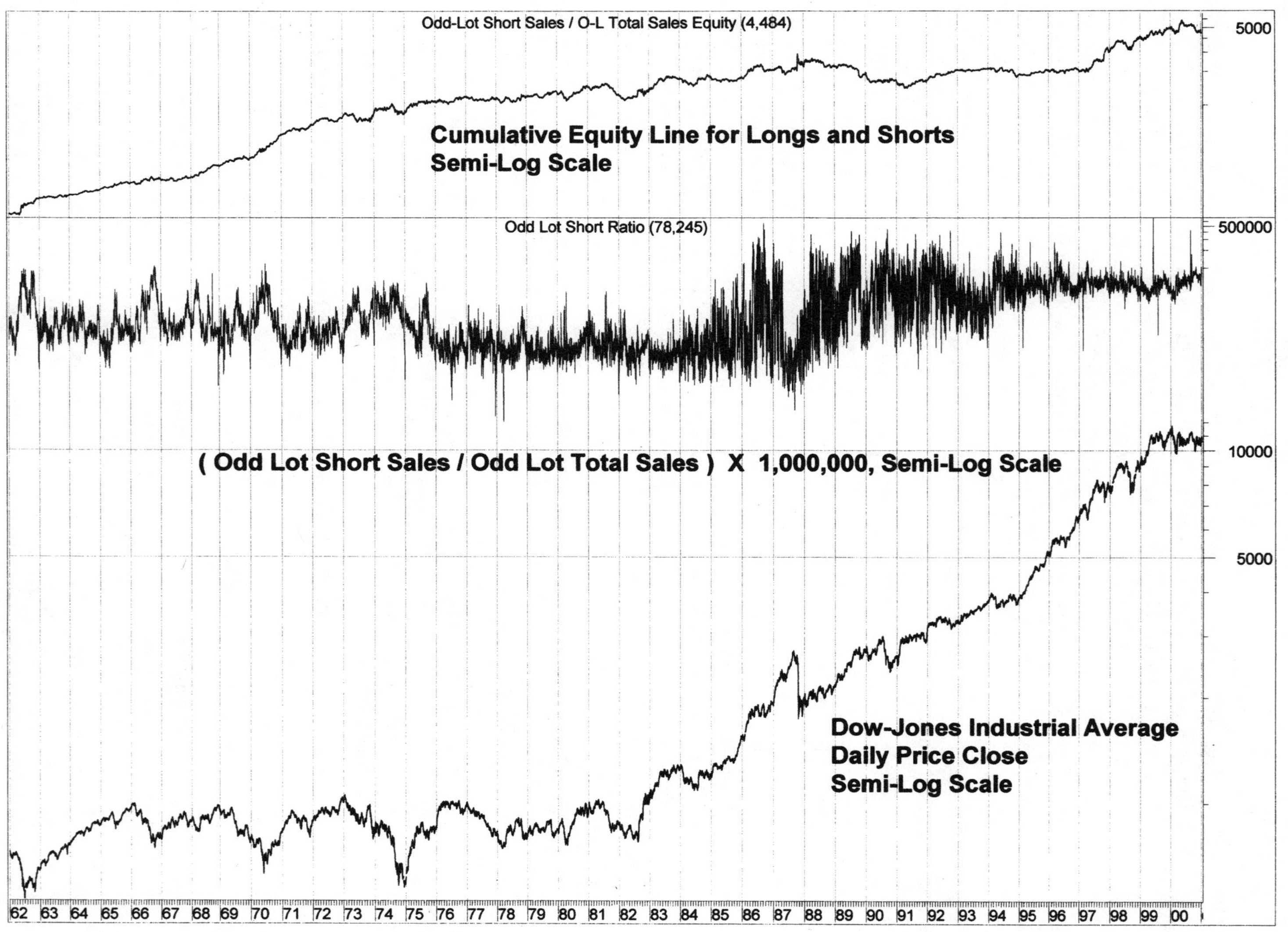
Odd-Lot Short Sales / O-L Total Sales Equity (4,484)
5000
Cumulative Equity Line for Longs and Shorts
Semi-Log Scale
Odd Lot Short Ratio (78,245)
500000
(Odd Lot Short Sales / Odd Lot Total Sales) X 1,000,000, Semi-Log Scale
10000
5000
Dow-Jones Industrial Average
Daily Price Close
Semi-Log Scale
62
63
64
65
66
67
68
69
70
71
72
73
74
75
76
77
78
79
80
81
82
83
84
85
86
87
88
89
90
91
92
93
94
95
96
97
98
99
00

Odd Lot Short Sales/(Odd Lot Total Sales), Long and Short

Total net profit	4384.41	Open position value	0	Net Profit / Buy&Hold %	221.06
Percent gain/loss	4384.41	Annual percent gain/loss	112.29	Annual Net % / B&H %	221.10
Initial investment	100	Interest earned	0		
Current position	Long	Date position entered	1/8/01		
Buy/Hold profit	1365.61	Days in test	14252	# of days per trade	3.34
Buy/Hold pct gain/loss	1365.61	Annual B/H pct gain/loss	34.97		
Total closed trades	4262	Commissions paid	0		
Avg profit per trade	1.03	Avg Win/Avg Loss ratio	1.14		
Total long trades	2131	Total short trades	2131	Long Win Trade %	51.06
Winning long trades	1088	Winning short trades	1048	Short Win Trade %	49.18
Total winning trades	2136	Total losing trades	2126	Total Win Trade %	50.12
Amount of winning trades	35542.98	Amount of losing trades	−31158.6	Net Profit Margin %	6.57
Average win	16.64	Average loss	−14.66	Average P. Margin %	6.33
Largest win	460.45	Largest loss	−277.99	% Net / (Win + Loss)	24.71
Average length of win	3.64	Average length of loss	2.96	(Win − Loss) / Loss %	22.97
Longest winning trade	41	Longest losing trade	29	(Win − Loss) / Loss %	41.38
Most consecutive wins	10	Most consecutive losses	10	(Win − Loss) / Loss %	0.00
Total bars out	6	Average length out	6		
Longest out period	6				
System close drawdown	−3.37	Profit/Loss index	12.34	% Net Profit / SODD	130101.19
System open drawdown	−3.37	Reward/Risk index	99.92	(Net P.-SODD)/Net P.	99.92
Max open trade drawdown	−293.5	Buy/Hold index	221.06	% SODD / Net Profit	−0.08

In the Equis MetaStock® "System Report" (profit and loss summary statistics), the *Total net profit* is the sum of profits minus the sum of losses, including open positions marked to the market. In contrast, the *Amount of Winning Trades* is the sum of realized profits (the total of all gains on closed-out trades only, excluding any open positions). Similarly, the *Amount of Losing Trades* is the sum of realized losses (the total of all losses on closed-out trades only, excluding any open positions). *System close drawdown* is the largest decline in the cumulative equity line below the initial investment, based on closed-out positions only. *System open drawdown (SODD)* is the largest decline in the cumulative equity line below the initial investment when a position is open. *Max open trade drawdown* is the largest decline in the cumulative equity line below the trade entry price during the worst single trade. The *Profit/Loss Index* is a complex calculation that relates the Amount of Winning Trades to the Amount of Losing Trades on a scale of −100 (worst possible performance) to +100 (best possible performance), with zero representing profits equal to losses. *Reward/Risk Index* is the Total net profit minus System open drawdown. The resulting difference is then divided by the Total net profit. The *Buy/Hold Index* is the Total net profit minus the buy-and-hold strategy's net profit. The resulting difference is then divided by the buy-and-hold net profit. In this exercise, initial equity is assumed to be $100. Both long and short positions are taken unless otherwise noted. Trades are executed at the closing price on the signal date. Transaction costs, interest expenses, and margins are not included in the statistics.

costs and no taxes. This would have been 221.06 percent greater than buy-and-hold. Short selling would have been profitable and was included in the strategy. The indicator still would have outperformed the passive buy-and-hold strategy without short selling. The Ratio of Daily Odd Lot Short Sales to Odd Lot Total Sales as an indicator would have given profitable buy signals slightly more than half of the time and profitable sell short signals slightly less than half of the time. Trading would have been extremely active at one trade every 3.34 calendar days. These results are contrary to traditional expectations.

The Equis International MetaStock® System Testing rules for the Ratio of Daily Odd Lot Short Sales to Odd Lot Total Sales (multiplied by 1,000,000 for scaling) is inserted into the field normally reserved for open interest, are written as follows:

Enter long: OI < Ref(Mov(OI ,opt1,E),-1)

Close long: OI > Ref(Mov(OI ,opt2,E),-1)

Enter short: OI > Ref(Mov(OI ,opt2,E),-1)

Close short: OI < Ref(Mov(OI ,opt1,E),-1)

OPT1 Current value: 1
OPT2 Current value: 18

Indicator Strategy Example for the Daily Ratio of Odd Lot Shorts to Purchases Plus Sales, Long and Short, Another Inverted Strategy

Using daily data, we divided odd lot short sales by odd lot total purchases plus odd lot total sales, then multiplied that ratio by 10,000 for scaling. Based on a 39-year file of these daily Odd Lot Short Ratios and daily closing price data for the DJIA from January 1962 to January 2001, we found that the following long and short parameters would have outperformed the passive buy-and-hold strategy on a purely mechanical trend-following signal basis with no subjectivity, no sophisticated technical analysis, and no judgement:

Enter Long (Buy) at the current daily price close of the DJIA when the latest Daily Ratio of Odd Lot Short Sales to Purchases plus Sales is below its previous day's value.

Close Long (Sell) at the current daily price close of the DJIA when the latest Daily Ratio of Odd Lot Short Sales to Purchases plus Sales is above its previous day's trailing 12-day EMA of the Daily Ratio of Odd Lot Short Sales to Purchases plus Sales.

Enter Short (Sell Short) at the current daily price close of the DJIA when the latest Daily Ratio of Odd Lot Short Sales to Purchases plus Sales is above its previous day's trailing 12-day EMA of the Daily Ratio of Odd Lot Short Sales to Purchases plus Sales.

Close Short (Cover) at the current daily price close of the DJIA when the latest Daily Ratio of Odd Lot Short Sales to Purchases plus Sales is below its previous day's value.

Starting with $100 and reinvesting profits, total net profits for this Daily Ratio of Odd Lot Short Sales to Purchases plus Sales Inverted Strategy would have been $3,199.85, assuming a fully invested strategy, reinvestment of profits, no transactions costs and no taxes. This would have been 134.32 percent greater than buy-and-hold. Short selling would have been profitable and was included in the strategy. The indicator still would have outperformed the passive buy-and-hold strategy without short selling. The Long-and-Short Daily Ratio of Odd Lot Short Sales to Purchases plus Sales as an indicator would have given profitable buy signals slightly more than half of the time and profitable sell short signals slightly less than half of the time. Trading would have been extremely active at one trade every 3.19 calendar days. These results are contrary to traditional expectations.

The Equis International MetaStock® System Testing rules for the Daily Ratio of Odd Lot Short Sales to Purchases plus Sales, where the ratio of Odd Lot Short Sales to Total Purchases plus Total Sales (multiplied by 10,000 for scaling) is inserted into the field normally reserved for open interest, are written as follows:

Enter long: OI < Ref(Mov(OI ,opt1,E),-1)

Close long: OI > Ref(Mov(OI ,opt2,E),-1)

Enter short: OI > Ref(Mov(OI ,opt2,E),-1)

Close short: OI < Ref(Mov(OI ,opt1,E),-1)

OPT1 Current value: 1
OPT2 Current value: 12

Indicator Strategy Example for the Daily Ratio of Odd Lot Short Sales to Purchases Plus Sales, Inverted Strategy, Long Only

Using the exact same parameters as the preceding, profit would have been 20% lower for the long-only strategy, with no short selling. It still would have outperformed the passive buy-and-hold strategy. The chart, on page 474, seems to show a milder equity drawdowns, especially from 1987 to 1991.

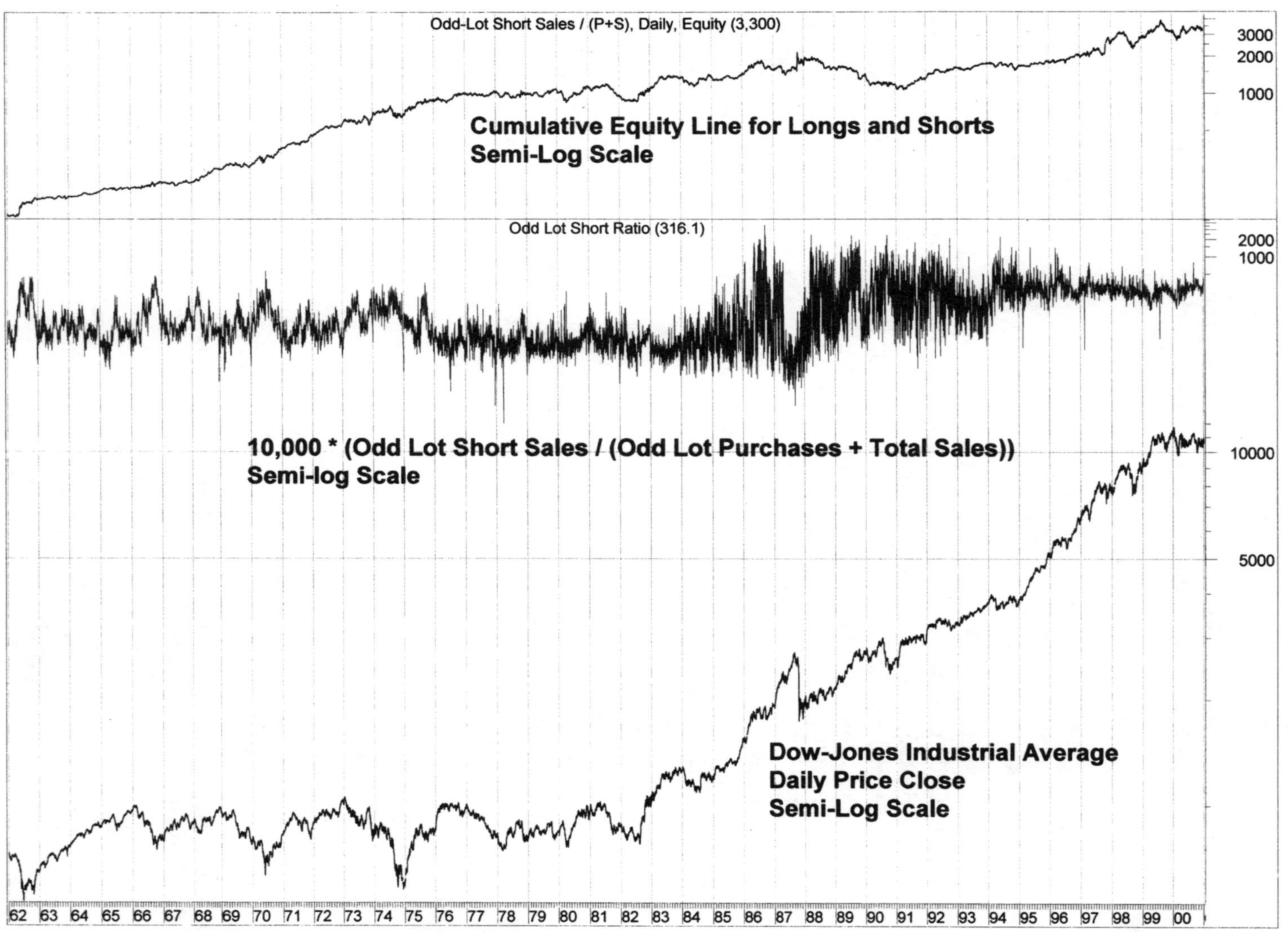
Odd-Lot Short Sales / (P+S), Daily, Equity (3,300)
Cumulative Equity Line for Longs and Shorts
Semi-Log Scale
3000
2000
1000
Odd Lot Short Ratio (316.1)
2000
1000
10,000 * (Odd Lot Short Sales / (Odd Lot Purchases + Total Sales))
Semi-log Scale
10000
5000
Dow-Jones Industrial Average
Daily Price Close
Semi-Log Scale
62 63 64 65 66 67 68 69 70 71 72 73 74 75 76 77 78 79 80 81 82 83 84 85 86 87 88 89 90 91 92 93 94 95 96 97 98 99 00

Odd Lot Short Sales/(Odd Lot Purchases + Sales)

Total net profit	3199.85	Open position value	0	Net Profit / Buy&Hold %	134.32
Percent gain/loss	3199.85	Annual percent gain/loss	81.95	Annual Net % / B&H %	134.34
Initial investment	100	Interest earned	0		
Current position	Short	Date position entered	1/8/01		
Buy/Hold profit	1365.61	Days in test	14252	# of days per trade	3.19
Buy/Hold pct gain/loss	1365.61	Annual B/H pct gain/loss	34.97		
Total closed trades	4463	Commissions paid	0		
Avg profit per trade	0.72	Avg Win/Avg Loss ratio	1.14		
Total long trades	2232	Total short trades	2231	Long Win Trade %	51.08
Winning long trades	1140	Winning short trades	1080	Short Win Trade %	48.41
Total winning trades	2220	Total losing trades	2243	Total Win Trade %	49.74
Amount of winning trades	28381.41	Amount of losing trades	−25181.54	Net Profit Margin %	5.97
Average win	12.78	Average loss	−11.23	Average P. Margin %	6.46
Largest win	342.99	Largest loss	−168.72	% Net / (Win + Loss)	34.06
Average length of win	3.53	Average length of loss	2.87	(Win − Loss) / Loss %	23.00
Longest winning trade	26	Longest losing trade	21	(Win − Loss) / Loss %	23.81
Most consecutive wins	9	Most consecutive losses	12	(Win − Loss) / Loss %	-25.00
Total bars out	6	Average length out	6		
Longest out period	6				
System close drawdown	−3.34	Profit/Loss index	11.27	% Net Profit / SODD	95803.89
System open drawdown	−3.34	Reward/Risk index	99.9	(Net P.-SODD)/Net P.	99.90
Max open trade drawdown	−175.12	Buy/Hold index	134.32	% SODD / Net Profit	−0.10

In the Equis MetaStock® "System Report" (profit and loss summary statistics), the *Total net profit* is the sum of profits minus the sum of losses, including open positions marked to the market. In contrast, the *Amount of Winning Trades* is the sum of realized profits (the total of all gains on closed-out trades only, excluding any open positions). Similarly, the *Amount of Losing Trades* is the sum of realized losses (the total of all losses on closed-out trades only, excluding any open positions). *System close drawdown* is the largest decline in the cumulative equity line below the initial investment, based on closed-out positions only. *System open drawdown (SODD)* is the largest decline in the cumulative equity line below the initial investment when a position is open. *Max open trade drawdown* is the largest decline in the cumulative equity line below the trade entry price during the worst single trade. The *Profit/Loss Index* is a complex calculation that relates the Amount of Winning Trades to the Amount of Losing Trades on a scale of −100 (worst possible performance) to +100 (best possible performance), with zero representing profits equal to losses. *Reward/Risk Index* is the Total net profit minus System open drawdown. The resulting difference is then divided by the Total net profit. The *Buy/Hold Index* is the Total net profit minus the buy-and-hold strategy's net profit. The resulting difference is then divided by the buy-and-hold net profit. In this exercise, initial equity is assumed to be $100. Both long and short positions are taken unless otherwise noted. Trades are executed at the closing price on the signal date. Transaction costs, interest expenses, and margins are not included in the statistics.

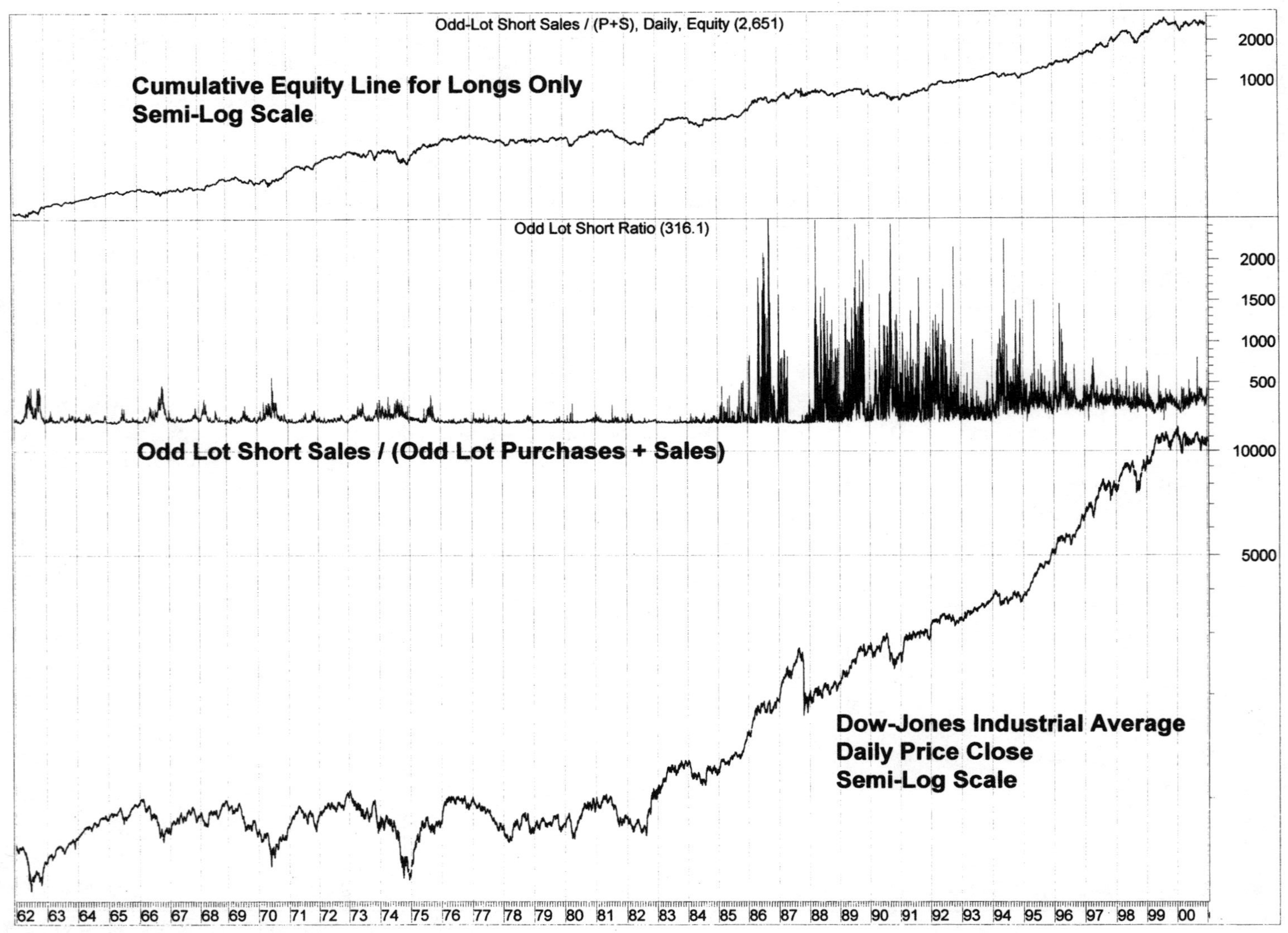

Odd-Lot Short Sales / (P+S), Daily, Equity (2,651)
Cumulative Equity Line for Longs Only
Semi-Log Scale
2000
1000
Odd Lot Short Ratio (316.1)
2000
1500
1000
500
Odd Lot Short Sales / (Odd Lot Purchases + Sales)
10000
5000
Dow-Jones Industrial Average
Daily Price Close
Semi-Log Scale
62 63 64 65 66 67 68 69 70 71 72 73 74 75 76 77 78 79 80 81 82 83 84 85 86 87 88 89 90 91 92 93 94 95 96 97 98 99 00

Odd Lot Short Sales/(Odd Lot Purchases + Sales), Long Only

Total net profit	2551.04	Open position value	N/A	Net Profit / Buy&Hold %	86.81
Percent gain/loss	2551.04	Annual percent gain/loss	65.33	Annual Net % / B&H %	86.82
Initial investment	100	Interest earned	0		
Current position	Out	Date position entered	1/8/01		
Buy/Hold profit	1365.61	Days in test	14252	# of days per trade	6.39
Buy/Hold pct gain/loss	1365.61	Annual B/H pct gain/loss	34.97		
Total closed trades	2232	Commissions paid	0		
Avg profit per trade	1.14	Avg Win/Avg Loss ratio	1.26		
Total long trades	2232	Total short trades	0	Long Win Trade %	51.08
Winning long trades	1140	Winning short trades	0	Short Win Trade %	#DIV/45
Total winning trades	1140	Total losing trades	1092	Total Win Trade %	51.08
Amount of winning trades	10586.88	Amount of losing trades	−8035.83	Net Profit Margin %	13.70
Average win	9.29	Average loss	−7.36	Average P. Margin %	11.59
Largest win	143.76	Largest loss	−129.77	% Net / (Win + Loss)	5.11
Average length of win	4.45	Average length of loss	3.46	(Win − Loss) / Loss %	28.61
Longest winning trade	26	Longest losing trade	21	(Win − Loss) / Loss %	23.81
Most consecutive wins	9	Most consecutive losses	10	(Win − Loss) / Loss %	-10.00
Total bars out	5438	Average length out	2.44		
Longest out period	6				
System close drawdown	−5.62	Profit/Loss index	24.1	% Net Profit / SODD	45392.17
System open drawdown	−5.62	Reward/Risk index	99.78	(Net P.-SODD)/Net P.	99.78
Max open trade drawdown	−140.96	Buy/Hold index	86.81	% SODD / Net Profit	−0.22

In the Equis MetaStock® "System Report" (profit and loss summary statistics), the *Total net profit* is the sum of profits minus the sum of losses, including open positions marked to the market. In contrast, the *Amount of Winning Trades* is the sum of realized profits (the total of all gains on closed-out trades only, excluding any open positions). Similarly, the *Amount of Losing Trades* is the sum of realized losses (the total of all losses on closed-out trades only, excluding any open positions). *System close drawdown* is the largest decline in the cumulative equity line below the initial investment, based on closed-out positions only. *System open drawdown (SODD)* is the largest decline in the cumulative equity line below the initial investment when a position is open. *Max open trade drawdown* is the largest decline in the cumulative equity line below the trade entry price during the worst single trade. The *Profit/Loss Index* is a complex calculation that relates the Amount of Winning Trades to the Amount of Losing Trades on a scale of −100 (worst possible performance) to +100 (best possible performance), with zero representing profits equal to losses. *Reward/Risk Index* is the Total net profit minus System open drawdown. The resulting difference is then divided by the Total net profit. The *Buy/Hold Index* is the Total net profit minus the buy-and-hold strategy's net profit. The resulting difference is then divided by the buy-and-hold net profit. In this exercise, initial equity is assumed to be $100. Both long and short positions are taken unless otherwise noted. Trades are executed at the closing price on the signal date. Transaction costs, interest expenses, and margins are not included in the statistics.

Indicator Strategy Example for the Weekly Ratio of Odd Lot Shorts to Total Shorts, Traditional Interpretation

Unfortunately, the weekly Odd-Lot Short Ratio contradicts the daily: it would have been profitable, going both long and short, to buy when the weekly reading crosses above trailing exponential moving average (EMA) smoothing lengths from 2 to 8 weeks, and sell when the weekly reading crosses below the EMA. This still would have underperformed buy and hold, however. Longer-length smoothings beyond 8 weeks would have been unprofitable.

As further refinement, based on a 55-year file of weekly ratios of Odd Lot Short Sales to Total Short Sales and weekly closing price data for the DJIA from January 1946 to December 2000, we found that the following parameters would have underperformed the passive buy-and-hold strategy but would have called the direction right five times out of eight, for longs only, on a purely mechanical trend-following signal basis with no subjectivity, no sophisticated technical analysis, and no judgement:

Enter Long (Buy) at the current weekly price close of the DJIA when the latest Odd Lot Short Ratio is 2.5% above its previous week's 2-week EMA of the Odd Lot Short Ratio.

Close Long (Sell) at the current weekly price close of the DJIA when the latest Odd Lot Short Ratio is 2.5% below its previous week's 10-week EMA of the Odd Lot Short Ratio.

Enter Short (Sell Short) never.

Starting with $100 and reinvesting profits, total net profits for this *long-only* weekly ratio of Odd Lot Short Sales to Total Short Sales contrary strategy would have been $1,853.61, assuming a fully invested strategy, reinvestment of profits, no transactions costs and no taxes. This would have been 64.48 percent less than buy-and-hold. No short selling would have been profitable, and no short selling was included in the strategy. *Short selling would have cut the profit by 84%, and short selling would have generated slightly more losing trades than profitable trades.* The *long-only* weekly ratio of Odd Lot Short Sales to Total Short Sales would have given profitable buy signals 62.97% of the time. Trading would have been moderately active at one trade every 31.76 calendar days. Note that this strategy considers end-of-week closing prices only while ignoring everything in between. These results are slightly supportive of traditional expectations, though not to justify the effort.

The Equis International MetaStock® System Testing rules for the weekly Odd Lot Short Ratio, where the ratio of Odd Lot Short Sales to Total Short Sales is inserted into the field normally reserved for open interest, are written as follows:

Enter long: OI>Ref(Mov(OI,opt1,E),-1) + ((opt2/1000))*Ref(Mov(OI,opt1,E),-1)

Close long: OI<Ref(Mov(OI,opt3,E),-1) − ((opt2/1000))*Ref(Mov(OI,opt3,E),-1)

OPT1 Current value: 2

OPT2 Current value: 25

OPT3 Current value: 10

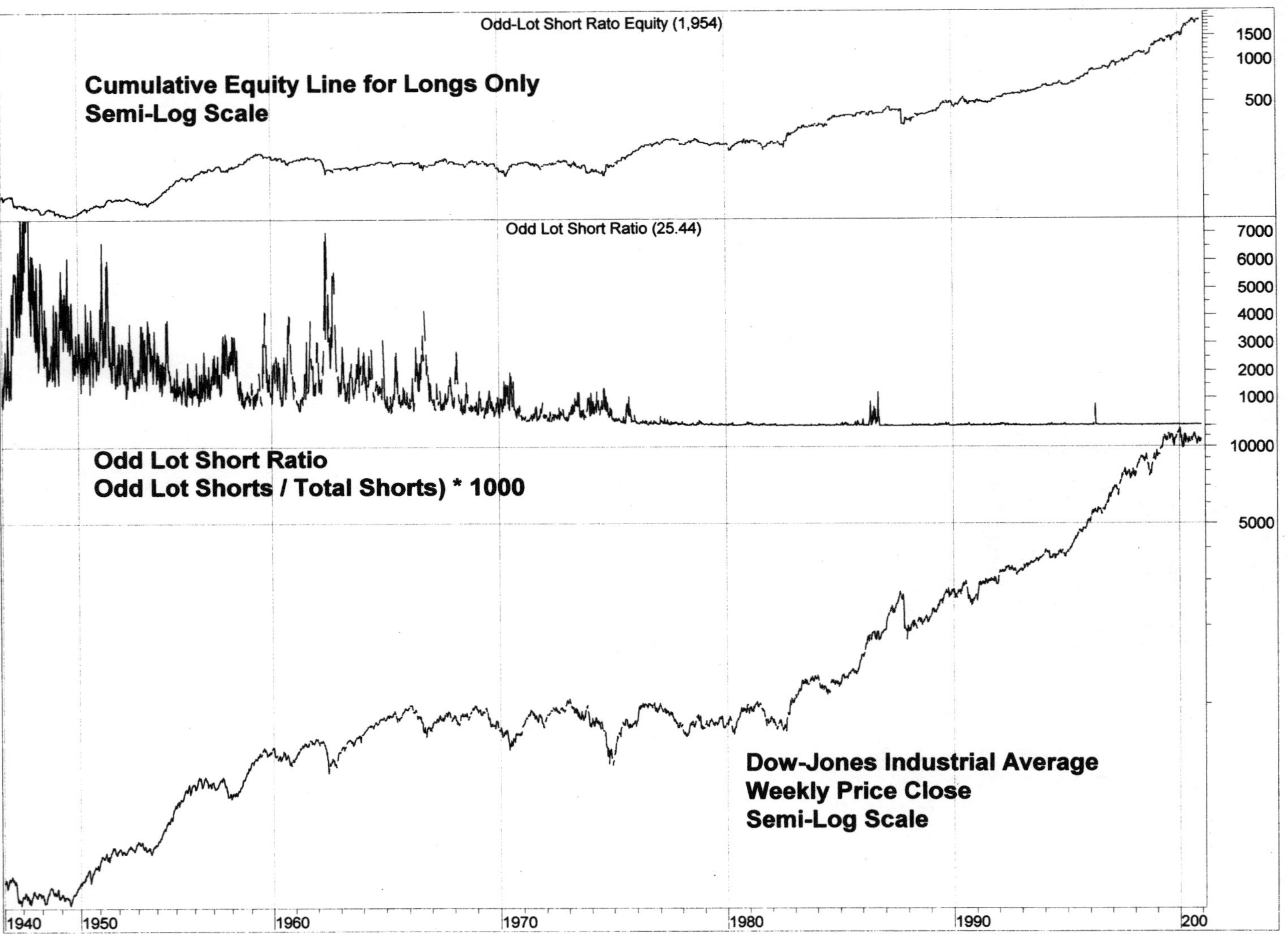
Odd-Lot Short Rato Equity (1,954)
Cumulative Equity Line for Longs Only
Semi-Log Scale
1500
1000
500
Odd Lot Short Ratio (25.44)
7000
6000
5000
4000
3000
2000
1000
Odd Lot Short Ratio
Odd Lot Shorts / Total Shorts) * 1000
10000
5000
Dow-Jones Industrial Average
Weekly Price Close
Semi-Log Scale
1940
1950
1960
1970
1980
1990
200

Odd Lot Short Ratio (Envelope)

Total net profit	1853.61	Open position value	N/A	Net Profit / Buy&Hold %	−64.48
Percent gain/loss	1853.61	Annual percent gain/loss	33.71	Annual Net % / B&H %	-64.47
Initial investment	100	Interest earned	0		
Current position	Out	Date position entered	12/22/00		
Buy/Hold profit	5217.78	Days in test	20070	# of days per trade	31.76
Buy/Hold pct gain/loss	5217.78	Annual B/H pct gain/loss	94.89		
Total closed trades	632	Commissions paid	0		
Avg profit per trade	2.93	Avg Win/Avg Loss ratio	1.28		
Total long trades	632	Total short trades	0	Long Win Trade %	62.97
Winning long trades	398	Winning short trades	0	Short Win Trade %	#DIV/0!
Total winning trades	398	Total losing trades	234	Total Win Trade %	62.97
Amount of winning trades	3433.61	Amount of losing trades	−1580	Net Profit Margin %	36.97
Average win	8.63	Average loss	−6.75	Average P. Margin %	12.22
Largest win	187.45	Largest loss	−94.08	% Net / (Win + Loss)	33.17
Average length of win	3.06	Average length of loss	3.83	(Win − Loss) / Loss %	-20.10
Longest winning trade	12	Longest losing trade	15	(Win − Loss) / Loss %	−20.00
Most consecutive wins	16	Most consecutive losses	5	(Win − Loss) / Loss %	220.00
Total bars out	2017	Average length out	3.19		
Longest out period	13				
System close drawdown	−27.45	Profit/Loss index	53.98	% Net Profit / SODD	6427.22
System open drawdown	−28.84	Reward/Risk index	98.47	(Net P.-SODD)/Net P.	98.44
Max open trade drawdown	−107.07	Buy/Hold index	−64.48	% SODD / Net Profit	−1.56

In the Equis MetaStock® "System Report" (profit and loss summary statistics), the *Total net profit* is the sum of profits minus the sum of losses, including open positions marked to the market. In contrast, the *Amount of Winning Trades* is the sum of realized profits (the total of all gains on closed-out trades only, excluding any open positions). Similarly, the *Amount of Losing Trades* is the sum of realized losses (the total of all losses on closed-out trades only, excluding any open positions). *System close drawdown* is the largest decline in the cumulative equity line below the initial investment, based on closed-out positions only. *System open drawdown (SODD)* is the largest decline in the cumulative equity line below the initial investment when a position is open. *Max open trade drawdown* is the largest decline in the cumulative equity line below the trade entry price during the worst single trade. The *Profit/Loss Index* is a complex calculation that relates the Amount of Winning Trades to the Amount of Losing Trades on a scale of −100 (worst possible performance) to +100 (best possible performance), with zero representing profits equal to losses. *Reward/Risk Index* is the Total net profit minus System open drawdown. The resulting difference is then divided by the Total net profit. The *Buy/Hold Index* is the Total net profit minus the buy-and-hold strategy's net profit. The resulting difference is then divided by the buy-and-hold net profit. In this exercise, initial equity is assumed to be $100. Both long and short positions are taken unless otherwise noted. Trades are executed at the closing price on the signal date. Transaction costs, interest expenses, and margins are not included in the statistics.

Ohama's 3-D Technique

Bill Ohama identified three futures markets that by logic and actual practice trade together: crude oil, heating oil, and gasoline. When prices of these three contracts diverge, Ohama enters a trade designed to take advantage of expected realignment. (See LeBeau, C. & Lucas, D. W. (1992). *Technical Traders Guide to Computer Analysis of the Futures Market.* Homewood, IL: Business One Irwin.)

In trading Intermarket Divergences, the trader initiates a trade when prices of financial instruments diverge, or do not move proportionately to a similar extent, or in a similar direction. He may buy one and short the other in an attempt to take advantage of possible price movement before these financial instruments come back into alignment.

The risk is that on occasion there is a good reason for the divergence and the misalignment persists or even intensifies. There are no guarantees on timely realignment. This risk hit, in a dramatic way, Long Term Capital Management, which quickly lost so many billions of dollars betting on *normality* that it required a massive government-sponsored financial bailout in 1998.

On-Balance Volume

(See Volume: On-Balance Volume (OBV).)

Open Interest

Open interest is the total commitment of longs or shorts in a futures market. Since the number of contracts held long must equal the number of contracts held short, open interest is either the number of contracts held long or the number of contracts held short. In other words, open interest is the number of contracts held long plus the number of contracts held short, divided by two.

In the conventional interpretation, when open interest is trending upward or rising, the prevailing price trend is confirmed—whatever it is, up, down or neutral. The prevailing price trend is likely to continue. Rising open interest means that new positions are being established that reinforce the existing trend. Open interest tends to enter an uptrend when the price of the underlying futures contract enters a directional trend, as new trend-following positions are attracted by the trend.

When open interest reverses trend from up to down, existing positions are liquidated or closed out faster than new positions enter the market. The prevailing price uptrend or downtrend is unsustainable.

Some complicate the analysis further by adding volume as another variable. Volume should be trending in the same direction as open interest in order to confirm the conclusion.

The following table expresses the relationships between price trends and open interest trends. The simple rule of thumb is that when both price and open interest are trending in the same direction, the future is bullish, so prices should trend higher. But when price and open interest are trending in opposite directions, the future is bearish, so prices should trend lower.

Trend of Price	*Trend of Open Interest*	*Interpretation*	*Implied Trend Prediction*
Up	Up	Long Buying	Up
Up	Neutral	Long Buying + Short Covering	Up
Up	Down	Short Covering	Down
Down	Up	Short Selling	Down
Down	Neutral	Long Selling + Short Selling	Down
Down	Down	Long Selling	Up
Neutral	Up	Long Buying + Short Shorting	Neutral
Neutral	Neutral	Offsetting, Balanced Activity	Neutral
Neutral	Down	Long Selling + Short Covering	Neutral

Indicator Strategy Example for Open Interest

For stock index futures, open interest follows a clear seasonal pattern four times a year (the third Friday of March, June, September, and December), rising sharply before expatriation and falling sharply after expiration. Based on an 18-year file of daily data for the entire history of the S&P 500 Composite Stock Price Index Futures Contract from 4/21/82 to 12/29/00 (*Perpetual Contract* data collected from www.csidata.com), we found that the following parameters would have produced a positive result on a purely mechanical overbought/oversold signal basis with no subjectivity, no sophisticated technical analysis, and no judgement:

Enter Long (Buy) at the current daily price close of the S&P 500 Composite Stock Price Index futures *Perpetual Contract* when this contract is above its previous day's 145-day EMA *and* this contract's current Open Interest is above its previous day's 314-day EMA. Alternately, buy when this contract is below its previous day's 145-day EMA *and* this contract's current Open Interest is below its previous day's 314-day EMA.

Close Long (Sell) at the current daily price close of the S&P 500 Composite Stock Price Index futures *Perpetual Contract* when this contract is below its previous day's 145-day EMA *and* this contract's current Open Interest is above its previous day's 314-day EMA. Alternately, sell when this contract is above its previous day's 145-day EMA *and* this contract's current Open Interest is below its previous day's 314-day EMA.

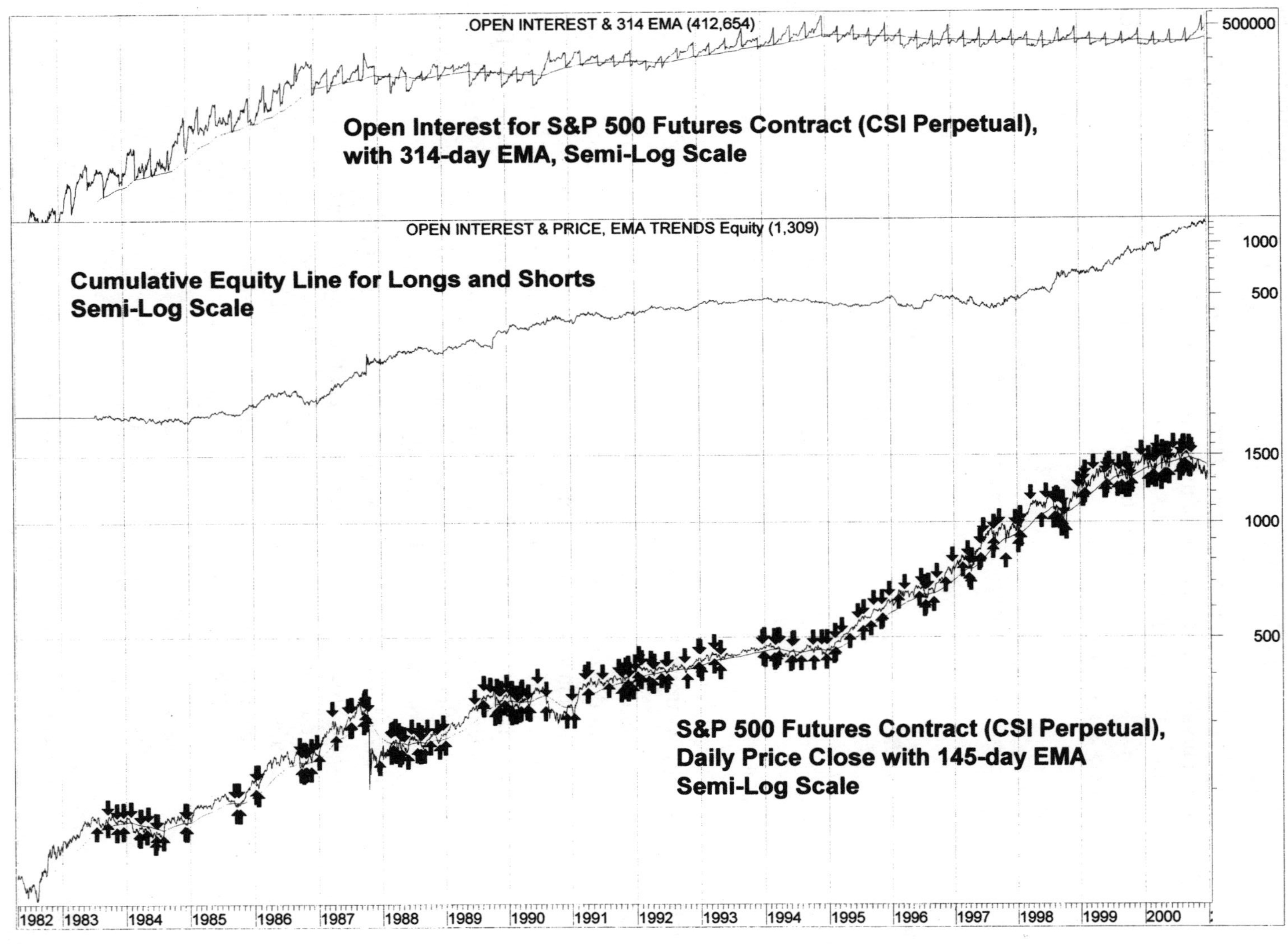

.OPEN INTEREST & 314 EMA (412,654)
500000
Open Interest for S&P 500 Futures Contract (CSI Perpetual),
with 314-day EMA, Semi-Log Scale
OPEN INTEREST & PRICE, EMA TRENDS Equity (1,309)
1000
500
Cumulative Equity Line for Longs and Shorts
Semi-Log Scale
1500
1000
500
S&P 500 Futures Contract (CSI Perpetual),
Daily Price Close with 145-day EMA
Semi-Log Scale
1982
1983
1984
1985
1986
1987
1988
1989
1990
1991
1992
1993
1994
1995
1996
1997
1998
1999
2000

Open Interest

Total net profit	1208.84	Open position value	98.82	Net Profit / Buy&Hold %	16.85
Percent gain/loss	1208.84	Annual percent gain/loss	64.62	Annual Net % / B&H %	16.85
Initial investment	100	Interest earned	0		
Current position	Short	Date position entered	9/29/00		
Buy/Hold profit	1034.49	Days in test	6828	# of days per trade	21.40
Buy/Hold pct gain/loss	1034.49	Annual B/H pct gain/loss	55.3		
Total closed trades	319	Commissions paid	0		
Avg profit per trade	3.48	Avg Win/Avg Loss ratio	1.51		
Total long trades	160	Total short trades	159	Long Win Trade %	65.00
Winning long trades	104	Winning short trades	80	Short Win Trade %	50.31
Total winning trades	184	Total losing trades	135	Total Win Trade %	57.68
Amount of winning trades	2156.06	Amount of losing trades	−1046.04	Net Profit Margin %	34.67
Average win	11.72	Average loss	−7.75	Average P. Margin %	20.39
Largest win	77.82	Largest loss	−68.12	% Net / (Win + Loss)	6.65
Average length of win	16.74	Average length of loss	11.76	(Win − Loss) / Loss %	42.35
Longest winning trade	186	Longest losing trade	65	(Win − Loss) / Loss %	186.15
Most consecutive wins	18	Most consecutive losses	11	(Win − Loss) / Loss %	63.64
Total bars out	315	Average length out	315		
Longest out period	315				
System close drawdown	−9.08	Profit/Loss index	53.61	% Net Profit / SODD	13313.22
System open drawdown	−9.08	Reward/Risk index	99.25	(Net P.-SODD)/Net P.	99.25
Max open trade drawdown	−68.12	Buy/Hold index	26.41	% SODD / Net Profit	−0.75

In the Equis MetaStock® "System Report" (profit and loss summary statistics), the *Total net profit* is the sum of profits minus the sum of losses, including open positions marked to the market. In contrast, the *Amount of Winning Trades* is the sum of realized profits (the total of all gains on closed-out trades only, excluding any open positions). Similarly, the *Amount of Losing Trades* is the sum of realized losses (the total of all losses on closed-out trades only, excluding any open positions). *System close drawdown* is the largest decline in the cumulative equity line below the initial investment, based on closed-out positions only. *System open drawdown (SODD)* is the largest decline in the cumulative equity line below the initial investment when a position is open. *Max open trade drawdown* is the largest decline in the cumulative equity line below the trade entry price during the worst single trade. The *Profit/Loss Index* is a complex calculation that relates the Amount of Winning Trades to the Amount of Losing Trades on a scale of −100 (worst possible performance) to +100 (best possible performance), with zero representing profits equal to losses. *Reward/Risk Index* is the Total net profit minus System open drawdown. The resulting difference is then divided by the Total net profit. The *Buy/Hold Index* is the Total net profit minus the buy-and-hold strategy's net profit. The resulting difference is then divided by the buy-and-hold net profit. In this exercise, initial equity is assumed to be $100. Both long and short positions are taken unless otherwise noted. Trades are executed at the closing price on the signal date. Transaction costs, interest expenses, and margins are not included in the statistics.

Enter Short (Sell Short) at the current daily price close of the S&P 500 Composite Stock Price Index futures *Perpetual Contract* when this contract is below its previous day's 145-day EMA *and* this contract's current Open Interest is above its previous day's 314-day EMA. Alternately, sell short when this contract is above its previous day's 145-day EMA *and* this contract's current Open Interest is below its previous day's 314-day EMA.

Close Short (Cover) at the current daily price close of the S&P 500 Composite Stock Price Index futures *Perpetual Contract* when this contract is above its previous day's 145-day EMA *and* this contract's current Open Interest is above its previous day's 314-day EMA. Alternately, buy when this contract is below its previous day's 145-day EMA *and* this contract's current Open Interest is below its previous day's 314-day EMA.

Starting with $100 and reinvesting profits, total net profits for this Open Interest strategy would have been $1208.84, assuming a fully invested strategy, reinvestment of profits, no transactions costs and no taxes. This would have been 16.85 percent better than buy-and-hold. Short selling would have been profitable and was included in the strategy. The Open Interest as a long and short strategy would have given profitable buy signals 57.68% of the time. Trading would have been moderately active at one trade every 21.40 calendar days.

The Equis International MetaStock® System Testing rules are written as follows:

Enter long:

```
(CLOSE > Ref(Mov(CLOSE,opt1,E),-1) AND
OI > Ref(Mov(OI,opt2,E),-1))
OR (CLOSE < Ref(Mov(CLOSE,opt1,E),-1) AND
OI < Ref(Mov(OI,opt2,E),-1))
```

Close long:

```
(CLOSE < Ref(Mov(CLOSE,opt1,E),-1) AND
OI > Ref(Mov(OI,opt2,E),-1))
OR (CLOSE > Ref(Mov(CLOSE,opt1,E),-1) AND
OI < Ref(Mov(OI,opt2,E),-1))
```

Enter short:

```
(CLOSE < Ref(Mov(CLOSE,opt1,E),-1) AND
OI > Ref(Mov(OI,opt2,E),-1))
OR (CLOSE > Ref(Mov(CLOSE,opt1,E),-1) AND
OI < Ref(Mov(OI,opt2,E),-1))
```

Close short:

```
(CLOSE > Ref(Mov(CLOSE,opt1,E),-1) AND
OI > Ref(Mov(OI,opt2,E),-1))
OR (CLOSE < Ref(Mov(CLOSE,opt1,E),-1) AND
OI < Ref(Mov(OI,opt2,E),-1))
```

OPT1 Current value: 145

OPT2 Current value: 314.

Open Interest, Larry Williams' Variation

Larry Williams has a different interpretation from the usual one. In his view, open interest is primarily an indicator of *short selling* by big commercials or the professional *smart money* players who dominate the futures markets, and who are usually right. Changes of 25% or more in open interest indicate that the big boys are making big bets, and we should bet with them.

When open interest rises, commercials are shorting. This is bearish, particularly in a contango market or a normal market, where the nearby contracts are trading at a discount to the far out dated contracts. Prices are likely to trend down.

On the other hand, open interest drops when commercials cover shorts. This is bullish, particularly in a backwardation and inverted market. Backwardation describes an abnormal market, where the nearby contracts are trading at a premium to the far-out dated contracts, expiring further into the future. Prices are likely to trend up.

In a strongly bullish price uptrend, if price falls sharply against the main trend while open interest falls sharply, commercials are covering their shorts into the price weakness, and that is bullish.

In a significant bearish price downtrend, if price rallies sharply against the main trend while open interest rises sharply, commercials are shorting into the price strength, and that is bearish.

For further discussion of this analysis by Larry R. Williams, see Robbins, Joel (1995). *High Performance Futures Trading.* Chicago, IL: Probus Publishing (pp 227–250).

Indicator Strategy Example for Larry Williams' Variation on Open Interest

For stock index futures, the *simplest* form of Larry Williams' interpretation, trading *against* the trend of Open Interest, produced a loss over all time frames. Whenever we find an unexpected, consistently negative result, we test for the opposite conditions. Indeed, trading *with* the trend of Open Interest produced a profit over all time frames. *(See Open Interest Trend-Following Strategy)*

Open Interest Trend-Following Strategy

For stock index futures, trading *with* the trend of Open Interest would have produced a profit over all time frames. *(See Open Interest.)*

Based on an 18-year file of daily data for the entire history of the S&P 500 Composite Stock Price Index futures *CSI Perpetual Contract* from 4/21/82 to 12/29/00 collected from www.csidata.com, we found that the following parameters would have produced a positive result on a purely mechanical overbought/oversold signal basis with no subjectivity, no sophisticated technical analysis, and no judgement:

> **Enter Long (Buy)** at the current daily price close of the S&P 500 Composite Stock Price Index futures *CSI Perpetual Contract* when this contract's current Open Interest is above its previous day's 665-day EMA.
>
> **Close Long (Sell)** at the current daily price close of the S&P 500 Composite Stock Price Index futures *CSI Perpetual Contract* when this contract's current Open Interest is below its previous day's 665-day EMA.
>
> **Enter Short (Sell Short)** at the current daily price close of the S&P 500 Composite Stock Price Index futures *CSI Perpetual Contract* when this contract's current Open Interest is below its previous day's 665-day EMA.
>
> **Close Short (Cover)** at the current daily price close of the S&P 500 Composite Stock Price Index futures *CSI Perpetual Contract* when this contract's current Open Interest is above its previous day's 665-day EMA.

Starting with $100 and reinvesting profits, total net profits for this Open Interest trend-following strategy would have been $1244.14, assuming a fully invested strategy, reinvestment of profits, no transactions costs and no taxes. This would have been 20.27 percent better than buy-and-hold. Short selling would have been profitable and was included in the strategy. Simply following the Open Interest trend as a long and short strategy would have given profitable buy signals 67.27% of the time. Trading would have been moderate at one trade every 62.07 calendar days.

The Equis International MetaStock® System Testing rules are written as follows:

> **Enter long:** OI > Ref(Mov(OI,opt1,E),-1)
>
> **Close long:** OI < Ref(Mov(OI,opt1,E),-1)
>
> **Enter short:** OI < Ref(Mov(OI,opt1,E),-1)
>
> **Close short:** OI > Ref(Mov(OI,opt1,E),-1)
>
> OPT1 Current value: 665

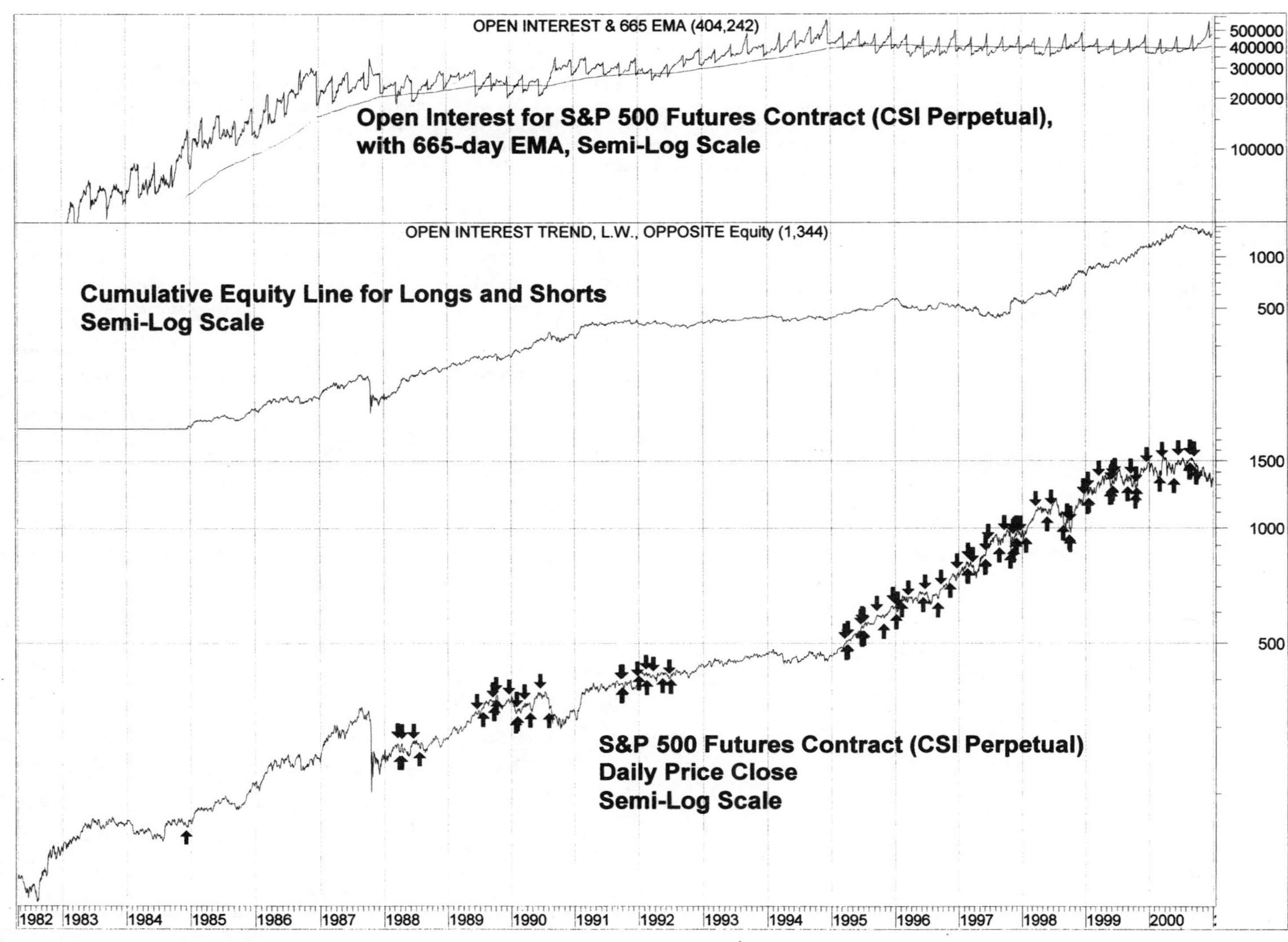
OPEN INTEREST & 665 EMA (404,242)
Open Interest for S&P 500 Futures Contract (CSI Perpetual),
with 665-day EMA, Semi-Log Scale
500000
400000
300000
200000
100000
OPEN INTEREST TREND, L.W., OPPOSITE Equity (1,344)
Cumulative Equity Line for Longs and Shorts
Semi-Log Scale
1000
500
S&P 500 Futures Contract (CSI Perpetual)
Daily Price Close
Semi-Log Scale
1500
1000
500
1982
1983
1984
1985
1986
1987
1988
1989
1990
1991
1992
1993
1994
1995
1996
1997
1998
1999
2000

Open Interest, trading with the trend

Total net profit	1244.14	Open position value	−119.54	Net Profit / Buy&Hold %	20.27
Percent gain/loss	1244.14	Annual percent gain/loss	66.51	Annual Net % / B&H %	20.27
Initial investment	100	Interest earned	0		
Current position	Long	Date position entered	9/29/00		
Buy/Hold profit	1034.49	Days in test	6828	# of days per trade	62.07
Buy/Hold pct gain/loss	1034.49	Annual B/H pct gain/loss	55.3		
Total closed trades	110	Commissions paid	0		
Avg profit per trade	12.4	Avg Win/Avg Loss ratio	1.89		
Total long trades	55	Total short trades	55	Long Win Trade %	78.18
Winning long trades	43	Winning short trades	31	Short Win Trade %	56.36
Total winning trades	74	Total losing trades	36	Total Win Trade %	67.27
Amount of winning trades	1837.42	Amount of losing trades	−473.75	Net Profit Margin %	59.00
Average win	24.83	Average loss	−13.16	Average P. Margin %	30.72
Largest win	151.63	Largest loss	−52.56	% Net / (Win + Loss)	48.52
Average length of win	46.24	Average length of loss	19.06	(Win − Loss) / Loss %	142.60
Longest winning trade	831	Longest losing trade	62	(Win − Loss) / Loss %	1240.32
Most consecutive wins	9	Most consecutive losses	4	(Win − Loss) / Loss %	125.00
Total bars out	666	Average length out	666		
Longest out period	666				
System close drawdown	0	Profit/Loss index	72.42	% Net Profit / SODD	401335.48
System open drawdown	−0.31	Reward/Risk index	99.98	(Net P.-SODD)/Net P.	99.98
Max open trade drawdown	−175.35	Buy/Hold index	8.71	% SODD / Net Profit	−0.02

In the Equis MetaStock® "System Report" (profit and loss summary statistics), the *Total net profit* is the sum of profits minus the sum of losses, including open positions marked to the market. In contrast, the *Amount of Winning Trades* is the sum of realized profits (the total of all gains on closed-out trades only, excluding any open positions). Similarly, the *Amount of Losing Trades* is the sum of realized losses (the total of all losses on closed-out trades only, excluding any open positions). *System close drawdown* is the largest decline in the cumulative equity line below the initial investment, based on closed-out positions only. *System open drawdown (SODD)* is the largest decline in the cumulative equity line below the initial investment when a position is open. *Max open trade drawdown* is the largest decline in the cumulative equity line below the trade entry price during the worst single trade. The *Profit/Loss Index* is a complex calculation that relates the Amount of Winning Trades to the Amount of Losing Trades on a scale of −100 (worst possible performance) to +100 (best possible performance), with zero representing profits equal to losses. *Reward/Risk Index* is the Total net profit minus System open drawdown. The resulting difference is then divided by the Total net profit. The *Buy/Hold Index* is the Total net profit minus the buy-and-hold strategy's net profit. The resulting difference is then divided by the buy-and-hold net profit. In this exercise, initial equity is assumed to be $100. Both long and short positions are taken unless otherwise noted. Trades are executed at the closing price on the signal date. Transaction costs, interest expenses, and margins are not included in the statistics.

Optimism/Pessimism Index (OP)

The Wyckoff Optimism/Pessimism Index (OP) is similar to On-Balance Volume except that it uses intraday price movement rather than just the direction of the daily closing prices to determine the sign (plus or minus) assigned to the volume during the time interval of the directional price movement, or price wave. OP is calculated by:

- assigning a plus sign to the volume on advancing intraday price waves and a minus sign to the volume on declining intraday price waves,
- summing the daily plus and minus volumes while respecting sign, then
- cumulating the daily sums into a cumulative total.

See *Technical Analysis of Stocks & Commodities,* www.traders.com, for a series of informative articles written on Richard D. Wyckoff's methods.

Option Activity by Public Customers: Customer Option Activity Index

Option Activity by Public Customers is a measure of public sentiment used as a contrary opinion indicator. It was developed by Arthur A. Merrill, CMT, "Customer Option Activity," *Technical Analysis of Stocks & Commodities,* Vol. 8:12, www.traders.com.

Merrill was inspired by Robert Nurock's measure of options activity by professionals. The necessary weekly data is derived from a weekly report by The Options Clearing Corporation, which includes the total volume of options bought and sold on all exchanges nationwide by customers, market makers, and firms. Merrill selects data for customers only, and he plugs the numbers into Nurock's basic formula, expressing a ratio as follows:

$$(\text{call buys} + \text{put sells} - \text{call sells} - \text{put buys}) / \\ (\text{call buys} + \text{put sells} + \text{call sells} + \text{put buys})$$

This ratio sums the public's net bullish activity and divides it by the total public activity. Next, Merrill multiplies the ratio by 100, then he smoothes it with a 33% EMA. As a benchmark, Merrill selects two thirds of a standard deviation from the mean to indicate unusually high and low data points. High index readings reflect public optimism and are bearish. Low index readings reflect public pessimism and are bullish.

In a ten year period from 1980 to 1990, Merrill measured the smoothed Customer Option Activity Index signals at his 2/3 standard deviation benchmarks for their accuracy in forecasting the direction of the DJIA. The 26-week forecast was correct 155 times and wrong 99 times, which was statistically highly significant.

Options

An option grants the owner of the option the right (but not the obligation) to buy (call) or sell (put) a specific underlying security at a specific price on or before a specific future date. Options are extremely dynamic and difficult to value. All of their relevant variables are constantly shifting: volatility, interest rates, investor sentiment, and liquidity. Any of these variables can fluctuate much more or much less than it ever has in the past.

Option valuation models are backward looking. They precisely quantify past behavior and project that compiled information forward into the unknown future. That is a very big mistake when the future deviates dramatically from the past.

Investors felt a confidence that was not grounded in reality when they used a precise mathematical formula for valuing options and derivatives developed by Nobel Prize winners Fischer Black and Myron Scholes. Both the Portfolio Insurance meltdown (October 1987) and the failure of Long Term Capital Management (August 1998) taught a costly lesson: precisely calculated derivatives strategies can go massively haywire if variables change dramatically and without warning. Even if the valuation formulas are useful *most* of the time, only one major deviation of the variables can quickly wipe out slowly accumulated capital.

Technical analysis was developed to gauge probable future changes in the critical shifting variables, and any attempt to trade without this tool is akin to flying in a fog without instruments.

For reference, here are the basic definitions behind the Greek letters that represent naïve forecasts of the future. One should not attempt to employ these concepts without intensive study.

- *Delta* is a naïve estimate of an option's possible price change stated as a percentage of the price change in the underlying security. A delta of 50 generally means that the option might move about half as much as the underlying security; therefore, delta changes with the distance of the market price of the underlying security from its contractually fixed strike price. This change can occur quickly. Delta for calls is stated as a positive number, while delta for puts is stated as a negative number.
- *Gamma* is a naïve estimate of the rate of change in delta for each one-point change in the underlying security. Supposing an option has a delta of 50 and a gamma of 10, then the option's expected delta might be 60 if the underlying security goes up one point. And that's a lot of *ifs*.
- *Theta* is the rate at which an option loses its time premium. Theta can be fast or slow, depending on sentiment and the action of the underlying security. Time is the enemy of the option buyer. As an option approaches expiration, the rate of time premium decay accelerates.

- *Vega* is the sensitivity of an option to changes in volatility, and no one knows what rapid changes the future might hold.
- *Rho* is the sensitivity of an option to changes in interest rates.
- *Life* is expressed as the number of days until expiration. Generally speaking, the shorter the time until expiration, then the less valuable the option—*other things being equal.* Keep in mind that there are absolutely no guarantees that other things will be equal.
- *Expiration* is the critical date when the option ceases to exist, and this is a sure thing. Trading activity and liquidity usually start to decline before expiration, so pay attention to the calendar. Watch volume and open interest. Generally, it pays to close out long positions more than a month before expiration because of the acceleration of time-premium decay factor as expiration approaches. Stock and stock index options expire on the Saturday following the third Friday of each month. The last day to trade is that Friday. Four times a year, stock options, index futures, and index options expire on the Saturday following the third Friday of March, June, September, and December. These dates, known as *triple witching days,* have been unusually volatile. Pay attention to days both *after* and, especially, *before* expiration.

Oscillators

Oscillators quantify velocity, and they express the speed at which a data series is moving. These versatile indicators are used to express the velocity of price, breadth, volume, sentiment, fundamental indicators, or any combination of variables.

Some of the more popular price oscillators include Stochastics, Relative Strength Index (RSI), and the ratio of or difference between two moving averages. *(See Price Oscillators: Moving Average Oscillators.)* They are usually constructed from market data covering the past one to four weeks; however, they may be adapted to any time frame.

An oscillator typically swings up and down around a median point that functions as an anchor and as an attractor. This typically may be zero, one, or fifty—depending how the oscillator formula is structured. This median point marks a neutral point and a dividing line between positive and negative momentum. The number is used as a signal threshold, although crossing the neutral zone will often be somewhat late in the price move.

There may be maximum and minimum limits built into the oscillator formula. Also, there are usually overbought and oversold thresholds, established based on historical observation.

A market can only move in three directions: up, down, or sideways. It is common knowledge among traders that most markets fluctuate within a trading range most of the time. More time is spent going sideways than trending higher or lower. In trading ranges, it pays to bet on reversals. In a trading range, price has a tendency to bounce from one extreme to an opposite extreme. The strategy that maximizes profits is "buy low, sell high." So the trader must sell near the high end of the trading range and buy near the lower end of the trading range. Oscillators are useful tools in identifying overbought and oversold extremes.

Short-term, contratrend trading works fine as long as prices stay within the trading range. If the price starts a powerful new trend, without advance notice, very large losses quickly accrue to those betting against the new trend. Weeks or months of small trading profits may be wiped out in days.

New major trends are the most powerful and dynamic when they are new. After a prolonged trading range, traders are conditioned to think the trends do not last. However, in a dynamic new trend, oscillators quickly hit overbought or oversold, and remain there while prices continue to surge or plummet in the direction of the new trend. When divergences do appear, they merely signify a slowing of the initial explosive velocity of a new trend. Oscillator traders continue to fade the trend, and their subsequent forced loss cutting feeds the continuation of the new trend. The oscillator mindset becomes a trap that will cause the trader to miss the bigger picture. Fighting a major trend based on some oscillator reading is a debilitating experience that has cost some leveraged traders everything. Oscillator trades contrary to a major trend can produce large equity drawdowns.

A major trend is perceived only through long-term chart analysis. It is not possible to see the big picture through the narrow lens of a short-term oscillator.

Oscillators can be interpreted in a variety of ways. The following are some of the typical criteria for the interpretation of oscillators:

- The oscillator and/or its own trailing moving average can be compared to certain high and low critical threshold levels, determined by observation of past oscillator behavior, to judge overbought and oversold levels. For example, overbought levels for RSI are typically defined as above 70, while oversold levels are typically below 30. This tends to work fine in a market confined to a sideways trading range, but it works very poorly when the market is in a powerful directional trend.
- The relative levels of the oscillator are compared to the relative levels of the raw price data to determine any positive or negative divergences between the two. Keep in mind that Divergence Analysis can be subjective and requires experienced good judgement to apply correctly.
- The oscillator is compared to a neutral threshold level, which is often zero or one or fifty, depending on how the data is manipulated by the indicator formula.

- The oscillator is compared to its own past trend, defined by its own moving average or trendline: above trend implies improving momentum while below trend implies deteriorating momentum.
- The latest direction of both the oscillator and/or its moving average can be considered: rising generally implies improving momentum while falling generally implies deteriorating momentum.
- The recent past trend of the oscillator may also be judged by its recent waves: a series of higher highs and higher lows would be bullish, while a series of lower highs and lower lows would be bearish.

When one or more to these criteria are present, it can be taken as a partial signal to buy or sell, subordinate to major trend analysis. When the criteria are mixed, more subtle judgements may be called for. Since oscillators may tempt the user to trade against the prevailing trend, they can be dangerous in the hands of a novice. Oscillators should be used only with confirmation by long-term trend technical analysis methods. For an example of an oscillator adapted to longer-term analysis, see *Oscillators: Moving Average Oscillators,* below.

Outside Day with an Outside Close

The outside day is characterized by the current day's price range entirely enveloping the previous day's range in both directions, that is, both a higher high and a lower low. Here, the closing price is also outside the previous day's range, beyond the boundary of the previous day's range. This pattern implies a volatile struggle where price pushes forcefully in one direction then the other, with the direction of the close pointing to the path of least resistance, and probable future trend. Therefore, on an outside day, buy a higher close, or short a lower close. Stops may be placed just beyond the range.

Buying and shorting outside days would have been an unprofitable trading strategy over 19-years of S&P 500 futures trading. The Equis International MetaStock® System Testing rules may be written as follows:

Enter long: L<Ref(LLV(L,opt1),-1) AND C>Ref(HHV(H,opt1),-1)

Close long: C<Ref(LLV(C,opt2),-1)

Enter short: H>Ref(HHV(H,opt1),-1) AND C<Ref(LLV(L,opt1),-1)

Close short: C>Ref(HHV(H,opt2),-1)

Overbought/Oversold Oscillators

Catching reversals of the minor trend *in trading ranges* or with the direction of the major trend can be profitable if the strategy is applied consistently and with perspective. Buying at bottoms and selling at tops is always alluring to traders and investors alike. Consequently, many indicators have been devised to signal price extremes. Stochastics and RSI are two of the more popular examples.

Overbought means significantly high readings on short-term oscillators, warning of possible vulnerability to downward price correction.

Oversold means significantly low readings on short-term oscillators, alerting to the potential for an upward price correction.

Oscillators are most useful when the market is in a trading range. Also, oscillators are useful for trading minor reactions in harmony with the direction of the major trend.

Oscillators are dangerous if used for fading trending markets. This cannot be emphasized enough. It is hazardous to your wealth to take positions opposite to the major trend. A major trend is an overwhelmingly powerful force and must be respected. A major trend can overshoot all objectives that may seem reasonable.

The ability of a market to register an overbought condition during a major uptrend is not a reason to fade that uptrend. Rather, the high oscillator reading should be taken as a positive sign of the vitality of the bullish trend.

Similarly, the ability of a market to register an oversold condition during a major bearish trend is not a reason to buy. Rather, a low oscillator reading should be taken as a negative indication, a sign of the vitality of the bear.

In a sideways or bearish major trend, the declining oscillator peaks and negative divergences on rallies usually indicate impending price weakness.

In a sideways or bullish major trend, a pattern of rising oscillator lows and positive divergences on price declines usually indicate impending price strength.

Note that overbought/oversold indicators should be employed only in conjunction with major trend analysis as an overriding filter. The direction of the major trend must be our major focus. If we lose this major trend focus, we are vulnerable to losing major dollars.

Parabolic Time/Price System

The Parabolic Time/Price System is a stop-setting entry and exit trading system described by J. Welles Wilder, Jr. (Wilder, Jr., J. W. (1978). *New Concepts In Technical Trading Systems.* McLeansville, NC: Trend Research). The system is designed to allow some leeway or tolerance for contratrend price fluctuation early in a new trade. As time in the trade goes forward, the Parabolic Time/Price System progressively tightens a protective trailing stop order.

To accomplish this, the system employs a series of progressively shorter, exponentially smoothed moving averages that follow the price trend. These averages change each period that price moves to a new extreme in the expected trend direction. The exponential smoothing constants, called *Acceleration Factors,* rise from an initial minimum of 0.02, and then increase by 0.02 each day the price trend makes progress in the expected direction, up to a maximum Acceleration Factor of 0.20.

This adaptive technique adjusts a trailing *Stop and Reverse Price (SAR)* progressively closer to the actual current price. This SAR gives the new trend the most breathing room when the trend is new. Then as time goes on, the protective stop tightens. The Parabolic Time/Price System rides the trend until the SAR is penetrated, then the existing position is closed out, and the opposite position is opened.

SAR calculations begin anew on each fresh SAR signal. For example, on the day of an initial buy signal, when a new long position is opened, the SAR is equal to the *Extreme Price (EP),* which is the lowest low recorded during the downward price movement that the Parabolic Time/Price System says has just ended. Thereafter, SAR is adjusted upward by an Acceleration Factor (AF) in the new expected trend direction.

For new buy signals, the initial SAR is equal to the lowest price recorded during the just closed short position. On the second day, and thereafter, the SAR is adjusted upward as follows:

$$S = P + A(H - P)$$

where

S = the long-side sell Stop and Reverse Price (SAR) at which we reverse our current long position by selling long and selling short.

P = the previous period's SAR.

A = an acceleration factor. A begins at .02 for the next period immediately after the initial SAR buy stop order opens the current long trade. The next period and each period thereafter, A is increased by .02 for each period that price rises to the highest high level (H) since the current long trade was opened. For periods when price does not set a new high within the current long trade time duration, A is left unchanged from its previous period's level.

H = the highest high price since the current long trade was opened on a buy stop order.

For new sell long and sell short signals, the initial SAR is equal to the highest price recorded during the just closed long position. On the second day, and thereafter, the SAR is adjusted downward as follows:

$$S = P - A(L - P)$$

where

S = the short-side buy Stop and Reverse Price (SAR) at which we reverse our current short position by covering our outstanding short sale and buying a new long position.

P = the previous period's SAR.

A = an acceleration factor. A begins at .02 for the next period immediately after the initial SAR sell stop order opens the current short-side trade. The next period and each period thereafter, A is increased by .02 for each period that price falls to the lowest low level (L) since the current short trade was opened. For periods when price does not set a new low within the current short trade time duration, A is left unchanged from its previous period's level.

L = the lowest low price since the current short trade was opened on a sell stop order.

On both sides of the market, long and short, the SAR must lie at or outside the latest two periods' high to low price ranges. The SAR must never be inside the latest two periods' price ranges. If it does fall within the latest two periods' high to low price ranges, it must be reset: to the lower of the two most recent lows, for long positions; to the higher of the two most recent highs, for short positions.

The table on the facing page offers an example of the calculations involved in the Parabolic Time/Price System.

Indicator Strategy Example for the Parabolic Time/Price System: Contrary SAR

Our testing failed to uncover any effectiveness whatsoever for the Parabolic Time/Price System as originally described by Wilder. When an indicator loses money consistently, we can reverse the rules, buying when the indicator signals sell, and selling when the indicator signals buy. That worked, but the equity drawdowns were large. A long-term EMA filter can reduce drawdowns, but it also reduces total profit. The MetaStock® Indicator Builder syntax for our contrary version is: SAR(0.04,0.22).

Based on daily data for the S&P 500 Stock Index Futures *CSI Perpetual Contract* (www.csidata.com) from 4/21/82 to 5/23/01, we found that trading contrarily to SAR signals, with an Acceleration Factor step size of 0.04 rising to a maximum of

Example of Parabolic Time Price-System Calculations (A: begin at .02, increment .02, maximum 0.2)

Position	*Year*	*NYSE Annual Prices*		*Extreme*												
	End			*High or*												
Long or Short	*Date*	*High*	*Low*	*Low Price**	−	*P*	=	*Diff*	×	*A*	=	*A* × *Diff*	+	*P*	=	*S*
Long	1973	65.87	48.71	65.87	−											
Short	1974	53.77	32.47	32.47	−	65.87	=	−33.40	×	.02	=	−.67	+	65.87	=	65.20
Short	1975	51.39	36.49	32.47	−	65.20	=	−32.73	×	.02	=	−.65	+	65.20	=	64.55
Short	1976	57.88	47.67	32.47	−	64.55	=	−32.08	×	.02	=	−.64	+	64.55	=	63.91
Short	1977	57.92	49.61	32.47	−	63.91	=	−31.44	×	.02	=	−.63	+	63.91	=	63.28
Short	1978	60.60	48.27	32.47	−	63.28	=	−30.81	×	.02	=	−.62	+	63.28	=	62.66
Long	1979	63.58	53.42	63.58	−	32.47	=	+31.11	×	.02	=	+.62	+	32.47	=	33.09
Long	1980	81.29	53.66	81.29	−	33.09	=	+48.20	×	.04	=	+1.93	+	33.09	=	35.02
Long	1981	79.44	63.75	81.29	−	35.02	=	+46.27	×	.04	=	+1.85	+	35.02	=	36.87
Long	1982	83.13	58.78	83.13	−	36.87	=	+46.26	×	.06	=	+2.78	+	36.87	=	39.65
Long	1983	99.63	79.63	99.63	−	39.65	=	+59.98	×	.08	=	+4.80	+	39.65	=	44.45
Long	1984	98.12	84.81	99.63	−	44.45	=	+55.18	×	.08	=	+4.41	+	44.45	=	48.86
Long	1985	122.44	94.41	122.44	−	48.86	=	+73.58	×	.10	=	+7.36	+	48.86	=	56.22
Long	1986	145.91	117.30	145.91	−	56.20	=	+89.69	×	.12	=	+10.76	+	56.22	=	66.98
Long	1987				−	66.98								66.98	=	

*During the duration of the position.

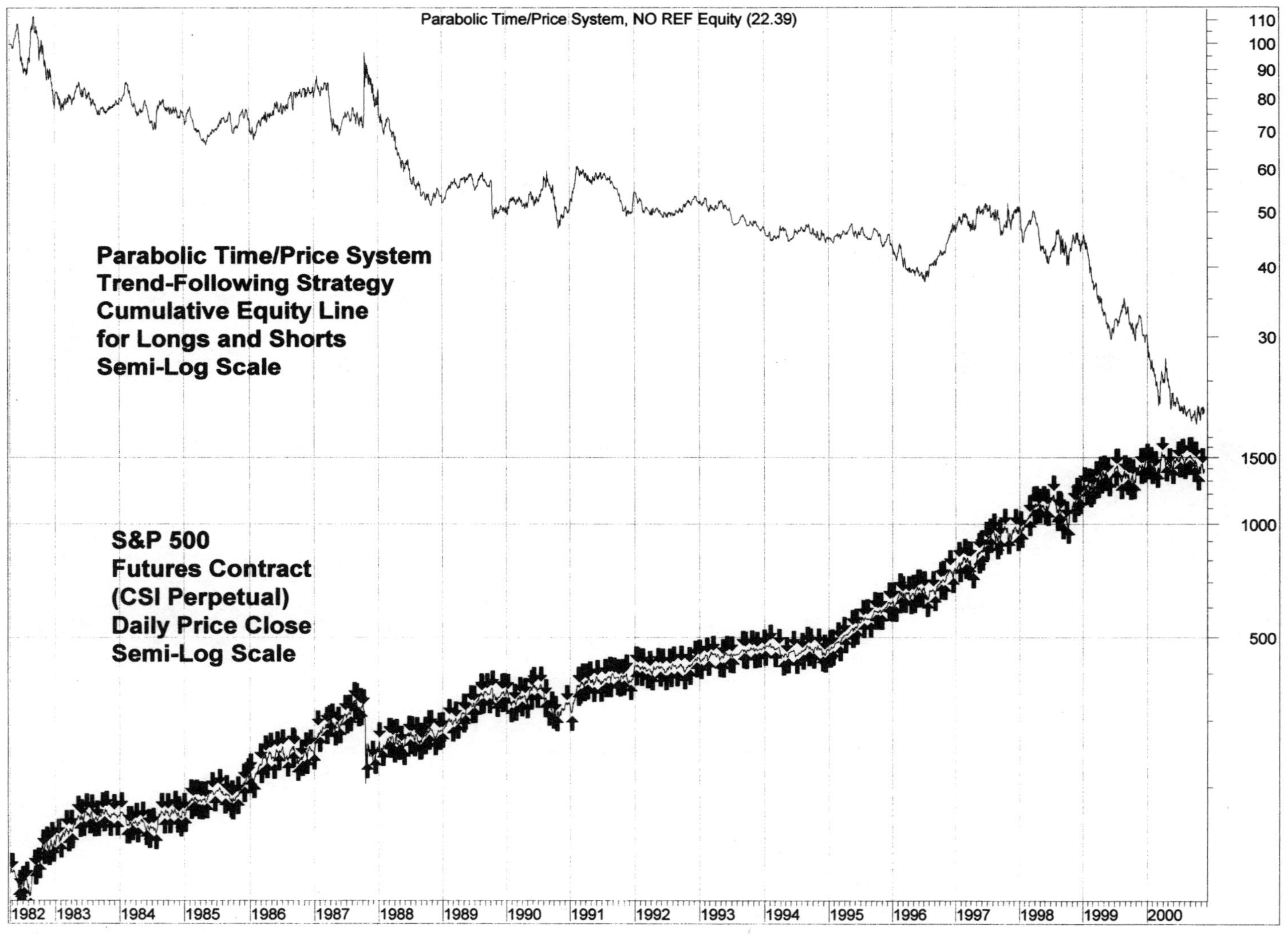

Parabolic Time/Price System, NO REF Equity (22.39)
Parabolic Time/Price System
Trend-Following Strategy
Cumulative Equity Line
for Longs and Shorts
Semi-Log Scale
S&P 500
Futures Contract
(CSI Perpetual)
Daily Price Close
Semi-Log Scale
110
100
90
80
70
60
50
40
30
1500
1000
500
1982
1983
1984
1985
1986
1987
1988
1989
1990
1991
1992
1993
1994
1995
1996
1997
1998
1999
2000

0.22, would have produced a positive result on a purely mechanical trend-fading signal basis with no subjectivity, no sophisticated technical analysis, and no judgement:

Enter Long (Buy) at the current daily price close of the S&P 500 Stock Index Futures *Perpetual Contract* when the daily high price is less than the SAR, with a SAR Acceleration Factor step size of 0.04 rising up to a maximum of 0.22.

Close Long (Sell) at the current daily price close of the S&P 500 Stock Index Futures *Perpetual Contract* when the daily low price is greater than the SAR, with a SAR Acceleration Factor step size of 0.04 rising up to a maximum of 0.22.

Enter Short (Sell Short) at the current daily price close of the S&P 500 Stock Index Futures *Perpetual Contract* when the daily low price is greater than the SAR, with a SAR Acceleration Factor step size of 0.04 rising up to a maximum of 0.22.

Close Short (Cover) at the current daily price close of the S&P 500 Stock Index Futures *Perpetual Contract* when the daily high price is less than the SAR, with a SAR Acceleration Factor step size of 0.04 rising up to a maximum of 0.22.

Starting with $100 and reinvesting profits, total net profits for this contrary, trend-fading strategy would have been would have been $1,199.66, assuming a fully invested strategy, reinvestment of profits, no transactions costs and no taxes. This would have been 20.19 percent greater than buy-and-hold. Short selling would have been only slightly unprofitable, and short selling was included in the strategy. This contrary indicator would have given profitable buy signals 67.66% of the time. Trading would have been active at one trade every 10.39 calendar days.

The chart shows how going against the trend can cause severe equity drawdowns in trending markets. This Contrary SAR indicator works on balance because the stock market is choppy in the short-term most of the time.

The Equis International MetaStock® System Testing rules for the Parabolic Time/Price System are written:

Enter long: H<SAR(0.01*opt1,0.01*opt2)

Close long: L>SAR(0.01*opt1,0.01*opt2)

Enter short: L>SAR(0.01*opt1,0.01*opt2)

Close short: H<SAR(0.01*opt1,0.01*opt2)

OPT1 Current value: 4
OPT2 Current value: 22

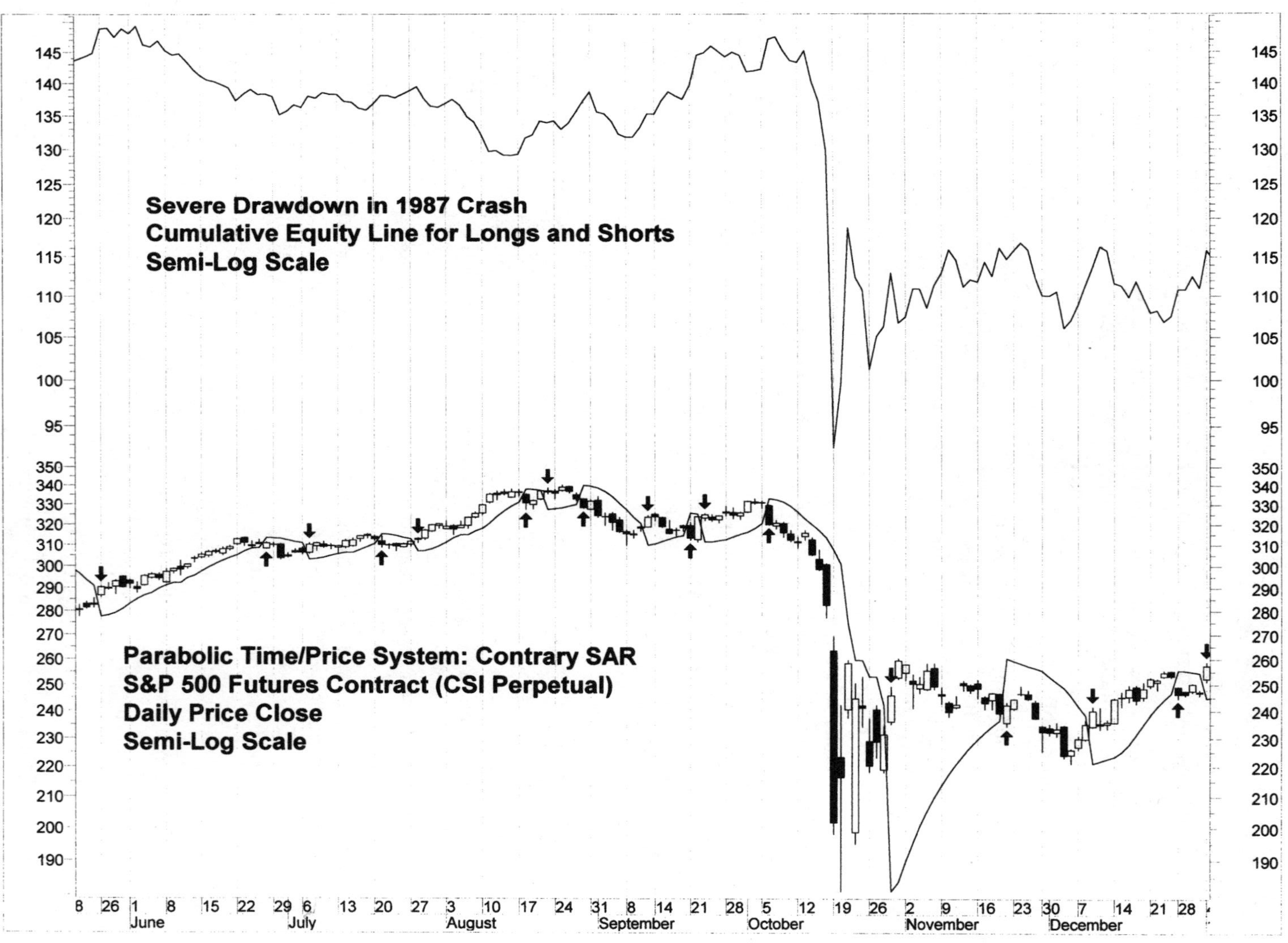

Severe Drawdown in 1987 Crash
Cumulative Equity Line for Longs and Shorts
Semi-Log Scale
Parabolic Time/Price System: Contrary SAR
S&P 500 Futures Contract (CSI Perpetual)
Daily Price Close
Semi-Log Scale
145
140
135
130
125
120
115
110
105
100
95
350
340
330
320
310
300
290
280
270
260
250
240
230
220
210
200
190
8
26
1
June
8
15
22
29
6
July
13
20
27
3
August
10
17
24
31
8
September
14
21
28
5
October
12
19
26
2
November
9
16
23
30
7
December
14
21
28

Parabolic Time/Price System: Contrary Stop and Reverse Price

Total net profit	1199.66	Open position value	−31.03	Net Profit / Buy&Hold %	20.19
Percent gain/loss	1199.66	Annual percent gain/loss	62.8	Annual Net % / B&H %	20.19
Initial investment	100	Interest earned	0		
Current position	Short	Date position entered	5/10/01		
Buy/Hold profit	998.13	Days in test	6973	# of days per trade	10.39
Buy/Hold pct gain/loss	998.13	Annual B/H pct gain/loss	52.25		
Total closed trades	671	Commissions paid	0		
Avg profit per trade	1.83	Avg Win/Avg Loss ratio	0.84		
Total long trades	336	Total short trades	335	Long Win Trade %	76.19
Winning long trades	256	Winning short trades	198	Short Win Trade %	59.10
Total winning trades	454	Total losing trades	217	Total Win Trade %	67.66
Amount of winning trades	2851.85	Amount of losing trades	−1621.16	Net Profit Margin %	27.51
Average win	6.28	Average loss	−7.47	Average P. Margin %	−8.65
Largest win	77.06	Largest loss	−100.49	% Net / (Win + Loss)	−13.20
Average length of win	6.14	Average length of loss	12.42	(Win − Loss) / Loss %	−50.56
Longest winning trade	17	Longest losing trade	33	(Win − Loss) / Loss %	−48.48
Most consecutive wins	9	Most consecutive losses	6	(Win − Loss) / Loss %	50.00
Total bars out	7	Average length out	7		
Longest out period	7				
System close drawdown	−13.6	Profit/Loss index	42.53	% Net Profit / SODD	6148.95
System open drawdown	−19.51	Reward/Risk index	98.4	(Net P.-SODD)/Net P.	98.37
Max open trade drawdown	−122.51	Buy/Hold index	17.08	% SODD / Net Profit	−1.63

In the Equis MetaStock® "System Report" (profit and loss summary statistics), the *Total net profit* is the sum of profits minus the sum of losses, including open positions marked to the market. In contrast, the *Amount of Winning Trades* is the sum of realized profits (the total of all gains on closed-out trades only, excluding any open positions). Similarly, the *Amount of Losing Trades* is the sum of realized losses (the total of all losses on closed-out trades only, excluding any open positions). *System close drawdown* is the largest decline in the cumulative equity line below the initial investment, based on closed-out positions only. *System open drawdown (SODD)* is the largest decline in the cumulative equity line below the initial investment when a position is open. *Max open trade drawdown* is the largest decline in the cumulative equity line below the trade entry price during the worst single trade. The *Profit/Loss Index* is a complex calculation that relates the Amount of Winning Trades to the Amount of Losing Trades on a scale of −100 (worst possible performance) to +100 (best possible performance), with zero representing profits equal to losses. *Reward/Risk Index* is the Total net profit minus System open drawdown. The resulting difference is then divided by the Total net profit. The *Buy/Hold Index* is the Total net profit minus the buy-and-hold strategy's net profit. The resulting difference is then divided by the buy-and-hold net profit. In this exercise, initial equity is assumed to be $100. Both long and short positions are taken unless otherwise noted. Trades are executed at the closing price on the signal date. Transaction costs, interest expenses, and margins are not included in the statistics.

Percentage of Stocks Above Their Own 30-Week and 10-Week Simple Moving Averages

The percentage of stocks in any defined universe that are above their own trailing key moving averages is a traditional breadth-momentum indicator followed by many technical analysts. We simply count the number of the stocks that are trading above their key moving averages, then divide that number by the total number of stocks examined. The resulting percentage shows the proportion of stocks that can be considered to be in uptrends. The indicator has been viewed as a momentum gauge with leading indicator characteristics, and it is also used to quantify overbought and oversold general market conditions. And like other momentum indicators, the Percentage may peak or trough before tops and bottoms in the price indexes.

Indicator Strategy Example for the Percentage of Stocks Above Their Own 30-Week Simple Moving Averages

Historical data for this indicator shows that the Percentage of Stocks Above Their Own 30-Week Simple Moving Averages can be an effective indicator on both the long and short sides, and particularly on the long side. Based on the weekly Percentage and the Dow-Jones Industrial Average (DJIA) for 33 years from January 1968 to January 2001, we found that the following parameters would have produced a significantly positive result on a purely mechanical trend-following signal basis with no subjectivity, no sophisticated technical analysis, and no judgement:

Enter Long (Buy) at the current weekly price close of the DJIA when the Percentage of Stocks Above Their Own 30-Week Simple Moving Averages as of the previous week is less than its own trailing 35-week Exponential Moving Average as of the previous week, and the current Percentage Above Their Own 30-Week SMA is greater than its own trailing 2-week Exponential Moving Average as of the previous week.

Close Long (Sell) at the current weekly price close of the DJIA when the Percentage of Stocks Above Their Own 30-Week Simple Moving Averages as of the previous week is greater than its own trailing 17-week Exponential Moving Average as of the previous week, and the current Percentage Above Their Own 30-Week SMA is less than its own trailing 41-week Exponential Moving Average as of the previous week.

Enter Short (Sell Short) at the current weekly price close of the DJIA when the Percentage of Stocks Above Their Own 30-Week Simple Moving Averages as of the previous week is greater than its own trailing

17-week Exponential Moving Average as of the previous week, and the current Percentage Above Their Own 30-Week SMA is less than its own trailing 41-week Exponential Moving Average as of the previous week.

Close Short (Cover) at the current weekly price close of the DJIA when the Percentage of Stocks Above Their Own 30-Week Simple Moving Averages as of the previous week is less than its own trailing 35-week Exponential Moving Average as of the previous week, and the current Percentage Above Their Own 30-Week SMA is greater than its own trailing 2-week Exponential Moving Average as of the previous week.

Starting with $100 and reinvesting profits, total net profits for this trend-following strategy would have been $5,548.81, assuming a fully invested strategy, reinvestment of profits, no transactions costs and no taxes. This would have been 467.45 percent better than buy-and-hold. Even short selling would have been profitable and was included in this strategy. The long-and-short strategy would have given profitable signals 54.30% of the time. Trading would have been relatively inactive at one trade every 68.65 calendar days.

The Equis International MetaStock® System Testing rules, where the Percentage of Stocks Above Their Own 30-Week Simple Moving Averages is inserted in the field normally reserved for open interest, are written as follows:

Enter long: Ref(OI,-1)<Ref(Mov(OI,opt1,E),-1) AND
OI>Ref(Mov(OI,opt2,E),-1)

Close long: Ref(OI,-1)>Ref(Mov(OI,opt3,E),-1) AND
OI<Ref(Mov(OI,opt4,E),-1)

Enter short: Ref(OI,-1)>Ref(Mov(OI,opt3,E),-1) AND
OI<Ref(Mov(OI,opt4,E),-1)

Close short: Ref(OI,-1)<Ref(Mov(OI,opt1,E),-1) AND
OI>Ref(Mov(OI,opt2,E),-1)

OPT1 Current value: 35

OPT2 Current value: 2

OPT3 Current value: 17

OPT4 Current value: 41

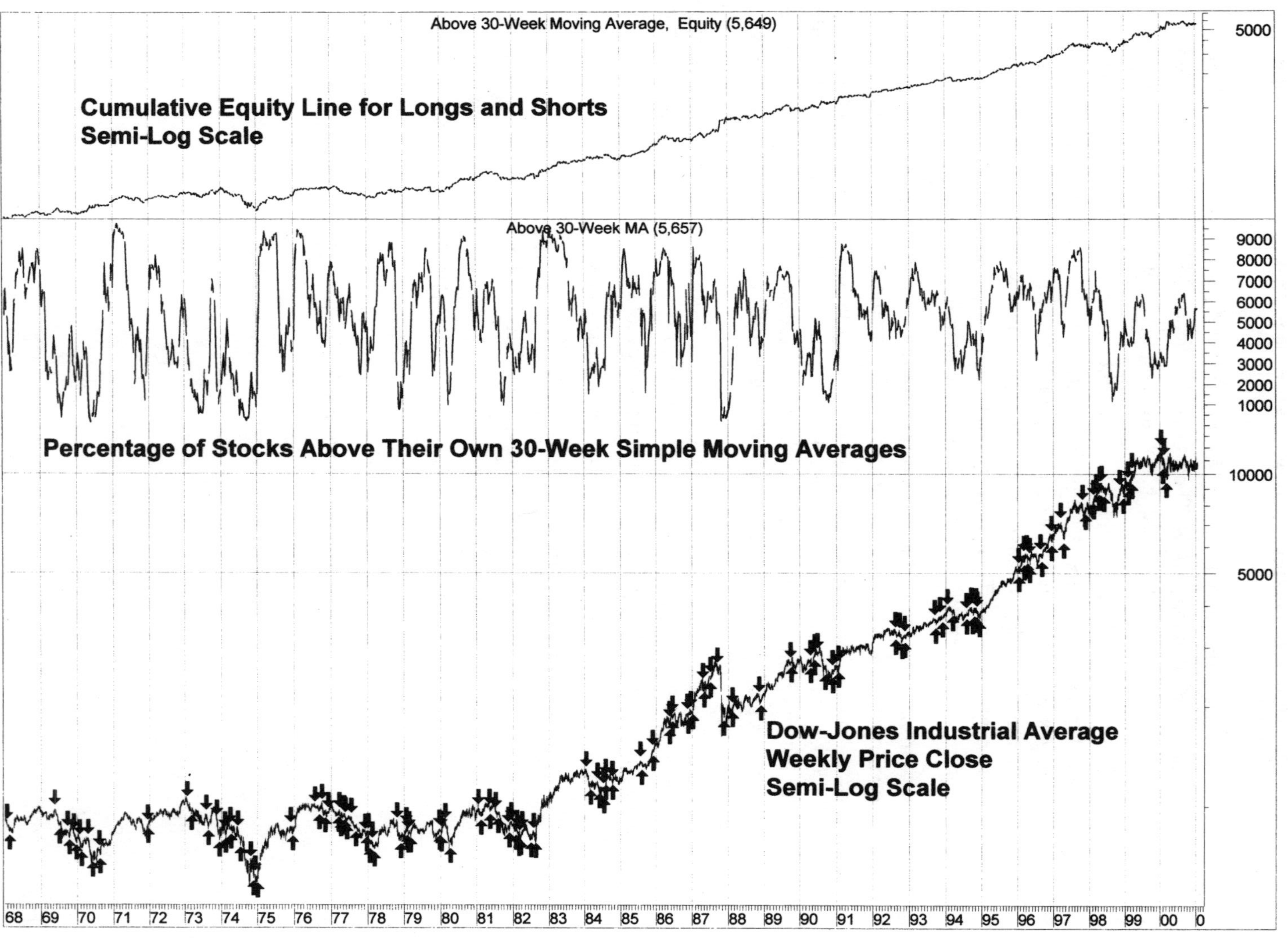

Above 30-Week Moving Average, Equity (5,649)
Cumulative Equity Line for Longs and Shorts
Semi-Log Scale
5000
Above 30-Week MA (5,657)
9000
8000
7000
6000
5000
4000
3000
2000
1000
Percentage of Stocks Above Their Own 30-Week Simple Moving Averages
10000
5000
Dow-Jones Industrial Average
Weekly Price Close
Semi-Log Scale
68
69
70
71
72
73
74
75
76
77
78
79
80
81
82
83
84
85
86
87
88
89
90
91
92
93
94
95
96
97
98
99
00
0

Percentage of Stocks Above Their Own 30-Week Simple Moving Averages

Total net profit	5548.81	Open position value	387.45	Net Profit / Buy&Hold %	467.45
Percent gain/loss	5548.81	Annual percent gain/loss	158.61	Annual Net % / B&H %	467.48
Initial investment	100	Interest earned	0		
Current position	Long	Date position entered	3/10/00		
Buy/Hold profit	977.85	Days in test	12769	# of days per trade	68.65
Buy/Hold pct gain/loss	977.85	Annual B/H pct gain/loss	27.95		
Total closed trades	186	Commissions paid	0		
Avg profit per trade	27.75	Avg Win/Avg Loss ratio	3.69		
Total long trades	93	Total short trades	93	Long Win Trade %	58.06
Winning long trades	54	Winning short trades	47	Short Win Trade %	50.54
Total winning trades	101	Total losing trades	85	Total Win Trade %	54.30
Amount of winning trades	6688.77	Amount of losing trades	−1527.4	Net Profit Margin %	62.82
Average win	66.23	Average loss	−17.97	Average P. Margin %	57.32
Largest win	804.28	Largest loss	−259.46	% Net / (Win + Loss)	51.22
Average length of win	13.52	Average length of loss	5.94	(Win − Loss) / Loss %	127.61
Longest winning trade	82	Longest losing trade	42	(Win − Loss) / Loss %	95.24
Most consecutive wins	6	Most consecutive losses	8	(Win − Loss) / Loss %	−25.00
Total bars out	94	Average length out	94		
Longest out period	94				
System close drawdown	−1.42	Profit/Loss index	78.41	% Net Profit / SODD	223742.34
System open drawdown	−2.48	Reward/Risk index	99.96	(Net P.-SODD)/Net P.	99.96
Max open trade drawdown	−576.86	Buy/Hold index	507.07	% SODD / Net Profit	−0.04

In the Equis MetaStock® "System Report" (profit and loss summary statistics), the *Total net profit* is the sum of profits minus the sum of losses, including open positions marked to the market. In contrast, the *Amount of Winning Trades* is the sum of realized profits (the total of all gains on closed-out trades only, excluding any open positions). Similarly, the *Amount of Losing Trades* is the sum of realized losses (the total of all losses on closed-out trades only, excluding any open positions). *System close drawdown* is the largest decline in the cumulative equity line below the initial investment, based on closed-out positions only. *System open drawdown (SODD)* is the largest decline in the cumulative equity line below the initial investment when a position is open. *Max open trade drawdown* is the largest decline in the cumulative equity line below the trade entry price during the worst single trade. The *Profit/Loss Index* is a complex calculation that relates the Amount of Winning Trades to the Amount of Losing Trades on a scale of −100 (worst possible performance) to +100 (best possible performance), with zero representing profits equal to losses. *Reward/Risk Index* is the Total net profit minus System open drawdown. The resulting difference is then divided by the Total net profit. The *Buy/Hold Index* is the Total net profit minus the buy-and-hold strategy's net profit. The resulting difference is then divided by the buy-and-hold net profit. In this exercise, initial equity is assumed to be $100. Both long and short positions are taken unless otherwise noted. Trades are executed at the closing price on the signal date. Transaction costs, interest expenses, and margins are not included in the statistics.

Indicator Strategy Example for the Percentage of Stocks Above Their Own 10-Week Simple Moving Averages

Using the same basic strategy as the 30-Week, above, the Percentage of Stocks Above Their Own 10-Week Simple Moving Averages would have been less effective as an indicator. We found that the following parameters would have produced a less positive result on a purely mechanical trend-following signal basis with no subjectivity, no sophisticated technical analysis, and no judgement:

Enter Long (Buy) at the current weekly price close of the DJIA when the Percentage of Stocks Above Their Own 10-Week Simple Moving Averages as of the previous week is less than its own trailing 18-week Exponential Moving Average as of the previous week, and the current Percentage Above Their Own 10-Week SMA is greater than its own trailing 34-week Exponential Moving Average as of the previous week.

Close Long (Sell) at the current weekly price close of the DJIA when the Percentage of Stocks Above Their Own 10-Week Simple Moving Averages as of the previous week is greater than its own trailing 7-week Exponential Moving Average as of the previous week, and the current Percentage Above Their Own 10-Week SMA is less than its own trailing 34-week Exponential Moving Average as of the previous week.

Enter Short (Sell Short) at the current weekly price close of the DJIA when the Percentage of Stocks Above Their Own 10-Week Simple Moving Averages as of the previous week is greater than its own trailing 7-week Exponential Moving Average as of the previous week, and the current Percentage Above Their Own 10-Week SMA is less than its own trailing 34-week Exponential Moving Average as of the previous week.

Close Short (Cover) at the current weekly price close of the DJIA when the Percentage of Stocks Above Their Own 10-Week Simple Moving Averages as of the previous week is less than its own trailing 18-week Exponential Moving Average as of the previous week, and the current Percentage Above Their Own 10-Week SMA is greater than its own trailing 34-week Exponential Moving Average as of the previous week.

Starting with $100 and reinvesting profits, total net profits for this trend-following strategy would have been $3,375.93, assuming a fully invested strategy, reinvestment of profits, no transactions costs and no taxes. This would have been 245.24 percent better than buy-and-hold. Even short selling slightly would have been profitable and was included in this strategy. The long-and-short strategy would have given profitable signals 52.05% of the time. Trading would have been relatively inactive at one trade every 87.46 calendar days.

The Equis International MetaStock® System Testing rules, where the Percentage of Stocks Above Their Own 10-Week Simple Moving Averages is inserted in the field normally reserved for volume, are written as follows:

Enter long: Ref(V,-1)<Ref(Mov(V,opt1,E),-1) AND
V>Ref(Mov(V,opt2,E),-1)

Close long: Ref(V,-1)>Ref(Mov(V,opt3,E),-1) AND
V<Ref(Mov(V,opt2,E),-1)

Enter short: Ref(V,-1)>Ref(Mov(V,opt3,E),-1) AND
V<Ref(Mov(V,opt2,E),-1)

Close short: Ref(V,-1)<Ref(Mov(V,opt1,E),-1) AND
V>Ref(Mov(V,opt2,E),-1)

OPT1 Current value: 18

OPT2 Current value: 34

OPT3 Current value: 7

OPT4 Current value: 34

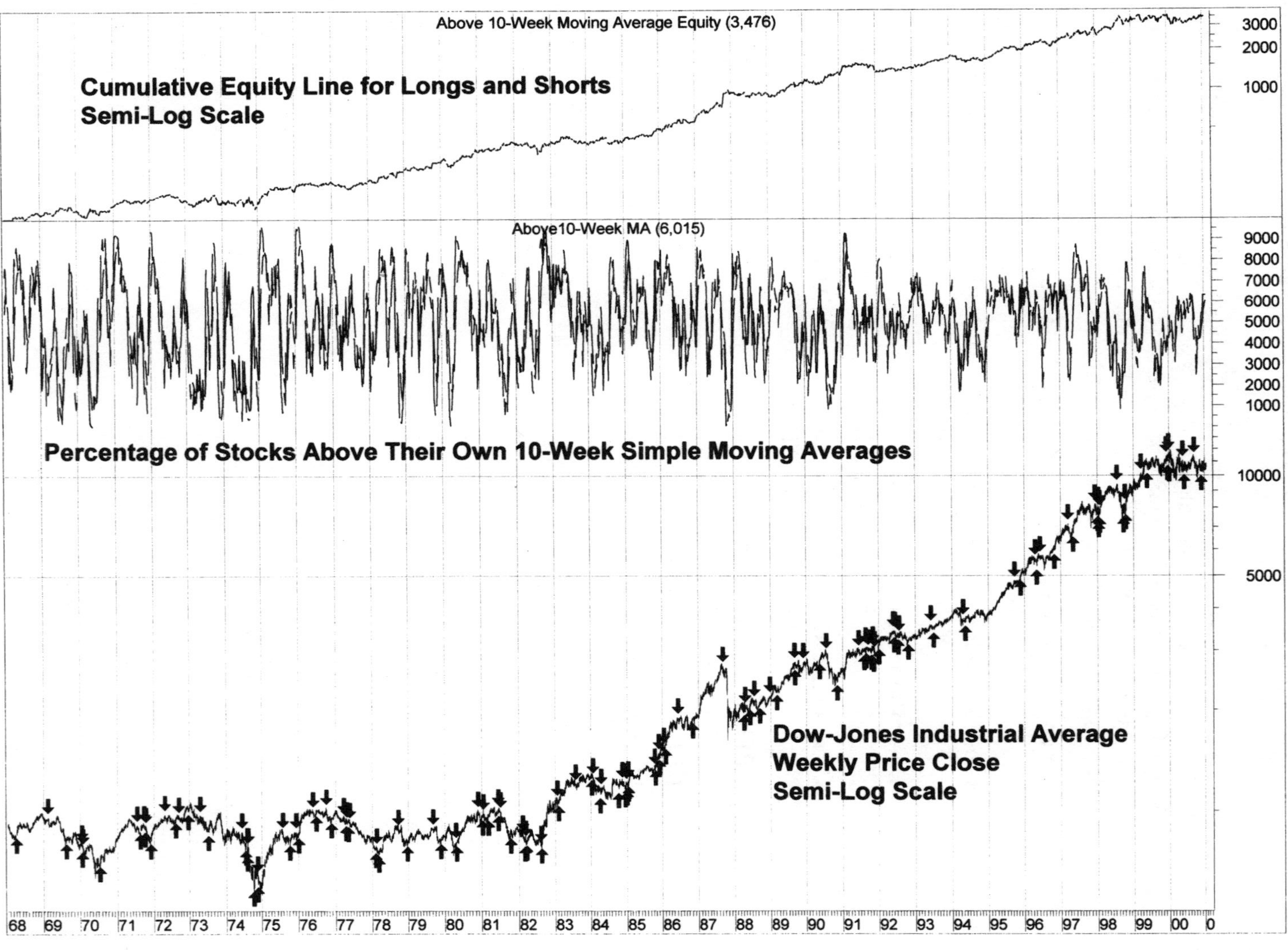

Above 10-Week Moving Average Equity (3,476)
Cumulative Equity Line for Longs and Shorts
Semi-Log Scale
3000
2000
1000
Above10-Week MA (6,015)
9000
8000
7000
6000
5000
4000
3000
2000
1000
Percentage of Stocks Above Their Own 10-Week Simple Moving Averages
10000
5000
Dow-Jones Industrial Average
Weekly Price Close
Semi-Log Scale
68
69
70
71
72
73
74
75
76
77
78
79
80
81
82
83
84
85
86
87
88
89
90
91
92
93
94
95
96
97
98
99
00
0

Percentage of Stocks Above Their Own 10-Week Simple Moving Averages

Total net profit	3375.93	Open position value	93.4	Net Profit / Buy&Hold %	245.24
Percent gain/loss	3375.93	Annual percent gain/loss	96.5	Annual Net % / B&H %	245.26
Initial investment	100	Interest earned	0		
Current position	Long	Date position entered	12/1/00		
Buy/Hold profit	977.85	Days in test	12769	# of days per trade	87.46
Buy/Hold pct gain/loss	977.85	Annual B/H pct gain/loss	27.95		
Total closed trades	146	Commissions paid	0		
Avg profit per trade	22.48	Avg Win/Avg Loss ratio	2.23		
Total long trades	73	Total short trades	73	Long Win Trade %	57.53
Winning long trades	42	Winning short trades	34	Short Win Trade %	46.58
Total winning trades	76	Total losing trades	70	Total Win Trade %	52.05
Amount of winning trades	5591.4	Amount of losing trades	−2308.87	Net Profit Margin %	41.55
Average win	73.57	Average loss	−32.98	Average P. Margin %	38.09
Largest win	529.68	Largest loss	−272.38	% Net / (Win + Loss)	32.08
Average length of win	16.95	Average length of loss	8.03	(Win − Loss) / Loss %	111.08
Longest winning trade	71	Longest losing trade	49	(Win − Loss) / Loss %	44.90
Most consecutive wins	6	Most consecutive losses	4	(Win − Loss) / Loss %	50.00
Total bars out	113	Average length out	113		
Longest out period	113				
System close drawdown	0	Profit/Loss index	59.39	% Net Profit / SODD	#DIV/0!
System open drawdown	0	Reward/Risk index	100	(Net P.-SODD)/Net P.	100.00
Max open trade drawdown	−504.93	Buy/Hold index	254.79	% SODD / Net Profit	0.00

In the Equis MetaStock® "System Report" (profit and loss summary statistics), the *Total net profit* is the sum of profits minus the sum of losses, including open positions marked to the market. In contrast, the *Amount of Winning Trades* is the sum of realized profits (the total of all gains on closed-out trades only, excluding any open positions). Similarly, the *Amount of Losing Trades* is the sum of realized losses (the total of all losses on closed-out trades only, excluding any open positions). *System close drawdown* is the largest decline in the cumulative equity line below the initial investment, based on closed-out positions only. *System open drawdown (SODD)* is the largest decline in the cumulative equity line below the initial investment when a position is open. *Max open trade drawdown* is the largest decline in the cumulative equity line below the trade entry price during the worst single trade. The *Profit/Loss Index* is a complex calculation that relates the Amount of Winning Trades to the Amount of Losing Trades on a scale of −100 (worst possible performance) to +100 (best possible performance), with zero representing profits equal to losses. *Reward/Risk Index* is the Total net profit minus System open drawdown. The resulting difference is then divided by the Total net profit. The *Buy/Hold Index* is the Total net profit minus the buy-and-hold strategy's net profit. The resulting difference is then divided by the buy-and-hold net profit. In this exercise, initial equity is assumed to be $100. Both long and short positions are taken unless otherwise noted. Trades are executed at the closing price on the signal date. Transaction costs, interest expenses, and margins are not included in the statistics.

Permission Filters, Permission Screens

To accept a signal from a sensitive, short-term indicator, there also must be a confirming signal from a slower, long-term indicator. For example, buy when the price close crosses above a trailing five-period moving average—but only if price is also above a trailing 200-period moving average. This kind of Permission Screening can filter out many trades against the larger trend and thus reduce trading frequency. (See: Kase, C. (1996). *Trading with the Odds: Using the Power of Probability to Profit in the Futures Market.* Irwin Professional Publishing. Adapted with permission.)

Pivot Point

A Pivot Point is an extreme price high or low that marks a turning point for a trend. To qualify as a Pivot Point, a turning point must be obvious and stand out on the chart.

Another definition of a Pivot Point is tomorrow's projected high and low. There are five steps to arrive at these forward projections:

1. Calculate today's average price (A), which is the sum today's high plus today's low plus today's close, then divide that sum by three. This is expressed in familiar symbols as, $A = (H + L + C) / 3$.
2. The next period's projected high is two times that average price minus today's low, or $2A - L$.
3. The next period's projected low is two times today's average price minus today's high, or $2A - H$.
4. The next period's extreme projected high is today's average price plus today's price range, or $A + (H - L)$.
5. The next period's extreme projected low is today's average price minus today's price range, or $A - (H - L)$.

(See LeBeau, C., & Lucas, D. W. (1992). *Technical Traders Guide to Computer Analysis of the Futures Market.* Homewood, IL: Business One Irwin.)

Pivot Point Reverse Trading System

The Pivot Point Reverse Trading System is a simple way to identify a change in minor trend direction. A top pivot point is defined as a high that is higher than both the previous period's high and the next period's high. A bottom pivot point is characterized by a low that is lower than both the previous period's low and the next period's low. Either one of these pivot points signals a reversal in minor trend direction. Furthermore, we found that requiring confirmation of trend change by the closing price improves the system.

Indicator Strategy Example for the Pivot Point Reverse Trading System

The Pivot Point Reverse Trading System can be an effective indicator on both the long and short sides, and particularly on the long side. Based on the daily DJIA for 101 years from January 1900 through December 2000, we found that the following parameters would have produced a significantly positive result on a purely mechanical trend-following signal basis with no subjectivity, no sophisticated technical analysis, and no judgement:

Enter Long (Buy) at the current daily price close of the DJIA when there appears a bottom pivot point with a closing price reversal confirmation; that is, a low yesterday that is lower than the previous day's low, a low today that is higher than yesterday's low, and a close today that is higher than yesterday's close.

Close Long (Sell) at the current daily price close of the DJIA when there appears a top pivot point with a closing price reversal confirmation; that is, a high yesterday that is higher than the previous day's high, a high today that is lower than yesterday's high, and a close today that is lower than yesterday's close.

Enter Short (Sell Short) at the current daily price close of the DJIA when there appears a top pivot point with a closing price reversal confirmation; that is, a high yesterday that is higher than the previous day's high, a high today that is lower than yesterday's high, and a close today that is lower than yesterday's close.

Close Short (Cover) at the current daily price close of the DJIA when there appears a bottom pivot point with a closing price reversal confirmation; that is, a low yesterday that is lower than the previous day's low, a low today that is higher than yesterday's low, and a close today that is higher than yesterday's close.

Starting with $100 and reinvesting profits, total net profits for this trend-following strategy would have been $2,912,550.50, assuming a fully invested strategy, reinvestment of profits, no transactions costs and no taxes. This would have been 13,463.27 percent better than buy-and-hold. Even short selling would have been profitable and was included in this strategy. The long-and-short Pivot Point Reverse Trading System would have given profitable signals 40.41% of the time. Trading would have been hyperactive at one trade every 5.35 calendar days.

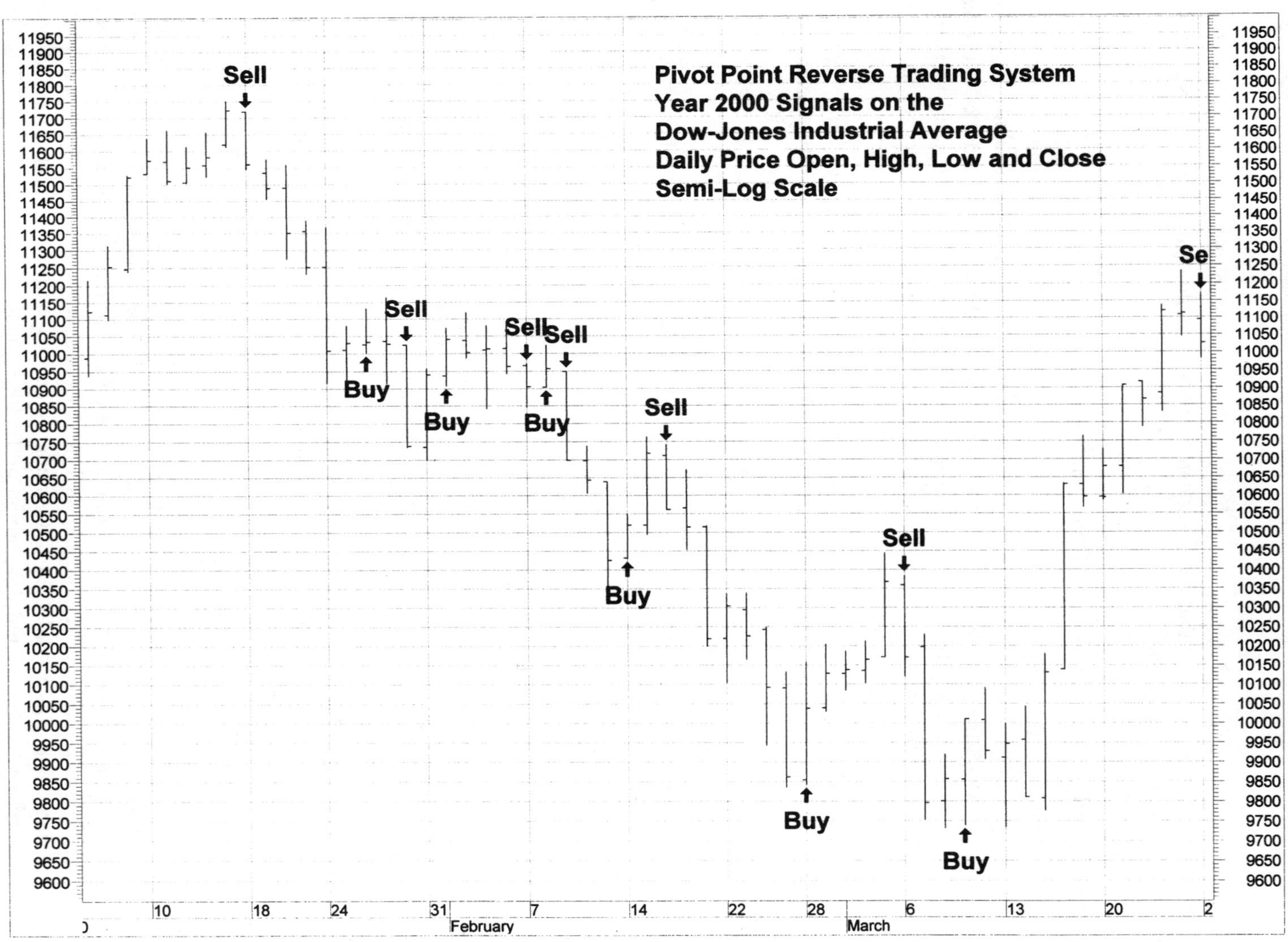

Pivot Point Reverse Trading System
Year 2000 Signals on the
Dow-Jones Industrial Average
Daily Price Open, High, Low and Close
Semi-Log Scale
Sell
Buy
Sell
Buy
Sell
Sell
Buy
Sell
Buy
Sell
Buy
Sell
Buy
Se
10
18
24
31
February
7
14
22
28
March
6
13
20
2

Pivot Point Reverse Trading System

Total net profit	2912550.5	Open position value	40853.84	Net Profit / Buy&Hold %	13463.27
Percent gain/loss	2912550.5	Annual percent gain/loss	28819.93	Annual Net % / B&H %	13462.96
Initial investment	100	Interest earned	0		
Current position	Long	Date position entered	12/22/00		
Buy/Hold profit	21473.8	Days in test	36887	# of days per trade	5.35
Buy/Hold pct gain/loss	21473.8	Annual B/H pct gain/loss	212.49		
Total closed trades	6896	Commissions paid	0		
Avg profit per trade	416.43	Avg Win/Avg Loss ratio	1.89		
Total long trades	3448	Total short trades	3448	Long Win Trade %	43.97
Winning long trades	1516	Winning short trades	1271	Short Win Trade %	36.86
Total winning trades	2787	Total losing trades	4109	Total Win Trade %	40.41
Amount of winning trades	13030242	Amount of losing trades	−10158552	Net Profit Margin %	12.38
Average win	4675.36	Average loss	−2472.27	Average P. Margin %	30.82
Largest win	304738.75	Largest loss	−230805	% Net / (Win + Loss)	13.81
Average length of win	6.89	Average length of loss	3.74	(Win − Loss) / Loss %	84.22
Longest winning trade	484	Longest losing trade	169	(Win − Loss) / Loss %	186.39
Most consecutive wins	9	Most consecutive losses	18	(Win − Loss) / Loss %	−50.00
Total bars out	3	Average length out	3		
Longest out period	3				
System close drawdown	−7.39	Profit/Loss index	22.28	% Net Profit / SODD	39412050.07
System open drawdown	−7.39	Reward/Risk index	100	(Net P.-SODD)/Net P.	100.00
Max open trade drawdown	−230805	Buy/Hold index	13653.52	% SODD / Net Profit	0.00

In the Equis MetaStock® "System Report" (profit and loss summary statistics), the *Total net profit* is the sum of profits minus the sum of losses, including open positions marked to the market. In contrast, the *Amount of Winning Trades* is the sum of realized profits (the total of all gains on closed-out trades only, excluding any open positions). Similarly, the *Amount of Losing Trades* is the sum of realized losses (the total of all losses on closed-out trades only, excluding any open positions). *System close drawdown* is the largest decline in the cumulative equity line below the initial investment, based on closed-out positions only. *System open drawdown (SODD)* is the largest decline in the cumulative equity line below the initial investment when a position is open. *Max open trade drawdown* is the largest decline in the cumulative equity line below the trade entry price during the worst single trade. The *Profit/Loss Index* is a complex calculation that relates the Amount of Winning Trades to the Amount of Losing Trades on a scale of −100 (worst possible performance) to +100 (best possible performance), with zero representing profits equal to losses. *Reward/Risk Index* is the Total net profit minus System open drawdown. The resulting difference is then divided by the Total net profit. The *Buy/Hold Index* is the Total net profit minus the buy-and-hold strategy's net profit. The resulting difference is then divided by the buy-and-hold net profit. In this exercise, initial equity is assumed to be $100. Both long and short positions are taken unless otherwise noted. Trades are executed at the closing price on the signal date. Transaction costs, interest expenses, and margins are not included in the statistics.

The Equis International MetaStock® System Testing rules for the Pivot Point Reverse Trading System are written:

Enter long: (Ref(L,-2)>Ref(L,-1)) AND (Ref(L,-1)<L) AND (Ref(C,-1)<C)

Close long: (Ref(H,-2)<Ref(H,-1)) AND (Ref(H,-1)>H) AND (Ref(C,-1)>C)

Enter short: (Ref(H,-2)<Ref(H,-1)) AND (Ref(H,-1)>H) AND (Ref(C,-1)>C)

Close short: (Ref(L,-2)>Ref(L,-1)) AND (Ref(L,-1)<L) AND (Ref(C,-1)<C)

Point and Figure Charts (P&F Charts)

Point and Figure Charts apply a price filter (consisting of a predefined box size and a predefined reversal amount) to price fluctuations for the purpose of filtering out and eliminating some of the noise in the data. Only substantial changes in prices are recorded on the chart. This allows the main trend to emerge as the dominant feature on the chart.

Like most charts, price movement is measured along the vertical y-axis on the graph. Unlike most charts, however, time does not determine progress along the horizontal x-axis. In fact, time plays no role whatsoever in the construction or development of the chart. Point and Figure Charts differ from most price charts in that they completely disregard time.

In time series charts, such as the popular bar charts and Candlestick charts, the passage of time moves the postings to the chart from left to right. In contrast, Point and Figure Charts move to a new column to the right not by the passage of time but only when price changes direction by some predefined *box size times reversal amount.*

If price does not change direction by that predefined box size times reversal amount, then the chart is posted in the same column whenever it moves by the predefined box size in the same direction as the already established current column. When the price does not move by either the box size or the reversal amount, then no new entry to the chart is posted. Thus, for a stock confined to a very small price range, there may be no new posting to the Point and Figure Chart for several days, weeks or even months.

In the traditional one-point reversal Point and Figure Chart, when price changes direction by a full *point* and actually trades at that the next, non-fractional, round-number point, at any time during the trading session, then a *figure* (which is the numeral that represents the latest price) is entered at that new price in the next column to the right. *Each price tick counts.* So, a volatile stock that fluctuates several full points in both directions in a single day might be posted in several columns for that day. Point and Figure purists insist that this is the only correct way to post Point and Figure Charts. This method obviously requires tick data and more time and attention to detail than most individual traders and investors are capable of giving to chart creation. Consequently, the one-point reversal method is used mainly by full-time professional analysts and traders. (See Wheelan, A. (1954). *Study Helps in Point and Figure Technique.* New York: Morgan Rodgers & Roberts.) For a complete array of professional-quality Point and Figure Charting services and other valuable data necessary for technical-analysis research, institutional investors may contact UST Securities Corporation, 5 Vaughn Drive, CN5209, Princeton, NJ 08543-5209, phone (201) 734-7747.

Box sizes and reversal amounts may be any size, depending on the price and volatility of the instrument. Practical experience reveals the most useful sizes. To keep the chart work simple and consistent, many traders use the one-point reversal Point and Figure Chart for all stocks. Here, both the box size and reversal size are one-point, using round numbers only and ignoring fractions. For example, for a stock that rises from 45 to 50, a current price reversal to a tick at 49 would be posted in a new column to the right. Then, the next round number price determines if the new column is to be an advancing price column or a declining price column. If the next round number price is 50, then the new column is an advancing price column. But if the next round number price is 48, then the new column is a declining price column.

For low-priced stocks under 20, Wheelan recommended a half-point box size. For high-priced stocks over 80, he suggested a three-point box size. UST Securities has developed an interesting semi-log scale to automatically adapt to changing levels in the price of the stock. UST, Art Merrill, and Ned Davis Research have experimented with percentage scaling. Ned Davis Research finds a four percent box size with an eight percent reversal amount to be useful in filtering the long-term trend of the DJIA.

Several less demanding, short-cut variations of Point and Figure Charting have evolved over the years. (See Cohen, A. *How to Use the Three-Point Reversal Method of Point & Figure Stock Market Trading.* Larchmont, NY: Chartcraft, www.chartcraft.com). Cohen's method uses a three-box reversal amount for all stocks and indexes. Chartcraft allows the box size to vary depending on the price level of the stock, as follows: for stocks priced at 5 and under, use a quarter-point box size; for stocks priced above 5 and under 21, use a half-point box size; for stocks priced at 21 to 100, use a full-point box size; and for stocks priced above 100, use a two-point box size.

MetaStock® software can construct Chartcraft's Three-Point Reversal Chart, but the user must specify the settings. When a stock price is in an uptrend, MetaStock® posts an "X" when price rises by the specified box size (commonly, one point). When the price trend reverses, as determined by the price declining by a pre-specified reversal amount (commonly, three boxes), then and only then does the software post an "O" in a new column, one column to the right. In a continuing downward column of Os, as long as prices continue to decline without moving up by the reversal amount, Os are posted in the same column, each subsequent O lower than the previous O. Only when prices advance by the reversal amount is an *X* posted in a new column to the right. When prices rise or fall by an amount that is less than the box size, no Xs or Os are posted to the chart. Each column may contain either Xs or Os—but never both. Each column must contain at least the reversal amount of boxes. MetaStock® software first checks if prices have moved in the current direction (that is, a higher high in a column of Xs, or a lower low in a column of Os) before it checks for a reversal in the opposite direction. The software thus posts continuation of the prevailing trend before reversal of the trend. Both P&F Charts shown here were produced by MetaStock® software.

The user may specify a box size and reversal amount of any magnitude. For any box size and reversal amount to change columns (either from a rising column of Xs to a declining column of Os, or from a declining column of Os to a rising column of Xs), prices must reverse by the reversal amount multiplied by the box size.

For example, as the chart of the DJIA illustrates, if the box size is set to 100 points and the reversal amount is set to 3 boxes, then prices must reverse direction 300 points (3 times 100) to change columns. When the current column is composed of rising Xs, the price must fall 300 points to change to a new column of falling Os. Conversely, when the current column is composed of declining Os, the price must rise 300 points to change to a new column of advancing Xs.

Thus, the changing of columns only signifies some specified minimal change in the short-term trend of prices. As the box size and reversal amount increase, we filter out more and more price fluctuations on the chart, leaving only the largest price movements as the box size and reversal amount become very large.

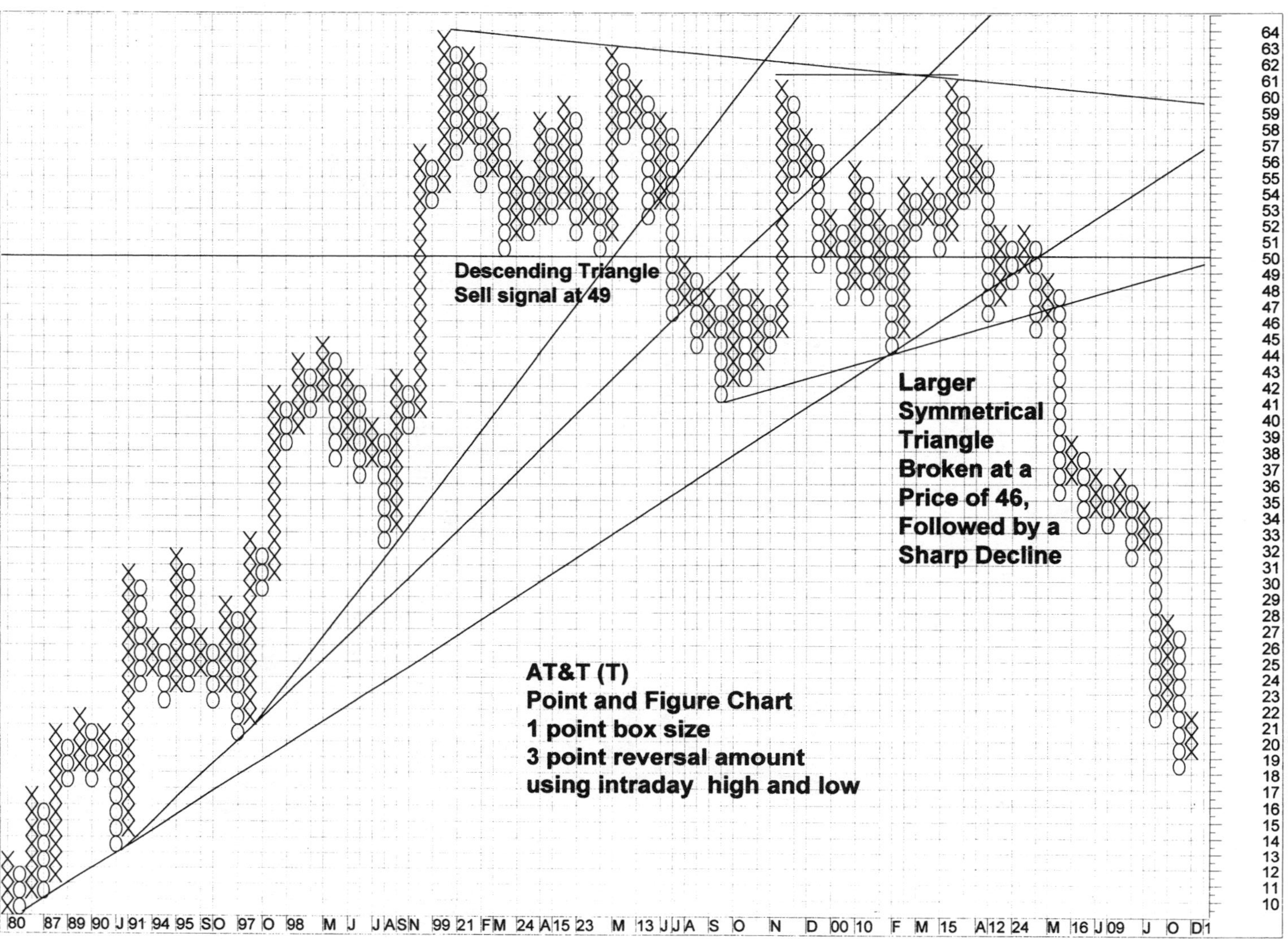

Descending Triangle
Sell signal at 49
Larger
Symmetrical
Triangle
Broken at a
Price of 46,
Followed by a
Sharp Decline
AT&T (T)
Point and Figure Chart
1 point box size
3 point reversal amount
using intraday high and low

It is the trend and patterns on the chart that have meaning. Trendlines, previous tops and bottoms, Head-and-Shoulders, Double and Triple Tops and Bottoms, Saucers, Triangles and many of the other useful chart patterns can be applied to P&F Charts. By filtering out some of the smaller price fluctuations on the Point and Figure Chart, the larger and more significant trends and patterns may become more recognizable.

Recall the Dow Theory, where a chart pattern of higher highs is a sign of a bull market, while lower lows is a sign of a bear market. Similarly, with the Chartcraft method, a mechanical buy signal is recognized when a column of X's rises above a previous column of X's. That is, of course, higher highs. Conversely, a mechanical sell signal is recognized when a column of O's falls below a previous column of O's, clearly pinpointing lower lows.

The 100 X 3 P&F Chart of the DJIA reveals some of the weaknesses and strengths of the Point and Figure Chart. Because the chart is determined solely by the point fluctuations, movements disappear when price is low. For example, the greatest bear market of all time, which saw the DJIA fall 89% from 1929 to 1932, totally disappeared from the 100 X 3 P&F Chart. This is because (using round number boxes) price fell from 300 to 100, only −200 points, or 100 points less than the −300 points required to register a reversal to a new down column of Os. Also, it may seem odd that all the price action from 1900 through 1997 takes up only as much horizontal space as year 2000 alone.

But other features really stand out on the Point and Figure Chart. The third fan line (trendline) up from an all-time low of 100 was broken in September 1999 at 10800, and then became resistance by the time the all-time high was hit at 11700 in March 2000. Also, it is clear that old resistance at 9600 (two tops in January and February 1999) functioned as support in year 2000. A breakdown to 9500 would complete a large reversal pattern that could lead to a test of support at 7500.

The 1 X 3 P&F Chart of AT&T on page 517 shows the Fan Principle in action: when three trendlines are broken, you have three strikes and you are out, the trend is over. This compressed 20-year picture also reveals two Triangle Reversal patterns: a Descending Triangle Reversal from the all time high of 64 to the failed Double Bottom at 51 is completely contained within a much larger Symmetrical Triangle Reversal. The latter was followed by a clear breakdown at 46, and that was preceded by the break of the third Fan line. The typical short-term bar chart of one year or less will miss this big picture.

An informal poll conducted at a 1997 meeting of the International Federation of Technical Analysts showed that about ten percent of the analysts present used Point and Figure Charts.

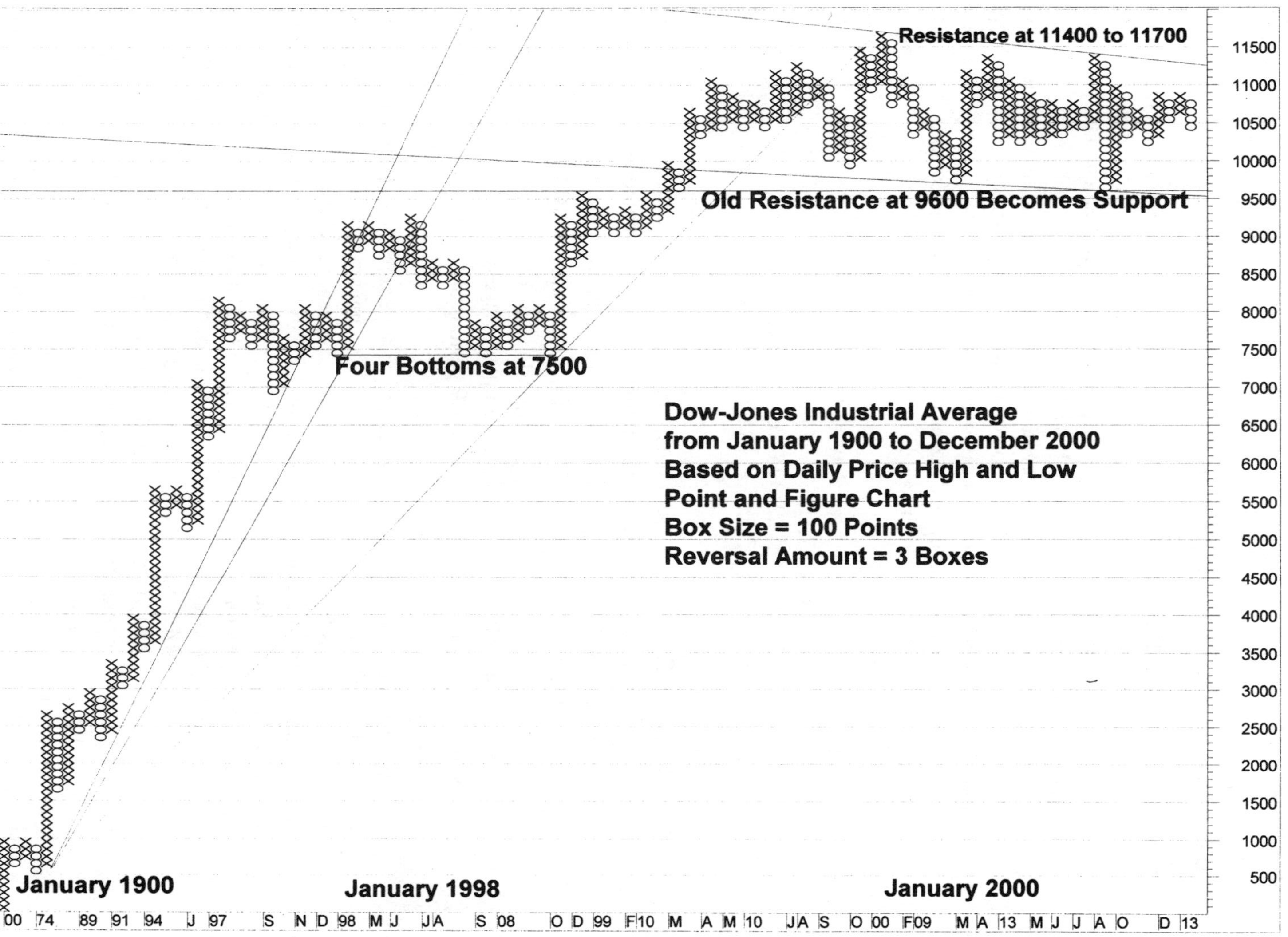

Resistance at 11400 to 11700
Old Resistance at 9600 Becomes Support
Four Bottoms at 7500
Dow-Jones Industrial Average
from January 1900 to December 2000
Based on Daily Price High and Low
Point and Figure Chart
Box Size = 100 Points
Reversal Amount = 3 Boxes
January 1900
January 1998
January 2000

Polarized Fractal Efficiency (PFE)

Polarized Fractal Efficiency (PFE) was introduced by Hans Hannula in the January 1994 issue of *Technical Analysis of Stocks & Commodities* (www.traders.com). The indicator was intended to quantify the efficiency of price movement and how trendy or choppy the recent past price action has been.

The article contains a highly elevated fog factor. The basic indicator at its core appears to be a highly complex variation of a price velocity oscillator, where a longer period change in the price close is divided by a shorter period average change in price. A companion article in the magazine offers the following MetaStock® Formula Language to express Polarized Fractal Efficiency:

```
Mov(If(C,>,Ref(C,-9),
Sqrt(Power(ROC(C,9,$), 2)+Power(10,2)) /
Sum(Sqrt(Power(ROC(C,1,$),2)+1),9),
−Sqrt(Power(ROC(C,9,$),2)+Power(10,2)) /
Sum(Sqrt(Power(ROC(C,1,$),2)+1),9))*100,5,E)
```

where

Mov(. . . ,5,E) = the five-period exponential moving average.

Sqrt = square root of the expression that follows in parentheses.

Power(ROC(C,9,$), 2) = the 10-day change in the closing price squared.

Power(10,2) = 10 raised to a power of 2, or ten squared, or 100.

ROC(C,9,$) = the rate of change of the close over the past 10 periods expressed in dollars (that is, points, not percentages).

Sum . . . 9 = the sum over the trailing 9 periods of the expression that follows in parentheses.

According to Hans Hannula, PFE readings above zero indicate that the trend has been up. The higher the PFE, the more efficient the upward movement. A straight-line price rise would be 100% efficient. Conversely, PFE readings below zero indicate that the trend has been down, and the lower the PFE the more efficient the downward movement. A straight-line price drop would be −100% efficient. Readings near zero indicate price congestion, choppy, trend-less, inefficient movement.

Using the MetaStock® predefined formula, PFE(DATA ARRAY,PERIODS, SMOOTHING PERIODS), and default parameters of *CLOSE* price for the data array, *ten* for the periods, and *five* for the smoothing, it appears that the S&P 500 futures *CSI Perpetual Contract* seldom trend efficiently. Moreover, it would appear that the ranges of the indicator have become more extreme in recent years. So, this indicator might benefit from being preprocessed and statistically normalized to compensate for changes in volatility. Moreover, it seems possible that the outputs may be inconsistent with the author's apparent stated intent. Therefore, caution is warranted when viewing this indicator.

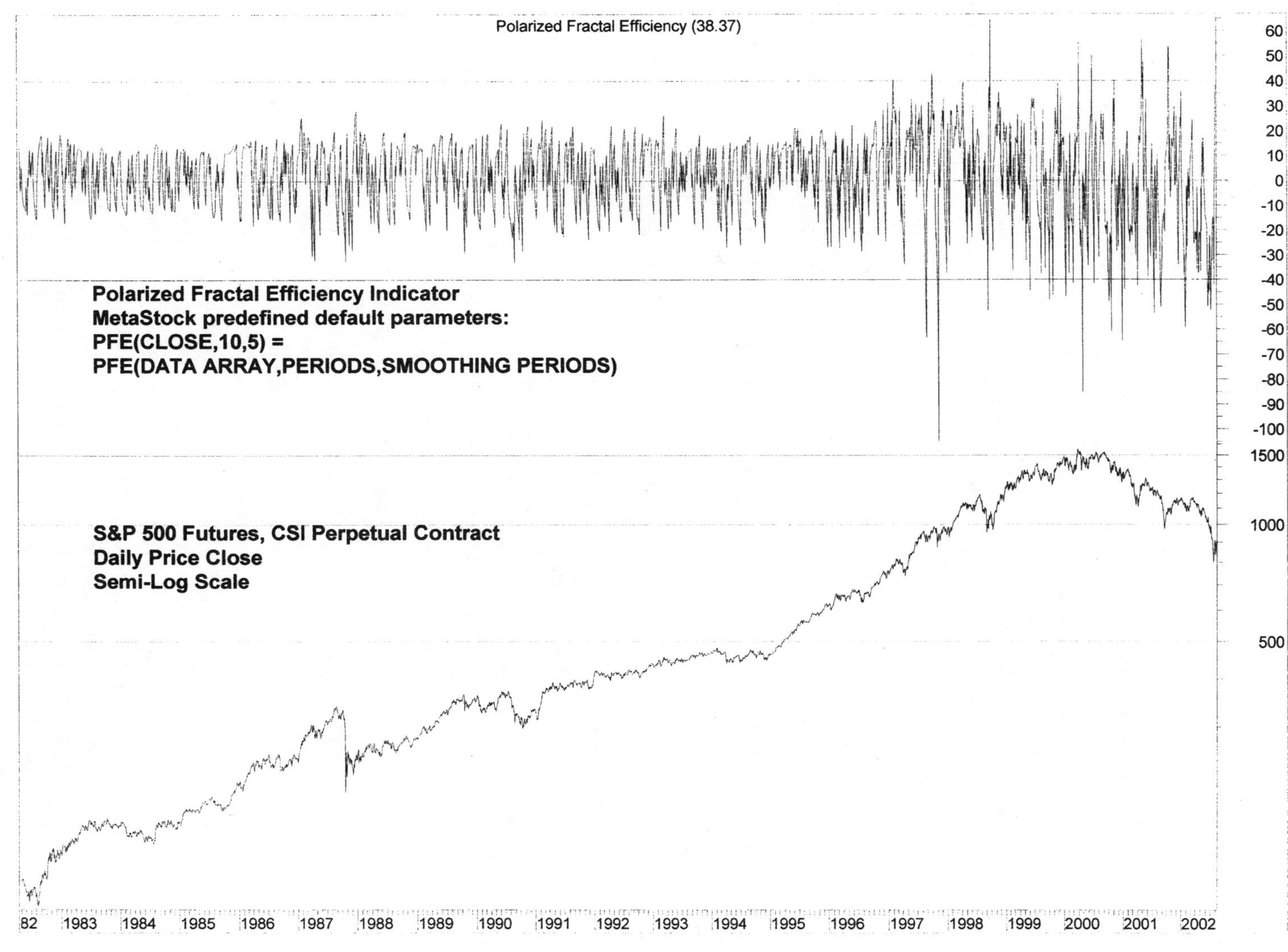

Polarized Fractal Efficiency (38.37)
Polarized Fractal Efficiency Indicator
MetaStock predefined default parameters:
PFE(CLOSE,10,5) =
PFE(DATA ARRAY,PERIODS,SMOOTHING PERIODS)
S&P 500 Futures, CSI Perpetual Contract
Daily Price Close
Semi-Log Scale
60
50
40
30
20
10
0
-10
-20
-30
-40
-50
-60
-70
-80
-90
-100
1500
1000
500
82
1983
1984
1985
1986
1987
1988
1989
1990
1991
1992
1993
1994
1995
1996
1997
1998
1999
2000
2001
2002

Positive Volume Index (PVI)

The Positive Volume Index (PVI), created by Paul Dysart, cumulates net price change fractional ratios for periods of increasing volume only. The volume itself is used only as a qualifier to determine whether or not to include the day's net price change fractional ratio in the cumulative total. Most often, PVI is defined as a cumulative total of daily price change ratios on rising volume days only. Also, PVI can be calculated for any other time interval, such as minutes, hourly, weekly, and monthly. Moreover, PVI can be calculated using any market index, stock or commodity, as long as there is data for closing price and volume.

The PVI is calculated in six simple steps:

1. Subtract the previous day's volume from today's volume, respecting sign.
2. If the Step 1 subtraction results in a positive number, then the current day's volume is greater than the previous day's volume. That is defined as a positive volume day.
3. If the Step 1 subtraction results in a negative number, then the current day's volume is less than the previous day's volume. That is defined as a negative volume day.
4. If it is a positive volume day then calculate the day's price change fraction by dividing the current day's price gain (assigned a plus sign) or the current day's price loss (assigned a minus sign) by the closing price of the previous day. Respect the sign.
5. If it is a negative volume day then the current day's price change fraction is set to zero.
6. Add the number found in Step 4 or Step 5 to a cumulative total.

In the MetaStock® Indicator Builder dialogue, PVI may be written:

Cum(If(V>Ref(V,-1),ROC(C,1,%),0))

The literal translation is: "Cumulate the following: If the current volume "V" is greater than the previous period's volume "Ref(V,-1)", then compute the Rate-of-Change "ROC" of the Closing price "C" for one period expressed as a percentage; otherwise (if the current volume is less than the previous volume), set the day's Rate-of-Change of the Closing price computation to zero before cumulating."

Norman Fosback (The Institute for Econometric Research, 3471 North Federal Highway, Forth Lauderdale, FL 33306) found that when PVI was above its own trailing 1-year moving average, it effectively indicated a bull market for stocks. Our independent testing confirmed Fosback's results.

We also found that when PVI was below its own trailing 1-year moving average, it paid to be out of the stock market. A negative PVI trend signaled a huge loss for the stock market from 1929 to 1932. On the whole, however, selling short on negative PVI trend signals did not pay.

Indicator Strategy Example for the Positive Volume Index (PVI)

Historical data shows that the Positive Volume Index is a moderately effective indicator on the long side. Based on the number of shares traded each day on the NYSE and the daily prices for the DJIA for 72 years from 1928 to 2000, we found that the following parameters would have produced a positive result on a purely mechanical trend-following signal basis with no subjectivity, no sophisticated technical analysis, and no judgement:

Enter Long (Buy) at the current daily price close of the DJIA when the current Positive Volume Index is greater than the previous day's 1-year (253-day) EMA of the Positive Volume Index.

Close Long (Sell) at the current daily price close of the DJIA when the current Positive Volume Index is less than the previous day's 1-year (253-day) EMA of the Positive Volume Index.

Enter Short (Sell Short) never.

Starting with $100 and reinvesting profits, total net profits for this Positive Volume Index strategy would have been $6,591.80, assuming a fully invested strategy, reinvestment of profits, no transactions costs and no taxes. This would have been 44.08 percent better than buy-and-hold. Only about a third of the 108 signals would have produced winning trades, and the average long trade would have lasted nearly a year. Short selling, which is not included in this strategy, would have lost money.

The Equis International MetaStock® System Testing rules are written as follows:

Enter long: PVI()>Ref(Mov(PVI(),opt1,E),-1)

Close long: PVI()<Ref(Mov(PVI(),opt1,E),-1)

OPT1 Current value: 253

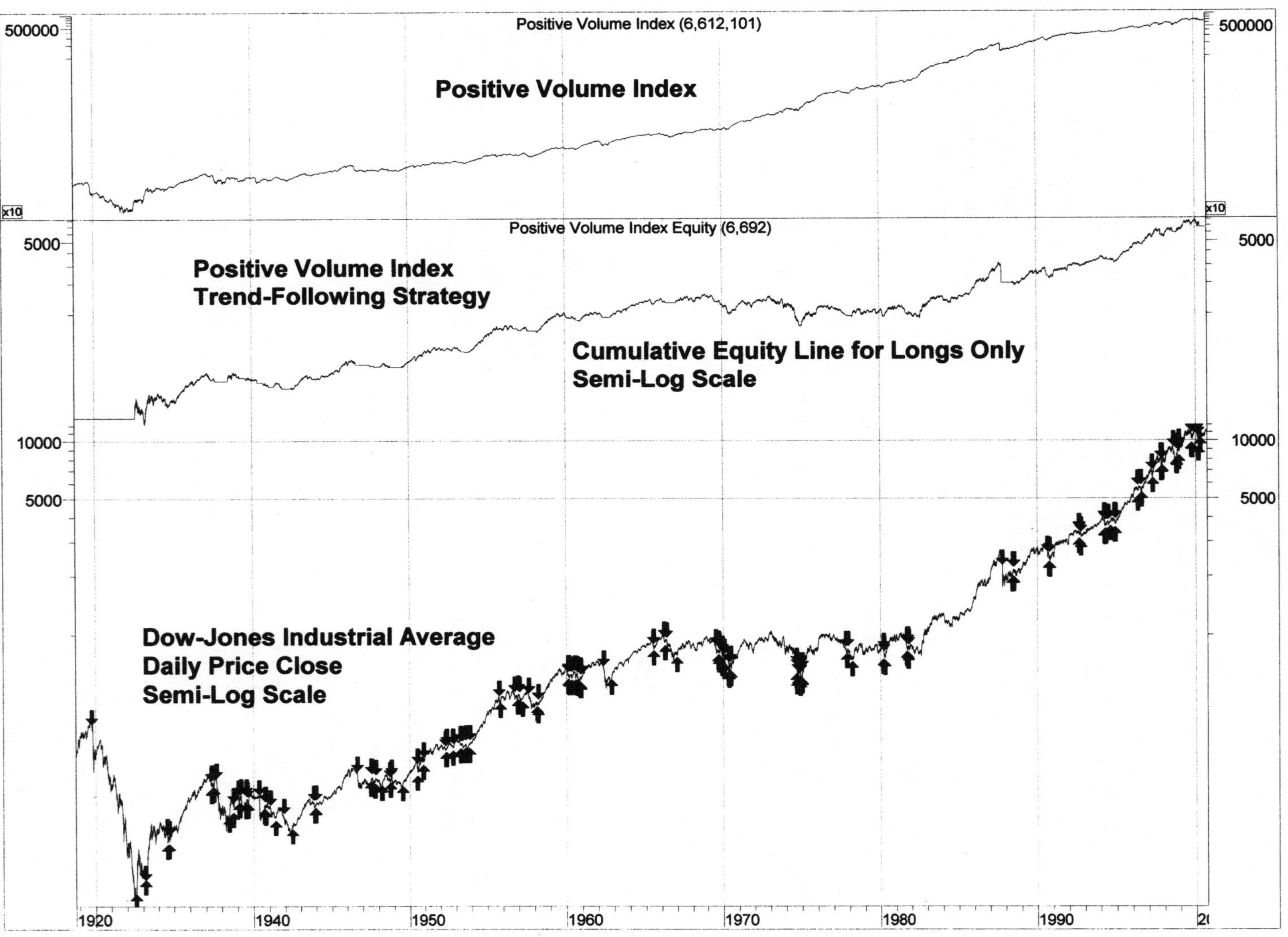

Positive Volume Index (6,612,101)
Positive Volume Index
500000
x10
Positive Volume Index Equity (6,692)
Positive Volume Index
Trend-Following Strategy
Cumulative Equity Line for Longs Only
Semi-Log Scale
5000
10000
5000
Dow-Jones Industrial Average
Daily Price Close
Semi-Log Scale
1920
1940
1950
1960
1970
1980
1990

Positive Volume Index: versus 1-year EMA

Total net profit	6591.8	Open position value	N/A	Net Profit / Buy&Hold %	44.08
Percent gain/loss	6591.8	Annual percent gain/loss	91.57	Annual Net % / B&H %	44.09
Initial investment	100	Interest earned	0		
Current position	Out	Date position entered	4/27/00		
Buy/Hold profit	4575.25	Days in test	26276	# of days per trade	243.30
Buy/Hold pct gain/loss	4575.25	Annual B/H pct gain/loss	63.55		
Total closed trades	108	Commissions paid	0		
Avg profit per trade	61.04	Avg Win/Avg Loss ratio	8.31		
Total long trades	108	Total short trades	0	Long Win Trade %	33.33
Winning long trades	36	Winning short trades	0	Short Win Trade %	#DIV/0!
Total winning trades	36	Total losing trades	72	Total Win Trade %	33.33
Amount of winning trades	8681.33	Amount of losing trades	−2089.53	Net Profit Margin %	61.20
Average win	241.15	Average loss	−29.02	Average P. Margin %	78.52
Largest win	1458.32	Largest loss	−336.63	% Net / (Win + Loss)	62.49
Average length of win	319.25	Average length of loss	39.04	(Win − Loss) / Loss %	717.75
Longest winning trade	1512	Longest losing trade	1046	(Win − Loss) / Loss %	44.55
Most consecutive wins	4	Most consecutive losses	9	(Win − Loss) / Loss %	−55.56
Total bars out	3975	Average length out	36.47		
Longest out period	957				
System close drawdown	−2.14	Profit/Loss index	75.93	% Net Profit / SODD	51903.94
System open drawdown	−12.7	Reward/Risk index	99.81	(Net P.-SODD)/Net P.	99.81
Max open trade drawdown	−336.63	Buy/Hold index	44.08	% SODD / Net Profit	−0.19

In the Equis MetaStock® "System Report" (profit and loss summary statistics), the *Total net profit* is the sum of profits minus the sum of losses, including open positions marked to the market. In contrast, the *Amount of Winning Trades* is the sum of realized profits (the total of all gains on closed-out trades only, excluding any open positions). Similarly, the *Amount of Losing Trades* is the sum of realized losses (the total of all losses on closed-out trades only, excluding any open positions). *System close drawdown* is the largest decline in the cumulative equity line below the initial investment, based on closed-out positions only. *System open drawdown (SODD)* is the largest decline in the cumulative equity line below the initial investment when a position is open. *Max open trade drawdown* is the largest decline in the cumulative equity line below the trade entry price during the worst single trade. The *Profit/Loss Index* is a complex calculation that relates the Amount of Winning Trades to the Amount of Losing Trades on a scale of −100 (worst possible performance) to +100 (best possible performance), with zero representing profits equal to losses. *Reward/Risk Index* is the Total net profit minus System open drawdown. The resulting difference is then divided by the Total net profit. The *Buy/Hold Index* is the Total net profit minus the buy-and-hold strategy's net profit. The resulting difference is then divided by the buy-and-hold net profit. In this exercise, initial equity is assumed to be $100. Both long and short positions are taken unless otherwise noted. Trades are executed at the closing price on the signal date. Transaction costs, interest expenses, and margins are not included in the statistics.

Pre-Holiday Seasonality

Stock prices tend to rise on the last trading day before holidays. Arthur A. Merrill, CMT, first revealed this phenomenon in the first edition of his book, Merrill, A. (1966). *Behavior of Prices on Wall Street.* Chappaqua, New York: Analysis Press. In his 1984 revised second edition, Merrill found that the pre-holiday session rose 67.9% of the time on average, based on 89-years of past history. This is 29.4% better than average, as only 52.5% of all trading days were rising days. The most bullish holiday was Labor Day, followed by Independence Day, Memorial Day, Christmas, New Year's, Good Friday, and Thanksgiving.

The only exception to the bullish holiday rule was Presidents' Day, which was actually down slightly more often than up. Only 48.9% of the President's Days rose, and that is 6.9% worse than the 89-year average of all trading days rising of 52.5%.

Name of Holiday	*% Rising Days*	*% up Average Days*	*% Above % Below (−) Average*
Labor Day	79.6%	52.5%	51.6%
Independence Day	75.3%	52.5%	43.4%
Memorial Day	75.0%	52.5%	42.9%
Christmas	72.2%	52.5%	37.5%
New Year's	70.8%	52.5%	34.9%
Good Friday	61.5%	52.5%	17.1%
Thanksgiving	60.2%	52.5%	14.7%
Presidents' Day	48.9%	52.5%	−6.9%
averages	67.9%	52.5%	29.4%

Presidential Election Cycle

Arthur A. Merrill, CMT, developed the study of seasonal behavior of stock market prices in his classic book, Merrill, A. (1984). *Behavior of Prices on Wall Street,* Second Edition. Chappaqua, NY: Analysis Press.

Merrill found that from 1886 through 1983, stock prices generally rose the month before a Presidential Election in the United States and continued through the following January until the President is actually sworn in. Immediately after the swearing in ceremony, prices tend to decline for the next 17 months through June of the second year of the Presidential term. Following that prolonged decline, stock prices generally rise until the next Presidential swearing in ceremony.

Yale Hirsch, publisher of the *Stock Traders Almanac* (www.stocktraders almanac.com), updates many of Merrill's studies each year. His published table (on page 139 of his 2001 edition) shows that since 1832, on average, stock prices perform much better in the final two years than in the first two years of the 4-year Presidential term of office. Preelection years were best, up 74% of the time. Election years were up 69% of the time, while midterm election years were up 60% of the time. In contrast, postelection years were down 61% of the time from 1832 to 1981, though this bearish tendency has totally reversed since 1985. Of the total net stock price gains since 1832, 74% were recorded in the final two years (preelection year and election year) of Presidential Administrations. This compares to only 26% of the total net market gain recorded in the first two years (postelection year and midterm election year) of Presidential Administrations.

Every preelection year (15 out of 15 years) since 1943 has seen a higher stock market. Double-digit gains have been recorded in 11 of these 15 years. The average annual gain for a preelection year has been 17% since 1943.

In Presidential Elections since the end of World War II, a Republican challenger won the White House from the ruling Democrats three times, and each time the DJIA declined in the postelection year. In contrast, when an incumbent Democratic President retained the White House, all three times the DJIA advanced in the post-election year. When the Democrats ousted Republicans, the market advanced two out of three times in the post-election year.

It is commonly assumed that the incumbent President is highly motivated to use his considerable powers to insure his own reelection and to keep his own political party in power.

Traditionally, U.S. citizens have been opposed to U.S. involvement in wars, particularly foreign wars. U.S. Presidents closely connected to war have suffered dire consequences.

1. Zachary Taylor, a career army officer elected on the strength of the victories he won in the Mexican War from May 13, 1846, to February 2, 1848, served as the 12th U.S. President but held the office for only 16 months, from his inauguration on March 5, 1849, to his death in office on July 9, 1850.
2. The South viewed the 1860 election of the 16th U.S. President, Abraham Lincoln, as a threat to slavery, and the U.S. Civil War began on April 12, 1861. Four years later, on April 15, 1865, Lincoln was the first U.S. President to be assassinated.
3. James A. Garfield, 20th U.S. President and former brigadier general for the Union Army in the Civil War, died in office on September 19, 1881, after being shot by an "embittered attorney".

4. William McKinley, 25th U.S. President during the 100-days Spanish-American War in 1898, was shot by a "deranged anarchist" on September 14, 1901.
5. Franklin D. Roosevelt, the 32nd U.S. President, died on April 12,1945, just two weeks before Germany surrendered in WWII.
6. In April, 1961, 35th U.S. President John F. Kennedy approved an amphibious landing of more than 1000 Cuban exiles at the Bay of Pigs. Kennedy also sent 16,000 military advisors to Vietnam from 1961 to 1963. JFK was assassinated on November 22, 1963, just 20 days after the assassination of South Vietnam President Diem on November 2, 1963.

In addition to death in office, there may be some tendency to vote out of office the party in power when war began or during war.

1. Woodrow Wilson's Democrats lost in 1920 following World War I (1914–1918).
2. Harry Truman was defeated for reelection in 1952 during the Korean War (1950–1953).
3. Dwight D. Eisenhower greatly increased U.S. military aid, including supplies and up to 700 military advisors, to the French in Vietnam to prevent a Communist victory. The Republican Party Presidential candidate was defeated in the 1960 election.
4. The Vietnam War was so divisive that Lyndon Johnson felt compelled not to run for reelection in 1968. By the end of 1968, U.S. troop levels reached 495,000, and American deaths rose to 30,000, with servicemen dying at the rate of more than a thousand a month. Johnson's Democratic Party Presidential candidate lost the 1968 election.
5. The 1968 election winner, Richard M. Nixon, was forced to resign on August 9, 1974, as Vietnam War dragged on.
6. On April 29, 1975, appointed U.S. President Gerald R. Ford ordered "Operation Frequent Wind", the helicopter evacuation of 7000 Americans and South Vietnamese from Saigon, thus ending the Vietnam War in defeat. Ford was defeated in 1976.
7. Operation Desert Storm in January, 1991, (reversing Iraq's seizure of Kuwait) occurred under Republican President George H. Bush, who was defeated for reelection in 1992.
8. In March, 1999, 42nd President Bill Clinton launched a campaign of air strikes against Serbian military targets in Yugoslavia. Clinton's Democratic Party candidate was defeated in 2000.

Could all of this be mere happenstance? Listen to someone who had substantial first-hand knowledge of war. "The United States never lost a soldier or a foot of ground in my administration. We kept the peace. People ask how it happened—by God, it didn't just happen, I'll tell you that," Dwight D. Eisenhower, Allied commander in Europe during World War II and 34th U.S. President, from January 20, 1953 to January 20, 1961. Ike gained credit for the Korean War truce in July, 1953, and he was rewarded with reelection in 1956.

But Ike forgot to mention that the first American deaths of the Vietnam War were during his second term, on July 8, 1959, when two U.S. military advisors were killed by Viet Minh guerrillas in South Vietnam. Eisenhower's Republican Party candidate lost the 1960 election.

Since 1840, seven U.S. Presidents elected at 20 year intervals in a year ending in zero have died in office. Only one U.S. President, Zachary Taylor, not elected at 20 year intervals in a year ending in zero died in office, but then he was a war President. Noted market analyst and astrologer Arch Crawford points out that the seven deaths all coincide with astrological conjunctions of Jupiter and Saturn in an Earth sign—Taurus, Virgo or Capricorn. Every time this conjunction occurred, the U.S. President died in office. Ronald Reagan was elected with Jupiter and Saturn conjunction in an Air sign, *not* an Earth sign, and he lived, even though he was shot and very seriously wounded by an armed assassin. In 2000, a U.S. President was elected with astrological conjunctions of Jupiter and Saturn in an Earth sign. (See Arch Crawford's monthly market newsletter, Crawford Perspectives, 6890 E. Sunrise Drive, #120-70, Tucson, Arizona 85750-0840, phone (520) 577-1158, fax (520) 577-1110, www.astromoney.com.)

					Dow Industrials % Change				
Died or Resigned in Office	*Elected*	*Party*	*Change in Party*	*Year Elected*	*Election Year*	*Post-Election Year*	*Mid-term Election Year*	*Pre-Election Year*	*Sums*
	Jackson	D		1832	5	−1	13	3	20
	Van Buren	D		1836	−12	−12	2	−12	−34
Died	Harrison, W.	W	Change	1840	6	−13	−18	45	20
	Polk	D	Change	1844	16	8	−15	1	10
Died	Taylor	W	Change	1848	−4	0	19	−3	12
	Pierce	D	Change	1852	20	−13	−30	2	−21
	Buchanan	D		1856	4	−31	14	−11	−24
	Lincoln	R	Change	1860	14	−2	55	38	105
Died	Lincoln	R		1864	6	−9	4	2	3
	Grant	R		1868	11	2	6	7	26
	Grant	R		1872	7	−13	3	−4	−7
	Hayes	R		1876	−18	−9	6	43	22
Died	Garfield	R		1880	19	3	−3	−9	10
	Cleveland	D	Change	1884	−19	20	12	−8	5
	Harrison, B.	R	Change	1888	5	6	−14	18	15

Continued

Died or Resigned in Office	Elected	Party	Change in Party	Year Elected	Dow Industrials % Change: Election Year	Post-Election Year	Mid-term Election Year	Pre-Election Year	Sums
	Cleveland	D	Change	1892	−7	−25	−1	2	−31
	McKinley	R	Change	1896	−2	21	23	9	51
Died	McKinley	R		1900	7	−9	0	−24	−26
	Roosevelt, T.	R		1904	42	38	−2	−38	40
	Taft	R		1908	47	15	−18	1	45
	Wilson	D	Change	1912	8	−10	−5	82	75
	Wilson	D		1916	−4	−22	11	31	16
Died	Harding	R	Change	1920	−33	13	22	−3	−1
	Coolidge	R		1924	26	30	0	29	85
	Hoover	R		1928	48	−17	−34	−53	−56
	Roosevelt, F.	D	Change	1932	−23	67	4	39	87
	Roosevelt, F.	D		1936	25	−33	28	−3	17
	Roosevelt, F.	D		1940	−13	−15	8	14	−6
Died	Roosevelt, F.	D		1944	12	27	−8	2	33
	Truman	D		1948	−2	13	18	14	43
	Eisenhower	R	Change	1952	8	−4	44	21	69
	Eisenhower	R		1956	2	−13	34	16	40
Died	Kennedy	D	Change	1960	−9	19	−11	17	16
	Johnson	D		1964	15	11	−19	15	22
	Nixon	R	Change	1968	4	−15	5	6	0
Resigned	Nixon	R		1972	15	−17	−28	38	9
	Carter	D	Change	1976	18	−17	−3	4	2
	Reagan	R	Change	1980	15	−9	20	20	46
	Reagan	R		1984	−4	28	23	2	49
	Bush, G. H.	R		1988	12	27	−4	20	55
	Clinton	D	Change	1992	4	14	2	34	54
	Clinton	D		1996	26	23	16	25	90
	Bush, G. W.	R	Change	2000	−6				−6
				Sums	291	75	178	434	978
				% of Gains	30%	8%	18%	44%	100%
				# Years Up	29	19	25	31	104
				# Years Down	13	23	17	11	64
				% Years Up	69%	45%	60%	74%	62%
				% Years Down	31%	55%	40%	26%	38%

This table reprinted here with permission of Yale Hirsch, *Stock Traders Almanac,* The Hirsch Organization, Inc., 184 Central Avenue, Old Tappan, NJ 07675, www.stocktradersalmanac.com. This *Almanac* provides annual updates on the Presidential Election Cycle as well as other curious and helpful calendar-based statistics updated each year.

Indicator Strategy Example for the Presidential Election Cycle

A strategy of buying stocks about two years before then selling just after the Presidential Election was suggested by David MacNeill in an edition of the *Stock Traders Almanac,* Old Tappan, NJ: Hirsch Organization, www.stocktradersalmanac.com.

Historical data shows that this Presidential Election Cycle strategy would have been quite accurate on the long side over the past 68 years. The only losing trades would have between the end of 1938 and the end of 1940, a time of unusual volatility due to war news. Based on the year-end closing prices for the DJIA for 68 years from the end of 1932 to the end of 2000, we found that the following parameters would have produced a positive result on a purely mechanical trend-following signal basis with no subjectivity, no sophisticated technical analysis, and no judgement:

Enter Long (Buy) at the year-end price close of the DJIA nearly 22 months before the Presidential Election.

Close Long (Sell) at the year-end price close of the DJIA nearly two months after the Presidential Election.

Enter Short (Sell Short) never.

Starting with $100 and reinvesting profits, total net profits for this Presidential Election Cycle strategy would have been $3688.03, assuming a fully invested strategy, reinvestment of profits, no transactions costs and no taxes. This would have been 73.63 percent less than buy-and-hold, but the strategy was exposed to market risk only half of the time. No allowance was made for any return on capital when out of the market after a sell signal. Only one of 17 signals would have been a loser, so 94.12% would have been winning trades. Short selling, which was not included in this strategy, would have lost money. This is a very simple strategy, and there is probably plenty of room for performance enhancement with the addition of more sophisticated filter rules.

The Equis International MetaStock® System Testing rules (where code numbers are inserted into the field normally reserved for Open Interest, as shown below) are written:

Enter long: OI=8888

Close long: OI=9999

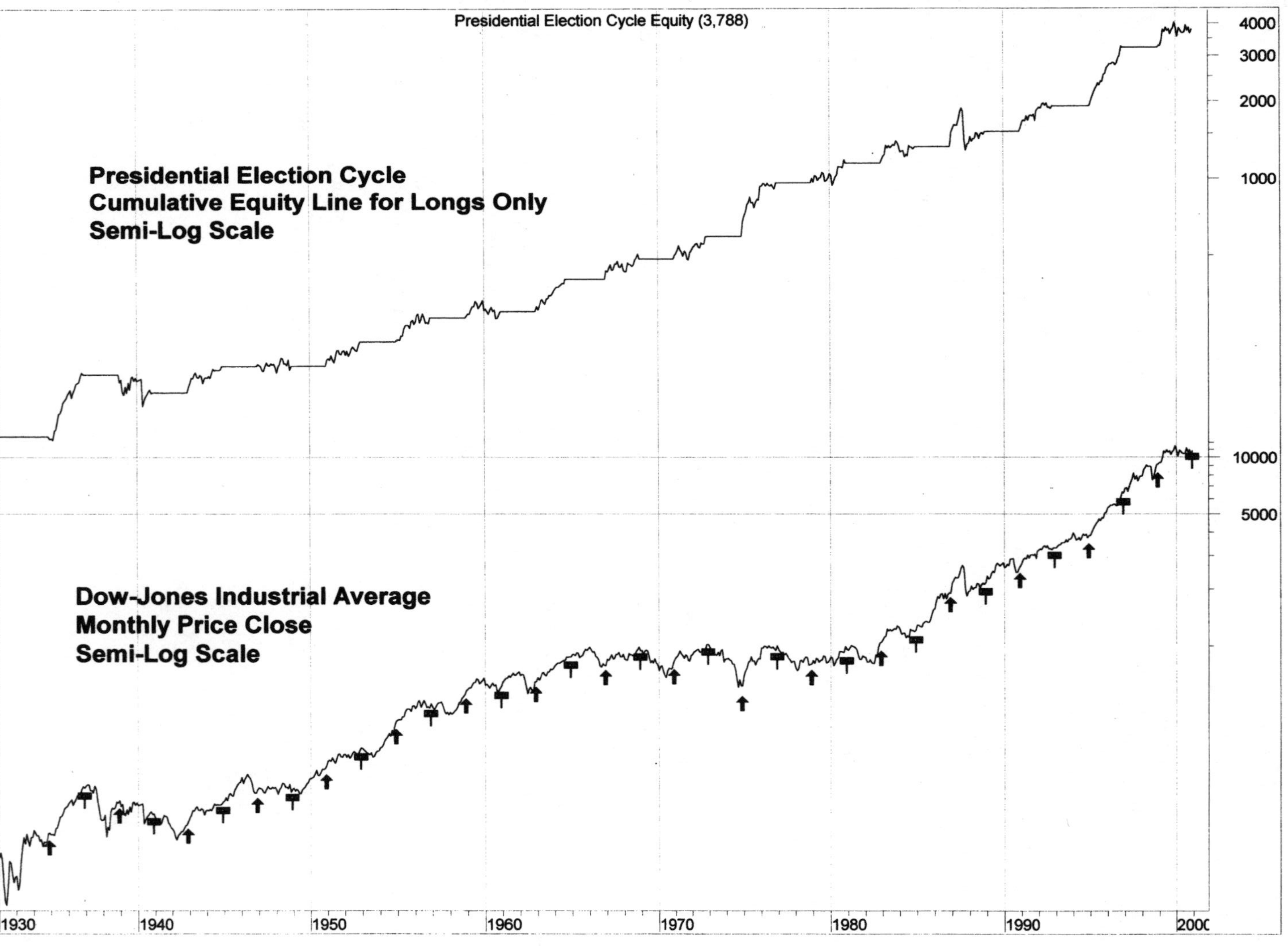
Presidential Election Cycle Equity (3,788)
Presidential Election Cycle
Cumulative Equity Line for Longs Only
Semi-Log Scale
Dow-Jones Industrial Average
Monthly Price Close
Semi-Log Scale
4000
3000
2000
1000
10000
5000
1930
1940
1950
1960
1970
1980
1990
200C

Presidential Election Cycle

Total net profit	3688.03	Open position value	N/A	Net Profit / Buy&Hold %	−73.63
Percent gain/loss	3688.03	Annual percent gain/loss	53.42	Annual Net % / B&H %	−73.62
Initial investment	100	Interest earned	0		
Current position	Out	Date position entered	12/29/00		
Buy/Hold profit	13983.54	Days in test	25200	# of days per trade	1482.35
Buy/Hold pct gain/loss	13983.54	Annual B/H pct gain/loss	202.54		
Total closed trades	17	Commissions paid	0		
Avg profit per trade	216.94	Avg Win/Avg Loss ratio	8.89		
Total long trades	17	Total short trades	0	Long Win Trade %	94.12
Winning long trades	16	Winning short trades	0	Short Win Trade %	#DIV/0!
Total winning trades	16	Total losing trades	1	Total Win Trade %	94.12
Amount of winning trades	3714.13	Amount of losing trades	−26.1	Net Profit Margin %	98.60
Average win	232.13	Average loss	−26.1	Average P. Margin %	79.79
Largest win	1306.85	Largest loss	−26.1	% Net / (Win + Loss)	96.08
Average length of win	25	Average length of loss	25	(Win − Loss) / Loss %	0.00
Longest winning trade	25	Longest losing trade	25	(Win − Loss) / Loss %	0.00
Most consecutive wins	15	Most consecutive losses	1	(Win − Loss) / Loss %	1400.00
Total bars out	437	Average length out	24.28		
Longest out period	36				
System close drawdown	0	Profit/Loss index	99.3	% Net Profit / SODD	119741.23
System open drawdown	−3.08	Reward/Risk index	99.92	(Net P.-SODD)/Net P.	99.92
Max open trade drawdown	−44.01	Buy/Hold index	−73.63	% SODD / Net Profit	−0.08

In the Equis MetaStock® "System Report" (profit and loss summary statistics), the *Total net profit* is the sum of profits minus the sum of losses, including open positions marked to the market. In contrast, the *Amount of Winning Trades* is the sum of realized profits (the total of all gains on closed-out trades only, excluding any open positions). Similarly, the *Amount of Losing Trades* is the sum of realized losses (the total of all losses on closed-out trades only, excluding any open positions). *System close drawdown* is the largest decline in the cumulative equity line below the initial investment, based on closed-out positions only. *System open drawdown (SODD)* is the largest decline in the cumulative equity line below the initial investment when a position is open. *Max open trade drawdown* is the largest decline in the cumulative equity line below the trade entry price during the worst single trade. The *Profit/Loss Index* is a complex calculation that relates the Amount of Winning Trades to the Amount of Losing Trades on a scale of −100 (worst possible performance) to +100 (best possible performance), with zero representing profits equal to losses. *Reward/Risk Index* is the Total net profit minus System open drawdown. The resulting difference is then divided by the Total net profit. The *Buy/Hold Index* is the Total net profit minus the buy-and-hold strategy's net profit. The resulting difference is then divided by the buy-and-hold net profit. In this exercise, initial equity is assumed to be $100. Both long and short positions are taken unless otherwise noted. Trades are executed at the closing price on the signal date. Transaction costs, interest expenses, and margins are not included in the statistics.

Price Channel Trading Range Breakout Rule

Price Channel indicators include the *N*-Day Rule, Donchian's Four-Week Rule, Keltner's Minor Trend Rule, Thrust Method, and the Turtle Trading method. This wheel has been reinvented several times, each time with great enthusiasm, and all these are different names for the same thing.

The idea is simple: buy when the price rises up above previous highs, and sell when the price falls below previous lows. The only parameter to consider is the time length of the look-back period. It is pure trend-following.

These Price Channel lines extend horizontally from price highs and lows into the future, out to the right on the chart. (See *Trend Channel* for a discussion of *sloping* Price Channel lines.)

Indicator Strategy Example for Price Channel

Our testing confirms that Price Channel can be an effective indicator. MetaStock® software executes all trades on the close and, therefore, Price Channel works better examining close-only data. Based on an 18.5-year file of S&P futures *CSI Perpetual Contract* (www.csidata.com) from April 21, 1982, to November 17, 2000, we found that the following parameters would have produced a positive result on a purely mechanical trend-following signal basis with no subjectivity, no sophisticated technical analysis, and no judgement:

Enter Long (Buy) at the current daily price close of the S&P 500 futures *CSI Perpetual Contract* when the close is greater than the close the previous period.

Close Long (Sell) at the current daily price close of the S&P 500 futures *CSI Perpetual Contract* when the close is less than any close over the previous 100 periods.

Enter Short (Sell Short) at the current daily price close of the S&P 500 futures *CSI Perpetual Contract* when the close is less than any close over the previous 100 periods.

Close Short (Cover) at the current daily price close of the S&P 500 futures *CSI Perpetual Contract* when the close is greater than the close the previous period.

Starting with $100 and reinvesting profits, total net profits for this Price Channel trend-following strategy would have been $1547.87, assuming a fully invested, always long-or-short strategy, reinvestment of profits, no transactions costs and no taxes. This would have been 45.96 percent better than buy-and-hold. Trading would have been relatively inactive, with 56 signals in 20 years, one every 130.5 days on average.

The Equis International MetaStock® System Testing rules for the Price Channel indicator are written:

Enter long: C>Ref(HHV(C,opt1),-1)

Close long: C<Ref(LLV(C,opt2),-1)

Enter short: C<Ref(LLV(C,opt2),-1)

Close short: C>Ref(HHV(C,opt1),-1)

OPT1 Current value: 1
OPT2 Current value: 100

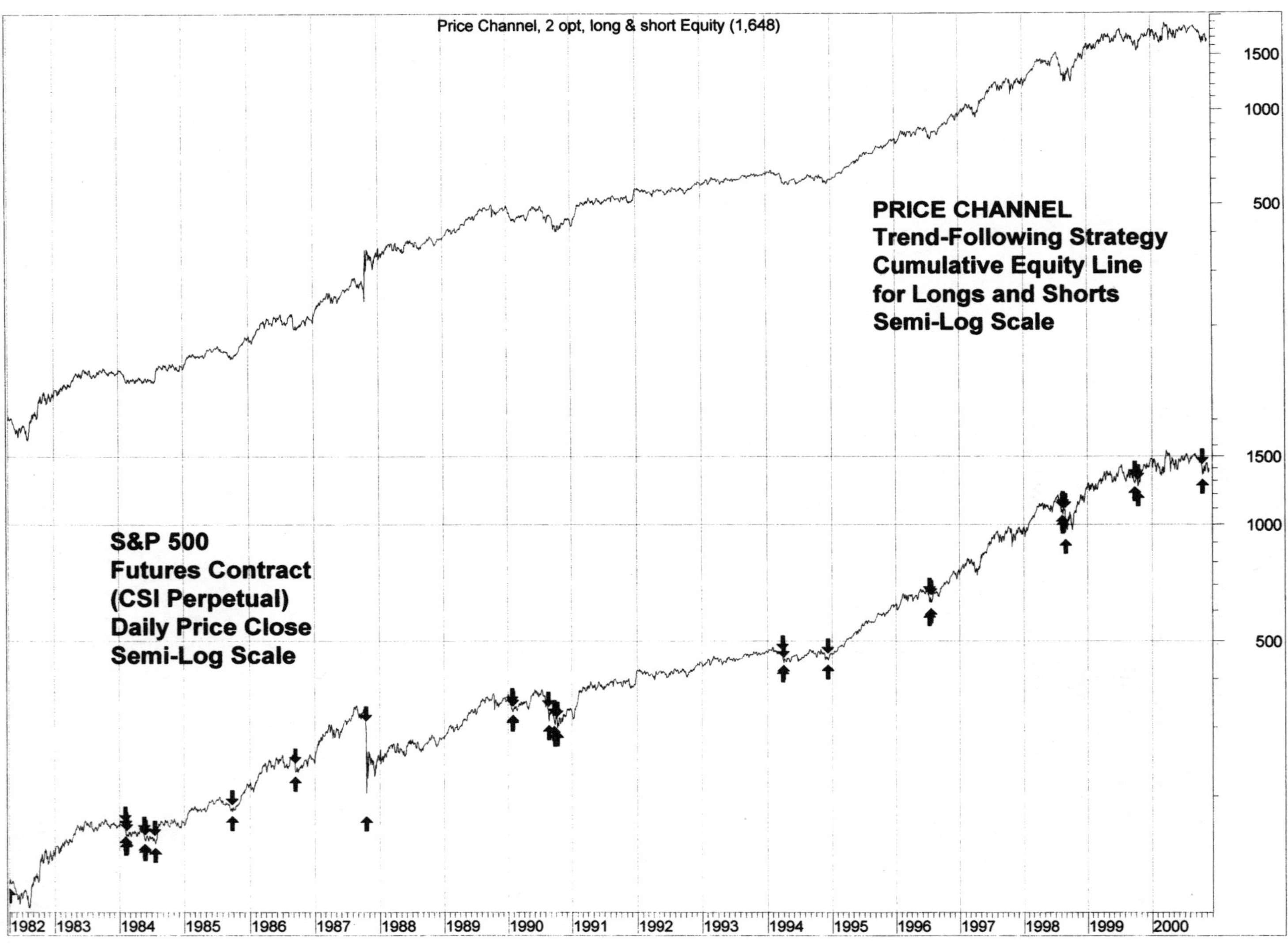

Price Channel, 2 opt, long & short Equity (1,648)
PRICE CHANNEL
Trend-Following Strategy
Cumulative Equity Line
for Longs and Shorts
Semi-Log Scale
S&P 500
Futures Contract
(CSI Perpetual)
Daily Price Close
Semi-Log Scale
1500
1000
500
1500
1000
500
1982
1983
1984
1985
1986
1987
1988
1989
1990
1991
1992
1993
1994
1995
1996
1997
1998
1999
2000

Price Channel

Total net profit	1547.87	Open position value	−18.04	Net Profit / Buy&Hold %	45.96
Percent gain/loss	1547.87	Annual percent gain/loss	83.26	Annual Net % / B&H %	45.97
Initial investment	100	Interest earned	0		
Current position	Long	Date position entered	10/13/00		
Buy/Hold profit	1060.46	Days in test	6786	# of days per trade	130.50
Buy/Hold pct gain/loss	1060.46	Annual B/H pct gain/loss	57.04		
Total closed trades	52	Commissions paid	0		
Avg profit per trade	30.11	Avg Win/Avg Loss ratio	10.42		
Total long trades	26	Total short trades	26	Long Win Trade %	38.46
Winning long trades	10	Winning short trades	8	Short Win Trade %	30.77
Total winning trades	18	Total losing trades	34	Total Win Trade %	34.62
Amount of winning trades	1912.73	Amount of losing trades	−346.82	Net Profit Margin %	69.30
Average win	106.26	Average loss	−10.2	Average P. Margin %	82.48
Largest win	561.82	Largest loss	−57.23	% Net / (Win + Loss)	81.51
Average length of win	232.89	Average length of loss	15.65	(Win − Loss) / Loss %	1388.12
Longest winning trade	876	Longest losing trade	173	(Win − Loss) / Loss %	406.36
Most consecutive wins	3	Most consecutive losses	5	(Win − Loss) / Loss %	−40.00
Total bars out	2	Average length out	2		
Longest out period	2				
System close drawdown	0	Profit/Loss index	81.7	% Net Profit / SODD	11373.03
System open drawdown	−13.61	Reward/Risk index	99.13	(Net P.-SODD)/Net P.	99.12
Max open trade drawdown	−57.23	Buy/Hold index	44.26	% SODD / Net Profit	−0.88

In the Equis MetaStock® "System Report" (profit and loss summary statistics), the *Total net profit* is the sum of profits minus the sum of losses, including open positions marked to the market. In contrast, the *Amount of Winning Trades* is the sum of realized profits (the total of all gains on closed-out trades only, excluding any open positions). Similarly, the *Amount of Losing Trades* is the sum of realized losses (the total of all losses on closed-out trades only, excluding any open positions). *System close drawdown* is the largest decline in the cumulative equity line below the initial investment, based on closed-out positions only. *System open drawdown (SODD)* is the largest decline in the cumulative equity line below the initial investment when a position is open. *Max open trade drawdown* is the largest decline in the cumulative equity line below the trade entry price during the worst single trade. The *Profit/Loss Index* is a complex calculation that relates the Amount of Winning Trades to the Amount of Losing Trades on a scale of −100 (worst possible performance) to +100 (best possible performance), with zero representing profits equal to losses. *Reward/Risk Index* is the Total net profit minus System open drawdown. The resulting difference is then divided by the Total net profit. The *Buy/Hold Index* is the Total net profit minus the buy-and-hold strategy's net profit. The resulting difference is then divided by the buy-and-hold net profit. In this exercise, initial equity is assumed to be $100. Both long and short positions are taken unless otherwise noted. Trades are executed at the closing price on the signal date. Transaction costs, interest expenses, and margins are not included in the statistics.

Price Channel Trading Range Breakout Rule, Dynamic

A dynamic variation of the basic trading range breakout system, with an adaptive length for the look-back period, has been suggested by Perry J. Kaufman (Kaufman, P. (1987). *The New Commodity Trading Systems and Methods.* New York: John Wiley & Sons. Page 213). For example, the number of days in the look-back period can be varied by multiplying the long-term historical optimal length by a ratio of long-term historical price volatility to recent price volatility. By placing recent volatility in the denominator of the fractional multiplier, as volatility rises, the multiplier declines, thus producing a smaller value for the look-back period, making the decision rule more sensitive, and speeding the response time when the market is volatile and on the move. Conversely, as volatility declines, the multiplier rises, thus producing a larger value for the look-back period, making the decision rule less sensitive, and slowing response time when the market is dull and quiet with low volatility.

Price Oscillators: Moving Average Oscillators

Moving average oscillators are most usefully set up as a percentage difference between a shorter and a longer moving average. Moving averages are widely used to smooth out raw market data. They tame at least some of the erratic short-term fluctuation that typically creates confusion.

All technical analysis computer software should be able to plot the percentage difference, ratio, or point difference between any two moving averages. Thoughtful technicians greatly prefer percentage difference or the ratio representations because these automatically adjust over time to large differences in price levels. For example, when the DJIA was at 1000, a 100-point price move was 10%, but when the DJIA was 10,000, a 100-point price swing was only 1%. While a point difference would show both movements as being of equal magnitude, a percentage difference (or ratio) more accurately portrays the comparative significance of each price movement.

For fine tuning a moving average oscillator, there are two parameters to be optimized: the time length, n, of a shorter moving average and the time length, p, of a longer one. When the percentage difference (or point difference) between the two moving averages crosses zero, a trend change, and thus a trade position change, is signaled in the direction of the crossing. (When the ratio of two moving averages crosses 1.00, that is exactly the same as the difference crossing zero.)

The number of observations (minutes, days, weeks, months) that should be included in a moving average designed to identify a trend depends on the length of the cyclical movements in the underlying raw time series data. Optimal values can determined by simple "brute force", a systematic trial-and-error procedure testing various combinations of lengths. For example, if we allow each length to range from 1 to 100 days, there would be 10,000 (100 x 100) combinations of two moving averages. That would take time to run on some computers, but we do not need to test every possible combination of averages. In actual practice, to make this task more manageable and faster, we would first approach it with broad-scan testing using large increments between tested variables. In our example, if we allow two moving averages to range between 5 to 100 days in increments of 5 days, we cut the number of combinations to 400 (20 x 20), a 96% reduction. This task can be completed in minutes. After that broad first pass, we can decrease both the increment and the range, focusing in on the most promising parameters for fine tuning.

The popularly followed relationship between the closing price and any moving average can also be displayed as an oscillator. The calculations are even simpler than a two moving average oscillator, since a moving average with a period length of one is simply the closing price itself.

For example, using the popular 40-week (200-day) moving average, subtract the 40-week moving average of Friday's closing prices from the latest Friday's closing price. Then, divide that difference by the 40-week moving average, and multiply by 100 to convert from decimals to percentages. When the resulting oscillator crosses above zero, the closing price moves above its own 40-week moving average, and that is interpreted as a buy signal. Conversely, when the closing price moves below its own 40-week moving average, the oscillator crosses below zero, and that is taken as a signal to close out long positions by selling.

There are three advantages to viewing moving average crossovers as percentage difference oscillators moving above and below zero:

1. We can often see crossings more clearly.
2. We can better anticipate crossings.
3. We can subjectively interpret momentum divergences from an oscillator chart. Such divergences may not be detected on a price with moving average chart without the oscillator.

Indicator Strategy Example for the Price Oscillator, Percentage Difference of Two Moving Averages

A Price Oscillator can be interpreted many ways, but the simplest way is pure trend following. Based on a 101-year file of weekly data for the DJIA from 1/2/1900 to 12/29/00, we found that the following parameters would have produced a positive result on a purely mechanical signal basis with no subjectivity, no sophisticated technical analysis, and no judgement:

> **Enter Long (Buy)** when the 1/40 oscillator turns positive; that is, buy at the current weekly price close of the DJIA when that closing price divided

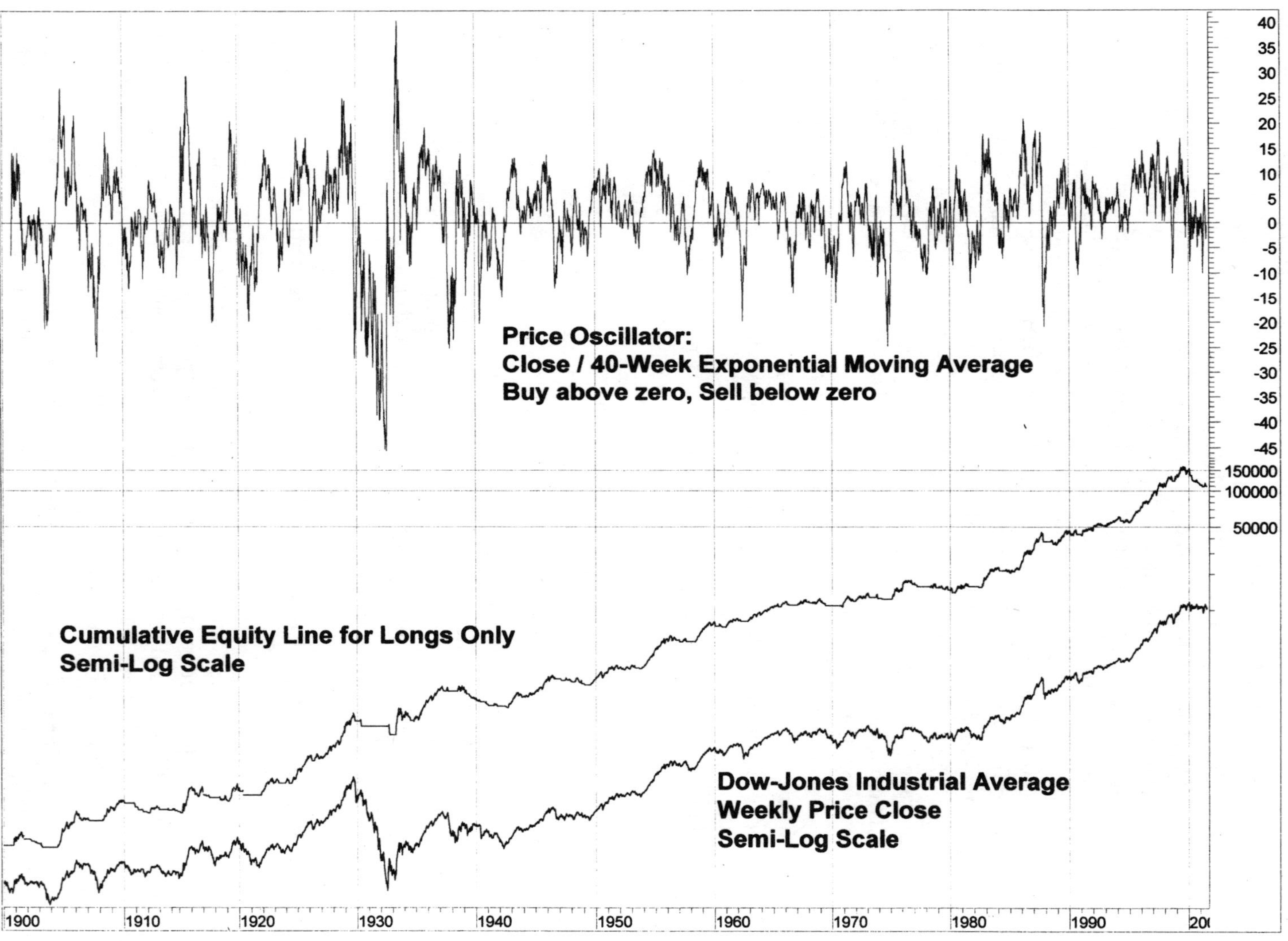

Price Oscillator:
Close / 40-Week Exponential Moving Average
Buy above zero, Sell below zero
Cumulative Equity Line for Longs Only
Semi-Log Scale
Dow-Jones Industrial Average
Weekly Price Close
Semi-Log Scale
40
35
30
25
20
15
10
5
0
-5
-10
-15
-20
-25
-30
-35
-40
-45
150000
100000
50000
1900
1910
1920
1930
1940
1950
1960
1970
1980
1990

Price Oscillator, Close/40-Week Exponential Moving Average

Total net profit	97517.16	Open position value	0	Net Profit / Buy&Hold %	331.86
Percent gain/loss	97517.16	Annual percent gain/loss	965.23	Annual Net % / B&H %	331.87
Initial investment	100	Interest earned	0		
Current position	Long	Date position entered	12/29/00		
Buy/Hold profit	22580.61	Days in test	36876	# of days per trade	208.34
Buy/Hold pct gain/loss	22580.61	Annual B/H pct gain/loss	223.5		
Total closed trades	177	Commissions paid	0		
Avg profit per trade	550.94	Avg Win/Avg Loss ratio	7.18		
Total long trades	177	Total short trades	0	Long Win Trade %	29.94
Winning long trades	53	Winning short trades	0	Short Win Trade %	#DIV/0!
Total winning trades	53	Total losing trades	124	Total Win Trade %	29.94
Amount of winning trades	144654.22	Amount of losing trades	−47137.06	Net Profit Margin %	50.85
Average win	2729.32	Average loss	−380.14	Average P. Margin %	75.55
Largest win	57516.2	Largest loss	−8538.57	% Net / (Win + Loss)	74.15
Average length of win	54.04	Average length of loss	5.52	(Win − Loss) / Loss %	878.99
Longest winning trade	192	Longest losing trade	21	(Win − Loss) / Loss %	814.29
Most consecutive wins	4	Most consecutive losses	15	(Win − Loss) / Loss %	−73.33
Total bars out	2054	Average length out	11.54		
Longest out period	122				
System close drawdown	−3.27	Profit/Loss index	67.41	% Net Profit / SODD	2982176.15
System open drawdown	−3.27	Reward/Risk index	100	(Net P.-SODD)/Net P.	100.00
Max open trade drawdown	−8538.57	Buy/Hold index	331.86	% SODD / Net Profit	0.00

In the Equis MetaStock® "System Report" (profit and loss summary statistics), the *Total net profit* is the sum of profits minus the sum of losses, including open positions marked to the market. In contrast, the *Amount of Winning Trades* is the sum of realized profits (the total of all gains on closed-out trades only, excluding any open positions). Similarly, the *Amount of Losing Trades* is the sum of realized losses (the total of all losses on closed-out trades only, excluding any open positions). *System close drawdown* is the largest decline in the cumulative equity line below the initial investment, based on closed-out positions only. *System open drawdown (SODD)* is the largest decline in the cumulative equity line below the initial investment when a position is open. *Max open trade drawdown* is the largest decline in the cumulative equity line below the trade entry price during the worst single trade. The *Profit/Loss Index* is a complex calculation that relates the Amount of Winning Trades to the Amount of Losing Trades on a scale of −100 (worst possible performance) to +100 (best possible performance), with zero representing profits equal to losses. *Reward/Risk Index* is the Total net profit minus System open drawdown. The resulting difference is then divided by the Total net profit. The *Buy/Hold Index* is the Total net profit minus the buy-and-hold strategy's net profit. The resulting difference is then divided by the buy-and-hold net profit. In this exercise, initial equity is assumed to be $100. Both long and short positions are taken unless otherwise noted. Trades are executed at the closing price on the signal date. Transaction costs, interest expenses, and margins are not included in the statistics.

by its own trailing 40-week EMA crosses above one, which also means that the percentage price oscillator crosses above zero.

Close Long (Sell) when the 1/40 oscillator turns negative; that is, sell at the current weekly price close of the DJIA when that closing price divided by its own trailing 40-week EMA crosses below one, which also means that the percentage price oscillator crosses below zero.

Enter Short (Sell Short) never.

Starting with $100 and reinvesting profits, total net profits for this trend-following strategy would have been $97,517.16, assuming a fully invested strategy, reinvestment of profits, no transactions costs and no taxes. This would have been 331.86 percent greater than buy-and-hold. Short selling would have been not profitable, and short selling was not included in the strategy. This Price Oscillator long-only strategy would have given profitable buy signals only 29.94% of the time. Note that this trend-following strategy, though wrong on most of its trades, would have enjoyed much bigger average gains than average losses. There would have been some equity drawdowns, but they appear to have been controlled. Trading would have been relatively inactive at one trade every 208.34 calendar days, on average.

The Equis International MetaStock® System Testing rules are written as follows:

Enter long: ((Mov(C,opt1,E)/Mov(C,opt2,E))-1)*100>0

Close long: ((Mov(C,opt1,E)/Mov(C,opt2,E))-1)*100<0

OPT1 Current value: 1
OPT2 Current value: 40

The Equis International MetaStock® Indicator Builder formula is written:

```
periods:=Input("Enter the shorter EMA periods: ",1,100,1);
multiplier:=Input("Enter the number of signal line periods: ",1,100,40);
((Mov(C,periods,E)/Mov(C,multiplier*periods,E))-1)*100;
Input("Plot a horizontal line at ",-100,100,0);
{Price Oscillator ((Mov(C,periods,E)/Mov(C,multiplier*periods,E))-1)*100}
```

Price Trend Channels, Sloping Upward or Downward

Price channels are among the oldest and most popular tools for swing trading. In an uptrend, draw a straight trendline sloping upward through the most recent obvious pivot-point lows for a lower channel line and support line where we look to buy. Next, draw a parallel straight line through the an intervening price high point for an upper channel line, resistance line, and upside price swing target where we look to sell, to take profits on the long side.

In a downtrend, draw a straight trendline sloping downward through the most recent obvious pivot-point highs for an upper channel line and resistance line where we look to sell short. Next, draw a parallel straight line through the an intervening price low point for a lower channel line, support line, and downside price swing target where we look to buy to cover short, to take profits on the short side.

Price often finds resistance and support at these parallel channel lines. In the case of a shortfall of a channel line, the prevailing trend may be losing momentum, losing power. In the case of overshoot of a channel line, the trend may be accelerating or growing more volatile.

Channels also can be projected mathematically, without the use of traditional charting methods, through the use of bands around moving averages or regression lines. Such bands are the basic line plus and minus fixed percentages or adaptive quantities based on trailing standard deviations or multiples of Average True Range. (See Bollinger Bands and Envelopes.)

Program Trading Volume

Program trading buying and selling volume reflects certain professional trading strategies, including stock index futures arbitrage against a basket of underlying stocks. Basically, when futures become cheap compared to the underlying stocks, buy futures and simultaneously sell stocks. When futures become expensive compared to the underlying stocks, buy stocks and simultaneously sell futures. Traders use sometimes complex variations of the Black-Scholes Options Pricing Model to determine what is expensive and cheap.

Ned Davis Research found that when the ratio of smoothed buy program trading volume divided by total program trading volume rises above 104.2, it is bullish for stocks. Conversely, when the ratio falls below 97, it is bearish. This strategy outperformed the market over the period shown on the chart.

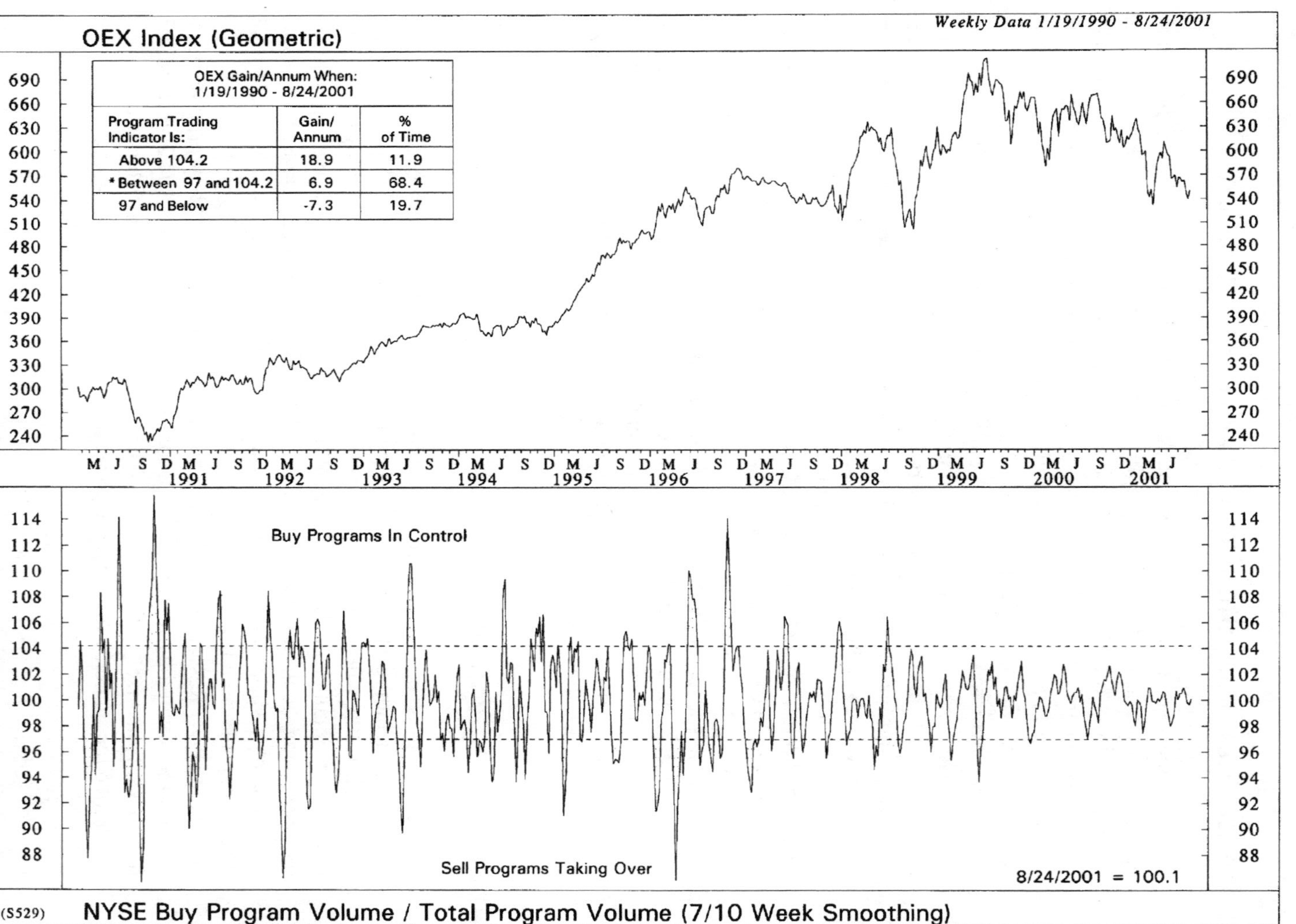

Chart by permission of Ned Davis Research.

Projection Bands

Projection Bands were originally introduced by Mel Widner in the July 1995 issue of *Technical Analysis of Stocks & Commodities* magazine (www.traders.com). These bands are conceptually similar to several better-known tools used to help identify trading range boundaries, such Price Channels, Envelopes, and Bollinger Bands.

Projection Bands are derived by first finding a linear regression line fitted through the closes over the past *n*-period look-back window. Then, two lines are drawn parallel to this linear regression line: one plotted though the lows and another plotted through the highs of the *n*-period look-back window. The relevant window moves forward every day such that the price is always contained within these minimum and maximum price boundaries.

The interpretation is simple: when price is at the upper band, it could be considered to be on resistance and overbought; when price is at the lower band, it could be considered to be oversold and on support.

Projection Bands are designed to help a trader buy low and sell high. They work best in a sideways, trading range market. During strongly trending markets, however, overbought/oversold indicators can go very wrong, as the trend overwhelms all resistance and support and price continues in the trend direction much farther than most traders expect.

Indicator Strategy Example for Projection Bands

Projection Bands require experience and judgement to use as Mel Widner intended. Even naïve testing assumptions suggest that Projection Bands may have some objective potential value as a purely mechanical, contra-trend technical indicator. The majority of oversold buy signals would have been profitable. Moreover, these buy signals would have been robust, with all lookback period lengths from 1 to 50 days profitable and right most of the time, for long trades only. Short lengths under 11-days would have been only slightly profitable.

As attractive as a high percentage of profitable trades may seem, however, it is important to note that this and other contra-trend overbought/oversold strategies failed to provide any protection in the Crash of '87. As the chart shows, there can be sharp equity drawdowns. Using Projection Bands for contra-trend oversold and overbought signals would have been a profitable strategy for long trades only. Short selling would not have been profitable in the past.

Based on a 18-year file of daily data for the entire history of the S&P 500 Composite Stock Price Index Futures from 4/21/82 to 12/22/00 (using *CSI Perpetual Contract* data collected from www.csidata.com), we found that the following parameters would have produced a positive result on a purely mechanical overbought/oversold signal basis with no subjectivity, no sophisticated technical analysis, and no judgement:

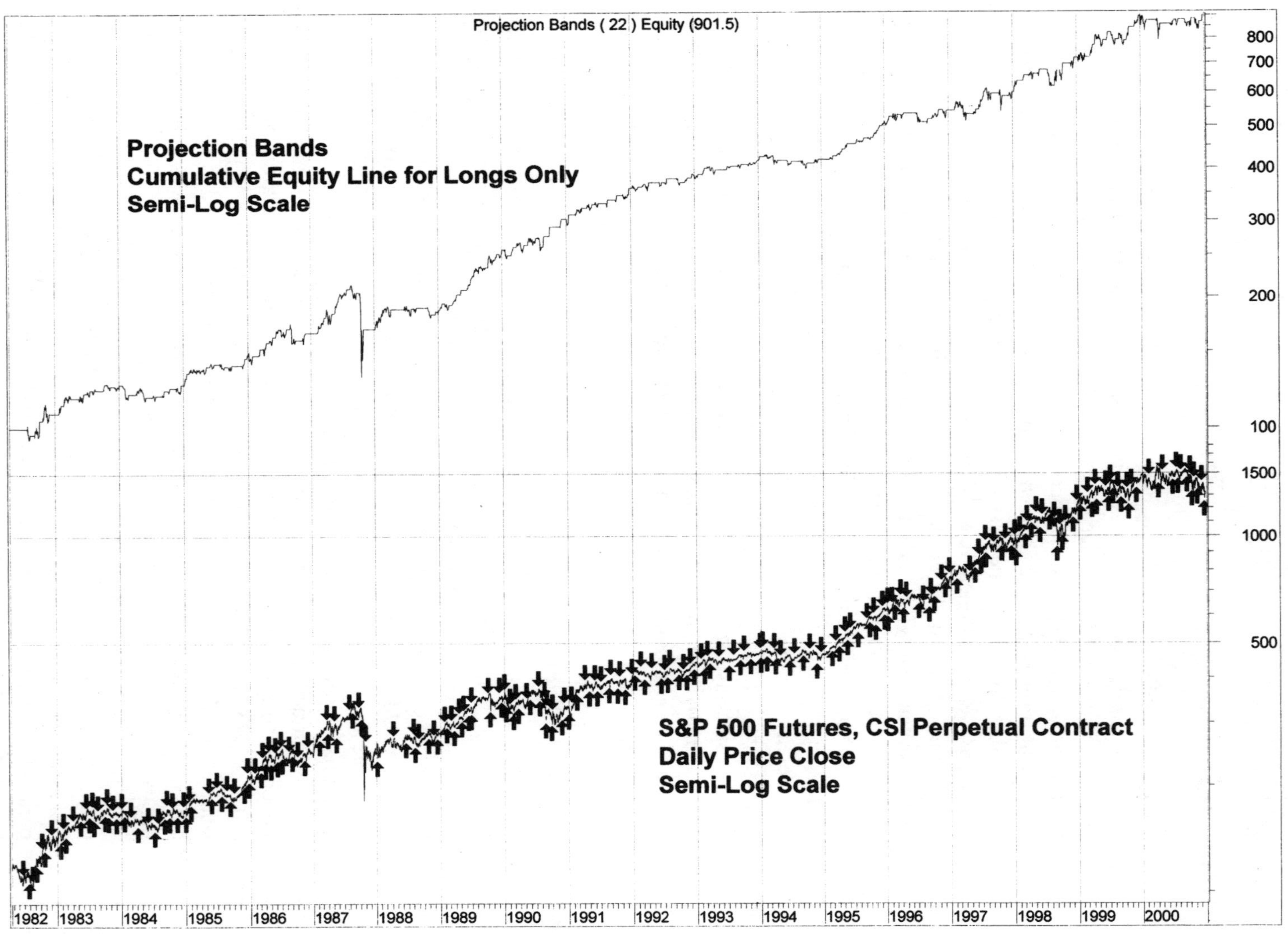
Projection Bands (22) Equity (901.5)
Projection Bands
Cumulative Equity Line for Longs Only
Semi-Log Scale
S&P 500 Futures, CSI Perpetual Contract
Daily Price Close
Semi-Log Scale
800
700
600
500
400
300
200
100
1500
1000
500
1982
1983
1984
1985
1986
1987
1988
1989
1990
1991
1992
1993
1994
1995
1996
1997
1998
1999
2000

Projection Bands

Total net profit	801.5	Open position value	32	Net Profit / Buy&Hold %	−21.99
Percent gain/loss	801.5	Annual percent gain/loss	42.89	Annual Net % / B&H %	−21.99
Initial investment	100	Interest earned	0		
Current position	Long	Date position entered	12/20/00	# of days per trade	35.90
Buy/Hold profit	1027.4	Days in test	6821		
Buy/Hold pct gain/loss	1027.4	Annual B/H pct gain/loss	54.98		
Total closed trades	123	Commissions paid	0		
Avg profit per trade	6.26	Avg Win/Avg Loss ratio	1.04		
Total long trades	123	Total short trades	0	Long Win Trade %	77.24
Winning long trades	95	Winning short trades	0	Short Win Trade %	#DIV/0!
Total winning trades	95	Total losing trades	28	Total Win Trade %	77.24
Amount of winning trades	1075.74	Amount of losing trades	−306.23	Net Profit Margin %	55.68
Average win	11.32	Average loss	−10.94	Average P. Margin %	1.71
Largest win	58.21	Largest loss	−55.7	% Net / (Win + Loss)	2.20
Average length of win	19.26	Average length of loss	20.64	(Win − Loss) / Loss %	−6.69
Longest winning trade	69	Longest losing trade	50	(Win − Loss) / Loss %	38.00
Most consecutive wins	12	Most consecutive losses	3	(Win − Loss) / Loss %	300.00
Total bars out	2559	Average length out	20.64		
Longest out period	69				
System close drawdown	−3.09	Profit/Loss index	72.36	% Net Profit / SODD	14135.80
System open drawdown	−5.67	Reward/Risk index	99.3	(Net P.-SODD)/Net P.	99.29
Max open trade drawdown	−87.71	Buy/Hold index	−18.87	% SODD / Net Profit	−0.71

In the Equis MetaStock® "System Report" (profit and loss summary statistics), the *Total net profit* is the sum of profits minus the sum of losses, including open positions marked to the market. In contrast, the *Amount of Winning Trades* is the sum of realized profits (the total of all gains on closed-out trades only, excluding any open positions). Similarly, the *Amount of Losing Trades* is the sum of realized losses (the total of all losses on closed-out trades only, excluding any open positions). *System close drawdown* is the largest decline in the cumulative equity line below the initial investment, based on closed-out positions only. *System open drawdown (SODD)* is the largest decline in the cumulative equity line below the initial investment when a position is open. *Max open trade drawdown* is the largest decline in the cumulative equity line below the trade entry price during the worst single trade. The *Profit/Loss Index* is a complex calculation that relates the Amount of Winning Trades to the Amount of Losing Trades on a scale of −100 (worst possible performance) to +100 (best possible performance), with zero representing profits equal to losses. *Reward/Risk Index* is the Total net profit minus System open drawdown. The resulting difference is then divided by the Total net profit. The *Buy/Hold Index* is the Total net profit minus the buy-and-hold strategy's net profit. The resulting difference is then divided by the buy-and-hold net profit. In this exercise, initial equity is assumed to be $100. Both long and short positions are taken unless otherwise noted. Trades are executed at the closing price on the signal date. Transaction costs, interest expenses, and margins are not included in the statistics.

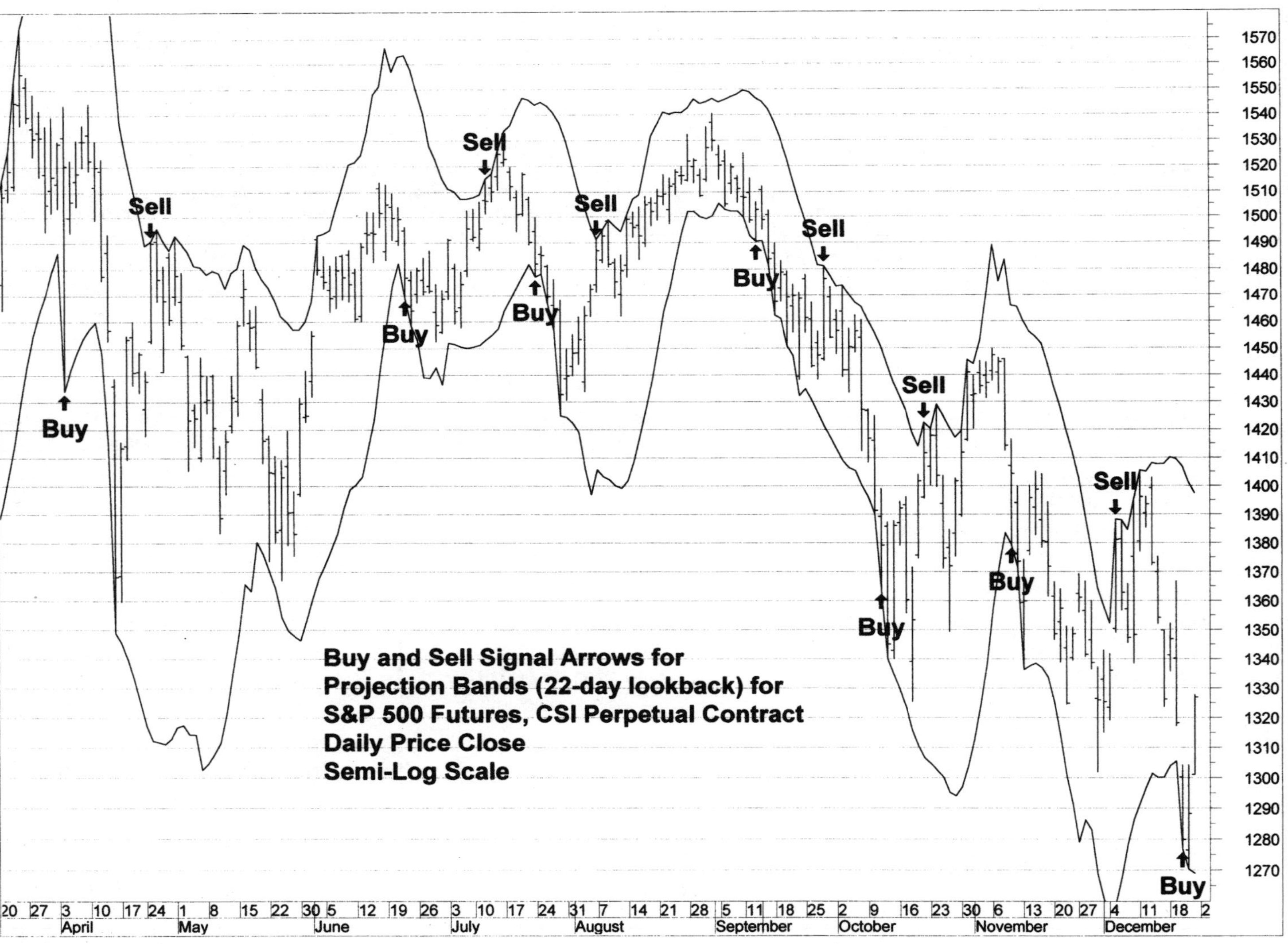
Buy and Sell Signal Arrows for
Projection Bands (22-day lookback) for
S&P 500 Futures, CSI Perpetual Contract
Daily Price Close
Semi-Log Scale
Buy
Sell
Buy
Buy
Sell
Buy
Sell
Buy
Sell
Sell
Buy
Buy
Sell
Buy
1570
1560
1550
1540
1530
1520
1510
1500
1490
1480
1470
1460
1450
1440
1430
1420
1410
1400
1390
1380
1370
1360
1350
1340
1330
1320
1310
1300
1290
1280
1270
20 27 3 10 17 24 1 8 15 22 30 5 12 19 26 3 10 17 24 31 7 14 21 28 5 11 18 25 2 9 16 23 30 6 13 20 27 4 11 18 2
April
May
June
July
August
September
October
November
December

Enter Long (Buy) at the current daily price close of the S&P 500 Composite Stock Price Index futures *CSI Perpetual Contract* when the daily low is equal to the 22 day look-back period Projection Band Bottom (Low).

Close Long (Sell) at the current daily price close of the S&P 500 Composite Stock Price Index futures *CSI Perpetual Contract* when the daily high is equal to the 22 day look-back period Projection Band Top (High).

Enter Short (Sell Short) never.

Starting with $100 and reinvesting profits, total net profits for this Projection Bands counter-trend strategy would have been $801.50, assuming a fully invested strategy, reinvestment of profits, no transactions costs and no taxes. This would have been 21.99 percent less than buy-and-hold. No short selling would have been profitable, and no short selling was included in the strategy. Short selling would have cut the profit further. The long-only Projection Bands as an indicator would have given profitable buy signals 77.24% of the time. Trading would have been only moderately active at one trade every 35.90 calendar days. Note that this strategy executes trades at closing prices only.

The Equis International MetaStock® System Testing rules are written:

Enter long: LOW=ProjBandBot(opt1)

Close long: HIGH=ProjBandTop(opt1)

Enter short: HIGH=ProjBandTop(opt1)

Close short: LOW=ProjBandBot(opt1)

OPT1 Current value: 22

Projection Oscillator

The Projection Oscillator was originally introduced by Mel Widner in the July 1995 issue of *Technical Analysis of Stocks & Commodities* magazine (www.traders.com). It is based on Projection Bands. It gives the location of the current close within the top and bottom bands, stated as a percentage of the current high-band minus low-band range. That percentage is smoothed with a 3-day EMA. The Projection Oscillator is conceptually somewhat similar to the better-known Stochastic, and it is interpreted in a similar manner.

The simplest way to use the Projection Oscillator is for overbought/oversold signals: buy when the oscillator falls below 30; sell when the oscillator rises above 70. The general idea is that high levels indicate excessive, unsustainable optimism, while low levels indicate excessive unsustainable pessimism. That works fine in a market confined to a sideways trading range, but it works very poorly when the market is in a powerful directional trend.

Like other oscillators, the Projection Oscillator may be used for Divergence Analysis. Here we consider selling when prices are making higher highs while the oscillator fails to surpass its own previous highs. We consider buying when prices are making lower lows while the oscillator fails to break its own previous lows. Keep in mind that Divergence Analysis is subjective and requires experienced good judgement to apply correctly. Since it may tempt the user to trade against the prevailing trend, it can be dangerous in the hands of a novice.

Indicator Strategy Example for Projection Oscillator

The Projection Oscillator requires experience and judgement to use as Mel Widner intended. Even naïve testing assumptions suggest that the Projection Oscillator may have some objective potential value as a purely mechanical, contra-trend technical indicator. The majority of oversold buy signals would have been profitable. Moreover, these buy signals would have been robust, with all lookback period lengths from 1 to 50 days profitable and right most of the time, for long trades only.

As attractive as a high percentage of profitable trades may seem, however, it is important to note that this and other contra-trend overbought/oversold strategies failed to provide any protection in the Crash of '87. As the chart shows, there can be sharp equity drawdowns. Using the Projection Oscillator for contra-trend oversold and overbought signals would have been a profitable strategy for long trades only. Short selling would not have been profitable in the past.

Based on a 18-year file of daily data for the entire history of the S&P 500 Composite Stock Price Index Futures from 4/21/82 to 12/22/00 (*CSI Perpetual Contract* data collected from www.csidata.com), we found that the following parameters would have produced a positive result on a purely mechanical overbought/oversold signal basis with no subjectivity, no sophisticated technical analysis, and no judgement:

> **Enter Long (Buy)** at the current daily price close of the S&P 500 Composite Stock Price Index futures *CSI Perpetual Contract* when the Projection Oscillator (the 3-day EMA of the 14-day look-back-period price close location within the Top minus Bottom Projection Bands) is less than 30.
>
> **Close Long (Sell)** at the current daily price close of the S&P 500 Composite Stock Price Index futures *CSI Perpetual Contract* when the Projection Oscillator (the 3-day EMA of the 14-day look-back-period price close location within the Top minus Bottom Projection Bands) is greater than 70.
>
> **Enter Short (Sell Short)** never.

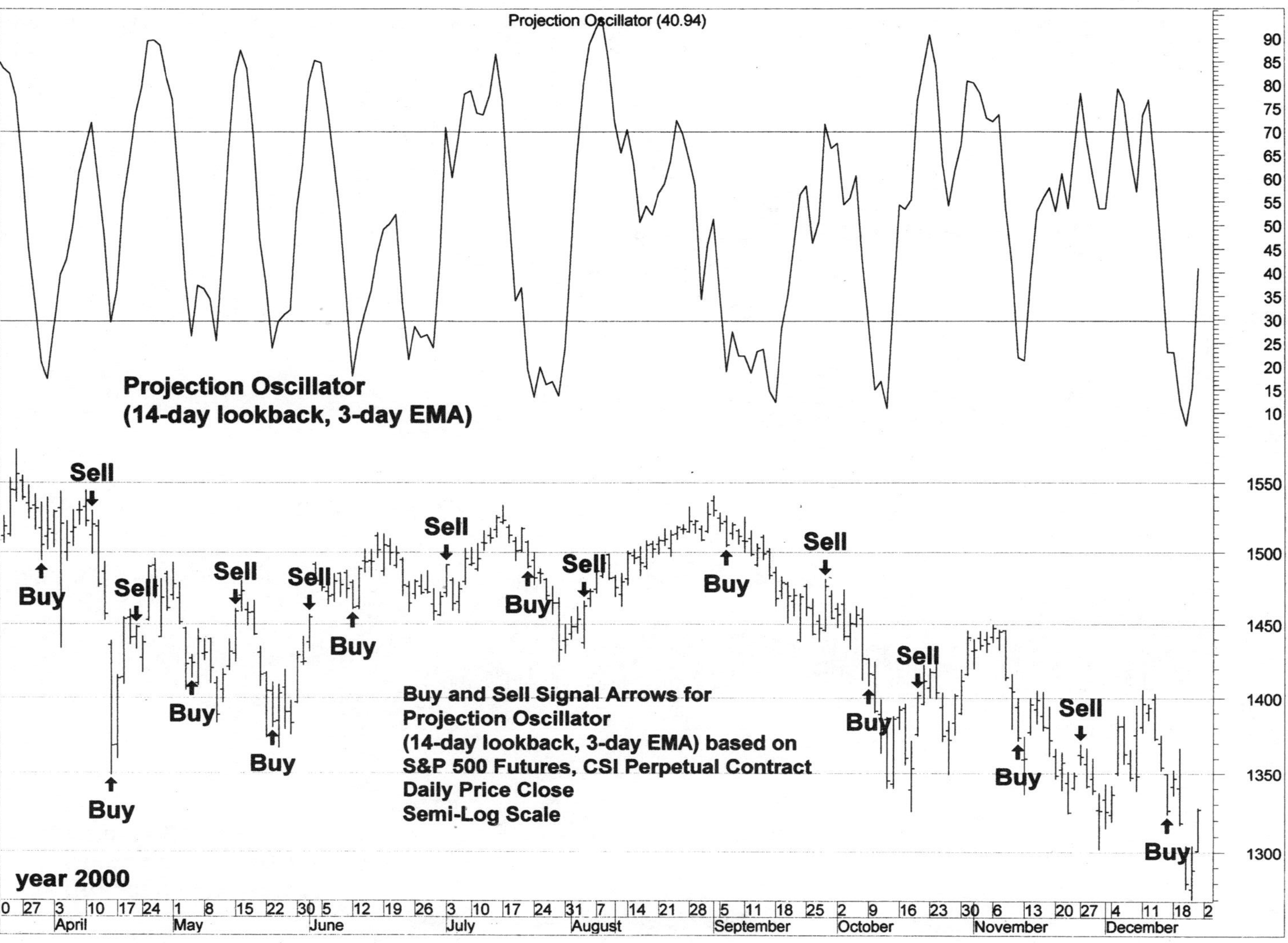
Projection Oscillator (40.94)
Projection Oscillator
(14-day lookback, 3-day EMA)
Buy and Sell Signal Arrows for
Projection Oscillator
(14-day lookback, 3-day EMA) based on
S&P 500 Futures, CSI Perpetual Contract
Daily Price Close
Semi-Log Scale
year 2000
Buy
Sell
April
May
June
July
August
September
October
November
December

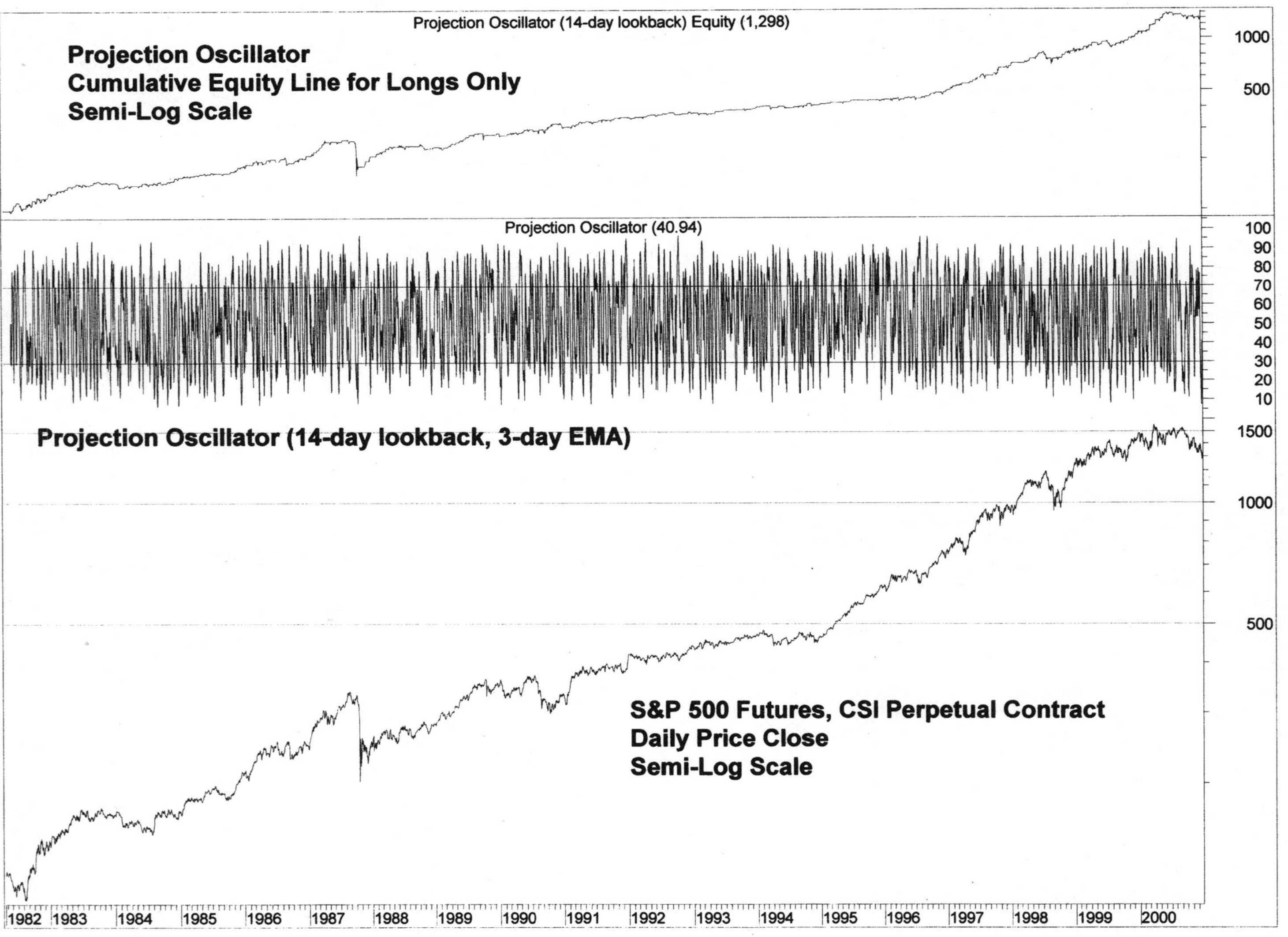

Projection Oscillator (14-day lookback) Equity (1,298)
Projection Oscillator
Cumulative Equity Line for Longs Only
Semi-Log Scale
1000
500
Projection Oscillator (40.94)
100
90
80
70
60
50
40
30
20
10
Projection Oscillator (14-day lookback, 3-day EMA)
1500
1000
500
S&P 500 Futures, CSI Perpetual Contract
Daily Price Close
Semi-Log Scale
1982
1983
1984
1985
1986
1987
1988
1989
1990
1991
1992
1993
1994
1995
1996
1997
1998
1999
2000

Projection Oscillator

Total net profit	1197.67	Open position value	0.68	Net Profit / Buy&Hold %	16.57
Percent gain/loss	1197.67	Annual percent gain/loss	64.09	Annual Net % / B&H %	16.57
Initial investment	100	Interest earned	0		
Current position	Long	Date position entered	12/15/00		
Buy/Hold profit	1027.4	Days in test	6821	# of days per trade	31.87
Buy/Hold pct gain/loss	1027.4	Annual B/H pct gain/loss	54.98		
Total closed trades	214	Commissions paid	0		
Avg profit per trade	5.59	Avg Win/Avg Loss ratio	1.14		
Total long trades	214	Total short trades	0	Long Win Trade %	76.64
Winning long trades	164	Winning short trades	0	Short Win Trade %	#DIV/0!
Total winning trades	164	Total losing trades	50	Total Win Trade %	76.64
Amount of winning trades	1636.41	Amount of losing trades	−439.42	Net Profit Margin %	57.66
Average win	9.98	Average loss	−8.79	Average P. Margin %	6.34
Largest win	78.59	Largest loss	−74.51	% Net / (Win + Loss)	2.66
Average length of win	9.47	Average length of loss	13.24	(Win − Loss) / Loss %	−28.47
Longest winning trade	33	Longest losing trade	27	(Win − Loss) / Loss %	22.22
Most consecutive wins	14	Most consecutive losses	4	(Win − Loss) / Loss %	250.00
Total bars out	2931	Average length out	13.63		
Longest out period	56				
System close drawdown	0	Profit/Loss index	73.16	% Net Profit / SODD	52994.25
System open drawdown	−2.26	Reward/Risk index	99.81	(Net P.-SODD)/Net P.	99.81
Max open trade drawdown	−96.33	Buy/Hold index	16.64	% SODD / Net Profit	−0.19

In the Equis MetaStock® "System Report" (profit and loss summary statistics), the *Total net profit* is the sum of profits minus the sum of losses, including open positions marked to the market. In contrast, the *Amount of Winning Trades* is the sum of realized profits (the total of all gains on closed-out trades only, excluding any open positions). Similarly, the *Amount of Losing Trades* is the sum of realized losses (the total of all losses on closed-out trades only, excluding any open positions). *System close drawdown* is the largest decline in the cumulative equity line below the initial investment, based on closed-out positions only. *System open drawdown (SODD)* is the largest decline in the cumulative equity line below the initial investment when a position is open. *Max open trade drawdown* is the largest decline in the cumulative equity line below the trade entry price during the worst single trade. The *Profit/Loss Index* is a complex calculation that relates the Amount of Winning Trades to the Amount of Losing Trades on a scale of −100 (worst possible performance) to +100 (best possible performance), with zero representing profits equal to losses. *Reward/Risk Index* is the Total net profit minus System open drawdown. The resulting difference is then divided by the Total net profit. The *Buy/Hold Index* is the Total net profit minus the buy-and-hold strategy's net profit. The resulting difference is then divided by the buy-and-hold net profit. In this exercise, initial equity is assumed to be $100. Both long and short positions are taken unless otherwise noted. Trades are executed at the closing price on the signal date. Transaction costs, interest expenses, and margins are not included in the statistics.

Starting with $100 and reinvesting profits, total net profits for this Projection Oscillator counter-trend strategy would have been $1197.67, assuming a fully invested strategy, reinvestment of profits, no transactions costs and no taxes. This would have been 16.57 percent greater than buy-and-hold. No short selling would have been profitable, and no short selling was included in the strategy. Short selling would have cut the profit to less than buy-and-hold. The long-only Projection Oscillator as an indicator would have given profitable buy signals 76.64% of the time. Trading would have been only moderately active at one trade every 31.87 calendar days. Note that this strategy executes trades at closing prices only.

The Equis International MetaStock® System Testing rules are written:

Enter long: ProjOsc(opt1,3)<30

Close long: ProjOsc(opt1,3)>70

OPT1 Current value: 14

Proprietary Indicators

Proprietary indicators are offered without documentation. The algorithm or formula need to calculate the result is not divulged. The quite understandable business reason for such non-disclosure is to preserve the uniqueness of the analysis, to prevent widespread imitation, and to maintain trade secrets.

Unfortunately for the user, such secrecy also prevents understanding and developing confidence in the indicator output. If a trader cannot understand exactly what a proprietary indicator is saying and why, then he is likely to abandon all discipline based on such a proprietary indicator after a few losing signals. Although strings of losing signals are common to most indicators, good indicators overcome this problem if the trader sticks with the discipline of following every signal.

Also, if the underlying assumptions on which a proprietary indicator relies should be changed by some powerful external development, the user would not be equipped to notice before substantial losses are incurred.

Furthermore, relying on a proprietary indicator does not contribute to intellectual development, enhanced trading skills or growth of wisdom of its user.

For these reasons, most thoughtful technicians avoid all proprietary indicators. There are, after all, many interesting and useful concepts to explore that are fully available for thorough analysis. And, no matter if an indicator is accepted or rejected, a thorough study of an indicator's construction and past performance can offer beneficial insights into the nature of market movements, making the student a better technical analyst.

Psychological Line, PI Opinion Oscillator, PI

The PI was designed by Japanese technical analysts as a simple way to identify overbought and oversold extremes in speculative markets. According to Ken Muranaka (writing in *Futures,* June, 2000, Volume 29, Number 6, page 48–50), PI is simply the number of days over the past 12 trading days that the price of a security went up. PI is computed by the following formula:

$$PI = (n / 12) * 100$$

where n is the number of days that the market price closed higher than the previous day, over a moving window of the past 12 consecutive trading days. (The 12-day look-back period could be varied to suit the particular characteristics of the market of interest.)

PI must always range between zero and one hundred. PI is zero when every day of the past twelve was a declining day. PI is 100 when every day of the past twelve was a advancing day. When PI is 75 or higher, meaning that price advanced nine or more times over the past 12 days, the market is overbought. When PI is 25 of lower, meaning that price advanced only three or fewer times over the past 12 days, the market is oversold. PI is generally used in conjunction with other technical tools.

Although you do not need a computer to compute PI, Ken Muranaka points out that PI is easy to compute with a spreadsheet, using the IF function to assign a value of one when today's closing price is higher than the close yesterday or zero when today's close is lower.

Public Short Ratio

Public short sales are whatever is left of total short sales after deducting member short selling. Thus, the Public Short Ratio is computed by subtracting total member short sales from total short sales, then dividing that difference by total short sales.

According to *Contrary Opinion* thinking, the public is *not* the smart money when it comes to stock trading, or anything else for that matter. So, when relatively unseasoned amateur traders are shorting, we want to be buying. When they are not shorting, we should be.

In other words, when the Public Short Ratio is high, the amateur traders are shorting heavily relative to the savvy members, and that has long been considered a bullish indicator for the future trend of stock prices.

Similarly, a low Public Short Ratio is bearish. The amateur traders are optimistic relative to the smart-money members. Thus, this indicator is interpreted in a manner similar to an inverted Overbought/Oversold Oscillator.

Short Selling is an aggressive trading strategy designed to take advantage of declining prices. Speculators may sell short a stock when they anticipate a price decline.

If the stock does drop, they may realize a profit equal to the difference between their sell-short price and the lower buy-back price. If they are wrong and the stock rises, their loss will equal the amount of the stock price appreciation, the difference between their sell-short price and the higher buy-back price.

Late each Friday, after the close, the NYSE releases summary statistics on the total volume of short sales, also separating short sales by stock exchange members from nonmembers (the public). Because the absolute levels of short selling have increased in all categories along with the general expansion in the total volume of trading activity, the data must be normalized somehow, hence, the various short sales ratios.

Indicator Strategy Example for Public Short Ratio

Based on a 55-year file of Public Short Ratios and weekly closing price data for the DJIA from January 1946 to December 2000, we found that the following parameters would have produced a positive result on a purely mechanical overbought/oversold signal basis with no subjectivity, no sophisticated technical analysis, and no judgement:

Enter Long (Buy) at the current weekly price close of the DJIA when the latest Public Short Ratio is more than 45.7% above its previous week's 50-week EMA of the Public Short Ratio.

Close Long (Sell) at the current weekly price close of the DJIA when the latest Public Short Ratio is more than 45.7% below its previous week's 50-week EMA of the Public Short Ratio.

Enter Short (Sell Short) at the current weekly price close of the DJIA when the latest Public Short Ratio is more than 45.7% below its previous week's 50-week EMA of the Public Short Ratio.

Close Short (Cover) at the current weekly price close of the DJIA when the latest Public Short Ratio is more than 45.7% above its previous week's 50-week EMA of the Public Short Ratio.

Starting with $100 and reinvesting profits, total net profits for this Public Short Ratio Envelope strategy would have been $11,646.27, assuming a fully invested strategy, reinvestment of profits, no transactions costs and no taxes. This would have been 123.20 percent greater than buy-and-hold. Short selling would have been moderately profitable and was included in the strategy. The Long-and-Short Public Short Ratio as an indicator would have given profitable buy signals 77.78% of the time. Trading would have been inactive at one trade every 557.50 calendar days. Note that this strategy considers week-end closing prices only while ignoring everything in between.

Curiously, this strategy has not given a signal since 6/6/86. It is quite apparent on a close examination of the chart that the raw data seems to have become less volatile since 1986. Since it is possible that the character of the underlying data may have changed, caution is warranted in attempting to apply this Public Short Ratio Envelope strategy to actual trading.

The Equis International MetaStock® System Testing rules for Public Short Ratio, where the ratio of Public Short Sales to Total Short Sales is inserted into the field normally reserved for volume, are written as follows:

Enter long: V> (Ref(Mov(V,opt1,E),−1)+
((opt2/1000))*Ref(Mov(V,opt1,E),-1))

Close long: V< (Ref(Mov(V,opt1,E),−1)−
((opt2/1000))*Ref(Mov(V,opt1,E),-1))

Enter short: V< (Ref(Mov(V,opt1,E),−1)−
((opt2/1000))*Ref(Mov(V,opt1,E),-1))

Close short: V> (Ref(Mov(V,opt1,E),−1)+
((opt2/1000))*Ref(Mov(V,opt1,E),−1))

OPT1 Current value: 50

OPT2 Current value: 457

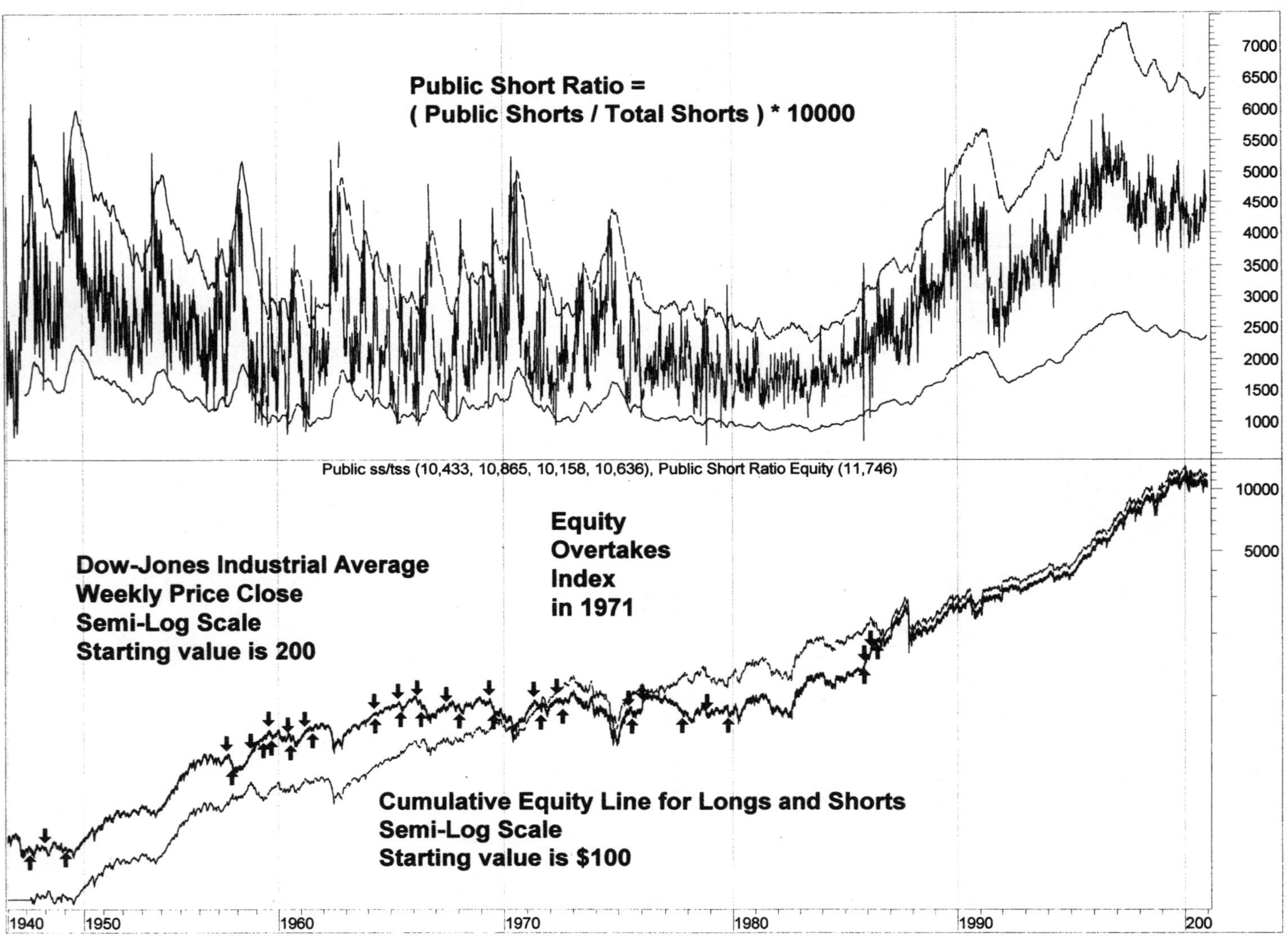
Public Short Ratio =
(Public Shorts / Total Shorts) * 10000
Public ss/tss (10,433, 10,865, 10,158, 10,636), Public Short Ratio Equity (11,746)
Dow-Jones Industrial Average
Weekly Price Close
Semi-Log Scale
Starting value is 200
Equity
Overtakes
Index
in 1971
Cumulative Equity Line for Longs and Shorts
Semi-Log Scale
Starting value is $100
7000
6500
6000
5500
5000
4500
4000
3500
3000
2500
2000
1500
1000
10000
5000
1940
1950
1960
1970
1980
1990
200

Public Short Ratio

Total net profit	11646.27	Open position value	9663.42	Net Profit / Buy&Hold %	123.20
Percent gain/loss	11646.27	Annual percent gain/loss	211.8	Annual Net % / B&H %	123.21
Initial investment	100	Interest earned	0		
Current position	Long	Date position entered	6/6/86		
Buy/Hold profit	5217.78	Days in test	20070	# of days per trade	557.50
Buy/Hold pct gain/loss	5217.78	Annual B/H pct gain/loss	94.89		
Total closed trades	36	Commissions paid	0		
Avg profit per trade	55.08	Avg Win/Avg Loss ratio	1.26		
Total long trades	18	Total short trades	18	Long Win Trade %	83.33
Winning long trades	15	Winning short trades	13	Short Win Trade %	72.22
Total winning trades	28	Total losing trades	8	Total Win Trade %	77.78
Amount of winning trades	2564.13	Amount of losing trades	−581.28	Net Profit Margin %	63.04
Average win	91.58	Average loss	−72.66	Average P. Margin %	11.52
Largest win	889.17	Largest loss	−319.55	% Net / (Win + Loss)	47.13
Average length of win	61.18	Average length of loss	46.25	(Win − Loss) / Loss %	32.28
Longest winning trade	438	Longest losing trade	151	(Win − Loss) / Loss %	190.07
Most consecutive wins	14	Most consecutive losses	2	(Win − Loss) / Loss %	600.00
Total bars out	62	Average length out	62		
Longest out period	62				
System close drawdown	0	Profit/Loss index	95.25	% Net Profit / SODD	254841.79
System open drawdown	−4.57	Reward/Risk index	99.96	(Net P.-SODD)/Net P.	99.96
Max open trade drawdown	−410.62	Buy/Hold index	308.41	% SODD / Net Profit	−0.04

In the Equis MetaStock® "System Report" (profit and loss summary statistics), the *Total net profit* is the sum of profits minus the sum of losses, including open positions marked to the market. In contrast, the *Amount of Winning Trades* is the sum of realized profits (the total of all gains on closed-out trades only, excluding any open positions). Similarly, the *Amount of Losing Trades* is the sum of realized losses (the total of all losses on closed-out trades only, excluding any open positions). *System close drawdown* is the largest decline in the cumulative equity line below the initial investment, based on closed-out positions only. *System open drawdown (SODD)* is the largest decline in the cumulative equity line below the initial investment when a position is open. *Max open trade drawdown* is the largest decline in the cumulative equity line below the trade entry price during the worst single trade. The *Profit/Loss Index* is a complex calculation that relates the Amount of Winning Trades to the Amount of Losing Trades on a scale of −100 (worst possible performance) to +100 (best possible performance), with zero representing profits equal to losses. *Reward/Risk Index* is the Total net profit minus System open drawdown. The resulting difference is then divided by the Total net profit. The *Buy/Hold Index* is the Total net profit minus the buy-and-hold strategy's net profit. The resulting difference is then divided by the buy-and-hold net profit. In this exercise, initial equity is assumed to be $100. Both long and short positions are taken unless otherwise noted. Trades are executed at the closing price on the signal date. Transaction costs, interest expenses, and margins are not included in the statistics.

Public/Specialist Short Ratio

The Public/Specialist Short Ratio is computed by dividing the total public (nonmember) short sales by the total specialist short sales.

Traditionally, the public (amateur traders) is assumed to be wrong, while the specialists (professional traders) are assumed to be right about the future direction of stock prices. Therefore, high Public/Specialist Short Ratios are bullish while low Ratios are bearish.

Short Selling is an aggressive trading strategy designed to take advantage of declining prices. Speculators may sell short a stock when they anticipate a price decline. If the stock does drop, they may realize a profit equal to the difference between their sell-short price and the lower buy-back price. If they are wrong and the stock rises, their loss will equal the amount of the stock price appreciation, the difference between their sell-short price and the higher buy-back price.

Late each Friday, after the close, the NYSE releases summary statistics on the total volume of short sales, also separating short sales by stock exchange members from nonmembers (the public). Because the absolute levels of short selling have increased in all categories along with the general expansion in the total volume of trading activity, the data must be normalized somehow, hence, the various short sales ratios.

Indicator Strategy Example for Public/Specialist Short Ratio

Based on a 55-year file of Public/Specialist Short Ratios and weekly closing price data for the DJIA from January 1946 to December 2000, we found that the following parameters would have produced a positive result on a purely mechanical overbought/oversold signal basis with no subjectivity, no sophisticated technical analysis, and no judgement:

Enter Long (Buy) at the current weekly price close of the DJIA when the latest Public/Specialist Short Ratio is more than 59% above its previous week's 4-week EMA of the Public/Specialist Short Ratio.

Close Long (Sell) at the current weekly price close of the DJIA when the latest Public/Specialist Short Ratio is more than 59% below its previous week's 4-week EMA of the Public/Specialist Short Ratio.

Enter Short (Sell Short) at the current weekly price close of the DJIA when the latest Public/Specialist Short Ratio is more than 59% below its previous week's 4-week EMA of the Public/Specialist Short Ratio.

Close Short (Cover) at the current weekly price close of the DJIA when the latest Public/Specialist Short Ratio is more than 59% above its previous week's 4-week EMA of the Public/Specialist Short Ratio.

Starting with $100 and reinvesting profits, total net profits for this Public/Specialist Short Ratio Envelope strategy would have been $8,431.27, assuming a fully invested strategy, reinvestment of profits, no transactions costs and no taxes. This would have been 61.59 percent greater than buy-and-hold. Short selling would have been moderately profitable and was included in the strategy. The Long-and-Short Public/Specialist Short Ratio as an indicator would have given profitable buy signals 90.00% of the time. Trading would have been inactive at one trade every 2,007.00 calendar days. Note that this strategy considers week-end closing prices only while ignoring everything in between.

Curiously, this strategy has not given a signal since 11/15/85. It is always possible that the behavior of the underlying data could change due to rule changes or evolution of business practices. In general, when the behavior of the underlying data changes, it is no longer appropriate to apply historical norms when making current decisions. Therefore, be cautious if you attempt to use this indicator.

The Equis International MetaStock® System Testing rules for Public/Specialist Short Ratio, where the ratio of Public Short Sales to Total Short Sales is inserted into the field normally reserved for volume, are written as follows:

Enter long: V> (Ref(Mov(V,opt1,E),−1)+
((opt2/1000))*Ref(Mov(V,opt1,E),−1))

Close long: V< (Ref(Mov(V,opt1,E),−1)−
((opt2/1000))*Ref(Mov(V,opt1,E),−1))

Enter short: V< (Ref(Mov(V,opt1,E),−1)−
((opt2/1000))*Ref(Mov(V,opt1,E),−1))

Close short: V> (Ref(Mov(V,opt1,E),−1)+
((opt2/1000))*Ref(Mov(V,opt1,E),−1))

OPT1 Current value: 4

OPT2 Current value: 590

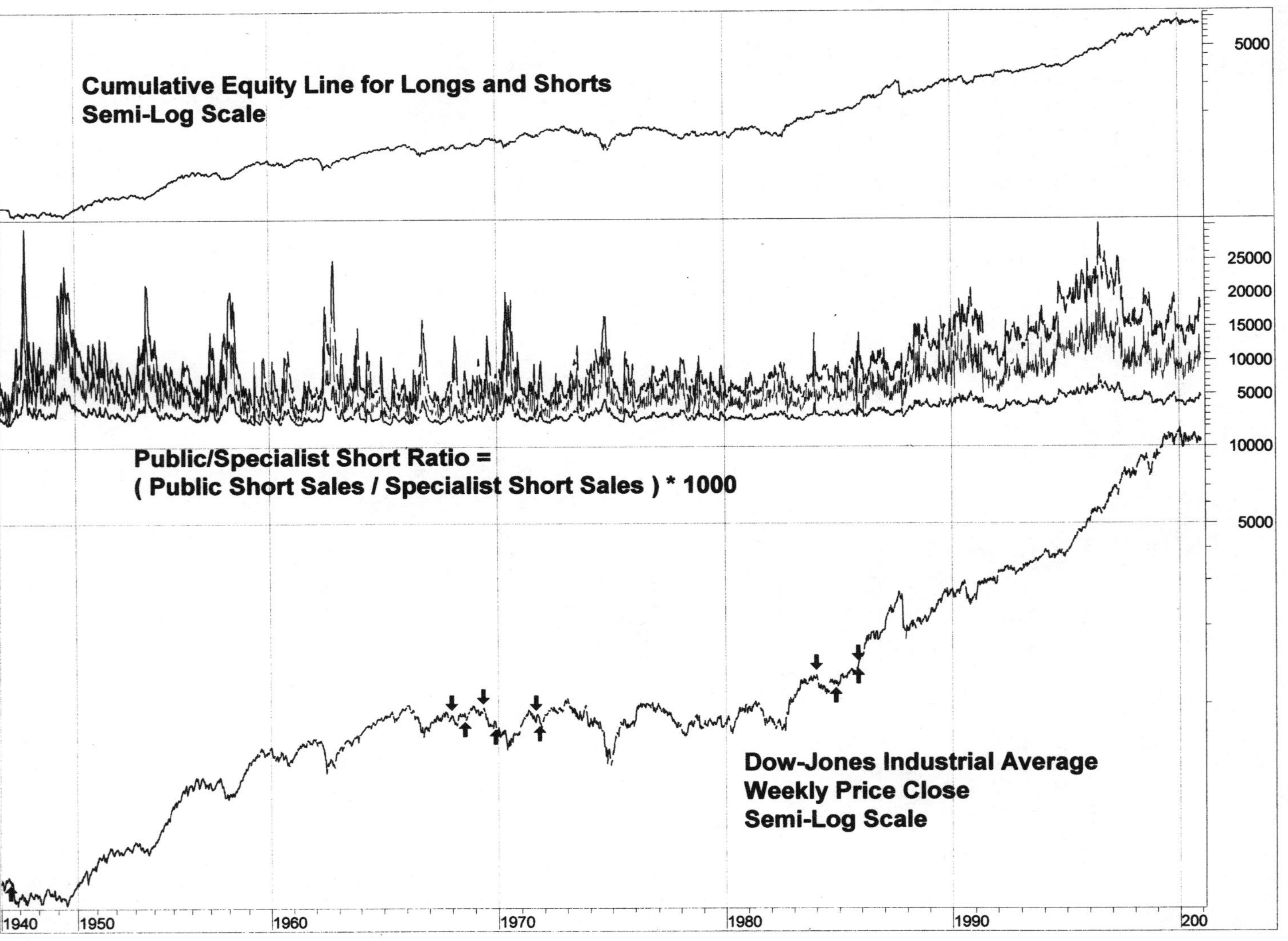

Cumulative Equity Line for Longs and Shorts
Semi-Log Scale
5000
25000
20000
15000
10000
5000
Public/Specialist Short Ratio =
(Public Short Sales / Specialist Short Sales) * 1000
10000
5000
Dow-Jones Industrial Average
Weekly Price Close
Semi-Log Scale
1940
1950
1960
1970
1980
1990
200

Public/Specialist Short Ratio

Total net profit	8431.27	Open position value	7380.11	Net Profit / Buy&Hold %	61.59
Percent gain/loss	8431.27	Annual percent gain/loss	153.33	Annual Net % / B&H %	61.59
Initial investment	100	Interest earned	0		
Current position	Long	Date position entered	11/15/85		
Buy/Hold profit	5217.78	Days in test	20070	# of days per trade	2007.00
Buy/Hold pct gain/loss	5217.78	Annual B/H pct gain/loss	94.89		
Total closed trades	10	Commissions paid	0		
Avg profit per trade	105.12	Avg Win/Avg Loss ratio	4.65		
Total long trades	5	Total short trades	5	Long Win Trade %	100.00
Winning long trades	5	Winning short trades	4	Short Win Trade %	80.00
Total winning trades	9	Total losing trades	1	Total Win Trade %	90.00
Amount of winning trades	1076.89	Amount of losing trades	−25.73	Net Profit Margin %	95.33
Average win	119.65	Average loss	−25.73	Average P. Margin %	64.60
Largest win	343.24	Largest loss	−25.73	% Net / (Win + Loss)	86.05
Average length of win	229	Average length of loss	2	(Win − Loss) / Loss %	11350.00
Longest winning trade	1121	Longest losing trade	2	(Win − Loss) / Loss %	55950.00
Most consecutive wins	9	Most consecutive losses	1	(Win − Loss) / Loss %	800.00
Total bars out	27	Average length out	27		
Longest out period	27				
System close drawdown	0	Profit/Loss index	99.7	% Net Profit / SODD	42410.81
System open drawdown	−19.88	Reward/Risk index	99.76	(Net P.-SODD)/Net P.	99.76
Max open trade drawdown	−197.47	Buy/Hold index	203.03	% SODD / Net Profit	−0.24

In the Equis MetaStock® "System Report" (profit and loss summary statistics), the *Total net profit* is the sum of profits minus the sum of losses, including open positions marked to the market. In contrast, the *Amount of Winning Trades* is the sum of realized profits (the total of all gains on closed-out trades only, excluding any open positions). Similarly, the *Amount of Losing Trades* is the sum of realized losses (the total of all losses on closed-out trades only, excluding any open positions). *System close drawdown* is the largest decline in the cumulative equity line below the initial investment, based on closed-out positions only. *System open drawdown (SODD)* is the largest decline in the cumulative equity line below the initial investment when a position is open. *Max open trade drawdown* is the largest decline in the cumulative equity line below the trade entry price during the worst single trade. The *Profit/Loss Index* is a complex calculation that relates the Amount of Winning Trades to the Amount of Losing Trades on a scale of −100 (worst possible performance) to +100 (best possible performance), with zero representing profits equal to losses. *Reward/Risk Index* is the Total net profit minus System open drawdown. The resulting difference is then divided by the Total net profit. The *Buy/Hold Index* is the Total net profit minus the buy-and-hold strategy's net profit. The resulting difference is then divided by the buy-and-hold net profit. In this exercise, initial equity is assumed to be $100. Both long and short positions are taken unless otherwise noted. Trades are executed at the closing price on the signal date. Transaction costs, interest expenses, and margins are not included in the statistics.

Put/Call Premium Ratio

The Put/Call Premium Ratio is the ratio of the average premiums on equity puts divided by the average premiums on equity calls. It is a sentiment indicator, interpreted according to the theory of *Contrary Opinion.* Options speculators are wrong about the direction of stock prices when they go to extremes.

When options speculators feel overly pessimistic, they bid up put prices excessively. This inflates put premiums and causes the Put/Call Premium Ratio rise to a relatively high level. Contrarily, this is bullish for the future of stock prices.

At the opposite extreme, when options speculators feel overly optimistic, they bid up call prices excessively. This inflates call premiums and causes the Put/Call Premium Ratio to fall to a relatively low level. Contrarily, this is bearish for the future of stock prices.

Technical analysts generally look to the levels of the Ratio to find signals. We have found it more useful to study the large changes in the Ratio from one week to the next. We get better signals when we see options speculators change their opinions suddenly and dramatically.

The data is compiled by the Options Clearing Corporation. Historical data for this indicator is available to institutional investors through UST Securities Corporation, 5 Vaughn Drive, CN5209, Princeton, NJ 08543-5209, phone (609) 734-7788.

Indicator Strategy Example for the Put/Call Premium Ratio Jump Strategy

Based on a 21-year file of weekly Put/Call Premium Ratios and weekly closing price data for the DJIA from August 1979 to November 2000, we found that the following parameters would have produced a positive result on a purely mechanical overbought/oversold signal basis with no subjectivity, no sophisticated technical analysis, and no judgement:

Enter Long (Buy) at the current weekly price close of the DJIA when the latest Put/Call Premium Ratio jumps more than 19.4% above its previous week's level.

Close Long (Sell) at the current weekly price close of the DJIA when the latest Put/Call Premium Ratio jumps more than 31.4% below its previous week's level.

Enter Short (Sell Short) at the current weekly price close of the DJIA Average when the latest Put/Call Premium Ratio jumps more than 31.4% below its previous week's level.

Close Short (Cover) at the current weekly price close of the DJIA when the latest Put/Call Premium Ratio jumps more than 19.4% above its previous week's level.

Starting with $100 and reinvesting profits, total net profits for this Put/Call Premium Ratio Jump Strategy would have been $2,769.00, assuming a fully invested strategy, reinvestment of profits, no transactions costs and no taxes. This would have been 143.47 percent greater than buy-and-hold. Short selling would have been moderately profitable and was included in the strategy. The Long-and-Short Put/Call Premium Ratio Jump Strategy would have given profitable signals 65.83% of the time. Trading would have been moderate at one trade every 64.88 calendar days. Note that this strategy considers week-end closing prices only while ignoring everything in between.

The Equis International MetaStock® System Testing rules for the Put/Call Premium Ratio, where the ratio of Put Premiums to Call Premiums is multiplied by 10000 (for scaling) and inserted into the field normally reserved for volume, are written as follows:

Enter long: V> (Ref(Mov(V,opt1,E),−1)+
((opt2/1000))*Ref(Mov(V,opt1,E),−1))

Close long: V< (Ref(Mov(V,opt1,E),−1)−
((opt3/1000))*Ref(Mov(V,opt1,E),−1))

Enter short: V< (Ref(Mov(V,opt1,E),−1)−
((opt3/1000))*Ref(Mov(V,opt1,E),−1))

Close short: V> (Ref(Mov(V,opt1,E),−1)+
((opt2/1000))*Ref(Mov(V,opt1,E),−1))

OPT1 Current value: 1

OPT2 Current value: 194

OPT3 Current value: 314

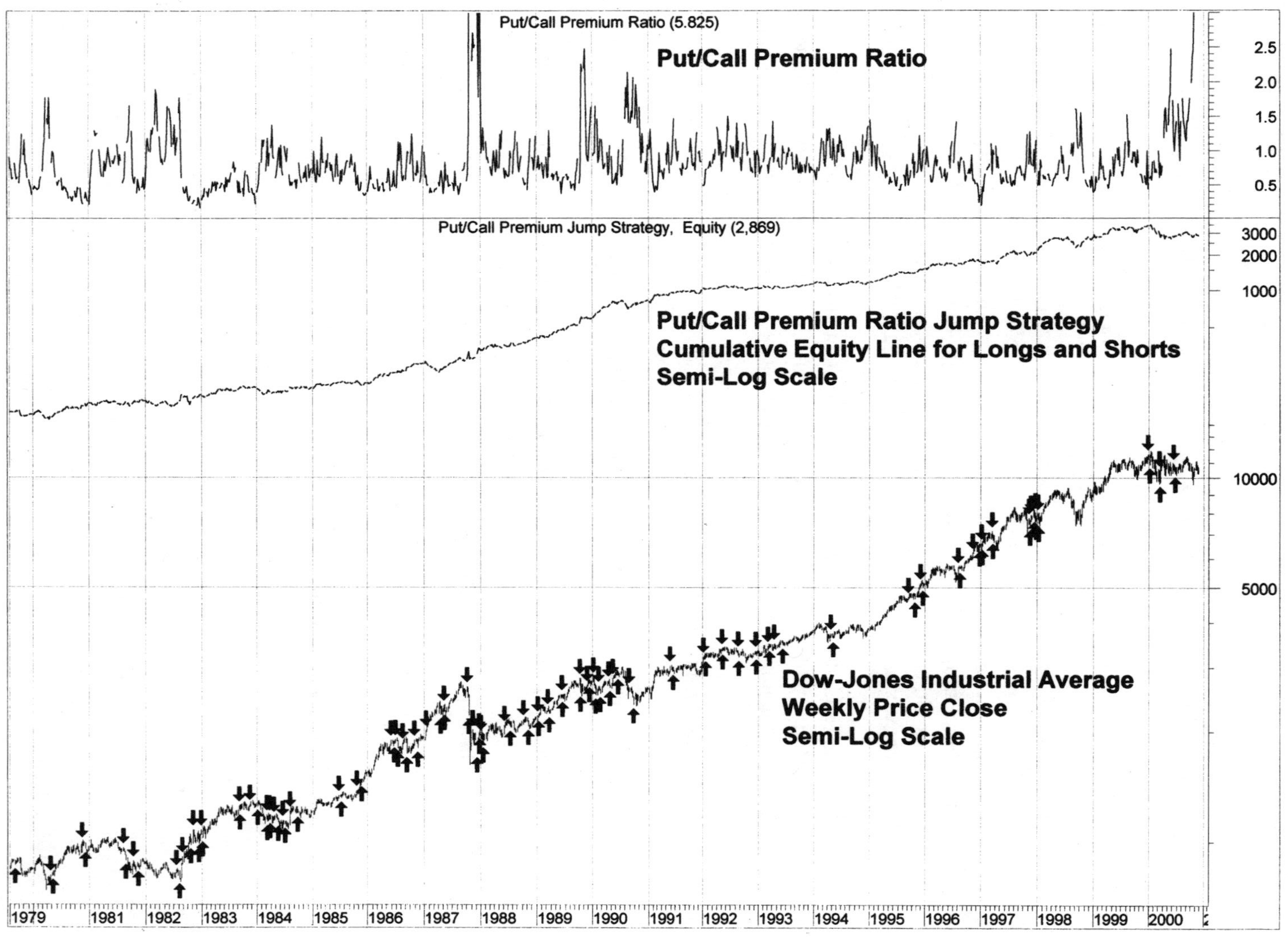

Put/Call Premium Ratio (5.825)
Put/Call Premium Ratio
2.5
2.0
1.5
1.0
0.5
Put/Call Premium Jump Strategy, Equity (2,869)
3000
2000
1000
Put/Call Premium Ratio Jump Strategy
Cumulative Equity Line for Longs and Shorts
Semi-Log Scale
10000
5000
Dow-Jones Industrial Average
Weekly Price Close
Semi-Log Scale
1979
1981
1982
1983
1984
1985
1986
1987
1988
1989
1990
1991
1992
1993
1994
1995
1996
1997
1998
1999
2000

Put/Call Premium Ratio Jump Strategy

Total net profit	2769	Open position value	17.94	Net Profit / Buy&Hold %	143.47
Percent gain/loss	2769	Annual percent gain/loss	129.82	Annual Net % / B&H %	143.47
Initial investment	100	Interest earned	0		
Current position	Long	Date position entered	6/23/00		
Buy/Hold profit	1137.32	Days in test	7785	# of days per trade	64.88
Buy/Hold pct gain/loss	1137.32	Annual B/H pct gain/loss	53.32		
Total closed trades	120	Commissions paid	0		
Avg profit per trade	22.93	Avg Win/Avg Loss ratio	1.68		
Total long trades	60	Total short trades	60	Long Win Trade %	76.67
Winning long trades	46	Winning short trades	33	Short Win Trade %	55.00
Total winning trades	79	Total losing trades	41	Total Win Trade %	65.83
Amount of winning trades	3979.09	Amount of losing trades	−1228.04	Net Profit Margin %	52.83
Average win	50.37	Average loss	−29.95	Average P. Margin %	25.42
Largest win	1185.42	Largest loss	−480.23	% Net / (Win + Loss)	42.34
Average length of win	11.34	Average length of loss	7.54	(Win − Loss) / Loss %	50.40
Longest winning trade	104	Longest losing trade	36	(Win − Loss) / Loss %	188.89
Most consecutive wins	7	Most consecutive losses	3	(Win − Loss) / Loss %	133.33
Total bars out	6	Average length out	6		
Longest out period	6				
System close drawdown	−8.33	Profit/Loss index	69.28	% Net Profit / SODD	21854.78
System open drawdown	−12.67	Reward/Risk index	99.54	(Net P.-SODD)/Net P.	99.54
Max open trade drawdown	−500.32	Buy/Hold index	145.04	% SODD / Net Profit	−0.46

In the Equis MetaStock® "System Report" (profit and loss summary statistics), the *Total net profit* is the sum of profits minus the sum of losses, including open positions marked to the market. In contrast, the *Amount of Winning Trades* is the sum of realized profits (the total of all gains on closed-out trades only, excluding any open positions). Similarly, the *Amount of Losing Trades* is the sum of realized losses (the total of all losses on closed-out trades only, excluding any open positions). *System close drawdown* is the largest decline in the cumulative equity line below the initial investment, based on closed-out positions only. *System open drawdown (SODD)* is the largest decline in the cumulative equity line below the initial investment when a position is open. *Max open trade drawdown* is the largest decline in the cumulative equity line below the trade entry price during the worst single trade. The *Profit/Loss Index* is a complex calculation that relates the Amount of Winning Trades to the Amount of Losing Trades on a scale of −100 (worst possible performance) to +100 (best possible performance), with zero representing profits equal to losses. *Reward/Risk Index* is the Total net profit minus System open drawdown. The resulting difference is then divided by the Total net profit. The *Buy/Hold Index* is the Total net profit minus the buy-and-hold strategy's net profit. The resulting difference is then divided by the buy-and-hold net profit. In this exercise, initial equity is assumed to be $100. Both long and short positions are taken unless otherwise noted. Trades are executed at the closing price on the signal date. Transaction costs, interest expenses, and margins are not included in the statistics.

Put/Call Ratio: Put/Call Volume Ratio

The Put/Call Ratio is a sentiment indicator interpreted in accordance with the theory of *Contrary Opinion.* Options speculators are wrong about the direction of stock prices when they go to extremes.

The Put/Call Ratio is calculated by dividing the daily volume of equity put options by the volume of equity call options. Daily Chicago Board Options Exchange (CBOE) data normally is used in the calculation. (Historical data for this indicator is available to institutional investors through UST Securities Corporation, 5 Vaughn Drive, CN5209, Princeton, NJ 08543-5209, phone (609) 734-7788.)

Extremely high Put/Call Ratios indicate that options speculators strongly feel that stocks prices will fall much lower. On the contrary, since options speculators are wrong when they go to emotional extremes, their pessimism is bullish for the future of stock prices.

At the opposite extreme, very low Put/Call Ratios indicate that options speculators feel strongly that stock prices are about to move much higher. Their optimism is bearish for the future of stock prices.

Technical analysts generally look to the levels of the Ratio to find signals. In this case, the levels appear to migrate over time. Therefore, we have found it more useful to study the large changes in the Ratio relative to a trailing exponential moving average of the raw data. We get better signals when we see options speculators change their opinions suddenly and dramatically, relative to where they have been.

Indicator Strategy Example for the Put/Call Volume Ratio Envelope Strategy

Based on a 22-year file of daily Put/Call Volume Ratios and daily closing price data for the DJIA from January 1978 to November 2000, we found that the following parameters would have produced a positive result on a purely mechanical overbought/oversold signal basis with no subjectivity, no sophisticated technical analysis, and no judgement:

Enter Long (Buy) at the current daily price close of the Dow-Jones Industrial Average (DJIA) when the latest Put/Call Volume Ratio jumps more than 19.5% above its own trailing 90-day exponential moving average (EMA) as of the previous day.

Close Long (Sell) at the current daily price close of the DJIA when the latest Put/Call Volume Ratio jumps more than 42.0% below its own trailing 90-day EMA as of the previous day.

Enter Short (Sell Short) at the current daily price close of the DJIA when the latest Put/Call Volume Ratio jumps more than 42.0% below its own trailing 90-day EMA as of the previous day.

Close Short (Cover) at the current daily price close of the DJIA when the latest Put/Call Volume Ratio jumps more than 19.5% above its own trailing 90-day EMA as of the previous day.

Starting with $100 and reinvesting profits, total net profits for this Put/Call Volume Ratio Envelope Strategy would have been $2,893.76, assuming a fully invested strategy, reinvestment of profits, no transactions costs and no taxes. This would have been 141.37 percent greater than buy-and-hold. Short selling would have been moderately profitable and was included in the strategy. The Long-and-Short Put/Call Volume Ratio Jump Strategy as an indicator would have given profitable buy signals 89.74% of the time. Trading would have been moderate at one trade every 215.56 calendar days.

The Equis International MetaStock® System Testing rules for the Put/Call Volume Ratio, where the ratio of Put Volume to Call Volume is multiplied by 10000 (for scaling) and inserted into the field normally reserved for volume, are written as follows:

Enter long: V > (Ref(Mov(V, opt1,E),−1)+
((opt2/1000))*Ref(Mov(V, opt1,E),−1))

Close long: V < (Ref(Mov(V, opt1,E),−1)−
((opt3/1000))*Ref(Mov(V, opt1,E),−1))

Enter short: V < (Ref(Mov(V, opt1,E),−1)−
((opt3/1000))*Ref(Mov(V, opt1,E),−1))

Close short: V > (Ref(Mov(V, opt1,E),−1)+
((opt2/1000))*Ref(Mov(V, opt1,E),−1))

OPT1 Current value: 90

OPT2 Current value: 195

OPT3 Current value: 420

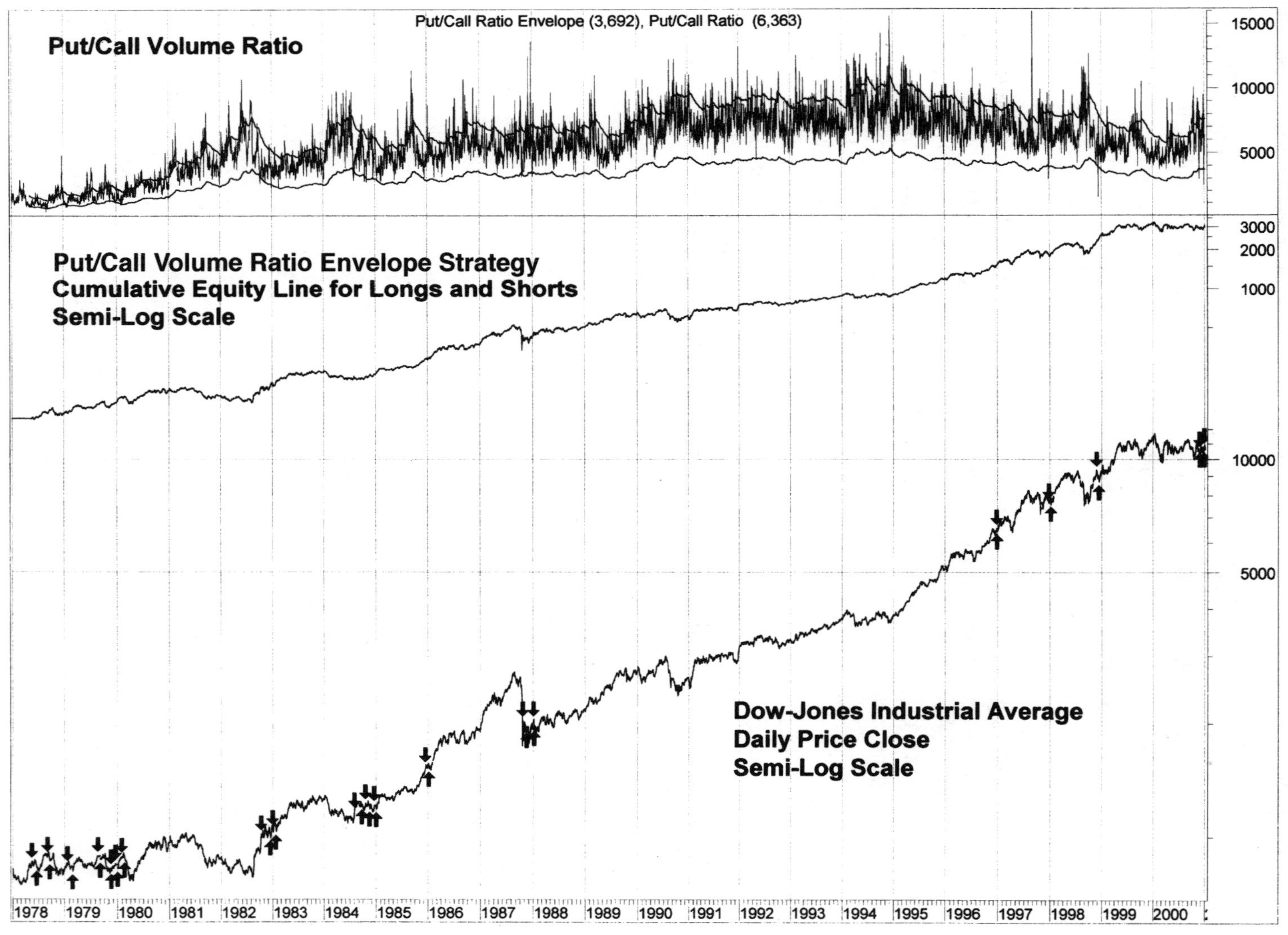
Put/Call Ratio Envelope (3,692), Put/Call Ratio (6,363)
Put/Call Volume Ratio
15000
10000
5000
Put/Call Volume Ratio Envelope Strategy
Cumulative Equity Line for Longs and Shorts
Semi-Log Scale
3000
2000
1000
10000
5000
Dow-Jones Industrial Average
Daily Price Close
Semi-Log Scale
1978
1979
1980
1981
1982
1983
1984
1985
1986
1987
1988
1989
1990
1991
1992
1993
1994
1995
1996
1997
1998
1999
2000

Put/Call Volume Ratio Envelope Strategy

Total net profit	2893.76	Open position value	−6.96	Net Profit / Buy&Hold %	141.37
Percent gain/loss	2893.76	Annual percent gain/loss	125.64	Annual Net % / B&H %	141.38
Initial investment	100	Interest earned	0		
Current position	Long	Date position entered	1/2/01		
Buy/Hold profit	1198.87	Days in test	8407	# of days per trade	215.56
Buy/Hold pct gain/loss	1198.87	Annual B/H pct gain/loss	52.05		
Total closed trades	39	Commissions paid	0		
Avg profit per trade	74.38	Avg Win/Avg Loss ratio	8.47		
Total long trades	19	Total short trades	20	Long Win Trade %	89.47
Winning long trades	17	Winning short trades	18	Short Win Trade %	90.00
Total winning trades	35	Total losing trades	4	Total Win Trade %	89.74
Amount of winning trades	2940.38	Amount of losing trades	−39.66	Net Profit Margin %	97.34
Average win	84.01	Average loss	−9.91	Average P. Margin %	78.90
Largest win	1077.3	Largest loss	−23.15	% Net / (Win + Loss)	95.79
Average length of win	159.49	Average length of loss	44.25	(Win − Loss) / Loss %	260.43
Longest winning trade	2268	Longest losing trade	85	(Win − Loss) / Loss %	2568.24
Most consecutive wins	17	Most consecutive losses	1	(Win − Loss) / Loss %	1600.00
Total bars out	94	Average length out	94		
Longest out period	94				
System close drawdown	0	Profit/Loss index	98.65	% Net Profit / SODD	202360.84
System open drawdown	−1.43	Reward/Risk index	99.95	(Net P.-SODD)/Net P.	99.95
Max open trade drawdown	−85.18	Buy/Hold index	140.79	% SODD / Net Profit	−0.05

In the Equis MetaStock® "System Report" (profit and loss summary statistics), the *Total net profit* is the sum of profits minus the sum of losses, including open positions marked to the market. In contrast, the *Amount of Winning Trades* is the sum of realized profits (the total of all gains on closed-out trades only, excluding any open positions). Similarly, the *Amount of Losing Trades* is the sum of realized losses (the total of all losses on closed-out trades only, excluding any open positions). *System close drawdown* is the largest decline in the cumulative equity line below the initial investment, based on closed-out positions only. *System open drawdown (SODD)* is the largest decline in the cumulative equity line below the initial investment when a position is open. *Max open trade drawdown* is the largest decline in the cumulative equity line below the trade entry price during the worst single trade. The *Profit/Loss Index* is a complex calculation that relates the Amount of Winning Trades to the Amount of Losing Trades on a scale of −100 (worst possible performance) to +100 (best possible performance), with zero representing profits equal to losses. *Reward/Risk Index* is the Total net profit minus System open drawdown. The resulting difference is then divided by the Total net profit. The *Buy/Hold Index* is the Total net profit minus the buy-and-hold strategy's net profit. The resulting difference is then divided by the buy-and-hold net profit. In this exercise, initial equity is assumed to be $100. Both long and short positions are taken unless otherwise noted. Trades are executed at the closing price on the signal date. Transaction costs, interest expenses, and margins are not included in the statistics.

Qstick

Qstick is a price momentum oscillator, a simple moving average of close minus open, that oscillates above and below zero. By focusing on the difference between the close and the open, Qstick is an attempt to quantify the implications of Japanese Candlestick Charts: when today's close is greater than today's open, it indicates buying pressure; but when today's close is less than today's open, it indicates selling pressure. Like other Oscillators, Qstick may be interpreted in a variety of ways. Qstick was presented by Tushar Chande and Stanley Kroll, *The New Technical Trader,* John Wiley & Sons, New York, 1994, 256 pages.

As originally presented and as still generally computed, Qstick levels expanded to higher highs and lower lows as stock market price levels increased more than ten fold over 18 years from 1982 to 2000. (To normalize the indicator, convert the basic Qstick to a percentage by dividing the close minus open difference by the close.)

Trend-Following Indicator Strategy Example for Qstick

Qstick may be used for trend following. Qstick values above zero indicate a majority of white candlesticks and a dominance of buying pressure over selling pressure for the time period measured by the moving average. Conversely, Qstick values below zero indicate a majority of black candlesticks and a dominance of selling pressure over buying pressure for the period measured by the moving average. Thus, crossing zero can be used to generate signals.

Also, the trend direction for Qstick may be used to generate signals. For example, a rising trend of Qstick may be considered bullish while a falling trend may be considered bearish.

Based on a 18-year file of daily data for the entire history of the S&P 500 Composite Stock Price Index futures from 4/21/82 to 12/22/00 (*CSI Perpetual Contract* collected from www.csidata.com), we found that the following parameters would have produced a positive result on a purely mechanical signal basis with no subjectivity, no sophisticated technical analysis, and no judgement:

Enter Long (Buy) at the current daily price close of the S&P 500 Composite Stock Price Index futures *CSI Perpetual Contract* when the 1-day Qstick (with no moving average smoothing) is greater than zero and rising.

Close Long (Sell) at the current daily price close of the S&P 500 Composite Stock Price Index futures *CSI Perpetual Contract* when the 1-day Qstick (with no moving average smoothing) is less than zero or falling.

Enter Short (Sell Short) never.

Starting with $100 and reinvesting profits, total net profits for this Qstick trend-following strategy would have been $222.76, assuming a fully invested strategy, reinvestment of profits, no transactions costs and no taxes. This would have been 78.32 percent less than buy-and-hold. No short selling would have been profitable, and no short selling was included in the strategy. This long-only Qstick variation would have given profitable buy signals 49.19% of the time. Trading would have been hyperactive at one trade every 4.83 calendar days.

The Equis International MetaStock® System Testing rules are written as follows:

Enter long: CLOSE-OPEN>0 AND
CLOSE-OPEN>Ref(CLOSE-OPEN,-1)

Close long: CLOSE-OPEN<0 OR
CLOSE-OPEN<Ref(CLOSE-OPEN,-1)

Counter-Trend Indicator Strategy Example for Qstick

Naïve testing assumptions suggest that Qstick may have some objective potential value as a purely mechanical, contra-trend technical indicator, buying below zero and selling above zero. The majority of buy signals would have been profitable. Moreover, these buy signals would have been robust, with all period lengths from 1 to 50 days profitable and right most of the time, again for long trades only. Short lengths of 6-days and less would have been the least profitable.

As attractive as a high percentage of profitable trades may seem, however, it is important to note that this and other contra-trend strategies failed to provide any protection in the Crash of '87, the decline of 1998 and other market price drops. As the chart shows, there are sharp equity drawdowns. Using Qstick for contra-trend signals out-performed the passive buy-and-hold strategy for long trades only. Short selling would not have been profitable in the past.

Based on a 18-year file of daily data for the entire history of the S&P 500 Composite Stock Price Index futures from 4/21/82 to 12/22/00 (*CSI Perpetual Contract* collected from www.csidata.com), we found that the following parameters would have produced a positive result on a purely mechanical overbought/oversold signal basis with no subjectivity, no sophisticated technical analysis, and no judgement:

Enter Long (Buy) at the current daily price close of the S&P 500 Composite Stock Price Index futures *CSI Perpetual Contract* when the 9-day simple moving average Qstick is less than zero.

Close Long (Sell) at the current daily price close of the S&P 500 Composite Stock Price Index futures *CSI Perpetual Contract* when the 9-day simple moving average Qstick is greater than zero.

Enter Short (Sell Short) never.

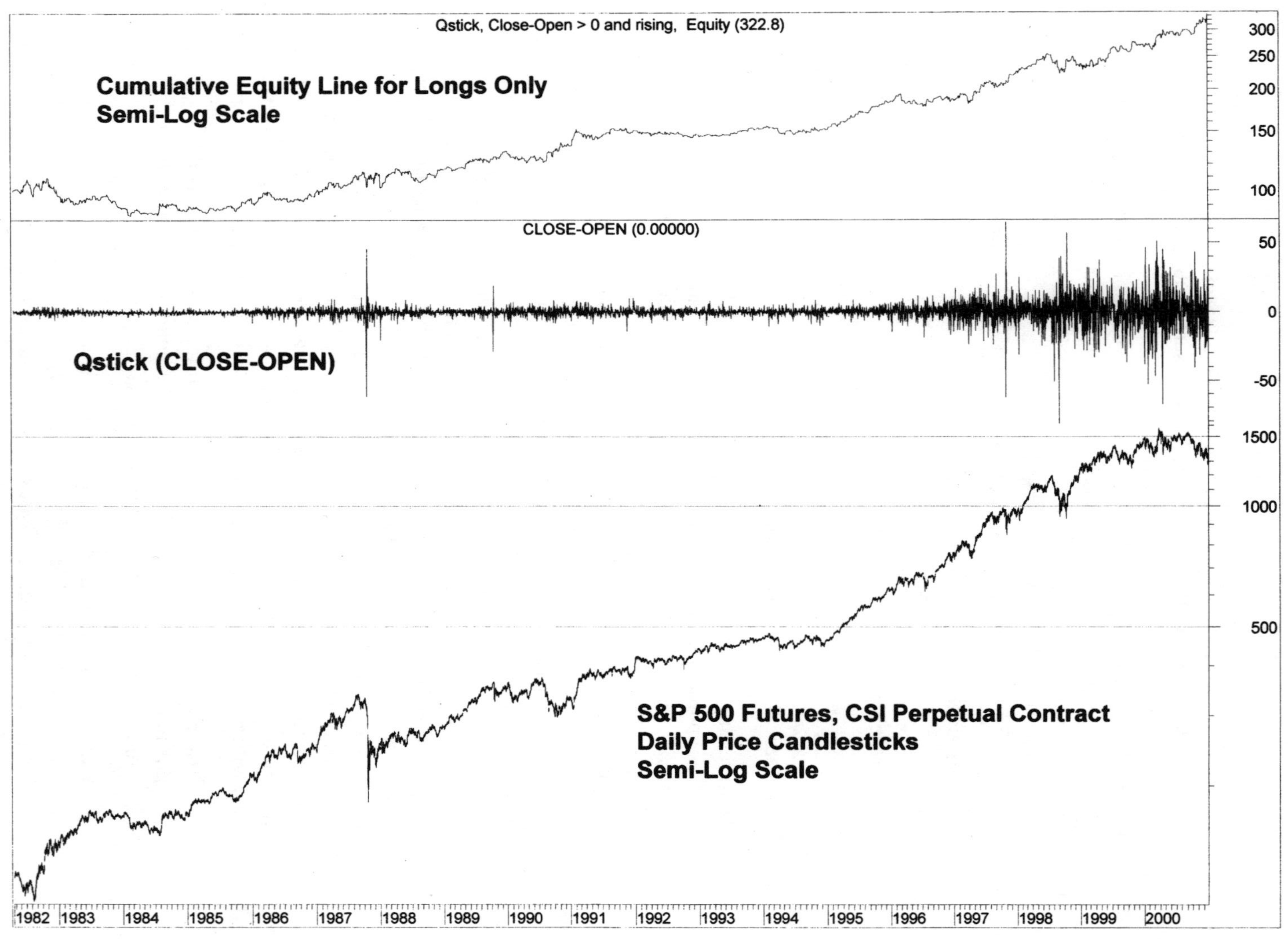
Qstick, Close-Open > 0 and rising, Equity (322.8)
Cumulative Equity Line for Longs Only
Semi-Log Scale
CLOSE-OPEN (0.00000)
Qstick (CLOSE-OPEN)
S&P 500 Futures, CSI Perpetual Contract
Daily Price Candlesticks
Semi-Log Scale
300
250
200
150
100
50
0
-50
1500
1000
500
1982
1983
1984
1985
1986
1987
1988
1989
1990
1991
1992
1993
1994
1995
1996
1997
1998
1999
2000

Qstick 1, Trend-Following

Total net profit	222.76	Open position value	9.41	Net Profit / Buy&Hold %	−78.32
Percent gain/loss	222.76	Annual percent gain/loss	11.92	Annual Net % / B&H %	−78.32
Initial investment	100	Interest earned	0		
Current position	Long	Date position entered	12/21/00		
Buy/Hold profit	1027.4	Days in test	6821	# of days per trade	4.83
Buy/Hold pct gain/loss	1027.4	Annual B/H pct gain/loss	54.98		
Total closed trades	1413	Commissions paid	0		
Avg profit per trade	0.15	Avg Win/Avg Loss ratio	1.32		
Total long trades	1413	Total short trades	0	Long Win Trade %	49.19
Winning long trades	695	Winning short trades	0	Short Win Trade %	#DIV/0!
Total winning trades	695	Total losing trades	718	Total Win Trade %	49.19
Amount of winning trades	982.03	Amount of losing trades	−768.68	Net Profit Margin %	12.19
Average win	1.41	Average loss	−1.07	Average P. Margin %	13.71
Largest win	15.13	Largest loss	−11.54	% Net / (Win + Loss)	13.46
Average length of win	2.52	Average length of loss	2.08	(Win − Loss) / Loss %	21.15
Longest winning trade	5	Longest losing trade	4	(Win − Loss) / Loss %	25.00
Most consecutive wins	8	Most consecutive losses	10	(Win − Loss) / Loss %	−20.00
Total bars out	4310	Average length out	3.05		
Longest out period	10				
System close drawdown	−16.47	Profit/Loss index	22.47	% Net Profit / SODD	1352.52
System open drawdown	−16.47	Reward/Risk index	93.11	(Net P.-SODD)/Net P.	92.61
Max open trade drawdown	−11.54	Buy/Hold index	−77.4	% SODD / Net Profit	−7.39

In the Equis MetaStock® "System Report" (profit and loss summary statistics), the *Total net profit* is the sum of profits minus the sum of losses, including open positions marked to the market. In contrast, the *Amount of Winning Trades* is the sum of realized profits (the total of all gains on closed-out trades only, excluding any open positions). Similarly, the *Amount of Losing Trades* is the sum of realized losses (the total of all losses on closed-out trades only, excluding any open positions). *System close drawdown* is the largest decline in the cumulative equity line below the initial investment, based on closed-out positions only. *System open drawdown (SODD)* is the largest decline in the cumulative equity line below the initial investment when a position is open. *Max open trade drawdown* is the largest decline in the cumulative equity line below the trade entry price during the worst single trade. The *Profit/Loss Index* is a complex calculation that relates the Amount of Winning Trades to the Amount of Losing Trades on a scale of −100 (worst possible performance) to +100 (best possible performance), with zero representing profits equal to losses. *Reward/Risk Index* is the Total net profit minus System open drawdown. The resulting difference is then divided by the Total net profit. The *Buy/Hold Index* is the Total net profit minus the buy-and-hold strategy's net profit. The resulting difference is then divided by the buy-and-hold net profit. In this exercise, initial equity is assumed to be $100. Both long and short positions are taken unless otherwise noted. Trades are executed at the closing price on the signal date. Transaction costs, interest expenses, and margins are not included in the statistics.

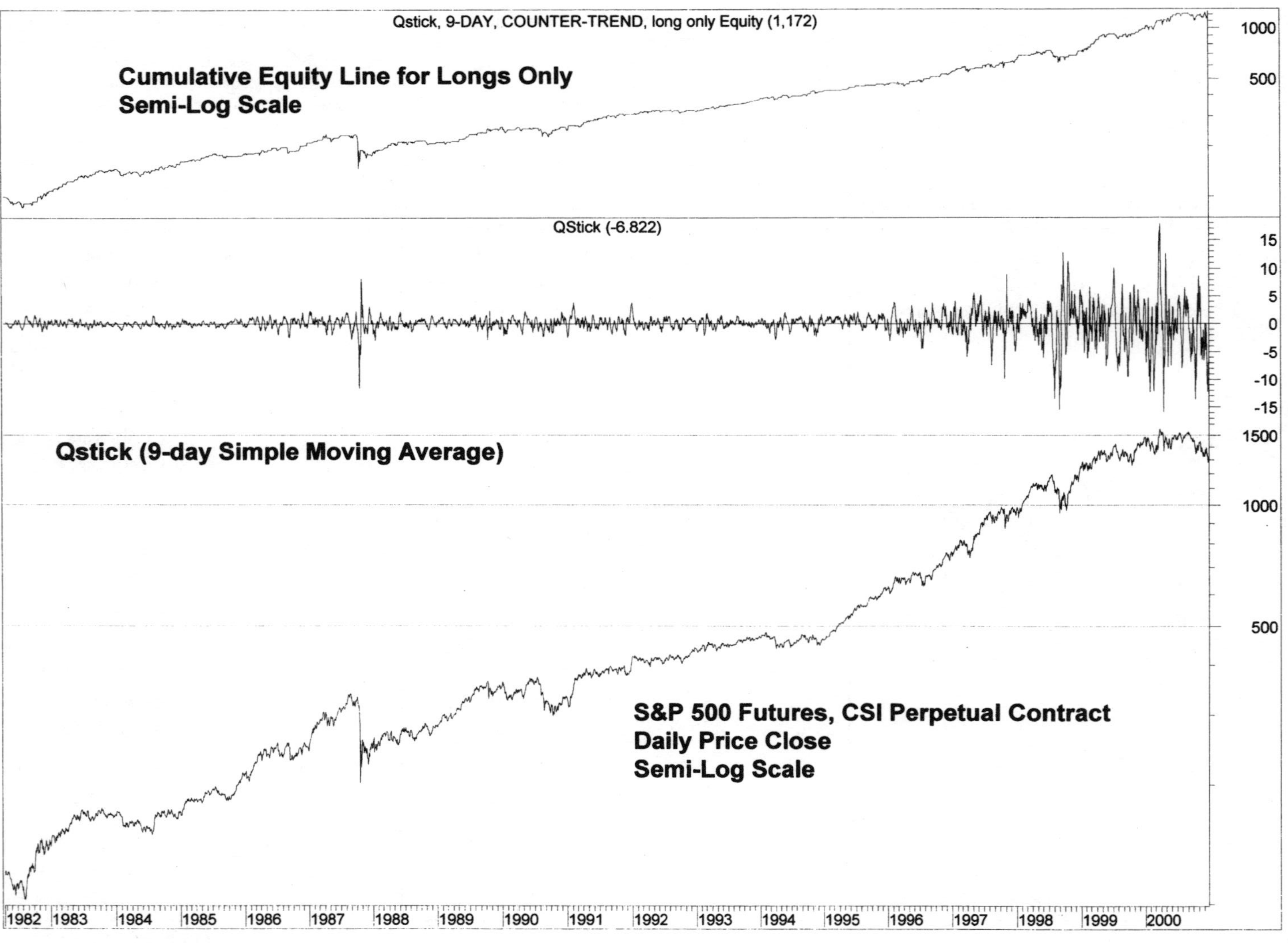

Qstick, 9-DAY, COUNTER-TREND, long only Equity (1,172)
Cumulative Equity Line for Longs Only
Semi-Log Scale
1000
500
QStick (-6.822)
15
10
5
0
-5
-10
-15
Qstick (9-day Simple Moving Average)
1500
1000
500
S&P 500 Futures, CSI Perpetual Contract
Daily Price Close
Semi-Log Scale
1982
1983
1984
1985
1986
1987
1988
1989
1990
1991
1992
1993
1994
1995
1996
1997
1998
1999
2000

Qstick 9, Counter-trend

Total net profit	1071.86	Open position value	−17.97	Net Profit / Buy&Hold %	4.33
Percent gain/loss	1071.86	Annual percent gain/loss	57.36	Annual Net % / B&H %	4.33
Initial investment	100	Interest earned	0		
Current position	Long	Date position entered	12/7/00		
Buy/Hold profit	1027.4	Days in test	6821	# of days per trade	18.64
Buy/Hold pct gain/loss	1027.4	Annual B/H pct gain/loss	54.98		
Total closed trades	366	Commissions paid	0		
Avg profit per trade	2.98	Avg Win/Avg Loss ratio	1.1		
Total long trades	366	Total short trades	0	Long Win Trade %	74.04
Winning long trades	271	Winning short trades	0	Short Win Trade %	#DIV/0!
Total winning trades	271	Total losing trades	95	Total Win Trade %	74.04
Amount of winning trades	1598.74	Amount of losing trades	−508.91	Net Profit Margin %	51.71
Average win	5.9	Average loss	−5.36	Average P. Margin %	4.80
Largest win	42.64	Largest loss	−55.26	% Net / (Win + Loss)	−12.89
Average length of win	5.44	Average length of loss	10.04	(Win − Loss) / Loss %	−45.82
Longest winning trade	27	Longest losing trade	28	(Win − Loss) / Loss %	−3.57
Most consecutive wins	19	Most consecutive losses	4	(Win − Loss) / Loss %	375.00
Total bars out	3017	Average length out	8.22		
Longest out period	65				
System close drawdown	−10.45	Profit/Loss index	67.81	% Net Profit / SODD	7537.69
System open drawdown	−14.22	Reward/Risk index	98.69	(Net P.-SODD)/Net P.	98.67
Max open trade drawdown	−91.09	Buy/Hold index	2.58	% SODD / Net Profit	−1.33

In the Equis MetaStock® "System Report" (profit and loss summary statistics), the *Total net profit* is the sum of profits minus the sum of losses, including open positions marked to the market. In contrast, the *Amount of Winning Trades* is the sum of realized profits (the total of all gains on closed-out trades only, excluding any open positions). Similarly, the *Amount of Losing Trades* is the sum of realized losses (the total of all losses on closed-out trades only, excluding any open positions). *System close drawdown* is the largest decline in the cumulative equity line below the initial investment, based on closed-out positions only. *System open drawdown (SODD)* is the largest decline in the cumulative equity line below the initial investment when a position is open. *Max open trade drawdown* is the largest decline in the cumulative equity line below the trade entry price during the worst single trade. The *Profit/Loss Index* is a complex calculation that relates the Amount of Winning Trades to the Amount of Losing Trades on a scale of −100 (worst possible performance) to +100 (best possible performance), with zero representing profits equal to losses. *Reward/Risk Index* is the Total net profit minus System open drawdown. The resulting difference is then divided by the Total net profit. The *Buy/Hold Index* is the Total net profit minus the buy-and-hold strategy's net profit. The resulting difference is then divided by the buy-and-hold net profit. In this exercise, initial equity is assumed to be $100. Both long and short positions are taken unless otherwise noted. Trades are executed at the closing price on the signal date. Transaction costs, interest expenses, and margins are not included in the statistics.

Starting with $100 and reinvesting profits, total net profits for this Qstick counter-trend strategy would have been $1071.86, assuming a fully invested strategy, reinvestment of profits, no transactions costs and no taxes. This would have been 4.33 percent greater than buy-and-hold. No short selling would have been profitable, and no short selling was included in the strategy. This long-only Qstick variation would have given profitable buy signals 74.04% of the time. Trading would have been only moderately active at one trade every 18.64 calendar days.

The Equis International MetaStock® System Testing rules are written as follows:

Enter long: Qstick(opt1)<0

Close long: Qstick(opt1)>0

OPT1 Current value: 9

R-squared

R-squared attempts to quantify the propensity of prices to trend in the established direction. The more closely prices move in a linear relationship with the passing of time, the stronger the trend has been, and the higher the r-squared. When r-squared is above its critical value and heading up, then it is said that we may be 95% confident that a strong trend has been present.

The following table shows the critical values of r-squared required for a 95% confidence level at various time periods. If the r-squared value is equal to or greater than the critical values shown, prices have shown a statistically significant trend. But if the r-squared value is less than the critical values shown, prices have shown no statistically significant trend.

Number of Periods	*r-squared Critical Value (95% confidence level)*
5	0.77
10	0.40
14	0.27
20	0.20
25	0.16
30	0.13
50	0.08
60	0.06
120	0.03

R-squared is commonly used with Linear Regression Slope. When critical r-squared values are accompanied by a positive Linear Regression Slope value, that is taken as a significant signal. Indeed, by adding a requirement of r-squared greater than 0.03, profitability of the 245-day Linear Regression Slope was enhanced slightly. See Linear Regression Slope.

Indicator Strategy Example for r-squared with Linear Regression Slope

R-squared combined with Linear Regression Slope is robust. We required r-squared critical values of 0.03 or greater combined Linear Regression Slope period lengths between 120 and 320 days. All would have been profitable for long trades only. No short selling strategy was profitable.

Based on an 18-year file of daily data for the entire history of the S&P 500 Composite Stock Price Index futures *CSI Perpetual Contract,* collected from www.csidata.com, from 4/21/82 to 12/22/00, we found that the following parameters

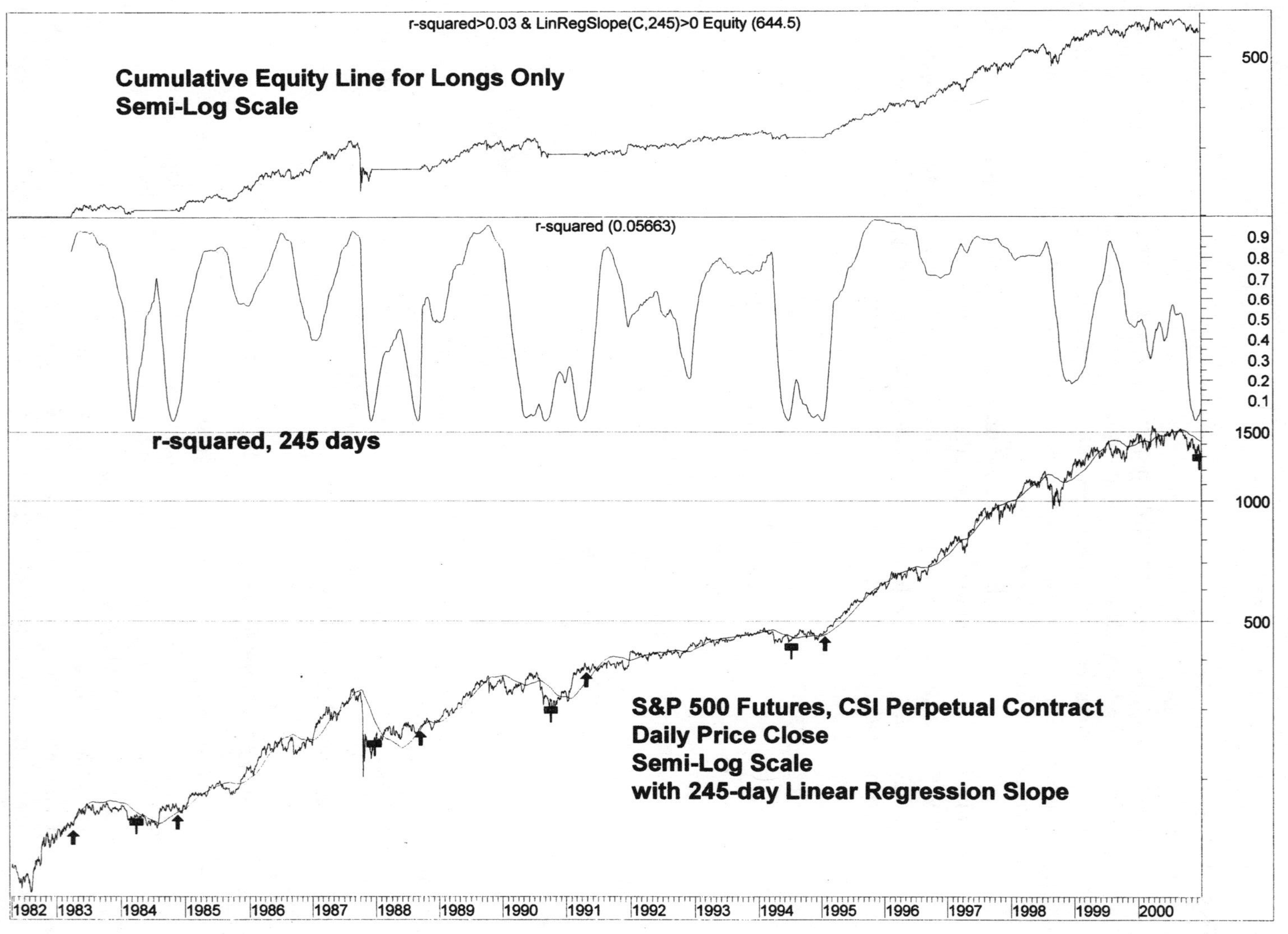

r-squared>0.03 & LinRegSlope(C,245)>0 Equity (644.5)
Cumulative Equity Line for Longs Only
Semi-Log Scale
500
r-squared (0.05663)
0.9
0.8
0.7
0.6
0.5
0.4
0.3
0.2
0.1
r-squared, 245 days
1500
1000
500
S&P 500 Futures, CSI Perpetual Contract
Daily Price Close
Semi-Log Scale
with 245-day Linear Regression Slope
1982
1983
1984
1985
1986
1987
1988
1989
1990
1991
1992
1993
1994
1995
1996
1997
1998
1999
2000

r-squared = 0.03 and Linear Regression Slope = 245 days

Total net profit	544.48	Open position value	N/A	Net Profit / Buy&Hold %	−47.00
Percent gain/loss	544.48	Annual percent gain/loss	29.14	Annual Net % / B&H %	−47.00
Initial investment	100	Interest earned	0		
Current position	Out	Date position entered	12/18/00		
Buy/Hold profit	1027.4	Days in test	6821	# of days per trade	1364.20
Buy/Hold pct gain/loss	1027.4	Annual B/H pct gain/loss	54.98		
Total closed trades	5	Commissions paid	0		
Avg profit per trade	108.9	Avg Win/Avg Loss ratio	N/A		
Total long trades	5	Total short trades	0	Long Win Trade %	100.00
Winning long trades	5	Winning short trades	0	Short Win Trade %	#DIV/0!
Total winning trades	5	Total losing trades	0	Total Win Trade %	100.00
Amount of winning trades	544.48	Amount of losing trades	0	Net Profit Margin %	100.00
Average win	108.9	Average loss	N/A	Average P. Margin %	#VALUE!
Largest win	420.18	Largest loss	0	% Net / (Win + Loss)	100.00
Average length of win	770.8	Average length of loss	N/A	(Win − Loss) / Loss %	#VALUE!
Longest winning trade	1492	Longest losing trade	0	(Win − Loss) / Loss %	#DIV/0!
Most consecutive wins	5	Most consecutive losses	0	(Win − Loss) / Loss %	#DIV/0!
Total bars out	879	Average length out	146.5		
Longest out period	245				
System close drawdown	0	Profit/Loss index	100	% Net Profit / SODD	#DIV/0!
System open drawdown	0	Reward/Risk index	100	(Net P.-SODD)/Net P.	100.00
Max open trade drawdown	−5.15	Buy/Hold index	−47	% SODD / Net Profit	0.00

In the Equis MetaStock® "System Report" (profit and loss summary statistics), the *Total net profit* is the sum of profits minus the sum of losses, including open positions marked to the market. In contrast, the *Amount of Winning Trades* is the sum of realized profits (the total of all gains on closed-out trades only, excluding any open positions). Similarly, the *Amount of Losing Trades* is the sum of realized losses (the total of all losses on closed-out trades only, excluding any open positions). *System close drawdown* is the largest decline in the cumulative equity line below the initial investment, based on closed-out positions only. *System open drawdown (SODD)* is the largest decline in the cumulative equity line below the initial investment when a position is open. *Max open trade drawdown* is the largest decline in the cumulative equity line below the trade entry price during the worst single trade. The *Profit/Loss Index* is a complex calculation that relates the Amount of Winning Trades to the Amount of Losing Trades on a scale of −100 (worst possible performance) to +100 (best possible performance), with zero representing profits equal to losses. *Reward/Risk Index* is the Total net profit minus System open drawdown. The resulting difference is then divided by the Total net profit. The *Buy/Hold Index* is the Total net profit minus the buy-and-hold strategy's net profit. The resulting difference is then divided by the buy-and-hold net profit. In this exercise, initial equity is assumed to be $100. Both long and short positions are taken unless otherwise noted. Trades are executed at the closing price on the signal date. Transaction costs, interest expenses, and margins are not included in the statistics.

would have produced a positive result on a purely mechanical signal basis with no subjectivity, no sophisticated technical analysis, and no judgement:

Enter Long (Buy) at the current daily price close of the S&P 500 Composite Stock Price Index futures *CSI Perpetual Contract* when the 245-day Linear Regression Slope is greater than zero and r-squared is equal to or greater than 0.03, indicating a significant price uptrend.

Close Long (Sell) at the current daily price close of the S&P 500 Composite Stock Price Index futures *CSI Perpetual Contract* when the 245-day Linear Regression Slope is less than zero and r-squared is equal to or greater than 0.03, indicating a significant price downtrend.

Enter Short (Sell Short) never.

Starting with $100 and reinvesting profits, total net profits for this r-squared combined with Linear Regression Slope trend-following strategy would have been $544.48, assuming a fully invested strategy, reinvestment of profits, no transactions costs and no taxes. This would have been 47.00 percent less than buy-and-hold. No short selling would have been profitable, and no short selling was included in the strategy. This long-only r-squared combined with Linear Regression Slope variation would have given profitable buy signals 100% of the time, though the sample size of only five trades is not significant. Trading would have been inactive at one trade every 1364.20 calendar days.

The Equis International MetaStock® System Testing rules are written as follows:

Enter long: LinRegSlope(C,opt1)>0 AND RSquared(C,opt1)>=opt2*0.001

Close long: LinRegSlope(C,opt1)<0 AND RSquared(C,opt1)>=opt2*0.001

OPT1 Current value: 245
OPT2 Current value: 30

Random Walk Hypothesis

The Random Walk Hypothesis holds that stock price movements are totally haphazard. The future movements of markets cannot be predicted by any method whatsoever. Both technical and fundamental analysis have no validity. An intelligent analyst with the best education, information and insight would still have no chance of earning extraordinary returns in the market. Active investors who have become enormously wealthy from their investments are mere statistical flukes. Ten thousand monkeys playing the investment game would produce similar proportions of winners and losers. Any evidence of anomalies contradicting the Random Walk Hypothesis are merely data or programming errors.

There never has been any actual evidence or proof to support the Random Walk Hypothesis, and its popularity is steadily fading. More academics are arguing that there is actual evidence of anomalies (non-random, inefficient stock price movement), that markets may be predictable to at least some degree, and even that efficient markets are an impossibility.

It is impossible to find a successful investor or trader who has any time for the Random Walk Hypothesis. Many simple and objective technical market indicators included in this book beat a passive buy-and-hold strategy very substantially on an absolute basis and particularly on a risk-adjusted basis. These impressive results would not be possible if the market were largely efficient or random.

Random Walk Index (RWI)

The Random Walk Index (RWI) is both a short-term overbought/oversold trend fading indicator and a long-term trend following indicator. RWI was introduced by E. Michael Poulos, "Of Trends And Random Walks", *Technical Analysis of Stocks & Commodities*, V. 9:2 pages 49-52, www.traders.com. The indicator identifies the maximum RWI value over the past *n*-days, separately for lows and highs, and separately for short term and long term.

RWI computes the difference between today's low and the high *n*-days ago, and that difference is divided by the *Average True Range* for the most recent past *n* days multiplied by the square root of the number of days, including today. By multiplying the divisor by the square root of the number of days, the indicator gives progressively less weight to the older data.

For example, first compare today's low to yesterday's high, then divide that by the product of the two days' Average True Range multiplied by the square root of 2. Second, compare today's low to the high two days ago, then divide that by the Average True Range for the past three days' average range multiplied by the square root of 3. Third, compare today's low to the high three days ago, then divide that by the Average True Range for the past four days' average range multiplied by the square root of 4. And so on. This process is carried out to an *n*-day lookback period. The largest value of RWI for the series of lookback lengths from one through *n*-periods is recorded. If any of these lookback lengths generate a value of greater than one, then the market is trending (lower in this example).

Also, RWI computes the difference between today's high and the low *n*-days ago, and that difference also is divided by the Average True Range for the most recent past *n* days multiplied by the square root of the number of days, including today.

The same process is repeated, subtracting each of the previous *n*-days' lows from today's high, then that difference is divided by these past days' Average True Range multiplied by the square root of the number of days being measured, including today. Fortunately, all of this calculating is done effortlessly with the preprogrammed indicator on the Metastock® software indicator menu.

RWI uses separate indicators for the short-term and the long term. SRWI is a short-term, 2- to 7-day RWI used for short-term overbought/oversold trend fading. SRWI above 1.0 is unsustainable. Peaks in the SRWI of highs coincide with short-term price peaks. Peaks in the SRWI of lows coincide with short-term price lows.

LRWI is a longer-term, 8- to 64-day RWI used for long-term trend following. LRWI of highs greater than 1.0 indicates a longer-term, sustainable uptrend. LRWI of lows greater than 1.0 indicates a longer-term, sustainable downtrend.

The author suggests that an effective trading system might be built that opens trades after short-term corrections against the direction of the long-term trend: close short and enter long when the long-term RWI of the highs is greater than 1.0 and the short-term RWI of lows peaks above 1.0; close long and enter short when the long-term RWI of the lows is greater than 1.0 and the short-term RWI of highs peaks above 1.0.

Indicator Strategy Example for the Random Walk Index

Based on an 18-year file of daily data for the entire history of the S&P 500 Composite Stock Price Index futures *CSI Perpetual Contract,* collected from www.csidata.com, from 4/21/82 to 12/22/00, we found that the following parameters would have produced a positive result on a purely mechanical signal basis with no subjectivity, no sophisticated technical analysis, and no judgement:

Enter Long (Buy) at the current daily price close of the S&P 500 Composite Stock Price Index futures *CSI Perpetual Contract* when the long-term RWI of the highs is greater than 1.0 and the short-term RWI of lows is greater than 1.0.

Close Long (Sell) at the current daily price close of the S&P 500 Composite Stock Price Index futures *CSI Perpetual Contract* when the short-term RWI of the highs is greater than 1.0 and the long-term RWI of lows is greater than 1.0.

Enter Short (Sell Short) never.

Starting with $100 and reinvesting profits, total net profits for this Random Walk Index strategy would have been $359.06, assuming a fully invested strategy, reinvestment of profits, no transactions costs and no taxes. This would have been

65.05 percent less than buy-and-hold. No short selling would have been profitable, and no short selling was included in the strategy. This long-only Random Walk Index strategy would have given profitable buy signals 53.19% of the time. Trading would have been only moderately active at one trade every 145.13 calendar days.

The Equis International MetaStock® System Testing rules are written as follows:

Enter long: RWIH(8,64)>1 AND RWIL(2,7)>1

Close long: RWIH(2,7)>1 AND RWIL(8,64)>1

MetaStock® System Testing rules for the Random Walk Index, with flexible parameters

We do not think of indicator parameters as given. Rather they can be allowed to change and evolve to fit the market traded. The following MetaStock® System Testing rules would offer the potential for greater flexibility and adaptability, and greater profits, for any market, using the same RWI system:

Enter long: RWIH(opt1*opt2,opt1*opt2*opt1*opt2)>1 AND RWIL(opt1,opt1*opt2)>1

Close long: RWIL(opt1*opt2,opt1*opt2*opt1*opt2)>1 AND RWIH(opt1,opt1*opt2)>1

Enter short: RWIL(opt1*opt2,opt1*opt2*opt1*opt2)>1 AND RWIH(opt1,opt1*opt2)>1

Close short: RWIH(opt1*opt2,opt1*opt2*opt1*opt2)>1 AND RWIL(opt1,opt1*opt2)>1

OPT1 Current value: 5

OPT2 Current value: 2

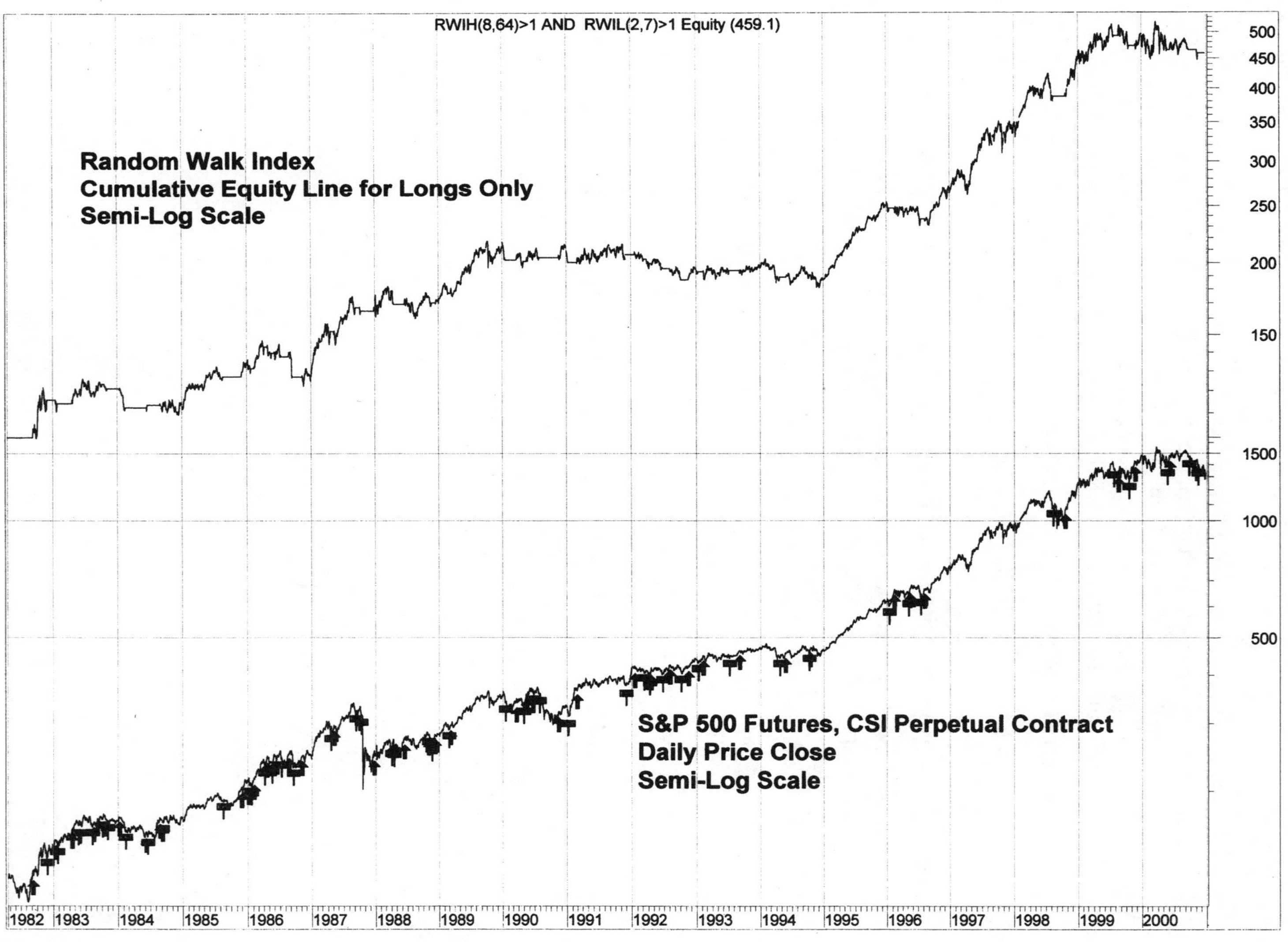
RWIH(8,64)>1 AND RWIL(2,7)>1 Equity (459.1)
Random Walk Index
Cumulative Equity Line for Longs Only
Semi-Log Scale
S&P 500 Futures, CSI Perpetual Contract
Daily Price Close
Semi-Log Scale
500
450
400
350
300
250
200
150
1500
1000
500
1982
1983
1984
1985
1986
1987
1988
1989
1990
1991
1992
1993
1994
1995
1996
1997
1998
1999
2000

Random Walk Index

Total net profit	359.06	Open position value	N/A	Net Profit / Buy&Hold %	−65.05
Percent gain/loss	359.06	Annual percent gain/loss	19.21	Annual Net % / B&H %	−65.06
Initial investment	100	Interest earned	0		
Current position	Out	Date position entered	11/14/00		
Buy/Hold profit	1027.4	Days in test	6821	# of days per trade	145.13
Buy/Hold pct gain/loss	1027.4	Annual B/H pct gain/loss	54.98		
Total closed trades	47	Commissions paid	0		
Avg profit per trade	7.64	Avg Win/Avg Loss ratio	3.49		
Total long trades	47	Total short trades	0	Long Win Trade %	53.19
Winning long trades	25	Winning short trades	0	Short Win Trade %	#DIV/0!
Total winning trades	25	Total losing trades	22	Total Win Trade %	53.19
Amount of winning trades	479.97	Amount of losing trades	−120.9	Net Profit Margin %	59.76
Average win	19.2	Average loss	−5.5	Average P. Margin %	55.47
Largest win	150.25	Largest loss	−19.49	% Net / (Win + Loss)	77.04
Average length of win	108.2	Average length of loss	35.95	(Win − Loss) / Loss %	200.97
Longest winning trade	506	Longest losing trade	160	(Win − Loss) / Loss %	216.25
Most consecutive wins	4	Most consecutive losses	4	(Win − Loss) / Loss %	0.00
Total bars out	1321	Average length out	27.52		
Longest out period	100				
System close drawdown	0	Profit/Loss index	74.81	% Net Profit / SODD	108806.06
System open drawdown	−0.33	Reward/Risk index	99.91	(Net P.-SODD)/Net P.	99.91
Max open trade drawdown	−25.88	Buy/Hold index	−65.05	% SODD / Net Profit	−0.09

In the Equis MetaStock® "System Report" (profit and loss summary statistics), the *Total net profit* is the sum of profits minus the sum of losses, including open positions marked to the market. In contrast, the *Amount of Winning Trades* is the sum of realized profits (the total of all gains on closed-out trades only, excluding any open positions). Similarly, the *Amount of Losing Trades* is the sum of realized losses (the total of all losses on closed-out trades only, excluding any open positions). *System close drawdown* is the largest decline in the cumulative equity line below the initial investment, based on closed-out positions only. *System open drawdown (SODD)* is the largest decline in the cumulative equity line below the initial investment when a position is open. *Max open trade drawdown* is the largest decline in the cumulative equity line below the trade entry price during the worst single trade. The *Profit/Loss Index* is a complex calculation that relates the Amount of Winning Trades to the Amount of Losing Trades on a scale of −100 (worst possible performance) to +100 (best possible performance), with zero representing profits equal to losses. *Reward/Risk Index* is the Total net profit minus System open drawdown. The resulting difference is then divided by the Total net profit. The *Buy/Hold Index* is the Total net profit minus the buy-and-hold strategy's net profit. The resulting difference is then divided by the buy-and-hold net profit. In this exercise, initial equity is assumed to be $100. Both long and short positions are taken unless otherwise noted. Trades are executed at the closing price on the signal date. Transaction costs, interest expenses, and margins are not included in the statistics.

Range: Upshaw's "Home On The Range" Price Projection Method (HOTR)

David L. Upshaw, CMT, (465 Hillcrest East, Lake Quivira, KS 66106), devised a simple way to make price range projections for a market. Using only the yearly high and low for the Dow-Jones Industrial Average (DJIA), divide the annual price low by the annual price high. Next, multiply that ratio by 100, to convert it to a percentage. Calculate a 20-year simple moving average of that percentage ratio. Compute the standard deviation; that is, the 20 percentage ratios (one for each year) minus their 20-year average, square these differences, divide by the number of observations (in this case 20), then take the square root. Most of the time, the annual price range in any year will be within one standard deviation of the average price range of the past 20 years.

The following is the custom formula for Upshaw's "Home On The Range" Price Projection Method in MetaStock® Formula Language:

```
Mov((((L/H)*100)),20,S); Stdev((L/H)*100,20)
```

Where Mov is Moving Average, L is Low for the year, H is High for the year, 20 is the number of years in the moving average, S is the symbol for Simple Moving Average, and Stdev is the Standard Deviation, again over 20 years.

This formula returns all the information we need for Upshaw's HOTR. It tells us that over the 20 years from 1980 through 2000, the low of the DJIA as a percentage of the high has averaged 79.6%. The standard deviation over the same period has been 6.2 percentage points. These numbers were fairly stable for 42 years, 1958 through 2000.

The same formula can be applied to any time period or any financial instrument. For example, substitute 99 years for 20 years in the formula, and we find that over 99 years, from 1901 to 2000, the low of the DJIA as a percentage of the high has averaged 76.3%. The standard deviation over the same period has been 10.4 percentage points. The wider range and higher standard deviation reflect the greater volatility the market exhibited in the 1920's and 1930's.

These formulas might seem to offer a readily workable rough guideline for projecting a price range. Once a year's high or low seems likely to have been established, it becomes a simple statistical exercise to project the opposite extreme of the range—just plug the numbers into the formula.

We might modify Upshaw's formula to look at annual rates-of-change of year-end closing prices, a popular pastime among forecasters. We would divide the last price of the year by the closing price one year earlier. Next, multiply that ratio fraction by 100, to convert it to a percentage. Calculate an n-period simple moving average of this percentage. Compute the standard deviation. Again, most of the time, the

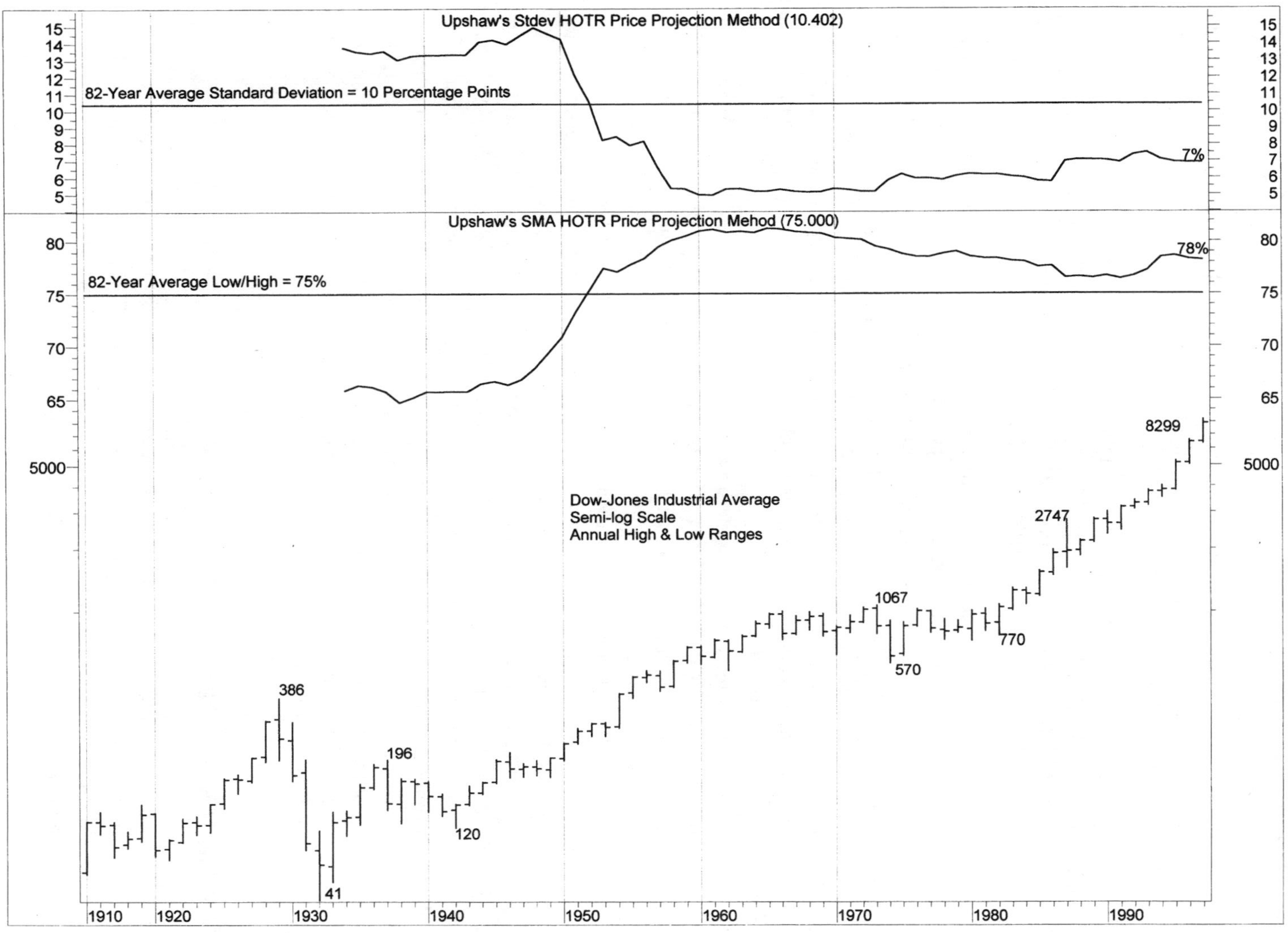

Upshaw's Stdev HOTR Price Projection Method (10.402)
82-Year Average Standard Deviation = 10 Percentage Points
7%
Upshaw's SMA HOTR Price Projection Mehod (75.000)
82-Year Average Low/High = 75%
78%
Dow-Jones Industrial Average
Semi-log Scale
Annual High & Low Ranges
386
41
196
120
1067
570
770
2747
8299
5000
65
70
75
80
5 6 7 8 9 10 11 12 13 14 15
1910
1920
1930
1940
1950
1960
1970
1980
1990

annual price change is within one standard deviation of the average price change of the past *n*-periods. The following is the custom formula using closing prices only in MetaStock® Formula Language:

```
Periods:= Input("Enter the number of periods",1,999,10);
((C/Ref(C,-1))*100)-100;
Mov((((C/Ref(C,-1))*100)-100),Periods,S);
Stdev(((C/Ref(C,-1))*100),Periods);
```

Where Periods is the number of periods you choose for the calculation, Periods are allowed to vary from one period to 999 periods (with a default value set at ten periods, since 10 years is an industry standard in performance measurement), C is the closing price, and Ref(C,-1) is the previous period's closing price.

The DJIA's rolling 10-year average annual rate of price appreciation was 16% from 1997 through 2000, an extreme level seen only once before, in 1928. That 16% growth rate was double the 99-year average of 8%. In other words, price performance was 100% above average.

The rolling 10-year standard deviation hovered around 12 percentage points from 1991 to 2000, well below the historical 89-year average of 20 and at the low end of the historical range of 38 to 10 percentage points. In other words, volatility was 40% below average.

So, the formula says that over the past century, the DJIA has gone up 8% a year on average, with a normal range of −12% to +28%, representing one standard deviation of 20 percentage points, based on 100-years of history.

This kind of simple observation is commonly mistaken for a forecast that may seem to be statistically reasonable but actually is completely naïve. Reality is a great deal more complex than a simple formula. Multiple cycles spanning a variety of time frames are continuously converging and diverging in non-linear combinations, defeating straight-line projections. Investors would be better served by technical indicators that do not even attempt to make forecasts, but rather effectively track trends to give timely signals of trend change that we can act upon to maximize our profits and minimize our losses.

The Range Indicator (TRI)

The Range Indicator (TRI) is designed to take advantage of an expanding normalized price range within an established long-term trend. TRI was introduced by Jack L. Weinberg in the June 1995 issue of *Technical Analysis of Stocks & Commodities* magazine, V13:6 (www.traders.com). TRI is based on a somewhat complex formula,

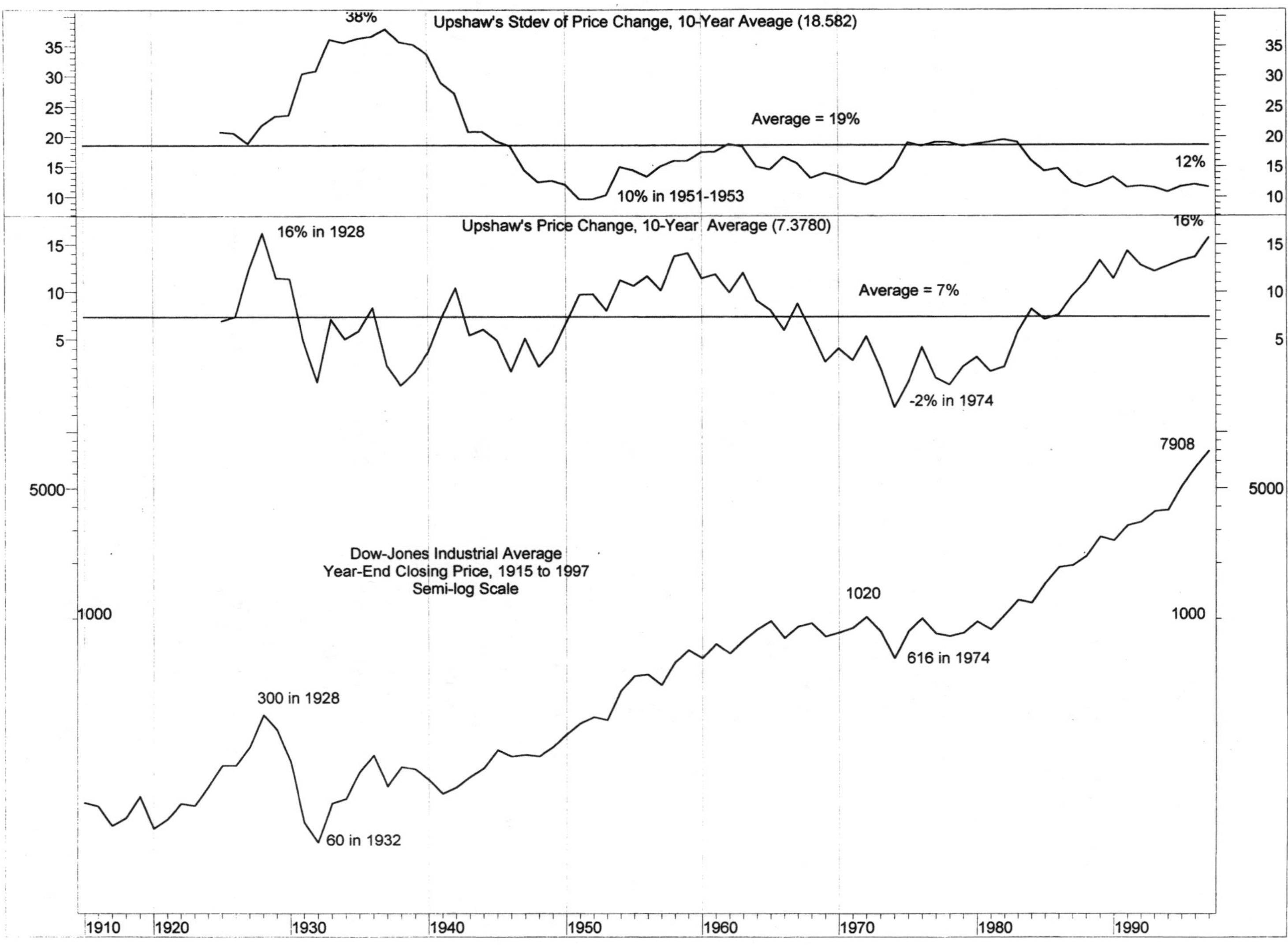

38%
Upshaw's Stdev of Price Change, 10-Year Aveage (18.582)
Average = 19%
12%
10% in 1951-1953
35
30
25
20
15
10
Upshaw's Price Change, 10-Year Average (7.3780)
16% in 1928
16%
Average = 7%
-2% in 1974
15
10
5
7908
5000
Dow-Jones Industrial Average
Year-End Closing Price, 1915 to 1997
Semi-log Scale
1020
1000
616 in 1974
300 in 1928
60 in 1932
1910
1920
1930
1940
1950
1960
1970
1980
1990

with if/then contingencies. Fortunately, the formula is a predefined function on the MetaStock® indicator menu. At its core, TRI is nothing more than a volatility measure, specifically, a normalized *Average True Range.* Used with a trend/momentum indicator, as Weinberg suggests, TRI jumps on accelerating short-term price volatility within a larger time-frame trend.

TRI is based on the basic observation that a large expansion in the average size of the daily high-low price range indicates the end of a trading range and the start of a new price trend in a market. Small daily price ranges often coincide with a dull, trend-less, trading-range bound, sideways price drift. On the other hand, a significant expansion in the daily price ranges often coincides with a new and dynamic directional price trend.

TRI may be expressed as follows:

R = the current day's True Range divided by the difference of the current closing price minus the previous day's closing price.

T = the True Range for the current day.

L = the lowest value of either T or R over the past *n* days.

H = the highest value of either T or R over the past *n* days.

C = current closing price.

P = the previous day's closing price.

n = the number of days in the calculation period.

x = the number of days in exponential moving average smoothing.

1. If C>P, then compute T/(C-P). That is, if the current closing price is greater than the previous day's closing price, then divide the current day's True Range by the current closing price minus the previous day's closing price.
2. If C<P, then calculate T. That is, if the current closing price is less than the previous day's closing price, then calculate the current day's True Range.
3. If the highest value of either Step 1 or Step 2 over the past *n* days is greater than the lowest value of either Step 1 or Step 2 over the past *n* days, then subtract the lowest value (L) from the value of either Step 1 or Step 2, whichever applies.
4. Divide the difference in Step 3 by H-L, that is, divide by the difference of H minus L.
5. Multiply the ratio from Step 4 by 100.
6. Smooth the value from Step 5 with an *x*-day exponential moving average.

Weinberg suggested interpreting TRI together with the use of an independent indicator of price trend, such as moving average crossover. Signals are taken when TRI crosses above and below certain arbitrarily defined levels. Those levels would depend on the volatility of each particular market being analyzed. The problem with that is that the number of combinations of parameters, fitted to each particular market, and allowing *n* and *x* to vary, could be staggering, making working with this indicator time consuming and complex. Moreover, we observed that the appropriate levels for TRI might drift over time, such that the user might have to adjust parameters frequently. A more adaptive approach might be to apply Moving Averages, Envelopes or Bollinger Bands to TRI to define signal thresholds. We used the simplest form, TRI above and below a trailing exponential moving average of itself, for signal generation in our Indicator Strategy Example, below.

In his published example, Weinberg used three days to compute the both of Average True Range and the Rate of Change of closing price. Weinberg used 10 days for an exponential moving average smoothing. Again, Weinberg noted that the actual appropriate number of days for basic measuring and smoothing would depend on the volatility of each particular market being analyzed.

In the predefined MetaStock® version of Range Indicator, default values are set to 10 periods for computing the normalized Average True Range and 10 days for exponential moving average smoothing. For the S&P futures, these default values appear to work better than the 3 periods Average True Range and 10-day smoothing used in Weinberg's example.

Indicator Strategy Example for the Range Indicator

A simplified version of The Range Indicator would have outperformed a simple trend-following indicator while cutting the number of losing trades in half. Based on an 18-year file of daily data for the entire history of the S&P 500 Composite Stock Price Index futures *CSI Perpetual Contract*, collected from www.csidata.com, from 4/21/82 to 12/22/00, we found that the following parameters would have produced a positive result on a purely mechanical signal basis with no subjectivity, no sophisticated technical analysis, and no judgement:

Enter Long (Buy) at the current daily price close of the S&P 500 Composite Stock Price Index futures *CSI Perpetual Contract* when it closes above its own previous day's 271-day trailing Exponential Moving Average of the closing prices and The Range Indicator (set to the MetaStock® default values of 10 periods and 10-day Exponential Smoothing) is above its previous day's 4-day trailing Exponential Moving Average of the TRI itself, thus indicating an expanding normalized price range.

Close Long (Sell) at the current daily price close of the S&P 500 Composite Stock Price Index futures *CSI Perpetual Contract* when it closes below its own previous day's 271-day trailing Exponential Moving Average of the closing prices and The Range Indicator (set to the MetaStock® default values of 10 periods and 10-day Exponential Smoothing) is above its

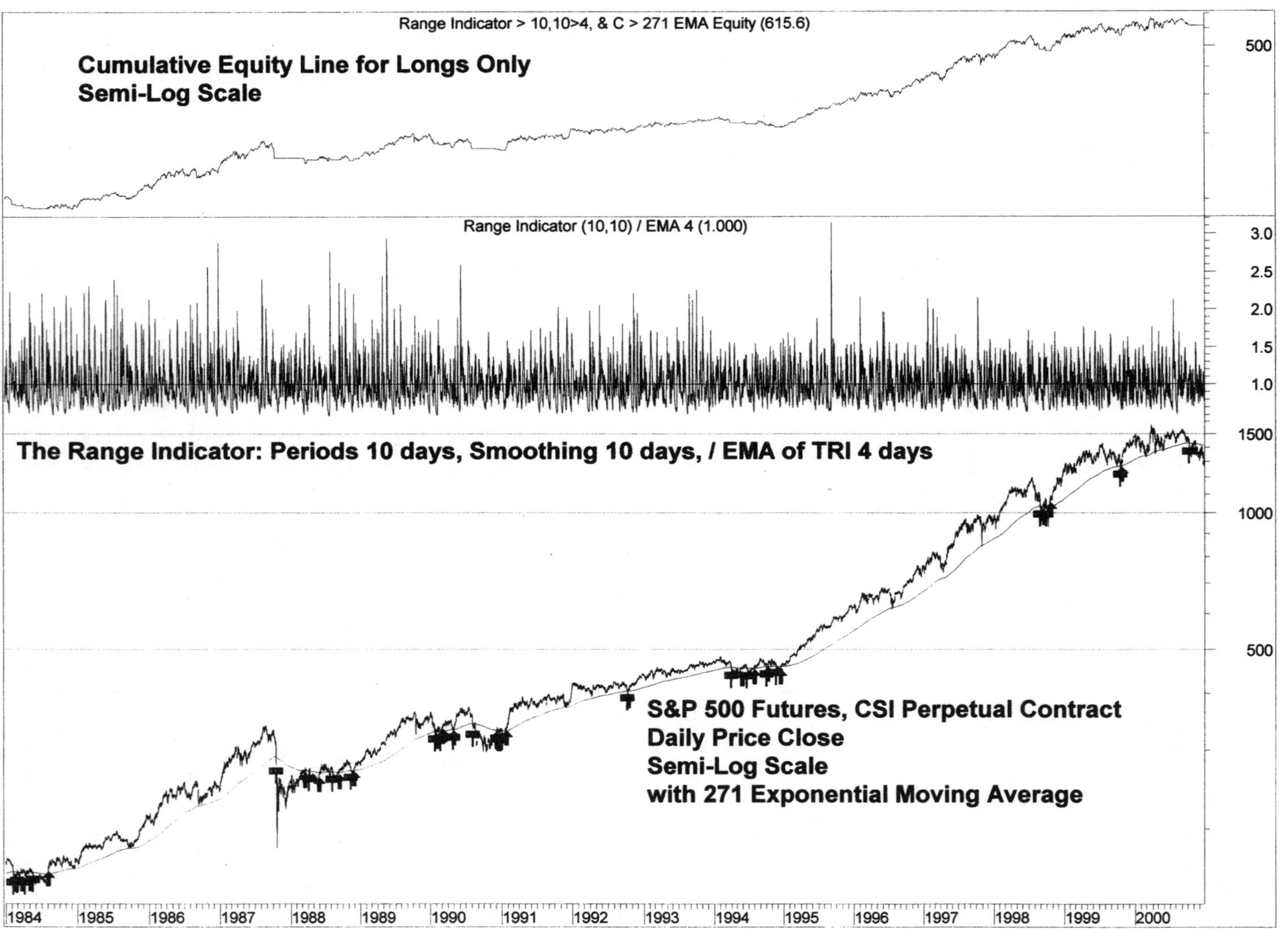

Range Indicator > 10,10>4, & C > 271 EMA Equity (615.6)
Cumulative Equity Line for Longs Only
Semi-Log Scale
500
Range Indicator (10,10) / EMA 4 (1.000)
3.0
2.5
2.0
1.5
1.0
The Range Indicator: Periods 10 days, Smoothing 10 days, / EMA of TRI 4 days
1500
1000
500
S&P 500 Futures, CSI Perpetual Contract
Daily Price Close
Semi-Log Scale
with 271 Exponential Moving Average
1984
1985
1986
1987
1988
1989
1990
1991
1992
1993
1994
1995
1996
1997
1998
1999
2000

The Range Indicator (10 & 10, Cross 4 EMA)

Total net profit	515.6	Open position value	N/A	Net Profit / Buy&Hold %	−49.82
Percent gain/loss	515.6	Annual percent gain/loss	27.59	Annual Net % / B&H %	−49.82
Initial investment	100	Interest earned	0		
Current position	Out	Date position entered	10/6/00		
Buy/Hold profit	1027.4	Days in test	6821	# of days per trade	284.21
Buy/Hold pct gain/loss	1027.4	Annual B/H pct gain/loss	54.98		
Total closed trades	24	Commissions paid	0		
Avg profit per trade	21.48	Avg Win/Avg Loss ratio	26.84		
Total long trades	24	Total short trades	0	Long Win Trade %	33.33
Winning long trades	8	Winning short trades	0	Short Win Trade %	#DIV/0!
Total winning trades	8	Total losing trades	16	Total Win Trade %	33.33
Amount of winning trades	557.1	Amount of losing trades	−41.51	Net Profit Margin %	86.13
Average win	69.64	Average loss	−2.59	Average P. Margin %	92.83
Largest win	265.27	Largest loss	−6.26	% Net / (Win + Loss)	95.39
Average length of win	421.25	Average length of loss	29.44	(Win − Loss) / Loss %	1330.88
Longest winning trade	934	Longest losing trade	185	(Win − Loss) / Loss %	404.86
Most consecutive wins	2	Most consecutive losses	6	(Win − Loss) / Loss %	−66.67
Total bars out	930	Average length out	37.2		
Longest out period	273				
System close drawdown	−9.13	Profit/Loss index	92.55	% Net Profit / SODD	5250.51
System open drawdown	−9.82	Reward/Risk index	98.13	(Net P.-SODD)/Net P.	98.10
Max open trade drawdown	−8.79	Buy/Hold index	−49.82	% SODD / Net Profit	−1.90

In the Equis MetaStock® "System Report" (profit and loss summary statistics), the *Total net profit* is the sum of profits minus the sum of losses, including open positions marked to the market. In contrast, the *Amount of Winning Trades* is the sum of realized profits (the total of all gains on closed-out trades only, excluding any open positions). Similarly, the *Amount of Losing Trades* is the sum of realized losses (the total of all losses on closed-out trades only, excluding any open positions). *System close drawdown* is the largest decline in the cumulative equity line below the initial investment, based on closed-out positions only. *System open drawdown (SODD)* is the largest decline in the cumulative equity line below the initial investment when a position is open. *Max open trade drawdown* is the largest decline in the cumulative equity line below the trade entry price during the worst single trade. The *Profit/Loss Index* is a complex calculation that relates the Amount of Winning Trades to the Amount of Losing Trades on a scale of −100 (worst possible performance) to +100 (best possible performance), with zero representing profits equal to losses. *Reward/Risk Index* is the Total net profit minus System open drawdown. The resulting difference is then divided by the Total net profit. The *Buy/Hold Index* is the Total net profit minus the buy-and-hold strategy's net profit. The resulting difference is then divided by the buy-and-hold net profit. In this exercise, initial equity is assumed to be $100. Both long and short positions are taken unless otherwise noted. Trades are executed at the closing price on the signal date. Transaction costs, interest expenses, and margins are not included in the statistics.

previous day's 4-day trailing Exponential Moving Average of the TRI itself, thus indicating an expanding normalized price range.

Enter Short (Sell Short) never.

Starting with $100 and reinvesting profits, total net profits for the Range Indicator strategy would have been $515.60, assuming a fully invested strategy, reinvestment of profits, no transactions costs and no taxes. This would have been 49.82 percent less than buy-and-hold. No short selling would have been profitable, and no short selling was included in the strategy. This long-only Range Indicator strategy would have given profitable buy signals 33.33% of the time. Trading would have been relatively inactive at one trade every 284.21 calendar days.

The Equis International MetaStock® System Testing rules are written as follows:

Enter long: CLOSE > Ref(Mov(CLOSE,opt1,E),-1) AND
RangeIndicator(opt2,opt3)>
Ref(Mov(RangeIndicator(opt2,opt3),opt4,E),-1)

Close long: CLOSE < Ref(Mov(CLOSE,opt1,E),-1) AND
RangeIndicator(opt2,opt3)>
Ref(Mov(RangeIndicator(opt2,opt3),opt4,E),-1)

OPT1 Current value: 271

OPT2 Current value: 10

OPT3 Current value: 10

OPT4 Current value: 4

Rate of Change (ROC)

Rate of Change is a common expression of price velocity, or "momentum". Generally, ROC is computed by dividing the current price by the price n-periods ago. For example, if the current price is 100 and the price 18-weeks ago was 80, then the 18-week Rate of Change is 100/80 or 1.25. Next, technicians commonly subtract 1.00 and multiply by 100 to change the scaling to percentage points of price change over the time interval selected. (Momentum is sometimes expressed as the current price *minus* the price n-weeks ago, but that creates problems with comparable scaling over time as price levels change.)

Commonly, when the percentage Rate of Change is greater than zero, that is taken as a signal that price velocity exhibits positive trend momentum and that is bullish. The point at which Rate of Change crosses above zero is taken as a buy signal. But when Rate of Change crosses below zero, that is a sell signal, and it means trend momentum has turned bearish.

The major problem with Rate of Change is that it jumps around erratically. It is as dependent on the old, obsolete data dropping off the moving *n*-period calculation window as it is sensitive to fresh data coming in. A large change in the market *n*-periods ago will cause the ROC to jump wildly even if the current market is unchanged. This is a big mistake. ROC produces more than its fair share of bad signals and is not recommended as a technical indicator. There are much better indicators to choose from.

Indicator Strategy Example for ROC

Based on a 101-year file of weekly data for the DJIA from January 1900 to December 2000, we found that the following parameters would have produced a positive result on a purely mechanical trend-following signal basis with no subjectivity, no sophisticated technical analysis, and no judgement:

Enter Long (Buy) at the current end-of-week price close of the DJIA when the ROC over the past 18 weeks is greater than zero.

Close Long (Sell) at the current end-of-week price close of the DJIA when the ROC over the past 18 weeks is less than zero.

Enter Short (Sell Short) never.

Starting with $100 and reinvesting profits, total net profits for this ROC trend-following strategy would have been $91,674.62, assuming a fully invested strategy, reinvestment of profits, no transactions costs and no taxes. This would have been 305.37 percent greater than buy-and-hold. No short selling would have been profitable, and no short selling was included in the strategy. Long-only ROC as an indicator would have given profitable buy signals 43.06% of the time. Trading would have been relatively inactive at one trade every 176.43 calendar days.

The Equis International MetaStock® System Testing rules are written as follows:

Enter long: ROC(C,opt1,%)>0

Close long: ROC(C,opt1,%)<0

OPT1 Current value: 18

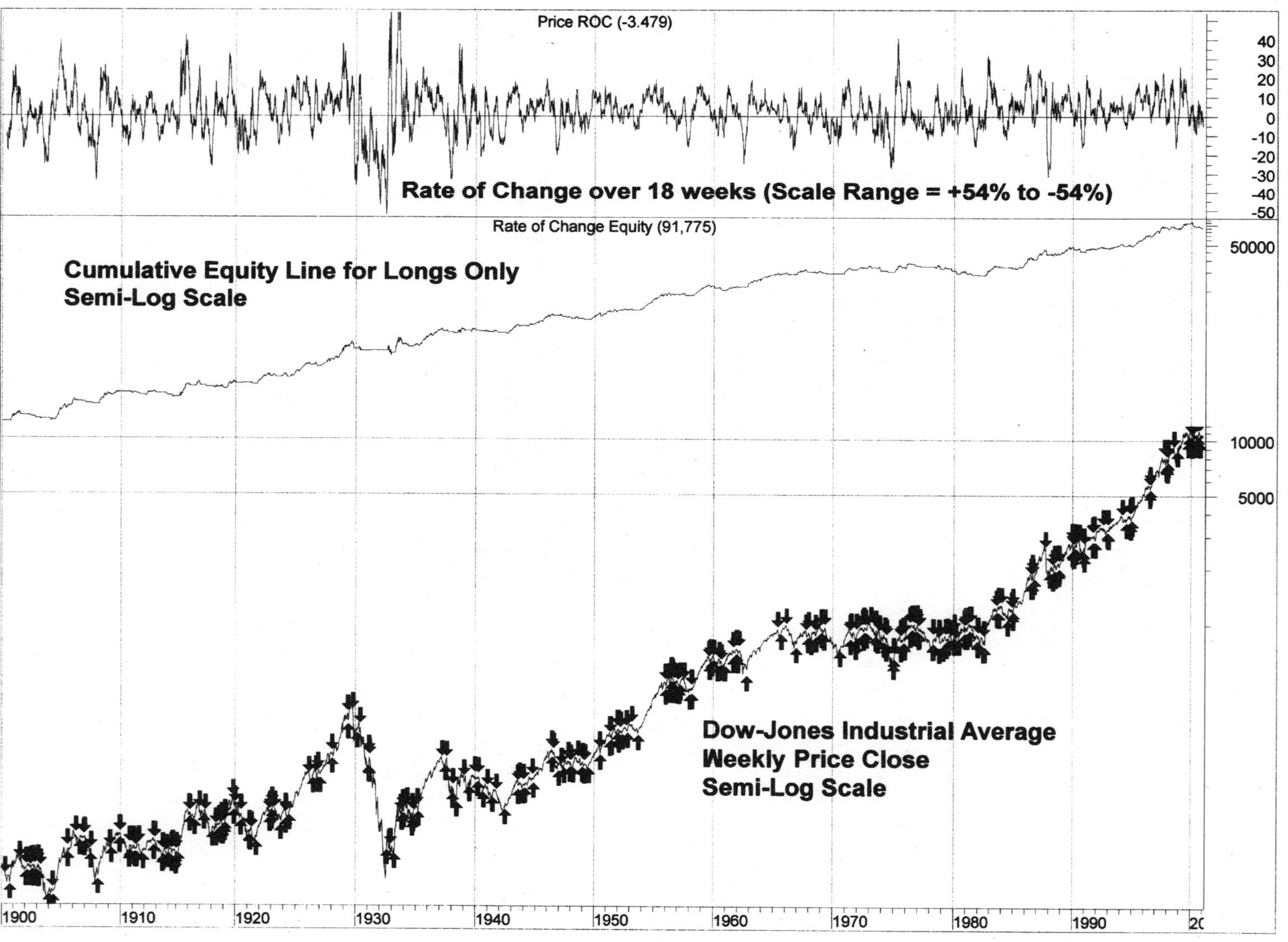

Price ROC (-3.479)
40
30
20
10
0
-10
-20
-30
-40
-50
Rate of Change over 18 weeks (Scale Range = +54% to -54%)
Rate of Change Equity (91,775)
Cumulative Equity Line for Longs Only
Semi-Log Scale
50000
10000
5000
Dow-Jones Industrial Average
Weekly Price Close
Semi-Log Scale
1900
1910
1920
1930
1940
1950
1960
1970
1980
1990

Rate of Change, 18 weeks

Total net profit	91674.62	Open position value	N/A	Net Profit / Buy&Hold %	305.37
Percent gain/loss	91674.62	Annual percent gain/loss	907.45	Annual Net % / B&H %	305.36
Initial investment	100	Interest earned	0		
Current position	Out	Date position entered	11/10/00		
Buy/Hold profit	22614.89	Days in test	36874	# of days per trade	176.43
Buy/Hold pct gain/loss	22614.89	Annual B/H pct gain/loss	223.86		
Total closed trades	209	Commissions paid	0		
Avg profit per trade	438.63	Avg Win/Avg Loss ratio	3.34		
Total long trades	209	Total short trades	0	Long Win Trade %	43.06
Winning long trades	90	Winning short trades	0	Short Win Trade %	#DIV/0!
Total winning trades	90	Total losing trades	119	Total Win Trade %	43.06
Amount of winning trades	151696.02	Amount of losing trades	−60021.39	Net Profit Margin %	43.30
Average win	1685.51	Average loss	−504.38	Average P. Margin %	53.94
Largest win	24342.23	Largest loss	−5507.92	% Net / (Win + Loss)	63.10
Average length of win	28.69	Average length of loss	7.18	(Win − Loss) / Loss %	299.58
Longest winning trade	137	Longest losing trade	26	(Win − Loss) / Loss %	426.92
Most consecutive wins	4	Most consecutive losses	8	(Win − Loss) / Loss %	−50.00
Total bars out	2230	Average length out	10.62		
Longest out period	75				
System close drawdown	0	Profit/Loss index	60.43	% Net Profit / SODD	#DIV/0!
System open drawdown	0	Reward/Risk index	100	(Net P.-SODD)/Net P.	100.00
Max open trade drawdown	−5507.92	Buy/Hold index	305.37	% SODD / Net Profit	0.00

In the Equis MetaStock® "System Report" (profit and loss summary statistics), the *Total net profit* is the sum of profits minus the sum of losses, including open positions marked to the market. In contrast, the *Amount of Winning Trades* is the sum of realized profits (the total of all gains on closed-out trades only, excluding any open positions). Similarly, the *Amount of Losing Trades* is the sum of realized losses (the total of all losses on closed-out trades only, excluding any open positions). *System close drawdown* is the largest decline in the cumulative equity line below the initial investment, based on closed-out positions only. *System open drawdown (SODD)* is the largest decline in the cumulative equity line below the initial investment when a position is open. *Max open trade drawdown* is the largest decline in the cumulative equity line below the trade entry price during the worst single trade. The *Profit/Loss Index* is a complex calculation that relates the Amount of Winning Trades to the Amount of Losing Trades on a scale of −100 (worst possible performance) to +100 (best possible performance), with zero representing profits equal to losses. *Reward/Risk Index* is the Total net profit minus System open drawdown. The resulting difference is then divided by the Total net profit. The *Buy/Hold Index* is the Total net profit minus the buy-and-hold strategy's net profit. The resulting difference is then divided by the buy-and-hold net profit. In this exercise, initial equity is assumed to be $100. Both long and short positions are taken unless otherwise noted. Trades are executed at the closing price on the signal date. Transaction costs, interest expenses, and margins are not included in the statistics.

Relative Strength (Ratio Analysis)

Relative strength analysis is a powerful tool for stock selection and timing. Two methods of analyzing relative strength are the traditional ratio method and the computerized screening method. The traditional ratio method precisely quantifies the price strength of each investment instrument or index compared to another instrument or index. Relative strength analysis is not limited to stock prices but also is applied to the prices of commodities, currencies, and anything that trades. Naturally, relative strength is productively applied to industry groups and broader sectors. *(See Sector Rotation.)*

The screening method compares and ranks each instrument or index to a much larger universe of all relevant instruments and indexes. The relative strength screening method is particularly flexible, since anything that trades can be compared to anything else that trades or to everything else that trades.

Published research studies conducted over many decades of actual historical stock price data show that a stock that is behaving well relative to the larger market probably will continue to outperform. Conversely, a stock that is behaving poorly relative to the market likely will continue to underperform.

The Traditional Ratio Method for Analysis of Relative Strength

As a common example of the ratio method, we simply divide a particular stock's price by a market index, mostly typically, the S&P 500 Composite Stock Price Index. Alternately, we may divide the stock's price by any index of significance to that stock, such as a related industry or sector index. The resulting ratio is plotted like a typical price/time line chart, but with relative strength on the vertical y-axis and time on the horizontal x-axis.

The resulting *relative strength ratio line* can be analyzed using all the established technical methods, including trendlines, moving averages, patterns, momentum oscillators, divergences, and so on. A rising relative strength trend simply tells us that the stock is outperforming the market. Note that a stock could actually go down in price while at the same time its relative strength ratio is rising, so long as the general market index (the ratio's denominator) goes down proportionately more than the stock's price (the ratio's numerator). This would imply that the stock has a better demand/supply balance than the general market. On the bearish side, a falling relative strength trend says that the that the stock has a worse demand/supply balance than the general market.

Technical analysts compare the pure price trend and momentum of a stock to its own relative strength line's trend and momentum, looking for either an "all-clear" confirmation of trend continuation or a "warning" divergence of possible trend

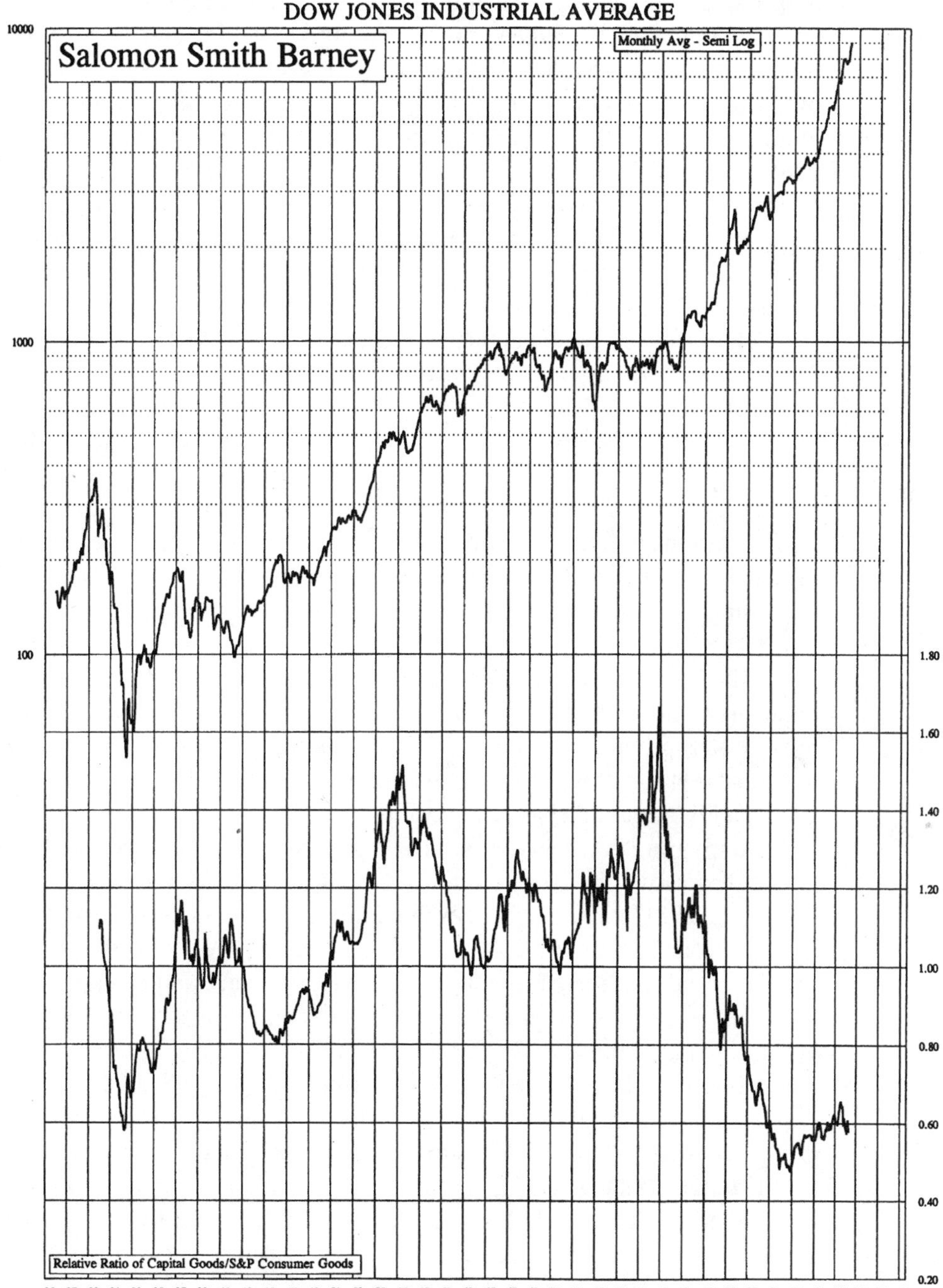

Chart by permission of Salomon Smith Barney.

change ahead. When both the pure price trend and the relative strength ratio line are both rising and making new highs, indications are all-clear, or in gear, for bullish trend continuation. But when price is making a new high and the relative strength ratio line fails to make a new high, that clearly says that investors prefer other stocks over that stock, and that can be an early warning of possible price trouble ahead. Aggressive traders will start to liquidate the stock at this first sign of trouble, while patient long-term holders may wait for the price trend to turn down as well, thus, confirming the deteriorating relative strength ratio line. Conversely, in bearish markets, when the relative strength ratio line turns upward, that is an early indication of a possible better price trend ahead, but again the odds of being correct are better when the price trend also confirms by turning upward.

There is a solid rational behind this analysis. In the later stages of a bear market, for example, "strong-hands" investors begin to accumulate the stocks they have the most confidence in, placing large bids that support the prices, so that the prices of the best, most desirable stocks stabilize before most other stocks. Thus, the best stocks begin to outperform a falling general market, causing their relative strength ratio lines to rise. Conversely, well into a bull market, "smart-money" investors anticipating future conditions will begin to offer out large quantities of the stocks they lack confidence in, putting lids on those stocks' price appreciation even as the general market is still rising. This supply causes the relative strength ratio lines of such stocks to turn down.

Alan R. Shaw, CMT, observes that relative strength often runs in long secular trends that can persist for many years. Stocks and industry groups in strong technical relative strength uptrends are likely to continue to outperform the market until both price and relative strength lose momentum and change direction on a major-trend basis. That kind of trend change generally takes months to develop. Conversely, stocks and groups in major negative relative strength trends can underperform the broad market for many years. Shaw divides the prices of stocks and industry group indexes by the S&P 500 Index, he analyzes these ratios in conjunction with the raw price data, and he constantly watches for tandem confirmation (suggesting the continuation of an existing trend) or divergence (suggesting a significant trend change).

One of Shaw's favorite relative strength charts appears on page 601. The upper half of the page shows a 72-year monthly price line chart of the DJIA from 1926 to 1998. The lower half of the page shows, from 1930 to 1998, a 68-year monthly traditional relative strength ratio line of the price of the S&P Capital Goods stock industry groups divided by the S&P Consumer Goods stock industry groups. Despite obvious cyclical noise (that is, the smaller swings lasting a few months), the persistence of long-term, secular relative strength trends is evident. The two longest lasting directional moves lasted 11 and 12 years. Four full cycles, low to low, lasted 14, 17, 8, and 21 years.

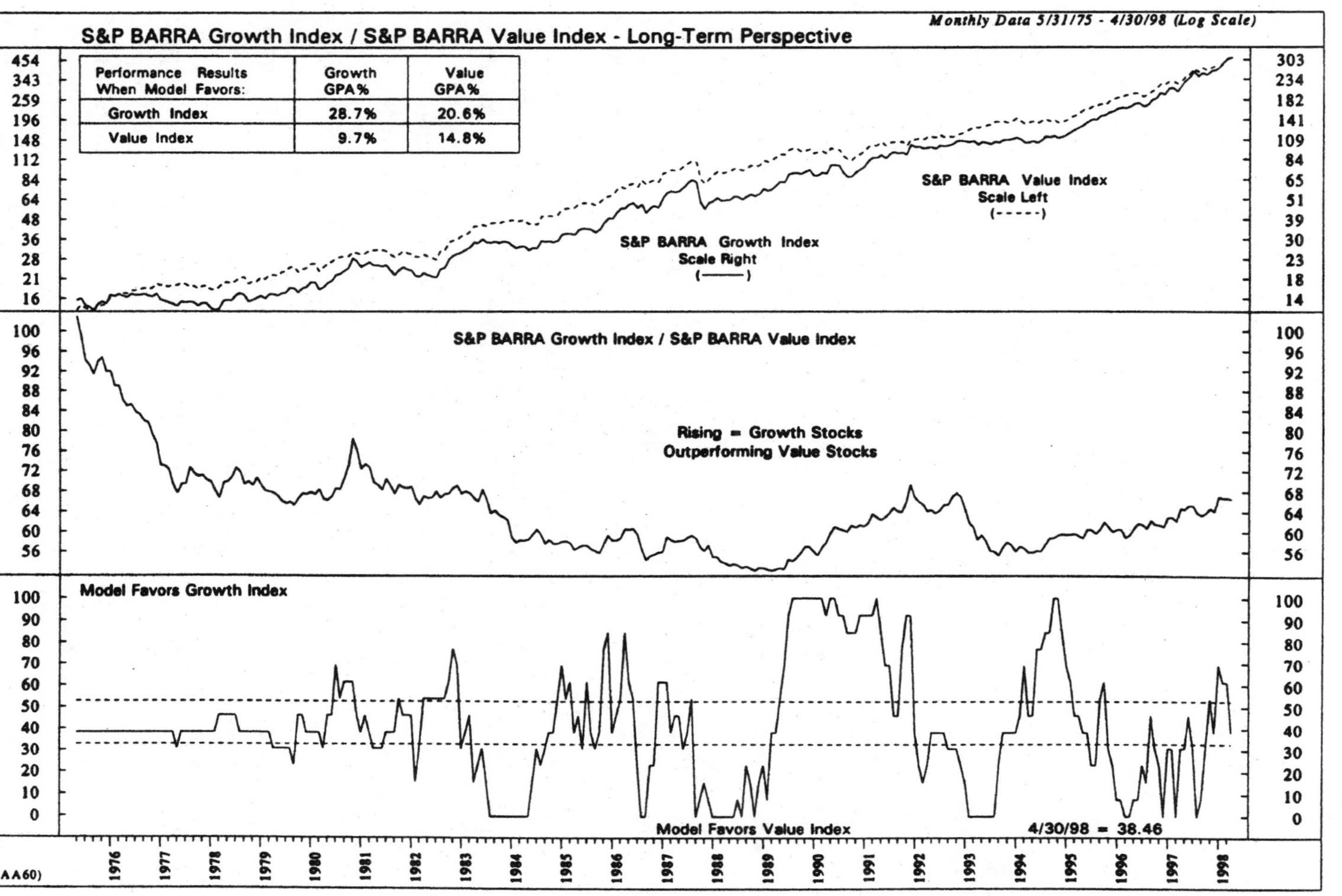
S&P BARRA Growth Index / S&P BARRA Value Index - Long-Term Perspective
Monthly Data 5/31/75 - 4/30/98 (Log Scale)
Performance Results When Model Favors:
Growth GPA%
Value GPA%
Growth Index 28.7% 20.6%
Value Index 9.7% 14.8%
S&P BARRA Value Index Scale Left (-----)
S&P BARRA Growth Index Scale Right (——)
454 343 259 196 148 112 84 64 48 36 28 21 16
303 234 182 141 109 84 65 51 39 30 23 18 14
S&P BARRA Growth Index / S&P BARRA Value Index
Rising = Growth Stocks Outperforming Value Stocks
100 96 92 88 84 80 76 72 68 64 60 56
Model Favors Growth Index
Model Favors Value Index
4/30/98 = 38.46
100 90 80 70 60 50 40 30 20 10 0
1976 1977 1978 1979 1980 1981 1982 1983 1984 1985 1986 1987 1988 1989 1990 1991 1992 1993 1994 1995 1996 1997 1998
(AA60)

Chart by permission of Ned Davis Research.

The Ned Davis Research chart on page 603 shows the relative strength ratio of growth stocks divided by value stocks. Growth stocks outperformed value stocks for many years until 1974 (not shown). Growth stocks underperformed value stocks for 14 years from 1974 to 1988. Then, growth stocks outperformed value stocks again for 12 years from 1988 to 2000. Clearly, major relative strength trends can run in long cycles.

This ratio method of analysis is most useful to professional technical analysts and portfolio managers, and it can be useful to anyone following a moderately sized universe of closely analyzed stocks. The ratio method may be time-consuming and impractical, however, for screening many thousands of stocks and other instruments using consistent and objective criteria. Moreover, the traditional technical methods of chart interpretation may be subject to the analyst's personal experiences, preferences, bias, and judgments. To overcome these deficiencies, technical analysts devised the computerized screening method for analyzing relative strength.

The Screening Method for Analysis of Relative Strength

Many analysts prefer the screening method over the ratio method. With the computerized screening method's predefined criteria programmed into a computer, any financial instrument can be quantitatively measured and ranked, quickly and objectively, against many thousands of competing instruments. For example, the entire universe of all stocks, all futures, all commodities and all currencies can be efficiently ranked form best to worst relative strength performance.

The most prominent advocate of the screening method is Charles D. Kirkpatrick, CMT. He is widely recognized for his research on relative strength, which he has studied intensively for several decades, since the late 1960's, when he and Robert A. Levy, Ph.D., worked together on a variety of experiments in technical forecasting. Kirkpatrick's current relative strength model, which he has published continuously since 1982, has outperformed the S&P 500 by more than four to one.

Kirkpatrick's screening method ranks 5,000 stocks each week by their relative strength, from strongest to weakest. Every stock's recent performance is compared against the whole universe of stocks, over a constant, pre-defined specific time period.

Kirkpatrick's method of measuring relative price performance is to divide the closing price each Thursday by the trailing 26-week moving average of those weekly prices. Then that ratio for each stock is ranked against the comparable calculations for all other stocks, forming a list of stocks ordered by performance from strongest to weakest. The top percentiles of the list represent the top performing stocks, those with the highest relative strength. Conversely, the bottom percentiles of the list represent the worst performing stocks, those with the lowest relative strength. The midpoint of the list shows the median past performance.

Kirkpatrick has found through exhaustive back-testing confirmed by long real-time experience that the time interval over which relative strength screening is calculated is critical. As he varied the time window, both shorter and longer, statistical significance declined. Particularly, the shortest time periods, less than six weeks, produce consistently negative results, thus confirming the established wisdom of the pioneer technicians, such as Charles Dow, who taught that the shorter-term trends are more noisy.

Focusing on the strongest stocks is the basis of the sometimes wildly popular "momentum investing," that is, buying those stocks with the highest upside price velocity without regard to any other considerations. This speculative style, taken to extremes, leads to Alan Greenspan's "irrational exuberance," or excessive stock price valuations. Precisely where the momentum game runs out of steam has proven to be difficult to pinpoint in actual practice. Kirkpatrick acknowledges that stock prices can be driven to unsustainable extremes. There is always some danger of buying at a top or selling at a bottom when following relative strength. Moreover, when the trend reverses, an extended stock can revert to its mean quickly, taking away months of price progress in a matter of days. Long observation suggests, however, that more often the strongest stocks remain strong to the very end of a bull market, even after the general market already has begun a cyclical decline. The strongest stocks often are the last to be hit by selling in the more advanced stages of a general market decline.

Kirkpatrick's method has been extensively tested and found to be statistically significant in academic literature. See Robert A. Levy, Ph.D., the *Journal of Finance,* December 1967, pages 595-610. More recently, the value of Kirkpatrick's screening method was recognized by Narasimhan Jegadeesh and Sheridan Titman, "Returns to Buying Winners and Selling Losers: Implications for Stock Market Efficiency," *Journal of Finance,* vol. XLVIII, No. 1, March 1993, pages 65–91.

Kirkpatrick's research is available through Kirkpatrick & Company, Inc., 7669 County Road 502, Bayfield, CO, 81122, e-mail: kirkco@capecod.net.

Relative Price Strength (RS) Ratings for thousands of stocks are available each day in *Investor's Business Daily* financial newspaper. According to publisher William J. O'Neil, he calculates each stock's price change over the latest year, then he ranks this price velocity against all other stocks. These RS ranks are expressed on a percentile scale, with 99 representing the strongest price performers and 1 the worst price velocity. For example, a stock with an 80 RS Rating outperformed 80% of all other stocks over the past year and, based on this above-average RS, is a possible buy candidate. Stocks dropping below a 70 RS Rating show weakening relative price performance and might be possible sell candidates. Stocks with high RS Ratings have greater upside potential, while stocks with low RS Ratings are more vulnerable to disappointments. The average RS Rating in O'Neil's models of the Greatest Stock Market Winners was 87 before these stocks made their biggest price advances. O'Neil has had best results combining RS with chart interpretation, catching stocks with high RS just as they are beginning to emerge from a base-building pattern. When RS is extremely high and the price is extended relative to its base, it is time to sell. (O'Neil, William J., *How to Make Money in Stocks: a Winning System in Good Times or Bad,* McGraw-Hill, New York, 1991, 248 pages.)

Published studies suggest that the strong tend to grow stronger and the weak tend to become weaker over long-term time intervals measured in months and years. Independent academic research confirms that momentum strategies are most profitable at the medium time horizon, 3 to 12 months, according to Conrad and Kaul, "An Anatomy of Trading Strategies", *The Review of Financial Studies,* volume 11, Fall 1998, pages 489–519.

Top-ranked stocks by relative price strength rose in price at a 70% annual rate over the past 15 years, four times faster than the 18% annual rate recorded by Value Line's top-ranked stocks (by both earnings and price momentum), and 4.5 times faster than the 15.6% annual price appreciation of the S&P 500 index, according to data provided by Samuel Eisenstadt, Research Chairman of the Value Line Investment Survey, *Value Line Selection & Opinion,* Value Line Publishing, Inc., 220 East 42nd Street, New York, NY 10017-5891, January 28, 2000, pages 5099-5114. The 35-year average performance of Value Line's top Timeliness stocks (highest earnings and price momentum) is more than 20%, compounded annually, 2.4 times faster than the S&P 500 market price appreciation of 8.4%. All data is exclusive of transactions costs, dividends and taxes.

Past performance is a good indicator of future performance, according to Jonathan Clements, "Hot Stocks Are Sizzling on Momentum", *The Wall Street Journal,* September 7, 1999, page C1. If a stock has dazzling performance one year, there is a good chance it will post better-than-average performance the next. "Winners continue to win, but losers really continue to lose," says Tobias Moskowitz, Professor of Finance at the University of Chicago. The reason may be that investors are slow to react to new information, and analysts tend to change their earnings estimates too gradually in an attempt to avoid the career risk of going too far out on a limb, according to John Bogel, Jr., president of Bogel Investment Management. Also, with mutual funds, last year's top-performing funds often continue to outperform, according to a study by Mark Carhart, co-head of quantitative research for Goldman Sachs Asset Management, published in the March 1997 *Journal of Finance.* This study was based on stock-fund performance for the 31 years ended December 1993. The top 10% funds in one year did noticeably better than average the next year. But funds in the bottom 10% lagged badly the subsequent year. The top performers earned an average of eight percentage points per year more than the worst performing funds. Moreover, there is a strong tendency for the worst performers to continue trailing, and this bad performance often persisted until the funds were liquidated or merged. The poor performers tended to be funds that charge high expenses and trade rapidly. Another study by Sheldon Jacobs, editor of *No-load Fund Investor* newsletter, found that buying the top diversified no-load fund each year returned 22.2% annually over the past 23 years, and that was 48% better than the 15% return of the average U.S. diversified fund. Mark Carhart suggests that persistence of relative performance of funds reflects more the continued momentum in the underlying stocks, rather than any particular actions by fund management. Clements concludes that investors need not be afraid to buy stocks that have performed well, and they should not be anxious to buy stocks that have been crushed.

"Keep momentum on your side, by hanging onto winning investments, while dumping your losers quickly. Academic research suggests that the best performing stocks and funds in any given year often enjoy good results in the year that follows. Meanwhile, losing positions tend to keep on losing," according to Jonathan Clements, "Rules for When You Shred the Rules", *The Wall Street Journal,* January 25, 2000, page C1. Clements quotes investment researcher James P. O'Shaughnessy, chairman of O'Shaughnessy Capital Management in Greenwich, CT, "Let the momentum work for you. If you've got five stocks and two are winning, sell the other three and concentrate your money on the ones that are winning. And the minute you see a break in the momentum, get out." Clements adds, "This is also the smartest tax strategy . . . By hanging onto your winners, you delay the capital-gains tax bill, while selling losers generates a loss that can be used to reduce your taxes."

The top investment strategies "buy stocks with the best relative price strength," O'Shaughnessy concludes. On a risk adjusted basis, the worst performing strategy is buying the stocks with the worst 1-year performance. "Avoid last year's biggest price losers at all costs—their record over the last 40 years is abysmal." For further details on his research and a detailed bibliography of serious books and papers on investment returns and risks, see O'Shaughnessy, James P., *What Works on Wall Street,* Revised Edition, McGraw-Hill, New York, 1998.

Kirkpatrick Finds that Relative Strength Substantially Outperforms the Market

Relative price strength works well with real-time, unseen data over the long-term, according to Charles D. Kirkpatrick II, CMT. (See Kirkpatrick, C. D., "Stock Selection: A Test of Relative Stock Values Reported over 17.5 Years", www.mta.org, 2001.)

In summary, in July 1982, Kirkpatrick established stock selection and deletion criteria and determined the performance measurement method (equally weighting each stock each week) for his first study, which he named "List 1". From July 1982 to December 31, 2000, List 1 had appreciated 5,086.6%, versus a 1,087.6% gain for the S&P 500, and a 221.9% gain for the Value Line Geometric. During that 17.5 year period, both List 1 and the S&P 500 suffered three down years, compared to seven down years for the Value Line Geometric. List 1 stock selection criteria included three variables: high relative price strength, high relative earnings growth, and a strong chart pattern.

In January 1999, Kirkpatrick started "List 2," which, as of December 31, 2000, had appreciated 137.3%, versus a gain of 7.41% for the S&P 500, and a loss of 9.99% for Value Line Geometric. List 2 had no down years, compared to one down year for the S&P and two down years for the Value Line Geometric. The selection criteria for List 2 also included three variables: high relative price strength, high earnings growth, and a low relative price-to-sales ratio (PSR). List 2 also substantially outperformed List 1, which gained 75.19% over the same 2-year period, 1999 and 2000.

Kirkpatrick's testing did not include dividends and transaction costs. Kirkpatrick published each list each week in *Kirkpatrick's Institutional Market Strategist,* Kirkpatrick & Company, Inc., 7669 County Road 502, Bayfield, CO, 81122, e-mail: kirkco@capecod.net.

List 2 was added in 1999 to supplement List 1, which continued on exactly as before. For List 1, the strong chart pattern criterion was designed to function as a stop-loss on negative price action, but later tests of the simple price pattern alone showed no discernible advantage was gained. So, List 2 was begun using an alternate risk-reduction approach, selecting only those stocks trading at low relative price to sales ratios. Compared to List 1, List 2 offered three advantages over the two years of real-time testing:

- Portfolio volatility declined nearly in half, with a portfolio beta consistently below one for List 2, versus a portfolio beta often approaching two for List 1.
- Turnover declined and average holding period more than doubled, to well over a year for List 2, up from 22 weeks for List 1.
- The size of the List 2 portfolio was considerably smaller and more manageable, 5 to 15 stocks for List 2, versus up to 80 stocks for List 1.

Relative Price Strength Rank was defined as each stock's price performance measured equally against all other stocks' price performance. The ratio of each stock's current price divided by its own trailing 26-week moving average was ranked against the equivalent ratios of all other stocks, with the highest ratios and the highest percentile ranks representing the highest relative strength. Thus, the 99th percentile represented the strongest stock and the 0 percentile represented the weakest. The closing price used each week was the Thursday close. A stock was eliminated from both lists when relative price strength declined to or below the 30th percentile.

Relative Earnings Growth was defined as the 1-year rate of change of a moving four-quarter average. As with relative price strength, the rate of change of earnings for each stock was ranked against the rate of change of earnings for all other stocks. High ranking stocks were chosen for both lists. A stock was eliminated from List 1 when relative earnings growth declined to or below the top 80th percentile. A stock was eliminated from List 2 when relative earnings growth declined to or below the 50th percentile.

For List 1 only, Chart Pattern was defined as *advancing* if the latest price directional movement was above the two most recent previous high price pivots, and only those advancing stocks were considered for selection. The Chart Pattern was *declining* if the latest price directional movement was below the two most recent low price pivots, and those declining stocks were eliminated.

For List 2 only, a requirement for addition to the list was a Relative Price/Sales Ratio (PSR) at or below the 30th percentile. The lower the PSR the greater the potential for positive surprise. The higher the PSR the higher the risk. O'Shaughnessy (1998) argues that the PSR is the most reliable method of selecting stocks for long term appreciation. (O'Shaughnessy, James P., *What Works on Wall Street: A Guide to the Best-Performing Investment Strategies of All Time,* McGraw-Hill, New York, 1998.) The basic PSR is the current weekly close price divided by the last reported four-quarters sales. PSR was not included in List 2 deletion criteria.

Each week the entire list of available U.S. stocks (usually around 5,000) was screened by the above criteria. Any stock not already on the list that met the selection criteria was added to the list.

For List 1 only, a stock was eliminated when relative price strength declined to or below the 30th percentile, when relative earnings growth declined to or below the top 80th percentile, or when the stock price chart pattern broke two previous lower reversal points.

For List 2 only, a stock was eliminated when relative price strength declined to or below the 30th percentile, or when relative earnings growth declined to or below the 50th percentile. (Relative Price/Sales Ratio was not included in deletion criteria.)

Relative Strength Index (RSI)

The Relative Strength Index (RSI) is one of the most popular price momentum indicators. RSI is misnamed, since it has nothing to do with the well-established technical analysis concept of Relative Strength, which compares the price of one financial instrument or index with another. RSI was first described by J. Welles Wilder, Jr., in his 1978 book, *New Concepts in Technical Trading Systems* (Trend Research, PO Box 128, McLeansville, NC 27301). Mathematically, RSI is represented as:

$$RSI = 100 - (100/(1+RS))$$

where

RS is the ratio of the exponentially smoothed moving average of n-period gains divided by the absolute value (i.e., ignoring sign) of the exponentially smoothed moving average of n-period losses.

An example calculating RSI follows on pages 616–617.

As you can see by the formula, RSI does not relate any security to any other security. Rather, RSI quantifies price momentum. It depends solely on the changes in closing prices. Despite its name, it has absolutely nothing in common with the traditional Relative Strength concept, whereby the price of a stock is divided by a broad market index (such as the Standard & Poor's 500 Index) to arrive at a ratio that shows the trend of a stock's performance relative to the general market. Instead, Wilder's RSI is actually a front-weighted price velocity ratio for only one item (a stock, a futures contract, or an index). And, in conformity with the standard interpretation of price velocity indicators generally, Wilder places considerable emphasis on confirmations and divergences of RSI compared to the underlying price series.

RSI's method of calculation, using Exponential Moving Averages, correctly avoids the problem of erratic movement caused solely by dropping off old data, that is, the problem of the "take away" number, a problem that plagues such popular indicators as short Simple Moving Averages, Rate of Change, and Stochastics. Exponential smoothing also eliminates the need to work with long columns of historical data each day. Obviously, the smaller n is, the shorter the period measured and the more sensitive the indicator, while the larger n is, the longer the period measured and the less sensitive the indicator. Wilder's suggested n-period length is 14 days. Other popular lengths are 20, 10, 8, 7, and 5 days. We found that the shortest one, 5 days produced the best result. The indicator can also be applied to any time frame, from minutes to months.

RSI's method of calculation, using ratios, tames the indicator's y-axis range to limits of 0 to 100. Due to its use of ratios, however, RSI seems to be subject to greater volatility and erratic movement than smoothed indicators that are not dependent on ratios.

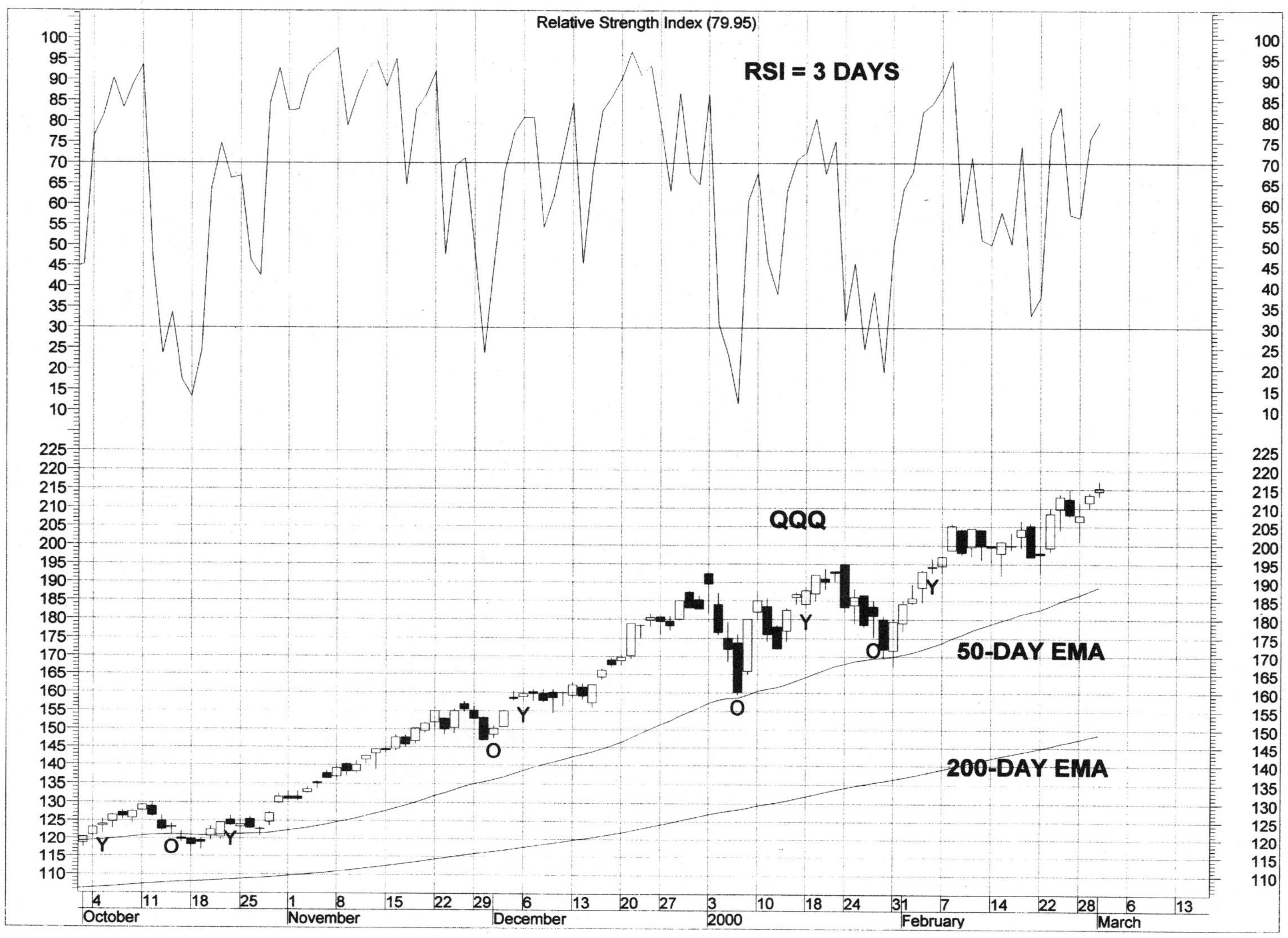
Relative Strength Index (79.95)
RSI = 3 DAYS
QQQ
50-DAY EMA
200-DAY EMA
October
November
December
2000
February
March

Example of Welles Wilder's RSI over Four Periods

Year End Date	*Price on the Close*	*Positive Change (Close Minus Previous Close)*	*Negative Change (Previous Close Minus Close)*	*P Previous*	*Multiplied by n − 1 =*	*Pp × 3*	*Add PC*	*Positive Sum*	*Divide by n for P*
	C	*PC*	*NC*	*Pp*	*× 3*	*Product*	*+ PC*	*PS*	*÷ 4 = P*
									P
1968	58.90	N/A	N/A						
1969	51.53	0.00	7.37						
1970	50.23	0.00	1.30						
1971	56.43	6.20	0.00						
1972	64.48	8.05	0.00	N/A	× 3	N/A	‡	‡	÷ 4 = 3.56‡
1973	51.82	0.00	12.66	3.56	× 3	= 10.68	+ 0.00	= 10.68	÷ 4 = 2.67
1974	36.13	0.00	15.69	2.67	× 3	= 8.01	+ 0.00	= 8.01	÷ 4 = 2.00
1975	47.64	11.51	0.00	2.00	× 3	= 6.00	+ 11.51	= 17.51	÷ 4 = 4.38
1976	57.88	10.24	0.00	4.38	× 3	= 13.14	+ 10.24	= 23.38	÷ 4 = 5.85
1977	52.50	0.00	5.38	5.85	× 3	= 17.55	+ 0.00	= 17.55	÷ 4 = 4.39
1978	53.62	1.12	0.00	4.39	× 3	= 13.17	+ 1.12	= 14.29	÷ 4 = 3.57
1979	61.95	8.33	0.00	3.57	× 3	= 10.71	+ 8.33	= 19.04	÷ 4 = 4.76
1980	77.86	15.91	0.00	4.76	× 3	= 14.28	+ 15.91	= 30.19	÷ 4 = 7.55
1981	71.11	0.00	6.75	7.55	× 3	= 22.65	+ 0.00	= 22.65	÷ 4 = 5.66
1982	81.03	9.92	0.00	5.66	× 3	= 16.98	+ 9.92	= 26.90	÷ 4 = 6.73
1983	95.18	14.15	0.00	6.73	× 3	= 20.19	+ 14.15	= 34.34	÷ 4 = 8.59
1984	96.38	1.20	0.00	8.59	× 3	= 25.77	+ 1.20	= 26.97	÷ 4 = 6.74
1985	121.58	25.20	0.00	6.74	× 3	= 20.22	+ 25.20	= 45.42	÷ 4 = 11.36
1986	138.58	17.00	0.00	11.35	× 3	= 34.05	+ 17.00	= 51.05	÷ 4 = 12.76

‡ Wilder uses an *n*-period simple moving average for the *n*th period. In this example, he would use a four-period simple moving average. Thereafter, Wilder smooths by multiplying the previous smoothed value by *n*–1 (in this case, 3), adding the current period's PC or NC, then dividing that sum by *n* (in this case, 4). This procedure is equivalent to exponential smoothing. Some computer software uses other variations of exponential smoothing which change RSI only insignificantly.

Indicator Strategy Example for RSI

RSI requires experience and judgement to use as Wilder intended. Even naïve testing assumptions suggest that RSI may have some objective potential value as a purely mechanical, contra-trend technical indicator. The great majority of oversold buy signals would have been profitable. Moreover, these buy signals would have been robust, with all RSI lengths from 2 to 21 days profitable and right most of the time, for long trades only.

Example of Welles Wilder's RSI over Four Periods *(continued)*

N *Previous* ------ *Np*	*Multi-* *plied* *by* *n − 1 =* ------ *× 3*	*Np × 3* ----- *Product*	*Add* *NC* ----- *+ NC*	*Negative* *Sum* ----- *NS*	*Divide* *by n* *for N* ----- *÷ 4 = N* ----- *N*	*Ratio* *of* *P ÷ N* ---- *RS*	*1* *Plus* *RS* ----- *1 + RS*	*100 ÷* *(1 + RS)* ------ *RR*	*100* *Minus* *RR* ---- *RSI*
N/A	× 3	N/A	‡	‡	÷ 4 = 2.17‡	1.64	2.64	37.88	62.12
2.17	× 3 =	6.51 +	12.66 =	19.17	÷ 4 = 4.79	0.56	1.56	64.10	35.90
4.79	× 3 =	14.37 +	15.69 =	30.06	÷ 4 = 7.52	0.27	1.27	78.74	21.26
7.52	× 3 =	22.56 +	0 =	22.56	÷ 4 = 5.64	0.78	1.78	56.18	43.82
5.64	× 3 =	16.92 +	0 =	16.92	÷ 4 = 4.23	1.38	2.38	42.02	57.98
4.23	× 3 =	12.69 +	5.38 =	18.07	÷ 4 = 4.52	0.97	1.97	50.76	49.24
4.52	× 3 =	13.56 +	0 =	13.56	÷ 4 = 3.39	1.05	2.05	48.78	51.22
3.39	× 3 =	10.17 +	0 =	10.17	÷ 4 = 2.54	1.87	2.87	34.84	65.16
2.54	× 3 =	9.62 +	0 =	7.62	÷ 4 = 1.91	3.95	4.95	20.20	79.80
1.91	× 3 =	5.73 +	6.75 =	12.48	÷ 4 = 3.12	1.81	2.81	35.59	64.41
3.12	× 3 =	9.36 +	0 =	9.36	÷ 4 = 2.34	2.88	3.88	25.77	74.23
2.34	× 3 =	7.02 +	0 =	7.02	÷ 4 = 1.76	4.88	5.88	17.01	82.99
1.76	× 3 =	5.28 +	0 =	5.28	÷ 4 = 1.32	5.11	6.11	16.37	83.63
1.32	× 3 =	3.96 +	0 =	3.96	÷ 4 = 0.99	11.64	12.64	7.91	92.09
0.99	× 3 =	2.97 +	0 =	2.97	÷ 4 = 0.74	17.24	18.24	5.48	94.52

As attractive as a high percentage of profitable trades may seem, however, it is important to note that this (like other contra-trend strategies) failed to provide any protection in the Crash of '87, the decline of 1998 and other market price drops. As the chart shows, there are sharp equity drawdowns. Using RSI for contra-trend oversold and overbought signals underperformed the passive buy-and-hold strategy for long trades only, while short selling would not have been profitable in the past.

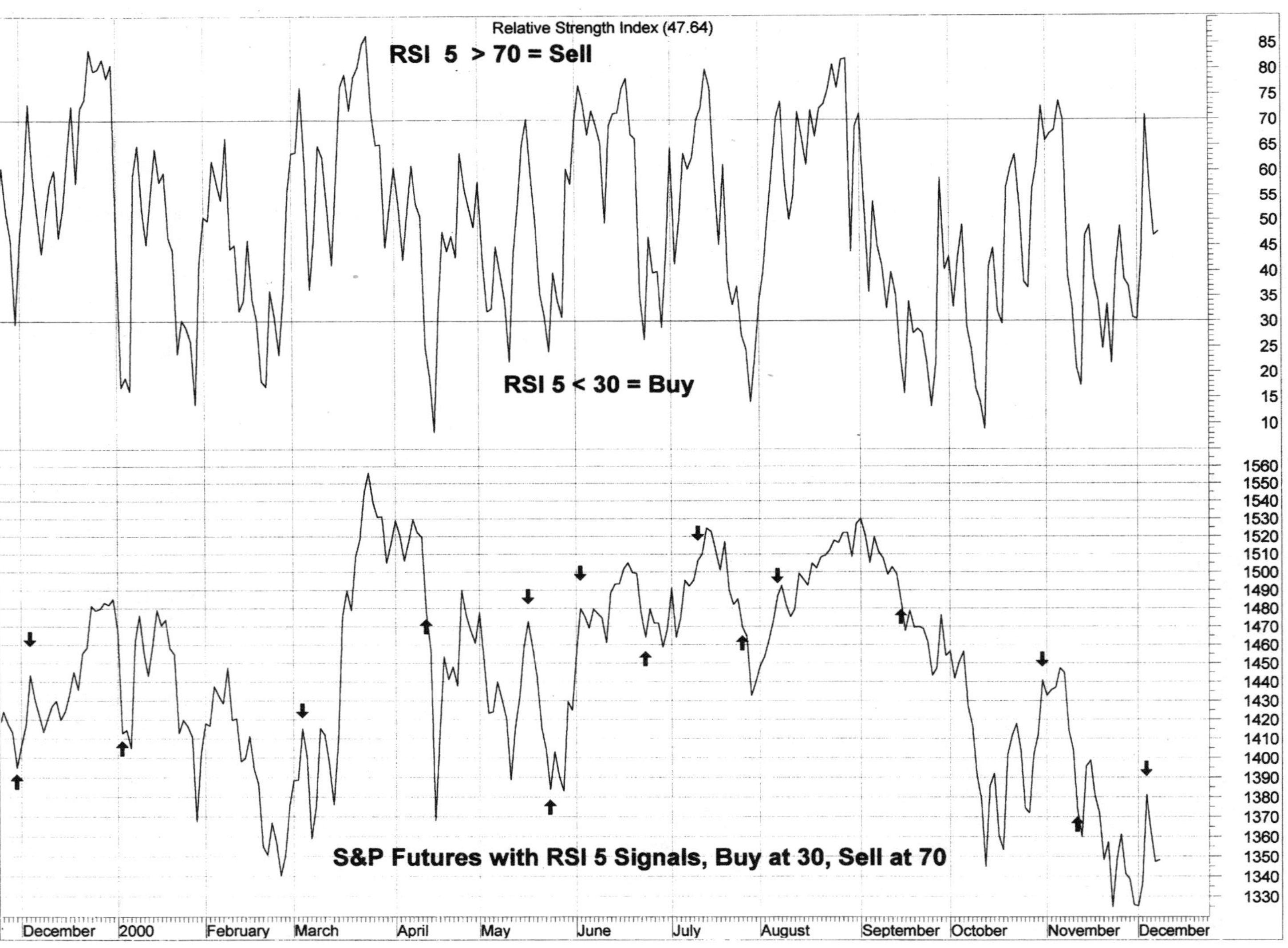
Relative Strength Index (47.64)
RSI 5 > 70 = Sell
RSI 5 < 30 = Buy
S&P Futures with RSI 5 Signals, Buy at 30, Sell at 70
85 80 75 70 65 60 55 50 45 40 35 30 25 20 15 10
1560 1550 1540 1530 1520 1510 1500 1490 1480 1470 1460 1450 1440 1430 1420 1410 1400 1390 1380 1370 1360 1350 1340 1330
December 2000 February March April May June July August September October November December

Based on an 18-year file of daily data for the entire history of the S&P 500 Composite Stock Price Index futures *CSI Perpetual Contract,* collected from www.csidata.com, from 4/21/82 to 12/08/00, we found that the following parameters would have produced a positive result on a purely mechanical signal basis with no subjectivity, no sophisticated technical analysis, and no judgement:

Enter Long (Buy) at the current daily price close of the S&P 500 Composite Stock Price Index futures *CSI Perpetual Contract* when the 5-day RSI(5) is less than 30.

Close Long (Sell) at the current daily price close of the S&P 500 Composite Stock Price Index futures *CSI Perpetual Contract* when the 5-day RSI(5) is greater than 70.

Enter Short (Sell Short) never.

Starting with $100 and reinvesting profits, total net profits for this RSI countertrend strategy would have been $717.36, assuming a fully invested strategy, reinvestment of profits, no transactions costs and no taxes. This would have been 31.39 percent less than buy-and-hold. No short selling would have been profitable, and no short selling was included in the strategy. Short selling would have cut the profit in half. Long-only RSI as an indicator would have given profitable buy signals 85.94% of the time. Trading would have been relatively inactive at one trade every 53.18 calendar days. Note that this strategy considers closing prices only while ignoring intraday highs and lows.

The Equis International MetaStock® System Testing rules for RSI are written as follows:

Enter long: RSI(opt1)<30

Close long: RSI(opt1)>70

OPT1 Current value: 5

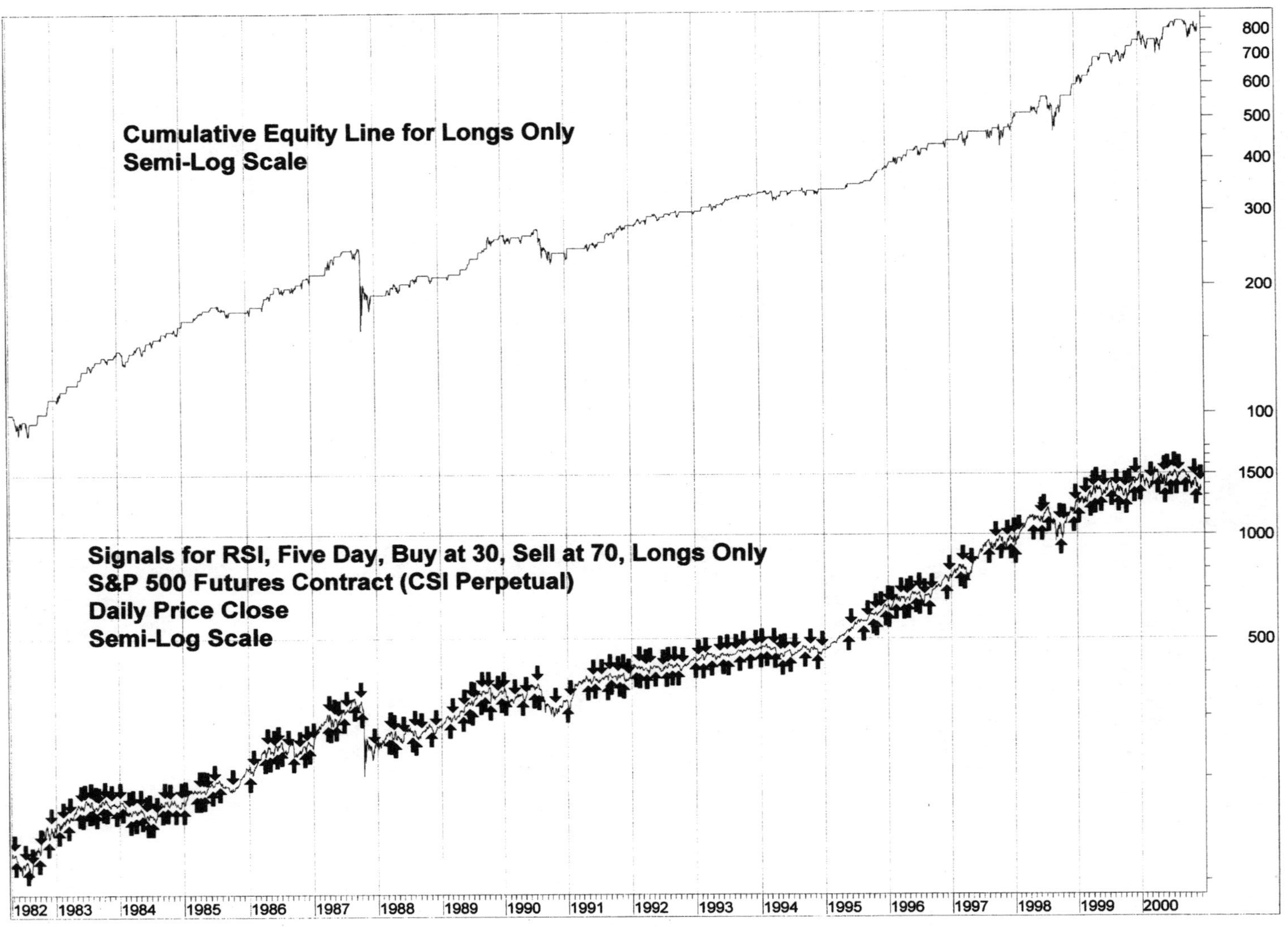
Cumulative Equity Line for Longs Only
Semi-Log Scale
Signals for RSI, Five Day, Buy at 30, Sell at 70, Longs Only
S&P 500 Futures Contract (CSI Perpetual)
Daily Price Close
Semi-Log Scale
800
700
600
500
400
300
200
100
1500
1000
500
1982
1983
1984
1985
1986
1987
1988
1989
1990
1991
1992
1993
1994
1995
1996
1997
1998
1999
2000

RSI, Five Day, Buy at 30, Sell at 70

Total net profit	717.36	Open position value	N/A	Net Profit / Buy&Hold %	−31.39
Percent gain/loss	717.36	Annual percent gain/loss	38.47	Annual Net % / B&H %	−31.38
Initial investment	100	Interest earned	0		
Current position	Out	Date position entered	12/5/00		
Buy/Hold profit	1045.54	Days in test	6807	# of days per trade	53.18
Buy/Hold pct gain/loss	1045.54	Annual B/H pct gain/loss	56.06		
Total closed trades	128	Commissions paid	0		
Avg profit per trade	5.6	Avg Win/Avg Loss ratio	0.75		
Total long trades	128	Total short trades	0	Long Win Trade %	85.94
Winning long trades	110	Winning short trades	0	Short Win Trade %	#DIV/0!
Total winning trades	110	Total losing trades	18	Total Win Trade %	85.94
Amount of winning trades	918.11	Amount of losing trades	−200.75	Net Profit Margin %	64.12
Average win	8.35	Average loss	−11.15	Average P. Margin %	−14.36
Largest win	52.19	Largest loss	−55.73	% Net / (Win + Loss)	−3.28
Average length of win	13.75	Average length of loss	30.56	(Win − Loss) / Loss %	−55.01
Longest winning trade	42	Longest losing trade	65	(Win − Loss) / Loss %	−35.38
Most consecutive wins	14	Most consecutive losses	2	(Win − Loss) / Loss %	600.00
Total bars out	2907	Average length out	22.53		
Longest out period	106				
System close drawdown	−4.47	Profit/Loss index	78.13	% Net Profit / SODD	6575.25
System open drawdown	−10.91	Reward/Risk index	98.5	(Net P.-SODD)/Net P.	98.48
Max open trade drawdown	−93.45	Buy/Hold index	−31.39	% SODD / Net Profit	−1.52

In the Equis MetaStock® "System Report" (profit and loss summary statistics), the *Total net profit* is the sum of profits minus the sum of losses, including open positions marked to the market. In contrast, the *Amount of Winning Trades* is the sum of realized profits (the total of all gains on closed-out trades only, excluding any open positions). Similarly, the *Amount of Losing Trades* is the sum of realized losses (the total of all losses on closed-out trades only, excluding any open positions). *System close drawdown* is the largest decline in the cumulative equity line below the initial investment, based on closed-out positions only. *System open drawdown (SODD)* is the largest decline in the cumulative equity line below the initial investment when a position is open. *Max open trade drawdown* is the largest decline in the cumulative equity line below the trade entry price during the worst single trade. The *Profit/Loss Index* is a complex calculation that relates the Amount of Winning Trades to the Amount of Losing Trades on a scale of −100 (worst possible performance) to +100 (best possible performance), with zero representing profits equal to losses. *Reward/Risk Index* is the Total net profit minus System open drawdown. The resulting difference is then divided by the Total net profit. The *Buy/Hold Index* is the Total net profit minus the buy-and-hold strategy's net profit. The resulting difference is then divided by the buy-and-hold net profit. In this exercise, initial equity is assumed to be $100. Both long and short positions are taken unless otherwise noted. Trades are executed at the closing price on the signal date. Transaction costs, interest expenses, and margins are not included in the statistics.

Relative Volatility Index (RVI)

The Relative Volatility Index (RVI) measures the direction of price volatility and is used as a filter to confirm an independent price momentum indicator. RVI was developed by Donald G. Dorsey and first introduced in the June 1993 issue of *Technical Analysis of Stocks and Commodities* magazine (www.traders.com). A revision to the indicator was covered in the September 1995 issue.

The RVI calculation is similar to the RSI *(See Relative Strength Index)* except that the RVI measures the standard deviation of daily price changes rather than absolute price changes. RSI separates each day's closing price net changes into positive changes and negative changes, then RSI smoothes and normalizes these changes by using ratios that produce a standard scale from zero to 100. The RVI uses the same basic formula but substitutes the 10-day standard deviation of the closing prices for the net changes.

RVI was designed to measure the direction of volatility. Dorsey reasoned that a trading system might be improved if a confirming indicator, used as a filter, were added to one of the price momentum indicators. This filter, the RVI, calculated strength by measuring volatility rather than price change, adding the diversification previously lacking in many systems. RVI was designed to be an indicator that could be used to confirm without duplicating signals from a trend-momentum indicator (such as RSI, MACD, Stochastics, Rate of Change, Price Oscillators such as a dual moving average crossover system, and so forth). As Dorsey asserts, "Because the RVI measures a different set of market dynamics than other indicators, it is often superior as a confirming indicator...The RVI's advantage is as a confirming indicator because it provides a level of diversification missing in the RSI."

Dorsey tested the profitability of a moving average crossover strategy and found that results could be improved by adding RVI rules for confirmation.

Indicator Strategy Example for RVI

Our testing confirmed that RVI does indeed filter out many signals, but profitability would not have been significantly better than the passive buy-and-hold strategy. Based on a merged 20-year file of adjusted daily data for the entire histories of the S&P 500 Depositary Receipts since 1993, the S&P futures from 1982 to 1993, and cash S&P 500 Stock Price Index from 1980 to 1982, we found that the following parameters would have produced the following result on a purely mechanical trend-following signal basis with no subjectivity, no sophisticated technical analysis, and no judgement:

Enter Long (Buy) at the current daily price close of the S&P when the 280-period RVI is greater than 50 and the current day's price close is greater than yesterday's 140-day EMA of the daily closing prices.

Close Long (Sell) at the current daily price close of the S&P when the 280-period RVI is less than 50 and the current day's price close is less than yesterday's 140-day EMA of the daily closing prices.

Enter Short (Sell Short) at the current daily price close of the S&P when the 280-period RVI is less than 50 and the current day's price close is less than yesterday's 140-day EMA of the daily closing prices.

Close Short (Cover) at the current daily price close of the S&P when the 280-period RVI is greater than 50 and the current day's price close is greater than yesterday's 140-day EMA of the daily closing prices.

Starting with $100 and reinvesting profits, total net profits for this RVI trend-following strategy would have been $867.42, assuming a fully invested strategy, reinvestment of profits, no transactions costs and no taxes. This would have been only 1.33 percent better than buy-and-hold. Trading would have been extremely inactive with only five signals in 20 years, making this indicator ineffective as a trading guide.

The Equis International MetaStock® System Testing rules for the pre-processed RVI indicator are written as follows:

Enter long: RVI(opt1) > 50 AND CLOSE > Ref(Mov(CLOSE,opt2,E),−1)

Close long: RVI(opt1) < 50 AND CLOSE < Ref(Mov(CLOSE,opt2,E),−1)

Enter short: RVI(opt1) < 50 AND CLOSE < Ref(Mov(CLOSE,opt2,E),−1)

Close short: RVI(opt1) > 50 AND CLOSE > Ref(Mov(CLOSE,opt2,E),−1)

OPT1 Current value: 280

OPT2 Current value: 140

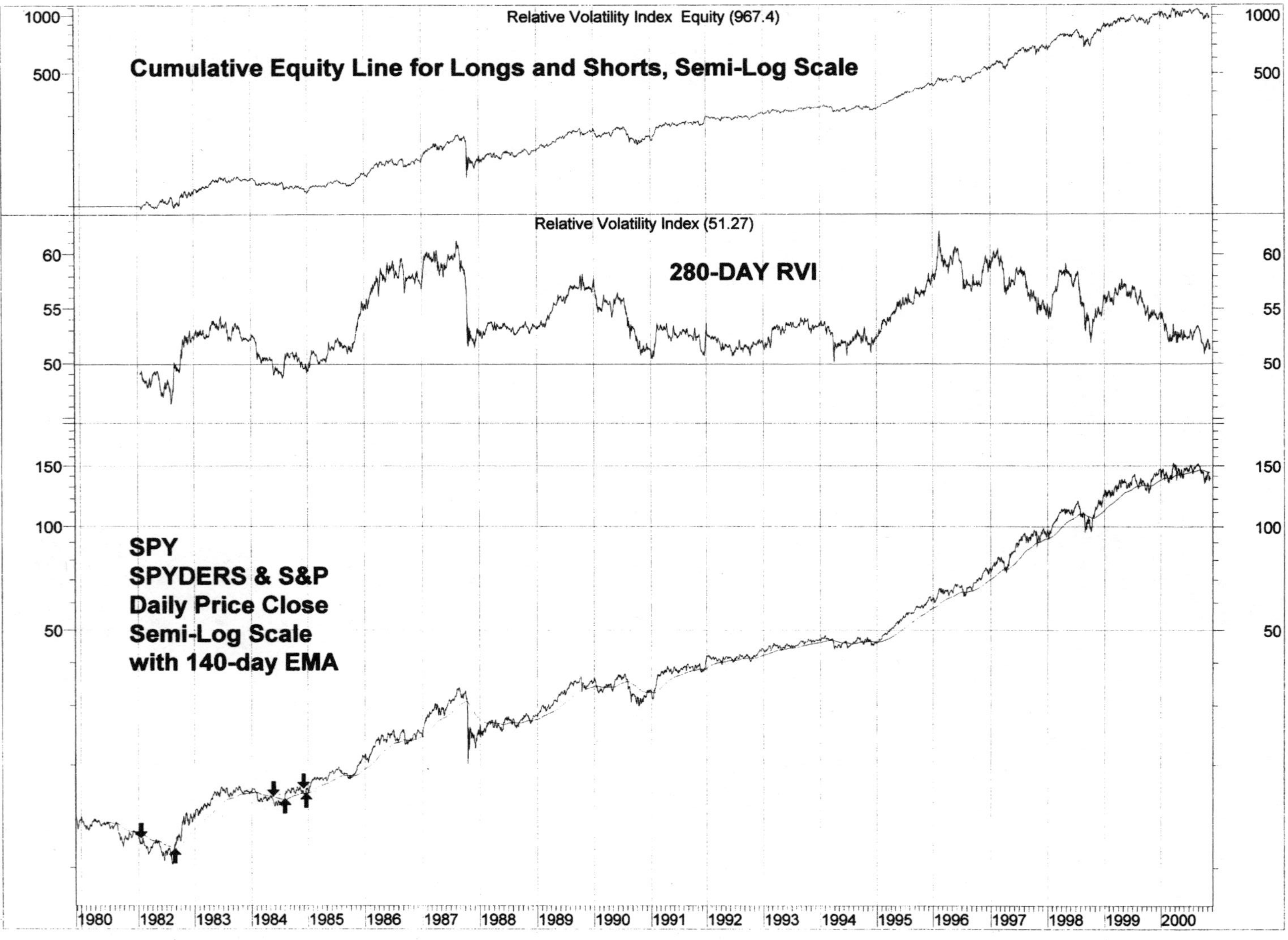

Relative Volatility Index Equity (967.4)
Cumulative Equity Line for Longs and Shorts, Semi-Log Scale
Relative Volatility Index (51.27)
280-DAY RVI
SPY
SPYDERS & S&P
Daily Price Close
Semi-Log Scale
with 140-day EMA
1000
500
60
55
50
150
100
50
1980
1982
1983
1984
1985
1986
1987
1988
1989
1990
1991
1992
1993
1994
1995
1996
1997
1998
1999
2000

Relative Volatility Index (RVI)

Total net profit	867.42	Open position value	846.99	Net Profit / Buy&Hold %	1.33
Percent gain/loss	867.42	Annual percent gain/loss	43.4	Annual Net % / B&H %	1.33
Initial investment	100	Interest earned	0		
Current position	Long	Date position entered	12/19/84		
Buy/Hold profit	856	Days in test	7295	# of days per trade	1459.00
Buy/Hold pct gain/loss	856	Annual B/H pct gain/loss	42.83		
Total closed trades	5	Commissions paid	0		
Avg profit per trade	4.09	Avg Win/Avg Loss ratio	4.12		
Total long trades	2	Total short trades	3	Long Win Trade %	100.00
Winning long trades	2	Winning short trades	0	Short Win Trade %	0.00
Total winning trades	2	Total losing trades	3	Total Win Trade %	40.00
Amount of winning trades	32.12	Amount of losing trades	−11.69	Net Profit Margin %	46.63
Average win	16.06	Average loss	−3.9	Average P. Margin %	60.92
Largest win	31.66	Largest loss	−6.74	% Net / (Win + Loss)	64.90
Average length of win	262	Average length of loss	73.33	(Win − Loss) / Loss %	257.29
Longest winning trade	440	Longest losing trade	153	(Win − Loss) / Loss %	187.58
Most consecutive wins	1	Most consecutive losses	1	(Win − Loss) / Loss %	0.00
Total bars out	289	Average length out	289		
Longest out period	289				
System close drawdown	−0.9	Profit/Loss index	98.67	% Net Profit / SODD	19405.37
System open drawdown	−4.47	Reward/Risk index	99.49	(Net P.-SODD)/Net P.	99.48
Max open trade drawdown	−7.12	Buy/Hold index	100.28	% SODD / Net Profit	−0.52

In the Equis MetaStock® "System Report" (profit and loss summary statistics), the *Total net profit* is the sum of profits minus the sum of losses, including open positions marked to the market. In contrast, the *Amount of Winning Trades* is the sum of realized profits (the total of all gains on closed-out trades only, excluding any open positions). Similarly, the *Amount of Losing Trades* is the sum of realized losses (the total of all losses on closed-out trades only, excluding any open positions). *System close drawdown* is the largest decline in the cumulative equity line below the initial investment, based on closed-out positions only. *System open drawdown (SODD)* is the largest decline in the cumulative equity line below the initial investment when a position is open. *Max open trade drawdown* is the largest decline in the cumulative equity line below the trade entry price during the worst single trade. The *Profit/Loss Index* is a complex calculation that relates the Amount of Winning Trades to the Amount of Losing Trades on a scale of −100 (worst possible performance) to +100 (best possible performance), with zero representing profits equal to losses. *Reward/Risk Index* is the Total net profit minus System open drawdown. The resulting difference is then divided by the Total net profit. The *Buy/Hold Index* is the Total net profit minus the buy-and-hold strategy's net profit. The resulting difference is then divided by the buy-and-hold net profit. In this exercise, initial equity is assumed to be $100. Both long and short positions are taken unless otherwise noted. Trades are executed at the closing price on the signal date. Transaction costs, interest expenses, and margins are not included in the statistics.

Renko Charts

The Japanese Renko Chart is a unique kind of a line chart designed to filter out minor, short-term market noise. It is similar to the western Point and Figure technique in that price movement (and not the passage of time) determines the progress along the horizontal x-axis. We make a chart entry (which is called a *renga* in Japanese, a *brick* in English) only when price moves by a fixed and predetermined amount, or box size, expressed in some obvious unit of local currency, such as one dollar.

A difference is that instead of using intraday high and low extremes like a western Point and Figure Chart, the Japanese Renko Chart uses the close to determine when to lay a new *renga* (brick). The current close is compared with the high and low of the previous brick. In an uptrend, when this close rises above the top of the previous brick by at least the box size (or a greater amount), then one or more white bricks are laid above and in the next column to the right. If the uptrend reverses, indicated by the current closing price falling below the bottom of the previous brick by at least the box size, then one or more black bricks are laid below and in the next column to the right.

Charting the S&P Depositary Receipts (SPY) for the full year 2000, January through December, using MetaStock® software, the two charts compare the 1 point box size Renko Chart to the similar 1 point box size and 1 point reversal Point and Figure Chart.

(See Nison, S. (1994). *Beyond Candlesticks.* New York: Wiley.)

Resistance

At the most basic level, Support and Resistance are previous lows and highs. Also, the sloping trendlines and price channels that contain the price action within orderly ascending or descending patterns offer moving points of Support and Resistance that function similarly to horizontal trading ranges. *(See Support and Resistance.)*

Resistance Index, Art Merrill's

The Resistance Index measures the difference between resistance to downward price swings and resistance to upward price swings. Resistance is defined as the NYSE volume required to move the Dow-Jones Industrial Average (DJIA) one point. This indicator was invented by Arthur A. Merrill, CMT.

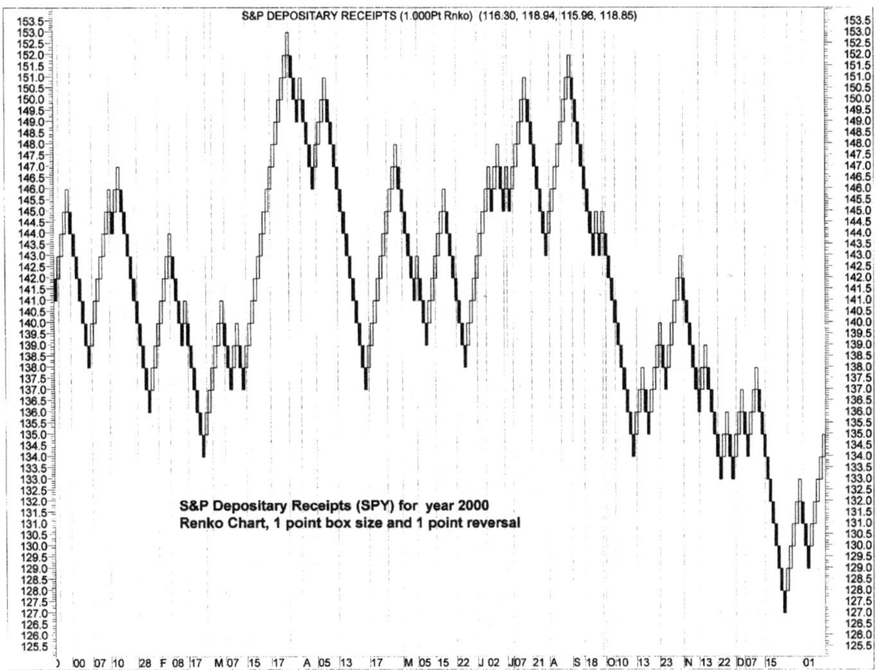
S&P DEPOSITARY RECEIPTS (1.000Pt Rnko) (116.30, 118.94, 115.96, 118.85)
S&P Depositary Receipts (SPY) for year 2000
Renko Chart, 1 point box size and 1 point reversal

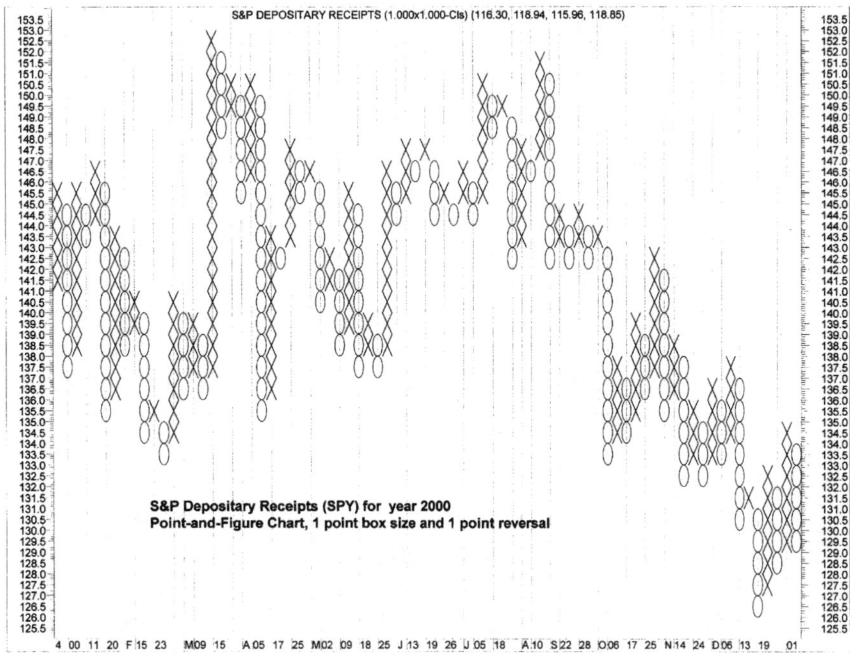
S&P DEPOSITARY RECEIPTS (1.000x1.000-Cls) (116.30, 118.94, 115.96, 118.85)
S&P Depositary Receipts (SPY) for year 2000
Point-and-Figure Chart, 1 point box size and 1 point reversal

Merrill's Resistance Index may be calculated and interpreted in ten steps.

1. Gather DJIA price and NYSE volume data for each hour of trading.
2. Calculate the DJIA total net points change each hour, respecting sign, plus or minus.
3. Total the plus point changes (from Step 2) for the week.
4. Total the volume for the hours with plus point changes for the week.
5. Divide the total weekly plus-point volume (from Step 4) by the total weekly plus point changes (from Step 3). This is *rise resistance.*
6. Repeat Steps 3, 4 and 5 substituting minus point changes and their associated volume. This is *decline resistance.*
7. Subtract rise resistance (from Step 5) from decline resistance (from Step 6). This is *net resistance.*
8. Smooth that net resistance (from Step 7) with a 13-week exponential moving average (EMA). This is the *Resistance Index.*
9. When the Resistance Index is more than 67% of one standard deviation below its mean, it is bullish.
10. When the Resistance Index is more than 67% of one standard deviation above its mean, it is bearish.

Measuring the 11 years from 1971 to 1982, over a 52-week forward window of time, Merrill found his Resistance Index correctly predicted the market direction 64% of the time. Statistically, this was highly significant. Over 26-weeks, it was right more often than not, but not significantly so. Over 5- and 1-weeks, it was wrong more often than right, though not significantly.

The Rule of Seven

The Rule of Seven is a guideline for roughly estimating price targets for a significant price move. It uses a multiple of the point price distance of the first wave in the move to estimate (usually three) tentative price objectives in advance.

For an uptrend, the Rule of Seven method first subtracts the highest high of the first wave up from the low that marked the beginning of the uptrend. This difference is expressed in points of price, not in percentages. This difference is multiplied by the ratio of the integer 7 divided by the integers 1 to 7. That product is then added to the original low to arrive at an upside objective. For example, the point size of the first up wave is multiplied by 7/3, then that product is added to the low price. When the S&P 500 rose from a low of 102.20 in August 1982 to a high of 337.90 in August 1987, the difference was 235.70 points. That difference multiplied by 7/3 (which is 2.33) is 549.97. Then that product added back to the original low of 102.20 equals 652.17, which is an upside objective. We can easily set up a spread sheet, as shown. The most probable upside objectives are 7/4, 7/3, and 7/2 times the price range of the first wave. These proved to be too conservative, in this case.

Similarly, for a downtrend, the price size in points of the first down wave is multiplied by a fraction, and that product is subtracted from the high to arrive at an downside objective. The most probable downside objectives are 7/5, 7/4 and 7/3 times the price range of the first wave. For example, the point size of the first down wave is multiplied by 7/5, then that product is subtracted from the high price. When the S&P 500 fell from a high of 1553.11 in March 2000 to a low of 1339.40 in April 2000, the difference was 213.71 points. That difference multiplied by 7/5 (which is 1.40) is 299.19. Then that product subtracted from the original high of 1553.11 equals 1253.92. The S&P 500 fell 1254.07 on December 21, 2000—almost a direct hit. After that, the S&P bounced up 10% to 1383.37 by January 31, 2001.

Subtract	*Upside*	*Upside*	*Upside*	*Upside*	*Upside*	*Upside*	*Upside*
High	Rule of 7	Additive	Divide	Given	Multiply	Given	Add
minus	Constant(C)	Sequence(S)	C/S	Range(R)	R*(C/S)	Low	Objectives
Low	7.00	1.00	7.00	235.70	1649.90	102.20	1752.10
337.90	7.00	2.00	3.50	235.70	824.95	102.20	927.15*
−102.20	7.00	3.00	2.33	235.70	549.97	102.20	652.17*
235.70	7.00	4.00	1.75	235.70	412.48	102.20	514.68*
	7.00	5.00	1.40	235.70	329.98	102.20	432.18
	7.00	6.00	1.17	235.70	274.98	102.20	377.18
	7.00	7.00	1.00	235.70	235.70	102.20	337.90

Subtract	*Downside*	*Downside*	*Downside*	*Downside*	*Downside*	*Downside*	*Downside*
High	Rule of 7	Additive	Divide	Given	Multiply	Given	Subtract
minus	Constant(C)	Sequence(S)	C/S	Range(R)	R*(C/S)	High	Objectives
Low	7.00	1.00	7.00	213.71	1495.97	1553.11	57.14
1553.11	7.00	2.00	3.50	213.71	747.99	1553.11	805.13
−1339.40	7.00	3.00	2.33	213.71	498.66	1553.11	1054.45*
213.71	7.00	4.00	1.75	213.71	373.99	1553.11	1179.12*
	7.00	5.00	1.40	213.71	299.19	1553.11	1253.92*
	7.00	6.00	1.17	213.71	249.33	1553.11	1303.78
	7.00	7.00	1.00	213.71	213.71	1553.11	1339.40
							Most Likely*

Santa Claus Rally

The Santa Claus Rally begins five trading days before New Year's Day and ends the second trading day of January. It has occurred 77% of the time, 37 of the past 48 years, from 1952 through 2000. It has taken the S&P 500 Index up 1.5% on average since 1952. This rally was first identified in 1972 by Yale Hirsch, editor of *Stock Traders Almanac,* The Hirsch Organization, Inc., 184 Central Avenue, Old Tappan, NJ 07675, page 114, www.stocktradersalmanac.com.

The Santa Claus Rally has failed to occur 23% of the time, 11 of the past 48 years. Hirsch says that when that happens, there are lower prices to come in the year ahead, if not an outright bear market. As he says, "If Santa Claus Rally should fail to call, bears may come to Broad and Wall." In other words, if there is no year-end rally, then look for selling pressure and lower prices on the NYSE, which is located at the corner of Broad and Wall Streets in lower Manhattan, New York, New York.

Schultz Advances/Total Issues Traded (A/T)

Schultz Advances/Total Issues Traded (A/T) is another variation of a market breadth indicator developed by John Schultz. The A/T is calculated by dividing the number of advancing issues by the total number of issues traded. Various moving averages may be used to smooth out erratic daily movements. Weekly data also may be used in a separate calculation. The Schultz A/T is usually calculated based on issues listed on the New York Stock Exchanges, and similar indicators may be calculated for other markets, such as the NASDAQ. The Schultz A/T can be expressed by the following basic formula, before applying any moving average for smoothing:

$$S = (A) / (A + D + U)$$

where

S = today's 1-day ratio of advances to total issues traded
A = number of advancing issues
D = number of declining issues
U = number of unchanged issues
A + D + U = total number of issues traded each day

The 68-year mean level of the Schultz A/T is 0.394. The chart shows that the typical levels appear to have narrowed in recent decades compared to the 1930's and 1940's. We multiplied S by 1000 to convert to three significant digits and avoid handling fractions.

Indicator Strategy Example for Schultz Advances/Total Issues Traded (A/T)

The trend of the Schultz A/T is an effective indicator, producing steadily rising cumulative profits over many decades. Based on a 68-year file of daily data for the number of shares advancing, declining, and unchanged each day on the NYSE and the DJIA since March 8, 1932, we found that a simple trend-following rule would have produced a positive result on a purely mechanical signal basis with no subjectivity, no sophisticated technical analysis, and no judgement:

Enter Long (Buy) at the current daily price close of the DJIA when the Schultz A/T crosses above its own previous day's trailing 7-day EMA.

Close Long (Sell) at the current daily price close of the DJIA when the Schultz A/T crosses below its own previous day's trailing 7-day EMA.

Enter Short (Sell Short) at the current daily price close of the DJIA when the Schultz A/T crosses below its own previous day's trailing 7-day EMA.

Close Short (Cover) at the current daily price close of the DJIA when the Schultz A/T crosses above its own previous day's trailing 7-day EMA.

Starting with $100 and reinvesting profits, total net profits for this Schultz A/T trend-following strategy would have been $473,954,592, assuming a fully invested strategy, reinvestment of profits, no transactions costs and no taxes. This would have been 3,779,846 percent better than buy-and-hold. Even short selling would have been profitable. Trading would have been hyperactive with one trade every 2.93 calendar days.

The Equis International MetaStock® System Testing rules, where the current Schultz A/T times 1000 is inserted into the data field normally reserved for Volume (V), are written as follows:

Enter long: V > Ref(Mov(V,opt1,E),-1)

Close long: V < Ref(Mov(V,opt1,E),-1)

Enter short: V < Ref(Mov(V,opt1,E),-1)

Close short: V > Ref(Mov(V,opt1,E),-1)

OPT1 Current value: 7

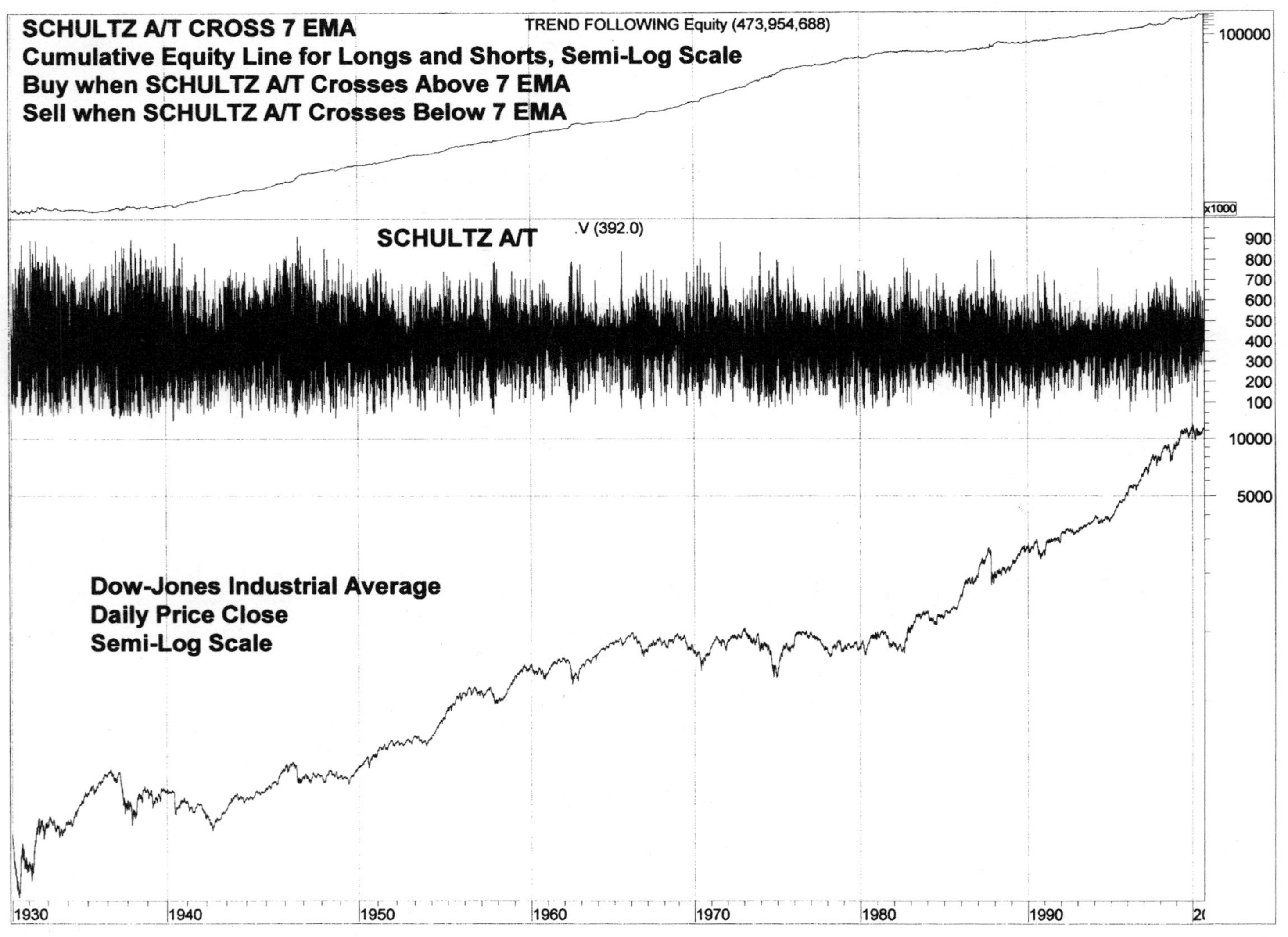

SCHULTZ A/T CROSS 7 EMA
Cumulative Equity Line for Longs and Shorts, Semi-Log Scale
Buy when SCHULTZ A/T Crosses Above 7 EMA
Sell when SCHULTZ A/T Crosses Below 7 EMA
TREND FOLLOWING Equity (473,954,688)
100000
x1000
SCHULTZ A/T
.V (392.0)
900
800
700
600
500
400
300
200
100
10000
5000
Dow-Jones Industrial Average
Daily Price Close
Semi-Log Scale
1930
1940
1950
1960
1970
1980
1990

Schultz A/T: 7-day EMA

Total net profit	473954592	Open position value	0	Net Profit / Buy&Hold %	3779846.12
Percent gain/loss	473954592	Annual percent gain/loss	6913653.03	Annual Net % / B&H %	3779918.06
Initial investment	100	Interest earned	0		
Current position	Short	Date position entered	9/8/00	# of days per trade	2.93
Buy/Hold profit	12538.66	Days in test	25022		
Buy/Hold pct gain/loss	12538.66	Annual B/H pct gain/loss	182.9		
Total closed trades	8036	Commissions paid	0		
Avg profit per trade	58978.92	Avg Win/Avg Loss ratio	1.51		
Total long trades	4018	Total short trades	4018	Long Win Trade %	53.56
Winning long trades	2152	Winning short trades	1738	Short Win Trade %	43.26
Total winning trades	3890	Total losing trades	4146	Total Win Trade %	48.41
Amount of winning trades	1.604E+09	Amount of losing trades	−1.13E+09	Net Profit Margin %	17.34
Average win	412327.49	Average loss	−272551.67	Average P. Margin %	20.41
Largest win	23307040	Largest loss	−16179232	% Net / (Win + Loss)	18.05
Average length of win	3.94	Average length of loss	2.6	(Win − Loss) / Loss %	51.54
Longest winning trade	12	Longest losing trade	11	(Win − Loss) / Loss %	9.09
Most consecutive wins	11	Most consecutive losses	16	(Win − Loss) / Loss %	−31.25
Total bars out	8	Average length out	8		
Longest out period	8				
System close drawdown	−25.05	Profit/Loss index	29.55	% Net Profit / SODD	1892034299.40
System open drawdown	−25.05	Reward/Risk index	100	(Net P.-SODD)/Net P.	100.00
Max open trade drawdown	−16179232	Buy/Hold index	3779846.95	% SODD / Net Profit	0.00

In the Equis MetaStock® "System Report" (profit and loss summary statistics), the *Total net profit* is the sum of profits minus the sum of losses, including open positions marked to the market. In contrast, the *Amount of Winning Trades* is the sum of realized profits (the total of all gains on closed-out trades only, excluding any open positions). Similarly, the *Amount of Losing Trades* is the sum of realized losses (the total of all losses on closed-out trades only, excluding any open positions). *System close drawdown* is the largest decline in the cumulative equity line below the initial investment, based on closed-out positions only. *System open drawdown (SODD)* is the largest decline in the cumulative equity line below the initial investment when a position is open. *Max open trade drawdown* is the largest decline in the cumulative equity line below the trade entry price during the worst single trade. The *Profit/Loss Index* is a complex calculation that relates the Amount of Winning Trades to the Amount of Losing Trades on a scale of −100 (worst possible performance) to +100 (best possible performance), with zero representing profits equal to losses. *Reward/Risk Index* is the Total net profit minus System open drawdown. The resulting difference is then divided by the Total net profit. The *Buy/Hold Index* is the Total net profit minus the buy-and-hold strategy's net profit. The resulting difference is then divided by the buy-and-hold net profit. In this exercise, initial equity is assumed to be $100. Both long and short positions are taken unless otherwise noted. Trades are executed at the closing price on the signal date. Transaction costs, interest expenses, and margins are not included in the statistics.

Second Hour Index

The Second Hour Index uses the relative strength of the market during the second hour of trading as a measure of future market potential. This indicator was invented by Arthur A. Merrill, CMT, who found that it was highly significant and bullish for the future performance of the Dow-Jones Industrial Average (DJIA) over the next 13-, 26-, and 52-weeks when the DJIA's performance during the during the second hour of trading was substantially stronger than its average performance of all the hours of the day. And he found that it was highly significant and bearish when second hour was weak relative to all hours.

Merrill's Second Hour Index may be calculated and interpreted in eight steps.

1. Each trading day, calculate the DJIA total net points change in the second hour.
2. Sum these daily points change (Step 1) for each day of the week.
3. Divide that sum (Step 2) by the number of days in the week, thereby averaging the daily second-hour price changes for the week as a whole.
4. To arrive at the average performance of all hours during the week, subtract the previous Friday's closing price from the current Friday's closing price, then divide that difference by the number of hours in the week. (Use Thursday's close in the case of a holiday. Also, adjust the hours in the week for holidays.)
5. Subtract the daily average performance of all hours during the week (Step 4) from the average second hour performance (Step 3).
6. Smooth that difference (Step 5) with a 26-week exponential moving average (EMA). This is the Second Hour Index.
7. When the Second Hour Index (Step 6) is more than 67% of one standard deviation above its mean, it is bullish.
8. When the Second Hour Index is more than 67% of one standard deviation below its mean, it is bearish.

Measuring the 11 years from 1971 to 1982, over a 52-week forward window of time, Merrill found his Second Hour Index correctly predicted the market direction 80% of the time. Over 26-weeks, it was right in 72% of the occurrences. Over 13-weeks, it was correct 64% of the time. Over 5-weeks, it was right 59% of the time. But for the week ahead, it was correct only 54% of the time. Therefore, the longer the time frame, the better this indicator works.

Secondary Offerings

Secondary offerings are additional public stock sales by corporations with a previously existing public market for their stock. Also, very large stockholders, such as corporate insiders, may sell some or all of their stock in a special offering, or they may join in a public stock offering by the corporation itself. Sometimes, such sales are said to be for diversification or estate purposes and, therefore, do not necessarily reflect an insider's opinion of the stock's prospects.

It used to be thought, with some logic, that a rise in secondary offerings generally to a relatively high level was an indication of well-informed insiders making their exits from an overvalued market heading for a decline. Conversely, a relatively low level of secondary offerings implied that stocks were considered by insiders to be too cheap to sell and, therefore, stock prices were heading for a major rally. As the chart on page 632 shows, this appears to have given timely signals until 1991, when secondary offerings rose to a high level and mostly stayed there as the major stock market price indexes doubled and then doubled again. One possible problem could be that there are a greater number of public corporations than in the past so, naturally, the number of secondary offerings ought to be higher. Thus, this data may need to be statistically normalized relative to the number of public corporations before it becomes useful again. *(See Insiders' Sell/Buy Ratio.)*

Sector Rotation

Relative Strength is the most important indicator for stock selection and timing. Relative Strength rotates sequentially from one industry sector to the next, depending on each sector's sensitivity to underlying fundamental cyclic economic forces and the stage of the economic cycle, according to Sam Stovall ("Top Down Investing with S&P's Sam Stovall", interviewed by Thom Hartle, *Technical Analysis of Stocks & Commodities,* V14:3, www.traders.com).

Economic expansions last about 51 months on average. The expansion can be divided into thirds of 17 months each, representing early, middle, and late stages of the economic expansion.

In the first stage of economic expansion, inflation is low and falling, interest rates are low, and the yield curve is steep (that is, short-term interest rates are well below long-term interest rates). Industrial Production has been low and falling but begins to turn upward. Transportation industries (Air Freight, Airlines, Railroads, Truckers) are the first to rebound. Later in this early stage of economic expansion, relative strength shifts to Technology.

In the second, middle stage of economic expansion, inflation bottoms out and short-term interest rates begin to rise moderately. Industrial Production is rising sharply. Relative strength shifts to Service industries then, later, into Capital Goods.

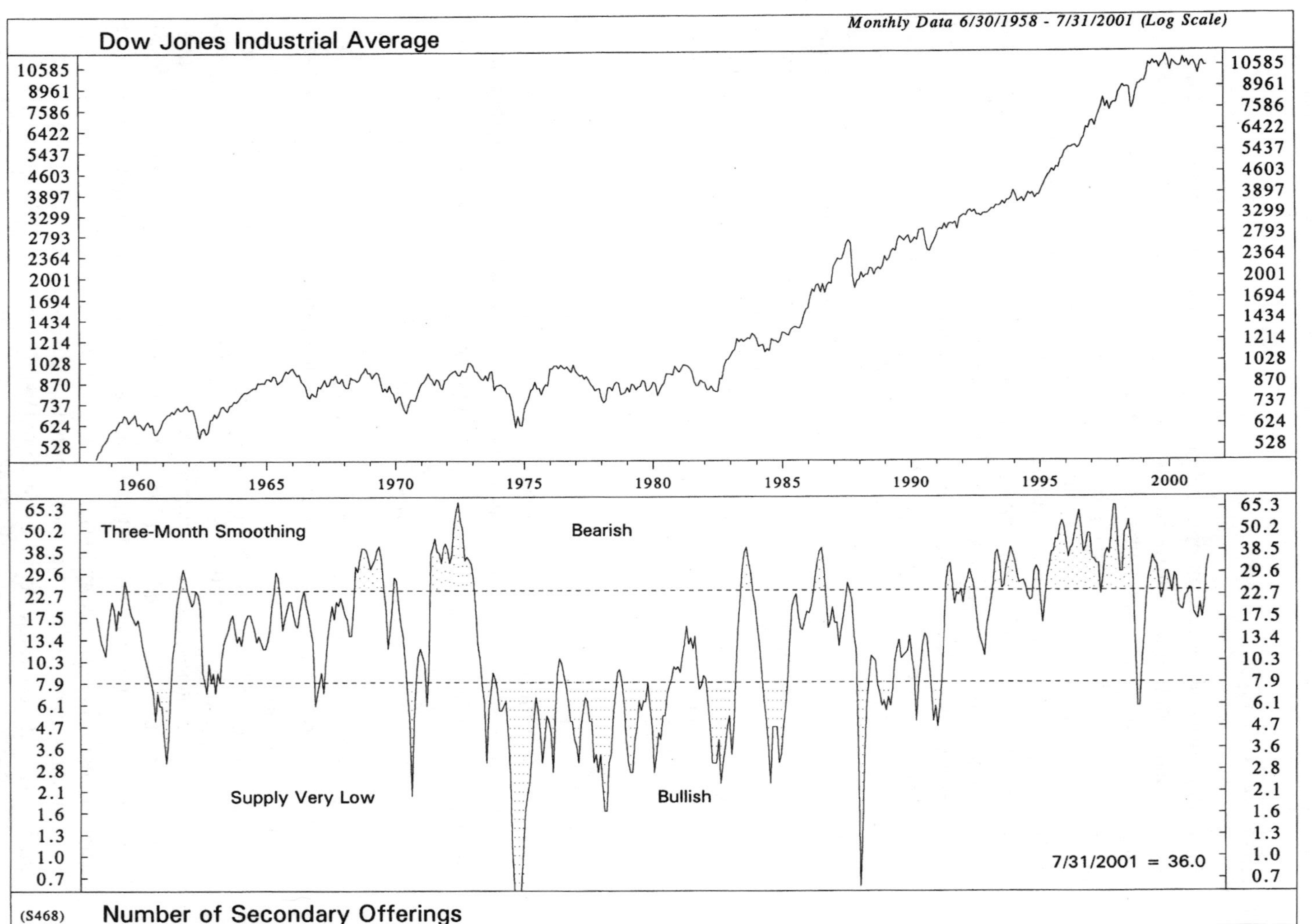

Chart by permission of Ned Davis Research.

The Capital Goods sector includes Aerospace, Containers, Electrical Equipment, Engineering and Construction, Machinery, Manufacturing, Office Equipment and supplies, Trucks and Parts, and Waste Management.

In the late stages of economic expansion, inflation rises, prompting Fed tightening. Interest rates rise. Consumer Expectations and Industrial Production top out. Relative strength shifts first into Basic Materials industries then later into Energy. Raw materials and assets in the ground have long been considered to be inflation hedges. Basic Materials include Agricultural Products, Aluminum, Chemicals, Containers & Paper Packaging, Gold and Precious Metals, Mining, Iron and Steel, Metals, and Paper, and Forest Products.

Economic contractions are much shorter, lasting only about 12 months on average. The contraction can be divided into two equal halves of 6 months each, representing early and late stages of the economic contraction.

In the early stage of economic contraction, inflation rates begin to stabilize, interest rates top out, and Industrial Production and Consumer Expectations are falling. Even when the economy is relatively poor, people still want to consume Consumer Staples, which are basic necessities, produced by industries such as Tobacco, Drugs, Food, Beverages, Broadcasting, Distributors (Food and Health), Personal Care, Restaurants, Retail Drug Stores, Retail Food Chains, Services, and Specialty Printing. So, relative strength shifts to these Consumer Staples, which are relatively insensitive to economic cycles and, therefore, are considered safe.

In the late stages of economic contraction, inflation rates and interest rates both are moving lower. Industrial Production and Consumer Expectations have already been declining but eventually begin to slow their rate of descent. As the late stage economic contraction unfolds, relative strength shifts first to the still relatively safe Utilities (Electric and Natural Gas). Later, as interest rates come down, relative strength rotates to Financials (Banks, Consumer Finance, Insurance, Brokers, Savings and Loan). Finally, relative strength shifts to Consumer Cyclicals as investors begin to anticipate that the worst of the economic contraction may be coming to a conclusion. The Consumer Cyclical Sector includes Automobile Manufacturers, Auto Parts and Equipment, Building Materials, Distributors of Durable Goods, Footwear, Gaming (Lottery and Pari-mutuel), Hardware and Tools, Homebuilding, Household Furnishings and Appliances, Leisure-Time Products, Lodging (Hotels), Photography/Imaging, Publishing, Newspapers, Retail, Services (Advertising and Marketing), Services (Commercial and Consumer), Textiles (Apparel), and Textiles (Home Furnishings).

Sentimeter

The Sentimeter expresses stock prices as multiplies of dividends. Sentimeter, a term coined by Edson Gould, is the Price/Dividend Ratio, the inverse of the Dividend

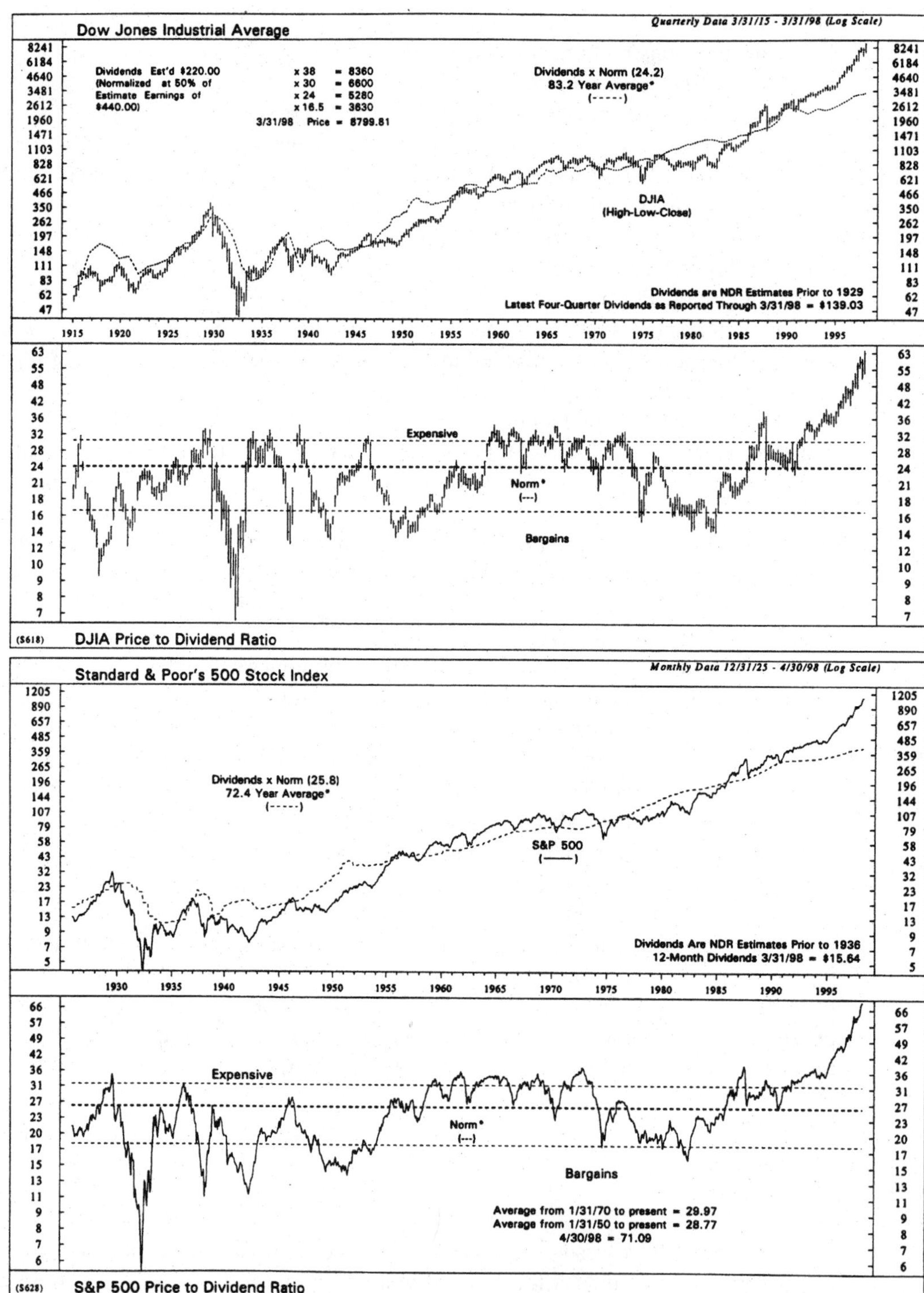

Chart by permission of Ned Davis Research.

Yield, on an index, such as the DJIA or the S&P 500. Gould's idea is that the Dividend Yield quantifies market sentiment:

A relatively high Sentimeter (low Dividend Yields) indicates general optimism toward the stock market and a possible overbought condition.

A relatively low Sentimeter (high Dividend Yields) indicates general pessimism toward the stock market and a possible oversold condition.

The Sentimeter is calculated by dividing a stock price index by the comparable total dividends (paid for all shares in the index) during the preceding 12 months. For example, if the market price index is 100 and the dividends per share paid during the latest 12 months is $4.50, the price/dividend ratio is 22.22 (100 divided by $4.50). The Dividend Yield would be the dividend divided by the price, 4.5%, which is $4.50 divided by 100.

The historical average Price/Dividend Ratio is 24.2 times dividends for the DJIA and 25.8 times dividends for the S&P 500 Index. Extremely low readings below 17 and 18 used to be thought to indicate undervaluation and the potential for stock prices to rise. Extremely high readings above 30 were thought to indicate overvaluation and the potential for stock prices to decline. It has become clear that these historical guidelines are no longer adequate for market timing since extreme readings have been substantially exceeded for years. The Sentimeter worked well as an indicator until the years 1991–2000, when the big bull market blew out all historical norms by a wide margin.

Changing fashions in corporate finance play a role in the recent unreliability of this indicator. Because of the double taxation of dividends, corporate and individual, companies have been retaining a larger share of their earnings to plow back into their business or to make promising external acquisitions to enhance future growth. Dividend payout ratios have fallen and seem unlikely to reverse anytime soon. This does not, however, explain recent extraordinarily low dividend yields because earnings yields also are low (and price/earnings ratios are high).

Sharpe Ratio

The Sharpe Ratio is a common estimate of the risk of a strategy. It is the excess average return divided by the standard deviation of that return. The excess average return is the average return minus the risk-free rate of return on U.S. Treasury bills.

There are very serious problems with this ratio making it an inappropriate measure of risk. One of the worst problems is that the Sharpe Ratio fails to distinguish between upside and downside volatility. That can lead to the ridiculous conclusion that a strategy with large upward jumps in returns but with no drawdowns is a riskier strategy than one with smaller fluctuations in both directions and the same endpoint. In addition, the Sharpe Ratio fails to distinguish between intermittent and consecutive losses.

For a detailed discussion of various performance measures, see Schwager, J. D., *Technical Analysis,* Wiley, New York, 1996, 775 pages.

Short Interest for Individual Stocks, Phil Erlanger's Indicators

Short selling is a measure of sentiment, an expression of strong opinion, that is useful for analyzing both individual stocks and the overall general stock market over the intermediate to long term, according to Phillip B. Erlanger, CMT, (www.erlanger2000.com). After many years of intense study, the world's foremost expert on Short Interest has arrived at the following conclusions:

The Short Interest Ratio must be normalized to adjust for short-term volume fluctuations. This ratio is the current short interest divided by the 1-month average daily trading volume. The problem with this ratio is that it could change substantially due to changes in the recent volume of trading activity, even while short interest has remained constant. That could lead to the wrong conclusion. The solution is the Erlanger Short Interest Ratio, which smoothes the average daily volume over a trailing 12-month period for more steady results.

To judge stocks one against another, the Short Interest Ratio must be normalized to adjust for the historical volatility of that ratio for each stock. Erlanger normalizes by quantifying the latest reading of a stock's short interest ratio position within its historical 5-year range. For example, if the current short interest ratio for a particular stock is 5.00, the 5-year high ratio is 6.00, and the 5-year low ratio is 2.00, then the Erlanger Short Intensity Rank would be $(5.00 - 2.00) / (6.00 - 2.00) = 75\%$. This normalized rank can then be compared to any other stock's rank.

High short interest must not be taken as an automatic signal to trade in the opposite direction. Sometimes, the short sellers are right and a weak stock continues to decline in price. Rather, it is most significant when there is both excessive bearish sentiment and positive relative strength. This is the formula for a short squeeze that can lead to a large price appreciation which can continue until the short interest dissipates.

Any database of historical short interest must be split adjusted to prevent distortion. Most databases fail to adjust for stock splits, resulting in a misleading upward bias. Adjusting for average daily volume alone is not sufficient. Split adjust both the short interest and the average daily volume data.

For big picture perspective, Erlanger computes simple averages of his ratios and ranks for all individual stocks in an industry group, a group sector and the general market. Price has an easier time rallying following high levels of adjusted and normalized short selling for an individual stock, an industry group, a group sector and the general market.

Short Interest Ratio

The Short Interest Ratio is a long-term, *Contrary Opinion* sentiment indicator. It is calculated by dividing the monthly short interest figure released by the New York Stock Exchange by the average volume of trading per day during that month.

When a relatively large amount of short selling activity is evident, traders obviously have speculated that stock prices are likely to move lower. A relatively high Short Interest Ratio adds to potential buying demand for stocks because bears must eventually cover their shorts (that is, they must buy the stock they previously sold short). This buying power is potential fuel for a rally.

Relatively low levels of short selling produce low Short Interest Ratio readings. These low levels are not bullish because they represent little buying power.

The Short Interest Ratio has changed its behavior substantially over the past two decades, with the dynamic growth of new derivative markets for options and futures. These, plus active mergers and acquisitions activity, have produced a proliferation of complex arbitrage strategies. In the early 1980's, less than 25% of the NYSE issues reporting short interest were affected by arbitrage transactions, but that rose to more than 50% later in that decade. We need an adaptive, evolving technical indicator to keep pace with these changing levels of activity.

Indicator Strategy Example for the Short Interest Ratio

Based on 69-years of monthly data for the Short Interest Ratio and the DJIA from January,1932, through December, 2000, we found that the following parameters would have produced a positive result on a purely mechanical trend-following signal basis with no subjectivity, no sophisticated technical analysis, and no judgement:

Enter Long (Buy) at the current month-end price close of the DJIA when the current Short Interest Ratio is greater than the previous month's 74-month EMA of the Short Interest Ratio.

Close Long (Sell) at the current month-end price close of the DJIA when the current Short Interest Ratio is less than the previous month's 74-month EMA of the Short Interest Ratio.

Enter Short (Sell Short) never.

Starting with $100 and reinvesting profits, total net profits for this Short Interest Ratio trend-following strategy would have been $5,888.84, assuming a fully

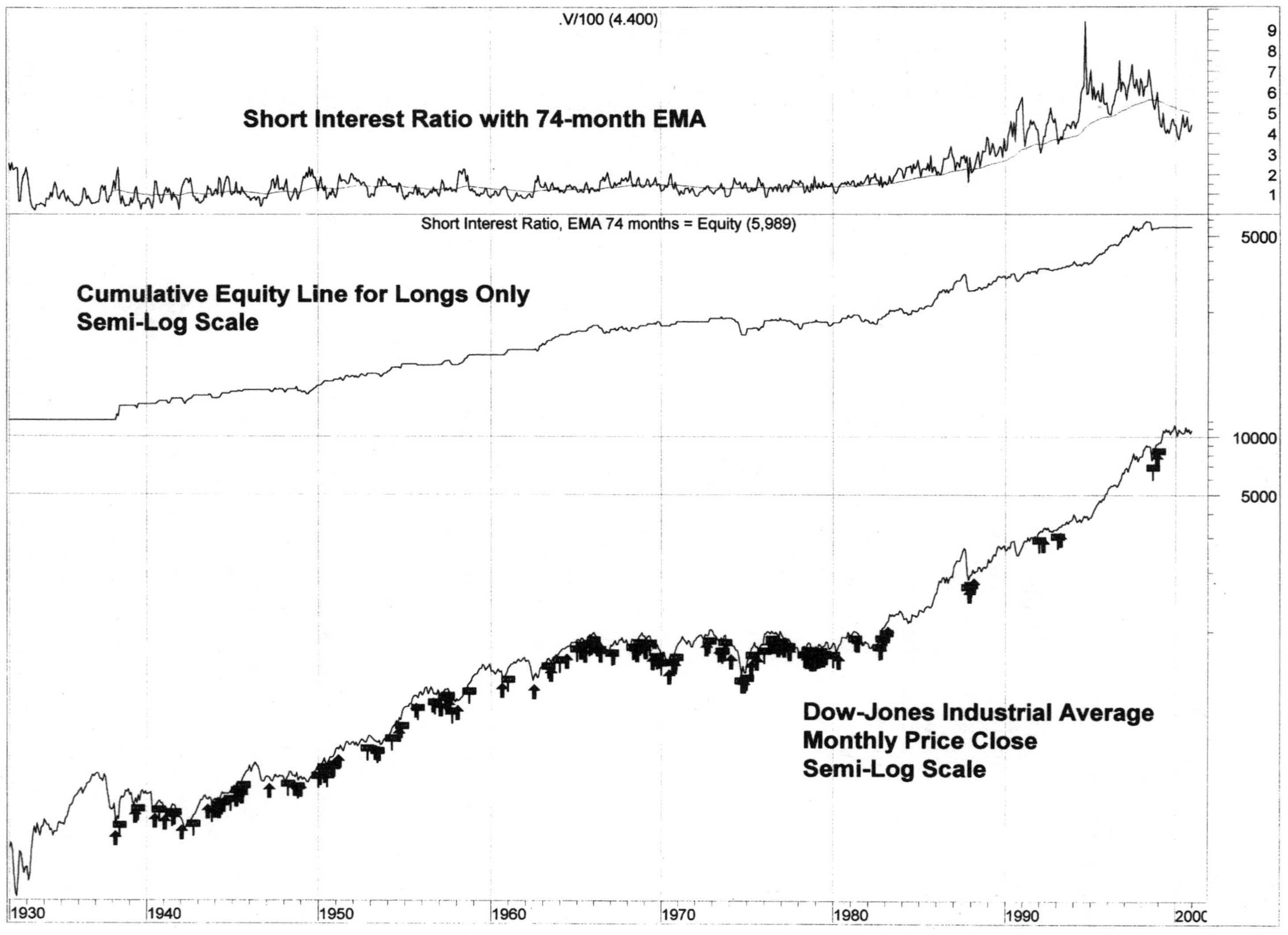

.V/100 (4.400)
Short Interest Ratio with 74-month EMA
9
8
7
6
5
4
3
2
1
Short Interest Ratio, EMA 74 months = Equity (5,989)
Cumulative Equity Line for Longs Only
Semi-Log Scale
5000
10000
5000
Dow-Jones Industrial Average
Monthly Price Close
Semi-Log Scale
1930
1940
1950
1960
1970
1980
1990
2000

Short Interest Ratio & 74-month EMA

Total net profit	5888.84	Open position value	N/A	Net Profit / Buy&Hold %	−57.89
Percent gain/loss	5888.84	Annual percent gain/loss	85.39	Annual Net % / B&H %	−57.89
Initial investment	100	Interest earned	0		
Current position	Out	Date position entered	1/1/99		
Buy/Hold profit	13983.54	Days in test	25172	# of days per trade	340.16
Buy/Hold pct gain/loss	13983.54	Annual B/H pct gain/loss	202.76		
Total closed trades	74	Commissions paid	0		
Avg profit per trade	79.58	Avg Win/Avg Loss ratio	3.85		
Total long trades	74	Total short trades	0	Long Win Trade %	72.97
Winning long trades	54	Winning short trades	0	Short Win Trade %	#DIV/0!
Total winning trades	54	Total losing trades	20	Total Win Trade %	72.97
Amount of winning trades	6515.41	Amount of losing trades	−626.57	Net Profit Margin %	82.45
Average win	120.66	Average loss	−31.33	Average P. Margin %	58.77
Largest win	3307.52	Largest loss	−257.95	% Net / (Win + Loss)	85.53
Average length of win	7.96	Average length of loss	4.45	(Win − Loss) / Loss %	78.88
Longest winning trade	66	Longest losing trade	16	(Win − Loss) / Loss %	312.50
Most consecutive wins	8	Most consecutive losses	2	(Win − Loss) / Loss %	300.00
Total bars out	457	Average length out	6.09		
Longest out period	75				
System close drawdown	0	Profit/Loss index	90.38	% Net Profit / SODD	#DIV/0!
System open drawdown	0	Reward/Risk index	100	(Net P.-SODD)/Net P.	100.00
Max open trade drawdown	−257.95	Buy/Hold index	−57.89	% SODD / Net Profit	0.00

In the Equis MetaStock® "System Report" (profit and loss summary statistics), the *Total net profit* is the sum of profits minus the sum of losses, including open positions marked to the market. In contrast, the *Amount of Winning Trades* is the sum of realized profits (the total of all gains on closed-out trades only, excluding any open positions). Similarly, the *Amount of Losing Trades* is the sum of realized losses (the total of all losses on closed-out trades only, excluding any open positions). *System close drawdown* is the largest decline in the cumulative equity line below the initial investment, based on closed-out positions only. *System open drawdown (SODD)* is the largest decline in the cumulative equity line below the initial investment when a position is open. *Max open trade drawdown* is the largest decline in the cumulative equity line below the trade entry price during the worst single trade. The *Profit/Loss Index* is a complex calculation that relates the Amount of Winning Trades to the Amount of Losing Trades on a scale of −100 (worst possible performance) to +100 (best possible performance), with zero representing profits equal to losses. *Reward/Risk Index* is the Total net profit minus System open drawdown. The resulting difference is then divided by the Total net profit. The *Buy/Hold Index* is the Total net profit minus the buy-and-hold strategy's net profit. The resulting difference is then divided by the buy-and-hold net profit. In this exercise, initial equity is assumed to be $100. Both long and short positions are taken unless otherwise noted. Trades are executed at the closing price on the signal date. Transaction costs, interest expenses, and margins are not included in the statistics.

invested strategy, reinvestment of profits, no transactions costs and no taxes. This would have been 57.89 percent less than buy-and-hold. No short selling would have been profitable, and no short selling was included in the strategy. Short selling would have cut the profit by more than half. The long-only Short Interest Ratio as an indicator would have given profitable buy signals 72.97% of the time. Trading would have been inactive at one trade every 340.16 calendar days. Note that this strategy considers month-end closing prices only, while ignoring all daily price movements.

The Equis International MetaStock® System Testing rules (where the Short Interest Ratio is inserted into the data field normally reserved for Volume) are written as follows:

Enter long: V > Ref(Mov(V,opt1,E),-1)

Close long: V < Ref(Mov(V,opt1,E),-1)

OPT1 Current value: 74

Sign of the Bear

This breadth momentum indicator was developed by market newsletter publisher and portfolio manager, Peter G. Eliades, *Stockmarket Cycles,* P. O. Box 6873, Santa Rosa, CA 95406-0873, phone (707) 769-4800, fax (707) 769-4803, e-mail: peter@eliades.net. There are three requirements for the Sign of the Bear:

1. There must be 21 to 27 consecutive trading days where the daily advance/decline ratio on the NYSE is both above 0.65 and below 1.95. This indicates a churning market that is going nowhere.
2. That 21 to 27 day quiet period must be broken by a one-daily advance/decline ratio below 0.65. This is the first sign of negative trend change.
3. Finally, the 2-day average of the advance/decline ratio must fall below 0.75. This 2-day average may include the initial day below 0.65 that triggers Requirement 2. This confirms negative trend change.

The advance/decline ratio is the number of advancing issues divided by the number of declining issues each day on the NYSE. A 2-day average is the current advance/decline ratio added to the previous day's advance/decline ratio, then that sum is divided by two.

The following table shows that there have been only seven signals for the Sign of the Bear since 1929. Some have been a few weeks before the final price high of the bull market. Each signal has been followed by a drop in the DJIA ranging from 21% to 89% and averaging 39%.

Date	*Drop*
7/22/29	−89%
12/14/61	−29%
1/31/66	−27%
10/25/68	−36%
12/12/72	−45%
4/6/98	−21%
9/18/00	−27%
Average	−39%

Indicator Example of the Advance/Decline Ratio Oscillator 2-day EMA Crossing 0.75

Eliades' Sign of the Bear lacks an exit rule, a buy signal to close out the sell signal. Breadth-Momentum Oscillators can be used as part of a complete trend-following strategy, however. Based on a 68-year file of daily data for the number of shares advancing and declining each day on the NYSE and the DJIA since March 8, 1932, we found that the following specific parameters would have produced a positive result on a purely mechanical signal basis with no subjectivity, no sophisticated technical analysis, and no judgement:

Enter Long (Buy) at the current daily price close of the DJIA when the 2-day EMA of the daily Advance/Decline Ratio rises to cross above 0.75.

Close Long (Sell) at the current daily price close of the DJIA when the 2-day EMA of the daily Advance/Decline Ratio falls to cross below 0.75.

Enter Short (Sell Short) at the current daily price close of the DJIA when the 2-day EMA of the daily Advance/Decline Ratio falls to cross below 0.75.

Close Short (Cover) at the current daily price close of the DJIA when the 2-day EMA of the daily Advance/Decline Ratio rises to cross above 0.75.

Starting with $100 and reinvesting profits, total net profits for this Breadth-Momentum Oscillator trend-following strategy would have been $10,533,586, assuming a fully invested strategy, reinvestment of profits, no transactions costs and no taxes. This would have been 83,908.87 percent better than buy-and-hold. Even short selling would have been profitable. Trading would have been very active with one trade every 6.76 calendar days.

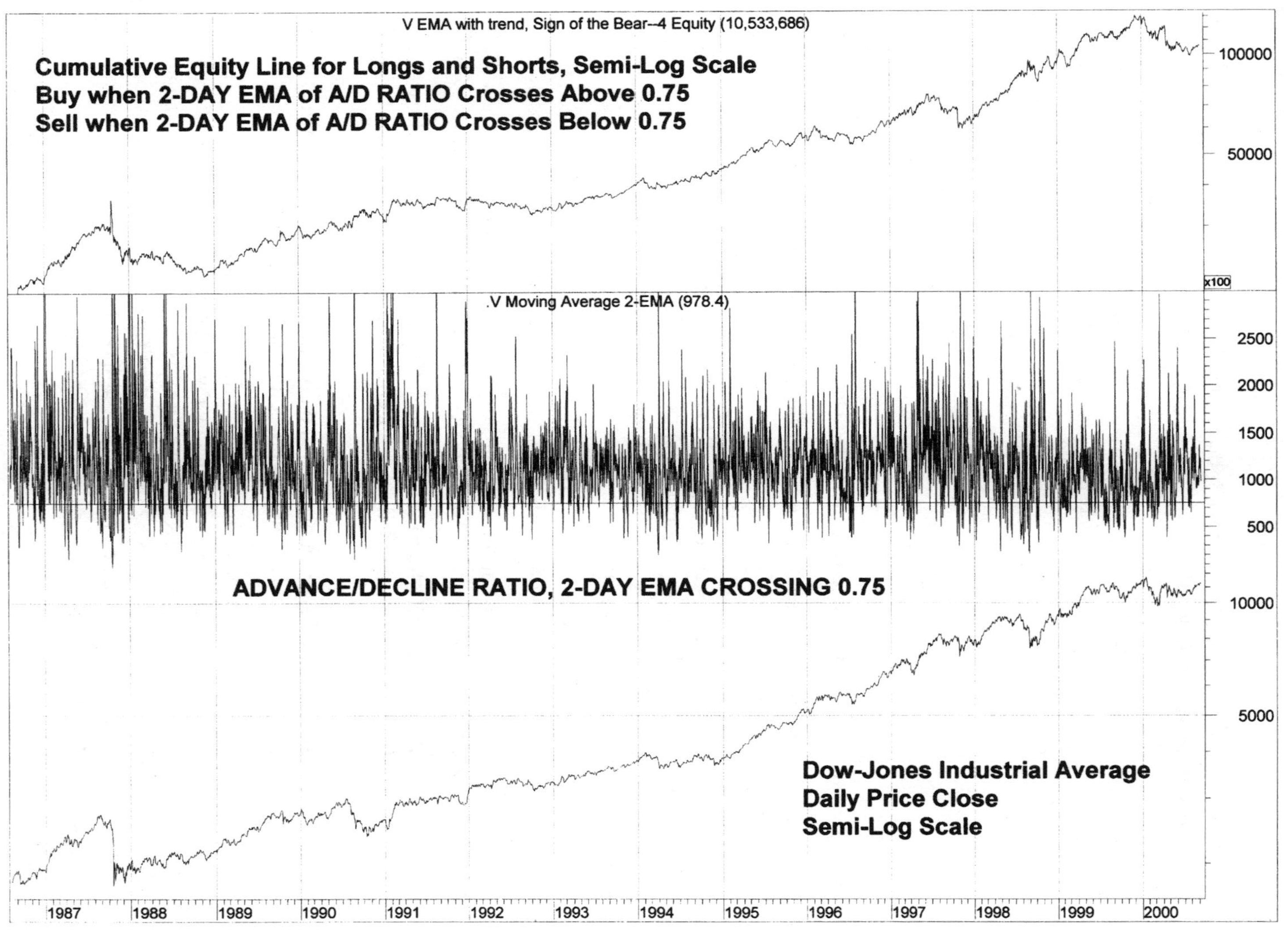
V EMA with trend, Sign of the Bear--4 Equity (10,533,686)
Cumulative Equity Line for Longs and Shorts, Semi-Log Scale
Buy when 2-DAY EMA of A/D RATIO Crosses Above 0.75
Sell when 2-DAY EMA of A/D RATIO Crosses Below 0.75
100000
50000
x100
.V Moving Average 2-EMA (978.4)
2500
2000
1500
1000
500
ADVANCE/DECLINE RATIO, 2-DAY EMA CROSSING 0.75
10000
5000
Dow-Jones Industrial Average
Daily Price Close
Semi-Log Scale
1987
1988
1989
1990
1991
1992
1993
1994
1995
1996
1997
1998
1999
2000

Advance / Decline Ratio Oscillator 2-day EMA Crossing 0.75

Total net profit	10533586	Open position value	655832.06	Net Profit / Buy&Hold %	83908.87
Percent gain/loss	10533586	Annual percent gain/loss	153655.14	Annual Net % / B&H %	83910.46
Initial investment	100	Interest earned	0		
Current position	Long	Date position entered	7/31/00		
Buy/Hold profit	12538.66	Days in test	25022	# of days per trade	6.76
Buy/Hold pct gain/loss	12538.66	Annual B/H pct gain/loss	182.9		
Total closed trades	3702	Commissions paid	0		
Avg profit per trade	2668.22	Avg Win/Avg Loss ratio	1.8		
Total long trades	1851	Total short trades	1851	Long Win Trade %	42.90
Winning long trades	794	Winning short trades	833	Short Win Trade %	45.00
Total winning trades	1627	Total losing trades	2075	Total Win Trade %	43.95
Amount of winning trades	33685556	Amount of losing trades	−23807786	Net Profit Margin %	17.18
Average win	20704.09	Average loss	−11473.63	Average P. Margin %	28.69
Largest win	1289721	Largest loss	−497100	% Net / (Win + Loss)	44.36
Average length of win	8.97	Average length of loss	3.45	(Win − Loss) / Loss %	160.00
Longest winning trade	66	Longest losing trade	22	(Win − Loss) / Loss %	200.00
Most consecutive wins	10	Most consecutive losses	10	(Win − Loss) / Loss %	0.00
Total bars out	2	Average length out	2		
Longest out period	2				
System close drawdown	−45.15	Profit/Loss index	30.67	% Net Profit / SODD	23330201.55
System open drawdown	−45.15	Reward/Risk index	100	(Net P.-SODD)/Net P.	100.00
Max open trade drawdown	−497100	Buy/Hold index	89139.36	% SODD / Net Profit	0.00

In the Equis MetaStock® "System Report" (profit and loss summary statistics), the *Total net profit* is the sum of profits minus the sum of losses, including open positions marked to the market. In contrast, the *Amount of Winning Trades* is the sum of realized profits (the total of all gains on closed-out trades only, excluding any open positions). Similarly, the *Amount of Losing Trades* is the sum of realized losses (the total of all losses on closed-out trades only, excluding any open positions). *System close drawdown* is the largest decline in the cumulative equity line below the initial investment, based on closed-out positions only. *System open drawdown (SODD)* is the largest decline in the cumulative equity line below the initial investment when a position is open. *Max open trade drawdown* is the largest decline in the cumulative equity line below the trade entry price during the worst single trade. The *Profit/Loss Index* is a complex calculation that relates the Amount of Winning Trades to the Amount of Losing Trades on a scale of −100 (worst possible performance) to +100 (best possible performance), with zero representing profits equal to losses. *Reward/Risk Index* is the Total net profit minus System open drawdown. The resulting difference is then divided by the Total net profit. The *Buy/Hold Index* is the Total net profit minus the buy-and-hold strategy's net profit. The resulting difference is then divided by the buy-and-hold net profit. In this exercise, initial equity is assumed to be $100. Both long and short positions are taken unless otherwise noted. Trades are executed at the closing price on the signal date. Transaction costs, interest expenses, and margins are not included in the statistics.

The Equis International MetaStock® System Testing rules, where the current Advance/Decline Ratio multiplied by 1000 (to avoid handling fractions) is inserted into the data field normally reserved for Volume (V), are written as follows:

Enter long: Mov(V,opt1,E)>opt2

Close long: Mov(V,opt1,E)<opt2

Enter short: Mov(V,opt1,E)<opt2

Close short: Mov(V,opt1,E)>opt2

OPT1 Current value: 2
OPT2 Current value: 750

Simple Moving Average (SMA): Moving Arithmetic Mean

Mathematically, a simple arithmetic mean formula is represented as:

$$M_k = \frac{1}{n} \sum_{i=k-n+1}^{k} C_i = (C_{k-n+1} + C_{k-n+2} + C_{k-n+3} + \ldots + C_k) \div n$$

where

M_k = the simple moving average arithmetic mean at period k.
C_i = the closing price for period i.
n = the total number of periods to be included in the moving mean calculation.
k = the number of the position of the period being studied within the total number of periods in the database (see example, page 649).

The Simple Moving Average (SMA) is probably the simplest, oldest, and most widely used statistical method applied to stock price data. For example, the 200-day simple moving average has been a popular and moderately effective guide to stock market transaction timing for many decades. To compute it, we simply add together the closing prices for the past 200 trading days, then divide that sum by 200. Before computers, technicians took a shortcut, adding up the weekly closing prices over 40 weeks, then dividing by 40. Assuming five trading days in a week, 200 days is 40 weeks (200/5=40). Or, if they were extremely computationally adverse, they added 10 month-end closing prices then divided by 10. Assuming twenty trading days in a month, 200 days is 10 months (200/20=10). All three methods produce nearly the same result, a result good enough to encourage increasing popularity of this major

Example of Simple Moving Average of Four Periods

Year End	*Price NYSE Close*	*Four-Period Moving Total (T)*	*Four-Period Simple Moving Average (T ÷ 4)*
1968	58.90		
1969	51.53		
1970	50.23		
1971	56.43	217.09	54.27
1972	64.48	222.67	55.67
1973	51.82	222.96	55.74
1974	36.13	208.86	52.22
1975	47.64	200.07	50.02
1976	57.88	193.47	48.37
1977	52.50	194.15	48.54
1978	53.62	211.64	52.91
1979	61.95	225.95	56.49
1980	77.86	245.93	61.48
1981	71.11	264.54	66.14
1982	81.03	291.95	72.99
1983	95.18	325.18	81.30
1984	96.38	343.70	85.93
1985	121.58	394.17	98.54
1986	138.58	451.72	112.93

trend following indicator over the decades. Despite its simplicity, the SMA is a useful tool for identifying and following price trends and smoothing data of all kinds.

Since only two prices affect the most recent SMA, updating the calculation can be accomplished quickly without a computer. For example, to maintain a 10-month SMA, at each month end, we would subtract the oldest data, now 11 months old, from our 10-month moving total. Then, we add the latest data to the moving total. Finally, we divide that new moving total by the number of periods averaged, which in this example of 10 periods simply involves placing the decimal point before the last digit of the moving total.

Indicator Strategy Example for the Simple Moving Average (SMA)

Based on the daily closing prices for the DJIA from 1900 to 2001, Simple Moving Average Crossover Strategies of all lengths from 1-day to 385 days would have been profitable and would have beaten the passive buy-and-hold strategy. The 1-, 4-, and 5-day SMA would have produced maximum net profits in the billions of dollars,

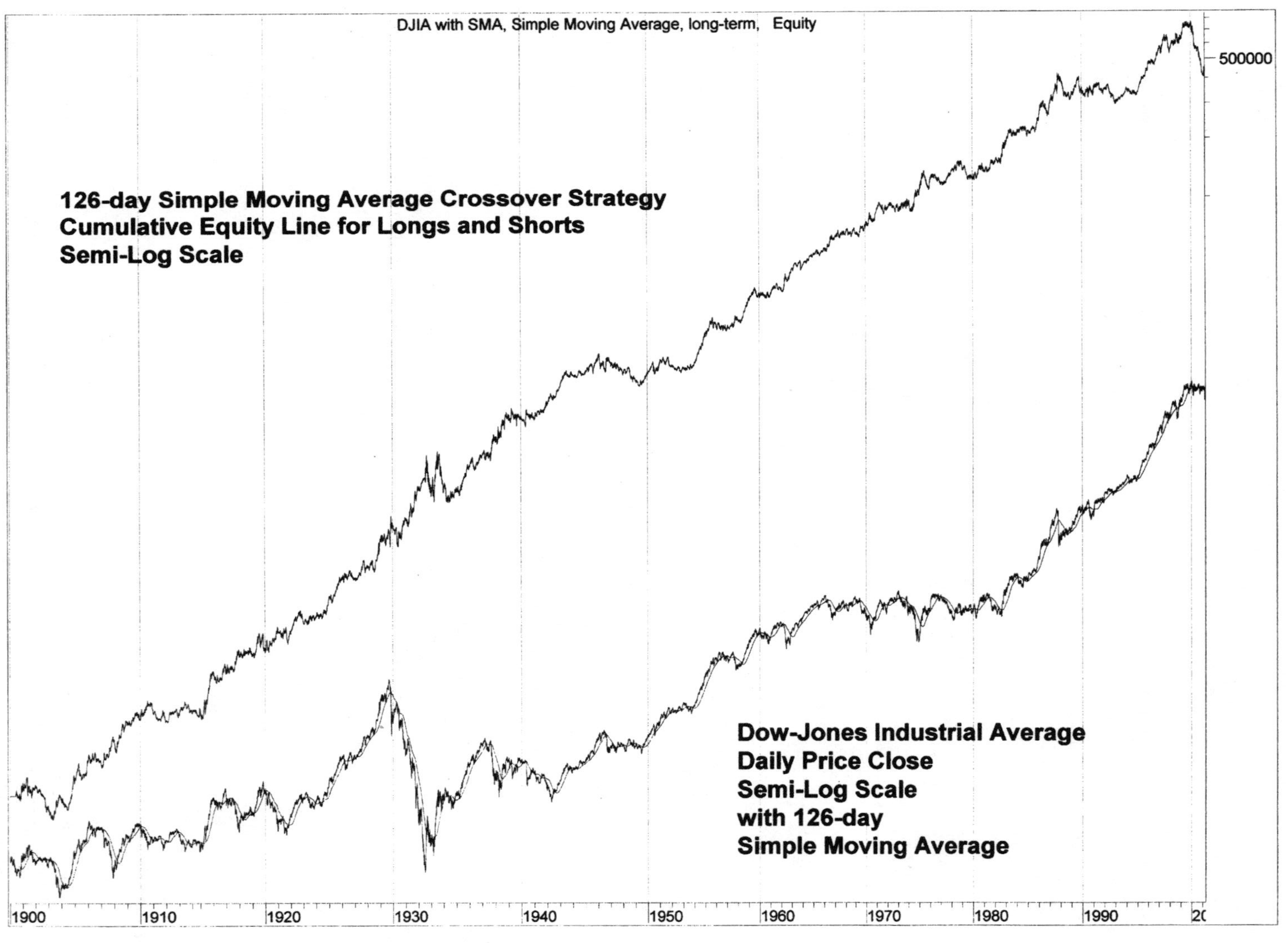
DJIA with SMA, Simple Moving Average, long-term, Equity
500000
126-day Simple Moving Average Crossover Strategy
Cumulative Equity Line for Longs and Shorts
Semi-Log Scale
Dow-Jones Industrial Average
Daily Price Close
Semi-Log Scale
with 126-day
Simple Moving Average
1900
1910
1920
1930
1940
1950
1960
1970
1980
1990

126-Day SMA Crossover Strategy

Total net profit	426745.59	Open position value	20677.37	Net Profit / Buy&Hold %	2022.54
Percent gain/loss	426745.59	Annual percent gain/loss	4211.04	Annual Net % / B&H %	2022.50
Initial investment	100	Interest earned	0		
Current position	Short	Date position entered	3/9/01		
Buy/Hold profit	20105.4	Days in test	36989	# of days per trade	41.75
Buy/Hold pct gain/loss	20105.4	Annual B/H pct gain/loss	198.4		
Total closed trades	886	Commissions paid	0		
Avg profit per trade	458.32	Avg Win/Avg Loss ratio	5.56		
Total long trades	443	Total short trades	443	Long Win Trade %	24.83
Winning long trades	110	Winning short trades	75	Short Win Trade %	16.93
Total winning trades	185	Total losing trades	701	Total Win Trade %	20.88
Amount of winning trades	1273965.75	Amount of losing trades	−867897.5	Net Profit Margin %	18.96
Average win	6886.3	Average loss	−1238.08	Average P. Margin %	69.52
Largest win	147373.22	Largest loss	−36365	% Net / (Win + Loss)	60.42
Average length of win	117.43	Average length of loss	9.65	(Win − Loss) / Loss %	1116.89
Longest winning trade	500	Longest losing trade	89	(Win − Loss) / Loss %	461.80
Most consecutive wins	4	Most consecutive losses	27	(Win − Loss) / Loss %	−85.19
Total bars out	127	Average length out	127		
Longest out period	127				
System close drawdown	−23.51	Profit/Loss index	32.96	% Net Profit / SODD	1787790.49
System open drawdown	−23.87	Reward/Risk index	99.99	(Net P.-SODD)/Net P.	99.99
Max open trade drawdown	−36365	Buy/Hold index	2125.39	% SODD / Net Profit	−0.01

In the Equis MetaStock® "System Report" (profit and loss summary statistics), the *Total net profit* is the sum of profits minus the sum of losses, including open positions marked to the market. In contrast, the *Amount of Winning Trades* is the sum of realized profits (the total of all gains on closed-out trades only, excluding any open positions). Similarly, the *Amount of Losing Trades* is the sum of realized losses (the total of all losses on closed-out trades only, excluding any open positions). *System close drawdown* is the largest decline in the cumulative equity line below the initial investment, based on closed-out positions only. *System open drawdown (SODD)* is the largest decline in the cumulative equity line below the initial investment when a position is open. *Max open trade drawdown* is the largest decline in the cumulative equity line below the trade entry price during the worst single trade. The *Profit/Loss Index* is a complex calculation that relates the Amount of Winning Trades to the Amount of Losing Trades on a scale of −100 (worst possible performance) to +100 (best possible performance), with zero representing profits equal to losses. *Reward/Risk Index* is the Total net profit minus System open drawdown. The resulting difference is then divided by the Total net profit. The *Buy/Hold Index* is the Total net profit minus the buy-and-hold strategy's net profit. The resulting difference is then divided by the buy-and-hold net profit. In this exercise, initial equity is assumed to be $100. Both long and short positions are taken unless otherwise noted. Trades are executed at the closing price on the signal date. Transaction costs, interest expenses, and margins are not included in the statistics.

assuming we start with one hundred dollars in 1900. Performance deteriorated as the moving average period length increased. All SMA period lengths of 1 to 100 days would have outperformed buy-and-hold by more than seven to one. Of the "intermediate-term" lengths, the 66-day SMA would have produced the best results, net profit of $639,933, which would have been more than 31 times the buy-and-hold strategy's $20,105. The popular 200-day SMA Crossover Strategy would have produced much less profit of $121,257, which would have been only six times the buy-and-hold-strategy's $20,105 net profit.

Of the "long-term" lengths, the 126-day SMA Crossover Strategy would have produced the maximum profit on a purely mechanical trend-following signal basis with no subjectivity, no sophisticated technical analysis, and no judgement:

Enter Long (Buy) at the current daily price close of the DJIA when this close is greater than the previous day's 126-day SMA of the daily closing prices.

Close Long (Sell) at the current daily price close of the DJIA when this close is less than the previous day's 126-day SMA of the daily closing prices.

Enter Short (Sell Short) at the current daily price close of the DJIA when this close is less than the previous day's 126-day SMA of the daily closing prices.

Close Short (Cover) at the current daily price close of the DJIA when this close is greater than the previous day's 126-day SMA of the daily closing prices.

Starting with $100 and reinvesting profits, total net profits for this 126-day SMA Crossover Strategy would have been $426,745.59, assuming a fully invested strategy, reinvestment of profits, no transactions costs and no taxes. This would have been 2,022.54 percent better than buy-and-hold. Short selling would have been profitable, but not since the Crash of '87. Trading frequency would have been moderate with one trade every 41.75 calendar days. There would have been 185 profitable trades and 701 losing trades, for a winning percentage of only 20.88% profitable. But because this trend-following strategy cuts losses and lets profits run, it would have made money despite being wrong on most of its signals. This is typical of the longer-term trend-following strategies. Such a strategy may be used alone, and it also can be useful as a filter to other trading systems.

The Equis International MetaStock® System Testing rules are written as follows:

Enter long: CLOSE > Ref(Mov(CLOSE,opt1,S),-1)

Close long: CLOSE < Ref(Mov(CLOSE,opt1,S),-1)

Enter short: CLOSE < Ref(Mov(CLOSE,opt1,S),-1)

Close short: CLOSE > Ref(Mov(CLOSE,opt1,S),-1)

OPT1 Current value: 126

Specialist Short Ratio

The Specialist Short Ratio is computed by dividing total specialist short sales by total short sales, which includes both member and public short sales. Because, the absolute levels of short selling have increased in all categories along with the general expansion in the total volume of trading activity, the data must be normalized somehow, hence, the various short sales ratios.

The data is released, with a 2-week lag, by the NYSE each week after the Friday close. This release includes summary data only for the exchange as a whole. It excludes data for individual stocks. (Suggestion: In this age of advanced data processing, it might be possible and contribute to an efficient, fair and orderly market if the NYSE would release this data without a lag and include data on individual stocks.)

Specialists are seasoned professional traders who own seats on the exchange, are backed by substantial trading capital, and have access to privileged and important market information, including the price and quantity of bids and offers above and below the market price for the stocks in which they make markets. For these reasons, specialists are considered to be *the smart money* when it comes to trading. If they are not market savvy, they will not be able to remain in the specialist business over the long run. Specialists are mostly right about the future trend of stock prices. Therefore, low specialist short selling is bullish, and high specialist shorting is bearish. Thus, this indicator is interpreted in a manner similar to an Overbought/Oversold Oscillator.

A *short sale* is a bet that a stock will fall. A trader will place an order to "Sell Short" a stock he has no existing position in when he feels confident that its price is likely to decline significantly. (The trader's broker seamlessly arranges for the trader to borrow the stock. Some illiquid stocks cannot be borrowed and, therefore, cannot be sold short.) Eventually, the trader must place a buy order to "Cover Short" to close out his short position: at a profit if the stock price declines as anticipated, or at a loss if the stock price rises unexpectedly.

Indicator Strategy Example for Specialist Short Ratio

Based on a 55-year file of Specialist Short Ratios and weekly closing price data for the DJIA from January 1946 to December 2000, we found that the following parameters would have slightly underperformed the passive buy-and-hold strategy but

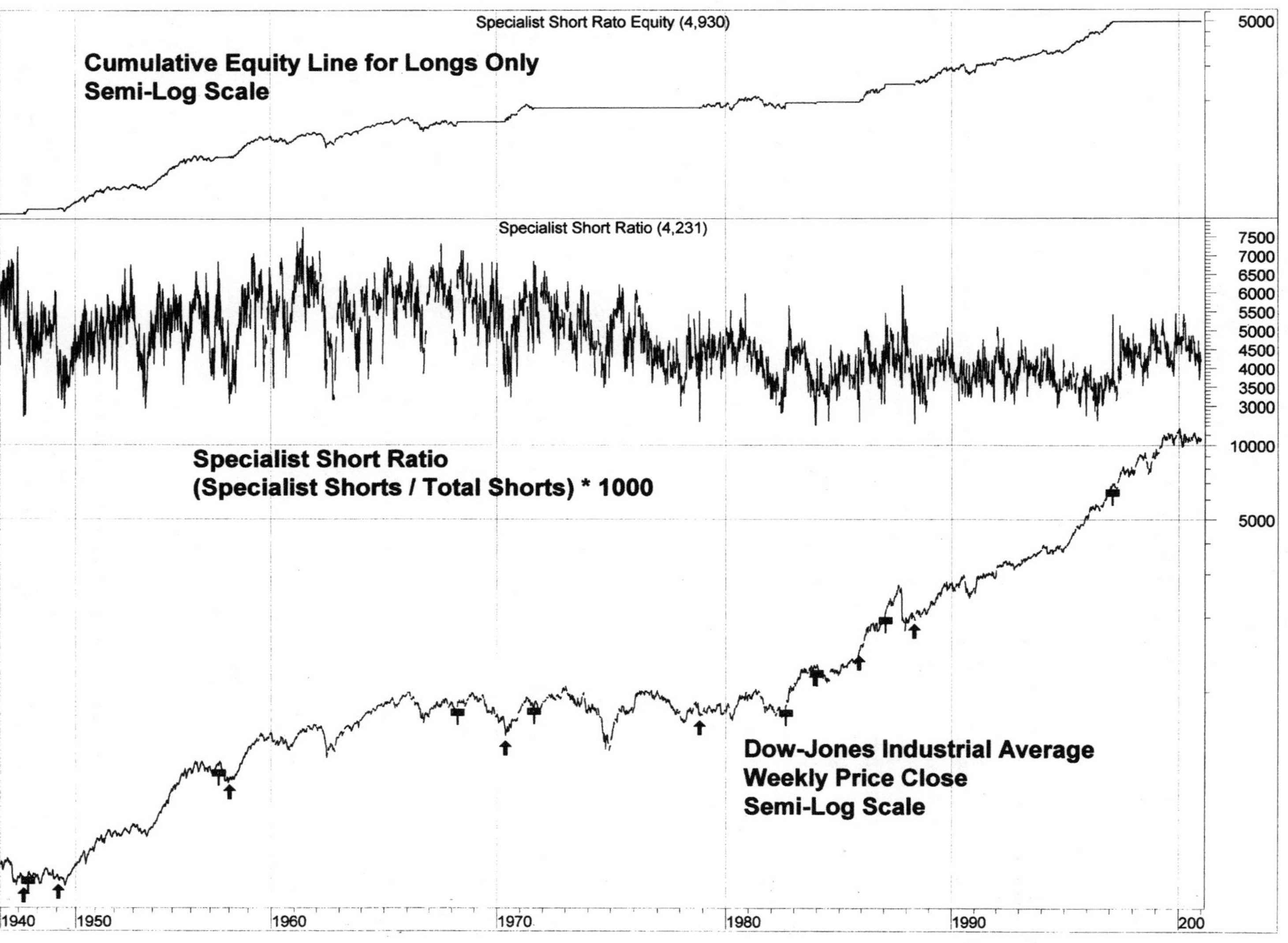

Specialist Short Rato Equity (4,930)
Cumulative Equity Line for Longs Only
Semi-Log Scale
5000
Specialist Short Ratio (4,231)
7500
7000
6500
6000
5500
5000
4500
4000
3500
3000
Specialist Short Ratio
(Specialist Shorts / Total Shorts) * 1000
10000
5000
Dow-Jones Industrial Average
Weekly Price Close
Semi-Log Scale
1940
1950
1960
1970
1980
1990
200

Specialist Short Ratio (Envelope)

Total net profit	4829.91	Open position value	N/A	Net Profit / Buy&Hold %	−7.43
Percent gain/loss	4829.91	Annual percent gain/loss	87.84	Annual Net % / B&H %	−7.43
Initial investment	100	Interest earned	0		
Current position	Out	Date position entered	2/14/97		
Buy/Hold profit	5217.78	Days in test	20070	# of days per trade	2508.75
Buy/Hold pct gain/loss	5217.78	Annual B/H pct gain/loss	94.89		
Total closed trades	8	Commissions paid	0		
Avg profit per trade	603.74	Avg Win/Avg Loss ratio	N/A		
Total long trades	8	Total short trades	0	Long Win Trade %	100.00
Winning long trades	8	Winning short trades	0	Short Win Trade %	#DIV/0!
Total winning trades	8	Total losing trades	0	Total Win Trade %	100.00
Amount of winning trades	4829.91	Amount of losing trades	0	Net Profit Margin %	100.00
Average win	603.74	Average loss	N/A	Average P. Margin %	#VALUE!
Largest win	3525.78	Largest loss	0	% Net / (Win + Loss)	100.00
Average length of win	221.88	Average length of loss	N/A	(Win − Loss) / Loss %	#VALUE!
Longest winning trade	535	Longest losing trade	0	(Win − Loss) / Loss %	#DIV/0!
Most consecutive wins	8	Most consecutive losses	0	(Win − Loss) / Loss %	#DIV/0!
Total bars out	1109	Average length out	123.22		
Longest out period	378				
System close drawdown	0	Profit/Loss index	100	% Net Profit / SODD	447213.89
System open drawdown	−1.08	Reward/Risk index	99.98	(Net P.-SODD)/Net P.	99.98
Max open trade drawdown	−47.65	Buy/Hold index	−7.43	% SODD / Net Profit	−0.02

In the Equis MetaStock® "System Report" (profit and loss summary statistics), the *Total net profit* is the sum of profits minus the sum of losses, including open positions marked to the market. In contrast, the *Amount of Winning Trades* is the sum of realized profits (the total of all gains on closed-out trades only, excluding any open positions). Similarly, the *Amount of Losing Trades* is the sum of realized losses (the total of all losses on closed-out trades only, excluding any open positions). *System close drawdown* is the largest decline in the cumulative equity line below the initial investment, based on closed-out positions only. *System open drawdown (SODD)* is the largest decline in the cumulative equity line below the initial investment when a position is open. *Max open trade drawdown* is the largest decline in the cumulative equity line below the trade entry price during the worst single trade. The *Profit/Loss Index* is a complex calculation that relates the Amount of Winning Trades to the Amount of Losing Trades on a scale of −100 (worst possible performance) to +100 (best possible performance), with zero representing profits equal to losses. *Reward/Risk Index* is the Total net profit minus System open drawdown. The resulting difference is then divided by the Total net profit. The *Buy/Hold Index* is the Total net profit minus the buy-and-hold strategy's net profit. The resulting difference is then divided by the buy-and-hold net profit. In this exercise, initial equity is assumed to be $100. Both long and short positions are taken unless otherwise noted. Trades are executed at the closing price on the signal date. Transaction costs, interest expenses, and margins are not included in the statistics.

would have produced 100% accurate signals, on a purely mechanical overbought/oversold signal basis with no subjectivity, no sophisticated technical analysis, and no judgement:

Enter Long (Buy) at the current weekly price close of the DJIA when the latest Specialist Short Ratio is 28.5% below its previous week's 21-week EMA of the Specialist Short Ratio.

Close Long (Sell) at the current weekly price close of the DJIA when the latest Specialist Short Ratio is 28.5% above its previous week's 13-week EMA of the Specialist Short Ratio.

Enter Short (Sell Short) never.

Starting with $100 and reinvesting profits, total net profits for this Specialist Short Ratio counter-trend strategy would have been $4,829.91, assuming a fully invested strategy, reinvestment of profits, no transactions costs and no taxes. This would have been 7.43 percent less than buy-and-hold. No short selling would have been profitable, and no short selling was included in the strategy. Short selling would have cut the profit by 58%. Long-only Specialist Short Ratio as an indicator would have given profitable buy signals 100% of the time. Trading would have been inactive at one trade every 2508.75 calendar days. Note that this strategy considers weekend closing prices only while ignoring everything in between.

The Equis International MetaStock® System Testing rules for Specialist Short Ratio, where the ratio of Specialist Short Sales to Total Short Sales is inserted into the field normally reserved for open interest, are written as follows:

Enter long: OI < (Ref(Mov(OI,opt1,E),-1) − ((opt2/1000))*Ref(Mov(OI,opt1,E),-1))

Close long: OI > Ref(Mov(OI,opt3,E),-1) + ((opt2/1000))*Ref(Mov(OI,opt3,E),-1)

OPT1 Current value: 21

OPT2 Current value: 285

OPT3 Current value: 13

Speed Resistance Lines

Speed Resistance Lines provide theoretical support and resistance. They were developed by Edson Gould, who published a technical analysis newsletter, *Findings & Forecasts,* which achieved great popularity and a wide following in the 1970s, thanks to a number of startlingly accurate market calls. Gould was educated as an engineer, and he used his knowledge, long experience, and intuition to conceptualize structures of market movements. Gould viewed market movements as the meaningful unfolding of underlying significant forces of accumulation and distribution.

Speed Resistance Lines move at a fraction of the pace of the preceding significant market price move. Rising Speed Resistance Lines move up at rates of speed that are one-third and two-thirds the rate of a previous notable advance from a significant low to a significant high. Falling Speed Resistance Lines move down at rates of speed that are one-third and two-thirds the rate of a previous notable decline from a significant high to a significant low. There are few turning points a year that really stand out on the chart, and these are the significant highs and lows.

To compute Rising Speed Resistance Lines, subtract the price at an outstanding low from the price at a subsequent important rally peak. Divide that difference into thirds. Add one-third and then two-thirds to the original low. On an arithmetically scaled chart, directly below and on the exact date of the outstanding rally peak, mark these two calculated points, at one-third and two-thirds of the total rally advance in price, from low to high. Draw straight lines from the low through these two points. These straight lines are the One-Third and Two-Thirds Speed Resistance Lines. The procedure is similar for falling Speed Resistance Lines, which are drawn down from a high through points one-third and two-thirds the distance above a subsequent low.

For downside corrections or reactions against a strong bullish trend, price should find support at the rising Two-Thirds Speed Resistance Line. If that support fails, however, price may then fall to the One-Third Speed Resistance Line, where it should find support. The chart shows that the Rising One-Third Speed Resistance Line from the 1982 low to the 1987 high provided precise support in the Crash of '87. The related rising Two-Thirds Speed Resistance Line provided six years of guidance reminiscent of a median line on the subsequent rising trend from 1988 to 1994.

In a bear market, oversold rallies and dead cat bounces should find resistance at the falling Two-Thirds Resistance Speed Line. If that resistance fails to stop the price recovery, however, price may then rise up to the One-Third Speed Resistance Line, where it should find resistance.

Note that MetaStock® software by Equis International (www.equis.com) also automatically draws a Three-Thirds Speed Resistance Line from low to high (or from high to low). This is not discussed much but appears to be interesting at times when extended out into the future. The 3/3, Three-Thirds Speed Resistance Line drawn from the 1982 low to the 1983 high was never exceeded but was fairly closely approached at the end of the steep bull market that ended in March 2000. Also, note that the 3/3, Three-Thirds Speed Resistance Line drawn from the December 1994 low to the May 1996 high seemed to provid structure to the subsequent bullish trend.

Springboard

A Springboard occurs when price breaks out above or below a resistance or support level but immediately reverses with a forceful move in the opposite direction. This *hooks* or *traps* trend-followers who went with the breakout. These trend-followers must now cut losses, which adds fuel to the new directional momentum.

Stage Analysis

Stage Analysis is a term coined by Stan Weinstein (See Weinstein, S. (1988). *Stan Weinstein's Secrets for Profiting in Bull and Bear Markets.* Homewood, IL: Irwin) to describe his observation that stocks pass through four stages in their complete bull through bear cycle.

Stage 1 is base-building, characterized by the stock price fluctuating sideways in a relatively narrow trading range. There is little interest in the stock and nothing seems to be happening. Something important is happening, however, and that is accumulation by the smart-money investors with the vision to see better things ahead. Volume has been light but begins to improve on rallies. In Stage 1, the stock price wanders aimlessly back and forth across its own trailing 50-day, 150-day, and

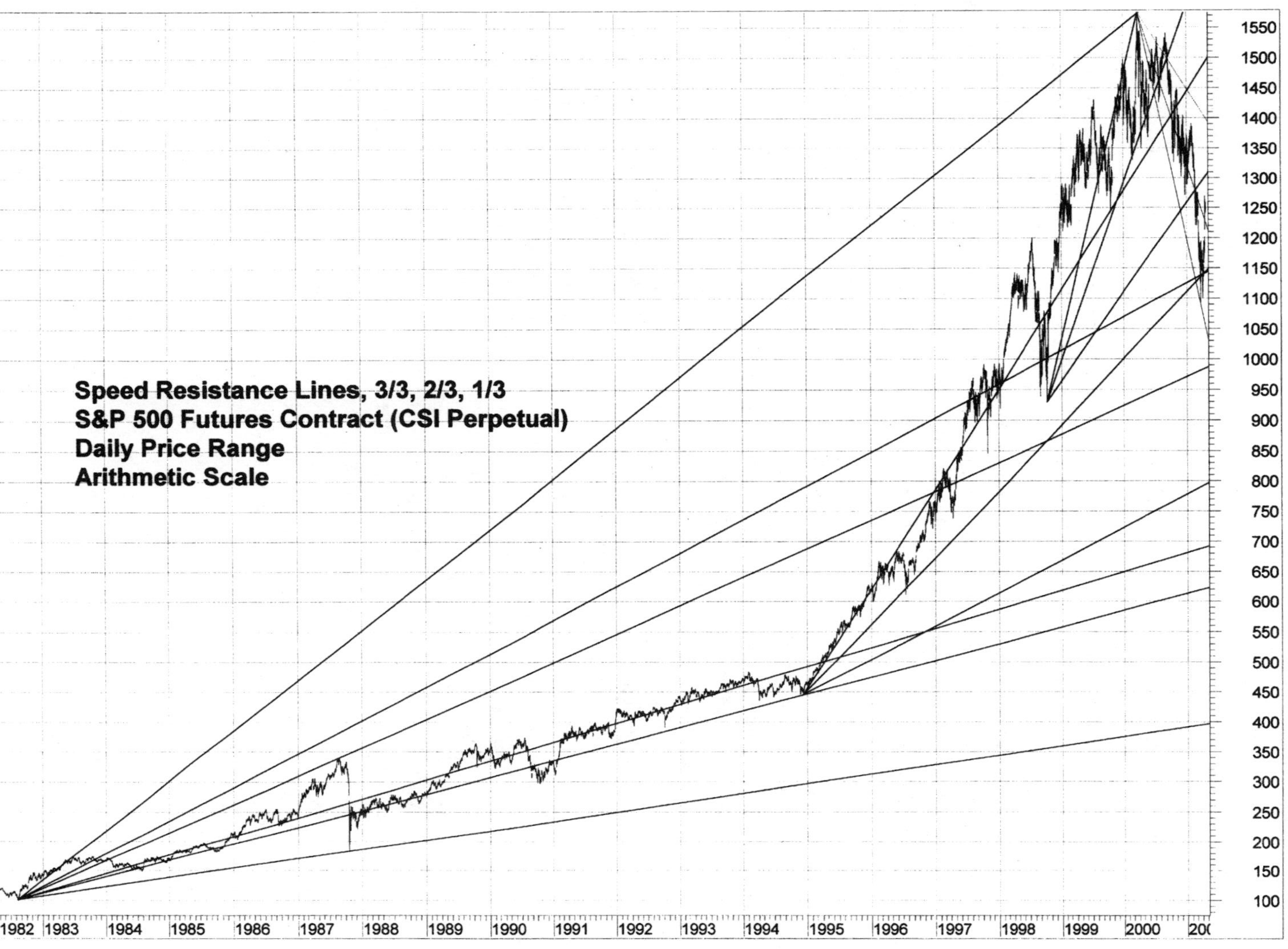

Speed Resistance Lines, 3/3, 2/3, 1/3
S&P 500 Futures Contract (CSI Perpetual)
Daily Price Range
Arithmetic Scale
1550 1500 1450 1400 1350 1300 1250 1200 1150 1100 1050 1000 950 900 850 800 750 700 650 600 550 500 450 400 350 300 250 200 150 100
1982 1983 1984 1985 1986 1987 1988 1989 1990 1991 1992 1993 1994 1995 1996 1997 1998 1999 2000

200-day moving averages. This is not the time for trend trading, since the whipsaws would eat into your capital. Stage 1 can drag out for many months or even years, so for the technical trader it is too early to buy. But the longer Stage 1 lasts, the greater the upside potential in the next Stage 2.

Stage 2 sees a breakout and a substantial price mark-up. The price moves above all moving averages and makes new 52-week highs. Volume jumps up on the breakout, rises on rallies, and falls on price dips. The moving averages are rising now. Corrective Secondary Waves or shake-outs temporarily may drop the stock below its own trailing 50-day moving average but not for long, as price springs back up quickly. The trailing 150-day and 200-day moving averages provide support on normal contra-trend reactions, periods of profit taking. Fundamental conditions begin to improve in Stage 2. Everyone is making money except the short sellers. It is a Bull Market.

Stage 3 is the top. The fundamental news is very positive and everyone is talking bullish. The stock price stalls out, however, and no longer responds to good news. Volume is high, but there is a seller for every buyer. Price slides sideways through rising trendlines. A potentially bearish chart pattern forms. Price begins to cross back and forth through the various moving averages. Toward the end of Stage 3, everyone who is going to buy has already bought, so the price has only one way to go, down.

Stage 4 is the breakdown followed by a major decline. The stock price drops below its Stage 3 trading range and below its own trailing 50-day, 150-day, and 200-day moving averages. These moving averages are pointing lower now, declining, and they provide resistance on normal contra-trend rallies, periods of short covering. In the early part of Stage 4, the fundamentals still look good, but the stock price fails to respond to good news or rallies only very briefly before declining again. As Stage 4 progresses, fundamentals begin to turn negative. At that point, everyone wants out, and the decline steepens. There may be a series of selling panics and selling climaxes on high volume as investors turn fearful. The decline usually goes further than anyone thought possible, until the stock is extremely oversold and undervalued. Eventually, everyone who is going to sell has already sold, and so the stock no longer drops to new lows on bad news. The crowd has been badly burned and consequently is totally disgusted with the stock, muttering, "Never again." At this point, the stage is set for an eventual new round of accumulation, and a new Stage 1 may begin, though that probably will take time.

Standard Deviation

Standard deviation is a statistical measurement of data dispersion, or scatter, or volatility. It is a quantification of the variability of the distribution of the raw data around a simple moving average. Standard deviation is calculated in six steps:

1. Compute a simple average of the raw data over the relevant time interval selected, by summing the observed values and then dividing by the total number of observations.
2. Compute the differences between each observation (the raw data for each time period) and the average of all observations (from the first step).
3. Compute the squares of these differences.
4. Sum the squares of the differences.
5. Divide this sum of squares by the number of observations to arrive at the *variance.*
6. Calculate the square root of this variance to arrive at the standard deviation, a quantification of the variability of the distribution of the raw data around the moving average.

Standard deviation is symbolized by the Greek letter *sigma,* σ. In many practical applications it is worth knowing whether the data points are clustered tightly around the mean or dispersed widely over a range and by how much. If the standard deviation is small, the individual data points are tightly clustered around the mean. But if the standard deviation is large, the individual data points are widely scattered around the mean. (See *Bollinger Bands,* for an example of a popular technical indicator that uses standard deviation.)

Statistics

The technical indicators in this book are simple mathematical models. Being simple, they are easy to understand, compute, and implement. Simplicity is a very important criterion for selecting an investment method.

A mathematical model is simply an idealized representation of reality in the form of a clearly defined formula, or more than one formula combined into a "system." Fortunately, though perhaps counter-intuitively, simple models actually work better than complex systems. If we can't understand it, we won't use it.

Technical analysts have long used simple statistics. There is no evidence that advanced, complex statistics work any better than the simplest statistics. In fact, experience strongly suggests that the opposite is true, that simple statistics work better than advanced and complex statistics.

Technicians use moving averages more than any other statistic. Moving averages are simple and easy-to-understand mathematical measures of the underlying trend. Raw market data can be noisy, and technical analysts recognized decades ago that moving averages can smooth the data enough to reveal the trend. Moving averages of the daily closing price reliably follow the price trend. Also, they often provide support and resistance.

Traditionally, for many decades, technicians have used moving averages covering windows of time of the past 10 months, 10 weeks, and 10 days to identify and follow long-, intermediate-, and short-term trends. To calculate a 10-period simple moving average, we simply add together the daily closing prices over the past 10 periods then divide that sum by 10. Curiously, ten months is slightly more than 200 trading days, which is the most popular moving average of the long-term, major trend. The computer can quickly add together the daily closing prices over the past 200 days and divide that sum by 200 to find the 200-day simple moving average. Then, if the current closing price is higher than the moving average, the long-term trend is assumed to be upward (bullish) and the financial instrument in question is a buy candidate. On the other hand, if the current closing price is lower than the 200-day moving average, then the main trend is downward (bearish) and the instrument is a sell candidate. Using simple moving averages covering all three time frames (10 months, 10 weeks, and 10 days) together offers confirmation and other advantages. *(See Multiple Time Frame Analysis.)*

Some technical indicators use the variability of the distribution of the data around the moving average. Sometimes, it may seem significant to know whether the data points are clustered tightly around the mean or dispersed widely over a range. The standard deviation is simply the square root of the mean of the squares of the deviations. In other words, we calculate the difference of each observed data point minus the mean or average of the recent past data points, we square these differences, then we divide these squared numbers by the number of observations under consideration (which is symbolized by the letter n). This standard deviation is traditionally designated by a forbidding Greek letter, sigma, but it is actually a very simple concept. If the standard deviation is small, the individual data points are tightly clustered around the mean. But if the standard deviation is large, the individual data points are widely scattered around the mean. The variance is simply the square of the standard deviation.

Correlation is a measure of relatedness. When two data series increase or decrease proportionately and simultaneously, they are correlated positively. A perfect positive correlation results in a coefficient of $+1$. At the opposite extreme, if one data series increases in the same proportion that the other decreases, the two are negatively correlated. A perfect negative correlation produces a coefficient of -1. A total absence of correlation would be a coefficient of 0. Intermediate values are interpreted by degree. A high positive correlation would be 0.75. A high negative correlation would be −0.75. A low positive correlation would be 0.25. A low negative correlation would be −0.25.

There are also tests of reliability designed to tell us whether an indicator is valid or not. Statisticians have devised several tests for the significance or reliability of data. One we refer to in this book is the chi-square test. Here, the deviations (observed indicator values minus expected random values) are squared, divided by the expected values, and summed. The value of chi-square is then compared with values in a standard statistical table to determine the significance of the deviations.

Back testing an indicator using substantial historical data going back many years yields a clear simulated record of buy and sell signals and a Cumulative Equity Curve. This curve can be compared against the record of the passive Buy-and-Hold Strategy. If the curve shows greater profit with less risk (that is, less negative variability, or fewer large losses), then it is clear that the indicator adds value to the investment decision making process. Usually, this will be obvious by simple visual inspection of the chart of Cumulative Equity versus the unmanaged underlying security. No number crunching is required.

Taking the time to learn to comfortably read charts pays unexpected dividends in being able to grasp the meaning of data in more powerful and insightful ways than any abstract statistic possibly could reveal. Experienced technical analysts develop a strong sense of statistical significance by simply inspecting a graph of the actual data. It is an art well worth cultivating.

STIX: The Polymetric Short-term Indicator

STIX is an exponentially smoothed, breadth-momentum oscillator developed by *The Polymetric Report.* A 9% (or 21-day) exponential smoothing constant applied to the number of advancing issues divided by the sum of the number of advancing issues plus the number of declining issues. STIX is usually calculated based on issues listed on the New York Stock Exchange, and similar indicators may be calculated for other markets, such as the NASDAQ. STIX may be expressed by the following formula:

$$S = (((A / (A + D)) * 0.09) + (P * 0.91)$$

where

S = today's STIX

A = number of advancing issues

D = number of declining issues

P = previous day's STIX

STIX is usually multiplied by 100 to avoid dealing with fractions. STIX oscillates around a perfectly balanced number of 50, where advances and declines are equal. One may start calculating STIX with an initial value of 50 at any point in time, ideally after a sideways market trend, although STIX will be accurate within a few weeks no matter when it is started.

Record ranges for STIX are from 28 to 69, low to high, both set in 1932. Traditionally, high levels above 58 were thought to indicate strong bullish breadth momentum, while low levels below 40 indicated bearish momentum. As the graph shows, however, breadth volatility has diminished in recent years, producing no signals for STIX based on thresholds of 40 and 58.

Trends, comparative levels, and divergences in STIX have been interpreted relative to a market price index in typical oscillator fashion. For example, a positive divergence in STIX on a re-test of previous price index lows is generally thought to indicate a diminishing imbalance of supply over demand, and that may be a bullish leading indicator of the short-term trend. On the other hand, a negative divergence in STIX on a re-test of previous price index highs indicates a diminishing imbalance of demand over supply, and that is a bearish leading indicator of the short-term trend.

Indicator Strategy Example for STIX

Based on a 68-year file of daily data for the number of shares advancing and declining each day on the NYSE and the DJIA since March 8, 1932, we found that a simple trend-following rule would have produced a positive result on a purely mechanical signal basis with no subjectivity, no sophisticated technical analysis, and no judgement:

Enter Long (Buy) at the current daily price close of the DJIA when STIX crosses above 49.

Close Long (Sell) at the current daily price close of the DJIA when STIX crosses below 49.

Enter Short (Sell Short) at the current daily price close of the DJIA when STIX crosses below 49.

Close Short (Cover) at the current daily price close of the DJIA when STIX crosses above 49.

Starting with $100 and reinvesting profits, total net profits for this STIX trend-following strategy would have been $240,013.89 , assuming a fully invested strategy, reinvestment of profits, no transactions costs and no taxes. This would have been 1,814.19 percent better than buy-and-hold. Even short selling would have been profitable. Trading would have been fairly active with one trade every 16.35 calendar days.

The Equis International MetaStock® System Testing rules, where one hundred times the ratio of advances divided by the sum of advances plus declines is inserted into the data field normally reserved for Volume (V), are written as follows:

Enter long: Mov(V,opt1,E)>opt2 AND Ref(Mov(V,opt1,E),-1)<opt2

Close long: Mov(V,opt1,E)<opt3 AND Ref(Mov(V,opt1,E),-1)>opt3

Enter short: Mov(V,opt1,E)<opt3 AND Ref(Mov(V,opt1,E),-1)>opt3

Close short: Mov(V,opt1,E)>opt2 AND Ref(Mov(V,opt1,E),-1)<opt2

OPT1 Current value: 21
OPT2 Current value: 49
OPT3 Current value: 49

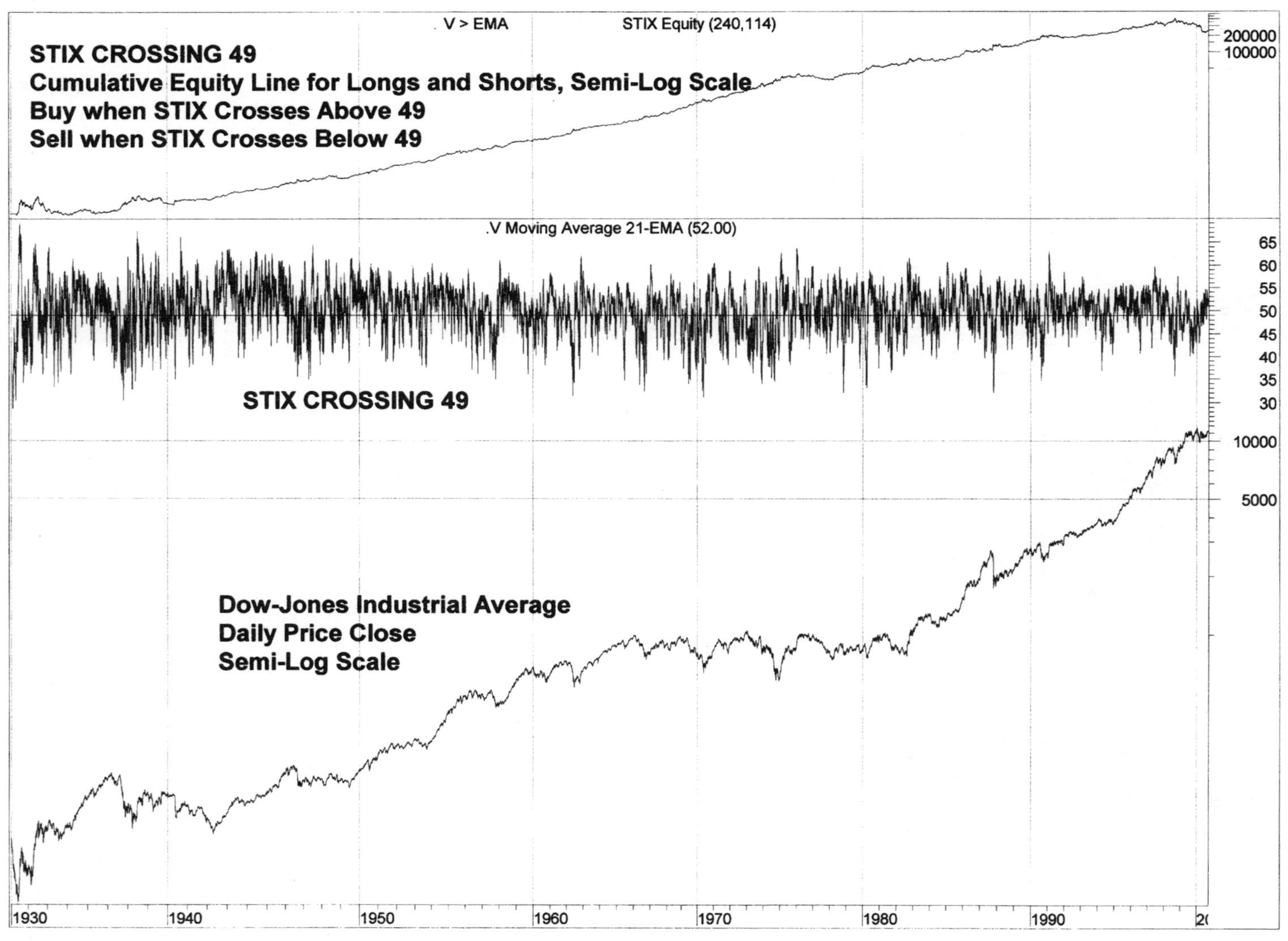
V > EMA
STIX Equity (240,114)
STIX CROSSING 49
Cumulative Equity Line for Longs and Shorts, Semi-Log Scale
Buy when STIX Crosses Above 49
Sell when STIX Crosses Below 49
200000
100000
.V Moving Average 21-EMA (52.00)
65
60
55
50
45
40
35
30
STIX CROSSING 49
10000
5000
Dow-Jones Industrial Average
Daily Price Close
Semi-Log Scale
1930
1940
1950
1960
1970
1980
1990
2(

STIX Crossing 49

Total net profit	240013.89	Open position value	14949.6	Net Profit / Buy&Hold %	1814.19
Percent gain/loss	240013.89	Annual percent gain/loss	3501.12	Annual Net % / B&H %	1814.23
Initial investment	100	Interest earned	0		
Current position	Long	Date position entered	7/31/00		
Buy/Hold profit	12538.66	Days in test	25022	# of days per trade	16.35
Buy/Hold pct gain/loss	12538.66	Annual B/H pct gain/loss	182.9		
Total closed trades	1530	Commissions paid	0		
Avg profit per trade	147.1	Avg Win/Avg Loss ratio	2.33		
Total long trades	765	Total short trades	765	Long Win Trade %	40.78
Winning long trades	312	Winning short trades	248	Short Win Trade %	32.42
Total winning trades	560	Total losing trades	970	Total Win Trade %	36.60
Amount of winning trades	874366.19	Amount of losing trades	−649302.13	Net Profit Margin %	14.77
Average win	1561.37	Average loss	−669.38	Average P. Margin %	39.99
Largest win	49665.41	Largest loss	−32085.47	% Net / (Win + Loss)	21.50
Average length of win	24.92	Average length of loss	5.73	(Win − Loss) / Loss %	334.90
Longest winning trade	152	Longest losing trade	60	(Win − Loss) / Loss %	153.33
Most consecutive wins	6	Most consecutive losses	15	(Win − Loss) / Loss %	−60.00
Total bars out	84	Average length out	84		
Longest out period	84				
System close drawdown	−6.05	Profit/Loss index	26.99	% Net Profit / SODD	3681194.63
System open drawdown	−6.52	Reward/Risk index	100	(Net P.-SODD)/Net P.	100.00
Max open trade drawdown	−32085.47	Buy/Hold index	1933.42	% SODD / Net Profit	0.00

In the Equis MetaStock® "System Report" (profit and loss summary statistics), the *Total net profit* is the sum of profits minus the sum of losses, including open positions marked to the market. In contrast, the *Amount of Winning Trades* is the sum of realized profits (the total of all gains on closed-out trades only, excluding any open positions). Similarly, the *Amount of Losing Trades* is the sum of realized losses (the total of all losses on closed-out trades only, excluding any open positions). *System close drawdown* is the largest decline in the cumulative equity line below the initial investment, based on closed-out positions only. *System open drawdown (SODD)* is the largest decline in the cumulative equity line below the initial investment when a position is open. *Max open trade drawdown* is the largest decline in the cumulative equity line below the trade entry price during the worst single trade. The *Profit/Loss Index* is a complex calculation that relates the Amount of Winning Trades to the Amount of Losing Trades on a scale of −100 (worst possible performance) to +100 (best possible performance), with zero representing profits equal to losses. *Reward/Risk Index* is the Total net profit minus System open drawdown. The resulting difference is then divided by the Total net profit. The *Buy/Hold Index* is the Total net profit minus the buy-and-hold strategy's net profit. The resulting difference is then divided by the buy-and-hold net profit. In this exercise, initial equity is assumed to be $100. Both long and short positions are taken unless otherwise noted. Trades are executed at the closing price on the signal date. Transaction costs, interest expenses, and margins are not included in the statistics.

Stochastics (Lane's Stochastics)

In statistics, the term "stochastic" refers to random variables. But that is the opposite of what George Lane has in mind. Lane's Stochastics is a short-term *price velocity* indicator, precisely defined and successfully popularized by George C. Lane (Investment Educators, PO Box 2354, Des Plaines, IL). Because Stochastics is based on a fixed period-to-period moving calculation that can jump around erratically due solely to data for the oldest period being dropped off the calculation as the data window (period of predefined length) moves forward in time, Lane's Stochastics is twice smoothed by moving averages. Lane's Stochastics may be calculated, as follows:

$$K = 100\,((C - L) / (H - L))$$

where

K = the location of the current price relative to the recent price range.

C = the latest closing price of the stock or contract.

L = the n-period low price of the stock or contract.

H = the n-period high price of the stock or contract.

n can be any number (Lane suggests 5 to 21 days).

Next, Lane smoothes K twice with 3-period simple moving averages: his %K is the 3-period simple moving average of K, and %D is the 3-period simple moving average of %K. After smoothing the data, K has no further use. Only the %K and %D lines are used for interpretation of signals.

Lane offers several guidelines for interpretation of Stochastics, including overbought/oversold preconditions, divergences, and crossovers. First, consider buy signals. In a downward price move, a precondition for a buy signal is recognized when %K becomes oversold below 25%. It is more significant when %K is extremely oversold below 15%. Note that these are only preconditions and not signals for action.

After an oversold precondition has been achieved, look for a positive divergence. When price moves down to a new low but the already oversold %K does not make a new low, this is a positive divergence, and we should be on alert for an upturn in the price trend. The actual buy signal comes when %K crosses above %D. Lane says that the buy signal is more reliable when %D has already turned up when %K crosses above %D. If the slower %D has been quietly carving out a pattern of higher lows as price makes lower lows, that is all the more reason to look for a buying opportunity on the next decline.

Considering sell signals, in a upward price move, a precondition for a sell signal is recognized when %K becomes overbought above 75%. It is more significant when %K is extremely overbought above 85%. Note that these are only preconditions and not signals for action.

After an overbought precondition has been achieved, look for a negative divergence. When price moves up to a new high but the already overbought %K does not make a new high, this is a negative divergence, and we should be on alert for a downturn in the price trend. The actual sell signal comes when %K crosses below %D. Lane says that the sell signal is more reliable when %D has already turned down when %K crosses below %D. If the slower %D has been quietly carving out a pattern of lower highs as price makes higher highs, that is all the more reason to look for a selling opportunity on the next rally.

Lane finds additional significance in *failures.* For example, following an overbought precondition, when %K has already crossed under %D, then %K rallies again and re-approaches %D, but %K fails to cross above %D, that is a good time to enter a trade on the short side.

Similarly, after a price drop to an oversold precondition and a minor upward price reaction causing %K to cross above %D, when %K falls again and re-approaches %D, but %K fails to cross under %D, that is a good time to enter a trade on the long side.

Lane analyzes the velocity of the %K and %D lines, and finds implications of trend change. A *warning* is given when %K makes an extreme turn and an unusually large move. This indicates at most two days remaining in the old trend.

When velocity slows, that is, when the speed of either the %K or %D lines flattens out, it indicates a price reversal on the next day. Lane calls this a *hinge.*

Lane says reliability is enhanced when %K is in an extreme overbought or oversold zone: for buy signals, %K is extremely oversold below 15%; for sell signals, %K is extremely overbought above 85%.

The most extreme %K levels near 100% and 0% indicate unusually powerful price velocity that is likely to continue in the prevailing trend direction. At times, %K can be nailed to 100% or 0% for many consecutive days in a strong move. Only after %K pulls back, tries again, but then fails to achieve its previous extreme reading does Lane recognize a worthwhile overbought/oversold precondition for a signal.

It is most important to note that Lane considers signals to be more reliable when they are in the same direction as the major trend. This implies that short-term Stochastics could be used with major trend indicators to filter its signals.

Indicator Strategy Example for Stochastics

Stochastics require experience and judgement to use as George Lane intended. His guidelines are too complex for simple computer testing. Still, even naïve testing assumptions suggest that Stochastics may have value as a purely mechanical indicator. Our tests found a majority of profitable signals, and results would have been robust for all %K period lengths from 4 to 50 days.

As attractive as a high percentage of profitable trades may seem, however, it is important to note that this and other contra-trend strategies failed to provide any protection in the Crash of '87, the decline of 1998 and other steep market price drops. As the chart shows, there are sharp equity drawdowns. Using Stochastics for contra-trend oversold and overbought signals would have outperformed the passive buy-and-hold strategy *for long trades only.* Short selling would not have been profitable in the past.

Based on a merged file of adjusted daily data for the entire history of the S&P 500 Stock Index Futures *CSI Perpetual Contract* (www.csidata.com) from inception on 4/21/82 to 5/10/01, and cash S&P 500 Stock Price Index from 11/28/80 to 4/21/82, we found that the following parameters would have produced a significantly positive result on a counter-trend, mechanical overbought/oversold signal basis with no subjectivity, no sophisticated technical analysis, and no judgement:

Enter Long (Buy) at the current daily price close of the S&P 500 Stock Index Futures *CSI Perpetual Contract* when %K Stochastic (with K equal to seven days, and smoothed by a 3-day SMA) is less than 30.

Close Long (Sell) at the current daily price close of the S&P 500 Stock Index Futures *CSI Perpetual Contract* when %K Stochastic (with K equal to seven days, and smoothed by a 3-day SMA) is greater than 70.

Enter Short (Sell Short) at the current daily price close of the S&P 500 Stock Index Futures *CSI Perpetual Contract* when %K Stochastic (with K equal to seven days, and smoothed by a 3-day SMA) is greater than 70.

Close Short (Cover) at the current daily price close of the S&P 500 Stock Index Futures *CSI Perpetual Contract* when %K Stochastic (with K equal to seven days, and smoothed by a 3-day SMA) is less than 30.

Starting with $100 and reinvesting profits, total net profits for this Stochastics counter-trend strategy would have been $1,215.35, assuming a fully invested strategy, reinvestment of profits, no transactions costs and no taxes. This would have been 52.12 percent greater than buy-and-hold. Short selling would have been slightly unprofitable, and short selling was included in this strategy. This long-and-short Stochastics as an indicator would have given profitable buy signals 70.64% of the time. Trading would have been active at one trade every 13.70 calendar days. Note that this counter-trend, overbought/oversold strategy would have suffered large equity drawdowns, the worst down 36% in the Crash of '87.

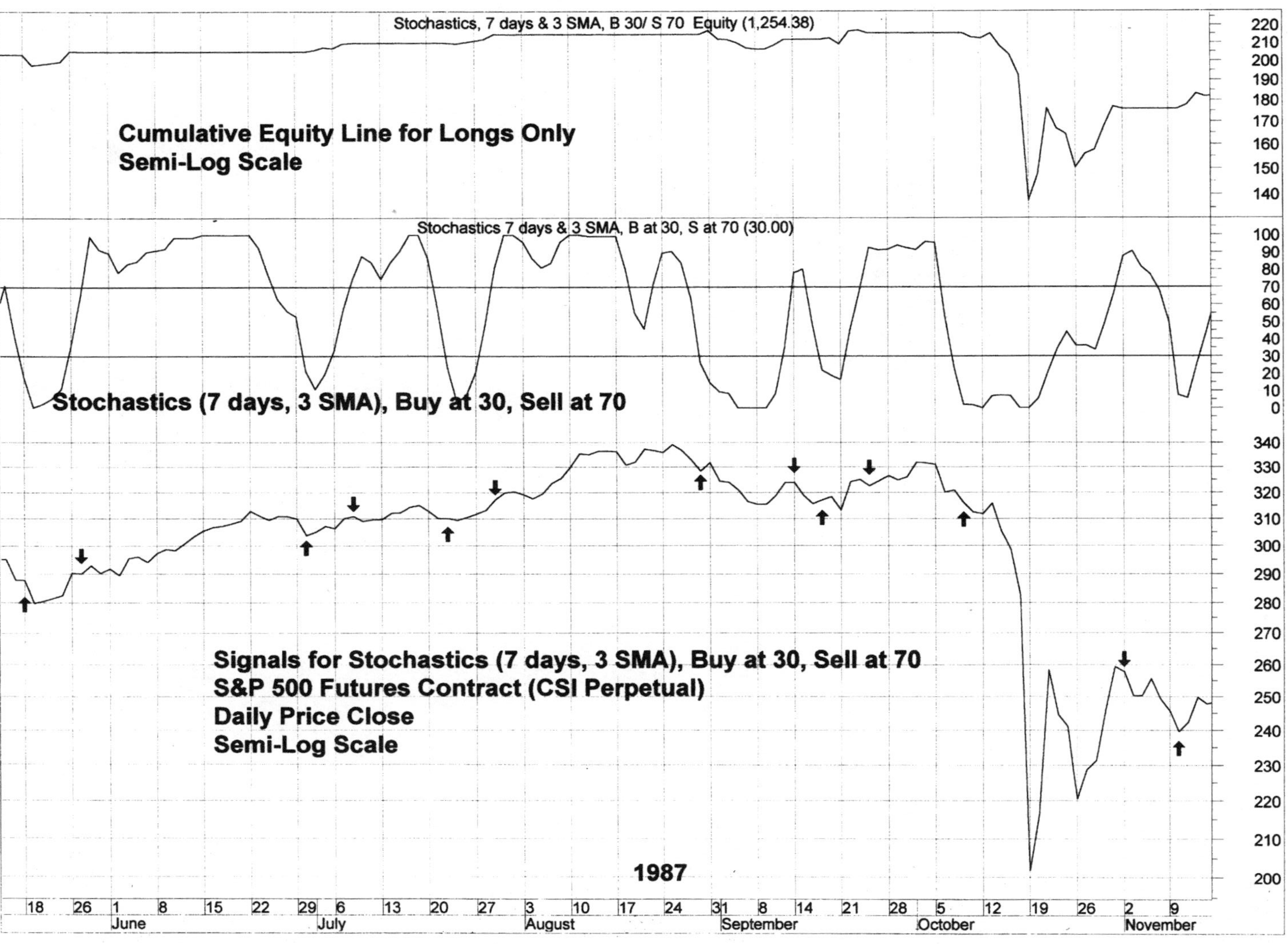

Stochastics, 7 days & 3 SMA, B 30/ S 70 Equity (1,254.38)
Cumulative Equity Line for Longs Only
Semi-Log Scale
Stochastics 7 days & 3 SMA, B at 30, S at 70 (30.00)
Stochastics (7 days, 3 SMA), Buy at 30, Sell at 70
Signals for Stochastics (7 days, 3 SMA), Buy at 30, Sell at 70
S&P 500 Futures Contract (CSI Perpetual)
Daily Price Close
Semi-Log Scale
1987
June
July
August
September
October
November

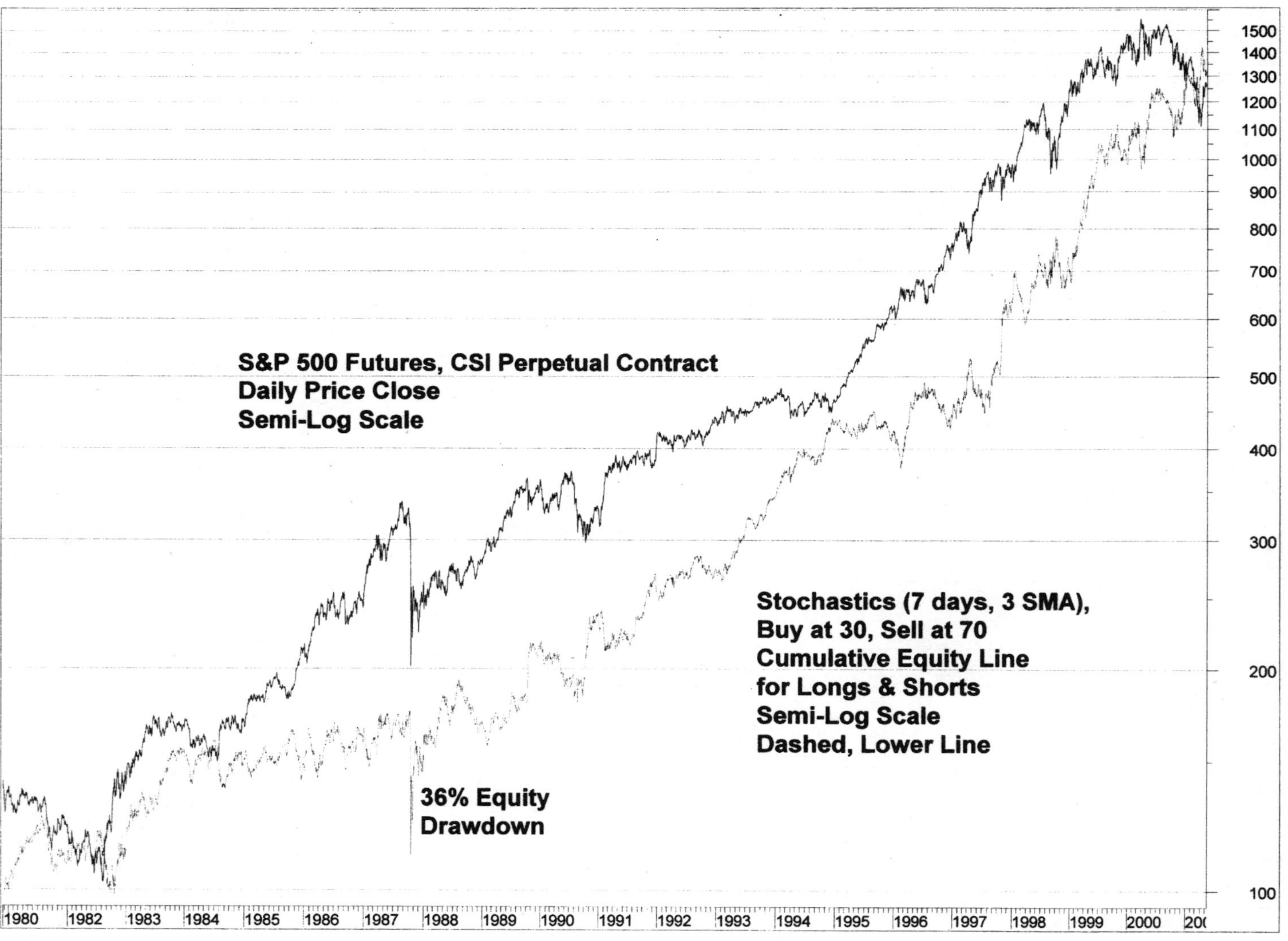
S&P 500 Futures, CSI Perpetual Contract
Daily Price Close
Semi-Log Scale
Stochastics (7 days, 3 SMA),
Buy at 30, Sell at 70
Cumulative Equity Line
for Longs & Shorts
Semi-Log Scale
Dashed, Lower Line
36% Equity
Drawdown
1500
1400
1300
1200
1100
1000
900
800
700
600
500
400
300
200
100
1980
1982
1983
1984
1985
1986
1987
1988
1989
1990
1991
1992
1993
1994
1995
1996
1997
1998
1999
2000

Stochastics (7 days, 3 SMA), Buy at 30, Sell at 70

Total net profit	1215.35	Open position value	−109.38	Net Profit / Buy&Hold %	52.12
Percent gain/loss	1215.35	Annual percent gain/loss	59.39	Annual Net % / B&H %	52.13
Initial investment	100	Interest earned	0		
Current position	Short	Date position entered	4/10/01		
Buy/Hold profit	798.93	Days in test	7469	# of days per trade	13.70
Buy/Hold pct gain/loss	798.93	Annual B/H pct gain/loss	39.04		
Total closed trades	545	Commissions paid	0		
Avg profit per trade	2.43	Avg Win/Avg Loss ratio	0.76		
Total long trades	273	Total short trades	272	Long Win Trade %	77.29
Winning long trades	211	Winning short trades	174	Short Win Trade %	63.97
Total winning trades	385	Total losing trades	160	Total Win Trade %	70.64
Amount of winning trades	2946.06	Amount of losing trades	−1621.33	Net Profit Margin %	29.00
Average win	7.65	Average loss	−10.13	Average P. Margin %	−13.95
Largest win	86.13	Largest loss	−102.19	% Net / (Win + Loss)	−8.53
Average length of win	7.5	Average length of loss	17.48	(Win − Loss) / Loss %	−57.09
Longest winning trade	24	Longest losing trade	51	(Win − Loss) / Loss %	−52.94
Most consecutive wins	11	Most consecutive losses	3	(Win − Loss) / Loss %	266.67
Total bars out	9	Average length out	9		
Longest out period	9				
System close drawdown	0	Profit/Loss index	42.84	% Net Profit / SODD	65341.40
System open drawdown	−1.86	Reward/Risk index	99.85	(Net P.-SODD)/Net P.	99.85
Max open trade drawdown	−133.61	Buy/Hold index	38.43	% SODD / Net Profit	−0.15

In the Equis MetaStock® "System Report" (profit and loss summary statistics), the *Total net profit* is the sum of profits minus the sum of losses, including open positions marked to the market. In contrast, the *Amount of Winning Trades* is the sum of realized profits (the total of all gains on closed-out trades only, excluding any open positions). Similarly, the *Amount of Losing Trades* is the sum of realized losses (the total of all losses on closed-out trades only, excluding any open positions). *System close drawdown* is the largest decline in the cumulative equity line below the initial investment, based on closed-out positions only. *System open drawdown (SODD)* is the largest decline in the cumulative equity line below the initial investment when a position is open. *Max open trade drawdown* is the largest decline in the cumulative equity line below the trade entry price during the worst single trade. The *Profit/Loss Index* is a complex calculation that relates the Amount of Winning Trades to the Amount of Losing Trades on a scale of −100 (worst possible performance) to +100 (best possible performance), with zero representing profits equal to losses. *Reward/Risk Index* is the Total net profit minus System open drawdown. The resulting difference is then divided by the Total net profit. The *Buy/Hold Index* is the Total net profit minus the buy-and-hold strategy's net profit. The resulting difference is then divided by the buy-and-hold net profit. In this exercise, initial equity is assumed to be $100. Both long and short positions are taken unless otherwise noted. Trades are executed at the closing price on the signal date. Transaction costs, interest expenses, and margins are not included in the statistics.

The Equis International MetaStock® System Testing rules are written as follows:

Enter long: Mov((C-LLV(C,opt1))/(HHV(C,opt1)-LLV(C,opt1)),opt2,S)< .5-.01*opt3

Close long: Mov((C-LLV(C,opt1))/(HHV(C,opt1)-LLV(C,opt1)),opt2,S)> .5+.01*opt3

Enter short: Mov((C-LLV(C,opt1))/(HHV(C,opt1)-LLV(C,opt1)),opt2,S)> .5+.01*opt3

Close short: Mov((C-LLV(C,opt1))/(HHV(C,opt1)-LLV(C,opt1)),opt2,S)< .5-.01*opt3

OPT1 Current value: 7

OPT2 Current value: 3

OPT3 Current value: 20

Another Indicator Strategy Example for Stochastics with Long-term EMA Filter

Based on a merged file of adjusted daily data for the entire history of the S&P 500 Stock Index Futures *CSI Perpetual Contract* collected from (www.csidata.com) from inception on 4/21/82 to 5/10/01, and cash S&P 500 Stock Price Index from 11/28/80 to 4/21/82, we found that the following parameters would have produced a significantly positive result on a filtered mechanical overbought/oversold signal basis with no subjectivity, no sophisticated technical analysis, and no judgement:

Enter Long (Buy) at the current daily price close of the S&P 500 Stock Index Futures *CSI Perpetual Contract* when %K Stochastic (with K equal to 7 days, and smoothed by a 3-day SMA) is less than 30 and the current day's price close is greater than today's 271-day EMA of the daily closing prices.

Close Long (Sell) at the current daily price close of the S&P 500 Stock Index Futures *CSI Perpetual Contract* when %K Stochastic (with K equal to 7 days, and smoothed by a 3-day SMA) is greater than 70 or the current day's price close is less than today's 271-day EMA of the daily closing prices.

Enter Short (Sell Short) at the current daily price close of the S&P 500 Stock Index Futures *CSI Perpetual Contract* when %K Stochastic (with K equal to 7 days, and smoothed by a 3-day SMA) is greater than 70 and the current day's price close is less than today's 271-day EMA of the daily closing prices.

Close Short (Cover) at the current daily price close of the S&P 500 Stock Index Futures *CSI Perpetual Contract* when %K Stochastic (with K equal to 7 days, and smoothed by a 3-day SMA) is less than 30 or the current day's price close is greater than today's 271-day EMA of the daily closing prices.

Starting with $100 and reinvesting profits, total net profits for this Stochastics counter-trend strategy would have been $ 825.49, assuming a fully invested strategy, reinvestment of profits, no transactions costs and no taxes. This would have been 3.32 percent greater than buy-and-hold. Even short selling would have been slightly profitable, and short selling was included in this strategy. This long-and-short Stochastics as an indicator would have given profitable buy signals 72.00% of the time. Trading would have been less active at one trade every 27.16 calendar days. Note that this filtered strategy would have enjoyed fewer and milder equity drawdowns. This is very important when considering the practical merits of any trading system.

The Equis International MetaStock® System Testing rules are written as follows:

Enter long: Mov((C-LLV(C,opt1))/(HHV(C,opt1)-LLV(C,opt1)),
opt2,S)<.5-.01*opt3 AND CLOSE > Mov(CLOSE,opt4,E)

Close long: Mov((C-LLV(C,opt1))/(HHV(C,opt1)-LLV(C,opt1)),
opt2,S)>.5+.01*opt3 OR CLOSE < Mov(CLOSE,opt4,E)

Enter short: Mov((C-LLV(C,opt1))/(HHV(C,opt1)-LLV(C,opt1)),
opt2,S)>.5+.01*opt3 AND CLOSE < Mov(CLOSE,opt4,E)

Close short: Mov((C-LLV(C,opt1))/(HHV(C,opt1)-LLV(C,opt1)),
opt2,S)<.5-.01*opt3 OR CLOSE > Mov(CLOSE,opt4,E)

OPT1 Current value: 7

OPT2 Current value: 3

OPT3 Current value: 20

OPT4 Current value: 271

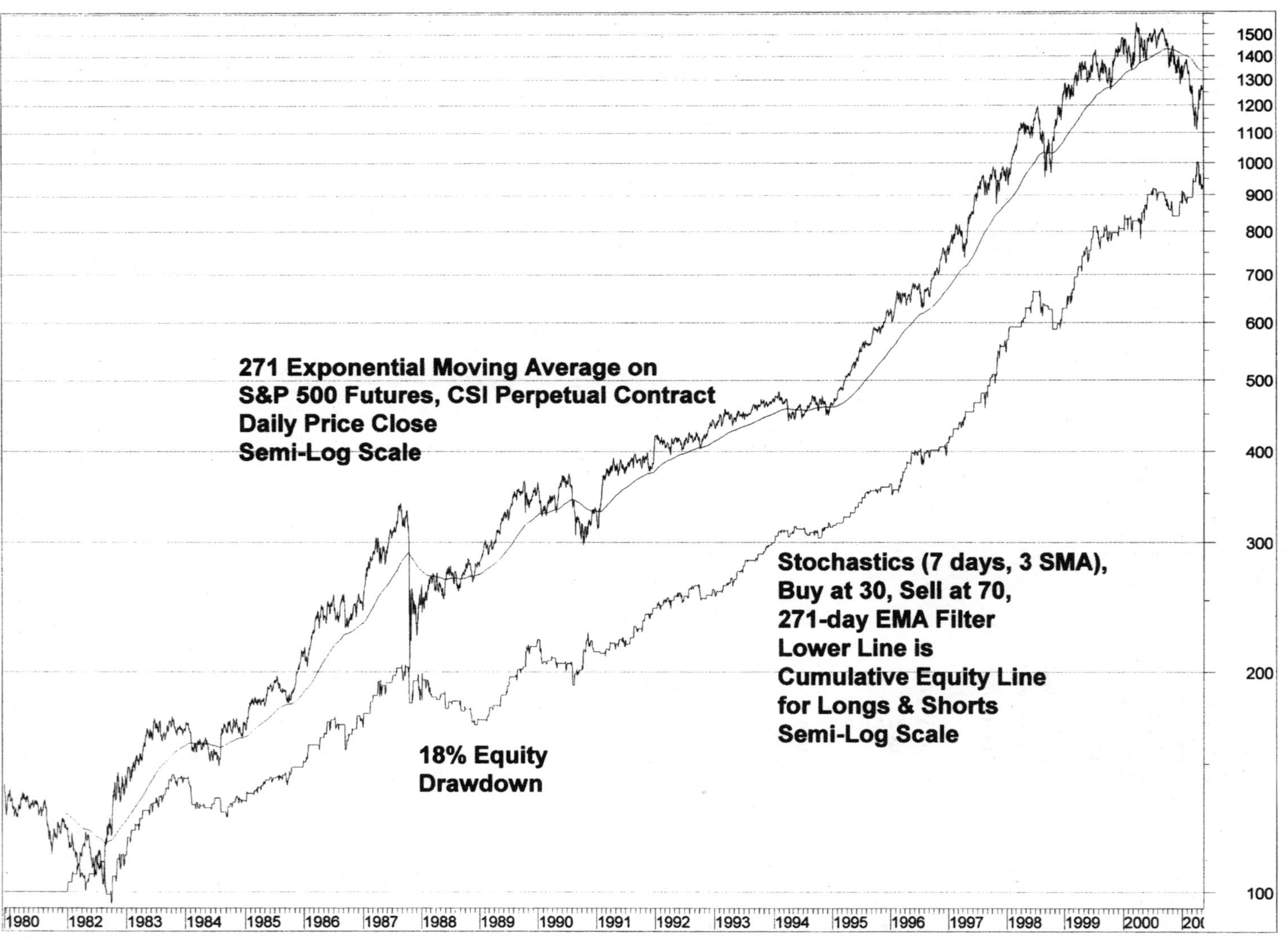
271 Exponential Moving Average on
S&P 500 Futures, CSI Perpetual Contract
Daily Price Close
Semi-Log Scale
Stochastics (7 days, 3 SMA),
Buy at 30, Sell at 70,
271-day EMA Filter
Lower Line is
Cumulative Equity Line
for Longs & Shorts
Semi-Log Scale
18% Equity
Drawdown
1500
1400
1300
1200
1100
1000
900
800
700
600
500
400
300
200
100
1980
1982
1983
1984
1985
1986
1987
1988
1989
1990
1991
1992
1993
1994
1995
1996
1997
1998
1999
2000

Stochastics with Long-term EMA Filter Rules

Total net profit	825.49	Open position value	−76.96	Net Profit / Buy&Hold %	3.32
Percent gain/loss	825.49	Annual percent gain/loss	40.34	Annual Net % / B&H %	3.33
Initial investment	100	Interest earned	0		
Current position	Short	Date position entered	4/10/01		
Buy/Hold profit	798.93	Days in test	7469	# of days per trade	27.16
Buy/Hold pct gain/loss	798.93	Annual B/H pct gain/loss	39.04		
Total closed trades	275	Commissions paid	0		
Avg profit per trade	3.28	Avg Win/Avg Loss ratio	1.15		
Total long trades	224	Total short trades	51	Long Win Trade %	78.13
Winning long trades	175	Winning short trades	23	Short Win Trade %	45.10
Total winning trades	198	Total losing trades	77	Total Win Trade %	72.00
Amount of winning trades	1363.24	Amount of losing trades	−460.78	Net Profit Margin %	49.48
Average win	6.89	Average loss	−5.98	Average P. Margin %	7.07
Largest win	64.07	Largest loss	−50.5	% Net / (Win + Loss)	11.84
Average length of win	6.53	Average length of loss	9.4	(Win − Loss) / Loss %	−30.53
Longest winning trade	18	Longest losing trade	21	(Win − Loss) / Loss %	−14.29
Most consecutive wins	13	Most consecutive losses	5	(Win − Loss) / Loss %	160.00
Total bars out	3681	Average length out	13.34		
Longest out period	277				
System close drawdown	−0.78	Profit/Loss index	64.18	% Net Profit / SODD	22371.00
System open drawdown	−3.69	Reward/Risk index	99.56	(Net P.-SODD)/Net P.	99.55
Max open trade drawdown	−86.92	Buy/Hold index	−6.31	% SODD / Net Profit	−0.45

In the Equis MetaStock® "System Report" (profit and loss summary statistics), the *Total net profit* is the sum of profits minus the sum of losses, including open positions marked to the market. In contrast, the *Amount of Winning Trades* is the sum of realized profits (the total of all gains on closed-out trades only, excluding any open positions). Similarly, the *Amount of Losing Trades* is the sum of realized losses (the total of all losses on closed-out trades only, excluding any open positions). *System close drawdown* is the largest decline in the cumulative equity line below the initial investment, based on closed-out positions only. *System open drawdown (SODD)* is the largest decline in the cumulative equity line below the initial investment when a position is open. *Max open trade drawdown* is the largest decline in the cumulative equity line below the trade entry price during the worst single trade. The *Profit/Loss Index* is a complex calculation that relates the Amount of Winning Trades to the Amount of Losing Trades on a scale of −100 (worst possible performance) to +100 (best possible performance), with zero representing profits equal to losses. *Reward/Risk Index* is the Total net profit minus System open drawdown. The resulting difference is then divided by the Total net profit. The *Buy/Hold Index* is the Total net profit minus the buy-and-hold strategy's net profit. The resulting difference is then divided by the buy-and-hold net profit. In this exercise, initial equity is assumed to be $100. Both long and short positions are taken unless otherwise noted. Trades are executed at the closing price on the signal date. Transaction costs, interest expenses, and margins are not included in the statistics.

Stochastic Pop Breakout: Popsteckle

Technical analysts have invented alternate ways to use George Lane's Stochastics. Jake Bernstein may have been the first to try buying rather than selling when Lane's Stochastics rises to 70. Writing in the August 2000 issue of *Technical Analysis of Stocks & Commodities* magazine (800-832-4642, www.traders.com), David Steckler (www.dsteckler@aol.com) devised the following specific setup conditions, which he claims telegraph a rapid appreciation in the price of a stock:

- Daily ADX below 20 (even better, below 15), indicating a non-trending market. (See *Directional Movement.*) ADX measures the strength of the recent trend, not its direction, up or down.
- Daily Stochastics %K above 70 (even better above 80) and rising. Set %K to a 3-period SMA of the raw ratio, K, which is set to 8 days.
- Weekly Stochastics %K above 50 and rising. Again, set %K to a 3-period SMA of the raw ratio, K, which is set to 8 weeks.
- Stock price breakout (see *Price Channel*), on above-average volume, with volume greater than a 50-day SMA of volume. Wait for the stock to trade higher than the recent congestion-range high, with higher volume on the breakout.
- Bullish market conditions, indicated by an appropriate general market price index and/or industry group price index trading above a trailing 50-day SMA or above a 20-day EMA for two consecutive trading days.
- Use an appropriate exit strategy and a money management methodology that works best with your trading style.

Stock Market Price Indexes

Price indexes are important for judging trends and measuring performance for the stock market in general. And, thanks to innovations over the past two decades, we can now buy and sell futures, options, trusts, and mutual funds constructed to match many of the most popular indexes. These new financial instruments are useful for speculators who want to "play the market" but do not have the time to conduct research on individual stocks. Indexes also offer the advantage of diversification over a large number of stocks, which reduces risk.

The oldest and most popular indexes are those published by Dow Jones & Co. Founder Charles Dow published his first market average on July 3, 1884, in his *Customer's Afternoon Letter,* the predecessor to *The Wall Street Journal.* This first group of stocks was comprised of 11 stocks, 9 railroads and 2 industrials.

On May 26, 1896, Dow published his first Dow Jones Industrial Average (also commonly referred to as *the Dow* or the *DJIA*), composed solely of 12 Industrials. On October 1, 1928, the Dow was expanded to 30 stocks, and it has remained at that number ever since. The component stocks have changed many times over the years, however, because of mergers, bankruptcies, and companies and whole industries rising and falling in economic power. The publisher tries to maintain a current list of 30 of the largest and most important blue-chip stocks. The only two names recognizable today from 1928 are General Electric and General Motors. Given current trends toward increasingly competitive financial capitalism and accelerating technological change, we might expect even more frequent changes of component stock issues in years ahead. The current list of stocks included in the Dow Averages can be found each day on page C3 of *The Wall Street Journal.*

For all practical purposes, the DJIA is remarkably representative of the general market. The 30 Dow stocks comprise only about 15% of the total market value of all U.S. stocks. Critics have long doubted that such a small sample could adequately represent the whole stock market, which is comprised of many thousands of stocks. And it is obvious that the Dow and the broader market sometimes go their separate ways for a while. Also, in the words of Arthur A. Merrill, CMT, a professional statistician as well as an expert technical market analyst, "Statisticians wince when they learn the weighting method" of the Dow-Jones averages. The arithmetic price average is price weighted, so a $100 stock has 10 times the influence of a $10 stock. Worse, if a stock splits two-for-one, its weight immediately drops in half. Finally, substitutions of stocks in the averages also have detracted from comparability of the averages to themselves over time. But despite these reasonable criticisms, statistics clearly show that the Dow Averages reflect the trends of the broad market very closely.

Looking at it with a microscope, we have noticed over the years a somewhat greater number of false signals (misleading breakouts and breakdowns) with the DJIA than with the better constructed indexes such as the Standard & Poor's or NYSE composites. In fact, when the DJIA diverges from the S&P 500, the DJIA is usually the one that proves to be wrong. That is why most technical analysts chart more than one general price index.

The Dow-Jones Transportation and Utility Averages suffer from the same weaknesses as the DJIA—price weighting, splits, substitutions, and small sample size (only 20 transportation stocks and 15 utilities). Takeover speculation in only one or two transportation equities can have a significant effect on the average. In 1980, when energy stocks were dominating the market, most of the utility average's movements were directly attributable to four natural gas stocks, rather than the staid electric utility equities most people think of when they consider the utility average.

Contrary to popular opinion, we've found that the Dow-Jones Transportation Average is not a reliable leading indicator for the general market. But the Dow-Jones

Utility Average is a fairly reliable leading indicator more often than not, although the lead may be long and variable.

The broad-based, capitalization-weighted Standard & Poor's (S&P) indexes and NYSE price indexes are measures of total market value. The most recent price of the hundreds of component stocks are multiplied by the number of shares outstanding. This product is then divided by a base date index number to make the index comparable over time. Splits have no impact, and substitutions of stocks are properly handled by adjusting the base date index number. Thus, valid and comparable market price data are available all the way back to 1873 for the S&P 500.

The NYSE Composite (symbol NYA) is composed of all 2,800 common stocks listed on the New York Stock Exchange. The NYA includes about 82% of the total market value of all U.S. stocks. The S&P Composite Index of the 500 biggest stocks (symbol SPX) is a subset of the NYSE Composite, and it comprises about 65% of the total market value of all U.S. stocks. The S&P 100 (OEX) index, used as the market index for a Chicago Board Options Exchange contract, is a subset of the S&P 500, listing the 100 largest stocks. As one might guess, there is a near perfect correlation between these capitalization-weighted indexes, all of which have the bulk of their weight in the 100 largest stocks.

The NASDAQ Composite (symbol COMP) is composed of 5500 unlisted stocks traded over-the-counter, and it comprises about 18% of the total market value of all U.S. stocks. The NASDAQ Technology Stock Index of 700 stocks is a subset of the COMP, and it comprises about 37% of the total market value of the COMP. NASDAQ stands for the National Association of Securities Dealers Automatic Quotation system.

The American Stock Exchange (AMEX) Market Value Index is properly capitalization weighted, but its entire capitalization does not match that of only one stock, IBM, so its significance is minuscule. Moreover, only 10 stocks account for about one third of the AMEX total weight, so price distortions are possible. Few technical analysts follow the AMEX index.

The Russell 3000 stock index is composed of 3000 common stocks, and it comprises about 98% of the total market value of all U.S. stocks. A subset, the Russell 1000 stock index, is the top third of the 3000 in terms of market capitalization. The Russell 1000 comprises about 90% of the total market value of the Russell 3000. The Russell 2000 stock index, which is the bottom two-thirds of the Russell 3000 in market capitalization, comprises about 10% of the total market value of the Russell 3000.

The Wilshire 5000 stock index is the most broadly based, capitalization-weighted index, comprising almost all of the total market value of all U.S. stocks. Originally composed of 5000 stocks, this index now covers approximately 7,000 U.S. equities, including all actively trading common stocks on the New York Stock Exchange, American Stock Exchange, and NASDAQ over-the-counter dealer market.

The Value Line Averages are unweighted geometric averages of 1665 stocks. The smallest stock has the same impact as the largest. According to Norman G. Fosback, in his 1976 book *Stock Market Logic* (Institute for Econometric Research, 3471 North Federal Highway, Fort Lauderdale, FL 33306), the geometric averaging method (based on logarithms) results in a negative, downward bias, so that the geometric average is always below the simple arithmetic average or mean. We have not found the Value Line composite useful in our technical work.

Fosback is also critical of the advance-decline line as a market barometer, for three very good reasons. First, no consideration is given to the extent of price or market value change, but only to the direction of price change, up or down. Academic studies have proven that average price advances are larger than average price declines, so the advance-decline line's failure to take into account the size of any price change means that the advance-decline must underperform the stock market price indexes, which it does. Second, the number of listed stocks has increased over the years, thus destroying the comparability of the advance-decline line over time. (This can be adjusted for by dividing advances minus declines by advances plus declines or by total issues traded.) Third, inclusion of preferred stocks, which fluctuate more with bond prices than with common stock prices, produces distortions, particularly when bond prices and common stock prices are trending in opposite directions, as they often have in the past. Given these substantial shortcomings, false divergences in the advance-decline line versus price indexes become more understandable.

On the positive side, Fosback holds unweighted total return indexes in high regard. These are based on Quotron's "QCHA," which is the average percentage price change for each common stock listed on the NYSE. Including dividend return as well as percentage price change gives a more realistic overall representation, according to Fosback, because more than half of the long-term total return of all common stocks through history has been from dividends.

Although Fosback has made a good case for unweighted, total return indexes, they still do not enjoy wide popularity. For one thing, the big institutions have difficulty trading large dollar amounts of small capitalization stocks, so they mostly stay with the big, high-capitalization stocks that dominate the S&P 500. Thus, they focus on that index. For another thing, unweighted total return indexes are not widely published in the popular press, and few people choose to spend the time necessary to make their own calculations.

In conclusion, like most technical researchers, we prefer the broad-based, capitalization-weighted indexes for our technical studies, specifically the S&P 500 or NYSE Composite, which for practical purposes are nearly the same. We use the Dow for many studies for the very practical reason that we happen to have the most daily data in computer readable form (back to 1900) for the Dow. Finally, the weight of tradition favoring the DJIA is heavy and demands respect.

Support and Resistance

At the most basic level, Support and Resistance are previous lows and highs. Price movements have a tendency to halt or at least react or hesitate at the previous lows and highs that stand out on the chart as obviously significant. Also, the sloping trendlines and price channels that contain the price action within orderly ascending or descending patterns offer moving points of Support and Resistance that function similarly to horizontal trading ranges.

A very useful property of Support and Resistance is the tendency of these levels to reverse roles once penetrated. Specifically, once a Support level below the current price is broken, that level becomes Resistance on future rally attempts. Similarly, once a Resistance level above the current price is broken, that level becomes Support on future downward price corrections.

The chart example of Texas Instruments shows that the 1.4 to 1.8 zone of support held all declines for 11 years from 1980 to 1991. The resistance around 3.5 to 3.7, encountered in 1983, 1988, and early 1993, reversed roles and functioned as support in late 1993. Also, the 1987-1994 resistance in the 5 to 5.5 zone reversed roles and functioned as support on three separate occasions in 1996. The very long, 15-year sideways trading range from 1980 to 1995 functioned as a powerful base of accumulation for a major price markup to 99.8 in 2000.

Inquiring minds always want to know why, of course, so here is a rationale, best illustrated by an example. Suppose a stock has been trading in a range of 50 to 55 for several months. Active followers of the stock have taken notice, so they buy on dips to Support at 50 then sell and short on rallies to Resistance at 55, a profitable business strategy. But orderly patterns do not last forever, and one day the price slices through 50 and closes at 48. The next day, it drops two more points. The third day it falls another point to 45. By this time, swing traders who bought at 50 and did not do the right thing and cut their loss quickly are down 10% and, consequently, are in a dysfunctional psychological state. They hope for a rally back to their buy price at 50. If they can only get their money back they will get out even. This is bad trading strategy, of course, but it is human nature to hate to be wrong, to feel pain on losing, to be slow to admit mistakes, and to hope for a lucky break that will allow them to undo their pain. So if the stock does bounce back to 50, all those suffering buyers hoping to get their money back will be relieved and happy to offer their long stock positions for sale at that 50 level, thereby putting a lid on the price and creating a resistance level that is hard for the stock to overcome. Also, bears, who covered shorts at 50 because it seemed like the lower end of a trading range, now would be happy to reestablish short positions at 50 if they get the chance.

Similarly, on the upside, following a long 50 to 55 trading range followed by a penetration of Resistance at 55 and a run to 60, the short sellers at 55 are now hoping

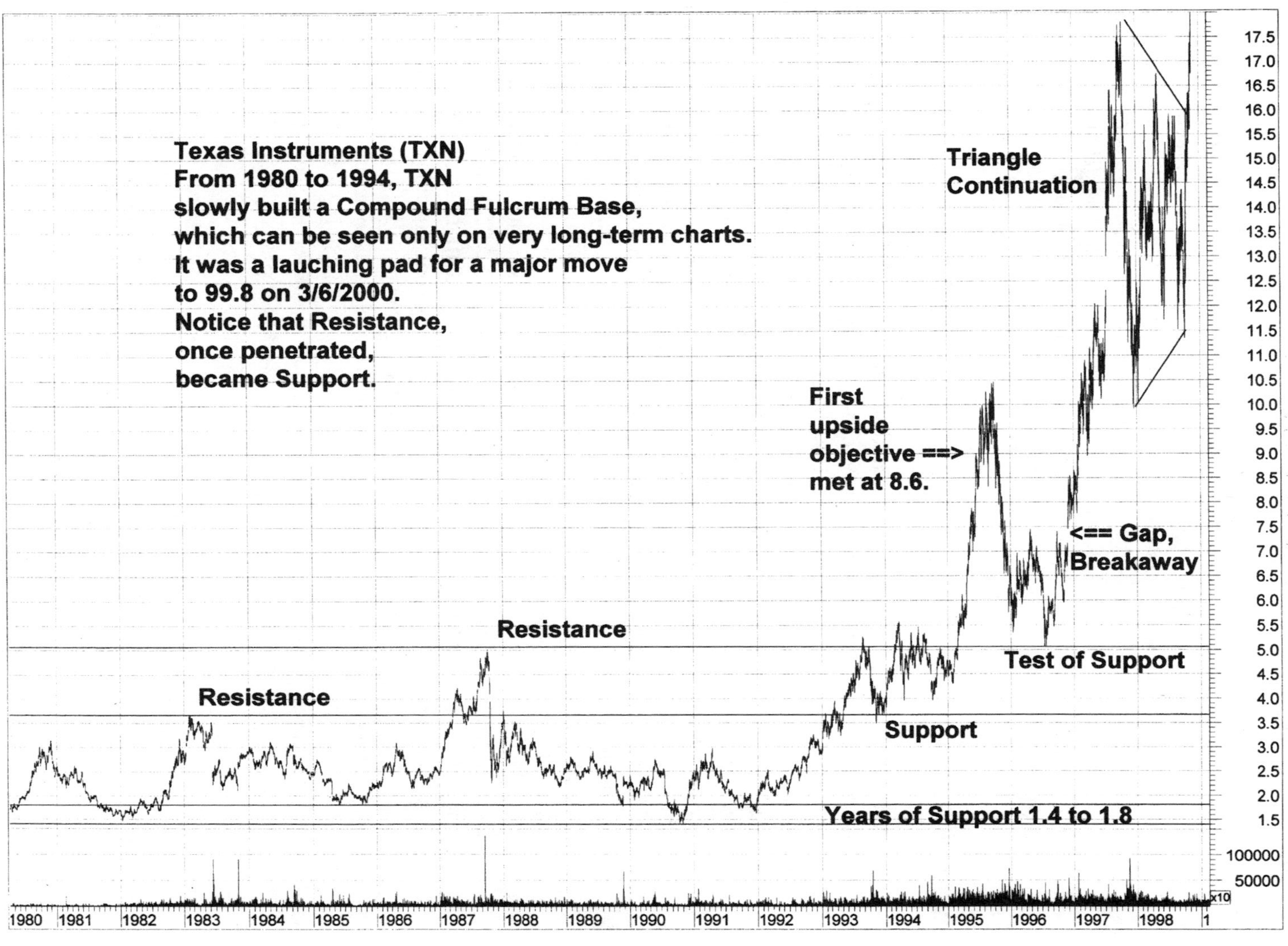
Texas Instruments (TXN)
From 1980 to 1994, TXN
slowly built a Compound Fulcrum Base,
which can be seen only on very long-term charts.
It was a lauching pad for a major move
to 99.8 on 3/6/2000.
Notice that Resistance,
once penetrated,
became Support.
Triangle
Continuation
First
upside
objective ==>
met at 8.6.
<== Gap,
Breakaway
Resistance
Resistance
Test of Support
Support
Years of Support 1.4 to 1.8
17.5
17.0
16.5
16.0
15.5
15.0
14.5
14.0
13.5
13.0
12.5
12.0
11.5
11.0
10.5
10.0
9.5
9.0
8.5
8.0
7.5
7.0
6.5
6.0
5.5
5.0
4.5
4.0
3.5
3.0
2.5
2.0
1.5
100000
50000
x10
1980
1981
1982
1983
1984
1985
1986
1987
1988
1989
1990
1991
1992
1993
1994
1995
1996
1997
1998

for a downward price correction so they can reduce their losses and their psychological discomfort at being wrong. They will be willing buyers at 55, their break-even point. Also, bulls on the stock who did not short but did take profits at 55, feel remorse at the potential profit they missed. These bulls also hope for a correction to 55, where they sold long, so they can undo their painful mistake and get another chance to reestablish their long positions. Thus, both groups, the bulls and the bears, will be bidding for the stock at 55, providing price support.

Swing Filter

A major challenge to traders is how to deal with noise in the data generated by free markets. There are many conceptually related techniques that attempt to filter out minor price movements, or *ripples* in Dow Theory terminology. Some simply ignore price movements less than a certain minimum size. The Point and Figure Charting method is an ancient and well-known example of such a filter.

Swing Filter is a simple idea: examine each high and low and filter out price reversals under a minimum percentage size. For example, some stock market analysts filter out and (thus ignore) movements of less than 3% or 4% or 8%. This cuts down on the amount of data to be considered, simplifying the decision-making process. The idea is that if we can cut out some of the minor noise, we can reduce the confusion and better focus on the main trend. The optimal size of the filter can be determined by back testing.

A good example of a Swing Filter is a slightly asymmetrical rule developed more than 12 years ago by Ned Davis Research. Buy the S&P 500 Index when it rises from an extreme closing price low by 8.4%. Hold long until the S&P 500 Index falls from an extreme closing price high by 7.2%, then sell long positions and switch into Commercial Paper. This simple filter would have given profitable signals 63% of the time, for long trades only. It would have outperformed a passive buy-and-hold strategy by 44.2% from 1969 to 1998, as the chart shows. This Swing Filter rule is always on the right side of the big price moves, has a built-in, loss-cutting stop loss point, and has an average gain four times larger than its average loss.

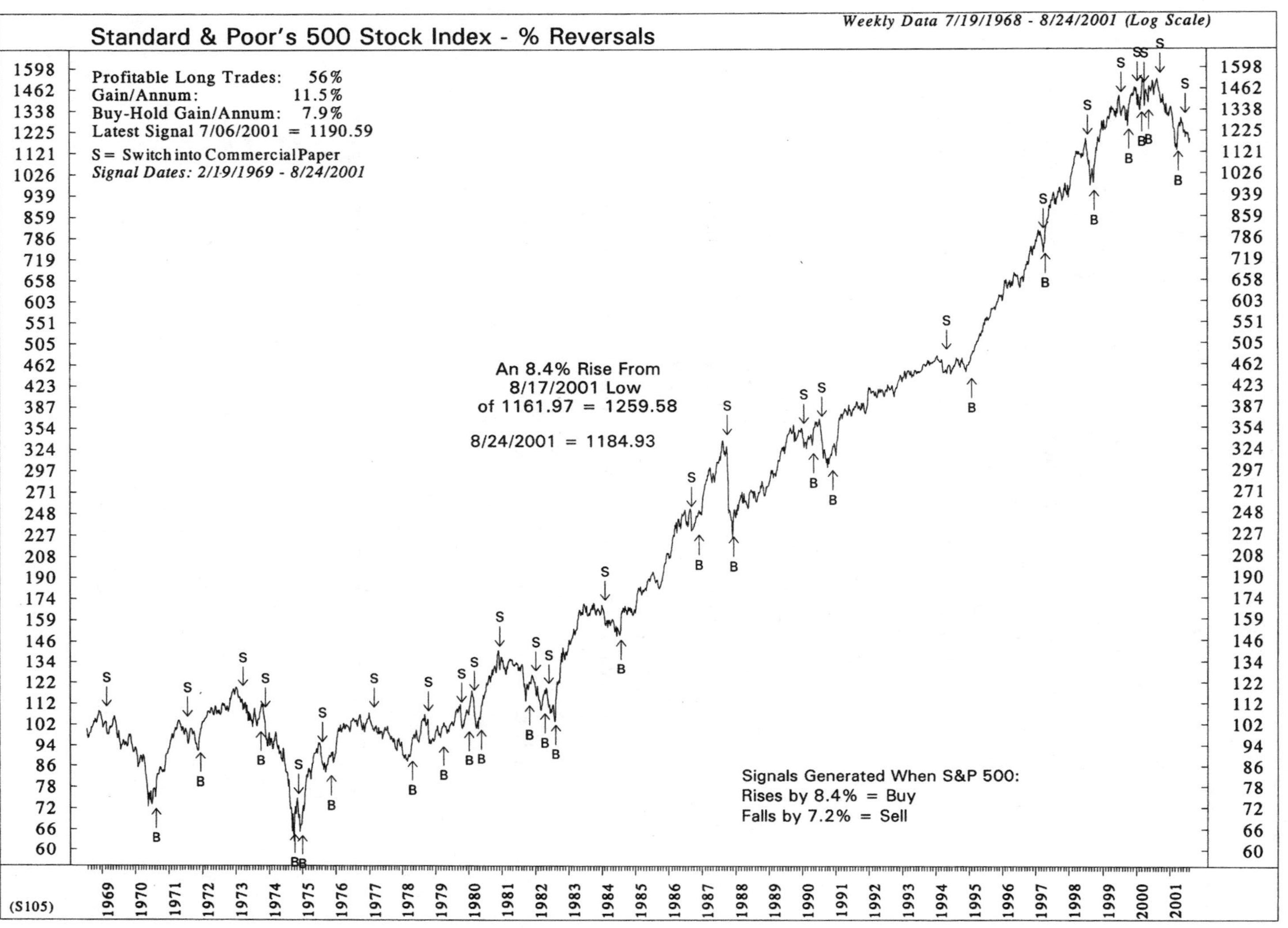

Standard & Poor's 500 Stock Index - % Reversals
Weekly Data 7/19/1968 - 8/24/2001 (Log Scale)
Profitable Long Trades: 56%
Gain/Annum: 11.5%
Buy-Hold Gain/Annum: 7.9%
Latest Signal 7/06/2001 = 1190.59
S = Switch into Commercial Paper
Signal Dates: 2/19/1969 - 8/24/2001
An 8.4% Rise From
8/17/2001 Low
of 1161.97 = 1259.58
8/24/2001 = 1184.93
Signals Generated When S&P 500:
Rises by 8.4% = Buy
Falls by 7.2% = Sell
1598
1462
1338
1225
1121
1026
939
859
786
719
658
603
551
505
462
423
387
354
324
297
271
248
227
208
190
174
159
146
134
122
112
102
94
86
78
72
66
60
1969
1970
1971
1972
1973
1974
1975
1976
1977
1978
1979
1980
1981
1982
1983
1984
1985
1986
1987
1988
1989
1990
1991
1992
1993
1994
1995
1996
1997
1998
1999
2000
2001
(S105)

Chart by permission of Ned Davis Research.

Swing Index (Wilder's)

Wilder's Swing Index (SI) is a complex trend-confirmation/divergence indicator published by J. Welles Wilder, Jr., in his 1978 book, *New Concepts in Technical Trading Systems* (Trend Research, PO Box 128, McLeansville, NC 27301). Wilder designed SI to be a better representation of the true market trend. SI compares relationships between the current prices (open, high, low, and close) and the previous period's prices. Mathematically, SI may be expressed as follows:

$$SI = ((50 * K) / M) * ((C - Cp) + .5 (C - O) + .25(Cp - Op)) / R)$$

where

K = the larger of H − Cp or L − Cp.
H = the highest price of the current period.
Cp = the closing price of the previous period.
L = the lowest price of the current period.
M = the value of a limit move set by the futures exchange.
C = the closing price of the current period.
O = the opening price of the current period.
Op = the opening price of the previous period.

R is defined by the following two steps:

Step 1: Determine which is the largest of the following three values:

H − Cp, *or*
L − Cp, *or*
H − L.

Step 2: Calculate R according to one of following three formulas:

If the largest value in Step 1 is H − Cp, then
$R = (H - Cp) - .5(L - C) + .25(Cp - Op)$.

If the largest value in Step 1 is L − Cp, then
$R = (L - Cp) - .5(H - C) + .25(Cp - Op)$.

If the largest value in Step 1 is H − L, then
$R = (H - L) + .25(Cp - Op)$.

Stocks do not have daily price movement limits. Therefore, when using MetaStock® software, we use the maximum number of 30,000 for the "limit move parameter."

The SI data can be plotted as an oscillator viewed with a variety of technical analysis methods. It is most productively viewed as the Accumulation Swing Index (ASI), which is a cumulative running total of the Swing Index. *(See Accumulation Swing Index.)*

Swing Retracement Levels

This Swing Retracement method subtracts the extreme low from the extreme high of any significant swing (price range), multiplies that difference by certain customary numbers long used by the trading community, then adds these products to the extreme low and subtracts them from the extreme high. The results are useful price targets as well as support and resistance levels.

W. D. Gann divided a price range into eighths: 0.125, 0.25, 0.375, 0.5, 0.625, 0.75, 0.875, and 1. Gann also projected whole number integer multiples of a price range: 0, 1, 2, 3, 4, 5, 6, 7, 8, 9, 10, etc. Gann marked off squares of integers: 4, 9, 16, 25, 36, 49, 64, 81, 100, 144, etc. Gann also used the range from the extreme high price down to zero. And independent of any past prices, Gann noted round numbers, especially those followed by zeros.

The most important Fibonacci ratios to multiply the past price ranges by are: 0.236, 0.382, 0.500, 0.618, 0.786, 1.000, 1.272, 1.618, 2.000, 2.618, and 4.236.

Dow Theorists emphasize thirds, that is, 0.333 and 0.667.

Tubb's Law of Proportion emphasizes common fractions, 1/2 or 0.5, 2/3 or 0.667, and 3/4 or 0.75, as the most important ratios.

This Swing Retracement method also may be applied to time intervals between swing highs and lows. For example, if a price upswing lasted 100 calendar days, from the date of the price low to the date of the price high, we might look for a downward price correction of that up-move to terminate at or near the following Fibonacci numbers of days from the top, rounded to whole numbers: 24, 38, 50, 62, 79, 100, 127, 162, 200, 262, and 424 calendar days. Finally, to cover all bases, we could mark off the thirds, 33 and 66 days, and all the Gann numbers.

To the uninitiated, unaware of the market's hidden structures, this exercise may seem arbitrary and illogical at first. But many experienced traders employ Swing Retracement because it often helps them determine *in advance* potential price levels and time junctures at which to be especially alert for price-trend change. They use these dates and price levels in conjunction with other technical indicators to pinpoint trend changes that otherwise would be impossible to identify. On occasion, they hit a future turning point with uncanny accuracy.

Taylor Book Method

The Taylor Book Method is a short-term, contrary, trend-fading strategy that attempts to capitalize on an observed tendency of the markets to move in price ripples of about 3 days in one direction before reversing. Basically, after three down days, look to buy any early weakness at or near the opening. If the market is not weak early, postpone action by a day. Look to take profits near previous daily highs. Conversely, after three up days, look to short any early strength at or near the opening. If the market is not strong early, postpone action by a day. Look to take profits near previous daily lows. Positions are closed out in one to 3 days. (See Taylor, George Douglas, *The Taylor Trading Technique,* 1950, Traders Press, PO Box 6206, Greenville, SC 29606, www.traderspressbookstore.com.)

TEMA

(See Triple Exponential Moving Averages.)

Three Line Break Charts

The Japanese Three Line Break Chart is a unique kind of a line chart designed to filter out minor, short-term market noise. It is named for the three line blocks used to construct the chart.

This method considers closing prices only and ignores all intraday highs and lows. A new white block is added to the chart in a new column to the right when the high of the previous block is exceeded. A new black block is added when the current close breaks the low of the previous block, and this new black block is drawn in the next column to the right from the bottom of the previous block. When there is neither a new high or low, nothing is added and the chart remains the same. Thus, like the western Point and Figure Technique, price movement (and not the passage of time) determines the progress along the horizontal *x*-axis.

Following a rally powerful enough to form three consecutive white blocks, a downside reversal is recognized only when the price falls below the lowest price of the most recent three consecutive white blocks. At that point, from the bottom of the highest white block, a black block is drawn down to this new price low.

Following a sell-off powerful enough to form three consecutive black blocks, an upside reversal is recognized only when the price rises above the highest price of the most recent three consecutive black blocks. At that point, from the top of the lowest black block, a white block is drawn up to this new price high.

The chart shows the Three Line Break Chart for the S&P Depositary Receipts (SPY) for the full year 2000, January through December, drawn with MetaStock® software. See *Renko Chart* to compare this chart to the similar 1 point box size Renko

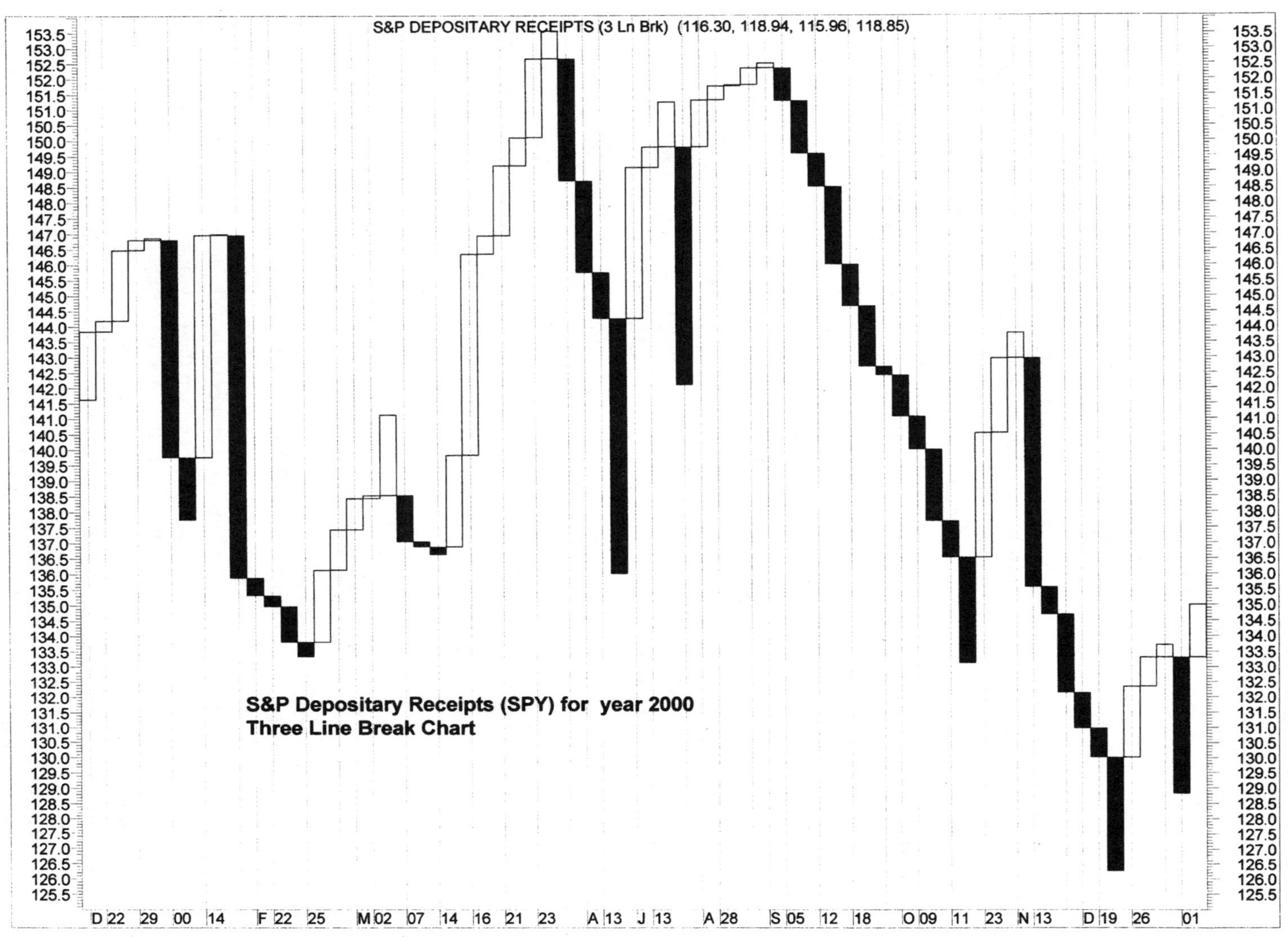
S&P DEPOSITARY RECEIPTS (3 Ln Brk) (116.30, 118.94, 115.96, 118.85)
S&P Depositary Receipts (SPY) for year 2000
Three Line Break Chart
D 22 29 00 14 F 22 25 M 02 07 14 16 21 23 A 13 J 13 A 28 S 05 12 18 O 09 11 23 N 13 D 19 26 01

Chart and to the 1 point box size and 1 point reversal *Point and Figure Chart* for the same stock over the same time.

Three Moving Average Crossover

Three Moving Average Crossover is a combination indicator that uses three moving averages of different lengths to generate trading signals. It combines fast and slow moving average signals in one indicator. Buy when the slope of the fast moving average is positive and the medium moving average is above the slow moving average. Sell when the slope of the fast moving average is negative and the medium moving average is below the slow moving average. One popular version uses 4-, 9-, and 18-trading days for the moving average lengths. These specific period lengths could be allowed to vary, of course, producing a very large number of possibilities. One possible MetaStock® System Test could be expressed as follows:

Enter long: Mov(CLOSE,opt1,E) > Ref(Mov(CLOSE,opt1,E),-1) AND Mov(CLOSE,2*opt1,E) > Mov(CLOSE,4*opt1,E)

Close long: Mov(CLOSE,opt1,E) < Ref(Mov(CLOSE,opt1,E),-1) AND Mov(CLOSE,2*opt1,E) < Mov(CLOSE,4*opt1,E)

Enter short: Mov(CLOSE,opt1,E) < Ref(Mov(CLOSE,opt1,E),-1) AND Mov(CLOSE,2*opt1,E) < Mov(CLOSE,4*opt1,E)

Close short: Mov(CLOSE,opt1,E) > Ref(Mov(CLOSE,opt1,E),-1) AND Mov(CLOSE,2*opt1,E) > Mov(CLOSE,4*opt1,E)

TICK

TICK is a snapshot of the market's trend at any specific time in the trading day. TICK reflects market strength (positive and rising) or weakness (negative and falling) at any moment during the trading day. TICK is the net difference between the number of NYSE stocks with their latest sales occurring on an uptick (a higher current price than the next most recent price) minus the number of NYSE stocks with last sales occurring on a downtick (a lower current price than the previous price). In essence, it is a moment-to-moment representation of net advancing issues, considering only the most recent price compared to the next most recent price.

TICK oscillates around zero. It can be interpreted in standard oscillator fashion.

Traders watch TICK to identify shifts in trends. When TICK goes from a large negative reading to a large positive reading, that indicates a bullish change in the market's demand and supply balance. Similarly, an equally dramatic negative swing, from a big plus TICK to a big minus TICK, indicates a bearish change.

Positive and negative divergences in TICK relative to an independent indicator, such as a market price index, indicate an impending price trend change. When TICK makes a series of lower highs while an independent market indicator makes higher highs, such a negative divergence warns of a possible bearish change in the prevailing trend. Similarly, when TICK makes a series of higher lows while an independent market indicator makes lower lows, such a positive divergence warns of a possible bullish change in the prevailing trend.

Generally, extremely high TICK readings indicate extremely positive momentum and unusual market strength. Such a strong trend often continues until momentum starts to dissipate on rallies. Some very aggressive short-term professional traders fade extreme momentum, expecting a return to more normal conditions. Generally, counter-trend trading tactics are not appropriate for long-term investors.

Extremely low TICK readings indicate unusual selling pressure. Again, it is risky to fade such momentum, but the best time to buck that negative trend is when there is a genuine Selling Climax on huge volume. Such a Selling Climax is often followed by an unsustainable Dead Cat Bounce that can be profitable for astute traders.

TICK has larger implications beyond day trading. The last price of the day, the closing price, has long been regarded as the single most important price of the day. The daily tug of war between bulls and bears is settled at one price at the end of the fray. When all is said and done at day's end, that closing price is where demand and supply balance. The close is a summary of the day's activity. Technicians usually apply various moving averages to closing TICK values to smooth out erratic movements and reveal any underlying trend. (We added 10,000 to closing TICK to avoid the more complicated handling negative numbers, so our graph oscillates around 10,000.)

Indicator Strategy Example for Closing TICK

TICK is a robust indicator, with all exponential moving average lengths tested (from one to 500 days) profitable for long and short trades. The cumulative equity line shows few drawdown periods. Based on a 35-year file from January 1966 to January 2001 (TICK at the end of each day and the DJIA daily closing price) the following parameters would have produced a positive result on a purely mechanical signal basis with no subjectivity, no sophisticated technical analysis, and no judgement:

Enter Long (Buy) at the current daily price close of the DJIA when current closing TICK is greater than its own trailing 11-day exponential moving average (EMA) as of the previous day, thereby signaling a rising trend of closing TICK.

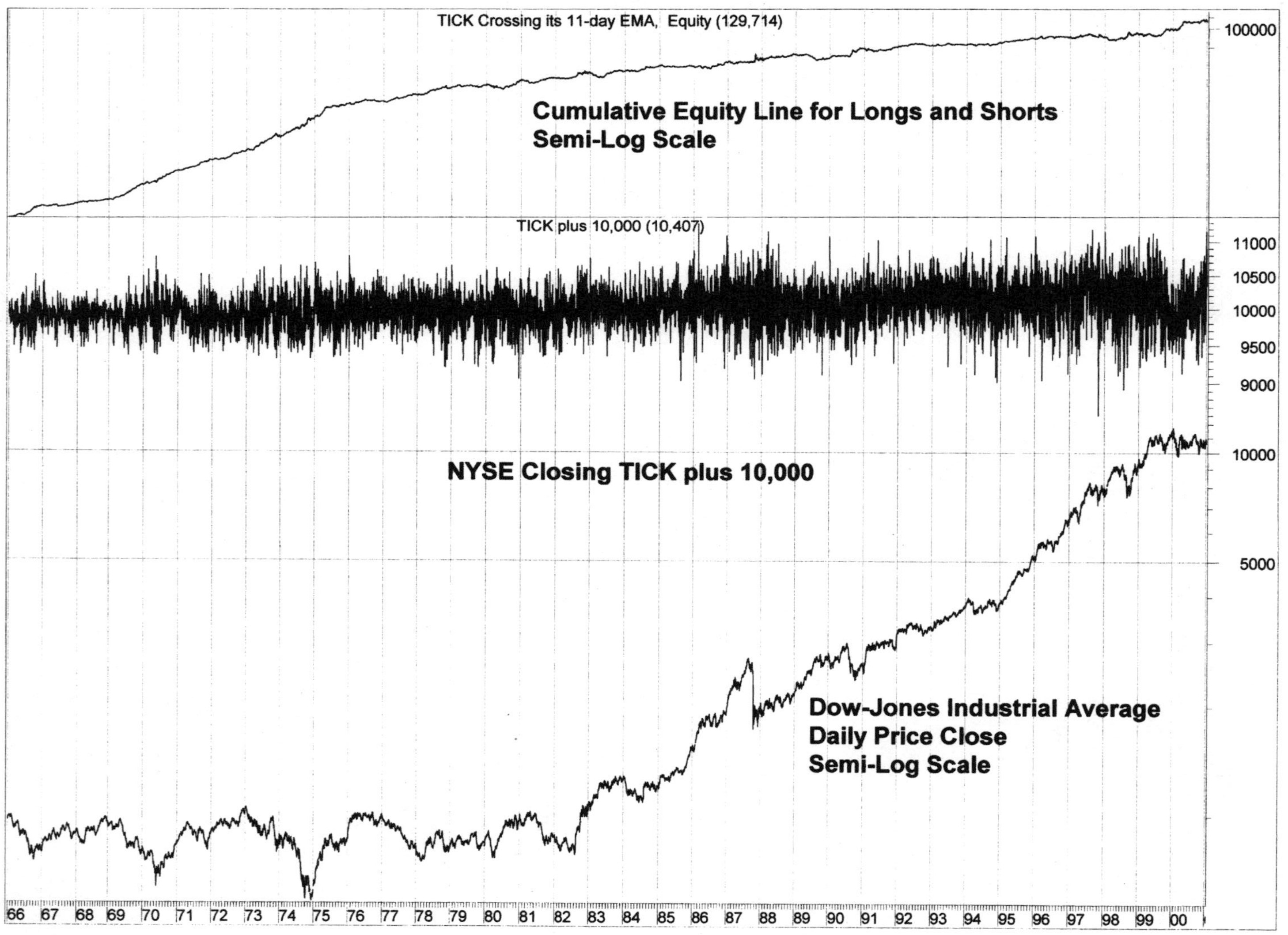

TICK Crossing its 11-day EMA, Equity (129,714)
100000
Cumulative Equity Line for Longs and Shorts
Semi-Log Scale
TICK plus 10,000 (10,407)
11000
10500
10000
9500
9000
NYSE Closing TICK plus 10,000
10000
5000
Dow-Jones Industrial Average
Daily Price Close
Semi-Log Scale
66 67 68 69 70 71 72 73 74 75 76 77 78 79 80 81 82 83 84 85 86 87 88 89 90 91 92 93 94 95 96 97 98 99 00

TICK Crossing 11-day EMA

Total net profit	129613.94	Open position value	492.06	Net Profit / Buy&Hold %	12905.09
Percent gain/loss	129613.94	Annual percent gain/loss	3698.91	Annual Net % / B&H %	12906.01
Initial investment	100	Interest earned	0		
Current position	Short	Date position entered	1/5/01		
Buy/Hold profit	996.64	Days in test	12790	# of days per trade	3.04
Buy/Hold pct gain/loss	996.64	Annual B/H pct gain/loss	28.44		
Total closed trades	4202	Commissions paid	0		
Avg profit per trade	30.73	Avg Win/Avg Loss ratio	1.26		
Total long trades	2101	Total short trades	2101	Long Win Trade %	51.88
Winning long trades	1090	Winning short trades	977	Short Win Trade %	46.50
Total winning trades	2067	Total losing trades	2135	Total Win Trade %	49.19
Amount of winning trades	708502.63	Amount of losing trades	−579380.56	Net Profit Margin %	10.03
Average win	342.77	Average loss	−271.37	Average P. Margin %	11.63
Largest win	9345.78	Largest loss	−4445.94	% Net / (Win + Loss)	35.53
Average length of win	3.64	Average length of loss	2.57	(Win − Loss) / Loss %	41.63
Longest winning trade	16	Longest losing trade	11	(Win − Loss) / Loss %	45.45
Most consecutive wins	13	Most consecutive losses	8	(Win − Loss) / Loss %	62.50
Total bars out	12	Average length out	12		
Longest out period	12				
System close drawdown	0	Profit/Loss index	18.28	% Net Profit / SODD	#DIV/0!
System open drawdown	0	Reward/Risk index	100	(Net P.-SODD)/Net P.	100.00
Max open trade drawdown	−4445.94	Buy/Hold index	12954.46	% SODD / Net Profit	0.00

In the Equis MetaStock® "System Report" (profit and loss summary statistics), the *Total net profit* is the sum of profits minus the sum of losses, including open positions marked to the market. In contrast, the *Amount of Winning Trades* is the sum of realized profits (the total of all gains on closed-out trades only, excluding any open positions). Similarly, the *Amount of Losing Trades* is the sum of realized losses (the total of all losses on closed-out trades only, excluding any open positions). *System close drawdown* is the largest decline in the cumulative equity line below the initial investment, based on closed-out positions only. *System open drawdown (SODD)* is the largest decline in the cumulative equity line below the initial investment when a position is open. *Max open trade drawdown* is the largest decline in the cumulative equity line below the trade entry price during the worst single trade. The *Profit/Loss Index* is a complex calculation that relates the Amount of Winning Trades to the Amount of Losing Trades on a scale of −100 (worst possible performance) to +100 (best possible performance), with zero representing profits equal to losses. *Reward/Risk Index* is the Total net profit minus System open drawdown. The resulting difference is then divided by the Total net profit. The *Buy/Hold Index* is the Total net profit minus the buy-and-hold strategy's net profit. The resulting difference is then divided by the buy-and-hold net profit. In this exercise, initial equity is assumed to be $100. Both long and short positions are taken unless otherwise noted. Trades are executed at the closing price on the signal date. Transaction costs, interest expenses, and margins are not included in the statistics.

Close Long (Sell) at the current daily price close of the DJIA when current closing TICK is less than its own trailing 11-day EMA as of the previous day, thereby signaling a falling trend of closing TICK.

Enter Short (Sell Short) at the current daily price close of the DJIA when current closing TICK is less than its own trailing 11-day EMA as of the previous day, thereby signaling a falling trend of closing TICK.

Close Short (Cover) at the current daily price close of the DJIA when current closing TICK is greater than its own trailing 11-day EMA as of the previous day, thereby signaling a rising trend of closing TICK.

Starting with $100 and reinvesting profits, total net profits for this TICK trend-following strategy would have been $129,613.94, assuming a fully invested strategy, reinvestment of profits, no transactions costs and no taxes. This would have been 12,905.09 percent greater than buy-and-hold. Short selling would have been profitable, and short selling was included in the strategy. Despite its high profitability, TICK would have been incorrect more often than it was right, with only 49.19% winning trades. Trading would have been hyperactive at one trade every 3.04 calendar days.

The Equis International MetaStock® System Testing rules for closing TICK, where we added 10,000 to closing TICK and inserted it into the data field normally reserved for volume, are written as follows:

Enter long: V > Ref(Mov(V,opt1,E),-1)

Close long: V < Ref(Mov(V,opt1,E),-1)

Enter short: V < Ref(Mov(V,opt1,E),-1)

Close short: V > Ref(Mov(V,opt1,E),-1)

OPT1 Current value: 11

Tick Volume Bar

A Tick Volume Bar is a bar chart with price on the vertical y-axis and n-tick intervals on the horizontal x-axis. Each price bar is defined by n number of ticks. For example, a tick volume bar of 10 would contain the price range measured over the past 10 transactions, a tick volume bar of 100 would contain the price range measured over the past 100 transactions, and so on.

Time Segmented Volume (TSV)

Time Segmented Volume (TSV) is a proprietary price and volume oscillator created by Don Worden (www.TC2000.com, Worden Brothers, Inc., 4950 Pine Cone Drive, Durham, North Carolina 27707, phone 800 776 4940). Worden typically uses an 18-, 26-, or 31-bar TSV; with the shorter the time period the more sensitive, and the longer the time period the less sensitive. Next, Worden smoothes this TSV data with an exponential moving average (of 13-days in his published example), which he overlays on the TSV. Worden has observed that TSV works better for some stocks than others, so he evaluates past performance of TSV for each stock to see how well TSV applies on a case by case basis.

TSV is interpreted much the same as any other oscillator: it is examined in a variety of ways to determine the relative balance of accumulation (buying) and distribution (selling) and the implied potential for sustained directional price movement.

- The oscillator is measured for its level relative to its own recent range, with high levels bullish and low levels bearish.
- The relative levels of the oscillator are compared to the relative levels of the raw price data to determine any positive or negative divergences between the two.
- The oscillator is compared to a critical threshold level, in this case the zero line. Above the threshold is bullish. Below the threshold is bearish.
- The oscillator's own exponential moving average is compared to the critical threshold level. Above the threshold is bullish. Below the threshold is bearish.
- The oscillator is compared to its own past trend, which in this case is defined by its own trailing exponential moving average. Above trend is bullish. Below trend is bearish.
- In contrast to many oscillators, TSV is not used to determine overbought and oversold levels.

When these criteria line up on one side, bullish or bearish, the implications for action are clear, and the stock is bought or sold. When the criteria are mixed, subtle judgements are called for.

Time Series Forecast (TSF), Moving Linear Regression, End Point Moving Average (EPMA)

Time Series Forecast (TSF) is the ending value of a Linear Regression trendline plus its slope. The addition of slope extends the Linear Regression trendline forward in time by one trading day, offering a naïve forecast of the next day's price. This assumes the trend continues in linear fashion (which it seldom does). TSF is designed to speed up trend change signals by reducing lag. TSF tracks the raw data more closely than Linear Regression trendlines or moving averages.

The term "End Point Moving Average" is a misnomer, strictly speaking, because this indicator is not computed like a moving average. But Patrick E. Lafferty ("The End Point Moving Average", *Technical Analysis of Stocks & Commodities,* V13, pages 413–417, www.traders.com), correctly pointed out that this indicator could be interpreted much the same as moving averages. He suggested a buy signal when TSF moves up and the value of the DJIA is higher than the value of the TSF. He suggested a sell signal when TSF moves down and the value of the DJIA is lower than the value of the TSF.

Total Issues Traded

Total issues traded includes all of the issues that traded at all on any given day, including the total number of stocks ending the day higher, lower, and unchanged. On the NYSE, total issues traded rose 1080% from 1940 to 1999. Such growth distorts the meaning of breadth (advances, declines, new highs, and new lows) indicators over time. *(See Number of Total Issues Traded.)*

Total Short Ratio

The Total Short Ratio is calculated by dividing total short sales by total volume. Monthly NYSE data is used. High readings reflect excessive shorting and are viewed as bullish. Low readings signify low levels of shorting and are considered bearish. *(See Short Interest Ratio.)*

Total Win Trade %, the Trader's Advantage

The Trader's Advantage is the Total Winning Trade Percentage, or "Total Win Trade %" in our tables. This is the number of profitable trades divided by the total number of trades. This statistic is generally accorded far more attention than it deserves. Many good trend-following indicators that work well in terms of outperforming Reward/Risk benchmarks, because they cut losses and let profits run, actually have relatively low Total Winning Trade Percentages. In contrast, some indicators that work poorly in terms of underperforming Reward/Risk benchmarks actually have relatively high Total Winning Trade Percentages. In practical terms, Total Win Trade % is unimportant relative to Reward/Risk considerations, which deserve most of our attention.

Trap: Bull Trap, Bear Trap

A Trap occurs when price breaks out above a resistance level or below a support level but then immediately reverses with a forceful move in the opposite direction. This traps or hooks trend-followers who went with the breakout. These trend-followers must now cut losses, which adds fuel to the new directional momentum. The resulting fast move is of interest to short-term traders. A Bull Trap is an upside breakout followed by a fast and violent reversal to the downside. A Bear Trap is a downside breakout followed by a fast and violent reversal to the upside. Traps are quite common and significant in short-term trading but are of little importance to long-term investing. A Trap is also known as a Springboard.

Trailing Reversal Trading System

The Trailing Reversal Trading System enters a long trade when the stock price rises *n* percent from a recent Pivot Point Low. The system sells long and sells short when the stock price falls *n* percent from a recent Pivot Point High. The only variable, *n* percent, depends on preferred time frame and trading frequency. Typically this percentage may vary from 1% to 5% for traders up to 7% to 15% for investors. (See *Swing Filter,* on page 680.)

Trend Channel

The Trend Channel is composed of two parallel lines moving forward in time. These two parallel lines contain most or all price fluctuations. The Trend Channel may slope upward or downward. A sideways trading range is a horizontal Trend Channel, also known as a Price Channel.

Once we have established a Trendline through at least two of the more recent price pivot extremes, we may draw a parallel line through intervening extreme prices in the opposite direction. This Channel Line can be used for setting price objectives for trading within the trend. Both the basic trendline and the parallel Trend Channel offer reasonable estimates of the limits of future price swings moving forward in time.

All good things must eventually come to an end. When the price moves outside the boundaries of the Channel, that signals new and more forceful price momentum. It could mean either trend acceleration (if price breaks out in the direction of the prevailing trend) or trend reversal (if price breaks out in the opposite direction to the prevailing trend). In either case, we assume that the balance of demand and supply is shifting for the financial instrument analyzed. The new price objective would be the width of the recent Channel plus or minus the breakout point.

Following a period when prices have been contained within a Channel, when the price moves toward one boundary but fails to reach it by a substantial margin, that may signal a change in momentum and a shift in the balance of demand and supply. The technical analyst goes on alert for a trend change, which would be confirmed by an actual break of the Trend Channel.

Trendlines, Trend Lines

Trendlines are a basic tool of technical analysis. They are simple to define and to draw on any price chart, bar, candlestick, and point-and-figure.

For an uptrend line, once the price has established a higher high and higher low, we can connect the lowest low with a more recent higher low. Alternately, we could judge that a better fit to the price trend could be accomplished by using the second and third higher lows for our trendline. In either case, we start with an obvious past price low that stands out on the chart, then we move our hand to the right (moving forward in time) and up (moving higher in price) to another obvious price low that was higher than the first low and happened at a later date. We connect these two points with a straight line. This is a tentative up trendline. When the price falls again and stops on that line, then the up trendline is confirmed as valid. It takes at least three points on a line to form a valid trendline.

Similarly for an downtrend line, after the price has already established a lower high and lower low, we start with an obvious past price high that stands out on the

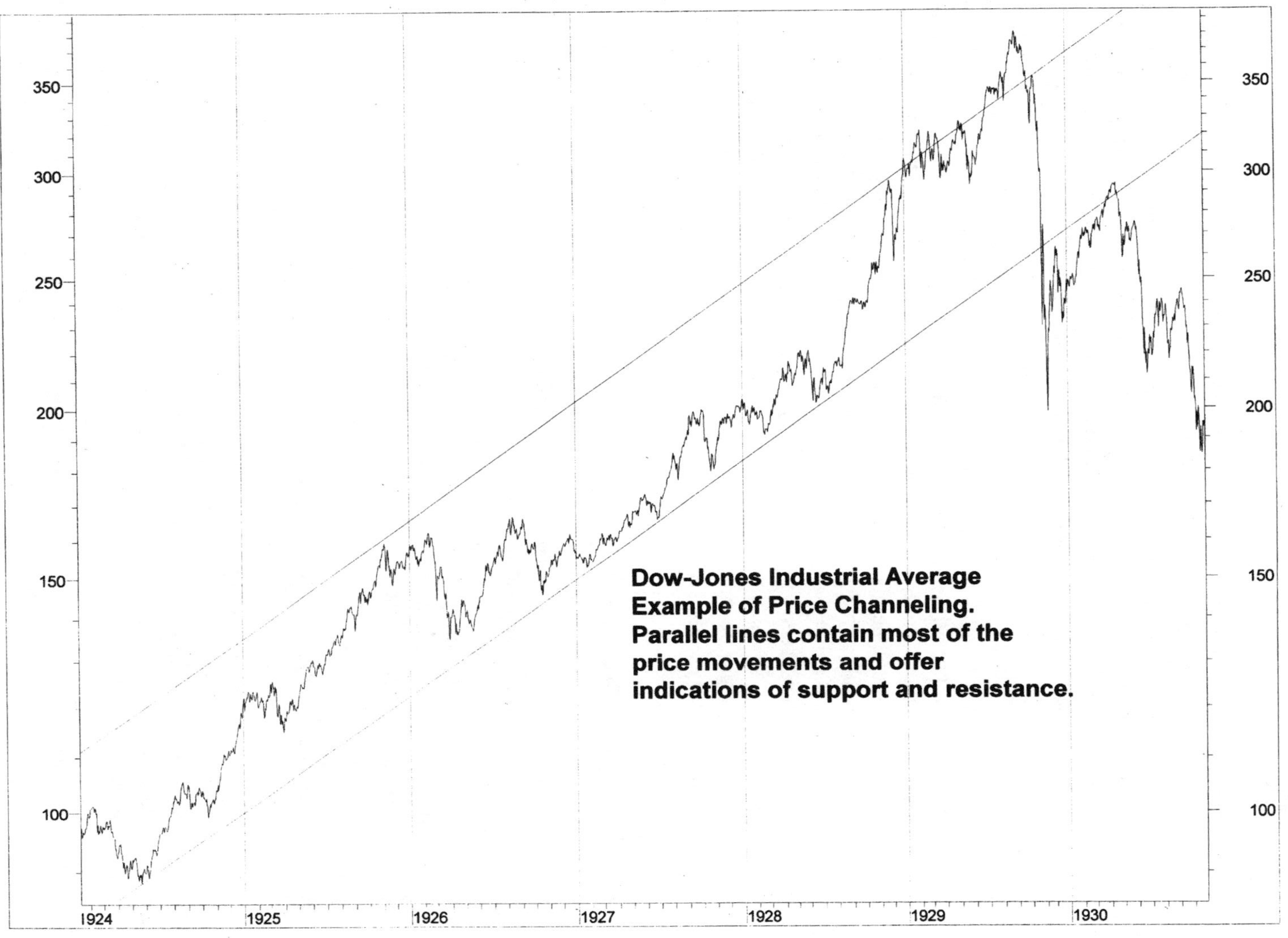
Dow-Jones Industrial Average
Example of Price Channeling.
Parallel lines contain most of the
price movements and offer
indications of support and resistance.
350
300
250
200
150
100
1924
1925
1926
1927
1928
1929
1930

chart. Next we move our hand to the right (moving forward in time) and down (moving lower in price) to another obvious price high that was lower than the first high and happened at a later date. Connect these two points with a straight line. This is a tentative down trendline. When the price rises again and stops on that line, then the down trendline is confirmed as valid. It takes three points on a line to form a valid trendline.

Horizontal trendlines drawn through obvious chart highs and lows are used to define the sideways price ranges that often turn into recognizable continuation or reversal chart patterns.

A trendline is generally considered to be more valid the longer it lasts (in time) and the more times the price touches the trendline and holds. Again we emphasize that it takes at least three points on a line to form a valid trendline. And the more price touches on a trendline, the more powerful and significant that trendline is.

If the trendline happens to coincide with another significant technical indicator, such as a key moving average or a Gann Angle, then that trendline is more powerful.

Trendlines seem to work better on arithmetic scale charts for short-to-intermediate-term analysis, covering minutes to weeks and even months. For multi-year trends, it may be more useful to use a semi-log scale, particularly if the financial instrument analyzed has had a very large price move.

Trident Commodity Trading System

The Trident Commodity Trading System looks for equality of price swing size in the direction of the main trend. This idea is related to Trend Channel. For example, in an uptrend, if the previous swing upward was 10% then, after a correction, we would look for the next upswing to be about 10%. Points could be used instead of percentage moves. Trident also places emphasis on half- and quarter-size swings for support, resistance and confirmation.

Triple Crossover Method

The Triple Crossover Method refers to the use of three moving averages of different lengths to signal the trend. Usually, for a buy signal, a short-period length moving average must rise above both an intermediate-term and a long-term period length moving average. Also, the intermediate may or may not be required to be above the long-length average. For a sell signal, the opposite conditions apply, a short-period length moving average must fall below both an intermediate-term and a long-term period length moving average. The best period lengths for each of three moving averages may be found by brute-force optimization. There are a very large number of possible combinations of period lengths. (See *Three Moving Average Crossover,* on page 686.)

Triple Exponential Moving Averages (TEMA)

Triple Exponential Moving Averages (TEMA) uses three different Exponential Moving Averages (EMAs) in an effort to speed up signals and achieve a faster response to price fluctuations. TEMA was introduced by Patrick G. Mulloy in 1994, " Smoothing Data With Less Lag", *Technical Analysis of Stocks & Commodities* magazine, V. 12:2 (www.traders.com).

TEMA uses single, double and triple EMAs. The first EMA smoothes the closing price, while the second EMA smoothes the first EMA and the third EMA smoothes the second EMA. Then, TEMA1 = 3EMA1 − 3EMA2 + EMA3. Thus, TEMA1 is a composite of single, double and triple Exponential Moving Averages.

In our independent observations, at short lengths, TEMA does appear to respond more effectively to changing new data than both an ordinary EMA and a Double EMA. At longer period lengths, however, TEMA responds much less effectively than the equivalent length EMA. As the table shows, TEMA underperformed a single EMA at lengths of 29 days and higher. Therefore, TEMA should not be assumed to be a substitute for any other moving average. Rather, it may best be considered to be an unfamiliar new tool to be approached with appropriately cautious respect. TEMA definitely cannot be used in place of traditional moving averages without testing.

The facing table shows a comparison of the signal performance of a standard moving average crossover rule using TEMA and an ordinary EMA of the same length, in days, as measured against the S&P 500 Composite Stock Price Index futures *CSI Perpetual Contract* from 4/21/82 to 12/29/00. The data reflects long trades only. It is apparent that TEMA would have been a more efficient signal generator than an ordinary EMA at very short time period lengths but much less effective at longer time period lengths of more than 28 days.

Indicator Strategy Example for TEMA

Based on a 18-year file of daily data for the entire history of the S&P 500 Composite Stock Price Index futures *CSI Perpetual Contract* (www.csidata.com) from 4/21/82 to 12/29/00, we found that the following parameters would have produced a positive result on a purely mechanical signal basis with no subjectivity, no sophisticated technical analysis, and no judgement:

Enter Long (Buy) at the current daily price close of the S&P 500 Composite Stock Price Index futures *CSI Perpetual Contract* when that price close is greater than the 6-day TEMA, signifying a short-term price uptrend.

Close Long (Sell) at the current daily price close of the S&P 500 Composite Stock Price Index futures *CSI Perpetual Contract* when that price close is less than the 6-day TEMA, signifying a short-term price downtrend.

Enter Short (Sell Short) never.

Starting with $100 and reinvesting profits, total net profits for this TEMA trend-following strategy would have been $815.33, assuming a fully invested strategy, reinvestment of profits, no transactions costs and no taxes. This would have been 21.19 percent less than buy-and-hold. No short selling would have been profitable, and no short selling was included in the strategy. This long-only TEMA would have given profitable buy signals 46.97% of the time. Trading would have been very active at one trade every 7.67 calendar days.

The Equis International MetaStock® System Testing rules are written as follows:

Enter long: CLOSE > Tema(CLOSE,opt1)

Close long: CLOSE < Tema(CLOSE,opt1)

OPT1 Current value: 6

TEMA Length in days	Total Net Profit	# of Trades Total	Win	Lose	% Wins	Avg Win/ Avg Loss	EMA Length in days	Total Net Profit	# of Trades Total	Win	Lose	% Wins	Avg Win/ Avg Loss
2	368.81	1406	697	709	49.57	1.32	2	311.97	917	382	535	41.66	2.01
3	362.96	1215	592	623	48.72	1.37	3	260.03	768	311	457	40.49	2.06
4	591.73	1089	529	560	48.58	1.53	4	182.53	669	261	408	39.01	2.09
5	709.75	985	474	511	48.12	1.72	5	139.26	606	226	380	37.29	2.15
6	815.33	890	418	472	46.97	1.79	6	136.28	563	208	355	36.94	2.17
7	572.61	852	383	469	44.95	1.78	7	115.31	538	195	343	36.25	2.22
8	506.42	793	358	435	45.15	1.73	8	116.75	508	179	329	35.24	2.32
9	430.09	760	334	426	43.95	1.79	9	105.67	480	161	319	33.54	2.45
10	349.62	737	318	419	43.15	1.86	10	106.24	454	145	309	31.94	2.63
11	379.11	698	304	394	43.55	1.87	11	87.03	443	134	309	30.25	2.77
12	445.87	666	293	373	43.99	1.87	12	76.94	422	122	300	28.91	2.90
13	383.79	648	276	372	42.59	2.03	13	61.87	415	117	298	28.19	2.93
14	401.87	611	264	347	43.21	2.06	14	67.75	395	111	284	28.10	3.01
15	271.20	600	251	349	41.83	1.96	15	91.22	376	109	267	28.99	3.02
16	272.77	577	241	336	41.77	1.97	16	121.09	359	102	257	28.41	3.27
17	209.18	564	233	331	41.31	1.88	17	105.64	359	104	255	28.97	3.10
18	205.47	541	224	317	41.40	1.88	18	117.50	348	100	248	28.74	3.20
19	162.50	527	216	311	40.99	1.85	19	108.23	343	99	244	28.86	3.15
20	166.94	514	204	310	39.69	1.99	20	111.52	334	95	239	28.44	3.23
21	138.26	502	194	308	38.65	2.03	21	115.76	329	93	236	28.27	3.29
22	150.41	489	179	310	36.61	2.27	22	123.31	318	89	229	27.99	3.33
23	160.52	481	174	307	36.17	2.35	23	144.92	305	86	219	28.20	3.41
24	179.98	466	174	292	37.34	2.29	24	140.92	299	85	214	28.43	3.34
25	204.81	458	168	290	36.68	2.42	25	168.71	290	80	210	27.59	3.59
26	188.61	460	168	292	36.52	2.40	26	160.97	283	79	204	27.92	3.54
27	165.65	461	165	296	35.79	2.41	27	161.95	272	76	196	27.94	3.58
28	165.32	456	163	293	35.75	2.41	28	143.82	263	73	190	27.76	3.54
29	140.41	451	159	292	35.25	2.42	29	158.53	258	76	182	29.46	3.36
30	121.60	441	158	283	35.83	2.32	30	152.09	254	76	178	29.92	3.23
31	115.55	431	150	281	34.80	2.42	31	137.96	250	73	177	29.20	3.29
32	95.56	431	145	286	33.64	2.43	32	147.56	244	72	172	29.51	3.33
33	65.52	431	139	292	32.25	2.46	33	146.94	242	69	173	28.51	3.50
34	68.38	425	136	289	32.00	2.52	34	154.00	239	67	172	28.03	3.64
35	85.06	414	134	280	32.37	2.57	35	150.03	238	67	171	28.15	3.58
36	99.71	397	129	268	32.49	2.62	36	170.23	234	71	163	30.34	3.32
37	76.79	401	129	272	32.17	2.54	37	179.24	231	70	161	30.30	3.40
38	87.67	401	129	272	32.17	2.58	38	183.09	225	69	156	30.67	3.41
39	89.48	394	128	266	32.49	2.56	39	169.90	221	66	155	29.86	3.48
40	74.36	386	124	262	32.12	2.54	40	172.92	219	61	158	27.85	3.88
41	61.43	378	121	257	32.01	2.52	41	176.51	217	63	154	29.03	3.68
42	55.95	374	121	253	32.35	2.44	42	173.62	216	63	153	29.17	3.60
43	66.44	371	121	250	32.61	2.48	43	175.03	212	60	152	28.30	3.76
44	67.58	363	118	245	32.51	2.50	44	193.24	208	58	150	27.88	3.93
45	77.54	361	116	245	32.13	2.61	45	223.81	203	57	146	28.08	4.09
46	84.87	355	114	241	32.11	2.65	46	236.39	202	57	145	28.22	4.17
47	100.90	341	111	230	32.55	2.68	47	252.03	195	57	138	29.23	4.07
48	96.72	336	106	230	31.55	2.78	48	276.33	189	59	130	31.22	3.91
49	89.70	330	103	227	31.21	2.80	49	290.37	187	58	129	31.02	4.03
50	77.76	332	98	234	29.52	2.95	50	274.66	180	53	127	29.44	4.20

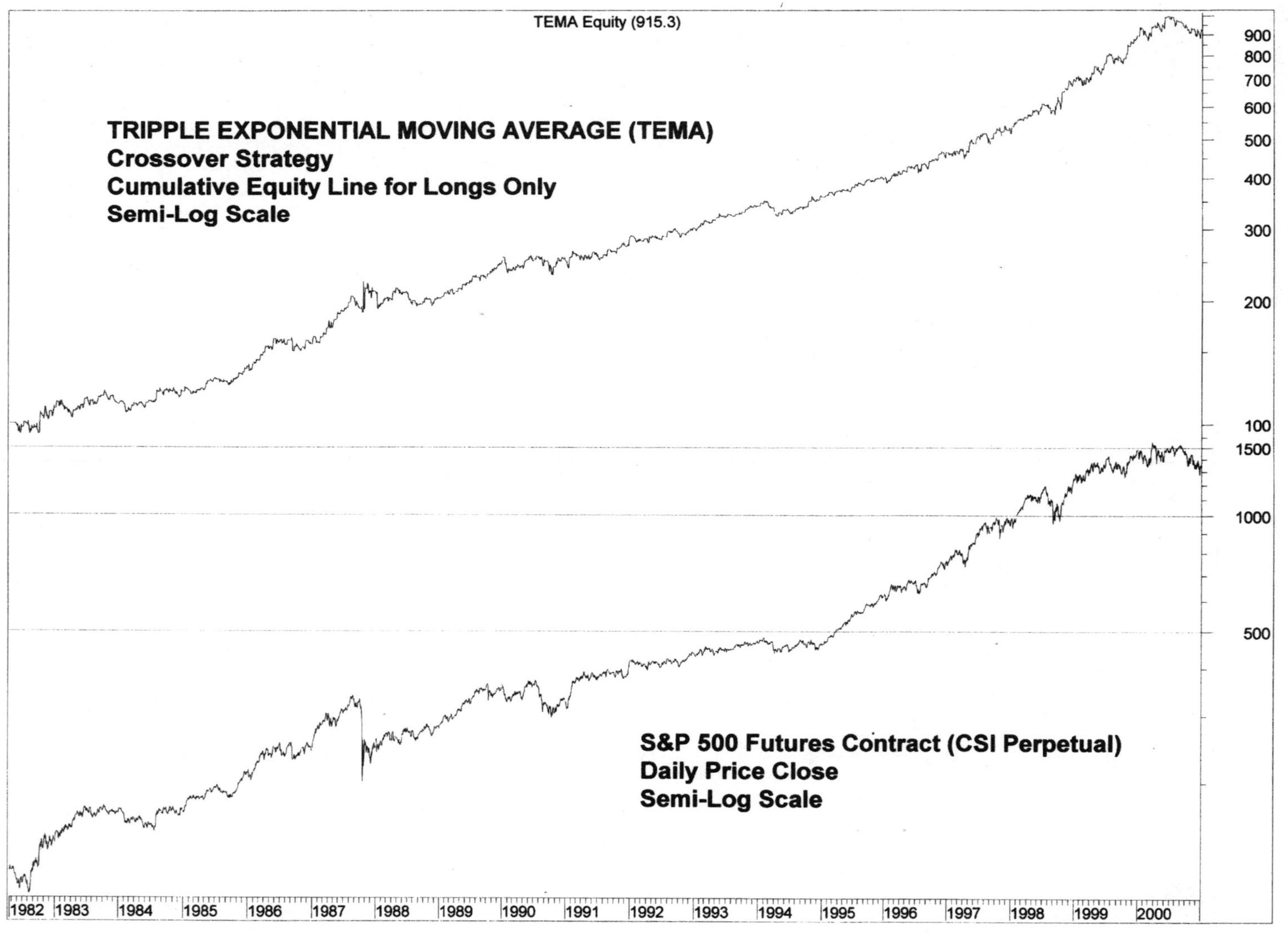
TEMA Equity (915.3)
TRIPPLE EXPONENTIAL MOVING AVERAGE (TEMA)
Crossover Strategy
Cumulative Equity Line for Longs Only
Semi-Log Scale
S&P 500 Futures Contract (CSI Perpetual)
Daily Price Close
Semi-Log Scale
900
800
700
600
500
400
300
200
100
1500
1000
500
1982
1983
1984
1985
1986
1987
1988
1989
1990
1991
1992
1993
1994
1995
1996
1997
1998
1999
2000

TEMA Crossover, 6 days

Total net profit	815.33	Open position value	N/A	Net Profit / Buy&Hold %	−21.19
Percent gain/loss	815.33	Annual percent gain/loss	43.58	Annual Net % / B&H %	−21.19
Initial investment	100	Interest earned	0		
Current position	Out	Date position entered	12/29/00		
Buy/Hold profit	1034.49	Days in test	6828	# of days per trade	7.67
Buy/Hold pct gain/loss	1034.49	Annual B/H pct gain/loss	55.3		
Total closed trades	890	Commissions paid	0		
Avg profit per trade	0.92	Avg Win/Avg Loss ratio	1.79		
Total long trades	890	Total short trades	0	Long Win Trade %	46.97
Winning long trades	418	Winning short trades	0	Short Win Trade %	#DIV/0!
Total winning trades	418	Total losing trades	472	Total Win Trade %	46.97
Amount of winning trades	2217.93	Amount of losing trades	−1402.6	Net Profit Margin %	22.52
Average win	5.31	Average loss	−2.97	Average P. Margin %	28.26
Largest win	48.56	Largest loss	−34.23	% Net / (Win + Loss)	17.31
Average length of win	4.64	Average length of loss	2.68	(Win − Loss) / Loss %	73.13
Longest winning trade	12	Longest losing trade	9	(Win − Loss) / Loss %	33.33
Most consecutive wins	6	Most consecutive losses	8	(Win − Loss) / Loss %	−25.00
Total bars out	3306	Average length out	3.71		
Longest out period	22				
System close drawdown	−5.67	Profit/Loss index	36.76	% Net Profit / SODD	14278.98
System open drawdown	−5.71	Reward/Risk index	99.3	(Net P.-SODD)/Net P.	99.30
Max open trade drawdown	−34.23	Buy/Hold index	−21.19	% SODD / Net Profit	−0.70

In the Equis MetaStock® "System Report" (profit and loss summary statistics), the *Total net profit* is the sum of profits minus the sum of losses, including open positions marked to the market. In contrast, the *Amount of Winning Trades* is the sum of realized profits (the total of all gains on closed-out trades only, excluding any open positions). Similarly, the *Amount of Losing Trades* is the sum of realized losses (the total of all losses on closed-out trades only, excluding any open positions). *System close drawdown* is the largest decline in the cumulative equity line below the initial investment, based on closed-out positions only. *System open drawdown (SODD)* is the largest decline in the cumulative equity line below the initial investment when a position is open. *Max open trade drawdown* is the largest decline in the cumulative equity line below the trade entry price during the worst single trade. The *Profit/Loss Index* is a complex calculation that relates the Amount of Winning Trades to the Amount of Losing Trades on a scale of −100 (worst possible performance) to +100 (best possible performance), with zero representing profits equal to losses. *Reward/Risk Index* is the Total net profit minus System open drawdown. The resulting difference is then divided by the Total net profit. The *Buy/Hold Index* is the Total net profit minus the buy-and-hold strategy's net profit. The resulting difference is then divided by the buy-and-hold net profit. In this exercise, initial equity is assumed to be $100. Both long and short positions are taken unless otherwise noted. Trades are executed at the closing price on the signal date. Transaction costs, interest expenses, and margins are not included in the statistics.

Triple Screen Trading System

The Triple Screen Trading System is a three-part composite indicator presented by Alexander Elder in his popular book, *Trading for a Living: Psychology, Trading Tactics, Money Management,* John Wiley & Sons, Inc., New York, 1993. With Triple Screen, Elder applies three screens before he accepts a trade: a long-term trend-following indicator, a short-term contra-trend indicator, and a very short-term trend-following indicator. All three indicators must be "go" before a transaction is warranted.

- Elder suggests a weekly *MACD Histogram* direction (rising is bullish, falling is bearish) as a longer term permission filter: trades may be entered only in harmony with that. When weekly MACDH is rising, only long trades may be initiated. When weekly MACDH is falling, only short trades may be entered. *(See Indicator Seasons.)*
- Triple Screen trades contrary to a daily overbought/oversold oscillator. Elder suggests his *Force Index, Elder-Ray,* or *Stochastics* to generate these signals. When the daily oscillator is oversold and weekly MACDH is rising, only long trades may be initiated. When the daily oscillator is overbought and weekly MACDH is falling, only short trades may be initiated.
- Finally, Triple Screen enters positions in harmony with intraday breakouts. For example, buy when the high today moves above the high of the previous day, assuming the first two conditions have already been met. Sell short when the low today moves below the low of the previous day, again assuming the first two conditions have already been met.

TRIX (triple exponential smoothing of the log of closing price)

TRIX is a price momentum oscillator introduced by Jack K. Hutson, "Good Trix", *Technical Analysis of Stocks & Commodities* magazine, V. 1:5, (www.traders.com). TRIX is the 1-day difference of the triple exponential smoothing of the log of closing price computed in six steps:

1. Compute the log of the daily price close.
2. Smooth the log with an exponential moving average (EMA).
3. Compute an EMA of the EMA from Step 2.
4. Compute an EMA of the EMA from Step 3.
5. Compute the 1-day difference between each day's output of the third smoothing; that is, subtract the result of Step 4 today from the result of Step 4 the previous day.
6. Multiply the result in Step 5 by 10,000 for scaling.

As with other indicators, varying the number of days in the EMA allows TRIX to adjust to fit the appropriate trading cycle.

Indicator Strategy Example for TRIX

There are many possible ways to interpret TRIX. *(See Oscillators.)* For relatively straight-forward trend-following, buy when TRIX changes direction from down to up. Sell when TRIX changes direction from up to down.

Based on a 18-year file of daily data for the entire history of the S&P 500 Composite Stock Price Index futures *CSI Perpetual Contract* (www.csidata.com) from 4/21/82 to 12/29/00, we found that the following parameters would have produced a positive result on a purely mechanical signal basis with no subjectivity, no sophisticated technical analysis, and no judgement:

Enter Long (Buy) at the current daily price close of the S&P 500 Composite Stock Price Index futures *CSI Perpetual Contract* when the 2-day TRIX is rising; that is, when TRIX (with daily time periods set to two) is greater than the previous day's 2-day TRIX.

Close Long (Sell) at the current daily price close of the S&P 500 Composite Stock Price Index futures *CSI Perpetual Contract* when the 2-day TRIX is falling; that is, when TRIX (with daily time periods set to two) is less than the previous day's 2-day TRIX.

Enter Short (Sell Short) never.

Starting with $100 and reinvesting profits, total net profits for this TRIX trend-following strategy would have been $694.55, assuming a fully invested strategy, reinvestment of profits, no transactions costs and no taxes. This would have been 32.86 percent less than buy-and-hold. No short selling would have been profitable, and no short selling was included in the strategy. This long-only TRIX would have given profitable buy signals 48.10% of the time. Trading would have been very active at one trade every 6.50 calendar days.

The Equis International MetaStock® System Testing rules are written as follows:

Enter long: TRIX(opt1)>Ref(TRIX(opt1),-1)

Close long: TRIX(opt1)<Ref(TRIX(opt1),-1)

OPT1 Current value: 2

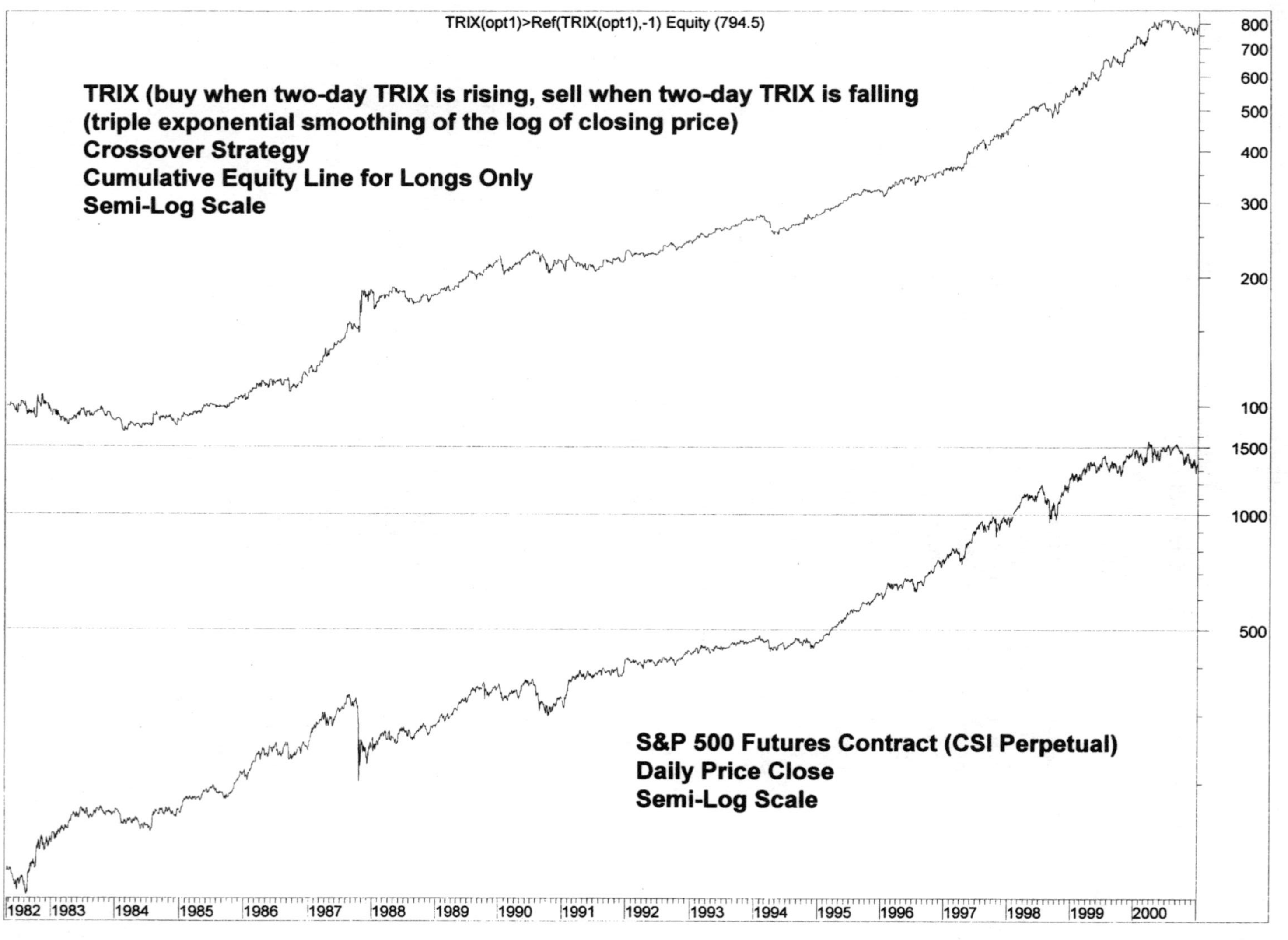

TRIX(opt1)>Ref(TRIX(opt1),-1) Equity (794.5)
TRIX (buy when two-day TRIX is rising, sell when two-day TRIX is falling
(triple exponential smoothing of the log of closing price)
Crossover Strategy
Cumulative Equity Line for Longs Only
Semi-Log Scale
S&P 500 Futures Contract (CSI Perpetual)
Daily Price Close
Semi-Log Scale
800
700
600
500
400
300
200
100
1500
1000
500
1982
1983
1984
1985
1986
1987
1988
1989
1990
1991
1992
1993
1994
1995
1996
1997
1998
1999
2000

TRIX (2)

Total net profit	694.55	Open position value	N/A	Net Profit / Buy&Hold %	−32.86
Percent gain/loss	694.55	Annual percent gain/loss	37.13	Annual Net % / B&H %	−32.86
Initial investment	100	Interest earned	0		
Current position	Out	Date position entered	12/28/00		
Buy/Hold profit	1034.49	Days in test	6828	# of days per trade	6.50
Buy/Hold pct gain/loss	1034.49	Annual B/H pct gain/loss	55.3		
Total closed trades	1050	Commissions paid	0		
Avg profit per trade	0.66	Avg Win/Avg Loss ratio	1.66		
Total long trades	1050	Total short trades	0	Long Win Trade %	48.10
Winning long trades	505	Winning short trades	0	Short Win Trade %	#DIV/0!
Total winning trades	505	Total losing trades	545	Total Win Trade %	48.10
Amount of winning trades	1983.84	Amount of losing trades	−1289.29	Net Profit Margin %	21.22
Average win	3.93	Average loss	−2.37	Average P. Margin %	24.76
Largest win	38.3	Largest loss	−27.35	% Net / (Win + Loss)	16.68
Average length of win	3.92	Average length of loss	2.46	(Win − Loss) / Loss %	59.35
Longest winning trade	8	Longest losing trade	6	(Win − Loss) / Loss %	33.33
Most consecutive wins	7	Most consecutive losses	8	(Win − Loss) / Loss %	−12.50
Total bars out	3508	Average length out	3.34		
Longest out period	10				
System close drawdown	−13.16	Profit/Loss index	35.01	% Net Profit / SODD	5277.74
System open drawdown	−13.16	Reward/Risk index	98.14	(Net P.-SODD)/Net P.	98.11
Max open trade drawdown	−27.35	Buy/Hold index	−32.86	% SODD / Net Profit	−1.89

In the Equis MetaStock® "System Report" (profit and loss summary statistics), the *Total net profit* is the sum of profits minus the sum of losses, including open positions marked to the market. In contrast, the *Amount of Winning Trades* is the sum of realized profits (the total of all gains on closed-out trades only, excluding any open positions). Similarly, the *Amount of Losing Trades* is the sum of realized losses (the total of all losses on closed-out trades only, excluding any open positions). *System close drawdown* is the largest decline in the cumulative equity line below the initial investment, based on closed-out positions only. *System open drawdown (SODD)* is the largest decline in the cumulative equity line below the initial investment when a position is open. *Max open trade drawdown* is the largest decline in the cumulative equity line below the trade entry price during the worst single trade. The *Profit/Loss Index* is a complex calculation that relates the Amount of Winning Trades to the Amount of Losing Trades on a scale of −100 (worst possible performance) to +100 (best possible performance), with zero representing profits equal to losses. *Reward/Risk Index* is the Total net profit minus System open drawdown. The resulting difference is then divided by the Total net profit. The *Buy/Hold Index* is the Total net profit minus the buy-and-hold strategy's net profit. The resulting difference is then divided by the buy-and-hold net profit. In this exercise, initial equity is assumed to be $100. Both long and short positions are taken unless otherwise noted. Trades are executed at the closing price on the signal date. Transaction costs, interest expenses, and margins are not included in the statistics.

True Range

True Range is the full price range of a period, including gaps. Gaps are price points where there were no actual trades executed. Gaps often occur overnight, and often in reaction to news events, although gaps can occur within any time interval and without any event.

J. Welles Wilder, Jr., in his 1978 book, *New Concepts in Technical Trading Systems* (Trend Research, PO Box 128, McLeansville, NC 27301), defined True Range as the largest value of the following three possibilities:

$$T = H - L$$
$$T = H - P$$
$$T = P - L$$

where

T = True Range.
H = the highest price of the current period.
L = the lowest price of the current period.
P = the closing price of the previous period.

Wilder defined Average True Range (ATR) as a exponential smoothing (or exponential moving average) of True Range. Most frequently, Wilder used examples with an exponential smoothing constant of 1/14, or 0.07143, which is roughly equivalent to a 27-day simple moving average. For his Volatility Index, Wilder uses an exponential smoothing constant of 1/7, or 0.14286, which is roughly equivalent to a 13-day simple moving average.

25-Day Plurality Index

The 25-Day Plurality Index is a market breadth indicator designed to show when the market is either active and on the move (extremely high readings) or complacent and doing nothing (extremely low readings). It is calculated in four steps:

1. Subtract the number of declining issues from the number of advancing issues each day.
2. Convert that difference to an absolute value by throwing away the sign, plus or minus.
3. Add together these absolute values for the past 25 days.
4. Repeat Steps 1, 2 and 3 each day to maintain a moving total of the absolute differences between advances and declines.

Traditionally, NYSE data is used in the calculation, but it might be adapted to data from other exchanges.

Absolute value ignores sign, plus or minus. So, for example, if the day's market movement is moderately bullish, with the number of advancing issues 1500 and the number of declining issues 1300, the day's 25-day Plurality Index input before summation is 200. On the other hand, if the next day's market trend is reversed to moderately bearish, with the number of advancing issues 1300 and the number of declining issues 1500, the day's input still equals 200, because absolute value only counts the difference without regard to whether the imbalance is to the advancing or declining side. In contrast most other breadth indicators assign a plus sign to advances and a minus sign to declines, and they retain the sign.

The graph shows that the levels of the 25-day Plurality Index have been increasing over time. The number of total issues traded on the NYSE grew 1080% over 59 years, from a low of 303 on 8/24/40 to a high of 3574 on 11/30/99. This growth can distort the meaning of a breadth indicator over time. The technical analyst must adapt, and we could convert this indicator to a percentage of the absolute value of net advances minus declines divided by total issues traded. *(See Absolute Breadth Index.)* Alternately, we could measure the 25-day Plurality Index against its own Bollinger Bands, which are adaptive envelops that automatically adjust to changes in levels over time.

The interesting observation behind the 25-day Plurality Index is that when the absolute difference between the number of advancing and declining stocks is extremely high, the market is more likely to be near a bottom. Significant market price lows are often more extreme, more intensely emotional, with most stocks affected by general pessimism, fear, and forced selling to meet margin calls. Prices are changing for most stocks near a market bottom.

Conversely, when the absolute difference between the number of advancing and declining stocks is low, the market is more likely to be near a market top. Significant market price tops are more likely to be dull, slowly unfolding affairs, as ready cash reserves for buying stock are gradually drawn down until they are eventually exhausted. Stock uptrends begin to stall out on an issue by issue basis, one by one, and the whole topping process stretches out over time. As the bull market wears out and the demand and supply for stock reaches equilibrium, stock prices are likely to be mixed.

Indicator Strategy Example for the 25-Day Plurality Index: The Old Standards are Obsolete

The 25-Day Plurality Index used to be interpreted as bullish for the stock market when it rose above the 12,000 level and bearish when it fell below 6,000. Of course, judging this indicator against absolute and fixed levels does not allow it to adapt to

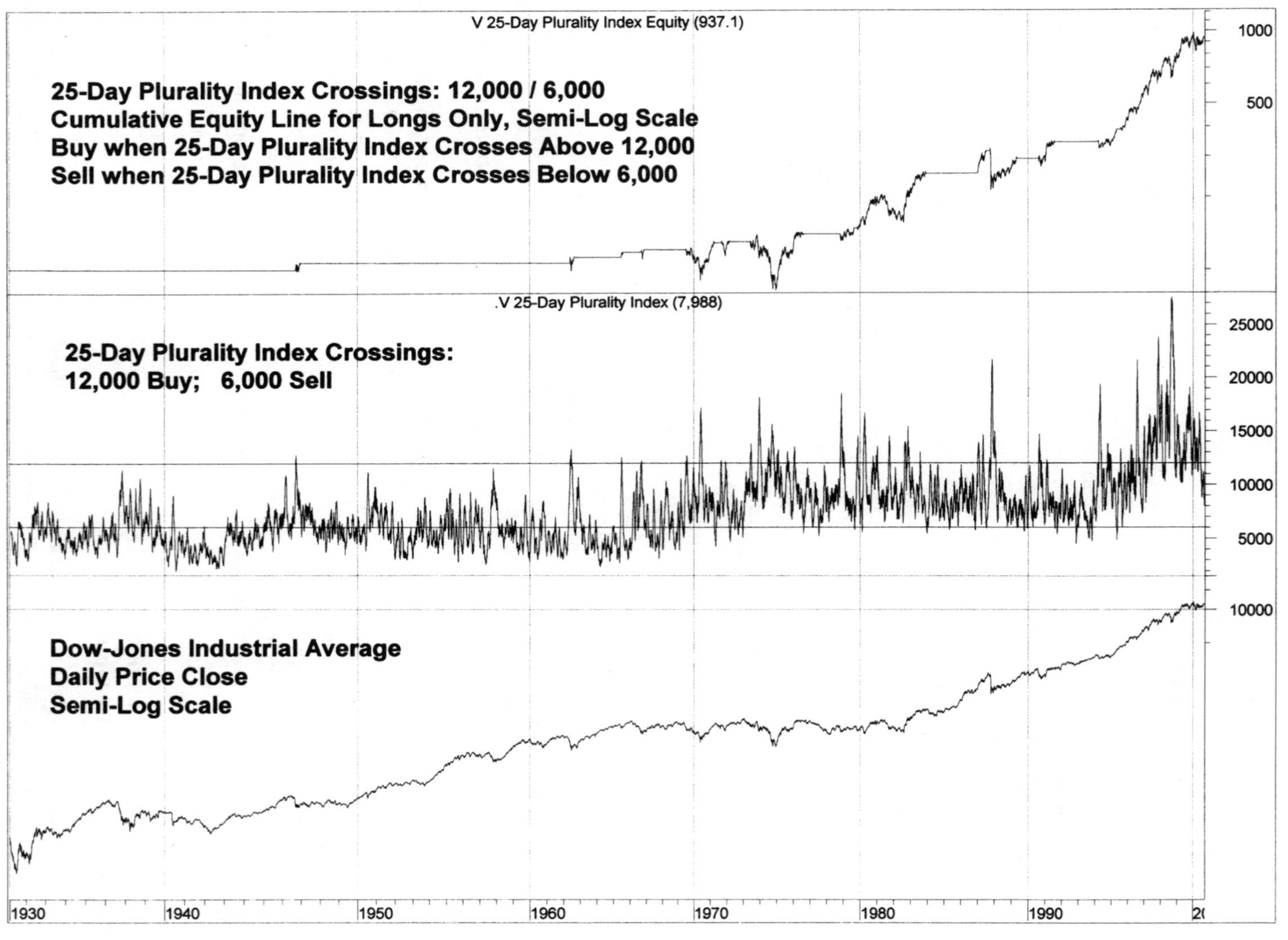
V 25-Day Plurality Index Equity (937.1)
25-Day Plurality Index Crossings: 12,000 / 6,000
Cumulative Equity Line for Longs Only, Semi-Log Scale
Buy when 25-Day Plurality Index Crosses Above 12,000
Sell when 25-Day Plurality Index Crosses Below 6,000
1000
500
.V 25-Day Plurality Index (7,988)
25-Day Plurality Index Crossings:
12,000 Buy; 6,000 Sell
25000
20000
15000
10000
5000
Dow-Jones Industrial Average
Daily Price Close
Semi-Log Scale
10000
1930
1940
1950
1960
1970
1980
1990

25-Day Plurality Index, Longs only

Total net profit	837.09	Open position value	549.45	Net Profit / Buy&Hold %	−93.32
Percent gain/loss	837.09	Annual percent gain/loss	12.21	Annual Net % / B&H %	−93.32
Initial investment	100	Interest earned	0		
Current position	Long	Date position entered	7/20/95		
Buy/Hold profit	12538.66	Days in test	25022	# of days per trade	1787.29
Buy/Hold pct gain/loss	12538.66	Annual B/H pct gain/loss	182.9		
Total closed trades	14	Commissions paid	0		
Avg profit per trade	20.55	Avg Win/Avg Loss ratio	1.04		
Total long trades	14	Total short trades	0	Long Win Trade %	92.86
Winning long trades	13	Winning short trades	0	Short Win Trade %	#DIV/0!
Total winning trades	13	Total losing trades	1	Total Win Trade %	92.86
Amount of winning trades	310.56	Amount of losing trades	−22.92	Net Profit Margin %	86.25
Average win	23.89	Average loss	−22.92	Average P. Margin %	2.07
Largest win	89.12	Largest loss	−22.92	% Net / (Win + Loss)	59.09
Average length of win	270.85	Average length of loss	411	(Win − Loss) / Loss %	−34.10
Longest winning trade	952	Longest losing trade	411	(Win − Loss) / Loss %	131.63
Most consecutive wins	11	Most consecutive losses	1	(Win − Loss) / Loss %	1000.00
Total bars out	12895	Average length out	859.67		
Longest out period	4325				
System close drawdown	0	Profit/Loss index	97.33	% Net Profit / SODD	4619.70
System open drawdown	−18.12	Reward/Risk index	97.88	(Net P.-SODD)/Net P.	97.84
Max open trade drawdown	−102.17	Buy/Hold index	−88.94	% SODD / Net Profit	−2.16

In the Equis MetaStock® "System Report" (profit and loss summary statistics), the *Total net profit* is the sum of profits minus the sum of losses, including open positions marked to the market. In contrast, the *Amount of Winning Trades* is the sum of realized profits (the total of all gains on closed-out trades only, excluding any open positions). Similarly, the *Amount of Losing Trades* is the sum of realized losses (the total of all losses on closed-out trades only, excluding any open positions). *System close drawdown* is the largest decline in the cumulative equity line below the initial investment, based on closed-out positions only. *System open drawdown (SODD)* is the largest decline in the cumulative equity line below the initial investment when a position is open. *Max open trade drawdown* is the largest decline in the cumulative equity line below the trade entry price during the worst single trade. The *Profit/Loss Index* is a complex calculation that relates the Amount of Winning Trades to the Amount of Losing Trades on a scale of −100 (worst possible performance) to +100 (best possible performance), with zero representing profits equal to losses. *Reward/Risk Index* is the Total net profit minus System open drawdown. The resulting difference is then divided by the Total net profit. The *Buy/Hold Index* is the Total net profit minus the buy-and-hold strategy's net profit. The resulting difference is then divided by the buy-and-hold net profit. In this exercise, initial equity is assumed to be $100. Both long and short positions are taken unless otherwise noted. Trades are executed at the closing price on the signal date. Transaction costs, interest expenses, and margins are not included in the statistics.

changes in the marketplace, specifically in this case, a 12-fold increase in the number of stocks traded over 59 years. The graph shows the very small $837.09 cumulative profits from following these parameters for buy and sell signals over the past 68 years, measured against the DJIA. Since March 8, 1932, we found that a simple 12,000 / 6,000 rule would have produced a sub-par result on a purely mechanical signal basis with no subjectivity, no sophisticated technical analysis, and no judgement:

Enter Long (Buy) at the current daily price close of the DJIA when the 25-Day Plurality Index crosses above 12,000.

Close Long (Sell) at the current daily price close of the DJIA when the 25-Day Plurality Index crosses below 6,000.

Enter Short (Sell Short) never.

Starting with $100 and reinvesting profits, total net profits for 25-Day Plurality Index strategy would have been $837.09, assuming a fully invested strategy, reinvestment of profits, no transactions costs and no taxes. This would have been 93.32 percent below buy-and-hold. Short selling would have been unprofitable and was not included in these statistics. Trading would have been extremely inactive with one trade every 1787.29 calendar days.

The Equis International MetaStock® System Testing rules, where the net value of advances minus declines is inserted into the data field normally reserved for Volume (V), are written as follows:

Enter long: ((Mov(Abs(V),25,S))*25)>12000

Close long: ((Mov(Abs(V),25,S))*25)<6000

Enter short: ((Mov(Abs(V),25,S))*25)<6000

Close short: ((Mov(Abs(V),25,S))*25)>12000

An Alternate Indicator Strategy Example: Bollinger Bands Perform Much Better with the 25-Day Plurality Index

Testing back to March 8, 1932, we found that Bollinger Bands above and below this indicator would have produced a far better result on a purely mechanical signal basis with no subjectivity, no sophisticated technical analysis, and no judgement:

Enter Long (Buy) at the current daily price close of the DJIA when the 25-Day Plurality Index crosses above the previous day's upper Bollinger Band set at two standard deviations above the 324-day exponential moving average of the 25-Day Plurality Index.

Close Long (Sell) at the current daily price close of the DJIA when the 25-Day Plurality Index crosses below the previous day's lower Bollinger Band set at two standard deviations below the 324-day exponential moving average of the 25-Day Plurality Index.

Enter Short (Sell Short) never.

Starting with $100 and reinvesting profits, total net profits for this 25-Day Plurality Index strategy would have been $18,257.66, assuming a fully invested strategy, reinvestment of profits, no transactions costs and no taxes. This would have been 45.61 percent better than buy-and-hold. Short selling would have been unprofitable and was not included in these statistics. Trading would have been extremely inactive with one trade every 1668.13 calendar days.

The Equis International MetaStock® System Testing rules, where the net value of advances minus declines is inserted into the data field normally reserved for Volume (V), are written as follows:

Enter long: ((Mov(Abs(V),25,S))*25)>Ref(BBandTop(((Mov(Abs(V), 25,S))*25),opt1,E,opt2),-1

Close long: ((Mov(Abs(V),25,S))*25) < Ref(BBandBot(((Mov (Abs(V),25,S))*25),opt1,E,opt2),-1)

OPT1 Current value: 324

OPT2 Current value: 2

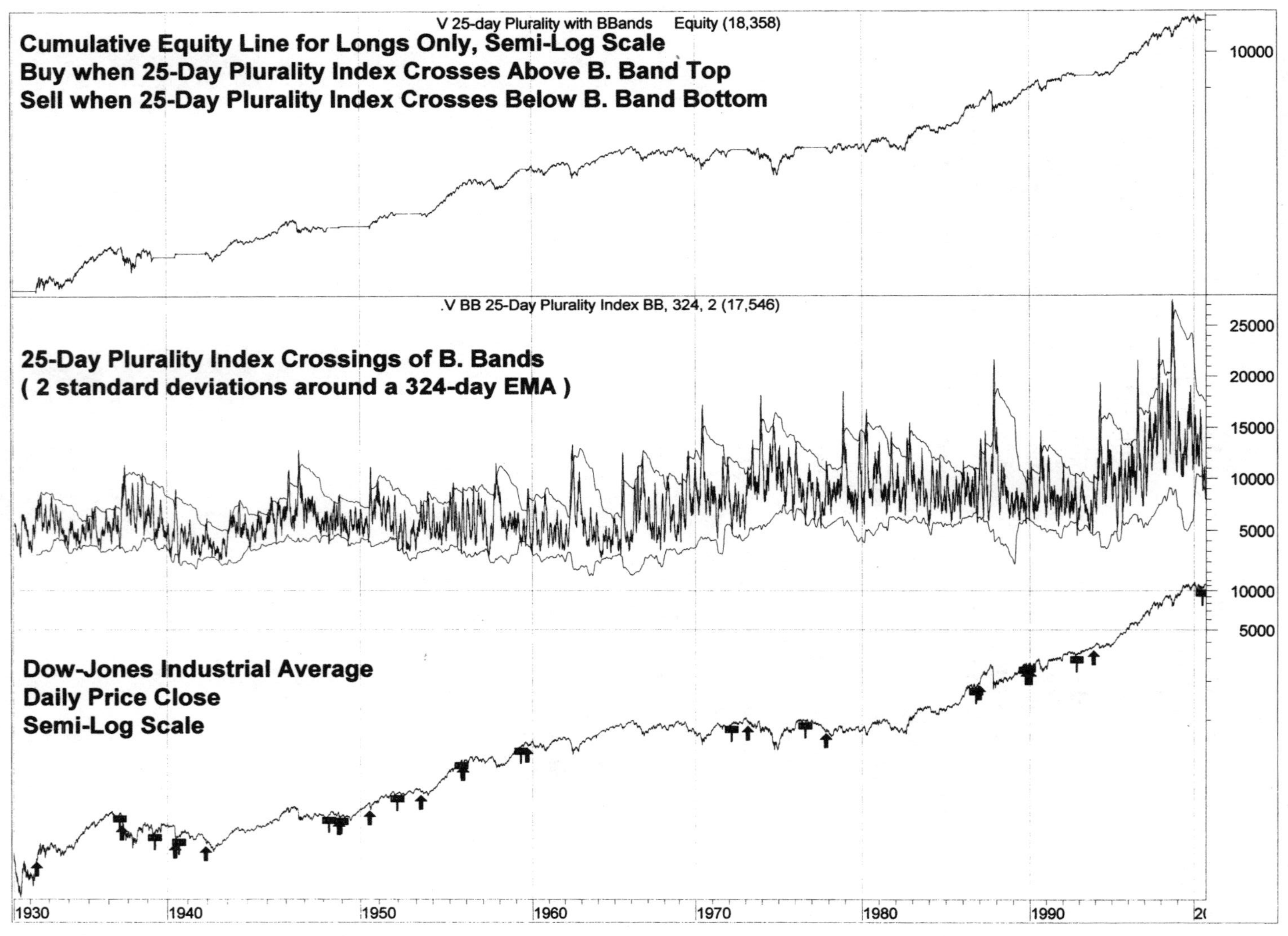
V 25-day Plurality with BBands Equity (18,358)
Cumulative Equity Line for Longs Only, Semi-Log Scale
Buy when 25-Day Plurality Index Crosses Above B. Band Top
Sell when 25-Day Plurality Index Crosses Below B. Band Bottom
10000
.V BB 25-Day Plurality Index BB, 324, 2 (17,546)
25-Day Plurality Index Crossings of B. Bands
(2 standard deviations around a 324-day EMA)
25000
20000
15000
10000
5000
Dow-Jones Industrial Average
Daily Price Close
Semi-Log Scale
10000
5000
1930
1940
1950
1960
1970
1980
1990
20

25-Day Plurality Index with Bollinger Bands (324, 2sd)

Total net profit	18257.66	Open position value	N/A	Net Profit / Buy&Hold %	45.61
Percent gain/loss	18257.66	Annual percent gain/loss	266.33	Annual Net % / B&H %	45.62
Initial investment	100	Interest earned	0		
Current position	Out	Date position entered	7/7/00		
Buy/Hold profit	12538.66	Days in test	25022	# of days per trade	1668.13
Buy/Hold pct gain/loss	12538.66	Annual B/H pct gain/loss	182.9		
Total closed trades	15	Commissions paid	0		
Avg profit per trade	1217.18	Avg Win/Avg Loss ratio	36.19		
Total long trades	15	Total short trades	0	Long Win Trade %	93.33
Winning long trades	14	Winning short trades	0	Short Win Trade %	#DIV/0!
Total winning trades	14	Total losing trades	1	Total Win Trade %	93.33
Amount of winning trades	18293.76	Amount of losing trades	−36.1	Net Profit Margin %	99.61
Average win	1306.7	Average loss	−36.1	Average P. Margin %	94.62
Largest win	11999.1	Largest loss	−36.1	% Net / (Win + Loss)	99.40
Average length of win	1034.21	Average length of loss	504	(Win − Loss) / Loss %	105.20
Longest winning trade	3117	Longest losing trade	504	(Win − Loss) / Loss %	518.45
Most consecutive wins	13	Most consecutive losses	1	(Win − Loss) / Loss %	1200.00
Total bars out	3144	Average length out	196.5		
Longest out period	433				
System close drawdown	0	Profit/Loss index	99.8	% Net Profit / SODD	558338.23
System open drawdown	−3.27	Reward/Risk index	99.98	(Net P.-SODD)/Net P.	99.98
Max open trade drawdown	−606.41	Buy/Hold index	45.61	% SODD / Net Profit	−0.02

In the Equis MetaStock® "System Report" (profit and loss summary statistics), the *Total net profit* is the sum of profits minus the sum of losses, including open positions marked to the market. In contrast, the *Amount of Winning Trades* is the sum of realized profits (the total of all gains on closed-out trades only, excluding any open positions). Similarly, the *Amount of Losing Trades* is the sum of realized losses (the total of all losses on closed-out trades only, excluding any open positions). *System close drawdown* is the largest decline in the cumulative equity line below the initial investment, based on closed-out positions only. *System open drawdown (SODD)* is the largest decline in the cumulative equity line below the initial investment when a position is open. *Max open trade drawdown* is the largest decline in the cumulative equity line below the trade entry price during the worst single trade. The *Profit/Loss Index* is a complex calculation that relates the Amount of Winning Trades to the Amount of Losing Trades on a scale of −100 (worst possible performance) to +100 (best possible performance), with zero representing profits equal to losses. *Reward/Risk Index* is the Total net profit minus System open drawdown. The resulting difference is then divided by the Total net profit. The *Buy/Hold Index* is the Total net profit minus the buy-and-hold strategy's net profit. The resulting difference is then divided by the buy-and-hold net profit. In this exercise, initial equity is assumed to be $100. Both long and short positions are taken unless otherwise noted. Trades are executed at the closing price on the signal date. Transaction costs, interest expenses, and margins are not included in the statistics.

Two Moving Average Crossover

Two Moving Average Crossover is a combination indicator that uses two moving averages of different lengths to generate trading signals. It combines one shorter (fast) and one longer (slow) moving average to generate buy and sell signals. Buy when the fast moving average crosses above the slow moving average. Sell when the fast moving average crosses below the slow moving average. The period lengths of each moving average could be allowed to vary in any way, producing a number of possibilities. One possible MetaStock® System Test could be expressed as follows:

Enter long: Mov(CLOSE,opt1,E) > Mov(CLOSE,opt1*opt2,E)

Close long: Mov(CLOSE,opt1,E) < Mov(CLOSE,opt1*opt2,E)

Enter short: Mov(CLOSE,opt1,E) < Mov(CLOSE,opt1*opt2,E)

Close short: Mov(CLOSE,opt1,E) > Mov(CLOSE,opt1*opt2,E)

Turtle Soup

Master trader Richard Dennis trained a group of raw recruits he named *Turtles*. One of their strategies reportedly was to trade in the direction of a breakout from a Price Channel, specifically, buy when price makes a new 20-day high and sell short when price makes a new 20-day low. The recipe for Turtle Soup is to fade the Turtles when price reverses immediately after such a breakout and, hopefully, collect fast profits when the trend followers cut losses. *(See Trap.)* Place a protective stop just beyond the entry bar extreme, and trail the stop if price moves in the right direction. (See Connors, Laurence A., and Raschke, Linda Bradford, *Street Smarts, High Probability Short-Term Trading Strategies,* M. Gordon Publishing Group, Malibu, California, 1995, 239 pages.)

Typical Price

The Typical Price is calculated by adding the high, low, and closing prices together, and then dividing by three. The result is thought to be a rough estimate of the average or typical price for the period. The Typical Price may be used with many indicators in the place of the closing price. But in our testing, the closing price produces better results.

Ultimate Oscillator

The Ultimate Oscillator is a time-weighted price momentum oscillator introduced by Larry Williams, "The Ultimate Oscillator", *Technical Analysis of Stocks & Commodities* magazine, V. 3:4, (www.traders.com). The Ultimate Oscillator uses time-weighted sums of three different oscillators, each of which is a sum of price change ratios over three different time periods, the First Cycle (short-term), the Second Cycle (intermediate-term) and the Third Cycle (long-term). First, calculate buying pressure each day, defined as the current closing price minus the lower of the current low or the previous period's low. Sum this buying pressure over three separate time periods: First Cycle, Williams suggests 7 days; Second Cycle, twice the first cycle or 14 days; and the Third Cycle twice the second cycle or 28 days. (Of course, any other time intervals, measured in days, minutes, weeks or months, could be adapted to the basic concept.) Next, these buying pressure sums are divided by similar sums using True Range. (These ratios may be thought of as the sums of buying pressure divided by the sums of buying pressure plus selling pressure.) Finally, those three ratios (buying pressure/total pressure over three different time frames) are weighted by 4 for the First Cycle, 2 for the Second Cycle and 1 for the Third Cycle.

Once calculated, the Ultimate Oscillator may be interpreted in six steps each for longs and shorts, according to Williams.

- For long positions:
  1. The oscillator must have established an oversold reading below 30.
  2. There must be a bullish divergence setup, where the security's price makes a lower low that is not confirmed by a lower low in the oscillator.
  3. The oscillator must break its downtrend line.
  4. When the oscillator establishes a pattern of higher highs from an oversold extreme low point below 30, there is confirmation of a new oscillator uptrend, new positive momentum, and a bullish change in the probable trend of the security's price.
  5. Take long-side profits when the oscillator moves to an extremely overbought level above 70.
  6. Close longs when the oscillator rises above 50 then falls below 45.
- For short positions:
  1. The oscillator must have established at least a mildly overbought reading above 50.
  2. There must be a bearish divergence setup, where the security's price makes a higher high that is not confirmed by a higher high in the oscillator.
  3. The oscillator must break its uptrend line.

4. When the oscillator establishes a pattern of lower lows from an overbought extreme high point, there is confirmation of a new oscillator downtrend, new negative momentum, and a bearish change in the probable trend of the security's price.
5. Take short side profits when the oscillator moves to an extremely oversold level below 30.
6. Close shorts when the oscillator rises above 65.

Indicator Strategy Example for the Ultimate Oscillator

There are many alternate ways to interpret the Ultimate Oscillator. *(See Oscillators.)* If we allow each of Williams' parameters to vary, there would be a staggering number of possibilities. One way to start might be to test the overbought/oversold parameters against observed data.

Based on a 18-year file of daily data for the entire history of the S&P 500 Composite Stock Price Index futures *CSI Perpetual Contract* (www.csidata.com) from 4/21/82 to 12/29/00, we found that the following parameters would have produced a positive result on a purely mechanical signal basis with no subjectivity, no sophisticated technical analysis, and no judgement:

Enter Long (Buy) at the current daily price close of the S&P 500 Composite Stock Price Index futures *CSI Perpetual Contract* when the Ultimate Oscillator is below 43.

Close Long (Sell) at the current daily price close of the S&P 500 Composite Stock Price Index futures *CSI Perpetual Contract* when the Ultimate Oscillator is above 73.

Enter Short (Sell Short) at the current daily price close of the S&P 500 Composite Stock Price Index futures *CSI Perpetual Contract* when the Ultimate Oscillator is above 74.

Close Short (Cover) at the current daily price close of the S&P 500 Composite Stock Price Index futures *CSI Perpetual Contract* when the Ultimate Oscillator is below 49.

Starting with $100 and reinvesting profits, total net profits for this Ultimate Oscillator strategy would have been $1,357.21, assuming a fully invested strategy, reinvestment of profits, no transactions costs and no taxes. This would have been 31.20 percent greater than buy-and-hold. Even short selling would have been slightly profitable, and short selling was included in the strategy. This long and short Ultimate Oscillator strategy would have given profitable buy signals 96.00% of the time and profitable sell short signals 57.14% of the time. Note that this contra-trend strategy does not include a stop loss, and there are occasional large equity drawdowns. Trading would have been relatively inactive at one trade every 148.43 calendar days.

The Equis International MetaStock® System Testing rules are written as follows:

Enter long: Ult(opt1,2*opt1,4*opt1)<50-opt2

Close long: Ult(opt1,2*opt1,4*opt1)>50+opt3

Enter short: Ult(opt1,2*opt1,4*opt1)>50+opt4

Close short: Ult(opt1,2*opt1,4*opt1)<50-opt5

OPT1 Current value: 7
OPT2 Current value: 7
OPT3 Current value: 23
OPT4 Current value: 24
OPT5 Current value: 1

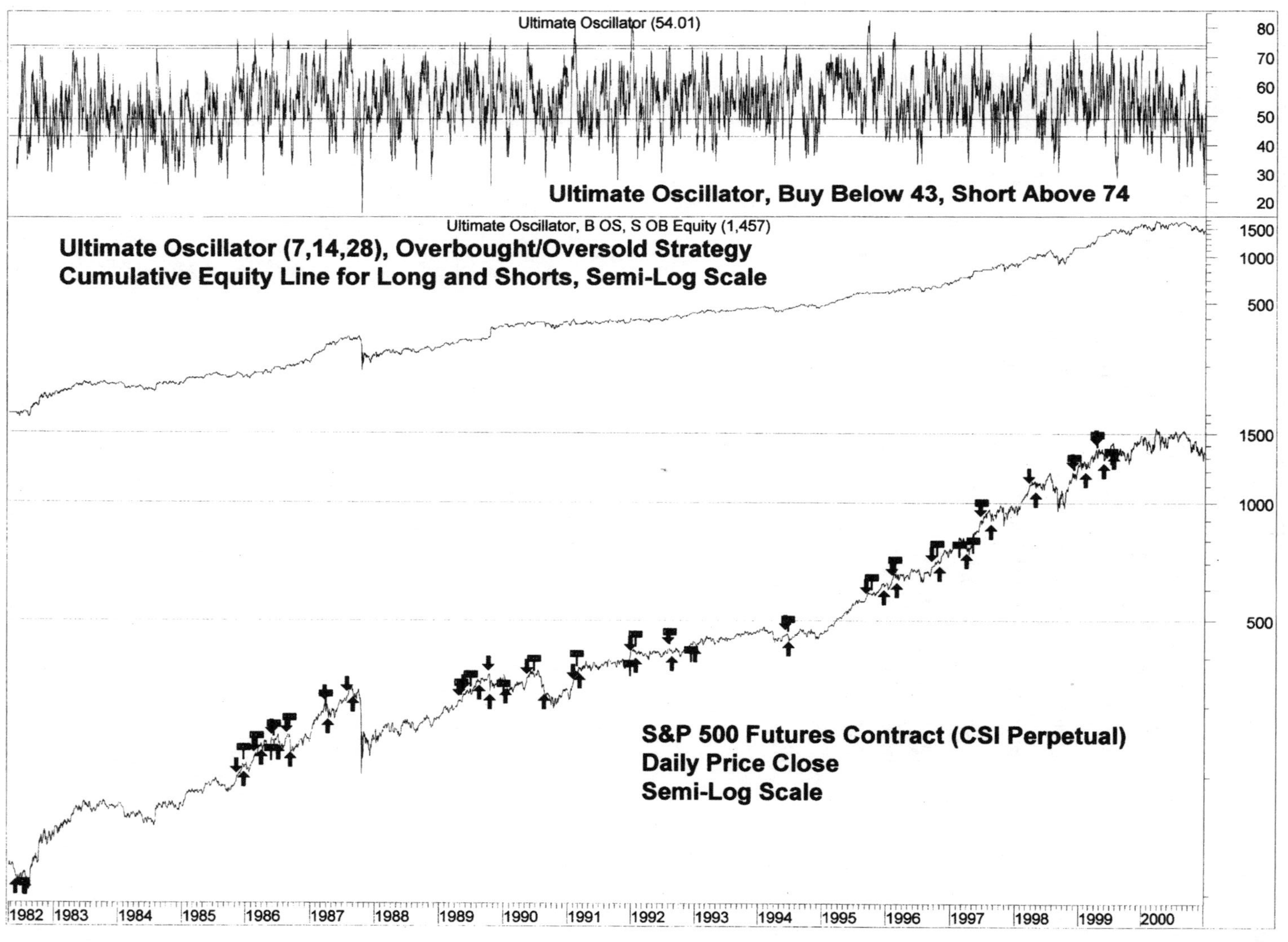

Ultimate Oscillator (54.01)
80
70
60
50
40
30
20
Ultimate Oscillator, Buy Below 43, Short Above 74
Ultimate Oscillator, B OS, S OB Equity (1,457)
Ultimate Oscillator (7,14,28), Overbought/Oversold Strategy
Cumulative Equity Line for Long and Shorts, Semi-Log Scale
1500
1000
500
1500
1000
500
S&P 500 Futures Contract (CSI Perpetual)
Daily Price Close
Semi-Log Scale
1982
1983
1984
1985
1986
1987
1988
1989
1990
1991
1992
1993
1994
1995
1996
1997
1998
1999
2000

Ultimate Oscillator, Long Below 43, Short Above 74

Total net profit	1357.21	Open position value	−30.99	Net Profit / Buy&Hold %	31.20
Percent gain/loss	1357.21	Annual percent gain/loss	72.55	Annual Net % / B&H %	31.19
Initial investment	100	Interest earned	0		
Current position	Long	Date position entered	7/23/99		
Buy/Hold profit	1034.49	Days in test	6828	# of days per trade	148.43
Buy/Hold pct gain/loss	1034.49	Annual B/H pct gain/loss	55.3		
Total closed trades	46	Commissions paid	0		
Avg profit per trade	30.18	Avg Win/Avg Loss ratio	4.17		
Total long trades	25	Total short trades	21	Long Win Trade %	96.00
Winning long trades	24	Winning short trades	12	Short Win Trade %	57.14
Total winning trades	36	Total losing trades	10	Total Win Trade %	78.26
Amount of winning trades	1487.17	Amount of losing trades	−98.97	Net Profit Margin %	87.52
Average win	41.31	Average loss	−9.9	Average P. Margin %	61.34
Largest win	181.41	Largest loss	−27.24	% Net / (Win + Loss)	73.89
Average length of win	92.58	Average length of loss	60.9	(Win − Loss) / Loss %	52.02
Longest winning trade	835	Longest losing trade	416	(Win − Loss) / Loss %	100.72
Most consecutive wins	10	Most consecutive losses	2	(Win − Loss) / Loss %	400.00
Total bars out	493	Average length out	18.26		
Longest out period	50				
System close drawdown	0	Profit/Loss index	93.2	% Net Profit / SODD	22887.18
System open drawdown	−5.93	Reward/Risk index	99.56	(Net P.-SODD)/Net P.	99.56
Max open trade drawdown	−127.35	Buy/Hold index	28.2	% SODD / Net Profit	−0.44

In the Equis MetaStock® "System Report" (profit and loss summary statistics), the *Total net profit* is the sum of profits minus the sum of losses, including open positions marked to the market. In contrast, the *Amount of Winning Trades* is the sum of realized profits (the total of all gains on closed-out trades only, excluding any open positions). Similarly, the *Amount of Losing Trades* is the sum of realized losses (the total of all losses on closed-out trades only, excluding any open positions). *System close drawdown* is the largest decline in the cumulative equity line below the initial investment, based on closed-out positions only. *System open drawdown (SODD)* is the largest decline in the cumulative equity line below the initial investment when a position is open. *Max open trade drawdown* is the largest decline in the cumulative equity line below the trade entry price during the worst single trade. The *Profit/Loss Index* is a complex calculation that relates the Amount of Winning Trades to the Amount of Losing Trades on a scale of −100 (worst possible performance) to +100 (best possible performance), with zero representing profits equal to losses. *Reward/Risk Index* is the Total net profit minus System open drawdown. The resulting difference is then divided by the Total net profit. The *Buy/Hold Index* is the Total net profit minus the buy-and-hold strategy's net profit. The resulting difference is then divided by the buy-and-hold net profit. In this exercise, initial equity is assumed to be $100. Both long and short positions are taken unless otherwise noted. Trades are executed at the closing price on the signal date. Transaction costs, interest expenses, and margins are not included in the statistics.

Unchanged Issues Index

The Unchanged Issues Index is calculated by dividing the total number of unchanged issues by the total number of issues traded. Most commonly, daily or weekly NYSE data is used in the calculation, and similar indicators could be applied to data from other exchanges.

The popular assumption behind the indicator is that stock prices tend to bottom out when the great majority of stocks are participating in a market decline. Therefore, the Unchanged Issues Index is low. Conversely, the popular interpretation is that the market tops out when the majority of stocks stall out due to full valuation, and the Unchanged Issues Index is high.

The popular interpretation does not hold up under objective testing, however. On the contrary, the data suggests that relatively high readings on the Unchanged Issues Index are bearish, while low readings are bullish. But the results are not strong.

Indicator Strategy Example of the Unchanged Issues Index

Based on a 68-year file of daily data for the Unchanged Issues Index (the total number of shares unchanged divided by the total number of shares traded each day on the NYSE) and the DJIA since 1932, we found that extreme moves below and above Bollinger Bands placed at two standard deviations around the previous day's 7-day exponential moving average *(See Bollinger Bands)* would have produced a mildly positive result on a purely mechanical signal basis with no subjectivity, no sophisticated technical analysis, and no judgement:

Enter Long (Buy) at the current daily price close of the DJIA when the Unchanged Issues Index falls below the previous day's lower Bollinger Band placed at two standard deviations below a 7-day exponential moving average (EMA) of the Unchanged Issues Index.

Close Long (Sell) at the current daily price close of the DJIA when the Unchanged Issues Index rises above the previous day's upper Bollinger Band placed at two standard deviations above a 7-day EMA of the Unchanged Issues Index.

Sell Long and Sell Short at the current daily price close of the DJIA when the Unchanged Issues Index rises above the previous day's upper Bollinger Band placed at two standard deviations above a 7-day EMA of the Unchanged Issues Index.

Cover Short and Buy Long at the current daily price close of the DJIA when the Unchanged Issues Index falls below the previous day's lower

Bollinger Band placed at two standard deviations below a 7-day EMA of the Unchanged Issues Index.

Starting with $100 and reinvesting profits, total net profits for the Unchanged Issues Index would have been $9,403.33, assuming a fully invested strategy, reinvestment of profits, no transactions costs and no taxes. This would have been 25.01 percent below buy-and-hold. Short selling would have been unprofitable and most of the short trades would have lost money. A long only strategy (not shown) beat buy-and-hold, and 59.38% of the long trades were winners.

The Equis International MetaStock® System Testing rules, where the Unchanged Issues Index is inserted into the data field normally reserved for Volume (V), are written as follows:

Enter long: V<Ref(BBandBot(V,opt1,E,opt2),-1)

Close long: V>Ref(BBandTop(V,opt1,E,opt2),-1)

Enter short: V>Ref(BBandTop(V,opt1,E,opt2),-1)

Close short: V<Ref(BBandBot(V,opt1,E,opt2),-1)

OPT1 Current value: 7

OPT2 Current value: 2

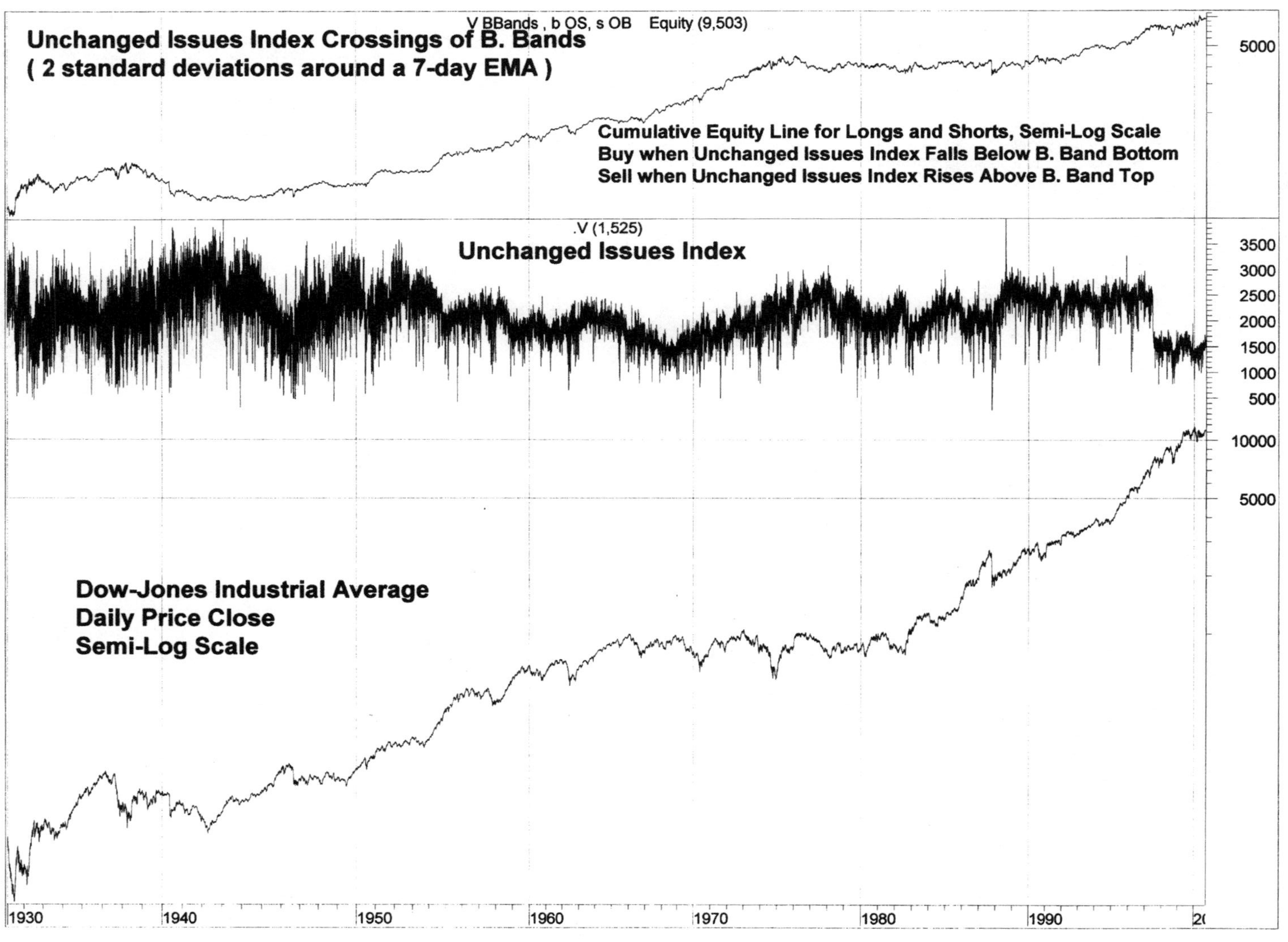

Unchanged Issues Index Crossings of B. Bands
(2 standard deviations around a 7-day EMA)
V BBands , b OS, s OB
Equity (9,503)
Cumulative Equity Line for Longs and Shorts, Semi-Log Scale
Buy when Unchanged Issues Index Falls Below B. Band Bottom
Sell when Unchanged Issues Index Rises Above B. Band Top
.V (1,525)
Unchanged Issues Index
Dow-Jones Industrial Average
Daily Price Close
Semi-Log Scale
5000
3500
3000
2500
2000
1500
1000
500
10000
5000
1930
1940
1950
1960
1970
1980
1990
2(

Unchanged Issues Index & BBands

Total net profit	9403.33	Open position value	4.66	Net Profit / Buy&Hold %	−25.01
Percent gain/loss	9403.33	Annual percent gain/loss	137.17	Annual Net % / B&H %	−25.00
Initial investment	100	Interest earned	0		
Current position	Long	Date position entered	8/31/00		
Buy/Hold profit	12538.66	Days in test	25022	# of days per trade	19.38
Buy/Hold pct gain/loss	12538.66	Annual B/H pct gain/loss	182.9		
Total closed trades	1291	Commissions paid	0		
Avg profit per trade	7.28	Avg Win/Avg Loss ratio	1.14		
Total long trades	645	Total short trades	646	Long Win Trade %	59.38
Winning long trades	383	Winning short trades	313	Short Win Trade %	48.45
Total winning trades	696	Total losing trades	595	Total Win Trade %	53.91
Amount of winning trades	37519.41	Amount of losing trades	−28120.75	Net Profit Margin %	14.32
Average win	53.91	Average loss	−47.26	Average P. Margin %	6.57
Largest win	1242.11	Largest loss	−1053.15	% Net / (Win + Loss)	8.23
Average length of win	15.47	Average length of loss	14.46	(Win − Loss) / Loss %	6.98
Longest winning trade	72	Longest losing trade	113	(Win − Loss) / Loss %	−36.28
Most consecutive wins	9	Most consecutive losses	7	(Win − Loss) / Loss %	28.57
Total bars out	11	Average length out	11		
Longest out period	11				
System close drawdown	−17.74	Profit/Loss index	25.06	% Net Profit / SODD	51751.95
System open drawdown	−18.17	Reward/Risk index	99.81	(Net P.-SODD)/Net P.	99.81
Max open trade drawdown	−1460.2	Buy/Hold index	−24.97	% SODD / Net Profit	−0.19

In the Equis MetaStock® "System Report" (profit and loss summary statistics), the *Total net profit* is the sum of profits minus the sum of losses, including open positions marked to the market. In contrast, the *Amount of Winning Trades* is the sum of realized profits (the total of all gains on closed-out trades only, excluding any open positions). Similarly, the *Amount of Losing Trades* is the sum of realized losses (the total of all losses on closed-out trades only, excluding any open positions). *System close drawdown* is the largest decline in the cumulative equity line below the initial investment, based on closed-out positions only. *System open drawdown (SODD)* is the largest decline in the cumulative equity line below the initial investment when a position is open. *Max open trade drawdown* is the largest decline in the cumulative equity line below the trade entry price during the worst single trade. The *Profit/Loss Index* is a complex calculation that relates the Amount of Winning Trades to the Amount of Losing Trades on a scale of −100 (worst possible performance) to +100 (best possible performance), with zero representing profits equal to losses. *Reward/Risk Index* is the Total net profit minus System open drawdown. The resulting difference is then divided by the Total net profit. The *Buy/Hold Index* is the Total net profit minus the buy-and-hold strategy's net profit. The resulting difference is then divided by the buy-and-hold net profit. In this exercise, initial equity is assumed to be $100. Both long and short positions are taken unless otherwise noted. Trades are executed at the closing price on the signal date. Transaction costs, interest expenses, and margins are not included in the statistics.

Upside/Downside Ratio

The Upside/Downside Ratio is the volume of advancing issues divided by the volume of declining issues. Daily NYSE data normally is used in the calculation.

The Upside/Downside Ratio was designed to measure buying and selling pressure. High readings indicate buying pressure, which is bullish. Low readings reflect selling pressure, which is bearish.

Martin Zweig (900 Third Avenue, New York, NY 10022, (212) 755-9860) found that a daily Upside/Downside Ratio of greater than 9 to 1 has been extremely bullish. Every bull market, and many strong intermediate up moves, have begun with a greater than 9 to 1 reading of the Upside/Downside Ratio.

Furthermore, in cases where two readings greater than 9 to 1 occurred within 3 months or less, average gains in stock prices were significant. From January 1960 to May 1985, 12 buy signals were given, by 2 days within a 3-month period having readings of greater than 9 to 1. In every case Zweig found that stock prices were higher 6 and 12 months later. The average gains after 6 and 12 months were 14% and 20.7%, respectively.

Updating Zweig's study since May 1985, there have been only four signals where two readings greater than 9 to 1 occurred within 3 months. On balance, the four signals that did occur were profitable, as measured from the second 9 to 1 signal date. The results are shown in the table below. There have not been two signals within 3 months since September 6, 1988.

Up/Down Volume > 9

Second 9/1 Signal Date	*Closing Price S&P 500*	*S&P 500 6 Months Later*	*% Change 6 Months S&P 500*	*S&P 500 12 Months Later*	*% Change 12 Months S&P 500*
11/20/86	242.05	278.20	14.93	242.00	−0.02
10/29/87	265.00	261.35	−1.38	278.55	5.11
5/31/88	262.15	272.50	3.95	320.50	22.26
9/6/88	265.60	294.80	10.99	349.25	31.49
Average			7.12		14.71

Indicator Strategy Example of the Upside/Downside Ratio

Based on a 16-year file of daily data for the Upside/Downside Ratio and the S&P 500 cash index since 1984, we found that a simple trend-following rule would have produced a positive result on a purely mechanical signal basis with no subjectivity, no sophisticated technical analysis, and no judgement:

Enter Long (Buy) at the current daily price close of the S&P 500 when the Upside/Downside Ratio crosses above its own previous day's trailing 3-day exponential moving average (EMA).

Close Long (Sell) at the current daily price close of the S&P 500 when the Upside/Downside Ratio crosses below its own previous day's trailing 3-day EMA.

Enter Short (Sell Short) at the current daily price close of the S&P 500 when the Upside/Downside Ratio crosses below its own previous day's trailing 3-day EMA.

Close Short (Cover) at the current daily price close of the S&P 500 when the Upside/Downside Ratio crosses above its own previous day's trailing 3-day EMA.

Starting with $100 and reinvesting profits, total net profits for this Upside/Downside Ratio trend-following strategy would have been $1,157.23, assuming a fully invested strategy, reinvestment of profits, no transactions costs and no taxes. This would have been 26.91 percent better than buy-and-hold. Even short selling would have been profitable. Trading would have been hyperactive with one trade every 2.80 calendar days.

The Equis International MetaStock® System Testing rules, where the current Upside/Downside Ratio times 10,000 is inserted into the data field normally reserved for Volume (V), are written as follows:

Enter long: V > Ref(Mov(V,opt1,E),-1)

Close long: V < Ref(Mov(V,opt1,E),-1)

Enter short: V < Ref(Mov(V,opt1,E),-1)

Close short: V > Ref(Mov(V,opt1,E),-1)

OPT1 Current value: 3

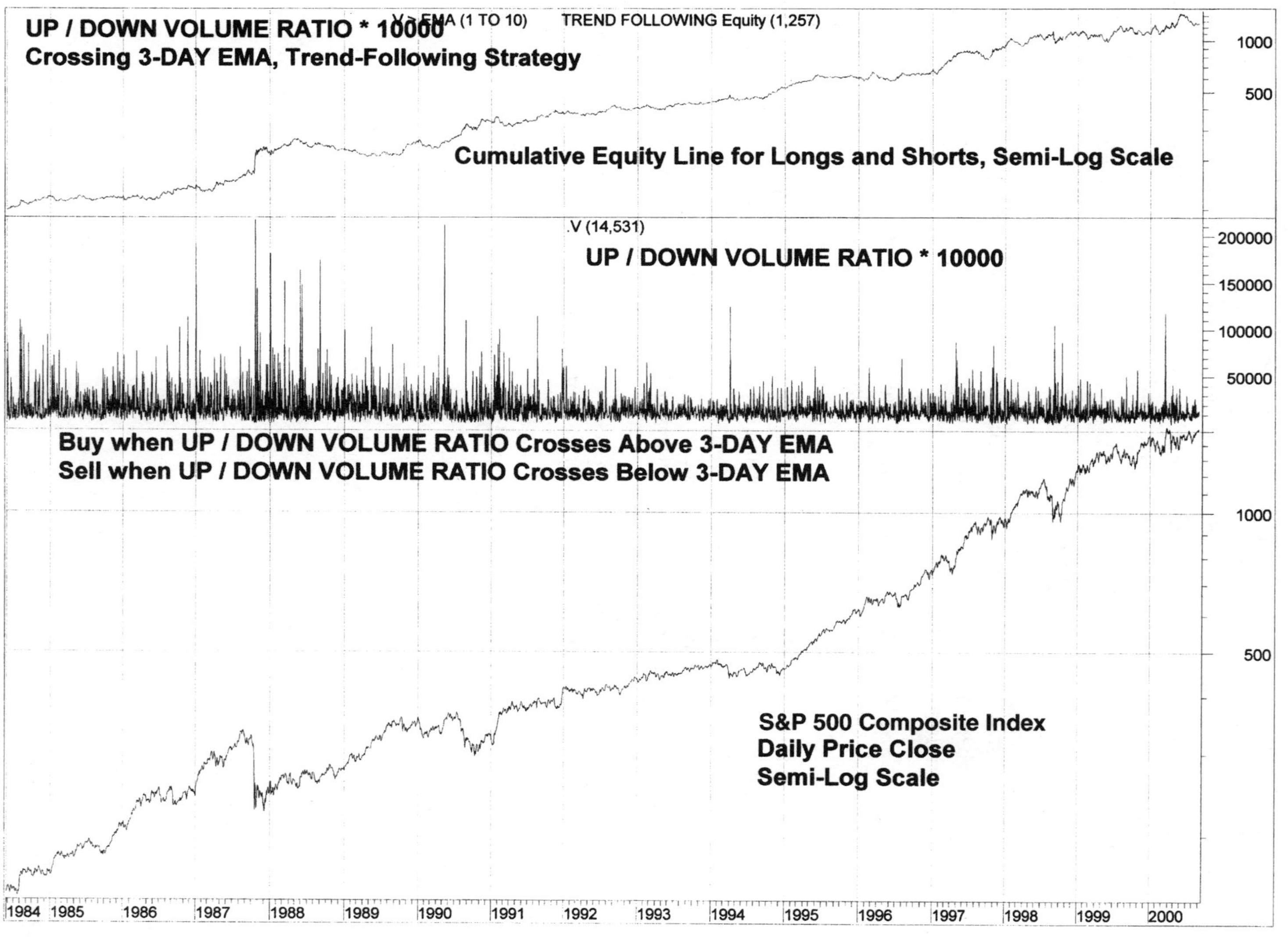
UP / DOWN VOLUME RATIO * 10000
Crossing 3-DAY EMA, Trend-Following Strategy
V > EMA (1 TO 10)
TREND FOLLOWING Equity (1,257)
Cumulative Equity Line for Longs and Shorts, Semi-Log Scale
1000
500
.V (14,531)
UP / DOWN VOLUME RATIO * 10000
200000
150000
100000
50000
Buy when UP / DOWN VOLUME RATIO Crosses Above 3-DAY EMA
Sell when UP / DOWN VOLUME RATIO Crosses Below 3-DAY EMA
1000
500
S&P 500 Composite Index
Daily Price Close
Semi-Log Scale
1984
1985
1986
1987
1988
1989
1990
1991
1992
1993
1994
1995
1996
1997
1998
1999
2000

Upside/Downside Ratio Crossing Trailing 3-day Exponential Moving Average

Total net profit	1157.23	Open position value	2.55	Net Profit / Buy&Hold %	26.91
Percent gain/loss	1157.23	Annual percent gain/loss	71.11	Annual Net % / B&H %	26.91
Initial investment	100	Interest earned	0		
Current position	Long	Date position entered	8/31/00		
Buy/Hold profit	911.82	Days in test	5940	# of days per trade	2.80
Buy/Hold pct gain/loss	911.82	Annual B/H pct gain/loss	56.03		
Total closed trades	2120	Commissions paid	0		
Avg profit per trade	0.54	Avg Win/Avg Loss ratio	1.38		
Total long trades	1060	Total short trades	1060	Long Win Trade %	54.72
Winning long trades	580	Winning short trades	428	Short Win Trade %	40.38
Total winning trades	1008	Total losing trades	1112	Total Win Trade %	47.55
Amount of winning trades	5697.51	Amount of losing trades	−4542.83	Net Profit Margin %	11.28
Average win	5.65	Average loss	−4.09	Average P. Margin %	16.02
Largest win	82.06	Largest loss	−78.08	% Net / (Win + Loss)	2.49
Average length of win	3.44	Average length of loss	2.48	(Win − Loss) / Loss %	38.71
Longest winning trade	9	Longest losing trade	7	(Win − Loss) / Loss %	28.57
Most consecutive wins	8	Most consecutive losses	9	(Win − Loss) / Loss %	−11.11
Total bars out	4	Average length out	4		
Longest out period	4				
System close drawdown	0	Profit/Loss index	20.3	% Net Profit / SODD	#DIV/0!
System open drawdown	0	Reward/Risk index	100	(Net P.-SODD)/Net P.	100.00
Max open trade drawdown	−78.08	Buy/Hold index	27.19	% SODD / Net Profit	0.00

In the Equis MetaStock® "System Report" (profit and loss summary statistics), the *Total net profit* is the sum of profits minus the sum of losses, including open positions marked to the market. In contrast, the *Amount of Winning Trades* is the sum of realized profits (the total of all gains on closed-out trades only, excluding any open positions). Similarly, the *Amount of Losing Trades* is the sum of realized losses (the total of all losses on closed-out trades only, excluding any open positions). *System close drawdown* is the largest decline in the cumulative equity line below the initial investment, based on closed-out positions only. *System open drawdown (SODD)* is the largest decline in the cumulative equity line below the initial investment when a position is open. *Max open trade drawdown* is the largest decline in the cumulative equity line below the trade entry price during the worst single trade. The *Profit/Loss Index* is a complex calculation that relates the Amount of Winning Trades to the Amount of Losing Trades on a scale of −100 (worst possible performance) to +100 (best possible performance), with zero representing profits equal to losses. *Reward/Risk Index* is the Total net profit minus System open drawdown. The resulting difference is then divided by the Total net profit. The *Buy/Hold Index* is the Total net profit minus the buy-and-hold strategy's net profit. The resulting difference is then divided by the buy-and-hold net profit. In this exercise, initial equity is assumed to be $100. Both long and short positions are taken unless otherwise noted. Trades are executed at the closing price on the signal date. Transaction costs, interest expenses, and margins are not included in the statistics.

Volatility, Introduction

Volatility is a measure of up and down price movement, without regard to trend direction. All measures of plain volatility are based on past price fluctuation, but what we really need to know is future volatility. There is no way to know what that will be, however. It seems to depend on investors' emotions. Plain volatility without trend direction is generally misleading.

There are many ways to compute volatility. Many use Greek symbols and are quite complex and difficult to understand. All methods attempt to quantify *how much* price fluctuation there has been. Volatility is often defined as a measure of a stock's tendency to move up and down in price, based on its daily price history over, say, the latest month or year or other period. As an example of perhaps the simplest possible approach to a difficult problem, volatility might be defined as the percentage price change or fluctuation over a given period of time. (Note that you would need to use percentage price changes rather than dollar or point price changes to allow proper comparisons over time because of dramatically changing price levels in the long bull market.)

We have experimented with many formulations of volatility and found that volatility is a coincident indicator that can change frequently, rapidly and unpredictably, or hardly at all, depending on the mood of the trading crowd. Price fluctuation alone, without consideration for price trend, appears to contain little useful information. And this is the weakness of strategies that depend on historical volatility, such as many past options and derivatives valuation attempts.

The use of complex measures of variance based on past volatility to construct portfolios and to value derivatives does not appear to have allowed users to outperform the benchmark S&P 500 Index buy-and-hold strategy. On the contrary, the complex mathematics of finance failed spectacularly at least twice in the past: Portfolio Insurance caused, or at least worsened, the Crash of 1987; and in August 1998 Long-Term Capital Management's failed derivatives strategies brought the entire U.S. financial system to the brink of disaster, which was only narrowly averted by timely intervention by Federal Reserve Board officials.

Mathematician Benoit Mandelbrot conjectured that stock price change distributions have infinite variance. Bill Eckhardt (Schwager, Jack D., *The New Market Wizards,* Harper Collins, New York, 1992, 493 pages) pointed out that if this variance is not finite, then sometime in the unforeseeable future there could be more extreme scenarios than we might be able to imagine. Even the 1-day, 20% S&P 500 Index price drop on October 19, 1987, might not be as extreme as it possibly could become. Also, if market prices do not have a finite variance, then any classically derived estimate of risk for the buy-and-hold strategy could be significantly understated.

In sum, historical measures of volatility, without consideration for trend direction, cannot be counted on. Volatility measurements taken over the past 30-days or a year, however popular, may prove badly misleading at the most critical times when we need good analysis the most.

Volatility, Chaikin's

Chaikin's Volatility, developed by veteran technical analyst Marc Chaikin, measures the smoothed velocity of the spread between a security's high and low prices. First, Chaikin subtracts the daily low from the high. Next, he calculates a 10-day exponential moving average of those daily differences. Finally, he computes a 10-day percentage rate-of-change of that exponential moving average.

Using 62-years of daily high-low data from 1928, we found that a marginal profit would have been made if we bought the DJIA when Chaikin's Volatility crossed below zero, indicating falling volatility, and we sold and sold short when it crossed above zero, indicating rising volatility. This strategy would have lost money since the Crash of '87, solely due to persistent losses on the short side in the record breaking bull market. A long-only strategy would have been profitable, but even that under performed buy-and-hold. The opposite strategy, buying rising volatility and selling falling volatility, would have lost heavily. Like other volatility indicators we have tested, Chaikin's Volatility does not appear particularly fruitful as a stand-alone indicator.

The MetaStock® indicator-builder formula for Chaikin's Volatility may be expressed as follows:

```
ROC(Mov(H-L,10,E),10,%);
Input("Plot a horizontal line at",-100,100,0);
```

Volatility, CBOE Volatility Index (VIX)

The CBOE's Volatility Index (VIX) is a relatively new volatility indicator that has gained popularity with some traders because it offers up-to-the-minute estimates of the stock market's implied volatility using real-time stock option bid/ask quotes. VIX is a weighted average of the implied volatilities of eight OEX calls and puts with an average time to maturity of 30 days. Implied volatility is the volatility percentage that explains the current market price of an option. Implied volatility reflects option speculators' emotions of greed and fear.

VIX shoots upward when options traders *fear* the market might collapse. Then VIX reverts to the mean when the selling panic is over and traders calm down. The 14.75-year average level of VIX is about 20. VIX jumped to a record 152.48 during the day on so-called *Black Monday* 10/19/87, the Crash of '87. It took 4 months for

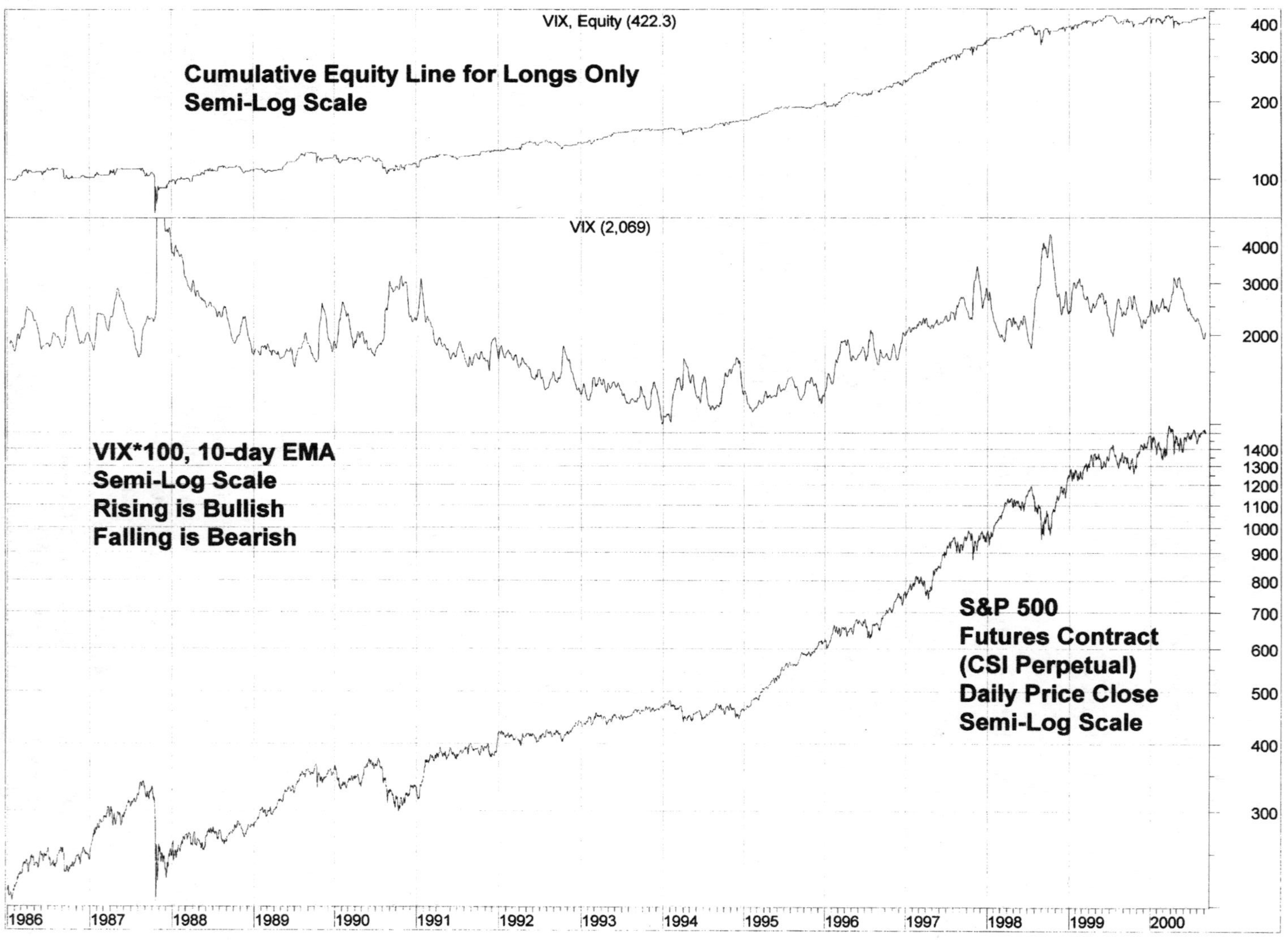
VIX, Equity (422.3)
Cumulative Equity Line for Longs Only
Semi-Log Scale
VIX (2,069)
VIX*100, 10-day EMA
Semi-Log Scale
Rising is Bullish
Falling is Bearish
S&P 500
Futures Contract
(CSI Perpetual)
Daily Price Close
Semi-Log Scale
400
300
200
100
4000
3000
2000
1400
1300
1200
1100
1000
900
800
700
600
500
400
300
1986
1987
1988
1989
1990
1991
1992
1993
1994
1995
1996
1997
1998
1999
2000

VIX versus 10-Day EMA

Total net profit	322.27	Open position value	−4.43	Net Profit / Buy&Hold %	−46.65
Percent gain/loss	322.27	Annual percent gain/loss	21.93	Annual Net % / B&H %	−46.66
Initial investment	100	Interest earned	0		
Current position	Long	Date position entered	9/5/00		
Buy/Hold profit	604.12	Days in test	5364	# of days per trade	12.42
Buy/Hold pct gain/loss	604.12	Annual B/H pct gain/loss	41.11		
Total closed trades	432	Commissions paid	0		
Avg profit per trade	0.76	Avg Win/Avg Loss ratio	1.09		
Total long trades	432	Total short trades	0	Long Win Trade %	63.43
Winning long trades	274	Winning short trades	0	Short Win Trade %	#DIV/0!
Total winning trades	274	Total losing trades	158	Total Win Trade %	63.43
Amount of winning trades	693.17	Amount of losing trades	−366.47	Net Profit Margin %	30.83
Average win	2.53	Average loss	−2.32	Average P. Margin %	4.33
Largest win	22.49	Largest loss	−27.84	% Net / (Win + Loss)	−10.63
Average length of win	4.85	Average length of loss	4.83	(Win − Loss) / Loss %	0.41
Longest winning trade	17	Longest losing trade	22	(Win − Loss) / Loss %	−22.73
Most consecutive wins	9	Most consecutive losses	7	(Win − Loss) / Loss %	28.57
Total bars out	2481	Average length out	5.73		
Longest out period	25				
System close drawdown	−7.35	Profit/Loss index	46.79	% Net Profit / SODD	1217.95
System open drawdown	−26.46	Reward/Risk index	92.41	(Net P.-SODD)/Net P.	91.79
Max open trade drawdown	−46.69	Buy/Hold index	−47.39	% SODD / Net Profit	−8.21

In the Equis MetaStock® "System Report" (profit and loss summary statistics), the *Total net profit* is the sum of profits minus the sum of losses, including open positions marked to the market. In contrast, the *Amount of Winning Trades* is the sum of realized profits (the total of all gains on closed-out trades only, excluding any open positions). Similarly, the *Amount of Losing Trades* is the sum of realized losses (the total of all losses on closed-out trades only, excluding any open positions). *System close drawdown* is the largest decline in the cumulative equity line below the initial investment, based on closed-out positions only. *System open drawdown (SODD)* is the largest decline in the cumulative equity line below the initial investment when a position is open. *Max open trade drawdown* is the largest decline in the cumulative equity line below the trade entry price during the worst single trade. The *Profit/Loss Index* is a complex calculation that relates the Amount of Winning Trades to the Amount of Losing Trades on a scale of −100 (worst possible performance) to +100 (best possible performance), with zero representing profits equal to losses. *Reward/Risk Index* is the Total net profit minus System open drawdown. The resulting difference is then divided by the Total net profit. The *Buy/Hold Index* is the Total net profit minus the buy-and-hold strategy's net profit. The resulting difference is then divided by the buy-and-hold net profit. In this exercise, initial equity is assumed to be $100. Both long and short positions are taken unless otherwise noted. Trades are executed at the closing price on the signal date. Transaction costs, interest expenses, and margins are not included in the statistics.

VIX to return to the 20s. As price ranges narrowed from 1991 to 1996, VIX spent most of its time in a below-average 11 to 19 range, as the chart on page 730 shows. VIX set its record low at 8.86 on 12/23/93.

Indicator Strategy Example for Volatility (VIX)

Historical data shows that Volatility (VIX) is bullish when in a rising trend. On the long side, the trend of VIX would have been profitable, though not as profitable as the buy-and-hold strategy, and right more often than wrong. On the short side, however, the trend of VIX would have been unprofitable across all daily time horizons and wrong more often than right.

Based on the VIX as posted on the CBOE web site and a 14.75-year file of daily data for the S&P 500 Composite Stock Price Index futures *CSI Perpetual Contract* from January 1986 to September 2000 collected from www.csidata.com, we found that the following parameters would have produced the following result on a purely mechanical trend-following signal basis with no subjectivity, no sophisticated technical analysis, and no judgement:

> **Enter Long (Buy)** at the current daily price close of the S&P 500 Composite Stock Price Index futures *CSI Perpetual Contract* when VIX today is greater than yesterday's 10-day EMA of VIX, indicting a rising trend of Volatility.
>
> **Close Long (Sell)** at the current daily price close of the S&P 500 Composite Stock Price Index futures *CSI Perpetual Contract* when VIX today is less than yesterday's 10-day EMA of VIX, indicting a falling trend of Volatility.
>
> **Sell Short** never.

Starting with $100 and reinvesting profits, total net profits for this VIX strategy would have been $ 322.27, assuming a fully invested strategy, reinvestment of profits, no transactions costs, and no taxes. This would have been 46.65% less than buy-and-hold. Short selling would have lost heavily and consistently and was not included. Trading would have been active, with one trade every 12.42 calendar days. This indicator would have been right more often than wrong for long trades, with 63.43% winning long-side trades.

The Equis International MetaStock® System Testing rules, where VIX is inserted into the data field normally reserved for volume, are written as follows:

Enter long: V > Ref(Mov(V,opt1,E),-1)

Close long: V < Ref(Mov(V,opt1,E),-1)

Enter short: V < Ref(Mov(V,opt1,E),-1)

Close short: V > Ref(Mov(V,opt1,E),-1)

OPT1 Current value: 10

Volatility Bands

Volatility bands around a moving average are a better approach to analyzing volatility. They can be usefully quantified and made to work in a trading system. *(See Bollinger Bands.)*

Bollinger Bands may be applied to Volatility (VIX) itself. The following parameters produced signals that were right more often than wrong but still did not keep pace with a passive buy-and-hold strategy. The Equis International MetaStock® System Testing rules, where VIX is inserted into the data field normally reserved for volume, are written as follows:

Enter long: Mov(V,opt3,E) > Ref(BBandTop(V,opt1,E,opt2),-1)

Close long: Mov(V,opt3,E) < Ref(BBandTop(V,opt1,E,opt2),-1)

Enter short: Mov(V,opt3,E) < Ref(BBandBot(V,opt1,E,opt2),-1)

Close short: Mov(V,opt3,E) > Ref(BBandBot(V,opt1,E,opt2),-1)

OPT1 Current value: 13
OPT2 Current value: 2
OPT3 Current value: 1

Volatility & Price Channel

Volatility & Price Channel is a combined indicator system, of which there are billions and billions. Here, when the price both breaks out of a trading range *and* price volatility increases on the breakout, a signal to buy or sell is recognized. Volatility can be described various ways, including *Average True Range,* which is an average of recent high minus low price ranges over some variable look-back period, such as 6 days. An increase in volatility indicates greater price movement, which implies greater intensity of buying or selling. This greater movement and intensity make the price action more significant than a price breakout alone without increasing volatility. Therefore, a price channel breakout with rising volatility triggers a signal to buy or sell in order to follow the direction of the breakout.

Indicator Strategy Example for a Volatility & Price Channel Trend-Following Strategy

Based on daily data for the S&P 500 Stock Index Futures *CSI Perpetual Contract* from 4/21/82 to 5/23/01 collected from www.csidata.com, we found that the following specific parameters would have produced a positive result on a purely mechanical trend-following signal basis with no subjectivity, no sophisticated technical analysis, and no judgement:

Enter Long (Buy) at the current daily price close of the S&P 500 Stock Index Futures *CSI Perpetual Contract* when the daily price close is greater than the previous day's close and the current daily high-low range is greater than 138% of the previous day's Average True Range with a look-back period of 6 days.

Close Long (Sell) at the current daily price close of the S&P 500 Stock Index Futures *CSI Perpetual Contract* when the daily price close is less than the lowest daily close over the trailing 84 trading days and the current daily high-low range is greater than 138% of the previous day's Average True Range with a look-back period of 6 days.

Enter Short (Sell Short) at the current daily price close of the S&P 500 Stock Index Futures *CSI Perpetual Contract* when the daily price close is less than the lowest daily close over the trailing 84 trading days and the current daily high-low range is greater than 138% of the previous day's Average True Range with a look-back period of 6 days.

Close Short (Cover) at the current daily price close of the S&P 500 Stock Index Futures *CSI Perpetual Contract* when the daily price close is greater than the previous day's close and the current daily high-low range is greater than 138% of the previous day's Average True Range with a look-back period of 6 days.

Starting with $100 and reinvesting profits, total net profits for this Volatility & Price Channel Trend-Following Strategy would have been would have been $2,089.03, assuming a fully invested strategy, reinvestment of profits, no transactions costs, and no taxes. This would have been 109.29 percent greater than buy-and-hold. Short selling would have been only slightly unprofitable, and short selling was included in the strategy. This contrary indicator would have given profitable buy signals 62.50% of the time. Trading would have been relatively inactive at one trade every 217.91 calendar days.

The chart shows how Cumulative Equity for this Volatility & Price Channel Trend-Following Strategy, which started lower (at 100) then crossed above the unmanaged S&P 500 Stock Index Futures *CSI Perpetual Contract* in the Crash of October '87 as the Volatility & Price Channel strategy profited while buy-and-hold lost heavily. Also, note milder equity drawdowns in general for the Volatility & Price Channel versus the unmanaged contract. Greater profitability with milder drawdowns are desirable qualities in an indicator.

The Equis International MetaStock® System Testing rules for this Volatility & Price Channel Trend-Following Strategy are written:

Enter long: CLOSE>Ref(HHV(C,opt1),-1) AND
(H-L)>Ref((ATR(opt2))*(opt4/100),-1)

Close long: CLOSE<Ref(LLV(C,opt3),-1) AND
(H-L)>Ref((ATR(opt2))*(opt4/100),-1)

Enter short: CLOSE<Ref(LLV(C,opt3),-1) AND
(H-L)>Ref((ATR(opt2))*(opt4/100),-1)

Close short: CLOSE>Ref(HHV(C,opt1),-1) AND
(H-L)>Ref((ATR(opt2))*(opt4/100),-1)

OPT1 Current value: 1

OPT2 Current value: 6

OPT3 Current value: 84

OPT4 Current value: 138

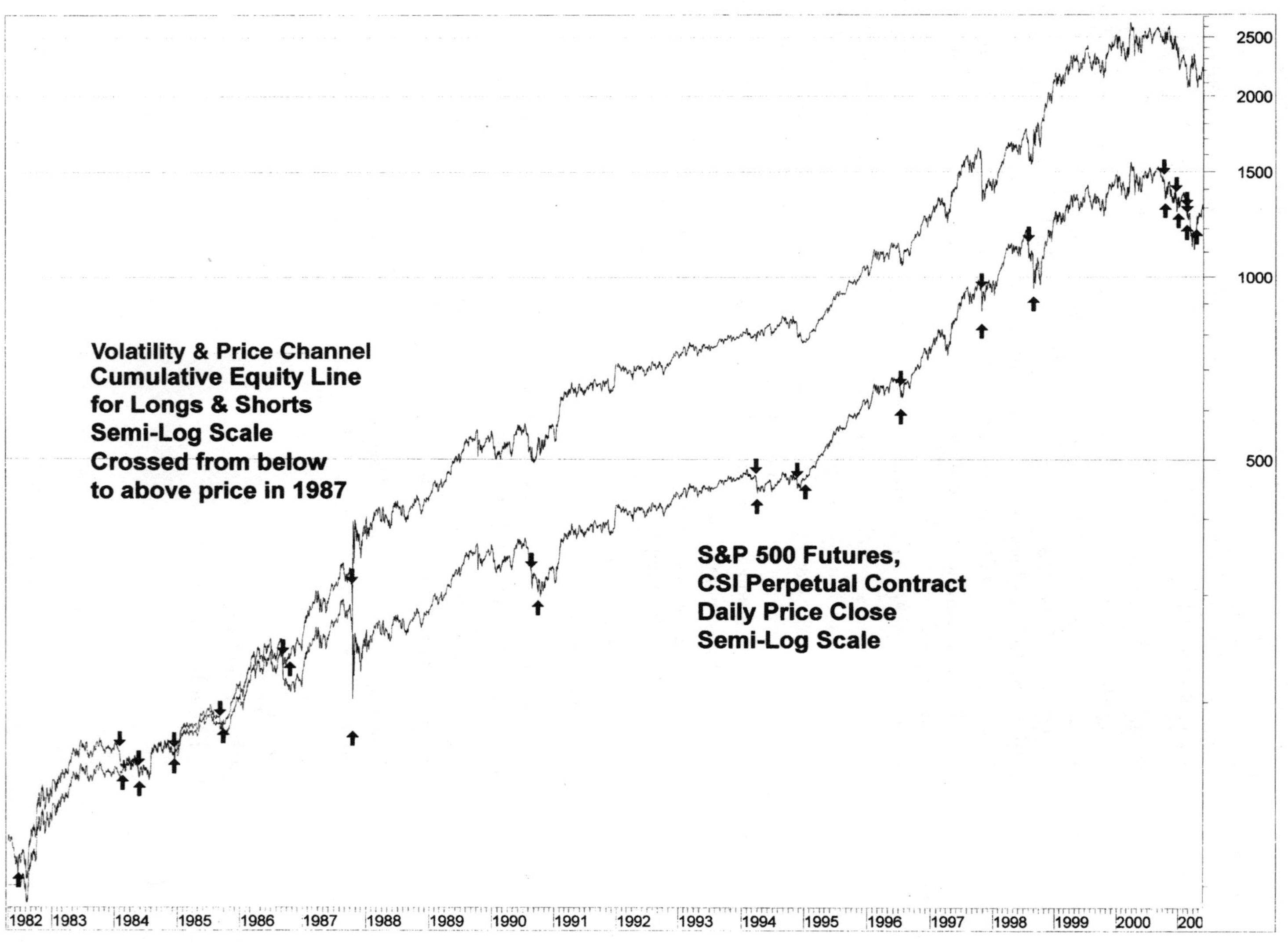

Volatility & Price Channel
Cumulative Equity Line
for Longs & Shorts
Semi-Log Scale
Crossed from below
to above price in 1987
S&P 500 Futures,
CSI Perpetual Contract
Daily Price Close
Semi-Log Scale
2500
2000
1500
1000
500
1982
1983
1984
1985
1986
1987
1988
1989
1990
1991
1992
1993
1994
1995
1996
1997
1998
1999
2000
200

Volatility & Price Channel Trend-Following Strategy

Total net profit	2089.03	Open position value	76.47	Net Profit / Buy&Hold %	109.29
Percent gain/loss	2089.03	Annual percent gain/loss	109.35	Annual Net % / B&H %	109.28
Initial investment	100	Interest earned	0		
Current position	Long	Date position entered	4/18/01		
Buy/Hold profit	998.13	Days in test	6973	# of days per trade	217.91
Buy/Hold pct gain/loss	998.13	Annual B/H pct gain/loss	52.25		
Total closed trades	32	Commissions paid	0		
Avg profit per trade	62.89	Avg Win/Avg Loss ratio	2.92		
Total long trades	16	Total short trades	16	Long Win Trade %	75.00
Winning long trades	12	Winning short trades	8	Short Win Trade %	50.00
Total winning trades	20	Total losing trades	12	Total Win Trade %	62.50
Amount of winning trades	2533.47	Amount of losing trades	−520.9	Net Profit Margin %	65.89
Average win	126.67	Average loss	−43.41	Average P. Margin %	48.95
Largest win	722.9	Largest loss	−170.69	% Net / (Win + Loss)	61.80
Average length of win	227.25	Average length of loss	20.33	(Win − Loss) / Loss %	1017.81
Longest winning trade	884	Longest losing trade	65	(Win − Loss) / Loss %	1260.00
Most consecutive wins	7	Most consecutive losses	5	(Win − Loss) / Loss %	40.00
Total bars out	44	Average length out	44		
Longest out period	44				
System close drawdown	0	Profit/Loss index	80.04	% Net Profit / SODD	31748.18
System open drawdown	−6.58	Reward/Risk index	99.69	(Net P.-SODD)/Net P.	99.69
Max open trade drawdown	−170.69	Buy/Hold index	116.96	% SODD / Net Profit	−0.31

In the Equis MetaStock® "System Report" (profit and loss summary statistics), the *Total net profit* is the sum of profits minus the sum of losses, including open positions marked to the market. In contrast, the *Amount of Winning Trades* is the sum of realized profits (the total of all gains on closed-out trades only, excluding any open positions). Similarly, the *Amount of Losing Trades* is the sum of realized losses (the total of all losses on closed-out trades only, excluding any open positions). *System close drawdown* is the largest decline in the cumulative equity line below the initial investment, based on closed-out positions only. *System open drawdown (SODD)* is the largest decline in the cumulative equity line below the initial investment when a position is open. *Max open trade drawdown* is the largest decline in the cumulative equity line below the trade entry price during the worst single trade. The *Profit/Loss Index* is a complex calculation that relates the Amount of Winning Trades to the Amount of Losing Trades on a scale of −100 (worst possible performance) to +100 (best possible performance), with zero representing profits equal to losses. *Reward/Risk Index* is the Total net profit minus System open drawdown. The resulting difference is then divided by the Total net profit. The *Buy/Hold Index* is the Total net profit minus the buy-and-hold strategy's net profit. The resulting difference is then divided by the buy-and-hold net profit. In this exercise, initial equity is assumed to be $100. Both long and short positions are taken unless otherwise noted. Trades are executed at the closing price on the signal date. Transaction costs, interest expenses, and margins are not included in the statistics.

Volatility Expansions

Volatility Expansions are data outliers, identified as price spikes away from the moving average of price. Outliers are unusual, aberrant data points that stray far from the mean. Outliers can offer trading opportunities. Several known trading systems attempt to take advantage of data outliers.

Statistics are commonly used to measure the variability of data around its central tendency, quantifying how far from the mean the observations stray and how much variability is normal and abnormal. Variability (the spread of the data) can be measured by the range, variance, and standard deviation.

Range is simply the high minus the low in the data sample and it includes all outliers, which might give one a distorted impression of the typical variability.

Variance measures the average variability around the mean by summing the squared deviations of each data point from the mean, then dividing that sum by the number of observations minus one, as expressed in the following formula:

$$s^2 = \frac{(\sum ((x - \bar{x})^2))}{n - 1} = (SUMMATION\ ((x - Mean)^2))\ /\ (n - 1)$$

Standard Deviation is the square root of the Variance. This may appear to be more useful than Variance because, by taking the square root of the average squared differences between observed data points and their mean, we thereby convert the measure of variability back into the same units of measure as the raw data we started with. In the case of stocks, for example, the unit of measure would be dollars per share.

The smaller the standard deviation, the more tightly the measurements in a sample cluster around the mean. A smaller standard deviation implies greater consistency.

A normal distribution, which is shaped like a symmetrical bell curve, contains approximately 67% of all the observed data within plus or minus one standard deviation around the mean. Approximately 95% of the data is within plus or minus two standard deviations around the mean. And approximately 99.7% of the data is within plus or minus three standard deviations around the mean.

Unfortunately, market data is not necessarily normally distributed. Rather, the distribution curve is often skewed to one side because of overbalance of data outliers in one direction. For example, in a sharply rising bull market, the distribution curve might be positively skewed, with a long tail to the right. In a prolonged and severe bear market, however, there might be a negative skew, with a long tail to the left.

The problem is that any statistics we may calculate are entirely dependent on *past* data rather than reflecting the unknown future data that we can only wish we had. That deficiency may not entirely preclude detection of some useful tendencies, other things being equal. Still, experience in sudden market jolts, such as the Crash of October 1987, suggests that reliance on past tendencies may be costly when investor emotions are running wild. Mechanical and statistical tools need to be filtered with sound technical analysis.

For a further discussion of the statistical approach to volatility expansions, see: Kase, Cynthia A., *Trading with the Odds: Using the Power of Probability to Profit in the Futures Market,* Irwin Professional Publishing, 1996, 149 pages.

Volatility Index, Art Merrill's Version

Arthur A. Merrill, CMT, has devised a simple measure of volatility for the DJIA by simply calculating the absolute value of the daily percentage price changes. He averages these daily changes for each full week (which is usually five trading days, except when there is a holiday). Then he smoothes this average weekly volatility with a 5-week EMA.

Merrill calculates plus and minus 67% of one standard deviation of the smoothed volatility. These should contain the middle quartiles, approximately. He interprets the 5-week exponentially smoothed volatility relative to its upper and lower 67% of one standard deviation bands as follows: a ratio above 67% of one standard deviation is bullish; a ratio below 67% of one standard deviation is bearish.

Using a chi-squared test of significance and a test period covering 1971 to 1982, Merrill found that this indicator correctly predicted the direction of the general market as measured by the DJIA 63% of the time over the next 13 weeks. This result was highly significant statistically. It predicted the market 60% of the time over the next 26 weeks, which was significant. It accurately predicted 57% of the time over the next 5 weeks, which was probably significant. Accuracy over the next one and 52 weeks was only a little better than 50%, which was insignificant statistically.

Volatility Ratios

Pure volatility measures that fail to distinguish upside price movement from downside price movement are of questionable value for market timing.

In the first edition of this encyclopedia, we tested weekly High/Low price ratios applied to the New York Stock Composite Index as a simple measure of volatility. We were not able to find any objective decision rule that offered consistent profitability. The distribution of profits over various time lengths assumed erratic patterns. There were losses in many time intervals. We concluded that using volatility as a market timing indicator did not appear to be fruitful.

For this second edition, we tested the absolute value of daily closing price percentage changes for the DJIA from 1900 to 2001 using our standard Exponential Moving Average Crossover model. Again, we were not able to find a timing rule that beat buy-and-hold. We wrote our Equis International MetaStock® System Testing rules as follows:

Enter long: Abs(ROC(C,opt1,%)) >
Ref(Mov(Abs(ROC(C,opt1,%)),opt2,E),-1)

Close long: Abs(ROC(C,opt1,%)) <
Ref(Mov(Abs(ROC(C,opt1,%)),opt2,E),-1)

Enter short: Abs(ROC(C,opt1,%)) <
Ref(Mov(Abs(ROC(C,opt1,%)),opt2,E),-1)

Close short: Abs(ROC(C,opt1,%)) >
Ref(Mov(Abs(ROC(C,opt1,%)),opt2,E),-1)

OPT1 Current value: 1

OPT2 Current value: 6

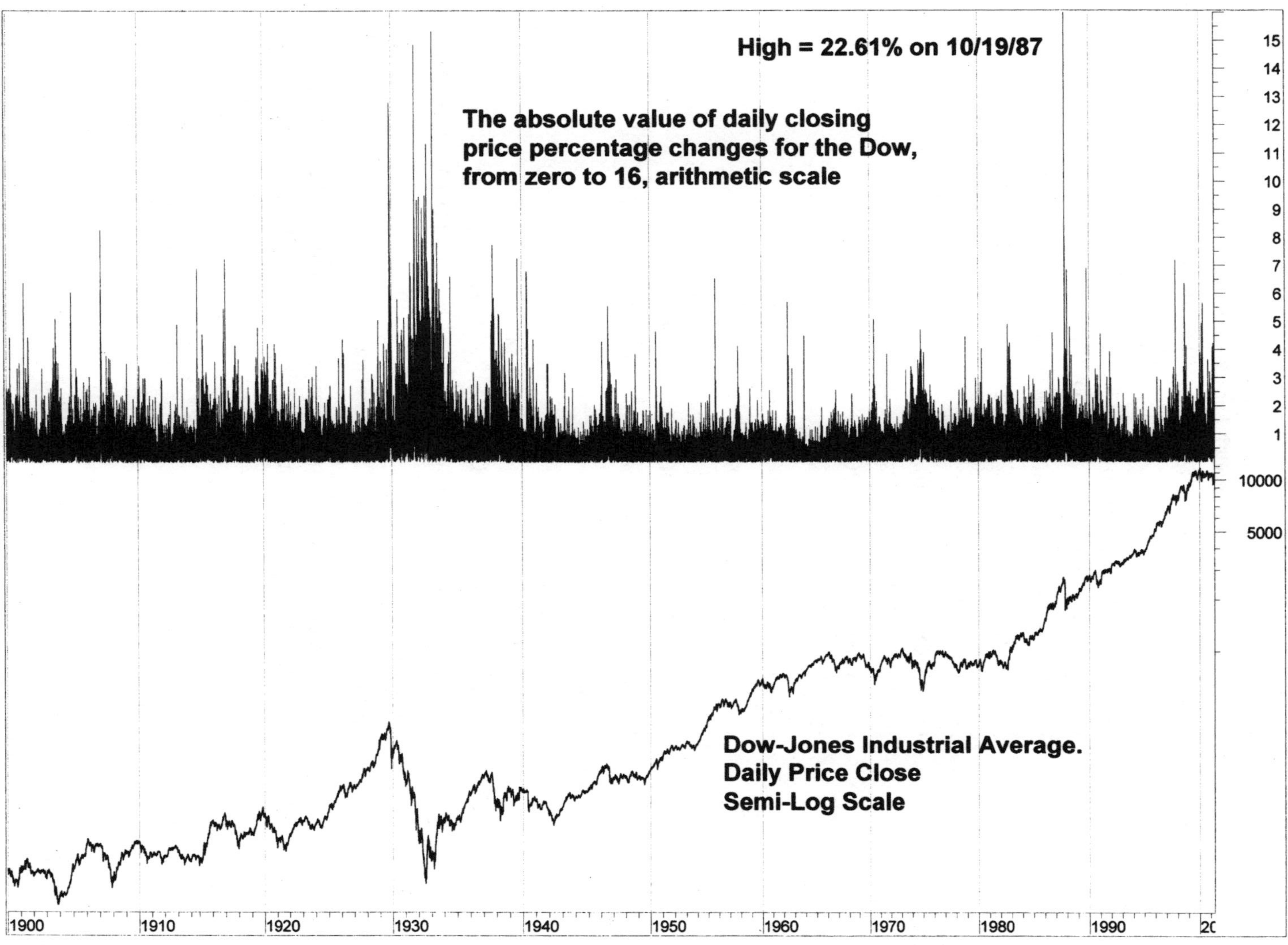

High = 22.61% on 10/19/87
The absolute value of daily closing
price percentage changes for the Dow,
from zero to 16, arithmetic scale
Dow-Jones Industrial Average.
Daily Price Close
Semi-Log Scale
15
14
13
12
11
10
9
8
7
6
5
4
3
2
1
10000
5000
1900
1910
1920
1930
1940
1950
1960
1970
1980
1990
20

We also tried an acceleration model, but we found even worse results. We wrote our Equis International MetaStock® System Testing rules as follows:

Enter long:

```
(Mov((Abs(ROC(C,1,%))),opt1,E)/
Ref(Mov((Abs(ROC(C,1,%))),opt2*opt1,E),-1))/
(Ref(Mov((Mov((Abs(ROC(C,1,%))),opt1,E)/
Ref(Mov((Abs(ROC(C,1,%))),opt2*opt1,E),-1)),opt1,E),-1))>= 1
```

Close long:

```
(Mov((Abs(ROC(C,1,%))),opt1,E)/
Ref(Mov((Abs(ROC(C,1,%))),opt2*opt1,E),-1))/
(Ref(Mov((Mov((Abs(ROC(C,1,%))),opt1,E)/
Ref(Mov((Abs(ROC(C,1,%))),opt2*opt1,E),-1)),opt1,E),-1))<1
```

Enter short:

```
(Mov((Abs(ROC(C,1,%))),opt1,E)/
Ref(Mov((Abs(ROC(C,1,%))),opt2*opt1,E),-1))/
(Ref(Mov((Mov((Abs(ROC(C,1,%))),opt1,E)/
Ref(Mov((Abs(ROC(C,1,%))),opt2*opt1,E),-1)),opt1,E),-1))<1
```

Close short:

```
(Mov((Abs(ROC(C,1,%))),opt1,E)/
Ref(Mov((Abs(ROC(C,1,%))),opt2*opt1,E),-1))/
(Ref(Mov((Mov((Abs(ROC(C,1,%))),opt1,E)/
Ref(Mov((Abs(ROC(C,1,%))),opt2*opt1,E),-1)),opt1,E),-1))>= 1
```

OPT1 Range: From 1 to 12 by 1, Current value: 2

OPT2 Range: From 1 to 12 by 1, Current value: 4

Finally, we switched to weekly price changes and again applied velocity, acceleration, and deceleration models. Results were discouraging for all approaches.

Volume

Volume is a key technical indicator serving an important analytical function. The volume of stock transactions, also known as *turnover* and *trading activity,* is the number of shares changing hands in a given period (hour, day, week, month, year, and so forth).

High and rising volume confirms the price trend in a bull market. Volume usually peaks before the final price top. Also, volume confirms breakouts: when price moves out of a sideways trading range, through a sloping *Trend Channel,* or through any support or resistance level, volume should increase to confirm the validity of the breakout.

When a stock breaks out upward, a pickup in volume indicates fresh buying interest, new demand, new buyers entering the market.

When a stock breaks out downward, a pickup in volume indicates fresh selling, new supply, new sellers entering the market.

A breakout lacking volume confirmation is not to be entirely trusted. Low volume indicates apathy, indecision, and lack of attraction to a stock on both sides, the buy side and the sell side. Then, price is more likely to drift aimlessly reflecting lack of investor interest in the stock. A breakout on low volume is more likely to be an aberration.

Occasionally, high volume can also signal a temporary excess, an overbought or oversold extreme. Extremely active trading is sometimes associated with minor price turning points, as in a buying or selling climax, when the irrational exuberance of the crowd reaches an unsustainable extreme. These junctures can be followed by price temporary corrections in the opposite direction to the prevailing trend. Generally, however, a major trend is not reversed by just one high-volume climax. Rather, it takes time and further testing to turn the Primary Tide.

A great old Wall Street saying is, "Volume is a weapon of the Bull—it takes fresh buying to push prices higher, but prices can fall of their own weight." True, it does take relatively strong demand from buyers versus supply from sellers to push prices higher. Prices move up when demand (buying) overbalances supply (supply). Also, in general, high volume is bullish more often than not. Since for every share that is sold a share is bought, high volume at least indicates that significant buying demand is present.

On the other hand, prices can fall a long distance on light volume. For example, well into a bear market, after investors realize that stock prices are in persistent downtrend, few want to buy stocks, so volume dries up. Prices can drift a long way down as sellers look for bids but do not find enough bids to absorb all their stock offerings. So, volume can remain relatively low while prices move lower and lower as sellers search for buyers willing to take the stock, to take the other side of the trade. When there are no bids nearby, the price may fall in a vacuum, dropping straight down with no volume at all, making a price gap on the chart.

There is no perfect indicator, and volume is subject to distortions that can boost or depress the total number of shares changing hands for reasons other than demand and supply. These distortions include holidays, seasonal patterns, buy and sell programs, arbitrage, dynamic hedging, block trades, and index fund position adjustments. When these distortions become significant, indicators weighted by volume suffer some instability.

Another great old Wall Street saying is, "In price there is knowledge." True, price most reliably and consistently reflects the demand and supply balance for stocks. Nevertheless, volume is a very useful confirming indicator that has proved itself over many decades of actual practice. Volume adds value to a complete technical analysis.

Indicator Strategy Example for Pure Volume Only

There are many indicators that incorporate volume, and they are covered in these pages. The best volume indicators combine volume with price. At the purest and most basic level, historical data shows that high volume is bullish and low volume is bearish. Based on the trend of the number of shares traded each day on the NYSE for 72 years from 1928 to 2000, we found that the following parameters would have produced a positive result on a purely mechanical trend-following signal basis with no subjectivity, no sophisticated technical analysis, and no judgement:

Enter Long (Buy) at the current daily price close of the DJIA when the NYSE Volume today is greater than yesterday's 220-day EMA of the daily volume.

Close Long (Sell) at the current daily price close of the DJIA when the NYSE Volume today is less than yesterday's 220-day EMA of the daily volume.

Enter Short (Sell Short) at the current daily price close of the DJIA when the NYSE Volume today is less than yesterday's 220-day EMA of the daily volume.

Close Short (Cover) at the current daily price close of the DJIA when the NYSE Volume today is greater than yesterday's 220-day exponential moving average of the daily volume.

Starting with $100 and reinvesting profits, total net profits for this Pure Volume Only strategy would have been $12,007.92, assuming a fully invested strategy, reinvestment of profits, no transactions costs, and no taxes. This would have been 177.21% better than the passive buy-and-hold strategy. There would have been more winning trades than losing trades for long trades, but the opposite would have been true for short sales. Curiously, the Volume trend-following strategy would not have been profitable over the past 14 years, due to losses on short sales.

The Equis International MetaStock® System Testing rules are written as follows:

Enter long: V > Ref(Mov(V,opt1,E),-1)

Close long: V < Ref(Mov(V,opt1,E),-1)

Enter short: V < Ref(Mov(V,opt1,E),-1)

Close short: V > Ref(Mov(V,opt1,E),-1)

OPT1 Current value: 220

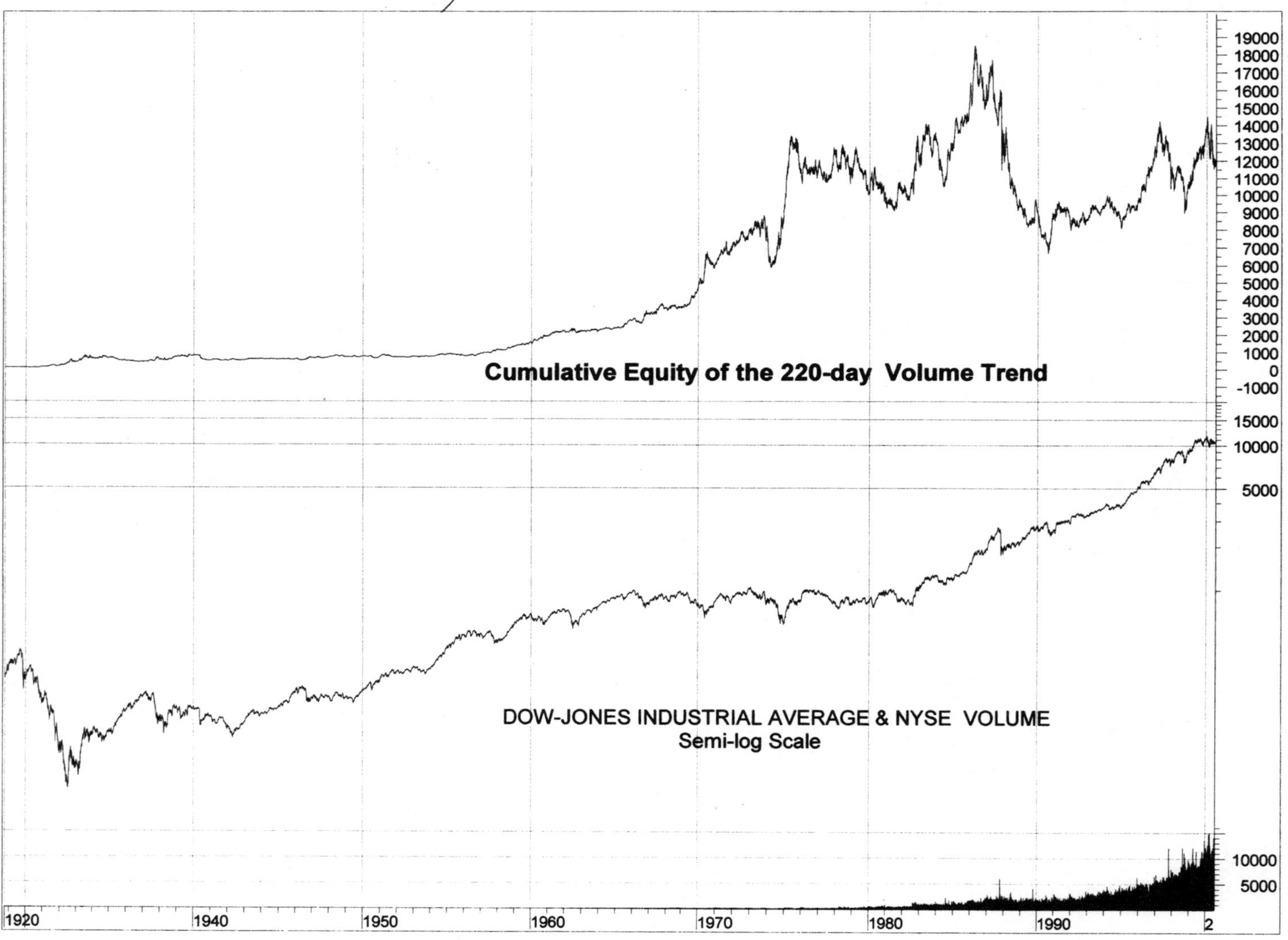

Cumulative Equity of the 220-day Volume Trend
DOW-JONES INDUSTRIAL AVERAGE & NYSE VOLUME
Semi-log Scale
19000 18000 17000 16000 15000 14000 13000 12000 11000 10000 9000 8000 7000 6000 5000 4000 3000 2000 1000 0 -1000
15000 10000 5000
10000 5000
1920 1940 1950 1960 1970 1980 1990 2

Volume versus 220-day EMA

Total net profit	12007.92	Open position value	0	Net Profit / Buy&Hold %	177.21
Percent gain/loss	12007.92	Annual percent gain/loss	167.2	Annual Net % / B&H %	177.19
Initial investment	100	Interest earned	0		
Current position	Short	Date position entered	7/7/00		
Buy/Hold profit	4331.67	Days in test	26213	# of days per trade	6.71
Buy/Hold pct gain/loss	4331.67	Annual B/H pct gain/loss	60.32		
Total closed trades	3907	Commissions paid	0		
Avg profit per trade	3.07	Avg Win/Avg Loss ratio	1.16		
Total long trades	1954	Total short trades	1953	Long Win Trade %	51.84
Winning long trades	1013	Winning short trades	870	Short Win Trade %	44.55
Total winning trades	1883	Total losing trades	2024	Total Win Trade %	48.20
Amount of winning trades	157402.39	Amount of losing trades	−145394.5	Net Profit Margin %	3.97
Average win	83.59	Average loss	−71.84	Average P. Margin %	7.56
Largest win	2965.13	Largest loss	−2630.35	% Net / (Win + Loss)	5.98
Average length of win	6.42	Average length of loss	4.75	(Win − Loss) / Loss %	35.16
Longest winning trade	94	Longest losing trade	66	(Win − Loss) / Loss %	42.42
Most consecutive wins	9	Most consecutive losses	9	(Win − Loss) / Loss %	0.00
Total bars out	221	Average length out	221		
Longest out period	221				
System close drawdown	−14.33	Profit/Loss index	7.63	% Net Profit / SODD	71475.71
System open drawdown	−16.8	Reward/Risk index	99.86	(Net P.-SODD)/Net P.	99.86
Max open trade drawdown	−4447.7	Buy/Hold index	177.21	% SODD / Net Profit	−0.14

In the Equis MetaStock® "System Report" (profit and loss summary statistics), the *Total net profit* is the sum of profits minus the sum of losses, including open positions marked to the market. In contrast, the *Amount of Winning Trades* is the sum of realized profits (the total of all gains on closed-out trades only, excluding any open positions). Similarly, the *Amount of Losing Trades* is the sum of realized losses (the total of all losses on closed-out trades only, excluding any open positions). *System close drawdown* is the largest decline in the cumulative equity line below the initial investment, based on closed-out positions only. *System open drawdown (SODD)* is the largest decline in the cumulative equity line below the initial investment when a position is open. *Max open trade drawdown* is the largest decline in the cumulative equity line below the trade entry price during the worst single trade. The *Profit/Loss Index* is a complex calculation that relates the Amount of Winning Trades to the Amount of Losing Trades on a scale of −100 (worst possible performance) to +100 (best possible performance), with zero representing profits equal to losses. *Reward/Risk Index* is the Total net profit minus System open drawdown. The resulting difference is then divided by the Total net profit. The *Buy/Hold Index* is the Total net profit minus the buy-and-hold strategy's net profit. The resulting difference is then divided by the buy-and-hold net profit. In this exercise, initial equity is assumed to be $100. Both long and short positions are taken unless otherwise noted. Trades are executed at the closing price on the signal date. Transaction costs, interest expenses, and margins are not included in the statistics.

Volume Acceleration

Volume Acceleration is a two-part indicator based on the Volume * Price Momentum Oscillator (V*PMO).

Volume Acceleration takes into consideration both the V*PMO position relative to zero (above or below) *and* whether V*PMO is rising or falling relative to its previous day's level.

When the *n*-period exponential moving average of V*PMO is positive and rising, momentum is bullish and accelerating, so we buy. We exit longs when momentum decelerates, thus indicating that the rally is losing steam.

When the *n*-period exponential moving average of V*PMO is negative and falling, momentum is bearish and accelerating to the downside, so we sell short. We exit short positions when negative momentum decelerates, thus indicating that the bear is losing its destructive power.

Indicator Strategy Example of Volume Acceleration

Historical data shows that, Volume Acceleration is a more effective indicator than the Volume * Price Momentum Oscillator (V*PMO) alone. Based on the number of shares traded each day on the NYSE and the daily prices for the DJIA for more than 72 years from 1928 to 2001, we found that the following parameters would have produced a significantly positive result on a purely mechanical trend-following signal basis with no subjectivity, no sophisticated technical analysis, and no judgement:

Enter Long (Buy) at the current daily price close of the DJIA when the 3-day EMA of the daily V*PMO is greater than zero and moving higher relative to its previous day's level.

Close Long (Sell) at the current daily price close of the DJIA when the 3-day EMA of the daily V*PMO is less than zero or when V*PMO moves lower relative to its previous day's level.

Enter Short (Sell Short) at the current daily price close of the DJIA when the 3-day EMA of the daily V*PMO is less than zero and moving lower relative to its previous day's level.

Close Short (Cover) at the current daily price close of the DJIA when the 3-day EMA of the daily V*PMO is greater than zero or when V*PMO moves higher relative to its previous day's level.

Starting with $100 and reinvesting profits, total net profits for this Volume Acceleration strategy would have been $72,812,288, assuming a fully invested strategy, reinvestment of profits, no transactions costs, and no taxes. This would have been

1,767,385.88% better than the passive buy-and-hold strategy. Short selling would have been profitable over the full 72 years, but unprofitable since 1987.

The Equis International MetaStock® System Testing rules are written as follows:

Enter long: Mov((C-Ref(C,-1))*V,opt1,E)>0 AND
(Mov((C-Ref(C,-1))*V,opt1,E)>Ref(Mov((C-Ref(C,-1))*V,opt1,E), −1))

Close long: Mov((C-Ref(C,-1))*V,opt1,E)<0 OR
(Mov((C-Ref(C,-1))*V,opt1,E)< Ref(Mov((C-Ref(C,-1))*V,opt1,E), −1))

Enter short: Mov((C-Ref(C,-1))*V,opt1,E)<0 AND
(Mov((C-Ref(C,-1))*V,opt1,E)< Ref(Mov((C-Ref(C,-1))*V,opt1,E), −1))

Close short: Mov((C-Ref(C,-1))*V,opt1,E)>0 OR
(Mov((C-Ref(C,-1))*V,opt1,E)> Ref(Mov((C-Ref(C,-1))*V,opt1,E), −1))

OPT1 Current value: 3

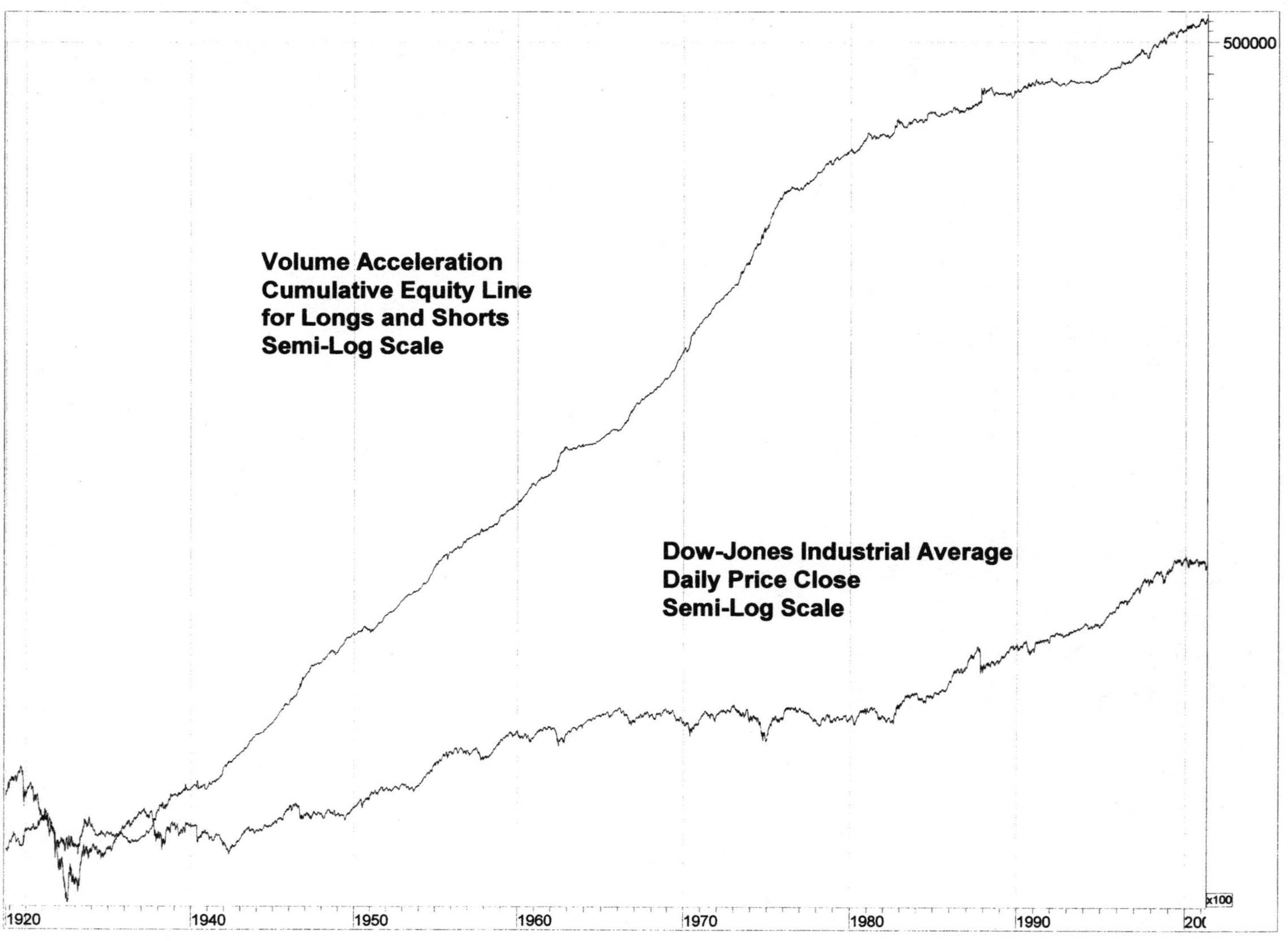

Volume Acceleration
Cumulative Equity Line
for Longs and Shorts
Semi-Log Scale
Dow-Jones Industrial Average
Daily Price Close
Semi-Log Scale
500000
x100
1920
1940
1950
1960
1970
1980
1990

Volume Acceleration

Total net profit	72812288	Open position value	0	Net Profit / Buy&Hold %	1767385.88
Percent gain/loss	72812288	Annual percent gain/loss	1003189.08	Annual Net % / B&H %	1767322.62
Initial investment	100	Interest earned	0		
Current position	Long	Date position entered	4/12/01		
Buy/Hold profit	4119.54	Days in test	26492	# of days per trade	3.61
Buy/Hold pct gain/loss	4119.54	Annual B/H pct gain/loss	56.76		
Total closed trades	7332	Commissions paid	0		
Avg profit per trade	9930.75	Avg Win/Avg Loss ratio	1.31		
Total long trades	3880	Total short trades	3452	Long Win Trade %	52.37
Winning long trades	2032	Winning short trades	1621	Short Win Trade %	46.96
Total winning trades	3653	Total losing trades	3679	Total Win Trade %	49.82
Amount of winning trades	313840384	Amount of losing trades	−241027680	Net Profit Margin %	13.12
Average win	85913.05	Average loss	−65514.46	Average P. Margin %	13.47
Largest win	4436074	Largest loss	−2108380	% Net / (Win + Loss)	35.57
Average length of win	2.95	Average length of loss	2.13	(Win − Loss) / Loss %	38.50
Longest winning trade	9	Longest losing trade	5	(Win − Loss) / Loss %	80.00
Most consecutive wins	16	Most consecutive losses	13	(Win − Loss) / Loss %	23.08
Total bars out	11676	Average length out	2.46		
Longest out period	8				
System close drawdown	−7.72	Profit/Loss index	23.2	% Net Profit / SODD	943164352.33
System open drawdown	−7.72	Reward/Risk index	100	(Net P.-SODD)/Net P.	100.00
Max open trade drawdown	−2108380	Buy/Hold index	1767385.03	% SODD / Net Profit	0.00

In the Equis MetaStock® "System Report" (profit and loss summary statistics), the *Total net profit* is the sum of profits minus the sum of losses, including open positions marked to the market. In contrast, the *Amount of Winning Trades* is the sum of realized profits (the total of all gains on closed-out trades only, excluding any open positions). Similarly, the *Amount of Losing Trades* is the sum of realized losses (the total of all losses on closed-out trades only, excluding any open positions). *System close drawdown* is the largest decline in the cumulative equity line below the initial investment, based on closed-out positions only. *System open drawdown (SODD)* is the largest decline in the cumulative equity line below the initial investment when a position is open. *Max open trade drawdown* is the largest decline in the cumulative equity line below the trade entry price during the worst single trade. The *Profit/Loss Index* is a complex calculation that relates the Amount of Winning Trades to the Amount of Losing Trades on a scale of −100 (worst possible performance) to +100 (best possible performance), with zero representing profits equal to losses. *Reward/Risk Index* is the Total net profit minus System open drawdown. The resulting difference is then divided by the Total net profit. The *Buy/Hold Index* is the Total net profit minus the buy-and-hold strategy's net profit. The resulting difference is then divided by the buy-and-hold net profit. In this exercise, initial equity is assumed to be $100. Both long and short positions are taken unless otherwise noted. Trades are executed at the closing price on the signal date. Transaction costs, interest expenses, and margins are not included in the statistics.

Volume Accumulation Oscillator, Volume Accumulation Trend

The Volume Accumulation Oscillator and Trend are volume momentum indicators developed by Marc Chaikin (177 E. 77th Street, New York, NY 10021). In their simplest forms, they are based on the running total of each day's volume times the difference between the daily closing price minus the midpoint of the daily price range. So, instead of measuring price change from the previous close, which is the more common practice, here we measure the day's price change from the day's median price, the mid point. Mathematically, the formula for the cumulative total of Volume Accumulation is expressed as follows:

Cum((C-(H+L)/2)*V)

where

Cum means cumulating a running total of the daily values of the expression that follows in parenthesis.

C = the closing price for a period.

H = the highest price for the same period.

L = the lowest price for the period.

V = the total volume of trading activity for the period.

For example, if the current period's highest price is 180, the lowest price 160, the close 165, and the volume 2000, then the day's closing price of 165 minus the midpoint of 170 is minus 5. Then, multiply −5 times the day's volume of 2000 to arrive at the day's Volume Accumulation of −10,000:

(C-(H+L)/2)*V = ((165-(180+160)/2)*2000 = (-5)*2000 = −10,000

Next, compute a running total of these daily calculations for the Volume Accumulation Cumulative Total. We can then plot that as a line, and we can measure the trend of that cumulative total of daily values in various ways, including chart patterns, trend lines, moving averages, etc. For example, the chart at the top of the facing page shows the Volume Accumulation Cumulative Total with a large rollover top (like a Complex Head-and-Shoulders Top) in 1999 and sharp drop in 2000, offering dramatic possibilities in chart interpretation. Note that with Volume Accumulation so negative, its followers might have been unprofitably bearish from October 1999 until the joint S&P and NASDAQ top in March 2000.

Alternately, we can convert this cumulative total into an oscillator by, for example, subtracting from it some moving average of itself. *(See Oscillators.)* The chart at the bottom of the facing page shows Volume Accumulation as a sensitive, short-term oscillator, computed by subtracting the current Volume Accumulation cumulative total minus its own previous day's 2-day EMA, then dividing that difference by the

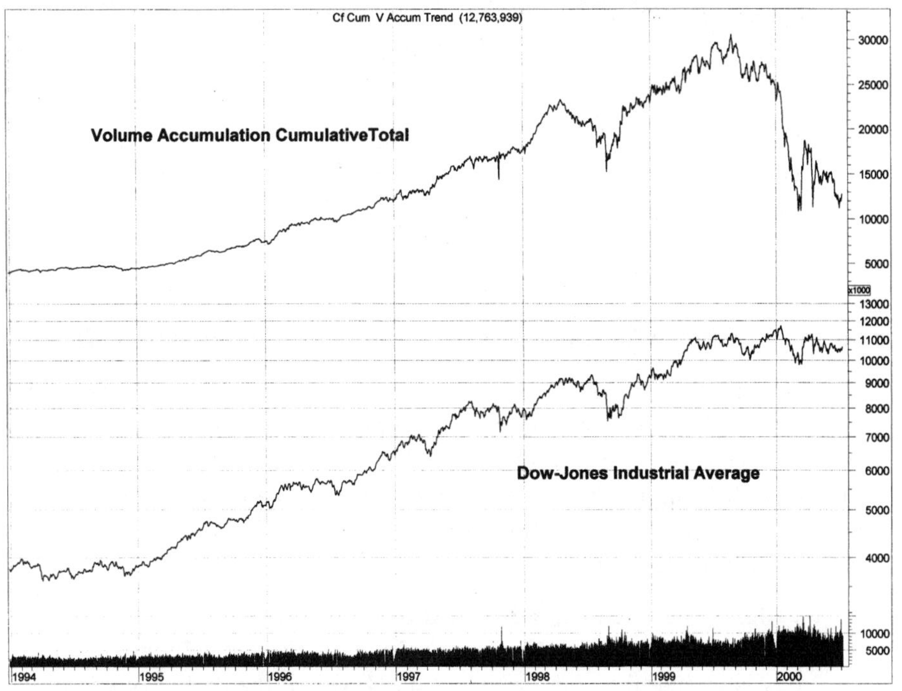
Cf Cum V Accum Trend (12,763,939)
Volume Accumulation CumulativeTotal
Dow-Jones Industrial Average
30000
25000
20000
15000
10000
5000
x1000
13000
12000
11000
10000
9000
8000
7000
6000
5000
4000
10000
5000
1994
1995
1996
1997
1998
1999
2000

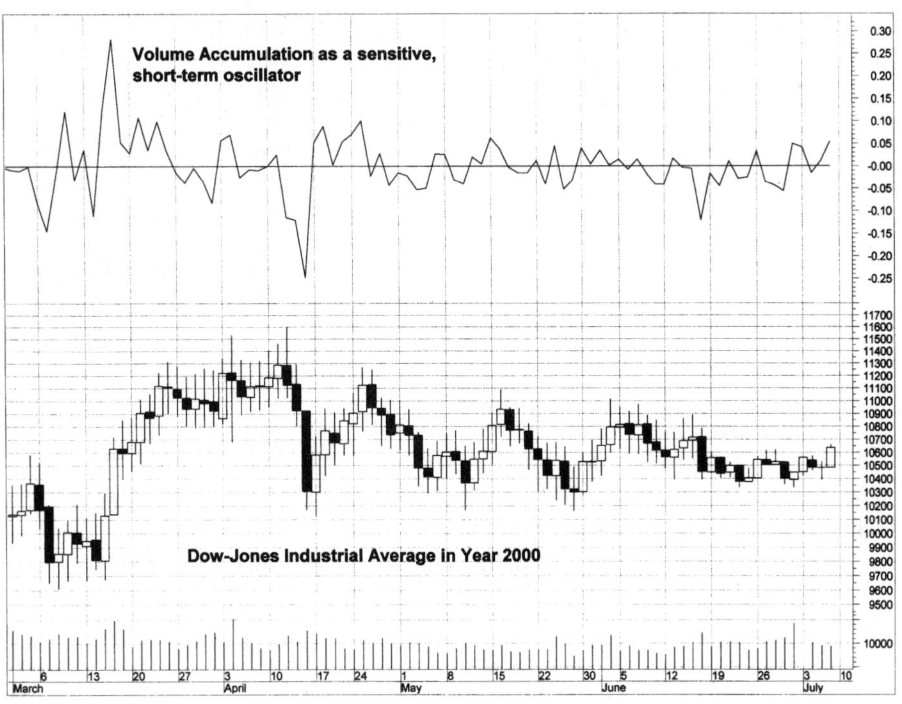
Volume Accumulation as a sensitive, short-term oscillator
Dow-Jones Industrial Average in Year 2000
0.30
0.25
0.20
0.15
0.10
0.05
-0.00
-0.05
-0.10
-0.15
-0.20
-0.25
11700
9500
10000
March
April
May
June
July

previous day's 2-day EMA, in order to normalize the scale. This Volume Accumulation Oscillator can be plotted with the following Equis MetaStock® Indicator Builder formula:

```
((Cum((C-(H+L)/2)*V))-
(Ref(Mov(Cum((C-(H+L)/2)*V),2,E),-1)))/
(Ref(Mov(Cum((C-(H+L)/2)*V),2,E),-1));
Input("Plot a horizontal line at",-0.25,0.25,0);
```

Indicator Strategy Example for the Volume Accumulation Oscillator and Trend

Historical data shows that Volume Accumulation can be an effective indicator, particularly on the long side. Based on the number of shares traded each day on the NYSE and the daily prices for the DJIA for 73 years from 1928 to 2001, we found that the following parameters would have produced a positive result on a purely mechanical trend-following signal basis with no subjectivity, no sophisticated technical analysis, and no judgement:

Enter Long (Buy) at the current daily price close of the DJIA when the Volume Accumulation Cumulative Line (that is, the daily running total) today is greater than yesterday's 2-day EMA of the daily Volume Accumulation Cumulative Line.

Close Long (Sell) at the current daily price close of the DJIA when the Volume Accumulation daily running total today is less than yesterday's 2-day EMA of the daily Volume Accumulation Cumulative Line.

Enter Short (Sell Short) at the current daily price close of the DJIA when the Volume Accumulation daily running total today is less than yesterday's 2-day EMA of the daily Volume Accumulation Cumulative Line.

Close Short (Cover) at the current daily price close of the DJIA when the Volume Accumulation daily running total today is greater than yesterday's 2-day EMA of the daily Volume Accumulation Cumulative Line.

Starting with $100 and reinvesting profits, total net profits for this Volume Accumulation Oscillator strategy would have been $18,863,680, assuming a fully invested strategy, reinvestment of profits, no transactions costs, and no taxes. This would have been 457,807.44% better than the passive buy-and-hold strategy. Despite these impressive numbers, however, this Volume Accumulation Oscillator trend-following strategy would not have been profitable since 1987, due to losses on short sales.

The Equis International MetaStock® System Testing rules are written as follows:

Enter long: Cum((C-(H+L)/2)*V)>
Ref(Mov(Cum((C-(H+L)/2)*V),opt1,E),-1)

Close long: Cum((C-(H+L)/2)*V)<
Ref(Mov(Cum((C-(H+L)/2)*V),opt1,E),-1)

Enter short: Cum((C-(H+L)/2)*V)<
Ref(Mov(Cum((C-(H+L)/2)*V),opt1,E),-1)

Close short: Cum((C-(H+L)/2)*V)>
Ref(Mov(Cum((C-(H+L)/2)*V),opt1,E),-1)

OPT1 Current value: 2

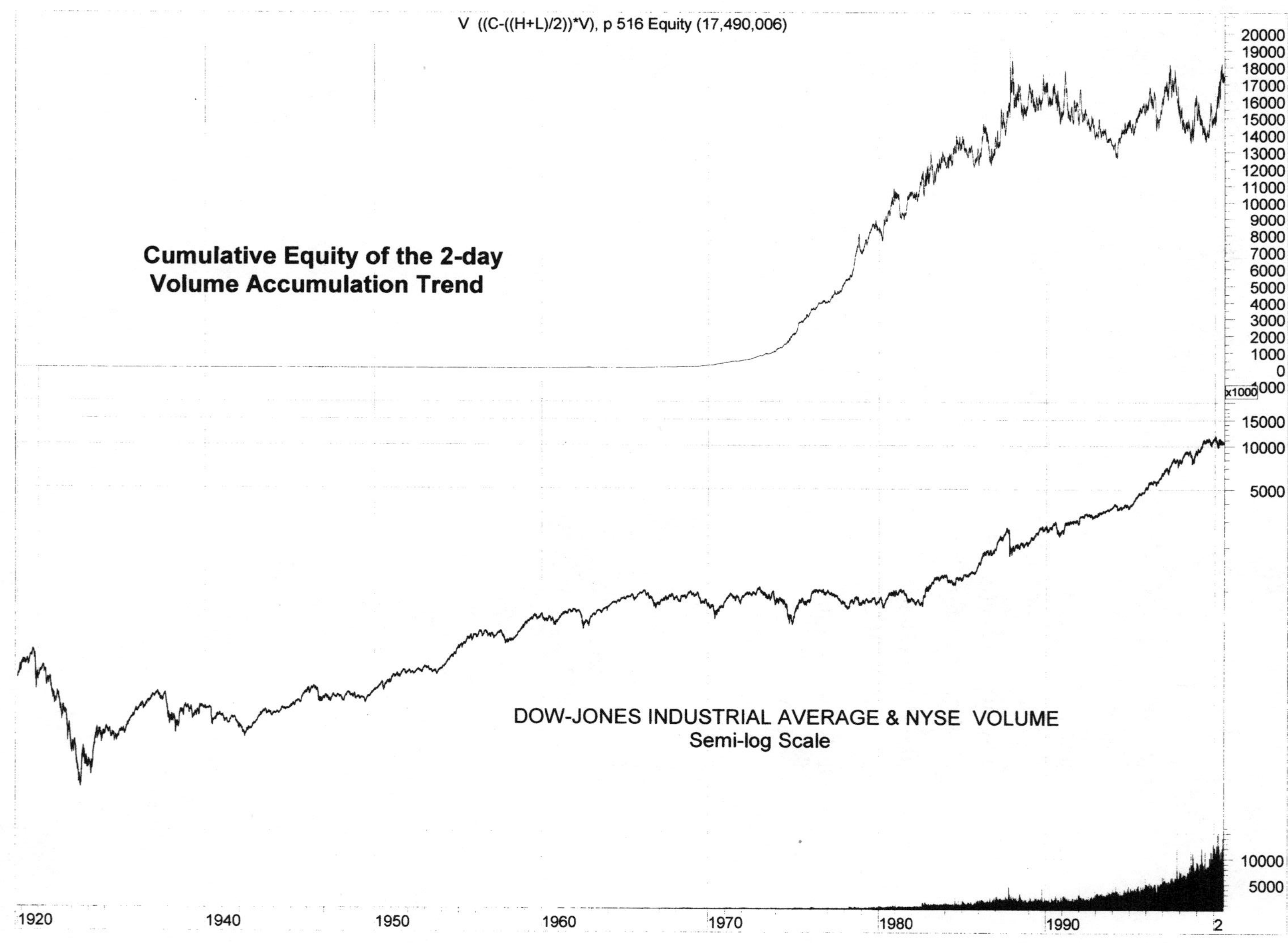
V ((C-((H+L)/2))*V), p 516 Equity (17,490,006)
Cumulative Equity of the 2-day
Volume Accumulation Trend
DOW-JONES INDUSTRIAL AVERAGE & NYSE VOLUME
Semi-log Scale
20000
19000
18000
17000
16000
15000
14000
13000
12000
11000
10000
9000
8000
7000
6000
5000
4000
3000
2000
1000
0
-1000
x1000
15000
10000
5000
10000
5000
1920
1940
1950
1960
1970
1980
1990
2

Volume Accumulation Oscillator and Trend

Total net profit	18863680	Open position value	0	Net Profit / Buy&Hold %	457807.44
Percent gain/loss	18863680	Annual percent gain/loss	259898.96	Annual Net % / B&H %	457791.05
Initial investment	100	Interest earned	0		
Current position	Long	Date position entered	4/12/01		
Buy/Hold profit	4119.54	Days in test	26492	# of days per trade	3.74
Buy/Hold pct gain/loss	4119.54	Annual B/H pct gain/loss	56.76		
Total closed trades	7074	Commissions paid	0		
Avg profit per trade	2666.62	Avg Win/Avg Loss ratio	1.33		
Total long trades	3537	Total short trades	3537	Long Win Trade %	49.22
Winning long trades	1741	Winning short trades	1484	Short Win Trade %	41.96
Total winning trades	3225	Total losing trades	3849	Total Win Trade %	45.59
Amount of winning trades	181530784	Amount of losing trades	−162667232	Net Profit Margin %	5.48
Average win	56288.62	Average loss	−42262.21	Average P. Margin %	14.23
Largest win	2881155	Largest loss	−1437708	% Net / (Win + Loss)	33.42
Average length of win	4.67	Average length of loss	2.66	(Win − Loss) / Loss %	75.56
Longest winning trade	23	Longest losing trade	14	(Win − Loss) / Loss %	64.29
Most consecutive wins	13	Most consecutive losses	15	(Win − Loss) / Loss %	−13.33
Total bars out	3	Average length out	3		
Longest out period	3				
System close drawdown	−78.15	Profit/Loss index	10.39	% Net Profit / SODD	24091545.34
System open drawdown	−78.3	Reward/Risk index	100	(Net P.-SODD)/Net P.	100.00
Max open trade drawdown	−1437708	Buy/Hold index	457807.21	% SODD / Net Profit	0.00

In the Equis MetaStock® "System Report" (profit and loss summary statistics), the *Total net profit* is the sum of profits minus the sum of losses, including open positions marked to the market. In contrast, the *Amount of Winning Trades* is the sum of realized profits (the total of all gains on closed-out trades only, excluding any open positions). Similarly, the *Amount of Losing Trades* is the sum of realized losses (the total of all losses on closed-out trades only, excluding any open positions). *System close drawdown* is the largest decline in the cumulative equity line below the initial investment, based on closed-out positions only. *System open drawdown (SODD)* is the largest decline in the cumulative equity line below the initial investment when a position is open. *Max open trade drawdown* is the largest decline in the cumulative equity line below the trade entry price during the worst single trade. The *Profit/Loss Index* is a complex calculation that relates the Amount of Winning Trades to the Amount of Losing Trades on a scale of −100 (worst possible performance) to +100 (best possible performance), with zero representing profits equal to losses. *Reward/Risk Index* is the Total net profit minus System open drawdown. The resulting difference is then divided by the Total net profit. The *Buy/Hold Index* is the Total net profit minus the buy-and-hold strategy's net profit. The resulting difference is then divided by the buy-and-hold net profit. In this exercise, initial equity is assumed to be $100. Both long and short positions are taken unless otherwise noted. Trades are executed at the closing price on the signal date. Transaction costs, interest expenses, and margins are not included in the statistics.

Volume: Cumulative Volume Index of Net Advancing Issues Minus Declining Issues

The Cumulative Volume Index is the running total of the daily differences between the Volume of Advancing Issues minus the Volume of Declining Issues. To calculate it, there are only two steps:

1. Compute daily net advancing volume by subtracting the Volume of Declining Issues from the Volume of Advancing Issues traded each day on the NYSE.
2. Add that daily net difference to the cumulative total of the daily net advancing volume as of the preceding day.

Historically, the interpretation of this indicator has been dependent on the chart reading skills of the technical analyst, who typically relies upon his judgements of trend, pattern, and divergence versus a stock price index, such as the S&P 500 or the DJIA.

Indicator Strategy Example for the Cumulative Volume Index

The Cumulative Volume Index can be an effective indicator viewed entirely objectively. Based on a 37-year file of daily data of the volume behind the number of shares advancing and declining each day on the NYSE and the DJIA, we found that the simplest possible trend-following rule would have produced a positive result on a purely mechanical signal basis with no subjectivity, no sophisticated technical analysis, and no judgement:

Enter Long (Buy) at the current daily price close of the DJIA when the Cumulative Volume Index rises relative to its level the previous day.

Close Long (Sell) at the current daily price close of the DJIA when the Cumulative Volume Index falls relative to its level the previous day.

Enter Short (Sell Short) at the current daily price close of the DJIA when the Cumulative Volume Index falls relative to its level the previous day.

Close Short (Cover) at the current daily price close of the DJIA when the Cumulative Volume Index rises relative to its level the previous day.

Starting with $100 and reinvesting profits, total net profits for this Cumulative Volume Index trend-following strategy would have been $852,743.19, assuming a fully invested strategy, reinvestment of profits, no transactions costs, and no taxes. This would have been 66,357.02% better than buy-and-hold. Short selling would have been profitable, but not since the bottom of 8/12/82. Trading would have been hyperactive with one trade every 3.59 calendar days. (See chart on page 760.)

The Equis International MetaStock® System Testing rules, where the current Cumulative Volume Index is inserted into the data field normally reserved for Volume (V), are written as follows:

Enter long: V > Ref(V,-1)

Close long: V < Ref(V,-1)

Enter short: V < Ref(V,-1)

Close short: V > Ref(V,-1)

Volume: Cumulative Volume Ratio

The Cumulative Volume Index, more often than not, produces a line with an upward bias. This is because it does not adjust for distortions that tend to inflate volume over time, namely, the ever growing number of issues listed, numerous stock splits, and derivatives arbitrage trading. To adjust the data in order to gain comparability, we could try the following transformation of the daily data before cumulating net volume in a running total:

$$V = (A - D) / (A + D)$$

where

V = today's 1-day Volume Index
A = Volume of Advancing Issues
D = Volume of Declining Issues

Curiously, this formula produces a chart line with a downward bias that is more misleading than the upward bias of the more popular Cumulative Volume Index. The reason behind these biases is that stocks tend to rise on high volume and fall on low volume. As the old saying goes, "It takes volume to push stocks higher, but they fall of their own weight."

Volume of Issues, Advancing

The volume of advancing issues is the total volume of advancing stocks, those stocks that end the current day at a higher price than their previous day's closing price. Data for the New York Stock Exchange is used most frequently, and data for the NASDAQ and American Stock Exchange is also widely available. Advancing volume offers an indication of buying pressure: it is bullish when advancing volume (or a moving

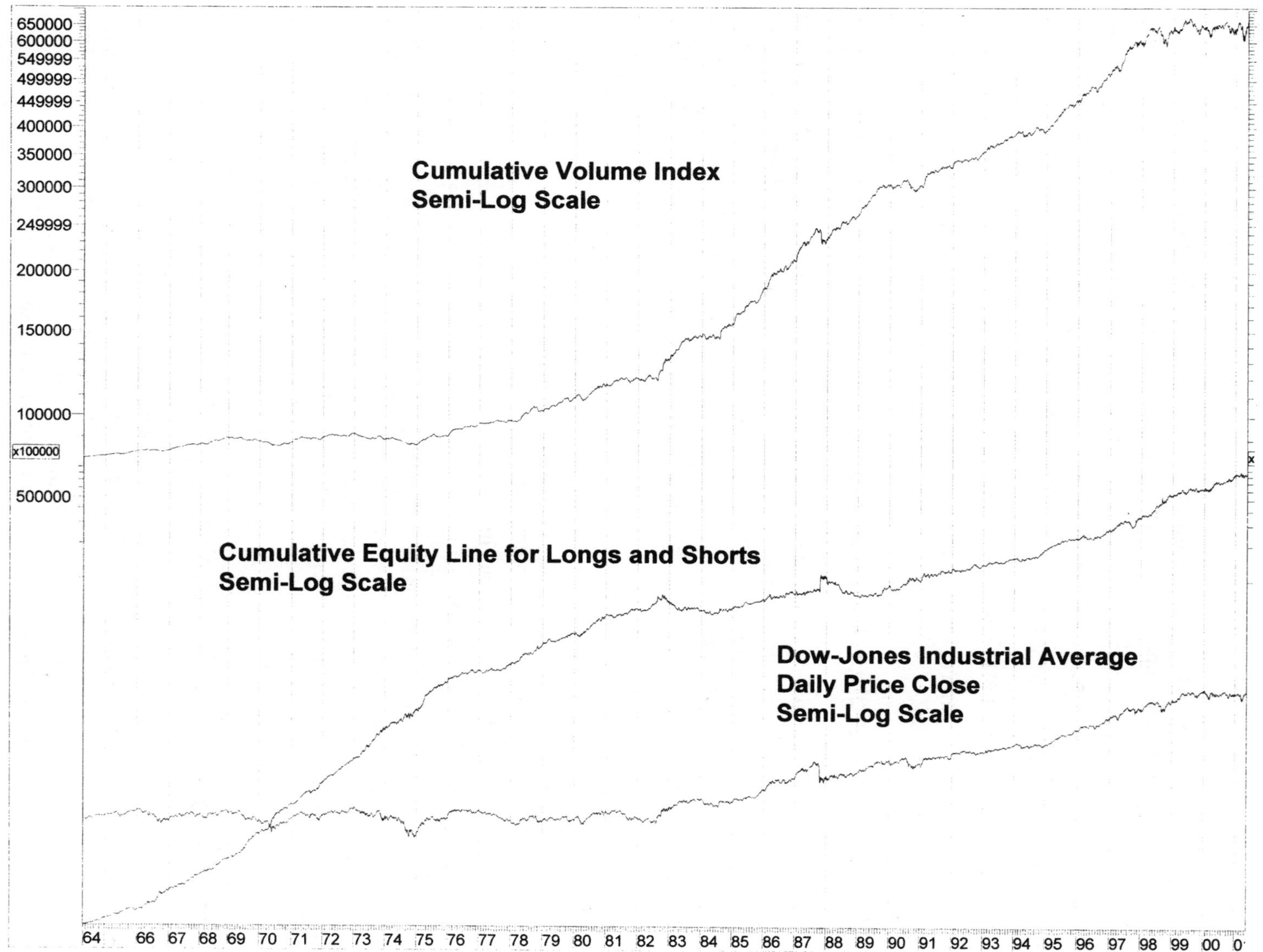

650000
600000
549999
499999
449999
400000
350000
300000
249999
200000
150000
100000
x100000
500000
Cumulative Volume Index
Semi-Log Scale
Cumulative Equity Line for Longs and Shorts
Semi-Log Scale
Dow-Jones Industrial Average
Daily Price Close
Semi-Log Scale
64
66
67
68
69
70
71
72
73
74
75
76
77
78
79
80
81
82
83
84
85
86
87
88
89
90
91
92
93
94
95
96
97
98
99
00
0

Cumulative Volume Index

Total net profit	852743.19	Open position value	32025.89	Net Profit / Buy&Hold %	66357.02
Percent gain/loss	852743.19	Annual percent gain/loss	23001.13	Annual Net % / B&H %	66358.05
Initial investment	100	Interest earned	0		
Current position	Long	Date position entered	5/14/01		
Buy/Hold profit	1283.15	Days in test	13532	# of days per trade	3.59
Buy/Hold pct gain/loss	1283.15	Annual B/H pct gain/loss	34.61		
Total closed trades	3772	Commissions paid	0		
Avg profit per trade	217.58	Avg Win/Avg Loss ratio	1.59		
Total long trades	1886	Total short trades	1886	Long Win Trade %	47.88
Winning long trades	903	Winning short trades	858	Short Win Trade %	45.49
Total winning trades	1761	Total losing trades	2011	Total Win Trade %	46.69
Amount of winning trades	2915657.25	Amount of losing trades	−2094938.5	Net Profit Margin %	16.38
Average win	1655.68	Average loss	−1041.74	Average P. Margin %	22.76
Largest win	42574.19	Largest loss	−27290.38	% Net / (Win + Loss)	21.88
Average length of win	4.57	Average length of loss	2.51	(Win − Loss) / Loss %	82.07
Longest winning trade	24	Longest losing trade	10	(Win − Loss) / Loss %	140.00
Most consecutive wins	11	Most consecutive losses	11	(Win − Loss) / Loss %	0.00
Total bars out	2	Average length out	2		
Longest out period	2				
System close drawdown	−0.14	Profit/Loss index	28.93	% Net Profit / SODD	609102278.57
System open drawdown	−0.14	Reward/Risk index	100	(Net P.-SODD)/Net P.	100.00
Max open trade drawdown	−27290.38	Buy/Hold index	68853.01	% SODD / Net Profit	0.00

In the Equis MetaStock® "System Report" (profit and loss summary statistics), the *Total net profit* is the sum of profits minus the sum of losses, including open positions marked to the market. In contrast, the *Amount of Winning Trades* is the sum of realized profits (the total of all gains on closed-out trades only, excluding any open positions). Similarly, the *Amount of Losing Trades* is the sum of realized losses (the total of all losses on closed-out trades only, excluding any open positions). *System close drawdown* is the largest decline in the cumulative equity line below the initial investment, based on closed-out positions only. *System open drawdown (SODD)* is the largest decline in the cumulative equity line below the initial investment when a position is open. *Max open trade drawdown* is the largest decline in the cumulative equity line below the trade entry price during the worst single trade. The *Profit/Loss Index* is a complex calculation that relates the Amount of Winning Trades to the Amount of Losing Trades on a scale of −100 (worst possible performance) to +100 (best possible performance), with zero representing profits equal to losses. *Reward/Risk Index* is the Total net profit minus System open drawdown. The resulting difference is then divided by the Total net profit. The *Buy/Hold Index* is the Total net profit minus the buy-and-hold strategy's net profit. The resulting difference is then divided by the buy-and-hold net profit. In this exercise, initial equity is assumed to be $100. Both long and short positions are taken unless otherwise noted. Trades are executed at the closing price on the signal date. Transaction costs, interest expenses, and margins are not included in the statistics.

average of advancing volume) rises; it is bearish when advancing volume falls. Advancing volume is most often used as a component of another indicator, such as Cumulative Volume Index, Arms' Short-Term Trading Index, Ninety Percent Days, and Upside/Downside Volume Ratio.

Volume of Issues, Declining

The volume of declining issues is the total volume of declining stocks, those stocks that end the current day at a lower price than their previous day's closing price. Declining volume offers an indication of selling pressure: it is bearish when declining volume (or a moving average of declining volume) rises; it is bullish when declining volume falls. Coupled with Advancing volume, Declining volume is most often used as a component of another indicator.

Volume: Klinger Oscillator (KO)

This volume-based oscillator was developed by Stephen J. Klinger. It is computed in seven steps:

1. Find the average price of the day by summing the high, low, and close, then dividing by three.
2. If today's average price is greater than the previous day's average price, assign a plus sign to today's volume.
3. If today's average price is less than the previous day's average price, assign a minus sign to today's volume.
4. Calculate a 34-period period exponential moving average of the signed volume from Steps 2 and 3.
5. Calculate a 55-period exponential moving average of the signed volume from Steps 2 and 3.
6. Subtract the 34-period exponential moving average from the 55-period exponential moving average, and plot this difference.
7. Calculate and plot a 13-period exponential moving average of the daily differences from Step 6.

When today's average price is greater than yesterday's average price, that is defined as *accumulation.* Conversely, when today's average price is less than yesterday's average price, that is defined as *distribution.* When the sums are equal, the forces of demand and supply are considered to be in balance. The average difference between the number of shares being accumulated and distributed each day is defined as the *volume force.* A rising trend of volume force is bullish, while a falling trend of volume force is bearish. The Klinger Oscillator also is compared to price to identify divergences.

Indicator Strategy Example for Klinger Oscillator

Based on a 18-year file of daily data for the entire history of the S&P 500 Composite Stock Price Index Futures *CSI Perpetual Contract* from 4/21/82 to 12/29/00 collected from www.csidata.com, we found that the following parameters would have produced below-average results on a purely mechanical overbought/oversold signal basis with no subjectivity, no sophisticated technical analysis, and no judgement:

Enter Long (Buy) at the current daily price close of the S&P 500 Composite Stock Price Index futures *CSI Perpetual Contract* when the current Klinger Oscillator (using the standard parameters, above) crosses above its own trailing 2-day EMA computed as of the previous day's close.

Close Long (Sell) at the current daily price close of the S&P 500 Composite Stock Price Index futures *CSI Perpetual Contract* when the current Klinger Oscillator (using the standard parameters, above) crosses below its own trailing 2-day EMA computed as of the previous day's close.

Enter Short (Sell Short) never.

Starting with $100 and reinvesting profits, total net profits would have been $261.46, assuming a fully invested strategy, reinvestment of profits, no transactions costs, and no taxes. This would have been 74.73 percent less than buy-and-hold. No short selling would have been profitable, and no short selling was included in the strategy. The long-only Klinger Oscillator as an indicator would have given profitable buy signals 46.30% of the time. Trading would have been active at one trade every 10.10 calendar days. This long-only Klinger Oscillator trend-following strategy got caught long at the wrong time in the crash of 1987, suffering an unusually large equity drawdown, as the chart clearly shows. Obviously, relatively low profitability with high equity drawdown make an unfavorable combination.

The Equis International MetaStock® System Testing rules are written as follows:

Enter long: KVO()>Ref(Mov(KVO(),opt1,E),-1)

Close long: KVO()<Ref(Mov(KVO(),opt1,E),-1)

OPT1 Current value: 2

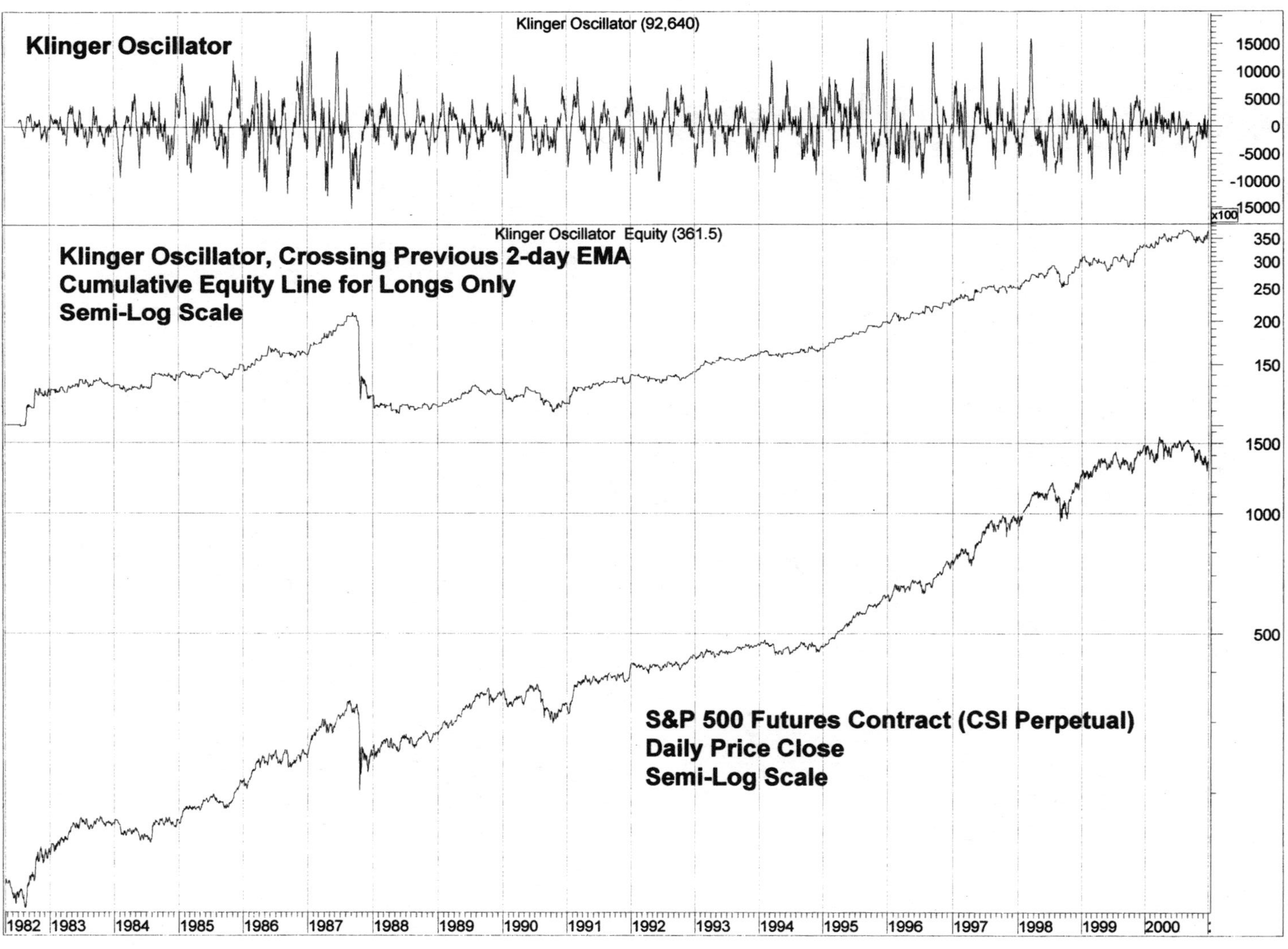

Klinger Oscillator
Klinger Oscillator (92,640)
15000
10000
5000
0
-5000
-10000
-15000
x100
Klinger Oscillator Equity (361.5)
Klinger Oscillator, Crossing Previous 2-day EMA
Cumulative Equity Line for Longs Only
Semi-Log Scale
350
300
250
200
150
1500
1000
500
S&P 500 Futures Contract (CSI Perpetual)
Daily Price Close
Semi-Log Scale
1982
1983
1984
1985
1986
1987
1988
1989
1990
1991
1992
1993
1994
1995
1996
1997
1998
1999
2000

Klinger Oscillator, Cross Previous 2-day EMA

Total net profit	261.46	Open position value	12.74	Net Profit / Buy&Hold %	−74.73
Percent gain/loss	261.46	Annual percent gain/loss	13.98	Annual Net % / B&H %	−74.72
Initial investment	100	Interest earned	0		
Current position	Long	Date position entered	12/21/00		
Buy/Hold profit	1034.49	Days in test	6828	# of days per trade	10.10
Buy/Hold pct gain/loss	1034.49	Annual B/H pct gain/loss	55.3		
Total closed trades	676	Commissions paid	0		
Avg profit per trade	0.37	Avg Win/Avg Loss ratio	1.57		
Total long trades	676	Total short trades	0	Long Win Trade %	46.30
Winning long trades	313	Winning short trades	0	Short Win Trade %	#DIV/0!
Total winning trades	313	Total losing trades	363	Total Win Trade %	46.30
Amount of winning trades	949.18	Amount of losing trades	−700.45	Net Profit Margin %	15.08
Average win	3.03	Average loss	−1.93	Average P. Margin %	22.18
Largest win	17.3	Largest loss	−55.62	% Net / (Win + Loss)	−52.55
Average length of win	5.84	Average length of loss	3.09	(Win − Loss) / Loss %	89.00
Longest winning trade	13	Longest losing trade	14	(Win − Loss) / Loss %	−7.14
Most consecutive wins	10	Most consecutive losses	9	(Win − Loss) / Loss %	11.11
Total bars out	3127	Average length out	4.62		
Longest out period	59				
System close drawdown	−0.97	Profit/Loss index	27.18	% Net Profit / SODD	26954.64
System open drawdown	−0.97	Reward/Risk index	99.63	(Net P.-SODD)/Net P.	99.63
Max open trade drawdown	−55.62	Buy/Hold index	−73.49	% SODD / Net Profit	−0.37

In the Equis MetaStock® "System Report" (profit and loss summary statistics), the *Total net profit* is the sum of profits minus the sum of losses, including open positions marked to the market. In contrast, the *Amount of Winning Trades* is the sum of realized profits (the total of all gains on closed-out trades only, excluding any open positions). Similarly, the *Amount of Losing Trades* is the sum of realized losses (the total of all losses on closed-out trades only, excluding any open positions). *System close drawdown* is the largest decline in the cumulative equity line below the initial investment, based on closed-out positions only. *System open drawdown (SODD)* is the largest decline in the cumulative equity line below the initial investment when a position is open. *Max open trade drawdown* is the largest decline in the cumulative equity line below the trade entry price during the worst single trade. The *Profit/Loss Index* is a complex calculation that relates the Amount of Winning Trades to the Amount of Losing Trades on a scale of −100 (worst possible performance) to +100 (best possible performance), with zero representing profits equal to losses. *Reward/Risk Index* is the Total net profit minus System open drawdown. The resulting difference is then divided by the Total net profit. The *Buy/Hold Index* is the Total net profit minus the buy-and-hold strategy's net profit. The resulting difference is then divided by the buy-and-hold net profit. In this exercise, initial equity is assumed to be $100. Both long and short positions are taken unless otherwise noted. Trades are executed at the closing price on the signal date. Transaction costs, interest expenses, and margins are not included in the statistics.

Volume: New York Stock Exchange versus Over-the-Counter

The smoothed ratio of the weekly volume on the NYSE divided by the volume Over-the-Counter is interpreted as an indicator of serious investment activity compared to speculative fever.

The stocks listed on the NYSE generally are considered to be more conservative, since they represent ownership shares in more seasoned, mature companies. In contrast, the stocks traded Over-the-Counter generally are considered to be more speculative and risky, since they represent ownership shares in younger, sometimes untested companies that may not have experienced many up and down business cycles. Of course, there are exceptions to these generalities, but they hold more often than not.

Ned Davis Research found that modestly above-average returns would have been gained for long trades only if we buy when the smoothed NYSE/OTC Volume Ratio rises above 102.12%, indicating a cautious, "quality" investment psychology, and then sell our long position when the NYSE/OTC Volume Ratio falls below 96.35%, indicating an excessively "speculative" mass mood.

Volume: On-Balance Volume (OBV)

On-Balance Volume (OBV) is a price and volume trend quantification popularized by Joseph E. Granville, author of *A New Strategy of Daily Stock Market Timing for Maximum Profit,* Prentice-Hall, Englewood Cliffs, NJ, 1976. It is easy to calculate: if the price close today is above the close yesterday, then the entire day's volume is assigned a plus sign; but if the price close today is below the close yesterday, then the entire day's volume is assigned a minus sign. Note that it does not matter how much the price changes today, a penny or ten dollars. Only the direction of the price change, up or down, determines the plus or minus sign assigned to the entire day's volume. Each day's OBV is cumulated in a running total that can be compared visually to the graph of the pure price trend for confirmation or divergence.

Mathematically, today's OBV input before cumulating can be computed as follows:

$$OBV = ((C-P) / | C-P |) * V$$

where

C = the current period's closing price.
P = the previous period's closing price.
| C-P | = the absolute value of the difference between the two closing prices.
V = the current period's volume.

Dow Jones Industrial Average
Weekly Data 6/01/79 - 5/22/98 (Log Scale)
Profitable Trades: 76%
Gain/Annum: 14.8%
Buy-Hold Gain/Annum: 13.5%
Latest Signal 9/13/96 = 5838.52
5/22/98 = 9114.44
Signals Generated When Volume Ratio:
Rises Above 102.12 = Buy
Falls Below 96.35 = Sell
9774
8421
7255
6251
5385
4640
3998
3444
2967
2557
2203
1898
1635
1409
1214
1046
901
776
669
1980 1981 1982 1983 1984 1985 1986 1987 1988 1989 1990 1991 1992 1993 1994 1995 1996 1997 1998
Relative Quality Volume
Relative Speculative Volume
5/22/98 = 97.66
(16/22-Week Smoothing)
108
107
106
105
104
103
102
101
100
99
98
97
96
95
94
93
92
91
90
89
(S523)
NYSE Volume / OTC Volume

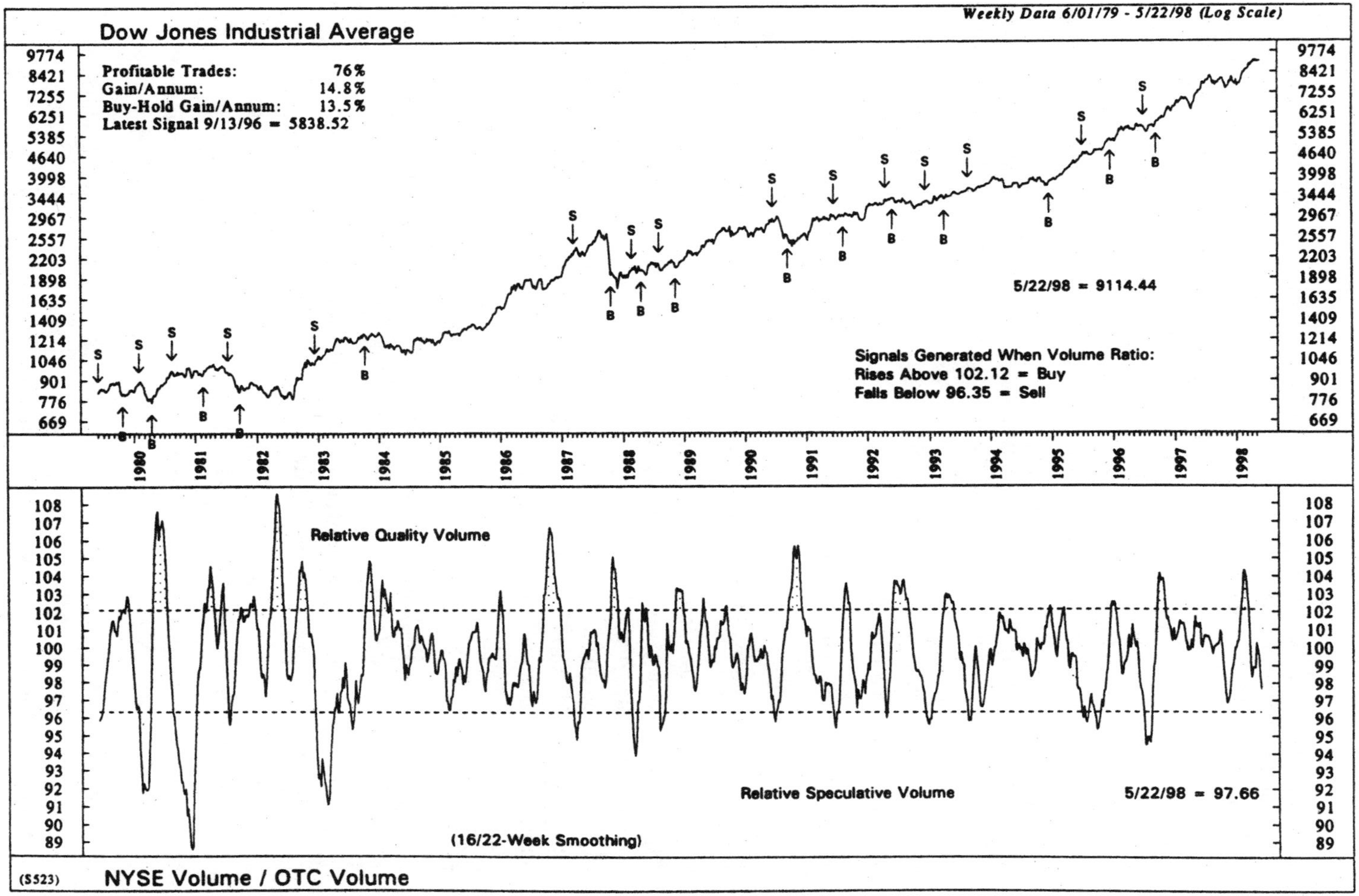

Chart by permission of Ned Davis Research.

Since any positive number divided by the absolute value of itself is one, the expression in parentheses serves only to determine the sign, plus or minus. Thus, if the current period's price change is positive (rising), with C greater than P, volume is assigned a plus sign for the period. But if C is less than P, the price has fallen and volume is assigned a minus sign for that period.

The cumulative running total of daily OBV respects the daily OBV plus or minus sign. This results in a cumulative OBV line that rises every day that price rises and that falls every day that price falls. The day's volume determines the amount of this rise or fall.

There are a variety of ways to analyze OBV using all the technical tools of trend assessment, overbought/oversold oscillators, and divergence analysis. By far the simplest way is to use a computer to find an objective trend-following decision rule.

The Equis International MetaStock® Indicator Builder formula for plotting Cumulative OBV is written as follows:

```
(If(C>Ref(C,-1),1,-1)*V)+PREV
```

Indicator Strategy Example for On-Balance Volume

Historical data shows that OBV is one of the better volume-based indicators. It beat buy-and-hold strategy by an extremely large margin. Still, it is a slightly less effective indicator than the *Volume * Price Momentum Oscillator (V*PMO),* particularly on the short side. Based on the number of shares traded each day on the NYSE and the daily prices for the DJIA for 72 years from 1928 to 2001, we found that the following parameters would have produced a positive result on a purely mechanical trend-following signal basis with no subjectivity, no sophisticated technical analysis, and no judgement:

Enter Long (Buy) at the current daily price close of the DJIA when the cumulative OBV line crosses above its previous day's 3-day EMA.

Close Long (Sell) at the current daily price close of the DJIA when the cumulative OBV line crosses below its previous day's 3-day EMA.

Enter Short (Sell Short) at the current daily price close of the DJIA when the cumulative OBV line crosses below its previous day's 3-day EMA.

Close Short (Cover) at the current daily price close of the DJIA when the cumulative OBV line crosses above its previous day's 3-day EMA.

Starting with $100 and reinvesting profits, total net profits for this OBV strategy would have been $47,999,352, assuming a fully invested strategy, reinvestment of profits, no transactions costs, and no taxes. This would have been 1,165,062.91

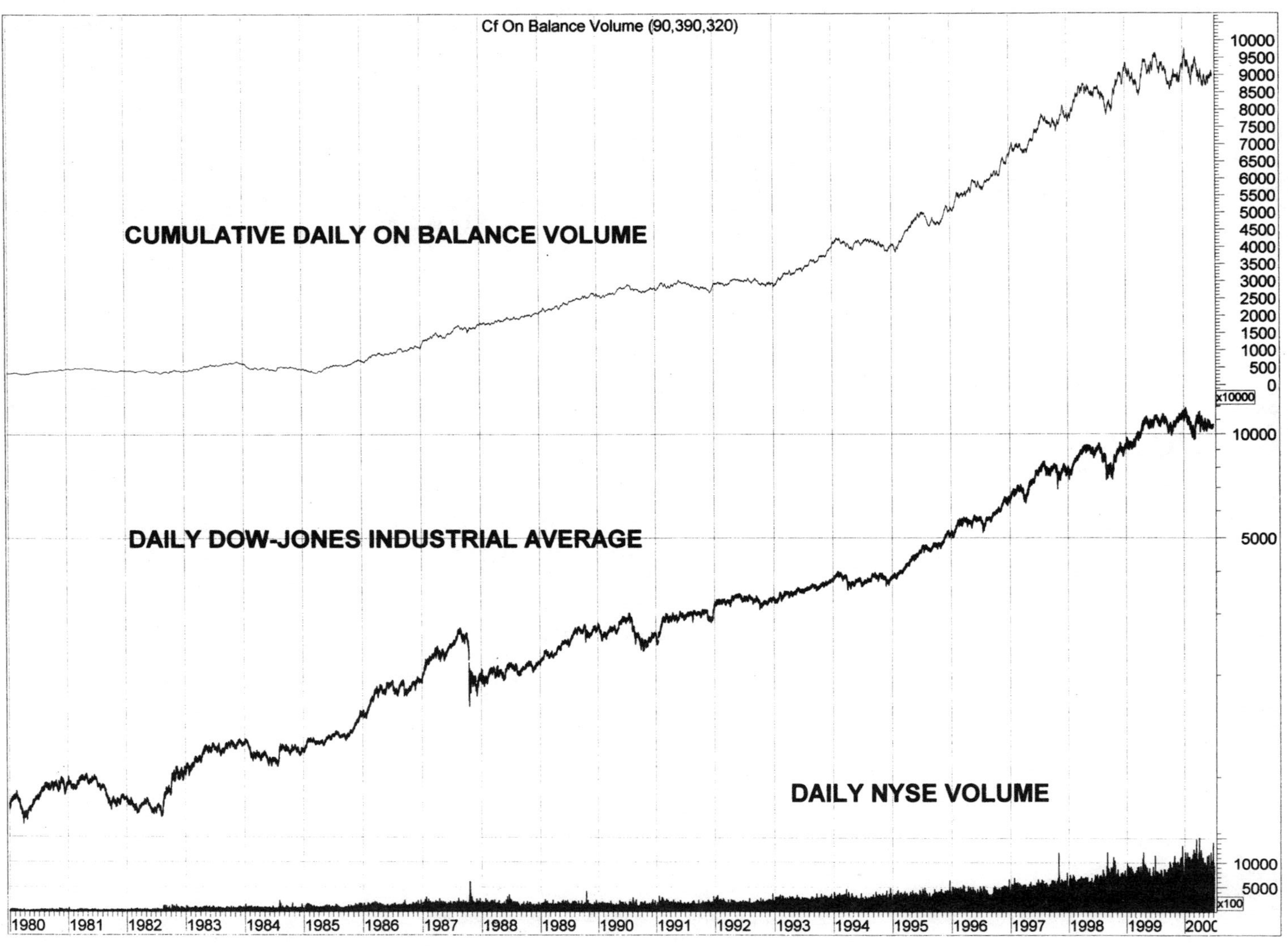

Cf On Balance Volume (90,390,320)
CUMULATIVE DAILY ON BALANCE VOLUME
DAILY DOW-JONES INDUSTRIAL AVERAGE
DAILY NYSE VOLUME
10000
9500
9000
8500
8000
7500
7000
6500
6000
5500
5000
4500
4000
3500
3000
2500
2000
1500
1000
500
0
x10000
10000
5000
10000
5000
x100
1980
1981
1982
1983
1984
1985
1986
1987
1988
1989
1990
1991
1992
1993
1994
1995
1996
1997
1998
1999
200C

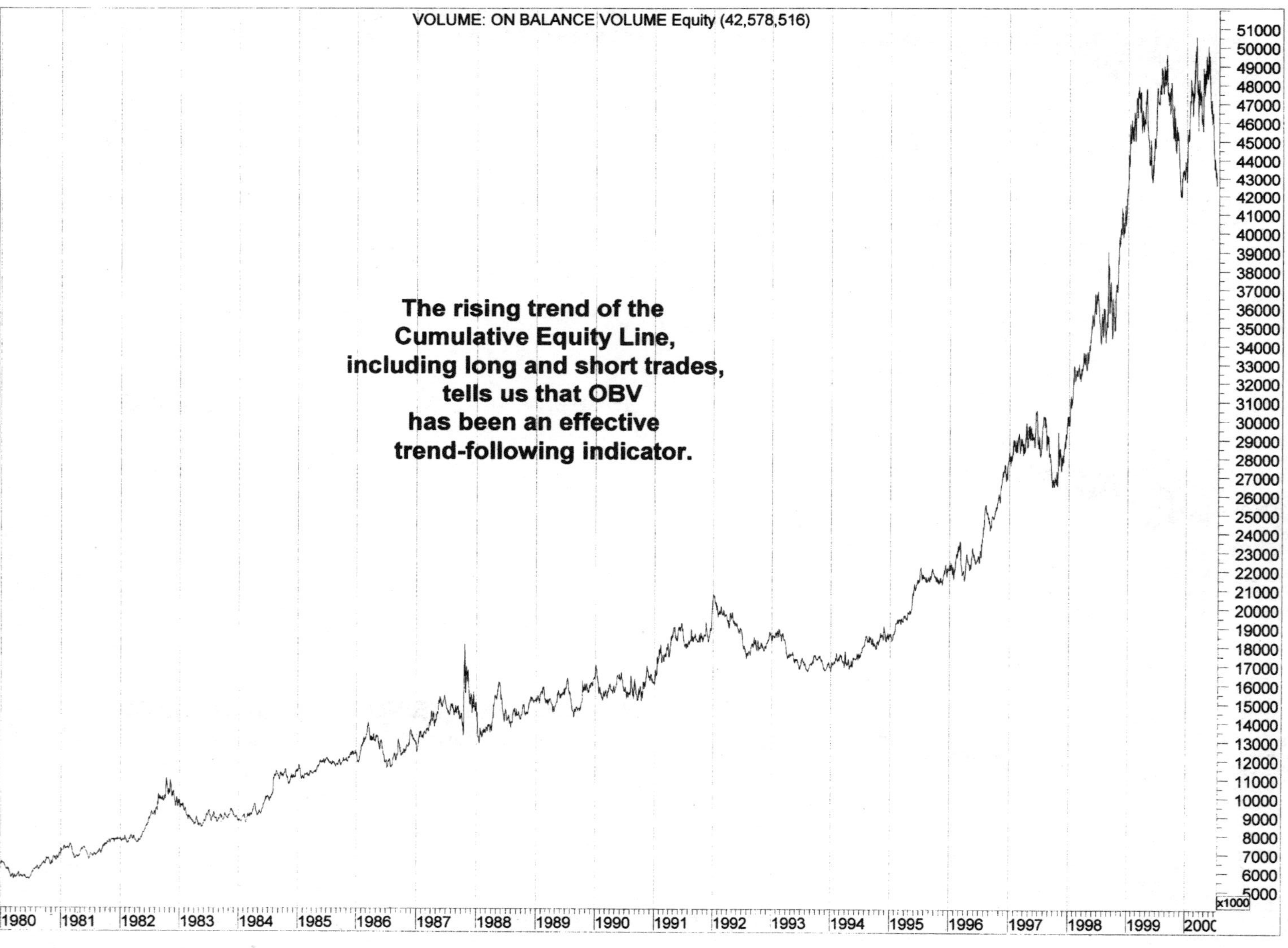
VOLUME: ON BALANCE VOLUME Equity (42,578,516)
The rising trend of the
Cumulative Equity Line,
including long and short trades,
tells us that OBV
has been an effective
trend-following indicator.
x1000
1980
1981
1982
1983
1984
1985
1986
1987
1988
1989
1990
1991
1992
1993
1994
1995
1996
1997
1998
1999
2000

Volume: OBV Cross EMA 3-day

Total net profit	47999352	Open position value	0	Net Profit / Buy&Hold %	1165062.91
Percent gain/loss	47999352	Annual percent gain/loss	661322.79	Annual Net % / B&H %	1165021.19
Initial investment	100	Interest earned	0		
Current position	Long	Date position entered	4/12/01		
Buy/Hold profit	4119.54	Days in test	26492	# of days per trade	3.50
Buy/Hold pct gain/loss	4119.54	Annual B/H pct gain/loss	56.76		
Total closed trades	7564	Commissions paid	0		
Avg profit per trade	6345.76	Avg Win/Avg Loss ratio	1.86		
Total long trades	3782	Total short trades	3782	Long Win Trade %	43.47
Winning long trades	1644	Winning short trades	1349	Short Win Trade %	35.67
Total winning trades	2993	Total losing trades	4571	Total Win Trade %	39.57
Amount of winning trades	270331232	Amount of losing trades	−222332048	Net Profit Margin %	9.74
Average win	90321.16	Average loss	−48639.7	Average P. Margin %	30.00
Largest win	3141108	Largest loss	−1480628	% Net / (Win + Loss)	35.93
Average length of win	4.95	Average length of loss	2.4	(Win − Loss) / Loss %	106.25
Longest winning trade	20	Longest losing trade	9	(Win − Loss) / Loss %	122.22
Most consecutive wins	13	Most consecutive losses	18	(Win − Loss) / Loss %	−27.78
Total bars out	5	Average length out	5		
Longest out period	5				
System close drawdown	−47.12	Profit/Loss index	17.76	% Net Profit / SODD	101866196.94
System open drawdown	−47.12	Reward/Risk index	100	(Net P.-SODD)/Net P.	100.00
Max open trade drawdown	−1480628	Buy/Hold index	1165062.34	% SODD / Net Profit	0.00

In the Equis MetaStock® "System Report" (profit and loss summary statistics), the *Total net profit* is the sum of profits minus the sum of losses, including open positions marked to the market. In contrast, the *Amount of Winning Trades* is the sum of realized profits (the total of all gains on closed-out trades only, excluding any open positions). Similarly, the *Amount of Losing Trades* is the sum of realized losses (the total of all losses on closed-out trades only, excluding any open positions). *System close drawdown* is the largest decline in the cumulative equity line below the initial investment, based on closed-out positions only. *System open drawdown (SODD)* is the largest decline in the cumulative equity line below the initial investment when a position is open. *Max open trade drawdown* is the largest decline in the cumulative equity line below the trade entry price during the worst single trade. The *Profit/Loss Index* is a complex calculation that relates the Amount of Winning Trades to the Amount of Losing Trades on a scale of −100 (worst possible performance) to +100 (best possible performance), with zero representing profits equal to losses. *Reward/Risk Index* is the Total net profit minus System open drawdown. The resulting difference is then divided by the Total net profit. The *Buy/Hold Index* is the Total net profit minus the buy-and-hold strategy's net profit. The resulting difference is then divided by the buy-and-hold net profit. In this exercise, initial equity is assumed to be $100. Both long and short positions are taken unless otherwise noted. Trades are executed at the closing price on the signal date. Transaction costs, interest expenses, and margins are not included in the statistics.

percent better than buy-and-hold. In contrast to most other volume-based indicators, OBV would have been significantly profitable since the Crash of '87, despite losses on unprofitable short sales in a record-breaking bull market. Not surprisingly, short sales would have been extremely unprofitable since 1982, while long-only trades would have been very profitable. Trading would have been hyperactive at one trade every 3.50 calendar days.

The Equis International MetaStock® System Testing rules are written as follows:

Enter long: OBV()>Ref(Mov(OBV(),opt1,E),-1)

Close long: OBV()<Ref(Mov(OBV(),opt1,E),-1)

Enter short: OBV()<Ref(Mov(OBV(),opt1,E),-1)

Close short: OBV()>Ref(Mov(OBV(),opt1,E),-1)

OPT1 Current value: 3

Volume Oscillator

Oscillators are effective in organizing, or *taming,* wild and raw market data for use in a systematic trading strategy or investment timing model. For example, we found that a 220-day EMA of Volume can be used to define active or inactive trading activity. By calculating the *percentage* deviation of volume from its 220-day trend, and graphing it, we can visually grasp *exactly how much* trading activity is above or below normal.

For example, we can readily comprehend with a glance at the following chart when stock turnover is, say, 50% above or below normal. Simply subtract from current volume its own trailing 220-day EMA, divide that difference by the 220-day EMA, then multiply that ratio by 100 in order to convert the ratio fraction to a percentage, as shown in the following Equis MetaStock® Indicator Builder formula:

```
(V-(Ref(Mov(V,220,E),-1)))
/(Ref(Mov(V,220,E),-1))*100;
Input("Plot a horizontal line at",-0.25,0.25,0);
```

where

V = the total volume of trading activity for the period.

(Ref(Mov(V,220,E),-1) = the previous day's 220-day EMA of Volume.

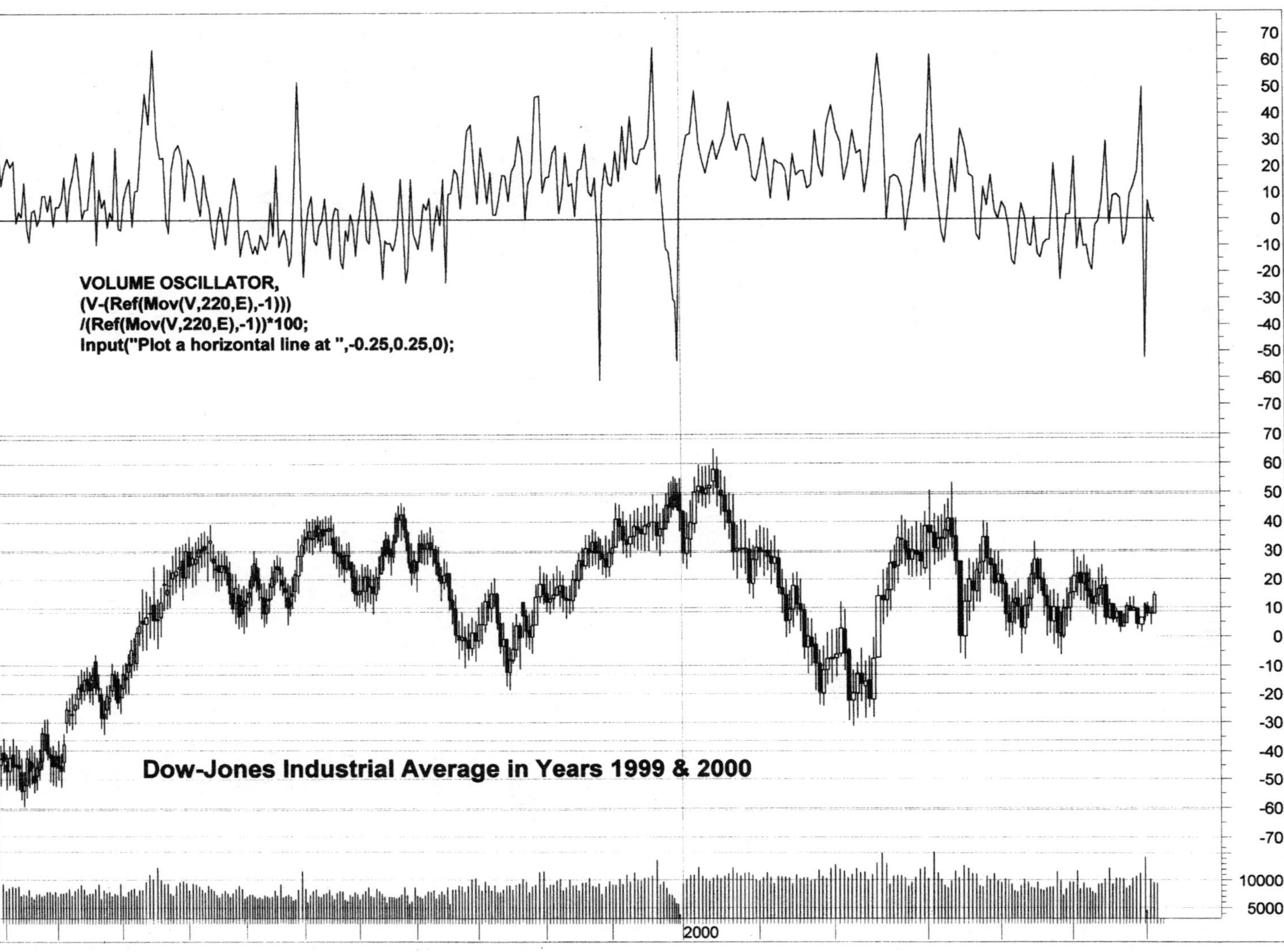
VOLUME OSCILLATOR,
(V-(Ref(Mov(V,220,E),-1)))
/(Ref(Mov(V,220,E),-1))*100;
Input("Plot a horizontal line at ",-0.25,0.25,0);
Dow-Jones Industrial Average in Years 1999 & 2000
2000

Volume * Price Momentum Oscillator (V*PMO)

Volume * Price Momentum Oscillator (V*PMO) is a price *and* volume momentum oscillator. Before applying a smoothing, the basic input value of a 1-day V*PMO is expressed as follows:

Today's Input Value for V*PMO = V * P

where

V = today's volume.

P = today's price change, close minus the previous day's close.

For example, if today's price change is a decline of 4 points and today's volume is 200, then today's V*PMO input value is −800.

Next, compute an exponential moving average of these daily price changes multiplied by volume. This smoothes the erratic daily data enough to allow us to plot a momentum oscillator useful for system development and, possibly, useful for subjective interpretation, including divergence analysis.

As with simple momentum indicators generally, when the *n*-period exponential moving average of V*PMO is positive, momentum is bullish, so we buy, entering or initiating a long position. But when the *n*-period exponential moving average of V*PMO is negative, we close out long positions and enter a short position.

Indicator Strategy Example for the Volume * Price Momentum Oscillator (V*PMO)

Historical data shows that the Volume * Price Momentum Oscillator (V*PMO) would have been an effective indicator, particularly on the long side. Based on the number of shares traded each day on the NYSE and the daily prices for the DJIA for 72 years from 1928 to 2001, we found that the following parameters would have produced a significantly positive result on a purely mechanical trend-following signal basis with no subjectivity, no sophisticated technical analysis, and no judgement:

Enter Long (Buy) at the current daily price close of the DJIA when the 3-day EMA of the daily V*PMO is greater than zero.

Close Long (Sell) at the current daily price close of the DJIA when the 3-day EMA of the daily V*PMO is less than zero.

Enter Short (Sell Short) at the current daily price close of the DJIA when the 3-day EMA of the daily V*PMO is less than zero.

Close Short (Cover) at the current daily price close of the DJIA when the 3-day EMA of the V*PMO is greater than zero.

Starting with $100 and reinvesting profits, total net profits for the Volume * Price Momentum Oscillator (V*PMO) strategy would have been $ 61,609,220, assuming a fully invested strategy, reinvestment of profits, no transactions costs, and no taxes. This would have been 1,495,436.39% better than the passive buy-and-hold strategy. Short selling would have been profitable over the full 72 years but unprofitable since December 1985. Trading would have been hyperactive at one trade every 5.29 calendar days.

The Equis International MetaStock® System Testing rules are written as follows:

Enter long: Mov((C-Ref(C,-1))*V,opt1,E)>0

Close long: Mov((C-Ref(C,-1))*V,opt1,E)<0

Enter short: Mov((C-Ref(C,-1))*V,opt1,E)<0

Close short: Mov((C-Ref(C,-1))*V,opt1,E)>0

OPT1 Current value: 3

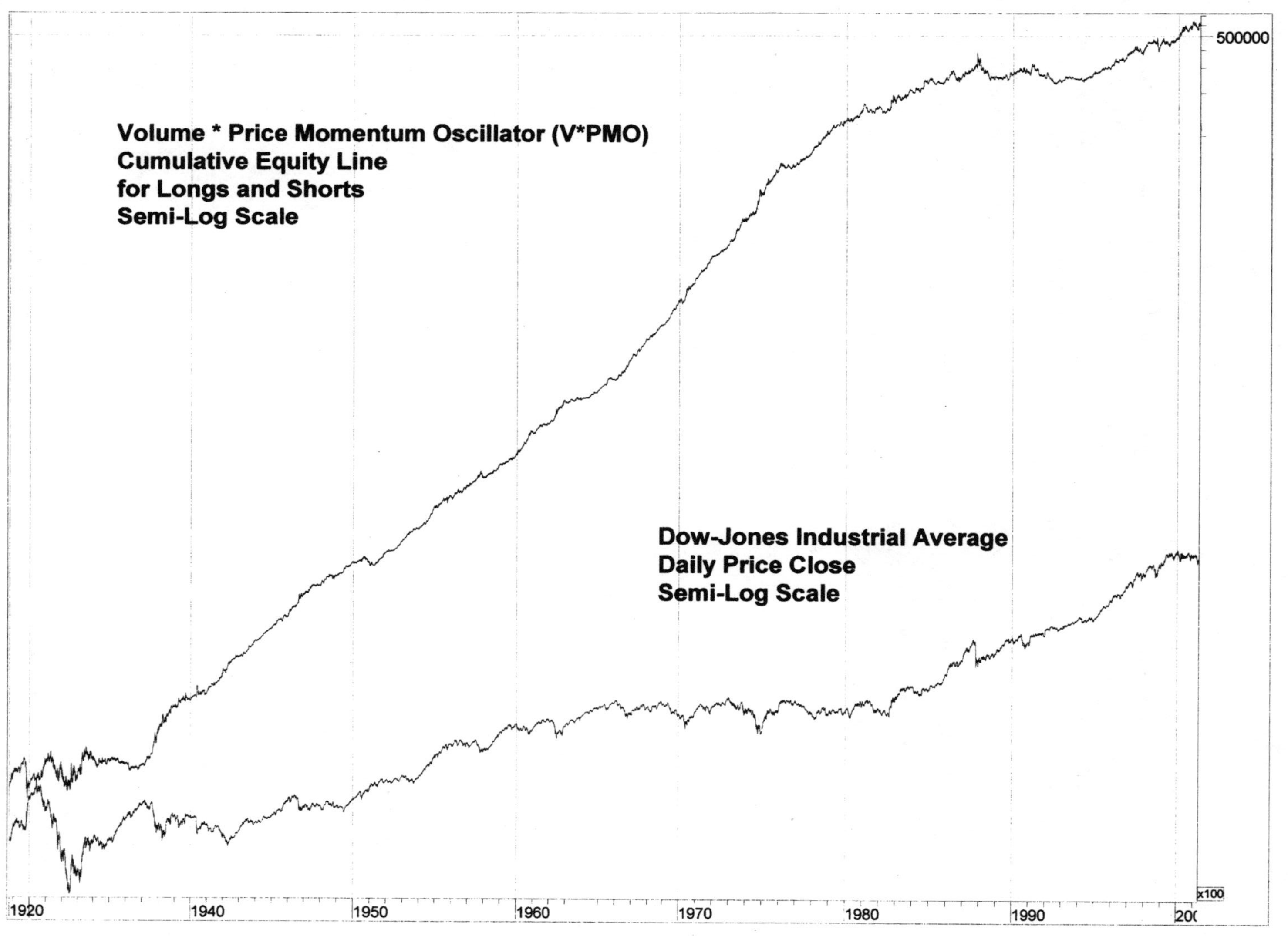

Volume * Price Momentum Oscillator (V*PMO)
Cumulative Equity Line
for Longs and Shorts
Semi-Log Scale
Dow-Jones Industrial Average
Daily Price Close
Semi-Log Scale
500000
x100
1920
1940
1950
1960
1970
1980
1990
20(

Volume * Price Momentum Oscillator (V*PMO)

Total net profit	61609220	Open position value	1270590.38	Net Profit / Buy&Hold %	1495436.39
Percent gain/loss	61609220	Annual percent gain/loss	848836.08	Annual Net % / B&H %	1495382.88
Initial investment	100	Interest earned	0		
Current position	Long	Date position entered	4/5/01		
Buy/Hold profit	4119.54	Days in test	26492	# of days per trade	5.29
Buy/Hold pct gain/loss	4119.54	Annual B/H pct gain/loss	56.76		
Total closed trades	5008	Commissions paid	0		
Avg profit per trade	12048.45	Avg Win/Avg Loss ratio	1.86		
Total long trades	2504	Total short trades	2504	Long Win Trade %	44.05
Winning long trades	1103	Winning short trades	893	Short Win Trade %	35.66
Total winning trades	1996	Total losing trades	3012	Total Win Trade %	39.86
Amount of winning trades	320391680	Amount of losing trades	−260053184	Net Profit Margin %	10.40
Average win	160516.87	Average loss	−86339.04	Average P. Margin %	30.05
Largest win	5003268	Largest loss	−2330460	% Net / (Win + Loss)	36.45
Average length of win	7.24	Average length of loss	2.91	(Win − Loss) / Loss %	148.80
Longest winning trade	26	Longest losing trade	11	(Win − Loss) / Loss %	136.36
Most consecutive wins	8	Most consecutive losses	11	(Win − Loss) / Loss %	−27.27
Total bars out	4	Average length out	4		
Longest out period	4				
System close drawdown	−1.32	Profit/Loss index	19.15	% Net Profit / SODD	3779706748.47
System open drawdown	−1.63	Reward/Risk index	100	(Net P.-SODD)/Net P.	100.00
Max open trade drawdown	−2330460	Buy/Hold index	1526278.67	% SODD / Net Profit	0.00

In the Equis MetaStock® "System Report" (profit and loss summary statistics), the *Total net profit* is the sum of profits minus the sum of losses, including open positions marked to the market. In contrast, the *Amount of Winning Trades* is the sum of realized profits (the total of all gains on closed-out trades only, excluding any open positions). Similarly, the *Amount of Losing Trades* is the sum of realized losses (the total of all losses on closed-out trades only, excluding any open positions). *System close drawdown* is the largest decline in the cumulative equity line below the initial investment, based on closed-out positions only. *System open drawdown (SODD)* is the largest decline in the cumulative equity line below the initial investment when a position is open. *Max open trade drawdown* is the largest decline in the cumulative equity line below the trade entry price during the worst single trade. The *Profit/Loss Index* is a complex calculation that relates the Amount of Winning Trades to the Amount of Losing Trades on a scale of −100 (worst possible performance) to +100 (best possible performance), with zero representing profits equal to losses. *Reward/Risk Index* is the Total net profit minus System open drawdown. The resulting difference is then divided by the Total net profit. The *Buy/Hold Index* is the Total net profit minus the buy-and-hold strategy's net profit. The resulting difference is then divided by the buy-and-hold net profit. In this exercise, initial equity is assumed to be $100. Both long and short positions are taken unless otherwise noted. Trades are executed at the closing price on the signal date. Transaction costs, interest expenses, and margins are not included in the statistics.

Volume Reversal

When volume increases and there is a clear directional price range expansion, then there is a Volume Reversal. Volume Reversal was developed by Mark A. Leibovit, a technical analyst who has specialized in transactional activity studies. Leibovit is editor of *The Volume Reversal Survey* (PO Box 1451, Sedona, AZ 86339), a semi-monthly market newsletter. Volume Reversal is based on the ancient technical analysis observation that volume should increase to confirm a change in directional price movement. Leibovit's Volume Reversal interpretation depends entirely on the following definitions:

- An *increase in volume* occurs when today's total transactional activity is greater than the previous day's volume of trade.
- A *Rally Day* occurs when the current intraday high is higher than the previous day's high and the current intraday low is the same or higher than the previous day's low.
- A *Reaction Day* occurs when the current intraday low is lower than the previous day's low and the current intraday high is the same or lower than the previous day's high.
- A *Positive Volume Reversal* occurs when a change from a Reaction Day to a Rally Day is accompanied by an increase in volume. It is time to buy.
- A *Negative Volume Reversal* occurs when a change from a Rally Day to a Reaction Day is accompanied by an increase in volume. It is time to sell.

Significantly, we should highlight what is specifically *ignored as not relevant* in Leibovit's Volume Reversal interpretation:

- An *Inside Day* occurs when the current intraday high is the same or lower than the previous day's high, and when the current intraday low is the same or higher than the previous day's low.
- An *Outside Day* occurs when the current intraday high is higher than the previous day's high, and when the current intraday low is lower than the previous day's low.
- The *Close* is the last price of the day, and it too counts for nothing.

A close examination of the buy and sell arrows on the chart on the facing page should make these definitions clear.

In our independent Indicator Strategy testing, this indicator underperformed a passive buy-and-hold strategy in recent years. As the chart of the S&P Depositary Recipts shows, a cumulative Volume Reversal indicator peaked out on July 22, 1997, which was too early for practical trading purposes. It appears that Leibovit's success depends on his good judgement based on his long experience, rather than on any simple, mechanical interpretation of this indicator.

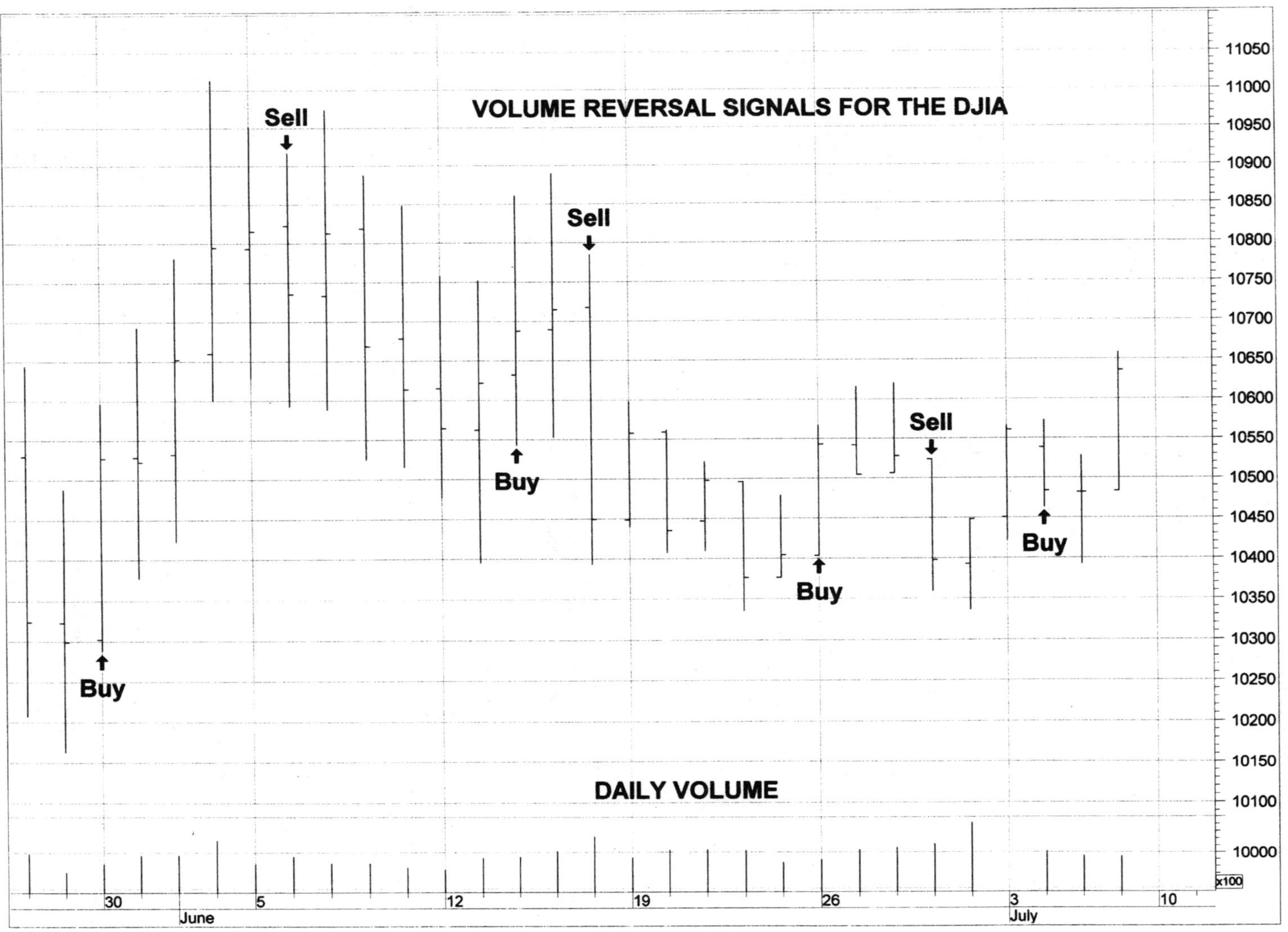
VOLUME REVERSAL SIGNALS FOR THE DJIA
Sell
Sell
Sell
Buy
Buy
Buy
Buy
DAILY VOLUME
11050
11000
10950
10900
10850
10800
10750
10700
10650
10600
10550
10500
10450
10400
10350
10300
10250
10200
10150
10100
10000
x100
30
June
5
12
19
26
3
July
10

The Equis International MetaStock® Indicator Builder Dialog for a cumulative Volume Reversal indicator (similar to On Balance Volume may be written as follows:

Cum ((If(H>Ref(H,-1)) AND (L>=Ref(L,-1)) AND (V>Ref(V,-1)),V,0))
+(If((H<=Ref(H,-1)) AND (L<Ref(L,-1)) AND (V>Ref(V,-1)),-V,0)))

The Equis International MetaStock® System Testing rules may be written as follows:

Enter long: H>Ref(H,-1) AND L>=Ref(L,-1) AND V>Ref(V,-1)

Close long: H<=Ref(H,-1) AND L<Ref(L,-1) AND V>Ref(V,-1)

Enter short: H<=Ref(H,-1) AND L<Ref(L,-1) AND V>Ref(V,-1)

Close short: H>Ref(H,-1) AND L>=Ref(L,-1) AND V>Ref(V,-1)

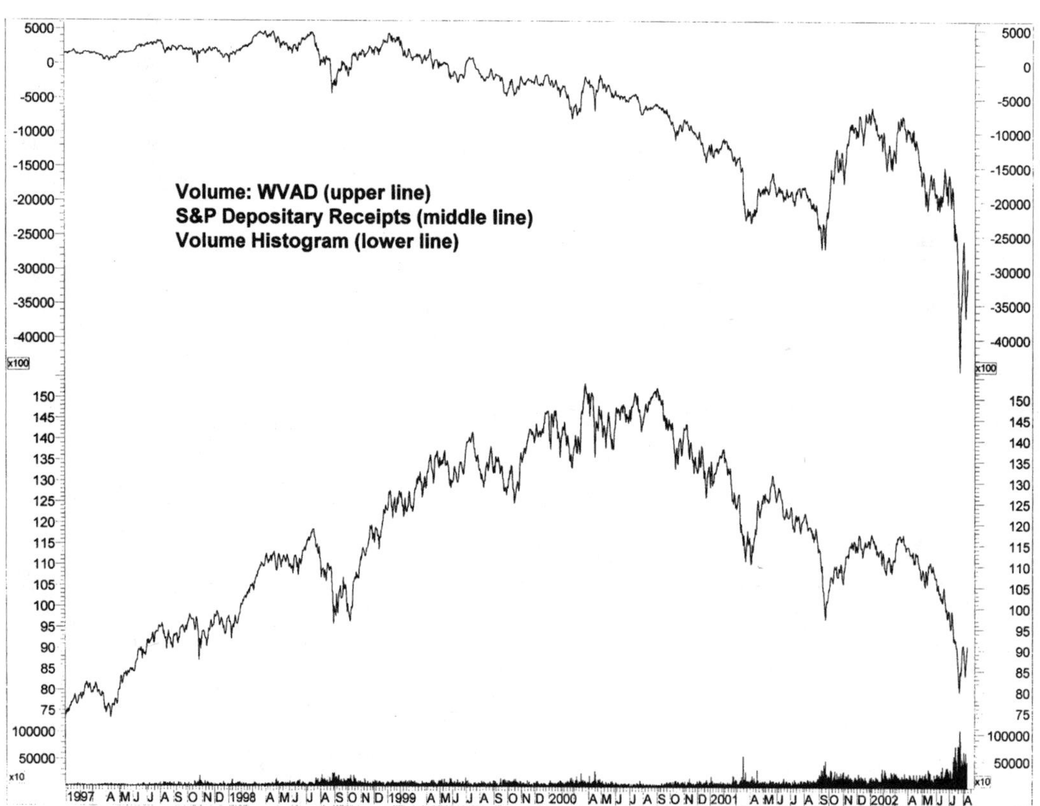

Volume Up Days/Down Days

The Volume Up Days/Down Days, developed by award-winning technical analyst, Arthur A. Merrill, CMT, is a ratio oscillator calculated by dividing the sum of the total daily volume on the latest five trading days that the price closed higher by the sum of the total daily volume on the most recent five trading days that the price closed lower. The following example should make it clear:

Day	Volume of Shares Traded	Price Close: Up or Down
1	183	Up
2	165	Down
3	177	Down
4	242	Up
5	234	Up
6	212	Down
7	195	Up
8	152	Down
9	145	Down
10	163	Down
11	159	Down
12	180	Up

$$\text{Volume Up Days/Down Days} = \frac{(183 + 242 + 234 + 195 + 180)}{(212 + 152 + 145 + 163 + 159)}$$

The result of the above calculation is 1.24. According to Art Merrill's research, readings above 1.05 are bullish, while readings below 0.95 are bearish.

Volume: Williams' Variable Accumulation Distribution (WVAD)

Williams' Variable Accumulation Distribution (WVAD) is a volume-weighted price momentum indicator, developed by Larry Williams. WVAD is based on the idea that the best measure of a day's buying power and selling pressure is dependent on the relationship between the number of points that the market has moved from its opening price to its closing price for the day. Specifically, it is calculated and interpreted in six steps:

1. Subtract the opening price from the closing price. Respect the sign, plus or minus.
2. Divide that difference (from Step 1) by the difference of the high minus the low.
3. Multiply that ratio (from Step 2) by the volume.
4. Average that product (from Step 3) over a moving window of *n*-days of time.
5. If the moving average (from Step 4) is positive, net buying pressure is dominant so a long position is initiated.
6. If the moving average (from Step 4) is negative, net selling pressure is dominant so a short position is initiated.

Mathematically, Steps 1 through 3 of the WVAD formula can be expressed as:

$$WVAD = (((C\text{-}O) / (H - L)) * V)$$

where

C = the current period's closing price.
O = the current period's opening price.
H = the current period's high price.
L = the current period's low price.
V = the current period's volume.

For example, if the current day's opening price was 175, the high was 180, the low was 160, the close was 165, and the volume was 2000 shares, then:

$$WVAD=(((165\text{-}175)/(180\text{-}160)) * 2000) = -1000$$

In Step 4, for a 4-period WVAD, for example, this −1000 would become an input for a 4-day moving average.

In our independent Indicator Strategy testing, this indicator underperformed a passive buy-and-hold strategy. As the chart of the S&P Depositary Receipts shows, such a cumulative WVAD indicator peaked out on April 3, 1998, which was too early for practical trading purposes. It appears that Williams' success depends on his good judgement based on his long experience, rather than on any simple, mechanical interpretation of this indicator.

The Equis International MetaStock® Indicator Builder Dialog for a cummulative WVAD indicator may be written: Cum(((C-O)/(H-L))*V).

The Equis International MetaStock® System Testing rules may be written as follows:

Enter long: Mov(((C-O)/(H-L))*V,opt1,E) > 0

Close long: Mov(((C-O)/(H-L))*V,opt1,E) < 0

Enter short: Mov(((C-O)/(H-L))*V,opt1,E) < 0

Close short: Mov(((C-O)/(H-L))*V,opt1,E) > 0

OPT1 Current value: 4

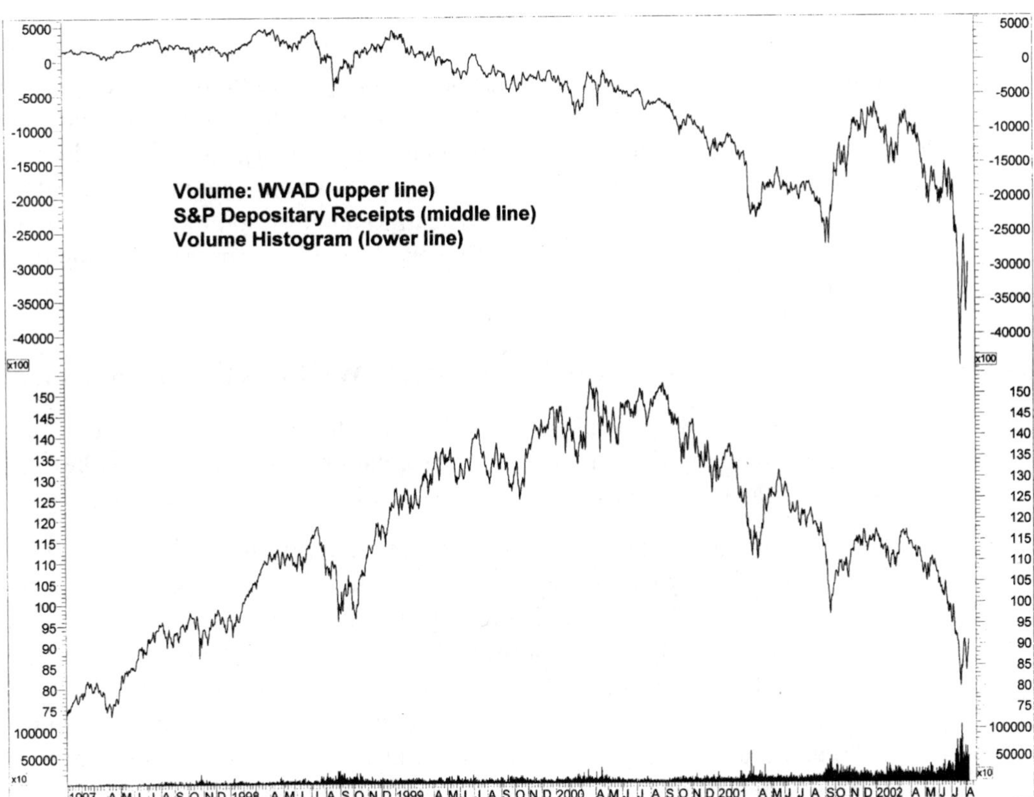

Wall $treet Week (W$W) Technical Market Index

The Wall $treet Week (W$W) Technical Market Index was once one of the most widely followed technical market indicators, thanks to the popularity of the PBS weekly television program. It was a consensus index of ten different stock market indicators, created by Robert J. Nurock, President/Market Strategist of Investor's Analysis, Inc., P.O. Box 460, Santa Fe, NM 87504-0460. Bob Nurock was the original "Chief Elf" and one of the original regular panelists for many years after the show's inception in 1970. When Bob Nurock gave up show business, his Index left Wall $treet Week with him. Still, Nurock's Wall $treet Week (W$W) Technical Market Index is an interesting example of a complex, combination indicator with a highly significant record of performance.

Introduced to the Wall $treet Week audience on October 6, 1972, the W$W Technical Market Index was based on the weekly interpretations of ten different technical market indicators. The Index ignored fundamental data on the economy, corporate earnings, and dividends. The ten technical market indicator readings were summed into one number designed to facilitate the perception of changes in investor psychology, market action, speculation, and monetary conditions that are often present at key market turning points. The Index attempted to identify intermediate to long-term market moves (lasting 3-to-6 months, or longer), rather than short-term swings. Nurock designed the Index to both confirm the continuation of a current trend (when the majority of its components are neutral) and also to provide early warning of a change in a prevailing trend (when five or more of its components swing to positive or negative).

How Nurock Constructed his Original Wall $treet Week (W$W) Technical Market Index

Nurock used the following ten Technical Market Indicators. Nurock stated his intention to update the specific formulas and interpretation levels annually. More current parameters are available separately under each indicator entry in this book.

1. Momentum Ratio measures the percentage difference between the DJIA and its 30-day simple moving average. Divide the DJIA's latest close by its most recent 30-day simple moving average. The resulting Momentum Oscillator flashes overbought/oversold warnings when the DJIA deviates more than three percent (3%) from its 30-day simple moving average. When the DJIA is more than three percent (3%) below its 30-day simple moving average, an extreme often registered at market bottoms, this indicator is positive and bullish. When the DJIA is more than three percent (3%) above its 30-day simple moving average, an extreme often registered at market tops, this indicator is negative and bearish.

2. Hi-Lo Index compares the total number of stocks attaining new highs versus the number dropping to new lows over the past 10 trading days on the NYSE. 10-day moving totals of both new highs and new lows are computed and compared. At significant market bottoms, few new highs are attained. At market tops, few new lows are registered. A reversal from either extreme confirms a change in market direction. When the number of new highs crosses above the number of new lows, it is positive and bullish. When the number of new highs crosses below the number of new lows, it is negative and bearish.
3. Market Breadth Indicator is a moving total of the net difference between daily advances and declines over the past 10 trading days. This breadth momentum quantifies the underlying strength of market moves by indicating whether or not the majority of stocks are moving in the same direction as the market averages, an important confirmation of general market strength or weakness. It is positive and bullish when this indicator rises from below to above +1000, and it remains positive until it declines 1000 points from its peak. It is negative and bearish when this indicator falls from above to below −1000, and it remains negative until it rises 1000 points from its trough. Readings between −1000 and +1000 are neutral.
4. Arms' Short-Term Trading Index uses NYSE data to compute a 10-day moving average of (Advances/Declines) / (Advancing Volume/Declining Volume). Readings above 1.20 indicate extreme pessimism and are positive. Readings below .80 indicate extreme optimism and are negative.
5. Percentage of NYSE Stocks Above Their Moving Averages is oversold and therefore positive when less than 30% of NYSE stocks are trading above their own 10-week moving averages and less than 40% of NYSE stocks are trading above their own 30-week moving averages. It is overbought and therefore negative when more than 70% of NYSE stocks are above their own 10-week averages and more than 60% are above their own 30-week moving averages.
6. Premium Ratio on Options divides the average premium on all listed put options by the average premium on all listed call options on a weekly basis. The raw data is from the Options Clearing Corporation (142 W. Jackson Blvd., Chicago, IL 60604). When the Premium Ratio is above 95.5%, it indicates investors are overly pessimistic, which is positive. When the Premium Ratio is below 42%, investors are bidding up call prices excessively and are therefore overly optimistic, which is negative.

7. Advisory Service Sentiment survey by Investor's Intelligence categorizes the forecasts of about 100 stock market newsletters as bullish, bearish, or expecting a market correction. When sentiment becomes distinctly one-sided, a contrary move in the market is anticipated. When the percentage of bears plus half of the percentage expecting a correction rises above 51.5%, it is positive and bullish. When the same calculation results in a reading below 35.5%, it is negative and bearish.
8. Low-Priced Activity Ratio relates the level of trading volume in Barron's Low-Priced Stock Index to volume in the blue-chip DJIA. A ratio above 7.59% indicates high speculative activity, which is negative and bearish. A ratio below 2.82% indicates low speculation and is positive and bullish.
9. Insider Activity Ratio is a ratio of insider sell transactions relative to buy transactions, as compiled weekly by Vickers Stock Research Corporation. A ratio above 3.61 to 1 means that sellers are significantly more numerous than buyers, and that indicates that key corporate insiders believe their stocks are overvalued and a downward price adjustment is likely. A ratio below 1.42 implies that insiders believe their stocks are undervalued and an upward price move is likely. Insiders are usually right.
10. Fed Policy provides a guide to the direction of Federal Reserve Board policy, as reflected by the level of the Federal Funds Rate relative to the Discount Rate. The daily closing bid price for Fed Funds is divided by the Discount Rate. These ratios are smoothed by a 4-day average for Friday, Monday, Tuesday, and Thursday each week. Wednesday readings are omitted as they are unusually volatile, due to end of the bank week transactions when individual banks even up reserve positions. The 4-day moving average is negative above 125%, indicating a high Fed Funds Rate relative to the Discount Rate and tight money, which usually slows the growth of business and chokes the stock market. The 4-day moving average is positive below 103%, since a low Fed Funds Rate relative to the Discount Rate indicates easy money, which fosters expansion of business and a rising stock market.

How the Wall Street Week (W$W) Technical Market Index is Compiled

The W$W Index is compiled once a week on Friday based on data available as of Thursday's close for each of the ten indicators.

- When an indicator reaches an extreme usually registered at market bottoms, it is positive and bullish, and therefore it is assigned a value of plus one.
- When an indicator reaches an extreme usually registered at market tops, it is negative and bearish, and therefore it is assigned a value of minus one.
- When an indicator is between extremes, it is neutral, and therefore it is assigned a value of zero.
- The first time an indicator moves directly from one extreme to another (from positive to negative, or from negative to positive), it is assigned a neutral value of zero. That zero value is maintained until a new plus or minus value is reached. This first-time exception allows for a more gradual dissipation of the initial strong momentum typical of a new trend.

Once this assignment of values (+1, 0, or −1) for each of the ten indicators is complete, the ten values are summed (respecting the sign, positive or negative) to arrive at the W$W Index reading for the week. For example, if four indicators are positive and bullish, five are neutral, and one is negative and bearish, the sum would be $4 + 0 - 1 = 3$. For another example, if two indicators are bullish, one is neutral, and seven are negative, the sum would be $2 + 0 - 7 = -5$.

How the Wall $treet Week (W$W) Technical Market Index is Interpreted

W$W Current Reading	Interpretation
10	Extremely Bullish
9	Extremely Bullish
8	Extremely Bullish
7	Extremely Bullish
6	Extremely Bullish
5	Extremely Bullish
4	Strongly Bullish
3	Bullish
2	Mildly Bullish
1	Neutral
0	Neutral
−1	Neutral
−2	Mildly Bearish
−3	Bearish
−4	Strongly Bearish
−5	Extremely Bearish
−6	Extremely Bearish
−7	Extremely Bearish
−8	Extremely Bearish
−9	Extremely Bearish
−10	Extremely Bearish

Performance Record of the Wall $treet Week (W$W) Technical Market Index Is Highly Significant

The W$W Index's ability to forecast the Dow Jones Industrial Average (DJIA) was independently verified by Arthur A. Merrill, CMT. Merrill examined all positive or bullish index readings of +5 or greater to determine whether or not the DJIA was higher 1, 5, 13, 26 and 52 weeks later. Also, Merrill checked all negative or bearish index readings of −5 or lower to see whether or not the DJIA was lower 1, 5, 13, 26 and 52 weeks later.

For the 12.2-year period from October 18, 1974 (the date of W$W Index's first revision) through December 31, 1986, the W$W Index correctly forecasted the DJIA 58.5% of the time 1 week in advance; 62.6% of the time 5 weeks in advance; 70.4% of the time 13 weeks in advance; 79.5% of the time 26 weeks in advance; and 81.6% of the time 52 weeks in advance. All are highly significant statistical readings.

Weighted Moving Average: Moving Position Weighted Arithmetic Mean

A weighted arithmetic mean weights each data observation proportionally by its position in time, with the most recent data assigned the highest weight and the oldest data assigned the lowest weight. The sum of the products (the daily values multiplied by each variable weight) is then divided by the sum of the weights.

For example, assume that the market has just closed, and we choose to calculate a 6-day weighted moving average of the daily closing prices for a hypothetical stock.

1. First, we number each of the 6 most recent past daily closing prices, such that the oldest data 5 days ago is numbered "day 1"; the data from 4 days ago is numbered "day 2"; the data from 3 days ago is numbered "day 3"; the data from 2 days ago is numbered "day 4"; the data from 1 day ago is numbered "day 5"; and the data from today is numbered "day 6". These assigned date position numbers (1, 2, 3, 4, 5, and 6) are our weights.
2. Using these weights, multiply the daily closing price 5 days ago by 1; multiply the daily closing price 4 days ago by 2; multiply the daily closing price 3 days ago by 3; multiply the daily closing price 2 days ago by 4; multiply the daily closing price 1 day ago by 5; and multiply the daily closing price today by 6.
3. Sum the 6 products (from Step 2). In this example, the sum of products is 1135.
4. Add up the sum of the weights, which is $1 + 2 + 3 + 4 + 5 + 6 = 21$. A shortcut formula for the sum of the weights is $0.5 \times n \times (n + 1)$, where n is the number of observations. In this example, the sum of the weights is $0.5 \times 6 \times (6 + 1) = 21$.
5. Divide the sum of products (from Step 3) by the sum of the weights (from Step 4). In this example, the sum of products divided by the sum of weights is 54.

6-day weighted moving average for a hypothetical stock

closing price from	*daily closing weights*	*multiply*	*price*	*equals*	*products*	*sum of products/ sum of weights*
5 days ago	1	×	50	=	50	
4 days ago	2	×	51	=	102	
3 days ago	3	×	53	=	159	
2 days ago	4	×	56	=	224	
1 day ago	5	×	60	=	300	
today	6	×	50	=	300	
sums	21				1135	54

Using a Microsoft Excel spreadsheet to calculate a 6-month weighted moving average for the month-end NYSE Composite, and assuming the price is in column B, the following formula is inserted into each cell of column H:

=(B6*1+B7*2+B8*3+B9*4+B10*5+B11*6)/21

6-month weighted moving average for the month-end NYSE Composite

	A	B	C	D	E	F	G	H
row	month-end date	closing price	multiply	weights	equals	products	moving sum of products	sum of products/ sum of weights
6	2/28/74	51.56	×	1	=	51.56		
7	3/29/74	50.21	×	2	=	100.42		
8	4/30/74	47.93	×	3	=	143.79		
9	5/31/74	45.92	×	4	=	183.68		
10	6/28/74	44.90	×	5	=	224.50		
11	7/31/74	41.55	×	6	=	249.30	953.25	45.39
12	8/30/74	37.70	×	1	=	37.70	939.39	42.73
13	9/30/74	33.45	×	2	=	66.90	905.87	39.52
14	10/31/74	38.97	×	3	=	116.91	878.99	38.68
15	11/29/74	37.13	×	4	=	148.52	843.83	37.74
16	12/31/74	36.13	×	5	=	180.65	799.98	36.93
17	1/31/75	40.91	×	6	=	245.46	796.14	37.91
18	2/28/75	43.07	×	1	=	43.07	801.51	39.54
19	3/31/75	44.21	×	2	=	88.42	823.03	41.23
20	4/30/75	46.19	×	3	=	138.57	844.69	42.98
21	5/30/75	48.46	×	4	=	193.84	890.01	45.03
22	6/30/75	50.85	×	5	=	254.25	963.61	47.23
23	7/31/75	47.52	×	6	=	285.12	1003.27	47.77
24	8/29/75	46.29	×	1	=	46.29	1006.49	47.65
25	9/30/75	44.49	×	2	=	88.98	1007.05	46.86
26	10/31/75	47.05	×	3	=	141.15	1009.63	46.79
27	11/28/75	48.24	×	4	=	192.96	1008.75	47.02
28	12/31/75	47.64	×	5	=	238.20	992.70	47.09
29	1/30/76	53.55	×	6	=	321.30	1028.88	48.99
30	2/27/76	53.35	×	1	=	53.35	1035.94	50.56
31	3/31/76	54.80	×	2	=	109.60	1056.56	52.20
32	4/30/76	54.11	×	3	=	162.33	1077.74	53.15
33	5/31/76	53.31	×	4	=	213.24	1098.02	53.54
34	6/30/76	55.71	×	5	=	278.55	1138.37	54.38
35	7/30/76	55.26	×	6	=	331.56	1148.63	54.70

Indicator Strategy Example for Weighted Moving Average Crossover Strategy

Based on daily closing prices for the DJIA from January 1900 to March 2001, we found that the following parameters would have produced a significantly positive result on a purely mechanical trend-following signal basis with no subjectivity, no sophisticated technical analysis, and no judgement:

Enter Long (Buy) at the current daily price close of the DJIA when this close is greater than yesterday's 6-day weighted moving average of the daily closing prices.

Close Long (Sell) at the current daily price close of the DJIA when this close is less than yesterday's 6-day weighted moving average of the daily closing prices.

Enter Short (Sell Short) at the current daily price close of the DJIA when this close is less than yesterday's 6-day weighted moving average of the daily closing prices.

Close Short (Cover) at the current daily price close of the DJIA when this close is greater than yesterday's 6-day weighted moving average of the daily closing prices.

Starting with $100 and reinvesting profits, total net profits for this Weighted Moving Average Crossover Strategy would have been $ 10,772,985,856.00, assuming a fully invested strategy, reinvestment of profits, no transactions costs and no taxes. This would have been 51,712,052.38 percent greater than the passive buy-and-hold strategy. Short selling would have been profitable and was included in this strategy. Only 38.48% of the trades would have been profitable, but this strategy cuts losses quickly and lets profits run. Trading would have been hyperactive at one trade every 5.89 calendar days.

The Equis International MetaStock® System Testing rules are written as follows:

Enter long: CLOSE > Ref(Mov(CLOSE,opt1,W),-1)

Close long: CLOSE < Ref(Mov(CLOSE,opt1,W),-1)

Enter short: CLOSE < Ref(Mov(CLOSE,opt1,W),-1)

Close short: CLOSE > Ref(Mov(CLOSE,opt1,W),-1)

OPT1 Current value: 6

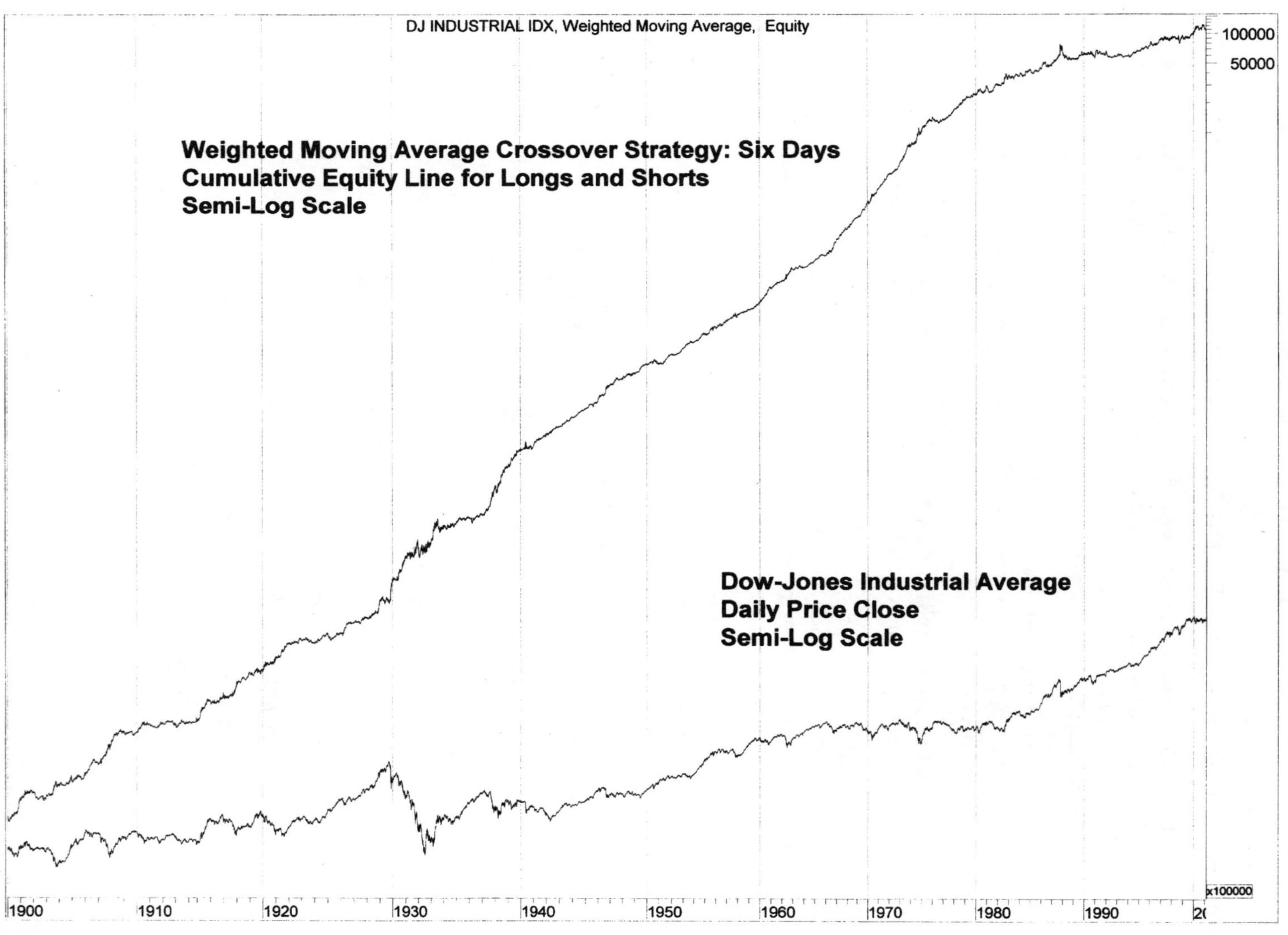
DJ INDUSTRIAL IDX, Weighted Moving Average, Equity
Weighted Moving Average Crossover Strategy: Six Days
Cumulative Equity Line for Longs and Shorts
Semi-Log Scale
Dow-Jones Industrial Average
Daily Price Close
Semi-Log Scale
100000
50000
x100000
1900
1910
1920
1930
1940
1950
1960
1970
1980
1990

Weighted Moving Average Crossover Strategy: 6 Days

Total net profit	10772985856	Open position value	29685260	Net Profit / Buy&Hold %	51712052.38
Percent gain/loss	10772985856	Annual percent gain/loss	106417857.6	Annual Net % / B&H %	51711770.15
Initial investment	100	Interest earned	0		
Current position	Short	Date position entered	2/28/01		
Buy/Hold profit	20832.6	Days in test	36950	# of days per trade	5.89
Buy/Hold pct gain/loss	20832.6	Annual B/H pct gain/loss	205.79		
Total closed trades	6278	Commissions paid	0		
Avg profit per trade	1711261.64	Avg Win/Avg Loss ratio	1.96		
Total long trades	3139	Total short trades	3139	Long Win Trade %	42.63
Winning long trades	1338	Winning short trades	1078	Short Win Trade %	34.34
Total winning trades	2416	Total losing trades	3862	Total Win Trade %	38.48
Amount of winning trades	58486444032	Amount of losing trades	−47743111168	Net Profit Margin %	10.11
Average win	24207965.25	Average loss	−12362276.33	Average P. Margin %	32.39
Largest win	1428177920	Largest loss	−463197184	% Net / (Win + Loss)	51.02
Average length of win	8.86	Average length of loss	3.26	(Win − Loss) / Loss %	171.78
Longest winning trade	39	Longest losing trade	24	(Win − Loss) / Loss %	62.50
Most consecutive wins	6	Most consecutive losses	18	(Win − Loss) / Loss %	−66.67
Total bars out	7	Average length out	7		
Longest out period	7				
System close drawdown	−9.63	Profit/Loss index	18.41	% Net Profit / SODD	111869012004.15
System open drawdown	−9.63	Reward/Risk index	100	(Net P.-SODD)/Net P.	100.00
Max open trade drawdown	−463197184	Buy/Hold index	51854547.61	% SODD / Net Profit	0.00

In the Equis MetaStock® "System Report" (profit and loss summary statistics), the *Total net profit* is the sum of profits minus the sum of losses, including open positions marked to the market. In contrast, the *Amount of Winning Trades* is the sum of realized profits (the total of all gains on closed-out trades only, excluding any open positions). Similarly, the *Amount of Losing Trades* is the sum of realized losses (the total of all losses on closed-out trades only, excluding any open positions). *System close drawdown* is the largest decline in the cumulative equity line below the initial investment, based on closed-out positions only. *System open drawdown (SODD)* is the largest decline in the cumulative equity line below the initial investment when a position is open. *Max open trade drawdown* is the largest decline in the cumulative equity line below the trade entry price during the worst single trade. The *Profit/Loss Index* is a complex calculation that relates the Amount of Winning Trades to the Amount of Losing Trades on a scale of −100 (worst possible performance) to +100 (best possible performance), with zero representing profits equal to losses. *Reward/Risk Index* is the Total net profit minus System open drawdown. The resulting difference is then divided by the Total net profit. The *Buy/Hold Index* is the Total net profit minus the buy-and-hold strategy's net profit. The resulting difference is then divided by the buy-and-hold net profit. In this exercise, initial equity is assumed to be $100. Both long and short positions are taken unless otherwise noted. Trades are executed at the closing price on the signal date. Transaction costs, interest expenses, and margins are not included in the statistics.

Weighting Different Technical Indicators

There is an overwhelmingly large number of possible technical indicator combinations. Assume we pick just ten indicators from this book and we choose to examine all combinations of these indicators. We would have to examine ten to the 10th power number of combinations, or ten billion combinations. The number of possibilities mushrooms when we assign variable weights to different indicators, for example, according to their historical effectiveness.

William Eckhardt (see Schwager, Jack, *The New Market Wizards,* HarperCollins Publishers, 10 E. 53rd Street, New York, NY 10022, page 109), a trader and mathematician, stated that assigning weights tends to be assumption-laden regarding the relationship among the indicators. The literature on robust statistics implies that the best strategy is not some optimized weighting scheme, but rather weighting each indicator by 1 or 0. In other words, accept or reject. If the indicator is good enough to be used at all, it's good enough to be weighted equally with the other ones. If it is not good enough, exclude it entirely.

An alternate approach is used by Arthur A. Merrill, CMT, who has many decades of experience as both a professional statistician and technical analyst. He observes that at any given time some indicators are bullish while others are bearish, and it is only human nature to see only those that confirm preconceived opinion. Merrill's solution to this problem is to objectively weight the indicators by past performance. First, he measures each indicator by its accuracy in forecasting the direction of the DJIA over 1, 5, 13, 26, and 52 weeks ahead, giving progressively greater weight to the longer time periods, which generally provide the most accurate forecasts. Merrill defines accuracy by the number of correct forecasts divided by the total number of forecasts. He further quantifies accuracy by the chi squared test of statistical significance with one degree of freedom. Merrill translates this significance data for all of his indicators into weights proportional to the logs of chi square, which is his own original innovation. Finally, he divides the sum of all bullish weights by the sums of all bullish plus all bearish weights for a totally objective weight of the statistical evidence he calls the Technical Trend Balance.

Criteria for including, excluding, and weighting indicators should be based on the investor's objectives, logic and common sense, and historical risk-adjusted returns simulated over many decades of unseen historical data. Also, each component indicator should be analyzed and followed separately to allow the technical analyst to perceive possible changes in each indicator's behavior. On occasion, such changes have been substantial over time for some indicators, due to structural changes in the trading environment.

Wilder's Smoothing

Wilder's Smoothing was developed by J. Welles Wilder, Jr., who may best be known as the developer of Directional Movement and RSI. Wilder used a formula for smoothing nearly identical to the more widely accepted exponential smoothing *(See Exponential Moving Average)*. When Wilder mentions dividing by a smoothing number of 14, for a very close approximation use an Exponential Moving Average number of days of 28. Both smoothing methods allocate decreasingly smaller weight each day to all historical data in the series.

Williams' Percent Range (%R)

This indicator, attributed to Larry Williams (P.O. Box 8162, Rancho Santa Fe, CA 92067), is the exact inverse of Stochastics, which is a more popular version of the same thing. *(See Stochastics.)*

Williams' Variable Accumulation Distribution (WVAD)

(See Volume: Williams' Variable Accumulation Distribution (WVAD).)

Wyckoff Wave

The Wyckoff Wave is a changing price index of eight important and active stocks. Recently, the eight stocks were: Bristol Myers (BMY), General Motors (GM), Dow Chemical (DOW), IBM (IBM), Exxon Mobil (XOM), Merrill Lynch (MER), General Electric (GE), and Union Pacific (UNP). *(See Technical Analysis of Stocks & Commodities*, www.traders.com, for a series of informative articles written on Richard D. Wyckoff's methods.)

About the Author

Robert W. Colby is an independent investment authority widely recognized for his objective and unbiased research. He has more than 30 years of professional experience as a research analyst, strategist, trader, portfolio manager, university instructor, consultant, public speaker, and author. He has served as a senior research analyst and vice president at one of the largest Wall Street firms and as an Instructor at The New York Institute of Finance and at New York University, where he created and taught intensive courses on investment methods. Currently, he consults with both individual and institutional investors, and he is a featured speaker on investment research methods and the investment outlook at conferences and seminars worldwide. He is a Chartered Market Technician (CMT), a member of the Market Technicians Association, and a colleague of the International Federation of Technical Analysts.

For his latest ongoing research, go to www.robertwcolby.com.

Special Discount Offer from MetaStock® and Robert W. Colby

- Flexible, customizable and advanced charting capabilities, including nine different charting styles.
- MetaStock Explorer™ can scan thousands of securities to find and rank the ones that meet your customizable criteria.
- Expert Systems, Expert Advisor™, Expert Alerts, Expert Commentary, and Expert Symbols offer guidance, tutoring, assessments, monitoring your securities, and flagging special conditions.
- MetaStock Performance Systems®, New Performance Systems™ and 10 Explorations are designed to increase profitability and decrease risk.
- Built-in extras include Web Browser, Online Trading Capability, Tutorial, Historical Data on CD, Training on CD, and Technical Support.
- MetaStock® offers two versions of their software: MetaStock®, an economical end-of-day data version (for longer-term investors); and MetaStock® Professional, a more expensive, real-time, live-data version (for active short-term traders).

I have designed and taught technical analysis courses for both professional traders and average investors. I always strongly encourage my students do their own research and to think for themselves. Useful tools such as MetaStock® help you do that.

For further details and to order MetaStock®, call toll-free 1-800-882-3040.

Be sure to mention "Offer Code COLBY" to receive your special discount.

Yours Truly,
Robert W. Colby

MetaStock® and MetaStock Performance Systems® are registered trademarks of Equis International, Inc., a Reuters company, 3950 South 700 East, Suite 100, Salt Lake City, Utah 84107, phone (800) 882-3040 or (801) 265-8886, fax (801) 265-3999, www.equis.com. All other product names are the property of their respective owners.

Robert W. Colby is an objective and independent researcher, investment manager, author, educator, consultant, and speaker. He is not an employee of any company that offers investment brokerage services or investment software products. He has not accepted and will not accept any advance compensation for recommending or for mentioning any service, product, or security.

For Robert W. Colby's latest thinking, updates, and recommendations go to www.robertwcolby.com

INDEX

C

D

E

F

G

H

I

J

M

N

O

P

Q

R

S

T

U

V

W

Y

Z